SO-ABD-820

Advance Praise for *American Literature*

The volumes of the Penguin Academic *American Literature* provide a compact, portable selection of American writers that represents the diversity of voices that make up our literature.

Terry Engebretsen
Idaho State University

The "Letters to the Readers" provide a useful and insightful introduction to the periods. I do find all of them appealing and think they do a good job of covering the content. I would definitely assign them.

Allan Charkin
Texas State University

The Letters do a great job of connecting literature to the forces that shape it. They also provide continuity between the developments of important writing traditions. These are some of the best overview chapters out there.

Sean Nighbert
St. Philips College

Strengths are the excellent sources listed at the end of the headnotes—bringing scholarship up to date for students and teacher, and the personal reader-friendly tone of the introductions, giving not just information but inviting the student and teacher to enter into a dialogue about this writer or this period.

Mary Ann Wilson
University of Louisiana at Lafayette

About the Author

William E. Cain is Mary Jewett Gaiser Professor of English and American Studies at Wellesley College, where he teaches courses in American literature, American studies, Shakespeare, and composition. Professor Cain received the B.A. degree in 1974 from Tufts University and both the M.A. (1976) and the Ph.D. (1978) from Johns Hopkins University. He became a member of the Wellesley faculty in 1978 and has taught in the American Studies program as well as in the English department.

The author of *The Crisis in Criticism* (1984) and *F. O. Matthiessen and the Politics of Criticism* (1988), Professor Cain has also edited many books, including *William Lloyd Garrison and the Fight Against Slavery: Selections from* The Liberator (1995), *The Blithedale Romance: A Cultural and Critical Edition* (1996), and *A Historical Guide to Henry David Thoreau* (2000). He is also the author of a study of American literary and cultural criticism, 1900–1950, included in *The Cambridge History of American Literature*, vol. 6. Professor Cain is a coeditor of *The Norton Anthology of Literary Theory and Criticism* (2001), and, with Sylvan Barnet, he has coauthored several books on literature and composition.

American Literature

Volume I

Edited by

William E. Cain
Wellesley College

Penguin Academics

PEARSON
Longman

New York   San Francisco   Boston
London   Toronto   Sydney   Tokyo   Singapore   Madrid
Mexico City   Munich   Paris   Cape Town   Hong Kong   Montreal

Vice President and Editor-in-Chief: Joseph P. Terry
Development Manager: Janet Lanphier
Senior Development Editor: Katharine Glynn
Senior Supplements Editor: Donna Campion
Media Supplements Editor: Nancy Garcia
Senior Marketing Manager: Melanie Craig
Production Manager: Eric Jorgensen
Project Coordination, Text Design, and Electronic Page Makeup: Electronic
    Publishing Services Inc., NYC
Cover Designer Manager: Wendy Ann Fredericks
Cover Illustration/Photo: "The King of the Turf," 'St. Julien', written by Orrin
    A. Hickok, 1880 (Lithograph), Currier, N. (1813–88) and Ives,
    J.M. (1824–95). Hall of Fame Trotter, New York, USA. BAL 8801
Manufacturing Buyer: Lucy Hebard
Printer and Binder: Courier Corporation - Westford
Cover Printer: Phoenix Color Corporation.

For permission to use copyrighted material, grateful acknowledgment is made
to the copyright holders on pp.1365–1366, which are hereby made part of this
copyright page.

Library of Congress Cataloguing-in-Publication Data
American literature / William E. Cain.
    p. cm.
    Includes bibliographical references (p.) and index.
    ISBN 0–321–11623–2 (v. 1) — ISBN 0–321–11624–0 (v. 2)
    1. American literature. 2. United States—Literary collections. I. Cain,
    William E., date–

PS507.A5753 2004
810.8—dc22

2003058108

Copyright © 2004 by Pearson Education, Inc.

All rights reserved. No part of this publication may be reproduced, stored in a
retrieval system, or transmitted, in any form or by any means, electronic,
mechanical, photocopying, recording, or otherwise, without the prior written
permission of the publisher. Printed in the United States.

Please visit us at www.ablongman.com

For more information about the Penguin Academics series, please contact us by
mail at Longman Publishers, attn. Marketing Department, 1185 Avenue of the
Americas, 25th Floor, New York, NY 10036, or by e-mail at www.ablongman.com

ISBN 0-321-11623-2

1234567890—CRW—06050403

Contents

PART 3   AMERICAN LITERATURE IN A DIVIDED NATION   843

Letter to the Reader: Slavery in America   845

Welcome: Suggestions for Students

It is my hope that you will enjoy and learn from the rich range of selections in this volume, and, for those of you taking a two-semester course, in the other volume of this two-volume set: the American literary tradition is filled with powerful and captivating writers and works.

One of the rewards for each of us of moving through an anthology like this is to rediscover authors we've always liked a lot even as we meet authors new to us who seize our attention right away. Another reward is encountering unfamiliar authors who may be less well known now than they were in their own era—the critic and novelist William Dean Howells comes to mind—but who produced important, influential work we can still find stimulating.

Still another, related kind of reward is meeting up with a selection that seems hard at first but that, for some of you at least, ends up sparking a lifelong enthusiasm. In my own case, I found the short-story writers and novelists Henry James and Gertrude Stein challenging when I first read them in college, and I felt the same way about the religious writer Jonathan Edwards, the essayist Ralph Waldo Emerson, and the poets Hart Crane and Wallace Stevens. Now, all of these authors, especially Emerson and James, are among my favorites. I'm glad I came across their work in my college courses, and glad, too, my teachers encouraged me to stick with them or (if that was not an appealing prospect!) to give them another chance in a year or two. My teachers urged me to figure out what these authors might have been aiming to accomplish in their writings even if I did not find them exciting or absorbing right away.

I recall in fact, with both embarrassment and gratitude, an exchange with one of my teachers about Henry James. Too fussy, complicated, hard to understand, tedious, I said about the selection we had been assigned. My teacher replied that there was a great deal of energy in my complaints and that she expected before too long I would be an admirer of James— and she was right.

Another of my teachers gave me a helpful specific suggestion for reading and studying literature that I'd like to pass along to you. Read with a dictionary nearby—a good one, with definitions of names and places as well as of words. As you'll see, I have annotated the selections in this volume, explaining references and allusions and terms. But you'll come across other things you are unsure about, and that's when you'll want to have the dictionary handy for consultation.

Are you a slow or a fast reader? Some of my students tell me they read slowly the first time they move through a selection, pausing to look up words, jotting down notes and questions in the margins; they mark up the pages paragraph by paragraph. Other students take a different approach; they read through the selection fairly quickly the first time, and then go back for slower-paced second and third readings. Some of these students mark up the pages of their books too. Others like to keep the book's pages free of markings and jottings and instead write their thoughts and questions in a notebook or a reading journal.

Of course nowadays we live and work in a computerized world. This doesn't mean books have lost their appeal. So far, I have not met anyone who says he or she enjoys reading lines and lines of text on a computer screen. For *reading*, books are much better. But having access to a computer and a connection to the Internet can provide you with many resources that will make your study of American literature, and your use of this volume, all the more productive and provocative.

Don't forget, by the way, that the Internet is not a replacement for the library. If you have to write a term paper on Hawthorne or Hemingway, you'll find good material on the Internet, but the major biographies, significant critical works, and most of the other key primary and secondary sources—you'll find these only in your library or through inter-library loan.

But it is true that the Internet can supply information and context for reading literature. When I'm rereading selections for class, I seem always to be catching sight of still more words whose definitions I need to know more fully, or place names I want to identify more accurately, and so on. I do plenty of marking and circling, and, as I proceed, I might consult a Web site such as www.bartleby.com, which offers an excellent dictionary and encyclopedias, a gazetteer (that is, an encyclopedia of geographical places) of North America, the King James Bible, and much more. Many of you no doubt have similar Web reference sites bookmarked that you make use of in your literary study and paperwriting.

What matters finally, however, are your responses to the literary works you are assigned or that you peruse on your own. And this leads me to offer another suggestion one of my teachers gave me. Be an active, question-asking reader, he said. It sounds so simple, so obvious—but this tip benefited me enormously. It made me realize I would get the most from my reading if I put a lot of *myself* into it—asking questions large and small, pushing myself to express in words what I was noticing, thinking, and feeling about a poem or story, or a specific passage in a longer work.

For a paper assignment in particular, often a good first step is jotting down in a notebook, or in a computer file, a sentence that begins like this, "What I really like about this poem is…" or, "The thing about this story that confuses me is…." From there, you can write more phrases and sentences (explain further, elaborate, clarify), and you can also return to the literary work itself, locating the passages in it that help you understand, and explain to yourself, why you have responded in the ways you have.

Ask lots of questions, work closely with the text: You can't go wrong if you follow these sound pieces of advice.

This is the first edition of this anthology, and while (with the help of my publisher's excellent staff) I have done my best on it, I know there's always room for improvement. I'd be grateful for your comments and suggestions, and I hope you'll feel free to contact me: wcain@wellesley.edu.

William E. Cain
English Department
Wellesley College
Wellesley MA 02481

To the Instructor

Dear Colleague,

You'll notice right away that this anthology is shorter than others that are available. The very big anthologies have an obvious advantage—they include a great deal from which you and I can choose. But for many of you, and for many students, these anthologies are too big—too much book to carry around, too many selections (and too little time during the semester to read them), and too expensive.

I have tried in this anthology to present a good range of selections for you and your students, but I've also taken the risk of being more selective. For my own students in a survey course, I think it's important to give them lots to read, discuss and debate, and respond to in short essays and research papers. But I also think that for many students, less can be more. A sharper focus, with a clearer kind of progress through the semester, often leads to a better educational result.

As I made my choices, I relied on recommendations I received from many instructors whom the publisher's staff and I consulted. There are selections that everyone wants included—Emerson's "The American Scholar" and Eliot's "The Love Song of J. Alfred Prufrock," for example. These are easy picks. But in other cases, the choices become harder. "Young Goodman Brown"— nearly everyone values this Hawthorne story highly. After that.... "Roger Malvin's Burial" is a favorite of mine, but instructors I contacted esteem it less highly than other stories. So, with some reluctance on my part, I left it out.

On the other hand, there is still plenty of Hawthorne in volume 1 of this anthology—several stories, plus *The Scarlet Letter* in its entirety. In the survey course I teach, I can achieve my goals for the weeks on Hawthorne effectively with what's included here.

You'll also see that I have tried for a different tone and approach in my headnotes, aiming once again for greater focus and clarity. I have done my best to keep the students in mind, and to give them tips for their reading of the story or play or poems that follow. It's an odd fact that in most anthologies, the lengthy headnotes make little or no reference to the selections. I have often been grateful for them, to be sure, in their degree of biographical detail, but I'm not certain that they quite succeed in telling our students, concisely, the key points and issues that matter for the literary works in the book.

A different tone and approach: I have made the same effort in the longer sections, three in each volume, that provide general commentary and overview. At first I attempted to write the usual period introductions, but I wasn't satisfied with what I was producing. It was too similar to the introductions I had encountered in other anthologies I have used in my courses—which, however much I benefited from them, my students found slow-going.

So I have written Letters rather than period introductions. Sometimes, I confess, I found myself thinking more about you as my audience than about the students—about the kind of conversation or scholarly exchange we might have. But I've aimed overall to pitch my Letters in the direction of our students, explaining and exploring ideas and topics that will stimulate their interest in American literature and make your work with them more enjoyable and productive.

The choice of selections, the headnotes, the Letters, the map, and the chronology: These features make this anthology different. It's an anthology that gives you a new option when you plan your syllabus and structure your assignments.

Because this is a new kind of anthology, and, even more, because this is its first edition, I would like very much to hear from you about it—what works well, what could be done better.

If I have one wish for this anthology, it's that it might bring me into closer touch with teachers of American literature—teachers who love the subject and who, in many instances, teach it in a demanding institutional setting. So many students to keep track of, so many papers and exams to read and correct—and all of those e-mails from students to answer! And if you're like me, you are probably busy with department and college or university tasks and committees. So time-consuming: often it can feel hard to be as much *inside* our favorite authors and books, and our favorite fields and topics, with so much else to take care of.

I feel some urgency about—as best I can—making contact, and staying in contact, with those of you who are teaching American literature courses, who are preserving and also diversifying and enriching the American literary tradition. There's a community of us out there, teaching American literature, making challenging decisions about which writers and works to highlight, pondering the best assignments for papers and the best questions to spark discussion in class. I think this anthology has turned out well, but I look forward to being in dialogue with you to make it better, and I welcome your suggestions and comments.

William E. Cain
wcain@wellesley.edu
English Department
Wellesley College
Wellesley, MA 02481

Acknowledgments

For his strong commitment to this project, I am grateful to Joe Terry. I have also benefited greatly from the advice and encouragement of Katharine Glynn and Janet Lanphier. The production of the book was handled with care and patience by Scott Hitchcock and the staff of Electronic Publishing Services Inc., Madeline Perri, and Eric Jorgensen.

For valuable help with research, I am indebted to a former Wellesley College student, Nicole Parent. The annotations gained enormously from the contributions of Kathryn Goodfellow. I also valued very much the astute suggestions offered by Sylvan Barnet, and the insightful comments and recommendations given by a number of reviewers, including Mark Baggett, Samford University; Laura Behling, Gustavis Adolphus College; Derek Bowe, Oakwood College; Vivien Brown, Laredo Community College; Mark Canada, University of North Carolina at Pembroke; Melvin Clark, South Texas Community College; Thomas Cooley, The Ohio State University; Jonathan S. Cullick, Northern Kentucky University; David Curtis, Belmont University; Dr. Bill Dynes, University of Indianapolis; David H. Evans, Dalhousie University; Betty Hart, University of Southern Illinois; Sylvia Henneberg, Morehead State University; Dr. David Lavery, Middle Tennessee State University; Paul Lehman, University of Central Oklahoma; Mary Magoulick, Georgia College and State University; Quentin Miller, Suffolk University; Kevin Morris, Greenville Technical College; Julia Nash, Merrimack College; Anne G. Myles, University of Iowa; Paul Petrie, Southern Connecticut State University; Teresa Purvis, Lansing Community College; James A. Sappenfield, University of Milwaukee; John Scott, Lexington Community College; Allison Singley, Gettysburg College; Debbie Stallings, Hinds Community College; and Teresa Trevathan, South Plains College. As always, Barbara Harman, and Julia and Isabel Harman Cain, provided me with steady support.

William E. Cain

Epigraphs

Don't say it, write it.
A book may be as great a thing as a battle.
The best part of a book is not the thought it contains but the thought it suggests.
You are known by the books you read.
A reading people will be a knowing people.

—AMERICAN PROVERBS

They knew they were pilgrims.
—WILLIAM BRADFORD, *HISTORY OF PLYMOUTH PLANTATION*, 1630—1651

For we must consider that we shall be as a city upon a hill.
—JOHN WINTHROP, *A MODEL OF CHRISTIAN CHARITY*, 1630

In the beginning all the world was America.
—JOHN LOCKE, *TWO TREATISES OF GOVERNMENT*, 1690

America is more wild and absurd than ever.
—EDMUND BURKE, LETTER TO LORD ROCKINGHAM,
SEPTEMBER 9, 1769

The cause of America is in a great measure the cause of all mankind.
—THOMAS PAINE, *COMMON SENSE*, 1776

E pluribus unum. ("Out of many, one.")
—MOTTO FOR THE UNITED STATES SEAL, 1776

What then is the American, this new man?
—MICHEL GUILLAUME JEAN DE CRÈVECOEUR, *LETTERS FROM
AN AMERICAN FARMER*, 1782

Who reads an American book, or goes to an American play, or looks at an American picture or statue?
—SYDNEY SMITH, IN THE *EDINBURGH REVIEW*, 1820

The United States themselves are essentially the greatest poem.
—WALT WHITMAN, PREFACE, *LEAVES OF GRASS*, 1855

America means opportunity, freedom, power.
—RALPH WALDO EMERSON, 1864, IN *UNCOLLECTED LECTURES*, 1932

I am a self-made woman.

—SOJOURNER TRUTH, 1882

PART I

From Exploration to New Nation

Contexts for Early American Literature

"The religious atmosphere of the country," wrote the French traveler Alexis de Tocqueville in *Democracy in America* (1835, 2 vols.), "was the first thing that struck me on arrival in the United States." Americans tolerated a wide range of religions, denominations, and sects, and many were involved in religion-based reforms, such as temperance and abolitionism, or had been won over to the spirit of revivalism sweeping across the land. Yet, Tocqueville noted, the religious commitments and passions of America's people did not endanger the nation's political stability:

> In the United States no religious doctrine displays the slightest hostility to democratic and republican institutions. The clergy of all the different sects there hold the same language; their opinions are in agreement with the laws, and the human mind flows onwards, so to speak, in one undivided current.

The new nation's Founders had rejected a national or state church. The Constitution of the United States (1787) does not refer to God, Christianity, or Providence; and the First Amendment begins, "Congress shall make no law respecting an establishment of religion, or prohibiting the free exercise thereof."

The relationship between religion and politics was complicated, however, as Tocqueville proceeded to explain:

> Religion in America takes no direct part in the government of society, but it must be regarded as

> the first of their political institutions.... I do not
> know whether all Americans have a sincere faith
> in their religion — for who can search the human
> heart? — but I am certain that they hold it to be
> indispensable to the maintenance of republican
> institutions. This opinion is not peculiar to a class
> of citizens or to a party, but it belongs to the
> whole nation and to every rank of society.

According to polls taken in 2002–2003, 95 percent of
Americans profess to believe in God or in some higher
spirit or power or source of truth; this is much higher
than the figure for European countries. Sixty to 70 percent of Americans identify themselves as members of a
church, temple, or mosque, and 50 percent say they
attend services weekly.

Americans today believe in and practice many religions, but the United States remains predominantly
Christian. In one poll, March 2002, 82 percent identified
themselves as Christian (that is, either Catholic or
Protestant). No other religious group recorded above
one percent. This fact to the side, perhaps the key conclusion of the poll was that the American public "over-
whelmingly sees religion's influence in the world and the
nation as a good thing."

Religion, especially as it pertains to the literature in
this anthology, is more than a matter of doctrines and
denominations. "Religion, whatever it is, is a man's total
reaction upon life," concluded the philosopher William
James in *The Varieties of Religious Experience* (1902). In
this broad sense, all of us are religious; all of us experience some kind of "total reaction" to the life we lead. We
seek to understand our place in the world, the nature of
our relationships to other persons and to Nature, and the

form of existence that might or might not await us when this earthly existence ends.

Religion is preoccupied with urgent, agonizing questions, and, as some have said, literature has an inherently religious element or dimension, absorbed as it is in its related array of ultimate questions. For many teachers and students, the study of American literature can take on something of a religious quest or mission, as American authors and texts impel us to reckon with who we are, individually and collectively, and who we wish to become. One is reminded here of the questions in the title of a Tahitian painting by the French post-impressionist Paul Gauguin: "D'où venons-nous? Que sommes-nous? Où allons-nous?" (Where did we come from? What are we? Where are we going?)

Literature courses highlight such questions, but it must be said that religion itself has not loomed large in recent years in American literature textbooks and classrooms. This was not the case decades ago, when every American literature survey opened with several weeks on the Puritan settlements in Plymouth and Massachusetts Bay in the early seventeenth century. These weeks set the stage for the entire semester, which climaxed with Nathaniel Hawthorne's evocation of mid-seventeenth-century Boston in *The Scarlet Letter* (1850), Herman Melville's fierce encounter with the Christian God (and much else) in *Moby-Dick* (1851), and Emily Dickinson's dynamic engagement with God in her poems of the 1850s and 1860s.

Perhaps we find religion hard to talk about in a twenty-first-century college classroom. We want to be respectful of everyone's religious belief, or lack of belief, and this goal may feel hard for us to achieve if religion — or, more precisely, Christianity — keeps coming to the fore.

The limited attention to religion in American literature courses may derive from another source—the poor reputation of the Puritans, of whom it is assumed no one with any sort of happy outlook on life could ever enjoy reading. If you consult a dictionary for "Puritanism," you'll find the following:

> Puritanism: Scrupulous moral rigor, especially hostility to social pleasures and indulgences: *"Puritanism is the source of our greatest hypocrisies and most crippling illusions"* (Molly Haskell, film critic).—*The American Heritage Dictionary of the English Language* (4th ed., 2000).

Earlier in the twentieth century, the cultural critic H. L. Mencken offered this barbed definition: "Puritanism—The haunting fear that someone, somewhere, may be happy." Puritanism, Mencken and others maintained, was repressive, hypocritical, pleasure-denying, and intolerant; it led to narrow-mindedness and to a moral and cultural rigidity that, centuries after Puritan doctrine itself had faded, still afflicts and distorts American society. Critics, intellectuals, and historians argued or implied that Puritanism was at odds with democracy and enlightenment, and that the Founders had to resist the dour legacy of Puritanism to create the United States.

In *The Cambridge History of American Literature* (1917–1921), the influential scholar Vernon Louis Parrington presented this negative picture of the Puritan era:

> New England Puritanism...is one of the fascinating *puzzles* in the history of the English people. It phrased its aspirations in so strange a dialect, and interpreted its programme in such esoteric terms, that it appears almost like an alien episode in the

records of a practical race. No other phase of Anglo-Saxon civilization seems so singularly remote from every-day reality, so little leavened by natural human impulses and promptings.... Strange, perverted, scarce intelligible beings those old Puritans seem to us—mere crabbed theologians disputing endlessly over Calvinistic dogma, or chilling the marrow of honest men and women with their tales of hell-fire.

Parrington was baffled by, and critical of, the leading Puritan ministers. Of Cotton Mather (included in this anthology), the author of some 450 works on religion, history, science, and other subjects, Parrington concluded:

Self-centered and self-righteous, the victim of strange asceticisms and morbid spiritual debauches, every circumstance of his life ripened and expanded the colossal egotism of his nature. His vanity was daily fattened by the adulation of silly women and the praise of foolish men, until the insularity of his thought and judgment grew into a disease.

Yet, as Parrington acknowledges, Puritanism was a pervasive fact and force in early American history, and Puritan themes and emphases, however qualified or adapted or challenged, appear in many later works of American literature. As the eminent literary historian (and one of the foremost twentieth-century scholars of Puritan writing) Perry Miller observed, "Without some understanding of Puritanism...there is no understanding of America."

Puritanism bears not only on the nature of religion in American culture, society, and literature, but also on its conception of "the other," of those—Native Americans above all, but other racial and ethnic groups as well — whom the white British settlers and colonialists encountered, interacted and worked with, exploited, and waged war against. It is connected to the issues of authority and power, both in the private or domestic and in the public spheres, that American writers have frequently considered. And it is tied as well to the quest for truth — about the self, the nation, God, Nature, the cosmos — that American writers have undertaken.

The Puritans were determined explorers, hardy and resilient visionaries, and tough-minded builders of settlements, communities, towns, and colonies. It is important for us to know who they were, what they believed, and what they said and did when they arrived in North America. The settlement of the Americas, with which this anthology begins, is an astounding story, in some respects thrilling and sublime, in others terrible and tragic.

For an anthology of American literature, the English settlements along the Atlantic seaboard, and particularly those in New England, are the most significant because of their impact on literature written in English. Perhaps one could term it "North American English literature" or "English literature of North America and, later, of the United States." Spanish settlements in the Caribbean, Central and South America, Florida, and the American Southwest, and French settlements in Canada — these and other settlements and colonies, to be sure, are crucial components of the full complex historical account of multicultural contact. Many languages, literatures, and cultures affected the development of American literature, so much so that some scholars, including Werner Sollors, Marc Shell, and Lawrence Rosenwald, have advocated a multilingual approach to American literature that would include texts written by Americans in Spanish, French, Dutch, German, and other non-English languages and dialects.

While this approach is provocative in theory, it demands a range and depth of expertise in foreign languages that few of us possess. One could argue, too, that however rich the results this approach might yield, it cannot displace the fact that English has been and remains the national language and, following from this, that American literature has been a literature written in English as an inevitable result of British settlement. There are occasions when this rule is broken; sometimes, as in two selections in this anthology, it seems essential to draw on a text first written in a language other than English. Nonetheless, it was "British America," as the historian Alan Taylor stated in *American Colonies* (2001) that "became the most populous, prosperous, and powerful colonial presence on the continent, a development that made the American Revolution possible and successful"—and, one could add, that made possible the development of American literature.

Jamestown, in Virginia, preceded Plymouth and the Massachusetts Bay Colony; founded in May 1607, Jamestown was the first permanent English colony in the Americas. But New England formed the religious, intellectual, and literary context for the emergence of American literature in the seventeenth and eighteenth centuries, and for the first great period of American writing, largely centered in New England and New York in the 1830s, 1840s, and 1850s—the period of Ralph Waldo Emerson, Henry David Thoreau, Nathaniel Hawthorne, Frederick Douglass, Herman Melville, Walt Whitman, and Emily Dickinson, major writers featured in the second half of this book.

The Puritan movement, which arose in sixteenth-century England, consisted of those who claimed that the Anglican Church—the state church of England—was tainted by remnants of Catholic belief and ritual and had to be purged of them and hence made "pure." At the center of Puritanism, according to the historian Charles L. Cohen in *God's Caress: The Psychology of Puritan Religious Experience* (1986), is an emphasis on "intense personal devotion and extreme ethical probity." The central influence was the sixteenth-century French-born Swiss theologian John Calvin, whose prolific works hammered home the omnipotence of God, the total depravity of humankind (resulting from original sin), and predestination (whereby a chosen few are elected by God for salvation).

As Cohen explains, Puritanism is focused on the experience of "conversion":

> During conversion those whom God elects to save (the saints) undergo a protracted spiritual experience in which they regret their sins, despair of obtaining eternal life, discover that they are redeemed by their faith in Christ alone, and celebrate their assurance that through him their salvation is absolutely secure.

This "new birth," says Cohen:

> instills in the elect feelings of spiritual power and a zeal to demonstrate their love to God and to fellow saints by carrying out the Lord's commands. Puritan piety was characterized by a veneration of the Bible as the rule for living righteously and a pervasive sense that God providentially supervises all human affairs.

The first Puritans to settle in America were the small band of Separatists or, as they were later called, Pilgrims, led by William Bradford (included in this anthology); they were "Separatists" because they sought to separate altogether from the Church of England, which they judged could never be wholly reformed. They sailed aboard the *Mayflower* and established Plymouth Colony in Massachusetts (their original destination was Virginia) in winter 1620–1621. Another, much larger, more moderate group was led by John Winthrop (also in this anthology); they arrived aboard the *Arbella* and other ships in 1630, settled in the Salem and Boston areas—a small group had preceded them to Salem in 1628—and established the Massachusetts Bay Colony. By midcentury, the second colony had grown to about 10,000 and extended into Maine, Connecticut, and other parts of New England. In 1691, the smaller Plymouth merged with Massachusetts Bay.

Puritanism was forthright but embattled, inspired by a conviction that God was guiding the faithful and by a fear of internal critics whose words and deeds would subvert the cause and endanger the community's spiritual coherence and prosperity. There were dissenters who challenged Puritan orthodoxy and religious and civil rule and suffered as a result—a feature of early American religious and cultural history that looks forward to the radical, dissenting, or skeptical views that such later writers as Emerson, Thoreau, Melville, and Dickinson expressed. Many American writers have been critics of convention and custom; they have been naysayers and iconoclasts who in their art have extended the boundaries of traditional form and acceptable content.

One of the Puritan dissenters was Roger Williams, who served in the early 1630s as a teacher and minister in Salem and then at Plymouth. He criticized Puritan government and appealed for more democracy in the church, thereby calling attention to an ongoing tension in Puritan belief and practice: Who should be admitted to formal membership in the church and allowed to receive the sacrament of communion? If only the "saved" should be admitted, how would their identity as saved souls be known? Because his views were judged subversive, Williams was forced to flee Salem, and in 1636 he and a band of followers founded a new settlement in Providence, in what later became the state of Rhode Island.

Though Puritans had themselves suffered persecution in England, their leaders were far from tolerant in America, as the response to Williams demonstrates. Another dissenter was Anne Hutchinson, who arrived in the Massachusetts Bay Colony in 1634. She preached a "covenant of grace" that, to an extent, anticipated the Transcendentalist philosophy Emerson articulated in the 1830s and 1840s. For Hutchinson, the individual could intuit God's love and grace directly, a claim that Puritan elders rejected as "antinomian"—that is, as an assertion that a Christian enlightened by God's grace is freed from obedience to religious and civil laws. Hutchinson stated that God had spoken to her "by the voice of his own spirit to my soul," whereas for the Puritan leadership God spoke through the Bible; Scripture was the repository of truth, not direct revelation.

In reference to Hutchinson, John Winthrop said:

> She walked by such a rule as cannot stand with peace of any state; for such bottomless revelations, as either came without any word, or without the sense of the word (which was framed to human capacity) if they be allowed in one thing must be admitted a rule in all things; for they being above reason and Scripture, they are not subject to control.

For her unorthodox opinions, Hutchinson was denounced and banished, and she relocated to Rhode Island, and later to Long Island and New York's Pelham Bay area, where in 1643 she was killed in an Indian raid. Her story illustrates the conflict between those American individuals and sects who seek, as the religious historian William G. McLoughlin stated (1965), to maintain "moral order," and, on the other side, those who profess their "moral freedom," their independence from or transcendence of civil and religious law and the authority to which others are bound. In *The Puritan Origins of the American Self* (1975), Sacvan Bercovitch makes a related point about the relevance of the Hutchinson case to American literary history, referring to the central "paradox" in American literature, focused in Emerson but reaching back as far as the dispute between Hutchinson and the Puritans—the paradox "of a literature devoted at once to the exaltation of the individual and the search for a perfect community."

Hutchinson's disagreement with the Puritan ministers also dramatizes the charged centrality of gender roles in American social and cultural history, which Anne Bradstreet, Mary Rowlandson, Margaret Fuller, and other women authors in this anthology in their different ways explore. One of Hutchinson's judges declared to her: "You have stepped out of your place, you have rather been a Husband than a Wife and a Preacher than a Hearer; and a Magistrate than a Subject."

The first periods of settlement in Plymouth and Massachusetts Bay were arduous. During the winter of 1620–1621, for example, half of Plymouth's colonists died; the following winter, they had little to eat, and the 1622 harvest was a failure, forcing them to subsist on shellfish, grains of corn, and small portions of bread. One is tempted simply to conclude it was a miracle the Puritan settlers survived, for that is how they interpreted their survival themselves. The religious scholar Edwin S. Gaustad has stressed that the Puritans perceived their "religious migrations as comparable to the Israelites' moving under God's direction into the Promised Land." As they saw it, God was with them in the midst of adversity, singling them out for special guidance and protection as performers of a luminous mission. As another scholar remarked, Puritanism was "a movement of religious protest, inspired by a driving zeal and an exalted religious devotion, which its enemies called fanaticism, but which to Puritans was an issue of life or death." These men and women possessed a stalwart sense of collective purpose, enacted under God's supervision, even as they were minutely watchful of any signs that God was displeased with their efforts. They studied the Bible, reading and rereading it in the light of their mission to America.

The probing psychological and emotional introspection we discern in Emerson, Hawthorne, and Dickinson, and in later writers such as Henry James, is rooted in—however much it departs from—the religious devotion and spiritual intensity of devout Puritans centuries earlier. The complicating issue for Emerson and the others is whether God is knowable or truly there at all. Is God present or absent from human consciousness and conscience? How is God experienced? The Puritan William Ames, in *Conscience with the Power and Cases Thereof* (Latin, 1632; English, 1643), defined conscience as "a man's judgment of himself, according to the judgment of God of him." Everything changes when the second phrase is omitted. For Emerson and, even more, for writers a century or more later, it could be liberating or terrifying, or both, to peer inward but not know, or not believe, or not care if God's power and providence saturated the self. Maybe the self was alone.

The Puritans believed they were not alone, and, as scrupulous readers of the Bible, they had keen awareness of and interest in "the Word," its meanings and implications. They would not have characterized themselves as "creative writers," since such a phrase implies an independence from God at odds with their religious beliefs. Still, as Kenneth B. Murdock stated in *Literature and Theology in Colonial New England* (1949), "the Puritan thought long and hard about the problems of prose style and tried consciously to discover for himself a system of rules for giving adequate expression to his ideas and beliefs." In a sense, the Puritans were America's first literary theorists, delving into and articulating the powers and properties of language as Emerson, Edgar Allan Poe, and Whitman would, for different purposes, two centuries later.

Here, for example, is Increase Mather, a Puritan preacher educated at Harvard (founded in 1636) and Trinity College, Dublin, writing in 1670 about his father, Richard Mather, a minister and teacher in the Boston area who had died in 1669:

> His way of preaching was plain, aiming to shoot his arrows not over his people's heads but into their hearts and consciences.... The Lord gave him an excellent faculty in making abstruse things plain, that in handling the deepest mysteries he would accommodate himself to vulgar capacities, that even the meanest might learn something.

Puritan ministers and scholars did not believe in literature for its own sake; literature made sense only if connected to the religious instruction of souls. If a speaker or a writer used language with care, diligence, and zeal, he could awaken and educate his audiences. The poet and minister Michael Wigglesworth noted (1650):

> For whereas our untractable nature refuseth to be drawn, and a stiff will scorns to be compelled, yet

by the power of well-composed speech, nature is drawn against the stream with delight, and the will after a sort compelled with its own consent. Although for a time it struggle and make resistance, yet at length it suffers itself to be vanquished and takes a secret contentment in being overcome.

The Puritans even allowed for (as we might describe it) an individual style, a handling of language distinctive to the writer or preacher. In his handbook for divinity students (1726), Cotton Mather said this:

After all, every man will have his own style which will distinguish him as much as his gait; and if you can attain to that which I have newly described, but always writing so as to give an easy conveyance unto your ideas, I would not have you by any scourging be driven out of your gait.

Puritans took life very seriously, as their attitude toward language suggests, and this made them suspicious of fiction, lyric poetry, and drama. They were critical of anything that seemed frivolous or wasteful, which impelled them to restrict or ban music, dance, theater, and the celebration of religious holidays (e.g., Christmas). Puritan magistrates regulated types and colors of clothing, and meted out punishments to those who did not attend church. Yet, as Perry Miller explained in *The New England Mind* (1939), there was more to them than denial and constraint:

They did feel that life was certainly grim, and never for a moment did they lose sight of its harshness, pain, and brutality.... [But] they remembered their cosmic optimism in the midst of anguish, and they were too busy waging war against sin, too intoxicated with the exultation of the conflict to find occasional reversals, however costly, any cause for deep discouragement.

"What shall we say," asked the Puritan preacher and author Thomas Shepard (1648),

> of the singular providence of God bringing so many shiploads of His people through so many dangers, as upon eagles' wings, with so much safety from year to year? The fatherly care of our God in feeding and clothing so many in a wilderness, giving such healthfulness and great increase of posterity?

Here is expressed the grand vision of America as a nation of destiny that shapes much political discourse and rhetoric even today. America then, and now the United States, is the pathfinder, the exemplar, the redeemer, among nations; its role in the world is to break from older social and political models, undemocratic and corrupt, and to spur reform and revolution everywhere—through its example, or, sometimes, through its military and economic might.

American writers have often contested this vision, even as they have voiced affirmative and celebratory sentiments about America as an idea and ideal. Emerson, Thoreau, Douglass—these writers, and others in this volume, criticize America deeply and rigorously, yet all the while they profess an American identity, a conception of themselves as Americans. As one reads the selections by them and others in this anthology, one wonders: Is it possible for an American writer to be patriotic, and if so, what would an authentically patriotic American literature look and sound like? American writers, grappling with this question, swing back and forth from fervent hope to despair, from optimism to pessimism, as they contemplate America's soaring prospects and huge shortcomings and persistent injustices.

A strong sense of religious mission—perhaps we could say, of patriotic destiny—thus inspired and fortified the Puritans. In "A Model of Christian Charity" (included in this anthology), Winthrop proclaimed, "For we must consider that we shall be as a city upon a hill. The eyes of all people are upon us."

Nothing is more frequent in the history of American literary, cultural, and political writing and speech than affirmations, like Winthrop's, of national mission— unless it is the expression of alarm about the nation's failure to fulfill its promise, its decline from its principles, and its desperate need to rededicate and renew itself. Winthrop's next sentences are: "So that if we deal falsely with our God in this work we have undertaken, and so cause him to withdraw his present help from us, we shall be made a story and a by-word throughout the world."

The rhythm of Winthrop's sentences anticipates the pattern of the Puritan jeremiad, a popular mid-seventeenth-century form that accented the falling off of the community since the time of the founders, the first settlers, the pioneering generation. The jeremiad—from Jeremiah, a Hebrew prophet of the seventh and sixth centuries B.C., whose lamentations are included in the Hebrew Bible and the Old Testament—describes the present as a period of affliction, misfortune, and mourning during which God's people suffer as a deserved punishment for their wrongdoing. The author of a jeremiad offers hope, however, that the chosen can recover their spiritual well-being by rejecting sin and appealing for God's forgiveness and restoration to his favor.

As Sacvan Bercovitch showed (1978), the jeremiad, full of fear and apprehension, is, finally, reassuring because it aims to convince the audience or readership that change and renewal are possible. The situation is dire, but not beyond redemption. The form the jeremiad took in America, Bercovitch says, "inverts the doctrine of vengeance into a promise of ultimate success, affirming to the world, and despite the world, the inviolability of the colonial cause." Its purpose, he continues, is "to direct an imperiled people of God toward the fulfillment of their destiny, to guide them individually toward salvation, and collectively toward the American city of God."

This interplay of peril and hope is also manifest in Puritan writings about the soul of each believer, though here the tone frequently is more uneasy and ominous. As David E. Stannard, in *The Puritan Way of Death* (1979), explained, "If the Puritans' sense of *national* mission was infused with an overwhelming and single-minded confidence, their sense of *individual* salvation was beset with agonizing insecurity." Who, after all, could be certain that he or she knew, with no shadow of doubt, he or she was saved? There was boundless joy in believing one was saved, but spiritual life among imperfect men and women was always tainted by original sin and therefore could never be steady. No one could afford to be at rest when the issue was the fate of one's soul.

Here is part of a letter (1637) from Margaret Winthrop to her husband John:

> Sad thoughts possess my spirits, and I cannot repulse them; which makes me unfit for any thing, wondering what the Lord means by all these troubles among us. Sure I am, that all shall work to the best to them that love God, or rather are loved of him. I know he will bring light out of obscurity, and make his righteousness shine forth as clear as the noonday. Yet I find in myself an adverse spirit, and a trembling heart, not so willing to submit to the will of God as I desire.

Mrs. Winthrop's words not only illustrate the Puritans' habit of self-scrutiny but also suggest the challenge that Puritan belief and practice posed to any effort to establish and secure a single unified church. The focus on the soul of each believer, on his or her depravity and possible regeneration and salvation, raised the possibility—the likelihood—that individuals and groups would become discontented, restless, and split away.

Puritanism hence functioned over time to both consolidate and unsettle authority. The community, the church, mattered greatly, yet salvation, ultimately, was each man's or woman's personal story. The type of self-reliance Emerson espoused in the 1830s would have shocked an earnest Puritan. Where in Emerson's ideas was God? But the shock might have carried a measure of recognition, for in Emerson—who traced his ancestors back to Thomas Emerson, who emigrated from England to America in 1635—there is an abiding concern for self-examination, renewal, and regeneration not wholly severed from the practices of the Puritans.

Between the Puritans and Emerson are the sermons and writings of Jonathan Edwards (included in this volume), who sought to revitalize Calvinist tenets in the eighteenth century.

Edwards stated in his "Personal Narrative" (1740; published 1765) that each person must "lie low before God, as in the dust; that I might be nothing, and that God might be all." A century later, in *Nature* (1836), Emerson wrote:

> Crossing a bare common, in snow puddles, at twilight, under a clouded sky, without having in my thoughts any occurrence of special good fortune, I have enjoyed a perfect exhilaration. I am glad to the brink of fear. In the woods too, a man casts off

his years, as the snake his slough, and at what period soever of life, is always a child. In the woods, is perpetual youth. Within these plantations of God, a decorum and sanctity reign, a perennial festival is dressed, and the guest sees not how he should tire of them in a thousand years.

As different from one another as Edwards and Emerson seem, there is a bond between them. "What is persistent," according to Perry Miller, "is the Puritan's effort to confront, face to face, the image of a blinding divinity in the physical universe, and to look upon that universe without the intermediacy of ritual, of ceremony, of the Mass and the confessional." In Miller's view, two crucial, intersecting questions constitute "the major theme of American literature" from the Puritans through Edwards and Emerson to the present: "What became of the sinners?" and "What became of the angry God?"

There is still more to the narrative of Puritan settlement and its effects on American life and literature, and it pertains also to the settlements the English, Dutch, Spanish, French, and Portuguese launched elsewhere in the Americas. On one level, it is correct to observe with Perry Miller that the Puritans "attached no significance a priori to their wilderness destination.... It was simply a void." The historian Darren Staloff has said much the same:

Few radical movements have enjoyed the auspicious conditions of the Puritan founders of Massachusetts. Far from the metropolitan authorities, the leaders of the settlement were able to inscribe their ideal holy commonwealth on the tabula rasa of the wilderness free from outside interference.

These, after all, are the very claims that Puritans in New England and Anglicans in Virginia made repeatedly. "In a vacant soil," reflected the minister John Cotton, "he that taketh possession of it, and bestoweth culture and husbandry upon it, his Right it is."

In the New England area, along the coast of Virginia in the Roanoke and Jamestown settlements, and in the Caribbean and in Central and South America, the land was already inhabited; it was *not* empty or vacant. As Francis Jennings noted in *The Invasion of America* (1975), "Europeans did not find a wilderness here.... They made one. Jamestown, Plymouth, Salem, Boston, Providence, New Amsterdam [the capital, at the tip of Manhattan, of the Dutch colony of New Netherland], Philadelphia—all grew upon sites previously occupied by Indian communities. So did Quebec and Montreal and Detroit and Chicago." "The so-called settlement of America," Jennings concludes, "was a *re*-settlement, a reoccupation of land made waste by the diseases and demoralization introduced by the newcomers."

The Puritans understood their arrival in very different terms. Robert Cushman, after a visit to Plymouth, reported, "The country is yet raw; the land untilled; the cities not builded, the cattle not settled. We are compassed about with a helpless and idle people, the natives of the country, which cannot, in any comely or comfortable manner, help themselves, much less us." Cushman omitted the fact that if the first Pilgrims had not received help from the local Indians, they would have perished almost immediately. Like others, he said that no one was present when the Puritans arrived. Giving reasons (1622) for emigration from England to America, Cushman maintained about the Indians: "To us, they cannot come: our land is full. To them, we may go; their land is empty." The Indians occupied the land, yet as far as Cushman was concerned, it had no one on it.

Starting at zero in 1606, the white population reached 3.2 million at the first federal census in the United States in 1790. Meanwhile, as the consequence of disease and warfare, the Indian population throughout the Americas declined dramatically. The exact figures are in dispute, but one reliable study by the geographer William Denevan indicates that the population of the Americas in 1492 was somewhere between 43 million and 65 million; for comparison, the population of the European countries in 1492 was in the range of 60 to 70 million. Denevan estimates that for North America, the figure is about 3.8 million, though others have proposed a figure closer to 5 million. The impact of European exploration and conquest on the Caribbean was devastating. By the 1530s, for example, "the Indians of Jamaica and Puerto Rico were almost extinct, and the Bahamas had none at all," Kenneth Maxwell has observed. "The European incursion into the Caribbean unquestionably had produced a holocaust with few parallels in world history."

In North America, the effect was less catastrophic but still disastrous. By 1800, the number of Indians in the United States and Canada had declined to 600,000. As specific case studies, Francis Jennings described the situation on Martha's Vineyard, off the Massachusetts coast, and Block Island, off the Rhode Island coast. When the English settled Martha's Vineyard in 1642, the population of the Wampanoag Indians was 3,000; by the mid-1760s, it was 300. On Block Island, the Indian population declined from 1,500 in the mid-1660s to 51 in the mid-1770s.

The Europeans announced that one of their main motives in exploring and settling the Americas was the imperative of bringing Christianity to the "savages." In his journal in 1492, Christopher Columbus (two letters he wrote are in this anthology) depicted one of the first moments of cultural encounter between the Old and New Worlds:

> In order that they would be friendly to us — because I recognized that they were people who would be better freed and converted to our Holy Faith by love than by force — to some of them I gave red caps, and glass beads which they put on their chests, and many other things of small value, in which they took so much pleasure and became so much our friends that it was a marvel.

Missionary work and conversion were typically performed not by gift-giving or reason or instruction but by force: Indians did not enjoy the option of refusing to be converted. As of 1514, the Spanish read the Requerimiento to the native inhabitants of the New World. Prepared by advisers to King Ferdinand, the text was written in Spanish, which Indians could not understand. It included the following passage, warning of the consequences if the Indians failed to welcome the Spanish and embrace the Catholic faith:

> If you do not do this or if you maliciously delay in doing it, I certify to you that with the help of God we shall forcefully enter into your country and shall make war against you in all ways and manners that we can, and shall subject you to the yoke and obedience of the Church and of their highnesses may command; and we shall take away your goods and shall do to you all the harm and damage that we can, as to vassals who do not obey and refuse to receive their lord and resist

and contradict him; and we protest that the deaths and losses which shall accrue from this are your fault, and not that of their highnesses, or ours, or of these soldiers who come with us.

The priest and protector of the Indians, Bartolomé de las Casas, in his *Brief Account of the Devastation of the Indies* (1542, excerpted in this anthology), surveyed the effects of Spanish exploration and conquest:

Acting like ravening beasts, killing, terrorizing, afflicting, torturing, and destroying the native peoples, doing all this with the strangest and most varied new methods of cruelty, never seen or heard of before, and to such a degree that this Island of Hispaniola once so populous (having a population that I estimated to be more than three million), has now a population of barely two hundred persons.

Las Casas's figure of 3 million may be high, but modern scholars agree that the population was at least 1 million, and by the mid-sixteenth century, it was a few hundred. "Within a decade or two of that," Kirkpatrick Sale added in *The Conquest of Paradise* (1492), the Indians of Hispaniola "were extinct."

In the early seventeenth century, many Indian tribes, speaking many languages and dialects, lived along the eastern seaboard. A tribe ranged in number from 2,000 to 20,000 and consisted of villages of 200 to 400 inhabitants; each village was ruled by a sachem (i.e., a chief). The Indians had a strong feeling for the land, for their territory, but not of exclusive ownership or private property in land. Few made use of a written alphabet; their body of literature was keyed to oral performances, and their cultural memory was based in song, dance, ritual, and recitation. In the southern sections of New England, the Indian population decreased as a consequence of war and epidemics from 120,000 in 1570 to 12,000 in 1670. Bloody battles between English settlers and Indian tribes also broke out in Virginia in the 1620s, and there, too, violence and disease decimated the native population, reducing it from 20,000 in 1610 to 2,000 in 1670.

In 1637, the settlers in the Connecticut Valley engaged in brutal conflict with the Pequot, which began when the Pequot murdered an English trader. As the literary historian Larzer Ziff (1973) stated: "For the Puritans the war came very rapidly to be a matter not of capturing and executing the Pequots who had committed criminal acts, but of exterminating the tribe altogether." More than 500 Pequot were killed when the English launched an assault on their fortified main village on the Mystic River. Those who survived fled north and west and were killed in later English attacks or else were captured and sold into slavery in the West Indies or New England.

An English commander, John Underhill, justified the ferocity of the attack by the Puritans and their band of Indian allies:

> It may be demanded, Why should you be so furious? (as some have said). Should not Christians have more mercy and compassion? But I would refer to David's war [i.e., the biblical King David of Israel]. When a people have grown to such a height of blood, and sin against God and man, and all confederates in the action, there he hath no respect towards persons, but harrows them, and saws them, and puts them to the sword, and the most terrible death that may be. Sometimes the scripture declares women and children must perish

with their parents. Sometimes the case alters; but we will not dispute it now. We had sufficient light from the word of God for our proceedings.

When hostilities ended, the colonists prohibited the Pequots from regrouping as a tribe, outlawing the name itself.

Even more harrowing was King Philip's War, 1675–1676. King Philip was chief of the Wampanoag; his Wampanoag name was Metacom, and he was the leader of a tribe whose population had decreased since the time of first contact with the English from 12,000 to about 1,000. Once more, amid a series of disputes over lands and guns, the precipitating event was a murder — not of an Englishman this time but of a Native American Christian, whom the Wampanoag believed was an informer. Three Wampanoag were arrested, tried for murder, and executed; in retaliation, King Philip's forces, including Wampanoag and other Indian allies, raided English settlements, burning properties and slaying many whites. Fierce warfare spread, reaching its climax in August 1676, when Philip's wife and son were captured and he was killed. His head was taken to Plymouth, mounted on a stake, and left there for twenty-five years. Justifying the war and its aftermath, Increase Mather concluded in *The History of King Philip's War* (1676), "We may truly say of Philip, and the Indians, who have fought to dispossess us of the land, which the Lord hath give to us…. I have not sinned against thee, but thou dost me wrong to war against me."

White American civilization, culture, and literature came into existence at the expense of the people who were already here. This is one of the bitter truths of American literary history, which the selections in this volume by Mary Rowlandson, Benjamin Franklin, Philip

Freneau, the Cherokee Citizens, Lydia Howard Huntley Sigourney, and William Apess from a variety of angles bear witness. While the Indians were already on the land, they did not possess, it was assumed, any real right to it. They were inferior; their lives were not informed by God's providential design. William Bradford, in *Of Plymouth Plantation* (begun 1630, completed 1651, excerpted in this volume) recalled that the Pilgrims felt "in continual danger of the savage people, who are cruel, barbarous, and most treacherous." At the close of the century, in *Magnalia Christi Americana* (1702, also excerpted here), Cotton Mather similarly depicted Indians as "doleful creatures who were the veriest ruins of mankind, who were to be found anywhere on the face of the earth." Even John Eliot, who labored as a missionary among Indians in Massachusetts, emphasized "the vast distance of natives from common civility, almost humanity itself."

Another momentous development was unfolding in the Americas during this time. Soon after Columbus's voyages, Indians were enslaved and transported from one Caribbean island to another in order to address the pressing need for workers. But there were not enough Indians (their numbers had fallen precipitously) to meet the demand, and by the first two decades of the sixteenth century, a vigorous, profitable trade in slaves captured from Africa was underway. African slave labor made possible an enormously profitable triangular commerce from England to Africa to the Caribbean and North America. Sugar, coffee, cotton, tobacco, rice, indigo: these commodities accounted for a major increase in European trade and commerce during the seventeenth and eighteenth centuries.

It is estimated that from the early sixteenth through the nineteenth centuries, 9.5 million Africans were forcibly transported from their native lands to the Americas. Of this total, 5 million were taken to South America; in excess of 4 million were taken to the West Indies; and 400,000 to 500,000 went to British North America. After their seizure in Africa, these men, women, and children were packed into ships under horrific conditions; 20 percent or more did not survive the journey across the Atlantic Ocean. By the late seventeenth century, propelled by the charter of Charles II for the Royal African Company, England had become the central force in this hideous trafficking in slaves. Said one contemporary, "The whole city of Liverpool was built by the blood of the poor Africans."

In the Southern coastal colonies, the first laborers were white indentured servants who worked for four- to five-year terms; 50 percent died while still indentured. The first blacks held in bondage were introduced in 1619—though scholars now believe they were, strictly speaking, not slaves but indentured servants—and for several decades their numbers remained small; in Virginia, for example, there were in 1650 about 500 slaves in a total population of 15,000. These first groups of slaves did not, for the most part, travel directly from Africa to British North America but settled first in the West Indies before later transport to the mainland.

Soon the numbers of slaves increased as more and more were purchased as workers. By 1700, the black population in Virginia had risen to 16,000. To make the point another way, from 1650 to 1700, the percentage of blacks in the population of Virginia jumped from 3 percent to 28 percent. North American slaves were oppressed, exploited, and brutalized, but in general the conditions they endured were less ghastly than those experienced by slaves in the sugar fields of the brutally hot, humid West Indies. By the 1720s, slaves in the

Maryland and Virginia areas began naturally to reproduce their numbers. No slave population in the Americas had done this before. Further south on the American mainland, in South Carolina, the black population by 1740 was 60 percent of the total, and by the 1770s, the figure for Georgia was nearly 50 percent.

Northern colonies made use of slave labor, but less extensively. By the early 1740s, there were 1,400 slaves in Boston—about 9 percent of the population—and in Newport, Rhode Island, as in New York City, the figure was 10 percent. Slaves were more important to the economy of the Southern colonies, large sections of which were based on a single lucrative export—tobacco, rice, or indigo, for example. From 1620 to 1640, the amount of tobacco exported per year from the Virginia and Maryland areas increased from 2,500 pounds to 3 million pounds; in 1700, the figure had reached nearly 30 million pounds.

By the eighteenth century, the vast majority of slaves arrived in North America directly from Africa, and the cultural interaction between African, African American, and Afro-Caribbean groups was complex and diverse. Another factor in the making of slave communities and kinship networks was the size and scale of the plantations and estates where slaves were held. During the 1780s, 50 percent of Virginia's slaves lived on farms consisting of ten or more slaves. The extensive, powerful, and wealthy Carter family of Virginia owned 2,300 slaves on holdings of 170,000 acres. By 1789, the year George Washington took the oath of office as the first president of the United States, there were slaves in the North and in the South—700,000 in all.

In a later Letter in this anthology, I review in greater detail the history of American slavery, and a number of selections in this volume, including those by John

Woolman, Phillis Wheatley, James Fenimore Cooper, Frederick Douglass, Harriet Jacobs, and Abraham Lincoln, focus on this topic. But slavery is implicit in, or pertinent to, our study of literary works by others in this anthology as well. When Franklin speaks of "the way to wealth"; when Crèvecoeur asks, "What is an American?"; when Emerson celebrates "the American scholar" and honors "self-reliance"; when Whitman sings his democratic "song of myself"—all of these texts—memorable, provocative, invigorating—carry as part of their meaning their relationship to Native Americans and African Americans. The existence of slavery does not discredit these authors' ideas, arguments, and insights, but it does complicate them. As the historian Edmund Morgan noted in *American Slavery, American Freedom* (1975), white Americans of the colonial and revolutionary eras possessed a vivid feeling for freedom, liberty, and independence "because they saw every day what life without them could be like."

When we learn about and reflect on historical contexts for American literature, including those that involve race and ethnicity and that lead us to wounding insights like Morgan's, we are not diminishing its value. Rather, we are trying to reach a richer, more complex understanding of it—of its authors, of its texts, and of the history within which American writers have done their work and American readers have responded to it. American literature must be approached with respect and admiration, and also in a critical spirit of inquiry and informed judgment.

I started this Letter by saying that reading and examining American literature can take on something of the nature of a religious quest or mission, and perhaps to some of you this may sound excessive or extreme: Literature, after all, is not the same thing as religion. But many of the writers included in this anthology, from Columbus and the Puritans to Edwards to Emerson, Hawthorne, and Dickinson, are directly or indirectly implicated in religious experience. The best of them, such as Hawthorne and Dickinson, were not only greatly gifted artists, extraordinarily adept in their resourceful uses of language, but were also seekers of truth—about the meaning of freedom, the nature of the self, God, America, history, Nature, the universe. By experiencing, delving into, and contesting the truths they articulate in their writings, we may come closer to discovering our own.

For further study: Sydney E. Ahlstrom, *A Religious History of the American People* (1972); and Peter W. Williams, *America's Religions: From Their Origins to the Twenty-first Century* (2002).

See also these books by Perry Miller: *The New England Mind: The Seventeenth Century* (1939); *The New England Mind: From Colony to Province* (1953); *Errand into the Wilderness* (1956); and *Nature's Nation* (1967).

Also stimulating: Darrett B. Rutman, *American Puritanism: Faith and Practice* (1970); Sacvan Bercovitch, *The Puritan Origins of the American Self* (1976) and *The American Jeremiad* (1978); Stephen Foster, *The Long Argument: English Puritanism and the Shaping of New England Culture, 1570–1700* (1991); and Janice Knight, *Orthodoxies in Massachusetts: Rereading American Puritanism* (1994).

Studies of Native American history include Francis Jennings, *The Invasion of America: Indians, Colonialism, and the Cant of Conquest* (1975); Kirkpatrick Sale, *The Conquest of Paradise: Christopher Columbus and the Columbian Legacy* (1990); Ted Morgan, *Wilderness at Dawn: The Settling of the North American Continent* (1993); Alfred Cave, *The Pequot War* (1996); Jill Lepore, *The Name of War: King Philip's War and the Origins of American Identity* (1998); James D. Drake, *King Philip's War: Civil*

War in New England, 1675–1676 (1999); Karen Ordahl Kupperman, *Indians and English: Facing Off in Early America* (2000); and Mary Beth Norton, *In the Devil's Snare: The Salem Witchcraft Crisis of 1692* (2002).

Surveys include Richard Middleton, *Colonial America: A History, 1607–1760* (1992); Mary Beth Norton, *Founding Mothers and Fathers: Gendered Power and the Forming of American Society* (1996); and Alan Taylor, *American Colonies* (2001).

Christopher Columbus

(1451–1506)

Christopher Columbus—his name in Italian is Cristoforo Colombo, and in Spanish it is Cristóbal Colón—did not "discover" America, but through his four transatlantic voyages (1492–1493, 1493–1496, 1498–1500, and 1502–1504) he inaugurated the era of European exploration, exploitation, and colonization of the Caribbean and of North and South America. Born near Genoa, Italy, Columbus by his early teens was making voyages as a seaman in both the Mediterranean Sea and the Atlantic Ocean. He was drawn all the more to travel and seafaring through the influence of his brother Bartolomeo, who was a mapmaker and a student of geography, and by the family of his wife, the daughter of a Portuguese navigator.

On August 3, 1492, with the support of King Ferdinand and Queen Isabella of Spain, Columbus departed from Palos, in southwestern Spain, on the Santa Maria *(about 90 feet long and 100 tons), with the* Nina *and the* Pinta, *in search of an Atlantic route to Asia. His crew numbered about forty; the other ships had crews of twenty to thirty. As a recent scholar noted, on this journey "there were no priests, no soldiers, and no settlers; this was a voyage of exploration and discovery."*

Columbus reached land on October 12, 1492, setting foot in the Bahamas on an island he called San Salvador and taking possession of its territory and its people. It is unclear today precisely which island it was; Columbus described it as "large and flat, with bright green trees and much water." For the next few months he continued his explorations, claiming other islands, including Cuba and Hispaniola (now Haiti and the Dominican Republic). In March 1493 he returned to Spain, appearing before the King and Queen in Barcelona and displaying to them spices, gold, exotic birds—and human captives. Acclaimed throughout Europe, Columbus now enjoyed the title Admiral of the Open Sea.

Columbus undertook a second voyage in September 1493, sailing with a fleet of seventeen ships and 1,400 colonists, exploring the Caribbean area and finally departing in March 1496 for the two-month journey home. This time, one of his purposes was to bring Christianity to the natives, and one of the consequences of this period of exploration, when laborers were needed for arduous work and settlement, was the institution of slavery.

In May 1498 Columbus set sail from Spain again, but this trip ended badly; he was accused of misrule as governor of Hispaniola and was sent back to Spain in manacles in late 1500. Humiliated, but persistent as ever, Columbus managed to gain royal support for a fourth voyage. After his third voyage, he said of the islands, "I believe that the Earthly Paradise lies here, which no one can enter except by God's leave." He maintained to Ferdinand and Isabella that a river he had found in Trinidad would lead him to the Red Sea and from there to Jerusalem, where he would recover the Holy Sepulchre, in which the body of Jesus lay between his burial and the Resurrection. The fourth voyage began in May 1502 and ended with his return to Spain in November 1504.

Eventually, Columbus's name became synonymous with grand adventure, courage at sea and on uncharted land, and the splendor of the "New World." One account of his life from the first decades of the twentieth century, for example, refers to him as a "man of genius," "a bold, skillful navigator," and a "deeply religious" figure "possessed of personal magnetism" and of "unusual resources and of unflinching determination."

But by 1992, the 500th anniversary of Columbus's first voyage, his name was tarnished as researchers and critics called attention to the ghastly price—massacre, slavery, death by disease—paid by the native people he encountered. The peaceful Taino, for instance, the Arawakan Indians who inhabited the islands of Puerto Rico, Hispaniola, Jamaica, and Cuba, numbered in the millions at the end of the fifteenth century, but as a result of Spanish conquest, cruel enslavement, dislocation, and disease, their population declined to a few thousand by 1520, and by midcentury they barely existed.

Columbus's first name means "bearer of Christ," and to him this gave his quest for a westward route to Asia a divine sanction: He was a man with a mission, "the Enterprise of the Indies," that God had inspired. To the day he died, he believed he had reached the verge of a passageway to the rich and fabled countries of India, Cathay (China), and Cipango (Japan). He never knew where he had been. The name of another Italian navigator, Amerigo Vespucci (1454–1512), a voyager to the Caribbean and along the coast of Brazil, became attached to the continents of the western hemisphere.

The first document below is a letter Columbus wrote to a Spanish merchant and court official; the second, dealing with events of the fourth voyage, he prepared for the Spanish king and queen.

As a good point of departure, consult The Christopher Columbus Encyclopedia, *ed. Silvio A. Bedini (1992). For a provocative range of critical response and interpretation: Claudia L. Bushman,* America Discovers Columbus: How an Italian Explorer Became an American Hero *(1992);* Confronting Columbus: An Anthology, *ed. John Yewell, Chris Dodge, and Jan DeSirey (1992); William D. Phillips Jr. and Carla Rahn Phillips,* The Worlds of Christopher Columbus *(1992); Ilan Stavans,* Imagining Columbus: The Literary Voyage *(1993); and Jonathan Hart,* Columbus, Shakespeare, and the Interpretation of the New World *(2003). See also James Axtell,* After Columbus: Essays in the Ethnohistory of Colonial North America *(1988) and* Beyond 1492: Encounters in Colonial North America *(1992).*

From Letter to Luis de Santangel[1] Regarding the First Voyage

[At sea, February 15, 1493]

Sir,

As I know that you will be pleased at the great victory with which Our Lord has crowned my voyage, I write this to you, from which you will learn how in thirty-three days, I passed from the Canary Islands to the Indies with the fleet which the most illustrious king and queen our sovereigns gave to me. And there I found very many islands filled with people innumerable, and of them all I have taken possession for their highnesses, by proclamation made and with the royal standard unfurled, and no opposition was offered to me. To the first island which I found I gave the name *San Salvador*,[2] in remembrance of the Divine Majesty, Who has marvelously bestowed all this; the Indians call it "Guanahani." To the second I gave the name *Isla de Santa María de Concepción*; to the third, *Fernandina*; to the fourth, *Isabella*[3]; to the fifth, *Isla Juana*,[4] and so to each one I gave a new name.

When I reached Juana I followed its coast to the westward, and I found it to be so extensive that I thought that it must be the mainland, the province of Catayo.[5] And since there were neither towns nor villages on the seashore, but only small hamlets, with the people of which I could not have speech because they all fled immediately, I went forward on the same course, thinking that I should not fail to find great cities and

---

[1]LUIS DE SANTANGEL: Santangel was a former merchant who, as minister of finance for the Spanish Crown, supported Columbus's proposal to King Ferdinand and Queen Isabella and helped finance the first voyage.

[2]SAN SALVADOR: The exact location and identity of this island, located in the Bahamas, is not known for certain.

[3]FERNANDINA; TO THE FOURTH, ISABELLA: Columbus named these islands after his patrons, King Ferdinand of Aragón (1452–1516) and Queen Isabella of Castile (1451–1504), the ruling monarchs of Spain.

[4]ISLA JUANA: Named for Ferdinand and Isabella's daughter, Juana (1479–1555), known as Joanna the Mad, who, after the untimely death of her brother, became heiress to the throne of Castile. The Isla Juana, present day Cuba, is the only island that can be identified for certain in this group Columbus cites.

[5]CATAYO: Also called "Cathay," "Cathayo," and "Cataya." Catayo was the old European name for China.

towns. And at the end of many leagues, seeing that there was no change and that the coast was bearing me northwards, which I wished to avoid since winter was already beginning and I proposed to make from it to the south, and as moreover the wind was carrying me forward, I determined not to wait for a change in the weather and retraced my path as far as a certain harbor known to me. And from that point I sent two men inland to learn if there were a king or great cities. They traveled three days' journey and found an infinity of small hamlets and people without number, but nothing of importance. For this reason they returned.

I understood sufficiently from other Indians, whom I had already taken, that this land was nothing but an island. And therefore I followed its coast eastwards for one hundred and seven leagues to the point where it ended. And from that cape I saw another island distant eighteen leagues from the former, to the east, to which I at once gave the name "Española.[6]" And I went there and followed its northern coast, as I had in the case of Juana, to the eastward for one hundred and eighty-eight great leagues in a straight line. This island and all the others are very fertile to a limitless degree, and this island is extremely so. In it there are many harbors on the coast of the sea, beyond comparison with others which I know in Christendom, and many rivers, good and large, which is marvelous. Its lands are high, and there are in it very many sierras and very lofty mountains, beyond comparison with the island of Tenerife.[7] All are most beautiful, of a thousand shapes, and all are accessible and filled with trees of a thousand kinds and tall, and they seem to touch the sky. And I am told that they never lose their foliage, as I can understand, for I saw them as green and as lovely as they are in Spain in May, and some of them were flowering, some bearing fruit, and some in another stage, according to their nature. And the nightingale was singing and other birds of a thousand kinds in the month of November there where I went. There are six or eight kinds of palm, which are a wonder to behold on account of their beautiful variety, but so are the other trees and fruits and plants. In it are marvelous pine groves, and there are very large tracts of cultivatable lands, and there is honey, and there are birds of many kinds and fruits in great diversity. In the interior are mines of metals, and the population is without number. Española is a marvel.

[1493]

[6]ESPAÑOLA: The island of Hispaniola, which today comprises Haiti and the Dominican Republic.
[7]TENERIFE: The largest of the Canary Islands.

From Letter to Ferdinand and Isabella Regarding the Fourth Voyage

[Jamaica, July 7, 1503]

Of Española,[1] Paria,[2] and the other lands, I never think without weeping. I believed that their example would have been to the profit of others; on the contrary, they are in an exhausted state; although they are not dead, the infirmity is incurable or very extensive; let him who brought them to this state come now with the remedy if he can or if he knows it; in destruction, everyone is an adept. It was always the custom to give thanks and promotion to him who imperiled his person. It is not just that he who has been so hostile to this undertaking should enjoy its fruits or that his children should. Those who left the Indies, flying from toils and speaking evil of the matter and of me, have returned with official employment.[3] So it has now been ordained in the case of Veragua.[4] It is an ill example and without profit for the business and for justice in the world.

The fear of this, with other sufficient reasons, which I saw clearly, led me to pray your highnesses before I went to discover these islands and Terra Firma, that you would leave them to me to govern in your royal name. It pleased you; it was a privilege and agreement, and under seal and oath, and you granted me the title of viceroy and admiral and governor general of all. And you fixed the boundary, a hundred leagues beyond the Azores and the Cape Verde Islands, by a line passing from pole to pole, and you gave me wide power over this and over all that I might further discover. The document states this very fully.

The other most important matter, which calls aloud for redress, remains inexplicable to this moment. Seven years I was at your royal court, where all to whom this undertaking was mentioned, unanimously declared it to be a delusion. Now all, down to the very tailors, seek permission to make discoveries. It can be believed that they go forth to plunder, and it is granted to them to do so, so that they greatly prejudice my

[1]ESPAÑOLA: The island of Hispaniola, which today comprises Haiti and the Dominican Republic. The letter, written in Jamaica, was carried by Diego Mendez, who accompanied Columbus on his fourth voyage aboard the *Santiago de Paulos* (more commonly known as the *Bermuda*).
[2]PARIA: The mainland region of modern Venezuela, near the island of Trinidad.
[3]OFFICIAL EMPLOYMENT: Columbus refers to enemies he has in the Spanish court; their identities are uncertain.
[4]VERAGUA: Modern Panama, where Columbus was shipwrecked earlier on his fourth voyage.

honor and do very great damage to the enterprise. It is well to give to God that which is His due and to Caesar that which belongs to him. This is a just sentiment and based on justice.

The lands which here obey Your Highnesses are more extensive and richer than all other Christian lands. After I, by the divine will, had placed them under your royal and exalted lordship, and was on the point of securing a very great revenue, suddenly, while I was waiting for ships to come to your high presence with victory and with great news of gold, being very secure and joyful, I was made a prisoner and with my two brothers was thrown into a ship, laden with fetters, stripped to the skin, very ill-treated, and without being tried or condemned. Who will believe that a poor foreigner could in such a place rise against Your Highnesses, without cause, and without the support of some other prince, and being alone among your vassals and natural subjects, and having all my children at your royal court?

I came to serve at the age of twenty-eight years, and now I have not a hair on my body that is not gray, and my body is infirm, and whatever remained to me from those years of service has been spent and taken away from me and sold, and from my brothers, down to my very coat, without my being heard or seen, to my great dishonor. It must be believed that this was not done by your royal command. The restitution of my honor, the reparation of my losses, and the punishment of him who did this, will spread abroad the fame of your royal nobility. The same punishment is due to him who robbed me of the pearls, and to him who infringed my rights as admiral.[5] Very great will be your merit, fame without parallel will be yours, if you do this, and there will remain in Spain a glorious memory of Your Highnesses, as grateful and just princes.

The pure devotion which I have ever borne to the service of Your Highnesses, and the unmerited wrong that I have suffered, will not permit me to remain silent, although I would fain do so; I pray Your Highnesses to pardon me. I am so ruined as I have said; hitherto I have wept for others; now, Heaven have mercy upon me, and may the earth weep for me. Of worldly goods, I have not even a blanca[6] for an offering in spiritual things. Here in the Indies I have become careless of the

---

[5]INFRINGED MY RIGHTS AS ADMIRAL: Columbus refers to Alonso de Ojeda (c. 1466–1508), who accompanied Columbus on his second voyage and was one of the first conquistadores. As a former member of Columbus's crew, Ojeda had access to the reports sent back to the Crown, some of which described the plentiful pearls found in Paria (Venezuela). Contrary to royal promises made to Columbus, Ojeda was granted license to explore this area with the understanding that he would share his profits with the Crown. He collected a considerable quantity of pearls in Paria before sailing to Española.

[6]BLANCA: A small Spanish coin of little value.

prescribed forms of religion. Alone in my trouble, sick, in daily expectation of death, and encompassed about by a million savages, full of cruelty and our foes, and so separated from the holy Sacraments of Holy Church, my soul will be forgotten if it here leaves my body. Weep for me, whoever has charity, truth, and justice.

I did not sail upon this voyage to gain honor or wealth; this is certain, for already all hope of that was dead. I came to Your Highnesses with true devotion and with ready zeal, and I do not lie. I humbly pray Your Highnesses that if it please God to bring me forth from this place, that you will be pleased to permit me to go to Rome and to other places of pilgrimage. May the Holy Trinity preserve your life and high estate, and grant you increase of prosperity.

Done in the Indies in the island of Jamaica, on the seventh of July, in the year one thousand five hundred and three.

[1505]

Bartolomé de las Casas

(1484–1566)

Bartolomé de las Casas, a priest, a Dominican missionary, and a prolific early Spanish historian, was a student of Latin and theology in Seville, Spain, when the news arrived in 1493 of Christopher Columbus's successful first voyage. A little more than a decade later, Casas took part in a journey to and exploration of Hispaniola (that is, Haiti and the Dominican Republic). But once he became a priest, probably in 1510, Casas increasingly came to regret his own moral blindness, and he called for an end to brutal exploitation and enslavement of the native peoples. The Spanish government named him "Protector of the Indians" and, in 1520–1522, he undertook a project off the coast of Venezuela to establish a model "town of free Indians." This venture, however, proved a failure, as Spain in the first decades of the sixteenth century extended its range of conquest and harsh rule.

Through appeal and negotiation, Casas did manage to gain support for reforms from the Pope and Charles V, Holy Roman Emperor and King of Spain. But these were nearly impossible to implement and sustain, and Charles V later revoked key laws and provisions on behalf of Indian peoples that Casas had argued for.

Below, is an excerpt from The Devastation of the Indies: A Brief Account *(1542–1546, published 1552), in which Casas describes horrible tortures imposed by the Spanish on the natives they encountered in Hispaniola.*

For biography and context, consult the following titles by Lewis Hanke: Bartolomé de las Casas: An Interpretation of His Life and Writings *(1951);* Bartolomé de las Casas: Bookman, Scholar, and Propagandist *(1952); and* Bartolomé de las Casas, Historian: An Essay in Spanish Historiography *(1952). See also Henry Raup Wagner and Helen Rand Parish,* The Life and Writings of Bartolomé de las Casas *(1967);* Bartolomé de las Casas in History: Toward an Understanding of the Man and His Work, *ed. Juan Friede and Benjamin Keen (1971);* Western Expansion and Indigenous Peoples: The Heritage of Las Casas, *ed. Elias Sevilla-Casas (1977); and Gustavo Gutiérrez,* Las Casas: In Search of the Poor of Jesus Christ, *trans. Robert R. Barr (1993).*

From The Devastation of the Indies: Hispaniola

This was the first land in the New World to be destroyed and depopulated by the Christians, and here they began their subjection of the women and children, taking them away from the Indians to use them and ill use them, eating the food they provided with their sweat and toil. The Spaniards did not content themselves with what the Indians gave them of their own free will, according to their ability, which was always too little to satisfy enormous appetites, for a Christian eats and consumes in one day an amount of food that would suffice to feed three houses inhabited by ten Indians for one month. And they committed other acts of force and violence and oppression which made the Indians realize that these men had not come from Heaven.[1] And some of the Indians concealed their foods while others concealed their wives and children and still others fled to the mountains to avoid the terrible transactions of the Christians.

And the Christians attacked them with buffets and beatings, until finally they laid hands on the nobles of the villages. Then they behaved with such temerity and shamelessness that the most powerful ruler of the islands had to see his own wife raped by a Christian officer.

From that time onward the Indians began to seek ways to throw the Christians out of their lands. They took up arms, but their weapons were very weak and of little service in offense and still less in defense. (Because of this, the wars of the Indians against each other are little more than games played by children.) And the Christians, with their horses and swords and pikes began to carry out massacres and strange cruelties against them. They attacked the towns and spared neither the children nor the aged nor pregnant women nor women in childbed, not only stabbing them and dismembering them but cutting them to pieces as if dealing with sheep in the slaughter house. They laid bets as to who, with one stroke of the sword, could split a man in two or could cut off his head or spill out his entrails with a single stroke of the pike. They took infants from their mothers' breasts, snatching them by the legs and pitching them headfirst against the crags or snatched them by the arms and threw them into the rivers, roaring with laughter and saying as the babies fell into the water, "Boil there, you offspring of the devil!" Other infants they put to the sword along with their mothers and anyone else who happened to be nearby. They made some low wide gallows on which the hanged victim's feet almost touched the ground, stringing up their victims in lots of thirteen, in memory of Our Redeemer and His twelve Apostles,[2] then set burning wood at their feet and thus burned them alive. To others they

---

[1]INDIANS REALIZE THAT THESE MEN HAD NOT COME FROM HEAVEN: Reports from early European voyagers relate that many native peoples believed the European sailors to be gods.
[2]THIRTEEN, IN MEMORY OF OUR REDEEMER AND HIS TWELVE APOSTLES: A reference to Jesus Christ and his twelve disciples.

attached straw or wrapped their whole bodies in straw and set them afire. With still others, all those they wanted to capture alive, they cut off their hands and hung them round the victim's neck, saying, "Go now, carry the message," meaning, Take the news to the Indians who have fled to the mountains. They usually dealt with the chieftains and nobles in the following way: they made a grid of rods which they placed on forked sticks, then lashed the victims to the grid and lighted a smoldering fire underneath, so that little by little, as those captives screamed in despair and torment, their souls would leave them.

I once saw this, when there were four or five nobles lashed on grids and burning; I seem even to recall that there were two or three pairs of grids where others were burning, and because they uttered such loud screams that they disturbed the captain's sleep, he ordered them to be strangled. And the constable, who was worse than an executioner, did not want to obey that order (and I know the name of that constable and know his relatives in Seville), but instead put a stick over the victims' tongues, so they could not make a sound, and he stirred up the fire, but not too much, so that they roasted slowly, as he liked. I saw all these things I have described, and countless others.

And because all the people who could do so fled to the mountains to escape these inhuman, ruthless, and ferocious acts, the Spanish captains, enemies of the human race, pursued them with the fierce dogs they kept which attacked the Indians, tearing them to pieces and devouring them. And because on few and far between occasions, the Indians justifiably killed some Christians, the Spaniards made a rule among themselves that for every Christian slain by the Indians, they would slay a hundred Indians.

[1542–1546, pub. 1552]

Iroquois Creation Story

Iroquois *is the name given to a member of the Iroquois Confederacy, a group of North American Indian tribes that speak a language—Cayuga, Cherokee, Huron, Mohawk, Oneida, Onondaga, Seneca, or Tuscarora—of the Iroquois family. The name itself ("rattlesnake") is not native to these people; it was bestowed upon them by rival tribes and by the French. They termed themselves* Haudenosaunee, *"the people of the long house," a reference to their favored dwelling, made of elm bark and 20 feet wide and from 50 to 200 feet long.*

The Iroquois lived in territories in what is now southern Canada, the upper Midwest, New York State, and Pennsylvania. According to the scholar Lee Sultzman:

> At its maximum in 1680, their empire extended west from the north shore of Chesapeake Bay through Kentucky to the junction of the Ohio and Mississippi Rivers; then north following the Illinois River to the south end of Lake Michigan; east across all of lower Michigan, southern Ontario and adjacent parts of southwestern Quebec; and finally south through northern New England west of the Connecticut River through the Hudson and upper Delaware Valleys across Pennsylvania back to the Chesapeake.

Iroquois men were hunters, fishers, traders, and farmers, and groups of women assisted them in agriculture. They lived in villages of several hundred persons, within a complex social organization (kinship was identified through the women, who also were the owners of property) that included the family/household, clans, half-tribes, tribes or nations, and the confederacy.

At some point in the sixteenth century the Iroquois Confederacy (or League of the Iroquois) was formed, bringing together tribes that had been engaged in war with one another. The structure they established called for representation, deliberation, and voting in order to reach a decision. Sultzman, like some other scholars, claims that "Europeans learned from the Iroquois, and the League, with its elaborate system of checks, balances, and supreme law, almost certainly influenced the American Articles of Confederation and Constitution." But while this view is intriguing, most researchers have rejected it.

Each Iroquois village had a council, and each drew upon a cosmology keyed to the myth of "a woman who fell from the sky." Iroquois men were brave, fierce warriors, and anthropologists have commented on the elements of cruelty, aggression, and violence in their beliefs and stories. They tortured enemies and practiced ritual cannibalism.

The Iroquois were powerful, yet their population was fairly small; in 1600, they numbered about 20,000, and this figure was cut in half by mid-century as a result of warfare and disease. The population recovered later in the century, but by the late eighteenth century, after the Iroquois's disastrous alliance with the British during the Revolutionary War, it had declined again to about 8,000.

There are many versions of the Iroquois creation story. The one given below was taken down by David Cusick in the late 1820s.

Two books by Daniel K. Richter are illuminating: The Ordeal of the Longhouse: The Peoples of the Iroquois League in the Era of European Colonization (1992) and Facing East from Indian Country: A Native History of Early America (2001). See also Extending the Rafters: Interdisciplinary Approaches to Iroquoian Studies, ed. Michael K. Foster, Jack Campisi, and Marianne Mithun (1984); and Beyond the Covenant Chain: The Iroquois and Their Neighbors in Indian North America, 1600–1800, ed. Daniel K. Richter and James H. Merrell (1987). For further reflections: Edmund Wilson, Apologies to the Iroquois, and Joseph Mitchell, The Mohawks in High Steel, published together, with a new introduction by William N. Fenton (1992).

A Tale of the Foundation of the Great Island, now North America:—The two Infants born, and the Creation of the Universe.

Among the ancients there were two worlds in existence. The lower world was in a great darkness; the possession of the great monster[1]; but the upper world was inhabited by mankind[2]; and there was a woman conceived[3] and would have the twin born. When her travail[4] drew near, and her situation seemed to produce a great distress on her mind, and she was induced by some of her relatives to lay herself on a mattress which was prepared, so as to gain refreshments to her wearied body; but while she was asleep the very place sunk down towards the dark

---

[1]GREAT MONSTER: Undefined creature that is not human.
[2]MANKIND: The sky people; humans possessing powers different from those of "real people" (see note 10).
[3]A WOMAN CONCEIVED: In most versions of this Iroquios creation tale, the woman in the story is of the second generation of sky women who become pregnant without sexual intercourse.
[4]TRAVAIL: Labor of childbirth.

world. The monsters[5] of the great water were alarmed at her appearance of descending to the lower world; in consequence, all the species of the creatures were immediately collected into where it was expected she would fall. When the monsters were assembled, and they made consultation, one of them was appointed in haste to search the great deep, in order to procure some earth, if it could be obtained; accordingly the monster descends, which succeeds, and returns to the place. Another requisition was presented, who would be capable to secure the woman from the terrors of the great water, but none was able to comply except a large turtle came forward and made proposal to them to endure her lasting weight, which was accepted. The woman was yet descending from a great distance. The turtle executes upon the spot, and a small quantity of earth was varnished on the back part of the turtle. The woman alights on the seat prepared, and she receives a satisfaction.[6] While holding her, the turtle increased every moment, and become a considerable island of earth, and apparently covered with small bushes. The woman remained in a state of unlimited darkness, and she was overtaken by her travail to which she was subject. While she was in the limits of distress one of the infants was moved by an evil opinion,[7] and he was determined to pass out under the side of the parent's arm, and the other infant in vain endeavored to prevent his design. The woman was in a painful condition during the time of their disputes, and the infants entered the dark world by compulsion, and their parent expired in a few moments. They had the power of sustenance without a nurse, and remained in the dark regions. After a time the turtle increased to a great Island, and the infants were grown up, and one of them possessed with a gentle disposition and named Enigorio,[8] i.e., the good mind. The other youth possessed an insolence of character, and was named Enigonhahetgea,[9] i.e., the bad mind. The good mind was not contented to remain in a dark situation, and he was anxious to create a great light in the dark world; but the bad mind was desirous that the world should remain in a natural

---

[5]MONSTERS: In other versions of this story, the monsters are identifiable animals.

[6]RECEIVES A SATISFACTION: She lands safely on the turtle's back.

[7]ONE OF THE INFANTS WAS MOVED BY AN EVIL OPINION…THE OTHER INFANT IN VAIN ENDEAVORED TO PREVENT HIS DESIGN: The woman is carrying twins, who are rivals representing good and evil. The evil twin decides not to be born naturally but to burst through his mother's side, killing her. The good twin vainly tries to prevent this. Thus, good and evil are born into the world.

[8]ENIGORIO: The good twin is also called Tharonhiawagon, meaning "sky grasper," "creator," or "upholder of heavens." Enigorio comes from a translation of the Tuscarora word for "good-minded" into Mohawk.

[9]ENIGONHAHETGEA: The evil twin is also called Tawiscaron, meaning "evil-minded," "patron of winter," "flint," or "ice." Enigonhahetgea comes from a translation of the Tuscarora word for "bad-minded" into Seneca or Onondaga.

state. The good mind determined to prosecute his designs, and therefore commences the work of creation. At first he took the parent's head,
(the deceased) of which he created an orb, and established it in the center of the firmament, and it became of a very superior nature to bestow
light to the new world, (now the sun) and again he took the remnant
of the body, and formed another orb, which was inferior to the light, (now
the moon.) In the orb a cloud of legs appeared to prove it was the body
of the good mind, (parent.) The former was to give light to the day, and
the latter to the night; and he also created numerous spots of light, (now
stars;) these were to regulate the days, nights, seasons, years, etc.
Whenever the light extended to the dark world the monsters were displeased and immediately concealed themselves in the deep places, lest
they should be discovered by some human beings. The good mind continued the works of creation, and he formed numerous creeks and rivers
on the Great Island, and then created numerous species of animals of
the smallest and greatest, to inhabit the forests, and fish of all kinds to
inhabit the waters. When he had made the universe he was in doubt
respecting some being to possess the Great Island; and he formed two
images of the dust of the ground in his own likeness, male and female,
and by his breathing into their nostrils he gave them the living souls, and
named them Ea-gwe-howe,[10] i.e., a real people; and he gave the Great
Island, all the animals of game for their maintenance; and he appointed
thunder to water the earth by frequent rains, agreeable to the nature of
the system; after this the Island became fruitful, and vegetation afforded
the animals subsistence. The bad mind, while his brother was making the
universe, went throughout the Island and made numerous high mountains and falls of water, and great steeps, and also creates various reptiles
which would be injurious to mankind; but the good mind restored the
Island to its former condition. The bad mind proceeded further in his
motives, and he made two images of clay in the form of mankind: but
while he was giving them existence they became apes; and when he had
not the power to create mankind he was envious against his brother;
and again he made two of clay. The good mind discovered his brother's
contrivances, and aided in giving them living souls. (It is said these had
the most knowledge of good and evil.) The good mind now accomplishes
the works of creation, notwithstanding the imaginations of the bad mind
were continually evil; and he attempted to enclose all the animals of game
in the earth, so as to deprive them from mankind; but the good mind

[10]EA-GWE-HOWE: Humans, who are earthly dwellers different from the sky people. Translated, it
means "real people," referring to the Native Americans themselves.

released them from confinement, (the animals were dispersed, and traces of them were made on the rocks near the cave where it was closed.) The good mind experiences that his brother was at variance with the works of creation, and feels not disposed to favor any of his proceedings, but gives admonitions of his future state. Afterwards the good mind requested his brother to accompany him, as he was proposed to inspect the game, etc., but when a short distance from their nominal residence, the bad mind became so unmanly that he could not conduct his brother any more.[11] The bad mind offered a challenge to his brother and resolved that who gains the victory should govern the universe; and appointed a day to meet the contest. The good mind was willing to submit to the offer, and he enters the reconciliation with his brother; which he falsely mentions that by whipping with flags would destroy his temporal life[12]; and he earnestly solicits his brother also to notice the instrument of death, which he manifestly relates by the use of deer horns, beating his body he would expire. On the day appointed the engagement commenced, which lasted for two days; after pulling up the trees and mountains as the track of a terrible whirlwind, at last the good mind gains the victory by using the horns, as mentioned the instrument of death, which he succeeded in deceiving his brother, and he crushed him in the earth; and the last words uttered from the bad mind were, that he would have equal power over the souls of mankind after death; and he sinks down to eternal doom, and became the Evil Spirit. After this tumult the good mind repaired to the battle ground, and then visited the people and retires from the earth.

[11]CONDUCT HIS BROTHER ANYMORE: The good twin can no longer manage his brother.
[12]DESTROY HIS TEMPORAL LIFE: The good twin falsely tells his brother that he can be killed by being beaten with rushes or reeds. The evil twin admits he can be killed by being beaten with antlers. Their temporal—or earthly—lives are distinguished from their spiritual ones.

John Smith

(1580–1631)

The explorer and colonizer John Smith, born in Lincolnshire, England, the son of a yeoman farmer, began his military career as a teenage soldier in armies on the European continent. Captured and enslaved while waging war against the Turks, he managed to kill his master and escape, traveling in eastern Europe and then to the northern coast of Africa.

When Smith was in his early twenties, the Virginia Company gave him an appointment as a captain in the garrison being readied for the Company's settlement in North America. Smith and the other settlers reached Jamestown, Virginia, in April 1607 and, according to legend, during one their explorations Smith was saved from execution at the hands of Indians by Pocahontas, the chief's twelve-year-old daughter.

Conditions for the settlers were harsh in the extreme; of the hundred people who arrived, only about forty were left six months later when the first supply ship arrived. In 1608 Smith was named president of the colony's council and he led the remaining settlers with a firm hand. Whenever negotiations failed, he also waged campaigns against the Indian tribes nearby.

Returning to England in October 1609, Smith made another voyage to North America in 1614, this time exploring the northern coast, the area of "New" England, as he termed it. His Description of New England *(1616), excerpted here, helped spark an interest in colonization that was taken up by William Bradford and the Pilgrims, who established Plymouth in 1620–1621, and John Winthrop and the Puritans, who settled in the Boston area over the same period. A prolific writer, publicist, and propagandist for North American settlement, Smith celebrates in the passages below the bounty that is in store for those who make the arduous trip across the Atlantic Ocean to the new world.*

Smith was disillusioned by his experiences in Jamestown, where the community suffered from mismanagement and dissension, as he indicated in A True Relation…in Virginia *(1608). In the New England areas, he hoped British colonists would create communities of craftsmen, farmers, and fishermen. In Smith's literary and historical writing, as the scholar Raymond F. Dolle remarked:*

> The dream of golden plunder by aristocratic European treasure-hunters gives way to a plan of social development by free, industrious colonists. For Smith, the New World is a place where the poor could earn a new social position by exploiting the natural riches and where heroic, self-made men could establish a new, more democratic society.

For biography and context: Bradford Smith, Captain John Smith: His Life and Legend *(1953); Everett H. Emerson,* Captain John Smith *(1971); A. T. Vaughan,* American Genesis: Captain John Smith and the Founding of Virginia *(1975); and J. A. Leo Lemay,* The American Dream of Captain John Smith *(1991).*

From A Description of New-England, by Captaine John Smith

Who can desire more content, that hath small meanes; or but only his merit to advance his fortune, then to tread, and plant that ground hee hath purchased by the hazard of his life? If he have but the taste of virtue, and magnanimitie,[1] what to such a minde can bee more pleasant, then planting and building a foundation for his Posteritie, gotte from the rude earth, by Gods blessing and his owne industrie, without prejudice[2] to any? If hee have any graine of faith or zeale in Religion, what can hee doe lesse hurtfull to any; or more agreeable to God, then to seeke to convert those poore Salvages to know Christ, and humanitie, whose labors with discretion will triple requite thy charge and paines? What so truely sutes with honour and honestie, as the discovering things unknowne? erecting Townes, peopling Countries, informing the ignorant, reforming things unjust, teaching virtue; and gaine to our Native mother-countrie[3] a kingdom to attend her; finde imployment for those that are idle, because they know not what to doe: so farre from wronging any, as to cause Posteritie to remember thee; and remembring thee, ever honour that remembrance with praise? Consider: What were the beginnings and endings of the Monarkies of the Chaldeans, the Syrians, the Grecians, and Romanes,[4] but this one rule; What was it they would not doe, for the good of the commonwealth, or their Mother-citie? For example: Rome, What made her such a Monarchesse, but onely the adventures of her youth, not in riots at home; but in dangers abroad? and the justice and

---

[1]MAGNANIMITIE: Magnanimity; nobility or generosity of spirit.
[2]PREJUDICE: Injury, harm, or damage.
[3]NATIVE MOTHER-COUNTRIE: England.
[4]MONARKIES OF THE CHALDEANS, THE SYRIANS, THE GRECIANS, AND ROMANES: Smith refers to four ancient civilizations, which he calls monarchies. The Chaldeans were a people of the southern portion of Babylonia, or lower Mesopotamia; the Syrians lived in an area northeast of Phoenicia that extended beyond the Euphrates and the Tigris rivers; the Greeks and Romans were those of the ancient world.

judgement out of their experience, when they grewe aged. What was their ruine and hurt, but this; The excesse of idlenesse, the fondnesse of Parents, the want of experience in Magistrates, the admiration of their undeserved honours, the contempt of true merit, their unjust jealosies, their politicke incredulities, their hypocriticall seeming goodnesse, and their deeds of secret lewdnesse? finally, in fine, growing onely formall temporists, all that their predecessors got in many years, they lost in few daies. Those by their pains and vertues became Lords of the world; they by their ease and vices became slaves to their servants. This is the difference betwixt the use of Armes in the field, and on the monuments of stones; the golden age and the leaden age, prosperity and miserie, justice and corruption, substance and shadowes, words and deeds, experience and imagination, making Commonwealths and marring Commonwealths, the fruits of vertue and the conclusions of vice.

...

For Gentlemen, what exercise should more delight them, then ranging dayly those unknowne parts, using fowling and fishing, for hunting and hauking? and yet you shall see the wilde haukes give you some pleasure, in seeing them stoope[5] (six or seaven after one another) an houre or two together, at the skuls[6] of fish in the faire harbours, as those ashore at a foule[7]; and never trouble nor torment your selves, with watching, mewing, feeding, and attending them: nor kill horse and man without running and crying, See you not a hauk?[8] For hunting also: the woods, lakes, and rivers, affoord not onely chase sufficient, for any that delights in that kinde of toyle, or pleasure; but such beasts to hunt, that besides the delicacy of their bodies for food, their skins are so rich, as may well recompence thy dayly labour, with a Captains pay.

For labourers, if those that sowe hemp, rape[9], turnups, parsnips, carrats, cabidge, and such like; give 20, 30, 40, 50 shillings yearely for an acre of ground, and meat drinke and wages to use it, and yet grow rich: when better, or at least as good ground, may be had and cost nothing but labour; it seemes strange to me, any such should there grow poore.

...

My purpose is not to perswade children from their parents; men from their wives; nor servants from their masters: onely, such as with

---

[5]STOOPE: Swoop down.
[6]SKULS: A skull is a large, shallow, oval or circular basket used to hold fish. Smith could be referring to the large quantities of fish in the harbor or to actual schools of fish.
[7]FOULE: Fowl.
[8]HAUK: Hawk. Smith contrasts the wild hawks of America with the hawks kept by falconers in England.
[9]RAPE: The rape plant, wild turnip, or field mustard.

free consent may be spared: But that each parish, or village, in Citie, or Countrey, that will but apparell their fatherlesse children, of thirteene or fourteene years of age, or young married people, that have small wealth to live on; heere by their labour may live exceeding well: provided alwaies that first there bee a sufficient power to command them, houses to receive them, meanes to defend them, and meet provisions for them; for, any place may bee overlain[10]: and it is most necessarie to have a fortresse (ere this grow to practice) and sufficient masters (as, Carpenters, Masons, Fishers, Fowlers, Gardiners, Husbandmen,[11] Sawyers,[12] Smiths, Spinsters,[13] Taylors, Weavers, and such like) to take ten, twelve, or twentie, or as ther is occasion, for Apprentises. The Masters by this may quicklie growe rich; these may learne their trades themselves, to doe the like; to a generall and an incredible benefit, for King, and Countrey, Master, and Servant.

[1616]

---

[10]OVERLAIN: Overcome.
[11]HUSBANDMEN: Farmers.
[12]SAWYERS: Workmen who saw timber.
[13]SPINSTERS: Women who spin wool or flax for making cloth.

William Bradford

(1590–1657)

The colonial governor and historian William Bradford was born in Austerfield in South Yorkshire, England, the son of a farmer, and he was largely self-educated. With other Separatist church members, Bradford moved in 1608–1609 to Amsterdam and then to Leyden, Holland, where this radical branch of Christians could practiced their faith relatively free from persecution. In 1620, about 100 church members journeyed across the Atlantic aboard the Mayflower *(90 feet long and 26 feet across at its widest), sailing off the coast of Cape Cod, Massachusetts, when stormy seas prevented them from reaching Virginia.*

After the male settlers signed the Mayflower Compact (establishing civil government, rule of law, and government by mutual consent) and elected John Carver governor, the passengers made their settlement in Plymouth. The devout, dedicated, resolute Bradford, whose wife in December 1620 had fallen from the Mayflower *and drowned, was elected governor in April 1621, a position he held (except for several years when he was an assistant) for more than three decades.*

Bradford's major work is Of Plimoth *[hereafter* Plymouth, *the modern spelling]* Plantation, *which he began writing in 1630. In the first part he describes the motives, goals, and challenges of these Christian voyagers to North America—Bradford named them "Pilgrims"—and he concludes with an account of the construction of the first house in Plymouth. In the mid-1640s, when the colony was undergoing a difficult period of backsliding and division, Bradford resumed his history, taking it up to the year 1646. As literary historian William J. Scheick has observed, "sadly intimating Bradford's despair over his sense of the colony's religious and social decline, the history ends in silence, with merely two dates listed without any commentary." It is unclear whether Bradford intended the work for publication; while widely read in manuscript, it did not appear in print until 1856. His later work includes poems and religious dialogues staged as discussions between older and younger colonists.*

Of Plymouth Plantation *is written in the third person in a plain, serious, and occasionally pungent style that shows the influence of the Geneva Bible (1560), the version (with annotations in the margins) favored by the Puritans. Drawing on Scriptural examples and parallels, Bradford praises the providence of God for leading the Pilgrims to their home in the New World.*

For further study: Bradford Smith, Bradford of Plymouth *(1951); Perry D. Westbrook,* William Bradford *(1978); and Douglas Anderson,* William Bradford's Books: Of Plimoth Plantation and the Printed Word *(2003).*

From *Of Plymouth Plantaion*

BOOK I, CHAPTER IX. OF THEIR VOYAGE, AND HOW THEY PASSED THE SEA; AND OF THEIR SAFE ARRIVAL AT CAPE COD

September 6.[1] These troubles being blown over,[2] and now all being compact together in one ship, they put to sea again with a prosperous wind, which continued divers days together, which was some encouragement unto them; yet, according to the usual manner, many were afflicted with seasickness. And I may not omit here a special work of God's providence. There was a proud and very profane young man, one of the seamen, of a lusty, able body, which made him the more haughty; he would always be contemning the poor people in their sickness and cursing them daily with grievous execrations; and did not let to tell them that he hoped to help to cast half of them overboard before they came to their journey's end, and to make merry with what they had; and if he were by any gently reproved, he would curse and swear most bitterly. But it pleased God before they came half seas over, to smite this young man with a grievous disease, of which he died in a desperate manner, and so was himself the first that was thrown overboard. Thus his curses light on his own head, and it was an astonishment to all his fellows for they noted it to be the just hand of God upon him.

After they had enjoyed fair winds and weather for a season, they were encountered many times with cross winds and met with many fierce storms with which the ship was shroudly[3] shaken, and her upper works

---

[1]SEPTEMBER 6: Julius Caesar established a solar calendar in 45 BCE with three common years containing 365 days and one year (leap year) containing 366 days every fourth year. The first day of the year, in accordance with Roman tradition, was March 25, the vernal equinox. March was considered the first month of the year (which explains why the names for September, October, November, and December correspond with the Latin roots for seven, eight, nine, and ten.) This calendar is referred to as the Julian or Old Style (O.S.) calendar. The calendar, however, was not completely accurate. In 1582, Pope Gregory XIII ordered ten days to be dropped from October, thus restoring the vernal equinox at least to an average of the 20th of March. Thus, October 4, 1582, was followed by October 15, 1582. The new calendar was adopted in Roman Catholic countries (most of Europe), but Protestant England (and, by extension, its American colonies) refused to make the switch, resulting in a ten-day gap. The Gregorian calendar wasn't adopted in England until 1752. Thus, by our modern calendar, Bradford would have written this letter on September 16, 1620.

[2]THESE TROUBLES BEING BLOWN OVER: Bradford refers to troubles experienced that August aboard the companion vessel to the *Mayflower*, the *Speedwell*, which proved unseaworthy, necessitating a transfer of everything and everyone to the *Mayflower*.

[3]SHROUDLY: Severely or sharply.

made very leaky; and one of the main beams in the midships was bowed and cracked, which put them in some fear that the ship could not be able to perform the voyage. So some of the chief of the company, perceiving the mariners to fear the sufficiency of the ship as appeared by their mutterings, they entered into serious consultation with the master and other officers of the ship, to consider in time of the danger, and rather to return than to cast themselves into a desperate and inevitable peril. And truly there was great distraction and difference of opinion amongst the mariners themselves; fain would they do what could be done for their wages' sake (being now near half the seas over) and on the other hand they were loath to hazard their lives too desperately. But in examining of all opinions, the master and others affirmed they knew the ship to be strong and firm under water; and for the buckling of the main beam, there was a great iron screw the passengers brought out of Holland, which would raise the beam into its place; the which being done, the carpenter and master affirmed that with a post put under it, set firm in the lower deck and otherways bound, he would make it sufficient. And as for the decks and upper works, they would caulk them as well as they could, and though with the working of the ship they would not long keep staunch,[4] yet there would otherwise be no great danger, if they did not overpress her with sails. So they committed themselves to the will of God and resolved to proceed.

In sundry of these storms the winds were so fierce and the seas so high, as they could not bear a knot of sail,[5] but were forced to hull[6] for divers[7] days together. And in one of them, as they thus lay at hull in a mighty storm, a lusty young man called John Howland, coming upon some occasion above the gratings was, with a seele[8] of the ship, thrown into sea; but it pleased God that he caught hold of the topsail halyards[9] which hung overboard and ran out at length. Yet he held his hold (though he was sundry fathoms under water) till he was hauled up by the same rope to the brim of the water, and then with a boat hook and other means got into the ship again and his life saved. And though he was something ill with it, yet he lived many years after and became a profitable member both in church and commonwealth. In all this voyage there died but

[4]STAUNCH: Watertight, dry.
[5]KNOT OF SAIL: The square footage of sail needed to increase the ship's speed by one nautical mile per hour.
[6]FORCED TO HULL: Drift or sail with only a short sail.
[7]DIVERS: Several to many.
[8]SEELE: Grate covering a hatch or vent on deck.
[9]HALYARDS: A rope used for raising or lowering a sail or flag.

one of the passengers, which was William Butten, a youth, servant to Samuel Fuller, when they drew near the coast.

But to omit other things (that I may be brief) after long beating at sea they fell with that land which is called Cape Cod; the which being made and certainly known to be it, they were not a little joyful. After some deliberation had amongst themselves and with the master of the ship, they tacked about and resolved to stand for the southward (the wind and weather being fair) to find some place about Hudson's River for their habitation. But after they had sailed that course about half the day, they fell amongst dangerous shoals and roaring breakers, and they were so far entangled therewith as they conceived themselves in great danger; and the wind shrinking upon them withal, they resolved to bear up again for the Cape and thought themselves happy to get out of those dangers before night overtook them, as by God's good providence they did. And the next day they got into the Cape Harbor[10] where they rid in safety.

A word or two by the way of this cape. It was thus first named by Captain Gosnold and his company, Anno[11] 1602, and after by Captain Smith was called Cape James; but it retains the former name amongst seamen. Also, that point which first showed those dangerous shoals unto them they called Point Care and Tucker's Terror; but the French and Dutch to this day call it Malabar by reason of those perilous shoals and the losses they have suffered there.

Being thus arrived in a good harbor, and brought safe to land, they fell upon their knees and blessed the God of Heaven who had brought them over the vast and furious ocean, and delivered them from all the perils and miseries thereof, again to set their feet on the firm and stable earth, their proper element. And no marvel if they were thus joyful, seeing wise Seneca[12]a was so affected with sailing a few miles on the coast of his own Italy, as he affirmed, that he had rather remain twenty years on his way by land than pass by sea to any place in a short time, so tedious and dreadful was the same unto him.

But here I cannot but stay and make a pause, and stand half amazed at this poor people's present condition; and so I think will the reader, too, when he well considers the same. Being thus passed the vast ocean, and a sea of troubles before in their preparation (as may be remembered by

---

[10]CAPE HARBOR: Provincetown Harbor.
[11]ANNO: In the year. (Latin)
[12]SENECA: Bradford references the *Moral Epistles to Lucilius*, Epistle 53, by Lucius Annaeus Seneca, also known as Seneca the Younger (c. 3 BCE–65CE), a Roman philosopher, statesman, and writer. His works include a satire, philosophical essays, letters dealing with moral issues, and ten tragedies. His plays strongly influenced Renaissance tragic drama, especially the literature of Elizabethan England.

that which went before), they had now no friends to welcome them nor inns to entertain or refresh their weatherbeaten bodies; no houses or much less towns to repair to, to seek for succour. It is recorded in Scripture as a mercy to the Apostle and his shipwrecked company,[13] that the barbarians showed them no small kindness in refreshing them, but these savage barbarians, when they met with them (as after will appear) were readier to fill their sides full of arrows than otherwise. And for the season it was winter, and they that know the winters of that country know them to be sharp and violent, and subject to cruel and fierce storms, dangerous to travel to known places, much more to search an unknown coast. Besides, what could they see but a hideous and desolate wilderness, full of wild beasts and wild men—and what multitudes there might be of them they knew not. Neither could they, as it were, go up to the top of Pisgah[14] to view from this wilderness a more goodly country to feed their hopes, for which way soever they turned their eyes (save upward to the heavens) they could have little solace or content in respect of any outward objects. For summer being done, all things stand upon them with a weather-beaten face, and the whole country, full of woods and thickets, represented a wild and savage hue. If they looked behind them, there was the mighty ocean which they had passed and was now as a main bar and gulf to separate them from all the civil parts of the world. If it be said they had a ship to succour them, it is true; but what heard they daily from the master and company? But that with speed they should look out a place (with their shallop[15]) where they would be, at some near distance; for the season was such as he would not stir from thence till a safe harbor was discovered by them, where they would be, and he might go without danger; and that victuals consumed apace but he must and would keep sufficient for themselves and their return. Yea, it was muttered by some that if they got not a place in time, they would turn them and their goods ashore and leave them. Let it also be considered what weak hopes of supply and succour they left behind them, that might bear up their minds in this sad condition and trials they were under; and they could not but be very small. It is true, indeed, the affections and love of their brethren at

---

[13]IT IS RECORDED IN SCRIPTURE AS A MERCY TO THE APOSTLE AND HIS SHIPWRECKED COMPANY: The Apostle Paul. A reference to Acts 28:1–2: "And when they were escaped, then they knew that the island was called Malta. And the barbarous people showed us no little kindness, for they kindled a fire, and received us every one, because of the present rain, and because of the cold."
[14]PISGAH: The mountain east of the Jordan River from which Moses viewed the promised land (Deuteronomy 34:1–4).
[15]SHALLOP: A small boat, with oars or a sail, used in shallow waters as a means of transportation from a larger vessel; a dinghy.

Leyden[16] was cordial and entire towards them, but they had little power to help them or themselves; and how the case stood between them and the merchants at their coming away hath already been declared.

What could now sustain them but the Spirit of God and His grace? May not and ought not the children of these fathers rightly say: "Our fathers were Englishmen which came over this great ocean, and were ready to perish in this wilderness; but they cried unto the Lord, and He heard their voice and looked on their adversity,"[17] etc. "Let them therefore praise the Lord, because He is good: and His mercies endure forever." "Yea, let them which have been redeemed of the Lord, shew how He hath delivered them from the hand of the oppressor. When they wandered in the desert wilderness out of the way, and found no city to dwell in, both hungry and thirsty, their soul was overwhelmed in them. Let them confess before the Lord His loving kindness and His wonderful works before the sons of men."[18]

[1630–1650]

BOOK I, CHAPTER X. SHOWING HOW THEY SOUGHT OUT A PLACE OF HABITATION; AND WHAT BEFELL THEM THEREABOUT

Being thus arrived at Cape Cod the 11th of November, and necessity calling them to look out a place for habitation (as well as the master's and mariners' importunity); they having brought a large shallop[1] with them out of England, stowed in quarters in the ship, they now got her out and set their carpenters to work to trim her up; but being much bruised

---

[16]LEYDEN: Leyden, the Netherlands, where a number of the English Separatists remained, having settled there around 1609.
[17]THE HEARD THEIR VOICE AND LOOKED ON THEIR ADVERSITY: A reference to Deuteronomy 26:6–8: "And when we cried unto the Lord God of our fathers, the Lord heard our voice, and looked on our affliction, and our labor and our oppression." Also a reference to Psalm 107 (see note 18).
[18]LET THEM THEREFORE PRAISE THE LORD, BECAUSE HE IS GOOD...HIS WONDERFUL WORKS BEFORE THE SONS OF MEN: A reference to Psalm 107:1–8, "O give thanks to the Lord, for he is good; for his steadfast love endures forever / Let the redeemed of the Lord say so, those he redeemed from the hand of the enemy / And gathered in from the lands, from the east and from the west, from the north and from the south. / Some wandered in desert wastes, finding no way to an inhabited town / hungry and thirsty, their soul fainted within them / Then they cried to the Lord in their trouble, and he delivered them from their distress / He led them by a straight way, until they reached an inhabited town. / Let them thank the LORD for his steadfast love, for his wonderful works to humankind."
[1]SHALLOP: A small boat, with oars or a sail, used in shallow waters as a means of transportation from a larger vessel; a dinghy.

and shattered in the ship with foul weather, they saw she would be long in mending. Whereupon a few of them tendered themselves to go by land and discover those nearest places, whilst the shallop was in mending; and the rather because as they went into that harbor there seemed to be an opening some two or three leagues off, which the master judged to be a river.[2] It was conceived there might be some danger in the attempt, yet seeing them resolute, they were permitted to go, being sixteen of them well armed under the conduct of Captain Standish,[3] having such instructions given them as was thought meet.

They set forth the 15th of November; and when they had marched about the space of a mile by the seaside, they espied five or six persons with a dog coming towards them, who were savages; but they fled from them and ran up into the woods, and the English followed them, partly to see if they could speak with them, and partly to discover if there might not be more of them lying in ambush. But the Indians seeing themselves thus followed, they again forsook the woods and ran away on the sands as hard as they could, so as they could not come near them but followed them by the track of their feet sundry miles and saw that they had come the same way. So, night coming on, they made their rendezvous and set out their sentinels, and rested in quiet that night; and the next morning followed their track till they had headed a great creek and so left the sands, and turned another way into the woods. But they still followed them by guess, hoping to find their dwellings; but they soon lost both them and themselves, falling into such thickets as were ready to tear their clothes and armor in pieces; but were most distressed for want of drink. But at length they found water and refreshed themselves, being the first New England water they drunk of, and was now in great thirst as pleasant unto them as wine or beer had been in foretimes.

Afterwards they directed their course to come to the other shore, for they knew it was a neck of land they were to cross over, and so at length got to the seaside and marched to this supposed river, and by the way found a pond[4] of clear fresh water, and shortly after a good quantity of

---

[2]WHICH THE MASTER JUDGED TO BE A RIVER: Samuel Eliot Morison (1887–1976), a naval officer and history professor of Harvard University, noted of this observation, "Looking south from Provincetown Harbor where the Pilgrims were, the high land near Plymouth looks like an island on clear days, suggesting that there is a river or arm of the sea between it and Cape Cod."

[3]CAPTAIN STANDISH: Myles Standish (1584–1656) a professional soldier from Lancashire, England. Although not a Separatist, he was chosen to be the military leader of the Plymouth Colony.

[4]FOUND A POND: Near Truro, Massachusetts.

clear ground where the Indians had formerly set corn, and some of their graves. And proceeding further they saw new stubble where corn had been set the same year; also they found where lately a house had been, where some planks and a great kettle was remaining, and heaps of sand newly paddled with their hands. Which, they digging up, found in them divers fair Indian baskets filled with corn, and some in ears, fair and good, of divers colors, which seemed to them a very goodly sight (having never seen any such before). This was near the place of that supposed river they came to seek, unto which they went and found it to open itself into two arms with a high cliff of sand in the entrance but more like to be creeks of salt water than any fresh, for aught they saw; and that there was good harborage for their shallop, leaving it further to be discovered by their shallop, when she was ready. So, their time limited them being expired, they returned to the ship lest they should be in fear of their safety; and took with them part of the corn and buried up the rest. And so, like the men from Eshcol, carried with them of the fruits of the land and showed their brethren[5]; of which, and their return, they were marvelously glad and their hearts encouraged.

After this, the shallop being got ready, they set out again for the better discovery of this place, and the master of the ship desired to go himself. So there went some thirty men but found it to be no harbor for ships but only for boats. There was also found two of their houses covered with mats, and sundry of their implements in them, but the people were run away and could not be seen. Also there was found more of their corn and of their beans of various colors; the corn and beans they brought away, purposing to give them full satisfaction when they should meet with any of them as, about some six months afterward they did, to their good content.

And here is to be noted a special providence of God, and a great mercy to this poor people, that here they got seed to plant them corn the next year, or else they might have starved, for they had none nor any likelihood to get any till the season had been past, as the sequel did manifest. Neither is it likely they had had this, if the first voyage had not been made, for the ground was now all covered with snow and hard frozen; but the Lord is never wanting unto His in their greatest needs; let His holy name have all the praise.

[5]ESHCOL, CARRIED WITH THEM OF THE FRUITS OF THE LAND AND SHOWED THEIR BRETHREN: A reference to Numbers 13:23–26: "And they came unto the brook of Eshcol, and cut down from thence a branch with one cluster of grapes, and they bare it between two upon a staff; and they brought of the pomegranates, and of the figs.... And they went and came to Moses, and to Aaron, and to all the congregation of the children of Israel, unto the wilderness of Paran, to Kadesh; and brought back word unto them, and unto all the congregation, and showed them the fruit of the land."

The month of November being spent in these affairs, and much foul weather falling in, the 6th of December they sent out their shallop again with ten of their principal men and some seamen, upon further discovery, intending to circulate that deep bay of Cape Cod. The weather was very cold and it froze so hard as the spray of the sea lighting on their coats, they were as if they had been glazed. Yet that night betimes they got down into the bottom of the bay, and as they drew near the shore[6] they saw some ten or twelve Indians very busy about something. They landed about a league or two from them, and had much ado to put ashore anywhere—it lay so full of flats. Being landed, it grew late and they made themselves a barricado with logs and boughs as well as they could in the time, and set out their sentinel and betook them to rest, and saw the smoke of the fire the savages made that night. When morning was come they divided their company, some to coast along the shore in the boat, and the rest marched through the woods to see the land, if any fit place might be for their dwelling. They came also to the place where they saw the Indians the night before, and found they had been cutting up a great fish like a grampus,[7] being some two inches thick of fat like a hog, some pieces whereof they had left by the way. And the shallop found two more of these fishes dead on the sands, a thing usual after storms in that place, by reason of the great flats of sand that lie off.

So they ranged up and down all that day, but found no people, nor any place they liked. When the sun grew low, they hasted out of the woods to meet with their shallop, to whom they made signs to come to them into a creek[8] hard by, the which they did at high water; of which they were very glad, for they had not seen each other all that day since the morning. So they made them a barricado as usually they did every night, with logs, stakes and thick pine boughs, the height of a man, leaving it open to leeward,[9] partly to shelter them from the cold and wind (making their fire in the middle and lying round about it) and partly to defend them from any sudden assaults of the savages, if they should surround them; so being very weary, they betook them to rest. But about midnight they heard a hideous and great cry, and their sentinel called "Arm! arm!" So they bestirred them and stood to their arms and shot off a couple of muskets, and then the noise ceased. They concluded it was

[6]AS THEY DREW NEAR THE SHORE: Near Eastham, Massachusetts.
[7]GRAMPUS: Probably a pilot whale (Globicephalus). Grampus was a popular name for various delphinoid cetaceans with high dorsal fins and rounded heads.
[8]INTO A CREEK: Probably the mouth of the Herring River in Eastham, Massachusetts.
[9]LEEWARD: The side turned away from the wind.

a company of wolves or such like wild beasts, for one of the seamen told them he had often heard such a noise in Newfoundland.

So they rested till about five of the clock in the morning; for the tide, and their purpose to go from thence, made them be stirring betimes. So after prayer they prepared for breakfast, and it being day dawning it was thought best to be carrying things down to the boat. But some said it was not best to carry the arms down, others said they would be the readier, for they had lapped them up in their coats from the dew; but some three or four would not carry theirs till they went themselves. Yet as it fell out, the water being not high enough, they laid them down on the bank side and came up to breakfast.

But presently, all on the sudden, they heard a great and strange cry, which they knew to be the same voices they heard in the night, though they varied their notes; and one of their company being abroad came running in and cried, "Men, Indians! Indians!" And withal, their arrows came flying amongst them. Their men ran with all speed to recover their arms, as by the good providence of God they did. In the meantime, of those that were there ready, two muskets were discharged at them, and two more stood ready in the entrance of their rendezvous but were commanded not to shoot till they could take full aim at them. And the other two charged again with all speed, for there were only four had arms there, and defended the barricado, which was first assaulted. The cry of the Indians was dreadful, especially when they saw the men run out of the rendezvous toward the shallop to recover their arms, the Indians wheeling about upon them. But some running out with coats of mail on, and cutlasses in their hands, they soon got their arms and let fly amongst them and quickly stopped their violence. Yet there was a lusty man, and no less valiant, stood behind a tree within half a musket shot, and let his arrows fly at them; he was seen [to] shoot three arrows, which were all avoided. He stood three shots of a musket, till one taking full aim at him and made the bark or splinters of the tree fly about his ears, after which he gave an extraordinary shriek and away they went, all of them. They[10] left some to keep the shallop and followed them about a quarter of a mile and shouted once or twice, and shot off two or three pieces, and so returned. This they did that they might conceive that they were not afraid of them or any way discouraged.

Thus it pleased God to vanquish their enemies and give them deliverance; and by His special providence so to dispose that not any one of

[10]THEY: That is, the English settlers.

them were either hurt or hit, though their arrows came close by them and on every side [of] them; and sundry of their coats, which hung up in the barricado, were shot through and through. Afterwards they gave God solemn thanks and praise for their deliverance, and gathered up a bundle of their arrows and sent them into England afterward by the master of the ship, and called that place the First Encounter.

From hence they departed and coasted all along but discerned no place likely for harbor; and therefore hasted to a place that their pilot (one Mr. Coppin who had been in the country before) did assure them was a good harbor, which he had been in, and they might fetch it before night; of which they were glad for it began to be foul weather.

After some hours' sailing it began to snow and rain, and about the middle of the afternoon the wind increased and the sea became very rough, and they broke their rudder, and it was as much as two men could do to steer her with a couple of oars. But their pilot bade them be of good cheer for he saw the harbor; but the storm increasing, and night drawing on, they bore what sail they could to get in, while they could see. But herewith they broke their mast in three pieces and their sail fell overboard in a very grown sea, so as they had like to have been cast away. Yet by God's mercy they recovered themselves, and having the flood with them,[11] struck into the harbor. But when it came to, the pilot was deceived in the place, and said the Lord be merciful unto them for his eyes never saw that place before; and he and the master's mate would have run her ashore in a cove full of breakers before the wind. But a lusty seaman which steered bade those which rowed, if they were men, about with her or else they were all cast away; the which they did with speed. So he bid them be of good cheer and row lustily, for there was a fair sound before them, and he doubted not but they should find one place or other where they might ride in safety. And though it was very dark and rained sore, yet in the end they got under the lee of a small island and remained there all that night in safety. But they knew not this to be an island till morning, but were divided in their minds; some would keep the boat for fear they might be amongst the Indians, others were so wet and cold they could not endure but got ashore, and with much ado got fire (all things being so wet); and the rest were glad to come to them, for after midnight, the wind shifted to the northwest and it froze hard.

But though this had been a day and night of much trouble and danger unto them, yet God gave them a morning of comfort and refreshing (as usually He doth to His children) for the next day was a fair, sunshining

---

[11]HAVING THE FLOOD WITH THEM: Flood tide; the rising or inflowing tide.

day, and they found themselves to be on an island secure from the Indians, where they might dry their stuff, fix their pieces[12] and rest themselves; and gave God thanks for His mercies in their manifold deliverances. And this being the last day of the week, they prepared there to keep the Sabbath.

On Monday they sounded[13] the harbor and found it fit for shipping, and marched into the land and found divers cornfields and little running brooks, a place (as they supposed) fit for situation.[14] At least it was the best they could find, and the season and their present necessity made them glad to accept of it. So they returned to their ship again with this news to the rest of their people, which did much comfort their hearts.

On the 15th of December they weighed anchor to go to the place they had discovered, and came within two leagues of it, but were fain to bear up again; but the 16th day, the wind came fair, and they arrived safe in this harbor. And afterwards took better view of the place, and resolved where to pitch their dwelling; and the 25th day began to erect the first house for common use to receive them and their goods.

[1630–1650]

Book II, Chapter XI. Anno Domini 1620: The Mayflower Compact

I shall a little return back, and begin with a combination[1] made by them before they came ashore; being the first foundation of their government in this place. Occasioned partly by the discontented and mutinous speeches that some of the strangers[2] amongst them had let fall from them in the ship: That when they came ashore they would use their own liberty, for none had power to command them, the patent they had being for Virginia and not for New England, which belonged to another government, with which the Virginia Company had nothing to do.[3] And partly that such an act by them done, this their condition considered, might be as firm as any patent,[4] and in some respects more sure.

---

[12]PIECES: Weaponry.
[13]SOUNDED: Measured the depth of the harbor.
[14]FIT FOR SITUATION: Suitable to set up a camp.
[1]COMBINATION: Union, association.
[2]STRANGERS: The passengers aboard the *Mayflower* were either Separatists (more commonly known as Pilgrims), who sought a life in the New World for religious reasons, or commercial adventurers seeking to forward business interests; they were called Strangers by the Separatists.
[3]WITH WHICH THE VIRGINIA COMPANY HAD NOTHING TO DO: The Strangers argue that they are out of the jurisdiction of the Virginia Company's charter and therefore at liberty to do as they will.
[4]PATENT: Official legal document, often awarded by a sovereign granting privileges or rights to those individuals named in it.

The form was as followeth

IN THE NAME OF GOD, AMEN.

We whose names are underwritten, the loyal subjects of our
dread Sovereign Lord King James,[5] by the Grace of God of Great
Britain, France, and Ireland King, Defender of the Faith, etc.
Having undertaken, for the Glory of God and advancement of
the Christian Faith and Honour of our King and Country, a
Voyage to plant the First Colony in the Northern Parts of Virginia,
do by these presents solemnly and mutually in the presence of God
and one of another, Covenant and Combine ourselves together into
a Civil Body Politic, for our better ordering and preservation and
furtherance of the ends aforesaid; and by virtue hereof to enact,
constitute and frame such just and equal Laws, Ordinances, Acts,
Constitutions and Offices, from time to time, as shall be thought
most meet and convenient for the general good of the Colony, unto
which we promise all due submission and obedience. In witness
whereof we have hereunder subscribed our names at Cape Cod,
the 11th of November, in the year of the reign of our Sovereign
Lord King James, of England, France and Ireland the eighteenth,
and of Scotland the fifty-fourth. Anno Domini[6] 1620.

After this they chose, or rather confirmed, Mr. John Carver[7] (a man
godly and well approved amongst them) their Governor for that year. And
after they had provided a place for their goods, or common store (which
were long in unlading[8] for want of boats, foulness of the winter weather
and sickness of divers[9]) and begun some small cottages for their habitation; as time would admit, they met and consulted of laws and orders,
both for their civil and military government as the necessity of their
condition did require, still adding thereunto as urgent occasion in several
times, and as cases did require.

In these hard and difficult beginnings they found some discontents and
murmurings arise amongst some, and mutinous speeches and carriages in
other; but they were soon quelled and overcome by the wisdom, patience,

---

[5]LORD KING JAMES: King James I of England (1566–1625), also James VI of Scotland. While the
Pilgrims wished for religious freedom and separation from the Church of England, they still wished to
be associated with the English body politic. By professing their loyalty to the English throne, they can
later claim protection or military aid from England should the need arise.
[6]ANNO DOMINI: In the year of the Lord. (Latin)
[7]JOHN CARVER: An original member (1575–1621) of the group of Separatists who first went to
Leyden, the Netherlands. He chartered the *Mayflower* for the voyage to the New World. Bradford
became governor after Carver's death, only five months after the Mayflower Compact was written.
[8]UNLADING: Unloading.
[9]DIVERS: Several to many.

and just and equal carriage of things, by the Governor and better part, which clave[10] faithfully together in the main.

[1630–1650]

BOOK II, CHAPTER XII. ANNO DOMINI 1621: FIRST THANKSGIVING

They began now to gather in the small harvest they had, and to fit up their houses and dwellings against winter, being all well recovered in health and strength and had all things in good plenty. For as some were thus employed in affairs abroad, others were exercised in fishing, about cod and bass and other fish, of which they took good store, of which every family had their portion. All the summer there was no want[1]; and now began to come in store of fowl, as winter approached, of which this place did abound when they came first (but afterward decreased by degrees). And besides waterfowl there was great store of wild turkeys, of which they took many, besides venison, etc. Besides they had about a peck a meal[2] a week to a person, or now since harvest, Indian corn to that proportion. Which made many afterwards write so largely of their plenty here to their friends in England, which were not feigned but true reports.

[1630–1650]

---

[10]CLAVE: The past tense of *cleave*; joined together or attached.
[1]NO WANT: Bradford relates that the Pilgrims had enjoyed a season of plenty, during which no one went hungry.
[2]PECK A MEAL: A peck is a unit of dry measure about the fourth part of a bushel, or two gallons. Meal is coarse flour or grain.

John Winthrop

(1588–1649)

Born a member of a privileged family and a graduate (after private tutoring) of Trinity College, Cambridge, John Winthrop, having been elected governor of the Massachusetts Bay Company, arrived aboard the Arbella *at Salem, Massachusetts, about 14 miles northeast of Boston, in June 1630. Four ships made the voyage, carrying about 700 passengers who soon relocated to Boston Harbor and areas nearby. Winthrop served as governor or deputy governor for nearly two decades and was regarded as the chief authority and leading citizen of the colony. The colonial historian and minister Cotton Mather honored him as "the Father of New England."*

Winthrop was a church reformer but, unlike William Bradford and the Pilgrim settlers at Plymouth, he was not a Separatist; he believed the English church could be reformed from within and cleansed of its "Catholic" doctrinal traces and elements of ritual. An eloquent witness for his faith, Winthrop described the model Christian commonwealth as a shining city on a hill, a conception of national mission that has inspired America's writers as well as its politicians and statesmen. Winthrop was not, however, a proponent of democracy. As one scholar noted, he envisioned a "benevolent despotism" in which upper-class leadership directed the people below.

Winthrop's important Journal *was published in two volumes as the* History of New England, 1630–49, *in 1825–1826. His best-known work,* A Model of Christian Charity, *below, was first published in 1838. Probably written during the journey across the ocean and delivered as a lay sermon, it identified the purpose of the colony and the duties and responsibilities of its residents. A figure of imposing integrity and resolve, Winthrop called for discipline and order undertaken in service to God. The most difficult period of his governorship took place during the Antinomian controversy of 1637, when he faced in Anne Hutchinson and her fellow "heretics" a gathering of the faithful who focused on the inner light, the presence of the spirit within, and who thereby challenged the primacy of Puritan ministers. Hutchinson was brought to trial and excommunicated; sentenced to exile, she fled to Rhode Island. The crisis, for Winthrop and his associates, dramatized the problem of dissent and the grave dangers they believed it posed to religious and civil authority. In its aftermath, Winthrop presented an argument in favor of limiting immigration to those who accepted Puritan orthodoxy.*

For biography and background: Edmund S. Morgan, The Puritan Dilemma: The Story of John Winthrop *(1958); Darrett B. Rutman,* Winthrop's Boston: Portrait of a Puritan Town, 1630–1649 *(1965); James G. Moseley,* John Winthrop's World: History as a Story, the Story as History *(1992); and Francis J. Bremer,* John Winthrop: America's Forgotten Founding Father *(2003). See also Edmund S. Morgan, "John*

Winthrop's 'Modell of Christian Charity' in a Wider Context,"
Huntington Library Quarterly *50 (Winter 1987): 145–151.*

A Model of Christian Charity

I

A MODEL HEREOF

God Almighty in His most holy and wise providence, hath so disposed of the condition of mankind, as in all times some must be rich, some poor, some high and eminent in power and dignity; others mean and in subjection.

THE REASON HEREOF

First, to hold conformity with the rest of His works, being delighted to show forth the glory of His wisdom in the variety and difference of the creatures; and the glory of His power, in ordering all these differences for the preservation and good of the whole; and the glory of His greatness, that as it is the glory of princes to have many officers, so this great King will have many stewards, counting Himself more honored in dispensing His gifts to man by man, than if He did it by His own immediate hands.

Secondly, that He might have the more occasion to manifest the work of His Spirit: first upon the wicked in moderating and restraining them, so that the rich and mighty should not eat up the poor, nor the poor and despised rise up against their superiors and shake off their yoke; secondly in the regenerate, in exercising His graces, in them, as in the great ones, their love, mercy, gentleness, temperance, etc., in the poor and inferior sort, their faith, patience, obedience, etc.

Thirdly, that every man might have need of other, and from hence they might be all knit more nearly together in the bonds of brotherly affection. From hence it appears plainly that no man is made more honorable than another or more wealthy, etc., out of any particular and singular respect to himself, but for the glory of his Creator and the common good of the creature, man. Therefore God still reserves the property of these gifts to Himself as [in] Ezekiel: 16.17. He there calls wealth His gold and His silver.[1] [In] Proverbs: 3.9, he claims their service as His

---

[1]HE THERE CALLS WEALTH HIS GOLD AND HIS SILVER: Ezekiel 16:17: "Thou has also taken thy fair jewels of my gold and of my silver, which I had given thee, and made to thyself images of men, and didst commit whoredom with them."

due[2]: honor the Lord with thy riches, etc. All men being thus (by divine providence) ranked into two sorts, rich and poor; under the first are comprehended all such as are able to live comfortably by their own means duly improved; and all others are poor according to the former distribution.

There are two rules whereby we are to walk one towards another: justice and mercy. These are always distinguished in their act and in their object, yet may they both concur in the same subject in each respect; as sometimes there may be an occasion of showing mercy to a rich man in some sudden danger of distress, and also doing of mere justice to a poor man in regard of some particular contract, etc.

There is likewise a double law by which we are regulated in our conversation one towards another in both the former respects: the law of nature and the law of grace, or the moral law or the law of the Gospel, to omit the rule of justice as not properly belonging to this purpose otherwise than it may fall into consideration in some particular cases. By the first of these laws man as he was enabled so withal [is] commanded to love his neighbor as himself.[3] Upon this ground stands all the precepts of the moral law, which concerns our dealings with men. To apply this to the works of mercy, this law requires two things: first, that every man afford his help to another in every want or distress; secondly, that he performed this out of the same affection which makes him careful of his own goods, according to that of our Savior. Matthew: "Whatsoever ye would that men should do to you."[4] This was practiced by Abraham and Lot in entertaining the Angels[5] and the old man of Gibeah.

The law of grace or the Gospel hath some difference from the former, as in these respects: First, the law of nature was given to man in the estate of innocency; this of the Gospel in the estate of regeneracy.[6] Secondly, the former propounds one man to another, as the same flesh

---

[2]HE CLAIMS THEIR SERVICE AS HIS DUE: Proverbs 3:9: "Honor the Lord with thy substance, and with the first fruits of all thine increase."
[3]HIS NEIGHBOR AS HIMSELF: Matthew 19:19: "Thou shalt love thy neighbor as thyself"; and 5:43: "Ye have heard that it hath been said, Thou shalt love thy neighbor, and hate thine enemy."
[4]WHATSOEVER YE WOULD THAT MEN SHOULD DO TO YOU: Matthew 7:12: "Therefore all things whatsoever ye would that men should do to you, do ye even so to them: for this is the law and the prophets."
[5]PRACTICED BY ABRAHAM AND LOT IN ENTERTAINING THE ANGELS: In Genesis 18, Abraham entertains angels: "And he lift up his eyes and looked, and, lo, three men stood by him: and when he saw them, he ran to meet them from the tent door, and bowed himself toward the ground." In Genesis 19, Lot, Abraham's nephew and a citizen of the ill-fated city of Sodom, also entertains two angels and protects them from an angry mob: "And there came two angels to Sodom at even; and Lot sat in the gate of Sodom: and Lot seeing them rose up to meet them; and he bowed himself with his face toward the ground." In Judges 19, an old man of Gibeah offers shelter to a traveling stranger.
[6]ESTATE OF REGENERACY: When Adam and Eve were expelled from the Garden of Eden for their sin, they entered an unregenerate state. Christ offered salvation from Adam and Eve's sin and, hence, a state of regeneration or of being reborn.

and image of God; this is a brother in Christ also, and in the communion of the same spirit and so teacheth us to put a difference between Christians and others. *Do good to all, especially to the household of faith*: Upon this ground the Israelites were to put a difference between the brethren of such as were strangers though not of Canaanites.[7] Thirdly, the law of nature could give no rules for dealing with enemies, for all are to be considered as friends in the state of innocency, but the Gospel commands love to an enemy. Proof. If thine Enemy hunger, feed him; Love your Enemies, do good to them that hate you. Matthew: 5.44.[8]

This law of the Gospel propounds likewise a difference of seasons and occasions. There is a time when a Christian must sell all and give to the poor, as they did in the Apostles' times.[9] There is a time also when a Christian (though they give not all yet) must give beyond their ability, as they of Macedonia,[10] Corinthians: 2.8. Likewise community of perils calls for extraordinary liberality, and so doth community in some special service for the Church. Lastly, when there is no other means whereby our Christian brother may be relieved in his distress, we must help him beyond our ability, rather than tempt God in putting him upon help by miraculous or extraordinary means.

This duty of mercy is exercised in the kinds,[11] *giving, lending* and *forgiving.—*

Quest. What rule shall a man observe in giving in respect of the measure?

Ans. If the time and occasion be ordinary, he is to give out of his abundance. Let him lay aside as God hath blessed him. If the time and occasion be extraordinary, he must be ruled by them; taking this withal, that then a man cannot likely do too much, especially if he may leave himself and his family under probable means of comfortable subsistence.

Objection. A man must lay up for posterity, the fathers lay up for posterity and children and he "is worse than an infidel" that "provideth not for his own."

---

[7]CANAANITES: People of the land of Canaan, the Israelites' Promised Land.
[8]IF THINE ENEMY HUNGER, FEED HIM...: Matthew 5:44: "But I say unto you, Love your enemies, bless them that curse you, do good to them that hate you, and pray for them which despitefully use you, and persecute you."
[9]APOSTLES' TIMES: A reference to Luke 18:22, in which Jesus answers the question of a rich man as to how to gain the kingdom of heaven: "...sell all that thou hast, and distribute unto the poor, and thou shalt have treasure in heaven: and come, follow me."
[10]MUST GIVE BEYOND THEIR ABILTY AS THEY OF MACEDONIA: The entire reference from 2 Corinthians 8:1–2 reads: "Moreover, brethren, we do you to wit of the grace of God bestowed on the churches of Macedonia; How that in a great trial of affliction, the abundance of their joy and their deep poverty abounded unto the riches of their liberality."
[11]KINDS: Qualities or characteristics.

Ans. For the first, it is plain that it being spoken by way of comparison, it must be meant of the ordinary and usual course of fathers and cannot extend to times and occasions extraordinary. For the other place, the Apostle[12] speaks against such as walked inordinately, and it is without question, that he is worse than an infidel who through his own sloth and voluptuousness shall neglect to provide for his family.

Objection. "The wise man's eyes are in his head" saith Solomon,[13] "and foreseeth the plague;" therefore we must forecast and lay up against evil times when he or his may stand in need of all he can gather.

Ans. This very argument Solomon useth to persuade to liberality, Ecclesiastes: "Cast thy bread upon the waters,"[14] and "for thou knowest not what evil may come upon the land." Luke: 16.9. "Make you friends of the riches of iniquity."[15] You will ask how this shall be? very well. For first he that gives to the poor, lends to the Lord and He will repay him even in this life an hundred fold to him or his—The righteous is ever merciful and lendeth and his seed enjoyeth the blessing; and besides we know what advantage it will be to us in the day of account when many such witnesses shall stand forth for us to witness the improvement of our talent.[16] And I would know of those who plead so much for laying up for time to come, whether they hold that to be Gospel, Matthew: 6.19: "Lay not up for yourselves treasures upon earth,"[17] etc. If they acknowledge it, what extent will they allow it? if only to those primitive times, let them consider the reason whereupon our Savior grounds it. The first is that they are subject to the moth, the rust, the thief. Secondly, they will steal away the heart; where

---

[12]THE APOSTLE: The apostle St. Paul.

[13]THE WISE MAN'S EYES ARE IN HIS HEAD, SAITH SOLOMON: Solomon (c. 950 BCE), the king of Israel and the son of King David and Bathsheba, was known for his extraordinary wisdom. His reign is described in 1 Kings 1–11 and 2 Chronicles 1–10. Winthrop references Ecclesiastes 2:14: "The wise man's eyes are in his head; but the fool walketh in darkness: and I myself perceived also that one event happeneth to them all."

[14]CAST THY BREAD UPON THE WATERS: Ecclesiastes 11:1–2: "Cast thy bread upon the waters: for thou shalt find it after many days. / Give a portion to seven, and also to eight; for thou knowest not what evil shall be upon the earth."

[15]MAKE YOU FRIENDS OF THE RICHES OF INIQUITY: Winthrop references the story in Luke 16:9–10 in which a servant, removed from managing his master's property, cuts the bills of his master's debtors in half. Instead of being upset, his master praises the servant for his shrewdness. "And I say unto you, Make to yourselves friends of the mammon of unrighteousness; that, when ye fail, they may receive you into everlasting habitations. / He that is faithful in that which is least is faithful also in much: and he that is unjust in the least is unjust also in much."

[16]THE IMPROVEMENT OF OUR TALENT: Wealth, riches, abundance. See Matthew 25:14–30.

[17]LAY NOT UP FOR YOURSELVES TREASURES UPON EARTH: Matthew 6:19–21: "Lay not up for yourselves treasures upon earth, where moth and rust doth corrupt, and where thieves break through and steal: / But lay up for yourselves treasures in heaven, where neither moth nor rust doth corrupt, and where thieves do not break through nor steal: / For where your treasure is, there will your heart be also."

the treasure is there will the heart be also. The reasons are of like force at all times. Therefore the exhortation must be general and perpetual, with always in respect of the love and affection to riches and in regard of the things themselves when any special service for the church or particular distress of our brother do call for the use of them; otherwise it is not only lawful but necessary to lay up as Joseph[18] did to have ready upon such occasions, as the Lord (whose stewards we are of them) shall call for them from us. Christ gives us an instance of the first, when he sent his disciples for the ass, and bids them answer the owner thus, the Lord hath need of him.[19] So when the tabernacle was to be built he sends to His people to call for their silver and gold, etc.; and yields them no other reason but that it was for His work. When Elisha comes to the widow of Sareptah[20] and finds her preparing to make ready her pittance for herself and family, He bids her first provide for Him; he challengeth first God's part which she must first give before she must serve her own family. All these teach us that the Lord looks that when He is pleased to call for His right in anything we have, our own interest we have must stand aside till His turn be served. For the other, we need look no further than to that of John: 1: "He who hath this world's goods and seeth his brother to need and shuts up his compassion from him, how dwelleth the love of God in him," which comes punctually to this conclusion: if thy brother be in want and thou canst help him, thou needst not make doubt, what thou shouldst do, if thou lovest God thou must help him.

Quest. What rule must we observe in lending?

Ans. Thou must observe whether thy brother hath present or probable, or possible means of repaying thee, if there be none of these, thou must give him according to his necessity, rather than lend him as he requires. If he hath present means of repaying thee, thou art to look at

---

[18]JOSEPH: Described in the book of Genesis, Joseph was the eleventh and favorite son of Jacob. He was sold into slavery in Egypt by his jealous brothers, but through wisdom and fortitude rose from slavery to a high office in Pharaoh's court, with the responsibility of distributing grain supplies during a time of famine, which he foresaw in a dream. When his brothers come to Egypt to escape the famine, he reveals himself as their brother, forgives them, and welcomes them.

[19]THE LORD HATH NEED OF HIM: A reference to Matthew 21:2–3, "[He said] unto them, Go into the village over against you, and straightway ye shall find an ass tied, and a colt with her: loose them, and bring them unto me. / And if any man say ought unto you, ye shall say, The Lord hath need of them; and straightway he will send them."

[20]WHEN ELISHA COMES TO THE WIDOW OF SAREPTAH: A reference to the story of Elisha and the widow in Sareptah in 1 Kings 17:8–24, in which Elisha asks a poor widow to make him a cake. She explains that she has but a handful of meal and oil left, and she and her son will die of starvation after it is gone. He tells her not to fear, she will be provided for, so she feeds him before her family. "For thus saith the Lord God of Israel, The barrel of meal shall not waste, neither shall the cruse of oil fail, until the day that the Lord sendeth rain upon the earth."

him not as an act of mercy, but by way of commerce, wherein thou art to walk by the rule of justice; but if his means of repaying thee be only probable or possible, then is he an object of thy mercy, thou must lend him, though there be danger of losing it, Deuteronomy: 15.7: "If any of thy brethren be poor,"[21] etc., "thou shalt lend him sufficient." That men might not shift off this duty by the apparent hazard, He tells them that though the year of Jubilee[22] were at hand (when he must remit it, if he were not able to repay it before) yet he must lend him and that cheerfully: "It may not grieve thee to give him" saith He; and because some might object; "why so I should soon impoverish myself and my family," he adds "with all thy work,"[23] etc; for our Savior, Matthew: 5.42: "From him that would borrow of thee turn not away."

Quest. What rule must we observe in forgiving?

Ans. Whether thou didst lend by way of commerce or in mercy, if he have nothing to pay thee, [you] must forgive, (except in cause where thou hast a surety or a lawful pledge) Deuteronomy: 15.2. Every seventh year the creditor was to quit that which he lent to his brother if he were poor as appears—verse 8: "Save when there shall be no poor with thee." In all these and like cases, Christ was a general rule, Matthew: 7.22: "Whatsoever ye would that men should do to you, do ye the same to them also."

Quest. What rule must we observe and walk by in cause of community of peril?

Ans. The same as before, but with more enlargement towards others and less respect towards ourselves and our own right. Hence it was that in the primitive church they sold all, had all things in common, neither did any man say that which he possessed was his own. Likewise in their return out of the captivity, because the work was great for the restoring of the church and the danger of enemies was common to all, Nehemiah exhorts the Jews to liberality and readiness in remitting their

---

[21]IF ANY OF THY BRETHREN BE POOR: Deuteronomy 15:7: "If there be among you a poor man of one of thy brethren within any of thy gates in thy land which the Lord thy God giveth thee, thou shalt not harden thine heart, nor shut thine hand from thy poor brother."

[22]JUBILEE: A Jewish year of release and restoration, which, according to Leviticus 25, was to be observed every fifty years. In the Jubilee year, fields were to be left uncultivated, Hebrew slaves were to be set free, and property sold reverted to former owners or their heirs.

[23]WHY SO I SHOULD SOON IMPOVERISH MYSELF AND MY FAMILY WITH ALL THY WORK: Winthrop says that Christians should give freely to those in need, regardless of the timing. A loan requested only a year before the Jubilee should still be granted, even though it will be more likely erased under the Jubilee mandates rather than repaid. Deuteronomy 15:9: "Beware that there be not a thought in thy wicked heart, saying, The seventh year, the year of release, is at hand; and thine eye be evil against thy poor brother, and thou givest him nought; and he cry unto the Lord against thee, and it be sin unto thee."

debts to their brethren,[24] and disposing liberally of his own to such as wanted, and stand not upon his own due, which he might have demanded of them. Thus did some of our forefathers in times of persecution in England, and so did many of the faithful of other churches, whereof we keep an honorable remembrance of them; and it is to be observed that both in Scriptures and later stories of the churches that such as have been most bountiful to the poor saints, especially in these extraordinary times and occasions, God hath left them highly commended to posterity, as Zacheus, Cornelius, Dorcas, Bishop Hooper, the Cuttler of Brussells[25] and divers[26] others. Observe again that the Scripture gives no caution to restrain any from being over liberal this way; but all men to the liberal and cheerful practice hereof by the sweetest promises; as to instance one for many, Isaiah: 58.6: "Is not this the fast I have chosen to loose the bonds of wickedness, to take off the heavy burdens, to let the oppressed go free and to break every yoke, to deal thy bread to the hungry and to bring the poor that wander into thy house, when thou seest the naked to cover them. And then shall thy light break forth as the morning, and thy health shall grow speedily, thy righteousness shall go before God, and the glory of the Lord shall embrace thee; then thou shalt call and the Lord shall answer thee" etc. [Verse] 10: "If thou pour out thy soul to the hungry, then shall thy light spring out in darkness, and the Lord shall guide thee continually, and satisfy thy soul in drought, and make fat thy bones; thou shalt be like a watered garden, and they shalt be of thee that shall build the old waste places" etc. On the contrary, most heavy curses are laid upon such as are straightened towards the Lord and His people, Judges: 5.[23]: "Curse ye Meroshe because ye came not to help the Lord," etc. Proverbs: [21.13]: "He who shutteth his ears from hearing the cry of the poor, he shall cry and shall not be heard." Matthew: 25: "Go ye cursed into everlasting fire" etc. "I was hungry and ye fed me not." 2 Corinthians: 9.6: "He that soweth sparingly shall reap sparingly."

Having already set forth the practice of mercy according to the rule of God's law, it will be useful to lay open the grounds of it also, being the other part of the commandment, and that is the affection from which

---

[24]NEHEMIAH EXHORTS THE JEWS TO LIBERALITY AND READINESS IN REMITTING THEIR DEBTS TO THEIR BRETHREN: Nehemiah was an Old Testament prophet who acted as governer of Judaea around 444 BCE. He rebuilt the walls of Jerusalem and repopulated it by drafts from the surrounding districts. He is credited with saving the city by convincing lenders to charge no interest, considering first the common good of the city.

[25]ZACHEUS, CORNELIUS, DORCAS, BISHOP HOOPER, THE CUTTLER OF BRUSSELLS: Christian martyrs.

[26]DIVERS: Many.

this exercise of mercy must arise. The apostle[27] tells us that this love is
the fulfilling of the law, not that it is enough to love our brother and so
no further; but in regard of the excellency of his parts giving any motion
to the other as the soul to the body and the power it hath to set all the
faculties on work in the outward exercise of this duty. As when we bid
one make the clock strike, he doth not lay hand on the hammer, which
is the immediate instrument of the sound, but sets on work the first mover
or main wheel, knowing that will certainly produce the sound which he
intends. So the way to draw men to works of mercy, is not by force of
argument from the goodness or necessity of the work; for though this
course may enforce a rational mind to some present act of mercy, as is
frequent in experience, yet it cannot work such a habit in a soul, as shall
make it prompt upon all occasions to produce the same effect, but by
framing these affections of love in the heart which will as natively bring
forth the other, as any cause doth produce effect.

The definition which the Scripture gives us of love is this: "Love
is the bond of perfection." First, it is a bond or ligament. Secondly it
makes the work perfect. There is no body but consists of parts and
that which knits these parts together gives the body its perfection,
because it makes each part so contiguous to others as thereby they do
mutually participate with each other, both in strength and infirmity,
in pleasure and pain. To instance in the most perfect of all bodies: Christ
and His church make one body. The several parts of this body, considered apart before they were united, were as disproportionate and
as much disordering as so many contrary qualities or elements, but
when Christ comes and by His spirit and love knits all these parts to
Himself and each to other, it is become the most perfect and best proportioned body in the world. Ephesians: 4.16: "Christ, by whom all the
body being knit together by every joint for the furniture thereof, according to the effectual power which is the measure of every perfection of
parts," "a glorious body without spot or wrinkle," the ligaments hereof
being Christ, or His love, for Christ is love (1 John: 4.8). So this definition is right: "Love is the bond of perfection."

From hence we may frame these conclusions. 1. First of all, true
Christians are of one body in Christ, 1 Corinthians: 12.12, 27: "Ye are
the body of Christ and members of their part." Secondly: The ligaments
of this body which knit together are love. Thirdly: No body can be perfect which wants its proper ligament. Fourthly. All the parts of this body

---

[27]THE APOSTLE: A reference to St. Paul's Epistle to the Romans 9:31.

being thus united are made so contiguous in a special relation as they must needs partake of each other's strength and infirmity; joy and sorrow, weal and woe. 1 Corinthians: 12.26: "If one member suffers, all suffer with it, if one be in honor, all rejoice with it." Fifthly. This sensibleness and sympathy of each other's conditions will necessarily infuse into each part a native desire and endeavor to strengthen, defend, preserve and comfort the other.

To insist a little on this conclusion being the product of all the former, the truth hereof will appear both by precept and pattern. 1 John: 3.10: "Ye ought to lay down your lives for the brethren." Galatians: 6.2: "bear ye one another's burthens and so fulfill the law of Christ." For patterns we have that first of our Savior who out of His good will in obedience to His father, becoming a part of this body, and being knit with it in the bond of love, found such a native sensibleness of our infirmities and sorrows as He willingly yielded Himself to death to ease the infirmities of the rest of His body, and so healed their sorrows. From the like sympathy of parts did the apostles and many thousands of the saints lay down their lives for Christ. Again, the like we may see in the members of this body among themselves. Romans: 9. Paul could have been contented to have been separated from Christ, that the Jews might not be cut off from the body. It is very observable what he professeth of his affectionate partaking with every member: "who is weak" saith he "and I am not weak? who is offended and I burn not[28];" and again, 2 Corinthians: 7.13. "therefore we are comforted because ye were comforted." Of Epaphroditus[29] he speaketh, Philippians: 2.30. that he regarded not his own life to do him service. So Phoebe[30] and others are called the servants of the church. Now it is apparent that they served not for wages, or by constraint, but out of love. The like we shall find in the histories of the church in all ages, the sweet sympathy of affections which was in the members of this body one towards another, their cheerfulness in serving and suffering together, how liberal they were without repining, harborers without grudging and helpful without reproaching; and all from hence, because they had fervent love amongst them, which only make the practice of mercy constant and easy.

[28]AND I AM NOT WEAK? WHO IS OFFENDED AND I BURN NOT: 2 Corinthians 11:29.
[29]OF EPAPHRODITUS: In a letter to the Philippians, St. Paul explains that while he is in prison in Rome, he has sent Epaphroditus to serve as their spiritual guide. "Yet I supposed it necessary to send to you Epaphroditus, my brother, and companion in labour, and fellow soldier, but your messenger, and he that ministered to my wants" (Philippians 2:25).
[30]SO PHOEBE: St. Paul praises Phoebe in his letter to the Romans: "I commend unto you Phoebe our sister, which is a servant of the church which is at Cenchrea. / That ye receive her in the Lord, as becometh saints, and that ye assist her in whatsoever business she hath need of you: for she hath been a succourer of many, and of myself also" (Romans 16:2).

   The next consideration is how this love comes to be wrought. Adam in his first estate[31] was a perfect model of mankind in all their generations, and in him this love was perfected in regard of the habit. But Adam rent himself from his creator, rent all his posterity also one from another; whence it comes that every man is born with this principle in him, to love and seek himself only, and thus a man continueth till Christ comes and takes possession of the soul and infuseth another principle, love to God and our brother. And this latter having continual supply from Christ, as the head and root by which he is united, gets the predomining in the soul, so by little and little expels the former. 1 John: 4.7. "love cometh of God and every one that loveth is borne of God," so that this love is the fruit of the new birth, and none can have it but the new creature. Now when this quality is thus formed in the souls of men, it works like the spirit upon the dry bones. Ezekiel: 37: "bone came to bone." It gathers together the scattered bones, of perfect old man Adam, and knits them into one body again in Christ, whereby a man is become again a living soul.

   The third consideration is concerning the exercise of this love which is twofold, inward or outward. The outward hath been handled in the former preface of this discourse. For unfolding the other we must take in our way that maxim of philosophy *simile simili gaudet*,[32] or like will to like; for as it is things which are turned with disaffection to each other, the ground of it is from a dissimilitude arising from the contrary or different nature of the things themselves; for the ground of love is an apprehension of some resemblance in things loved to that which affects it. This is the cause why the Lord loves the creature, so far as it hath any of His image in it; He loves His elect because they are like Himself, He beholds them in His beloved son. So a mother loves her child, because she thoroughly conceives a resemblance of herself in it. Thus it is between the members of Christ. Each discerns, by the work of the spirit, his own image and resemblance in another, and therefore cannot but love him as he loves himself. Now when the soul, which is of a sociable nature, finds anything like to itself, it is like Adam when Eve was brought to him. She must have it one with herself. This is flesh of my flesh (saith the soul) and bone of my bone.[33] She conceives a great delight in it, therefore she desires nearness and familiarity with it. She hath a great propensity to do it good and receives such content in it, as fearing the miscarriage of her beloved she

---

[31]ADAM IN HIS FIRST ESTATE: In his innocence, before the fall.
[32]SIMILE SIMILI GAUDET: A medieval proverb meaning "like rejoices in like." (Latin)
[33]THIS IS FLESH OF MY FLESH AND BONE OF MY BONE: In Genesis 2:23, God creates Eve from a rib taken from the sleeping Adam. "And Adam said, This is now bone of my bones, and flesh of my flesh: she shall be called Woman, because she was taken out of Man."

bestows it in the inmost closet of her heart. She will not endure that it shall want any good which she can give it. If by occasion she be withdrawn from the company of it, she is still looking towards the place where she left her beloved. If she heard it groan, she is with it presently. If she find it sad and disconsolate, she sighs and moans with it. She hath no such joy as to see her beloved merry and thriving. If she see it wronged, she cannot hear it without passion. She sets no bounds to her affections, nor hath any thought of reward. She finds recompense enough in the exercise of her love towards it. We may see this acted to life in Jonathan and David.[34] Jonathan a valiant man endowed with the spirit of Christ, so soon as he discovers the same spirit in David had presently his heart knit to him by this lineament of love so that it is said he loved him as his own soul. He takes so great pleasure in him, that he strips himself to adorn his beloved. His father's kingdom was not so precious to him as his beloved David. David shall have it with all his heart, himself desires no more but that he may be near to him to rejoice in his good. He chooseth to converse with him in the wilderness even to the hazard of his own life, rather than with the great courtiers in his father's palace. When he sees danger towards him, he spares neither rare pains nor peril to direct it. When injury was offered his beloved David, he would not bear it, though from his own father; and when they must part for a season only, they thought their hearts would have broke for sorrow, had not their affections found vent by abundance of tears. Other instances might be brought to show the nature of this affection, as of Ruth and Naomi,[35] and many others; but this truth is cleared enough.

If any shall object that it is not possible that love should be bred or upheld without hope of requital, it is granted; but that is not our cause; for this love is always under reward. It never gives, but it always receives with advantage; first, in regard that among the members of the same body, love and affection are reciprocal in a most equal and sweet kind of commerce. Secondly, in regard of the pleasure and content that the exercise

---

[34]JONATHAN AND DAVID: A reference to the story of the great friendship between David and Jonathan, Saul's son, in 1 Samuel 19. Saul, the first king of the Israelites, became jealous of David, his son-in-law, and asked Jonathan kill him. Jonathan refused, defending David with a compelling argument and convincing Saul to relent.

[35]RUTH AND NAOMI: After their husbands die, Naomi encourages her daughters-in-law, Ruth and Orpah, to return to their parental homes, for she has nothing to offer them. Ruth refuses to leave her mother-in-law, pledging her devotion: "Entreat me not to leave thee, or to return from following after thee: for whither thou goest, I will go; and where thou lodgest, I will lodge: thy people shall be my people, and thy God my God" (Ruth 1:16).

of love carries with it, as we may see in the natural body. The mouth is at all the pains to receive and mince the food which serves for the nourishment of all the other parts of the body, yet it hath no cause to complain; for first the other parts send back by several passages a due proportion of the same nourishment, in a better form for the strengthening and comforting the mouth. Secondly, the labor of the mouth is accompanied with such pleasure and content as far exceeds the pains it takes. So is it in all the labor of love among Christians. The party loving, reaps love again, as was showed before, which the soul covets more than all the wealth in the world. Thirdly: Nothing yields more pleasure and content to the soul than when it finds that which it may love fervently, for to love and live beloved is the soul's paradise, both here and in heaven. In the state of wedlock there be many comforts to bear out the troubles of that condition; but let such as have tried the most, say if there be any sweetness in that condition comparable to the exercise of mutual love.

From former consideration arise these conclusions.

First: This love among Christians is a real thing, not imaginary.

Secondly: This love is as absolutely necessary to the being of the body of Christ, as the sinews and other ligaments of a natural body are to the being of that body.

Thirdly: This love is a divine, spiritual nature free, active, strong, courageous, permanent; undervaluing all things beneath its proper object; and of all the graces, this makes us nearer to resemble the virtues of our Heavenly Father.

Fourthly: It rests in the love and welfare of its beloved. For the full and certain knowledge of these truths concerning the nature, use, and excellency of this grace, that which the Holy Ghost hath left recorded, 1 Corinthians: 13, may give full satisfaction, which is needful for every true member of this lovely body of the Lord Jesus, to work upon their hearts by prayer, meditation, continual exercise at least of the special [influence] of His grace, till Christ be formed in them and they in Him, all in each other, knit together by this bond of love.

II

It rests now to make some application of this discourse by the present design, which gave the occasion of writing of it. Herein are four things to be propounded: first the persons, secondly the work, thirdly the end, fourthly the means.

First, For the persons. We are a company professing ourselves fellow members of Christ, in which respect only though we were absent from each other many miles, and had our employments as far distant, yet we ought to account ourselves knit together by this bond of love, and live in the exercise of it, if we would have comfort of our being in Christ. This was notorious in the practice of the Christians in former times; as is testified of the Waldenses,[36] from the mouth of one of the adversaries *Æneas Sylvius*[37] "mutuo [ament] penè antequam norunt,"[38] they used to love any of their own religion even before they were acquainted with them.

Secondly, for the work we have in hand. It is by a mutual consent, through a special overvaluing providence and a more than an ordinary approbation of the Churches of Christ, to seek out a place of cohabitation and consortship under a due form of government both civil and ecclesiastical. In such cases as this, the care of the public must oversway all private respects, by which, not only conscience, but mere civil policy, doth bind us. For it is a true rule that particular estates cannot subsist in the ruin of the public.

Thirdly. The end is to improve our lives to do more service to the Lord; the comfort and increase of the body of Christ whereof we are members; that ourselves and posterity may be the better preserved from the common corruptions of this evil world, to serve the Lord and work out our salvation under the power and purity of His holy ordinances.

Fourthly, for the means whereby this must be effected. They are twofold, a conformity with the work and end we aim at. These we see are extraordinary, therefore we must not content ourselves with usual ordinary means. Whatsoever we did or ought to have done when we lived in England, the same must we do, and more also, where we go. That which the most in their churches maintain as a truth in profession only, we must bring into familiar and constant practice, as in this duty of love. We must love brotherly without dissimulation; we must love one another with a pure heart fervently. We must bear one another's burthens. We must not look only on our own things, but also on the things of our brethren, neither must we think that the Lord will bear with such failings at our hands as he doth from those among whom we have lived; and that for three reasons.

---

[36]WALDENSES: A Protestant religious group organized by Peter Valdes (Waldo) in the late twelfth century . Its members proclaimed the Bible as the sole rule of life and faith, rejecting many of the institutions of the Catholic church. Their worship services consisted of Bible readings, the Lord's Prayer, and sermons, which they believed could be preached by all Christians.
[37]AENEAS SYLVIUS: Aeneas Sylvius Piccolomini (1405–1464), who was Pope Pius II.
[38]MUTUO AMENT PENÈ ANTEQUAM NORUNT: A more accurate approximation of this Latin phrase would be "mutuo solent amare pene antequam norint."

First, In regard of the more near bond of marriage between Him and us, where-in He hath taken us to be His after a most strict and peculiar manner, which will make Him the more jealous of our love and obedience. So He tells the people of Israel, you only have I known of all the families of the earth, therefore will I punish you for your transgressions. Secondly, because the Lord will be sanctified in them that come near Him. We know that there were many that corrupted the service of the Lord, some setting up altars before His own, others offering both strange fire and strange sacrifices also; yet there came no fire from heaven or other sudden judgment upon them, as did upon Nadab and Abihu,[39] who yet we may think did not sin presumptuously. Thirdly. When God gives a special commission He looks to have it strictly observed in every article. When He gave Saul a commission to destroy Amaleck,[40] He indented with him upon certain articles, and because he failed in one of the least, and that upon a fair pretense, it lost him the kingdom which should have been his reward if he had observed his commission.

Thus stands the cause between God and us. We are entered into covenant[41] with Him for this work. We have taken out a commission, the Lord hath given us leave to draw our own articles. We have professed to enterprise these actions, upon these and those ends, we have hereupon besought Him of favor and blessing. Now if the Lord shall please to hear us, and bring us in peace to the place we desire, then hath He ratified this covenant and sealed our commission, [and] will expect a strict performance of the articles contained in it; but if we shall neglect the observation of these articles which are the ends we have propounded, and, dissembling with our God, shall fall to embrace this present world and prosecute our carnal intentions, seeking great things for ourselves and our posterity, the Lord will surely break out in wrath against us; be revenged of such a perjured people and make us know the price of the breach of such a covenant.

---

[39]NADAB AND ABIHU: Two of the fours sons of Aaron, the high priest of the Hebrews; they were burned by a fire they offered to God, as described in Leviticus 10:1–2: "And Nadab and Abihu, the sons of Aaron, took either of them his censer, and put fire therein, and put incense thereon, and offered strange fire before the Lord, which he commanded them not. / And there went out fire from the Lord, and devoured them, and they died before the Lord." It is likely that they were destroyed because the fire was "strange"—that is, not taken from the great brazen altar (Leviticus 6:9)—and because they committed the offense while intoxicated (Leviticus 10:9).

[40]HE GAVE SAUL A COMMISSION TO DESTROY AMALECK: Saul, the first elected king of the Israelites, was instructed by God to destroy the Amalekites and all they owned, but he spared their sheep and oxen under the pretense of making them a burnt offering to the Lord. The prophet Samuel explained that it is more important to follow the Lord's commands than to make him burnt offerings. Saul lost his throne for this transgression.

[41]WE ARE ENTERED INTO COVENANT: A contract with God. The Israelites entered into a covenant with God in which he promised to protect them if they kept his commandments and were faithful to him.

Now the only way to avoid this shipwreck, and to provide for our posterity, is to follow the counsel of Micah,[42] to do justly, to love mercy, to walk humbly with our God. For this end, we must be knit together in this work as one man. We must entertain each other in brotherly affection, we must be willing to abridge ourselves of our superfluities, for the supply of other's necessities. We must uphold a familiar commerce together in all meekness, gentleness, patience and liberality. We must delight in each other, make other's conditions our own, rejoice together, mourn together, labor and suffer together, always having before our eyes our commission and community in the work, our community as members of the same body. So shall we keep the unity of the spirit in the bond of peace. The Lord will be our God, and delight to dwell among us as His own people, and will command a blessing upon us in all our ways, so that we shall see much more of His wisdom, power, goodness and truth, than formerly we have been acquainted with. We shall find that the God of Israel is among us, when ten of us shall be able to resist a thousand of our enemies; when He shall make us a praise and glory that men shall say of succeeding plantations, "the Lord make it like that of NEW ENGLAND." For we must consider that we shall be as a city upon a hill.[43] The eyes of all people are upon us, so that if we shall deal falsely with our God in this work we have undertaken, and so cause Him to withdraw His present help from us, we shall be made a story and a by-word through the world. We shall open the mouths of enemies to speak evil of the ways of God, and all professors for God's sake. We shall shame the faces of many of God's worthy servants, and cause their prayers to be turned into curses upon us till we be consumed out of the good land whither we are agoing.

And to shut up this discourse with that exhortation of Moses, that faithful servant of the Lord,[44] in his last farewell to Israel, Deuteronomy 30. Beloved, there is now set before us life and good, death and evil, in that we are commanded this day to love the Lord our God, and to love

[42]MICAH: A prophet (735–665 BCE) from southwest Judah whose writings attacked social injustices against the poor. He predicted the fall of Jerusalem because its inhabitants failed to uphold their covenant with God.
[43]FOR WE MUST CONSIDER THAT WE SHALL BE AS A CITY UPON A HILL: A reference to Matthew 5.14: "Ye are the light of the world. A city that is set on a hill cannot be hid."
[44]THAT EXHORTATION OF MOSES, THAT FAITHFUL SERVANT OF THE LORD: "And it shall come to pass, when all these things are come upon thee, the blessing and the curse, which I have set before thee, and thou shalt call them to mind among all the nations, whither the Lord thy God hath driven thee, / And shalt return unto the Lord thy God, and shalt obey his voice according to all that I command thee this day, thou and thy children, with all thine heart, and with all thy soul; / That then the Lord thy God will turn thy captivity, and have compassion upon thee, and will return and gather thee from all the nations, whither the Lord thy God hath scattered thee" (Deuteronomy 30:1–3).

one another, to walk in His ways and to keep His commandments and His ordinance and His laws, and the articles of our covenant with Him, that we may live and be multiplied, and that our Lord our God may bless us in the land whither we go to possess it. But if our hearts shall turn away, so that we will not obey, but shall be seduced, and worship other gods, our pleasures and profits, and serve them; it is propounded unto us this day, we shall surely perish out of the good land whither we pass over this vast sea to possess it.

> *Therefore let us choose life,*
> *that we and our seed*
> *may live by obeying His*
> *voice and cleaving to Him,*
> *for He is our life and our prosperity.*

[1630, 1838]

Anne Bradstreet

(1612–1672)

The poet Anne Bradstreet was born Anne Dudley in Northampton, England, and was tutored by her father. She married Simon Bradstreet in 1628, and in 1630 she, her husband, and her parents journeyed to the Massachusetts Bay Colony, sailing with John Winthrop and other Puritan notables and settling in the early 1640s in North Andover in northeastern Massachusetts on the Merrimack River. Bradstreet, the mother of eight children, began writing poetry in earnest (as a girl, she had composed some poems for her father) sometime in the early 1630s. Life in the colony was hard, and Bradstreet suffered frequently from illness. Her husband was an important jurist and diplomatic and political figure, which meant all the more that the labor and burden of the home fell on her.

Bradstreet's first volume of poetry, The Tenth Muse Lately Sprung Up in America, By a Gentlewoman in Those Parts, *was published (by her brother-in-law, without her permission) in London in 1650; showing the influence of Spenser, Sidney, Donne, Quarles, Herbert, and other English poets,* The Tenth Muse *was the first book of verse by a person residing anywhere in the British North American colonies— though its authorship was given as "anonymous" on the title page. In 1664 Bradstreet assembled a collection of her prose writings and published them with the title* Meditations. *Two years later she revised all of her poems for a collected edition, which was issued after her death.*

As a poet, Bradstreet is engaging and accessible in both style and subject, at her best when treating domestic scenes and relationships plainly and directly and without the strangeness, ornate difficulty, and bold imagery that characterize the verse of the later Puritan poet Edward Taylor. (Bradstreet's book was the only volume of English poetry Taylor included in his library.) One can glimpse in her work the rewards and special challenges that a woman, and a woman writer, experienced in early to mid-seventeenth century New England.

Bradstreet was a devout Christian and a dutiful daughter, wife, and mother, but also a woman and a poet who shows some resistance to the expectations of male authorities, secular and religious. Sometimes in her verse she seems to deny in herself the ambitions and aspirations to which her literary efforts—her acts as a writer—bear witness. Bradstreet is more of a creator, is more independent-minded, than she is willing to acknowledge openly. A sign perhaps of her ambivalence is her statement that her first gathering of poems was "the fruit but of some few hours curtailed from her sleep and other refreshments."

There is also this revealing passage from a letter to her children, left at her death with her poems, which catches the rhythm of both her doubt and resolve:

> *I have often been perplexed that I have not found that constant joy in my pilgrimage and refreshing which I supposed most of the servants of God have…. Many times hath Satan troubled me concerning the verity of the scriptures, many times by atheism how I could know whether there was a God: I never saw any miracles to confirm me, and those I read of did I know but they were feigned. That there is a God my reason would soon tell me by the wondrous works that I see, the vast frame of the heaven and the earth, the order of all things night and day, summer and winter, spring and autumn, the daily providing for this great household upon the earth.*

For biographical and critical discussion: Elizabeth Wade White, Anne Bradstreet: The Tenth Muse *(1971); Ann Stanford,* Anne Bradstreet, The Worldly Puritan: An Introduction to Her Poetry *(1975); Wendy Martin,* An American Triptych: Anne Bradstreet, Emily Dickinson, Adrienne Rich *(1984); and* Critical Essays on Anne Bradstreet, *ed. Pattie Cowell and Ann Stanford (1983).*

The Prologue

1

To sing of wars, of captains, and of kings,[1]
Of cities founded, commonwealths begun,
For my mean[2] pen are too superior things:
Or how they all or each their dates have run,
Let poets and historians set these forth,   5
My obscure lines shall not so dim their worth.

2

But when my wond'ring eyes and envious heart
Great Bartas'[3] sugar'd lines do but read o'er
Fool I do grudge the Muses[4] did not part

---

[1]TO SING OF WARS…: The themes of epic poetry.
[2]MEAN: Inferior, humble.
[3]GREAT BARTAS: Guillaume du Bartas (1544–1590), a French Calvinist poet who wrote for the French court. His most famous work is *The Divine Weeks and Works*, an epic poem about great moments in Christian history, translated in 1606 by Joshua Sylvester (1562–1618).
[4]MUSES: In Greek mythology, the nine goddesses who inspired the arts and sciences were collectively called *muses*; their names were Calliope, Clio, Erato, Euterpe, Melpomene, Polyhymnia, Terpsichore, Thalia, and Urania.

'Twixt him and me that overfluent store;   10
A Bartas can do what a Bartas will,
But simple I according to my skill.

3

From schoolboy's tongue no rhet'ric we expect,
Nor yet a sweet consort⁵ from broken strings,
Nor perfect beauty where's a main defect: 15
My foolish, broken, blemish'd Muse so sings,
And this to mend, alas, no art is able,
'Cause nature made it so irreparable.

4

Nor can I, like that fluent sweet tongu'd Greek,⁶
Who lisp'd at first, in future times speak plain;   20
By art he gladly found what he did seek,
A full requital of his striving pain.
Art can do much, but this maxim's most sure:
A weak or wounded brain admits no cure.

5

I am obnoxious⁷ to each carping tongue   25
Who says my hand a needle better fits,
A poet's pen all scorn I should thus wrong,
For such despite they cast on female wits:
If what I do prove well, it won't advance,
They'll say it's stol'n, or else it was by chance.   30

6

But sure the antique Greeks were far more mild,
Else of our sex, why feigned they those Nine,
And poesy made Calliope's⁸ own child;
So 'mongst the rest they placed the arts divine
But this weak knot, they will full soon untie,   35
The Greeks did nought, but play the fools and lie.

---

⁵SWEET CONSORT: The harmony of several instruments or voices together.
⁶SWEET TONGU'D GREEK: A reference to the Greek orator Demosthenes (383–322 BCE), known
for his passionate speeches.
⁷OBNOXIOUS: Exposed to possible harm or injury.
⁸CALLIOPE: The eldest and most distinguished of the Muses, Calliope ("beautiful voice") is the goddess of epic poetry.

7

Let Greeks be Greeks, and women what they are,
Men have precedency and still excel,
It is but vain unjustly to wage war;
Men can do best, and women know it well.   40
Preeminence in all and each is yours;
Yet grant some small acknowledgment of ours.

8

And oh ye high flown quills⁹ that soar the skies,
And ever with your prey still catch your praise,
If e'er you deign these lowly lines your eyes,   45
Give thyme or parsley wreath, I ask no bays;
This mean and unrefined ore of mine
Will make your glist'ring gold but more to shine.

[1650]

The Author to Her Book

Thou ill-form'd offspring of my feeble brain,
Who after birth did'st by my side remain,
Till snatcht from thence by friends,¹ less wise than true,
Who thee abroad expos'd to public view,
Made thee in rags halting to th' press to trudge,   5
Where errors were not lessened (all may judge).
At thy return my blushing was not small,
My rambling brat² (in print) should mother call;
I cast thee by as one unfit for light,
Thy visage was so irksome in my sight;   10
Yet being mine own, at length affection would
Thy blemishes amend, if so I could:

---

⁹QUILLS: Pens made from the feathers of a goose or other large bird.
¹TILL SNATCHED FROM THENCE BY FRIENDS: Bradstreet refers to the first printing of this edition of her poems, to which this preface was added for the second edition, which was published by her brother-in-law, John Trowbridge, without her knowledge.
²BRAT: Offspring or poor child. In the seventeenth century, this word, while not derogatory, implied a child of insignificance, such as a "beggar's brat."
³EVEN FEET: Metrical feet.

I wash'd thy face, but more defects I saw,
And rubbing off a spot, still made a flaw.
I stretcht thy joints to make thee even feet,[3]   15
Yet still thou run'st more hobbling than is meet;
In better dress to trim thee was my mind,
But nought save homespun cloth i' th' house I find;
In this array, 'mongst vulgars[4] may'st thou roam,
In critic's hands, beware thou dost not come;   20
And take thy way where yet thou art not known,
If for thy father asked, say thou had'st none:
And for thy mother, she alas is poor,
Which caus'd her thus to send thee out of door.

[1678]

Before the Birth of One of Her Children

All things within this fading world hath end,
Adversity doth still our joys attend;
No ties so strong, no friends so dear and sweet,
But with death's parting blow is sure to meet.
The sentence past is most irrevocable,   5
A common thing, yet oh inevitable;
How soon, my dear, death may my steps attend,
How soon't may be thy lot to lose thy friend,[1]
We both are ignorant, yet love bids me
These farewell lines to recommend to thee,   10
That when that knot's untied that made us one,
I may seem thine, who in effect am none.
And if I see not half my days that's due,[2]
What nature would, God grant to yours and you;

---

[4]VULGARS: People of the common class, usually uneducated.
[1]HOW SOON'T MAY BE THY LOT TO LOSE THY FRIEND: Bradstreet addresses her husband,
Simon, wistfully telling him that she might die in childbirth, depriving him of his wife, or "friend."
[2]AND IF I SEE NOT HALF MY DAYS THAT'S DUE: Childbirth may cut her normal lifespan in half.

The many faults that well you know I have,   15
Let be interr'd in my oblivion's grave;
If any worth or virtue were in me,
Let that live freshly in thy memory,
And when thou feel'st no grief, as I no harms,
Yet love thy dead, who long lay in thine arms: 20
And when thy loss shall be repaid with gains,
Look to my little babes, my dear remains.
And if thou love thy self, or loved'st me,
These O protect from step-dame's injury.[3]
And if chance to thine eyes shall bring this verse,   25
With some sad sighs honor my absent hearse;
And kiss the paper for thy love's dear sake,
Who with salt tears this last farewell did take.

[1678]

To My Dear and Loving Husband

If ever two were one, then surely we.
If ever man were loved by wife, then thee;
If ever wife was happy in a man,
Compare with me, ye women, if you can.
I prize thy love more than whole mines of gold   5
Or all the riches that the East doth hold.
My love is such that rivers cannot quench,
Nor ought but love from thee, give recompense.
Thy love is such I can no way repay,
The heavens reward thee manifold, I pray.   10
Then while we live, in love let's so persevere
That when we live no more, we may live ever.

[1678]

---

[3]THESE O PROTECT FROM STEP-DAME'S INJURY: A stepmother, who may prefer her own children to those of their husband's departed wife.

In Memory of My Dear Grandchild Elizabeth Bradstreet, Who Deceased August, 1665, Being a Year and a Half Old

1

Farewell dear babe, my heart's too much content,
Farewell sweet babe, the pleasure of mine eye,
Farewell fair flower that for a space was lent,
Then ta'en away unto eternity.
Blest babe, why should I once bewail thy fate,   5
Or sigh thy days so soon were terminate,
Sith[1] thou art settled in an everlasting state.

2

By nature trees do rot when they are grown,
And plums and apples thoroughly ripe do fall,
And corn and grass are in their season mown,   10
And time brings down what is both strong and tall.
But plants new set to be eradicate,
And buds new blown to have so short a date,
Is by His hand alone that guides nature and fate.

[1678]

[1]SITH: Since.

In Memory of My Dear Grandchild Anne Bradstreet, Who Deceased June 20, 1669, Being Three Years and Seven Months Old

With troubled heart and trembling hand I write,
The heavens have changed to sorrow my delight.
How oft with disappointment have I met,
When I on fading things my hopes have set.
Experience might 'fore this have made me wise, 5
To value things according to their price.
Was ever stable joy yet found below?
Or perfect bliss without mixture of woe?
I knew she was but as a withering flower,
That's here today, perhaps gone in an hour; 10
Like as a bubble, or the brittle glass,
Or like a shadow turning as it was.
More fool then I to look on that was lent
As if mine own, when thus impermanent.
Farewell dear child, thou ne'er shall come to me, 15
But yet a while, and I shall go to thee;
Meantime my throbbing heart's cheered up with this:
Thou with thy Savior art in endless bliss.

(1678)

Mary Rowlandson

(1635–1711)

Mary Rowlandson, born Mary White in Somersetshire, England, immigrated to America at an early age with her parents. They lived first in Salem, Massachusetts, and then in Lancaster, in the central part of the state. There she met Joseph Rowlandson, a minister, and they married in 1656.

On a February morning in 1676, members of the Pocasset, Nimpuc, and Wampanoag tribes, led by Metacom, attacked Lancaster, burning it to the ground and taking captive Rowlandson, her three children, and about twenty other inhabitants of the town. This was the first of many Indians raids on colonial settlements during the years 1675–1676. These raids are known collectively as King Philip's War— Philip was the name by which the colonists knew Metacom—and their immediate cause was the execution in Plymouth, Massachusetts, of three members of the Wampanoag tribe. By the war's end, thousands of Indians and hundreds of colonists had been killed and many homes destroyed. Metacom was killed, and his wife and children were sent into slavery in the West Indies.

Rowlandson was held captive for eleven weeks, moving from place to place over a distance of 150 miles; she was released after her husband paid a ransom of twenty pounds. The two of them then secured the freedom of the two children who remained alive (the third had died during the captivity). After they were released, the family moved to Wethersfield in north-central Connecticut. Rowlandson's husband died in 1678. Rowlandson remarried in 1679 and lived in Wethersfield until her death.

In The Sovereignty and Goodness of God, Together with the Faithfulness of His Promises Displayed *(1682), Rowlandson describes the details of her capture and captivity, a "lively resemblance of hell." She shows courage, determination, and a powerful, enduring faith in God. Her heroism amid physical and emotional trials, which she vividly depicts, made the book a popular success in America and England.*

Rowlandson is a devout Christian, yet at times her expressions of faith and citations from Scripture seem in tense, even ambivalent, relation to her account of her experiences. A similar tension may be glimpsed in her descriptions of the Indians: she appears to gain a new understanding of them, even as she still identifies them as heathen savages assigned by God to test the Puritans' faith.

Feminist critics and literary historians have explored the insights The Sovereignty and Goodness of God *offers into the ordinary, yet extraordinary, late-seventeenth-century life of a New England wife and mother. The first of many "captivity narratives," Rowlandson's book* has been seen by scholars as an influence on James Fenimore Cooper's The Last of the Mohicans *(1826) and even on William Faulkner's* Sanctuary *(1931), about the kidnapping of a Mississippi college girl.* Widely studied, discussed, and debated, The Sovereignty and Goodness of God *is one of the classic works of colonial literature.*

For critical interpretation and context: Mitchell Robert Breitwieser, American Puritanism and the Defense of Mourning: Religion, Grief, and Ethnology in Mary White Rowlandson's Captivity Narrative *(1990); Susan Howe,* The Birth-Mark: Unsettling the Wilderness in American Literary History *(1993); Kathryn and James Derounian and Arthur Levernier,* Indian Captivity Narrative, 1550–1900 *(1993); and Rebecca Blevins Faery,* Cartographies of Desire: Captivity, Race, and Sex in the Shaping of an American Nation *(1999). See also: Tara Fitzpatrick, "The Figure of Captivity: The Cultural Work of the Puritan Captivity Narrative,"* American Literary History *3:1 (Spring 1991), 1–26.*

A True History of the Captivity and Restoration of Mrs. Mary Rowlandson

THE PREFACE TO THE READER

It was on Tuesday *Feb.* 1. 1675. *in the afternoon, when the* Narrhagansets *Quarters (in or toward the* Nipmug *Country, whither they were now retired for fear of the* English *Army lying in their own Country) were the second time beaten up by the Forces of the United Colonies who thereupon soon betook themselves to flight, and were all the next day pursued by the* English, *some overtaken and destroyed. But on* Thursday *Feb.* 3. *the* English *having now been six days on their March, from their Headquarters at* Wickford, *in the Narrhaganset Country, toward, and after the Enemy, and Provision grown exceeding short; insomuch that they were fain to kill some Horses for the supply, especially of their* Indian *Friends, they were necessitated to consider what was best to be done; and about noon (having hitherto followed the Chase as hard as they might) a Council was called, and though some few were of another mind, yet it was concluded by far the greater part of the Council of War, that the Army should desist the pursuit, and retire: The Forces of* Plimouth *and the* Bay *to the next Town of the* Bay, *and* Connecticut *Forces to their own next Towns: which determination was immediately put in execution. The consequent whereof, as it was not difficult to be foreseen by those that knew the cause-less enmity of these* Barbarians *against the* English, *and the malicious and revengeful spirit of these Heathen; so it soon proved dismal.*

The Narrhagansets *were now driven quite from their own Country, and all their Provisions there hoarded up, to which they durst not at present return, and being so numerous as they were, soon devoured those to whom they went, whereby both the one and the other were now reduced to extream straits, and so necessitated to take the first and best opportunity for supply, and very glad no doubt of such an opportunity as this, to provide for themselves, and make spoile of the* English *at once; and seeing themselves thus discharged of their pursuers, and a little refreshed after their flight, the very next week on* Thursday Feb. 10. *they fell with mighty force and fury upon* Lancaster: *which small Town, remote from aid of others, and not being Garrison'd as it might, the Army being now come in, and as the time indeed required (the design of the* Indians *against that place being known to the English some time before was not able to make effectual resistance; but notwithstanding the utmost endeavour of the Inhabitants, most of the buildings were turned into ashes; many People (Men, Women and Children) slain, and others captivated. The most solemn and remarkable part of this Tragedy, may that justly be reputed, which fell upon the Family of that Reverend Servant of God, Mr.* Joseph Rowlandson, *the faithful Pastor of the Church of Christ in that place, who being gone down to the Council of the* Massachusets, *to seek aid for the defence of the place; at his return found the Town in flames, or smoke, his own house being set on fire by the Enemy, through the disadvantage of a defective Fortification and all in it consumed: His precious yoke-fellow, and dear Children, wounded and captivated (as the issue evidenced, and the following Narrative declares) by these cruel and barbarous Salvages. A sad Catastrophe! Thus all things come alike to all: None knows either love or hatred by all that is before him. 'Tis no new thing for Gods precious ones to drink as deep as others, of the Cup of common Calamity: take just* Lot *(yet captivated) for instance, beside others. But it is not my business[1] to dilate on these things, but only in few words introductively to preface to the following script, which is a Narrative of the wonderfully awful, wise, holy, powerful, and gracious providence of God, toward that worthy and precious Gentlewoman, the dear Consort of the said Reverend Mr.* Rowlandson, *and her Children with her, as in casting of her into such a waterless pit, so in preserving, supporting, and carrying through so many such extream hazards, unspeakable difficulties and disconsolateness, and*

---

[1]MY BUSINESS: This preface was written by a Puritan clergyman, probably Increase Mather (1639–1723).

at last delivering her out of them all, and her surviving Children also. It was a strange and amazing dispensation, that the Lord should so afflict his precious Servant, and Hand-maid: It was as strange, if not more, that he should so bear up the spirits of his Servant under such bereavements, and of his Hand-maid under such Captivity, travels, and hardships (much too hard for flesh and blood) as he did, and at length deliver and restore. But he was their Saviour, who hath said, When thou passest through the Waters, I will be with thee, and through the Rivers, they shall not overflow thee: when thou walkest through the Fire, thou shalt not be burnt, nor shall the flame kindle upon thee, *Isai.* 43. *Ver.* 3. *and again,* He woundeth, and his hands make whole, He shall deliver thee in six troubles, yea in seven there shall no evil touch thee: In Famine he shall redeem thee from death; and in War from the power of the sword, *Job.* 5. 18, 19, 20. *Methinks this dispensation doth bear some resemblance to those of* Joseph, David *and* Daniel, *yea and of the three Children too, the stories whereof do represent us with the excellent textures of divine providence, curious pieces of divine work: And truly so doth this, and therefore not to be forgotten, but worthy to be exhibited to, and viewed, and pondered by all, that disdain not to consider the operation of his hands.*

The works of the Lord (not only of Creation, but of Providence also, especially those that do more peculiarly concern his dear ones, that are as the apple of his eye, as the signet upon his hand, the delight of his eyes, and the object of his tenderest care) are great, sought out of all those that have pleasure therein. And of these, verily this is none of the least.

This Narrative *was Penned by the Gentlewoman her self, to be to her a* Memorandum *of Gods dealing with her, that she might never forget, but remember the same, and the several circumstances thereof, all the daies of her life. A pious scope, which deserves both commendation and imitation. Some Friends having obtained a sight of it, could not but be so much affected with the many passages of working providence discovered therein, as to judge it worthy of publick view, and altogether unmeet that such works of God should be hid from present and future Generation: and therefore though this Gentlewomans modesty would not thrust it into the Press, yet her gratitude unto God, made her not hardly perswadable to let it pass, that God might have his due glory, and others benefit by it as well as her selfe.*

I hope by this time none will cast any reflection upon this Gentlewoman, on the score of this publication of her Affliction and Deliverance. If any should, doubtless they may be reckoned with the nine Lepers, of whom it is said, Were there not ten cleansed, where are the nine? *but one returning to give God thanks. Let such further know, that this was a dispensation of publick note, and of Universal concernment;*

and so much the more, by how much the nearer this Gentlewoman stood related to that faithful Servant of God whose capacity and employment was publick, in the House of God, and his Name on that account of a very sweet savour in the Churches of Christ. Who is there of a true Christian spirit, that did not look upon himself much concerned in this bereavement, this Captivity in the time thereof, and in this deliverance when it came, yea more than in many others? and how many are there to whom, so concerned, it will doubtless be a very acceptable thing, to see the way of God with this Gentlewoman in the aforesaid dispensation, thus laid out and portrayed before their eyes.

To conclude, Whatever any coy phantasies may deem, yet it highly concerns those that have so deeply tasted how good the Lord is, to enquire with David, What shall I render to the Lord for all his benefits to me? *Psal.* 116. 12. *He thinks nothing too great: yea, being sensible of his own disproportion to the due praises of God, he calls in help;* O magnifie the Lord with me, let us exalt his Name together, Psal. 34. 3. *And it is but reason, that our praises should hold proportion with our prayers; and that as many have helped together by prayer for the obtaining of this mercy, so praises should be returned by many on this behalf; and forasmuch as not the general but particular knowledge of things makes deepest impression upon the affections, this Narrative particularizing the several passages of this providence, will not a little conduce thereunto: and therefore holy* David, *in order to the attainment of that end, accounts himself concerned to declare what God had done for his Soul,* Psal. 66. 16. Come and hear, all ye that fear God, and I will declare what God hath done for my Soul, *i. e. for his Life: See Ver.* 9, 10. He holdeth our soul in life, and suffers not our feet to be moved; for thou our God hast proved us: thou hast tried us, as silver is tried. *Life-mercies are heart-affecting-mercies; of great impression and force, to enlarge pious hearts in the praises of God, so that such know not how but to talk of Gods acts, and to speak of and publish his wonderful works. Deep troubles, when the waters come in unto the Soul, are wont to produce vows:* Vows must be paid, It is better not vow, than to vow and not pay. *I may say, that as none knows what it is to fight and pursue such an enemy as this, but they that have fought and pursued them: so none can imagine, what it is to be captivated, and enslaved to such Atheistical, proud, wild, cruel, barbarous, brutish, (in one word) diabolical Creatures as these, the worst of the heathen; nor what difficulties, hardships, hazards, sorrows, anxieties, and perplexities, do unavoidably wait upon such a condition, but those that have tried it. No serious spirit then (especially knowing any thing of this Gentlewomans Piety) can imagine but that the vows of God are upon her. Excuse her than if she come thus into the pub-lick, to pay those Vows. Come and hear what she hath to say.*

I am confident that no Friend of divine Providence, will ever repent his time and pains spent in reading over these sheets; but will judge them worth perusing again and again.

Here Reader, *you may see an instance of the Soveraignty of God, who doth what he will with his own as well as others; and who may say to him,* what dost thou? *Here you may see an instance of the Faith and Patience of the Saints, under the most heart-sinking Tryals: here you may see, the Promises are breasts full of Consolation, when all the World besides is empty, and gives nothing but sorrow. That God is indeed the supream Lord of the World: ruling the most unruly, weakening the most cruel and salvage: granting his People mercy in the sight of the most unmerciful: curb-ing the lusts of the most filthy, holding the hands of the violent, delivering the prey from the mighty, and gathering together the out-casts of Israel. Once and again, you have heard, but here you may see, that power belongeth unto God: that our God is the God of Salvation: and to him belong the issues from Death. That our God is in the Heavens, and doth what ever pleases him. Here you have* Samsons *Riddle exemplified, and that great promise,* Rom. 8. 28. *verified:* Out of the Eater comes forth meat, and sweet-ness out of the strong; *The worst of evils working together for the best good. How evident is it that the Lord hath made this Gentlewoman a gainer by all this Affliction, that she can say, 'tis good for her, yea better that she hath been, than she should not have been, thus afflicted.*

Oh how doth God shine forth in such things as these!

Reader, if thou gettest no good by such a Declaration as this, the fault must needs be thine own. Read therefore, peruse, ponder, and from hence lay up something from the experience of another, against thine own turn comes: that so thou also through patience and consolation of the Scripture mayest have hope,

Per Amicum.[2]

A NARRATIVE OF THE CAPTIVITY AND RESTORATION OF MRS. MARY ROWLANDSON.

On the tenth of *February,* 1675.[1] came the *Indians* with great numbers upon *Lancaster.* Their first coming was about Sun-rising. Hearing the noise of some Guns, we looked out; several Houses were burning, and the

---

[2]PER AMICUM: "By a friend." (Latin)
[1]TENTH OF FEBRUARY, 1675: A Thursday. By a modern (Gregorian) calendar, the date of abduc-tion was February 20, 1676. The Gregorian calendar wasn't adopted in England until 1752.

Smoke ascending to Heaven. There were five Persons taken in one House, the Father, and the Mother, and a sucking Child they knock'd on the head[2]; the other two they took, and carried away alive. There were two others, who being out of their Garrison upon some occasion, were set upon; one was knock'd on the head, the other escaped. Another there was who running along was shot and wounded, and fell down; he begged of them his Life, promising them Money (as they told me); but they would not hearken to him, but knock'd him on the head, stripped him naked, and split open his Bowels. Another seeing many of the *Indians* about his Barn, ventured and went out, but was quickly shot down. There were three others belonging to the same Garrison who were killed. The *Indians* getting up upon the Roof of the Barn, had advantage to shoot down upon them over their Fortification. Thus these murtherous Wretches went on, burning and destroying before them.

At length they came and beset our own House, and quickly it was the dolefullest day that ever mine eyes saw. The House stood upon the edge of a Hill; some of the *Indians* got behind the Hill, others into the Barn, and others behind any thing that would shelter them: from all which Places they shot against the House, so that the Bullets seemed to fly like Hail: and quickly they wounded one Man among us, then another, and then a third. About two Hours (according to my observation in that amazing time) they had been about the House, before they could prevail to fire it, (which they did with Flax and Hemp which they brought out of the Barn, and there being no Defence about the House, onely two Flankers,[3] at two opposite Corners, and one of them not finished.) They fired it once, and one ventured out and quenched it; but they quickly fired it again, and that took. Now is that dreadful Hour come, that I have often heard of, (in the time of the War, as it was the Case of others) but now mine Eyes see it. Some in our House were fighting for their Lives, others wallowing in their Blood; the House on fire over our Heads, and the bloody Heathen ready to knock us on the Head if we stirred out. Now might we hear Mothers and Children crying out for themselves, and one another, *Lord, what shall we do!* Then I took my Children[4] (and one of my Sisters,[5] here) to go forth and leave the House: But as soon as we came to the Door and appeared, the *Indians* shot so thick; that the Bullets ratled against the House, as if one had taken

---

[2]KNOCK'D ON THE HEAD: Killed by a severe blow to the head.
[3]FLANKERS: Projections on garrison houses that permit gunfire from within the building while providing protection from attackers outside the building.
[4]CHILDREN: Joseph (b. 1661), Mary (b. 1665), and Sarah (1669–1676), who died during Rowlandson's captivity.
[5]SISTERS: An unknown child of Hannah Divol's.

an handful of Stones and threw them; so that we were fain to give back. We had six stout Dogs belonging to our Garrison, but none of them would stir, though another time, if an *Indian* had come to the Door, they were ready to fly upon him, and tear him down. The Lord hereby would make us the more to acknowledge his Hand, and to see that our Help is always in him. But out we must go, the Fire increasing, and coming along behind us roaring, and the *Indians* gaping before us with their Guns, Spears, and Hatchets, to devour us. No sooner were we out of the House, but my Brother-in-Law (being before wounded, in defending the House, in or near the Throat) fell down dead, whereat the *Indians* scornfully shouted, and hallowed, and were presently upon him, stripping off his Clothes. The Bullets flying thick, one went thorow my Side, and the same (as would seem) thorow the Bowels and Hand of my dear Child in my Arms. One of my eldest Sisters[6] Children (named *William*) had then his Leg broken, which the *Indians* perceiving, they knock'd him on the head. Thus were we butchered by those merciless Heathen, standing amazed, with the Blood running down to our Heels. My elder Sister being yet in the House, and seeing those woful Sights, the Infidels haling Mothers one way, and Children another, and some wallowing in their Blood, and her elder son telling her that (her Son) *William* was dead, and my self was wounded; she said, And *Lord, let me die with them:* Which was no sooner said, but she was struck with a Bullet, and fell down dead over the Threshold. I hope she is reaping the Fruit of her good Labours, being faithful to the Service of God in her Place. In her younger years she lay under much trouble upon Spiritual accounts, till it pleased God to make that precious Scripture take hold of her Heart, 2 *Cor.* 12. 9. *And he said unto me, My grace is sufficient for thee.* More than twenty years after I have heard her tell, how sweet and comfortable that Place was to her. But to return: The *Indians* laid hold of us, pulling me one way, and the Children another, and said, *Come, go along with us:* I told them, they would kill me: They answered, *If I were willing to go along with them, they would not hurt me.*

O the doleful Sight that now was to behold at this House! *Come, behold the works of the Lord, what desolation he has made in the Earth.*[7] Of thirty seven Persons who were in this one House, none escaped either present Death, or a bitter Captivity, save onely one, who might say as he, *Job* 1. 15. *And I onely am escaped alone to tell the News.* There were twelve killed, some shot, some stabb'd with their Spears, some knock'd down with

[6]ELDEST SISTER: Elizabeth Kelly.
[7]COME, BEHOLD THE WORKS OF THE LORD, WHAT DESOLATION HE HAS MADE IN THE EARTH: Psalm 46:8.

their Hatchets. When we are in prosperity, Oh the Little that we think of such dreadful Sights, and to see our dear Friends and Relations lie bleeding out their Heart-blood upon the Ground! There was one who was chopp'd into the Head with a Hatchet, and stripp'd naked, and yet was crawling up and down. It is a solemn Sight to see so many Christians lying in their Blood, some here, and some there, like a company of Sheep torn by Wolves. All of them stript naked by a company of hell-hounds, roaring, singing, ranting and insulting, as if they would have torn our very hearts out, yet the Lord by his Almighty power, preserved a number of us from death, for there were twenty four of us taken alive: and carried Captive.

I had often before this said, that if the *Indians* should come, I should chuse rather to be killed by them, than taken alive: but when it came to the trial my mind changed: their glittering Weapons so daunted my Spirit, that I chose rather to go along with those (as I may say) ravenous Bears, than that moment to end my daies. And that I may the better declare what happened to me during that grievous Captivity, I shall particularly speak of the several Removes[8] we had up and down the Wilderness.

The first Remove. Now away we must go with those Barbarous Creatures, with our bodies wounded and bleeding, and our hearts no less than our bodies. About a mile we went that night; up upon a hill within sight of the Town where they intended to lodge. There was hard by a vacant house (deserted by the English before, for fear of the *Indians*) I asked them whether I might not lodge in the house that night? to which they answered, what will you love *English-men* still? this was the dolefullest night that ever my eyes saw. Oh the roaring, and singing, and dancing, and yelling of those black creatures in the night, which made the place a lively resemblance of hell: And as miserable was the waste that was there made, of Horses, Cattle, Sheep, Swine, Calves, Lambs, Roasting Pigs, and Fowls (which they had plundered in the Town) some roasting, some lying and burning, and some boyling, to feed our merciless Enemies; who were joyful enough though we were disconsolate. To add to the dolefulness of the former day, and the dismalness of the present night, my thoughts ran upon my losses and sad bereaved condition. All was gone, my Husband gone[9] (at least separated from me, he being in the Bay; and to add to my grief, the *Indians* told me they would kill him as he came homeward) my Children gone, my Relations and Friends gone, our house and home, and

---

[8]REMOVES: Rowlandson uses the word *remove* to indicate departures from one location to the next. The narrative includes 20 removes.
[9]MY HUSBAND GONE: Warned of a possible attack, Joseph Rowlandson had gone to Boston to seek military assistance for Lancaster.

all our comforts within door, and without, all was gone (except my life) and I knew not but the next moment that might go too.

There remained nothing to me but one poor wounded Babe, and it seemed at present worse than death, that it was in such a pitiful condition, bespeaking Compassion, and I had no refreshing for it, nor suitable things to revive it. Little do many think, what is the savageness and bruitishness of this barbarous Enemy, aye even those that seem to profess more than others among them, when the *English* have fallen into their hands.

Those seven that were killed at *Lancaster* the summer before upon a Sabbath day, and the one that was afterward killed upon a week day, were slain and mangled in a barbarous manner, by one-ey'd *John*,[10] and *Marlberough's* Praying *Indians*,[11] which Capt. *Mosely* brought to *Boston*, as the *Indians* told me.

The second Remove. But now (the next morning) I must turn my back upon the Town, and travel with them into the vast and desolate Wilderness, I know not whither. It is not my tongue, or pen can express the sorrows of my heart, and bitterness of my spirit, that I had at this departure: But God was with me, in a wonderful manner, carrying me along, and bearing up my Spirit, that it did not quite fail. One of the *Indians* carried my poor wounded Babe upon a horse: it went moaning all a long, I shall die, I shall die. I went on foot after it, with sorrow that cannot be exprest. At length I took it off the Horse, and carried it in my arms, till my strength failed, and I fell down with it. Then they set me upon a horse, with my wounded Child in my lap, and there being no Furniture[12] upon the horse back; as we were going down a steep hill, we both fell over the horses head, at which they like inhuman creatures laught, and rejoiced to see it, though I thought we should there have ended our dayes, as overcome with so many difficulties. But the Lord renewed my strength still, and carried me along, that I might see more of his power, yea, so much that I could never have thought of, had I not experienced it.

After this it quickly began to Snow, and when night came on, they stopt: and now down I must sit in the Snow, by a little fire, and a few boughs behind me, with my sick Child in my lap; and calling much for water, being now (thorough the wound) fallen into a violent Fever. My

[10]ONE-EY'D JOHN: John Monoco, chief of the Nashoway, who led an attack on Lancaster the year before.
[11]MARLBEROUGH'S PRAYING INDIANS: Christianized Indians. In August 1675, Captain Samuel Mosely arrested and brought to Boston 15 "praying" Indians from Marlborough, Massachusetts, and accused them of the August 1675 attack on Lancaster.
[12]FURNITURE: A saddle.

own wound also growing so stiff, that I could scarce sit down or rise up, yet so it must be, that I must sit all this cold winter night, upon the cold snowy ground, with my sick Child in my arms, looking that every hour would be the last of its life; and having no Christian Friend near me, either to comfort or help me. Oh I may see the wonderful power of God, that my Spirit did not utterly sink under my affliction; still the Lord upheld me with his gracious and merciful Spirit, and we were both alive to see the light of the next morning.

The third Remove. The morning being come, they prepared to go on their way: one of the *Indians* got up upon a horse, and they set me up behind him with my poor sick Babe in my lap. A very wearisome and tedious day I had of it; what with my own wound, and my Childs being so exceeding sick, and in a lamentable Condition with her wound. It may easily be judged what a poor feeble condition we were in, there being not the least crumb of refreshing that came within either of our mouths, from Wednesday night to Saturday night, except only a little cold water. This day in the afternoon, about an hour by Sun, we came to the place where they intended, *viz.* an *Indian Town* called *Wenimesset*,[13] Northward of *Quabaug*. When we were come, Oh the Number of *Pagans* (now merciless Enemies) that there came about me, that I may say as *David*, Psal. 27. 13. *I had fainted, unless I had believed*, &c.[14] The next day was the Sabbath: I then remembered how careless I had been of Gods holy time: how many Sabbaths I had lost and mispent, and how evilly I had walked in Gods sight; which lay so close upon my Spirit, that it was easie for me to see how righteous it was with God to cut off the thread of my life, and cast me out of his presence for ever. Yet the Lord still shewed mercy to me, and upheld me; and as he wounded me with one hand, so he healed me with the other. This day there came to me one *Robert Pepper*[15] (a Man belonging to *Roxbury*) who was taken in Capt. *Beers*[16] his fight; and had been now a considerable time with the

---

[13]WENIMESSET: A Native American village on the Ware River.

[14]I HAD FAINTED, UNLESS I HAD BELIEVED: Psalm 27:13–14: "I had fainted, unless I had believed to see the goodness of the Lord in the land of the living. / Wait on the Lord: be of good courage, and he shall strengthen thine heart: wait, I say, on the Lord."

[15]ROBERT PEPPER: Robert Pepper had been taken captive by the Indians in a raid a year before on Northfield, Massachusetts (see note 16).

[16]CAPT. BEERS: Captain Richard Beers, who had attempted to save the garrison of Northfield, Massachusetts, which was attacked by John Monoco (see note 10) in September 1675.

[17]KING PHILIP: King Philip (1639–1676), also known as Metcom or Metacomet, was the son of Massasoit, the Wampanoag leader. In 1675–1676, the most devastating war (King Philip's War) between the colonists and the Native Americans (specifically the Wampanoag, Nipmuck, and Narragansett tribes) in New England erupted, stemming from growing hostilities related to the theft of and forced sale of Native American lands. The English eventually defeated the poorly organized Native American forces in April 1676, when Philip was killed in Mt. Hope, Rhode Island. Over 12 settlements had been destroyed and countless Native American and English lives taken before the end of the war, which also resulted in the virtual extermination of Native American life in southern New England.

Indians; and up with them almost as far as *Albany* to see King *Philip*,[17] as he told me, and was now very lately come with them into these parts. Hearing I say that I was in this *Indian* Town he obtained leave to come and see me. He told me he himself was wounded in the Leg at Capt. *Beers* his fight; and was not able sometime to go, but as they carried him, and that he took oaken leaves and laid to his wound, and through the blessing of God, he was able to travel again. Then I took Oaken leaves and laid to my side, and with the blessing of God it cured me also; yet before the cure was wrought, I may say as it is in *Psal.* 38. 5, 6. *My wounds stink*[18] *and are corrupt, I am troubled, I am bowed down greatly, I go mourning all the day long.* I sate much alone with a poor wounded Child in my lap, which moaned night and day, having nothing to revive the body, or cheer the Spirits of her: but instead of that, sometimes one Indian would come and tell me, one hour, and your Master will knock your Child in the head, and then a second, and then a third, your Master will quickly knock your child in the head.

This was the Comfort I had from them; miserable comforters are ye all, as he said. Thus nine dayes I sat upon my knees, with my babe in my lap, till my flesh was raw again: my child being even ready to depart this sorrowful world, they bade me carry it out, to another Wigwam: (I suppose because they would not be troubled with such spectacles.) Whither I went with a very heavy heart, and down I sate with the picture of death in my lap. About two hours in the Night, my sweet Babe like a Lamb departed this life, on *Feb.* 18. 1675. it being about six years and five months old. It was nine dayes (from the first wounding) in this Miserable condition, without any refreshing of one nature or other, except a little cold water. I cannot but take notice, how at another time I could not bear to be in the room where any dead person was, but now the case is changed: I must and could lye down by my dead Babe, side by side, all the night after. I have thought since of the wonderful goodness of God to me, in preserving me so in the use of my reason and senses, in that distressed time, that I did not use wicked and violent means to end my own miserable life. In the morning, when they understood that my child was dead, they sent for me home to my Masters Wigwam: (by my Master in this writing must be understood *Quannopin*,[19] who was a Saggamore and married King *Philips* wives Sister[20]; not that he first took me, but I was sold to him by another *Narrhaganset Indian*, who took me when first

---

[18]MY WOUNDS STINK....: Job 16:2.
[19]QUANNOPIN: A Narragansett chief who led the attack on Lancaster.
[20]KING PHILIPS WIVES SISTER: Known as Whettimore or Weetamoo. Rowlandson later becomes her servant.

I came out of the Garrison) I went to take up my dead Child in my arms to carry it with me, but they bid me let it alone: there was no resisting, but go I must and leave it. When I had been a while at my Masters wigwam, I took the first opportunity I could get, to go look after my dead child: when I came I asked them what they had done with it? they told me it was upon the hill: then they went and shewed me where it was, where I saw the ground was newly digged, and there they told me they had buried it, there I left that child in the Wilderness, and must commit it, and my self also in this Wilderness condition, to him who is above all. God having taken away this dear child, I went to see my daughter *Mary*, who was at this same *Indian Town*, at a Wigwam not very far off, though we had little liberty or opportunity to see one another: she was about ten years old, and taken from the door at first by a Praying *Indian*, and afterward sold for a gun. When I came in sight she would fall a weeping; at which they were provoked, and would not let me come near her, but bade me be gone: which was a heart-cutting word to me. *I* had one child dead, another in the wilderness, I knew not where, the third they would not let me come near to: *Me* (as he said) *have ye bereaved of my Children, Joseph is not, and Simeon is not, and ye will take Benjamin also, all these things are against me.*[21] I could not sit still in this condition, but kept walking from one place to another. And as I was going along, my heart was even overwhelmed with the thoughts of my condition, and that I should have Children, and a Nation which I knew not ruled over them. Whereupon I earnestly intreated the Lord, that he would consider my low estate, and shew me a token for good, and if it were his blessed will, some sign and hope of some relief. And indeed quickly the Lord answered, in some measure, my poor Prayer: For as I was going up and down mourning and lamenting my condition, my Son came to me, and asked me how I did? I had not seen him before, since the destruction of the Town: and I knew not where he was, till I was informed by himself, that he was amongst a smaller parcel of *Indians*, whose place was about six miles off; with tears in his eyes, he asked me whether his Sister *Sarah* was dead? and told me he had seen his Sister *Mary*; and prayed me, that I would not be troubled in reference to himself. The occasion of his coming to see me at this time was this: There was, as I said, about six miles from us, a small Plantation of *Indians*, where it seems he had been during his Captivity: and at this time, there were some Forces of the *Indians* gathered out of our company, and some also from them

---

[21]ME HAVE YE BEREAVED OF MY CHILDREN: Jacob's lament to his sons who have returned from Egypt without his youngest son, Benjamin (Genesis 42:36).

(amongst whom was my Sons Master) to go to assault and burn *Medfield*[22]: in this time of the absence of his Master, his Dame brought him to see me. I took this to be some gracious Answer, to my earnest and unfeigned desire. The next day, *viz.* to this, the *Indians* returned from *Medfield:* (all the Company, for those that belonged to the other smaller company, came thorow the Town that now we were at) But before they came to us, Oh the outrageious roaring and hooping that there was! They began their din about a mile before they came to us. By their noise and hooping they signified how many they had destroyed: (which was at that time twenty three) Those that were with us at home, were gathered together as soon as they heard the hooping, and every time that the other went over their number, these at home gave a shout, that the very Earth rang again. And thus they continued till those that had been upon the expedition were come up to the Saggamores Wigwam; and then, Oh, the hideous insulting and triumphing that there was over some *English-mens* Scalps, that they had taken (as their manner is) and brought with them. I cannot but take notice of the wonderful mercy of God to me in those afflictions, in sending me a bible: one of the *Indians* that came from *Medfield* fight and had brought some plunder; came to me, and asked me, if I would have a Bible, he had got one in his Basket, I was glad of it, and asked him, whether he thought the *Indians* would let me read? He answered yes: so I took the bible, and in that melancholy time, it came into my mind to read first the 28 *Chapter of Deuteronomie*,[23] which I did, and when I had read it, my dark heart wrought on this manner, that there was no mercy for me, that the blessings were gone, and the curses came in their room, and that I had lost my opportunity. But the Lord helped me still to go on reading, till I came to *Chap.* 30. the seven first verses: where I found there was mercy promised again, if we would return to him, by repentance[24]: and though we were scattered from one end of the earth to the other, yet the Lord would gather us together, and turn all those curses upon our Enemies. I do not desire to live to forget this Scripture, and what comfort it was to me.

Now the *Indians* began to talk of removing from this place, some one way, and some another. There were now besides my self nine *English* Captives in this place (all of them Children, except one Woman) I got an opportunity to go and take my leave of them; they being to go one

---

[22]MEDFIELD: Medfield, Massachusetts, which was attacked on February 21, 1676.
[23]28 CHAPTER OF DEUTERONOMIE: Deuteronomy 28 focuses on blessings from God for obedience and curses for disobedience.
[24]REPENTANCE: Deuteronomy 30:3: "That then the Lord thy God will turn thy captivity, and have compassion upon thee, and will return and gather thee from all the nations."

way, and I another. I asked them whether they were earnest with God for deliverance; they all told me, they did as they were able; and it was some comfort to me, that the Lord stirred up Children to look to him. The Woman, *viz.* Goodwife *Joslin*[25] told me, she should never see me again, and that she could find in her heart to run away: I wisht her not to run away by any means, for we were near thirty miles from any *English* Town, and she very big with Child and had but one week to reckon: and another Childe, in her Arms, two years old, and bad rivers there were to go over, and we were feeble with our poor and course entertainment. I had my Bible with me, I pulled it out, and asked her, whether she would read; we opened the Bible, and lighted on *Psal.* 27. in which Psalm we especially took notice of that, *ver. ult.*[26] *Wait on the Lord, be of good courage, and he shall strengthen thine Heart, wait I say on the Lord.*

The fourth Remove. And now must I part with that little company that I had. Here I parted from my daughter *Mary,* (whom I never saw again till I saw her in *Dorchester,* returned from Captivity) and from four little Cousins and Neighbours, some of which I never saw afterward, the Lord only knows the end of them. Amongst them also was that poor woman before mentioned, who came to a sad end, as some of the company told me in my travel: she having much grief upon her Spirit, about her miserable condition, being so near her time, she would be often asking the *Indians* to let her go home; they not being willing to that, and yet vexed with her importunity, gathered a great company together about her, and stript her naked, and set her in the midst of them: and when they had sung and danced about her (in their hellish manner) as long as they pleased: they knockt her on the head, and the child in her arms with her: when they had done that, they made a fire and put them both into it: and told the other Children that were with them, that if they attempted to go home they would serve them in like manner: The Children said she did not shed one tear, but prayed all the while. But to return to my own Journey: we travelled about half a day or a little more, and came to a desolate place in the Wilderness; where there were no Wigwams or Inhabitants before: we came about the middle of the afternoon to this place; cold, and wet, and snowy, and hungry, and weary, and no refreshing (for man) but the cold ground to sit on, and our poor *Indian cheer.*

Heart-aking thoughts here I had about my poor Children, who were scattered up and down amongst the wild Beasts of the Forest: my head was light and dizzy (either through hunger, or hard lodging, or trouble,

---

[25]GOODWIFE JOSLIN: *Goodwife* is equivalent to the modern "Mrs." in designating a married woman. Ann Joslin and her child were later killed in March 1676.
[26]VER. ULT.: The last verse of Psalm 27 (14). (Latin abbreviation)

or all together) my knees feeble, my body raw by sitting double night and day, that I cannot express to man the affliction that lay upon my Spirit, but the Lord helped me at that time to express it to himself. I opened my Bible to read, and the Lord brought that precious Scripture to me, *Jer.* 31. 16. *Thus saith the Lord, refrain thy voice from weeping, and thine eyes from tears, for thy work shall be rewarded, and they shall come again from the land of the Enemy.* This was a sweet Cordial to me, when I was ready to faint; many and many a time, have I sate down and wept sweetly over this Scripture. At this place we continued about four days.

The fifth Remove. The occasion (as I thought) of their moving at this time, was, the *English Army* its being near and following them: For they went as if they had gone for their lives, for some considerable way; and then they made a stop, and chose out some of their stoutest men, and sent them back to hold the *English* Army in play whilst the rest escaped; and then like *Jehu* they marched on furiously,[27] with their old, and with their young: some carried their old decrepit Mothers, some carried one, and some another. Four of them carried a great *Indian* upon a Bier; but going through a thick Wood with him they were hindered, and could make no haste; whereupon they took him upon their backs, and carried him, one at a time, till we came to *Bacquaug* River. Upon a Friday a little after noon we came to this River. When all the Company was come up, and were gathered together, I thought to count the number of them, but they were so many, and being somewhat in motion, it was beyond my skill. In this Travel, because of my wound, I was somewhat favoured in my load; I carried only my knitting-work, and two quarts of parched Meal: Being very faint I asked my Mistress[28] to give me one spoonful of the Meal, but she would not give me a taste. They quickly fell to cutting dry trees, to make rafts to carry them over the River: and soon my turn came to go over: By the advantage of some brush which they had laid upon the Raft to sit on; I did not wet my foot (when many of themselves at the other end were mid-leg-deep) which cannot but be acknowledged as a favour of God to my weakened body, it being a very cold time. I was not before acquainted with such kind of doings or dangers. *When thou passest through the waters I will be with thee, and through the rivers they shall not overflow thee.* Isai. 43. 2. A certain number of us got over the river that night, but it was the night after the Sabbath before all the company was got over. On

---

[27]JEHU THEY MARCHED ON FURIOUSLY: Jehu (c. 842–815 BCE) led a military coup against Jehoram for the throne of Israel, described in II Kings 9:20.
[28]MISTRESS: See note 20.

the Saturday they boyled an old Horses leg (which they had got) and so we drank of the broth; as soon as they thought it was ready, and when it was almost all gone, they filled it up again.

The first week of my being among them, I hardly ate any thing; the second week I found my stomach grow very faint for want of something; and yet 'twas very hard to get down their filthy trash: but the third week (though I could think how formerly my stomach would turn against this or that, and I could starve and die before I could eat such things, yet) they were pleasant and savoury to my taste. I was at this time knitting a pair of white Cotton Stockins for my Mistriss: and I had not yet wrought upon the Sabbath day: when the Sabbath came they bade me go to work; I told them it was Sabbath-day, and desired them to let me rest, and told them I would do as much more to morrow: to which they answered me, they would break my face. And here I cannot but take notice of the strange providence of God in preserving the Heathen: They were many hundreds, old and young, some sick and some lame, many had *Papooses*[29] at their backs, the greatest number (at this time with us) were *Squaws*[30]: and they travelled with all they had, bag and baggage, and yet they got over this River aforesaid: and on Monday they set their Wigwams on fire, and away they went: on that very day came the *English* Army after them to this River, and saw the smoke of their Wigwams; and yet this River put a stop to them. God did not give them courage or activity to go over after us: we were not ready for so great a mercy as victory and deliverance: if we had been, God would have found out a way for the *English* to have passed this River, as well as for the *Indians* with their *Squaws* and *Children*, and all their *Luggage*. *Oh that my people had hearkened to me, and Israel had walked in my wayes, I should soon have subdued their Enemies, and turned my hand against their Adversaries*, Psal. 81. 13, 14.

The sixth Remove. On Monday (as I said) they set their Wigwams on fire, and went away. It was a cold morning; and before us was a great Brook with Ice on it: some waded through it, up to the knees and higher: but others went till they came to a Beaver-Dam, and I amongst them, where thorough the good providence of God, I did not wet my foot. I went along that day, mourning and lamenting, leaving farther my own Countrey, and travelling into the vast and howling wilderness; and I

---

[29]PAPOOSES: Babies.
[30]SQUAWS: Married Native American women.
[31]LOTS WIFE'S TEMPATION: As she and her family fled the doomed city of Sodom, Lot's wife was turned into a pillar of salt for disobeying God's command that no one look back on the destruction behind them (Genesis 19:24).

understood something of *Lots* Wife's Temptation,[31] when she looked back: we came that day to a great Swamp; by the side of which we took up our lodging that night. When I came to the brow of the hill, that looked toward the Swamp, I thought we had been come to a great *Indian Town*, (though there were none but our own Company) the *Indians* were as thick as the Trees; it seemed as if there had been a thousand Hatchets going at once: if one looked before one, there was nothing but *Indians*, and behind one, nothing but *Indians*; and so on either hand: I my self in the midst, and no Christian Soul near me, and yet how hath the Lord preserved me in safety! Oh the experience that I have had of the goodness of God, to me and mine!

The seventh Remove. After a restless and hungry night there, we had a wearisome time of it the next day. The Swamp by which we lay, was as it were, a deep Dungeon, and an exceeding high and steep hill before it. Before I got to the top of the hill, I thought my heart and legs and all would have broken, and failed me. What through faintness and soreness of Body, it was a grievous day of Travel to me. As we went along, I saw a place where *English* Cattle had been: that was a comfort to me, such as it was: quickly after that we came to an *English* path, which so took with me, that I thought I could there have freely lyen down and died. That day, a little after noon, we came to *Squakheag*; where the *Indians* quickly spread themselves over the deserted *English* Fields, gleaning what they could find; some pickt up Ears of Wheat, that were crickled down; some found ears of *Indian Corn*; some found Ground-nuts, and others sheaves of Wheat, that were frozen together in the Shock, and went to threshing of them out. My self got two Ears of *Indian Corn*, and whilst I did but turn my back, one of them was stollen from me, which much troubled me. There came an *Indian* to them at that time, with a Basket of *Horse-liver*: I asked him to give me a piece: what (sayes he) can you eat Horse-liver? I told him, I would try, if he would give a piece; which he did: and I laid it on the coals to roast; but before it was half ready, they got half of it away from me; so that I was fain to take the rest and eat it as it was with the blood about my mouth, and yet a savoury bit it was to me: For to the hungry Soul every bitter thing is sweet.[32] A solemn sight methought it was, to see whole fields of Wheat, and Indian Corn forsaken and spoiled: and the remanders of them to be food for our merciless Enemies. That night we had a mess of Wheat for our supper.

[32]FOR TO THE HUNGRY SOUL....: Proverbs 27:7.

The eighth Remove. On the morrow morning we must go over the River, *i.e. Connecticot,* to meet with King *Philip,* two Cannoos full, they had carried over, the next turn I my self was to go; but as my foot was upon the Cannoo to step in, there was a sudden outcry among them, and I must step back: and instead of going over the River, I must go four or five miles up the River farther northward. Some of the *Indians* ran one way, and some another. The cause of this rout was as I thought their espying some *English* Scouts, who were thereabout.

In this travel up the River; about noon the Company made a stop, and sate down; some to eat, and others to rest them. As I sate amongst them, musing of things past, my Son *Joseph* unexpectedly came to me: we asked of each others welfare; bemoaning our doleful condition, and the change that had come upon us: we had Husband and Father, and Children and Sisters, and Friends and Relations, and House, and Home, and many Comforts of this life: but now we might say as *Job, Naked came I out of my mothers womb, and naked shall I return, The Lord gave, and the Lord hath taken away; blessed be the Name of the Lord.*[33] I asked him whether he would read? He told me, he earnestly desired it. I gave him my Bible, and he lighted upon that comfortable Scripture, *Psal.* 118. 17, 18. *I shall not die but live, and declare the works of the Lord: The Lord hath chastened me sore, yet he hath not given me over to death.* Look here *Mother,* (sayes he) did you read this? And here I may take occasion to mention one principal ground of my setting forth these few Lines; even as the Psalmist sayes, To declare the works of the Lord, and his wonderful power in carrying us along, preserving us in the Wilderness, while under the Enemies hand, and returning of us in safety again. And his goodness in bringing to my hand so many comfortable and suitable Scriptures in my distress. But to Return: We travelled on till night; and in the morning we must go over the River to *Philip*'s Crew. When I was in the Cannoo, I could not but be amazed at the numerous Crew of Pagans, that were on the Bank on the other side. When I came ashore, they gathered all about me, I sitting alone in the midst: I observed they asked one another Questions, and laughed, and rejoyced over their Gains and Victories. Then my heart began to faile: and I fell a weeping; which was the first time to my remembrance, that I wept before them. Although I had met with so much Affliction, and my heart was many times ready to break, yet could I not shed one tear in their sight; but rather had been all this while in a maze, and like one astonished; but now I may say, as *Psal.* 137. 1. *By the Rivers of* Babylon, *there we sate down, yea, we*

---

[33]NAKED CAME I OUT OF MY MOTHERS WOMB....: Job 1:21.

wept when we remembered Zion. There one of them asked me, why I wept; I could hardly tell what to say; yet I answered, they would kill me: No, said he, none will hurt you. Then came one of them, and gave me two spoonfuls of Meal (to comfort me) and another gave me half a pint of Pease, which was more worth than many Bushels at another time. Then I went to see King *Philip;* he bade me come in, and sit down, and asked me whether I would smoak (an usual Complement now a days amongst Saints and Sinners.[34]) But this no way suited me. For though I had formerly used Tobacco, yet I had left it ever since I was first taken. *It seems to be a Bait the Devil layes to make men lose their precious time:* I remember with shame, how formerly, when I had taken two or three Pipes, I was presently ready for another, such a bewitching thing it is: But I thank God, he has now given me power over it; surely there are many who may be better imployed, than to lye sucking a stinking Tobacco-pipe.

Now the *Indians* gather their Forces to go against *Northampton:* over night one went about yelling and hooting to give notice of the design. Whereupon they fell to boyling of Ground Nuts, and parching of Corn, (as many as had it) for their Provision: and in the morning away they went. During my abode in this place *Philip* spake to me to make a shirt for his Boy, which I did; for which he gave me a shilling; I offered the money to my Master, but he bade me keep it: and with it I bought a piece of Horse-flesh. Afterwards I made a Cap for his Boy, for which he invited me to Dinner: I went, and he gave me a Pancake, about as big as two fingers; it was made of parched Wheat, beaten and fryed in Bears grease, but I thought I never tasted pleasanter meat in my life. There was a Squaw who spake to me to make a shirt for her Sannup[35]; for which she gave me a piece of Bear. Another asked me to knit a pair of Stockins, for which she gave me a quart of Pease. I Boyled my Pease and Bear together, and invited my Master and Mistress to Dinner: but the proud Gossip,[36] because I served them both in one Dish, would eat nothing, except one bit that he gave her upon the point of his Knife. Hearing that my Son was come to this place, I went to see him, and found him lying flat upon the ground: I asked him how he could sleep so? He answered me, that he was not asleep, but at Prayer; and lay so, that they might not observe what he was doing. I pray God, he may remember these things now he is returned in safety. At this place (the Sun now getting higher) what with the beams and heat of the Sun, and the smoak of the Wigwams, I thought I should

[34]SAINTS AND SINNERS: Christians and unbelievers.
[35]SANNUP: Husband.
[36]GOSSIP: Her mistress.

have been blind: I could scarce discern one Wigwam from another. There was here one *Mary Thurston* of *Medfield*, who seeing how it was with me, lent me a Hat to wear; but as soon as I was gone, the Squaw (who owned that *Mary Thurston*) came running after me, and got it away again. Here there was a Squaw who gave me one spoonful of Meal, I put it in my Pocket[37] to keep it safe: yet notwithstanding some body stole it, but put five *Indian Corns* in the room of it: which Corns were the greatest Provision I had in my travel for one day.

The *Indians* returning from *North-hampton*, brought with them some Horses and Sheep, and other things which they had taken; I desired them, that they would carry me to *Albany* upon one of those Horses, and sell me for Powder; for so they had sometimes discoursed. I was utterly hopeless of getting home on foot, the way that I came. I could hardly bear to think of the many weary steps I had taken, to come to this place.

The ninth Remove. But instead of going either to *Albany* or homeward we must go five miles up the River, and then go over it. Here we abode a while. Here lived a sorry *Indian*, who spake to me to make him a shirt, when I had done it, he would pay me nothing. But he living by the River side, where I often went to fetch water, I would often be putting him in mind, and calling for my pay: at last, he told me, if I would make another shirt, for a Papoos not yet born, he would give me a knife, which he did, when I had done it. I carried the knife in, and my Master asked me to give it him, and I was not a little glad that I had any thing that they would accept of, and be pleased with. When we were at this place my Masters Maid came home, she had been gone three Weeks into the *Narrhaganset Country*; to fetch Corn, where they had stored up some in the ground: she brought home about a peck and half of Corn. This was about the time that their great Captain (*Naananto*[38]) was killed in the *Narrhaganset* Country.

My Son being now about a mile from me, I asked liberty to go and see him, they bade me go, and away I went; but quickly lost my self, travelling over Hills and through Swamps, and could not find the way to him. And I cannot but admire at the wonderful power and goodness of God to me, in that though I was gone from home, and met with all sorts of *Indians*, and those I had no knowledge of, and there being no *Christian Soul* near me; yet not one of them offered the least imaginable miscarriage to me. I turned homeward again, and met with my Master; he shewed me the way to my Son. When I came to him I found him not well; and withal he had a Boyl on his side, which much troubled him: we

[37]POCKET: Not a pocket that was part of Rowlandson's clothing, but more like a small bag or sack.
[38]NAANANTO: In April 1676, the Narragansett were completely defeated soon after their chief, Canonchet (also known as Naananto), was killed.

bemoaned one another a while, as the Lord helped us, and then I returned again. When I was returned, I found my self as unsatisfied as I was before. I went up and down moaning and lamenting: and my spirit was ready to sink, with the thoughts of my poor Children: my Son was ill, and I could not but think of his mournful looks: and no *Christian Friend* was near him, to do any office of love for him, either for Soul or Body. And my poor Girl, I knew not where she was, nor whether she was sick, or well, or alive, or dead. I repaired under these thoughts to my Bible (my great comforter in that time) and that Scripture came to my hand, *Cast thy burden upon the Lord and he shall sustain thee*, Psal. 55. 22.

But I was fain to go and look after something to satisfie my hunger: and going among the Wigwams, I went into one, and there found a Squaw who shewed her self very kind to me, and gave me a piece of Bear. I put it into my pocket, and came home; but could not find an opportunity to broil it, for fear they would get it from me, and there it lay all that day and night in my stinking pocket. In the morning I went again to the same Squaw, who had a Kettle of Ground-nuts boyling: I asked her to let me boyle my piece of Bear in her Kettle, which she did, and gave me some Ground-nuts to eat with it, and I cannot but think how pleasant it was to me. I have seen Bear baked very handsomely amongst the *English*, and some liked it, but the thoughts that it was Bear, made me tremble: but now that was savoury to me that one would think was enough to turn the stomach of a bruit-Creature.

One bitter cold day, I could find no room to sit down before the fire: I went out, and could not tell what to do, but I went into another Wigwam where they were also sitting round the fire: but the Squaw laid a skin for me, and bid me sit down; and gave me some Ground-nuts, and bade me come again; and told me they would buy me if they were able; and yet these were Strangers to me that I never knew before.

The tenth Remove. That day a small part of the Company removed about three quarters of a mile, intending farther the next day. When they came to the place where they intended to lodge, and had pitched their Wigwams; being hungry, I went again back to the place we were before at, to get something to eat: being incouraged by the Squaws kindness, who bade me come again; when I was there, there came an *Indian* to look after me: who when he had found me, kickt me all along: I went home and found Venison roasting that night, but they would not give me one bit of it. Sometimes I met with Favour, and sometimes with nothing but Frowns.

[39]THE ELEVENTH REMOVE: Rowlandson is now around Chesterfield, New Hampshire, as far north as she will journey.

The eleventh Remove.[39] The next day in the morning they took their Travel, intending a dayes journey up the River, I took my load at my back, and quickly we came to wade over a River: and passed over tiresome and wearisome Hills. One Hill was so steep, that I was fain to creep up, upon my knees: and to hold by the twigs and bushes to keep my self from falling backward. My head also was so light, that I usually reeled as I went, but I hope all those wearisome steps that I have taken, are but a forwarding of me to the Heavenly rest. *I know, O Lord, that thy Judgments are right, and that thou in faithfulness hast afflicted me,* Psal. 119. 75.

The twelfth Remove. It was upon a Sabbath day morning, that they prepared for their Travel. This morning, I asked my Master whether he would sell me to my Husband? he answered *Nux*[40]: which did much rejoyce my spirit. My Mistriss, before we went, was gone to the burial of a *Papoos;* and returning, she found me sitting, and reading in my Bible: she snatched it hastily out of my hand, and threw it out of doors; I ran out, and catcht it up, and put it into my pocket, and never let her see it afterward. Then they packed up their things to be gone, and gave me my load, I complained it was too heavy, whereupon she gave me a slap in the face, and bade me go: I lifted up my heart to God, hoping the Redemption was not far off: and the rather because their insolency grew worse and worse.

But the thoughts of my going homeward (for so we bent our course) much cheared my Spirit, and made my burden seem light, and almost nothing at all. But (to my amazement and great perplexity) the scale was soon turned: for when we had gone a little way, on a sudden my Mistriss gives out, she would go no further, but turn back again, and said *I* must go back again with her, and she called her Sannup, and would have had him gone back also, but he would not, but said, he would go on, and come to us again in three dayes. My Spirit was upon this (I confess) very impatient and almost outragious. I thought I could as well have died as went back. I cannot declare the trouble that I was in about it: but yet back again I must go. As soon as I had an opportunity, I took my Bible to read, and that quieting Scripture came to my hand, *Psal.* 46. 10. *Be still, and know that I am God;* which stilled my spirit for the present: but a sore time of trial I concluded I had to go through. My Master being gone, who seemed to me the best Friend that I had of an *Indian,* both in cold and hunger, and quickly so it proved. Down I sat, with my Heart as full as it could hold, and yet so hungry that I could not sit

---

[40]NUX: Yes.

neither: but going out to see what I could find, and walking among the Trees, I found six Acorns and two Chesnuts, which were some refreshment to me. Towards night I gathered me some sticks for my own comfort, that I might not lye a Cold: but when we came to lye down, they bade me go out and lye somewhere else, for they had company (they said) come in more than their own: I told them I could not tell where to go, they bade me go look: I told them, if I went to another *Wigwam* they would be angry, and send me home again. Then one of the Company drew his Sword, and told me he would run me through if I did not go presently. Then was I fain to stoop to this rude fellow, and to go out in the Night, I knew not whither. Mine eyes have seen that Fellow afterwards walking up and down in *Boston,* under the appearance of a *Friend-Indian:* and several others of the like Cut. I went to one *Wigwam,* and they told me they had no room. Then I went to another, and they said the same: at last an old *Indian* bade me come to him, and his Squaw gave me some Ground-nuts: she gave me also something to lay under my Head, and a good Fire we had: and through the good Providence of God, I had a comfortable lodging that Night. In the morning another *Indian* bade me come at night, and he would give me six Ground-nuts, which I did. We were at this place and time about two miles from *Connecticut River.* We went in the morning (to gather Ground-nuts) to the River, and went back again at Night. I went with a great load at my back (for they when they went, though but a little way, would carry all their trumpery with them) I told them the skin was off my back, but I had no other comforting answer from them than this, that it would be no matter if my Head were off too.

The thirteenth Remove. Instead of going toward the Bay (which was that I desired) I must go with them five or six miles down the River, into a mighty Thicket of Brush: where we abode almost a fortnight. Here one asked me to make a shirt for her Papoos, for which she gave me a mess of Broth, which was thickened with meal made of the Bark of a Tree: and to make it the better she had put into it about a handful of Pease, and a few rosted Ground-nuts. I had not seen my Son a pretty while, and here was an *Indian* of whom I made inquiry after him, and asked him when he saw him? He answered me that such a time his Master roasted him; and that himself did eat a piece of him, as big as his two fingers, and that he was very good meat: but the Lord upheld my Spirit, under his discouragement; and I considered their horrible addictedness to lying, and that there is not one of them that makes the least conscience of speaking the truth. In this place on a cold night as I lay by the fire, I removed a stick which kept the heat from me, a Squaw moved it down again, at which I lookt up, and she threw an handful of ashes in my eyes; I thought I should have been quite blinded and have never seen more: but lying down, the Water run out of my eyes, and carried the dirt with it, that by the morning, I recovered my sight again. Yet upon this, and the like occasions, I hope it is not too much to say with *Job, Have pity upon me, have pity upon me, Oh ye my Friends, for the hand of the Lord has touched me.*[41] And here I cannot but remember how many times sitting in their Wigwams, and musing on things past, I should suddenly leap up and run out, as if I had been at home, forgetting where I was, and what my condition was: But when I was without, and saw nothing but Wilderness, and Woods, and a company of barbarous Heathen; my mind quickly returned to me, which made me think of that, spoken concerning *Sampson*, who said, *I will go out and shake my self as at other times, but he wist not that the Lord was departed from him.*[42] About this time, I began to think that all my hopes of Restoration would come to nothing. I thought of the *English* Army, and hoped for their coming, and being retaken by them, but that failed. I hoped to be carried to *Albany*, as the *Indians* had discoursed, but that failed also. I thought of being sold to my Husband, as my Master spake; but instead of that, my Master himself was gone, and I left behind: so that my spirit was now quite ready to sink. I asked them to let me go out, and pick up some sticks, that I might get alone, and pour out my heart unto the Lord. Then also I took my Bible to read, but I found no comfort here neither: yet I can say, that in all my sorrows and afflictions, God did not leave me to have my impatience work towards himself, as if his ways were unrighteous; but I knew that he laid upon me less then I deserved. Afterward, before this doleful time ended with me, I was turning the leaves of my Bible, and the Lord brought to me some Scriptures, which did a little revive me, as that *Isai.* 55. 8. *For my thoughts are not your thoughts, neither are your ways my ways, saith the Lord.* And also that, *Ps.* 37, 5. *Commit thy way unto the Lord, trust also in him, and he shall bring it to pass.*

About this time they came yelping from *Hadly*, having there killed three *English-men*, and brought one Captive with them, *viz. Thomas Read.*[43] They all gathered about the poor Man, asking him many Questions. I desired also to go and see him; and when I came he was crying bitterly: supposing they would quickly kill him. Whereupon I asked one of them, whether they intended to kill him? he answered me,

---

[41]JOB, HAVE PITY ON ME....: Job 19:21.
[42]I WILL GO OUT AND SHAKE MY SELF....: Judges 16:20.
[43]THOMAS READ: A soldier.

they would not: He being a little cheared with that, *I* asked him about the welfare of my Husband, he told me he saw him such a time in the *Bay*, and he was well, but very Melancholly. By which I certainly understood (though I suspected it before) that whatsoever the *Indians* told me respecting him, was vanity and lies. Some of them told me, he was dead, and they had killed him: some said he was Married again, and that the Governour wished him to Marry; and told him he should have his choice, and that all perswaded him I was dead. So like were these barbarous creatures to him who was a liar from the beginning.

As I was sitting once in the Wigwam here, *Philips* Maid came in with the Child in her arms, and asked me to give her a piece of my Apron, to make a flap for it, I told her I would not: then my Mistress had me give it, but still I said no. The Maid told me, if I would not give her a piece, she would tear a piece off it: I told her I would tear her Coat then: with that my Mistress rises up: and takes up a stick big enough to have killed me, and struck at me with it, but I stept out, and she struck the stick into the Mat of the Wigwam. But while she was pulling of it out, I ran to the Maid and gave her all my Apron, and so that storm went over.

Hearing that my Son was come to this place, I went to see him, and told him his Father was well, but very melancholly: he told me he was as much grieved for his Father as for himself; I wondered at his speech, for I thought I had enough upon my spirit in reference to my self, to make me mindless of my Husband and every one else: they being safe among their Friends. He told me also, that a while before, his Master (together with other *Indians*) were going to the *French* for Powder[44]; but by the way the *Mohawks*[45] met with them, and killed four of their Company, which made the rest turn back again: for which I desire that my self and he may bless the Lord; for it might have been worse with him, had he been sold to the *French*, than it proved to be in his remaining with the *Indians*.

I went to see an *English* Youth in this place, one *John Gilberd* of *Springfield*. I found him lying without doors, upon the ground; I asked him how he did? He told me was very sick of a flux,[46] with eating so much blood. They had turned him out of the Wigwam, and with him an *Indian Papoos*, almost dead (whose Parents had been killed) in a bitter cold day, without fire or clothes: the young man himself had noth-

[44]POWDER: Gunpowder.
[45]MOHAWKS: Although King Philip had asked the Mohawks to join his battle against New England, they allied themselves with the English.
[46]FLUX: Dysentery.

ing on, but his shirt and wastcoat: This sight was enough to melt a heart of flint. There they lay quivering in the Cold, the youth round like a dog; the *Papoos* stretcht out, with his eyes, and nose, and mouth full of dirt, and yet alive, and groaning. I advised *John* to go and get to some fire: he told me he could not stand, but I perswaded him still, lest he should ly there and die. And with much ado I got him to a fire, and went my self home. As soon as I was got home, his Masters Daughter came after me, to know what I had done with the *English-man*? I told her I had got him to a fire in such a place. Now had I need to pray *Pauls* prayer, *2 Thess.* 3. 2. *That we may be delivered from unreasonable and wicked men.* For her satisfaction I went along with her, and brought her to him; but before I got home again, it was noised about, that I was running away, and getting the *English* youth along with me: that as soon as I came in, they began to rant and domineer: asking me where I had been? and what I had been doing? and saying they would knock me in the head: I told them, I had been seeing the *English Youth:* and that I would not run away: they told me I lied, and taking up a Hatchet, they came to me, and said, they would knock me down if I stirred out again: and so confined me to the Wigwam. Now may I say with *David, 2 Sam.* 24. 14. *I am in a great strait.* If I keep in, I must dye with hunger, and if I go out, I must be knockt in the head. This distressed condition held that day, and half the next; and then the Lord remembered me, whose mercies are great. Then came an *Indian* to me, with a pair of Stockins which were too big for him; and he would have me ravel them out, and knit them fit for him. I shrewed my self willing, and bid him ask my Mistress, if I might go along with him a little way: She said yes, I might, but I was not a little refresht with that news, that I had my liberty again. Then I went along with him, and he gave me some roasted Ground-nuts, which did again revive my feeble stomach.

Being got out of her sight, I had time and liberty again to look into my Bible: which was my guide by day, and my Pillow by night. Now that comfortable Scripture presented it self to me, *Isai.* 54. 7. *For a small moment have I forsaken thee: but with great mercies will I gather thee.* Thus the Lord carried me along from one time to another: and made good to me this precious promise, and many others. Then my Son came to see me, and I asked his Master to let him stay a while with me: that I might comb his head, and look over him for he was almost overcome with lice. He told me, when I had done, that he was very hungry, but I had nothing to relieve him; but bid him go into the Wigwams as he went along, and see if he could get any thing among them. Which he did, and (it seems) tarried a little too long; for his Master was angry with him, and beat him, and then sold him. Then he came running to tell me he had a new Master, and that he had given him some Ground-nuts already. Then I went along with him to his new Master, who told me he loved him: and he should not want. So his Master carried him away, and I never saw him afterward: till I saw him at *Pascataqua* in *Portsmouth*.

That night they bade me go out of the Wigwam again: my Mistresses *Papoos* was sick, and it died that night; and there was one benefit in it, that there was more room. I went to a Wigwam, and they bade me come in, and gave me a skin to lye upon, and a mess of Venison and Ground-nuts; which was a choice Dish among them. On the morrow they buried the *Papoos*: and afterward, both morning and evening, there came a company to mourn and howl with her: though I confess, I could not much condole with them. Many sorrowful days I had in this place: often getting alone; *like a Crane or a Swallow so did I chatter; I did mourn as a Dove, mine eyes fail with looking upward. Oh Lord I am oppressed, undertake for me*, Isai. 38. 14. I could tell the Lord, as *Hezechiah*, ver. 3. *Remember now, O Lord, I beseech thee, how I have walked before thee in truth.* Now had I time to examine all my wayes: my Conscience did not accuse me of unrighteousness toward one or other: yet I saw how in my walk with God, I had been a careless creature. As *David* said, *Against thee, thee only have I sinned*[47]*:* and I might say with the poor Publican, *God be merciful unto me a sinner.* On the Sabbath days I could look upon the Sun, and think how People were going to the house of God, to have their Souls refresht; and then home, and their Bodies also: but I was destitute of both; and might say as the poor Prodigal, *he would fain have filled his belly with the husks that the Swine did eat, and no man gave unto him*, Luke 15. 16. For I must say with him, *Father I have sinned against Heaven, and in thy sight*, ver. 21. I remembered how on the night before and after the Sabbath, when my Family was about me, and Relations and Neighbours with us, we could pray and sing, and then refresh our bodies with the good creatures of God: and then have a comfortable Bed to ly down on: but instead of all this, I had only a little Swill for the body, and then like a Swine, must ly down on the Ground: I cannot express to man the sorrow that lay upon my Spirit, the Lord knows it. Yet that comfortable Scripture would often come to my mind, *For a small moment have I forsaken thee, but with great mercies I will gather thee.*[48]

The fourteenth Remove. Now must we pack up and be gone from this Thicket, bending our course towards the Bay-Towns. I having nothing

---

[47]AGAINST THEE, THEE ONLY I HAVE SINNED: Psalm 51:4.
[48]FOR A SMALL MOMENT HAVE I FORSAKEN THEE....: Isaiah 54:7.

to eat by the way this day, but a few crumbs of Cake, that an *Indian* gave my Girl, the same day we were taken. She gave it me, and I put it into my pocket: there it lay till it was so mouldy (for want of good baking) that one could not tell what it was made of; it fell all to crumbs, and grew so dry and hard, that it was like little flints; and this refreshed me many times, when I was ready to faint. It was in my thoughts when I put it into my mouth, that if ever I returned, I would tell the World, what a blessing the Lord gave to such mean food. As we went along, they killed a *Deer*, with a young one in her: they gave me a piece of the *Fawn*, and it was so young and tender, that one might eat the bones as well as the flesh, and yet I thought it very good. When night came on we sate down, it rained, but they quickly got up a Bark Wigwam, where I lay dry that night. I looked out in the morning, and many of them had lain in the rain all night, I saw by their Reeking.[49] Thus the Lord dealt mercifully with me many times: and I fared better than many of them. In the morning they took the blood of the *Deer*, and put it into the Paunch, and so boiled it I could eat nothing of that, though they ate it sweetly. And yet they were so nice[50] in other things, that when I had fetcht water, and had put the Dish I dipt the water with, into the Kettle of water which I brought, they would say, they would knock me down; for they said, it was a sluttish[51] trick.

The fifteenth Remove. We went on our travel. I having got one handful of Ground-nuts, for my support that day: they gave me my load, and I went on cheerfully (with the thoughts of going homeward) having my burden more on my back than my spirit: we came to *Baquaug* River again that day, near which we abode a few days. Sometimes one of them would give me a Pipe, another a little Tobacco, another a little Salt: which I would change for a little Victuals. I cannot but think what a Wolvish appetite persons have in a starving condition: for many times when they gave me that which was hot, I was so greedy, that I should burn my mouth, that it would trouble me hours after; and yet I should quickly do the same again. And after I was throughly hungry, I was never again satisfied. For though sometimes it fell out, that I got enough, and did eat till I could eat no more, yet I was as unsatisfied as I was when I began. And now could I see that Scripture verified (there being many Scriptures which we do not take notice of, or understand till we are afflicted) *Mic.* 6. 14. *Thou shalt eat and not be satisfied.* Now might I

---

[49]REEKING: Damp and steaming.
[50]NICE: Particular.
[51]SLUTTISH: Untidy or unclean.

see more than ever before, the miseries that sin hath brought upon us. Many times I should be ready to run out against the Heathen, but that Scripture would quiet me again, *Amos* 3. 6. *Shall there be evil in the City, and the Lord hath not done it?* The Lord help me to make a right improvement of his word, and that I might learn that great lesson, *Mic.* 6. 8, 9. *He hath shewed thee, O Man, what is good; and what doth the Lord require of thee, but to do justly, and love mercy, and walk humbly with thy God? Hear ye the rod, and who hath appointed it.*

The sixteenth Remove. We began this Remove with wading over *Baquaug* River. The Water was up to the knees, and the stream very swift, and so cold that I thought it would have cut me in sunder. I was so weak and feeble, that I reeled as I went along, and thought there I must end my days at last, after my bearing and getting through so many difficulties. The *Indians* stood laughing to see me staggering along, but in my distress the Lord gave me experience of the truth and goodness of that promise, *Isai.* 43. 2. *When thou passest thorough the waters, I will be with thee, and through the Rivers, they shall not overflow thee.* Then I sate down to put on my stockins and shoes, with the tears running down my eyes, and many sorrowful thoughts in my heart: but I gat up to go along with them. Quickly there came up to us an *Indian*, who informed them, that I must go to *Wachuset* to my Master: for there was a Letter come from the Council to the *Saggamores*,[52] about redeeming the Captives, and that there would be another in fourteen days, and that I must be there ready. My heart was so heavy before that I could scarce speak, or go in the path; and yet now so light, that I could run. My strength seemed to come again, and to recruit my feeble knees, and aking heart: yet it pleased them to go but one mile that night, and there we stayed two days. In that time came a company of *Indians* to us, near thirty, all on Horse back. My heart skipt within me, thinking they had been *English-men* at the first sight of them: for they were dressed in *English* Apparel, with Hats, white Neck-cloths, and Sashes about their wasts, and Ribbons upon their shoulders: but when they came near, there was a vast difference between the lovely Faces of *Christians*, and the foul looks of those *Heathens:* which much damped my spirit again.

The seventeenth Remove. A comfortable Remove it was to me, because of my hopes. They gave me my pack, and along we went cheerfully: but quickly my Will proved more than my strength; having little or no refresh-

[52]LETTER COME FROM THE COUNCIL TO THE SAGGAMORES: A letter from Massachusetts Bay Colony Governor John Leverett (1616–1679), dated March 31, 1676.

ing my strength failed, and my spirits were almost quite gone. Now may I say as *David, Psal.* 109. 22, 23, 24. *I am poor and needy, and my heart is wounded within me. I am gone like the shadow when it declineth: I am tossed up and down like the Locust: my knees are weak through fasting, and my flesh faileth of fatness.* At night we came to an *Indian Town*, and the *Indians* sate down by a Wigwam discoursing, but I was almost spent, and could scarce speak. I laid down my load, and went into the Wigwam, and there sate an *Indian* boiling of *Horses feet:* (they being wont to eat the flesh first, and when the feet were old and dried, and they had nothing else, they would cut off the feet and use them) I asked him to give me a little of his Broth, or Water they were boiling in: he took a Dish, and gave me one spoonful of Samp[53] and bid me take as much of the Broth as I would. Then I put some of the hot water to the Samp, and drank it up, and my spirit came again. He gave me also a piece of the Ruffe or Ridding[54] of the small Guts, and I broiled it on the coals; and now may I say with *Jonathan, See I pray you how mine eyes have been enlightened, because I tasted a little of this honey;* 1 Sam. 14. 29. Now is my Spirit revived again: though means be never to inconsiderable, yet if the Lord bestow his blessing upon them, they shall refresh both Soul and Body.

The eighteenth Remove. We took up our packs, and along we went. But a wearisome day I had of it. As we went along, I saw an *Englishman* stript naked, and lying dead upon the ground, but knew not who it was. Then we came to another *Indian Town*, where we stayed all night. In this Town, there were four *English Children*, Captives: and one of them my own Sisters. I went to see how she did, and she was well, considering her Captive condition. I would have tarried that night with her, but they that owned her would not suffer it. Then I went to another Wigwam, where they were boiling Corn and Beans, which was a lovely sight to see, but I could not get a taste thereof. Then I went into another Wigwam, where there were two of the *English Children:* The Squaw was boiling horses feet, then she cut me off a little piece, and gave one of the *English Children* a piece also. Being very hungry, I had quickly eat up mine: but the Child could not bite it, it was so tough and sinewy, but lay sucking, gnawing, chewing, and slobbering it in the Mouth and Hand, then I took it of the Child, and eat it my self; and savoury it was to my taste.

That I may say as *Job, Chap.* 6. 7. *The things that my Soul refused to touch, are as my sorrowful meat.* Thus the Lord made that pleasant and refreshing, which another time would have been an Abomination.

---

[53]SAMP: A porridge made of Indian corn.
[54]RUFFE OR RIDDING: Scraps; that which he intended to discard.

Then I went home to my Mistresses Wigwam: and they told me I disgraced My Master with begging: and if I did so any more, they would knock me on the Head: I told them, they had as good knock me on the Head, as starve me to death.

The nineteenth Remove. They said, when we went out, that we must travel to *Wachuset* this day. But a bitter weary day I had of it; travelling now three dayes together, without resting any day between. At last, after many weary steps, I saw *Wachuset* hills, but many miles off. Then we came to a great Swamp, through which we travelled up to the knees in mud and water, which was heavy going to one tired before. Being almost spent, I thought I should have sunk down at last, and never got out; but I may say, as in *Psal.* 94. 18. *When my foot slipped, thy mercy, O Lord, held me up.* Going along, having indeed my life, but little Spirit, *Philip,* (who was in the Company) came up, and took me by the hand, and said, *Two weeks more, and you shall be Mistriss again.* I asked him if he speak true? he answered, Yes, and quickly you shall come to your Master again: who had been gone from us three weeks. After many weary steps we came to *Wachuset,* where he was; and glad I was to see him. He asked me, when I washt me? I told him not this moneth; then he fetch me some water himself, and bid me wash, and gave me the Glass to see how I lookt, and bid his Squaw give me something to eat. So she gave me a mess of Beans and meat, and a little Ground-nut Cake. I was wonderfully revived with this favour shewed me, *Psal.* 106. 46. *He made them also to be pitied of all those that carried them Captives.*

My Master had three Squaws: living sometimes with one, and sometimes with another. One, this old Squaw at whose Wigwam I was, and with whom my Master had been those three weeks. Another was *Wettimore,* with whom I had lived and served all this while. A severe and proud Dame she was; bestowing every day in dressing her self near as much time as any of the Gentry of the land: powdering her hair and painting her face, going with her Neck-laces, with Jewels in her ears, and bracelets upon her hands. When she had dressed her self, her Work was to make Girdles of Wampom and Beads. The third Squaw was a younger one, by whom he had two Papooses. By that time I was refresht by the old Squaw, with whom my Master was, *Wettimores* Maid came to call me home, at which I fell a weeping; then the old Squaw told me, to encourage me, that if I wanted victuals, I should come to her, and that I should lye there in her Wigwam. Then I went with the Maid, and quickly came again and lodged there. The Squaw laid a Mat under me, and a good Rugg over me; the first time I had any such Kindness shewed me. I understood that *Wettimore* thought, that if she should let me go and serve with the old Squaw, she would be in danger to lose not only my service but the redemption-pay also. And I was not a little glad to hear this; being by it raised in my hopes, that in Gods due time there would be an end of this sorrowful hour. Then came an *Indian*, and asked me to knit him three pair of Stockins, for which I had a Hat, and a silk Handkerchief. Then another asked me to make her a shift, for which she gave me an Apron.

Then came *Tom and Peter*,[55] with the second Letter from the Council, about the Captives. Though they were *Indians*, I gat them by the hand, and burst out into Tears; my heart was so full that I could not speak to them: but recovering my self, I asked them how my Husband did? and all my Friends and Acquaintance? They said, they were well, but very Melancholy. They brought me two Biskets, and a pound of Tobacco. The Tobacco I quickly gave away: when it was all gone, one asked me to give him a pipe of Tobacco, I told him all was gone; then began he to rant and threaten; I told him when my Husband came, I would give him some: Hang him Rogue (says he) I will knock out his brains, if he comes here. And then again in the same breath, they would say, that if there should come an hundred without Guns they would do them no hurt. So unstable and like mad men they were: So that fearing the worst, I durst not send to my Husband; though there were some thoughts of his coming to Redeem and fetch me, not knowing what might follow; for there was little more trust to them than to the Master they served. When the Letter was come, the Saggamores met to consult about the Captives, and called me to them to enquire how much my Husband would give to redeem me: When I came, I sate down among them, as I was wont to do, as their manner is: Then they bade me stand up, and said, they were the *General Court.*[56] They bid me speak what I thought he would give. Now knowing that all we had was destroyed by the *Indians*, I was in a great strait. I thought if I should speak of but a little, it would be slighted, and hinder the matter; if of a great Sum, I knew not where it would be procured: yet at a venture, I said *Twenty pounds*,[57] yet desired them to take less: but they would not hear of that, but sent that message to *Boston*, that for *twenty pounds* I should be redeemed. It was a Praying *Indian* that wrote their Letter for them. There was another Praying *Indian*, who told me, that he had a Brother, that would not eat Horse; his Conscience was so tender and scrupulous, (though as large

---

[55]TOM AND PETER: Tom Dublet and Peter Conway, Christianized Nipmucks.
[56]GENERAL COURT: An imitation of the colonial assembly of Massachusetts Bay Colony.
[57]TWENTY POUNDS: A substantial sum for a ransom at this time. To put this amount in perspective, a servant was paid around 10 pounds a year in seventeenth-century New England.

as Hell, for the destruction of poor *Christians*). Then he said, he read that Scripture to him, 2 *King*. 6. 25. *There was a Famine in* Samaria, *and behold they besieged it, until an Asses head was sold for four-score pieces of silver, and the fourth part of a Kab of Doves dung, for five pieces of silver.* He expounded this place to his Brother, and shewed him that it was lawful to eat that in a Famine, which is not at another time. And now, says he, he will eat Horse with any *Indian* of them all. There was another Praying *Indian*, who when he had done all the Mischief that he could, betrayed his own Father into the *Englishes* hands, thereby to purchase his own Life. Another Praying *Indian* was at *Sudbury* Fight,[58] though, as he deserved, he was afterward hanged for it. There was another Praying *Indian*, so wicked and cruel, as to wear a string about his neck, strung with *Christian* Fingers. Another Praying *Indian*, when they went to *Sudbury* Fight, went with them, and his Squaw also with him, with her Papoos at her back: before they went to that Fight, they got a company together to *Powaw*[59]: the manner was as followeth. There was one that kneeled upon a *Deer-skin*, with the Company round him in a Ring, who kneeled, striking upon the Ground with their hands, and with sticks, and muttering or humming with their Mouths. Besides him who kneeled in the Ring, there also stood one with a Gun in his hand: Then he on the Deer-skin made a speech, and all manifested assent to it; and so they did many times together. Then they bade him with the Gun go out of the Ring, which he did; but when he was out they called him in again; but he seemed to make a stand; then they called the more earnestly, till he returned again. Then they all sang. Then they gave him two Guns, in either hand one. And so he on the Deer-skin began again; and at the end of every Sentence in his speaking, they all assented, humming or muttering with their Mouthes, and striking upon the Ground with their Hands. Then they bade him with the two Guns go out of the Ring again: which he did a little way. Then they called him in again, but he made a stand, so they called him with earnestness: but he stood reeling and wavering, as if he knew not whether he should stand or fall, or which way to go. Then they called him with exceeding great vehemency, all of them, one and another: after a little while, he turned in, staggering as he went, with his Arms stretched out; in either hand a Gun. As soon as he came in, they all sang and rejoyced exceedingly a while. And then he upon the Deer-skin, made another speech, until which they all assented in a rejoycing manner: and so they ended their business, and forthwith went

[58]SUDBURY FIGHT: A reference to an attack on Sudbury, Massachusetts, on April 18, 1676.
[59]POWAW: Pow-wow; confer or deliberate.

to *Sudbury* Fight. To my thinking they went without any scruple but that they should prosper and gain the Victory. And they went out not so rejoycing, but that they came home with as great a Victory. For they said they had killed two Captains, and almost an hundred men. One *Englishman* they brought alive with them; and he said it was too true, for they had made sad work at *Sudbury;* as indeed it proved. Yet they came home without that rejoycing and triumphing over their Victory, which they were wont to shew at other times: but rather like Dogs, (as they say) which have lost their Ears. Yet I could not perceive that it was for their own loss of Men: they said they had not lost about five or six: and I missed none, except in one Wigwam. When they went, they acted as if the Devil had told them that they should gain the Victory: and now they acted, as if the Devil had told them that they should have a fall. Whether it were so or no, I cannot tell, but so it proved: for quickly they began to fall, and so held on that Summer, till they came to utter ruine. They came home on a Sabbath day, and the Powaw[60] that kneeled upon the Deer-skin, came home (I may say without any abuse) as black as the Devil. When my Master came home, he came to me and bid me make a shirt for his Papoos of a Hollandlaced Pillowbeer.[61] About that time there came an *Indian* to me, and bade me come to his *Wigwam* at night, and he would give me some Pork and Ground-nuts. Which I did, and as I was eating, another *Indian* said to me, he seems to be your good Friend, but he killed two *English-men* at *Sudbury;* and there lye their Cloaths behind you: I looked behind me, and there I saw bloody-Cloathes, with Bullet-holes in them: yet the Lord suffered not this Wretch to do me any hurt. Yea, instead of that, he many times refresht me: five or six times did he and his Squaw refresh my feeble Carcass. If I went to their *Wigwam* at any time, they would always give me something, and yet they were strangers that I never saw before. Another *Squaw* gave me a piece of fresh Pork, and a little Salt with it: and lent me her Frying pan to fry it in: and I cannot but remember what a sweet, pleasant and delightful relish that bit had to me, to this day. So little do we prize common mercies, when we have them to the full.

The twentieth Remove. It was their usual manner to remove, when they had done any mischeif, lest they should be found out: and so they did at this time. We went about three or four miles, and there they built a great *Wigwam*, big enough to hold an hundred *Indians*, which they did in preparation to a great day of Dancing. They would say now amongst themselves, that the *Governour* would be so angry for his loss at

---

[60]POWAW: In this case, Rowlandson is probably referring to the shaman or tribal medicine man.
[61]PILLOWBEER: Pillowcase.
[62]MY SISTER: Hannah Divoll.

Sudbury, that he would send no more about the Captives, which made me grieve and tremble. My Sister[62] being not far from the place where we now were, and hearing that I was here, desired her Master let her come and see me, and he was willing to it, and would go with her; but she being ready before him, told him she would go before, and was come within a Mile or two of the place: Then he overtook her, and began to rant as if he had been mad, and made her go back again in the Rain; so that I never saw her till I saw her in *Charlstown*. But the Lord requited many of their ill-doings, for this *Indian*, her Master, was hanged after at *Boston*. The *Indians* now began to come from all quarters against the merry dancing day. Amongst some of them came one Goodwife *Kettle*. I told her that my Heart was so heavy that it was ready to break: so is mine too, said she, but yet said, I hope we shall hear some good news shortly. I could hear how earnestly my Sister desired to see me, and I as earnestly desired to see her; and yet neither of us could get an opportunity. My Daughter was also now but about a Mile off: and I had not seen her in nine or ten Weeks, as I had not seen my Sister since our first taking. I earnestly desired them to let me go and see them: yea, I intreated, begged, and perswaded them, but to let me see my Daughter: and yet so hard-hearted were they, that they would not suffer it. They made use of their Tyrannical Power whilst they had it: but through the Lords wonderful mercy, their time was now but short.

On a Sabbath-day, the Sun being about an hour high, in the Afternoon, came Mr. *John Hoar*,[63] (the Council permitting him, and his own forward spirit inclining him) together with the two forementioned *Indians*, *Tom* and *Peter*, with the third Letter from the Council. When they came near, I was abroad; though I saw them not, they presently called me in, and bade me sit down, and not stir. Then they catched up their Guns, and away they ran, as if an Enemy had been at hand: and the Guns went off apace. I manifested some great trouble, and they asked me what was the matter? I told them I thought they had killed the *English-man* (for they had in the mean time informed me that an *English-man* was come) they said No; they shot over his Horse, and under, and before his Horse; and they pusht him this way and that way, at their pleasure: shewing what they could do. Then they let them come to their Wigwams. I begged of them to let me see the *English-man*, but they would not. But there was I fain to sit their pleasure. When they had talked their fill with him, they suffered me to go to him. We asked each other of our welfare, and how my Husband did? and all my Friends? He told me they were all well, and would be glad to see me. Amongst other

---

[63]JOHN HOAR: Hoar, from Concord, Massachusetts, was delegated by Rowlandson's husband to represent him and negotiate Rowlandson's ransom.

things which my Husband sent me, there came a pound of *Tobacco:* which I sold for nine shillings in Money: for many of the *Indians* for want of *Tobacco,* smoked *Hemlock,* and *Ground-Ivy.* It was a great mistake in any, who thought I sent for *Tobacco:* for through the favour of God, that desire was overcome. I now asked them, whether I should go home with Mr. *Hoar?* they answered No, one and another of them: and it being Night, we lay down with that Answer: in the Morning Mr. *Hoar* invited the *Saggamores* to Dinner: but when we went to get it ready, we found that they had stollen the greatest part of the Provision Mr. *Hoar* had brought out of his Bags in the Night. And we may see the wonderful power of God, in that one passage, in that when there was such a great number of the *Indians* together, and so greedy of a little good Food; and no *English* there, but Mr. *Hoar,* and my self: that there they did not knock us in the Head, and take what we had: there being not only some Provision, but also Trading Cloth,[64] a part of the twenty pounds agreed upon: But instead of doing us any mischief, they seemed to be ashamed of the Fact, and said, it were some *Matchit*[65] *Indians* that did it. O that we could believe that there is nothing too hard for God! God shewed his power over the Heathen in this, as he did over the hungry Lions when *Daniel* was cast into the Den.[66] Mr. *Hoar* called them betime to Dinner; but they ate very little, they being so busie in dressing themselves, and getting ready for their Dance: which was carried on by eight of them; four Men and four Squaws: my Master and Mistriss being two. He was dressed in his Holland Shirt,[67] with great Laces sewed at the tail of it; he had his silver Buttons, his white Stockings, his Garters were hung round with Shillings, and he had Girdles of Wampon upon his Head and Shoulders. She had a Kersey Coat,[68] and covered with Girdles of Wampom from the Loins and upward. Her Arms from her Elbows to her Hands were covered with Bracelets; there were handfuls of Neck-laces about her Neck, and several sorts of Jewels in her Ears. She had fine red Stockins, and white Shoos, her Hair powdered, and her Face painted Red, that was always before Black. And all the Dancers were after the same manner. There were two other singing and knocking on a Kettle for their Musick. They kept hopping up and down one after another, with a Kettle of Water in the midst, standing warm upon some Embers, to drink of when they were a dry. They held on, till it was almost night, throwing out Wampom to the standers

---

[64]TRADING CLOTH: Cloth used for bartering.
[65]MATCHIT: Bad form.
[66]DANIEL WAS CAST INTO THE DEN: The prophet Daniel was cast into a den of lions, who would not harm him by the grace of God (Daniel 6:1–29).
[67]HOLLAND SHIRT: A shirt made of linen fabric.
[68]KERSEY: Coarse ribbed cloth usually woven from long wool.

by. At night I asked them again, if I should go home? they all as one said no, except[69] my Husband would come for me. When we were lain down, my Master went out of the Wigwam, and by and by sent in an *Indian*, called *James*, the *PRINTER*,[70] who told Mr. *Hoar*, that my Master would let me go home tomorrow, if he would let him have one pint of *Liquors*. Then Mr. *Hoar* called his own *Indians*, *Tom* and *Peter*: and bid them all go, and see whether he would promise it before them three: and if he would, he should have it; which he did, and had it. Then *Philip*[71] smelling the business, called me to him, and asked me what I would give him, to tell me some good news, and to speak a good word for me, that I might go home to morrow? I told him I could not tell what to give him; I would give any thing I had, and asked him what he would have? He said two Coats, and twenty shillings in Money, and half a bushel of Seed-Corn, and some Tobacco. I thanked him for his love: but I knew the good news as well as that crafty Fox. My Master, after he had had his Drink, quickly came ranting into the Wigwam again, and called for Mr. *Hoar*, drinking to him, and saying he was a good man; and then again he would say, Hang him Rogue. Being almost drunk, he would drink to him, and yet presently say he should be hanged. Then he called for me; I trembled to hear him, yet I was fain to go to him; and he drunk to me, shewing no incivility. He was the first *Indian*, I saw drunk all the while that I was amongst them. At last his Squaw ran out, and he after her, round the Wigwam, with his money gingling at his knees: but she escaped him; but having an old Squaw, he ran to her: and so through the Lords mercy, we were no more troubled with him that night. Yet I had not a comfortable nights rest: for I think I can say, I did not sleep for three nights together. The night before the Letter came from the Council, I could not rest, I was so full of fears and troubles (God many times leaving us most in the dark, when deliverance is nearest) yea at this time I could not rest night nor day. The next night I was over-joyed, Mr. *Hoar* being come, and that with such good Tydings. The third night I was even swallowed up with the thoughts of things; *viz.* that ever I should go home again: and that I must go, leaving my Children behind me in the Wilderness; so that sleep was now almost departed from mine eyes.

On *Tuesday* morning they called their General Court (as they stiled it) to consult and determine, whether I should go home or no: And they all as one man did seemingly consent to it, that I should go home: except *Philip*, who would not come among them.

---

[69]EXCEPT: Unless.
[70]PRINTER: James Printer, King Philip's secretary and chief translator.
[71]PHILIP: Not to be mistaken for King Philip, this was the Native American who aided Rowlandson earlier on the journey during the eighth remove.

But before I go any further, I would take leave to mention a few remarkable passages of Providence; which I took notice of in my afflicted time.

1. Of the fair opportunity lost in the long March, a little after the Fort-fight,[72] when our *English* Army was so numerous, and in pursuit of the Enemy; and so near as to overtake several, and destroy them: and the Enemy in such distress for Food, that our men might track them by their rooting in the Earth for Ground-nuts, whilst they were flying for their lives: I say, that then our Army should want Provision, and be forced to leave their pursuit, and return homeward: and the very next week the Enemy came upon our Town, like Bears bereft of their whelps, or so many ravenous Wolves, rending us and our Lambs to death. But what shall I say? God seemed to leave his People to themselves; and ordered all things for his own holy ends. *Shall there be evil in the City and the Lord hath not done it? They are not grieved for the affliction of Joseph, therefore they shall go Captive, with the first that go Captive. It is the Lords doing, and it should be marvellous in our Eyes.*[73]

2. I cannot but remember, how the *Indians* derided the slowness, and dulness of the *English* Army, in its setting out. For after the desolations at *Lancaster* and *Medfield*, as I went along with them, they asked me when I thought the *English* Army would come after them? I told them I could not tell: it may be they will come in *May*, said they. Thus did they scoffe at us, as if the *English* would be a quarter of a Year getting ready.

3. Which also I have hinted before; when the *English* Army with new supplies were sent forth to pursue after the Enemy, and they understanding it; fled before them till they came to *Baquaug River*, where they forthwith went over safely: that that River should be impassable to the *English*, I cannot but admire to see the wonderful providence of God in preserving the Heathen for farther affliction to our poor Country. They could go in great numbers over, but the *English* must stop: God had an over-ruling hand in all those things.

4. It was thought, if their Corn were cut down, they would starve and die with hunger: and all their Corn that could be found, was destroyed, and they driven from that little they had in store, into the Woods, in the midst of Winter; and yet how to admiration did the Lord preserve them for his holy ends, and the destruction of many still amongst the *English*! Strangely did the Lord provide for them: that I

[72]FORT-FIGHT: Referring to a English victory over the Narragansett in December 1675.
[73]SHALL THERE BE EVIL IN THE CITY....: Amos 3:6.

did not see (all the time I was among them) one Man, or Woman, or Child, die with Hunger.

Though many times they would eat that, that a Hog or a Dog would hardly touch: yet by that God strengthened them to be a scourge to his People.

Their chief and commonest food was Ground-nuts: they eat also Nuts, and Acorns, Hartychoaks, Lilly-roots, Ground-beans, and several other weeds and roots that I know not.

They would pick up old bones, and cut them in pieces at the joynts, and if they were full of worms and magots, they would scald them over the fire to make the vermine come out; and then boyle them, and drink up the Liquor, and then beat the great ends of them in a Morter, and so eat them. They would eat Horses guts and ears, and all sorts of wild birds which they could catch: Also Bear, Venison, Beavers, Tortois, Frogs, Squirils, Dogs, Skunks, Rattle-snakes: yea, the very Barks of Trees; besides all sorts of Creatures, and provision which they plundered from the *English*, I cannot but stand in admiration to see the wonderful power of God, in providing for such a vast number of our Enemies in the Wilderness, where there was nothing to be seen, but from hand to mouth. Many times in the morning, the generality of them, would eat up all they had, and yet have some farther supply against they wanted. It is said, *Psal. 81. 13. 14. Oh that my people had hearkened to me, and Israel had walked in my wayes; I should soon have subdued their Enemies, and turned my hand against their adversaries.* But now our perverse and evil carriages in the sight of the Lord, have so offended him; that instead of turning his hand against them, the Lord feeds and nourishes them up to be a scourge to the whole Land.

5. Another thing that I would observe is, the strange providence of God in turning things about when the *Indians were at the highest*, and the *English at the lowest*. I was with the Enemy eleven weeks and five days; and not one Week passed without the fury of the Enemy, and some desolation by fire and sword upon one place or other. They mourned (with their black faces) for their own losses: yet triumphed and rejoyced in their inhumane (and many times devilish cruelty) to the *English*. They would boast much of their Victories; saying, that in two hours time, they had destroyed such a Captain, and his Company, in such a place; and such a Captain, and his Company, in such a place; and such a Captain, and his Company, in such a place: and boast how many Towns they had destroyed, and then scoff, and say, they had done them a good turn, to send them to Heaven so soon. Again they would say, this Summer they

would knock all the Rogues in the head, or drive them into the Sea, or make them flie the Country: thinking surely, *Agag-like, The bitterness of Death is past.*[74] Now the *Heathen* begin to think that all is their own, and the poor *Christians* hopes to fail (as to man) and now their eyes are more to God, and their hearts sigh heaven-ward: and to say in good earnest, *Help Lord, or we perish*[75] when the Lord had brought his People to this, that they saw no help in any thing but himself; then he takes the quarrel into his own hand: and though they had made a pit (in their own imaginations) as deep as hell for the *Christians* that Summer; yet the Lord hurll'd themselves into it. And the Lord had not so many wayes before, to preserve them, but now he hath as many to destroy them.

But to return again to my going home: where we may see a remarkable change of Providence: at first they were all against it, except my Husband would come for me; but afterwards they assented to it, and seemed much to rejoyce in it: some asking me to send them some Bread, others some Tobacco, others shaking me by the hand, offering me a Hood and Scarf to ride in; not one moving hand or tongue against it. Thus hath the Lord answered my poor desires, and the many earnest requests of others put up unto God for me. In my Travels an *Indian* came to me, and told me, if I were willing, he and his Squaw would run away, and go home along with me. I told him, No, I was not willing to run away, but desired to wait Gods time, that I might go home quietly, and without fear. And now God hath granted me my desire. O the wonderful power of God that I have seen, and the experiences that I have had! I have been in the midst of those roaring Lions, and Salvage Bears, that feared neither God, nor Man, nor the Devil, by night and day, alone and in company, sleeping all sorts together; and yet not one of them ever offered the least abuse of unchastity to me, in word or action. Though some are ready to say, I speak it for my own credit; but I speak it in the presence of God, and to his Glory. Gods power is as great now, and as sufficient to save, as when he preserved *Daniel* in the Lions Den, or the three Children in the Fiery Furnace.[76] I may well say, as he, *Psal.* 107. 1, 2. *Oh give thanks unto the Lord, for he is good, for his mercy endureth for ever. Let the Redeemed of the Lord say so, whom he hath redeemed from the hand of the Enemy;* especially that I should come away in the midst of

---

[74]THE BITTERNESS OF DEATH IS PAST: Agag was the king of Amalek, who, after he was defeated but spared by Saul, was killed by the prophet Samuel (Samuel 15).
[75]HELP LORD, OR WE PERISH: Samuel 16:32.
[76]THREE CHILDREN IN THE FIERY FURNACE: Daniel 3:13–30 relates how Shadrach, Meshach, and Abednego refused to worship false gods and were thrown into a fiery furnace, but were saved by an angel sent by God.

so many hundreds of Enemies, quietly and peaceably, and not a Dog moving his tongue. So I took my leave of them, and in coming along my heart melted into Tears, more than all the while I was with them, and I was almost swallowed up with the thoughts that ever I should go home again. About the Suns going down, Mr. *Hoar,* and my self, and the two *Indians* came to *Lancaster,* and a solemn sight it was to me. There had I lived many comfortable years amongst my Relations and Neighbours; and now not one *Christian* to be seen, nor one House left standing. We went on to a Farm-house that was yet standing, where we lay all night; and a comfortable lodging we had, though nothing but straw to lye on. The Lord preserved us in safety that night, and raised us up again in the morning, and carried us along, that before noon we came to *Concord.* Now was I full of joy, and yet not without sorrow: joy, to see such a lovely sight, so many *Christians* together, and some of them my Neighbours: There I met with my Brother, and my Brother in Law, who asked me, if I knew where his Wife was? Poor heart! He had helped to bury her, and knew it not; she being shot down by the house, was partly burnt: so that those who were at *Boston* at the desolation of the Town, and came back afterward, and buried the dead, did not know her. Yet I was not without sorrow, to think how many were looking and longing, and my own Children amongst the rest, to enjoy that deliverance that I had now received; and I did not know whether ever I should see them again. Being recruited[77] with Food and Raiment, we went to *Boston* that day, where I met with my dear Husband, but the thoughts of our dear Children, one being dead, and the other we could not tell where, abated our comfort each in other. I was not before so much hem'd in with the merciless and cruel *Heathen,* but now as much with pitiful, tender-hearted, and compassionate *Christians.* In that poor, and distressed, and beggarly condition, I was received in, I was kindly entertained in several houses: so much love I received from several, (some of whom I knew, and others I knew not) that I am not capable to declare it. But the Lord knows them all by name: the Lord reward them seven-fold into their bosoms of his spirituals for their temporals.[78] The twenty pounds, the price of my Redemption, was raised by some *Boston* Gentlewomen, and M. *Usher,* whose bounty and religious charity I would not forget to make mention of. Then Mr. *Thomas Shepherd*[79] of *Charlestown* received us into his House, where we continued eleven weeks; and a Father and Mother they

---

[77]RECRUITED: Refreshed and strengthened.
[78]TEMPORALS: Worldly goods.
[79]THOMAS SHEPHERD: Thomas Shepard II.

were unto us. And many more tender-hearted Friends we met with in that place. We were now in the midst of love, yet not without much and frequent heaviness of heart, for our poor Children, and other Relations, who were still in affliction.

The week following, after my coming in, the Governour and Council sent forth to the *Indians* again; and that not without success: for they brought in my Sister, and Goodwife *Kettle:* Then not knowing where our Children were, was a sore trial to us still, and yet we were not without secret hopes that we should see them again. That which was dead lay heavier upon my spirit than those which were alive amongst the *Heathen:* thinking how it suffered with its wounds, and I was no way able to relieve it: and how it was buried by the *Heathen* in the Wilderness, from amongst all *Christians.* We were hurried up and down in our thoughts; sometimes we should hear a report that they were gone this way, and sometimes that: and that they were come in, in this place or that: we kept inquiring and listening to hear concerning them, but no certain news as yet. About this time the Council had ordered a day of publick *Thanks-giving:* though I thought I had still cause of mourning; and being unsettled in our minds, we thought we would ride toward the Eastward, to see if we could hear any thing concerning our Children. And as we were riding along (God is the wise disposer of all things) between *Ipswich* and *Rowly* we met with Mr *William Hubbard*,[80] who told us our Son *Joseph* was come in to Major *Waldrens*,[81] and another with him, which was my Sisters Son. I asked him how he knew it? he said the Major himself told me so. So along we went till we came to *Newbury*; and their Minister being absent, they desired my Husband to Preach the *Thanks-giving* for them; but he was not willing to stay there that night, but would go over to *Salisbury*, to hear farther, and come again in the morning; which he did: and Preached there that day. At night, when he had done, one came and told him that his Daughter was come in at *Providence:* here was mercy on both hands. Now hath God fulfilled that precious Scripture, which was such a comfort to me in my distressed condition. When my heart was ready to sink into the Earth (my Children being gone I could not tell whither) and my knees trembled under me, and I was walking through the valley of the shadow of death: then the Lord brought, and now has fulfilled that reviving word unto me: *Thus saith the Lord, Refrain thy voice from weeping, and thy eyes from tears, for thy work shall be rewarded, saith the Lord, and they shall*

---

[80]MR. WILLIAM HUBBARD: Reverend William Hubbard of Ipswich was a historian noted for his recounting of the Indian Wars.
[81]MAJOR WALDRENS: Richard Waldren of Dover, New Hampshire.

come again from the Land of the Enemy.[82] Now we were between them, the one on the East, and the other on the West: our Son being nearest, we went to him first, to *Portsmouth;* where we met with him, and with the Major also: who told us he had done what he could, but could not redeem him under seven pounds, which the good People thereabouts were pleased to pay. The Lord reward the Major, and all the rest, though unknown to me, for their labour of love. My Sisters Son was redeemed for four pounds, which the Council gave order for the payment of. Having now received one of our Children, we hastened towards the other: going back through *Newbury;* my Husband preached there on the Sabbath day: for which they rewarded him manifold.

On Monday we came to *Charlestown;* where we heard that the Governour of *Road-Island*[83] had sent over for our Daughter, to take care of her, being now within his Jurisdiction: which should not pass without our acknowledgments. But she being nearer *Rehoboth* than *Road-Island,* Mr. *Newman* went over, and took care of her, and brought her to his own house. And the goodness of God was admirable to us in our low estate; in that he raised up compassionate[84] Friends on every side to us; when we had nothing to recompence any for their love. The *Indians* were now gone that way, that it was apprehended dangerous to go to her: but the Carts which carried Provision to the *English* Army, being guarded, brought her with them to *Dorchester,* where we received her safe: blessed be the Lord for it, *for great is his power, and he can do whatsoever seemeth him good.* Her coming in was after this manner: she was travelling one day with the *Indians,* with her basket at her back: the company of *Indians* were got before her, and gone out of sight, all except one Squaw: she followed the Squaw till night, and then both of them lay down: having nothing over them but the Heavens; nor under them but the Earth. Thus she travelled three days together, not knowing whither she was going: having nothing to eat or drink but water, and green *Hirtleberries.*[85] At last they came into *Providence,* where she was kindly entertained by several of that Town. The *Indians* often said, that I should never have her under twenty pounds: but now the Lord hath brought her in upon free cost, and given her to me the second time. The Lord make us a blessing indeed, each to others. Now have I seen that Scripture also fulfilled, *Deut.* 30. 4, 7. *If any of thine be driven out to the utmost parts of heaven, from thence will the Lord*

---

[82]THUS SAITH THE LORD, REFRAIN THY VOICE FROM WEEPING....: Jeremiah 31:16.
[83]GOVERNOUR OF ROAD-ISLAND: William Coddington (1601–1678), one of the founders of Rhode Island and governor of its colony in 1674, 1675, and 1678.
[84]COMPASSIONATE: Kind, sympathetic.
[85]HIRTLEBERRIES: Berries related to huckleberries.

thy God gather thee, and from thence will he fetch thee. And the Lord thy God will put all these curses upon thine enemies, and on them which hate thee, which persecuted thee. Thus hath the Lord brought me and mine out of that horrible pit, and hath set us in the midst of tender-hearted and compassionate Christians. 'Tis the desire of my soul that we may walk worthy of the mercies received, and which we are receiving.

Our Family being now gathered together (those of us that were living) the South Church in *Boston* hired an house for us: then we removed from Mr. *Shephards*, those cordial Friends, and went to *Boston*, where we continued about three quarters of a year: Still the Lord went along with us, and provided graciously for us. I thought it somewhat strange to set up House-keeping with bare walls, but, as *Solomon* says, *Money answers all things*[86]: and that we had through the benevolence of *Christian* friends, some in this Town, and some in that, and others, and some from *England*, that in a little time we might look, and see the house furnished with love. The Lord hath been exceeding good to us in our low estate, in that when we had neither house nor home, nor other necessaries, the Lord so moved the hearts of these and those towards us; that we wanted neither food, nor rayment, for our selves or ours, Prov. 18. 24. *There is a Friend which sticketh closer than a Brother.* And how many such Friends have we found, and now living amongst! And truly such a Friend have we found him to be unto us, in whose house we lived, *viz.* Mr. *James Whitcomb*,[87] a Friend unto us near hand, and afar off.

I can remember the time, when I used to sleep quietly without workings in my thoughts, whole nights together: but now it is otherwise with me. When all are fast about me, and no eye open, but his who ever waketh, my thoughts are upon things past, upon the awful dispensations of the Lord towards us: upon his wonderful power and might in carrying us through so many difficulties, in returning us in safety, and suffering none to hurt us. I remember in the night season, how the other day I was in the midst of thousands of enemies, and nothing but death before me: it was then hard work to perswade my self that ever I should be satisfied with bread again. But now we are fed with the finest of the Wheat, and (as I may so say) with honey out of the rock[88]: instead of the husks, we have the fatted Calf[89]: the thoughts of these things in the

---

[86]MONEY ANSWERS ALL THINGS: Ecclesiastes 10:19.
[87]MR. JAMES WHITCOMB: A wealthy trader.
[88]HONEY OUT OF THE ROCK: Psalm 81:16: "He should have fed them also with the finest of the wheat: and with honey out of the rock should I have satisfied thee."
[89]FATTED CALF: A reference to the prodigal son in Luke 15:23: "And bring hither the fatted calf, and kill it, and let us eat and be merry."

particulars of them, and of the love and goodness of God towards us, make it true of me, what *David* said of himself, *Psal.* 6. 6. *I water my Couch with my tears.* Oh the wonderful power of God that mine eyes have seen, affording matter enough for my thoughts to run in, that when others are sleeping mine eyes are weeping.

I have seen the extream vanity of this World: one hour I have been in health, and wealth, wanting nothing: but the next hour in sickness, and wounds, and death, having nothing but sorrow and affliction.

Before I knew what affliction meant, I was ready sometimes to wish for it. When I lived in prosperity; having the comforts of this World about me, my Relations by me, and my heart chearful: and taking little care for any thing; and yet seeing many (whom I preferred before my self) under many trials and afflictions, in sickness, weakness, poverty, losses, crosses, and cares of the World, I should be sometimes jealous least I should have my portion in this life; and that Scripture would come to my mind, *Heb.* 12. 6. *For whom the Lord loveth he chasteneth, and scourgeth every Son whom he receiveth:* but now I see the Lord had his time to scourge and chasten me. The portion of some is to have their Affliction by drops, now one drop and then another: but the dregs of the Cup, the wine of astonishment, like a sweeping rain that leaveth no food, did the Lord prepare to be my portion. Affliction I wanted, and Affliction I had, full measure (I thought) pressed down and running over: yet I see when God calls a person to any thing, and through never so many difficulties, yet he is fully able to carry them through, and make them see and say they have been gainers thereby. And I hope I can say in some measure, as *David* did, *It is good for me that I have been afflicted.*[90] The Lord hath shewed me the vanity of these outward things, that they are the *Vanity of vanities, and vexation of spirit*[91]; that they are but a shadow, a blast, a bubble, and things of no continuance; that we must rely on God himself, and our whole dependance must be upon him. If trouble from smaller matters begin to arise in me, I have something at hand to check my self with, and say why I am troubled? It was but the other day, that if I had had the world, I would have given it for my Freedom, or to have been a Servant to a *Christian.* I have learned to look beyond present and smaller troubles, and to be quieted under them, as *Moses* said, *Exod.* 14. 13. *Stand still, and see the salvation of the Lord.*

[1682]

[90]IT IS GOOD FOR ME THAT I HAVE BEEN AFFLICTED: Psalm 119:71: "It is good for me that I have been afflicted; that I might learn thy statutes."
[91]VANITY OF VANITIES....: Ecclesiastes 1:2.

Edward Taylor

(1642?–1729)

The Puritan poet and minister Edward Taylor, born in England and raised on a farm, immigrated to Boston in 1688. After completing his training at Harvard College in 1671 he began his ministry in Westfield in western Massachusetts, establishing a church there in 1679. His period of service lasted fifty years. Taylor was married twice; his first wife gave birth to eight children, five of whom died in infancy; and his second gave birth to six more.

A prolific yet private poet, Taylor chose not to publish his verse (or, for that matter, his many sermons) during his lifetime, and he instructed "that his heirs should never publish it." A grandson, Ezra Stiles, placed a number of manuscripts in the Yale University library, but they were not found until 1937. The scholar Thomas H. Johnson prepared The Poetical Works of Edward Taylor *in 1939; later, prose writings and additional poems were published.*

Taylor is valued in particular for God's Determinations Touching His Elect, *a thirty-five poem sequence that describes Christ's opposition to Satan and explores the themes of conversion and fellowship among the elect in God's church; and for* Preparatory Meditations, *217 in all (two are given below), which he crafted to help discipline himself for his administering of the sacrament of communion.*

The seventeenth-century English religious poets John Donne, George Herbert, and Richard Crashaw are among Taylor's significant literary precursors. His imagery is colorful, his passion for God is fervent, and his literary language is witty, colloquial, and sometimes daring, even extravagant. Taylor also was a master of the dramatic turn of phrase and paradox. Furthermore, he developed a complex form of typology—the notion that certain events in the Old Testament anticipate those in the New Testament (the anticipations are the "types," and the fulfillments are the "antitypes").

Taylor's poems are intense, on occasion tormented and anguished, acts of spiritual self-examination that explore, as one critic stated, "the sweetness of God's grace, the degradation of natural man by original sin, the humility and weakness of man before the glory of an absolutely powerful, sovereign God, the delights of heaven, the horrors of hell, the mystery of the incarnation, atonement and redemption, and the hope of salvation."

For a good overview: Norman S. Grabo, Edward Taylor *(1961). See also, William J. Scheick* The Will and the Word: The Poetry of Edward Taylor *(1974); Karen E. Rowe,* Saint and Singer: Edward Taylor's Typology and the Poetics of Meditation *(1986); John Gatta,* Gracious Laughter: The Meditative Wit of Edward Taylor *(1989); and Thomas M. Davis,* A Reading of Edward Taylor *(1992).*

Meditation 22 (First Series)

Philippians 2.9. God hath highly exalted Him.[1]

When Thy Bright Beams, my Lord, do strike mine Eye,
    Methinks I then could truly Chide outright
My Hide-bound Soul that stands so niggardly[2]
    That scarce a thought gets glorified by't.
    My Quaintest[3] metaphors are ragged Stuff,   5
    Making the Sun seem like a Mullipuff.[4]

It's my desire, Thou shouldst be glorified:
    But when Thy Glory shines before mine eye,
I pardon Crave, lest my desire be Pride,
    Or bed Thy Glory in a Cloudy Sky.   10
    The Sun grows wan; and Angels palefaced shrink,
    Before Thy Shine, which I besmear with Ink.

But shall the Bird sing forth Thy Praise, and shall
    The little Bee present her thankful Hum?
But I who see Thy shining Glory fall   15
    Before mine Eyes, stand Blockish, Dull, and Dumb?
    Whether I speak, or speechless stand, I spy,
    I fail Thy Glory: therefore pardon Cry.

But this I find; My Rhymes do better suit
    Mine own Dispraise than tune forth praise to Thee.   20
Yet being Chid, whether Consonant,[5] or Mute,
    I force my Tongue to tattle, as You see.
    That I Thy glorious Praise may Trumpet right,
    Be Thou my Song, and make, Lord, me Thy pipe.

This shining Sky will fly away apace,   25
    When Thy bright Glory splits the same to make

[1]PHILIPPIANS 2.9. GOD HATH HIGHLY EXALTED HIM: Philippians 2:5–11: "Let this mind be in you, which was also in Christ Jesus: / Who, being in the form of God, thought it not robbery to be equal with God: / But made himself of no reputation, and took upon him the form of a servant, and was made in the likeness of men: / And being found in fashion as a man, he humbled himself, and became obedient unto death, even the death of the cross. / Wherefore God also hath highly exalted him, and given him a name which is above every name: / That at the name of Jesus every knee should bow, of things in heaven, and things in earth, and things under the earth; / And that every tongue should confess that Jesus Christ is Lord, to the glory of God the Father."
[2]NIGGARDLY: Scanty.
[3]QUAINTEST: Wisest, cleverest; usually pertaining to the skilled use of language.
[4]MULLIPUFF: Fuzz ball; used as a term of contempt.
[5]CONSONANT: Harmonious agreement of sounds.

Thy Majesty a Pass, whose Fairest Face
    Too foul a Path is for Thy Feet to take.
    What Glory then, shall tend Thee through the Sky
    Draining the Heaven much of Angels dry?   30

What Light then flame will in Thy Judgment Seat,
    Fore which all men and Angels shall appear?
How shall Thy Glorious Righteousness them treat,
    Rend'ring to each after his Works done here?
    Then Saints with Angels Thou wilt glorify: 35
    And burn Lewd[6] Men, and Devils Gloriously.

One glimpse, my Lord, of Thy bright Judgment Day,
    And Glory piercing through, like fiery Darts,
All Devils, doth me make for Grace to pray,
    For filling Grace had I ten thousand Hearts.   40
    I'd through ten Hells to see Thy Judgment Day
    Wouldst Thou but gild my Soul with Thy bright Ray.

[June 12, 1687]

Meditation 38 (First Series)

I John 2.1. An Advocate with the Father.[1]

Oh! What a thing is Man? Lord, Who am I?
    That Thou shouldst give him Law[2] (Oh! golden line)
To regulate his Thoughts, Words, Life thereby.
    And judge him Wilt thereby too in Thy time.
    A Court of Justice Thou in Heaven holdst   5
    To try his Case while he's here housed on mold.[3]

How do Thy Angels lay before Thine eye
    My Deeds both White and Black I daily do?
How doth Thy Court Thou Panelist[4] there them try?
    But flesh complains. What right for this? let's know.   10

---

[6]LEWD: Wicked, base, unprincipled.
[1]I JOHN 2.1. AN ADVOCATE WITH THE FATHER: 1 John 2:1–2: "My little children, these things write I unto you, that ye sin not. And if any man sin, we have an advocate with the Father, Jesus Christ the righteous: / And he is the propitiation for our sins: and not for ours only, but also for the sins of the whole world."
[2]LAW: Scriptural law; God's commandments.
[3]MOLD: As a body decays in the grave.
[4]PANELIST: Jury member.

For right, or wrong I can't appear unto't.
　　And shall a sentence Pass on such a suit?

Soft; blemish not this golden Bench, or place.
　　Here is no Bribe, nor Colorings[5] to hide,
Nor Pettifogger[6] to befog the Case,　　　　　　　　　　15
　　But justice hath Her Glory here well tried.
　　Her spotless Law all spotted Cases tends.
　　Without Respect or Disrespect them ends.

God's Judge Himself: and Christ Attorney is,
　　The Holy Ghost Registerer[7] is found.　　　　　　　　20
Angels the Sergeants[8] are, all Creatures kiss
　　The Book,[9] and do as Evidences[10] abound.
　　All Cases pass according to pure Law
　　And in the sentence is no Fret,[11] nor flaw.

What sayst, my Soul? Here all thy Deeds are tried.　　25
　　Is Christ thy Advocate to plead thy Cause?
Art thou His Client? Such shall never slide.
　　He never lost His Case: He pleads such Laws
　　As Carry do the same, nor doth refuse
　　The Vilest sinner's Case that doth Him Choose.　　30

This is His honor, not Dishonor: nay,
　　No Habeas-Corpus[12] against His Clients came.
For all their Fines His Purse doth make down pay.
　　He Non-Suits Satan's Suit or Casts[13] the Same.
　　He'll plead thy Case, and not accept a Fee.　　　　　35
　　He'll plead Sub Forma Pauperis[14] for thee.

My Case is bad. Lord, be my Advocate.
　　My sin is red: I'm under God's Arrest.

---

[5]COLORINGS: Used figuratively to mean giving a fair or pleasant appearance to something that is bad.
[6]PETTIFOGGER: Slang expression for a lawyer, usually of inferior status, who tends to try petty cases with legal trickery.
[7]REGISTERER: Court recorder.
[8]SERGEANTS: Officers who maintain order in the court and whose duty is to enforce judgments made by the court.
[9]THE BOOK: The Bible.
[10]EVIDENCES: Witnesses who give evidence.
[11]FRET: Malice.
[12]HABEAS-CORPUS: "You should have the body." (Latin) Legal term for the doctrine that no person should be incarcerated without quickly being told the charge against him.
[13]CASTS: Dismisses.
[14]SUB FORMA PAUPERIS: "According to the form of poverty." (Latin) Legal term for the procedure that allows a poor person to sue a wealthy one regardless of ability to pay the court costs should the case be lost.

Thou hast the Hint of Pleading; plead my State.
  it's bad Thy Plea will make it best.   40
  If Thou wilt plead my Case before the King:
  I'll Wagonloads of Love and Glory bring.

                [July 6, 1690]

Huswifery[1]

Make me, O Lord, Thy Spinning Wheel[2] complete.
  Thy Holy Word my Distaff make for me.
Make mine Affections Thy Swift Flyers neat
  And make my Soul Thy holy Spool to be.
  My conversation make to be Thy Reel   5
  And reel the yarn thereon spun of Thy Wheel.

Make me Thy Loom then, knit therein this Twine:
  And make Thy Holy Spirit, Lord, wind quills:[3]
Then weave the Web Thyself. The yarn is fine.
  Thine Ordinances make my Fulling Mills.[4]   10
  Then dye the same in Heavenly Colors Choice,
  All pinked with Varnished[5] Flowers of Paradise.

Then clothe therewith mine Understanding, Will,
  Affections, Judgment, Conscience, Memory,
My Words, and Actions, that their shine may fill   15
  My ways with glory and Thee glorify.
  Then mine apparel shall display before Ye
  That I am Clothed in Holy robes for glory.

                  [1939]

---

[1]HUSWIFERY: Housekeeping.
[2]WHEEL: A spinning wheel: the distaff holds raw wool, the flyers control the spinning of the wheel, the spool twists the yarn, and the reel holds the spun thread.
[3]QUILLS: Pieces of reed or other hollow stem on which spun thread is wound from the wheel, a bobbin.
[4]FULLING MILLS: A place where raw cloth is beaten to clean and thicken it to prepare it for use.
[5]PINKED WITH VARNISHED: adorned with brilliant or shiny details.

Cotton Mather

(1663–1728)

*In the late 1680s, the minister Cotton Mather inquired into the disturbing
behavior of four children, born to a mason in Boston named John
Goodwin, and he reached the conclusion that all were the victims of the
witchcraft of Mary Glover, an Irishwoman. He assembled the results of his
investigation in* Memorable Providences Relating to Witchcraft and
Possessions *(1689) and vowed that he would "never use but one grain of
patience with any man that shall go to impose upon me a Denial of Devils,
or of Witches."*

*Soon, in the early 1690s, the Salem witchcraft trials began, and as
they continued, with numbers of persons confessing they were witches,
Mather concluded, "An Army of Devils is horribly broke in upon the
place which is our center." God's Day of Judgment was near, he
declared in a sermon in August 1692, and, he claimed, he and other
religious authorities, ministers, and scholars had been appointed by
God to expose and punish witches—agents of the Devil—and support
their execution. In* The Wonders of the Invisible World *(1692),
excerpted below, Mather, drawing upon court records, tells the story of
this unnerving episode in colonial history—an episode that soon grew
more complicated and deeply disquieting when some of the witches
recanted their testimony.*

*Born in Boston, the son and grandson of esteemed ministers, Mather
entered Harvard College at the age of twelve. After receiving his bachelor's and master's degrees, he took a position as assistant to his father in
Boston's North Church. This tireless preacher, writer, researcher, and
scholar produced well over 400 works; his twentieth-century bibliogra-
pher needed three volumes, published in 1940, to list them all.*

*Prolific and hugely accomplished, Mather possessed, in the words of
Benjamin Peirce, author of* A History of Harvard University *(1833), a
flawed, difficult personality: "It is evident that his judgment was not
equal to his other faculties; that his passions, which were naturally
strong and violent, were not always under proper regulation; that he
was weak, credulous, enthusiastic, and superstitious." The distinguished literary historian Perry Miller, while acknowledging that
Mather was "the greatest intellectual in the land," felt obliged to add
that he was "nauseous human being."*

Mather's other major publications include The Present State of New
England *(1690);* The Short History of New England *(1694); and*
Magnalia Christi Americana *(1702), an 800-page history of the Church
in New England, celebrating "the great achievements of Christ in
America" and urging contemporary Puritans to revive the zealous spirit
of the colony's founders, such as William Bradford (see below) and John*

*Winthrop. Mather was a critic of the slave trade, yet he also favored
the extermination of Indians who had not converted to Christianity.*

In The Wonders of the Invisible World, *Mather examines witches,
their evil deeds, and their relation to the supernatural in general, as
well as the strenuous efforts made in Salem to root them out and bring
them to justice. According to the scholar Mary Beth Norton, legal
action was taken against at least 144 people; there were 54 confessions
of witchcraft, 19 hangings, and one "pressing to death by heavy
stones." She argues, furthermore, that these events are best understood
in the context of King William's War, which the American colonists
referred to as the Second Indian War. In her view, the frightening warfare on the frontier crucially contributed to the witchcraft fears. Devils,
witches, Indians—all three converged in the fearful mind of New
England's religious and civil authorities, leading, as one scholar has
said, to "the worst excess of Calvinism in America."*

For a brief overview, see Babette M. Levy, Cotton Mather *(1979).
For detailed biography: Robert Middlekauff,* The Mathers: Three
Generations of Puritan Intellectuals, 1596–1728 *(1971); David Levin,*
Cotton Mather: The Young Life of the Lord's Remembrancer,
1663–1703 *(1978); and Kenneth Silverman,* The Life and Times of
Cotton Mather *(1984). Also enlightening: Sacvan Bercovitch,* The
Puritan Origins of the American Self *(1975); and Christopher Felker,*
Reinventing Cotton Mather in the American Renaissance: *Magnalia
Christi Americana* in Hawthorne, Stowe, and Stoddard *(1993).*

From The Wonders of the Invisible World

[A PEOPLE OF GOD IN THE DEVIL'S TERRITORIES]

The New Englanders are a people of God settled in those, which were once
the devil's territories: and it may easily be supposed that the devil was
exceedingly disturbed, when he perceived such a people here accomplishing the promise of old made unto our blessed Jesus, that He should have the
utmost parts of the earth for His possession.[1] There was not a greater uproar

---

[1]HE SHOULD HAVE THE UTMOST PARTS OF THE EARTH FOR HIS POSSESSION: A reference
to Jesus's fasting in the desert, where Satan tempted him and offered him the kingdoms of the earth:
"And the devil, taking him up into an high mountain, shewed unto him all the kingdoms of the world
in a moment of time. / And the devil said unto him, All this power will I give thee, and the glory of
them: for that is delivered unto me; and to whomsoever I will I give it. / If thou therefore wilt worship
me, all shall be thine" (Luke 4:5–7).

among the Ephesians,[2] when the Gospel was first brought among them, than there was among the powers of the air (after whom those Ephesians walked) when first the silver trumpets of the Gospel here made the joyful sound. The devil thus irritated, immediately tried all sorts of methods to overturn this poor plantation: and so much of the church, as was fled into this wilderness, immediately found the serpent cast out of his mouth a flood for the carrying of it away. I believe that never were more satanical devices used for the unsettling of any people under the sun, than what have been employed for the extirpation of the vine which God has here planted, casting out the heathen, and preparing a room before it, and causing it to take deep root, and fill the land, so that it sent its boughs unto the Atlantic Sea eastward, and its branches unto the Connecticut River westward, and the hills were covered with a shadow thereof. But all those attempts of hell have hitherto been abortive, many an Ebenezer[3] has been erected unto the praise of God, by his poor people here; and having obtained help from God, we continue to this day. Wherefore the devil is now making one attempt more upon us; an attempt more difficult, more surprising, more snarled with unintelligible circumstances than any that we have hitherto encountered; an attempt so critical, that if we get well through, we shall soon enjoy halcyon days with all the vultures of hell trodden under our feet. He has wanted his incarnate legions to persecute us, as the people of God have in the other hemisphere been persecuted: he has therefore drawn forth his more spiritual ones to make an attack upon us. We have been advised by some credible Christians yet alive, that a malefactor, accused of witchcraft as well as murder, and executed in this place more than forty years ago, did then give notice of an horrible plot against the country by witchcraft, and a foundation of witchcraft then laid, which if it were not seasonably discovered, would probably blow up, and pull down all the churches in the country. And we have now with horror seen the discovery of such a witchcraft! An army of devils is horribly broke in upon the place which is the center, and after a sort, the first-born of our English settlements: and the houses of the good people there are filled with the doleful shrieks of their children and servants, tormented by invisible hands,[4] with tortures altogether preternatural. After

---

[2]EPHESIANS: Ephesus was located in the western part of Asia Minor, where many Jews lived. The apostle Paul, around 51 CE, visited this city to spread the message of the Gospel. While the Ephesians at first resisted his efforts to convert them, he eventually succeeded, and several Christian churches were founded in the area in his lifetime.

[3]EBENEZER: "Stone of help." (Hebrew) The name of the stone monument erected by Samuel after the victory of Mizpeh (1 Samuel 7:12).

[4]THE HOUSES OF THE GOOD PEOPLE THERE ARE FILLED WITH THE DOLEFUL SHRIEKS OF THEIR CHILDREN AND SERVANTS, TORMENTED BY INVISIBLE HANDS: Mather refers to the "afflictions" of the young women (and a few men) from Salem Village (Danvers), Massachusetts, in 1692. They claimed to be tormented by the spectral forms of witches, many of whom were their neighbors.

the mischiefs there endeavored, and since in part conquered, the terrible plague of evil angels hath made its progress into some other places, where other persons have been in like manner diabolically handled. These our poor afflicted neighbors, quickly after they become infected and infested with these demons, arrive to a capacity of discerning those which they conceive the shapes of their troublers; and notwithstanding the great and just suspicion that the demons might impose the shapes of innocent persons in their spectral exhibitions upon the sufferers (which may perhaps prove no small part of the witch-plot in the issue), yet many of the persons thus represented, being examined, several of them have been convicted of a very damnable witchcraft: yea, more than one [and] twenty have confessed, that they have signed unto a book, which the devil showed them, and engaged in his hellish design of bewitching and ruining our land. We know not, at least I know not, how far the delusions of Satan may be interwoven into some circumstances of the confessions; but one would think all the rules of understanding human affairs are at an end, if after so many most voluntary harmonious confessions, made by intelligent persons of all ages, in sundry towns, at several times, we must not believe the main strokes wherein those confessions all agree: especially when we have a thousand preternatural things every day before our eyes, wherein the confessors do acknowledge their concernment, and give demonstration of their being so concerned. If the devils now can strike the minds of men with any poisons of so fine a composition and operation, that scores of innocent people shall unite, in confessions of a crime, which we see actually committed, it is a thing prodigious, beyond the wonders of the former ages, and it threatens no less than a sort of a dissolution upon the world. Now, by these confessions 'tis agreed that the devil has made a dreadful knot of witches in the country, and by the help of witches has dreadfully increased that knot: that these witches have driven a trade of commissioning their confederate spirits to do all sorts of mischiefs to the neighbors, whereupon there have ensued such mischievous consequences upon the bodies and estates of the neighborhood, as could not otherwise be accounted for: yea, that at prodigious witch-meetings, the wretches have proceeded so far as to concert and consult the methods of rooting out the Christian religion from this country, and setting up instead of it perhaps a more gross diabolism than ever the world saw before. And yet it will be a thing little short of miracle, if in so spread a business as this, the devil should not get in some of his juggles,[5] to confound the discovery of all the rest. . . .

[5]JUGGLES: Fancy tricks.

But I shall no longer detain my reader from his expected entertainment, in a brief account of the trials which have passed upon some of the male-factors lately executed at Salem, for the witchcrafts whereof they stood convicted. For my own part, I was not present at any of them; nor ever had I any personal prejudice at the persons thus brought upon the stage; much less at the surviving relations of those persons, with and for whom I would be as hearty a mourner as any man living in the world: The Lord comfort them! But having received a command[6] so to do, I can do no other than shortly relate the chief matters of fact, which occurred in the trials of some that were executed, in an abridgment collected out of the court papers on this occasion put into my hands. You are to take the truth, just as it was; and the truth will hurt no good man. There might have been more of these, if my book would not thereby have swollen too big; and if some other worthy hands did not perhaps intend something further in these collections; for which cause I have only singled out four or five, which may serve to illustrate the way of dealing, wherein witchcrafts use to be concerned; and I report matters not as an advocate, but as an historian.

[THE TRIAL OF MARTHA CARRIER]

AT THE COURT OF OYER AND TERMINER, HELD BY ADJOURN-MENT AT SALEM, AUGUST 2, 1692.

I. Martha Carrier[7] was indicted for the bewitching certain persons, according to the form usual in such cases, pleading not guilty to her indictment; there were first brought in a considerable number of the bewitched persons who not only made the court sensible[8] of an horrid witchcraft committed upon them, but also deposed that it was Martha Carrier, or her shape, that grievously tormented them, by biting, pricking, pinching and choking of them. It was further deposed that while this Carrier was on her examination before the magistrates, the poor people were so tortured that every one expected their death upon the very spot, but that upon the binding of Carrier they were eased. Moreover

[6]COMMAND: Mather refers to a request made by the judges at the Salem trials to publically explain the sentencing of the people accused of witchcraft.
[7]MARTHA CARRIER: Carrier (1654–1692) was among the first people accused by the "afflicted children" of witchcraft. In May 1692 she was brought before the magistrates, who found suitable evidence to bring her to trial in August. She was found guilty of the crime of witchcraft. She is recorded as saying, "I am wronged. It is a shameful thing that you should mind these folks that are out of their wits." On August 19, 1692, Carrier, along with four other people, was hanged on Gallows Hill.
[8]SENSIBLE: Aware.

the look of Carrier then laid the afflicted people for dead: and her touch, if her eye at the same time were off them, raised them again: which things were also now seen upon her trial. And it was testified that upon the mention of some having their necks twisted almost round, by the shape of this Carrier, she replied, "It's no matter though their necks had been twisted quite off."

II. Before the trial of this prisoner, several of her own children had frankly and fully confessed not only that they were witches themselves, but that this their mother had made them so. This confession they made with great shows of repentance, and with much demonstration of truth. They related place, time, occasion; they gave an account of journeys, meetings and mischiefs by them performed, and were very credible in what they said. Nevertheless, this evidence was not produced against the prisoner at the bar,[9] inasmuch as there was other evidence enough to proceed upon.

III. Benjamin Abbot gave his testimony that last March was a twelve-month, this Carrier was very angry with him, upon laying out some land near her husband's: her expressions in this anger were that she would stick as close to Abbot as the bark stuck to the tree; and that he should repent of it afore seven years came to an end, so as Doctor Prescot should never cure him. These words were heard by others besides Abbot himself; who also heard her say, she would hold his nose as close to the grindstone as ever it was held since his name was Abbot. Presently after this, he was taken with a swelling in his foot, and then with a pain in his side, and exceedingly tormented. It bred into a sore, which was lanced by Doctor Prescot, and several gallons of corruption[10] ran out of it. For six weeks it continued very bad, and then another sore bred in the groin, which was also lanced by Doctor Prescot. Another sore than bred in his groin, which was likewise cut, and put him to very great misery: he was brought unto death's door, and so remained until Carrier was taken, and carried away by the constable, from which very day he began to mend, and so grew better every day, and is well ever since.

Sarah Abbot also, his wife, testified that her husband was not only all this while afflicted in his body, but also that strange, extraordinary and unaccountable calamities befell his cattle; their death being such as they could guess at no natural reason for.

[9]BAR: Court.
[10]CORRUPTION: Infected or putrid matter; pus.

IV. Allin Toothaker testified that Richard, the son of Martha Carrier, having some difference with him, pulled him down by the hair of the head. When he rose again he was going to strike at Richard Carrier but fell down flat on his back to the ground, and had not power to stir hand or foot, until he told Carrier he yielded; and then he saw the shape of Martha Carrier go off his breast.

This Toothaker had received a wound in the wars; and he now testified that Martha Carrier told him he should never be cured. Just afore the apprehending of Carrier, he could thrust a knitting needle into his wound four inches deep; but presently after her being seized, he was thoroughly healed.

He further testified that when Carrier and he some times were at variance, she would clap her hands at him, and say he should get nothing by it; whereupon he several times lost his cattle, by strange deaths, whereof no natural causes could be given.

V. John Rogger also testified that upon the threatening words of this malicious Carrier, his cattle would be strangely bewitched; as was more particularly then described.

VI. Samuel Preston testified that about two years ago, having some difference with Martha Carrier, he lost a cow in a strange, preternatural, unusual manner; and about a month after this, the said Carrier, having again some difference with him, she told him he had lately lost a cow, and it should not be long before he lost another; which accordingly came to pass; for he had a thriving and well-kept cow, which without any known cause quickly fell down and died.

VII. Phebe Chandler testified that about a fortnight before the apprehension of Martha Carrier, on a Lordsday, while the Psalm was singing in the Church, this Carrier then took her by the shoulder and shaking her, asked her, where she lived: she made her no answer, although as Carrier, who lived next door to her father's house, could not in reason but know who she was. Quickly after this, as she was at several times crossing the fields, she heard a voice, that she took to be Martha Carrier's, and it seemed as if it was over her head. The voice told her she should within two or three days be poisoned. Accordingly, within such a little time, one half of her right hand became greatly swollen and very painful; as also part of her face: whereof she can give no account how it came. It continued very bad for some days; and several times since she has had a great pain in her breast; and been so seized on her legs that she has hardly been able to go. She added that lately, going well to the house of God, Richard, the son of Martha Carrier, looked very earnestly upon her, and immediately her hand, which had formerly been poisoned, as is abovesaid, began to pain her greatly, and she had a strange burning at her stomach; but was then struck deaf, so that she could not hear any of the prayer, or singing, till the two or three last words of the Psalm.

VIII. One Foster, who confessed her own share in the witchcraft for which the prisoner stood indicted, affirmed that she had seen the prisoner at some of their witch-meetings, and that it was this Carrier, who persuaded her to be a witch. She confessed that the devil carried them on a pole to a witch-meeting; but the pole broke, and she hanging about Carrier's neck, they both fell down, and she then received an hurt by the fall, whereof she was not at this very time recovered.

IX. One Lacy, who likewise confessed her share in this witchcraft, now testified, that she and the prisoner were once bodily present at a witch-meeting in Salem Village; and that she knew the prisoner to be a witch, and to have been at a diabolical sacrament, and that the prisoner was the undoing of her and her children by enticing them into the snare of the devil.

X. Another Lacy, who also confessed her share in this witchcraft, now testified, that the prisoner was at the witch-meeting, in Salem Village, where they had bread and wine administered unto them.

XI. In the time of this prisoner's trial, one Susanna Sheldon[11] in open court had her hands unaccountably tied together with a wheel-band[12] so fast that without cutting, it could not be loosed: it was done by a specter; and the sufferer affirmed it was the prisoner's.

Memorandum. This rampant hag, Martha Carrier, was the person of whom the confessions of the witches, and of her own children among the rest, agreed that the devil had promised her she should be Queen of Hebrews.

[1692, 1693]

11SUSANNA SHELDON: Sheldon was an eighteen-year-old woman from Salem Village (Danvers), Massachusetts, and one of the original "afflicted children."
12WHEEL-BAND: A strap that goes around a wheel, such as a spinning wheel.

From Magnalia Christi Americana[1]
Galeacius Secundus[2]: The Life of William Bradford, Esq.,[3] Governor of Plymouth Colony

Omnium Somnos illius vigilantia defendit; omnium otium, illius Labor; omnium Delicias, illius Industria; omnium vacationem, illius occupatio.[4]

It has been a matter of some observation, that although Yorkshire be one of the largest shires in England; yet for all the fires of martyrdom which were kindled in the days of Queen Mary,[5] it afforded no more fuel than one poor leaf; namely, John Leaf, an apprentice, who suffered for the doctrine of the Reformation at the same time and stake with the famous John Bradford.[6] But when the reign of Queen Elizabeth[7] would not admit the reformation of worship to proceed unto those degrees, which were proposed and pursued by no small number of the faithful in those days, Yorkshire was not the least of the shires in England that afforded suffering witnesses thereunto. The churches there gathered were quickly molested with such a raging persecution, that if the spirit

---

[1]MAGNALIA CHRISTI AMERICANA: "A History of the Wonderful Works of Christ in America" [Latin]. The life of William Bradford is included in the second book of Mather's seven-volume history.
[2]GALEACIUS SECUNDUS: The second Galeazzo [Latin]. Galeazzo Caraccioli (1517–1586) was a nobleman from Naples, Italy who left his home to follow John Calvin (1509–64), a French Protestant theologian, in Geneva. The Separatist group Bradford led to New England also embraced many of the religious doctrines, practices, and teachings put forth by Calvin.
[3]WILLIAM BRADFORD: William Bradford (1590–1657) was governor of Plymouth Colony. As a young man, Bradford joined a separatist sect of Puritans in Scrooby, England, and emigrated in 1609 with many members of this group to Holland in search of religious toleration. In 1620, he sailed to New England on the *Mayflower*, and was elected governor in 1621 after the death of the group's leader, John Carver. Bradford, who was reelected governor 30 times, held the post for most of his lifetime.
[4]OMINIUM SOMNOS ILLIUS VIGILANTIA...ILLIUS OCCUPATIO: "His vigilance defends the sleep of all; his industry, their pleasures; and his diligence, their leisure." [Latin].
[5]QUEEN MARY: After the pope refused to grant English King Henry VIII (1491–1547) a divorce in 1534, the incensed king severed all ties with the Roman Catholic Church by declaring the Act of Supremacy, making himself head of the Church of England. When his daughter, Mary Tudor (1516–58) became queen in 1553, she restored Roman Catholicism as the official religion of England. Over 300 Protestants were burned at the stake as heretics for refusing to renounce their faith.
[6]JOHN BRADFORD: John Bradford (1510–1555) was burned at the stake with John Leaf (1537–1555) for heresy during the reign of Queen Mary I.
[7]QUEEN ELIZABETH: Elizabeth I (1533–1603) became queen of England after the death of her older sister Mary I. She reinstated the Act of Uniformity that required all English subjects to be members of the Church of England. Some Protestant sects left England for Holland in search of religious toleration.

of separation in them did carry them unto a further extreme than it should have done, one blamable cause thereof will be found in the extremity of that persecution. Their troubles made that cold country too hot for them, so that they were under a necessity to seek a retreat in the Low Countries;[8] and yet the watchful malice and fury of their adversaries rendered it almost impossible for them to find what they sought. For them to leave their native soil, their lands and their friends, and go into a strange place, where they must hear foreign language, and live meanly[9] and hardly, and in other employments than that of husbandry, wherein they had been educated, these must needs have been such discouragements as could have been conquered by none, save those who sought first the kingdom of God, and the righteousness thereof. But that which would have made these discouragements the more unconquerable unto an ordinary faith, was the terrible zeal of their enemies to guard all ports, and search all ships, that none of them should be carried off. I will not relate the sad things of this kind then seen and felt by this people of God; but only exemplify those trials with one short story. Divers of these people having hired a Dutchman, then lying at Hull, to carry them over to Holland, he promised faithfully to take them in, between Grimsby and Hull; but they coming to the place a day or two too soon, the appearance of such a multitude alarmed the officers of the town adjoining, who came with a great body of soldiers to seize upon them. Now it happened that one boat full of men had been carried aboard, while the women were yet in a bark that lay aground in a creek at low water. The Dutchman perceiving the storm that was thus beginning ashore, swore by the sacrament that he would stay no longer for any of them; and so taking the advantage of a fair wind then blowing, he put out to sea for Zeeland.[10] The women thus left near Grimsby-common, bereaved of their husbands, who had been hurried from them, and forsaken of their neighbors, of whom none durst in this fright stay with them, were a very rueful spectacle; some crying for fear, some shaking for cold, all dragged by troops of armed and angry men from one Justice to another, till not knowing what to do with them, they even dismissed them to shift as well as they could for themselves. But by their singular afflictions, and by their Christian behaviors, the cause for which they exposed themselves did gain considerably. In the meantime, the men at sea found reason to be glad that their families were not with them, for

---

[8]LOW COUNTRIES: The area that encompassed the Netherlands, Belgium, and the Grand Duchy of Luxembourg.
[9]MEANLY: In poverty.
[10]ZEELAND: A province of the Netherlands bordering on Belgium in the south.

they were surprised with an horrible tempest, which held them for fourteen days together, in seven whereof they saw not sun, moon or star, but were driven upon the coast of Norway. The mariners often despaired of life, and once with doleful shrieks gave over all, as thinking the vessel was foundered: but the vessel rose again, and when the mariners with sunk hearts often cried out, "We sink! we sink!" the passengers, without such distraction of mind, even while the water was running into their mouths and ears, would cheerfully shout, "Yet, Lord, thou canst save! Yet, Lord, thou canst save!" And the Lord accordingly brought them at last safe unto their desired haven: and not long after helped their distressed relations thither after them, where indeed they found upon almost all accounts a new world, but a world in which they found that they must live like strangers and pilgrims.

Among these devout people was our William Bradford, who was born *Anno*[11] 1588, in an obscure village called Austerfield, where the people were as unacquainted with the Bible, as the Jews do seem to have been with part of it in the days of Josiah[12]: a most ignorant and licentious people, and like unto their priest. Here, and in some other places, he had a comfortable inheritance left him of his honest parents, who died while he was yet a child, and cast him on the education,[13] first of his grandparents, and then of his uncles, who devoted him, like his ancestors, unto the affairs of husbandry.[14] Soon a long sickness kept him, as he would afterwards thankfully say, from the vanities of youth, and made him the fitter for what he was afterwards to undergo. When he was about a dozen years old, the reading of the Scriptures began to cause great impressions upon him; and those impressions were much assisted and improved, when he came to enjoy Mr. Richard Clifton's[15] illuminating ministry, not far from his abode; he was then also further befriended, by being brought into the company and fellowship of such as were then called professors;[16] though the young man that brought him into it did after become a profane and wicked apostate[17] Nor could the wrath of his uncles, nor the scoff of his neighbors, now turned upon him, as one of the Puritans, divert him from his pious inclinations.

---

[11]ANNO: In the year. (Latin)
[12]JOSIAH: Josiah was the King of Judah. In the 18th year of his reign, the book of the law of the God of Israel (probably Deuteronomy) was discovered in the Temple, and he began a reform movement that made Jerusalem the center of all religious activity (2 Kings 22).
[13]CAST HIM ON THE EDUCATION: Made his education dependent upon.
[14]HUSBANDRY: The business of agriculture and farming.
[15]MR. RICHARD CLIFTON: Richard Clifton (d. 1616) was a Puritan pastor from Scrooby, Nottinghamshire, who settled in Amsterdam with the Scrooby Separatists.
[16]PROFESSORS: One who makes an open declaration of religious beliefs.
[17]WICKED APOSTATE: One who publicly forsakes religious faith or beliefs.

At last, beholding how fearfully the evangelical and apostolical churchform, whereinto the churches of the primitive times were cast by the good spirit of God, had been deformed by the apostacy of the succeeding times; and what little progress the Reformation had yet made in many parts of Christendom towards its recovery, he set himself by reading, by discourse, by prayer, to learn whether it was not his duty to withdraw from the communion of the parish-assemblies, and engage with some society of the faithful, that should keep close unto the written Word of God, as the rule of their worship. And after many distresses of mind concerning it, he took up a very deliberate and understanding resolution, of doing so; which resolution he cheerfully prosecuted, although the provoked rage of his friends tried all the ways imaginable to reclaim him from it, unto all whom his answer was:

> Were I like to endanger my life, or consume my estate by any ungodly courses, your counsels to me were very seasonable; but you know that I have been diligent and provident in my calling, and not only desirous to augment what I have, but also to enjoy it in your company; to part from which will be as great a cross as can befall me. Nevertheless, to keep a good conscience, and walk in such a way as God has prescribed in His Word; is a thing which I must prefer before you all, and above life itself. Wherefore, since 'tis for a good cause that I am like to suffer the disasters which you lay before me, you have no cause to be either angry with me, or sorry for me; yea, I am not only willing to part with every thing that is dear to me in this world for this cause, but I am also thankful that God has given me an heart so to do, and will accept me so to suffer for Him.

Some lamented him, some derided him, all dissuaded him: nevertheless, the more they did it, the more fixed he was in his purpose to seek the ordinances of the Gospel, where they should be dispensed with most of the commanded purity; and the sudden deaths of the chief relations which thus lay at him,[18] quickly after convinced him what a folly it had been to have quitted his profession, in expectation of any satisfaction from them. So to Holland he attempted a removal.

Having with a great company of Christians hired a ship to transport them for Holland, the master perfidiously betrayed them into the hands of those persecutors, who rifled and ransacked their goods, and clapped

---

[18]LAY AT HIM: Tried to make him change his religious convictions.

their persons into prison at Boston,[19] where they lay for a month together. But Mr. Bradford being a young man of about eighteen, was dismissed sooner than the rest, so that within a while he had opportunity with some others to get over to Zeeland, through perils, both by land and sea not inconsiderable; where he was not long ashore ere a viper seized on his hand—that is, an officer—who carried him unto the magistrates, unto whom an envious passenger had accused him as having fled out of England. When the magistrates understood the true cause of his coming thither, they were well satisfied with him; and so he repaired joyfully unto his brethren at Amsterdam, where the difficulties to which he afterwards stooped in learning and serving of a Frenchman at the working of silks, were abundantly compensated by the delight wherewith he sat under the shadow of our Lord, in His purely dispensed ordinances. At the end of two years, he did, being of age to do it, convert his estate in England into money; but setting up for himself, he found some of his designs by the Providence of God frowned upon, which he judged a correction bestowed by God upon him for certain decays of internal piety, whereinto he had fallen; the consumption of his estate he thought came to prevent a consumption in his virtue. But after he had resided in Holland about half a score years, he was one of those who bore a part in that hazardous and generous enterprise of removing into New England, with part of the English church at Leyden,[20] where, at their first landing, his dearest consort[21] accidently falling overboard, was drowned in the harbor; and the rest of his days were spent in the services, and the temptations, of that American wilderness.

Here was Mr. Bradford, in the year 1621, unanimously chosen the governor of the plantation; the difficulties whereof were such, that if he had not been a person of more than ordinary piety, wisdom and courage, he must have sunk under them. He had, with a laudable industry, been laying up a treasure of experiences, and he had now occasion to use it; indeed, nothing but an experienced man could have been suitable to the necessities of the people. The potent nations of the Indians, into whose country they were come, would have cut them off, if the blessing of God upon his conduct had not quelled them; and if his prudence, justice and moderation had not overruled them, they had been ruined by their own distempers. One specimen of his demeanor is to this day particularly

---

[19]BOSTON: Boston, England.
[20]LEYDEN: Leyden, Holland.
[21]HIS DEAREST CONSORT: Bradford's wife, Dorothy (May) Bradford (1597–1620) fell overboard and drowned in Cape Cod harbor.

spoken of. A company of young fellows that were newly arrived were very unwilling to comply with the governor's order for working abroad on the public account; and therefore on Christmas Day, when he had called upon them, they excused themselves, with a pretense that it was against their conscience to work such a day.[22] The governor gave them no answer, only that he would spare them till they were better informed; but by and by he found them all at play in the street, sporting themselves with various diversions; whereupon commanding the instruments of their games to be taken from them, he effectually gave them to understand that it was against his conscience that they should play whilst others were at work, and that if they had any devotion to the day, they should show it at home in the exercises of religion, and not in the streets with pastime and frolics; and this gentle reproof put a final stop to all such disorders for the future.

For two years together after the beginning of the colony, whereof he was now governor, the poor people had a great experiment of "man's not living by bread alone[23]"; for when they were left all together without one morsel of bread for many months, one after another, still the good Providence of God relieved them, and supplied them, and this for the most part out of the sea. In this low condition of affairs, there was no little exercise for the prudence and patience of the governor, who cheerfully bore his part in all; and, that industry might not flag, he quickly set himself to settle propriety[24] among the new planters, foreseeing that while the whole country labored upon a common stock, the husbandry and business of the plantation could not flourish, as Plato[25] and others long since dreamed that it would if a community were established. Certainly, if the spirit which dwelt in the old Puritans, had not inspired these new planters, they had sunk under the burden of these difficulties; but our Bradford had a double portion of that spirit.

The plantation was quickly thrown into a storm that almost overwhelmed it, by the unhappy actions of a minister sent over from England by the adventurers[26] concerned for the plantation; but by the blessing of Heaven on the conduct of the governor, they weathered out that storm.

---

[22]AGAINST THEIR CONSCIENCE TO WORK SUCH A DAY: The Puritans did not observe Christmas as a holiday. In fact, in 1659, the General Court of the Massachusetts Bay Colony banned the observance of Christmas: "It is therefore ordered by this court...that whosoever shall be found observing any such day as Christmas or the like, either by forbearing of labor, feasting, or any other way...shall pay for every such offence five shilling as a fine to the county."

[23]"MAN'S NOT LIVING BY BREAD ALONE": Luke 4:4, "And Jesus answered him, saying, It is written, That man shall not live by bread alone, but by every word of God."

[24]PROPRIETY: Property.

[25]PLATO: Greek philosopher (427?–347 BCE).

[26]THE ADVENTURERS: English investors.

Only the adventurers, hereupon breaking to pieces, threw up all their concernments with the infant colony; whereof they gave this as one reason, that the planters dissembled with his Majesty and their friends in their petition, wherein they declared for a church discipline, agreeing with the French and others of the reforming churches in Europe.[27] Whereas 'twas now urged, that they had admitted into their communion a person who at his admission utterly renounced the churches of England, (which person, by the way, was that very man who had made the complaints against them) and therefore, though they denied the name of Brownists,[28] yet they were the thing. In answer hereunto, the very words written by the governor were these:

> Whereas you tax us with dissembling about the French discipline, you do us wrong, for we both hold and practice the discipline of the French and other Reformed Churches (as they have published the same in the Harmony of Confessions) according to our means, in effect and substance. But whereas you would tie us up to the French discipline in every circumstance, you derogate from the liberty we have in Christ Jesus. The Apostle Paul would have none to follow him in any thing, but wherein he follows Christ; much less ought any Christian or church in the world to do it. The French may err, we may err, and other churches may err, and doubtless do in many circumstances. That honor therefore belongs only to the infallible Word of God, and pure Testament of Christ, to be propounded and followed as the only rule and pattern for direction herein to all churches and Christians. And it is too great arrogancy for any man or church to think that he or they have so sounded the Word of God unto the bottom, as precisely to set down the church's discipline without error in substance or circumstance, that no other without blame may digress or differ in any thing from the same. And it is not difficult to show that the reformed churches differ in many circumstances among themselves.

By which words it appears how far he was free from that rigid spirit of separation, which broke to pieces the Separatists themselves in the Low

---

[27]REFORMING CHURCHES IN EUROPE: In Europe, countries assumed "official" religious positions (Protestant or Catholic), which were often enforced under threat of death. In 1598, French King Henry IV restored peace in France, with the Edict of Nantes, which defined the rights of the French Protestants (Huguenots) to worship according to their conscience without denying the authority of the Crown.

[28]BROWNISTS: Robert Browne (1550–1633) was an English clergyman who led a group of early separatists known as Brownists. He is considered the founder of Congregationalism.

Countries, unto the great scandal of the reforming churches.[29] He was indeed a person of a well-tempered spirit, or else it had been scarce possible for him to have kept the affairs of Plymouth in so good a temper for thirty-seven years together; in every one of which he was chosen their governor, except the three years wherein Mr. Winslow,[30] and the two years wherein Mr. Prince,[31] at the choice of the people, took a turn with him.

The leader of a people in a wilderness had need be a Moses;[32] and if a Moses had not led the people of Plymouth Colony, where this worthy person was the governor, the people had never with so much unanimity and importunity still called him to lead them. Among many instances thereof, let this one piece of self-denial be told for a memorial of him, wheresoever this history shall be considered: the patent of the colony was taken in his name, running in these terms: "To William Bradford, his heirs, associates, and assigns," but when the number of the freemen[33] was much increased, and many new townships erected, the General Court there desired of Mr. Bradford that he would make a surrender of the same into their hands, which he willingly and presently assented unto, and confirmed it according to their desire by his hand and seal, reserving no more for himself than was his proportion, with others, by agreement. But as he found the Providence of Heaven many ways recompensing his many acts of self-denial, so he gave this testimony to the faithfulness of the Divine Promises: that he had forsaken friends, houses and lands for the sake of the Gospel, and the Lord gave them him again. Here he prospered in his estate; and besides a worthy son which he had by a former wife, he had also two sons and a daughter by another, whom he married in this land.

He was a person for study as well as action; and hence, notwithstanding the difficulties through which he passed in his youth, he attained unto a notable skill in languages: the Dutch tongue was become almost as vernacular to him as the English; the French tongue he could also manage; the Latin and the Greek he had mastered; but the Hebrew he most of all studied, because he said he would see with his own eyes the ancient oracles of God in their native beauty. He was also well skilled in history, in antiquity, and in philosophy; and for theology he became so versed in it, that he was an irrefragable disputant against the errors, especially those

---

[29]CHURCHES: Arguments between the various separatist sects about which was the most pure caused fragmentation of the reformed churches.
[30]MR. WINSLOW: Edward Winslow (1596–1655).
[31]MR. PRINCE: Thomas Prince (1600–1673).
[32]MOSES: The leader of the Hebrews who led them from slavery in Egypt to the Promised Land.
[33]FREEMEN: Not indentured servants.

of Anabaptism,[34] which with trouble he saw rising in his colony; wherefore he wrote some significant things for the confutation of those errors. But the crown of all was his holy, prayerful, watchful, and fruitful walk with God, wherein he was very exemplary.

At length he fell into an indisposition of body, which rendered him unhealthy for a whole winter; and as the spring advanced, his health yet more declined; yet he felt himself not what he counted sick, till one day, in the night after which, the God of Heaven so filled his mind with ineffable consolations, that he seemed little short of Paul, rapt up unto the unutterable entertainments of Paradise.[35] The next morning he told his friends that the good spirit of God had given him a pledge of his happiness in another world, and the first fruits of his eternal glory; and on the day following he died, May 9, 1657, in the 69th year of his age— lamented by all the colonies of New England as a common blessing and father to them all.

O mihi si Similis Contingat Clausula Vitae![36]

Plato's brief description of a governor, is all that I will now leave as his character, in an

EPITAPH.

Νομεὺς Τροψὸς ἀγέλης ἀνθρωπίνης[37]

> Men are but flocks: Bradford beheld their need,
> And long did them at once both rule and feed.

[1702]

---

[34]ANABAPTISM: The name given to Protestant sects that opposed infant baptism and advocated the separation of church and state.

[35]PARADISE: A reference to 2 Corinthians 12:2: "How that he was caught up into paradise, and heard unspeakable words, which it is not lawful for a man to utter."

[36]O MIHI SI SIMILIS CONTINGAT CLAUSULA VITAE: "Oh, that such an to end of life might come to me." (Latin)

[37]*Νομεὺς Τροψὸς ἀγέλης ἀνθρωπίνης*: "Shepherd and provider to the human flock." (Greek)

Jonathan Edwards

(1703–1758)

Born in East Windsor, Connecticut, the brilliant son of a Congregational minister and the grandson of a minister even more eminent, Jonathan Edwards received his bachelor's degree at Yale—which he had entered at age thirteen—and in 1726 he became a minister himself. His first position was in Northampton in western Massachusetts on the Connecticut River. But Edwards suffered dismissal in 1750 because of a disagreement with members of his congregation over the standards for admission to the church. He maintained that the sacrament of communion should be given only to those who had experienced religious conversion—a standard the members of his congregation by a vote of 200 to 20 found too strict. Edwards then took his ministry to the town of Stockbridge, Massachusetts, in the Berkshire Mountains.

Early in 1758 Edwards began an appointment as president of the College of New Jersey (now Princeton University), but in late March he died after being inoculated for smallpox.

Edwards was an extraordinary preacher and scholar. He produced an intellectually complex and powerful body of work dealing not only with theology but also with psychology, ethics, and metaphysics. A modern theologian summarized Edwards's views in these terms:

> *The root of human sinfulness was antagonism toward God; God was justified in condemning sinners who scorned the work of Christ on their behalf; conversion meant a radical change of the heart; true Christianity involved not just an understanding of God and the facts of Scripture but a new "sense" of divine beauty, holiness, and truth.*

Edwards was the author of impassioned sermons and publications, including "God Glorified in the Work of Redemption" (1731); "A Divine and Supernatural Light" (1734); "The Excellency of Christ" (c. 1730s); and "Sinners in the Hands of an Angry God" (1741), in which he describes the horror of sin and the might and majesty of God. Sinfulness, Edwards believed, is the basic first fact of a person's life, which justifies eternal punishment—damnation to hell—unless God makes possible mercy and salvation.

Edwards also produced A Careful and Strict Enquiry into the Modern Prevailing Notions of that Freedom of Will, Which is Supposed to be Essential to Moral Agency, Virtue and Vice, Reward and Punishment, Praise and Blame *(1754), commonly known as* Freedom of the Will. *Here he argued that "will" is best understood in connection to the deepest motives of a person; "willing" an action thus is an expression, at a fundamental level, of who a person is. Human beings are profoundly responsible for their acts of will, for their choice to love and obey God or not. But the crucial point, for Edwards, is that each person is dependent on God for the regeneration of the will; by renewing and revitalizing the sinful heart, God makes repentance and an acceptance of the divine possible. In* Original Sin, *which was published in 1758 after Edwards's death, he defended and developed the concepts of human sinfulness and predestination treated in* Freedom of the Will.

Edwards was, furthermore, a major contributor to the wave of religious revivalism, the "Great Awakening," that took place in the 1730s through the 1740s. Among the writings that laid out his understanding of religious experience and the realization of God's kingdom are A Faithful Narrative of the Surprising Work of God *(1737);* Some Thoughts Concerning the Present Revival of Religion in New England *(1743); and* A History of the Work of Redemption *(1744). His fullest exploration and analysis of this topic is* A Treatise Concerning Religious Affections *(1746). Edwards's final published text in his lifetime was* The Great Christian Doctrine of Original Sin Defended *(1758).*

In addition to "Sinners in the Hands of an Angry God," below, is reprinted Edwards's "Personal Narrative," written a year or two earlier but not published until 1765, which recounts his conversion experience. Both texts vividly, and with high drama, show the insecurity and precariousness of a person's sense of conversion. A person must cling to faith because while conversion is a real experience, no one can be certain that a secure, steadily advancing spiritual life will follow. For Edwards, as he once explained, there is a difference between reading the word "fire" and being burned, and it is the intensity of actual religious feeling in these two works, and in others, that Edwards is determined to evoke.

A scholar in the early nineteenth-century wrote in tribute:

> *[Edwards] was the greatest of theologians; combining in a degree that is quite unexampled, the profoundly intellectual with the devotedly spiritual and sacred, and realizing in his own person a most rare, yet most beautiful, harmony between the simplicity of the Christian pastor on the one hand, and on the other, all the strength and prowess of a giant in philosophy.*

For biography and context: Perry Miller, Jonathan Edwards *(1949); David Levin,* Jonathan Edwards: A Profile *(1969); and George M. Marsden,* Jonathan Edwards: A Life *(2003). See also William J. Scheick,* The Writings of Jonathan Edwards: Theme, Motif, and Style *(1975);* Critical Essays on Jonathan Edwards, *ed. William J. Scheick (1980); and* Benjamin Franklin, Jonathan Edwards, and the Representation of American Culture, *ed. Barbara B. Oberg and Harry S. Stout (1993).*

Personal Narrative

I had a variety of concerns and exercises about my soul from my childhood; but had two more remarkable seasons of awakening[1] before I met with that change, by which I was brought to those new dispositions, and that new sense of things, that I have since had. The first time was when I was a boy, some years before I went to college,[2] at a time of remarkable awakening in my father's congregation.[3] I was then very much affected[4] for many months, and concerned about the things of religion, and my soul's salvation; and was abundant in duties. I used to pray five times a day in secret, and to spend much time in religious talk with other boys; and used to meet with them to pray together. I experienced I know not what kind of delight in religion. My mind was much engaged in it, and had much self-righteous pleasure; and it was my delight to abound in religious duties. I, with some of my schoolmates joined together, and built a booth in a swamp, in a very secret and retired place, for a place of prayer. And besides, I had particular secret places of my own in the woods, where I used to retire by myself; and used to be from time to time much affected. My affections seemed to be lively and easily moved, and I seemed to be in my element, when engaged in religious duties. And I am ready to think, many are deceived with such affections, and such a kind of delight, as I then had in religion, and mistake it for grace.

But in process of time, my convictions and affections wore off; and I entirely lost all those affections and delights, and left off secret prayer, at least as to any constant performance of it; and returned like a dog to his vomit,[5] and went on in ways of sin.

Indeed, I was at some times very uneasy, especially towards the latter part of the time of my being at college. Till it pleased God, in my last year at college, at a time when I was in the midst of many uneasy thoughts about the state of my soul, to seize me with a pleurisy;[6] in which he brought me nigh to the grave, and shook me over the pit of hell.

But yet, it was not long after my recovery, before I fell again into my old ways of sin. But God would not suffer me to go on with any quietness; but I had great and violent inward struggles: till after many conflicts

[1]AWAKENING: A spiritual awakening or sense of increased religious awareness.
[2]BEFORE I WENT TO COLLEGE: In 1716, when he was 13, Edwards was admitted to Yale College. He remained in New Haven, Connecticut, to study theology until 1620.
[3]FATHER'S CONGREGATION: That of Reverend Timothy Edwards.
[4]AFFECTED: Emotionally moved.
[5]RETURNED LIKE A DOG TO HIS VOMIT: A reference to Proverbs 26:11: "As a dog returneth to his vomit, so a fool returneth to his folly."
[6]PLEURISY: A respiratory disease featuring pain in the chest or side, fever, and physical wasting; usually occurs as a complication of a bad cold or other disease.

with wicked inclinations, and repeated resolutions, and bonds that I laid myself under by a kind of vows to God, I was brought wholly to break off all former wicked ways, and all ways of known outward sin; and to apply myself to seek my salvation, and practice the duties of religion: but without that kind of affection and delight, that I had formerly experienced. My concern now wrought more by inward struggles and conflicts, and self-reflections. I made seeking my salvation the main business of my life. But yet it seems to me, I sought after a miserable manner: which has made me sometimes since to question, whether ever it issued in that which was saving;[7] being ready to doubt, whether such miserable seeking was ever succeeded. But yet I was brought to seek salvation, in a manner that I never was before. I felt a spirit to part with all things in the world, for an interest in Christ. My concern continued and prevailed, with many exercising things and inward struggles; but yet it never seemed to be proper to express my concern that I had, by the name of terror.

From my childhood up, my mind had been wont to be full of objections against the doctrine of God's sovereignty, in choosing whom He would to eternal life and rejecting whom he pleased;[8] leaving them eternally to perish, and be everlastingly tormented in hell. It used to appear like a horrible doctrine to me. But I remember the time very well, when I seemed to be convinced, and fully satisfied, as to this sovereignty of God, and his justice in thus eternally disposing of men, according to his sovereign pleasure. But never could give an account, how, or by what means, I was thus convinced; not in the least imagining, in the time of it, nor a long time after, that there was any extraordinary influence of God's Spirit in it: but only that now I saw further, and my reason apprehended the justice and reasonableness of it. However, my mind rested in it; and it put an end to all those cavils and objections, that had till then abode with me, all the preceeding part of my life. And there has been a wonderful alteration in my mind, with respect to the doctrine of God's sovereignty, from that day to this; so that I scarce ever have found so much as the rising of an objection against God's sovereignty, in the most absolute sense, in showing mercy on whom he will show mercy, and hardening and eternally damning whom he will.[9] God's absolute sovereignty, and justice, with respect to

[7]SAVING: Spiritually redeeming.
[8]THE DOCTRINE OF GODS SOVEREIGNTY, IN CHOOSING WHOM HE WOULD TO ETERNAL LIFE AND REJECTING WHOM HE PLEASED: The doctrine of predestination, which, taken in its widest meaning, instructs that God, owing to his infallible knowledge of the future, has appointed and ordained all events. It applies to salvation in that God has already decided who will be saved and who will be damned, despite free will, which has no influence on the final outcome. The doctrine was put forth by the Protestant reformer John Calvin (1509–1564) that faith itself was a "divine gift" from God, and this gift was awarded only to a few people, known as the "elect." The elect were the only ones predestined to be granted salvation.
[9]AND DAMNING WHOM HE WILL: A reference to Romans 9:18: "Therefore hath he mercy on whom he will have mercy, and whom he will be hardeneth."

salvation and damnation, is what my mind seems to rest assured of, as much as of anything that I see with my eyes; at least it is so at times. But I have oftentimes since that first conviction, had quite another kind of sense of God's sovereignty, than I had then. I have often since, not only had a conviction, but a delightful conviction. The doctrine of God's sovereignty has very often appeared, an exceeding pleasant, bright and sweet doctrine to me: and absolute sovereignty is what I love to ascribe to God. But my first conviction was not with this.

The first that I remember that ever I found anything of that sort of inward, sweet delight in God and divine things, that I have lived much in since, was on reading those words, 1 Tim. 1.17, "Now unto the King eternal, immortal, invisible, the only wise God, be honor and glory for ever and ever, Amen." As I read the words, there came into my soul, and was as it were diffused through it, a sense of the glory of the divine being, a new sense, quite different from anything I ever experienced before. Never any words of Scripture seemed to me as these words did. I thought with myself, how excellent a Being that was; and how happy I should be, if I might enjoy that God, and be wrapt[10] up to God in heaven, and be as it were swallowed up in him. I kept saying, and as it were singing over these words of Scripture to myself; and went to prayer, to pray to God that I might enjoy him; and prayed in a manner quite different from what I used to do, with a new sort of affection. But it never came into my thought, that there was anything spiritual, or of a saving nature in this.

From about that time, I began to have a new kind of apprehensions and ideas of Christ, and the work of redemption, and the glorious way of salvation by him. I had an inward, sweet sense of these things, that at times came into my heart; and my soul was led away in pleasant views and contemplations of them. And my mind was greatly engaged, to spend my time in reading and meditating on Christ; and the beauty and excellency of his person, and the lovely way of salvation, by free grace[11] in him. I found no books so delightful to me, as those that treated of these subjects. Those words (Cant. 2:1) used to be abundantly with me: "I am the rose of Sharon, the lily of the valleys." The words seemed to me, sweetly to represent, the loveliness and beauty of Jesus Christ. And the whole book of Canticles[12] used to be pleasant to me; and I used to be much in reading it, about that time. And found, from time to time, an inward sweetness, that used, as it were, to carry me away in my contemplations; in what I know

---

[10]WRAPT: Lifted, transported.
[11]SALVATION, BY FREE GRACE: The belief that salvation is a gift of God's free grace and cannot be earned, obtained, or influenced by any virtue or work (also see note 8). References to free grace include Romans 3:24; Ephesians 2:8, 9; Acts 20:21; and Titus 3:5.
[12]CANTICLES: The Song of Solomon.

not how to express otherwise, than by a calm, sweet abstraction of soul from all the concerns o[f] this world; and a kind of vision, or fixed ideas and imaginations, of being alone in the mountains, or some solitary wilderness, far from all mankind, sweetly conversing with Christ, and wrapt and swallowed up in God. The sense I had of divine things, would often of a sudden as it were, kindle up a sweet burning in my heart; an ardor of my soul, that I know not how to express.

Not long after I first began to experience these things, I gave an account to my father, of some things that had passed in my mind. I was pretty much affected by the discourse we had together. And when the discourse was ended, I walked abroad alone, in a solitary place in my father's pasture, for contemplation. And as I was walking there, and looked up on the sky and clouds; there came into my mind, a sweet sense of the glorious majesty and grace of God, that I know not how to express. I seemed to see them both in a sweet conjunction: majesty and meekness joined together: it was a sweet and gentle, and holy majesty; and also a majestic meekness; an awful sweetness; a high, and great, and holy gentleness.

After this my sense of divine things gradually increased, and became more and more lively, and had more of that inward sweetness. The appearance of everything was altered: there seemed to be, as it were, a calm, sweet cast, or appearance of divine glory, in almost everything. God's excellency, his wisdom, his purity and love, seemed to appear in everything; in the sun, moon and stars; in the clouds, and blue sky; in the grass, flowers, trees; in the water, and all nature; which used greatly to fix my mind. I often used to sit and view the moon, for a long time; and so in the daytime, spent much time in viewing the clouds and sky, to behold the sweet glory of God in these things: in the meantime, singing forth with a low voice, my contemplations of the Creator and Redeemer. And scarce anything, among all the works of nature, was so sweet to me as thunder and lightning. Formerly, nothing had been so terrible to me. I used to be a person uncommonly terrified with thunder: and it used to strike me with terror, when I saw a thunderstorm rising. But now, on the contrary, it rejoiced me. I felt God at the first appearance of a thunderstorm. And used to take the opportunity at such times, to fix myself to view the clouds, and see the lightnings play, and hear the majestic and awful voice of God's thunder: which often times was exceeding entertaining, leading me to sweet contemplations of my great and glorious God. And while I viewed, used to spend my time, as it always seemed natural to me, to sing or chant forth my meditations; to speak my thoughts in soliloquies, and speak with a singing voice.

I felt then a great satisfaction as to my good estate. But that did not content me. I had vehement longings of soul after God and Christ, and after more holiness; wherewith my heart seemed to be full, and ready to break: which often brought to my mind, the words of the Psalmist, Ps. 119:28, "My soul breaketh for the longing it hath." I often felt a mourning and lamenting in my heart, that I had not turned to God sooner, that I might have had more time to grow in grace. My mind was greatly fixed on divine things; I was almost perpetually in the contemplation of them. Spent most of my time in thinking of divine things, year after year. And used to spend abundance of my time, in walking alone in the woods, and solitary places, for meditation, soliloquy and prayer, and converse with God. And it was always my manner, at such times, to sing forth my contemplations. And was almost constantly in ejaculatory prayer, wherever I was. Prayer seemed to be natural to me; as the breath, by which the inward burnings of my heart had vent.

The delights which I now felt in things of religion, were of an exceeding different kind, from those forementioned, that I had when I was a boy. They were totally of another kind; and what I then had no more notion or idea of, than one born blind has of pleasant and beautiful colors. They were of a more inward, pure, soul-animating and refreshing nature. Those former delights, never reached the heart; and did not arise from any sight of the divine excellency of the things of God; or any taste of the soul-satisfying, and life-giving good, there is in them.

My sense of divine things seemed gradually to increase, till I went to preach at New York; which was about a year and a half after they began. While I was there, I felt them, very sensibly, in a much higher degree, than I had done before. My longings after God and holiness, were much increased. Pure and humble, holy and heavenly Christianity, appeared exceeding amiable to me. I felt in me a burning desire to be in everything a complete Christian; and conformed to the blessed image of Christ: and that I might live in all things, according to the pure, sweet and blessed rules of the gospel. I had an eager thirsting after progress in these things. My longings after it, put me upon pursuing and pressing after them. It was my continual strife day and night, and constant inquiry, how I should be more holy, and live more holily, and more becoming a child of God, and disciple of Christ. I sought an increase of grace and holiness, and that I might live an holy life, with vastly more earnestness, than ever I sought grace, before I had it. I used to be continually examining myself, and studying and contriving for likely ways and means, how I should live holily, with far greater diligence and earnestness, than ever I pursued anything in my life: but with too great a dependence on my own strength, which afterwards proved a great damage to me. My experience had not then taught me, as it has done since, my extreme feebleness and impotence, every manner of way; and the innumerable and bottomless depths of secret corruption and deceit, that there was in my heart. However, I went on with my eager pursuit after more holiness; and sweet conformity to Christ.

The Heaven I desired was a heaven of holiness; to be with God, and to spend my eternity in divine love, and holy communion with Christ. My mind was very much taken up with contemplations on heaven, and the enjoyments of those there; and living there in perfect holiness, humility and love. And it used at that time to appear a great part of the happiness of heaven, that there the saints could express their love to Christ. It appeared to me a great clog and hindrance and burden to me, that what I felt within, I could not express to God, and give vent to, as I desired. The inward ardor of my soul, seemed to be hindered and pent up, and could not freely flame out as it would. I used often to think, how in heaven, this sweet principle should freely and fully vent and express itself. Heaven appeared to me exceeding delightful as a world of love. It appeared to me, that all happiness consisted in living in pure, humble, heavenly, divine love.

I remember the thoughts I used then to have of holiness. I remember I then said sometimes to myself, I do certainly know that I love holiness, such as the gospel prescribes. It appeared to me, there was nothing in it but what was ravishingly lovely. It appeared to me, to be the highest beauty and amiableness, above all other beauties: that it was a divine beauty; far purer than anything here upon earth; and that everything else, was like mire, filth and defilement, in comparison of it.

Holiness, as I then wrote down some of my contemplations on it, appeared to me to be of a sweet, pleasant, charming, serene, calm nature. It seemed to me, it brought an inexpressible purity, brightness, peacefulness and ravishment to the soul: and that it made the soul like a field or garden of God, with all manner of pleasant flowers; that is all pleasant, delightful and undisturbed; enjoying a sweet calm, and the gently vivifying beams of the sun. The soul of a true Christian, as I then wrote my meditations, appeared like such a little white flower, as we see in the spring of the year; low and humble on the ground, opening its bosom, to receive the pleasant beams of the sun's glory; rejoicing as it were, in a calm rapture; diffusing around a sweet fragrancy; standing peacefully and lovingly, in the midst of other flowers round about; all in like manner opening their bosoms, to drink in the light of the sun.

There was no part of creature-holiness, that I then, and at other times, had so great a sense of the loveliness of, as humility, brokenness of heart and poverty of spirit: and there was nothing that I had such a spirit to long for. My heart, as it were, panted after this to lie low before GOD, and in the dust; that I might be nothing, and that God might be all; that I might become as a little child.[13]

While I was there at New York, I sometimes was much affected with reflections on my past life, considering how late it was, before I began to be truly religious; and how wickedly I had lived till then: and once so as to weep abundantly, and for a considerable time together.

On January 12, 1722–3, I made a solemn dedication of myself to God, and wrote it down; giving up myself, and all that I had to God; to be for the future in no respect my own; to act as one that had no right to himself, in any respect. And solemnly vowed to take God for my whole portion and felicity; looking on nothing else as any part of my happiness, nor acting as if it were: and his law for the constant rule of my obedience; engaging to fight with all my might, against the world, the flesh and the devil, to the end of my life. But have reason to be infinitely humbled, when I consider, how much I have failed of answering my obligation.

I had then abundance of sweet religious conversation in the family where I lived, with Mr. John Smith, and his pious mother. My heart was knit in affection to those, in whom were appearances of true piety; and I could bear the thoughts of no other companions, but such as were holy, and the disciples of the blessed Jesus.

I had great longings for the advancement of Christ's kingdom in the world. My secret prayer used to be in great part taken up in praying for it. If I heard the least hint of anything that happened in any part of the world, that appeared to me, in some respect or other, to have a favorable aspect on the interest of Christ's kingdom, my soul eagerly catched[14] at it; and it would much animate and refresh me. I used to be earnest to read public news-letters, mainly for that end; to see if I could not find some news favorable to the interest of religion in the world.

I very frequently used to retire into a solitary place, on the banks of Hudson's River, at some distance from the city, for contemplation on divine things, and secret converse with God; and had many sweet hours there. Sometimes Mr. Smith and I walked there together, to converse of the things of God; and our conversation used much to turn on the advancement of Christ's kingdom in the world, and the glorious things that God would accomplish for his church in the latter days.

I had then, and at other times, the greatest delight in the holy Scriptures, of any book whatsoever. Oftentimes in reading it, every word seemed to touch my heart. I felt an harmony between something in my

---

[13]THAT I MIGHT BECOME AS A LITTLE CHILD: A reference to Mark 10:15: "Verily I say unto you, Whosoever shall not receive the kingdom of God as a little child, he shall not enter therein."
[14]CATCHED: Grabbed.

heart, and those sweet and powerful words. I seemed often to see so much light, exhibited by every sentence, and such a refreshing ravishing food communicated, that I could not get along in reading. Used oftentimes to dwell long on one sentence, to see the wonders contained in it; and yet almost every sentence seemed to be full of wonders.

I came away from New York in the month of April 1723, and had a most bitter parting with Madam Smith and her son. My heart seemed to sink within me, at leaving the family and city, where I had enjoyed so many sweet and pleasant days. I went from New York to Weathersfield[15] by water. As I sailed away, I kept sight of the city as long as I could; and when I was out of sight of it, it would affect me much to look that way, with a kind of melancholy mixed with sweetness. However, that night after this sorrowful parting, I was greatly comforted in God at Westchester,[16] where we went ashore to lodge: and had a pleasant time of it all the voyage to Saybrook.[17] It was sweet to me to think of meeting dear Christians in heaven, where we should never part more. At Saybrook we went ashore to lodge on Saturday, and there kept sabbath; where I had a sweet and refreshing season, walking alone in the fields.

After I came home to Windsor, remained much in a like frame of my mind, as I had been in at New York; but only sometimes felt my heart ready to sink, with the thoughts of my friends at New York. And my refuge and support was in contemplations on the heavenly state; as I find in my diary of May 1, 1723. It was my comfort to think of that state, where there is fulness of joy; where reigns heavenly, sweet, calm and delightful love, without alloy; where there are continually the dearest expressions of this love; where is the enjoyment of the persons loved, without ever parting; where these persons that appear so lovely in this world, will really be inexpressibly more lovely, and full of love to us. And how sweetly will the mutual lovers join together to sing the praises of God and the Lamb![18] How full will it fill us with joy, to think, that this enjoyment, these sweet exercises will never cease or come to an end; but will last to all eternity!

Continued much in the same frame in the general, that I had been in at New York, till I went to New Haven, to live there as Tutor of the College; having some special season of uncommon sweetness; particularly once at Bolton, in a journey from Boston, walking out alone in the fields. After I went to New Haven, I sunk in religion; my mind being diverted from my eager and violent pursuits after holiness, by some affairs that greatly perplexed and distracted my mind.

---

[15]WETHERSFIELD: Wethersfield, Connecticut, near Edwards's father's home in Windsor.
[16]WESTCHESTER: Westchester, New York.
[17]SAYBROOK: Saybrook, Connecticut.
[18]THE LAMB: The lamb is a symbol for Jesus Christ, who is also known as the lamb of God.

In September 1725, was taken ill at New Haven; and endeavoring to go home to Windsor, was so ill at the North Village, that I could go no further: where I lay sick for about a quarter of a year. And in this sickness, God was pleased to visit me again with the sweet influences of his spirit. My mind was greatly engaged there on divine, pleasant contemplations, and longings of soul. I observed that those who watched with me, would often be looking out for the morning, and seemed to wish for it. Which brought to my mind those words of the Psalmist, which my soul with sweetness made its own language, "My soul waiteth for the Lord more than they that watch for the morning: I say, more than they that watch for the morning" [Ps. 130:6]. And when the light of the morning came, and the beams of the sun came in at the windows, it refreshed my soul from one morning to another. It seemed to me to be some image of the sweet light of God's glory.

I remember, about that time, I used greatly to long for the conversion of some that I was concerned with. It seemed to me, I could gladly honor them, and with delight be a servant to them, and lie at their feet, if they were but truly holy.

But sometime after this, I was again greatly diverted in my mind, with some temporal concerns, that exceedingly took up my thoughts, greatly to the wounding of my soul: and went on through various exercises, that it would be tedious to relate, that gave me much more experience of my own heart, than ever I had before.

Since I came to this town, I have often had sweet complacency[19] in God in views of his glorious perfections, and the excellency of Jesus Christ. God has appeared to me, a glorious and lovely being, chiefly on the account of his holiness. The holiness of God has always appeared to me the most lovely of all his attributes. The doctrines of God's absolute sovereignty, and free grace, in showing mercy to whom he would show mercy; and man's absolute dependence on the operations of God's Holy Spirit, have very often appeared to me as sweet and glorious doctrines. These doctrines have been much my delight. God's sovereignty has ever appeared to me, as great part of his glory. It has often been sweet to me to go to God, and adore him as a sovereign God, and ask sovereign mercy of him.

I have loved the doctrines of the gospel: they have been to my soul like green pastures. The gospel has seemed to me to be the richest treasure; the treasure that I have most desired, and longed that it might dwell richly in me. The way of salvation by Christ, has appeared in a general way, glorious and excellent, and most pleasant and beautiful. It has often seemed to me, that it would in a great measure spoil heaven, to receive it in any other way. That text has often been affecting and delightful to

---

[19]COMPLACENCY: Pleasurable satisfaction, contentment.

me, Is. 32:2, "A man shall be an hiding place from the wind, and a covert from the tempest," etc.

It has often appeared sweet to me, to be united to Christ; to have him for my head, and to be a member of his body: and also to have Christ for my teacher and prophet. I very often think with sweetness and longings and pantings of soul, of being a little child, taking hold of Christ, to be led by him through the wilderness of this world. That text, Matt. 18 at the beginning, has often been sweet to me, "Except ye be converted, and become as little children," etc. I love to think of coming to Christ, to receive salvation of him, poor in spirit, and quite empty of self; humbly exalting him alone; cut entirely off from my own root, and to grow into, and out of Christ: to have God in Christ to be all in all; and to live by faith in the Son of God, a life of humble, unfeigned confidence in him. That Scripture has often been sweet to me, Ps. 115:1, "Not unto us, O Lord, not unto us, but unto thy name give glory, for thy mercy, and for thy truth's sake." And those words of Christ, Luke 10:21, "In that hour Jesus rejoiced in spirit, and said, I thank thee, O Father, Lord of heaven and earth, that thou hast hid these things from the wise and prudent, and hast revealed them unto babes: even so Father, for so it seemed good in thy sight." That sovereignty of God that Christ rejoiced in, seemed to me to be worthy to be rejoiced in; and that rejoicing of Christ, seemed to me to show the excellency of Christ, and the spirit that he was of.

Sometimes only mentioning a single word, causes my heart to burn within me: or only seeing the name of Christ, or the name of some attribute of God. And God has appeared glorious to me, on account of the Trinity. It has made me have exalting thoughts of God, that he subsists in three persons; Father, Son, and Holy Ghost.

The sweetest joys and delights I have experienced, have not been those that have arisen from a hope of my own good estate; but in a direct view of the glorious things of the gospel. When I enjoy this sweetness, it seems to carry me above the thoughts of my own safe estate. It seems at such times a loss that I cannot bear, to take off my eye from the glorious, pleasant object I behold without me, to turn my eye in upon myself, and my own good estate.

My heart has been much on the advancement of Christ's kingdom in the world. The histories of the past advancement of Christ's kingdom, have been sweet to me. When I have read histories of past ages, the pleasantest thing in all my reading has been, to read of the kingdom of Christ being promoted. And when I have expected in my reading, to come to any such thing, I have lotted[20] upon it all the way as I read. And my mind has been much entertained and delighted, with the Scripture promises and prophecies, of the future glorious advancement of Christ's kingdom on earth.

[20]LOTTED: Rejoiced.

I have sometimes had a sense of the excellent fullness of Christ, and his meetness and suitableness as a Savior; whereby he has appeared to me, far above all, the chief of ten thousands.[21] And his blood and atonement has appeared sweet, and his righteousness sweet; which is always accompanied with an ardency of spirit, and inward strugglings and breathings and groanings, that cannot be uttered, to be emptied of myself, and swallowed up in Christ.

Once, as I rid out into the woods for my health, anno 1737; and having lit from my horse in a retired place, as my manner commonly has been, to walk for divine contemplation and prayer; I had a view, that for me was extraordinary, of the glory of the Son of God; as mediator between God and man; and his wonderful, great, full, pure and sweet grace and love, and meek and gentle condescension. This grace, that appeared to me so calm and sweet, appeared great above the heavens. The person of Christ appeared ineffably excellent, with an excellency great enough to swallow up all thought and conception. Which continued, as near as I can judge, about an hour; which kept me, the bigger part of the time, in a flood of tears, and weeping aloud. I felt withal, an ardency of soul to be, what I know not otherwise how to express, than to be emptied and annihilated; to lie in the dust, and to be full of Christ alone; to love him with a holy and pure love; to trust in him; to live upon him; to serve and follow him, and to be totally wrapt up in the fullness of Christ; and to be perfectly sanctified and made pure, with a divine and heavenly purity. I have several other times, had views very much of the same nature, and that have had the same effects.

I have many times had a sense of the glory of the third person in the Trinity, in his office of Sanctifier; in his holy operations communicating divine light and life to the soul. God in the communications of his Holy Spirit, has appeared as an infinite fountain of divine glory and sweetness; being full and sufficient to fill and satisfy the soul: pouring forth itself in sweet communications, like the sun in its glory, sweetly and pleasantly diffusing light and life.

I have sometimes had an affecting sense of the excellency of the word of God, as a word of life; as the light of life; a sweet, excellent, life-giving word: accompanied with a thirsting after that word, that it might dwell richly in my heart.

I have often since I lived in this town, had very affecting views of my own sinfulness and vileness; very frequently so as to hold me in a kind of loud weeping, sometimes for a considerable time together: so that I have

[21]THE CHIEF OF TEN THOUSANDS: A reference to the Song of Solomon 5:10: "My beloved is white and ruddy, the chiefest among ten thousand."

often been forced to shut myself up.[22] I have had a vastly greater sense of my wickedness, and the badness of my heart, since my conversion, than ever I had before. It has often appeared to me, that if God should mark iniquity against me, I should appear the very worst of all mankind; of all that have been since the beginning of the world of this time: and that I should have by far the lowest place in hell. When others that have come to talk with me about their soul concerns, have expressed the sense they have had of their own wickedness, by saying that it seemed to them, that they were as bad as the devil himself; I thought their expressions seemed exceeding faint and feeble, to represent my wickedness. I thought I should wonder, that they should content themselves with such expressions as these, if I had any reason to imagine, that their sin bore any proportion to mine. It seemed to me, I should wonder at myself, if I should express my wickedness in such feeble terms as they did.

My wickedness, as I am in myself, has long appeared to me perfectly ineffable, and infinitely swallowing up all thought and imagination; like an infinite deluge, or infinite mountains over my head. I know not how to express better, what my sins appear to me to be, than by heaping infinite upon infinite, and multiplying infinite by infinite. I go about very often, for this many years, with these expressions in my mind, and in my mouth, "Infinite upon infinite. Infinite upon infinite!" When I look into my heart, and take a view of my wickedness, it looks like an abyss infinitely deeper than hell. And it appears to me, that were it not for free grace, exalted and raised up to the infinite height of all the fullness and glory of the great Jehovah,[23] and the arm of his power and grace stretched forth, in all the majesty of his power, and in all the glory of his sovereignty; I should appear sunk down in my sins infinitely below hell itself, far beyond sight of everything, but the piercing eye of God's grace, that can pierce even down to such a depth, and to the bottom of such an abyss.

And yet, I ben't in the least inclined to think, that I have a greater conviction of sin than ordinary. It seems to me, my conviction of sin is exceeding small, and faint. It appears to me enough to amaze me, that I have no more sense of my sin. I know certainly, that I have very little sense of my sinfulness. That my sins appear to me so great, don't seem to me to be, because I have so much more conviction of sin than other Christians, but because I am so much worse, and have so much more wickedness to be convinced of. When I have had these turns of weeping and crying for my sins, I thought I knew in the time of it, that my repentance was nothing to my sin.

---

[22]SHUT MYSELF UP: Withdraw alone.
[23]JEHOVAH: The English and common European phrasing, since the sixteenth century, of the Hebrew divine name "Yhwh" [Yahweh].

I have greatly longed of late, for a broken heart, and to lie low before God. And when I ask for humility of God, I can't bear the thoughts of being no more humble, than other Christians. It seems to me, that though their degrees of humility may be suitable for them; yet it would be a vile self-exaltation in me, not to be the lowest in humility of all mankind. Others speak of their longing to be humbled to the dust. Though that may be a proper expression for them, I always think for myself, that I ought to be humbled down below hell. 'Tis an expression that it has long been natural for me to use in prayer to God. I ought to lie infinitely low before God.

It is affecting to me to think, how ignorant I was, when I was a young Christian, of the bottomless, infinite depths of wickedness, pride, hypocrisy and deceit left in my heart.

I have vastly a greater sense, of my universal, exceeding dependence on God's grace and strength, and mere good pleasure, of late, than I used formerly to have; and have experienced more of an abhorrence of my own righteousness. The thought of any comfort or joy, arising in me, on any consideration, or reflection on my own amiableness, or any of my performances or experiences, or any goodness of heart or life, is nauseous and detestable to me. And yet I am greatly afflicted with a proud and self-righteous spirit; much more sensibly, than I used to be formerly. I see that serpent rising and putting forth its head, continually, everywhere, all around me.

Though it seems to me, that in some respects I was a far better Christian, for two or three years after my first conversion, than I am now; and lived in a more constant delight and pleasure: yet of late years, I have had a more full and constant sense of the absolute sovereignty of God, and a delight in that sovereignty; and have had more of a sense of the glory of Christ, as a mediator, as revealed in the Gospel. On one Saturday night in particular, had a particular discovery of the excellency of the gospel of Christ, above all other doctrines; so that I could not but say to myself; "This is my chosen light, my chosen doctrine": and of Christ, "This is my chosen prophet." It appeared to me to be sweet beyond all expression, to follow Christ, and to be taught and enlightened and instructed by him; to learn of him, and live to him.

Another Saturday night, January 1738–9, had such a sense, how sweet and blessed a thing it was, to walk in the way of duty, to do that which was right and meet to be done, and agreeable to the holy mind of God; that it caused me to break forth into a kind of a loud weeping, which held me some time; so that I was forced to shut myself up, and fasten the doors. I could not but as it were cry out, "How happy are they which do that which is right in the sight of God! They are blessed indeed, they are the happy ones!" I had at the same time, a very affecting sense, how meet and suitable it was that God should govern the world, and order all things according to his own pleasure; and I rejoiced in it, that God reigned, and that his will was done.

[c. 1740]

Sinners in the Hands of An Angry God

Their foot shall slide in due time—Deut. 32:35[1]

In this verse is threatened the vengeance of God on the wicked unbelieving Israelites, who were God's visible people, and who lived under the means of grace[2]; but who, notwithstanding all God's wonderful works towards them, remained (as ver. 28.[3]) void of counsel, having no understanding in them. Under all the cultivations of heaven, they brought forth bitter and poisonous fruit; as in the two verses next preceding the text.[4] The expression I have chosen for my text, "Their foot shall slide in due time," seems to imply the following doings, relating to the punishment and destruction to which these wicked Israelites were exposed.

1. That they were always exposed to *destruction*; as one that stands or walks in slippery places is always exposed to fall. This is implied in the manner of their destruction coming upon them, being represented by their foot sliding. The same is expressed, Psalm 73:18–19. "Surely thou didst set them in slippery places; thou castedst them down into destruction."

2. It implies, that they were always exposed to sudden unexpected destruction. As he that walks in slippery places is every moment liable to fall, he cannot foresee one moment whether he shall stand or fall the next; and when he does fall, he falls at once without warning: Which is also expressed in Psalm 73:18–19. "Surely thou didst set them in slippery places; thou castedst them down into destruction: How are they brought into desolation as in a moment!"

[1]THEIR FOOT SHALL SLIDE IN DUE TIME: A reference to Deuteronomy 32:35–36, which warns, "To me belongeth vengeance and recompence; their foot shall slide in due time: for the day of their calamity is at hand, and the things that shall come upon them make haste. / For the LORD shall judge his people."
[2]AND WHO LIVED UNDER THE MEANS OF GRACE: The Ten Commandments, which dictated moral law, are described in Exodus 19:10–25 as part of the covenant between God and the Hebrews.
[3]VER. 28.: "For they are a nation void of counsel, neither is there any understanding in them" (Deuteronomy 32:28).
[4]AS IN THE TWO VERSES NEXT PRECEDING THE TEXT: "For their vine is of the vine of Sodom, and of the fields of Gomorrah: their grapes are grapes of gall, their clusters are bitter. / Their wine is the poison of dragons, and the cruel venom of asps" (Deuteronomy 32:32–33).

3. Another thing implied is, that they are liable to fall *of themselves*, without being thrown down by the hand of another; as he that stands or walks on slippery ground needs nothing but his own weight to throw him down.

4. That the reason why they are not fallen already, and do not fall now, is only that God's appointed time is not come. For it is said, that when that due time, or appointed time comes, *their foot shall slide*. Then they shall be left to fall, as they are inclined by their own weight. God will not hold them up in these slippery places any longer, but will let them go; and then at that very instant, they shall fall into destruction; as he that stands on such slippery declining ground, on the edge of a pit, he cannot stand alone, when he is let go he immediately falls and is lost.

The observation from the words that I would now insist upon is this. "There is nothing that keeps wicked men at any one moment out of hell, but the mere pleasure of God." By the mere pleasure of God, I mean his sovereign pleasure, his arbitrary will, restrained by no obligation, hindered by no manner of difficulty, any more than if nothing else but God's mere will had in the least degree, or in any respect whatsoever, any hand in the preservation of wicked men one moment. The truth of this observation may appear by the following considerations.

1. There is no want of *power* in God to cast wicked men into hell at any moment. Men's hands cannot be strong when God rises up. The strongest have no power to resist him, nor can any deliver out of his hands. He is not only able to cast wicked men into hell, but he can most easily do it. Sometimes an earthly prince meets with a great deal of difficulty to subdue a rebel, who has found means to fortify himself, and has made himself strong by the numbers of his followers. But it is not so with God. There is no fortress that is any defense from the power of God. Though hand join in hand, and vast multitudes of God's enemies combine and associate themselves, they are easily broken in pieces. They are as great heaps of light chaff[5] before the whirlwind; or large quantities of dry stubble before devouring flames. We find it easy to tread on and crush a worm that we see crawling on the earth; so it is easy for us to cut or singe a slender thread that any thing hangs by: thus easy is it for God, when he pleases, to cast his enemies down to hell. What are we, that we should think to stand before him, at whose rebuke the earth trembles, and before whom the rocks are thrown down?

2. They *deserve* to be cast into hell; so that divine justice never stands in the way, it makes no objection against God's using his power at any moment to destroy them. Yea, on the contrary, justice calls aloud for an infinite punishment of their sins. Divine justice says of the tree that brings

[5]CHAFF: Inedible husks or hulls of grain separated by the threshing process.

forth such grapes of Sodom,[6] "Cut it down, why cumbereth it the ground?" Luke 13:7. The sword of divine justice is every moment brandished over their heads, and it is nothing but the hand of arbitrary mercy, and God's mere will, that holds it back.

3. They are already under a sentence of *condemnation* to hell. They do not only justly deserve to be cast down thither, but the sentence of the law of God, that eternal and immutable rule of righteousness that God has fixed between him and mankind, is gone out against them, and stands against them; so that they are bound over already to hell. John 3:18. "He that believeth not is condemned already." So that every unconverted man properly belongs to hell; that is his place; from thence he is, John 8:23. "Ye are from beneath." And thither he is bound; it is the place that justice, and God's word, and the sentence of his unchangeable law assign to him.

4. They are now the objects of that very same anger and wrath of God, that is expressed in the torments of hell. And the reason why they do not go down to hell at each moment, is not because God, in whose power they are, is not then very angry with them; as he is with many miserable creatures now tormented in hell, who there feel and bear the fierceness of his wrath. Yea, God is a great deal more angry with great numbers that are now on earth: yea, doubtless, with many that are now in this congregation, who it may be are at ease, than he is with many of those who are now in the flames of hell.

So that it is not because God is unmindful of their wickedness, and does not resent it, that he does not let loose his hand and cut them off. God is not altogether such an one as themselves, though they may imagine him to be so. The wrath of God burns against them, their damnation does not slumber; the pit is prepared, the fire is made ready, the furnace is now hot, ready to receive them; the flames do now rage and glow. The glittering sword is whet,[7] and held over them, and the pit hath opened its mouth under them.

5. The *devil* stands ready to fall upon them, and seize them as his own, at what moment God shall permit him. They belong to him; he has their souls in his possession, and under his dominion. The scripture represents them as his goods, Luke 11:12.[8] The devils watch them; they are ever by them at their right hand; they stand waiting for them, like greedy hungry lions that see their prey, and expect to have it, but are

---

[6]SODOM: Sodom and Gomorrah were wicked cities destroyed by God in Genesis 19:24.
[7]WHET: Sharpen.
[8]LUKE 11:12: See Luke 11:11–13: "If a son shall ask bread of any of you that is a father, will he give him a stone? or if he ask a fish, will he for a fish give him a serpent? / Or if he shall ask an egg, will he offer him a scorpion? / If ye then, being evil, know how to give good gifts unto your children: how much more shall your heavenly Father give the Holy Spirit to them that ask him?"

for the present kept back. If God should withdraw his hand, by which they are restrained, they would in one moment fly upon their poor souls. The old serpent is gaping for them; hell opens its mouth wide to receive them; and if God should permit it, they would be hastily swallowed up and lost.

6. There are in the souls of wicked men those hellish principles reigning, that would presently kindle and flame out into hell fire, if it were not for God's restraints. There is laid in the very nature of carnal men, a foundation for the torments of hell. There are those corrupt principles, in reigning power in them, and in full possession of them, that are seeds of hell fire. These principles are active and powerful, exceeding violent in their nature, and if it were not for the restraining hand of God upon them, they would soon break out, they would flame out after the same manner as the same corruptions, the same enmity does in the hearts of damned souls, and would beget the same torments as they do in them. The souls of the wicked are in scripture compared to the troubled sea, Isa. 57:20.[9] For the present, God restrains their wickedness by his mighty power, as he does the raging waves of the troubled sea, saying, "Hitherto shalt thou come, but no further;" but if God should withdraw that restraining power, it would soon carry all before it. Sin is the ruin and misery of the soul; it is destructive in its nature; and if God should leave it without restraint, there would need nothing else to make the soul perfectly miserable. The corruption of the heart of man is immoderate and boundless in its fury; and while wicked men live here, it is like fire pent up by God's restraints, whereas if it were let loose, it would set on fire the course of nature; and as the heart is now a sink of sin, so if sin was not restrained, it would immediately turn the soul into a fiery oven, or a furnace of fire and brimstone.

7. It is no security to wicked men for one moment, that there are no visible means of death at hand. It is no security to a natural[10] man, that he is now in health, and that he does not see which way he should now immediately go out of the world by any accident, and that there is no visible danger in any respect in his circumstances. The manifold and continual experience of the world in all ages, shows this is no evidence, that a man is not on the very brink of eternity, and that the next step will not be into another world. The unseen, unthought-of ways and means of persons going suddenly out of the world are innumerable and inconceivable.

---

[9]ISA. 57:20: Isaiah 57:20–21: "But the wicked are like the troubled sea, when it cannot rest, whose waters cast up mire and dirt. / There is no peace, saith my God, to the wicked."
[10]NATURAL: Unsaved.

Unconverted men walk over the pit of hell on a rotten covering, and there are innumerable places in this covering so weak that they will not bear their weight, and these places are not seen. The arrows of death fly unseen at noon-day[11]; the sharpest sight cannot discern them. God has so many different unsearchable ways of taking wicked men out of the world and sending them to hell, that there is nothing to make it appear, that God had need to be at the expense of a miracle, or go out of the ordinary course of his providence, to destroy any wicked man, at any moment. All the means that there are of sinners going out of the world, are so in God's hands, and so universally and absolutely subject to his power and determination, that it does not depend at all the less on the mere will of God, whether sinners shall at any moment go to hell, than if means were never made use of, or at all concerned in the case.

8. Natural men's prudence[12] and care to preserve their own lives, or the care of others to preserve them, do not secure them a moment. To this, divine providence and universal experience do also bear testimony. There is this clear evidence that men's own wisdom is no security to them from death; that if it were otherwise we should see some difference between the wise and politic men of the world, and others, with regard to their liableness to early and unexpected death: but how is it in fact? Eccles. 2:16.[13] "How dieth the wise man? even as the fool."

9. All wicked men's pains and *contrivance* which they use to escape hell, while they continue to reject Christ, and so remain wicked men, do not secure them from hell one moment. Almost every natural man that hears of hell, flatters himself that he shall escape it; he depends upon himself for his own security; he flatters himself in what he has done, in what he is now doing, or what he intends to do. Every one lays out matters in his own mind how he shall avoid damnation, and flatters himself that he contrives well for himself, and that his schemes will not fail. They hear indeed that there are but few saved, and that the greater part of men that have died heretofore are gone to hell; but each one imagines that he lays out matters better for his own escape than others have done. He does not intend to come to that place of torment; he says within himself, that he intends to take effectual care, and to order matters so for himself as not to fail.

---

[11]THE ARROWS OF DEATH FLY UNSEEN AT NOON-DAY: Psalm 91:5: "Thou shalt not be afraid for the terror by night; nor for the arrow that flieth by day."
[12]PRUDENCE: Discretion.
[13]ECCLES. 2:16: A reference to Ecclesiastes 2:16: "For there is no remembrance of the wise more than of the fool for ever; seeing that which now is in the days to come shall all be forgotten. And how dieth the wise man? as the fool."

But the foolish children of men miserably delude themselves in their own schemes, and in confidence in their own strength and wisdom; they trust to nothing but a shadow. The greater part of those who heretofore have lived under the same means of grace, and are now dead, are undoubtedly gone to hell; and it was not because they were not as wise as those who are now alive: it was not because they did not lay out matters as well for themselves to secure their own escape. If we could speak with them, and inquire of them, one by one, whether they expected, when alive, and when they used to hear about hell ever to be the subjects of that misery, we doubtless, should hear one and another reply, "No, I never intended to come here: I had laid out matters otherwise in my mind; I thought I should contrive well for myself: I thought my scheme good. I intended to take effectual care; but it came upon me unexpected; I did not look for it at that time, and in that manner; it came as a thief: Death outwitted me: God's wrath was too quick for me. Oh, my cursed foolishness! I was flattering myself, and pleasing myself with vain dreams of what I would do hereafter; and when I was saying, Peace and safety, then suddenly destruction came upon me."

10. God has laid himself under *no obligation*, by any promise to keep any natural man out of hell one moment. God certainly has made no promises either of eternal life, or of any deliverance or preservation from eternal death, but what are contained in the covenant of grace,[14] the promises that are given in Christ, in whom all the promises are yea and amen. But surely they have no interest in the promises of the covenant of grace who are not the children of the covenant, who do not believe in any of the promises, and have no interest in the Mediator of the covenant.[15]

So that, whatever some have imagined and pretended[16] about promises made to natural men's earnest seeking and knocking, it is plain and manifest, that whatever pains a natural man takes in religion, whatever prayers he makes, till he believes in Christ, God is under no manner of obligation to keep him a moment from eternal destruction.

So that, thus it is that natural men are held in the hand of God, over the pit of hell; they have deserved the fiery pit, and are already sentenced to it; and God is dreadfully provoked, his anger is as great towards them

---

[14]COVENANT OF GRACE: The original covenant (agreement), the Covenant of Works, was between Adam and God, in which God judged Adam by his actions. The Covenant of Grace, also called the second covenant, Christ made with humanity, which declared that belief in Jesus Christ was the key to salvation.
[15]MEDIATOR OF THE COVENANT: That is, Christ, who took upon himself the sins of the world and atoned for them through his death on the cross.
[16]PRETENDED: Claimed.

as to those that are actually suffering the executions of the fierceness of his wrath in hell, and they have done nothing in the least to appease or abate that anger, neither is God in the least bound by any promise to hold them up one moment; the devil is waiting for them, hell is gaping for them, the flames gather and flash about them, and would fain lay hold on them, and swallow them up; the fire pent up in their own hearts is struggling to break out: and they have no interest in any Mediator, there are no means within reach that can be any security to them. In short, they have no refuge, nothing to take hold of; all that preserves them every moment is the mere arbitrary will, and uncovenanted, unobliged forbearance of an incensed God.

APPLICATION

The use of this awful[17] subject may be for awakening unconverted persons in this congregation. This that you have heard is the case of every one of you that are out of Christ. That world of misery, that lake of burning brimstone, is extended abroad under you. There is the dreadful pit of the glowing flames of the wrath of God; there is hell's wide gaping mouth open; and you have nothing to stand upon, nor any thing to take hold of, there is nothing between you and hell but the air; it is only the power and mere pleasure of God that holds you up.

You probably are not sensible[18] of this; you find you are kept out of hell, but do not see the hand of God in it; but look at other things, as the good state of your bodily constitution, your care of your own life, and the means you use for your own preservation. But indeed these things are nothing; if God should withdraw his hand, they would avail no more to keep you from falling, than the thin air to hold up a person that is suspended in it.

Your wickedness makes you as it were heavy as lead, and to tend downwards with great weight and pressure towards hell; and if God should let you go, you would immediately sink and swiftly descend and plunge into the bottomless gulf, and your healthy constitution, and your own care and prudence, and best contrivance, and all your righteousness, would have no more influence to uphold you and keep you out of hell, than a spider's web would have to stop a falling rock. Were it not for the sovereign pleasure of God, the earth would not bear you one moment;

[17]AWFUL: Awe-inspiring; deserving of reverential respect.
[18]SENSIBLE: Conscious.

for you are a burden to it; the creation groans with you; the creature is made subject to the bondage of your corruption, not willingly; the sun does not willingly shine upon you to give you light to serve sin and Satan; the earth does not willingly yield her increase to satisfy your lusts; nor is it willingly a stage for your wickedness to be acted upon; the air does not willingly serve you for breath to maintain the flame of life in your vitals, while you spend your life in the service of God's enemies. God's creatures are good, and were made for men to serve God with, and do not willingly subserve to any other purpose, and groan when they are abused to purposes so directly contrary to their nature and end. And the world would spew you out, were it not for the sovereign hand of him who hath subjected it in hope. There are black clouds of God's wrath now hanging directly over your heads, full of the dreadful storm, and big with thunder; and were it not for the restraining hand of God, it would immediately burst forth upon you. The sovereign pleasure of God, for the present, stays his rough wind; otherwise it would come with fury, and your destruction would come like a whirlwind, and you would be like the chaff of the summer threshing floor.

The wrath of God is like great waters that are dammed for the present; they increase more and more, and rise higher and higher, till an outlet is given; and the longer the stream is stopped, the more rapid and mighty is its course, when once it is let loose. It is true, that judgment against your evil works has not been executed hitherto; the floods of God's vengeance have been withheld; but your guilt in the mean time is constantly increasing, and you are every day treasuring up more wrath; the waters are constantly rising, and waxing more and more mighty; and there is nothing but the mere pleasure of God, that holds the waters back, that are unwilling to be stopped, and press hard to go forward. If God should only withdraw his hand from the flood-gate, it would immediately fly open, and the fiery floods of the fierceness and wrath of God, would rush forth with inconceivable fury, and would come upon you with omnipotent power; and if your strength were ten thousand times greater than it is, yea, ten thousand times greater than the strength of the stoutest, sturdiest devil in hell, it would be nothing to withstand or endure it.

The bow of God's wrath is bent, and the arrow made ready on the string, and justice bends the arrow at your heart, and strains the bow, and it is nothing but the mere pleasure of God, and that of an angry God, without any promise or obligation at all, that keeps the arrow one moment from being made drunk with your blood. Thus all you that never passed under a great change of heart, by the mighty power of the Spirit of God upon your souls; all you that were never born again, and made new creatures, and raised from being dead in sin, to a state of new, and before altogether unexperienced light and life, are in the hands of an angry God. However you may have reformed your life in many things, and may have had religious affections, and may keep up a form of religion in your families and closets,[19] and in the house of God, it is nothing but his mere pleasure that keeps you from being this moment swallowed up in everlasting destruction. However unconvinced you may now be of the truth of what you hear, by and by you will be fully convinced of it. Those that are gone from being in the like circumstances with you, see that it was so with them; for destruction came suddenly upon most of them; when they expected nothing of it, and while they were saying, Peace and safety: now they see, that those things on which they depended for peace and safety, were nothing but thin air and empty shadows.

The God that holds you over the pit of hell, much as one holds a spider, or some loathsome insect over the fire, abhors you, and is dreadfully provoked: his wrath towards you burns like fire; he looks upon you as worthy of nothing else, but to be cast into the fire; he is of purer eyes than to bear to have you in his sight; you are ten thousand times more abominable in his eyes, than the most hateful venomous serpent is in ours. You have offended him infinitely more than ever a stubborn rebel did his prince; and yet it is nothing but his hand that holds you from falling into the fire every moment. It is to be ascribed to nothing else, that you did not go to hell the last night; that you was suffered to awake again in this world, after you closed your eyes to sleep. And there is no other reason to be given, why you have not dropped into hell since you arose in the morning, but that God's hand has held you up. There is no other reason to be given why you have not gone to hell, since you have sat here in the house of God, provoking his pure eyes by your sinful wicked manner of attending his solemn worship. Yea, there is nothing else that is to be given as a reason why you do not this very moment drop down into hell.

O sinner! Consider the fearful danger you are in: it is a great furnace of wrath, a wide and bottomless pit, full of the fire of wrath, that you are held over in the hand of that God, whose wrath is provoked and incensed as much against you, as against many of the damned in hell. You hang by a slender thread, with the flames of divine wrath flashing about it, and ready every moment to singe it, and burn it asunder; and you have no interest in any Mediator, and nothing to lay hold of to save yourself, nothing to keep off the flames of wrath, nothing of your own, nothing that you ever have done, nothing that you can do, to induce God to spare you one moment. And consider here more particularly

[19]CLOSETS: Small rooms for privacy; private rooms used for meditation.

1. *Whose* wrath it is: it is the wrath of the infinite God. If it were only the wrath of man, though it were of the most potent prince, it would be comparatively little to be regarded. The wrath of kings is very much dreaded, especially of absolute monarchs, who have the possessions and lives of their subjects wholly in their power, to be disposed of at their mere will. Prov. 20:2. "The fear of a king is as the roaring of a lion: Whoso provoketh him to anger, sinneth against his own soul." The subject that very much enrages an arbitrary prince, is liable to suffer the most extreme torments that human art can invent, or human power can inflict. But the greatest earthly potentates in their greatest majesty and strength, and when clothed in their greatest terrors, are but feeble, despicable worms of the dust, in comparison of the great and almighty Creator and King of heaven and earth. It is but little that they can do, when most enraged, and when they have exerted the utmost of their fury. All the kings of the earth, before God, are as grasshoppers; they are nothing, and less than nothing: both their love and their hatred is to be despised. The wrath of the great King of kings, is as much more terrible than theirs, as his majesty is greater. Luke 12:4–5. "And I say unto you, my friends, Be not afraid of them that kill the body, and after that, have no more that they can do. But I will forewarn you whom you shall fear: fear him, which after he hath killed, hath power to cast into hell: yea, I say unto you, Fear him."

2. It is the *fierceness* of his wrath that you are exposed to. We often read of the fury of God; as in Isaiah 59:18. "According to their deeds, accordingly he will repay fury to his adversaries." So Isaiah 66:15. "For behold, the Lord will come with fire, and with his chariots like a whirlwind, to render his anger with fury, and his rebuke with flames of fire." And in many other places. So, Rev. 19:15, we read of "the wine press of the fierceness and wrath of Almighty God."[20] The words are exceeding terrible. If it had only been said, "the wrath of God," the words would have implied that which is infinitely dreadful: but it is "the fierceness and wrath of God." The fury of God! the fierceness of Jehovah![21] Oh, how dreadful must that be! Who can utter or conceive what such expressions carry in them! But it is also "the fierceness and wrath of *Almighty* God." As though there would be a very great manifestation of his

---

[20]THE WINE PRESS OF THE FIERCENESS AND WRATH OF ALMIGHTY GOD: A reference to Revelation 19:15: "And out of his mouth goeth a sharp sword, that with it he should smite the nations: and he shall rule them with a rod of iron: and he treadeth the winepress of the fierceness and wrath of Almighty God."

[21]JEHOVAH: The English and common European phrasing, since the sixteenth century, of the Hebrew divine name "Yhwh" [Yaweh].

almighty power in what the fierceness of his wrath should inflict, as though omnipotence should be as it were enraged, and exerted, as men are wont to exert their strength in the fierceness of their wrath. Oh! then, what will be the consequence! What will become of the poor worms that shall suffer it! Whose hands can be strong? And whose heart can endure? To what a dreadful, inexpressible, inconceivable depth of misery must the poor creature be sunk who shall be the subject of this!

Consider this, you that are here present, that yet remain in an unregenerate state. That God will execute the fierceness of his anger, implies, that he will inflict wrath without any pity. When God beholds the ineffable extremity of your case, and sees your torment to be so vastly disproportioned to your strength, and sees how your poor soul is crushed, and sinks down, as it were, into an infinite gloom; he will have no compassion upon you, he will not forbear the executions of his wrath, or in the least lighten his hand; there shall be no moderation or mercy, nor will God then at all stay his rough wind; he will have no regard to your welfare, nor be at all careful lest you should suffer too much in any other sense, than only that you shall *not suffer beyond what strict justice requires*. Nothing shall be withheld, because it is so hard for you to bear. Ezek. 8:18. "Therefore will I also deal in fury: mine eye shall not spare, neither will I have pity; and though they cry in mine ears with a loud voice, yet I will not hear them." Now God stands ready to pity you; this is a day of mercy; you may cry now with some encouragement of obtaining mercy. But when once the day of mercy is past, your most lamentable and dolorous cries and shrieks will be in vain; you will be wholly lost and thrown away of God, as to any regard to your welfare. God will have no other use to put you to, but to suffer misery; you shall be continued in being to no other end; for you will be a vessel of wrath fitted to destruction; and there will be no other use of this vessel, but to be filled full of wrath. God will be so far from pitying you when you cry to him, that it is said he will only "laugh and mock,"[22] Prov. 1:25–26, &c.

How awful are those words, Isa. 63:3, which are the words of the great God. "I will tread them in mine anger, and will trample them in my fury, and their blood shall be sprinkled upon my garments, and I will stain all my raiment." It is perhaps impossible to conceive of words that carry in them greater manifestations of these three things, *viz.* contempt,

---

[22]LAUGH AND MOCK: A reference to Proverbs 1:24–26: "Because I have called, and ye refused; I have stretched out my hand, and no man regarded; / But ye have set at nought all my counsel, and would none of my reproof: / I also will laugh at your calamity; I will mock when your fear cometh."

and hatred, and fierceness of indignation. If you cry to God to pity you, he will be so far from pitying you in your doleful case, or showing you the least regard or favour, that instead of that, he will only tread you under foot. And though he will know that you cannot bear the weight of omnipotence treading upon you, yet he will not regard that, but he will crush you under his feet without mercy; he will crush out your blood, and make it fly, and it shall be sprinkled on his garments, so as to stain all his raiment. He will not only hate you, but he will have you, in the utmost contempt: no place shall be thought fit for you, but under his feet to be trodden down as the mire of the streets.

The misery you are exposed to is that which God will inflict to that end, that he might show what that wrath of Jehovah is. God hath had it on his heart to show to angels and men, both how excellent his love is, and also how terrible his wrath is. Sometimes earthly kings have a mind to show how terrible their wrath is, by the extreme punishments they would execute on those that would provoke them. Nebuchadnezzar, that mighty and haughty monarch of the Chaldean empire, was willing to show his wrath when enraged with Shadrach, Meshech, and Abednego[23]; and accordingly gave orders that the burning fiery furnace should be heated seven times hotter than it was before; doubtless, it was raised to the utmost degree of fierceness that human art could raise it. But the great God is also willing to show his wrath, and magnify his awful majesty and mighty power in the extreme sufferings of his enemies. Rom. 9:22. "What if God, willing to show his wrath, and to make his power known, endure with much long-suffering the vessels of wrath fitted to destruction?" And seeing this is his design, and what he has determined, even to show how terrible the unrestrained wrath, the fury and fierceness of Jehovah is, he will do it to effect. There will be something accomplished and brought to pass that will be dreadful with a witness. When the great and angry God hath risen up and executed his awful vengeance on the poor sinner, and the wretch is actually suffering the infinite weight and power of his indignation, then will God call upon the whole universe to behold that awful majesty and mighty power that is to be seen in it. Isa. 33:12–14. "And the people shall be as the burnings of lime, as thorns cut up shall they be burnt in the fire. Hear ye that are far off, what I have done; and ye that are near, acknowledge my might. The sinners in Zion are afraid; fearfulness hath surprised the hypocrites," &c.

[23]NEBUCHADNEZZAR, THAT MIGHTY...SHADRACH, MESHECH, AND ABEDNEGO: Nebuchadnezzar (630–562 BCE) was king of Babylon for 43 years. He destroyed Jerusalem in 586 BCE and removed most of its citizens to Chaldea, and then forbid them to worship their god. Daniel 3:13–30 relates how Shadrach, Meshach, and Abednego refused to worship false gods and were thrown into a fiery furnace, but were saved by an angel.

Thus it will be with you that are in an unconverted state, if you continue in it; the infinite might, and majesty, and terribleness of the omnipotent God shall be magnified upon you, in the ineffable strength your torments. You shall be tormented in the presence of the holy angels, and in the presence of the Lamb; and when you shall be in this state of suffering, the glorious inhabitants of heaven shall go forth and look on the awful spectacle, that they may see what the wrath and fierceness of the Almighty is; and when they have seen it, they will fall down and adore that great power and majesty. Isa. 66:23–24. "And it shall come to pass, that from one new moon to another, and from one sabbath to another, shall all flesh come to worship before me, saith the Lord. And they shall go forth and look upon the carcasses of the men that have transgressed against me; for their worm shall not die, neither shall their fire be quenched, and they shall be an abhorring unto all flesh."

4. It is *everlasting* wrath. It would be dreadful to suffer this fierceness and wrath of Almighty God one moment; but you must suffer it to all eternity. There will be no end to this exquisite horrible misery. When you look forward, you shall see a long forever, a boundless duration before you, which will swallow up your thoughts, and amaze your soul; and you will absolutely despair of ever having any deliverance, any end, any mitigation, any rest at all. You will know certainly that you must wear out long ages, millions of millions of ages, in wrestling and conflicting with this almighty merciless vengeance; and then when you have so done, when so many ages have actually been spent by you in this manner, you will know that all is but a point to what remains. So that your punishment will indeed be infinite. Oh, who can express what the state of a soul in such circumstances is! All that we can possibly say about it, gives but a very feeble, faint representation of it; it is inexpressible and inconceivable: For "who knows the power of God's anger?"[24]

How dreadful is the state of those that are daily and hourly in the danger of this great wrath and infinite misery! But this is the dismal case of every soul in this congregation that has not been born again, however moral and strict, sober and religious, they may otherwise be. Oh that you would consider it, whether you be young or old! There is reason to think, that there are many in this congregation now hearing this discourse, that will actually be the subjects of this very misery to all eternity. We know not who they are, or in what seats they sit, or what thoughts they now have. It may be they are now at ease, and hear all

---

[24]WHO KNOWS THE POWER OF GOD'S ANGER: A reference to Psalms 90:11–12: "Who knoweth the power of thine anger? even according to thy fear, so is thy wrath. / So teach us to number our days, that we may apply our hearts unto wisdom."

these things without much disturbance, and are now flattering themselves that they are not the persons, promising themselves that they shall escape. If we knew that there was one person, and but one, in the whole congregation, that was to be the subject of this misery, what an awful thing would it be to think of! If we knew who it was, what an awful sight would it be to see such a person! How might all the rest of the congregation lift up a lamentable and bitter cry over him! But, alas! instead of one, how many is it likely will remember this discourse in hell? And it would be a wonder, if some that are now present should not be in hell in a very short time, even before this year is out. And it would be no wonder if some persons, that now sit here, in some seats of this meeting-house, in health, quiet and secure, should be there before to-morrow morning. Those of you that finally continue in a natural condition, that shall keep out of hell longest will be there in a little time! your damnation does not slumber; it will come swiftly, and, in all probability, very suddenly upon many of you. You have reason to wonder that you are not already in hell. It is doubtless the case of some whom you have seen and known, that never deserved hell more than you, and that heretofore appeared as likely to have been now alive as you. Their case is past all hope; they are crying in extreme misery and perfect despair; but here you are in the land of the living and in the house of God, and have an opportunity to obtain salvation. What would not those poor damned hopeless souls give for one day's opportunity such as you now enjoy!

And now you have an extraordinary opportunity, a day wherein Christ has thrown the door of mercy wide open, and stands in calling and crying with a loud voice to poor sinners; a day wherein many are flocking to him, and pressing into the kingdom of God. Many are daily coming from the east, west, north and south; many that were very lately in the same miserable condition that you are in, are now in a happy state, with their hearts filled with love to him who has loved them, and washed them from their sins in his own blood, and rejoicing in hope of the glory of God. How awful is it to be left behind at such a day! To see so many others feasting, while you are pining and perishing! To see so many rejoicing and singing for joy of heart, while you have cause to mourn for sorrow of heart, and howl for vexation of spirit! How can you rest one moment in such a condition? Are not your souls as precious as the souls of the people at Suffield[25], where they are flocking from day to day to Christ?

[25]SUFFIELD: A nearby town.

Are there not many here who have lived long in the world, and are not to this day born again? and so are aliens from the commonwealth of Israel,[26] and have done nothing ever since they have lived, but treasure up wrath against the day of wrath? Oh, sirs, your case, in an especial manner, is extremely dangerous. Your guilt and hardness of heart is extremely great. Do you not see how generally persons of your years are passed over and left, in the present remarkable and wonderful dispensation of God's mercy? You had need to consider yourselves, and awake thoroughly out of sleep. You cannot bear the fierceness and wrath of the infinite God. And you, young men, and young women, will you neglect this precious season which you now enjoy, when so many others of your age are renouncing all youthful vanities, and flocking to Christ? You especially have now an extraordinary opportunity; but if you neglect it, it will soon be with you as with those persons who spent all the precious days of youth in sin, and are now come to such a dreadful pass in blindness and hardness. And you, children, who are unconverted, do not you know that you are going down to hell, to bear the dreadful wrath of that God, who is now angry with you every day and every night? Will you be content to be the children of the devil, when so many other children in the land are converted, and are become the holy and happy children of the King of kings?

And let every one that is yet out of Christ, and hanging over the pit of hell, whether they be old men and women, or middle-aged, or young people, or little children, now hearken to the loud calls of God's word and providence. This acceptable year of the Lord, a day of such great favours to some, will doubtless be a day of as remarkable vengeance to others. Men's hearts harden, and their guilt increases apace at such a day as this, if they neglect their souls; and never was there so great danger of such persons being given up to hardness of heart and blindness of mind. God seems now to be hastily gathering in his elect in all parts of the land; and probably the greater part of adult persons that ever shall be saved, will be brought in now in a little time, and that it will be as it was on the great out-pouring of the Spirit upon the Jews in the apostles' days[27]; the election will obtain, and the rest will be blinded. If this should be the case with you, you will

[26]ALIENS FROM THE COMMONWEALTH OF ISRAEL: That is, the unsaved; those not of God's chosen people.
[27]THE APOSTLES' DAYS: Referring to the day Peter baptizes a crowd, as described in Acts 2:40 "Then they that gladly received his word were baptized: and the same day there were added unto them about three thousand souls."

eternally curse this day, and will curse the day that ever you was born, to see such a season of the pouring out of God's Spirit, and will wish that you had died and gone to hell before you had seen it. Now undoubtedly it is, as it was in the days of John the Baptist, the axe is in an extraordinary manner laid at the root of the trees,[28] that every tree which brings not forth good fruit, may be hewn down and cast into the fire.

Therefore, let every one that is out of Christ, now awake and fly from the wrath to come. The wrath of Almighty God is now undoubtedly hanging over a great part of this congregation: Let every one fly out of Sodom: "Haste and escape for your lives, look not behind you, escape to the mountain, lest you be consumed."[29]

[1741]

---

[28]ROOT OF THE TREES: A reference to Matthew 3:10: "And now also the axe is laid unto the root of the trees: therefore every tree which bringeth not forth good fruit is hewn down, and cast into the fire."
[29]HASTE AND ESCAPE FOR YOUR LIVES, LOOK NOT BEHIND YOU, ESCAPE TO THE MOUNTAIN, LEST YOU BE CONSUMED: The command God gives Lot as he and his family flee the doomed city of Sodom in Genesis 19:17.

Benjamin Franklin

(1706–1790)

Born in Boston, the fifteenth son in a family of seventeen children, Benjamin Franklin, a printer's apprentice at age twelve after only two years of school, ran away in 1723 to live in Philadelphia. The following year he moved to London, returning to Philadelphia two years later. He then opened a printing shop; he became publisher of the Pennsylvania Gazette *(which grew to be one of the best newspapers in the colonies); he founded in 1731 the first circulating library; and in 1732 he began publication of* Poor Richard: An Almanac, *a yearly compilation of advice for achieving success through thrift, patience, and hard work.*

Postmaster, scientist, and inventor, member of the Pennsylvania Assembly, philanthropist and educator, president (elected 1769) of the American Philosophical Society, member of the Continental Congress and signer of the Declaration of Independence, distinguished diplomat, president of the Pennsylvania Society for Promoting the Abolition of Slavery, delegate to the Constitutional Convention in 1787—Franklin is one of the most remarkable, multi-talented figures in American literary, cultural, and political history. John Adams wrote of him:

> *Franklin's reputation was more universal than that of Leibniz or Newton, Frederick [Frederick the Great, King of Prussia] or Voltaire, and his character more beloved and esteemed than any or all of them…. His name was familiar to government and people, to kings, courtiers, nobility, clergy, and philosophers, as well as plebians…. When they spoke of him they seemed to think he was to restore the golden age.*

A modern biographer, Carl Van Doren, offered a similar assessment: "His mind was a federation of purposes, working harmoniously together…. His mind grew as his world grew…. He seems to have been more than any single man: a harmonious human being."

However, others were suspicious of this self-educated and self-made man, adroit and witty writer, canny businessman, keen creator of a good impression, and dispenser of so much sound advice ("Early to bed, early to rise, makes a man healthy, wealthy and wise," "God helps those who help themselves," "Little strokes fell great oaks," "Write your injuries in dust, your benefits in marble," "An apple a day keeps the doctor away"). The English poet John Keats, in a letter of 1818, referred to Franklin as "a philosophical Quaker full of mean and thrifty maxims." A century later, the novelist and critic D. H. Lawrence, chafing at Franklin's charm, urbanity, and ironic detachment, concluded: "And now, I, at least, know why I can't stand Benjamin. He tries to take away my wholeness and my dark forest, my freedom." More appreciatively, but still with reservations, the cultural historian J. W. Ward noted, "We admire the lusty good sense of the man who triumphs in the world that he accepts, yet at the same time we are uneasy with the man who wears so many masks that we are never sure who is behind them."

The selections below include "The Way to Wealth," an essay for the twenty-fifth anniversary of the Almanac, which was launched in 1732 under the fictitious editorship of "Richard Saunders"; "Remarks Concerning the Savages of North America"; and excerpts from the unfinished Autobiography.

Franklin's astoundingly productive life has sometimes caused his distinction as a writer to be overlooked. Accomplished in many genres, an entertainer, satirist, polemicist, and sage, Franklin stands, as one scholar has said, "as the American equal of such 18th century prose masters as Jonathan Swift and Samuel Johnson." Pithy, plain, and colloquial, direct and wry, pointed and pungent, Franklin, an avid reader, developed a fine feeling for the use of language as a means of expression and, even more, of persuasion. "Nothing should be expressed in two words that can be as well-expressed in one," he stated in a note on writing. "The whole should be as short as possible, consistent with clearness. The words should be so placed as to be agreeable to the ear in reading; summarily, it should be smooth, clear, and short."

Franklin is, on the one hand, the embodiment of the Age of Reason, and yet, on the other hand, he is decidedly modern, a masterfully agile performer of parts and manager of language who (in the words of one critic) "envisaged the process of what might be called self-creation as the conscious playing of a series of calculated roles."

Biographical studies: *Carl Van Doren*, Benjamin Franklin *(1938)*; *Robert Middlekauff*, Benjamin Franklin and His Enemies *(1996)*; *H. W. Brands*, The First American: The Life and Times of Benjamin Franklin *(2000)*; *Edmund S. Morgan*, Benjamin Franklin *(2002)*; *and Walter Isaacson*, Benjamin Franklin: An American Life *(2003)*. *See also* Critical Essays on Benjamin Franklin, *ed. Melvin H. Buxbaum (1987)*; *Ormond Seavey*, Becoming Benjamin Franklin: The Autobiography and the Life *(1988)*; *and* Benjamin Franklin, Jonathan Edwards, and the Representation of American Culture, *ed. Barbara B. Oberg and Harry S. Stout (1993)*.

The Way to Wealth

PREFACE TO POOR RICHARD IMPROVED

Courteous Reader,

I have heard that nothing gives an Author so great Pleasure, as to find his Works respectfully quoted by other learned Authors. This Pleasure I have seldom enjoyed; for tho' I have been, if I may say it without Vanity, an *eminent Author* of Almanacks annually now a full Quarter of a Century, my Brother Authors in the same Way, for what Reason I know not, have ever been very sparing in their Applauses; and no other Author has taken the least Notice of me, so that did not my Writings produce me some solid *Pudding*, the great Deficiency of *Praise* would have quite discouraged me.

I concluded at length, that the People were the best Judges of my Merit; for they buy my Works; and besides, in my Rambles, where I am not personally known, I have frequently heard one or other of my Adages repeated, with, *as Poor Richard says*, as the End on't; this gave me some Satisfaction, as it showed not only that my Instructions were regarded, but discovered likewise some Respect for my Authority; and I own, that to encourage the Practice of remembering and repeating those wise Sentences, I have sometimes *quoted myself* with great Gravity.

Judge then how much I must have been gratified by an Incident I am going to relate to you. I stopt my Horse lately where a great Number of People were collected at a Vendue[1] of Merchant Goods. The Hour of Sale not being come, they were conversing on the Badness of the Times, and one of the Company call'd to a plain clean old Man, with white Locks, *Pray, Father* Abraham, *what think you of the Times? Won't these heavy Taxes quite ruin the Country? How shall we ever be able to pay them? What would you advise us to?*—Father *Abraham* stood up, and reply'd, If you'd have my Advice, I'll give it you in short, for a *Word to the Wise is enough*, and *many Words won't fill a Bushel*, as *Poor Richard says*. They join'd in desiring him to speak his Mind, and gathering round him, he proceeded as follows;

"Friends," says he, "and Neighbours, the Taxes are indeed very heavy, and if those laid on by the Government were the only Ones we had to pay, we might more easily discharge them; but we have many others, and much more grievous to some of us. We are taxed twice as much by our

---

[1]VENDUE: Public sale or auction.

Idleness, three times as much by our *Pride*, and four times as much by our *Folly*; and from these Taxes the Commissioners cannot ease or deliver us by allowing an Abatement. However let us hearken to good Advice, and something may be done for us; *God helps them that help themselves*, as *Poor Richard* says, in his Almanack of 1733.

"It would be thought a hard Government that should tax its People one tenth Part of their *Time*, to be employed in its Service. But *Idleness* taxes many of us much more, if we reckon all that is spent in absolute *Sloth*, or doing of nothing, with that which is spent in idle Employments or Amusements, that amount to nothing. *Sloth*, by bringing on Diseases, absolutely shortens Life. *Sloth, like Rust, consumes faster than Labour wears, while the used Key is always bright*, as *Poor Richard* says. But *dost thou love Life, then do not squander Time, for that's the Stuff Life is made of*, as *Poor Richard* says.—How much more than is necessary do we spend in Sleep! forgetting that *The sleeping Fox catches no Poultry*, and that *there will be sleeping enough in the Grave*, as *Poor Richard* says. If Time be of all Things the most precious, *wasting Time* must be, as *Poor Richard* says, *the greatest Prodigality*; since, as he elsewhere tells us, *Lost Time is never found again*; and what we call *Time-enough, always proves little enough*. Let us then up and be doing, and doing to the Purpose; so by Diligence shall we do more with less Perplexity. *Sloth makes all Things difficult, but Industry all easy*, as *Poor Richard* says; and *He that riseth late, must trot all Day, and shall scarce overtake his Business at Night*. While *Laziness travels so slowly, that Poverty soon overtakes him*, as we read in *Poor Richard*, who adds, *Drive thy Business, let not that drive thee*; and *Early to Bed, and early to rise, makes a Man healthy, wealthy, and wise*.

"So what signifies *wishing* and *hoping* for better Times. We may make these Times better if we bestir ourselves. *Industry need not wish*, as *Poor Richard* says, and *He that lives upon Hope will die fasting*. *There are no Gains, without Pains*; then *Help Hands, for I have no Lands*, or if I have, they are smartly taxed. And, as *Poor Richard* likewise observes, *He that hath a Trade hath an Estate*, and *He that hath a Calling hath an Office of Profit and Honour*; but then the *Trade* must be worked at, and the *Calling* well followed, or neither the *Estate*, nor the *Office*, will enable us to pay our Taxes.—If we are industrious we shall never starve; for, as *Poor Richard* says, *At the working Man's House* Hunger *looks in, but dares not enter*. Nor will the Bailiff or the Constable enter, for *Industry pays Debts, while Despair encreaseth them*, says *Poor Richard*.—What though you have found no Treasure, nor has any rich Relation left you a Legacy, *Diligence is the Mother of Good-luck*, as *Poor Richard* says, *and God gives all Things to Industry*. Then *plough deep, while Sluggards sleep, and you shall have Corn to sell and to keep*, says *Poor Dick*. Work while it is called To-day, for you know not how much you may be hindered To-morrow, which makes *Poor Richard* say, *One To-day is worth two To-morrows*; and farther, *Have you somewhat to do To-morrow, do it To-day*. If you were a Servant, would you not be ashamed that a good Master should catch you idle? Are you then your own Master, *be ashamed to catch yourself idle*, as *Poor Dick* says. When there is so much to be done for yourself, your Family, your Country, and your gracious King, be up by Peep of Day; *Let not the Sun look down and say, Inglorious here he lies*. Handle your Tools without Mittens; remember that *the Cat in Gloves catches no Mice*, as *Poor Richard* says. 'Tis true there is much to be done, and perhaps you are weak handed, but stick to it steadily, and you will see great Effects, for *constant Dropping wears away Stones*, and by *Diligence and Patience the Mouse ate in two the Cable*; and *little Strokes fell great Oaks*, as *Poor Richard* says in his Almanack, the Year I cannot just now remember.

"Methinks "I hear some of you say, *Must a Man afford himself no Leisure?*—I will tell thee, my Friend, what *Poor Richard* says, *Employ thy Time well if thou meanest to gain Leisure*; and, *since thou art not sure of a Minute, throw not away an Hour*. Leisure, is Time for doing something useful; this Leisure the diligent Man will obtain, but the lazy Man never; so that, as *Poor Richard* says, a *Life of Leisure and a Life of Laziness are two Things*. Do you imagine that Sloth will afford you more Comfort than Labour? No, for as *Poor Richard* says, *Trouble springs from Idleness, and grievous Toil from needless Ease. Many without Labour, would live by their Wits only, but they break for want of Stock*. Whereas Industry gives Comfort, and Plenty, and Respect: *Fly Pleasures, and they'll follow you. The diligent Spinner has a large Shift*,[2] and *now I have a Sheep and a Cow, every Body bids me Good morrow*; all which is well said by *Poor Richard*.

"But with our Industry, we must likewise be *steady, settled* and *careful*, and oversee our own Affairs *with our own Eyes*, and not trust too much to others; for, as *Poor Richard* says,

> *I never saw an oft removed Tree,*
> *Nor yet an oft removed Family,*
> *That throve so well as those that settled be.*

[2]SHIFT: Wardrobe.

"And again, *Three Removes*[3] *is as bad as a Fire;* and again, *Keep thy Shop, and thy Shop will keep thee;* and again, *If you would have your Business done, go; If not, send.* And again,

> He that by the Plough would thrive,
> Himself must either hold or drive.

"And again, *The Eye of a Master will do more Work than both his Hands;* and again, *Want of Care does us more Damage than Want of Knowledge;* and again, *Not to oversee Workmen, is to leave them your Purse open.* Trusting too much to others Care is the Ruin of many; for, as the *Almanack* says, *In the Affairs of this World, Men are saved, not by Faith, but by the Want of it;* but a Man's own Care is profitable; for, saith *Poor Dick, Learning is to the Studious,* and *Riches to the Careful,* as well as *Power to the Bold,* and *Heaven to the Virtuous.* And farther, *If you would have a faithful Servant, and one that you like, serve yourself.* And again, he adviseth to Circumspection and Care, even in the smallest Matters, because sometimes *a little Neglect may breed great Mischief;* adding, *For want of a Nail the Shoe was lost; for want of a Shoe the Horse was lost; and for want of a Horse the Rider was lost,* being overtaken and slain by the Enemy, all for want of Care about a Horseshoe Nail.

"So much for Industry, my Friends, and Attention to one's own Business; but to these we must add *Frugality,* if we would make our *Industry* more certainly successful. A Man may, if he knows not how to save as he gets, *keep his Nose all his Life to the Grindstone,* and die not worth a *Groat*[4] at last. *A fat Kitchen makes a lean Will,* as *Poor Richard* says; and,

> Many Estates are spent in the Getting,
> Since Women for Tea forsook Spinning and Knitting,
> And Men for Punch forsook Hewing and Splitting.

"*If you would be wealthy,* says he, in another Almanack, *think of Saving as well as of Getting: The* Indies *have not made* Spain *rich, because her* Outgoes are greater than her Incomes. Away then with your expensive Follies, and you will not have so much Cause to complain of hard Times, heavy Taxes, and chargeable Families; for, as *Poor Dick* says,

> Women and Wine, Game and Deceit,
> Make the Wealth small, and the Wants great.

[3]REMOVES: Moves.
[4]GROAT: A coin equal to four pence. The groat ceased to be issued for circulation in 1662.

"And farther, *What maintains one Vice, would bring up two Children.* You may think perhaps, That a *little* Tea, or a *little* Punch now and then, Diet a *little* more costly, Clothes a *little* finer, and a *little* Entertainment now and then, can be no *great* Matter; but remember what *Poor Richard* says, *Many a* Little *makes a Mickle*,[5] and farther, *Beware of* little *Expences; a small Leak will sink a great Ship*; and again, *Who Dainties love, shall Beggars prove*; and moreover, *Fools make Feasts, and wise Men eat them.*

"Here you are all got together at this Vendue of *Fineries and Knicknacks.* You call them *Goods,* but if you do not take Care, they will prove *Evils* to some of you. You expect they will be sold *cheap,* and perhaps they may for less than they cost; but if you have no Occasion for them, they must be *dear* to you. Remember what *Poor Richard* says, *Buy what thou hast no Need of, and ere long thou shalt sell thy Necessaries.* And again, *At a great Pennyworth pause a while:* He means, that perhaps the Cheapness is *apparent* only, and not *real;* or the Bargain, by straitning thee in thy Business, may do thee more Harm than Good. For in another Place he says, *Many have been ruined by buying good Pennyworths.* Again, *Poor Richard* says, *'Tis foolish to lay out Money in a Purchase of Repentance;* and yet this Folly is practised every Day at Vendues, for want of minding the Almanack. *Wise Men,* as *Poor Dick* says, *learn by others Harms, Fools scarcely by their own;* but, *Felix quem faciunt aliena Pericula cautum.*[6] Many a one, for the Sake of Finery on the Back, have gone with a hungry Belly, and half starved their Families; *Silks and Sattins, Scarlet and Velvets,* as *Poor Richard* says, *put out the Kitchen Fire.* These are not the *Necessaries* of Life; they can scarcely be called the *Conveniencies,* and yet only because they look pretty, how many *want* to *have* them. The *artificial* Wants of Mankind thus become more numerous than the *natural;* and, as *Poor Dick* says, *For one poor Person, there are an hundred* indigent. By these, and other Extravagancies, the Genteel are reduced to Poverty, and forced to borrow of those whom they formerly despised, but who through *Industry* and *Frugality* have maintained their Standing; in which Case it appears plainly, that a *Ploughman on his Legs is higher than a Gentleman on his Knees,* as *Poor Richard* says. Perhaps they have had a small Estate left them, which they knew not the Getting of; they think *'tis Day, and will never be Night;* that a little to be spent out of *so much,* is not worth minding; (*a Child and a Fool,* as *Poor Richard*

[5]MICKLE: A lot.
[6]FELIX QUEM FACIUNT ALIENA PERICULA CAUTUM: A proverb, literally translated as "Happy he whom dangers make wary." (Latin)

says, *imagine* Twenty Shillings *and Twenty Years can never be spent*) but, *always taking out of the Meal-tub, and never putting in, soon comes to the Bottom*; then, as *Poor Dick* says, *When the Well's dry, they know the Worth of Water.* But this they might have known before, if they had taken his Advice; *If you would know the Value of Money, go and try to borrow some*; for, *he that goes a borrowing goes a sorrowing*; and indeed so does he that lends to such People, when he goes *to get it in again.*—*Poor Dick* farther advises, and says,

> *Fond Pride of Dress, is sure a very Curse;*
> *E'er Fancy you consult, consult your Purse.*

"And again, *Pride is as loud a Beggar as Want, and a great deal more saucy.* When you have bought one fine Thing you must buy ten more, that your Appearance may be all of a Piece; but *Poor Dick* says, *'Tis easier to* suppress *the first Desire, than to* satisfy *all that follow it.* And 'tis as truly Folly for the Poor to ape the Rich, as for the Frog to swell, in order to equal the Ox.

> *Great Estates may venture more,*
> *But little Boats should keep near Shore.*

"'Tis however a Folly soon punished; for *Pride that dines on Vanity sups on Contempt,* as *Poor Richard* says. And in another Place, *Pride breakfasted with Plenty, dined with Poverty, and supped with Infamy.* And after all, of what Use is this *Pride of Appearance,* for which so much is risked, so much is suffered? It cannot promote Health, or ease Pain; it makes no Increase of Merit in the Person, it creates Envy, it hastens Misfortune.

> *What is a Butterfly? At best*
> *He's but a Caterpillar drest.*
> *The gaudy Fop's his Picture just,*

as poor Richard says.

"But what Madness must it be to run in Debt for these Superfluities! We are offered, by the Terms of this Vendue, *Six Months Credit*; and that perhaps has induced some of us to attend it, because we cannot spare the ready Money, and hope now to be fine without it. But, ah, think what you do when you run in Debt; *You give to another Power over your Liberty.* If you cannot pay at the Time, you will be ashamed to see your Creditor; you will be in Fear when you speak to him; you will make poor pitiful sneaking Excuses, and by Degrees come to lose your Veracity, and sink into base downright lying; for, as *Poor Richard* says, *The second Vice* is lying, the first is running in Debt. And again, to the same Purpose, *Lying rides upon Debt's back.* Whereas a freeborn *Englishman* ought not to be ashamed or afraid to see or speak to any Man living. But Poverty often deprives a Man of all Spirit and Virtue: *'Tis hard for an empty Bag to stand upright*, as Poor Richard truly says. What would you think of that Prince, or that Government, who should issue an Edict forbidding you to dress like a Gentleman or a Gentlewoman, on Pain of Imprisonment or Servitude? Would you not say, that you are free, have a Right to dress as you please, and that such an Edict would be a Breach of your Privileges, and such a Government tyrannical? And yet you are about to put yourself under that Tyranny when you run in Debt for such Dress! Your Creditor has Authority at his Pleasure to deprive you of your Liberty, by confining you in Gaol[7] for Life, or to sell you for a Servant, if you should not be able to pay him! When you have got your Bargain, you may, perhaps, think little of Payment; but *Creditors, Poor Richard* tells us, *have better Memories than Debtors*; and in another Place says, *Creditors are a superstitious Sect, great Observers of set Days and Times.* The Day comes round before you are aware, and the Demand is made before you are prepared to satisfy it. Or if you bear your Debt in Mind, the Term which at first seemed so long, will, as it lessens, appear extremely short. Time will seem to have added Wings to his Heels as well as Shoulders. *Those have a short Lent,*[8] saith *Poor Richard, who owe Money to be paid at Easter.* Then since, as he says, *The Borrower is a Slave to the Lender, and the Debtor to the Creditor, disdain the Chain*, preserve your Freedom; and maintain your Independency: Be *industrious* and *free*; be *frugal* and *free*. At present, perhaps, you may think yourself in thriving Circumstances, and that you can bear a little Extravagance without Injury; but,

> *For Age and Want, save while you may;*
> *No Morning Sun lasts a whole Day*,

"As *Poor Richard* says.—Gain may be temporary and uncertain, but ever while you live, Expence is constant and certain; and *'tis easier to build two Chimnies than to keep one in Fuel*, as *Poor Richard* says. So *rather go to Bed supperless than rise in Debt.*

> *Get what you can, and what you get hold;*
> *'Tis the Stone that will turn all your lead into Gold,*

as *Poor Richard* says. And when you have got the Philosopher's Stone,[9] sure you will no longer complain of bad Times, or the Difficulty of paying Taxes.

---

[7]GAOL: Jail, prison.
[8]LENT: The period including 40 weekdays extending from Ash Wednesday to the eve of Easter Sunday, observed as a time of fasting and penitence by many Christian groups.
[9]PHILOSOPHER'S STONE: A substance believed by medieval alchemists to possess the power to change base metal, such as lead, into gold or silver.

"This Doctrine, my Friends, is *Reason* and *Wisdom*, but after all, do not depend too much upon your own *Industry*, and *Frugality*, and *Prudence*, though excellent Things, for they may all be blasted without the Blessing of Heaven; and therefore ask that Blessing humbly, and be not uncharitable to those that at present seem to want it, but comfort and help them. Remember *Job*[10] suffered, and was afterwards prosperous.

"And now to conclude, *Experience keeps a dear*[11] *School, but Fools will learn in no other, and scarce in that;* for it is true, *we may give Advice, but we cannot give Conduct*, as *Poor Richard* says: However, remember this, *They that won't be counselled, can't be helped*, as *Poor Richard* says: And farther, That *if you will not hear Reason, she'll surely rap your Knuckles."*

Thus the old Gentleman ended his Harangue. The People heard it, and approved the Doctrine, and immediately practised the contrary, just as if it had been a common Sermon; for the Vendue opened, and they began to buy extravagantly, notwithstanding all his Cautions, and their own Fear of Taxes.—I found the good Man had thoroughly studied my Almanacks, and digested all I had dropt on those Topicks during the Course of Five-and-twenty Years. The frequent Mention he made of me must have tired any one else, but my Vanity was wonderfully delighted with it, though I was conscious that not a tenth Part of this Wisdom was my own which he ascribed to me, but rather the *Gleanings* I had made of the Sense of all Ages and Nations. However, I resolved to be the better for the Echo of it; and though I had at first determined to buy Stuff for a new Coat, I went away resolved to wear my old One a little longer. *Reader*, if thou wilt do the same, thy Profit will be as great as mine.

> *I am, as ever,*
> *Thine to serve thee,*
> RICHARD SAUNDERS.

[July 7, 1757]

---

[10]JOB: Patriarch in the Old Testament whose faith is tested by great suffering.
[11]DEAR: Expensive.

Remarks Concerning the Savages of North America

Savages we call them, because their Manners differ from ours, which we think the Perfection of Civility; they think the same of theirs.

Perhaps, if we could examine the Manners of different Nations with Impartiality, we should find no People so rude, as to be without any Rules of Politeness; nor any so polite, as not to have some Remains of Rudeness.

The Indian Men, when young, are Hunters and Warriors; when old, Counsellors; for all their Government is by Counsel of the Sages; there is no Force, there are no Prisons, no Officers to compel Obedience, or inflict Punishment. Hence they generally study Oratory, the best Speaker having the most Influence. The Indian Women till the Ground, dress the Food, nurse and bring up the Children, and preserve and hand down to Posterity the Memory of public Transactions. These Employments of Men and Women are accounted natural and honourable. Having few artifical Wants, they have abundance of Leisure for Improvement by Conversation. Our laborious Manner of Life, compared with theirs, they esteem slavish and base; and the Learning, on which we value ourselves, they regard as frivolous and useless. An Instance of this occurred at the Treaty of Lancaster, in Pennsylvania, *anno*[1] 1744, between the Government of Virginia and the Six Nations.[2] After the principal Business was settled, the Commissioners from Virginia acquainted the Indians by a Speech, that there was at Williamsburg a College,[3] with a Fund for Educating Indian youth; and that, if the Six Nations would send down half a dozen of their young Lads to that College, the Government would take care that they should be well provided for, and instructed in all the Learning of the White People. It is one of the Indian Rules of Politeness not to answer a public Proposition the same day that it is made; they think it would be treating it as a light matter, and that they show it Respect by taking time to consider it, as of a Matter important. They therefore deferr'd their Answer till the Day following; when their Speaker began, by expressing their deep Sense of the kindness of the Virginia Government, in making them that Offer; "for we know," says he, "that you highly esteem the kind of Learning taught in those Colleges, and that

[1]ANNO: In the year. (Latin)
[2]SIX NATIONS: The Iroquois Confederation (the Confederation of the Haudenosaunee) comprised of six Native American tribes—Seneca, Cayuga, Oneida, Onondaga, Mohawk, and Tuscarora.
[3]WILLIAMSBURG A COLLEGE: The College of William and Mary.

the Maintenance of our young Men, while with you, would be very expensive to you. We are convinc'd, therefore, that you mean to do us Good by your Proposal; and we thank you heartily. But you, who are wise, must know that different Nations have different Conceptions of things; and you will therefore not take it amiss, if our Ideas of this kind of Education happen not to be the same with yours. We have had some Experience of it; Several of our young People were formerly brought up at the Colleges of the Northern Provinces; they were instructed in all your Sciences; but, when they came back to us, they were bad Runners, ignorant of every means of living in the Woods, unable to bear either Cold or Hunger, knew neither how to build a Cabin, take a Deer, or kill an Enemy, spoke our Language imperfectly, were therefore neither fit for Hunters, Warriors, nor Counsellors; they were totally good for nothing. We are however not the less oblig'd by your kind Offer, tho' we decline accepting it; and, to show our grateful Sense of it, if the Gentlemen of Virginia will send us a Dozen of their Sons, we will take great Care of their Education, instruct them in all we know, and make *Men* of them."

Having frequent Occasions to hold public Councils, they have acquired great Order and Decency in conducting them. The old Men sit in the foremost Ranks, the Warriors in the next, and the Women and Children in the hindmost. The Business of the Women is to take exact Notice of what passes, imprint it in their Memories (for they have no Writing), and communicate it to their Children. They are the Records of the Council, and they preserve Traditions of the Stipulations in Treaties 100 Years back; which, when we compare with our Writings, we always find exact. He that would speak, rises. The rest observe a profound Silence. When he has finish'd and sits down, they leave him 5 to 6 Minutes to recollect, that, if he has omitted anything he intended to say, or has any thing to add, he may rise again and deliver it. To interrupt another, even in common Conversation, is reckon'd highly indecent. How different this is from the conduct of a polite British House of Commons, where scarce a day passes without some Confusion, that makes the Speaker hoarse in calling *to Order*; and how different from the Mode of Conversation in many polite Companies of Europe, where, if you do not deliver your Sentence with great Rapidity, you are cut off in the middle of it by the Impatient Loquacity of those you converse with, and never suffer'd to finish it!

The Politeness of these Savages in Conversation is indeed carried to Excess, since it does not permit them to contradict or deny the Truth of what is asserted in their Presence. By this means they indeed avoid Disputes; but then it becomes difficult to know their Minds, or what Impression you make upon them. The Missionaries who have attempted to convert them to Christianity, all complain of this as one of the great

Difficulties of their Mission. The Indians hear with Patience the Truths of the Gospel explain'd to them, and give their usual Tokens of Assent and Approbation; you would think they were convinc'd. No such matter. It is mere Civility.

A Swedish Minister, having assembled the chiefs of the Susquehanah Indians, made a Sermon to them, acquainting them with the principal historical Facts on which our Religion is founded; such as the Fall of our first Parents by eating an Apple, the coming of Christ to repair the Mischief, his Miracles and Suffering, &c. When he had finished, an Indian Orator stood up to thank him. "What you have told us," says he, "is all very good. It is indeed bad to eat Apples. It is better to make them all into Cyder. We are much oblig'd by your kindness in coming so far, to tell us these Things which you have heard from your Mothers. In return, I will tell you some of those we had heard from ours. In the Beginning, our Fathers had only the Flesh of Animals to subsist on; and if their Hunting was unsuccessful, they were starving. Two of our young Hunters, having kill'd a Deer, made a Fire in the Woods to broil some Part of it. When they were about to satisfy their Hunger, they beheld a beautiful young Woman descend from the Clouds, and seat herself on that Hill, which you see yonder among the blue Mountains. They said to each other, it is a Spirit that has smelt our broiling Venison, and wishes to eat of it; let us offer some to her. They presented her with the Tongue; she was pleas'd with the Taste of it, and said, 'Your kindness shall be rewarded; come to this Place after thirteen Moons, and you shall find something that will be of great Benefit in nourishing you and your Children to the latest Generations.' They did so, and, to their Surprise, found Plants they had never seen before; but which, from that ancient time, have been constantly cultivated among us, to our great Advantage. Where her right Hand had touched the Ground, they found Maize; where her left hand had touch'd it, they found Kidney-Beans; and where her Backside had sat on it, they found Tobacco." The good Missionary, disgusted with this idle Tale, said, "What I delivered to you were sacred Truths; but what you tell me is mere Fable, Fiction, and Falshood." The Indian, offended, reply'd, "My brother, it seems your Friends have not done you Justice in your Education; they have not well instructed you in the Rules of common Civility. You saw that we, who understand and practise those Rules, believ'd all your stories; why do you refuse to believe ours?"

When any of them come into our Towns, our People are apt to crowd round them, gaze upon them, and incommode them, where they desire to be private; this they esteem great Rudeness, and the Effect of the Want of Instruction in the Rules of Civility and good Manners. "We have," say they, "as much Curiosity as you, and when you come into our Towns, we wish for Opportunities of looking at you; but for this purpose we hide ourselves behind Bushes, where you are to pass, and never intrude ourselves into your Company."

Their Manner of entering one another's village has likewise its Rules. It is reckon'd uncivil in travelling Strangers to enter a Village abruptly, without giving Notice of their Approach. Therefore, as soon as they arrive within hearing, they stop and hollow,[4] remaining there till invited to enter. Two old Men usually come out to them, and lead them in. There is in every Village a vacant Dwelling, called *the Strangers' House.* Here they are plac'd, while the old Men go round from Hut to Hut, acquainting the Inhabitants, that Strangers are arriv'd, who are probably hungry and weary; and every one sends them what he can spare of Victuals, and Skins to repose on. When the Strangers are refresh'd, Pipes and Tobacco are brought; and then, but not before, Conversation begins, with Enquiries who they are, whither bound, what News, etc.; and it usually ends with offers of Service, if the Strangers have occasion of Guides, or any Necessaries for continuing their journey; and nothing is exacted for the Entertainment.

The same Hospitality, esteem'd among them as a principal Virtue, is practis'd by private Persons; of which Conrad Weiser, our Interpreter, gave me the following Instance. He had been naturaliz'd among the Six Nations, and spoke well the Mohock Language. In going thro' the Indian Country, to carry a Message from our Governor to the Council at Onondaga, he call'd at the Habitation of Canassatego, an old Acquaintance, who embrac'd him, spread Furs for him to sit on, plac'd before him some boil'd Beans and Venison, and mix'd some Rum and Water for his Drink. When he was well refresh'd, and had lit his Pipe, Canassatego began to converse with him; ask'd how he had far'd the many Years since they had seen each other; whence he then came; what occasion'd the journey, etc. Conrad answered all his Questions; and when the Discourse began to flag, the Indian, to continue it, said, "Conrad, you have lived long among the white People, and know something of their Customs; I have been sometimes at Albany, and have observed, that once in Seven Days they shut up their Shops, and assemble all in the great House; tell me what it is for? What do they do there?" "They meet there," says Conrad, "to hear and learn *good Things.* " "I do not doubt," says the Indian, "that they tell you so; they have told me the same; but I doubt the Truth of what they say, and I will tell you my Reasons. I went lately to Albany to sell my Skins and buy Blankets, Knives, Powder, Rum, &c. You know I us'd generally to deal with Hans Hanson; but I was a little inclin'd this time to try some other Merchant. However, I call'd first upon Hans, and asked him what he would give for Beaver. He said he could not give any more than four Shillings a

Pound; 'but,' says he, 'I cannot talk on Business now; this is the Day when we meet together to learn *Good Things*, and I am going to the Meeting.' So I thought to myself, 'Since we cannot do any Business to-day, I may as well go to the meeting too,' and I went with him. There stood up a Man in Black, and began to talk to the People very angrily. I did not understand what he said; but, perceiving that he look'd much at me and at Hanson, I imagin'd he was angry at seeing me there; so I went out, sat down near the House, struck Fire, and lit my Pipe, waiting till the Meeting should break up. I thought too, that the Man had mention'd something of Beaver, and I suspected it might be the Subject of their Meeting. So, when they came out, I accosted my Merchant. 'Well, Hans,' says I, 'I hope you have agreed to give more than four Shillings a Pound.' 'No,' says he, 'I cannot give so much; I cannot give more than three shillings and sixpence.' I then spoke to several other Dealers, but they all sung the same song,—Three and sixpence,—Three and sixpence. This made it clear to me, that my Suspicion was right; and, that whatever they pretended of meeting to learn *good Things*, the real purpose was to consult how to cheat Indians in the Price of Beaver. Consider but a little, Conrad, and you must be of my Opinion. If they met so often to learn *good Things*, they would certainly have learnt some before this time. But they are still ignorant. You know our Practice. If a white Man, in travelling thro' our Country, enters one of our Cabins, we all treat him as I treat you; we dry him if he is wet, we warm him if he is cold, we give him Meat and Drink, that he may allay his Thirst and Hunger; and we spread soft Furs for him to rest and sleep on; we demand nothing in return. But, if I go into a white Man's House at Albany, and ask for Victuals and Drink, they say, 'Where is your Money?' and if I have none, they say, 'Get out, you Indian Dog.' You see they have not yet learned those little *Good Things*, that we need no Meetings to be instructed in, because our Mothers taught them to us when we were Children; and therefore it is impossible their Meetings should be, as they say, for any such purpose, or have any such Effect; they are only to contrive *the Cheating of Indians in the Price of Beaver.*"5

[1784]

5THE CHEATING OF INDIANS IN THE PRICE OF BEAVER: Franklin notes of this line, "It is remarkable that in all ages and countries hospitality has been allowed as the virtue of those whom the civilized were pleased to call barbarians. The Greeks celebrated the Scythians for it. The Saracens possessed it eminently, and it is to this day the reigning virtue of the wild Arabs. St. Paul too, in the relation of his voyage and shipwreck on the island of Melité says the barbarous people showed us no little kindness; for they kindled a fire, and received us every one, because of the present rain, and because of the cold." The Scythians were a group of ancient nomadic tribes of southeastern Europe known for their plundering and excellent horsemanship. The Greeks used the word *Saracen* to describe nomadic Syrians, and later Arabs; the word later was used by Europeans to describe any Muslim. Acts 28 recounts St. Paul's visit to Melita.

From The Autobiography

[PART ONE]

Twyford, at the Bishop of St. Asaph's 1771.[1]

Dear Son,

I have ever had a Pleasure in obtaining any little Anecdotes of my Ancestors. You may remember the Enquiries I made among the Remains of my Relations[2] when you were with me in England; and the Journey I took for that purpose. Now imagining it may be equally agreeable to you to know the Circumstances of *my* Life, many of which you are yet unacquainted with; and expecting a Week's uninterrupted Leisure in my present Country Retirement, I sit down to write them for you. To which I have besides some other Inducements. Having emerg'd from the Poverty and Obscurity in which I was born and bred, to a State of Affluence and some Degree of Reputation in the World, and having gone so far thro' Life with a considerable Share of Felicity, the conducting Means I made use of, which, with the Blessing of God, so well succeeded, my Posterity may like to know, as they may find some of them suitable to their own Situations, and therefore fit to be imitated. That Felicity, when I reflected on it, has induc'd me sometimes to say that were it offer'd to my Choice, I should have no Objection to a Repetition of the same Life from its Beginning, only asking the Advantage Authors have in a second Edition to correct some Faults of the first. So would I if I might, besides correcting the Faults, change some sinister Accidents and Events of it for others more favorable, but tho' this were denied, I should still accept the Offer. However, since such a Repetition is not to be expected, the Thing most like living one's Life over again, seems to be a *Recollection* of that Life; and to make that Recollection as durable as possible, the putting it down in Writing. Hereby, too, I shall indulge the Inclination so natural in old Men, to be talking of themselves and their own past Actions, and I shall indulge it, without being troublesome to others who thro' respect to Age might think themselves oblig'd to give me a Hearing, since this may be read or not as any one pleases. And lastly, (I may as well confess it, since my Denial of it will be believ'd by no body) perhaps I shall a good deal gratify my own *Vanity*. Indeed I scarce ever

[1]TWYFORD, AT THE BISHOP OF ST. ASAPH'S 1771: Franklin wrote the first part of his autobiography, addressed to his son, William (1731–1813), while visiting the home of Bishop Jonathan Shipley at Twyford, Berkshire, England (about 50 miles outside of London).
[2]REMAINS OF MY RELATIONS: Living relatives. Franklin had traveled to England with his son in 1758.

heard or saw the introductory Words, *Without Vanity I may say*, etc. but some vain thing immediately follow'd. Most People dislike Vanity in others whatever Share they have of it themselves, but I give it fair Quarter wherever I meet with it, being persuaded that it is often productive of Good to the Possessor and to others that are within his Sphere of Action: And therefore in many Cases it would not be quite absurd if a Man were to thank God for his Vanity among the other Comforts of Life.

And now I speak of thanking God, I desire with all Humility to acknowledge, that I owe the mention'd Happiness of my past Life to his kind Providence, which led me to the Means I us'd and gave them Success. My Belief of This, induces me to *hope*, tho' I must not *presume*, that the same Goodness will still be exercis'd towards me in continuing that Happiness, or in enabling me to bear a fatal Reverso,[3] which I may experience as others have done, the Complexion of my future Fortune being known to him only: and in whose Power it is to bless to us even our Afflictions.

The Notes one of my Uncles (who had the same kind of Curiosity in collecting Family Anecdotes) once put into my Hands, furnish'd me with several Particulars, relating to our Ancestors. From those Notes I learned that the Family had liv'd in the same Village, Ecton in Northamptonshire, for 300 Years, and how much longer he knew not, (perhaps from the Time when the Name *Franklin*[4] that before was the Name of an Order of People, was assum'd by them for a Surname, when others took Surnames all over the Kingdom) on a Freehold of about 30 Acres, aided by the Smith's Business which had continued in the Family till his Time, the eldest Son being always bred to that Business. A Custom which he and my Father both followed as to their eldest Sons. When I search'd the Register at Ecton, I found an Account of their Births, Marriages and Burials, from the Year 1555 only, there being no Register kept in that Parish at any time preceding. By that Register I perceiv'd that I was the youngest Son of the youngest Son for 5 Generations back. My Grandfather Thomas, who was born in 1598, lived at Ecton till he grew too old to follow Business longer, when he went to live with his Son John, a Dyer at Banbury in Oxfordshire, with whom my Father serv'd an Apprenticeship. There my Grandfather died and lies buried. We saw his Gravestone in 1758. His eldest Son Thomas liv'd in the House at Ecton, and left it with the Land to his only Child, a

---

[3]REVERSO: A backhanded stroke used in fencing.
[4]NAME FRANKLIN: The word "franklin" means freeholder, a designation of a class of landowners in the middle ages, of free but not of noble birth.

Daughter, who with her Husband, one Fisher of Wellingborough, sold it to Mr. Isted, now Lord of the Manor there.

My Grandfather had 4 Sons that grew up, viz., Thomas, John, Benjamin and Josiah. I will give you what Account I can of them at this distance from my Papers, and if those are not lost in my Absence, you will among them find many more Particulars. Thomas was bred a Smith under his Father, but being ingenious, and encourag'd in Learning (as all his Brothers likewise were,) by an Esquire[5] Palmer then the principal Gentleman in that Parish, he qualified himself for the Business of Scrivener,[6] became a considerable Man in the County Affairs, was a chief Mover of all public Spirited Undertakings for the County or Town of Northampton and his own Village, of which many Instances were told us at Ecton, and he was much taken Notice of and patroniz'd by the then Lord Halifax. He died in 1702, Jan. 6, old Stile,[7] just 4 Years to a Day before I was born. The Account we receiv'd of his Life and Character from some old People at Ecton, I remember struck you as something extraordinary from its Similarity to what you knew of mine. Had he died on the same Day, you said one might have suppos'd a Transmigration.

John was bred a Dyer, I believe of Woollens. Benjamin was bred a Silk Dyer, serving an Apprenticeship at London. He was an ingenious Man. I remember him well, for when I was a Boy he came over to my Father in Boston, and lived in the House with us some Years. He lived to a great Age. His Grandson Samuel Franklin now lives in Boston. He left behind him two Quarto Volumes,[8] Manuscript of his own Poetry, consisting of little occasional Pieces address'd to his Friends and Relations, of which the following sent to me, is a Specimen. He had form'd a Shorthand of his own, which he taught me, but never practicing it I have now forgot it. I was nam'd after this Uncle, there being a particular Affection between him and my Father. He was very pious, a great Attender of Sermons of the best Preachers, which he took down in his Shorthand and had with him many Volumes of them. He was also much of a Politician, too much perhaps for his Station. There fell lately into

[5]ESQUIRE: A young man of noble birth, usually from the higher order of English gentry.
[6]SCRIVENER: A professional copyist usually employed in legal professions.
[7]STILE: According to the Julian, or "Old Stile" calendar, the first day of the year was March 25, the vernal equinox. The calendar, however, was not completely accurate with matching solar years. In 1582, Pope Gregory XIII ordered ten days to be dropped from October, restoring the vernal equinox at least to an average of the 20th of March, and made January 1 the first day of the year. The "New Style" calendar was adopted in Roman Catholic countries (most of Europe) but Protestant England (and by extension its American colonies), refused to make the switch resulting in a ten-day gap. In 1752, the English relented, and they skipped eleven days in order to adopt the new calendar. Thus, Franklin's birthday is either January 6, 1705 ("Old Stile") or January 17, 1706, New Style.
[8]QUARTO VOLUMES: Books composed of paper of single sheets folded twice, thus forming four leaves.

my Hands in London a Collection he had made of all the principal Pamphlets relating to Public Affairs from 1641 to 1717. Many of the Volumes are wanting, as appears by the Numbering, but there still remains 8 Volumes Folio, and 24 in Quarto and Octavo. A Dealer in old Books met with them, and knowing me by my sometimes buying of him, he brought them to me. It seems my Uncle must have left them here when he went to America, which was above 50 Years since. There are many of his Notes in the Margins.

This obscure Family of ours was early in the Reformation, and continu'd Protestants thro' the Reign of Queen Mary,[9] when they were sometimes in Danger of Trouble on Account of their Zeal against Popery.[10] They had got an English Bible,[11] and to conceal and secure it, it was fastened open with Tapes under and within the Frame of a Joint Stool.[12] When my Great Great Grandfather read in it to his Family, he turn'd up the Joint Stool upon his Knees, turning over the Leaves then under the Tapes. One of the Children stood at the Door to give Notice if he saw the Apparitor[13] coming, who was an Officer of the Spiritual Court. In that Case the Stool was turn'd down again upon its feet, when the Bible remain'd conceal'd under it as before. This Anecdote I had from my Uncle Benjamin. The Family continu'd all of the Church of England till about the End of Charles the Second's Reign,[14] when some of the Ministers that had been outed for Nonconformity, holding Conventicles[15] in Northamptonshire, Benjamin and Josiah adher'd to them, and so continu'd all their Lives. The rest of the Family remain'd with the Episcopal Church.

Josiah, my Father, married young, and carried his Wife with three Children unto New England, about 1682. The Conventicles having been forbidden by Law, and frequently disturbed, induced some considerable Men of his Acquaintance to remove to that Country, and he was prevail'd with to accompany them thither, where they expected to enjoy their Mode of Religion with Freedom. By the same Wife he had 4 Children more born there, and by a second Wife ten more, in all 17, of which I

---

[9]QUEEN MARY: The English Reformation. After the Pope refused to grant English King Henry VIII (1491–1547) a divorce in 1534, the incensed king severed all ties with the Roman Catholic Church by declaring the Act of Supremacy, making him head of the Church of England. When his daughter, Mary Tudor (1516–58) became queen in 1553, she restored Roman Catholicism as the official religion of England. Many Protestants suffered during her reign.
[10]POPERY: Catholicism.
[11]ENGLISH BIBLE: The "Geneva" version of the Bible, used by the Puritans, translated by Calvinist Protestants living in Geneva, Switzerland.
[12]JOINT STOOL: A four-legged stool.
[13]APPARITOR: An officer of an ecclesiastical court who investigated suspected cases of heresy.
[14]CHARLES THE SECOND'S REIGN: Charles II (1630–1685) reigned from 1660 to his death in 1685.
[15]CONVENTICLES: Secret and illegal meetings of nonconformists who refused to acknowledge the authority of the Church of England.

remember 13 sitting at one time at his Table, who all grew up to be Men and Women, and married. I was the youngest Son and the youngest Child but two, and was born in Boston, New England.

My Mother the second Wife was Abiah Folger, a Daughter of Peter Folger, one of the first Settlers of New England, of whom honorable mention is made by Cotton Mather,[16] in his Church History of that Country, (entitled Magnalia Christi Americana) as a *godly learned Englishman*, if I remember the Words rightly.[17] I have heard that he wrote sundry small occasional Pieces, but only one of them was printed which I saw now many Years since. It was written in 1675, in the homespun Verse of that Time and People, and address'd to those then concern'd in the Government there. It was in favor of Liberty of Conscience, and in behalf of the Baptists, Quakers, and other Sectaries,[18] that had been under Persecution; ascribing the Indian Wars and other Distresses that had befallen the Country to that Persecution, as so many Judgments of God, to punish so heinous an Offence; and exhorting a Repeal of those uncharitable Laws. The whole appear'd to me as written with a good deal of Decent Plainness and manly Freedom. The six last concluding Lines I remember, tho' I have forgotten the two first of the Stanza, but the Purport of them was that his Censures proceeded from *Goodwill*, and therefore he would be known as the Author,

> because to be a Libeler, *(says he)*
> I hate it with my Heart.
> From Sherburne Town[19] where now I dwell,
> My Name I do put here,
> Without Offence, you real Friend,
> It is Peter Folgier.

My elder Brothers were all put Apprentices to different Trades. I was put to the Grammar School at Eight Years of Age, my Father intending to devote me as the Tithe[20] of his Sons to the Service of the Church. My early Readiness in learning to read (which must have been very early, as I do not remember when I could not read) and the Opinion of all his Friends that I should certainly make a good Scholar, encourag'd him in this Purpose of his. My Uncle Benjamin too approv'd of it, and propos'd to give me all his Shorthand Volumes of Sermons, I suppose as a Stock

---

[16]COTTON MATHER: (1663–1728) an American Puritan clergyman who published *Magnalia Christi Americana* (*The Wonderful Work of Christ in America*) in 1702 detailing the ecclesiastical history of New England.
[17]WORDS RIGHTLY: The exact quotation was "an Able Godly Englishman."
[18]SECTARIES: Members of various sects, most commonly applied to the English Protestant Dissenters.
[19]SHERBURNE TOWN: In the Island of Nantucket [Franklin's note].
[20]TITHE: A tenth of one's income traditionally given to the church.

to set up with, if I would learn his Character.[21] I continu'd however at the Grammar School not quite one Year; tho' in that time I had risen gradually from the Middle of the Class of that Year to be the Head of it, and farther was remov'd into the next Class above it, in order to go with that into the third at the End of the Year. But my Father in the meantime, from a View of the Expense of a College Education which, having so large a Family, he could not well afford, and the mean Living many so educated were afterwards able to obtain, Reasons that he gave to his Friends in my Hearing, altered his first Intention, took me from the Grammar School, and sent me to a School for Writing and Arithmetic kept by a then famous Man, Mr. George Brownell, very successful in his Profession generally, and that by mild encouraging Methods. Under him I acquired fair Writing pretty soon, but I fail'd in the Arithmetic, and made no Progress in it.

At Ten Years old, I was taken home to assist my Father in his Business, which was that of a Tallow Chandler and Soap-Boiler.[22] A Business he was not bred to, but had assumed on his Arrival in New England and on finding his Dying Trade would not maintain his Family, being in little Request. Accordingly I was employed in cutting Wick for the Candles, filling the Dipping Mold, and the Molds for cast Candles, attending the Shop, going of Errands, etc. I dislik'd the Trade and had a strong Inclination for the Sea; but my Father declar'd against it; however, living near the Water, I was much in and about it, learned early to swim well, and to manage Boats, and when in a Boat or Canoe with other Boys I was commonly allow'd to govern, especially in any case of Difficulty; and upon other Occasions I was generally a Leader among the Boys, and sometimes led them into Scrapes, of which I will mention one Instance, as it shows an early projecting public Spirit, tho' not then justly conducted. There was a Salt Marsh that bounded part of the Mill Pond, on the Edge of which at Highwater, we us'd to stand to fish for Minnows. By much Trampling, we had made it a mere Quagmire. My Proposal was to build a Wharf there fit for us to stand upon, and I show'd my Comrades a large Heap of Stones which were intended for a new House near the Marsh, and which would very well suit our Purpose. Accordingly in the Evening when the Workmen were gone, I assembled a Number of my Playfellows, and working with them diligently like so many Emmets,[23] sometimes two or three to a Stone, we brought them all away

---

[21]CHARACTER: Letters, i.e., his system of shorthand.
[22]TALLOW CHANDLER AND SOAPBOILER: A maker of candles and soap.
[23]EMMETS: Ants.

and built our little Wharf. The next Morning the Workmen were surpris'd at Missing the Stones; which were found in our Wharf; Enquiry
was made after the Removers; we were discovered and complain'd of;
several of us were corrected by our Fathers; and tho' I pleaded the
Usefulness of the Work, mine convinc'd me that nothing was useful
which was not honest.

I think you may like to know something of his Person and Character.
He had an excellent Constitution of Body, was of middle Stature, but well
set and very strong. He was ingenious, could draw prettily, was skill'd
a little in Music and had a clear pleasing Voice, so that when he play'd
Psalm Tunes on his Violin and sung withal as he some times did in an
Evening after the Business of the Day was over, it was extremely agreeable to hear. He had a mechanical Genius too, and on occasion was very
handy in the Use of other Tradesmen's Tools. But his great Excellence lay
in a sound Understanding, and solid Judgment in prudential Matters,
both in private and public Affairs. In the latter indeed he was never
employed, the numerous Family he had to educate and the Straitness
of his Circumstances, keeping him close to his Trade, but I remember well
his being frequently visited by leading People, who consulted him for
his Opinion on Affairs of the Town or of the Church he belong'd to and
show'd a good deal of Respect for his Judgment and Advice. He was
also much consulted by private Persons about their Affairs when any
Difficulty occur'd, and frequently chosen an Arbitrator between contending Parties. At his Table he lik'd to have as often as he could, some
sensible Friend or Neighbor, to converse with, and always took care to
start some ingenious or useful Topic for Discourse, which might tend to
improve the Minds of his Children. By this means he turn'd our Attention
to what was good, just, and prudent in the Conduct of Life; and little
or no Notice was ever taken of what related to the Victuals on the Table,
whether it was well or ill drest, in or out of season, of good or bad flavor, preferable or inferior to this or that other thing of the kind; so that
I was brought up in such a perfect Inattention to those Matters as to be
quite Indifferent what kind of Food was set before me; and so unobser-
vant of it, that to this Day, if I am ask'd I can scarce tell, a few Hours
after Dinner, what I din'd upon. This has been a Convenience to me in
traveling, where my Companions have been sometimes very unhappy for
want of a suitable Gratification of their more delicate because better
instructed Tastes and Appetites.

My Mother had likewise an excellent Constitution. She suckled all her
10 children. I never knew either my Father or Mother to have any
Sickness but that of which they died, he at 89 and she at 85 Years of age.

They lie buried together at Boston, where I some Years since plac'd a Marble stone over their Grave with this Inscription:

> *Josiah Franklin*
> *And Abiah his Wife*
> *Lie here interred.*
> *They lived lovingly together in Wedlock*
> *Fifty-five Years.*
> *Without an Estate or any gainful Employment,*
> *By constant Labor and Industry,*
> *With God's Blessing,*
> *They maintained a large Family*
> *Comfortably;*
> *And brought up thirteen Children,*
> *And seven Grandchildren*
> *Reputably.*
> *From this Instance, Reader,*
> *Be encouraged to Diligence in thy Calling,*
> *And distrust not Providence.*
> *He was a pious and prudent Man,*
> *She a discreet and virtuous Woman.*
> *Their youngest Son,*
> *In filial Regard to their Memory,*
> *Places this Stone.*
> *J.F. born 1655—Died 1744. Ætat[24] 89*
> *A.F. born 1667—died 1752—85.*

By my rambling Digressions I perceive myself to be grown old. I us'd to write more methodically. But one does not dress for private Company as for a public Ball. 'Tis perhaps only Negligence.

To return. I continu'd thus employ'd in my Father's Business for two Years, that is till I was 12 Years old; and my Brother John[25] who was bred to that Business having left my Father, married and set up for himself at Rhode Island, there was all Appearance that I was destin'd to supply his Place and be a Tallow Chandler. But my Dislike to the Trade continuing, my Father was under Apprehensions that if he did not find one for me more agreeable, I should break away and get to Sea, as his Son Josiah had done to his great Vexation. He therefore sometimes took me to walk with him, and see Joiners, Bricklayers, Turners, Braziers,[26] etc.

---

[24]AETAT: Aged.
[25]BROTHER JOHN: Franklin's favorite older brother, John Franklin (1690–1756).
[26]JOINERS . . . BRAZIERS: Woodworkers, brick masons, lathe (one who works wood while turning a lathe) workers, brass workers.

at their Work, that he might observe my Inclination, and endeavor to fix it on some Trade or other on Land. It has ever since been a Pleasure to me to see good Workmen handle their Tools; and it has been useful to me, having learned so much by it, as to be able to do little Jobs myself in my House, when a Workman could not readily be got; and to construct little Machines for my Experiments while the Intention of making the Experiment was fresh and warm in my Mind. My Father at last fix'd upon the Cutler's Trade,[27] and my Uncle Benjamin's Son Samuel who was bred to that Business in London being about that time establish'd in Boston, I was sent to be with him some time on liking. But his Expectations of a Fee with me displeasing my Father, I was taken home again.

From a Child I was fond of Reading, and all the little Money that came into my Hands was ever laid out in Books. Pleas'd with the Pilgrim's Progress, my first Collection was of John Bunyan's[28] Works, in separate little Volumes I afterwards sold them to enable me to buy R. Burton's[29] Historical Collections; they were small Chapmen's Books[30] and cheap, 40 or 50 in all. My Father's little Library consisted chiefly of Books in polemic Divinity, most of which I read, and have since often regretted, that at a time when I had such a Thirst for Knowledge, more proper Books had not fallen in my Way, since it was now resolv'd I should not be a Clergyman. Plutarch's Lives[31] there was, in which I read abundantly, and I still think that time spent to great Advantage. There was also a Book of Defoe's called an Essay on Projects[32] and another of Dr. Mather's call'd Essays to do Good,[33] which perhaps gave me a Turn of Thinking that had an Influence on some of the principal future Events of my Life.

This Bookish Inclination at length determin'd my Father to make me a Printer, tho' he had already one Son, (James) of that Profession. In 1717 my Brother James return'd from England with a Press and Letters[34] to set up his Business in Boston. I lik'd it much better than

---

[27]CUTLER'S TRADE: The knife-making trade. Children were traditionally apprenticed, for a fee paid by their parents to the master tradesman, around the age of fourteen and were bound to work until twenty-one. During their apprenticeship, they lived with the master's family.

[28]JOHN BUNYAN: English author John Bunyan (1628–1688) published the enormously popular *Pilgrim's Progress* in 1678, which tells the tale of the journey of Christian to the Celestial City.

[29]R. BURTON: Robert Burton (R.B.) was the pseudonym of London author and publisher Nathaniel Crouch (c. 1632–1725).

[30]CHAPMEN'S BOOKS: Popular pulp literature printed in small pamphlets of popular tales, ballads, and political tracts.

[31]PLUTARCH'S LIVES: Plutarch (c.46–120?) was a Greek biographer noted for his book *The Parallel Lives* describing the lives of famous Greeks and Romans.

[32]ESSAY ON PROJECTS: Daniel Defoe's (1659?–1731) *Essay on Projects* (1697) provided instruction on financial economy.

[33]ESSAYS TO DO GOOD: Cotton Mather's *Bonifacius: An Essay on the Good* (1710).

[34]PRESS AND LETTERS: Type face.

that of my Father, but still had a Hankering for the Sea. To prevent the apprehended Effect of such an Inclination, my Father was impatient to have me bound to my Brother.[35] I stood out some time, but at last was persuaded and signed the Indentures,[36] when I was yet but 12 Years old. I was to serve as an Apprentice till I was 21 Years of Age, only I was to be allow'd Journeyman's Wages[37] during the last Year. In a little time I made great Proficiency in the Business, and became a useful Hand to my Brother. I now had Access to better Books. An Acquaintance with the Apprentices of Booksellers enabled me sometimes to borrow a small one, which I was careful to return soon and clean. Often I sat up in my Room reading the greatest Part of the Night, when the Book was borrow'd in the Evening and to be return'd early in the Morning lest it should be miss'd or wanted. And after some time an ingenious Tradesman who had a pretty[38] Collection of Books, and who frequented our Printing-House took Notice of me, invited me to his Library, and very kindly lent me such Books as I chose to read. I now took a Fancy to Poetry, and made some little Pieces. My Brother, thinking it might turn to account encourag'd me, and put me on composing two occasional Ballads. One was called the *Light House Tragedy*,[39] and contain'd an Account of the drowning of Capt. Worthilake with his Two Daughters; the other was a Sailor Song on the Taking of *Teach* or Blackbeard the Pirate.[40] They were wretched Stuff, in the Grubstreet Ballad Style,[41] and when they were printed he sent me about the Town to sell them. The first sold wonderfully, the Event being recent, having made a great Noise. This flatter'd my Vanity. But my Father discourag'd me, by ridiculing my Performances, and telling me Verse-makers were generally Beggars; so I escap'd being a Poet, most

[35]BOUND TO MY BROTHER: Apprenticed (see note 37). James Franklin (1697–1735) had learned the printer's trade in England.
[36]INDENTURES: A legally binding contract to work for a period of years, usually seven, but in Franklin's case, nine. The term "indenture" refers to the fact that the contract was "indented," or torn in half, with each party keeping a portion of the signed copy.
[37]JOURNEYMAN'S WAGES: That is, paid for each day's work following his apprenticeship.
[38]PRETTY: Exceptionally fine.
[39]LIGHT HOUSE TRAGEDY: The story of lighthouse keeper George Worthylake, who drowned with his wife and daughter in 1718 after their boat capsized near Beacon Island (also called Little Brewster Island) in Boston Harbor. Franklin was twelve years old at the time he composed his poem based on the disaster.
[40]TAKING OF TEACH OR BLACKBEARD THE PIRATE: Edward Teach (d. 1718), a.k.a., "Blackbeard." He began his career as a privateer during the War of the Spanish Succession (1701–14) but turned pirate, preying on ships bound for coastal settlements of the West Indies and the Atlantic coast. Notorious for his cruelty, he was killed off the Carolina coast by a British naval force from Virginia.
[41]GRUBSTREET BALLAD STYLE: Grub Street was the name of an avenue near Moorfields in London (modern Milton Street), inhabited by struggling writers who penned ballad-style poems that capitalized on sensational happenings, much like modern tabloid writers. The term became synonymous for a literary hack.

probably a very bad one. But as Prose Writing has been of great Use to me in the Course of my Life, and was a principal Means of my Advancement, I shall tell you how in such a Situation I acquir'd what little Ability I have in that Way.

There was another Bookish Lad in the Town, John Collins by Name, with whom I was intimately acquainted. We sometimes disputed, and very fond we were of Argument, and very desirous of confuting one another. Which disputatious Turn, by the way, is apt to become a very bad Habit, making People often extremely disagreeable in Company, by the Contradiction that is necessary to bring it into Practice, and thence, besides souring and spoiling the Conversation, is productive of Disgusts and perhaps Enmities where you may have occasion for Friendship. I had caught it by reading my Father's Books of Dispute about Religion. Persons of good Sense, I have since observ'd, seldom fall into it, except Lawyers, University Men, and Men of all Sorts that have been bred at Edinburgh.[42] A Question was once some how or other started between Collins and me, of the Propriety of educating the Female Sex in Learning, and their Abilities for Study. He was of Opinion that it was improper; and that they were naturally unequal to it. I took the contrary Side, perhaps a little for Dispute sake. He was naturally more eloquent, had a ready Plenty of Words, and sometimes as I thought bore me down more by his Fluency than by the Strength of his Reasons. As we parted without settling the Point, and were not to see one another again for some time, I sat down to put my Arguments in Writing, which I copied fair and sent to him. He answer'd and I replied. Three or four Letters of a Side had pass'd, when my Father happen'd to find my Papers, and read them. Without entering into the Discussion, he took occasion to talk to me about the Manner of my Writing, observ'd that tho' I had the Advantage of my Antagonist in correct Spelling and pointing[43] (which I ow'd to the Printing-House) I fell far short in elegance of Expression, in Method and in Perspicuity, of which he convinc'd me by several Instances. I saw the Justice of his Remarks, and thence grew more attentive to the *Manner* in Writing, and determin'd to endeavor at Improvement.

About this time I met with an odd Volume of the Spectator.[44] I had never before seen any of them. I bought it, read it over and over, and was much delighted with it. I thought the Writing excellent, and wish'd if

---

[42]EDINBURGH: Scottish Presbyterians were known for their argumentative natures.
[43]POINTING: Punctuation.
[44]VOLUME OF THE SPECTATOR: An English periodical that aimed to "enliven morality with wit" published daily as the *Spectator* (1711–12) and the *New Spectator* (1714), featuring the essays of English poet and statesman Joseph Addison (1672–1719) and Richard Steele (1672–1729).

possible to imitate it. With that View, I took some of the Papers, and making short Hints of the Sentiment in each Sentence, laid them by a few Days, and then without looking at the Book, tried to complete the Papers again, by expressing each hinted Sentiment at length and as fully as it had been express'd before, in any suitable Words that should come to hand.

Then I compar'd my Spectator with the Original, discover'd some of my Faults and corrected them. But I found I wanted a Stock of Words or a Readiness in recollecting and using them, which I thought I should have acquir'd before that time, if I had gone on making Verses, since the continual Occasion for Words of the same Import but of different Length, to suit the Measure,[45] or of different Sound for the Rhyme, would have laid me under a constant Necessity of searching for Variety, and also have tended to fix that Variety in my Mind, and make me Master of it. Therefore I took some of the Tales and turn'd them into Verse: And after a time, when I had pretty well forgotten the Prose, turn'd them back again. I also sometimes jumbled my Collections of Hints into Confusion, and after some Weeks, endeavor'd to reduce them into the best Order, before I began to form the full Sentences, and complete the Paper. This was to teach me Method in the Arrangement of Thoughts. By comparing my Work afterwards with the original, I discover'd many faults and amended them; but I sometimes had the Pleasure of Fancying that in certain Particulars of small Import, I had been lucky enough to improve the Method or the Language and this encourag'd me to think I might possibly in time come to be a tolerable English Writer, of which I was extremely ambitious.

My Time for these Exercises and for Reading, was at Night after Work, or before Work began in the Morning; or on Sundays, when I contrived to be in the Printing-House alone, evading as much as I could the common Attendance on public Worship, which my Father used to exact of me when I was under his Care: And which indeed I still thought a Duty; tho' I could not, as it seemed to me, afford the Time to practice it.

When about 16 Years of Age, I happen'd to meet with a Book written by one Tryon,[46] recommending a Vegetable Diet. I determined to go into it. My Brother being yet unmarried, did not keep House, but boarded himself and his Apprentices in another Family. My refusing to eat Flesh occasioned an Inconveniency, and I was frequently chid for my singularity. I made myself acquainted with Tryon's Manner of preparing some of his Dishes, such as Boiling Potatoes or Rice, making Hasty Pudding,[47]

---

[45]MEASURE: Meter.
[46]TRYON: *The way to health, long life and happiness* (1682), by Thomas Tryon (1634–1703), a prominent vegetarian of the late 17th century.
[47]HASTY PUDDING: Cornmeal or oatmeal porridge.

and a few others, and then propos'd to my Brother, that if he would give me Weekly half the Money he paid for my Board, I would board myself. He instantly agreed to it, and I presently found that I could save half what he paid me. This was an additional Fund for buying Books: But I had another Advantage in it. My Brother and the rest going from the Printing-House to their Meals, I remain'd there alone, and dispatching presently my light Repast, (which often was no more than a Biscuit or a Slice of Bread, a Handful of Raisins or a Tart from the Pastry Cook's, and a Glass of Water) had the rest of the Time till their Return, for Study, in which I made the greater Progress from that greater Clearness of Head and quicker Apprehension which usually attend Temperance in Eating and Drinking. And now it was that being on some Occasion made asham'd of my Ignorance in Figures, which I had twice fail'd in learning when at School, I took Cocker's Book of Arithmetic,[48] and went thro' the whole by myself with great Ease. I also read Seller's and Sturmy's Books of Navigation,[49] and became acquainted with the little Geometry they contain, but never proceeded far in that Science. And I read about this Time Locke on Human Understanding[50] and the Art of Thinking by Messrs. du Port Royal.[51]

While I was intent on improving my Language, I met with an English Grammar (I think it was Greenwood's[52]) at the End of which there were two little Sketches of the Arts of Rhetoric and Logic, the latter finishing with a Specimen of a Dispute in the Socratic Method.[53] And soon after I procur'd Xenophon's Memorable Things of Socrates,[54] wherein there are many Instances of the same Method. I was charm'd with it, adopted it, dropped my abrupt Contradiction and positive Argumentation, and put on the humble Enquirer and Doubter. And

[48]COCKER'S BOOK OF ARITHMETIC: Edward Cocker's (1631–1677) *Arithmetic* (1677) ran over sixty editions.
[49]SELLER'S AND STURMY'S BOOKS OF NAVIGATION: Nautical cartographer John Seller (c. 1630-1697), *An Epitome of the Art of Navigation* (1681). Captain Samuel Sturmy (1633-1669), *The Mariner's Magazine: Or Sturmy's Mathematical and Practical Arts* (1699).
[50]LOCKE ON HUMAN UNDERSTANDING: John Locke (1632–1704), English philosopher who published *An Essay Concerning Human Understanding* in 1690.
[51]ART OF THINKING BY MESSRS. DU PORT ROYAL: *Logic: Or the Art of Thinking* (1687) by Antoine Arnauld (1612–1694) and Pierre Nicole (1625–1695) of Port Royal, an abbey located 17 miles west of Paris.
[52]GREENWOOD'S: James Greenwood, *An Essay towards a Practical English Grammar* (1711).
[53]SOCRATIC METHOD: A method of debate in which one person leads the discussion through a series of questions, with the result that the participants arrive at an answer through considering the questions or become aware of the faulty nature of their assumptions.
[54]XENOPHON'S MEMORABLE THINGS OF SOCRATES: Xenophon (c.430 BCE–355 BCE), Greek historian and disciple of Socrates who wrote *The Memorable Things of Socrates*, translated by Edward Bysshe in 1712.

being then, from reading Shaftesbury and Collins,[55] became a real
Doubter in many Points of our Religious Doctrine, I found this Method
safest for myself and very embarrassing to those against whom I used
it, therefore I took a Delight in it, practic'd it continually and grew very
artful and expert in drawing People even of superior Knowledge into
Concessions the Consequences of which they did not foresee, entangling
them in Difficulties out of which they could not extricate themselves,
and so obtaining Victories that neither myself nor my Cause always
deserved. I continu'd this Method some few Years, but gradually left
it, retaining only the Habit of expressing myself in Terms of modest
Diffidence, never using when I advance any thing that may possibly
be disputed, the Words, *Certainly, undoubtedly,* or any others that give
the Air of Positiveness to an Opinion; but rather say, *I conceive,* or *I
apprehend* a Thing to be so or so, *It appears to me,* or *I should think
it so or so for such and such Reasons,* or *I imagine* it to be so, or *it is
so* if *I am not mistaken.* This Habit I believe has been of great
Advantage to me, when I have had occasion to inculcate my Opinions
and persuade Men into Measures that I have been from time to time
engag'd in promoting. And as the chief Ends of Conversation are to
inform, or to be *informed,* to *please* or to *persuade,* I wish well-meaning sensible Men would not lessen their Power of doing Good by a
Positive assuming Manner that seldom fails to disgust, tends to create
Opposition, and to defeat every one of those Purposes for which Speech
was given us, to wit, giving or receiving Information, or Pleasure: For
if you would *inform,* a positive dogmatical Manner in advancing your
Sentiments, may provoke Contradiction and prevent a candid
Attention. If you wish Information and Improvement from the
Knowledge of others and yet at the same time express yourself as firmly
fix'd in your present Opinions, modest sensible Men, who do not love
Disputation, will probably leave you undisturb'd in the Possession of
your Error; and by such a Manner you can seldom hope to recommend
yourself in *pleasing* your Hearers, or to persuade those whose
Concurrence you desire. Pope[56] says, judiciously.

> *Men should be taught as if you taught them not,*
> *And things unknown propos'd as things forgot,*

---

[55]SHAFTESBURY AND COLLINS: Religious skeptic and philosopher Anthony Ashley Cooper, third
earl of Shaftesbury (1671–1713), who wrote *Characteristics of Men, Manners, Opinions, Times*
(1711). Anthony Collins (1676–1729) was an English theologian who defended the cause of rational
theology in his *Discourse of Free Thinking* (1713).
[56]POPE: Alexander Pope (1688–1744), English poet who wrote *An Essay on Criticism* (1711).

farther recommending it to us,

> *To speak tho' sure, with seeming Diffidence.*[57]

And he might have coupled with this Line that which he has coupled with another, I think less properly,

> *For want of Modesty is want of Sense.*

If you ask why *less properly*, I must repeat the Lines;

> Immodest Words admit of no Defence;
> *For* Want of Modesty is Want of Sense.[58]

Now is not *Want of Sense*, (where a Man is so unfortunate as to want it) some Apology for his *Want of Modesty?* and would not the Lines stand more justly thus?

> Immodest Words admit *but this* Defence,
> That Want of Modesty is Want of Sense.

This however I should submit to better Judgments.

My Brother had in 1720 or 21, begun to print a Newspaper. It was the second[59] that appear'd in America, and was called *The New England Courant*. The only one before it, was *The Boston News Letter*. I remember his being dissuaded by some of his Friends from the Undertaking, as not likely to succeed, one Newspaper being in their Judgment enough for America. At this time 1771 there are not less than five and twenty. He went on however with the Undertaking, and after having work'd in composing the Types and printing off the Sheets I was employ'd to carry the Papers[60] thro' the Streets to the Customers. He had some ingenious Men among his Friends who amus'd themselves by writing little Pieces for this Paper, which gain'd it Credit, and made it more in Demand; and these Gentlemen often visited us. Hearing their Conversations, and their Accounts of the Approbation their Papers were receiv'd with, I was excited

---

[57]TO SPEAK THO' SURE, WITH SEEMING DIFFIDENCE: Franklin quotes Pope from memory. The lines read, "Men must be taught as if you taught them not, and things unknown propos'd as things forgot" and "And speak, tho' sure, with seeming Diffidence."

[58]IMMODEST WORDS ADMIT...IS WANT OF SENSE: These lines are taken from English poet Wentworth Dillon, 4th earl of Roscommon (1633? –1685), not from Alexander Pope, appearing in *Essay on Translated Verse* (1684), lines 113–114. The second line should read, "For want of decency is want of sense."

[59]IT WAS THE SECOND: James Franklin's newspaper was actually the fifth published in America and the third Boston paper, appearing on August 7, 1721. The four preceding newspapers were: *Publick Occurrences, Both Foreign and Domestick* (1690), *Boston News-Letter* (1704), the *Boston Gazette* (1719), and the *Weekly Mercury* (1719).

[60]PAPERS: *The Silence Dogood Letters* (April 12-October 8 1722), a series of essays penned by a fictitious and opinionated widow of a country minister.

to try my Hand among them. But being still a Boy, and suspecting that my Brother would object to printing any Thing of mine in his Paper if he knew it to be mine, I contriv'd to disguise my Hand, and writing an anonymous Paper I put it in at Night under the Door of the Printing-House.

It was found in the Morning and communicated to his Writing Friends when they call'd in as Usual. They read it, commented on it in my Hearing, and I had the exquisite Pleasure, of finding it met with their Approbation, and that in their different Guesses at the Author none were named but Men of some Character among us for Learning and Ingenuity. I suppose now that I was rather lucky in my Judges: And that perhaps they were not really so very good ones as I then esteem'd them. Encourag'd however by this, I wrote and convey'd in the same Way to the Press several more Papers, which were equally approv'd, and I kept my Secret till my small Fund of Sense for such Performances was pretty well exhausted, and then I discovered[61] it; when I began to be considered a little more by my Brother's Acquaintance, and in a manner that did not quite please him, as he thought, probably with reason, that it tended to make me too vain. And perhaps this might be one Occasion of the Differences that we began to have about this Time. Tho' a Brother, he considered himself as my Master, and me as his Apprentice; and accordingly expected the same Services from me as he would from another; while I thought he demean'd me too much in some he requir'd of me, who from a Brother expected more Indulgence, Our Disputes were often brought before our Father, and I fancy I was either generally in the right, or else a better Pleader, because the Judgment was generally in my favor. But my Brother was passionate and had often beaten me, which I took extremely amiss; and thinking my Apprenticeship very tedious, I was continually wishing for some Opportunity of shortening it, which at length offered in a manner unexpected.[62]

One of the Pieces in our Newspaper, on some political Point which I have now forgotten, gave Offence to the Assembly. He was taken up, censur'd and imprison'd[63] for a Month by the Speaker's Warrant, I suppose because he would not discover his Author. I too was taken up and examin'd before

---

[61]DISCOVERED: Revealed.

[62]MANNER UNEXPECTED: "I fancy his harsh and tyrannical Treatment of me, might be as a means of impressing me with that Aversion to arbitrary Power that has stuck to me thro' my whole Life" [Franklin's note].

[63]IMPRISON'D: On June 11, 1722, James Franklin published an editorial criticizing the government for its failure to curtail the activities of pirates harassing merchant ships off the New England coast, hinting at a possible collusion. He was sent to prison for almost a month. When James Franklin was forbidden to publish his newspaper, he changed the masthead to bear the name of his brother Benjamin (whom he formally discharged as his apprentice) as the editor and publisher. After an argument with James, the now legally free thirteen year old Benjamin ran away to New York and then to Philadelphia.

the Council; but tho' I did not give them any Satisfaction, they contented themselves with admonishing me, and dismiss'd me; considering me perhaps as an Apprentice who was bound to keep his Master's Secrets. During my Brother's Confinement, which I resented a good deal, notwithstanding our private Differences, I had the Management of the Paper, and I made bold to give our Rulers some Rubs[64] in it, which my Brother took very kindly, while others began to consider me in an unfavorable Light, as a young Genius that had a Turn for Libeling and Satire.[65] My Brother's Discharge was accompanied with an Order of the House, (a very odd one) *that James Franklin should no longer print the Paper called the New England Courant.* There was a Consultation held in our Printing-House among his Friends what he should do in this Case. Some propos'd to evade the Order by changing the Name of the Paper; but my Brother seeing Inconveniences in that, it was finally concluded on as a better Way, to let it be printed for the future under the Name of *Benjamin Franklin.* And to avoid the Censure of the Assembly that might fall on him, as still printing it by his Apprentice, the Contrivance was, that my old Indenture should be return'd to me with a full Discharge on the Back of it, to be shown on Occasion; but to secure to him the Benefit of my Service I was to sign new Indentures for the Remainder of the Term, which were to be kept private. A very flimsy Scheme it was, but however it was immediately executed, and the Paper went on accordingly under my Name for several Months.[66] At length a fresh Difference arising between my Brother and me, I took upon me to assert my Freedom, presuming that he would not venture to produce the new Indentures. It was not fair in me to take this Advantage, and this I therefore reckon one of the first Errata[67] of my Life: But the Unfairness of it weigh'd little with me, when under the Impressions of Resentment, for the Blows his Passion too often urg'd him to bestow upon me. Tho' he was otherwise not an ill-natur'd Man: Perhaps I was too saucy and provoking.

When he found I would leave him, he took care to prevent my getting Employment in any other Printing-House of the Town, by going round and speaking to every Master, who accordingly refus'd to give me Work. I then thought of going to New York as the nearest Place where there was a Printer: and I was the rather inclin'd to leave Boston, when I reflected that I had already made myself a little obnoxious to the governing Party;

---

[64]RULERS SOME RUBS: Insults.
[65]TURN FOR LIBELING AND SATIRE: Satirizing.
[66]NAME FOR SEVERAL MONTHS: *The New England Courant* continued to be published under Benjamin's name until 1726.
[67]ERRATA: A printer's term for "errors." (Latin)

and from the arbitrary Proceedings of the Assembly in my Brother's Case it was likely I might if I stay'd soon bring myself into Scrapes; and farther that my indiscreet Disputations about Religion began to make me pointed at with Horror by good People, as an Infidel or Atheist; I determin'd on the Point: but my Father now siding with my Brother, I was sensible that if I attempted to go openly, Means would be used to prevent me. My Friend Collins therefore undertook to manage a little for me. He agreed with the Captain of a New York Sloop for my Passage, under the Notion of my being a young Acquaintance of his that had got a naughty Girl with Child, whose Friends would compel me to marry her, and therefore I could not appear or come away publicly. So I sold some of my Books to raise a little Money, was taken on board privately, and as we had a fair Wind, in three Days I found myself in New York near 300 Miles from home, a Boy of but 17, without the least Recommendation to or Knowledge of any Person in the Place, and with very little Money in my Pocket.

My Inclinations for the Sea, were by this time worn out, or I might now have gratified them. But having a Trade, and supposing myself a pretty good Workman, I offer'd my Service to the Printer of the Place, old Mr. William Bradford.[68] He could give me no Employment, having little to do, and Help enough already: But, says he, my Son at Philadelphia has lately lost his principal Hand, Aquila Rose, by Death. If you go thither I believe he may employ you. Philadelphia was 100 Miles farther. I set out, however, in a Boat for Amboy;[69] leaving my Chest and Things to follow me round by Sea. In crossing the Bay we met with a Squall that tore our rotten Sails to pieces, prevented our getting into the Kill,[70] and drove us upon Long Island. In our Way a drunken Dutchman, who was a Passenger too, fell overboard; when he was sinking I reach'd thro' the Water to his shock Pate[71] and drew him up so that we got him in again. His Ducking sober'd him a little, and he went to sleep, taking first out of his Pocket a Book which he desir'd I would dry for him. It prov'd to be my old favorite Author Bunyan's Pilgrim's Progress in Dutch, finely printed on good Paper with copper Cuts,[72] a Dress better than I had ever seen it wear in its own Language. I have since found that it has been translated into most of the Languages of Europe, and suppose it has been

---

[68]WILLIAM BRADFORD: William Bradford (1663–1752) was an American printer and the father of Andrew Bradford (1686–1742), editor of the Philadelphia newspaper the *American Weekly Mercury* (see note 59).
[69]AMBOY: Perth Amboy, New Jersey.
[70]KILL: The narrow channel that separates New York's Staten Island from New Jersey.
[71]SHOCK PATE: His shaggy head of hair.
[72]CUTS: Engravings.

more generally read than any other Book except perhaps the Bible. Honest John was the first that I know of who mix'd Narration and Dialogue, a Method of Writing very engaging to the Reader, who in the most interesting Parts finds himself as it were brought into the Company, and present at the Discourse. Defoe in his Crusoe, his Moll Flanders, Religious Courtship, Family Instructor,[73] and other Pieces, has imitated it with Success. And Richardson has done the same in his Pamela,[74] etc.

When we drew near the Island we found it was at a Place where there could be no Landing, there being a great Surf on the stony Beach. So we dropped Anchor and swung round towards the Shore. Some People came down to the Water Edge and hallow'd to us, as we did to them. But the Wind was so high and the Surf so loud, that we could not hear so as to understand each other. There were Canoes on the Shore, and we made Signs and hallow'd that they should fetch us, but they either did not understand us, or thought it impracticable. So they went away, and Night coming on, we had no Remedy but to wait till the Wind should abate, and in the mean time the Boatman and I concluded to sleep if we could, and so crowded into the Scuttle[75] with the Dutchman who was still wet, and the Spray beating over the Head of our Boat, leak'd thro' to us, so that we were soon almost as wet as he. In this Manner we lay all Night with very little Rest. But the Wind abating the next Day, we made a Shift to reach Amboy before Night, having been 30 hours on the Water without Victuals, or any Drink but a Bottle of filthy Rum: The Water we sail'd on being salt.

In the Evening I found myself very feverish, and went ill to Bed. But having read somewhere that cold Water drank plentifully was good for a Fever, I follow'd the Prescription, sweat plentifully most of the Night, my Fever left me, and in the Morning crossing the Ferry, proceeded on my Journey, on foot, having 50 Miles to Burlington,[76] where I was told I should find Boats that would carry me the rest of the Way to Philadelphia.

It rain'd very hard all the Day, I was thoroughly soak'd, and by Noon a good deal tir'd, so I stopped at a poor Inn, where I stayed all Night, beginning now to wish I had never left home. I cut so miserable a Figure

---

[73]DEFOE IN HIS CRUSOE, HIS MOLL FLANDERS, RELIGIOUS COURTSHIP, FAMILY INSTRUC-TOR: Daniel Defoe published the *Family Instructor* in 1715, *Robinson Crusoe* in 1719, and *Moll Flanders* and *Religious Courtship* in 1722.
[74]RICHARDSON HAS DONE THE SAME IN HIS PAMELA: English novelist Samuel Richardson (1689–1761) published *Pamela; or, Virtue Rewarded* in 1740. In 1744, Franklin reprinted Richardson's novel, making it the first novel to be published in America.
[75]SCUTTLE: A hole or opening in a ship's deck with movable cover or lid.
[76]BURLINGTON: In New Jersey, about eighteen miles north of Philadelphia.

too, that I found by the Questions ask'd me I was suspected to be some runaway Servant, and in danger of being taken up on that Suspicion. However I proceeded the next Day, and got in the Evening to an Inn within 8 or 10 Miles of Burlington, kept by one Dr. Browne.[77]

He entered into Conversation with me while I took some Refreshment, and finding I had read a little, became very sociable and friendly. Our Acquaintance continu'd as long as he liv'd. He had been, I imagine, an itinerant Doctor, for there was no Town in England, or Country in Europe, of which he could not give a very particular Account. He had some Letters,[78] and was ingenious, but much of an Unbeliever, and wickedly undertook some Years after to travesty the Bible in doggerel Verse as Cotton had done Virgil.[79] By this means he set many of the Facts in a very ridiculous Light, and might have hurt weak minds if his Work had been publish'd: but it never was. At his House I lay that Night, and the next Morning reach'd Burlington.—But had the Mortification to find that the regular Boats were gone a little before my coming, and no other expected to go till Tuesday, this being Saturday. Wherefore I return'd to an old Woman in the Town of whom I had bought Gingerbread to eat on the Water, and ask'd her Advice; she invited me to lodge at her House till a Passage by Water should offer; and being tired with my foot Traveling, I accepted the Invitation. She understanding I was a Printer, would have had me stay at that Town and follow my Business, being ignorant of the Stock necessary to begin with. She was very hospitable, gave me a Dinner of Ox Cheek with great Goodwill, accepting only of a Pot of Ale in return. And I thought myself fix'd till Tuesday should come. However walking in the Evening by the Side of the River a Boat came by, which I found was going towards Philadelphia with several People in her. They took me in, and as there was no Wind, we row'd all the Way; and about Midnight not having yet seen the City, some of the Company were confident we must have pass'd it, and would row no farther, the others knew not where we were, so we put towards the Shore, got into a Creek, landed near an old Fence with the Rails of which we made a Fire, the Night being cold, in October, and there we remain'd till Daylight. Then one of the Company knew the Place to be Cooper's Creek a little above Philadelphia, which we saw as soon as we got out of the Creek, and arriv'd there about 8 or 9 aClock, on the Sunday morning, and landed at the Market Street Wharf.

[77]DR. BROWNE: John Browne (c. 1667–1737), a physician and innkeeper in Burlington.
[78]LETTERS: Education.
[79]VIRGIL: Charles Cotton's (1630–1687) *Scarronides* (1664) parodied the Roman poet Virgil's (70–19 BCE) epic, the *Aeneid*.

I have been the more particular in this Description of my Journey, and shall be so of my first Entry into that City, that you may in your Mind compare such unlikely Beginning with the Figure I have since made there. I was in my working Dress, my best Clothes being to come round by Sea. I was dirty from my Journey; my Pockets were stuff'd out with Shirts and Stockings; I knew no Soul, nor where to look for Lodging. I was fatigu'd with Traveling, Rowing and Want of Rest. I was very hungry, and my whole Stock of Cash consisted of a Dutch Dollar and about a Shilling in Copper. The latter I gave the People of the Boat for my Passage, who at first refus'd it on Account of my Rowing; but I insisted on their taking it, a Man being sometimes more generous when he has but a little Money than when he has plenty, perhaps thro' Fear of being thought to have but little. Then I walk'd up the Street, gazing about, till near the Market House I met a Boy with Bread. I had made many a Meal on Bread, and inquiring where he got it, I went immediately to the Baker's he directed me to in Second Street; and ask'd for Biscuit, intending such as we had in Boston, but they it seems were not made in Philadelphia, then I ask'd for a three-penny Loaf, and was told they had none such: so not considering or knowing the Difference of Money and the greater Cheapness nor the Names of his Bread, I bad him give me three pennyworth of any sort. He gave me accordingly three great Puffy Rolls. I was surpris'd at the Quantity, but took it, and having no Room in my Pockets, walk'd off, with a Roll under each Arm, and eating the other. Thus I went up Market Street as far as Fourth Street, passing by the Door of Mr. Read, my future Wife's Father, when she standing at the Door saw me, and thought I made as I certainly did a most awkward ridiculous Appearance. Then I turn'd and went down Chestnut Street and part of Walnut Street, eating my Roll all the Way, and coming round found myself again at Market Street Wharf, near the Boat I came in, to which I went for a Drought of the River Water, and being fill'd with one of my Rolls, gave the other two to a Woman and her Child that came down the River in the Boat with us and were waiting to go farther. Thus refresh'd I walk'd again up the Street, which by this time had many clean dress'd People in it who were all walking the same Way; I join'd them, and thereby was led into the great Meeting House of the Quakers near the Market. I sat down among them, and after looking round a while and hearing nothing said, being very drowsy thro' Labor and want of Rest the preceding Night, I fell fast asleep, and continu'd so till the Meeting broke up, when one was kind enough to rouse me. This was therefore the first House I was in or slept in, in Philadelphia.

Walking again down towards the River, and looking in the Faces of People, I met a young Quaker Man whose Countenance I lik'd, and accosting him requested he would tell me where a Stranger could get Lodging. We were then near the Sign of the Three Mariners. Here, says he, is one Place that entertains Strangers, but it is not a reputable House; if thee wilt walk with me, I'll show thee a better. He brought me to the Crooked Billet in Water Street. Here I got a Dinner. And while I was eating it, several sly Questions were ask'd me, as it seem'd to be suspected from my youth and Appearance, that I might be some Runaway. After Dinner my Sleepiness return'd: and being shown to a Bed, I lay down without undressing, and slept till Six in the Evening; was call'd to Supper; went to Bed again very early and slept soundly till the next Morning. Then I made myself as tidy as I could, and went to Andrew Bradford the Printer's. I found in the Shop the old Man his Father, whom I had seen at New York, and who traveling on horse back had got to Philadelphia before me. He introduc'd me to his Son, who receiv'd me civilly, gave me a Breakfast, but told me he did not at present want a Hand, being lately supplied with one. But there was another Printer in town lately set up, one Keimer,[80] who perhaps might employ me; if not, I should be welcome to lodge at his House, and he would give me a little Work to do now and then till fuller Business should offer.

The old Gentleman said, he would go with me to the new Printer: And when we found him, Neighbor, says Bradford, I have brought to see you a young Man of your Business, perhaps you may want such a One. He ask'd me a few Questions, put a Composing Stick[81] in my Hand to see how I work'd, and then said he would employ me soon, tho' he had just then nothing for me to do. And taking old Bradford whom he had never seen before, to be one of the Townspeople that had a Goodwill for him, enter'd into a Conversation on his present Undertaking and Prospects; while Bradford not discovering that he was the other Printer's Father; on Keimer's Saying he expected soon to get the greatest Part of the Business into his own Hands, drew him on by artful Questions and starting little Doubts, to explain all his Views, what Interest he relied on, and in what manner he intended to proceed. I who stood by and heard all, saw immediately that one of them was a crafty old Sophister,[82] and the other a mere Novice. Bradford left me with Keimer, who was greatly surpris'd when I told him who the old Man was.

---

[80]KEIMER: Samuel Keimer (c. 1688–1742).
[81]COMPOSING STICK: An instrument of adjustable width used to set type before placing it in the galley tray.
[82]SOPHISTER: Experienced trickster.

Keimer's Printing-House I found, consisted of an old shatter'd Press and one small worn-out Font[83] of English, which he was then using himself, composing in it an Elegy on Aquila Rose[84] before-mentioned, an ingenious young Man of excellent Character much respected in the Town, Clerk of the Assembly, and a pretty Poet. Keimer made Verses, too, but very indifferently. He could not be said to write them, for his Manner was to compose them in the Types directly out of his Head; so there being no Copy, but one Pair of Cases,[85] and the Elegy likely to require all the Letter, no one could help him. I endeavor'd to put his Press (which he had not yet us'd, and of which he understood nothing) into Order fit to be work'd with; and promising to come and print off his Elegy as soon as he should have got it ready, I return'd to Bradford's who gave me a little Job to do for the present, and there I lodged and dieted.[86] A few Days after Keimer sent for me to print off the Elegy. And now he had got another Pair of Cases, and a Pamphlet to reprint, on which he set me to work.

These two Printers I found poorly qualified for their Business. Bradford had not been bred to it, and was very illiterate; and Keimer tho' something of a Scholar, was a mere Compositor,[87] knowing nothing of Presswork. He had been one of the French Prophets[88] and could act their enthusiastic Agitations. At this time he did not profess any particular Religion, but something of all on occasion; was very ignorant of the World, and had, as I afterwards found, a good deal of the Knave in his Composition. He did not like my Lodging at Bradford's while I work'd with him. He had a House indeed, but without Furniture, so he could not lodge me: But he got me a Lodging at Mr. Read's before-mentioned, who was the Owner of his House. And my Chest and Clothes being come by this time, I made rather a more respectable Appearance in the Eyes of Miss Read, than I had done when she first happen'd to see me eating my Roll in the Street.

I began now to have some Acquaintance among the young People of the Town, that were Lovers of Reading with whom I spent my Evenings

[83]WORN-OUT FONT OF ENGLISH: Oversized typeface.
[84]ELEGY ON AQUILA ROSE: Aquila Rose (1695–1723) was a journeyman printer who had worked for Andrew Bradford. Later, Franklin would take Rose's son, Joseph, as an apprentice.
[85]PAIR OF CASES: Two shallow cases that hold upper and lower case typeface.
[86]DIETED: Boarded.
[87]COMPOSITOR: Typesetter.
[88]FRENCH PROPHETS: After French King Louis XIV (1638–1715) revoked the Edict of Nantes in 1685 (which had granted religious freedom to the French Protestants), a small group of Huguenots fled to the Cevennes mountains where they experienced miracles of prophecy and speaking in tongues. Called the Camisards, they were persecuted by the king and many fled to England between 1601-1610, where they were mockingly referred to as the French Prophets. Others, such as the compositor Franklin mentions, fled to America.

very pleasantly and gaining Money by my Industry and Frugality, I lived very agreeably, forgetting Boston as much as I could, and not desiring that any there should know where I resided except my Friend Collins who was in my Secret, and kept it when I wrote to him. At length an Incident happened that sent me back again much sooner than I had intended.

I had a Brother-in-law, Robert Homes,[89] Master of a Sloop that traded between Boston and Delaware. He being at New Castle 40 Miles below Philadelphia, heard there of me, and wrote me a Letter, mentioning the Concern of my Friends in Boston at my abrupt Departure, assuring me of their Goodwill to me, and that everything would be accommodated to my Mind if I would return, to which he exhorted me very earnestly. I wrote an Answer to his Letter, thank'd him for his Advice, but stated my Reasons for quitting Boston fully, and in such a Light as to convince him I was not so wrong as he had apprehended. Sir William Keith[90] Governor of the Province, was then at New Castle, and Captain Homes happening to be in Company with him when my Letter came to hand, spoke to him of me, and show'd him the Letter. The Governor read it, and seem'd surpris'd when he was told my Age. He said I appear'd a young Man of promising Parts, and therefore should be encouraged: The Printers at Philadelphia were wretched ones, and if I would set up there, he made no doubt I should succeed; for his Part, he would procure me the public Business, and do me every other Service in his Power. This my Brother-in-Law afterwards told me in Boston. But I knew as yet nothing of it; when one Day Keimer and I being at Work together near the Window, we saw the Governor and another Gentleman (which prov'd to be Colonel French, of New Castle) finely dress'd, come directly across the Street to our House, and heard them at the Door.

Keimer ran down immediately, thinking it a Visit to him. But the Governor enquir'd for me, came up, and with a Condescension[91] and Politeness I had been quite unus'd to, made me many Compliments, desired to be acquainted with me, blam'd me kindly for not having made myself known to him when I first came to the Place, and would have me away with him to the Tavern where he was going with Colonel French to taste as he said some excellent Madeira. I was not a little surpris'd, and Keimer star'd like a Pig poison'd. I went however with the Governor

[89]ROBERT HOMES: Homes (b.1694) was the husband of Franklin's sister Mary. A ship's captain, he died at sea sometime before 1743.
[90]SIR WILLIAM KEITH: William Keith (1687–1749) was lieutenant-governor of Pennsylvania and Delaware. After his replacement as governor in March of 1728, he left the province, fleeing secretly from New Castle, Delaware to England to avoid his creditors.
[91]CONDESCENSION: Disregard for social status or rank.

and Colonel French, to a Tavern the Corner of Third Street, and over the Madeira he propos'd my Setting up my Business, laid before me the Probabilities of Success, and both he and Colonel French assur'd me I should have their Interest and Influence in procuring the Public-Business of both Governments. On my doubting whether my Father would assist me in it, Sir William said he would give me a Letter to him, in which he would state the Advantages, and he did not doubt of prevailing with him. So it was concluded I should return to Boston in the first Vessel with the Governor's Letter recommending me to my Father.

In the meantime the Intention was to be kept secret, and I went on working with Keimer as usual, the Governor sending for me now and then to dine with him, a very great Honor I thought it, and conversing with me in the most affable, familiar, and friendly manner imaginable. About the End of April 1724, a little Vessel offer'd for Boston. I took Leave of Keimer as going to see my Friends. The Governor gave me an ample Letter, saying many flattering things of me to my Father, and strongly recommending the Project of my setting up at Philadelphia, as a Thing that must make my Fortune. We struck on a Shoal in going down the Bay and sprung a Leak, we had a blustring time at Sea, and were oblig'd to pump almost continually, at which I took my Turn. We arriv'd safe however at Boston in about a Fortnight. I had been absent Seven Months and my Friends had heard nothing of me, for my Brother Homes was not yet return'd; and had not written about me. My unexpected Appearance surpris'd the Family; all were however very glad to see me and made me Welcome, except my Brother.

I went to see him at his Printing-House: I was better dress'd than ever while in his Service, having a genteel new Suit from Head to foot, a Watch, and my Pockets lin'd with near Five Pounds Sterling in Silver. He receiv'd me not very frankly, look'd me all over, and turn'd to his Work again. The Journeymen were inquisitive where I had been, what sort of a Country it was, and how I lik'd it? I prais'd it much, and the happy Life I led in it; expressing strongly my Intention of returning to it; and one of them asking what kind of Money we had there, I produc'd a handful of Silver and spread it before them, which was a kind of Raree-Show[92] they had not been us'd to, Paper being the Money of Boston. Then I took an Opportunity of letting them see my Watch: and lastly, (my Brother still grum and sullen) I gave them a Piece of Eight to drink[93] and took my Leave. This Visit of mine offended him extremely. For when

[92]RAREE-SHOW: Sidewalk peep show in a box.
[93]PIECE OF EIGHT TO DRINK: A Spanish coin marked with a figure 8 that they used to buy drinks.

my Mother some time after spoke to him of a Reconciliation, and of her Wishes to see us on good Terms together, and that we might live for the future as Brothers, he said, I had insulted him in such a Manner before his People that he could never forget or forgive it. In this however he was mistaken.

My Father receiv'd the Governor's Letter with some apparent Surprise; but said little of it to me for some Days; when Captain Homes returning, he show'd it to him, ask'd if he knew Keith, and what kind of a Man he was: Adding his Opinion that he must be of small Discretion, to think of setting a Boy up in Business who wanted yet 3 Years of being at Man's Estate. Homes said what he could in favor of the Project; but my Father was clear in the Impropriety of it; and at last gave a flat Denial to it. Then he wrote a civil Letter to Sir William thanking him for the Patronage he had so kindly offered me, but declining to assist me as yet in Setting up, I being in his Opinion too young to be trusted with the Management of a Business so important; and for which the Preparation must be so expensive.

My Friend and Companion Collins, who was a Clerk at the Post-Office, pleas'd with the Account I gave him of my new Country, determin'd to go thither also: And while I waited for my Father's Determination, he set out before me by Land to Rhode Island, leaving his Books which were a pretty Collection of Mathematics and Natural Philosophy, to come with mine and me to New York where he propos'd to wait for me. My Father, tho' he did not approve Sir William's Proposition, was yet pleas'd that I had been able to obtain so advantageous a Character from a Person of such Note where I had resided, and that I had been so industrious and careful as to equip myself so handsomely in so short a time: therefore seeing no Prospect of an Accommodation between my Brother and me, he gave his Consent to my Returning again to Philadelphia, advis'd me to behave respectfully to the People there, endeavor to obtain the general Esteem, and avoid lampooning and libeling to which he thought I had too much Inclination; telling me, that by steady Industry and a prudent Parsimony, I might save enough by the time I was One and Twenty to set me up, and that if I came near the Matter he would help me out with the Rest. This was all I could obtain, except some small Gifts as Tokens of his and my Mother's Love, when I embark'd again for New York, now with their Approbation and their Blessing.

The Sloop putting in at Newport, Rhode Island, I visited my Brother John, who had been married and settled there some Years. He received me very affectionately, for he always lov'd me. A Friend of his, one

Vernon, having some Money due to him in Pennsylvania, about 35 Pounds Currency, desired I would receive it for him, and keep it till I had his Directions what to remit it in. Accordingly he gave me an Order. This afterwards occasion'd me a good deal of Uneasiness. At Newport we took in a Number of Passengers for New York: Among which were two young Women, Companions, and a grave, sensible Matron-like Quaker-Woman with her Attendants. I had shown an obliging Readiness to do her some little Services which impress'd her I suppose with a degree of Goodwill towards me. Therefore when she saw a daily growing Familiarity between me and the two Young Women, which they appear'd to encourage, she took me aside and said, Young Man, I am concern'd for thee, as thou has no Friend with thee, and seems not to know much of the World, or of the Snares Youth is expos'd to; depend upon it those are very bad Women, I can see it in all their Actions, and if thee art not upon thy Guard, they will draw thee into some Danger: they are Strangers to thee, and I advise thee in a friendly Concern for thy Welfare, to have no Acquaintance with them. As I seem'd at first not to think so ill of them as she did, she mention'd some Things she had observ'd and heard that had escap'd my Notice; but now convinc'd me she was right. I thank'd her for her kind Advice, and promis'd to follow it. When we arriv'd at New York, they told me where they liv'd, and invited me to come and see them: but I avoided it. And it was well I did: For the next Day, the Captain miss'd a Silver Spoon and some other Things that had been taken out of his Cabin, and knowing that these were a Couple of Strumpets, he got a Warrant to search their Lodgings, found the stolen Goods, and had the Thieves punish'd. So tho' we had escap'd a sunken Rock which we scrap'd upon in the Passage, I thought this Escape of rather more Importance to me.

At New York I found my Friend Collins, who had arriv'd there some Time before me. We had been intimate from Children,[94] and had read the same Books together. But he had the Advantage of more time for Reading, and Studying and a wonderful Genius for Mathematical Learning in which he far outstripped me. While I liv'd in Boston most of my Hours of Leisure for Conversation were spent with him, and he continu'd a sober as well as an industrious Lad; was much respected for his Learning by several of the Clergy and other Gentlemen, and seem'd to promise making a good Figure in Life: but during my Absence he had acquir'd a Habit of Sotting with Brandy; and I found by his own Account and what I heard from others, that he had been drunk every day since his Arrival

[94]FROM CHILDREN: Since we were children.

at New York, and behav'd very oddly. He had gam'd too and lost his Money, so that I was oblig'd to discharge[95] his Lodgings, and defray his Expences to and at Philadelphia: Which prov'd extremely inconvenient to me. The then Governor of New York, Burnet,[96] Son of Bishop Burnet, hearing from the Captain that a young Man, one of his Passengers, had a great many Books, desired he would bring me to see him. I waited upon him accordingly, and should have taken Collins with me but that he was not sober. The Governor treated me with great Civility, show'd me his Library, which was a very large one, and we had a good deal of Conversation about Books and Authors. This was the second Governor who had done me the Honor to take Notice of me, which to a poor Boy like me was very pleasing.

We proceeded to Philadelphia. I received on the Way Vernon's Money, without which we could hardly have finish'd our Journey. Collins wish'd to be employ'd in some Counting House; but whether they discover'd his Dramming by his Breath, or by his Behavior, tho' he had some Recommendations, he met with no Success in any Application, and continu'd Lodging and Boarding at the same House with me and at my Expense. Knowing I had that Money of Vernon's he was continually borrowing of me, still promising Repayment as soon as he should be in Business. At length he had got so much of it, that I was distress'd to think what I should do, in case of being call'd on to remit it. His Drinking continu'd, about which we sometimes quarrel'd, for when a little intoxicated he was very fractious. Once in a Boat on the Delaware with some other young Men, he refused to row in his Turn: I will be row'd home, says he. We will not row you, says I. You must, says he, or stay all Night on the Water, just as you please. The others said, Let us row; What signifies it? But my Mind being soured with his other Conduct, I continu'd to refuse. So he swore he would make me row, or throw me overboard; and coming along stepping on the Thwarts[97] towards me, when he came up and struck at me, I clapped my Hand under his Crotch, and rising, pitch'd him headforemost into the River. I knew he was a good Swimmer, and so was under little Concern about him; but before he could get round to lay hold of the Boat, we had with a few Strokes pull'd her out of his Reach. And ever when he drew near the Boat, we ask'd if he would row, striking a few Strokes to slide her away from him. He was ready to die with Vexation, and obstinately would not promise to row; however seeing him

---

[95]TO DISCHARGE: Pay his bills.
[96]BURNET: William Burnet (1688–1729), governor of New York and New Jersey from 1720–1728 and of Massachusetts from 1728–1729.
[97]THWARTS: Oarsman's seat.

at last beginning to tire, we lifted him in; and brought him home dripping wet in the Evening. We hardly exchang'd a civil Word afterwards; and a West India Captain who had a Commission to procure a Tutor for the Sons of a Gentleman at Barbados, happening to meet with him, agreed to carry him thither. He left me then, promising to remit me the first Money he should receive in order to discharge the Debt. But I never heard of him after.

The Breaking into this Money of Vernon's was one of the first great Errata of my Life. And this Affair show'd that my Father was not much out in his Judgment when he suppos'd me too Young to manage Business of Importance. But Sir William, on reading his Letter, said he was too prudent. There was great Difference in Persons, and Discretion did not always accompany Years, nor was Youth always without it. And since he will not set you up, says he, I will do it myself. Give me an Inventory of the Things necessary to be had from England, and I will send for them. You shall repay me when you are able; I am resolv'd to have a good Printer here, and I am sure you must succeed. This was spoken with such an Appearance of Cordiality, that I had not the least doubt of his meaning what he said. I had hitherto kept the Proposition of my Setting up a Secret in Philadelphia, and I still kept it. Had it been known that I depended on the Governor, probably some Friend that knew him better would have advis'd me not to rely on him, as I afterwards heard it as his known Character to be liberal of Promises which he never meant to keep. Yet unsolicited as he was by me, how could I think his generous Offers insincere? I believ'd him one of the best Men in the World.

I presented him an Inventory of a little Printing-House, amounting by my Computation to about 100 Pounds Sterling. He lik'd it, but ask'd me if my being on the Spot in England to choose the Types and see that everything was good of the kind, might not be of some Advantage. Then, says he, when there, you may make Acquaintances and establish Correspondences in the Bookselling, and Stationery Way. I agreed that this might be advantageous. Then says he, get yourself ready to go with Annis;[98] which was the annual Ship, and the only one at that Time usually passing between London and Philadelphia. But it would be some Months before Annis sail'd, so I continu'd working with Keimer, fretting about the Money Collins had got from me, and in daily Apprehensions of being call'd upon by Vernon, which however did not happen for some Years after.

---

[98]ANNIS: Thomas Annis was captain of the *London Hope*, the ship on which Franklin sailed to London in 1724.

I believe I have omitted mentioning that in my first Voyage from Boston, being becalm'd off Block Island,[99] our People set about catching Cod and haul'd up a great many. Hitherto I had stuck to my Resolution of not eating animal Food; and on this Occasion, I consider'd with my Master Tryon, the taking every Fish as a kind of unprovok'd Murder, since none of them had or ever could do us any Injury that might justify the Slaughter. All this seem'd very reasonable. But I had formerly been a great Lover of Fish, and when this came hot out of the Frying Pan, it smelt admirably well. I balanc'd some time between Principle and Inclination: till I recollected, that when the Fish were opened, I saw smaller Fish taken out of their Stomachs: Then, thought I, if you eat one another, I don't see why we mayn't eat you. So I din'd upon Cod very heartily and continu'd to eat with other People, returning only now and then occasionally to a vegetable Diet. So convenient a thing it is to be a *reasonable Creature*, since it enables one to find or make a Reason for everything one has a mind to do.

Keimer and I liv'd on a pretty good familiar Footing and agreed tolerably well: for he suspected nothing of my Setting up. He retain'd a great deal of his old Enthusiasms, and lov'd an Argumentation. We therefore had many Disputations. I us'd to work him so with my Socratic Method,[100] and had trapann'd him so often by Questions apparently so distant from any Point we had in hand, and yet by degrees led to the Point, and brought him into Difficulties and Contradictions, that at last he grew ridiculously cautious, and would hardly answer me the most common Question, without asking first, *What do you intend to infer from that?* However it gave him so high an Opinion of my Abilities in the Confuting Way, that he seriously propos'd my being his Colleague in a Project he had of setting up a new Sect. He was to preach the Doctrines, and I was to confound all Opponents. When he came to explain with me upon the Doctrines, I found several Conundrums[101] which I objected to, unless I might have my Way a little too, and introduce some of mine. Keimer wore his Beard at full Length, because somewhere in the Mosaic Law it is said, *thou shalt not mar the Corners of thy Beard.*[102] He likewise kept the seventh-day Sabbath; and these two Points were Essentials with him. I dislik'd both, but agreed to admit them upon Condition of his adopting the Doctrine of using no animal Food. I doubt, says he,

---

[99]BLOCK ISLAND: Off the coast of Rhode Island.
[100]SOCRATIC METHOD: See note 53.
[101]CONUNDRUMS: Puzzles.
[102]THOU SHALT NOT MAR THE CORNERS OF THY BEARD: Leviticus 19:27: "Ye shall not round the corners of your heads, neither shalt thou mar the corners of thy beard."

my Constitution will not bear that. I assur'd him it would, and that he would be the better for it. He was usually a great Glutton, and I promis'd myself some Diversion in half-starving him. He agreed to try the Practice if I would keep him Company. I did so and we held it for three Months. We had our Victuals dress'd and brought to us regularly by a Woman in the Neighborhood, who had from me a List of 40 Dishes to be prepar'd for us at different times, in all which there was neither Fish Flesh nor Fowl, and the Whim suited me the better at this time from the Cheapness of it, not costing us about 18 Pence Sterling each, per Week. I have since kept several Lents[103] most strictly, leaving the common Diet for that, and that for the common, abruptly, without the least Inconvenience: So that I think there is little in the Advice of making those Changes by easy Gradations. I went on pleasantly, but Poor Keimer suffer'd grievously, tir'd of the Project, long'd for the Flesh Pots of Egypt,[104] and order'd a roast Pig. He invited me and two Women Friends to dine with him, but it being brought too soon upon table, he could not resist the Temptation, and ate it all up before we came.

I had made some Courtship during this time to Miss Read. I had a great Respect and Affection for her, and had some Reason to believe she had the same for me: but as I was about to take a long Voyage, and we were both very young, only a little above 18, it was thought most prudent by her Mother to prevent our going too far at present, as a Marriage if it was to take place would be more convenient after my Return, when I should be as I expected set up in my Business. Perhaps too she thought my Expectations not so well founded as I imagined them to be.

My chief Acquaintances at this time were, Charles Osborne, Joseph Watson, and James Ralph;[105] All Lovers of Reading. The two first were Clerks to an eminent Scrivener or Conveyancer in the Town, Charles Brockden;[106] the other was Clerk to a Merchant. Watson was a pious sensible young Man, of great integrity. The others rather more lax in their Principles of Religion, particularly Ralph, who as well as Collins had been unsettled by me, for which they both made me suffer. Osborne was sensible, candid, frank, sincere, and affectionate to his Friends; but in literary Matters too fond of Criticizing. Ralph, was ingenious, genteel in his

---

[103]LENTS: 40-day fasts.
[104]FLESH POTS OF EGYPT: Exodus 16:3: "And the children of Israel said unto them, Would to God we had died by the hand of the LORD in the land of Egypt, when we sat by the flesh pots, and when we did eat bread to the full; for ye have brought us forth into this wilderness, to kill this whole assembly with hunger."
[105]CHARLES OSBORNE, JOSEPH WATSON, AND JAMES RALPH: Osborne's dates are unknown. Watson died around 1728 and Ralph (c.1695–1762) became a political journalist in London.
[106]CHARLES BROCKDEN: Charles Brockden (1683–1769).

Manners, and extremely eloquent; I think I never knew a prettier Talker. Both of them great Admirers of Poetry, and began to try their Hands in little Pieces. Many pleasant Walks we four had together, on Sundays into the Woods near Skuylkill,[107] where we read to one another and conferr'd on what we read. Ralph was inclin'd to pursue the Study of Poetry, not doubting but he might become eminent in it and make his Fortune by it, alledging that the best Poets must when they first began to write, make as many Faults as he did. Osborne dissuaded him, assur'd him he had no Genius for Poetry, and advis'd him to think of nothing beyond the Business he was bred to; that in the mercantile way tho' he had no Stock, he might by his Diligence and Punctuality recommend himself to Employment as a Factor,[108] and in time acquire wherewith to trade on his own Account. I approv'd the amusing oneself with Poetry now and then, so far as to improve one's Language, but no farther. On this it was propos'd that we should each of us at our next Meeting produce a Piece of our own Composing, in order to improve by our mutual Observations, Criticisms and Corrections. As Language and Expression was what we had in View, we excluded all Considerations of Invention,[109] by agreeing that the Task should be a Version of the 18th Psalm, which describes the Descent of a Deity.[110] When the Time of our Meeting drew nigh, Ralph call'd on me first, and let me know his Piece was ready. I told him I had been busy, and having little Inclination had done nothing. He then show'd me his Piece for my Opinion; and I much approv'd it, as it appear'd to me to have great Merit. Now, says he, Osborne never will allow the least Merit in any thing of mine, but makes 1000 Criticisms out of mere Envy. He is not so jealous of you. I wish therefore you would take this Piece, and produce it as yours. I will pretend not to have had time, and so produce nothing. We shall then see what he will say to it. It was agreed, and I immediately transcrib'd it that it might appear in my own hand. We met.

Watson's Performance was read: there were some Beauties in it: but many Defects. Osborne's was read: It was much better. Ralph did it Justice, remark'd some Faults, but applauded the Beauties. He himself had nothing to produce. I was backward, seem'd desirous of being excus'd, had not had sufficient Time to correct; etc., but no Excuse could be admitted, produce I must. It was read and repeated; Watson and

---

[107]SKUYLKILL: Schuylkill River, Philadelphia.
[108]FACTOR: A business agent.
[109]CONSIDERATIONS OF INVENTION: Originality.
[110]DESCENT OF A DEITY: "He bowed the heavens also, and came down: and darkness was under his feet. / And he rode upon a cherub, and did fly: yea, he did fly upon the wings of the wind" (Psalms 18:9-10).

Osborne gave up the Contest; and join'd in applauding it immoderately. Ralph only made some Criticisms and propos'd some Amendments, but I defended my Text. Osborne was against Ralph, and told him he was no better a Critic than Poet; so he dropped the Argument. As they two went home together, Osborne express'd himself still more strongly in favor of what he thought my Production, having restrain'd himself before as he said, lest I should think it Flattery. But who would have imagin'd, says he, that Franklin had been capable of such a Performance; such Painting, such Force! such Fire! He has even improv'd the Original! In his common Conversation, he seems to have no Choice of Words; he hesitates and blunders; and yet, good God, how he writes!

When we next met, Ralph discover'd the Trick we had played him, and Osborne was a little laughed at. This Transaction fix'd Ralph in his Resolution of becoming a Poet. I did all I could to dissuade him from it, but he continu'd scribbling Verses, till *Pope*[111] cur'd him. He became however a pretty good Prose Writer. More of him hereafter. But as I may not have occasion again to mention the other two, I shall just remark here, that Watson died in my Arms a few Years after, much lamented, being the best of our Set. Osborne went to the West Indies, where he became an eminent Lawyer and made Money, but died young. He and I had made a serious Agreement, that the one who happen'd first to die, should if possible make a friendly Visit to the other, and acquaint him how he found things in that separate State. But he never fulfill'd his Promise.

The Governor, seeming to like my Company, had me frequently to his House; and his Setting me up was always mention'd as a fix'd thing. I was to take with me Letters recommendatory to a Number of his Friends, besides the Letter of Credit to furnish me with the necessary Money for purchasing the Press and Types, Paper, etc. For these Letters I was appointed to call at different times, when they were to be ready, but a future time was still named. Thus we went on till the ship whose Departure too had been several times postponed was on the Point of sailing. Then when I call'd to take my Leave and receive the Letters, his Secretary, Dr. Bard,[112] came out to me and said the Governor was extremely busy, in writing, but would be down at New Castle before the Ship, and there the Letters would be delivered to me.

Ralph, tho' married and having one Child, had determined to accompany me in this Voyage. It was thought he intended to establish a

---

[111]POPE: In his 1728 edition of the *Dunciad*, Alexander Pope responded to a disparaging remark Ralph made against him: "Silence, ye Wolves; while Ralph to Cynthia howls. / And makes Night hideous—Answer him ye Owls" (book 3, lines 159–160).
[112]DR. BARD: Patrick Bard (or Baird) came to Philadelphia sometime after 1720.

Correspondence, and obtain Goods to sell on Commission. But I found afterwards, that thro' some Discontent with his Wife's Relations, he purposed to leave her on their Hands, and never return again. Having taken leave of my Friends, and interchang'd some Promises with Miss Read, I left Philadelphia in the Ship, which anchor'd at New Castle. The Governor was there. But when I went to his Lodging, the Secretary came to me from him with the civilest Message in the World, that he could not then see me being engag'd in Business of the utmost Importance, but should send the Letters to me on board, wish'd me heartily a good Voyage and a speedy Return, etc. I return'd on board, a little puzzled, but still not doubting.

Mr. Andrew Hamilton,[113] a famous Lawyer of Philadelphia, had taken Passage in the same Ship for himself and Son: and with Mr. Denham[114] a Quaker Merchant, and Messrs. Onion and Russel Masters of an Iron Work in Maryland, had engag'd the Great Cabin; so that Ralph and I were forc'd to take up with a Berth in the Steerage: And none on board knowing us, were considered as ordinary Persons. But Mr. Hamilton and his Son (it was James, since Governor) return'd from New Castle to Philadelphia the Father being recall'd by a great Free to plead for a seized Ship. And just before we sail'd Colonel French coming on board, and showing me great Respect, I was more taken Notice of, and with my Friend Ralph invited by the other Gentlemen to come into the Cabin, there being now Room. Accordingly we remov'd thither.

Understanding that Colonel French had brought on board the Governor's Dispatches, I ask'd the Captain for those Letters that were to be under my Care. He said all were put into the Bag together; and he could not then come at them; but before we landed in England, I should have an Opportunity of picking them out. So I was satisfied for the present, and we proceeded on our Voyage. We had a sociable Company in the Cabin, and lived uncommonly well, having the Addition of all Mr. Hamilton's Stores, who had laid in plentifully. In this Passage Mr. Denham contracted a Friendship for me that continued during his Life. The Voyage was otherwise not a pleasant one, as we had a great deal of bad Weather.

When we came into the Channel, the Captain kept his Word with me, and gave me an Opportunity of examining the Bag for the Governor's

---

[113]ANDREW HAMILTON: Andrew Hamilton (c. 1678–1741), known as "the Philadelphia Lawyer," was famous for his successful defense of John Peter Zenger, the German publisher of the *New York Weekly Journal* in 1735. Zenger was on trial for libel against New York colonial governor William Cosby. The verdict, handed down by an American jury, helped establish the freedom of the press in the colonies. Hamilton's son, James, became governor of Pennsylvania four times between 1748 and 1773. [114]MR. DENHAM: Thomas Denham (d. 1628) was an English merchant who had settled in America in 1615.

Letters. I found none upon which my Name was put, as under my Care; I pick'd out 6 or 7 that by the Handwriting I thought might be the promis'd Letters, especially as one of them was directed to Basket[115] the King's Printer, and another to some Stationer. We arriv'd in London the 24th of December, 1724. I waited upon the Stationer who came first in my Way, delivering the Letter as from Governor Keith. I don't know such a Person, says he: but opening the Letter, O, this is from Riddlesden;[116] I have lately found him to be a complete Rascal, and I will have nothing to do with him, nor receive any Letters from him. So putting the Letter into my Hand, he turn'd on his Heel and left me to serve some Customer. I was surprised to find these were not the Governor's Letters. And after recollecting and comparing Circumstances, I began to doubt his Sincerity. I found my Friend Denham, and opened the whole Affair to him. He let me into Keith's Character, told me there was not the least Probability that he had written any Letters for me, that no one who knew him had the smallest Dependence on him, and he laughed at the Notion of the Governor's giving me a Letter of Credit, having as he said no Credit to give. On my expressing some Concerns about what I should do: He advis'd me to endeavor getting some Employment in the Way of my Business. Among the Printers here, says he, you will improve yourself; and when you return to America, you will set up to greater Advantage.

We both of us happen'd to know, as well as the Stationer, that Riddlesden the Attorney, was a very Knave. He had half ruin'd Miss Read's Father by drawing him in to be bound[117] for him. By his Letter it appear'd, there was a secret Scheme on foot to the Prejudice of Hamilton, (Suppos'd to be then coming over with us,) and that Keith was concern'd in it with Riddlesden. Denham, who was a Friend of Hamilton's, thought he ought to be acquainted with it. So when he arriv'd in England, which was soon after, partly from Resentment and Ill-Will to Keith and Riddlesden, and partly from Goodwill to him: I waited on him, and gave him the Letter. He thank'd me cordially, the Information being of Importance to him. And from that time he became my Friend, greatly to my Advantage afterwards on many Occasions.

But what shall we think of a Governor's playing such pitiful Tricks, and imposing so grossly on a poor ignorant Boy! It was a Habit he had acquired. He wish'd to please everybody; and having little to give, he gave

---

[115]BASKET: John Baskett (d. 1742).
[116]RIDDLESDEN: William Riddlesden (d. before 1733) known in Maryland as a man of "infamy."
[117]BOUND: He cosigned a document in which he assumed responsibility for Riddlesden's debts should he be unable to pay them.

Expectations. He was otherwise an ingenious sensible Man, a pretty good Writer, and a good Governor for the People, tho' not for his Constituents the Proprietaries,[118] whose Instructions he sometimes disregarded. Several of our best Laws were of his Planning, and pass'd during his Administration.

Ralph and I were inseparable Companions. We took Lodgings together in Little Britain[119] at 3 shillings 6 pence per Week, as much as we could then afford. He found some Relations, but they were poor and unable to assist him. He now let me know his Intentions of remaining in London, and that he never meant to return to Philadelphia. He had brought no Money with him, the whole he could muster having been expended in paying his Passage. I had 15 Pistoles.[120] So he borrowed occasionally of me, to subsist while he was looking out for Business. He first endeavor'd to get into the Playhouse, believing himself qualified for an Actor; but Wilkes,[121] to whom he applied, advis'd him candidly not to think of that Employment, as it was impossible he should succeed in it. Then he propos'd to Roberts, a Publisher in Paternoster Row,[122] to write for him a Weekly Paper like the Spectator, on certain Conditions, which Roberts did not approve. Then he endeavor'd to get Employment as a Hackney Writer[123] to copy for the Stationers and Lawyers about the Temple[124] but could find no Vacancy.

I immediately got into Work at Palmer's, then a famous Printing-House in Bartholomew Close;[125] and here I continu'd near a Year. I was pretty diligent; but spent with Ralph a good deal of my Earnings in going to Plays and other Places of Amusement. We had together consum'd all my Pistoles, and now just rubb'd on from hand to mouth. He seem'd quite to forget his Wife and Child, and I by degrees my Engagements with Miss Read, to whom I never wrote more than one Letter, and that was to let her know I was not likely soon to return. This was another of the great Errata of my Life, which I should wish to

---

[118]CONSTITUENTS THE PROPRIETARIES: The Penn family. In 1681, English Quaker William Penn (1644–1718), was granted proprietary rights to most of Pennsylvania and a large section of Delaware by King James II as payment for a royal debt. The Penn family, as legal owners of the colony, appointed the governor.
[119]LITTLE BRITAIN: A street in London near St. Paul's Cathedral.
[120]PISTOLES: A Spanish gold coin worth about eighteen shillings.
[121]WILKES: Irish actor Robert Wilkes (1665?–1732).
[122]PATERNOSTER ROW: Paternoster Row was the center of London's printing industry.
[123]HACKNEY WRITER: Writer for hire.
[124]LAWYERS ABOUT THE TEMPLE: The Inns of Court were four sets of buildings in London (the Inner Temple, the Middle Temple, Lincoln's Inn, and Gray's Inn) belonging to the four legal societies in London, and thus centers for the legal profession.
[125]BARTHOLOMEW CLOSE: A square known for its printers and typesetters.

correct if I were to live it over again. In fact, by our Expenses, I was constantly kept unable to pay my Passage.

At Palmer's I was employ'd in Composing for the second Edition of Wollaston's Religion of Nature.[126] Some of his Reasonings not appearing to me well-founded, I wrote a little metaphysical Piece, in which I made Remarks on them. It was entitled, *A Dissertation on Liberty and Necessity, Pleasure and Pain*.[127] I inscrib'd it to my Friend Ralph. I printed a small Number. I occasion'd my being more consider'd by Mr. Palmer, as a young Man of some Ingenuity, tho' he seriously expostulated with me upon the Principles of my Pamphlet which to him appear'd abominable. My printing this Pamphlet was another Erratum.

While I lodg'd in Little Britain I made an Acquaintance with one Wilcox a Bookseller, whose Shop was at the next Door. He had an immense Collection of second-hand Books. Circulating Libraries were not then in Use; but we agreed that on certain reasonable Terms which I have now forgotten, I might take, read and return any of his Books. This I esteem'd a great Advantage, and I made as much Use of it as I could.

My Pamphlet by some means falling into the Hands of one Lyons,[128] a Surgeon, Author of a Book entitled *The Infallibility of Human Judgment*, it occasioned an Acquaintance between us; he took great Notice of me, call'd on me often, to converse on these Subjects, carried me to the Horns a pale Ale-House in [blank] Lane, Cheapside, and introduc'd me to Dr. Mandeville,[129] Author of the Fable of the Bees who had a Club there, of which he was the Soul, being a most facetious entertaining Companion. Lyons too introduc'd me to Dr. Pemberton,[130] at Batson's Coffee House,[131] who promis'd to give me an Opportunity some time or other of seeing Sir Isaac Newton,[132] of which I was extremely desirous; but this never happened.

I had brought over a few Curiosities among which the principal was a Purse made of the Asbestos, which purifies by Fire. Sir Hans Sloane[133]

---

[126]WOLLASTON'S RELIGION OF NATURE: William Wollaston's (1659–1724) *The Religion of Nature Delineated* was first printed in 1722. Franklin set the type for the fourth edition published in 1726.

[127]A DISSERTATION ON LIBERTY AND NECESSITY, PLEASURE AND PAIN: In his essay, Franklin rejects the existence of virtue and vice. He was criticized for its publication and faced accusations of atheism.

[128]LYONS: William Lyons, author of *The Infallibility, Dignity and Excellency of Human Judgement* (1719).

[129]DR. MANDEVILLE: Bernard Mandeville (1670–1733) was a Dutch physician living in London who wrote *The Fable of the Bees* (1714).

[130]DR. PEMBERTON: Henry Pemberton (1694–1771).

[131]BATSON'S COFFEE HOUSE: Batson's coffee house in Cornhill was a favorite meeting place for London physicians.

[132]SIR ISAAC NEWTON: Sir Isaac Newton (1642–1727), English scientist and mathematician best known for his laws of light and motion.

[133]SIR HANS SLOANE: Hans Sloane's (1660–1753) Cabinet of Curiosities, was purchased by the British government in 1753 to form the foundation collection of the British Museum.

heard of it, came to see me, and invited me to his House in Bloomsbury Square; where he show'd me all his Curiosities, and persuaded me to let him add that to the Number, for which he paid me handsomely.

In our House there lodg'd a young Woman, a Millener,[134] who I think had a shop in the Cloisters.[135] She had been genteelly bred, was sensible and lively, and of most pleasing Conversation. Ralph read Plays to her in the Evenings, they grew intimate, she took another Lodging, and he follow'd her. They liv'd together some time, but he being still out of Business, and her Income not sufficient to maintain them with her Child, he took a Resolution of going from London, to try for a Country School, which he thought himself well qualified to undertake, as he wrote an excellent Hand, and was a Master of Arithmetic and Accounts. This however he deem'd a Business below him, and confident of future better Fortune when he should be unwilling to have it known that he once was so meanly employ'd, he chang'd his Name, and did me the Honor to assume mine. For I soon after had a Letter from him, acquainting me, that he was settled in a small Village in Berkshire, I think it was, where he taught reading and writing to 10 or a dozen Boys at 6 pence each per Week, recommending Mrs. T. to my Care, and desiring me to write to him directing for Mr. Franklin Schoolmaster at such a Place. He continu'd to write frequently, sending me large Specimens of an Epic Poem, which he was then composing, and desiring my Remarks and Corrections. These I gave him from time to time, but endeavor'd rather to discourage his Proceeding. One of Young's Satires[136] was then just publish'd. I copied and sent him a great Part of it, which set in a strong Light the Folly of pursuing the Muses with any Hope of Advancement by them. All was in vain. Sheets of the Poem continu'd to come by every Post. In the mean time Mrs. T. having on his Account lost her Friends and Business, was often in Distresses, and us'd to send for me, and borrow what I could spare to help her out of them. I grew fond of her Company, and being at this time under no Religious Restraints, and presuming on my Importance to her, I attempted Familiarities, (another Erratum) which she repuls'd with a proper Resentment, and acquainted him with my Behavior. This made a Breach between us, and when he return'd again to London, he let me know he thought I had cancel'd all the Obligations he had been under to me. So I found I was never to expect his Repaying me what I lent to him or advanc'd for him. This was however not then

---

[134]A MILLENER: A maker of women's hats.
[135]CLOISTERS: Probably near St. Bartholomew's Church in London.
[136]YOUNG'S SATIRES: Edward Young (1683–1765), author of *Love of Fame, the Universal Passion* (1725).

of much Consequence, as he was totally unable. And in the Loss of his Friendship I found myself reliev'd from a Burden. I now began to think of getting a little Money beforehand; and expecting better Work, I left Palmer's to work at Watts's[137] near Lincoln's Inn Fields, a still greater Printing-House. Here I continu'd all the rest of my Stay in London.

At my first Admission into this Printing-House, I took to working at Press, imagining I felt a Want of the Bodily Exercise I had been us'd to in America, where Presswork is mix'd with Composing. I drank only Water; the other Workmen, near 50 in Number, were great Guzzlers of Beer. On occasion I carried up and down Stairs a large Form of Types[138] in each hand, when others carried but one in both Hands. They wonder'd to see from this and several Instances that the Water-American as they call'd me was *stronger* than themselves who drunk *strong* Beer. We had an Alehouse Boy who attended always in the House to supply the Workmen. My Companion at the Press drank every day a Pint before Breakfast, a Pint at Breakfast with his Bread and Cheese; a Pint between Breakfast and Dinner; a Pint at Dinner; a Pint in the Afternoon about Six o'clock, and another when he had done his Day's Work. I thought it a detestable Custom. But it was necessary, he suppos'd, to drink *strong* Beer that he might be *strong* to labor. I endeavor'd to convince him that the Bodily Strength afforded by Beer could only be in proportion to the Grain or Flour of the Barley dissolved in the Water of which it was made; that there was more Flour in a Penny-worth of Bread, and therefore if he would eat that with a Pint of Water, it would give him more Strength than a Quart of Beer. He drank on however, and had 4 or 5 Shillings to pay out of his Wages every Saturday Night for that muddling Liquor; an Expense I was free from. And thus these poor Devils keep themselves always under.[139]

Watts after some Weeks desiring to have me in the Composing-Room, I left the Pressmen. A new *Bienvenu*[140] or Sum for Drink, being 5 Shillings, was demanded of me by the Compositors. I thought it an Imposition, as I had paid below. The Master thought so too, and forbad my Paying it. I stood out two or three Weeks, was accordingly considered as an Excommunicate, and had so many little Pieces of private Mischief done me, by mixing my Sorts,[141] transposing my Pages, breaking my Matter,[142] etc., etc. if I were ever so little out of the Room, and all ascrib'd to the Chapel[143] Ghost, which they said ever haunted those not regularly

[137]WATTS'S: John Watts (c. 1678–1763).
[138]FORM OF TYPES: Type that has been set and locked in a frame.
[139]ALWAYS UNDER: They remain poor.
[140]BIENVENU: Welcome. (French)
[141]SORTS: Type, letters.
[142]MATTER: Type set up for printing.
[143]CHAPEL: "A Printing House is always called a Chapel by the Workmen" [Franklin's note].

admitted, that notwithstanding the Master's Protection, I found myself oblig'd to comply and pay the Money; convinc'd of the Folly of being on ill Terms with those one is to live with continually. I was now on a fair Footing with them, and soon acquir'd considerable Influence. I propos'd some reasonable Alterations in their Chapel Laws, and carried them against all Opposition. From my Example a great Part of them, left their muddling Breakfast of Beer and Bread and Cheese, finding they could with me be supplied from a neighboring House with a large Porringer of hot Water-gruel, sprinkled with Pepper, crumb'd with Bread, and a Bit of Butter in it, for the Price of a Pint of Beer, viz., three halfpence. This was a more comfortable as well as cheaper Breakfast, and kept their Heads clearer. Those who continu'd sotting with Beer all day, were often, by not paying, out of Credit at the Alehouse, and us'd to make Interest with me to get Beer, *their Light*, as they phras'd it, *being out*. I watch'd the Pay table on Saturday Night, and collected what I stood engag'd for them, having to pay some times near Thirty Shillings a Week on their Accounts. This and my being esteem'd a pretty good Riggite,[144] that is a jocular verbal Satirist, supported my Consequence in the Society. My constant Attendance, (I never making a St. Monday[145]), recommended me to the Master; and my uncommon Quickness at Composing, occasion'd my being put upon all Work of Dispatch, which was generally better paid. So I went on now very agreeably.

My Lodging in Little Britain being too remote, I found another in Duke Street opposite to the Romish Chapel.[146] It was two pair of Stairs backwards at an Italian Warehouse. A Widow Lady kept the House; she had a Daughter and a Maid Servant, and a Journeyman who attended the Warehouse, but lodg'd abroad. After sending to enquire my Character at the House where I last lodg'd, she agreed to take me in at the same Rate, 3 Shillings 6 Pence per Week, cheaper as she said from the Protection she expected in having a Man lodge in the House. She was a Widow, an elderly Woman, been bred a Protestant, being a Clergyman's Daughter, but was converted to the Catholic Religion by her Husband, whose Memory she much revered, had lived much among People of Distinction, and knew a 1000 Anecdotes of them as far back as the Times of Charles the second. She was lame in her Knees with the Gout,[147] and therefore seldom stirr'd out of her Room, so sometimes wanted Company; and hers was so highly amusing to me that I was sure to spend an Evening with her whenever she desired it. Our

[144]RIGGITE: One who mocks others.
[145]ST. MONDAY: Taking Monday off as if it were a bank holiday.
[146]ROMISH CHAPEL: The Roman Catholic Chapel of St. Anselm and St. Cecilia.
[147]GOUT: A painful disease of the joints.

Supper was only half an Anchovy each, on a very little Strip of Bread and Butter, and half a Pint of Ale between us. But the Entertainment was in her Conversation. My always keeping good Hours, and giving little Trouble in the Family, made her unwilling to part with me; so that when I talk'd of a Lodging I had heard of, nearer my Business, for 2 Shillings a Week, which, intent as I now was on saving Money, made some Difference; she bid me not think of it, for she would abate me two Shillings a Week for the future, so I remain'd with her at 1 Shilling 6 Pence as long as I stayed in London.

In a Garret of her House there lived a Maiden Lady of 70 in the most retired Manner, of whom my Landlady gave me this Account, that she was a Roman Catholic, had been sent abroad when young and lodg'd in a Nunnery with an Intent of becoming a Nun: but the Country not agreeing with her, she return'd to England, where there being no Nunnery, she had vow'd to lead the Life of a Nun as near as might be done in those Circumstances: Accordingly She had given all her Estate to charitable Uses, reserving only Twelve Pounds a year to live on, and out of this Sum she still gave a great deal in Charity, living herself on Watergruel[148] only, and using no Fire but to boil it. She had lived many Years in that Garret, being permitted to remain there gratis by successive catholic Tenants of the House below, as they deem'd it a Blessing to have her there. A Priest visited her, to confess her every Day. I have ask'd her, says my Landlady, how she, as she liv'd, could possibly find so much Employment for a Confessor? O, says she, it is impossible to avoid *vain Thoughts*. I was permitted once to visit her: She was cheerful and polite, and convers'd pleasantly. The Room was clean, but had no other Furniture than a Mattress, a Table with a Crucifix and Book, a Stool, which she gave me to sit on, and a Picture over the Chimney of *St. Veronica*,[149] displaying her Handkerchief with the miraculous Figure of Christ's bleeding Face on it, which she explain'd to me with great Seriousness. She look'd pale, but was never sick, and I give it as another Instance on how small an Income Life and Health may be supported.

At Watts's Printing-House I contracted an Acquaintance with an ingenious young Man, one Wygate, who having wealthy Relations, had been better educated than most Printers, was a tolerable Latinist, spoke French, and lov'd Reading. I taught him, and a Friend of his, to swim at twice going into the River, and they soon became good Swimmers.

---

[148]WATERGRUEL: A thin gruel made with water rather than milk.
[149]ST. VERONICA: The legend of St. Veronica relates that as Christ carried the cross on his way to Golgotha, the place of his crucifixion, Veronica used her veil to wipe the blood from his face. The cloth retained his image upon it, and was cherished as a holy relic preserved at St. Peter's Church in Rome.

They introduc'd me to some Gentlemen from the Country who went to Chelsea by Water to see the College and Don Saltero's Curiosities.[150] In our Return, at the Request of the Company, whose Curiosity Wygate had excited, I stripped and leaped into the River, and swam from near Chelsea to Blackfriars,[151] performing on the Way many Feats of Activity both upon and under Water, that surpris'd and pleas'd those to whom they were Novelties. I had from a Child been ever delighted with this Exercise, had studied and practic'd all Thevenot's[152] Motions and Positions, added some of my own, aiming at the graceful and easy, as well as the Useful. All these I took this Occasion of exhibiting to the Company, and was much flatter'd by their Admiration. And Wygate, who was desirous of becoming a Master, grew more and more attach'd to me on that account, as well as from the Similarity of our Studies. He at length propos'd to me traveling all over Europe together, supporting ourselves every where by working at our Business. I was once inclin'd to it. But mentioning it to my good Friend Mr. Denham, with whom I often spent an Hour when I had Leisure, he dissuaded me from it; advising me to think only of returning to Pennsylvania, which he was now about to do.

I must record one Trait of this good Man's Character. He had formerly been in Business at Bristol, but fail'd in Debt to a Number of People, compounded[153] and went to America. There, by a close Application to Business as a Merchant, he acquir'd a plentiful Fortune in a few Years. Returning to England in the Ship with me, He invited his old Creditors to an Entertainment, at which he thank'd them for the easy Composition[154] they had favor'd him with, and when they expected nothing but the Treat,[155] every Man at the first Remove[155] found under his Plate an Order on a Banker for the full Amount of the unpaid Remainder with Interest.

He now told me he was about to return to Philadelphia, and should carry over a great Quantity of Goods in order to open a Store there: He propos'd to take me over as his Clerk, to keep his Books (in which he would instruct me), copy his Letters, and attend the Store. He added,

[150]DON SALTERO'S CURIOSITIES: James Salter, a former valet of Sir Hans Sloane (see note 132), was a collector of supposed holy relics, including Job's tears and pieces of the true cross. He operated a museum and tavern in Chelsea. Salter was dubbed Don Saltero by the London *"Tatler"* which described him as "a sage of thin and meagre countenance of that sect which the ancients called *"gingivistae"* - in our language, a toothdrawer..."
[151]CHELSEA TO BLACKFRIARS: About three miles.
[152]THEVENOT'S: Melchisedec Thevenot's *The Art of Swimming* (1699).
[153]COMPOUNDED: Partially settled his debts.
[154]COMPOSITION: The settling of a debt by a mutual arrangement.
[155]TREAT: An entertainment of food and drink, given without any expense to the recipient.
[156]REMOVE: When the plates are removed after the first course of a meal.

that as soon as I should be acquainted with mercantile Business he would promote me by sending me with a Cargo of Flour and Bread, etc., to the West Indies, and procure me Commissions from others; which would be profitable, and if I manag'd well, would establish me handsomely. The Thing pleas'd me, for I was grown tired of London, remember'd with Pleasure the happy Months I had spent in Pennsylvania, and wish'd again to see it. Therefore I immediately agreed, on the Terms of Fifty Pounds a Year, Pennsylvania Money; less indeed than my then Gettings as a Compositor, but affording a better Prospect.

I now took Leave of Printing, as I thought for ever, and was daily employ'd in my new Business; going about with Mr. Denham among the Tradesmen, to purchase various Articles, and see them pack'd up, doing Errands, calling upon Workmen to dispatch, etc., and when all was on board, I had a few Days' Leisure. On one of these Days I was to my Surprise sent for by a great Man I knew only by Name, a Sir William Wyndham[157] and I waited upon him. He had heard by some means or other of my Swimming from Chelsey to Blackfriars, and of my teaching Wygate and another young Man to swim in a few Hours. He had two Sons about to set out on their Travels; he wish'd to have them first taught Swimming; and propos'd to gratify me handsomely if I would teach them. They were not yet come to Town and my Stay was uncertain, so I could not undertake it. But from this Incident I thought it likely, that if I were to remain in England and open a Swimming School, I might get a good deal of Money. And it struck me so strongly, that had the Overture been sooner made me, probably I should not so soon have returned to America. After Many Years, you and I had something of more Importance to do with one of these Sons of Sir William Wyndham, become Earl of Egremont, which I shall mention in its Place.[158]

Thus I spent about 18 Months in London. Most Part of the Time, I work'd hard at my Business, and spent but little upon myself except in seeing Plays, and in Books. My Friend Ralph had kept me poor. He owed me about 27 Pounds; which I was now never likely to receive; a great Sum out of my small Earnings. I lov'd him notwithstanding, for he had many amiable Qualities. Tho' I had by no means improv'd my Fortune, I had pick'd up some very ingenious Acquaintance whose Conversation was of great Advantage to me, and I had read considerably.

[157]SIR WILLIAM WYNDHAM: William Wyndham (1687–1740) was the Tory leader of the English Parliament and Chancellor of the Exchequer.
[158]PLACE: Charles Wyndham, Earl of Egremont (1710–1763), is not mentioned in any other part of Franklin's autobiography.

We sail'd from Gravesend on the 23d of July 1726. For The Incidents of the Voyage, I refer you to my Journal, where you will find them all minutely related. Perhaps the most important Part of that Journal is the *Plan*[159] to be found in it which I formed at Sea for regulating my future Conduct in Life. It is the more remarkable, as being form'd when I was so young, and yet being pretty faithfully adhered to quite thro' to old Age. We landed in Philadelphia the 11th of October, where I found sundry Alterations. Keith was no longer Governor, being superseded by Major Gordon:[160] I met him walking the Streets as a common Citizen. He seem'd a little asham'd at seeing me, but pass'd without saying anything. I should have been as much asham'd at seeing Miss Read, had not her Friends despairing with Reason of my Return, after the Receipt of my Letter, persuaded her to marry another, one Rogers, a Potter, which was done in my Absence. With him however she was never happy, and soon parted from him, refusing to cohabit with him, or bear his Name. It being now said that he had another Wife. He was a worthless Fellow tho' an excellent Workman which was the Temptation to her Friends. He got into Debt, and ran away in 1727 or 28, went to the West Indies, and died there. Keimer had got a better House, a Shop well supplied with Stationery, plenty of new Types, a number of Hands tho' none good, and seem'd to have a great deal of Business.

Mr. Denham took a Store in Water Street, where we open'd our Goods. I attended the Business diligently, studied Accounts, and grew in a little Time expert at selling. We lodg'd and boarded together, he counsel'd me as a Father, having a sincere Regard for me: I respected and lov'd him: and we might have gone on together very happily: But in the Beginning of February 1726/7 when I had just pass'd my 21st Year, we both were taken ill. My Distemper was a Pleurisy,[161] which very nearly carried me off: I suffered a good deal, gave up the Point[162] in my own mind, and was rather disappointed when I found myself recovering; regretting in some degree that I must now sometime or other have all that disagreeable Work to do over again. I forget what his Distemper was. It held him a long time, and at length carried him off. He left me a small Legacy in a nuncupative Will[163], as a Token of his Kindness for me, and he left me once more to the wide World. For the Store was taken into the Care of his Executors,

---

[159]PART OF THAT JOURNAL IS THE PLAN: Only the "Outline" and "Preamble" survive of this document.
[160]MAJOR GORDON: Patrick Gordon (1644–1736), governor of Pennsylvania from 1726 to 1736.
[161]PLEURISY: A respiratory disease with by pain in the chest or side, fever, and physical wasting, usually occurring as a complication of a bad cold or other disease.
[162]POINT: Point of death.
[163]NUNCUPATIVE WILL: An oral will, from the Latin, *testamentum nuncupativum.*

and my Employment under him ended: My Brother-in-law Homes, being now at Philadelphia, advis'd my Return to my Business. And Keimer tempted me with an Offer of large Wages by the Year to come and take the Management of his Printing-House that he might better attend his Stationer's Shop. I had heard a bad Character of him in London, from his Wife and her Friends, and was not fond of having any more to do with him. I tried for farther Employment as a Merchant's Clerk; but not readily meeting with any, I clos'd again with Keimer.

I found in *his* House these Hands; Hugh Meredith[164] a Welsh-Pennsylvanian, 30 Years of Age, bred to Country Work: honest, sensible, had a great deal of solid Observation, was something of a Reader, but given to drink: Stephen Potts,[165] a young Country Man of full Age, bred to the Same, of uncommon natural Parts[166] and great Wit and Humor, but a little idle. These he had agreed with at extreme low Wages, per Week, to be rais'd a Shilling every 3 Months, as they would deserve by improving in their Business, and the Expectation of these high Wages to come on hereafter was what he had drawn them in with. Meredith was to work at Press, Potts at Bookbinding, which he by Agreement, was to teach them, tho' he knew neither one nor t'other. John—— a wild Irishman brought up to no Business, whose Service for 4 Years Keimer had purchas'd[167] from the Captain of a Ship. He too was to be made a Pressman. George Webb,[168] an Oxford Scholar, whose Time for 4 Years he had likewise bought, intending him for a Compositor: of whom more presently. And David Harry,[169] a Country Boy, whom he had taken Apprentice. I soon perceiv'd that the Intention of engaging me at Wages so much higher than he had been us'd to give, was to have these raw cheap Hands form'd thro' me, and as soon as I had instructed them, then, they being all articled to him, he should be able to do without me. I went on however, very cheerfully; put his Printing-House in Order, which had been in great Confusion, and brought his Hands by degrees to mind their Business and to do it better.

It was an odd Thing to find an Oxford Scholar in the Situation of a bought Servant. He was not more than 18 Years of Age, and gave me this

---

[164]HUGH MEREDITH: Hugh Meredith (c. 1696–1749) later became one of Franklin's business partners.
[165]STEPHEN POTTS: Stephen Potts (c. 1705–1758) was from Pennsylvania, and a member of Franklin's Junto club.
[166]UNCOMMON NATURAL PARTS: Uncommonly handsome.
[167]PURCHAS'D: Keimer had paid for John's passage in exchange for his service for four years.
[168]GEORGE WEBB: George Webb (1708–1736?) was a fellow printer and member of Franklin's Junto club.
[169]DAVID HARRY: David Harry (1708–1760) was a Welsh Quaker who later become the first printer in Barbados.

Account of himself; that he was born in Gloucester, educated at a Grammar School there, had been distinguish'd among the Scholars for some apparent Superiority in performing his Part when they exhibited Plays; belong'd to the Witty Club there, and had written some Pieces in Prose and Verse which were printed in the Gloucester Newspapers. Thence he was sent to Oxford; there he continu'd about a Year but not well-satisfied, wishing of all things to see London and become a Player. At length receiving his Quarterly Allowance of 15 Guineas, instead of discharging his Debts, he walk'd out of Town, hid his Gown in a Furz Bush,[170] and footed it to London, where having no Friend to advise him, he fell into bad Company, soon spent his Guineas, found no means of being introduc'd among the Players, grew necessitous, pawn'd his Clothes and wanted Bread. Walking the Street very hungry, and not knowing what to do with himself, a Crimp's Bill[171] was put into his Hand, offering immediate Entertainment and Encouragement to such as would bind themselves to serve in America. He went directly, sign'd the Indentures, was put into the Ship and came over; never writing a Line to acquaint his Friends what was become of him. He was lively, witty, good-natur'd and a pleasant Companion, but idle, thoughtless and imprudent to the last Degree.

John the Irishman soon ran away. With the rest I began to live very agreeably; for they all respected me, the more as they found Keimer incapable of instructing them, and that from me they learned something daily. We never work'd on a Saturday, that being Keimer's Sabbath. So I had two Days for Reading. My Acquaintance with ingenious People in the Town increased. Keimer himself treated me with great Civility and apparent Regard; and nothing now made me uneasy but my Debt to Vernon, which I was yet unable to pay, being hitherto but a poor Economist. He however kindly made no Demand of it.

Our Printing-House often wanted Sorts, and there was no Letter Founder in America. I had seen Types cast at James's in London,[172] but without much Attention to the Manner: However I now contriv'd a Mold, made use of the Letters we had as Puncheons,[173] struck the Matrices[174] in Lead, and thus supplied in a pretty tolerable way all Deficiencies. I also engrav'd several Things on occasion. I made the Ink, I was Warehouse-man and everything, in short quite a Factotum.[175]

[170]FURZ BUSH: He hid his academic gown (worn by Oxford students) in an evergreen bush.
[171]CRIMP'S BILL: An advertisement offering free passage to America in exchange for service as an indentured servant.
[172]JAMES'S IN LONDON: The foundry of Thomas James in London.
[173]PUNCHEONS: Stamping tools.
[174]MATRICES: Metal blocks in which characters are stamped or engraved to form a mould for casting type.
[175]FACTOTUM: A man of all work, one who does everything.

But however serviceable I might be, I found that my Services became every Day of less Importance, as the other Hands improv'd in the Business. And when Keimer paid my second Quarter's Wages, he let me know that he felt them too heavy, and thought I should make an Abatement. He grew by degrees less civil, put on more of the Master, frequently found Fault, was captious and seem'd ready for an Out-breaking. I went on nevertheless with a good deal of Patience, thinking that his encumber'd Circumstances were partly the Cause. At length a Trifle snapped our Connection. For a great Noise happening near the Courthouse, I put my Head out of the Window to see what was the Matter. Keimer being in the Street look'd up and saw me, call'd out to me in a loud Voice and angry Tone to mind my Business, adding some reproachful Words, that nettled me the more for their Publicity, all the Neighbors who were looking out on the same Occasion being Witnesses how I was treated. He came up immediately into the Printing-House, continu'd the Quarrel, high Words pass'd on both Sides, he gave me the Quarter's Warning we had stipulated, expressing a Wish that he had not been oblig'd to so long a Warning: I told him his Wish was unnecessary for I would leave him that Instant; and so taking my Hat walk'd out of Doors; desiring Meredith whom I saw below to take care of some Things I left, and bring them to my Lodging.

Meredith came accordingly in the Evening, when we talk'd my Affair over. He had conceiv'd a great Regard for me, and was very unwilling that I should leave the House while he remain'd in it. He dissuaded me from returning to my native Country[176] which I began to think of. He reminded me that Keimer was in debt for all he possess'd, that his Creditors began to be uneasy, that he kept his Shop miserably, sold often without Profit for ready Money, and often trusted without keeping Account. That he must therefore fail; which would make a Vacancy I might profit of. I objected my Want of Money. He then let me know, that his Father had a high Opinion of me, and from some Discourse that had pass'd between them, he was sure would advance Money to set us up, if I would enter into Partnership with him. My Time, says he, will be out with Keimer in the Spring. By that time we may have our Press and Types in from London: I am sensible I am no Workman. If you like it, Your Skill in the Business shall be set against the Stock I furnish; and we will share the Profits equally.— The Proposal was agreeable, and I consented. His Father was in Town, and approv'd of it, the more as he saw I had great Influence with his Son, had prevail'd on him to abstain

<hr />

[176]COUNTRY: Boston.

long from Dramdrinking,[177] and he hop'd might break him of that
wretched Habit entirely, when we came to be so closely connected. I gave
an Inventory to the Father, who carried it to a Merchant; the Things were
sent for; the Secret was to be kept till they should arrive, and in the mean
time I was to get Work if I could at the other Printing-House. But I found
no Vacancy there, and so remain'd idle a few Days, when Keimer, on a
Prospect of being employ'd to print some Paper-money, in New Jersey,
which would require Cuts and various Types that I only could supply, and
apprehending Bradford might engage me and get the Job from him, sent
me a very civil Message, that old Friends should not part for a few Words,
the Effect of sudden Passion, and wishing me to return. Meredith persuaded me to comply, as it would give more Opportunity for his
Improvement under my daily Instructions. So I return'd, and we went on
more smoothly than for some time before. The New Jersey Job was
obtain'd. I contriv'd a Copper-Plate Press for it, the first that had been
seen in the Country. I cut several Ornaments and Checks for the Bills. We
went together to Burlington,[178] where I executed the Whole to
Satisfaction, and he received so large a Sum for the Work, as to be
enabled thereby to keep his Head much longer above Water.

At Burlington I made an Acquaintance with many principal People of
the Province. Several of them had been appointed by the Assembly a
Committee to attend the Press, and take Care that no more Bills were
printed than the Law directed. They were therefore by Turns constantly
with us, and generally he who attended brought with him a Friend or two
for Company. My Mind having been much more improv'd by Reading
than Keimer's, I suppose it was for that Reason my Conversation seem'd
to be more valu'd. They had me to their Houses, introduc'd me to their
Friends and show'd me much Civility, while he, tho' the Master, was a
little neglected. In truth he was an odd Fish, ignorant of common Life,
fond of rudely opposing receiv'd Opinions, slovenly to extreme dirti-
ness, enthusiastic[179] in some Points of Religion, and a little Knavish[180]
withal. We continu'd there near 3 Months, and by that time I could
reckon among my acquired Friends, Judge Allen, Samuel Bustill, the
Secretary of the Province, Isaac Pearson, Joseph Cooper and several of
the Smiths, Members of Assembly, and Isaac Decow the Surveyor
General. The latter was a shrewd sagacious old Man, who told me that
he began for himself when young by wheeling Clay for the Brickmakers,

[177]DRAM DRINKING: Frequent drinking of small amounts of alcohol.
[178]BURLINGTON: New Jersey.
[179]ENTHUSIASTIC: Highly emotional.
[180]KNAVISH: Vulgar and obscene.

learned to write after he was of Age, carried the Chain for Surveyors, who taught him Surveying, and he had now by his Industry acquir'd a good Estate; and says he, I foresee, that you will soon work this Man out of his Business and make a Fortune in it at Philadelphia. He had not then the least Intimation of my Intention to set up there or anywhere. These Friends were afterwards of great Use to me, as I occasionally was to some of them. They all continued their Regard for me as long as they lived.

Before I enter upon my public Appearance in Business, it may be well to let you know the then State of my Mind, with regard to my Principles and Morals, that you may see how far those influenc'd the future Events of my Life. My Parents had early given me religious Impressions, and brought me through my Childhood piously in the Dissenting Way.[181] But I was scarce 15 when, after doubting by turns of several Points as I found them disputed in the different Books I read, I began to doubt of Revelation itself. Some Books against Deism[182] fell into my Hands; they were said to be the Substance of Sermons preached at Boyle's Lectures.[183] It happened that they wrought an Effect on me quite contrary to what was intended by them: For the Arguments of the Deists which were quoted to be refuted, appeared to me much Stronger than the Refutations. In short I soon became a thorough Deist. My Arguments perverted some others, particularly Collins and Ralph: but each of them having afterwards wrong'd me greatly without the least Compunction, and recollecting Keith's Conduct towards me, (who was another Free-thinker) and my own towards Vernon and Miss Read which at Times gave me great Trouble, I began to suspect that this Doctrine tho' it might be true, was not very useful. My London pamphlet, which had for its Motto those Lines of Dryden[184]

> ——Whatever is, is right
> Tho' purblind Man Sees but a Part of
> The Chain, the nearest Link,
> His Eyes not carrying to the equal Beam,
> That poizes all, above.[185]

---

[181]DISSENTING WAY: Presbyterian or Congregationalist, as opposed to the Anglican Church of England.
[182]DEISM: The doctrine that acknowledges a supreme being as the source of creation, but rejects the supernatural doctrines of many organized religions.
[183]BOYLE'S LECTURES: Robert Boyle (1627–1691), English physicist and chemist, who endowed annual lectures against "infidels."
[184]DRYDEN: John Dryden (1631–1700), English poet and dramatist.
[185]THAT POIZES ALL, ABOVE: The first line of this passage is actually from Alexander Pope's *Essay on Man* (1733), Epistle I, line 294. Dryden's line reads, "Whatever is, is in its Causes Just." The rest of the passage is from Dryden's *Oedipus* (1679) Act 3, Scene 1, lines 244-48.

And from the Attributes of God, his infinite Wisdom, Goodness and Power concluded that nothing could possibly be wrong in the World, and that Vice and Virtue were empty Distinctions, no such Things existing: appear'd now not so clever a Performance as I once thought it; and I doubted whether some Error had not insinuated itself unperceiv'd into my Argument, so as to infect all that follow'd, as is common in metaphysical Reasonings. I grew convinc'd that *Truth, Sincerity* and *Integrity* in Dealings between Man and Man, were of the utmost Importance to the Felicity of Life, and I form'd written Resolutions, (which still remain in my Journal Book) to practice them ever while I lived. Revelation had indeed no weight with me as such; but I entertain'd an Opinion, that tho' certain Actions might not be bad *because* they were forbidden by it, or good *because* it commanded them; yet probably those Actions might be forbidden *because* they were bad for us, or commanded *because* they were beneficial to us, in their own Natures, all the Circumstances of things considered. And this Persuasion, with the kind hand of Providence, or some guardian Angel, or accidental favorable Circumstances and Situations, or all together, preserved me (thro' this dangerous Time of Youth and the hazardous Situations I was sometimes in among Strangers, remote from the Eye and Advice of my Father) without any *willful* gross Immorality or Injustice that might have been expected from my Want of Religion. I say *willful*, because the Instances I have mentioned, had something of *Necessity* in them, from my Youth, Inexperience, and the Knavery of others. I had therefore a tolerable Character to begin the World with, I valued it properly, and determin'd to preserve it.

We had not been long return'd to Philadelphia, before the New Types arriv'd from London. We settled with Keimer, and left him by his Consent before he heard of it. We found a House to hire near the Market, and took it. To lessen the Rent, (which was then but 24 Pounds a Year tho' I have since known it let for 70) we took in Thomas Godfrey a Glazier,[186] and his Family, who were to pay a considerable Part of it to us, and we to board with them. We had scarce opened our Letters and put our Press in Order, before George House, an Acquaintance of mine, brought a Countryman to us; whom he had met in the Street enquiring for a Printer. All our Cash was now expended in the Variety of Particulars we had been obliged to procure, and this Countryman's Five Shillings, being our First Fruits and coming so seasonably, gave me more Pleasure than any

[186]THOMAS GODFREY A GLAZIER: Thomas Godfrey (1704–1749) was a glass setter for window-panes.

Crown[187] I have since earn'd; and from the Gratitude I felt towards House, has made me often more ready than perhaps I should otherwise have been to assist young Beginners.

There are Croakers in every Country always boding its Ruin. Such a one then lived in Philadelphia, a Person of Note, an elderly Man, with a wise Look and very grave Manner of Speaking. His Name was Samuel Mickle. This Gentleman, a Stranger to me, stopped one Day at my Door, and ask'd me if I was the young Man who had lately opened a new Printing-House: Being answer'd in the Affirmative; He said he was sorry for me; because it was an expensive Undertaking, and the Expense would be lost, for Philadelphia was a sinking[188] Place, the People already half Bankrupts or near being so; all Appearances of the contrary such as new Buildings and the Rise of Rents, being to his certain Knowledge fallacious, for they were in fact among the Things that would soon ruin us. And he gave me such a Detail of Misfortunes now existing or that were soon to exist, that he left me half-melancholy. Had I known him before I engag'd in this Business, probably I never should have done it. This Man continu'd to live in this decaying Place, and to declaim in the same Strain, refusing for many Years to buy a House there, because all was going to Destruction, and at last I had the Pleasure of seeing him give five times as much for one as he might have bought it for when he first began his Croaking.

I should have mention'd before, that in the Autumn of the preceding Year, I had form'd most of my ingenious Acquaintance into a Club, for mutual Improvement, which we call'd the Junto.[189] We met on Friday Evenings. The Rules I drew up, requir'd that every Member in his Turn should produce one or more Queries on any Point of Morals, Politics or Natural Philosophy, to be discuss'd by the Company, and once in three Months produce and read an Essay of his own Writing on any Subject he pleased. Our Debates were to be under the Direction of a President, and to be conducted in the sincere Spirit of Enquiry after Truth, without fondness for Dispute, or Desire of Victory; and to prevent Warmth, all expressions of Positiveness in Opinion, or of direct Contradiction, were after some time made contraband and prohibited under small pecuniary Penalties. The first Members were, Joseph Breintnall,[190] a Copier of Deeds for the Scriveners; a good-natur'd friendly middle-ag'd Man, a great

---

[187]CROWN: An English coin worth five shillings.
[188]SINKING: Economically declining.
[189]JUNTO: From the Spanish word, *junta*, meaning "fraternity," a club or group united by a common purpose.
[190]JOSEPH BREINTNALL: Joseph Breintnal, (d. 1746).

Lover of Poetry, reading all he could meet with, and writing some that was tolerable; very ingenious in many little Nicknackeries, and of sensible Conversation. Thomas Godfrey, a self-taught Mathematician, great in his Way, and afterwards Inventor of what is now call'd Hadley's Quadrant.[191] But he knew little out of his way, and was not a pleasing Companion, as like most Great Mathematicians I have met with, he expected unusual Precision in everything said, or was forever denying or distinguishing upon Trifles, to the Disturbance of all Conversation. He soon left us. Nicholas Scull,[192] a Surveyor, afterwards Surveyor-General, Who lov'd Books, and sometimes made a few Verses. William Parsons,[193] bred a Shoemaker, but loving Reading, had acquir'd a considerable Share of Mathematics, which he first studied with a View to Astrology that he afterwards laughed at. He also became Surveyor General. William Maugridge, a Joiner,[194] and a most exquisite Mechanic,[195] and a solid sensible Man. Hugh Meredith, Stephen Potts, and George Webb, I have Characteris'd before. Robert Grace,[196] a young Gentleman of some Fortune, generous, lively and witty, a Lover of Punning and of his Friends. And William Coleman,[197] then a Merchant's Clerk, about my Age, who had the coolest clearest Head, the best Heart, and the exactest Morals, of almost any Man I ever met with. He became afterwards a Merchant of great Note, and one of our Provincial Judges: Our Friendship continued without Interruption to his Death, upwards of 40 Years. And the Club continu'd almost as long and was the best School of Philosophy, Morals and Politics that then existed in the Province; for our Queries which were read the Week preceding their Discussion, put us on reading with Attention upon the several Subjects, that we might speak more to the purpose: and here too we acquired better Habits of Conversation, everything being studied in our Rules which might prevent our disgusting each other. From hence the long Continuance of the Club, which I shall have frequent Occasion to speak farther of hereafter; But my giving this Account of it here, is to show something of the Interest I had, everyone of these exerting themselves in recommending Business to us.

---

[191]HADLEY'S QUADRANT: An instrument used to measure altitude in navigation and astronomy, named for English scientist and optician John Hadley (1682–1744).
[192]NICHOLAS SCULL: Nicolas Scull (1687–1761) later became a surveyor.
[193]WILLIAM PARSONS: William Parsons (1701–1757), who was a cobbler when he joined the Junto, later became surveyor general in 1741.
[194]JOINER: A wood worker who does more ornamental or delicate work than a carpenter; a cabinet-maker.
[195]MECHANIC: A manual laborer, in this case, a skilled tradesman.
[196]ROBERT GRACE: Robert Grace was Franklin's landlord and a gentleman.
[197]WILLIAM COLEMAN: William Coleman (1704–1769).

Breintnall particularly procur'd us from the Quakers, the Printing 40 Sheets of their History, the rest being to be done by Keimer: and upon this we work'd exceeding hard, for the Price was low. It was a Folio, Pro Patria Size, in Pica with Long Primer Notes.[198] I compos'd of it a Sheet a Day, and Meredith work'd it off at Press. It was often 11 at Night and sometimes later, before I had finish'd my Distribution for the next day's Work: For the little Jobs sent in by our other Friends now and then put us back. But so determin'd I was to continue doing a Sheet a Day of the Folio, that one Night when having impos'd my Forms, I thought my Day's Work over, one of them by accident was broken and two Pages reduc'd to Pie,[199] I immediately distributed and compos'd it over again before I went to bed. And this Industry visible to our Neighbors began to give us Character and Credit; particularly I was told, that mention being made of the new Printing Office at the Merchants' Every-night-Club, the general Opinion was that it must fail, there being already two Printers in the Place, Keimer and Bradford; but Doctor Baird (whom you and I saw many Years after at his native Place, St. Andrews in Scotland) gave a contrary Opinion; for the Industry of that Franklin, says he, is superior to anything I ever saw of the kind: I see him still at work when I go home from Club; and he is at Work again before his Neighbors are out of bed. This struck the rest, and we soon after had Offers from one of them to supply us with Stationery. But as yet we did not choose to engage in Shop Business.

I mention this Industry the more particularly and the more freely, tho' it seems to be talking in my own Praise, that those of my Posterity who shall read it, may know the Use of that Virtue, when they see its Effects in my Favor throughout this Relation.

George Webb, who had found a Friend that lent him wherewith to purchase his Time of Keimer, now came to offer himself as a Journeyman to us. We could not then employ him, but I foolishly let him know, as a Secret, that I soon intended to begin a Newspaper, and might then have Work for him. My Hopes of Success as I told him were founded on this, that the then only Newspaper,[200] printed by Bradford was a paltry thing, wretchedly manag'd, no way entertaining; and yet was profitable to him. I therefore thought a good Paper could scarcely fail of good Encouragement. I requested Webb not to mention it, but he told it to Keimer, who immediately, to be beforehand with me, published Proposals

[198]FOLIO…LONG PRIMER NOTES: A large book with the main text in twelve point, and the notes in ten point type.
[199]PIE: A jumbled pile.
[200]NEWSPAPER: The *American Weekly Mercury*.

for Printing one himself, on which Webb was to be employ'd. I resented this, and to counteract them, as I could not yet begin our Paper, I wrote several Pieces of Entertainment for Bradford's Paper, under the Title of the Busy Body which Breintnall continu'd some Months.[201] By this means the Attention of the Public was fix'd on that Paper, and Keimer's Proposals which we burlesqu'd and ridicul'd, were disregarded. He began his Paper however, and after carrying it on three Quarters of a Year, with at most only 90 Subscribers, he offer'd it to me for a Trifle, and I having been ready some time to go on with it, took it in hand directly, and it prov'd in a few Years extremely profitable to me.[202]

I perceive that I am apt to speak in the singular Number, though our Partnership still continu'd. The Reason may be, that in fact the whole Management of the Business lay upon me. Meredith was no Compositor, a poor Pressman, and seldom sober. My Friends lamented my Connection with him, but I was to make the best of it.

Our first Papers made a quite different Appearance from any before in the Province, a better Type and better printed: but some spirited Remarks of my Writing on the Dispute then going on between Governor Burnet and the Massachusetts Assembly, struck the principal People, occasion'd the Paper and the Manager of it to be much talk'd of, and in a few Weeks brought them all to be our Subscribers. Their Example was follow'd by many, and our Number went on growing continually. This was one of the first good Effects of my having learned a little to scribble. Another was, that the leading Men, seeing a Newspaper now in the hands of one who could also handle a Pen, thought it convenient to oblige and encourage me. Bradford still printed the Votes and Laws and other Public Business. He had printed an Address of the House[203] to the Governor in a coarse blundering manner; We reprinted it elegantly and correctly, and sent one to every Member. They were sensible of the Difference, it strengthen'd the Hands of our Friends in the House, and they voted us their Printers for the Year ensuing.

Among my Friends in the House I must not forget Mr. Hamilton before-mentioned, who was then returned from England and had a Seat in it. He interested himself[204] for me strongly in that Instance, as he did in many others afterwards, continuing his Patronage till his Death. Mr.

[201]MONTHS: From February 4, 1728 to September 25, 1729.
[202]EXTREMELY PROFITABLE TO ME: In October of 1729, Franklin took over the publication of Keimer's *The Universal Instructor in All Arts and Sciences: and Pennsylvania Gazette*, shortening the name to the *Pennsylvania Gazette*.
[203]HOUSE: The Pennsylvania Assembly.
[204]INTERESTED HIMSELF: "I got his Son once £500" [Franklin's note].

Vernon about this time put me in mind of the Debt I ow'd him: but did not press me. I wrote him an ingenuous Letter of Acknowledgments, crav'd his Forbearance a little longer which he allow'd me, and as soon as I was able I paid the Principal with Interest and many Thanks. So that Erratum was in some degree corrected.

But now another Difficulty came upon me, which I had never the least Reason to expect. Mr. Meredith's Father, who was to have paid for our Printing-House according to the Expectations given me, was able to advance only one Hundred Pounds, Currency, which had been paid, and a Hundred more was due to the Merchant; who grew impatient and su'd us all. We gave Bail, but saw that if the Money could not be rais'd in time, the Suit must come to a Judgment and Execution, and our hopeful Prospects must with us be ruined, as the Press and Letters must be sold for Payment, perhaps at half-Price. In this Distress two true Friends whose Kindness I have never forgotten nor ever shall forget while I can remember anything, came to me separately unknown to each other, and without any Application from me, offering each of them to advance me all the Money that should be necessary to enable me to take the whole Business upon myself if that should be practicable, but they did not like my continuing the Partnership with Meredith, who as they said was often seen drunk in the Streets, and playing at low Games in Alehouses, much to our Discredit. These two Friends were *William Coleman* and *Robert Grace*.

I told them I could not propose a Separation while any Prospect remain'd of the Merediths fulfilling their Part of our Agreement. Because I thought myself under great Obligations to them for what they had done and would do if they could. But if they finally fail'd in their Performance, and our Partnership must be dissolv'd, I should then think myself at Liberty to accept the Assistance of my Friends. Thus the matter rested for some time. When I said to my Partner, perhaps your Father is dissatisfied at the Part you have undertaken in this Affair of ours, and is unwilling to advance for you and me what he would for you alone: If that is the Case, tell me, and I will resign the whole to you and go about my Business. No—says he, my Father has really been disappointed and is really unable; and I am unwilling to distress him farther. I see this is a Business I am not fit for. I was bred a Farmer, and it was a Folly in me to come to Town and put myself at 30 Years of Age an Apprentice to learn a new Trade. Many of our Welsh People are going to settle in North Carolina where Land is cheap: I am inclin'd to go with them, and follow my old Employment. You may find Friends to assist you. If you will take the Debts of the Company upon you, return to my Father the hundred Pound he has advanc'd, pay my little personal Debts, and give me

Thirty Pounds and a new Saddle, I will relinquish the Partnership and leave the whole in your Hands. I agreed to this Proposal. It was drawn up in Writing, sign'd and seal'd immediately. I gave him what he demanded and he went soon after to Carolina; from whence he sent me next Year two long Letters, containing the best Account that had been given of that Country, the Climate, Soil, Husbandry, etc., for in those Matters he was very judicious. I printed them in the Papers,[205] and they gave great Satisfaction to the Public.

As soon as he was gone, I recurr'd to my two Friends; and because I would not give an unkind Preference to either, I took half what each had offered and I wanted, of one, and half of the other; paid off the Company Debts, and went on with the Business in my own Name, advertising that the Partnership was dissolved. I think this was in or about the Year 1729.

About this Time there was a Cry among the People for more Paper-Money, only 15,000 Pounds being extant in the Province and that soon to be sunk.[206] The wealthy Inhabitants oppos'd any Addition, being against all Paper Currency, from an Apprehension that it would depreciate as it had done in New England to the Prejudice of all Creditors. We had discuss'd this Point in our Junto, where I was on the Side of an Addition, being persuaded that the first small Sum struck in 1723 had done much good, by increasing the Trade, Employment, and Number of Inhabitants in the Province, since I now saw all the old Houses inhabited, and many new ones building, where as I remember'd well, that when I first walk'd about the Streets of Philadelphia, eating my Roll, I saw most of the Houses in Walnut Street between Second and Front Streets with Bills[207] on their Doors, to be let; and many likewise in Chestnut Street, and other Streets; which made me then think the Inhabitants of the City were one after another deserting it. Our Debates possess'd me so fully of the Subject, that I wrote and printed an anonymous Pamphlet on it, entitled, *The Nature and Necessity of a Paper Currency*.[208] It was well receiv'd by the common People in general; but the Rich Men dislik'd it; for it increas'd and strengthen'd the Clamor for more Money; and they happening to have no Writers among them that were able to answer it, their Opposition slacken'd, and the Point was carried by a Majority in the House. My Friends there, who conceiv'd I had been of some Service,

---

[205]PAPERS: The *Pennsylvania Gazette*, May 6 and May 13, 1732.
[206]SUNK: Destroyed. The Pennsylvania Assembly issued paper money secured by real estate mortgages. When the mortgages were paid off, the money was "sunk." In 1729, however, the actual value of the paper currency was so low that the money was recalled before the mortgages were paid off.
[207]BILLS: Signs.
[208]THE NATURE AND NECESSITY OF A PAPER CURRENCY: The full title was *A Modest Inquiry into the Nature and Necessity of a Paper Currency* (April 3, 1729).

thought fit to reward me, by employing me in printing the Money,[209] a very profitable Job, and a great Help to me. This was another Advantage gain'd by my being able to write. The Utility of this Currency became by Time and Experience so evident, as never afterwards to be much disputed, so that it grew soon to 55,000 Pounds, and in 1739 to 80,000 Pounds, since which it arose during War to upwards of 350,000 Pounds— Trade, Building and Inhabitants all the while increasing. Tho' I now think there are Limits beyond which the Quantity may be hurtful.

I soon after obtain'd, thro' my Friend Hamilton, the Printing of the New Castle Paper Money,[210] another profitable Job, as I then thought it; small Things appearing great to those in small Circumstances. And these to me were really great Advantages, as they were great Encouragements. He procured me also the Printing of the Laws and Votes of that Government which continu'd in my Hands as long as I follow'd the Business.

I now open'd a little Stationer's Shop.[211] I had in it Blanks of all Sorts the correctest that ever appear'd among us, being assisted in that by my Friend Breintnall; I had also Paper, Parchment, Chapmen's Books, etc. One Whitmarsh[212] a Compositor I had known in London, an excellent Workman now came to me and work'd with me constantly and diligently, and I took an Apprentice the Son of Aquila Rose. I began now gradually to pay off the Debt I was under for the Printing-House. In order to secure my Credit and Character as a Tradesman, I took care not only to be in *Reality* Industrious and frugal, but to avoid all *Appearances* of the contrary. I dressed plainly; I was seen at no Places of idle Diversion; I never went out a-fishing or shooting; a Book, indeed, sometimes debauch'd me from my Work; but that was seldom, snug, and gave no Scandal: and to show that I was not above my Business, I sometimes brought home the Paper I purchas'd at the Stores, thro' the Streets on a Wheelbarrow. Thus being esteem'd an industrious thriving young Man, and paying duly for what I bought, the Merchants who imported Stationery solicited my Custom, others propos'd supplying me with Books, and I went on swimmingly. In the mean time Keimer's Credit and Business declining daily, he was at last forc'd to sell his Printing-House to satisfy his Creditors. He went to Barbados, and there lived some Years, in very poor Circumstances.

---

[209]MONEY: Franklin was contracted to print paper currency in 1731.
[210]NEW CASTLE PAPER MONEY: New Castle, Delaware, which had a separate legislature but shared Pennsylvania's governor.
[211]STATIONER'S SHOP: In July 1730.
[212]WHITMARSH: Thomas Whitmarsh (d. 1733) left Philadelphia for South Carolina a year later, where he started the eighth newspaper in America, the *South-Carolina Gazette*, in 1732.

His Apprentice David Harry, whom I had instructed while I work'd with him, set up in his Place at Philadelphia, having bought his Materials. I was at first apprehensive of a powerful Rival in Harry, as his Friends were very able, and had a good deal of Interest. I therefore propos'd a Partnership to him; which he, fortunately for me, rejected with Scorn. He was very proud, dress'd like a Gentleman, liv'd expensively, took much Diversion and Pleasure abroad, ran in debt, and neglected his Business, upon which all Business left him; and finding nothing to do, he follow'd Keimer to Barbados; taking the Printing-House with him. There this Apprentice employ'd his former Master as a Journeyman. They quarrel'd often. Harry went continually behind-hand, and at length was forc'd to sell his Types, and return to his Country Work in Pennsylvania. The Person that bought them employ'd Keimer to use them, but in a few years he died. There remain'd now no Competitor with me at Philadelphia, but the old one, Bradford, who was rich and easy, did a little Printing now and then by straggling Hands, but was not very anxious about the Business. However, as he kept the Post Office, it was imagined he had better Opportunities of obtaining News, his Paper was thought a better Distributer of Advertisements than mine, and therefore had many more, which was a profitable thing to him and a Disadvantage to me. For tho' I did indeed receive and send Papers by the Post, yet the public Opinion was otherwise; for what I did send was by Bribing the Riders[213] who took them privately: Bradford being unkind enough to forbid it: which occasion'd some Resentment on my Part; and I thought so meanly of him for it, that when I afterwards came into his Situation,[214] I took care never to imitate it.

I had hitherto continu'd to board with Godfrey who lived in Part of my House with his Wife and Children, and had one Side of the Shop for his Glazier's Business, tho' he work'd little, being always absorb'd in his Mathematics. Mrs. Godfrey projected a Match for me with a Relation's Daughter, took Opportunities of bringing us often together, till a serious Courtship on my Part ensu'd, the Girl being in herself very deserving. The old Folks encourag'd me by continual Invitations to Supper, and by leaving us together, till at length it was time to explain. Mrs. Godfrey manag'd our little Treaty. I let her know that I expected as much Money with their Daughter as would pay off my Remaining Debt for the Printing-House, which I believe was not then above a

[213]BRIBING THE RIDERS: Franklin bribed the postal carriers to have his papers delivered on the same day as Bradford's.
[214]SITUATION: In October of 1737, Franklin became Philadelphia's post master, Bradford's former office.

Hundred Pounds.[215] She brought me Word they had no such Sum to spare. I said they might mortgage their House in the Loan Office. The Answer to this after some Days was, that they did not approve the Match; that on Enquiry of Bradford they had been inform'd the Printing Business was not a profitable one, the Types would soon be worn out and more wanted, that S. Keimer and D. Harry had fail'd one after the other, and I should probably soon follow them; and therefore I was forbidden the House, and the Daughter shut up.

Whether this was a real Change of Sentiment, or only Artifice, on a Supposition of our being too far engag'd in Affection to retract, and therefore that we should steal a Marriage, which would leave them at Liberty to give or withhold what they pleas'd, I know not: But I suspected the latter, resented it, and went no more. Mrs. Godfrey brought me afterwards some more favorable Accounts of their Disposition, and would have drawn me on again: But I declared absolutely my Resolution to have nothing more to do with that Family. This was resented by the Godfreys, we differ'd, and they removed, leaving me the whole House, and I resolved to take no more Inmates. But this Affair having turn'd my Thoughts to Marriage, I look'd round me, and made Overtures of Acquaintance in other Places; but soon found that the Business of a Printer being generally thought a poor one, I was not to expect Money with a Wife unless with such a one, as I should not otherwise think agreeable. In the mean time, that hard-to-be-govern'd Passion of Youth, had hurried me frequently into Intrigues with low Women that fell in my Way, which were attended with some Expense and great Inconvenience, besides a continual Risk to my Health by a Distemper[216] which of all Things I dreaded, tho' by great good Luck I escaped it.

A friendly Correspondence as Neighbors and old Acquaintances, had continued between me and Mrs. Read's Family who all had a Regard for me from the time of my first Lodging in their House. I was often invited there and consulted in their Affairs, wherein I sometimes was of Service. I pitied poor Miss Read's unfortunate Situation, who was generally dejected, seldom cheerful, and avoided Company. I consider'd my Giddiness and Inconstancy when in London as in a great degree the Cause of her Unhappiness; tho' the Mother was good enough to think the Fault more her own than mine, as she had prevented our Marrying before I went thither, and persuaded the other Match in my Absence. Our mutual Affection was revived, but there were now great Objections to our

[215]HUNDRED POUNDS: Deborah Read's dowry, the money or property a wife brings her husband upon marriage.
[216]DISTEMPER: An illness, probably syphilis, a sexually transmitted disease.

Union. That Match was indeed look'd upon as invalid, a preceding Wife being said to be living in England; but this could not easily be prov'd, because of the Distance, etc. And tho' there was a Report of his Death, it was not certain. Then, tho' it should be true, he had left many Debts which his Successor might be call'd upon to pay. We ventured however, over all these Difficulties, and I took her to Wife Sept. 1, 1730.[217] None of the Inconveniencies happened that we had apprehended, she prov'd a good and faithful Helpmate, assisted me much by attending the Shop, we throve together, and have ever mutually endeavor'd to make each other happy. Thus I corrected that great Erratum as well as I could.

About this Time our Club meeting, not at a Tavern, but in a little Room of Mr. Grace's set apart for that Purpose; a Proposition was made by me, that since our Books were often referr'd to in our Disquisitions upon the Queries, it might be convenient to us to have them all together where we met, that upon Occasion they might be consulted; and by thus clubbing our Books to a common Library, we should, while we lik'd to keep them together, have each of us the Advantage of using the Books of all the other Members, which would be nearly as beneficial as if each owned the whole. It was lik'd and agreed to, and we fill'd one End of the Room with such Books as we could best spare. The Number was not so great as we expected; and tho' they had been of great Use, yet some Inconveniencies occurring for want of due Care of them, the Collection after about a Year was separated, and each took his Books home again.

And now I set on foot my first Project of a public Nature, that for a Subscription Library. I drew up the Proposals, got them put into Form by our great Scrivener Brockden, and by the help of my Friends in the Junto, procur'd Fifty Subscribers of 40 Shillings each to begin with and 10 Shillings a Year for 50 Years, the Term our Company was to continue. We afterwards obtain'd a Charter, the Company being increas'd to 100. This was the Mother of all the North American Subscription Libraries now so numerous. It is become a great thing itself, and continually increasing. These Libraries have improv'd the general Conversation of the Americans, made the common Tradesmen and Farmers as intelligent as most Gentlemen from other Countries, and perhaps have contributed in some degree to the Stand so generally made throughout the Colonies in Defense of their Privileges.

MEMO.

Thus far was written with the Intention express'd in the Beginning and therefore contains several little family Anecdotes of no

---

[217]WIFE SEPT 1, 1730: Because Deborah Read could not prove that her first husband was dead, she and Franklin entered a common-law marriage without a civil ceremony.

Importance to others. What follows was written many Years after in compliance with the Advice contain'd in these Letters, and accordingly intended for the Public. The Affairs of the Revolution occasion'd the Interruption.

[1771]

From The Autobiography

[PART TWO]

LETTER FROM MR. ABEL JAMES,[1] WITH NOTES ON MY LIFE, (RECEIVED IN PARIS.[2])

My dear & honored Friend.

I have often been desirous of writing to thee, but could not be reconciled to the Thought that the Letter might fall into the Hands of the British,[3] lest some Printer or busy Body should publish some Part of the Contents and give our Friends Pain and myself Censure.

Some Time since there fell into my Hands to my great Joy about 23 Sheets in thy own hand-writing containing an Account of the Parentage and Life of thyself, directed to thy Son ending in the Year 1730 with which there were Notes[4] likewise in thy writing, a Copy of which I enclose in Hopes it may be a means if thou continuedst it up to a later period, that the first and latter part may be put together; and if it is not yet continued, I hope thou wilt not delay it. Life is uncertain as the Preacher tells us, and what will the World say if kind, humane and benevolent Ben Franklin should leave his Friends and the World deprived of so pleasing and profitable a Work, a Work which would be useful and entertaining not only to a few, but to millions.

The Influence Writings under that Class have on the Minds of Youth is very great, and has no where appeared so plain as in our public Friends' Journals. It almost insensibly leads the Youth into the Resolution of endeavoring to become as good and as eminent as the Journalist. Should thine for Instance when published, and I think it could not fail of it, lead the Youth to equal the Industry and Temperance of thy early Youth, what a Blessing

---

[1]MR. ABEL JAMES: A Quaker merchant (1726–1790) living in Philadelphia.
[2]PARIS: In September 1783, Franklin was sent to Paris as the American representative negotiating the peace treaty with Great Britain. He remained until July 1785, when Thomas Jefferson replaced him as minister.
[3]HANDS OF THE BRITISH: James writes his letter in 1782, when Great Britain and the American Colonies are still at war.
[4]NOTES: Franklin's outline for his autobiography.

with that Class would such a Work be. I know of no Character living nor many of them put together, who has so much in his Power as Thyself to promote a greater Spirit of Industry and early Attention to Business, Frugality and Temperance with the American Youth. Not that I think the Work would have no other Merit and Use in the World, far from it, but the first is of such vast Importance, that I know nothing that can equal it.

The foregoing letter and the minutes accompanying it being shown to a friend, I received from him the following:

LETTER FROM MR. BENJAMIN VAUGHAN[5]

Paris, January 31, 1783.

My Dearest Sir,

When I had read over your sheets of minutes of the principal incidents of your life, recovered for you by your Quaker acquaintance; I told you I would send you a letter expressing my reasons why I thought it would be useful to complete and publish it as he desired. Various concerns have for some time past prevented this letter being written, and I do not know whether it was worth any expectation: happening to be at leisure however at present, I shall by writing at least interest and instruct myself; but as the terms I am inclined to use may tend to offend a person of your manners, I shall only tell you how I would address any other person, who was as good and as great as yourself, but less diffident. I would say to him, Sir, I *solicit* the history of your life from the following motives.

Your history is so remarkable, that if you do not give it, somebody else will certainly give it; and perhaps so as nearly to do as much harm, as your own management of the thing might do good.

It will moreover present a table of the internal circumstances of your country, which will very much tend to invite to it settlers of virtuous and manly minds. And considering the eagerness with which such information is sought by them, and the extent of your reputation, I do not know of a more efficacious advertisement than your Biography would give.

All that has happened to you is also connected with the detail of the manners and situation of *a rising* people; and in this respect I do not think that the writings of Caesar and Tacitus[6] can be more interesting to a true judge of human nature and society.

But these, Sir, are small reasons in my opinion, compared with the chance which your life will give for the forming of future great men;

---

[5]MR. BENJAMIN VAUGHAN: The private secretary (1751–1835) to Lord Shelburne. He served as Franklin's personal emissary during the Paris peace talks.
[6]CAESAR AND TACITUS: Julius Caesar (100–44 BCE), a Roman general and ruler. Publius Cornelius Tacitus (55–120 CE), a Roman historian.

and in conjunction with your *Art of Virtue*,[7] (which you design to publish) of improving the features of private character, and consequently of aiding all happiness both public and domestic.

The two works I allude to, Sir, will in particular give a noble rule and example of *self-education*. School and other education constantly proceed upon false principles, and show a clumsy apparatus pointed at a false mark; but your apparatus is simple, and the mark a true one; and while parents and young persons are left destitute of other just means of estimating and becoming prepared for a reasonable course in life, your discovery that the thing is in many a man's private power, will be invaluable!

Influence upon the private character late in life, is not only an influence late in life, but a weak influence. It is in *youth* that we plant our chief habits and prejudices; it is in youth that we take our party[8] as to profession, pursuits, and matrimony. In youth therefore the turn is given; in youth the education even of the next generation is given; in youth the private and public character is determined: and the term of life extending from youth to age, life ought to begin well from youth; and more especially *before* we take our party as to our principal objects.

But your Biography will not merely teach self-education, but the education of *a wise man*; and the wisest man will receive lights and improve his progress, by seeing detailed the conduct of another wise man. And why are weaker men to be deprived of such helps, when we see our race has been blundering on in the dark, almost without a guide in this particular, from the farthest trace of time. Shew then, Sir, how much is to be done, *both to sons and fathers*; and invite all wise men to become like yourself; and other men to become wise.

When we see how cruel statesmen and warriors can be to the humble race, and how absurd distinguished men can be to their acquaintance, it will be instructive to observe the instances multiply of pacific acquiescing manners; and to find how compatible it is to be great and *domestic*; enviable and yet *good-humored*.

The little private incidents which you will also have to relate, will have considerable use, as we want above all things, *rules of prudence in ordinary affairs*; and it will be curious to see how you have acted in these. It will be so far a sort of key to life, and explain many things that all men ought to have once explained to them, to give them a chance of becoming wise by foresight.

The nearest thing to having experience of one's own, is to have other people's affairs brought before us in a shape that is interesting; this is sure

---

[7]ART OF VIRTUE: Vaughan refers to a book Franklin proposed to write for children.
[8]TAKE OUR PARTY: Make our decision.

to happen from your pen. Your affairs and management will have an air of simplicity or importance that will not fail to strike; and I am convinced you have conducted them with as much originality as if you had been conducting discussions in politics or philosophy; and what more worthy of experiments and system, (its importance and its errors considered) than human life!

Some men have been virtuous blindly, others have speculated fantastically, and others have been shrewd to bad purposes; but you, Sir, I am sure, will give under your hand, nothing but what is at the same moment, wise, practical, and good.

Your account of yourself (for I suppose the parallel I am drawing for Dr. Franklin, will hold not only in point of character but of private history), will shew that you are ashamed of no origin; a thing the more important, as you prove how little necessary all origin is to happiness, virtue, or greatness.

As no end likewise happens without a means, so we shall find, Sir, that even you yourself framed a plan by which you became considerable; but at the same time we may see that though the event is flattering, the means are as simple as wisdom could make them; that is depending upon nature, virtue, thought, and habit.

Another thing demonstrated will be the propriety of every man's waiting for his time for appearing upon the stage of the world. Our sensations being very much fixed to the moment, we are apt to forget that more moments are to follow the first, and consequently that man should arrange his conduct so as to suit the *whole* of a life. Your attribution appears to have been applied to your *life*, and the passing moments of it have been enlivened with content and enjoyment, instead of being tormented with foolish impatience or regrets. Such a conduct is easy for those who make virtue and themselves their standard, and who try to keep themselves in countenance by examples of other truly great men, of whom patience is so often the characteristic.

Your Quaker correspondent, Sir, (for here again I will suppose the subject of my letter resembling Dr. Franklin,) praised your frugality, diligence, and temperance, which he considered as a pattern for all youth: but it is singular that he should have forgotten your modesty, and your disinterestedness, without which you never could have waited for your advancement, or found your situation in the mean time comfortable; which is a strong lesson to show the poverty of glory, and the importance of regulating our minds.

If this correspondent had known the nature of your reputation as well as I do, he would have said; your former writings and measures would secure attention to your Biography, and Art of Virtue; and your Biography and Art of Virtue, in return, would secure attention to them. This is an advantage attendant upon a various character, and which brings all that belongs to it into greater play; and it is the more useful, as perhaps more persons are at a loss for the *means* of improving their minds and characters, than they are for the time or the inclination to do it.

But there is one concluding reflection, Sir, that will show the use of your life as a mere piece of biography. This style of writing seems a little gone out of vogue, and yet it is a very useful one; and your specimen of it may be particularly serviceable, as it will make a subject of comparison with the lives of various public cut-throats and intriguers, and with absurd monastic self-tormentors, or vain literary triflers. If it encourages more writings of the same kind with your own, and induces more men to spend lives fit to be written; it will be worth all Plutarch's Lives put together.

But being tired of figuring to myself a character of which every feature suits only one man in the world, without giving him the praise of it; I shall end my letter, my dear Dr. Franklin, with a personal application to your proper self.

I am earnestly desirous then, my dear Sir, that you should let the world into the traits of your genuine character, as civil broils may otherwise tend to disguise or traduce it. Considering your great age, the caution of your character, and your peculiar style of thinking, it is not likely that any one besides yourself can be sufficiently master of the facts of your life, or the intentions of your mind.

Besides all this, the immense revolution of the present period, will necessarily turn our attention towards the author of it; and when virtuous principles have been pretended in it, it will be highly important to show that such have really influenced; and, as your own character will be the principal one to receive a scrutiny, it is proper (even for its effects upon your vast and rising country, as well as upon England and upon Europe), that it should stand respectable and eternal. For the furtherance of human happiness, I have always maintained that it is necessary to prove that man is not even at present a vicious and detestable animal; and still more to prove that good management may greatly amend him; and it is for much the same reason, that I am anxious to see the opinion established, that there are fair characters existing among the individuals of the race; for the moment that all men, without exception, shall be conceived abandoned, good people will cease efforts deemed to be hopeless, and perhaps think of taking their share in the scramble of life, or at least of making it comfortable principally for themselves.

Take then, my dear Sir, this work most speedily into hand: show yourself good as you are good, temperate as you are temperate; and above all things, prove yourself as one who from your infancy have loved justice, liberty, and concord, in a way that has made it natural and consistent for you to have acted, as we have seen you act in the last seventeen years of your life. Let Englishmen be made not only to respect, but even to love you. When they think well of individuals in your native country, they will go nearer to thinking well of your country; and when your countrymen see themselves well thought of by Englishmen, they will go nearer to thinking well of England. Extend your views even further; do not stop at those who speak the English tongue, but after having settled so many points in nature and politics, think of bettering the whole race of men.

As I have not read any part of the life in question, but know only the character that lived it, I write somewhat at hazard. I am sure however, that the life, and the treatise I allude to (on the *Art of Virtue*), will necessarily fulfil the chief of my expectations; and still more so if you take up the measure of suiting these performances to the several views above stated. Should they even prove unsuccessful in all that a sanguine admirer of yours hopes from them, you will at least have framed pieces to interest the human mind; and whoever gives a feeling of pleasure that is innocent to man, has added so much to the fair side of a life otherwise too much darkened by anxiety, and too much injured by pain.

In the hope therefore that you will listen to the prayer addressed to you in this letter, I beg to subscribe myself, my dearest Sir, etc., etc.

[Signed] BENJ. VAUGHAN.

CONTINUATION OF THE ACCOUNT OF MY LIFE.

BEGUN AT PASSY,[9] 1784

It is some time since I receiv'd the above Letters, but I have been too busy till now to think of complying with the Request they contain. It might too be much better done if I were at home among my Papers, which would aid my Memory and help to ascertain Dates. But my Return being uncertain, and having just now a little Leisure, I will endeavour to recollect and write what I can; if I live to get home, it may there be corrected and improv'd.

Not having any Copy here of what is already written, I know not whether an Account is given of the means I used to establish the Philadelphia public Library, which from a small Beginning is now become so considerable, though I remember to have come down to near the Time of that Transaction, 1730. I will therefore begin here, with an Account of it, which may be struck out if found to have been already given.

[9]PASSY: Franklin was staying at the Hôtel de Valentenois in the Paris suburb of Passy.

At the time I establish'd my self in Pensylvania, there was not a good Bookseller's Shop in any of the Colonies to the Southward of Boston. In New York and Philadelphia the Printers were indeed Stationers, they sold only Paper, etc., Almanacs, Ballads, and a few common School Books. Those who lov'd Reading were oblig'd to send for their Books from England. The Members of the Junto had each a few. We had left the Alehouse where we first met, and hired a Room to hold our Club in. I propos'd that we should all of us bring our Books to that Room, where they would not only be ready to consult in our Conferences, but become a common Benefit, each of us being at Liberty to borrow such as he wish'd to read at home. This was accordingly done, and for some time contented us. Finding the Advantage of this little Collection, I propos'd to render the Benefit from Books more common by commencing a Public Subscription Library. I drew a Sketch of the Plan and Rules that would be necessary, and got a skillful Conveyancer, Mr. Charles Brockden[10] to put the whole in Form of Articles of Agreement to be subscribed; by which each Subscriber engag'd to pay a certain Sum down for the first Purchase of Books and an annual Contribution for increasing them. So few were the Readers at that time in Philadelphia, and the Majority of us so poor, that I was not able with great Industry to find more than Fifty Persons, mostly young Tradesmen, willing to pay down for this purpose Forty shillings each, and Ten Shillings per Annum. On this little Fund we began. The Books were imported. The Library was open one Day in the Week for lending them to the Subscribers, on their Promisory Notes to pay Double the Value if not duly returned. The Institution soon manifested its Utility, was imitated by other Towns and in other Provinces, the Librarys were augmented by Donations, Reading became fashionable, and our People having no public Amusements to divert their Attention from Study became better acquainted with Books, and in a few Years were observ'd by Strangers to be better instructed and more intelligent than People of the same Rank generally are in other Countries.

When we were about to sign the above-mentioned Articles, which were to be binding on us, our Heirs, etc. for fifty Years, Mr. Brockden, the Scrivener, said to us, "You are young Men, but it is scarce probable that any of you will live to see the Expiration of the Term fix'd in this Instrument." A Number of us, however, are yet living: But the Instrument was after a few Years rendered null by a Charter that incorporated and gave Perpetuity to the Company.

---

[10]MR. CHARLES BROCKDEN: Brockden (1683–1769) was an attorney ("conveyancer") from Philadelphia who specialized in the transfer of real estate. He was that city's leading drafter of legal documents in the first half of the eighteenth century.

The Objections, and Reluctances I met with in Soliciting the Subscriptions, made me soon feel the Impropriety of presenting one's self as the Proposer of any useful Project that might be suppos'd to raise one's Reputation in the smallest degree above that of one's Neighbors, when one has need of their Assistance to accomplish that Project. I therefore put myself as much as I could out of sight, and stated it as a Scheme of a *Number of Friends*, who had requested me to go about and propose it to such as they thought Lovers of Reading. In this way my Affair went on more smoothly, and I ever after practis'd it on such Occasions; and from my frequent Successes, can heartily recommend it. The present little Sacrifice of your Vanity will afterwards be amply repaid. If it remains a while uncertain to whom the Merit belongs, some one more vain than yourself will be encourag'd to claim it, and then even Envy will be dispos'd to do you justice, by plucking those assum'd Feathers, and restoring them to their right Owner.

This Library afforded me the means of Improvement by constant Study, for which I set apart an Hour or two each Day; and thus repair'd in some Degree the Loss of the Learned Education my Father once intended for me. Reading was the only Amusement I allow'd my self. I spent no time in Taverns, Games, or Frolicks of any kind. And my Industry in my Business continu'd as indefatigable as it was necessary. I was in debt for my Printing-House, I had a young Family[11] coming on to be educated, and I had to contend with for Business two Printers who were establish'd in the Place before me. My Circumstances however grew daily easier: my original Habits of Frugality continuing. And my Father having among his Instructions to me when a Boy, frequently repeated a Proverb of Solomon,[12] *"Seest thou a Man diligent in his Calling, he shall stand before Kings, he shall not stand before mean Men."* I from thence consider'd Industry as a Means of obtaining Wealth and Distinction, which encourag'd me, tho' I did not think that I should ever literally stand before Kings, which however has since happened; for I have stood before five,[13] and even had the honor of sitting down with one, the King of Denmark, to Dinner.

We have an English Proverb that says,

> He that would thrive
> Must ask his Wife;[14]

---

[11]I HAD A YOUNG FAMILY: Franklin had three children, William, Francis, and Sarah.
[12]PROVERB OF SOLOMON: Proverbs 22:29.
[13]FOR I HAVE STOOD BEFORE FIVE: Franklin met the French kings Louis XV and Louis XVI, the British kings George II and George III, and the Danish king Christian VI.
[14]HE THAT WOULD THRIVE / MUST ASK HIS WIFE: More commonly, "He that will thrive, must first ask his wife."

It was lucky for me that I had one as much dispos'd to Industry and Frugality as myself. She assisted me cheerfully in my Business, folding and stitching Pamphlets, tending Shop, purchasing old Linen Rags for the Paper-makers, etc., etc. We kept no idle Servants, our Table was plain and simple, our furniture of the cheapest. For instance my Breakfast was a long time Bread and Milk, (no Tea) and I ate it out of a two penny earthen Porringer[15] with a Pewter Spoon. But mark how Luxury will enter Families, and make a Progress, in Spite of Principle. Being Call'd one Morning to Breakfast, I found it in a China Bowl with a Spoon of Silver. They had been bought for me without my Knowledge by my Wife, and had cost her the enormous Sum of three and twenty Shillings, for which she had no other Excuse or Apology to make, but that she thought *her* Husband deserv'd a Silver Spoon and China Bowl as well as any of his Neighbors. This was the first Appearance of Plate[16] and China in our House, which afterwards in a Course of Years as our Wealth increas'd augmented gradually to several Hundred Pounds in Value.

I had been religiously educated as a Presbyterian; and tho' some of the Dogmas of that Persuasion, such as the Eternal Decrees of God, Election, Reprobation,[17] etc. appear'd to me unintelligible, others doubtful, I early absented myself from the Public Assemblies of the Sect, Sunday being my Studying-Day, I never was without some religious Principles; I never doubted, for instance, the Existence of the Deity, that he made the World, and govern'd it by his Providence; that the most acceptable Service of God was the doing Good to Man; that our Souls are immortal; and that all Crime will be punished and Virtue rewarded either here or hereafter; these I esteem'd the Essentials of every Religion, and being to be found in all the Religions we had in our Country I respected them all, tho' with different degrees of Respect as I found them more or less mix'd with other Articles which without any Tendency to inspire, promote or confirm Morality, serv'd principally to divide us and make us unfriendly to one another. This Respect to all, with an Opinion that the worst had some good Effects, induc'd me to avoid all Discourse that might tend to lessen the good Opinion another might have of his own Religion; and as our Province increas'd in People and new Places of worship were continually wanted, and generally erected by voluntary Contribution, my Mite[18] for such purpose, whatever might be the Sect, was never refused.

Tho' I seldom attended any Public Worship, I had still an Opinion of its Propriety, and of its Utility when rightly conducted, and I regularly paid

---

[15]PORRINGER: A small bowl usually used to serve soup or porridge to children.
[16]PLATE: Silverware.
[17]REPROBATION: Punishment or rejection.
[18]MITE: Small amount.

my annual Subscription for the Support of the only Presbyterian Minister or Meeting we had in Philadelphia. He us'd to visit me sometimes as a Friend, and admonish me to attend his Administrations, and I was now and then prevail'd on to do so, once for five Sundays successively. Had he been, *in my Opinion*, a good Preacher perhaps I might have continued, notwithstanding the occasion I had for the Sunday's Leisure in my Course of Study: But his Discourses were chiefly either polemic Arguments, or Explications of the peculiar Doctrines of our Sect, and were all to me very dry, uninteresting and unedifying, since not a single moral Principle was inculcated or enforc'd their Aim seeming to be rather to make us Presbyterians than good Citizens. At length he took for his Text that Verse of the 4th Chapter of Philippians, *Finally, Brethren, Whatsoever Things are true, honest, just, pure, lovely, or of good report, if there be any virtue, or any praise, think on these Things*[19]; and I imagin'd in a Sermon on such a Text, we could not miss of having some Morality: But he confin'd himself to five Points only as meant by the Apostle, viz. 1. Keeping holy the Sabbath Day. 2. Being diligent in Reading the Holy Scriptures. 3. Attending duly the Public Worship. 4. Partaking of the Sacrament. 5. Paying a due Respect to God's Ministers. These might be all good Things, but as they were not the kind of good Things that I expected from that Text, I despaired of ever meeting with them from any other, was disgusted, and attended his Preaching no more. I had some Years before compos'd a little Liturgy or Form of Prayer for my own private Use, viz., in 1728, entitled, *Articles of Belief and Acts of Religion*.[20] I return'd to the Use of this, and went no more to the public Assemblies. My Conduct might be blameable, but I leave it without attempting farther to excuse it, my present purpose being to relate Facts, and not to make Apologies for them.

It was about this time that I conceiv'd the bold and arduous Project of arriving at moral Perfection. I wish'd to live without committing any Fault at anytime; I would conquer all that either Natural Inclination, Custom, or Company might lead me into. As I knew, or thought I knew, what was right and wrong, I did not see why I might not *always* do the one and avoid the other. But I soon found I had undertaken a Task of more Difficulty than I had imagined! While my care was employ'd in guarding against one Fault, I was often surpris'd by another. Habit took

---

[19]FINALLY, BRETHREN...THINK ON THESE THINGS: Paraphrase of Philippians 4.8: "Finally, brethren, whatsoever things are true, whatsoever things are honest, whatsoever things are just, whatsoever things are pure, whatsoever things are lovely, whatsoever things are of good report; if there be any virtue, and if there be any praise, think on these things."
[20]ARTICLES OF BELIEF AND ACTS OF RELIGION: Only the first section of Franklin's "Articles of Belief and Acts of Religion" survives.

the Advantage of Inattention. Inclination was sometimes too strong for Reason. I concluded at length, that the mere speculative Conviction that it was our Interest to be completely virtuous, was not sufficient to prevent our Slipping, and that the contrary Habits must be broken and good Ones acquired and established, before we can have any Dependence on a steady uniform Rectitude of Conduct. For this purpose I therefore contriv'd the following Method.

In the various Enumerations of the moral Virtues I had met with in my Reading, I found the Catalog more or less numerous, as different Writers included more or fewer Ideas under the same Name. Temperance, for Example, was by some confin'd to Eating and Drinking, while by others it was extended to mean the moderating every other Pleasure, Appetite, Inclination or Passion, bodily or mental, even to our Avarice and Ambition. I propos'd to myself, for the sake of Clearness, to use rather more Names with fewer Ideas annex'd to each, than a few Names with more Ideas; and I included under Thirteen Names of Virtues all that at that time occurr'd to me as necessary or desirable, and annex'd to each a short Precept, which fully express'd the Extent I gave to its Meaning.

These Names of Virtues with their Precepts were

1. TEMPERANCE.

Eat not to Dullness. Drink not to Elevation.

2. SILENCE.

Speak not but what may benefit others or yourself. Avoid trifling Conversation.

3. ORDER.

Let all your Things have their Places. Let each Part of your Business have its Time.

4. RESOLUTION.

Resolve to perform what you ought. Perform without fail what you resolve.

5. FRUGALITY.

Make no Expense but to do good to others or yourself: i.e., Waste nothing.

6. INDUSTRY.

Lose no Time. Be always employ'd in something useful. Cut off all unnecessary Actions.

7. SINCERITY.

Use no hurtful Deceit. Think innocently and justly; and, if you speak, speak accordingly.

8. JUSTICE.

Wrong none, by doing Injuries or omitting the Benefits that are your Duty.

9. MODERATION.

Avoid Extremes. Forbear resenting Injuries so much as you think they deserve.

10. CLEANLINESS.

Tolerate no Uncleanness in Body, Clothes or Habitation.

11. TRANQUILITY.

Be not disturbed at Trifles, or at Accidents common or unavoidable.

12. CHASTITY.

Rarely use Venery but for Health or Offspring: Never to Dullness, Weakness, or the Injury of your own or another's Peace or Reputation.

13. HUMILITY.

Imitate Jesus and Socrates.

My Intention being to acquire the *Habitude*[21] of all these Virtues, I judg'd it would be well not to distract my Attention by attempting the whole at once, but to fix it on one of them at a time, and when I should be Master of that, then to proceed to another, and so on till I should have gone thro' the thirteen. And as the previous Acquisition of some might facilitate the Acquisition of certain others, I arrang'd them with that View as they stand above. *Temperance* first, as it tends to produce that Coolness and Clearness of Head, which is so necessary where constant Vigilance was to be kept up, and Guard maintained, against the unremitting Attraction of ancient Habits, and the Force of perpetual Temptations. This being acquir'd and establish'd, *Silence* would be more easy, and my Desire being to gain Knowledge at the same time that I improv'd in Virtue, and considering that in Conversation it was obtain'd rather by use of the Ears than of the Tongue, and therefore wishing to break a Habit I was getting into of Prattling, Punning and Joking, which only made me acceptable to trifling Company, I gave *Silence* the second Place. This, and the next, *Order*, I expected would allow me more Time for attending to my Project and my Studies; RESOLUTION, once become habitual, would keep me firm in my Endeavors to obtain all the subsequent Virtues; *Frugality* and *Industry*, by freeing me from my remaining Debt, and producing Affluence and Independence, would make more easy the Practice

---

[21]HABITUDE: Part of one's inherent or essential character; disposition.

of *Sincerity* and *Justice*, etc. Conceiving then that agreable to the Advice of Pythagoras in his Golden Verses[22] daily Examination would be necessary, I contriv'd the following Method for conducting that Examination.

I made a little Book in which I allotted a Page for each of the Virtues. I rul'd each Page with red Ink, so as to have seven Columns, one for each Day of the Week, marking each Column with a Letter for the Day. I cross'd these Columns with thirteen red Lines, marking the Beginning of each Line with the first Letter of one of the Virtues, on which Line and in its proper Column I might mark by a little black Spot every Fault I found upon Examination to have been committed respecting that Virtue upon that Day.

FORM OF THE PAGES

	TEMPERANCE					
	Eat not to Dulness. *Drink not to Elevation.*					
	S	M	T	W	T	F	S
T							
S	●	●		●		●	
O	●	●	●			●	●
R		●					
F		●				●	
I			●				
S							
J							
M							
Cl.							
T							
Ch							
H							

I determined to give a Week's strict Attention to each of the Virtues successively. Thus in the first Week my great Guard was to avoid every

[22]ADVICE OF PYTHAGORAS IN HIS GOLDEN VERSES: Pythagoras (6th century BCE) was a Greek philosopher and mathematician. Franklin added a note indicating he wished to include these translated verses: "Let not the stealing God of Sleep surprize, Nor creep in Slumbers on thy weary Eyes, Ere ev'ry Action of the former Day, Strictly thou dost, and righteously survey. With Rev'rence at thy own Tribunal stand, And answer justly to thy own Demand. Where have I been? In what have I transgrest? What Good or Ill has this Day's Life exprest? Where have I fail'd in what I ought to do? In what to GOD, to Man, or to myself I owe? Inquire severe whate'er from first to last, From Morning's Dawn till Ev'nings Gloom has past. If Evil were thy Deeds, repenting mourn, And let thy Soul with strong Remorse be torn: If Good, the Good with Peace of Mind repay, And to thy secret Self with Pleasure say, Rejoice, my Heart, for all went well to Day."

the least Offence against Temperance, leaving the other Virtues to their ordinary Chance, only marking every Evening the Faults of the Day. Thus if in the first Week I could keep my first Line marked T clear of Spots, I suppos'd the Habit of that Virtue so much strengthen'd and its opposite weaken'd, that I might venture extending my Attention to include the next, and for the following Week keep both Lines clear of Spots. Proceeding thus to the last, I could go thro' a Course compleat in Thirteen Weeks, and four Courses in a year. And like him who having a Garden to weed, does not attempt to eradicate all the bad Herbs at once, which would exceed his Reach and his Strength, but works on one of the Beds at a time, and having accomplish'd the first proceeds to a Second; so I should have, (I hoped) the encouraging Pleasure of seeing on my Pages the Progress I made in Virtue, by clearing successively my Lines of their Spots, till in the End by a Number of Courses, I should be happy in viewing a clean Book after a thirteen Weeks daily Examination.

This my little Book had for its Motto these Lines from *Addison's Cato*,[23]

> *Here will I hold: If there is a Pow'r above us,*
> *(And that there is, all Nature cries aloud*
> *Thro' all her Works) he must delight in Virtue,*
> *And that which he delights in must be happy.*

Another from Cicero[24]:

> *O Vitæ Philosophia Dux! O Virtutum indagatrix, expultrixque vitiorum! Unus dies bene, et ex preceptis tuis actus, peccanti immortalitati est anteponendus.*[25]

Another from the Proverbs of Solomon speaking of Wisdom or Virtue;

> Length of Days is in her right hand, and in her Left Hand Riches and Honours; Her Ways are Ways of Pleasantness, and all her Paths are Peace.[26] III, 16, 17

And conceiving God to be the Fountain of Wisdom, I thought it right and necessary to solicit his Assistance for obtaining it; to this End I form'd the following little Prayer, which was prefix'd to my Tables of Examination, for daily Use.

> *O Powerful Goodness! bountiful Father! merciful Guide! Increase in me that Wisdom which discovers my truest Interests; Strengthen*

---

[23]ADDISON'S CATO: *Cato* (1713; Act 5.1, lines 15–18) a tragedy by Joseph Addison (1672–1719).
[24]CICERO: Marcus Tullius Cicero (106–43 BCE), a Roman philosopher and orator.
[25]O VITAE PHILOSPHIA DUX...ANTEPONENDUS: "O Philosophy, leader of life! O seeker of virtue, and critic of vice! From your teachings, a single day of good is preferred to an eternity of sin. (Latin) From *Tusculan Disputations*.
[26]LENGTH OF DAYS IS IN HER RIGHT HAND...PEACE: Proverbs 3:16–17.

my Resolutions to perform what that Wisdom dictates. Accept my kind Offices to thy other Children, as the only Return in my Prayer for thy continual Favors to me.

I us'd also sometimes a little Prayer which I took from Thomson's *Poems,*[27] viz.,

> *Father of Light and Life, thou Good supreme,*
> *O teach me what is good, teach me thy self!*
> *Save me from Folly, Vanity and Vice,*
> *From every low Pursuit, and fill my Soul*
> *With Knowledge, conscious Peace, and Virtue pure,*
> *Sacred, substantial, neverfading Bliss!*

The Precept of *Order* requiring that *every Part of my Business should have its allotted Time,* one Page in my little Book contain'd the following Scheme of Employment for the Twenty-four Hours of a natural Day.

The Morning Question, What Good Shall I do this Day?	5 6 7 8	Rise, wash, and address *Powerful Goodness;* contrive Day's Business and take the Resolution of the Day; prosecute the present Study: and breakfast.—
	9 10 11	Work.
	12 1	Read, or overlook my Accounts, and dine.
	2 3 4 5	Work.
Evening Question, What Good have I done to day?	6 7 8 9	Put Things in their Places, Supper, Musick, or Diversion, or Conversation, Examination of the Day.
	10 11 12 1 2 3 4	Sleep—

---

[27]THOMSON'S POEMS: From the poem "Winter," lines 218–23, in *The Seasons* (1730, revised 1744), by James Thomson (1700–1748).

I enter'd upon the Execution of this Plan for Self-Examination, and continu'd it with occasional Intermissions for some time. I was surpris'd to find myself so much fuller of Faults than I had imagined, but I had the Satisfaction of seeing them diminish. To avoid the Trouble of renewing now and then my little Book, which by scraping out the Marks on the Paper of old Faults to make room for new Ones in a new Course, became full of Holes: I transferr'd my Tables and Precepts to the Ivory Leaves of a Memorandum Book, on which the Lines were drawn with red Ink that made a durable Stain, and on those Lines I mark'd my Faults with a black Lead Pencil, which Marks I could easily wipe out with a wet Sponge. After a while I went thro' one Course only in a Year, and afterwards only one in several Years; till at length I omitted them entirely, being employ'd in Voyages and Business abroad with a Multiplicity of Affairs, that interfered. But I always carried my little Book with me.

My scheme of ORDER, gave me the most Trouble, and I found, that tho' it might be practicable where a Man's Business was such as to leave him the Disposition of his Time, that of a Journeyman Printer for instance, it was not possible to be exactly observ'd by a Master, who must mix with the World, and often receive People of Business at their own Hours. *Order* too, with regard to Places for Things, Papers, etc., I found extremely difficult to acquire. I had not been early accustomed to it, and having an exceeding good Memory, I was not so sensible of the Inconvenience attending Want of Method. This Article therefore cost me so much painful Attention and my Faults in it vex'd me so much, and I made so little Progress in Amendment, and had such frequent Relapses, that I was almost ready to give up the Attempt, and content myself with a faulty Character in that respect. Like the Man who in buying an Ax of a Smith my neighbor, desired to have the whole of its Surface as bright as the Edge; the Smith consented to grind it bright for him if he would turn the Wheel. He turn'd while the Smith press'd the broad Face of the Ax hard and heavily on the Stone, which made the Turning of it very fatiguing. The Man came every now and then from the Wheel to see how the Work went on; and at length would take his Ax as it was without farther Grinding. No, says the Smith, Turn on, turn on; we shall have it bright by and by; as yet 'tis only speckled. Yes, says the Man; but—*I think I like a speckled Ax best.*—And I believe this may have been the Case with many who having for want of some such Means as I employ'd found the Difficulty of obtaining good, and breaking bad Habits, in other Points of Vice and Virtue, have given up the Struggle, and concluded that *a speckled Ax was best.* For something that pretended to be Reason was every now and then suggesting to me, that such extreme Nicety as I exacted of myself might be a kind of Foppery in Morals, which if it were known would make me ridiculous; that a perfect Character might be attended with the Inconvenience of being envied and hated; and that a benevolent Man should allow a few Faults in himself, to keep his Friends in Countenance.

In Truth I found myself incorrigible with respect to *Order;* and now I am grown old, and my Memory bad, I feel very sensibly the want of it. But on the whole, tho' I never arrived at the Perfection I had been so ambitious of obtaining, but fell far short of it, yet I was by the Endeavor a better and a happier Man than I otherwise should have been, if I had not attempted it; As those who aim at perfect Writing by imitating the engraved Copies, tho' they never reach the wish'd for Excellence of those Copies, their Hand is mended by the Endeavor, and is tolerable while it continues fair and legible.

And it may be well my Posterity should be informed, that to this little Artifice, with the Blessing of God, their Ancestor ow'd the constant Felicity of his Life down to his 79th Year in which this is written. What Reverses may attend the Remainder is in the Hand of Providence: But if they arrive, the Reflection on past Happiness enjoy'd ought to help his Bearing them with more Resignation. To *Temperance* he ascribes his long-continu'd Health, and what is still left to him of a good Constitution. To *Industry* and *Frugality* the early Easiness of his Circumstances, and Acquisition of his Fortune, with all that Knowledge which enabled him to be an useful Citizen, and obtain'd for him some Degree of Reputation among the Learned. To *Sincerity* and *Justice* the Confidence of his Country, and the honorable Employs it conferr'd upon him. And to the joint Influence of the whole Mass of the Virtues, even in the imperfect State he was able to acquire them, all that Evenness of Temper, and that Cheerfulness in Conversation which makes his Company still sought for, and agreable even to his younger Acquaintance. I hope therefore that some of my Descendants may follow the Example and reap the Benefit.

It will be remark'd that, tho' my Scheme was not wholly without Religion there was in it no Mark of any of the distinguishing Tenets of any particular Sect. I had purposely avoided them; for being fully persuaded of the Utility and Excellency of my Method, and that it might be serviceable to People in all Religions, and intending some time or other to publish it, I would not have any thing in it that should prejudice any one of any Sect against it. I purposed writing a little Comment on each Virtue, in which I would have shown the Advantages of possessing it, and the Mischiefs attending its opposite Vice; and I should have called my Book the ART of *Virtue*, because it would have shown the *Means and Manner* of obtaining Virtue; which would have distinguish'd it from the mere

Exhortation to be good, that does not instruct and indicate the Means; but is like the Apostle's Man of verbal Charity, who only, without showing to the Naked and the Hungry *how* or where they might get Clothes or Victuals, exhorted them to be fed and clothed. *James II*, 15, 16.[28]

But it so happened that my Intention of writing and publishing this Comment was never fulfilled. I did indeed, from time to time put down short Hints of the Sentiments, Reasonings, etc., to be made use of in it; some of which I have still by me: But the necessary close Attention to private Business in the earlier part of Life, and public Business since, have occasioned my postponing it. For it being connected in my Mind with a *great and extensive Project* that required the whole Man to execute, and which an unforeseen Succession of Employs prevented my attending to, it has hitherto remain'd unfinish'd.

In this Piece it was my Design to explain and enforce this Doctrine, that vicious Actions are not hurtful because they are forbidden, but forbidden because they are hurtful, the Nature of Man alone consider'd: That it was therefore every one's Interest to be virtuous, who wish'd to be happy even in this World. And I should from this Circumstance (there being always in the World a Number of rich Merchants, Nobility, States and Princes, who have need of honest Instruments for the Management of their Affairs, and such being so rare) have endeavored to convince young Persons, that no Qualities were so likely to make a poor Man's Fortune as those of Probity and Integrity.

My List of Virtues contain'd at first but twelve: But a Quaker Friend having kindly inform'd me that I was generally thought proud; that my Pride show'd itself frequently in Conversation; that I was not content with being in the right when discussing any Point, but was overbearing and rather insolent; of which he convinc'd me by mentioning several Instances; I determined endeavouring to cure myself if I could of this Vice or Folly among the rest, and I added *Humility* to my List, giving an extensive Meaning to the Word. I cannot boast of much Success in acquiring the *Reality* of this Virtue; but I had a good deal with regard to the *Appearance* of it. I made it a Rule to forbear all direct Contradiction to the Sentiments of others, and all positive Assertion of my own. I even forbid myself, agreeable to the old Laws of our Junto, the Use of every Word or Expression in the Language that imported a fix'd Opinion; such as *certainly, undoubtedly*, etc., and I adopted instead of them, I *conceive,*

---

[28]JAMES II, 15,16: "If a brother or sister be naked, and destitute of daily food, / And one of you say unto them, Depart in peace, be ye warmed and filled; notwithstanding ye give them not those things which are needful to the body; what doth it profit?" From chapter two of the Epistle of James.

I *apprehend*, or I *imagine* a thing to be so or so, or it so appears to me at present. When another asserted something that I thought an Error, I denied myself the Pleasure of contradicting him abruptly, and of showing immediately some Absurdity in his Proposition; and in answering I began by observing that in certain Cases or Circumstances his Opinion would be right, but that in the present case there *appear'd* or *seem'd* to me some Difference, etc., I soon found the Advantage of this Change in my Manners. The Conversations I engag'd in went on more pleasantly. The modest way in which I propos'd my Opinions, procur'd them a readier Reception and less Contradiction; I had less Mortification when I was found to be in the wrong, and I more easily prevail'd with others to give up their Mistakes and join with me when I happen'd to be in the right. And this Mode, which I at first put on, with some violence to natural Inclination, became at length so easy and so habitual to me, that perhaps for these Fifty Years past no one has ever heard a dogmatical Expression escape me. And to this Habit (after my Character of Integrity) I think it principally owing, that I had early so much Weight with my Fellow Citizens, when I proposed new Institutions, or Alterations in the old; and so much Influence in public Councils when I became a Member. For I was but a bad Speaker, never eloquent, subject to much Hesitation in my choice of Words, hardly correct in Language, and yet I generally carried my Points.

In reality there is perhaps no one of our natural Passions so hard to subdue as *Pride*. Disguise it, struggle with it, beat it down, stifle it, mortify it as much as one pleases, it is still alive, and will every now and then peep out and show itself. You will see it perhaps often in this History. For even if I could conceive that I had completely overcome it, I should probably be proud of my Humility.

Thus far written at Passy, 1784.

John Woolman

(1720–1772)

Described by one scholar as "the purest and sweetest flowering of the Quaker spirit," John Woolman was born in Burlington County, New Jersey. He was the fourth child (and the eldest son) in a family of thirteen children. At age sixteen he underwent a conversion experience, a surge of feeling that profoundly connected him to God. Several years later Woolman learned the tailor's trade, even as he became increasingly involved in the meetings and preaching activities of the Society of Friends, or Quakers (the term comes from an early leader's injunction to "tremble at the word of the Lord"). Woolman married at age twenty-nine; he and his wife had one child.

When Woolman was in his twenties, he was asked by his employer to prepare a bill of sale for a slave; he did this once, but never again, telling his employer that slavery was "a practice inconsistent with the Christian religion." Like other early critics of slavery—they were few in number in the American colonies—Woolman emphasized that not only was slavery cruel and unjust toward the slaves but it was also spiritually perilous for the masters, corrupting their souls. No human being should be given total authority and power over another, Woolman maintained, for there is one true master alone to whom all are bound, and that is God himself.

On a trip through the Carolinas, where he spoke with slave owners, Woolman recorded in his Journal*:*

> *After some further conversation I said that men having power too often misapplied it; that though we made slaves of the Negroes, and the Turks made slaves of the Christians, I believed that liberty was the natural right of all men equally.*

During this same journey, he called attention as well to the misguided nature of the complaints—lazy, shiftless, irresponsible—that owners of slaves so often cast at the persons whom they held in bondage.

> *Free men whose minds were properly on their business, found a satisfaction in the improving, cultivating, and providing for their families; but Negroes, laboring to support those who claim them as their property, and expecting nothing but slavery during life, had not the like inducement to be industrious.*

Thanks in large measure to Woolman's efforts, the Quakers were leaders in the long and difficult fight against slavery. In contrast to the Puritans and their successors, who stressed the doctrine of predestination, the Quakers believed that Jesus had died to redeem all mankind—that all men and women could be saved—and thus their ways toward all persons were tolerant, peaceful, mild.

Woolman also spoke against the harsh treatment of sailors and on behalf of Native Americans. "I was early convinced in my mind," he recalled, "that true religion consisted of an inward life. I found no narrowness respecting sects and opinions, but believed that sincere, upright-hearted people in every society who truly love God, were accepted by him." A frequent traveler, Woolman sought whenever possible to put his convictions into practice. Knowing, for example, that slave labor was used to make dyes for clothes, he wore undyed clothing. On his trips to the South, he gave money to slaveholders with whom he stayed, saying that it should be given to the slaves who were laboring while he resided there. Woolman, according to one scholar, was "the greatest Quaker of the nineteenth century and perhaps the most Christlike individual that Quakerism has ever produced."

A classic of religious experience and reflection, Woolman's Journal, *which he began in the mid-1750s, is his best-known work. But his pioneering antislavery essay,* Some Considerations upon the Keeping of Negroes *(1756, excerpted below), is also memorable. As the historian Dwight Lowell Dumond noted, Woolman's essay was "the most widely distributed antislavery work before the Revolution," and "it still occupies an honored place upon the shelves of scholars."*

For a survey of the life and career: Paul Rosenblatt, John Woolman *(1969). See also Janet Whitney,* John Woolman: American Quaker *(1942); and Catherine Owen Peare,* John Woolman: Child of Light *(1954).*

From The Journal of John Woolman

[EARLY LIFE AND VOCATION]

I have often felt a motion of love to leave some hints in writing of my experience of the goodness of God, and now, in the thirty-sixth year of my age, I begin this work. I was born in Northampton, in Burlington County in West Jersey, A.D. 1720, and before I was seven years old I began to be acquainted with the operations of divine love. Through the care of my parents, I was taught to read near as soon as I was capable of it, and as I went from school one Seventh Day,[1] I remember, while my

---

[1]SEVENTH DAY: Saturday. Quakers (The Religious Society of Friends) substituted numbers for the traditional names of the days of the week to avoid recognizing pagan gods (e.g. Wednesday and Friday were named in honor of the Norse deities Woden and Freya, respectively.)

companions went to play by the way, I went forward out of sight; and sitting down, I read the twenty-second chapter of the Revelations: "He showed me a river of water, clear as crystal, proceeding out of the throne of God and the Lamb, etc." And in reading it my mind was drawn to seek after that pure habitation which I then believed God had prepared for His servants. The place where I sat and the sweetness that attended my mind remains fresh in my memory.

This and the like gracious visitations[2] had that effect upon me, that when boys used ill language it troubled me, and through the continued mercies of God I was preserved from it. The pious instructions of my parents were often fresh in my mind when I happened amongst wicked children, and was of use to me. My parents, having a large family of children, used frequently on First Days after meeting[3] to put us to read in the Holy Scriptures or some religious books, one after another, the rest sitting by without much conversation, which I have since often thought was a good practice. From what I had read and heard, I believed there had been in past ages people who walked in uprightness before God in a degree exceeding any that I knew, or heard of, now living; and the apprehension of there being less steadiness and firmness amongst people in this age than in past ages often troubled me while I was a child.

I had a dream about the ninth year of my age as follows: I saw the moon rise near the west and run a regular course eastward, so swift that in about a quarter of an hour she reached our meridian, when there descended from her a small cloud on a direct line to the earth, which lighted on a pleasant green about twenty yards from the door of my father's house (in which I thought I stood) and was immediately turned into a beautiful green tree. The moon appeared to run on with equal swiftness and soon set in the east, at which time the sun arose at the place where it commonly does in the summer, and shining with full radiance in a serene air, it appeared as pleasant a morning as ever I saw.

All this time I stood still in the door in an awful[4] frame of mind, and I observed that as heat increased by the rising sun, it wrought so powerfully on the little green tree that the leaves gradually withered; and before noon it appeared dry and dead. There then appeared a being, small of size, full of strength and resolution, moving swift from the north, southward, called a sun worm.[5]

2VISITATIONS: Moments in which he felt God's presence.
3MEETING: The Quaker service is called a "meeting" and the place that they gather is called the "meetinghouse." Worshippers remain silent until someone is moved by the spirit to speak.
4AWFUL: Full of amazement.
5SUN WORM: An imaginary creature, also called a sun snake.

Another thing remarkable in my childhood was that once, going to a neighbor's house, I saw on the way a robin sitting on her nest; and as I came near she went off, but having young ones, flew about and with many cries expressed her concern for them. I stood and threw stones at her, till one striking her, she fell down dead. At first I was pleased with the exploit, but after a few minutes was seized with horror, as having in a sportive way killed an innocent creature while she was careful for her young. I beheld her lying dead and thought those young ones for which she was so careful must now perish for want of their dam to nourish them; and after some painful considerations on the subject, I climbed up the tree, took all the young birds and killed them, supposing that better than to leave them to pine away and die miserably, and believed in this case that Scripture proverb was fulfilled, "The tender mercies of the wicked are cruel."[6] I then went on my errand, but for some hours could think of little else but the cruelties I had committed, and was much troubled.

Thus He whose tender mercies are over all His works hath placed a principle in the human mind which incites to exercise goodness toward every living creature; and this being singly attended to, people become tender-hearted and sympathizing, but being frequently and totally rejected, the mind shuts itself up in a contrary disposition.

About the twelfth year of my age, my father being abroad, my mother reproved me for some misconduct, to which I made an undutiful reply; and the next First Day as I was with my father returning from meeting, he told me he understood I had behaved amiss to my mother and advised me to be more careful in future. I knew myself blameable, and in shame and confusion remained silent. Being thus awakened to a sense of my wickedness, I felt remorse in my mind, and getting home I retired and prayed to the Lord to forgive me, and do not remember that I ever after that spoke unhandsomely[7] to either of my parents, however foolish in other things.

Having attained the age of sixteen years, I began to love wanton[8] company, and though I was preserved from profane language or scandalous conduct, still I perceived a plant in me which produced much wild grapes. Yet my merciful Father forsook me not utterly, but at times through His grace I was brought seriously to consider my ways, and the sight of my backsliding affected me with sorrow. But for want of rightly attending to the reproofs of instruction, vanity was added to vanity, and repentance

[6]THE TENDER MERCIES OF THE WICKED ARE CRUEL: Proverbs 12:10: "A righteous man regardeth the life of his beast: but the tender mercies of the wicked are cruel."
[7]UNHANDSOMELY: Inappropriately, discourteously.
[8]WANTON: Rebellious or reckless behavior.

to repentance; upon the whole my mind was more and more alienated from the Truth,[9] and I hastened toward destruction. While I meditate on the gulf toward which I traveled and reflect on my youthful disobedience, for these things I weep; mine eye runneth down with water.

Advancing in age the number of my acquaintance increased, and thereby my way grew more difficult. Though I had heretofore found comfort in reading the Holy Scriptures and thinking on heavenly things, I was now estranged therefrom. I knew I was going from the flock of Christ and had no resolution to return; hence serious reflections were uneasy to me and youthful vanities and diversions my greatest pleasure. Running in this road I found many like myself, and we associated in that which is reverse to true friendship.

But in this swift race it pleased God to visit me with sickness, so that I doubted of recovering. And then did darkness, horror, and amazement with full force seize me, even when my pain and distress of body was very great. I thought it would have been better for me never to have had a being than to see the day which I now saw. I was filled with confusion, and in great affliction both of mind and body I lay and bewailed myself. I had not confidence to lift up my cries to God, whom I had thus offended, but in a deep sense of my great folly I was humbled before Him, and at length that Word which is as a fire and a hammer broke and dissolved my rebellious heart. And then my cries were put up in contrition, and in the multitude of His mercies I found inward relief, and felt a close engagement that if He was pleased to restore my health, I might walk humbly before Him.

After my recovery this exercise remained with me a considerable time; but by degrees giving way to youthful vanities, they gained strength, and getting with wanton young people I lost ground. The Lord had been very gracious and spoke peace to me in the time of my distress, and I now most ungratefully turned again to folly, on which account at times I felt sharp reproof but did not get low enough to cry for help. I was not so hardy as to commit things scandalous, but to exceed in vanity and promote mirth was my chief study. Still I retained a love and esteem for pious people, and their company brought an awe upon me.

My dear parents several times admonished me in the fear of the Lord, and their admonition entered into my heart and had a good effect for a season, but not getting deep enough to pray rightly, the tempter when he came found entrance. I remember once, having spent a part of the day in wantonness, as I went to bed at night there lay in a window near my

[9]TRUTH: That is, the ideals and doctrines put forth by the Religious Society of Friends.

bed a Bible, which I opened, and first cast my eye on the text, "We lie down in our shame, and our confusion covers us."[10] This I knew to be my case, and meeting with so unexpected a reproof, I was somewhat affected with it and went to bed under remorse of conscience, which I soon cast off again.

Thus time passed on; my heart was replenished with mirth and wantonness, while pleasing scenes of vanity were presented to my imagination till I attained the age of eighteen years, near which time I felt the judgments of God in my soul like a consuming fire, and looking over my past life the prospect was moving. I was often sad and longed to be delivered from those vanities; then again my heart was strongly inclined to them, and there was in me a sore conflict. At times I turned to folly, and then again sorrow and confusion took hold of me. In a while I resolved totally to leave off some of my vanities, but there was a secret reserve in my heart of the more refined part of them, and I was not low enough to find true peace. Thus for some months I had great trouble, there remaining in me an unsubjected will which rendered my labors fruitless, till at length through the merciful continuance of heavenly visitations I was made to bow down in spirit before the Lord.

I remember one evening I had spent some time in reading a pious author, and walking out alone I humbly prayed to the Lord for His help, that I might be delivered from all those vanities which so ensnared me. Thus being brought low, He helped me; and as I learned to bear the cross I felt refreshment to come from His presence; but not keeping in that strength which gave victory, I lost ground again, the sense of which greatly affected me; and I sought deserts and lonely places and there with tears did confess my sins to God and humbly craved help of Him. And I may say with reverence He was near to me in my troubles, and in those times of humiliation opened my ear to discipline.

I was now led to look seriously at the means by which I was drawn from the pure Truth, and learned this: that if I would live in the life which the faithful servants of God lived in, I must not go into company as heretofore in my own will, but all the cravings of sense must be governed by a divine principle. In times of sorrow and abasement these instructions were sealed upon me, and I felt the power of Christ prevail over selfish desires, so that I was preserved in a good degree of steadiness. And being young and believing at that time that a single life was best for

[10]WE LIE DOWN IN OUR SHAME, AND OUR CONFUSION COVERS US: Jeremiah 3:25: "We lie down in our shame, and our confusion covereth us: for we have sinned against the LORD our God, we and our fathers, from our youth even unto this day, and have not obeyed the voice of the LORD our God."

me, I was strengthened to keep from such company as had often been a snare to me.

I kept steady to meetings, spent First Days after noon chiefly in reading the Scriptures and other good books, and was early convinced in my mind that true religion consisted in an inward life, wherein the heart doth love and reverence God the Creator and learn to exercise true justice and goodness, not only toward all men but also toward the brute creatures; that as the mind was moved on an inward principle to love God as an invisible, incomprehensible being, on the same principle it was moved to love Him in all His manifestations in the visible world; that as by His breath the flame of life was kindled in all animal and sensitive creatures, to say we love God as unseen and at the same time exercise cruelty toward the least creature moving by His life, or by life derived from Him, was a contradiction in itself.

I found no narrowness respecting sects and opinions, but believed that sincere, upright-hearted people in every Society who truly loved God were accepted of Him.

As I lived under the cross and simply followed the openings of Truth,[11] my mind from day to day was more enlightened; my former acquaintance was left to judge of me as they would, for I found it safest for me to live in private and keep these things sealed up in my own breast.

While I silently ponder on that change wrought in me, I find no language equal to it nor any means to convey to another a clear idea of it. I looked upon the works of God in this visible creation and an awfulness covered me; my heart was tender and often contrite, and a universal love to my fellow creatures increased in me. This will be understood by such who have trodden in the same path. Some glances of real beauty may be seen in their faces who dwell in true meekness. There is a harmony in the sound of that voice to which divine love gives utterance, and some appearance of right order in their temper and conduct whose passions are fully regulated. Yet all these do not fully show forth that inward life to such who have not felt it, but this white stone and new name is known rightly to such only who have it.[12]

Now though I had been thus strengthened to bear the cross, I still found myself in great danger, having many weaknesses attending me and strong temptations to wrestle with, in the feelings whereof I frequently

[11]OPENINGS OF TRUTH: Receiving direct messages from God.
[12]SUCH ONLY WHO HAVE IT: Revelation 2:17: "He that hath an ear, let him hear what the Spirit saith unto the churches; To him that overcometh will I give to eat of the hidden manna, and will give him a white stone, and in the stone a new name written, which no man knoweth saving he that receiveth it."

withdrew into private places and often with tears besought the Lord to help me, whose gracious ear was open to my cry.

All this time I lived with my parents and wrought[13] on the plantation, and having had schooling pretty well for a planter, I used to improve in winter evenings and other leisure times. And being now in the twenty-first year of my age, a man in much business shopkeeping and baking asked me if I would hire with him to tend shop and keep books. I acquainted my father with the proposal, and after some deliberation it was agreed for me to go.

At home I had lived retired, and now having a prospect of being much in the way of company, I felt frequent and fervent cries in my heart to God, the Father of Mercies, that He would preserve me from all taint and corruption, that in this more public employ I might serve Him, my gracious Redeemer, in that humility and self-denial with which I had been in a small degree exercised in a very private life.

The man who employed me furnished a shop in Mount Holly, about five miles from my father's house and six from his own, and there I lived alone and tended his shop. Shortly after my settlement here I was visited by several young people, my former acquaintance, who knew not but vanities would be as agreeable to me now as ever; and at these times I cried to the Lord in secret for wisdom and strength, for I felt myself encompassed with difficulties and had fresh occasion to bewail the follies of time past in contracting a familiarity with a libertine[14] people. And as I had now left my father's house outwardly, I found my Heavenly Father to be merciful to me beyond what I can express.

By day I was much amongst people and had many trials to go through, but in evenings I was mostly alone and may with thankfulness acknowledge that in those times the spirit of supplication was often poured upon me, under which I was frequently exercised and felt my strength renewed.

In a few months after I came here, my master bought[15] several Scotch menservants from on board a vessel and brought them to Mount Holly to sell, one of which was taken sick and died. The latter part of his sickness he, being delirious, used to curse and swear most sorrowfully, and after he was buried I was left to sleep alone the next night in the same

---

[13]WROUGHT: Worked.
[14]LIBERTINE: One who holds free opinions about religion, usually not restrained by moral and social laws.
[15]MASTER BOUGHT: Purchased the remaining years of service as outlined in an indenture contract. An indentured servant signed a contract to work for a period of years, usually seven, in return for passage to America, clothing, room, and board. The term "indenture" refers to the fact that the contract was "indented," or torn in half, with each party keeping a portion of the signed copy.

chamber where he died. I perceived in me a timorousness. I knew, however, I had not injured the man but assisted in taking care of him according to my capacity, and was not free to ask anyone on that occasion to sleep with me. Nature was feeble, but every trial was a fresh incitement to give myself up wholly to the service of God, for I found no helper like Him in times of trouble.

After a while my former acquaintance gave over expecting me as one of their company, and I began to be known to some whose conversation was helpful to me. And now, as I had experienced the love of God through Jesus Christ to redeem me from many pollutions and to be a succor to me through a sea of conflicts, with which no person was fully acquainted, and as my heart was often enlarged in this heavenly principle, I felt a tender compassion for the youth who remained entangled in snares like those which had entangled me. From one month to another this love and tenderness increased, and my mind was more strongly engaged for the good of my fellow creatures.

I went to meetings in an awful frame of mind and endeavored to be inwardly acquainted with the language of the True Shepherd. And one day being under a strong exercise of spirit, I stood up and said some words in a meeting, but not keeping close to the divine opening,[16] I said more than was required of me; and being soon sensible of my error, I was afflicted in mind some weeks without any light or comfort, even to that degree that I could take satisfaction in nothing. I remembered God and was troubled, and in the depth of my distress He had pity upon me and sent the Comforter. I then felt forgiveness for my offense, and my mind became calm and quiet, being truly thankful to my gracious Redeemer for His mercies. And after this, feeling the spring of divine love opened and a concern[17] to speak, I said a few words in a meeting, in which I found peace. This I believe was about six weeks from the first time, and as I was thus humbled and disciplined under the cross, my understanding became more strengthened to distinguish the language of the pure Spirit which inwardly moves upon the heart[18] and taught [me] to wait in silence sometimes many weeks together, until I felt that rise which prepares the creature to stand like a trumpet through which the Lord speaks to His flock.

---

[16]DIVINE OPENING: Woolman means that he did not speak because divine spirit moved him, but that he spoke with "worldly wisdom."

[17]CONCERN: When moved by the spirit of divine love, a Quaker is compelled to speak, almost against his or her will.

[18]HEART: Woolman grew better at distinguishing between his personal desires and the revelations that stemmed from true inner light.

From an inward purifying, and steadfast abiding under it, springs a lively operative desire for the good of others. All faithful people are not called to the public ministry, but whoever are, are called to minister of that which they have tasted and handled spiritually. The outward modes of worship are various, but wherever men are true ministers of Jesus Christ it is from the operation of His spirit upon their hearts, first purifying them and thus giving them a feeling sense of the conditions of others. This truth was early fixed in my mind, and I was taught to watch the pure opening and to take heed lest while I was standing to speak, my own will should get uppermost and cause me to utter words from worldly wisdom and depart from the channel of the true gospel ministry.

In the management of my outward affairs I may say with thankfulness I found Truth to be my support, and I was respected in my master's family, who came to live in Mount Holly within two year after my going there.

About the twenty-third year of my age, I had many fresh and heavenly openings in respect to the care and providence of the Almighty over his creatures in general, and over man as the most noble amongst those which are visible. And being clearly convinced in my judgment that to place my whole trust in God was best for me, I felt renewed engagements that in all things I might act on an inward principle of virtue and pursue worldly business no further than as Truth opened my way therein.

About the time called Christmas I observed many people from the country and dwellers in town who, resorting to the public houses, spent their time in drinking and vain sports, tending to corrupt one another, on which account I was much troubled. At one house in particular there was much disorder, and I believed it was a duty laid on me to go and speak to the master of that house. I considered I was young and that several elderly Friends in town had opportunity to see these things, and though I would gladly have been excused, yet I could not feel my mind clear.

The exercise was heavy, and as I was reading what the Almighty said to Ezekiel[19] respecting his duty as a watchman, the matter was set home more clearly; and then with prayer and tears I besought the Lord for His assistance, who in loving-kindness gave me a resigned heart. Then at a suitable opportunity I went to the public house, and seeing the man amongst a company, I went to him and told him I wanted to speak with him; so we went aside, and there in the fear and dread of the Almighty I expressed to him what rested on my mind, which he took kindly, and

---

[19]EZEKIEL: Ezekiel was an Old Testament prophet. The Book of Ezekiel is a collection of prophecies he preached to Jews of the Babylonian captivity from 593 BCE to 563 BCE. "Son of man, I have made thee a watchman unto the house of Israel: therefore hear the word at my mouth, and give them warning from me." (Ezekiel 3:17)

afterward showed more regard to me than before. In a few years after, he died middle-aged, and I often thought that had I neglected my duty in that case it would have given me great trouble, and I was humbly thankful to my gracious Father, who had supported me herein.

My employer, having a Negro woman, sold her and directed me to write a bill of sale, the man being waiting who bought her. The thing was sudden, and though the thoughts of writing an instrument of slavery for one of my fellow creatures felt uneasy, yet I remembered I was hired by the year, that it was my master who directed me to do it, and that it was an elderly man, a member of our Society, who bought her; so through weakness I gave way and wrote it, but at the executing it, I was so afflicted in my mind that I said before my master and the Friend that I believed slavekeeping to be a practice inconsistent with the Christian religion. This in some degree abated my uneasiness, yet as often as I reflected seriously upon it I thought I should have been clearer if I had desired to be excused from it as a thing against my conscience, for such it was. And some time after this a young man of our Society spake to me to write an instrument of slavery, he having lately taken a Negro into his house. I told him I was not easy to write it, for though many kept slaves in our Society, as in others, I still believed the practice was not right, and desired to be excused from writing [it]. I spoke to him in good will, and he told me that keeping slaves was not altogether agreeable to his mind, but that the slave being a gift made to his wife, he had accepted of her.

[1774]

From *Some Considerations on the Keeping of Negroes*

RECOMMENDED TO THE PROFESSORS[1] OF CHRISTIANITY OF EVERY DENOMINATION

INTRODUCTION

Customs generally approved and opinions received by youth from their superiors become like the natural produce of a soil, especially when they are suited to favourite inclinations. But as the judgments of God are without partiality, by which the state of the soul must be tried, it would be

---

[1]PROFESSORS: Believers, the faithful.

the highest wisdom to forego customs and popular opinions, and try the treasures of the soul by the infallible standard: Truth.

Natural affection needs a careful examination. Operating upon us in a soft manner, it kindles desires of love and tenderness, and there is danger of taking it for something higher. To me it appears an instinct like that which inferior creatures have; each of them, we see, by the ties of nature love self best. That which is a part of self they love by the same tie or instinct. In them it in some measure does the offices of reason, by which, among other things, they watchfully keep and orderly feed their helpless offspring. Thus natural affection appears to be a branch of self-love, good in the animal race, in us likewise with proper limitations, but otherwise is productive of evil by exciting desires to promote some by means prejudicial to others.

Our blessed Saviour seems to give a check to this irregular fondness in nature and, at the same time, a precedent for us: "Who is my mother, and who are my brethren?"[2]—thereby intimating that the earthly ties of relationship are, comparatively, inconsiderable to such who, through a steady course of obedience, have come to the happy experience of the Spirit of God bearing witness with their spirits that they are his children: "And he stretched forth his hands towards his disciples and said, 'Behold my mother and my brethren; for whosoever shall do the will of my Father which is in heaven (arrives at the more noble part of true relationship[3]) the same is my brother, and sister, and mother.'" Mt. 12:48 [–50].

This doctrine agrees well with a state truly complete, where love necessarily operates according to the agreeableness of things or principles unalterable and in themselves perfect. If endeavouring to have my children eminent amongst men after my death be that which no reasons grounded on those principles can be brought to support, then to be temperate in my pursuit after gain and to keep always within the bounds of those principles is an indispensable duty, and to depart from it a dark unfruitful toil.

In our present condition, to love our children is needful; but except this love proceeds from the true heavenly principle which sees beyond earthly treasures, it will rather be injurious than of any real advantage to them. Where the fountain is corrupt, the streams must necessarily be impure.

That important injunction of our Saviour (Mt. 6:33[4]), with the promise annexed, contains a short but comprehensive view of our duty

---

[2]WHO IS MY MOTHER, AND WHO ARE MY BRETHREN?: Matthew 12:48.
[3]ARRIVES AT THE MORE NOBLE PART OF TRUE RELATIONSHIP: Woolman inserts this phrase into the quotation from Matthew 12:48.
[4]MT. 6:33: "But seek ye first the kingdom of God, and his righteousness; and all these things shall be added unto you" (Matthew).

and happiness. If then the business of mankind in this life is to first seek another, if this cannot be done but by attending to the means, if a summary of the means is not to do that to another which (in like circumstances) we would not have done unto us, then these are points of moment and worthy of our most serious consideration.

What I write on this subject is with reluctance, and the hints given are in as general terms as my concern would allow. I know it is a point about which in all its branches men that appear to aim well are not generally agreed, and for that reason I chose to avoid being very particular. If I may happily have let drop anything that may excite such as are concerned in the practice to a close thinking on the subject treated of, the candid amongst them may easily do the subject such further justice as, on an impartial enquiry, it may appear to deserve; and such an enquiry I would earnestly recommend.

SOME CONSIDERATIONS ON THE KEEPING OF NEGROES

"Forasmuch as ye did it to the least of these my brethren, ye did it unto me."

MT. 25:40.

As many times there are different motives to the same actions, and one does that from a generous heart which another does for selfish ends, the like may be said in this case.

There are various circumstances amongst them that keep Negroes, and different ways by which they fall under their care; and, I doubt not, there are many well-disposed persons amongst them who desire rather to manage wisely and justly in this difficult matter than to make gain of it. But the general disadvantage which these poor Africans lie under in an enlightened Christian country having often filled me with real sadness, and been like undigested matter on my mind, I now think it my duty, through divine aid, to offer some thoughts thereon to the consideration of others.

When we remember that all nations are of one blood (Gen. 3:20[5]); that in this world we are but sojourners; that we are subject to the like afflictions and infirmities of body, the like disorders and frailties in mind, the like temptations; the same death and the same judgment; and that the All-wise Being is judge and Lord over us all, it seems to raise an idea of a general brotherhood and a disposition easy to be touched with

---

[5]GEN. 3:20: "And Adam called his wife's name Eve; because she was the mother of all living things" (Genesis).

a feeling of each other's afflictions. But when we forget those things and look chiefly at our outward circumstances, in this and some ages past, constantly retaining in our minds the distinction betwixt us and them with respect to our knowledge and improvement in things divine, natural, and artificial, our breasts being apt to be filled with fond notions of superiority, there is danger of erring in our conduct toward them.

We allow them to be of the same species with ourselves; the odds is we are in a higher station and enjoy greater favours than they. And when it is thus that our Heavenly Father endoweth some of his children with distinguished gifts, they are intended for good ends. But if those thus gifted are thereby lifted up above their brethren, not considering themselves as debtors to the weak nor behaving themselves as faithful stewards, none who judge impartially can suppose them free from ingratitude. When a people dwell under the liberal distribution of favours from heaven, it behooves them carefully to inspect their ways and consider the purposes for which those favours were bestowed, lest through forgetfulness of God and misusing his gifts they incur his heavy displeasure, whose judgments are just and equal, who exalteth and humbleth to the dust as he seeth meet.

It appears by Holy Record that men under high favours have been apt to err in their opinions concerning others. Thus Israel, according to the description of the prophet (Is. 65:5), when exceedingly corrupted and degenerated, yet remembered they were the chosen people of God and could say, "Stand by thyself; come not near me, for I am holier than thou." That this was no chance language, but their common opinion of other people, more fully appears by considering the circumstances which attended when God was beginning to fulfill his precious promises concerning the gathering of the Gentiles.

The Most High, in a vision, undeceived Peter, first prepared his heart to believe, and at the house of Cornelius showed him of a certainty that God was no respecter of persons. The effusion of the Holy Ghost upon a people with whom they, the Jewish Christians, would not so much as eat was strange to them. All they of the circumcision were astonished to see it, and the apostles and brethren of Judea contended with Peter about it, till he having rehearsed the whole matter and fully shown that the Father's love was unlimited, they are thereat struck with admiration and cry out, "Then hath God also to the Gentiles granted repentance unto life!" [Acts 11:18].

The opinion of peculiar favours being confined to them was deeply rooted, or else the above instance had been less strange to them, for these reasons: First, they were generally acquainted with the writings of the prophets, by whom this time was repeatedly spoken of and pointed at. Secondly, our blessed Lord shortly before expressly said, "I have other sheep, not of this fold; them also must I bring," etc. [Jn. 10:16]. Lastly, his words to them after his resurrection, at the very time of his ascension, "Ye shall be witnesses to me not only in Jerusalem, Judea, and Samaria, but to the uttermost parts of the earth" [Acts 1:8].

Those concurring circumstances, one would think, might have raised a strong expectation of seeing such a time. Yet when it came, it proved matter of offense and astonishment.

To consider mankind otherwise than brethren, to think favours are peculiar to one nation and exclude others, plainly supposes a darkness in the understanding. For as God's love is universal, so where the mind is sufficiently influenced by it, it begets a likeness of itself and the heart is enlarged towards all men. Again, to conclude a people froward,[6] perverse, and worse by nature than others (who ungratefully receive favours and apply them to bad ends), this will excite a behavior toward them unbecoming the excellence of true religion.

To prevent such error let us calmly consider their circumstances, and, the better to do it, make their case ours. Suppose, then, that our ancestors and we have been exposed to constant servitude in the more servile and inferior employments of life; that we had been destitute of the help of reading and good company; that amongst ourselves we had had few wise and pious instructors; that the religious amongst our superiors seldom took notice of us; that while others in ease have plentifully heaped up the fruit of our labour, we had received barely enough to relieve nature, and being wholly at the command of others had generally been treated as a contemptible, ignorant part of mankind. Should we, in that case, be less abject than they now are? Again, if oppression be so hard to bear that a wise man is made mad by it (Eccles. 7:7), then a series of those things altering the behaviour and manners of a people is what may reasonably be expected.

When our property is taken contrary to our mind by means appearing to us unjust, it is only through divine influence and the enlargement of heart from thence proceeding that we can love our reputed oppressors. If the Negroes fall short in this, an uneasy, if not a disconsolate, disposition will be awakened and remain like seeds in their minds, producing sloth and many other habits appearing odious to us, with which being free men they perhaps had not been chargeable. These and other circumstances, rightly considered, will lessen that too great disparity which some make between us and them.

---

[6]FROWARD: Difficult to deal with; contrary.

Integrity of heart hath appeared in some of them, so that if we continue in the world of Christ (previous to discipleship, Jn. 8:31[7]) and our conduct towards them be seasoned with his love, we may hope to see the good effect of it, the which, in a good degree, is the case with some into whose hands they have fallen. But that too many treat them otherwise, not seeming conscious of any neglect, is, alas! too evident.

When self-love presides in our minds our opinions are biased in our own favour. In this condition, being concerned with a people so situated that they have no voice to plead their own cause, there's danger of using ourselves to an undisturbed partiality till, by long custom, the mind becomes reconciled with it and the judgment itself infected.

To humbly apply to God for wisdom, that we may thereby be enabled to see things as they are and ought to be, is very needful; hereby the hidden things of darkness may be brought to light and the judgment made clear. We shall then consider mankind as brethren. Though different degrees and a variety of qualifications and abilities, one dependent on another, be admitted, yet high thoughts will be laid aside, and all men treated as becometh the sons of one Father, agreeable to the doctrine of Christ Jesus.

> *He hath laid down the best criterion by which mankind ought to judge of their own conduct, and others judge for them of theirs, one towards another—viz., "Whatsoever ye would that men should do unto you, do ye even so to them." I take it that all men by nature are equally entitled to the equality of this rule and under the indispensable obligations of it. One man ought not to look upon another man or society of men as so far beneath him but that he should put himself in their place in all his actions towards them, and bring all to this test—viz., How should I approve of this conduct were I in their circumstances and they in mine?—Arscott's* Considerations,[8] *Part III, Fol. 107.*

This doctrine, being of a moral unchangeable nature, hath been likewise inculcated in the former dispensation[9]: "If a stranger sojourn with thee in your land, ye shall not vex him; but the stranger that

---

[7]PREVIOUS TO DISCIPLESHIP, JN. 8:31: "Then said Jesus to those Jews which believed on him, If ye continue in my word, then are ye my disciples indeed" (John).

[8]ARSCOTT'S CONSIDERATIONS: Alexander Arscott (1676–1737), an educator and Quaker. The slightly altered quote Woolman cites comes from Arscott's 1734 volume entitled *Some considerations relating to the present state of the Christian religion: wherein the nature and design of Christianity, as well as the principle evidence of the truth of it, are explained and recommended out of the Holy Scriptures; with a general appeal to the experience of all men for confirmation thereof, Part III.*

[9]DISPENSATION: Order.

dwelleth with you shall be as one born amongst you, and thou shalt love him as thyself." Lev. 19:33, 34. Had these people come voluntarily and dwelt amongst us, to have called them strangers would be proper. And their being brought by force, with regret and a languishing mind, may well raise compassion in a heart rightly disposed. But there is nothing in such treatment which upon a wise and judicious consideration will any ways lessen their right of being treated as strangers. If the treatment which many of them meet with be rightly examined and compared with those precepts, "Thou shalt not vex him nor oppress him; he shall be as one born amongst you, and thou shalt love him as thyself" (Lev. 19:33; Deut. 27:19), there will appear an important difference betwixt them.

It may be objected there is cost of purchase and risk of their lives to them who possess 'em, and therefore needful that they make the best use of their time. In a practice just and reasonable such objections may have weight; but if the work be wrong from the beginning, there's little or no force in them. If I purchase a man who hath never forfeited his liberty, the natural right of freedom is in him. And shall I keep him and his posterity in servitude and ignorance? How should I approve of this conduct were I in his circumstances and he in mine? It may be thought that to treat them as we would willingly be treated, our gain by them would be inconsiderable; and it were, in diverse respects, better that there were none in our country.

We may further consider that they are now amongst us, and those of our nation the cause of their being here, that whatsoever difficulty accrues thereon we are justly chargeable with, and to bear all inconveniences attending it with a serious and weighty concern of mind to do our duty by them is the best we can do. To seek a remedy by continuing the oppression because we have power to do it and see others do it, will, I apprehend, not be doing as we would be done by.

How deeply soever men are involved in the most exquisite difficulties, sincerity of heart and upright walking before God, freely submitting to his providence, is the most sure remedy. He only is able to relieve not only persons but nations in their greatest calamities. David, in a great strait when the sense of his past error and the full expectation of an impending calamity as the reward of it were united to the aggravating his distress, after some deliberation saith, "Let me fall now into the hands of the Lord, for very great are his mercies; let me not fall into the hand of man." I Chron. 21:13.

To act continually with integrity of heart above all narrow or selfish motives is a sure token of our being partakers of that salvation which God hath appointed for walls and bulwarks[10] (Is. 5:26; Rom. 15:8), and is, beyond all contradiction, a more happy situation than can ever be promised by the utmost reach of art and power united, not proceeding from heavenly wisdom.

A supply to nature's lawful wants, joined with a peaceful, humble mind, is the truest happiness in this life. And if here we arrive to this and remain to walk in the path of the just, our case will be truly happy. And though herein we may part with or miss of some glaring shows of riches and leave our children little else but wise instructions, a good example, and the knowledge of some honest employment, these, with the blessing of providence, are sufficient for their happiness, and are more likely to prove so than laying up treasures for them which are often rather a snare than any real benefit, especially to them who, instead of being exampled to temperance, are in all things taught to prefer the getting of riches and to eye the temporal distinctions they give as the principal business of this life. These readily overlook the true happiness of man as it results from the enjoyment of all things in the fear of God, and miserably substituting an inferior good, dangerous in the acquiring and uncertain in the fruition, they are subject to many disappointments; and every sweet carries its sting.

It is the conclusion of our blessed Lord and his apostles, as appears by their lives and doctrines, that the highest delights of sense or most pleasing objects visible ought ever to be accounted infinitely inferior to that real intellectual happiness suited to man in his primitive innocence and now to be found in true renovation of mind, and that the comforts of our present life, the things most grateful to us, ought always to be received with temperance and never made the chief objects of our desire, hope, or love, but that our whole heart and affections be principally looking to that city "which hath foundations, whose maker and builder is God" [Heb. 11:10].

Did we so improve the gifts bestowed on us that our children might have an education suited to these doctrines, and our example to confirm it, we might rejoice in hopes of their being heirs of an inheritance incorruptible. This inheritance, as Christians, we esteem the most valuable; and how then can we fail to desire it for our children? Oh, that we were consistent with ourselves in pursuing means necessary to obtain it!

It appears by experience that where children are educated in fullness,[11] ease, and idleness, evil habits are more prevalent than is common

---

[10]BULWARKS: Defensive constructions; fortifications.
[11]FULLNESS: Abundance or affluence.

amongst such who are prudently employed in the necessary affairs of life. And if children are not only educated in the way of so great temptation, but have also the opportunity of lording it over their fellow creatures and being masters of men in their childhood, how can we hope otherwise than that their tender minds will be possessed with thoughts too high for them?—which by continuance, gaining strength, will prove like a slow current, gradually separating them from (or keeping from acquaintance with) that humility and meekness in which alone lasting happiness can be enjoyed....

[1754]

J. Hector St. John de Crèvecoeur
(1735–1813)

Born in Normandy, France, J. Hector St. John de Crèvecoeur traveled to
England when he was nineteen and lived there with relatives. The follow-
ing year he journeyed to Canada, where he served in the Canadian militia
and worked as a surveyor and map-maker. He made extended trips
through the American colonies in the 1760s before settling down in 1769,
newly married, as an American farmer in Orange County in the Hudson
River Valley of New York.

When the American Revolution began, Crèvecoeur decided to make
his way back to France. But when he tried to embark at New York City,
he was arrested as a rebel spy—a strange turn of events, given that he
was more sympathetic to the Tories than he was to the American revolu-
tionaries. Crèvecoeur finally reached London and then crossed the
Channel to take up residence in France. In 1783 he returned to the
United States, only to discover that an Indian raid had destroyed his
farm, that his wife was dead, and that his children were living with peo-
ple whom he did not know. In two years' time, despite success as a diplo-
mat, Crèvecoeur returned to France, where he remained until his death.

Crèvecoeur's Letters from an American Farmer *was first published*
in 1782—it was very popular and led to a friendship with Thomas
Jefferson and correspondence with George Washington and Benjamin
Franklin—and then in an expanded French edition in 1784. Through
his narrator, Farmer James, Crèvecoeur gives an impassioned, affirma-
tive account of the opportunities that exist for immigrants to America,
an extraordinary land where persons are made "new." They own prop-
erty, work under mild laws, and live in harmony with Nature.

In one of the Letters, Crèvecoeur takes disturbing note of slavery—
this Eden is imperfect after all. The final Letter in the series presents
Farmer James, fearing the violence caused by the Revolution, making
plans to move to the frontier and hoping there to find again the peace
and fulfillment imperiled by the war.

Crèvecoeur had come to the New World, the scholar Annette
Kolodny observed, "saturated with the Enlightenment's faith that here,
in an uncontaminated environment, Europe might produce the kind of
society it had only dreamt of on the old continent." In Letters from an
American Farmer, *Crèvecoeur pays tribute to this fervent hope, the*
American dream, even as he touches as well on its precariousness: the
splendid world of "new" men and women, the Americans, might prove
difficult to maintain and nurture.

For biography and interpretation: Thomas Philbrick, St. John de
Crèvecoeur *(1970); and Gay Wilson Allen and Roger Asselineau*, St.
John de Crèvecoeur: The Life of an American Farmer *(1987).*

From Letters from an American Farmer: Letter III. What Is an American?

I wish I could be acquainted with the feelings and thoughts which must agitate the heart and present themselves to the mind of an enlightened Englishman when he first lands on this continent. He must greatly rejoice that he lived at a time to see this fair country discovered and settled; he must necessarily feel a share of national pride when he views the chain of settlements which embellish these extended shores. When he says to himself, "This is the work of my countrymen, who, when convulsed by factions,[1] afflicted by a variety of miseries and wants, restless and impatient, took refuge here. They brought along with them their national genius,[2] to which they principally owe what liberty they enjoy and what substance they possess." Here he sees the industry of his native country displayed in a new manner and traces in their works the embryos of all the arts, sciences, and ingenuity which flourish in Europe. Here he beholds fair cities, substantial villages, extensive fields, an immense country filled with decent houses, good roads, orchards, meadows, and bridges where an hundred years ago all was wild, woody, and uncultivated! What a train of pleasing ideas this fair spectacle must suggest; it is a prospect which must inspire a good citizen with the most heart-felt pleasure. The difficulty consists in the manner of viewing so extensive a scene. He is arrived on a new continent; a modern society offers itself to his contemplation, different from what he had hitherto seen. It is not composed, as in Europe, of great lords who possess everything and of a herd of people who have nothing. Here are no aristocratical families, no courts, no kings, no bishops, no ecclesiastical dominion, no invisible power giving to a few a very visible one, no great manufactures employing thousands, no great refinements of luxury. The rich and the poor are not so far removed from each other as they are in Europe. Some few towns excepted, we are all tillers of the earth, from Nova Scotia to West Florida. We are a people of cultivators scattered over an immense territory, communicating with each other by means of good roads and navigable rivers, united by the silken bands of mild government, all respecting the laws without dreading their power, because they are equitable. We are all animated with the spirit of an industry which is unfettered and unrestrained,

[1]FACTIONS: Disputes.
[2]GENIUS: Distinctive national character.

because each person works for himself. If he travels through our rural districts, he views not the hostile castle and the haughty mansion, contrasted with the clay-built hut and miserable cabin, where cattle and men help to keep each other warm and dwell in meanness, smoke, and indigence. A pleasing uniformity of decent competence appears throughout our habitations. The meanest of our log-houses is a dry and comfortable habitation. Lawyer or merchant are the fairest titles our towns afford; that of a farm is the only appellation of the rural inhabitants of our country. It must take some time ere he can reconcile himself to our dictionary, which is but short in words of dignity and names of honour. There, on a Sunday, he sees a congregation of respectable farmers and their wives, all clad in neat homespun,[3] well mounted, or riding in their own humble wagons. There is not among them an esquire, saving the unlettered magistrate. There he sees a parson as simple as his flock, a farmer who does not riot[4] on the labour of others. We have no princes for whom we toil, starve, and bleed; we are the most perfect society now existing in the world. Here man is free as he ought to be, nor is this pleasing equality so transitory as many others are. Many ages will not see the shores of our great lakes replenished with inland nations, nor the unknown bounds of North America entirely peopled. Who can tell how far it extends? Who can tell the millions of men whom it will feed and contain? For no European foot has as yet travelled half the extent of this mighty continent!

The next wish of this traveller will be to know whence came all these people. They are a mixture of English, Scotch, Irish, French, Dutch, Germans, and Swedes. From this promiscuous breed, that race now called Americans have arisen. The eastern provinces[5] must indeed be excepted as being the unmixed descendants of Englishmen. I have heard many wish that they had been more intermixed also; for my part, I am no wisher and think it much better as it has happened. They exhibit a most conspicuous figure in this great and variegated picture; they too enter for a great share in the pleasing perspective displayed in these thirteen provinces. I know it is fashionable to reflect on them,[6] but I respect them for what they have done; for the accuracy and wisdom with which they have settled their territory; for the decency of their manners; for their early love of letters; their ancient college,[7] the first in this hemisphere; for

---

[3]HOMESPUN: Cloth made at home—usually simple, rustic woolen cloth.
[4]RIOT: Revel or indulge to excess.
[5]EASTERN PROVINCES: New England.
[6]REFLECT ON THEM: Cast blame.
[7]ANCIENT COLLEGE: Harvard College, founded in 1636.

their industry, which to me who am but a farmer is the criterion of everything. There never was a people, situated as they are, who with so ungrateful a soil have done more in so short a time. Do you think that the
monarchical ingredients which are more prevalent in other governments
have purged them from all foul stains? Their histories assert the contrary.

In this great American asylum, the poor of Europe have by some
means met together, and in consequence of various causes; to what purpose should they ask one another what countrymen they are? Alas, two
thirds of them had no country. Can a wretch who wanders about, who
works and starves, whose life is a continual scene of sore affliction or
pinching penury[8]—can that man call England or any other kingdom
his country? A country that had no bread for him, whose fields procured him no harvest, who met with nothing but the frowns of the rich,
the severity of the laws, with jails and punishments, who owned not a single foot of the extensive surface of this planet? No! Urged by a variety
of motives, here they came. Everything has tended to regenerate them:
new laws, a new mode of living, a new social system; here they are
become men: in Europe they were as so many useless plants, wanting veg-
etative mould and refreshing showers; they withered, and were mowed
down by want, hunger, and war; but now, by the power of transplantation, like all other plants they have taken root and flourished! Formerly
they were not numbered in any civil lists[9] of their country, except in those
of the poor; here they rank as citizens. By what invisible power hath
this surprising metamorphosis been performed? By that of the laws and
that of their industry. The laws, the indulgent laws, protect them as they
arrive, stamping on them the symbol of adoption; they receive ample
rewards for their labours; these accumulated rewards procure them lands;
those lands confer on them the title of freemen, and to that title every benefit is affixed which men can possibly require. This is the great operation daily performed by our laws. Whence proceed these laws? From the
government. Whence that government? It is derived from the original
genius and strong desire of the people ratified and confirmed by the crown.
This is the great chain which links us all, this is the picture which every
province exhibits, Nova Scotia excepted. There the crown has done all[10];
either there were no people who had genius or it was not much attended
to; the consequence is that the province is very thinly inhabited indeed;

---

[8]PENURY: State of want or poverty.
[9]CIVIL LISTS: Employees of the civil government—judges, officials, ambassadors, and so on.
[10]NOVA SCOTIA EXCEPTED...THERE THE CROWN HAS DONE ALL: Originally owned by
France, Nova Scotia, under a garrison government, was added to the British Empire in 1713. In
1755, the British banished the French Acadians from the area.

the power of the crown in conjunction with the musketos has prevented men from settling there. Yet some parts of it flourished once, and it contained a mild, harmless set of people. But for the fault of a few leaders, the whole was banished. The greatest political error the crown ever committed in America was to cut off men from a country which wanted nothing but men!

What attachment can a poor European emigrant have for a country where he had nothing? The knowledge of the language, the love of a few kindred as poor as himself, were the only cords that tied him; his country is now that which gives him his land, bread, protection, and consequence. *Ubi panis ibi patria*[11] is the motto of all emigrants. What, then, is the American, this new man? He is either an European or the descendant of an European; hence that strange mixture of blood, which you will find in no other country. I could point out to you a family whose grandfather was an Englishman, whose wife was Dutch, whose son married a French woman, and whose present four sons have now four wives of different nations. *He* is an American, who, leaving behind him all his ancient prejudices and manners, receives new ones from the new mode of life he has embraced, the new government he obeys, and the new rank he holds. He becomes an American by being received in the broad lap of our great Alma Mater.[12] Here individuals of all nations are melted into a new race of men, whose labours and posterity will one day cause great changes in the world. Americans are the western pilgrims who are carrying along with them that great mass of arts, sciences, vigour, and industry which began long since in the East; they will finish the great circle. The Americans were once scattered all over Europe; here they are incorporated into one of the finest systems of population which has ever appeared, and which will hereafter become distinct by the power of the different climates they inhabit. The American ought therefore to love this country much better than that wherein either he or his forefathers were born. Here the rewards of his industry follow with equal steps the progress of his labour; his labour is founded on the basis of nature, self-interest; can it want a stronger allurement? Wives and children, who before in vain demanded of him a morsel of bread, now, fat and frolicsome, gladly help their father to clear those fields whence exuberant crops are to arise to feed and to clothe them all, without any part being claimed, either by a despotic prince, a rich abbot, or a mighty lord. Here religion demands but little of him: a small voluntary salary to the minister

---

[11]UBI PANIS IBI PATRIA: "Where there is bread, there is one's fatherland." (Latin)
[12]ALMA MATER: Dear mother. (Latin)

and gratitude to God; can he refuse these? The American is a new man, who acts upon new principles; he must therefore entertain new ideas and form new opinions. From involuntary idleness, servile dependence, penury, and useless labour, he has passed to toils of a very different nature, rewarded by ample subsistence. This is an American....

Andrew[13] arrived at my house a week before I did, and I found my wife, agreeably to my instructions, had placed the axe in his hands as his first task. For some time, he was very awkward, but he was so docile, so willing, and grateful, as well as his wife, that I foresaw he would succeed. Agreeably to my promise, I put them all with different families, where they were well liked, and all parties were pleased. Andrew worked hard, lived well, grew fat, and every Sunday came to pay me a visit on a good horse, which Mr. P.R. lent him. Poor man, it took him a long time ere he could sit on the saddle and hold the bridle properly. I believe he had never before mounted such a beast, though I did not choose to ask him that question, for fear it might suggest some mortifying ideas. After having been twelve months at Mr. P.R.'s and having received his own and his family's wages, which amounted to eighty-four dollars, he came to see me on a weekday and told me that he was a man of middle age and would willingly have land of his own in order to procure him a home as a shelter against old age, that whenever this period should come, his son, to whom he would give his land, would then maintain him, and thus live altogether; he therefore required my advice and assistance. I thought his desire very natural and praiseworthy, and told him that I should think of it, but that he must remain one month longer with Mr. P.R., who had 3,000 rails to split. He immediately consented. The spring was not far advanced enough yet for Andrew to begin clearing any land, even supposing that he had made a purchase, as it is always necessary that the leaves should be out in order that this additional combustible may serve to burn the heaps of brush more readily.

A few days after, it happened that the whole family of Mr. P.R. went to meeting, and left Andrew to take care of the house. While he was at the door, attentively reading the Bible, nine Indians just come from the mountains suddenly made their appearance and unloaded their packs of furs on the floor of the piazza. Conceive, if you can, what was Andrew's consternation at this extraordinary sight! From the singular appearance of these people, the honest Hebridean[14] took them for a lawless band come to rob his master's house. He therefore, like a faithful

---

[13]ANDREW: An immigrant from Scotland.
[14]HEBRIDEAN: An individual from the Hebrides, a group of islands off the west coast of Scotland.

guardian, precipitately withdrew and shut the doors; but as most of our houses are without locks, he was reduced to the necessity of fixing his knife over the latch, and then flew upstairs in quest of a broadsword he had brought from Scotland. The Indians, who were Mr. P.R.'s particular friends, guessed at his suspicions and fears; they forcibly lifted the door and suddenly took possession of the house, got all the bread and meat they wanted, and sat themselves down by the fire. At this instant, Andrew, with his broadsword in his hand, entered the room, the Indians earnestly looking at him and attentively watching his motions. After a very few reflections, Andrew found that his weapon was useless when opposed to nine tomahawks, but this did not diminish his anger; on the contrary, it grew greater on observing the calm impudence with which they were devouring the family provisions. Unable to resist, he called them names in broad Scotch and ordered them to desist and be gone, to which the Indians (as they told me afterwards) replied in their equally broad idiom. It must have been a most unintelligible altercation between this honest Barra[15] man and nine Indians who did not much care for anything he could say. At last he ventured to lay his hands on one of them in order to turn him out of the house. Here Andrew's fidelity got the better of his prudence, for the Indian, by his motions, threatened to scalp him, while the rest gave the war whoop. This horrid noise so effectually frightened poor Andrew that, unmindful of his courage, of his broadsword, and his intentions, he rushed out, left them masters of the house, and disappeared. I have heard one of the Indians say since that he never laughed so heartily in his life. Andrew, at a distance, soon recovered from the fears which had been inspired by this infernal yell and thought of no other remedy than to go to the meeting-house, which was about two miles distant. In the eagerness of his honest intentions, with looks of affright still marked on his countenance, he called Mr. P.R. out and told him with great vehemence of style that nine monsters were come to his house—some blue, some red, and some black; that they had little axes in their hands out of which they smoked; and that like highlanders, they had no breeches; that they were devouring all his victuals; and that God only knew what they would do more. "Pacify yourself," said Mr. P.R.; "my house is as safe with these people as if I was there myself; as for the victuals, they are heartily welcome, honest Andrew; they are not people of much ceremony; they help themselves thus whenever they are among their friends; I do so too in their wigwams,

---

[15]BARRA: An island off of the west coast of Scotland.

whenever I go to their village; you had better therefore step in and hear the remainder of the sermon, and when the meeting is over, we will all go back in the wagon together."

At their return, Mr. P.R., who speaks the Indian language very well, explained the whole matter; the Indians renewed their laugh and shook hands with honest Andrew, whom they made to smoke out of their pipes; and thus peace was made and ratified according to the Indian custom, by the calumet.[16]

[1782]

---

[16]CALUMET: A pipe with a bowl made of clay or stone and a long stem often ornamented with feathers, used by Native Americans to symbolize peace or friendship.

John Adams

(1735–1826)

*John Adams wrote the letter below (the ellipses in it are in the original
text) to his wife, Abigail, while he was serving as a delegate to the
Continental Congress in Philadelphia. In early June 1776 a Virginian,
Richard Henry Lee, had advanced the motion (seconded by Adams) "that
these United Colonies are, and of right ought to be, Free and Independent
States." The motion was debated, and it carried on July 2. Thomas
Jefferson, with the advice of a committee that included Adams, drafted a
preamble to Lee's resolution, and it was adopted on July 4, 1776. This
preamble is the document now known as the Declaration of Independence.*

*Adams was born in Braintree, Massachusetts. He graduated in
1755 from Harvard College (he was the first in his family to attend college) and then undertook a career in law, which proceeded slowly for
him. He married Abigail Smith in 1764, and they had five children, one
of whom was John Quincy Adams, the future statesman and sixth president. Abigail Adams was a strong-minded person in her own right, a
wide-ranging reader, and a skillful letter-writer, and scholars have
studied this prominent, gifted woman's letters, experiences, and views
for insight into gender roles in America in the eighteenth century.*

*In 1770 Adams took on the case of British soldiers who had killed
five townspeople in the "Boston Massacre"; a man of strong convictions,
he believed the accused always has the right to a full and fair defense.
But Adams already had been critical of British rule, and by the early
1770s he was well underway in the campaign against the British, convinced that the mother country was denying and conspiring against the
freedoms of its colonies. A key member of many committees, his important writings of this period include* Novanglus *(1774) and* Thoughts on
Government *(1776), seminal texts in the Revolutionary cause and in
the development of a plan for the colonies' transformation into a government of independent states. During the Revolution, Adams served as
U.S. Commissioner to France, and he was a member of the delegation
that negotiated the Treaty of Paris that brought the war to an end.*

*Adams then served as U.S. minister to Great Britain (1785–1788);
as vice president under George Washington (1789–1797)—"My country," Adams said, "has in its wisdom contrived for me the most insignificant office that ever the invention of man contrived or his imagination
conceived"; and as the nation's second president (1797–1801). One of
his main political rivals was Jefferson, and Adams was deeply hurt by
and resentful of the voters who rejected him in favor of Jefferson in the
presidential election of 1800.*

*"Vanity," Adams remarked, "I am sensible, is my cardinal vice and
cardinal folly." Cranky, conservative by nature and temperament, energetic, ambitious, easily and highly agitated, Adams "was terribly open,*

earnest and direct," noted the Boston reformer and scholar Theodore Parker, *"and could not keep his mouth shut."*

Later, however, Adams and Jefferson renewed their relationship, maintaining a rich, vivid correspondence. Jefferson saw Adams's shortcomings, yet deeply respected him, writing in 1787 to James Madison that Adams *"is vain, irritable, and a bad calculator of the force and probable effect of the motives which govern men. This is all the ill which can possibly be said of him. He is as disinterested as the Being who made him."* Adams died on the same day Jefferson did, July 4, 1826, the fiftieth anniversary of the Continental Congress's unanimous approval of the Declaration of Independence.

For biography and context: John Ferling, John Adams: A Life *(1992); Joseph J. Ellis*, Passionate Sage: The Character and Legacy of John Adams *(1993); and David McCullough*, John Adams *(2001). See also Charles W. Akers*, Abigail Adams: An American Woman *(1980); and Phyllis Lee Levin*, Abigail Adams: A Biography *(1987). Also valuable: John Ferling*, Setting the World Ablaze: Washington, Adams, Jefferson, and the American Revolution *(2000); and Richard Brookhiser*, America's First Dynasty: The Adamses, 1735–1918 *(2002).*

John Adams to Abigail Adams

Philadelphia July 3d. 1776

Had a Declaration of Independency been made seven Months ago, it would have been attended with many great and glorious Effects[1]....We might before this Hour, have formed Alliances with foreign States.—We should have mastered Quebec and been in Possession of Canada....You will perhaps wonder, how such a Declaration would have influenced our Affairs, in Canada, but if I could write with Freedom I could easily convince you, that it would, and explain to you the manner how.—Many Gentlemen in high Stations and of great Influence have been duped, by the ministerial Bubble of Commissioners to treat[2]....And in real, sincere Expectation of this Event, which they so fondly wished, they have been slow and languid, in promoting Measures for the Reduction[3] of that

---

[1]GLORIOUS EFFECTS: On June 7, 1776, Richard Henry Lee (1732–1794), a delegate to the Continental Congress from Virginia, moved that "These United Colonies are, and of right ought to be, Free and Independent States." His motion was carried on July 2, 1776. To draft the formal declaration of this decision, a committee was created, of which Thomas Jefferson was a member and the primary author.
[2]TREAT: Negotiate.
[3]REDUCTION: Conquest.

Province. Others there are in the Colonies who really wished that our Enterprise in Canada would be defeated, that the Colonies might be brought into Danger and Distress between two Fires, and be thus induced to submit. Others really wished to defeat the Expedition to Canada, lest the Conquest of it, should elevate the Minds of the People too much to hearken to those Terms of Reconciliation which they believed would be offered Us. These jarring Views, Wishes and Designs, occasioned an opposition to many salutary Measures, which were proposed for the Support of that Expedition, and caused Obstructions, Embarrassments and studied Delays, which have finally, lost Us the Province.

All these Causes however in Conjunction would not have disappointed Us, if it had not been for a Misfortune, which could not be foreseen, and perhaps could not have been prevented, I mean the Prevalence of the small Pox among our Troops....This fatal Pestilence compleated our Destruction.—It is a Frown of Providence upon Us, which We ought to lay to heart.

But on the other Hand, the Delay of this Declaration to this Time, has many great Advantages attending it.—The Hopes of Reconciliation, which were fondly entertained by Multitudes of honest and well meaning tho weak and mistaken People, have been gradually and at last totally extinguished.—Time has been given for the whole People, maturely to consider the great Question of Independence and to ripen their Judgments, dissipate their Fears, and allure their Hopes, by discussing it in News Papers and Pamphletts, by debating it, in Assemblies, Conventions, Committees of Safety and Inspection, in Town and County Meetings, as well as in private Conversations, so that the whole People in every Colony of the 13, have now adopted it, as their own Act.—This will cement the Union, and avoid those Heats and perhaps Convulsions which might have been occasioned, by such a Declaration Six Months ago.

But the Day is past. The Second Day of July 1776, will be the most memorable Epocha, in the History of America.[4]—I am apt to believe that it will be celebrated, by succeeding Generations, as the great anniversary Festival. It ought to be commemorated, as the Day of Deliverance by solemn Acts of Devotion to God Almighty. It ought to be solemnized with Pomp and Parade, with Shews, Games, Sports, Guns, Bells, Bonfires and Illuminations from one End of this Continent to the other from this Time forward forever more.

---

[4]THE SECOND DAY OF JULY 1776, WILL BE THE MOST MEMORABLE EPOCHA, IN THE HISTORY OF AMERICA: Adams believed that July 2, 1776, the day the Continental Congress adopted the resolution to sever its ties to Great Britain, would be the celebrated day, rather than the day the Declaration of Independence was ratified, July 4.

You will think me transported with Enthusiasm but I am not.—I am well aware of the Toil and Blood and Treasure, that it will cost Us to maintain this Declaration, and support and defend these States.—Yet through all the Gloom I can see the Rays of ravishing[5] Light and Glory. I can see that the End is more than worth all the Means. And that Posterity will tryumph in that Days Transaction, even altho We should rue[6] it, which I trust in God We shall not.

[1776]

[5]RAVISHING: Transporting.
[6]RUE: Regret or wish one had acted otherwise.

Thomas Paine

(1737–1809)

Thomas Paine was born in Thetford, England, the son of Quakers. In his mid-thirties, his career plans unsettled, he met Benjamin Franklin, who urged him to emigrate to America and recommended him to friends in Philadelphia as an "ingenious, worthy young man."

Paine reached America in 1774 and found work in Philadelphia as coeditor of the Pennsylvania Magazine; *one of his own writings was a controversial antislavery pamphlet,* African Slavery in America *(1775). Strongly critical of the British's Parliament's taxation policies, he also maintained that the American colonies should break free from their dependence on Great Britain. In* Common Sense *(1776), which quickly sold hundreds of thousands of copies, Paine declared that simple facts and plain arguments ("common sense") made momentously clear that the colonies' time for independence had arrived.*

When the Revolutionary War began, Paine joined the Continental Army and launched his series of American Crisis *papers, sixteen in all, published between 1776 and 1783. Paine denounced the belief in a hereditary monarchy and endorsed equal rights for all of a country's citizens. A passionate and effective propagandist, he succeeded in rallying and uniting America's patriots.*

From the late 1770s to the late 1780s Paine held a position in the Pennsylvania Assembly. He traveled to England in 1787 and became involved in the agitation stirred up by the French Revolution. During 1791–1792 Paine published the two parts of The Rights of Man, *a defense of the Revolution against the attack on it that Edmund Burke had presented in* Reflections on the Revolution in France *(1790). Because of Paine's forthright critique of the monarchy, his book was banned in England.*

Paine fled to France and, honored for his defense of the Revolution, he was made a French citizen by the National Assembly. He was, however, later imprisoned for a year (he barely escaped a death sentence) for voting in the National Assembly against the execution of King Louis XVI. In 1802 he returned to the United States, but by this point his reputation had suffered. Some had simply forgotten his contributions decades earlier to the American Revolution, while others were enraged by his study of the Enlightenment, The Age of Reason *(1794), in which he attacked traditional religion. Paine's critics misrepresented his views, saying he scorned belief in God when, in fact, Paine professed his belief in God on the first page and throughout the book. "I believe in one God," he asserted. "The world is my country, all mankind are my brethren, and to do good is my religion." But the attacks took hold, and in the final years of his life Paine was impoverished and ostracized.*

Below are an excerpt from Common Sense, *the first of the*
American Crisis *papers, and chapter one of* The Age of Reason. *The
first of these was published anonymously in Philadelphia in January
1776 and then republished the following month, this time under
Paine's name. He made the case forcefully that the American colonies
possessed a right to independence and that their moral duty to the
world was to affirm and fight for it. The second, an inspiring piece
written at a low point in the Continental Army's struggle against the
British, was avidly read by soldiers and countless men and women
throughout the colonies. For the third, protesting religious creeds and
institutions, Paine was widely criticized.*

*"Without the pen of Paine," the statesman and second U.S. presi-
dent John Adams said, "the sword of [George] Washington would have
been wielded in vain." Adams had reservations about Paine's fiery style
and militant point of view, but he acknowledged in 1805 that no "man
in the world has had more influence on its inhabitants and affairs for
the last thirty years than Tom Paine." "While leading a revolution on
the political front," the biographer David Freeman Hawke noted, Paine
"also initiated one in polemic literature."*

For biography: David Freeman Hawke, Paine *(1974); Jack
Fruchtman Jr.,* Thomas Paine: Apostle of Freedom *(1994); and John
Keane,* Tom Paine: A Political Life *(1995). See also Eric Foner,* Tom
Paine and Revolutionary America *(1976); A. Owen Aldridge,* Thomas
Paine's American Ideology *(1984); and Gregory Claeys,* Thomas Paine:
Social and Political Thought *(1989).*

From *Common Sense*[1]: Introduction, & Parts I–II

INTRODUCTION

Perhaps the sentiments contained in the following pages, are not yet
sufficiently fashionable to procure them general favor; a long habit of not
thinking a thing wrong, gives it a superficial appearance of being right,
and raises at first a formidable outcry in defence of custom. But tumult
soon subsides. Time makes more converts than reason.

---

[1]COMMON SENSE: Paine's full title reads *Common Sense: Addressed to the Inhabitants of America,
on the following Interesting Subjects: viz: I. Of the Origin and Design of Government in General; with
Concise Remarks on the English Constitution. II. Of Monarchy and Hereditary Succession. III.
Thoughts on the Present State of American Affairs. IV. Of the Present Ability of America; with some
Miscellaneous Reflections.*

As a long and violent abuse of power is generally the means of calling the right of it in question, (and in matters too which might never have been thought of, had not the sufferers been aggravated into the inquiry,) and as the king of England hath undertaken in his own right, to support the parliament in what he calls theirs, and as the good people of this country are grievously oppressed by the combination, they have an undoubted privilege to inquire into the pretensions of both, and equally to reject the usurpation of either.

In the following sheets, the author hath studiously avoided every thing which is personal among ourselves. Compliments as well as censure to individuals make no part thereof. The wise and the worthy need not the triumph of a pamphlet; and those whose sentiments are injudicious or unfriendly, will cease of themselves, unless too much pains is bestowed upon their conversion.

The cause of America is, in a great measure, the cause of all mankind. Many circumstances have, and will arise, which are not local, but universal, and through which the principles of all lovers of mankind are affected, and in the event of which, their affections are interested. The laying a country desolate with fire and sword, declaring war against the natural rights of all mankind, and extirpating the defenders thereof from the face of the earth, is the concern of every man to whom nature hath given the power of feeling; of which class, regardless of party censure, is

The author.[2]
Philadelphia, Feb. 14, 1776.

THOUGHTS ON THE PRESENT STATE OF AMERICAN AFFAIRS

In the following pages I offer nothing more than simple facts, plain arguments, and common sense; and have no other preliminaries to settle with the reader, than that he will divest himself of prejudice and prepossession, and suffer his reason and his feelings to determine for themselves; that he will put on, or rather that he will not put off the true character of a man, and generously enlarge his views beyond the present day.

Volumes have been written on the subject of the struggle between England and America. Men of all ranks have embarked in the controversy, from different motives, and with various designs; but all have been ineffectual, and the period of debate is closed. Arms, as the last resource, decide the contest; the appeal was the choice of the king, and the continent hath accepted the challenge.

[2]THE AUTHOR: Paine published the pamphlet anonymously.

It hath been reported of the late Mr. Pelham[3] (who tho' an able minister was not without his faults) that on his being attacked in the house of commons, on the score, that his measures were only of a temporary kind, replied, "they will last my time." Should a thought so fatal and unmanly possess the colonies in the present contest, the name of ancestors will be remembered by future generations with detestation.

The sun never shined on a cause of greater worth. 'Tis not the affair of a city, a country, a province, or a kingdom, but of a continent—of at least one eighth part of the habitable globe. 'Tis not the concern of a day, a year, or an age; posterity are virtually involved in the contest, and will be more or less affected, even to the end of time, by the proceedings now. Now is the seed time of continental union, faith and honor. The least fracture now will be like a name engraved with the point of a pin on the tender rind of a young oak; the wound will enlarge with the tree, and posterity read it in full grown characters.

By referring the matter from argument to arms, a new area for politics is struck; a new method of thinking hath arisen. All plans, proposals, etc. prior to the nineteenth of April, i.e., to the commencement of hostilities,[4] are like the almanacs of the last year; which, though proper then, are superseded and useless now. Whatever was advanced by the advocates on either side of the question then, terminated in one and the same point, viz., a union with Great Britain; the only difference between the parties was the method of effecting it; the one proposing force, the other friendship; but it hath so far happened that the first hath failed, and the second hath withdrawn her influence.

As much hath been said of the advantages of reconciliation, which, like an agreeable dream, hath passed away and left us as we were, it is but right, that we should examine the contrary side of the argument, and inquire into some of the many material injuries which these colonies sustain, and always will sustain, by being connected with, and dependent on Great Britain. To examine that connection and dependence, on the principles of nature and common sense, to see what we have to trust to, if separated, and what we are to expect, if dependent.

I have heard it asserted by some, that as America hath flourished under her former connection with Great Britain, that the same connection is necessary towards her future happiness, and will always have the same effect. Nothing can be more fallacious than this kind of argument. We may as well assert, that because a child has thrived upon milk, that

---

[3]MR. PELHAM: Henry Pelham (1696–1754), prime minister of Great Britain from 1743 to 1754.
[4]HOSTILITIES: Paine refers to April 19, 1775, when the Massachusetts militia (the Minutemen) and the British engaged in the first armed conflict of the American Revolution at Lexington and Concord.

it is never to have meat; or that the first twenty years of our lives is to become a precedent for the next twenty. But even this is admitting more than is true, for I answer roundly, that America would have flourished as much, and probably much more, had no European power had any thing to do with her. The commerce by which she hath enriched herself are the necessaries of life, and will always have a market while eating is the custom of Europe.

But she has protected us, say some. That she hath engrossed[5] us is true, and defended the continent at our expense as well as her own is admitted, and she would have defended Turkey from the same motive, viz., the sake of trade and dominion.

Alas! we have been long led away by ancient prejudices and made large sacrifices to superstition. We have boasted the protection of Great Britain, without considering, that her motive was interest not attachment; that she did not protect us from our enemies on our account, but from her enemies on her own account, from those who had no quarrel with us on any other account, and who will always be our enemies on the same account. Let Britain wave her pretensions to the continent, or the continent throw off the dependance, and we should be at peace with France and Spain were they at war with Britain. The miseries of Hanover's last war,[6] ought to warn us against connections.

It hath lately been asserted in Parliament, that the colonies have no relation to each other but through the parent country, i.e., that Pennsylvania and the Jerseys,[7] and so on for the rest, are sister colonies by the way of England; this is certainly a very roundabout way of proving relationship, but it is the nearest and only true way of proving enmity (or enemyship, if I may so call it). France and Spain never were, nor perhaps ever will be our enemies as Americans, but as our being the subjects of Great Britain.

But Britain is the parent country, say some. Then the more shame upon her conduct. Even brutes do not devour their young; nor savages make war upon their families; wherefore the assertion, if true, turns to her reproach; but it happens not to be true, or only partly so, and the phrase parent or mother country hath been jesuitically[8] adopted by the king and his parasites, with a low papistical design of gaining an unfair

---

[5]ENGROSSED: Having exclusive possession of, especially with relation to trade privileges and property; monopolized.
[6]HANOVER'S LAST WAR: Great Britain's King George III (1738–1820; reign 1760–1820) was a descendant of the Prussian house of Hanover. Paine refers to the Seven Years' War (1756–1763), which began as a conflict between Prussia and Austria but grew to involve all the major European powers. American colonists were involved in the conflict through the French and Indian Wars and suffered many casualties, although Britain eventually won.
[7]JERSEYS: Originally, New Jersey was separated into East and West Jersey.
[8]JESUITICALLY: Cunningly. Many Protestants stereotyped Catholic Jesuits as plotters and sly tricksters.

bias on the credulous weakness of our minds. Europe, and not England, is the parent country of America. This new world hath been the asylum for the persecuted lovers of civil and religious liberty from every part of Europe. Hither have they fled, not from the tender embraces of the mother, but from the cruelty of the monster; and it is so far true of England, that the same tyranny which drove the first emigrants from home pursues their descendants still.

In this extensive quarter of the globe, we forget the narrow limits of three hundred and sixty miles (the extent of England) and carry our friendship on a larger scale; we claim brotherhood with every European Christian, and triumph in the generosity of the sentiment.

It is pleasant to observe by what regular gradations we surmount the force of local prejudice, as we enlarge our acquaintance with the world. A man born in any town in England divided into parishes, will naturally associate most with his fellow parishioners (because their interests in many cases will be common) and distinguish him by the name of neighbor; if he meet him but a few miles from home, he drops the narrow idea of a street, and salutes him by the name of townsman; if he travels out of the county, and meet him in any other, he forgets the minor divisions of street and town, and calls him countryman; i.e., countyman; but if in their foreign excursions they should associate in France or any other part of Europe, their local remembrance would be enlarged into that of Englishmen. And by a just parity of reasoning, all Europeans meeting in America, or any other quarter of the globe, are countrymen; for England, Holland, Germany, or Sweden, when compared with the whole, stand in the same places on the larger scale, which the divisions of street, town, and county do on the smaller ones; distinctions too limited for continental minds. Not one third of the inhabitants, even of this province, are of English descent.[9] Wherefore, I reprobate the phrase of parent or mother country applied to England only, as being false, selfish, narrow and ungenerous.

But admitting that we were all of English descent, what does it amount to? Nothing. Britain, being now an open enemy, extinguishes every other name and title: And to say that reconciliation is our duty, is truly farcical. The first king of England, of the present line (William the Conqueror[10]) was a Frenchman, and half the peers of England are

---

[9]ENGLISH DESCENT: Paine refers to Pennsylvania, which had a large German population.
[10]WILLIAM THE CONQUEROR: William of Normandy, (1027–1087), was born in Falaise, Normandy, France, the illegitimate child of Robert I, Duke of Normandy. He became King of England after defeating British forces in 1066; he claimed the throne through Edward the Confessor, whose mother was a sister of William's grandfather.

descendants from the same country; wherefore by the same method of reasoning, England ought to be governed by France.

Much hath been said of the united strength of Britain and the colonies, that in conjunction they might bid defiance to the world. But this is mere presumption; the fate of war is uncertain, neither do the expressions mean anything; for this continent would never suffer itself to be drained of inhabitants to support the British arms in either Asia, Africa, or Europe.

Besides, what have we to do with setting the world at defiance? Our plan is commerce, and that, well attended to, will secure us the peace and friendship of all Europe; because it is the interest of all Europe to have America a free port. Her trade will always be a protection, and her barrenness of gold and silver secure her from invaders.

I challenge the warmest advocate for reconciliation, to show, a single advantage that this continent can reap, by being connected with Great Britain. I repeat the challenge; not a single advantage is derived. Our corn[11] will fetch its price in any market in Europe, and our imported goods must be paid for buy them where we will.

But the injuries and disadvantages we sustain by that connection, are without number; and our duty to mankind at large, as well as to ourselves, instruct us to renounce the alliance: Because, any submission to, or dependence on Great Britain, tends directly to involve this continent in European wars and quarrels; and sets us at variance with nations, who would otherwise seek our friendship, and against whom, we have neither anger nor complaint. As Europe is our market for trade, we ought to form no partial connection with any part of it. It is the true interest of America to steer clear of European contentions, which she never can do, while by her dependance on Britain, she is made the make-weight in the scale of British politics.

Europe is too thickly planted with kingdoms to be long at peace, and whenever a war breaks out between England and any foreign power, the trade of America goes to ruin, because of her connection with Britain. The next war[12] may not turn out like the last, and should it not, the advocates for reconciliation now will be wishing for separation then, because, neutrality in that case, would be a safer convoy than a man of war. Every thing that is right or natural pleads for separation. The blood of the slain, the weeping voice of nature cries, 'tis time to part. Even the distance at which the Almighty hath placed England and America, is a strong and natural proof, that the authority of the one, over the other, was never

---

[11]CORN: Grain.
[12]THE NEXT WAR: The Seven Years' War (see note 6).

the design of Heaven. The time likewise at which the continent was dis-covered, adds weight to the argument, and the manner in which it was peopled increases the force of it. The reformation was preceded by the discovery of America, as if the Almighty graciously meant to open a sanc-tuary to the persecuted in future years, when home should afford nei-ther friendship nor safety.

The authority of Great Britain over this continent, is a form of gov-ernment, which sooner or later must have an end: And a serious mind can draw no true pleasure by looking forward, under the painful and pos-itive conviction, that what he calls "the present constitution" is merely temporary. As parents, we can have no joy, knowing that this government is not sufficiently lasting to ensure any thing which we may bequeath to posterity: And by a plain method of argument, as we are running the next generation into debt, we ought to do the work of it, otherwise we use them meanly and pitifully. In order to discover the line of our duty rightly, we should take our children in our hand, and fix our station a few years farther into life; that eminence will present a prospect, which a few pre-sent fears and prejudices conceal from our sight.

Though I would carefully avoid giving unnecessary offence, yet I am inclined to believe, that all those who espouse the doctrine of reconcili-ation, may be included within the following descriptions:

Interested men, who are not to be trusted; weak men who cannot see; prejudiced men who will not see; and a certain set of moderate men, who think better of the European world than it deserves; and this last class by an ill-judged deliberation, will be the cause of more calamities to this continent than all the other three.

It is the good fortune of many to live distant from the scene of pre-sent sorrow; the evil is not sufficiently brought to their doors to make them feel the precariousness with which all American property is possessed. But let our imaginations transport us for a few moments to Boston, that seat of wretchedness[13] will teach us wisdom, and instruct us for ever to renounce a power in whom we can have no trust. The inhabitants of that unfortunate city, who but a few months ago were in ease and affluence, have now no other alternative than to stay and starve, or turn out to beg. Endangered by the fire of their friends if they continue within the city, and plundered by the soldiery if they leave it. In their present condition they are prisoners without the hope of redemption, and in a general attack for their relief, they would be exposed to the fury of both armies.

---

[13]BOSTON, THAT SEAT OF WRETCHEDNESS: Boston was under British military blockade imme-diately following the battles of Lexington and Concord.

Men of passive tempers look somewhat lightly over the offenses of Britain, and, still hoping for the best, are apt to call out, "Come, we shall be friends again for all this." But examine the passions and feelings of mankind. Bring the doctrine of reconciliation to the touchstone of nature, and then tell me, whether you can hereafter love, honor, and faithfully serve the power that hath carried fire and sword into your land? If you cannot do all these, then are you only deceiving yourselves, and by your delay bringing ruin upon posterity. Your future connection with Britain, whom you can neither love nor honor, will be forced and unnatural, and being formed only on the plan of present convenience, will in a little time fall into a relapse more wretched than the first. But if you say, you can still pass the violations over, then I ask, Hath your house been burnt? Hath your property been destroyed before your face? Are your wife and children destitute of a bed to lie on, or bread to live on? Have you lost a parent or a child by their hands, and yourself the ruined and wretched survivor? If you have not, then are you not a judge of those who have. But if you have, and can still shake hands with the murderers, then are you unworthy the name of husband, father, friend, or lover, and whatever may be your rank or title in life, you have the heart of a coward, and the spirit of a sycophant.

This is not inflaming or exaggerating matters, but trying them by those feelings and affections which nature justifies, and without which, we should be incapable of discharging the social duties of life, or enjoying the felicities of it. I mean not to exhibit horror for the purpose of provoking revenge, but to awaken us from fatal and unmanly slumbers, that we may pursue determinately some fixed object. It is not in the power of Britain or of Europe to conquer America, if she do not conquer herself by delay and timidity. The present winter is worth an age if rightly employed, but if lost or neglected, the whole continent will partake of the misfortune; and there is no punishment which that man will not deserve, be he who, or what, or where he will, that may be the means of sacrificing a season so precious and useful.

It is repugnant to reason, to the universal order of things, to all examples from the former ages, to suppose, that this continent can longer remain subject to any external power. The most sanguine in Britain does not think so. The utmost stretch of human wisdom cannot, at this time compass a plan short of separation, which can promise the continent even a year's security. Reconciliation is now a fallacious dream. Nature hath deserted the connection, and Art cannot supply her place. For, as Milton wisely expresses, "never can true reconcilement grow where wounds of deadly hate have pierced so deep."[14]

Every quiet method for peace hath been ineffectual. Our prayers have been rejected with disdain; and only tended to convince us, that nothing flatters vanity, or confirms obstinacy in kings more than repeated petitioning—and nothing hath contributed more than that very measure to make the kings of Europe absolute: Witness Denmark and Sweden. Wherefore since nothing but blows will do, for God's sake, let us come to a final separation, and not leave the next generation to be cutting throats, under the violated unmeaning names of parent and child.

To say, they will never attempt it again is idle and visionary, we thought so at the repeal of the stamp act, yet a year or two undeceived us; as well may we suppose that nations, which have been once defeated, will never renew the quarrel.

As to government matters, it is not in the powers of Britain to do this continent justice: The business of it will soon be too weighty, and intricate, to be managed with any tolerable degree of convenience, by a power, so distant from us, and so very ignorant of us; for if they cannot conquer us, they cannot govern us. To be always running three or four thousand miles with a tale or a petition, waiting four or five months for an answer, which when obtained requires five or six more to explain it in, will in a few years be looked upon as folly and childishness—there was a time when it was proper, and there is a proper time for it to cease.

Small islands not capable of protecting themselves, are the proper objects for kingdoms to take under their care; but there is something very absurd, in supposing a continent to be perpetually governed by an island. In no instance hath nature made the satellite larger than its primary planet, and as England and America, with respect to each other, reverses the common order of nature, it is evident they belong to different systems: England to Europe—America to itself.

I am not induced by motives of pride, party, or resentment to espouse the doctrine of separation and independence; I am clearly, positively, and conscientiously persuaded that it is the true interest of this continent to be so; that every thing short of that is mere patchwork, that it can afford no lasting felicity,—that it is leaving the sword to our children, and

---

[14]"NEVER CAN TRUE RECONCILEMENT GROW WHERE WOUNDS OF DEADLY HATE HAVE PIERCED SO DEEP": From *Paradise Lost* (1667; 4:98–99), by John Milton (1608–1674).

shrinking back at a time, when, a little more, a little farther, would have rendered this continent the glory of the earth.

As Britain hath not manifested the least inclination towards a compromise, we may be assured that no terms can be obtained worthy the acceptance of the continent, or any ways equal to the expense of blood and treasure we have been already put to.

The object contended for, ought always to bear some just proportion to the expense. The removal of North, or the whole detestable junto,[15] is a matter unworthy the millions we have expended. A temporary stoppage of trade, was an inconvenience, which would have sufficiently balanced the repeal of all the acts complained of, had such repeals been obtained; but if the whole continent must take up arms, if every man must be a soldier, it is scarcely worth our while to fight against a contemptible ministry only. Dearly, dearly, do we pay for the repeal of the acts,[16] if that is all we fight for; for in a just estimation, it is as great a folly to pay a Bunker Hill price[17] for law, as for land. As I have always considered the independency of this continent, as an event, which sooner or later must arrive, so from the late rapid progress of the continent to maturity, the event could not be far off. Wherefore, on the breaking out of hostilities, it was not worth the while to have disputed a matter, which time would have finally redressed, unless we meant to be in earnest; otherwise, it is like wasting an estate of a suit at law, to regulate the trespasses of a tenant, whose lease is just expiring. No man was a warmer wisher for reconciliation than myself, before the fatal nineteenth of April, 1775 (Massacre at Lexington),[18] but the moment the event of that day was made known, I rejected the hardened, sullen tempered Pharaoh of England for ever; and disdain the wretch, that with the pretended title of FATHER OF HIS PEOPLE, can unfeelingly hear of their slaughter, and composedly sleep with their blood upon his soul.

But admitting that matters were now made up, what would be the event? I answer, the ruin of the continent. And that for several reasons:

First. The powers of governing still remaining in the hands of the king, he will have a negative over the whole legislation of this continent. And as he hath shown himself such an inveterate enemy to liberty, and discovered such a thirst for arbitrary power, is he, or is he not, a proper man to say to these colonies, "You shall make no laws but what I please?"

---

[15]JUNTO: A group or body joined for a common purpose, especially of a political nature. Lord North (1732–1792) was the British Prime Minister (1770–1782) during the American Revolution.
[16]THE ACTS: The Stamp Act (1765) and the Townshend Acts (1767).
[17]BUNKER HILL PRICE: Paine refers to the Battle of Bunker Hill (the Battle of Breed's Hill), which took place on June 17, 1775. The British lost 226 soldiers during the battle, and another 828 were wounded. The American patriots lost 145 men, and another 274 were wounded.
[18]FATAL NINETEENTH OF APRIL....: See note 4.

And is there any inhabitants in America so ignorant, as not to know, that according to what is called the present constitution, that this continent can make no laws but what the king gives leave to? and is there any man so unwise, as not to see, that (considering what has happened) he will suffer no Law to be made here, but such as suit his purpose? We may be as effectually enslaved by the want of laws in America, as by submitting to laws made for us in England. After matters are made up (as it is called) can there be any doubt but the whole power of the crown will be exerted, to keep this continent as low and humble as possible? Instead of going forward we shall go backward, or be perpetually quarrelling or ridiculously petitioning. We are already greater than the king wishes us to be, and will he not hereafter endeavor to make us less? To bring the matter to one point. Is the power who is jealous of our prosperity, a proper power to govern us? Whoever says No to this question is an independent, for independency means no more, than, whether we shall make our own laws, or whether the king, the greatest enemy this continent hath, or can have, shall tell us, "there shall be laws but such as I like."

But the king you will say has a negative in England; the people there can make no laws without his consent. In point of right and good order, there is something very ridiculous, that a youth of twenty-one (which hath often happened) shall say to several millions of people, older and wiser than himself, I forbid this or that act of yours to be law. But in this place I decline this sort of reply, though I will never cease to expose the absurdity of it, and only answer, that England being the king's residence, and America not so, makes quite another case. The king's negative here is ten times more dangerous and fatal than it can be in England, for there he will scarcely refuse his consent to a bill for putting England into as strong a state of defence as possible, and in America he would never suffer such a bill to be passed.

America is only a secondary object in the system of British politics— England consults the good of this country, no farther than it answers her own purpose. Wherefore, her own interest leads her to suppress the growth of ours in every case which doth not promote her advantage, or in the least interferes with it. A pretty state we should soon be in under such a second-hand government, considering what has happened! Men do not change from enemies to friends by the alteration of a name; and in order to show that reconciliation now is a dangerous doctrine, I affirm, that it would be policy in the kingdom at this time, to repeal the acts for the sake of reinstating himself in the government of the provinces; in order, that he may accomplish by craft and subtlety, in the long run, what he cannot do by force and violence in the short one. Reconciliation and ruin are nearly related.

Secondly. That as even the best terms, which we can expect to obtain, can amount to no more than a temporary expedient, or a kind of government by guardianship, which can last no longer than till the colonies come of age, so the general face and state of things, in the interim, will be unsettled and unpromising. Emigrants of property will not choose to come to a country whose form of government hangs but by a thread, and who is every day tottering on the brink of commotion and disturbance; and numbers of the present inhabitants would lay hold of the interval, to dispose of their effects, and quit the continent.

But the most powerful of all arguments, is, that nothing but independence, i.e., a continental form of government, can keep the peace of the continent and preserve it inviolate from civil wars. I dread the event of a reconciliation with Britain now, as it is more than probable, that it will be followed by a revolt somewhere or other, the consequences of which may be far more fatal than all the malice of Britain.

Thousands are already ruined by British barbarity; (thousands more will probably suffer the same fate.) Those men have other feelings than us who have nothing suffered. All they now possess is liberty, what they before enjoyed is sacrificed to its service, and having nothing more to lose, they disdain submission. Besides, the general temper of the colonies, towards a British government, will be like that of a youth, who is nearly out of his time, they will care very little about her. And a government which cannot preserve the peace, is no government at all, and in that case we pay our money for nothing; and pray what is it that Britain can do, whose power will be wholly on paper, should a civil tumult break out the very day after reconciliation? I have heard some men say, many of whom I believe spoke without thinking, that they dreaded an independence, fearing that it would produce civil wars. It is but seldom that our first thoughts are truly correct, and that is the case here; for there are ten times more to dread from a patched up connection than from independence. I make the sufferers case my own, and I protest, that were I driven from house and home, my property destroyed, and my circumstances ruined, that as a man, sensible of injuries, I could never relish the doctrine of reconciliation, or consider myself bound thereby.

The colonies have manifested such a spirit of good order and obedience to continental government, as is sufficient to make every reasonable person easy and happy on that head. No man can assign the least pretence for his fears, on any other grounds, that such as are truly childish and ridiculous, viz., that one colony will be striving for superiority over another.

Where there are no distinctions there can be no superiority, perfect equality affords no temptation. The republics of Europe are all (and we may say always) in peace. Holland and Switzerland are without wars, foreign or domestic; monarchical governments, it is true, are never long at rest: the crown itself is a temptation to enterprising ruffians at home; and that degree of pride and insolence ever attendant on regal authority swells into a rupture with foreign powers, in instances where a republican government, by being formed on more natural principles, would negotiate the mistake.

If there is any true cause of fear respecting independence, it is because no plan is yet laid down. Men do not see their way out; wherefore, as an opening into that business I offer the following hints; at the same time modestly affirming, that I have no other opinion of them myself, than that they may be the means of giving rise to something better. Could the straggling thoughts of individuals be collected, they would frequently form materials for wise and able men to improve to useful matter.

Let the assemblies be annual, with a President only. The representation more equal. Their business wholly domestic, and subject to the authority of a continental congress.

Let each colony be divided into six, eight, or ten, convenient districts, each district to send a proper number of delegates to congress, so that each colony send at least thirty. The whole number in congress will be at least three hundred ninety. Each congress to sit and to choose a president by the following method. When the delegates are met, let a colony be taken from the whole thirteen colonies by lot, after which let the whole congress choose (by ballot) a president from out of the delegates of that province. In the next Congress, let a colony be taken by lot from twelve only, omitting that colony from which the president was taken in the former congress, and so proceeding on till the whole thirteen shall have had their proper rotation. And in order that nothing may pass into a law but what is satisfactorily just, not less than three fifths of the congress to be called a majority. He that will promote discord, under a government so equally formed as this, would have joined Lucifer[19] in his revolt.

But as there is a peculiar delicacy, from whom, or in what manner, this business must first arise, and as it seems most agreeable and consistent, that it should come from some intermediate body between the governed and the governors, that is between the congress and the people, let a Continental Conference be held, in the following manner, and for the following purpose:

A committee of twenty-six members of congress, viz., two for each colony. Two members for each house of assembly, or provincial convention;

[19]LUCIFER: The devil, who sought to dethrone God.

and five representatives of the people at large, to be chosen in the capital city or town of each province, for, and in behalf of the whole province, by as many qualified voters as shall think proper to attend from all parts of the province for that purpose; or, if more convenient, the representatives may be chosen in two or three of the most populous parts thereof. In this conference, thus assembled, will be united, the two grand principles of business, knowledge and power. The members of Congress, Assemblies, or Conventions, by having had experience in national concerns, will be able and useful counsellors, and the whole, being empowered by the people will have a truly legal authority.

The conferring members being met, let their business be to frame a Continental Charter, or Charter of the United Colonies; (answering to what is called the Magna Charta of England[20]) fixing the number and manner of choosing members of Congress, members of Assembly, with their date of sitting, and drawing the line of business and jurisdiction between them: always remembering, that our strength is continental, not provincial: Securing freedom and property to all men, and above all things, the free exercise of religion, according to the dictates of conscience; with such other matter as is necessary for a charter to contain. Immediately after which, the said conference to dissolve, and the bodies which shall be chosen conformable to the said charter, to be the legislators and governors of this continent for the time being: Whose peace and happiness, may God preserve, Amen.

Should any body of men be hereafter delegated for this or some similar purpose, I offer them the following extracts from that wise observer on governments Dragonetti. "The science" says he, "of the politician consists in fixing the true point of happiness and freedom. Those men would deserve the gratitude of ages, who should discover a mode of government that contained the greatest sum of individual happiness, with the least national expense."—Dragonetti on Virtue and Rewards.[21]

But where says some is the king of America? I'll tell you Friend, he reigns above, and doth not make havoc of mankind like the Royal Brute of Britain. Yet that we may not appear to be defective even in earthly honors, let a day be solemnly set apart for proclaiming the charter; let it be brought forth placed on the divine law, the word of God; let a crown be placed thereon, by which the world may know, that so far as we approve of monarchy, that in America the law is king. For as in absolute

---

[20]MAGNA CHARTA: The Great Charter of English liberty, granted by King John (under considerable pressure from his nobles) at Runnymede on June 15, 1215. It established the principle that no one, including the king and lawmakers, is above the law.
[21]REWARDS: *A Treatise of Virtues and Rewards*, by Giacinto Dragonetti (1738–1818), was published in an English translation in 1769.

governments the king is law, so in free countries the law ought to be king; and there ought to be no other. But lest any ill use should afterwards arise, let the crown at the conclusion of the ceremony be demolished, and scattered among the people whose right it is.

A government of our own is our natural right: And when a man seriously reflects on the precariousness of human affairs, he will become convinced, that it is infinitely wiser and safer, to form a constitution of our own in a cool deliberate manner, while we have it in our power, than to trust such an interesting event to time and chance. If we omit it now, some Massenello[22] may hereafter arise, who laying hold of popular disquietudes, may collect together the desperate and the discontented, and by assuming to themselves the powers of government, may sweep away the liberties of the continent like a deluge. Should the government of America return again into the hands of Britain, the tottering situation of things, will be a temptation for some desperate adventurer to try his fortune; and in such a case, what relief can Britain give? Ere she could hear the news the fatal business might be done, and ourselves suffering like the wretched Britons under the oppression of the Conqueror.[23] Ye that oppose independence now, ye know not what ye do; ye are opening a door to eternal tyranny, by keeping vacant the seat of government. There are thousands and tens of thousands; who would think it glorious to expel from the continent, that barbarous and hellish power, which hath stirred up the Indians and Negroes to destroy us; the cruelty hath a double guilt, it is dealing brutally by us, and treacherously by them.

To talk of friendship with those in whom our reason forbids us to have faith, and our affections, wounded through a thousand pores instruct us to detest, is madness and folly. Every day wears out the little remains of kindred between us and them, and can there be any reason to hope, that as the relationship expires, the affection will increase, or that we shall agree better, when we have ten times more and greater concerns to quarrel over than ever?

Ye that tell us of harmony and reconciliation, can ye restore to us the time that is past? Can ye give to prostitution its former innocence? Neither can ye reconcile Britain and America. The last cord now is bro-

---

[22]MASSENELLO: "Thomas Anello, otherwise Massenello, a fisherman of Naples, who after spiriting up his countrymen in the public market place, against the oppression of the Spaniards, to whom the place was then subject, prompted them to revolt, and in the space of a day became king." (Paine's note)

[23]LIKE THE WRETCHED BRITONS UNDER THE OPPRESSION OF THE CONQUEROR: After securing the British throne at the Battle of Hastings in 1066, William the Conqueror of Normandy confiscated English land, declared it his personal property, and distributed it among his Norman followers. French become the official language of England. Eventually, Normans replaced the entire Anglo-Saxon aristocracy.

ken, the people of England are presenting addresses against us. There are injuries which nature cannot forgive; she would cease to be nature if she did. As well can the lover forgive the ravisher of his mistress, as the continent forgive the murders of Britain. The Almighty hath implanted in us these inextinguishable feelings for good and wise purposes. They are the guardians of his image in our hearts. They distinguish us from the herd of common animals. The social compact would dissolve, and justice be extirpated the earth, or have only a casual existence were we callous to the touches of affection. The robber and the murderer, would often escape unpunished, did not the injuries which our tempers sustain, provoke us into justice.

O ye that love mankind! Ye that dare oppose, not only the tyranny, but the tyrant, stand forth! Every spot of the old world is overrun with oppression. Freedom hath been hunted round the globe. Asia, and Africa, have long expelled her. Europe regards her like a stranger, and England hath given her warning to depart. O! receive the fugitive, and prepare in time an asylum for mankind.

[1776]

From *The American Crisis: Number I*

These are the times that try men's souls. The summer soldier and the sunshine patriot will, in this crisis, shrink from the service of their country; but he that stands it *now*, deserves the love and thanks of man and woman. Tyranny, like hell, is not easily conquered; yet we have this consolation with us, that the harder the conflict, the more glorious the triumph. What we obtain too cheap, we esteem too lightly: 'Tis dearness only that gives every thing its value. Heaven knows how to set a proper price upon its goods; and it would be strange indeed if so celestial an article as FREEDOM should not be highly rated. Britain, with an army to enforce her tyranny, has declared that she has a right *(not only to TAX)* but "to BIND *us in* ALL CASES WHATSOEVER,"[1] and if being *bound in that manner*, is not slavery, then is there not such a thing as slavery upon

---

[1] "TO BIND US IN ALL CASES WHATSOEVER": "The present winter is worth an age, if rightly employed; but, if lost or neglected, the whole continent will partake of the evil; and there is no punishment that man does not deserve, be he who, or what, or where he will, that may be the means of sacrificing a season so precious and useful." (Paine's note)

earth. Even the expression is impious; for so unlimited a power can belong only to God.

Whether the independence of the continent was declared too soon, or delayed too long, I will not now enter into as an argument; my own simple opinion is, that had it been eight months earlier, it would have been much better. We did not make a proper use of last winter, neither could we, while we were in a dependent state. However, the fault, if it were one, was all our own, we have none to blame but ourselves. But no great deal is lost yet. All that Howe[2] has been doing for this month past, is rather a ravage than a conquest, which the spirit of the Jerseys,[3] a year ago, would have quickly repulsed, and which time and a little resolution will soon recover.

I have as little superstition in me as any man living, but my secret opinion has ever been, and still is, that God Almighty will not give up a people to military destruction, or leave them unsupportedly to perish, who have so earnestly and so repeatedly sought to avoid the calamities of war, by every decent method which wisdom could invent. Neither have I so much of the infidel in me, as to suppose that He has relinquished the government of the world, and given us up to the care of devils; and as I do not, I cannot see on what grounds the king of Britain can look up to heaven for help against us: a common murderer, a highwayman, or a housebreaker, has as good a pretense as he.

'Tis surprising to see how rapidly a panic will sometimes run through a country. All nations and ages have been subject to them: Britain has trembled like an ague[4] at the report of a French fleet of flat bottomed boats; and in the fourteenth century[5] the whole English army, after ravaging the kingdom of France, was driven back like men petrified with fear; and this brave exploit was performed by a few broken forces collected and headed by a woman, Joan of Arc.[6] Would that heaven might inspire some Jersey maid to spirit up her countrymen, and save her fair fellow sufferers from ravage and ravishment! Yet panics, in some cases, have their uses; they produce as much good as hurt. Their duration is always short; the mind soon grows through them; and acquires a firmer habit than before. But their peculiar advantage is, that they are the touchstones of sincerity and hypocrisy, and bring things and men to light,

---

[2]HOWE: William Howe (1729–1814), commander of the British forces in America from 1775 to 1778. He was recalled for not fighting the war aggressively enough.
[3]JERSEYS: Originally, New Jersey was separated into East and West Jersey.
[4]AGUE: An acute or violent fever, marked with shivering and shaking.
[5]FOURTEENTH CENTURY: Paine incorrectly cites the date for Joan of Arc's conquest of the English forces (see note 6).
[6]JOAN OF ARC: The young woman (1412–1431) who led the French to victory over the English in 1429.

which might otherwise have lain forever undiscovered. In fact, they have the same effect on secret traitors, which an imaginary apparition would have upon a private murderer. They sift out the hidden thoughts of man, and hold them up in public to the world. Many a disguised Tory[7] has lately shown his head, that shall penitentially solemnize with curses the day on which Howe arrived upon the Delaware.

As I was with the troops at Fort Lee,[8] and marched with them to the edge of Pennsylvania, I am well acquainted with many circumstances, which those who live at a distance know but little or nothing of. Our situation there was exceedingly cramped, the place being on a narrow neck of land between the North River[9] and the Hackensack. Our force was inconsiderable, being not one fourth so great as Howe could bring against us. We had no army at hand to have relieved the garrison, had we shut ourselves up and stood on our defence. Our ammunition, light artillery, and the best part of our stores, had been removed, on the apprehension that Howe would endeavor to penetrate the Jerseys, in which case Fort Lee could be of no use to us; for it must occur to every thinking man, whether in the army or not, that these kinds of field forts are only for temporary purposes, and last in use no longer than the enemy directs his force against the particular object, which such forts are raised to defend. Such was our situation and condition at Fort Lee on the morning of the 20th of November, when an officer arrived with information that the enemy with 200 boats had landed about seven miles above: Major General Green,[10] who commanded the garrison, immediately ordered them under arms, and sent express to his Excellency General Washington at the town of Hackensack, distant by the way of the ferry, six miles. Our first object was to secure the bridge over the Hackensack, which laid up the river between the enemy and us, about six miles from us, and three from them. General Washington arrived in about three quarters of an hour, and marched at the head of the troops towards the bridge, which place I expected we should have a brush for; however, they did not choose to dispute it with us, and the greatest part of our troops

---

[7]TORY: A supporter of British interests; one loyal to the king.

[8]FORT LEE: On November 16, 1776, New York's Fort Washington fell to an overwhelming assault by Howe's British forces; over 2,000 American troops were captured. The Continental Army crossed the Hudson River and scaled the Palisades to regroup near Fort Lee. On November 20, the British General Cornwallis ferried between 6,000 and 8,000 men across the Hudson River north of Fort Lee. When the American general George Washington heard of this influx of British troops, he ordered the evacuation of Fort Lee and an immediate retreat. Most of the American supplies and artillery had to be left behind, leading to a period of severe hardship for the Continental Army.

[9]NORTH RIVER: Hudson River.

[10]GENERAL GREEN: Nathanael Green (1742–1786), a major-general under whom Paine served as aide-de-camp.

went over the bridge, the rest over the ferry, except some which passed at a mill on a small creek, between the bridge and the ferry, and made their way through some marshy grounds up to the town of Hackensack, and there passed the river. We brought off as much baggage as the wagons could contain, the rest was lost. The simple object was to bring off the garrison, and march them on till they could be strengthened by the Jersey or Pennsylvania militia, so as to be enabled to make a stand. We stayed four days at Newark, collected in our out-posts with some of the Jersey militia, and marched out twice to meet the enemy, on being informed that they were advancing, though our numbers were greatly inferior to theirs. Howe, in my little opinion, committed a great error in generalship in not throwing a body of forces off from Staten Island through Amboy, by which means he might have seized all our stores at Brunswick, and intercepted our march into Pennsylvania; but if we believe the power of hell to be limited, we must likewise believe that their agents are under some providential control.

I shall not now attempt to give all the particulars of our retreat to the Delaware; suffice it for the present to say, that both officers and men, though greatly harassed and fatigued, frequently without rest, covering, or provision, the inevitable consequences of a long retreat, bore it with a manly and a martial spirit. All their wishes centered in one, which was, that the country would turn out and help them to drive the enemy back. Voltaire[11] has remarked that king William never appeared to full advantage but in difficulties and in action; the same remark may be made on General Washington, for the character fits him. There is a natural firmness in some minds which cannot be unlocked by trifles, but which, when unlocked, discovers a cabinet[12] of fortitude; and I reckon it among those kind of public blessings, which we do not immediately see, that God hath blessed him with uninterrupted health, and given him a mind that can even flourish upon care.

I shall conclude this paper with some miscellaneous remarks on the state of our affairs; and shall begin with asking the following question, Why is it that the enemy hath left the New-England provinces, and made these middle ones the seat of war? The answer is easy: New-England is not infested with Tories, and we are. I have been tender in raising the cry against these men, and used numberless arguments to show them their danger, but it will not do to sacrifice a world to either their folly

---

[11]VOLTAIRE: Pseudonym of François Marie Arouet (1694–1778). Voltaire was a French writer and a leader of the eighteenth century's Enlightenment movement. His ideas greatly influenced the intellectual climate in Paris, leading to the French Revolution.
[12]CABINET: Repository.

or their baseness. The period is now arrived, in which either they or we must change our sentiments, or one or both must fall. And what is a Tory? Good God! what is he? I should not be afraid to go with a hundred Whigs[13] against a thousand Tories, were they to attempt to get into arms. Every Tory is a coward; for servile, slavish, self-interested fear is the foundation of Toryism; and a man under such influence, though he may be cruel, never can be brave.

But, before the line of irrecoverable separation be drawn between us, let us reason the matter together: Your conduct is an invitation to the enemy, yet not one in a thousand of you has heart enough to join him. Howe is as much deceived by you as the American cause is injured by you. He expects you will all take up arms, and flock to his standard, with muskets on your shoulders. Your opinions are of no use to him, unless you support him personally, for 'tis soldiers, and not Tories, that he wants.

I once felt all that kind of anger, which a man ought to feel, against the mean principles that are held by the Tories: a noted one, who kept a tavern at Amboy,[14] was standing at his door, with as pretty a child in his hand, about eight or nine years old, as I ever saw, and after speaking his mind as freely as he thought was prudent finished with this unfatherly expression, *"Well! give me peace in my day."* Not a man lives on the continent but fully believes that a separation must some time or other finally take place, and a generous parent should have said, *"If there must be trouble, let it be in my day, that my child may have peace"*; and this single reflection, well applied, is sufficient to awaken every man to duty. Not a place upon earth might be so happy as America. Her situation is remote from all the wrangling world, and she has nothing to do but to trade with them. A man may easily distinguish in himself between temper and principle, and I am as confident, as I am that God governs the world, that America will never be happy till she gets clear of foreign dominion. Wars, without ceasing, will break out till that period arrives, and the continent must in the end be conqueror; for though the flame of liberty may sometimes cease to shine, the coal never can expire.

America did not, nor does not want force; but she wanted a proper application of that force. Wisdom is not the purchase of a day, and it is no wonder that we should err at the first setting off. From an excess of tenderness, we were unwilling to raise an army, and trusted our cause to the temporary defence of a well-meaning militia. A summer's experience has now taught us better; yet with those troops, while they were collected,

---

[13]WHIGS: Supporters of the American Revolution.
[14]AMBOY: The town of Perth Amboy, New Jersey.

we were able to set bounds to the progress of the enemy, and, thank God! they are again assembling. I always considered a militia as the best troops in the world for a sudden exertion, but they will not do for a long campaign. Howe, it is probable, will make an attempt on this city,[15] should he fail on this side the Delaware, he is ruined: if he succeeds, our cause is not ruined. He stakes all on his side against a part of ours; admitting he succeeds, the consequence will be, that armies from both ends of the continent will march to assist their suffering friends in the middle states; for he cannot go everywhere, it is impossible. I consider Howe as the greatest enemy the Tories have; he is bringing a war into their country, which, had it not been for him and partly for themselves, they had been clear of. Should he now be expelled, I wish with all the devotion of a Christian, that the names of Whig and Tory may never more be mentioned; but should the Tories give him encouragement to come, or assistance if he come, I as sincerely wish that our next year's arms may expel them from the continent, and the congress appropriate their possessions to the relief of those who have suffered in well-doing. A single successful battle next year will settle the whole. America could carry on a two years war by the confiscation of the property of disaffected persons, and be made happy by their expulsion. Say not that this is revenge, call it rather the soft resentment of a suffering people, who, having no object in view but the *good* of *all*, have staked their *own all* upon a seemingly doubtful event. Yet it is folly to argue against determined hardness; eloquence may strike the ear, and the language of sorrow draw forth the tear of compassion, but nothing can reach the heart that is steeled with prejudice.

Quitting this class of men, I turn with the warm ardor of a friend to those who have nobly stood, and are yet determined to stand the matter out: I call not upon a few, but upon all: not on *this* state or *that* state, but on *every* state: up and help us; lay your shoulders to the wheel; better have too much force than too little, when so great an object is at stake. Let it be told to the future world, that in the depth of winter, when nothing but hope and virtue could survive, that the city and the country, alarmed at one common danger, came forth to meet and to repulse it. Say not that thousands are gone, turn out your tens of thousands[16]; throw not the burden of the day upon Providence, but *"show your faith by your works,"*[17] that God may bless you. It matters not where you live, or what

---

[15]THIS CITY: The reference is to Philadelphia.
[16]SAY NOT THAT THOUSANDS ARE GONE, TURN OUT YOUR TENS OF THOUSANDS: A reference to 1 Samuel 18:7: "Saul hath slain his thousands, and David his ten thousands.
[17]SHOW YOUR FAITH BY YOUR WORKS: James 2:18: "Shew me thy faith without thy works, and I will shew thee my faith by my works."

rank of life you hold, the evil or the blessing will reach you all. The far and the near, the home counties and the back, the rich and the poor, will suffer or rejoice alike. The heart that feels not now, is dead: the blood of his children shall curse his cowardice, who shrinks back at a time when a little might have saved the whole, and made *them* happy. I love the man that can smile in trouble, that can gather strength from distress, and grow brave by reflection. 'Tis the business of little minds to shrink; but he whose heart is firm, and whose conscience approves his conduct, will pursue his principles unto death. My own line of reasoning is to myself as straight and clear as a ray of light. Not all the treasures of the world, so far as I believe, could have induced me to support an offensive war, for I think it murder; but if a thief breaks into my house, burns and destroys my property, and kills or threatens to kill me, or those that are in it, and to *"bind me in all cases whatsoever"*[18] to his absolute will, am I to suffer it? What signifies it to me, whether he who does it is a king or a common man; my countryman or not my countryman; whether it be done by an individual villain, or an army of them? If we reason to the root of things we shall find no difference; neither can any just cause be assigned why we should punish in the one case and pardon in the other. Let them call me rebel, and welcome, I feel no concern from it; but I should suffer the misery of devils, were I to make a whore of my soul by swearing allegiance to one whose character is that of a sottish, stupid, stubborn, worthless brutish man. I conceive likewise a horrid idea in receiving mercy from a being, who at the last day shall be shrieking to the rocks and mountains to cover him, and fleeing with terror from the orphan, the widow, and the slain of America.

There are cases which cannot be overdone by language, and this is one. There are persons, too, who see not the full extent of the evil which threatens them; they solace themselves with hopes that the enemy, if he succeed, will be merciful. It is the madness of folly, to expect mercy from those who have refused to do justice; and even mercy, where conquest is the object, is only a trick of war; the cunning of the fox is as murderous as the violence of the wolf, and we ought to guard equally against both. Howe's first object is, partly by threats and partly by promises, to terrify or seduce the people to deliver up their arms and receive mercy. The ministry recommended the same plan to Gage,[19] and this is what the Tories will call making their peace, *"a peace which*

---

[18]BIND ME IN ALL CASES WHATSOEVER: A reference to the Declaratory Act of Parliament, February 24, 1766, which asserted British authority over the American colonies.
[19]GAGE: Thomas Gage (1721–1787), a general in the British army who commanded its forces in America from 1763 to 1775.

passeth all understanding" indeed![20] A peace which would be the immediate forerunner of a worse ruin than any we have yet thought of. Ye men
of Pennsylvania, do reason upon these things! Were the back counties
to give up their arms, they would fall an easy prey to the Indians, who
are all armed: this perhaps is what some Tories would not be sorry for.
Were the home counties to deliver up their arms, they would be exposed
to the resentment of the back counties, who would then have it in their
power to chastise their defection at pleasure. And were any one state to
give up its arms, *that* state must be garrisoned by all Howe's army of
Britons and Hessians[21] to preserve it from the anger of the rest. Mutual
fear is a principal link in the chain of mutual love, and woe be to that
state that breaks the compact. Howe is mercifully inviting you to barbarous destruction, and men must be either rogues or fools that will not
see it. I dwell not upon the vapors of imagination; I bring reason to your
ears, and, in language as plain as A, B, C, hold up truth to your eyes.

I thank God that I fear not. I see no real cause for fear. I know our
situation well, and can see the way out of it. While our army was collected, Howe dared not risk a battle; and it is no credit to him that he
decamped from the White Plains,[22] and waited a mean opportunity to
ravage the defenceless Jerseys; but it is great credit to us, that, with a
handful of men, we sustained an orderly retreat for near an hundred
miles, brought off our ammunition, all our field pieces, the greatest part
of our stores, and had four rivers to pass. None can say that our retreat
was precipitate, for we were near three weeks in performing it, that the
country[23] might have time to come in. Twice we marched back to meet
the enemy, and remained out till dark. The sign of fear was not seen
in our camp, and had not some of the cowardly and disaffected inhabitants spread false alarms through the country, the Jerseys had never
been ravaged. Once more we are again collected and collecting; our
new army at both ends of the continent is recruiting fast, and we shall
be able to open the next campaign with sixty thousand men, well armed
and clothed. This is our situation, and who will may know it. By perseverance and fortitude we have the prospect of a glorious issue; by cowardice and submission, the sad choice of a variety of evils—a ravaged
country—a depopulated city—habitations without safety, and slavery

[20]A PEACE WHICH PASSETH ALL UNDERSTANDING, INDEED: A reference to Philippians 4:7:
"And the peace of God, which passeth all understanding, shall keep your hearts and minds through
Christ Jesus."
[21]HESSIANS: German mercenaries hired by the British.
[22]WHITE PLAINS: The town in New York where General Howe succeeded in overcoming
Washington's troops. Howe failed to capitalize on his victory, and the Continental Army escaped.
[23]THE COUNTRY: People living in the rural areas.

without hope—our homes turned into barracks[24] and bawdyhouses[25] for Hessians, and a future race to provide for, whose fathers we shall doubt of. Look on this picture and weep over it! and if there yet remains one thoughtless wretch who believes it not, let him suffer it unlamented.

[1776]

From The Age of Reason

PART ONE: THE AUTHOR'S PROFESSION OF FAITH

It has been my intention, for several years past, to publish my thoughts upon religion; I am well aware of the difficulties that attend the subject, and from that consideration had reserved it to a more advanced period of life. I intended it to be the last offering I should make to my fellow citizens of all nations, and that at a time when the purity of the motive that induced me to it could not admit of a question, even by those who might disapprove the work.

The circumstance that has now taken place in France, of the total abolition of the whole national order of priesthood, and of everything appertaining to compulsive systems of religion, and compulsive articles of faith, has not only precipitated my intention, but rendered a work of this kind exceedingly necessary lest, in the general wreck of superstition, of false systems of government, and false theology, we lose sight of morality, of humanity, and of the theology that is true.

As several of my colleagues and others of my fellow citizens of France have given me the example of making their voluntary and individual profession of faith, I also will make mine; and I do this with all that sincerity and frankness with which the mind of man communicates with itself.

I believe in one God, and no more; and I hope for happiness beyond this life.

I believe the equality of man, and I believe that religious duties consist in doing justice, loving mercy, and endeavoring to make our fellow creatures happy.

But, lest it should be supposed that I believe many other things in addition to these, I shall, in the progress of this work, declare the things I do not believe, and my reasons for not believing them.

[24]BARRACKS: Buildings that house military troops.
[25]BAWDYHOUSES: Brothels.

I do not believe in the creed professed by the Jewish church, by the Roman church, by the Greek church, by the Turkish church, by the Protestant church, nor by any church that I know of. My own mind is my own church.

All national institutions of churches, whether Jewish, Christian, or Turkish, appear to me no other than human inventions set up to terrify and enslave mankind, and monopolize power and profit.

I do not mean by this declaration to condemn those who believe otherwise; they have the same right to their belief as I have to mine. But it is necessary to the happiness of man that he be mentally faithful to himself. Infidelity does not consist in believing, or in disbelieving; it consists in professing to believe what he does not believe.

It is impossible to calculate the moral mischief, if I may so express it, that mental lying has produced in society. When a man has so far corrupted and prostituted the chastity of his mind as to subscribe his professional belief to things he does not believe, he has prepared himself for the commission of every other crime. He takes up the trade of a priest for the sake of gain, and, in order to qualify himself for that trade, he begins with a perjury. Can we conceive anything more destructive to morality than this?

Soon after I had published the pamphlet *Common Sense*, in America, I saw the exceeding probability that a revolution in the system of government would be followed by a revolution in the system of religion. The adulterous connection of church and state, wherever it had taken place, whether Jewish, Christian, or Turkish, had so effectually prohibited, by pains and penalties, every discussion upon established creeds and upon first principles of religion, that until the system of government should be changed, those subjects could not be brought fairly and openly before the world; but that whenever this should be done, a revolution in the system of religion would follow. Human inventions and priestcraft would be detected; and man would return to the pure, unmixed, and unadulterated belief of one God, and no more . . . .

[1794]

Thomas Jefferson

(1743–1826)

On the evening of April 30, 1962, President John F. Kennedy welcomed forty-nine Nobel Prize winners to the White House: "I think this is the most extraordinary collection of human talent, of human knowledge, that has ever been gathered at the White House—with the possible exception of when Thomas Jefferson dined alone."

Author of the Declaration of Independence—author, too, of the Statute of Virginia for Religious Freedom—third president of the United States, and founder of the University of Virginia, Jefferson was born in Albemarle County in the colony of Virginia. His father was a surveyor and a planter, and his mother was a member of a prominent family. Jefferson himself became, as one scholar remarked, the "embodiment of the ideal of the eighteenth-century enlightened gentleman."

Jefferson was a student (1760–1762) at the College of William and Mary, a lawyer, a magistrate, a county lieutenant, and a member (elected in 1768) of Virginia's House of Burgesses. In 1772 he married Martha Wayles Skelton; they had a number of children, but only two lived into their adult years. Martha died a decade later, and Jefferson did not remarry.

From his inheritance, Jefferson came into the possession of slaves. Though the number varied somewhat, Jefferson in later years maintained about 200 slaves annually; most were at his home, Monticello, and the rest were at other locations nearby. He freed only a handful of slaves, and—the exact truth is still unclear—he may have fathered a child or children by one of his slaves, Sally Hemings. This is the most disquieting dimension of Jefferson's career: he celebrated freedom yet owned slaves.

Having secured his reputation with A Summary View of the Rights of British America *(1774), Jefferson in 1775–1776 was a member of the Continental Congress, and he was chosen to write the draft of the Declaration of Independence. Below is the text, taken from Jefferson's* Autobiography. *The underlined passages were deleted from Jefferson's draft, and the words and phrases printed here in the margins were inserted into the text. In the final section, the left-hand column is the draft and the right hand column is the final version.*

As Jefferson acknowledged, the Declaration of Independence is not original in its ideas. He read, learned from, and adapted the writings of the seventeenth-century English philosopher John Locke and of the philosophers of the Scottish Enlightenment, such as Francis Hutcheson, an eighteenth-century professor of moral philosophy at

Glasgow University. But Jefferson nonetheless produced a revolution-ary document, astounding in its implications, as Abraham Lincoln stated (1859) in a tribute: "The principles of Jefferson are the defini-tions and axioms of free society."

Returning to Virginia, Jefferson served as member of the legislature and then as governor (1779–1781). A noteworthy work of this period (and his only book) was Notes on the State of Virginia *(1784, excerpted below), which includes Jefferson's treatment of slavery and race; unwilling to free the slaves he owned, he nonetheless stated, "I tremble for my coun-try when I reflect that God is just; that his justice cannot sleep forever." In subsequent years Jefferson was minister to France (1784–1789), secretary of state (1790–1793), and vice president (1797–1801). In 1800 he was elected president, and he was reelected in 1804.*

Interested in and curious about art, architecture, philosophy, sci-ence, agriculture, and much else, Jefferson spent his final years working on and improving his home at Monticello, accumulating major debts in the process. He died on July 4, 1826, at almost the same time that another of the nation's founders, John Adams, died as well.

Jefferson was deeply concerned about the impact of slavery on the United States, but, nonetheless, he was optimistic about the nation's prospects. Human beings, he believed, are "endowed with a sense of right and wrong," which is "as much a part of man as his leg or arm." "With all the imperfections of our present government," he stated in 1787, "it is without comparison the best existing, or that ever did exist." "We, too, shall encounter follies," he wrote in a letter (1806), "but if great, they will be short, if long, they will be light; and the vigor of our country will get the better of them." "The system of government," he noted in another letter (1810), "which shall keep us afloat amidst the wreck of the world, will be immortalized in his-tory." More than anyone among the revolutionary generation, Jefferson was committed to the individual, the common man and woman. He was, as the French visitor Alexis de Tocqueville said in the mid-1830s, "the greatest democrat whom the democracy of America has yet produced."

For biography: Noble E. Cunningham Jr., In Pursuit of Reason: The Life of Thomas Jefferson *(1987); Willard Sterne Randall,* Thomas Jefferson: A Life *(1993); Andrew Burstein,* The Inner Jefferson: Portrait of a Grieving Optimist *(1995). See also Garry Wills,* Inventing America: Jefferson's Declaration of Independence *(1978);* Jeffersonian Legacies, *ed. Peter Onuf (1993); Joseph J. Ellis,* American Sphinx: The Character of Thomas Jefferson *(1996); and John Ferling,* Setting the World Ablaze: Washington, Adams, Jefferson, and the American Revolution *(2000).*

From *The Autobiography of Thomas Jefferson*

THE DECLARATION OF INDEPENDENCE[1]

It appearing in the course of these debates, that the colonies of New York, New Jersey, Pennsylvania, Delaware, Maryland, and South Carolina were not yet matured for falling from the parent stem, but that they were fast advancing to that state, it was thought most prudent to wait a while for them, and to postpone the final decision to July 1st; but, that this might occasion as little delay as possible, a committee was appointed to prepare a Declaration of Independence. The committee were John Adams, Dr. Franklin, Roger Sherman, Robert R. Livingston, and myself. Committees were also appointed, at the same time, to prepare a plan of confederation for the colonies, and to state the terms proper to be proposed for foreign alliance. The committee for drawing the Declaration of Independence, desired me to do it. It was accordingly done, and being approved by them, I reported it to the House on Friday, the 28th of June, when it was read, and ordered to lie on the table. On Monday, the 1st of July, the House resolved itself into a committee of the whole, and resumed the consideration of the original motion made by the delegates of Virginia, which, being again debated through the day, was carried in the affirmative by the votes of New Hampshire, Connecticut, Massachusetts, Rhode Island, New Jersey, Maryland, Virginia, North Carolina and Georgia. South Carolina and Pennsylvania voted against it. Delaware had but two members present, and they were divided. The delegates from New York declared they were for it themselves, and were assured their constituents were for it; but that their instructions having been drawn near a twelve-month before, when reconciliation was still the general object, they were enjoined by them to do nothing which should impede that object. They, therefore, thought themselves not justifiable in voting on either side, and asked leave to withdraw from the question: which was given them. The committee rose and reported their resolution to

---

[1]THE DECLARATION OF INDEPENDENCE: On June 7, 1776, Richard Henry Lee (1732–1794), a delegate to the Continental Congress from Virginia, moved that "These United Colonies are, and of right ought to be, Free and Independent States." His motion was carried on July 2, 1776. To draft the formal declaration of this decision, a committee was created, of which Thomas Jefferson was a member and the primary author. The Declaration itself was adopted on July 4, 1776.

the House. Mr. Edward Rutledge, of South Carolina, then requested the determination might be put off to the next day, as he believed his colleagues, though they disapproved of the resolution, would then join in it for the sake of unanimity. The ultimate question, whether the House would agree to the resolution of the committee, was accordingly postponed to the next day, when it was again moved, and South Carolina concurred in voting for it. In the meantime, a third member had come post[2] from the Delaware counties, and turned the vote of that colony in favor of the resolution. Members of a different sentiment attending that morning from Pennsylvania also, her vote was changed, so that the whole twelve colonies who were authorized to vote at all, gave their voices for it; and, within a few days, the convention of New York approved of it, and thus supplied the void occasioned by the withdrawing of her delegates from the vote.

Congress proceeded the same day to consider the Declaration of Independence, which had been reported and lain on the table the Friday preceding, and on Monday referred to a committee of the whole. The pusillanimous idea that we had friends in England worth keeping terms with, still haunted the minds of many. For this reason, those passages which conveyed censures on the people of England were struck out, lest they should give them offense. The clause too, reprobating the enslaving the inhabitants of Africa, was struck out in complaisance to South Carolina and Georgia, who had never attempted to restrain the importation of slaves, and who, on the contrary, still wished to continue it. Our northern brethren also, I believe, felt a little tender under those censures; for though their people had very few slaves themselves, yet they had been pretty considerable carriers of them to others. The debates, having taken up the greater parts of the 2d, 3d, and 4th days of July, were, on the evening of the last, closed; the Declaration was reported by the committee, agreed to by the House, and signed by every member present, except Mr. Dickinson.[3] As the sentiments of men are known not only by what they receive, but what they reject also, I will state the form of the Declaration as originally reported. The parts struck out by Congress shall be distinguished by a black line drawn under them, and those inserted by them shall be placed in the margin, or in a concurrent column.

[2]POST: Rapidly; as quickly as possible.
[3]MR. DICKINSON: John Dickinson (1732–1808), a delegate from Pennsylvania, opposed the language "these united Colonies are, and of right ought to be, free and independent states." He believed a compromise was still possible and that a complete separation from the British government was unwise.

A DECLARATION BY THE REPRESENTATIVES OF THE UNITED STATES OF AMERICA, IN GENERAL CONGRESS ASSEMBLED.

When, in the course of human events, it becomes necessary for one people to dissolve the political bands which have connected them with another, and to assume among the powers of the earth the separate and equal station to which the laws of nature and of nature's God entitle them, a decent respect to the opinions of mankind requires that they should declare the causes which impel them to the separation.

We hold these truths to be self evident: that all men are created equal[4]; that they are endowed by their Creator with <u>inherent</u> <u>and</u> inalienable rights; that among these are life, liberty, and the pursuit of happiness[5]; that to secure these rights, governments are instituted among men, deriving their just powers from the consent of the governed; that whenever any form of government becomes destructive of these ends, it is the right of the people to alter or to abolish it, and to institute new government, laying its foundation on such principles, and organizing its powers in such form, as to them shall seem most likely to effect their safety and happiness. Prudence, indeed, will dictate that governments long established should not be changed for light and transient causes; and accordingly all experience hath shown that mankind are more disposed to suffer while evils are sufferable, than to right themselves by abolishing the forms to which they are accustomed. But when a long train of abuses and usurpations, <u>begun at a distinguished</u>[6] <u>period and</u> pursuing invariably the same object, evinces a design to reduce them under absolute despotism, it is their right, it is their duty to throw off such government, and to provide new guards for their future security. Such has been the patient sufferance of these colonies; and such is now the necessity which constrains them to <u>expunge</u> their former systems of government. The history of the present king of Great Britain[7] is a history of <u>unremitting</u> injuries and usurpations, <u>among which appears no solitary fact to contradict the uniform tenor of the rest, but all</u>

[margin notes:] certain · alter · re-peated · all having

[4]EQUAL: Presidential biographer and scholar Garry Wills notes that Jefferson probably meant equal in possessing a moral sense, not equal in every sense.
[5]PURSUIT OF HAPPINESS: The English philosopher John Locke (1632–1704), in his *Second Treatise on Government* (1689), defined men's natural rights as, "life, liberty, and property." Jefferson meant for this expression to include the right to the "pursuit of happiness"—perhaps meaning, says Garry Wills, "a goal of human virtue."
[6]DISTINGUISHED: Specific.
[7]GREAT BRITAIN: King George III of England (1738–1820).

<u>have</u> in direct object the establishment of an absolute tyranny over these states. To prove this, let facts be submitted to a candid world <u>for the truth of which we pledge a faith yet unsullied by falsehood</u>.

He has refused his assent to laws the most wholesome and necessary for the public good.

He has forbidden his governors to pass laws of immediate and pressing importance, unless suspended in their operation till his assent should be obtained; and, when so suspended, he has utterly neglected to attend to them.

He has refused to pass other laws for the accommodation of large districts of people, unless those people would relinquish the right of representation to the legislature, a right inestimable to them, and formidable to tyrants only.

He has called together legislative bodies at places unusual, uncomfortable, and distant from the depository of their public records, for the sole purpose of fatiguing them into compliance with his measures.

He has dissolved representative houses repeatedly <u>and continually</u> for opposing with manly firmness his invasions on the rights of the people.

He has refused for a long time after such dissolutions to cause others to be elected, whereby the legislative powers, incapable of annihilation, have returned to the people at large for their exercise, the state remaining, in the meantime, exposed to all the dangers of invasion from without and convulsions within.

He has endeavored to prevent the population of these states; for that purpose obstructing the laws for naturalization of foreigners, refusing to pass others to encourage their migrations hither, and raising the conditions of new appropriations of lands.

obstructed by   He has <u>suffered</u> the administration of justice <u>totally to cease in some of these states</u> refusing his assent to laws for establishing judiciary powers.

He has made <u>our</u> judges dependent on his will alone for the tenure of their offices, and the amount and payment of their salaries.

He has erected a multitude of new offices, <u>by a self-assumed power</u> and sent hither swarms of new officers to harass our people and eat out their substance.

He has kept among us in times of peace standing armies <u>and ships of war</u> without the consent of our legislatures.

He has affected to render the military independent of, and superior to, the civil power.

He has combined with others[8] to subject us to a jurisdiction foreign to our constitutions and unacknowledged by our laws, giving his assent to their acts of pretended legislation for quartering large bodies of armed troops among us; for protecting them by a mock trial from punishment for any murders which they should commit on the inhabitants of these states; for cutting off our trade with all parts of the world; for imposing taxes on us without our consent; for depriving us [ ] of the benefits of trial by jury; for transporting us beyond seas to be tried for pretended offenses; for abolishing the free system of English laws in a neighboring province,[9] establishing therein an arbitrary government, and enlarging its boundaries, so as to render it at once an example and fit instrument for introducing the same absolute rule into these <u>states</u>; for taking away our charters, abolishing our most valuable laws, and altering fundamentally the forms of our governments; for suspending our own legislatures, and declaring themselves invested with power to legislate for us in all cases whatsoever. *in many cases* *colonies*

He has abdicated government here <u>withdrawing his governors, and declaring us out of his allegiance and protection.</u> *by declaring us out of his protection, and waging war against us*

He has plundered our seas, ravaged our coasts, burnt our towns, and destroyed the lives of our people.

He is at this time transporting large armies of foreign mercenaries[10] to complete the works of death, desolation and tyranny already begun with circumstances of cruelty and perfidy [ ] unworthy the head of a civilized nation. *scarcely paralleled in the most barbarous ages, and totally*

He has constrained our fellow citizens taken captive on the high seas, to bear arms against their country, to become the executioners of their friends and brethren, or to fall themselves by their hands.

He has [ ] endeavored to bring on the inhabitants of our frontiers, the merciless Indian savages, whose known rule of warfare is an undistinguished destruction of all ages, sexes and conditions <u>of existence</u>. *excited domestic insurrection among us, and has*

<u>He has incited treasonable insurrections of our fellow citizens, with the allurements of forfeiture and confiscation of our property.</u>

<u>He has waged cruel war against human nature itself, violating its most sacred rights of life and liberty in the persons of a distant people who never offended him, captivating and carrying them into</u>

---

[8]HE HAS COMBINED WITH OTHERS: The British Parliament and ministers of trade.
[9]PROVINCE: Jefferson refers to the Quebec Act of 1774, which restored French civil law to Quebec and recognized the Roman Catholic Church in the territory. It was identified as one of the "intolerable acts."
[10]TRANSPORTING LARGE ARMIES OF FOREIGN MERCENARIES: The reference is to the Hessians, German soldiers hired to supplement the British military forces in America.

slavery in another hemisphere, or to incur miserable death in their transportation thither. This piratical warfare, the opprobrium of INFIDEL powers, is the warfare of the CHRISTIAN king of Great Britain. Determined to keep open a market where MEN should be bought and sold, he has prostituted his negative for suppressing every legislative attempt to prohibit or to restrain this execrable commerce. And that this assemblage of horrors might want no fact of distinguished die, he is now exciting those very people to rise in arms among us, and to purchase that liberty of which he has deprived them, by murdering the people on whom he also obtruded them: thus paying off former crimes committed against the LIBERTIES of one people, with crimes which he urges them to commit against the LIVES of another.

In every stage of these oppressions we have petitioned for redress in the most humble terms: our repeated petitions have been answered only by repeated injuries.

A prince whose character is thus marked by every act which *free* may define a tyrant is unfit to be the ruler of a [ ] people who mean to be free. Future ages will scarcely believe that the hardiness of one man adventured, within the short compass of twelve years only, to lay a foundation so broad and so undisguised for tyranny over a people fostered and fixed in principles of freedom.

Nor have we been wanting in attentions to our British brethren. We have warned them from time to time of attempts by their legislature to extend a jurisdiction over these our states. We have reminded *an unwar-* them of the circumstances of our emigration and settlement here, *rantable/* no one of which could warrant so strange a pretension: that these *us* were effected at the expense of our own blood and treasure, unassisted by the wealth or the strength of Great Britain: that in constituting indeed our several forms of government, we had adopted one common king, thereby laying a foundation for perpetual league and amity with them: but that submission to their parliament was no part of our constitution, nor ever in idea, if history may be credited: and, we [ ] appealed to their native justice and magnanimity as well as *have* to the ties of our common kindred to disavow these usurpations which *and we* were likely to interrupt our connection and correspondence. They too *have con-* have been deaf to the voice of justice and of consanguinity, and when *jured them* occasions have been given them, by the regular course of their laws, *by* of removing from their councils the disturbers of our harmony, they *would* have, by their free election, reestablished them in power. At this very *inevitably* time too, they are permitting their chief magistrate to send over not only soldiers of our common blood, but Scotch and foreign mercenaries to invade and destroy us. These facts have given the last stab

of agonizing affection, and manly spirit bids us to renounce forever these unfeeling brethren. We must endeavor to forget our former love for them, and hold them as we hold the rest of mankind,
enemies in war, in peace friends. We might have been a free and
we a great people together; but a communication of grandeur and
must of freedom, it seems, is below their dignity. Be it so, since they will
there-
fore have it. The road to happiness and to glory is open to us, too.
We will tread it apart from them, and acquiesce in the necessity
which denounces[11] our eternal separation. [ ]!

(margin note: and hold them as we hold the rest mankind, enemies in war, in peace, friends.)

We therefore the representatives of the United States of
America in General Congress
assembled, do in the name, and by
the authority of the good people of
these states reject and renounce all
allegiance and subjection to the
kings of Great Britain and all others who may hereafter claim by,
through or under them: we utterly
dissolve all political connection
which may heretofore have subsisted between us and the people
or parliament of Great Britain:
and finally we do assert and
declare these colonies to be free
and independent states, and that
as free and independent states,
they have full power to levy war,
conclude peace, contract alliances,
establish commerce, and to do all
other acts and things which independent states may of right do.

And for the support of this declaration, we mutually pledge to
each other our lives, our fortunes,
and our sacred honor.

We, therefore, the representatives of the United States of America
in General Congress assembled,
appealing to the supreme judge of
the world for the rectitude of our
intentions, do in the name, and by
the authority of the good people of
these colonies, solemnly publish and
declare, that these united colonies
are, and of right ought to be free
and independent states; that they
are absolved from all allegiance to
the British crown, and that all political connection between them and
the state of Great Britain is, and
ought to be, totally dissolved; and
that as free and independent states,
they have full power to levy war,
conclude peace, contract alliances,
establish commerce, and to do all
other acts and things which independent states may of right do.

And for the support of this declaration, with a firm reliance on the protection of divine providence, we
mutually pledge to each other our lives,
our fortunes, and our sacred honor.

The Declaration thus signed on the 4th, on paper, was engrossed[12]
on parchment, and signed again on the 2d of August.

[1821, 1829]

[11]DENOUNCES: Declares, announces.

From *Notes on the State of Virginia*, Query V. Cascades

NATURAL BRIDGE[1]

The *Natural bridge*, the most sublime of Nature's works, though not comprehended under the present head, must not be pretermitted.[2] It is on the ascent of a hill, which seems to have been cloven through its length by some great convulsion. The fissure, just at the bridge, is by some admeasurements, 270 feet deep, by others only 205. It is about 45 feet wide at the bottom, and 90 feet at the top; this of course determines the length of the bridge, and its height from the water. Its breadth in the middle, is about 60 feet, but more at the ends, and the thickness of the mass at the summit of the arch, about 40 feet. A part of this thickness is constituted by a coat of earth, which gives growth to many large trees. The residue, with the hill on both sides, is one solid rock of limestone. The arch approaches the Semi-elliptical form; but the larger axis of the ellipsis, which would be the cord of the arch, is many times longer than the semi-axis which gives its height. Though the sides of this bridge are provided in some parts with a parapet of fixed rocks, yet few men have resolution to walk to them and look over into the abyss. You involuntarily fall on your hands and feet, creep to the parapet and peep over it. Looking down from this height about a minute gave me a violent headache. This painful sensation is relieved by a short, but pleasing view of the Blue ridge along the fissure downwards, and upwards by that of the Short hills, which, with the Purgatory mountain is a divergence from the North ridge; and, descending then to to the valley below, the sensation becomes delightful in the extreme. It is impossible for the emotions, arising from the sublime,[3] to be felt beyond what they are here: so beautiful an arch, so elevated, so light, and springing, as it were, up to heaven, the rapture of the Spectator is really indescribable! The fissure continues deep and narrow and, following the margin of the stream upwards about three eighths of a mile you arrive at a limestone cavern, less remarkable, however, for height and extent than those before described. Its

---

[12]ENGROSSED: Written in legal form; addressed in an official, legal document.
[1]NATURAL BRIDGE: Jefferson owned the land near Lexington, Virginia, on which the Natural Bridge stands.
[2]PRETERMITTED: Overlooked; passed by.
[3]SUBLIME: Overwhelming feeling of awe and reverence, inspired by sheer beauty or grandeur.

entrance into the hill is but a few feet above the bed of the stream. This bridge is in the county of Rockbridge, to which it has given name, and affords a public and commodious passage over a valley, which cannot be crossed elsewhere for a considerable distance. The stream passing under it is called Cedar Creek. It is a water of James River, and sufficient in the driest seasons to turn a grist-mill,[4] though its fountain is not more than two miles above.

[1787]

From *Notes on the State of Virginia*, Query VI. Productions Mineral, Vegetable, and Animal

The opinion advanced by the Count de Buffon[1] is 1. That the animals common both to the old and new world are smaller in the latter. 2. That those peculiar to the new are on a smaller scale. 3. That those which have been domesticated in both have degenerated in America. and 4. That on the whole it exhibits fewer species. And the reason he thinks is that the heats of America are less; that more waters are spread over its surface by nature, and fewer of these drained off by the hand of man. In other words, that *heat* is friendly, and *moisture* adverse to the production and development of large quadrupeds. I will not meet this hypothesis on its first doubtful ground, whether the climate of America be comparatively more humid? Because we are not furnished with observations sufficient to decide this question. And though, till it be decided, we are as free to deny, as others are to affirm, the fact, yet for a moment let it be supposed. The hypothesis, after this supposition, proceeds to another; that *moisture* is unfriendly to animal growth. The truth of this is inscrutable to us by reasonings a priori.[2] Nature has hidden from us her modus agendi.[3] Our only appeal on such questions is to experience; and I think that experience is against the supposition. It is by the assis-

---

[4]GRIST-MILL: Mill that grinds grain, usually by means of a water wheel.
[1]COUNT DE BUFFON: Georges Louis Leclerc (1707–1788), a French naturalist.
[2]A PRIORI: Done before any special examination; presumptively without prior knowledge.
[3]MODUS AGENDI: Operating procedure. (Latin)

tance of *heat* and *moisture* that vegetables are elaborated from the elements of earth, air, water, and fire. We accordingly see the more humid climates produce the greater quantity of vegetables. Vegetables are mediately or immediately the food of every animal: and in proportion to the quantity of food, we see animals not only multiplied in their numbers, but improved in their bulk, as far as the laws of their nature will admit. Of this opinion is the Count de Buffon himself in another part of his work: "in general it seems that somewhat cold countries are better suited to our oxen than hot countries, and they are the heavier and bigger in proportion as the climate is damper and more abounding in pasture lands. The oxen of Denmark, of Podolie,[4] of the Ukraine, and of Tartary[5] which is inhabited by the Calmouques,[6] are the largest of all." Here then a race of animals, and one of the largest too, has been increased in its dimensions by *cold* and *moisture*, in direct opposition to the hypothesis, which supposes that these two circumstances diminish animal bulk, and that it is their contraries *heat* and *dryness* which enlarge it. But when we appeal to experience, we are not to rest satisfied with a single fact. Let us therefore try our question on more general ground. Let us take our portions of the earth, Europe and America for instance, sufficiently extensive to give operation to general causes; let us consider the circumstances peculiar to each, and observe their effect on animal nature. America, running through the torrid as well as temperate zone, has more *heat*, collectively taken, than Europe. But Europe, according to our hypothesis, is the *dryest*. They are equally adapted then to animal productions; each being endowed with one of those causes which befriend animal growth, and with one which opposes it. If it be thought unequal to compare Europe with America, which is so much larger, I answer, not more so than to compare America with the whole world. Besides, the purpose of the comparison is to try an hypothesis, which makes the size of animals depend on the *heat* and *moisture* of climate. If therefore we take a region, so extensive as to comprehend a sensible distinction of climate, and so extensive too as that local accidents, or the intercourse of animals on its borders, may not materially affect the size of those in its interior parts, we shall comply with those conditions which the hypothesis may reasonably demand. The objection would be the weaker in the present case, because any intercourse of

---

[4]PODOLIE: Town in northeast India.
[5]TARTARY: Central Asia, whence came the Tartars, as the Mongols, Tartars, and Turks were collectively known in the West. Under the leadership of Genghis Khan (1162–1227), this group controlled much of Asia and Eastern Europe in the thirteenth century.
[6]CALMOUQUES: The Kalmuks, a Mongolian people living near the northwest shores of the Caspian Sea.

animals which may take place on the confines of Europe and Asia, is
to the advantage of the former, Asia producing certainly larger animals
than Europe . . . .

Hitherto I have considered this hypothesis as applied to brute animals
only, and not in its extension to the man of America, whether aboriginal
or transplanted. It is the opinion of Mons. de Buffon that the former furnishes no exception to it: "Although the savage of the new world is about
the same height as man in our world, this does not suffice for him to constitute an exception to the general fact that all living nature has become
smaller on that continent. The savage is feeble, and has small organs of generation; he has neither hair nor beard, and no ardor whatever for his female;
although swifter than the European because he is better accustomed to running, he is, on the other hand, less strong in body; he is also less sensitive,
and yet more timid and cowardly; he has no vivacity, no activity of mind;
the activity of his body is less an exercise, a voluntary motion, than a necessary action caused by want; relieve him of hunger and thirst, and you
deprive him of the active principle of all his movements; he will rest stupidly upon his legs or lying down entire days. There is no need for seeking further the cause of the isolated mode of life of these savages and their
repugnance for society: the most precious spark of the fire of nature has
been refused to them; they lack ardor for their females, and consequently
have no love for their fellow men: not knowing this stongest and most tender of all affections, their other feelings are also cold and languid; they
love their parents and children but little; the most intimate of all ties, the
family connection, binds them therefore but loosely together; between family and family there is no tie at all; hence they have no communion, no commonwealth, no state of society. Physical love constitutes their only morality;
their heart is icy, their society cold, and their rule harsh. They look upon
their wives only as servants for all work, or as beasts of burden, which
they load without consideration with the burden of their hunting, and which
they compel without mercy, without gratitude, to perform tasks which are
often beyond their strength. They have only few children, and they take
little care of them. Everywhere the original defect appears: they are indifferent because they have little sexual capacity, and this indifference to the
other sex is the fundamental defect which weakens their nature, prevents
its development, and—destroying the very germs of life—uproots society at
the same time. Man is here no exception to the general rule. Nature, by
refusing him the power of love, has treated him worse and lowered him
deeper than any animal." An afflicting picture indeed, which, for the honor
of human nature, I am glad to believe has no original. Of the Indian of South
America I know nothing; for I would not honor with the appellation of

knowledge, what I derive from the fables published of them. These I believe to be just as true as the fables of Aesop.[7] This belief is founded on what I have seen of man, white, red, and black, and what has been written of him by authors, enlightened themselves, and writing admidst an enlightened people. The Indian of North America being more within our reach, I can speak of him somewhat from my own knowledge, but more from the information of others better acquainted with him, and on whose truth and judgment I can rely. From these sources I am able to say, in contradiction to this representation, that he is neither more defective in ardor, nor more impotent with his female, than the white reduced to the same diet and exercise: that he is brave, when an enterprise depends on bravery; education with him making the point of honor consist in the destruction of an enemy by stratagem, and in the preservation of his own person free from injury; or perhaps this is nature; while it is education which teaches us to honor force more than finesse; that he will defend himself against an host of enemies, always choosing to be killed, rather than to surrender, though it be to the whites, who he knows will treat him well: that in other situations also he meets death with more deliberation, and endures tortures with a firmness unknown almost to religious enthusiasm with us: that he is affectionate to his children, careful of them, and indulgent in the extreme: that his affections comprehend his other connections, weakening, as with us, from circle to circle, as they recede from the center: that his friendships are strong and faithful to the uttermost extremity: that his sensibility is keen, even the warriors weeping most bitterly on the loss of their children, though in general they endeavor to appear superior to human events: that his vivacity and activity of mind is equal to ours in the same situation; hence his eagerness for hunting, and for games of chance. The women are submitted to unjust drudgery. This I believe is the case with every barbarous people. With such, force is law. The stronger sex therefore imposes on the weaker. It is civilization alone which replaces women in the enjoyment of their natural equality. That first teaches us to subdue the selfish passions, and to respect those rights in others which we value in ourselves. Were we in equal barbarism, our females would be equal drudges. The man with them is less strong than with us, but their woman stronger than ours; and both for the same obvious reason: because our man and their woman is habituated to labor, and formed by it. With both races the sex which is indulged with ease is least athletic. An Indian man is small in the hand

[7]AESOP: The legendary Greek author of a series of tales wherein animals were used to demonstrate moral topics. Probably written by many authors, the stories were popularized by the Roman poet Phaedrus in the first century CE.

and wrist for the same reason for which a sailor is large and strong in the arms and shoulders, and a porter in the legs and thighs.—They raise fewer children than we do. The causes of this are to be found, not in a difference of nature, but of circumstance. The women frequently attending the men in their parties of war and of hunting, childbearing becomes extremely inconvenient to them. It is said therefore, that they have learnt the practice of procuring abortion by the use of some vegetable; and that it even extends to prevent conception for a considerable time after. During these parties they are exposed to numerous hazards, to excessive exertions, to the greatest extremities of hunger. Even at their homes the nation depends for food, through a certain part of every year, on the gleanings of the forest; that is, they experience a famine once in every year. With all animals, if the female be badly fed, or not fed at all, her young perish: and if both male and female be reduced to like want, generation becomes less active, less productive. To the obstacles then of want and hazard, which nature has opposed to the multiplication of wild animals, for the purpose of restraining their numbers within certain bounds; those of labor and of voluntary abortion are added with the Indian. No wonder then if they multiply less than we do. Where food is regularly supplied, a single farm will show more of cattle, than a whole country of forests can of buffaloes. The same Indian women, when married to white traders, who feed them and their children plentifully and regularly, who exempt them from excessive drudgery, who keep them stationary and unexposed to accident, produce and raise as many children as the white women. Instances are known, under these circumstances, of their rearing a dozen children. An inhuman practice once prevailed in this country of making slaves of the Indians. (This practice commenced with the Spaniards with the first discovery of America). It is a fact well known with us, that the Indian women so enslaved produced and raised as numerous families as either the whites or blacks among whom they lived.—It has been said, that Indians have less hair than the whites, except on the head. But this is a fact of which fair proof can scarcely be had. With them it is disgraceful to be hairy on the body. They say it likens them to hogs. They therefore pluck the hair as fast as it appears. But the traders who marry their women, and prevail on them to discontinue this practice, say, that nature is the same with them as with the whites. Nor, if the fact be true, is the consequence necessary which has been drawn from it. Negroes have notoriously less hair than the whites; yet they are more ardent. But if cold and moisture be the agents of nature for diminishing the races of animals, how comes she all at once to suspend their operation as to the physical man of the new world, whom the Count acknowledges to be "about the same size as the man of our hemisphere," and to let loose their influence on his moral faculties? How has this "combination of the elements and other physical causes, so contrary to the enlargement of animal nature in this new world, these obstacles to the development and formation of great germs," been arrested and suspended, so as to permit the human body to acquire its just dimensions, and by what inconceivable process has their action been directed on his mind alone? To judge of the truth of this, to form a just estimate of their genius and mental powers, more facts are wanting, and great allowance to be made for those circumstances of their situation which call for a display of particular talents only. This done, we shall probably find that they are formed in mind as well as in body, on the same module with the "Homo sapiens Europaeus."[8] The principles of their society forbidding all compulsion, they are to be led to duty and to enterprise by personal influence and persuasion. Hence eloquence in council, bravery and address in war, become the foundations of all consequence with them. To these acquirements all their faculties are directed. Of their bravery and address in war we have multiplied proofs, because we have been the subjects on which they were exercised. Of their eminence in oratory we have fewer examples, because it is displayed chiefly in their own councils. Some, however, we have of very superior luster. I may challenge the whole orations of Demosthenes[9] and Cicero,[10] and of any more eminent orator, if Europe has furnished more eminent, to produce a single passage, superior to the speech of Logan, a Mingo chief,[11] to Lord Dunmore,[12] when governor of this state. And, as a testimony of their talents in this line, I beg leave to introduce it, first stating the incidents necessary for understanding it. In the spring of the year 1774, a robbery and murder were committed on an inhabitant of the frontiers of Virginia, by two Indians of the Shawnee tribe. The neighbouring whites, according to their custom, undertook to punish this outrage in a summary way. Col. Cresap, a man infamous for the many murders he had committed on those much-injured people, collected a party, and proceeded down the Kanhaway in quest of vengeance. Unfortunately a canoe of women and children, with one man only, was seen coming from the opposite chore, unarmed, and unsuspecting an

[8]HOMO SAPIENS EUROPAEUS: European human. (Latin)
[9]DEMOSTHENES: The Greek orator Demosthenes (383–322 BCE), known for his passionate speeches.
[10]CICERO: Marcus Tullius Cicero (106–43 BCE), great Roman orator, statesman, and writer.
[11]LOGAN, A MINGO CHIEF: In 1774, a white settler was killed by two Shawnees. A mob in search of vengeance, led by Michael Cresap (1742–1775), came upon an unarmed canoe filled with women and children and killed every person in it. It happened to be the family of Logan (Tal-ga-yee-ta), the Mingo chief of the Cayugas, who had enjoyed a strong relationship with the white settlers. Joined by the Shawnees and the Delawares, Logan organized a war against white settlers that was put down by the Virginia militia. He delivered, by a messenger, a speech to Lord Dunmore, the Governor of Virginia, which Jefferson later quotes.
[12]LORD DUNMORE: John Murray (1732–1809), Earl of Dunmore, who served as Virginia governor from 1771–1775. See note 11.
[13]CAPTAIN MICHAEL CRESAP: See note 11.

hostile attack from the whites. Cresap and his party concealed themselves on the bank of the river, and the moment the canoe reached the shore, singled out their objects, and, at one fire, killed every person in it. This happened to be the family of Logan, who had long been distinguished as a friend of the whites. This unworthy return provoked his vengeance. He accordingly signalized himself in the war which ensured. In the autumn of the same year, a decisive battle was fought at the mouth of the Great Kanhaway, between the collected forces of the Shawanees, Mingoes, and Delawares, and a detachment of the Virginia militia. The Indians were defeated, and sued for peace. Logan however disdained to be seen among the suppliants. But, lest the sincerity of a treaty should be distrusted, from which so distinguished a chief absented himself, he sent by a messenger the following speech to be delivered to Lord Dunmore.

"I appeal to any white man to say, if ever he entered Logan's cabin hungry, and he gave him not meat; if ever he came cold and naked, and he clothed him not. During the course of the last long and bloody war, Logan remained idle in his cabin, an advocate for peace. Such was my love for the whites, that my countrymen pointed as they passed, and said, 'Logan is the friend of white men.' I had even thought to have lived with you, but for the injuries of one man. Col. Cresap, the last spring, in cold blood, and unprovoked, murdered all the relations of Logan, not sparing even my women and children. There runs not a drop of my blood in the veins of any living creature. This called on me for revenge. I have sought it: I have killed many: I have fully glutted my vengeance. For my country, I rejoice at the beams of peace. But do not harbor a thought that mine is the joy of fear. Logan never felt fear. He will not turn on his heel to save his life. Who is there to mourn for Logan?—Not one."

Before we condemn the Indians of this continent as wanting genius,[15] we must consider that letters have not yet been introduced among them. Were we to compare them in their present state with the Europeans North of the Alps, when the Roman arms and arts first crossed those mountains, the comparison would be unequal, because, at that time, those parts of Europe were swarming with numbers; because numbers produce emulation, and multiply the chances of improvement, and one improvement begets another. Yet I may safely ask, How many good poets, how many able mathematicians, how many great inventors in arts or sciences had Europe North of the Alps then produced? And it was sixteen centuries

---

[14]SHAWANESE, MINGOES, AND DELAWARES: Native American tribes (see note 11).
[15]GENIUS: Natural ability or intellectual capacity.

after this before a Newton[16] could be formed. I do not mean to deny, that there are varieties in the race of man, distinguished by their powers both of body and mind. I believe there are, as I see to be the case in the races of other animals. I only mean to suggest a doubt, whether the bulk and faculties of animals depend on the side of the Atlantic on which their food happens to grow, or which furnishes the elements of which they are compounded? Whether nature has enlisted herself as a Cis[17] or Transatlantic partisan? I am induced to suspect, there has been more eloquence than sound reasoning displayed in support of this theory; that it is one of those cases where the judgment has been seduced by a glowing pen: and whilst I render every tribute of honor and esteem to the celebrated zoologist, who has added, and is still adding, so many precious things to the treasures of science, I must doubt whether in this instance he has not cherished error also, by lending her for a moment his vivid imagination and bewitching language.

[1787]

From *Notes on the State of Virginia*, Query XI. Aborigines, Original Condition and Origin

When the first effectual settlement of our colony was made, which was in 1607, the country from the sea-coast to the mountains, and from Patowmac to the most southern waters of James river, was occupied by upwards of forty different tribes of Indians. Of these the *Powhatans*, the *Mannahoacs*, and *Monacans*, were the most powerful. Those between the sea-coast and falls of the rivers, were in amity with one another, and attached to the *Powhatans* as their link of union. Those between the falls of the rivers and the mountains, were divided into two confederacies; the tribes inhabiting the head waters of Patowmac and Rappahanoc being attached to the *Mannahoacs*; and those on the upper parts of James river to the *Monacans*. But the *Monacans* and their friends

[16]NEWTON: Sir Isaac Newton (1643–1727), mathematician noted for developing the laws of gravity and motion.
[17]CIS: On this side of. (Latin)

were in amity with the *Mannahoacs* and their friends, and waged joint and perpetual war against the *Powhatans*. We are told that the *Powhatans*, *Mannahoacs*, and *Monacans*, spoke languages so radically different, that interpreters were necesary when they transacted business. Hence we may conjecture, that this was not the case between all the tribes, and probably that each spoke the language of the nation to which it was attached; which we know to have been the case in many particular instances. Very possibly there may have been anciently three different stocks, each of which multiplying in a long course of time, had separated into so many little societies. This practice results from the circumstance of their having never submitted themselves to any laws, any coercive power, any shadow of government. Their only controls are their manners, and that moral sense of right and wrong, which, like the sense of tasting and feeling, in every man makes a part of his nature. An offence against these is punished by contempt, by exclusion from society, or, where the case is serious, as that of murder, by the individuals whom it concerns. Imperfect as this species of coercion may seem, crimes are very rare among them: insomuch that were it made a question, whether no law, as among the savage Americans, or too much law, as among the civilized Europeans, submits man to the greatest evil, one who has seen both conditions of existence would pronounce it to be the last: and that the sheep are happier of themselves, than under care of the wolves. It will be said, that great societies cannot exist without government. The Savages therefore break them into small ones....

I know of no such thing existing as an Indian monument: for I would not honour with that name arrow points, stone hatchets, stone pipes, and half-shapen images. Of labour on the large scale, I think there is no remain as respectable as would be a common ditch for the draining of lands: unless indeed it be the Barrows,[1] of which many are to be found all over this country. These are of different sizes, some of them constructed of earth, and some of loose stones. That they were repositories of the dead, has been obvious to all: but on what particular occasion constructed, was matter of doubt. Some have thought they covered the bones of those who have fallen in battles fought on the spot of interment. Some ascribed them to the custom, said to prevail among the Indians, of collecting, at certain periods, the bones of all their dead, wheresoever deposited at the time of death. Others again supposed them the general sepulchres for towns, conjectured to have been on or near these grounds; and this opinion was supported by the quality of the lands in which

[1]BARROWS: Burial mounds.

they are found, (those constructed of earth being generally in the softest and most fertile meadow-grounds on river sides) and by a tradition, said to be handed down from the Aboriginal Indians, that, when they settled in a town, the first person who died was placed erect, and earth put about him, so as to cover and support him; that, when another died, a narrow passage was dug to the first, the second reclined against him, and the cover of earth replaced, and so on. There being one of these in my neighbourhood, I wished to satisfy myself whether any, and which of these opinions were just. For this purpose I determined to open and examine it thoroughly. It was situated on the low grounds of the Rivanna, about two miles above its principle fork, and opposite to some hills, on which had been an Indian town. It was of a spheroidical form, of about 40 feet in diameter at the base, and had been of about twelve feet altitude, though now reduced by the plough to seven and a half, having been under cultivation about a dozen years. Before this it was covered with trees of twelve inches diameter, and round the base was an excavation of five feet depth and width, from whence the earth had been taken of which the hillock was formed. I first dug superficially in several parts of it, and came to collections of human bones, at different depths, from six inches to three feet below the surface. These were lying in the utmost confusion, some vertical, some oblique, some horizontal, and directed to every point of the compass, entangled, and held together in clusters by the earth. Bones of the most distant parts were found together, as, for instance, the small bones of the foot in the hollow of a scull, many sculls would sometimes be in contact, lying on the face, on the side, on the back, top or bottom, so as, on the whole to give the idea of bones emptied promiscuously from a bag or basket, and covered over with earth, without any attention to their order. The bones of which the greatest numbers remained, were sculls, jaw-bones, teeth, the bones of the arms, thighs, legs, feet and hands. A few ribs remained, some vertebrae of the neck and spine, without their processes, and one instance only of the bone which serves as a base to the vertebral column. The sculls were so tender, that they generally fell to pieces on being touched. The other bones were stronger. There were some teeth which were judged to be smaller than those of an adult; a scull, which, on a slight view, appeared to be that of an infant, but it fell to pieces on being taken out, so as to prevent satisfactory examination; a rib, and a fragment of the under-jaw of a person about half grown; another rib of an infant; and part of the jaw of a child, which had not yet cut its teeth. This last furnishing the most decisive proof of the burial of children here, I was particular in my attention to it. It was part of the right-half of the under-jaw. The processes, by which it was articulated to the temporal bones, were entire; and the bone itself firm to where it had been broken off, which, as nearly as I could judge, was about the place of the eye-tooth. Its upper edge, wherein would have been the sockets of the teeth, was perfectly smooth. Measuring it with that of an adult, by placing their hinder processes together, its broken end extended to the penultimate grinder of the adult. This bone was white, all the others of a sand colour. The bones of infants being soft, they probably decay sooner, which might be the cause so few were found here. I proceeded then to make a perpendicular cut through the body of the barrow, that I might examine its internal structure. This passed about three feet from its center, was opened to the former surface of the earth, and was wide enough for a man to walk through and examine its sides. At the bottom, that is, on the level of the circumjacent plain, I found bones; above these a few stones, brought from a cliff a quarter of a mile off, and from the river one-eighth of a mile off; then a large interval of earth, then a stratum of bones, and so on. At one end of the section were four strata of bones plainly distinguishable; at the other, three; the strata in one part not ranging with those in another. The bones nearest the surface were least decayed. No holes were discovered in any of them, as if made with bullets, arrows, or other weapons. I conjectured that in this barrow might have been a thousand skeletons. Every one will readily seize the circumstances above related, which militate against the opinion, that it covered the bones only of persons fallen in battle; and against the tradition also, which would make it the common sepulchre of a town, in which the bodies were placed upright, and touching each other. Appearances certainly indicate that it has derived both origin and growth from the accustomary collection of bones, and deposition of them together; that the first collection had been deposited on the common surface of the earth, a few stones put over it, and then a covering of earth, that the second had been laid on this, had covered more or less of it in proportion to the number of bones, and was then also covered with earth; and so on. The following are the particular circumstances which give it this aspect. 1. The number of bones. 2. Their confused position. 3. Their being in different strata. 4. The strata in one part having no correspondence with those in another. 5. The different states of decay in these strata, which seem to indicate a difference in the time of inhumation. 6. The existence of infant bones among them.

But on whatever occasion they may have been made, they are of considerable notoriety among the Indians: for a party passing, about thirty years ago, through the part of the country where this barrow is, went through the woods directly to it, without any instructions or enquiry, and having staid about it some time, with expressions which were construed to be those of sorrow, they returned to the high road, which they had left about half a dozen miles to pay this visit, and pursued their journey. There is another barrow, much resembling this in the low grounds of the South branch of Shenandoah, where it is crossed by the road leading from the Rock-fish gap to Staunton. Both of these have, within these dozen years, been cleared of their trees and put under cultivation, are much reduced in their height, and spread in width, by the plough, and will probably disappear in time. There is another on a hill in the Blue ridge of mountains, a few miles North of Wood's gap, which is made up of small stones thrown together. This has been opened and found to contain human bones, as the others do. There are also many others in other parts of the country.

Great question has arisen from whence came those aboriginal inhabitants of America? Discoveries, long ago made, were sufficient to shew that a passage from Europe to America was always practicable, even to the imperfect navigation of ancient times. In going from Norway to Iceland, from Iceland to Groenland,[2] from Groenland to Labrador, the first traject[3] is the widest: and this having been practised from the earliest times of which we have any account of that part of the earth, it is not difficult to suppose that the subsequent trajects may have been sometimes passed. Again, the late discoveries of Captain Cook, coasting from Kamschatka[4] to California, have proved that, if the two continents of Asia and America be separated at all, it is only by a narrow streight. So that from this side also, inhabitants may have passed into America: and the resemblance between the Indians of America and the Eastern inhabitants of Asia, would induce us to conjecture, that the former are the descendants of the latter, or the latter of the former: excepting indeed the Eskimaux,[5] who, from the same circumstance of resemblance, and from identity of language, must be derived from the Groenlanders, and these probably from some of the northern parts of the old continent. A knowledge of their several languages would be the most certain evidence of their derivation which could be produced. In fact, it is the best proof of the affinity of nations which ever can be referred to. How many ages have elapsed since the English, the Dutch, the Germans, the Swiss, the Norwegians, Danes and Swedes have separated from their common stock? Yet how many more must elapse before the proofs of their common

[2]GROENLAND: Greenland.
[3]TRAJECT: Place to cross.
[4]KAMSCHATKA: A peninsula in Siberia.
[5]ESKIMAUX: Inuits, not Eskimos, were responsible for colonizing Greenland.

origin, which exist in their several languages, will disappear? It is to be lamented then, very much to be lamented, that we have suffered so many of the Indian tribes already to extinguish, without our having previously collected and deposited in the records of literature, the general rudiments at least of the languages they spoke. Were vocabularies formed of all the languages spoken in North and South America, preserving their appellations of the most common objects in nature, of those which must be present to every nation barbarous or civilised, with the inflections of their nouns and verbs, their principles of regimen and concord, and these deposited in all the public libraries, it would furnish opportunities to those skilled in the languages of the old world to compare them with these, now, or at any future time, and hence to construct the best evidence of the derivation of this part of the human race....

[1787]

From *Notes on the State of Virginia*, Query XVIII. Manners [Effect of Slavery]

It is difficult to determine on the standard by which the manners of a nation may be tried, whether *catholic*,[1] or *particular*. It is more difficult for a native to bring to that standard the manners of his own nation, familiarized to him by habit. There must doubtless be an unhappy influence on the manners of our people produced by the existence of slavery among us. The whole commerce between master and slave is a perpetual exercise of the most boisterous passions, the most unremitting despotism on the one part, and degrading submissions on the other. Our children see this, and learn to imitate it; for man is an imitative animal. This quality is the germ of all education in him. From his cradle to his grave he is learning to do what he sees others do. If a parent could find no motive either in his philanthropy or his self-love, for restraining the intemperance of passion towards his slave, it should always be a sufficient one that his child is present. But generally it is not sufficient. The parent storms, the child looks on, catches the lineaments of wrath, puts on the same airs in the circle of smaller

[1]CATHOLIC: Universal.

slaves, gives a loose to his worst of passions, and thus nursed, educated, and daily exercised in tyranny, cannot but be stamped by it with odious peculiarities. The man must be a prodigy who can retain his manners and morals undepraved by such circumstances. And with what execration[2] should the statesman be loaded, who permitting one half the citizens thus to trample on the rights of the other, transforms those into despots, and these into enemies, destroys the morals of the one part, and the amor patriæ[3] of the other. For if a slave can have a country in this world, it must be any other in preference to that in which he is born to live and labour for another: in which he must lock up the faculties of his nature, contribute as far as depends on his individual endeavours to the evanishment of the human race, or entail his own miserable condition on the endless generations proceeding from him. With the morals of the people, their industry also is destroyed. For in a warm climate, no man will labour for himself who can make another labour for him. This is so true, that of the proprietors of slaves a very small proportion indeed are ever seen to labour. And can the liberties of a nation be thought secure when we have removed their only firm basis, a conviction in the minds of the people that these liberties are of the gift of God? That they are not to be violated but with his wrath? Indeed I tremble for my country when I reflect that God is just: that his justice cannot sleep for ever: that considering numbers, nature and natural means only, a revolution of the wheel of fortune, an exchange of situation, is among possible events: that it may become probable by supernatural interference! The Almighty has no attribute which can take side with us in such a contest—But it is impossible to be temperate and to pursue this subject through the various considerations of policy, of morals, of history natural and civil. We must be contented to hope they will force their way into every one's mind. I think a change already perceptible, since the origin of the present revolution. The spirit of the master is abating, that of the slave rising from the dust, his condition mollifying,[4] the way I hope preparing, under the auspices of heaven, for a total emancipation, and that this is disposed, in the order of events, to be with the consent of the masters, rather than by their extirpation.

[1787]

---

[2]EXECRATION: Curse.
[3]AMOR PATRIAE: Love of country. (Latin)
[4]MOLLIFYING: Improving.

From *Notes on the State of Virginia*, Query XIX. Manufactures

We never had an interior trade of any importance. Our exterior commerce has suffered very much from the beginning of the present contest. During this time we have manufactured within our families the most necessary articles of clothing. Those of cotton will bear some comparison with the same kinds of manufacture in Europe; but those of wool, flax and hemp are very coarse, unsightly, and unpleasant: and such is our attachment to agriculture, and such our preference for foreign manufactures, that be it wise or unwise, our people will certainly return as soon as they can, to the raising raw materials, and exchanging them for finer manufactures than they are able to execute themselves.

The political economists of Europe have established it as a principle that every state should endeavor to manufacture for itself: and this principle, like many others, we transfer to America, without calculating the difference of circumstance which should often produce a difference of result. In Europe the lands are either cultivated, or locked up against the cultivator. Manufacture must therefore be resorted to of necessity not of choice, to support the surplus of their people. But we have an immensity of land courting the industry of the husbandman.[1] Is it best then that all our citizens should be employed in its improvement, or that one half should be called off from that to exercise manufactures and handicraft arts for the other? Those who labor in the earth are the chosen people of God, if ever He had a chosen people, whose breasts He has made his peculiar deposit for substantial and genuine virtue. It is the focus in which He keeps alive that sacred fire, which otherwise might escape from the face of the earth. Corruption of morals in the mass of cultivators is a phenomenon of which no age nor nation has furnished an example. It is the mark set on those, who not looking up to heaven, to their own soil and industry, as does the husbandman, for their subsistence, depend for it on the casualties and caprice of customers. Dependence begets subservience and venality,[2] suffocates the germ of virtue, and prepares fit tools for the designs of ambition. This, the natural progress and

[1]HUSBANDMAN: Farmer.
[2]VENALITY: Inclination to sin; the wasting of talent for base motives.

consequence of the arts, has sometimes perhaps been retarded by accidental circumstances: but, generally speaking, the proportion which the aggregate of the other classes of citizens bears in any state to that of its husbandmen is the proportion of its unsound to its healthy parts, and is a good enough barometer whereby to measure its degree of corruption. While we have land to labor then, let us never wish to see our citizens occupied at a workbench, or twirling a distaff.[3] Carpenters, masons, smiths are wanting in husbandry: but for the general operations of manufacture, let our workshops remain in Europe. It is better to carry provisions and materials to workmen there, than bring them to the provisions and materials, and with them their manners and principles. The loss by the transportation of commodities across the Atlantic will be made up in happiness and permanence of government. The mobs of great cities add just so much to the support of pure government as sores do to the strength of the human body. It is the manners and spirit of a people which preserve a republic in vigor. A degeneracy in these is a canker which soon eats to the heart of its laws and constitution.

[1787]

---

[3]DISTAFF: The rod on a spinning wheel around which thread or yarn is wound.

James Madison

(1751–1836)

Born in Port Conway, Virginia, James Madison graduated from the College of New Jersey (Princeton) in 1771 and during the 1770s was a delegate to the Virginia Convention, where he argued for religious freedom and toleration as a right (and not merely as a matter of law) and served as an adviser to Virginia's governors. Shy, short in stature, and scholarly, Madison served in the Continental Congress and the Virginia House of Delegates in the 1780s, working with his friend Thomas Jefferson. From 1789 to 1797 he was a member of the U.S. House of Representatives; he was secretary of state in Jefferson's administration, 1801–1809; and from 1809 to 1817 he served two terms as president.

Madison secured his central place in American politics and literature, however, during the late 1780s, when he wrote the draft of the Virginia Plan that, with revisions and modifications, formed the basis for the U.S. Constitution. He then played a crucial role in the ratification process. With Alexander Hamilton (whose idea it was) and John Jay, Madison collaborated on the Federalist *Papers, termed by one recent scholar "the most important American contribution to political theory." Madison wrote twenty-nine of the eighty-five essays; most were written by Hamilton, and a handful by Jay.*

Published under the name "Publius," the essays—first published in New York City newspapers and then gathered in two volumes in 1788—sought to engage and counter criticisms of the Constitution advanced by opponents of ratification. Hamilton cogently argued in the first number that Americans must address and decide 'the important question, whether societies of men are really capable or not, of establishing good government from reflection and choice, or whether they are forever destined to depend, for their political constitutions, on accident and force." The Federalist *Papers as a whole emphasized the importance of establishing and preserving a union of the states; highlighted the shortcomings of the Articles of Confederation; and indicated the advantages of the various provisions of the Constitution. Jefferson, writing to Madison, concluded they amounted to "the best commentary on the principles of government which was ever written."*

Madison emphasized the restraints the Constitution placed on the federal government. He called attention, for example, to the frequency of free elections and to the system of checks and balances ensured by the separation of powers into executive, legislative, and judicial branches. He noted, too, the positive tension that would exist between state and federal governments, and, in Federalist *number 10, below, he described the healthy kind of conflict that would occur among interest groups—which, he maintained, would function in a large republic to ward off factional disorder and preserve political stability. No single group or organization would succeed in gaining sway over others amid the counterbalancing of many interests.*

Ironically, the Federalist Papers *failed in their immediate purpose, which was to persuade New Yorkers to elect delegates who supported the Constitution to the convention where ratification would be debated and voted on; the fear of a loss of states' rights and of a threat to the liberty of individuals remained intense. Two-thirds of the delegates were at first opposed to ratification, though New York eventually did vote in favor by a slim margin. But the* Federalist Papers *provided advocates for ratification throughout the country with their main arguments, and, in Madison's case, readied him for the coming political struggle in his home state of Virginia, where he out-argued Patrick Henry and won a victory on behalf of ratification. Soon thereafter, during George Washington's first term, Madison was the central figure in the process that led to the Bill of Rights—which, ratified by the necessary number of states in 1791, was added to the Constitution as its first ten amendments.*

Known as the "father of the Constitution" and as one of the nation's foremost statesman and political theorists, Madison also is the author of the most extensive notes and records of the Constitutional Convention. He organized and prepared them for release, and, a few years after his death, they were published—he had withheld them in part because he wanted to wait until the framers (whose opinions he had recorded) were no longer alive.

Summing up Madison's career, the eminent orator, diplomat, and U.S. senator Daniel Webster said, "He had as much to do as any man in framing the Constitution, and as much to do as any man in administering it." Yet in his retirement Madison often regretted that the Constitution had become, on slavery (he owned nearly 100 slaves himself) and other topics, less a source of national consensus than an interpretive battleground. Competing interests fought over its true meaning, and on some occasions Madison was abruptly told he did not understand the nature of the document he had so crucially helped create and argue for. Time and again, the Union seemed on the verge of breaking apart, and in 1861 a war was waged to ensure its preservation. Yet despite decades, now centuries, of debate, controversy, bitter disagreement, and bloodshed, the U.S. Constitution remains in force, and the Union endures.

For a cogent survey: Garry Wills, James Madison *(2002). See also Ralph Ketcham,* James Madison: A Biography *(1971; rpt. 1990); and Richard B. Morris,* Witnesses at the Creation: Hamilton, Madison, Jay, and the Constitution *(1985). On* The Federalist Papers: *Garry Wills,* Explaining America: The Federalist *(1981); and Morton White,* Philosophy, The Federalist, and the Constitution *(1987). Also illuminating: Drew R. McCoy,* The Last of the Fathers: James Madison and the Republican Legacy *(1989); and Lance Banning,* The Sacred Fire of Liberty: James Madison and the Founding of the Federal Republic *(1995). An excellent resource:* James Madison and the American Nation, 1751–1836: An Encyclopedia, *ed. Robert A. Rutland (1994).*

The Federalist No. 10

November 22, 1787

To the People of the State of New York.

Among the numerous advantages promised by a well-constructed Union, none deserves to be more accurately developed than its tendency to break and control the violence of faction. The friend of popular governments, never finds himself so much alarmed for their character and fate, as when he contemplates their propensity to this dangerous vice. He will not fail therefore to set a due value on any plan which, without violating the principles to which he is attached, provides a proper cure for it. The instability, injustice and confusion introduced in the public councils, have in truth been the mortal diseases under which popular governments have everywhere perished; as they continue to be the favorite and fruitful topics from which the adversaries to liberty derive their most specious[1] declamations. The valuable improvements made by the American constitutions on the popular models, both ancient and modern, cannot certainly be too much admired; but it would be an unwarrantable partiality, to contend that they have as effectually obviated the danger on this side as was wished and expected. Complaints are everywhere heard from our most considerate and virtuous citizens, equally the friends of public and private faith, and of public and personal liberty; that our governments are too unstable; that the public good is disregarded in the conflicts of rival parties; and that measures are too often decided, not according to the rules of justice, and the rights of the minor party; but by the superior force of an interested and over-bearing majority. However anxiously we may wish that these complaints had no foundation, the evidence of known facts will not permit us to deny that they are in some degree true. It will be found indeed, on a candid review of our situation, that some of the distresses under which we labor, have been erroneously charged on the operation of our governments; but it will be

---

[1]SPECIOUS: Untrue; seemingly plausible but lacking truth or sincerity.

found, at the same time, that other causes will not alone account for many of our heaviest misfortunes; and particularly, for that prevailing and increasing distrust of public engagements, and alarm for private rights, which are echoed from one end of the continent to the other. These must be chiefly, if not wholly, effects of the unsteadiness and injustice, with which a factious spirit tainted our public administrations.

By a faction I understand a number of citizens, whether amounting to a majority or minority of the whole, who are united and actuated by some common impulse of passion, or of interest, adverse to the rights of other citizens, or to the permanent and aggregate interests of the community.

There are two methods of curing the mischiefs of faction: the one, by removing its causes; the other, by controling its effects.

There are again two methods of removing the causes of faction: the one by destroying the liberty which is essential to its existence; the other, by giving to every citizen the same opinions, the same passions, and the same interests.

It could never be more truly said than of the first remedy, that it is worse than the disease. Liberty is to faction, what air is to fire, an aliment[2] without which it instantly expires. But it could not be a less folly to abolish liberty, which is essential to political life, because it nourishes faction, than it would be to wish the annihilation of air, which is essential to animal life, because it imparts to fire its destructive agency.

The second expedient is as impracticable, as the first would be unwise. As long as the reason of man continues fallible, and he is at liberty to exercise it, different opinions will be formed. As long as the connection subsists between his reason and his self-love, his opinions and his passions will have a reciprocal influence on each other; and the former will be objects to which the latter will attach themselves. The diversity in the faculties of men from which the rights of property originate, is not less an insuperable obstacle to a uniformity of interests. The protection of these faculties is the first object of Government. From the protection of different and unequal faculties of acquiring property, the possession of degrees and kinds of property immediately results; and from the influence of these on the sentiments and views of the respective proprietors, ensues a division of the society into different interests and parties.

The latent causes of faction are thus sown in the nature of man; and we see them everywhere brought into different degrees of activity, according to the different circumstances of civil society. A zeal for dif-

[2]ALIMENT: Sustenance, support.

ferent opinions concerning religion, concerning Government and many other points, as well of speculation as of practice; an attachment to different leaders ambitiously contending for pre-eminence and power; or to persons of other descriptions whose fortunes have been interesting to the human passions, have in turn divided mankind into parties, inflamed them with mutual animosity, and rendered them much more disposed to vex and oppress each other, than to cooperate for their common good. So strong is this propensity of mankind to fall into mutual animosities, that where no substantial occasion presents itself, the most frivolous and fanciful distinctions have been sufficient to kindle their unfriendly passions, and excite their most violent conflicts. But the most common and durable source of factions, has been the various and unequal distribution of property. Those who hold, and those who are without property, have ever formed distinct interests in society. Those who are creditors, and those who are debtors, fall under a like discrimination. A landed interest, a manufacturing interest, a mercantile interest, a monied interest, with many lesser interests, grow up of necessity in civilized nation, and divide them into different classes, actuated by different sentiments and views. The regulation of these various and interfering interests forms the principal task of modern Legislation, and involved the spirit of party and faction in the necessary and ordinary operations of Government.

No man is allowed to be a judge in his own cause; because his interest would certainly bias his judgment, and, not improbably, corrupt his integrity. With equal, nay with greater reason, a body of men, are unfit to be both judges and parties, at the same time; yet, what are many of the most important acts of legislation, but so many judicial determinations, not indeed concerning the rights of single persons, but concerning the rights of large bodies of citizens; and what are the different classes of legislators, but advocates and parties to the causes which they determine? Is a law proposed concerning private debts? It is a question to which the creditors are parties on one side, and the debtors on the other. Justice ought to hold the balance between them. Yet the parties are and must be themselves the judges; and the most numerous party, or in other words, the most powerful faction must be expected to prevail. Shall domestic manufactures be encouraged, and in what degree, by restrictions on foreign manufactures? are questions which would be differently decided by the landed and the manufacturing classes; and probably by neither, with a sole regard to justice and the public good. The apportionment of taxes on the various descriptions of poverty, is an act which seems to require the most exact impartiality; yet, there is perhaps no legislative act in which greater opportunity and temptation are given to a predominant party, to trample on the rules of justice. Every shilling with which they over-burden the inferior number, is a shilling saved to their own pockets.

It is in vain to say, that enlightened statesmen will be able to adjust these clashing interests, and render them all subservient to the public good. Enlightened statesmen will not always be at the helm: Nor, in many cases, can such an adjustment be made at all, without taking into view indirect and remote considerations, which will rarely prevail over the immediate interest which one party may find in disregarding the rights of another, or the good of the whole.

The inference to which we are brought, is, that the causes of faction cannot be removed; and that relief is only to be sought in the means of controling its *effects*.

If a faction consists of less than a majority, relief is supplied by the republican principle, which enables the majority to defeat its sinister views by regular vote: it may clog the administration, it may convulse the society; but it will be unable to execute and mask its violence under the forms of the Constitution. When a majority is included in a faction, the form of popular government on the other hand enables it to sacrifice to its ruling passion or interest, both the public good and the rights of other citizens. To secure the public good, and private rights, against the danger of such a faction, and at the same time to preserve the spirit and the form of popular government, is then the great object to which our enquiries are directed: Let me add that it is the great desideratum,[3] by which alone this form of government can be rescued from the opprobrium under which it has so long labored, and be recommended to the esteem and adoption of mankind.

By what means is this object attainable? Evidently by one of two only. Either the existence of the same passion or interest in a majority at the same time, must be prevented; or the majority, having such co-existent passion or interest, must be rendered, by their number and local situation, unable to concert[4] and carry into effect schemes of oppression. If the impulse and the opportunity be suffered to coincide, we well know that neither moral nor religious motives can be relied on as an adequate control. They are not found to be such on the injustice and violence of individuals, and lose their efficacy in proportion to the number combined together; that is, in proportion as their efficacy becomes needful.

---

[3]DESIDERATUM: Something for which a desire or longing is felt.
[4]CONCERT: Join for a common purpose or goal.

From this view of the subject, it may be concluded, that a pure Democracy, by which I mean, a Society, consisting of a small number of citizens, who assemble and administer the Government in person, can admit of no cure for the mischiefs of faction. A common passion or interest will, in almost every case, be felt by a majority of the whole; a communication and concern results from the form of Government itself; and there is nothing to check the inducements to sacrifice the weaker party, or an obnoxious individual. Hence it is, that such Democracies have ever been spectacles of turbulence and contention; have ever been found incompatible with personal security, or the rights of property; and have in general been as short in their lives, as they have been violent in their deaths. Theoretic politicians, who have patronized this species of Government, have erroneously supposed, that by reducing mankind to a perfect equality in their political rights, they would at the same time, be perfectly equalized and assimilated in their possessions, their opinions, and their passions.

A Republic, by which I mean a Government in which the scheme of representation takes place, opens a different prospect, and promises the cure for which we are seeking. Let us examine the points in which it varies from pure Democracy, and we shall comprehend both the nature of the cure, and the efficacy which it must derive from the Union.

The two great points of difference between a Democracy and a Republic are, first, the delegation of the Government, in the latter, to a small number of citizens elected by the rest: secondly, the greater number of citizens, and greater sphere of country, over which the latter may be extended.

The effect of the first difference is, on the one hand to refine and enlarge the public views, by passing them through the medium of a chosen body of citizens, whose wisdom may best discern the true interest of their country, and whose patriotism and love of justice, will be least likely to sacrifice it to temporary or partial considerations. Under such a regulation, it may well happen that the public voice pronounced by the representatives of the people, will be more consonant to the public good, than if pronounced by the people themselves convened for the purpose. On the other hand, the effect may be inverted. Men of factious tempers, of local prejudices, or of sinister designs, may by intrigue, by corruption or by other means, first obtain the suffrages,[5] and then betray the interests of the people. The question resulting is, whether small or extensive Republics are most favorable to the election of proper guardians of the public weal[6]; and it is clearly decided in favor of the latter by two obvious considerations.

[5]SUFFRAGES: Votes.
[6]WEAL: Welfare.

In the first place it is to be remarked that however small the Republic may be, the Representatives must be raised to a certain number, in order to guard against the cabals[7] of a few; and that however large it may be, they must be limited to a certain number, in order to guard against the confusion of a multitude. Hence the number of Representatives in the two cases, not being in proportion to that of the Constituents, and being proportionally greatest in the small Republic, it follows, that if the proportion of fit characters, be not less, in the large than in the small Republic, the former will present a greater option, and consequently a greater probability of a fit choice.

In the next place, as each Representative will be chosen by a greater number of citizens in the large than in the small Republic, it will be more difficult for unworthy candidates to practise with success the vicious arts, by which elections are too often carried; and the suffrages of the people being more free, will be more likely to centre on men who possess the most attractive merit, and the most diffusive and established characters.

It must be confessed, that in this, as in most other cases, there is a mean, on both sides of which inconveniencies will be found to lie. By enlarging too much the number of electors, you render the representative too little acquainted with all their local circumstances and lesser interests; as by reducing it too much, you render him unduly attached to these, and too little fit to comprehend and pursue great and national objects. The Federal Constitution forms a happy combination in this respect; the great and aggregate interests being referred to the national, the local and particular, to the state legislatures.

The other point of difference is, the greater number of citizens and extent of territory which may be brought within the compass of Republican, than of Democratic Government[8]; and it is this circumstance principally which renders factious combinations less to be dreaded in the former, than in the latter. The smaller the society, the fewer probably will be the distinct parties and interests composing it; the fewer the distinct parties and interests, the more frequently will a majority be found of the same party; and the smaller the numbers of individuals composing a majority, and the smaller the compass within which they are placed, the more easily will they concert and execute their plans of oppression. Extend the sphere, and you take in a greater variety of parties and interests; you make it less probable that a majority of the whole will have a common motive to invade the rights of other citizens; or if such a common motive

---

[7]CABALS: Intrigues or conspiracies.

[8]REPUBLICAN, THAN OF DEMOCRATIC GOVERNMENT: Republicans, known in Madison's time as Federalists, were willing to have an elected few represent the whole. Democrats opposed this Federalist view, defending the individual's right to vote.

exists, it will be more difficult for all who feel it to discover their own strength, and to act in unison with each other. Besides other impediments, it may be remarked, that where there is a consciousness of unjust or dishonorable purposes, communication is always checked by distrust, in proportion to the number whose concurrence is necessary.

Hence it clearly appears, that the same advantage, which a Republic has over a Democracy, in controling the effects of faction, is enjoyed by a large over a small Republic—is enjoyed by the Union over the States composing it. Does this advantage consist in the substitution of Representatives, whose enlightened views and virtuous sentiments render them superior to local prejudices, and to schemes of injustice? It will not be denied, that the Representation of the Union will be most likely to possess these requisite endowments. Does it consist in the greater security afforded by a greater variety of parties, against the event of any one party being able to outnumber and oppress the rest? In an equal degree does the encreased variety of parties, comprised within the Union, encrease this security? Does it, in fine,[9] consist in the greater obstacles opposed to the concert and accomplishment of the secret wishes of an unjust and interested majority? Here, again, the extent of the Union gives it the most palpable advantage.

The influence of factious leaders may kindle a flame within their particular States but will be unable to spread a general conflagration through the other States: a religious sect, may degenerate into a political faction in a part of the confederacy; but the variety of sects dispersed over the entire face of it, must secure the national Councils against any danger from that source: a rage for paper money, for an abolition of debts, for an equal division of property, or for any other improper or wicked project, will be less apt to pervade the whole body of the Union, than a particular member of it; in the same proportion as such a malady is more likely to taint a particular county or district, than an entire State.

In the extent and proper structure of the Union, therefore, we behold a Republican remedy for the diseases most incident[10] to Republican Government. And according to the degree of pleasure and pride, we feel in being Republicans, ought to be our zeal in cherishing the spirit, and supporting the character of Federalists.

PUBLIUS.[11]

[1787]

---

[9]IN FINE: In conclusion.
[10]INCIDENT: A consequence of.
[11]PUBLIUS: The collective pseudonym adopted by Alexander Hamilton (1757–1804), John Jay (1745–1829), and Madison as authors of *The Federalist*.

Philip Freneau

(1752–1832)

Known in his era and afterward as "the Poet of the Revolution," Philip Freneau, born in New York City, was an undergraduate at Princeton University, where his roommate was the future statesman and president James Madison. Freneau first studied theology in preparation for a career as a minister, but taking part in a literary society, the Plain Dealing Club, he soon displayed his talent as a poet and a satirist. With a classmate, H. H. Brackenridge, he coauthored a comic narrative, Father Bombo's Pilgrimage to Mecca in Arabia; *and with Madison and Brackenridge he compiled* Satires Against the Tories. *Again with Brackenridge, he collaborated on a long patriotic poem, "The Rising Glory of America," a prophecy of the nation's future rule from the Atlantic to the Pacific oceans. A heady evocation of the spirit of independence that depicted America as a "new Jerusalem," the poem was read by Brackenridge at Princeton's commencement in 1771.*

After graduation, Freneau taught for two years but disliked it, and he was no more contented with further studies he pursued in theology. He wrote satiric verses about the British but then, surprisingly, left the colonies for the Caribbean, where he remained, mostly on St. Croix, for two years, composing Nature poetry and learning the art of navigation. Upon his return to the colonies he joined the militia and took to the sea on a ship conveying supplies through the British naval blockade. Imprisoned for six weeks in early 1780 aboard a British vessel, he became all the more a fierce enemy of British rule, and in the early 1780s, as editor in Philadelphia of the Freeman's Journal, *he produced much sharp, angry anti-British political writing.*

When the Revolutionary War ended, Freneau spent six years as a sea captain while continuing to write and publish satiric and romantic verse. But at the behest of his friends Madison and Thomas Jefferson, he reentered politics to establish a newspaper, the National Gazette, *in Philadelphia. From 1791 to the paper's demise in 1793, Freneau supported Jefferson's views and argued against those expressed by Alexander Hamilton, John Adams, and other Federalists; he even dared to criticize George Washington, which led Washington to refer to him as "that rascal Freneau."*

During the mid- to late 1790s, Freneau contributed to newspapers in New York and Philadelphia, but once Jefferson was elected to the presidency in 1800, Freneau retired from public life. He farmed, sailed, and remained intermittently active as an author of prose and poetry.

Freneau produced a sizable body of work: 500 poems, 1,100 prose pieces, and a number of short fictions. But much of it, while important in historical terms, lacks enduring literary interest. "The Indian Burying Ground" and "On the Religion of Nature," below, are two of

his best poems. They "break bravely from formalized poetic tradition,"
the Freneau scholar Lewis Leary observed, "to forecast, twelve years
before Wordsworth's Lyrical Ballads, the renaissance of wonder that
characterized the Romantic movement." While uneven in accomplish-
ment and limited in vision and depth, Freneau nonetheless must be val-
ued as one of the first authentically American voices in literature.

For a brief survey: Mary Weatherspoon Bowden, Philip Freneau
(1976). See also Lewis Leary, That Rascal Freneau: A Study in Literary
Failure (1941); Jacob Axelrad, Philip Freneau: Champion of
Democracy (1967); and Richard C. Vitzthum, Land and Sea: The Lyric
Poetry of Philip Freneau (1978).

The Indian Burying Ground

In spite of all the learned have said,
I still my old opinion keep;
The posture, that we give the dead,
Points out the soul's eternal sleep.

Not so the ancients of these lands—   5
The Indian, when from life released,
Again is seated with his friends,
And shares again the joyous feast.

His imaged birds, and painted bowl,
And venison,[1] for a journey dressed,[2]   10
Bespeak the nature of the soul,
Activity, that knows no rest.

His bow, for action ready bent,
And arrows, with a head of stone,
Can only mean that life is spent,   15
And not the old ideas gone.

Thou, stranger, that shalt come this way,
No fraud[3] upon the dead commit—
Observe the swelling turf, and say
They do not lie, but here they sit.   20

[1]VENISON: Deer meat.
[2]FOR A JOURNEY DRESSED: "The North American Indians bury their dead in a sitting posture;
decorating the corpse with wampum, the images of birds, quadrupeds, etc.: And (if that of a warrior)
with bows, arrows, tomahawks, and other military weapons." (Freneau's note)
[3]FRAUD: Deceit; theft of the grave's contents.

Here still a lofty rock remains,
On which the curious eye may trace
(Now wasted, half, by wearing rains)
The fancies of a ruder⁴ race.

Here still an aged elm aspires,   25
Beneath whose far-projecting shade
(And which the shepherd still admires)
The children of the forest played!

There oft a restless Indian queen
(Pale Sheba,⁵ with her braided hair)   30
And many a barbarous form is seen
To chide the man that lingers there.

By midnight moons, o'er moistening dews;
In habit for the chase arrayed,
The hunter still the deer pursues,   35
The hunter and the deer, a shade!

And long shall timorous fancy see
The painted chief, and pointed spear,
And Reason's self shall bow the knee
To shadows and delusions here.   40

[1788]

On the Religion of Nature

The power, that gives with liberal hand
    The blessings man enjoys, while here,
And scatters through a smiling land
    Abundant products of the year;
        That power of nature, ever blessed,   5
        Bestowed religion with the rest.

Born with ourselves, her early sway
    Inclines the tender mind to take
The path of right, fair virtue's way

---

⁴RUDER: Redder, more ruddy.
⁵PALE SHEBA: A reference to the Queen of Sheba, who visited King Solomon to test his wisdom, as described in 1 Kings 10:1–13.

Its own felicity to make.   10
　　This universally extends
　　And leads to no mysterious ends.

Religion, such as nature taught,
　　With all divine perfection suits;
Had all mankind this system sought   15
　　Sophists[1] would cease their vain disputes,
　　　　And from this source would nations know
　　　　All that can make their heaven below.

This deals not curses on mankind,
　　Or dooms them to perpetual grief,   20
If from its aid no joys they find,
　　It damns them not for unbelief;
　　　　Upon a more exalted plan
　　　　Creatress nature dealt with man—

Joy to the day, when all agree   25
　　On such grand systems to proceed,
From fraud, design, and error free,
　　And which to truth and goodness lead:
　　　　Then persecution will retreat
　　　　And man's religion be complete.   30

[1815]

---

[1]SOPHISTS: One who makes showy displays of knowledge, usually engaging in circular arguments.

Phillis Wheatley

(1753–1784)

*One of the best-known poets in America during the late eighteenth cen-
tury, the African female who became Phillis Wheatley was born on the
west coast of Africa and then captured and sold into slavery—transported
to America aboard the slave ship "Phillis"—when she was about seven
years old. In July 1761, John Wheatley, a prosperous tailor in Boston,
bought the girl, intending to make her an attendant for his wife. But soon,
despite her slave status, she found acceptance as a member of the family
and was raised alongside the Wheatleys' two children.*

*Unlike most slaves, especially those in the South but in the North as
well, Wheatley was taught to read and write. Tutored by Mrs.
Wheatley, she was a quick learner, and after a short time she grew
familiar with the Bible, the British literary tradition (her favorite poets
were John Milton, Alexander Pope, and Thomas Gray), the basics of
Latin and some Greek, and other subjects.*

Mr. Wheatley later wrote:

> *PHILLIS was brought from Africa to America, in the Year 1761,
> between seven and eight Years of Age. Without any Assistance from
> School Education, and by only what she was taught in the Family,
> she, in sixteen Months Time from her Arrival, attained the English
> language, to which she was an utter Stranger before, to such a
> degree, as to read any, the most difficult Parts of the Sacred
> Writings, to the great Astonishment of all who heard her.*

*Wheatley published her first poem in December 1767, in the Newport,
Rhode Island, Mercury, and six or seven more followed in the next two
years. She made her reputation in 1770 with "On the Death of the Rev.
Mr. George Whitefield," which was published in editions in Boston,
Philadelphia, and other cities in the colonies, and in London.*

*Wheatley gathered enough poems for a book, but no one in Boston
was willing to publish it. With the help of the Wheatleys, she
arranged for the book to be published in London, and she spent six
weeks in London in mid-1773 to help prepare its publication. Later
that year,* Poems on Various Subjects, Religious and Moral *appeared,
the first volume of poetry by an African American. About one-third of
the poems were elegies, and the others were keyed to religious, classical, and other topics. Wheatley, a devout Christian, took the message
of salvation as a central theme.*

*Not everyone believed that an African slave was the author of these
poems. The publisher thus included a note:*

> *AS it has been repeatedly suggested to the Publisher, by
> Persons, who have seen the Manuscript, that Numbers would be*

*ready to suspect they were not really the Writings of PHILLIS, he
has procured the following Attestation, from the most respectable
Characters in Boston, that none might have the least Ground for
disputing their Original.*

*WE whose Names are underwritten, do assure the World, that
the POEMS specified in the following Page, were (as we verily
believe) written by Phillis, a young Negro Girl, who was but a few
Years since, brought an uncultivated Barbarian from Africa, and
has ever since been, and now is, under the Disadvantage of serving
as a Slave in a Family in this Town. She has been examined by
some of the best Judges, and is thought qualified to write them.*

His Excellency THOMAS HUTCHINSON, Governor.

The Hon. ANDREW OLIVER, Lieutenant-Governor.

*[Sixteen others signed, including John Hancock, the American
patriot leader who signed his name with such a bold flourish on the
Declaration of Independence.]*

Soon after the publication of Poems, Mr. Wheatley granted Phillis
her freedom. She married a free black man, John Peters, and had three
children, all of whom died at an early age. She herself died in poverty
at the age of thirty-one. She was working on a second volume of poems
at the time and may have completed it, but it was lost after her death
and has never been located. Her work faded from view until the 1830s,
when members of the abolitionist movement called attention to it as
evidence of the intelligence and imagination of slaves.

Wheatley is a significant figure in historical terms; the scholar
Henry Louis Gates termed her "the progenitor of the black literary tradition." But her work has also been criticized because of its lack of
direct attention to racism and slavery. Only a phrase or two explicitly
mentions the oppression slaves experienced, as when Wheatley
observes, "Some view our sable race with scornful eye." Still, as the
feminist theorist and critic Frances Smith Foster emphasized:

Wheatley imbued her poetry with the sensitivity and passion of a
slave woman as she revised traditional poetic forms and language to
accommodate new messages…. Phillis Wheatley not only spoke but
also deliberately spoke as an African. Her poetry was a political act.

Below are four poems: "On the Death of the Rev. Mr. George
Whitefield," an esteemed English minister and preacher and leader of
religious revivals, and the chaplain to the Countess of Huntington,
whom Wheatley addresses in the text; "On Being Brought from Africa to
America"; "To S. M., A Young African Painter, On Seeing His Works,"
addressed to Scipio Moorhead, a slave in Boston; and "To His
Excellency General Washington." Wheatley sent the letter and poem to
Washington, the leader of the Revolutionary army, as a sign of her patriotism; he thanked her and proposed that she visit him, which she did in

*March 1776. Below, too, is a letter to Samson Occom (1723–1792), a
Native American, Dartmouth college graduate, and Presbyterian minister who criticized Christian ministers who owned slaves.*

For texts and contexts: William H. Robinson, Phillis Wheatley and
Her Writings *(1984); and* The Collected Works of Phillis Wheatley, *ed.
and with an essay by John C. Shields (1988). See also William H.
Robinson,* Phillis Wheatley: A Bio-Bibliography *(1981). For critical
responses:* Critical Essays on Phillis Wheatley, *ed. William H.
Robinson (1982).*

On the Death of the Rev. Mr. George Whitefield[1] 1770

Hail, happy saint, on thine immortal throne,
Possest of glory, life, and bliss unknown;
We hear no more the music of thy tongue,
Thy wonted auditories cease to throng.
Thy sermons in unequall'd accents flow'd,   5
And ev'ry bosom with devotion glow'd;
Thou didst in strains of eloquence refin'd
Inflame the heart, and captivate the mind.
Unhappy we the setting sun deplore,
So glorious once, but ah! it shines no more.   10

Behold the prophet in his tow'ring flight!
He leaves the earth for heav'n's unmeasur'd height,
And worlds unknown receive him from our sight.
There *Whitefield* wings with rapid course his way,
And sails to *Zion*[2] through vast seas of day.   15
Thy pray'rs, great saint, and thine incessant cries
Have pierc'd the bosom of thy native skies.
Thou moon hast seen, and all the stars of light,
How he has wrestled with his God by night.
He pray'd that grace in ev'ry heart might dwell,   20
He long'd to see *America* excel;
He charg'd its youth that ev'ry grace divine

[1]GEORGE WHITEFIELD: The Reverend George Whitefield (1714–1770) was a English Protestant
evangelist and follower of John Wesley who made several trips to America to assist in the Wesley mission there, including the construction of an orphanage.
[2]ZION: The heavenly city of God.

Should with full lustre in their conduct shine;
That Saviour, which his soul did first receive,
The greatest gift that ev'n a God can give,   25
He freely offer'd to the num'rous throng,
That on his lips with list'ning pleasure hung.

"Take him, ye wretched, for your only good,
"Take him[,] ye starving sinners, for your food;
  "Ye thirsty, come to this life-giving stream,   30
"Ye preachers, take him for your joyful theme;
"Take him[,] my dear *Americans*,["] he said,
"Be your complaints on his kind bosom laid:
"Take him, ye *Africans*, he longs for you,
  "*Impartial Saviour* is his title due: 35
"Wash'd in the fountain of redeeming blood,
"You shall be son, and kings, and priests to God."

Great *Countess*,[3] we *Americans* revere
Thy name, and mingle in thy grief sincere;
New England deeply feels, the *Orphans*[4] mourn,   40
Their more than father will no more return.

But, though arrested by the hand of death,
Whitefield no more exerts his lab'ring breath,
Yet let us view him in th'eternal skies,
Let ev'ry heart to this bright vision rise;   45
While the tomb safe retains its sacred trust,
Till life divine re-animates his dust.

[1770]

---

[3]GREAT COUNTESS: Selina Shirley Hastings (1707–1791), Countess of Huntington, a supporter of
Whitefield's activities. Wheatley visited her in England in 1773. Wheatley notes of this reference,
"The Countess of Huntingdon, to whom Mr. Whitefield was Chaplain."
[4]ORPHANS: Wheatley refers to the children in the Savannah, Georgia, orphanage sponsored by
Whitefield (see note 1).

On Being Brought from Africa to America

'Twas mercy brought me from my *Pagan*[1] land,
Taught my benighted soul to understand
That there's a God, that there's a *Saviour* too:
Once I redemption neither sought nor knew.
Some view our sable[2] race with scornful eye,   5
"Their colour is a diabolic die."[3]
Remember, *Christians*, *Negros*, black as *Cain*,[4]
May be refin'd, and join th'angelic train.

[1773]

To S. M.,[1] a Young African Painter, on Seeing His Works.

To show the lab'ring bosom's deep intent,
And thought in living characters to paint,
When first thy pencil did those beauties give,
And breathing figures learnt from thee to live,
How did those prospects give my soul delight,   5
A new creation rushing on my sight?
Still, wond'rous youth! each noble path pursue,
On deathless glories fix thine ardent view:
Still may the painter's and the poet's fire
To aid thy pencil, and thy verse conspire!   10
And may the charms of each seraphic[2] theme
Conduct thy footsteps to immortal fame!

[1]PAGAN: The tribes of West and Central Africa, whence Wheatley was abducted, worshiped multiple deities.
[2]SABLE: Dark.
[3]DIABOLIC DIE: Dye from the devil; mark of evil. Wheatley challenges those who argued that Africans were spiritually inferior.
[4]CAIN: The book of Genesis recounts how Cain slew his brother Abel and was then marked by God for his sin (Genesis 4:1–15).
[1]S.M.: Scipio Moorhead, a slave to Reverend John Moorhead of Boston.
[2]SERAPHIC: Angelic.

High to the blissful wonders of the skies
Elate thy soul, and raise thy wishful eyes.
Thrice happy, when exalted to survey   15
That splendid city, crown'd with endless day,
Whose twice six gates³ on radiant hinges ring:
Celestial Salem⁴ blooms in endless spring.

Calm and serene thy moments glide along,
And may the muse inspire each future song!   20
Still, with the sweets of contemplation bless'd,
May peace with balmy wings your soul invest!
But when these shades of time are chas'd away,
And darkness ends in everlasting day,
On what seraphic pinions shall we move,   25
And view the landscapes in the realms above?
There shall thy tongue in heav'nly murmurs flow,
And there my muse with heav'nly transport glow:
No more to tell of Damon's⁵ tender sighs,
Or rising radiance of Aurora's⁶ eyes,   30
For nobler themes demand a nobler strain,
And purer language on th' ethereal plain.
Cease, gentle muse! the solemn gloom of night
Now seals the fair creation from my sight.

[1773]

To His Excellency General Washington

Sir,

I Have taken the freedom to address your Excellency in the enclosed poem, and entreat your acceptance, though I am not insensible of its inaccuracies. Your being appointed by the Grand Continental Congress to be Generalissimo¹ of the armies of North

---

³TWICE SIX GATES: Heaven, like the city of Jerusalem, was thought to have twelve gates.
⁴CELESTIAL SALEM: Heavenly Jerusalem.
⁵DAMON: A reference to the Greek myth of the friends Damon and Pythias. When Pythias is condemned to death, Damon pledges to die in his place. This act of devotion earns the freedom of both.
⁶AURORA: In Roman mythology, the goddess of the dawn.
¹GENERALISSIMO: Washington had recently been appointed commander of the Continental Army.

America, together with the fame of your virtues, excite sensations not easy to suppress. Your generosity, therefore, I presume, will pardon the attempt. Wishing your Excellency all possible success in the great cause you are so generously engaged in. I am,

Your Excellency's most obedient humble servant,

PHILLIS WHEATLEY.

Providence, Oct. 26, 1775.
His Excellency Gen. Washington.

Celestial choir! enthron'd in realms of light,
Columbia's[2] scenes of glorious toils I write.
While freedom's cause her anxious breast alarms,
She flashes dreadful in refulgent arms.
See mother earth her offspring's fate bemoan,   5
And nations gaze at scenes before unknown!
See the bright beams of heaven's revolving light
Involved in sorrows and the veil of night!
 The goddess comes, she moves divinely fair,
Olive and laurel binds her golden hair: 10
Wherever shines this native of the skies,
Unnumber'd charms and recent graces rise.
 Muse! bow propitious while my pen relates
How pour her armies through a thousand gates,
As when Eolus[3] heaven's fair face deforms,   15
Enwrapp'd in tempest and a night of storms;
Astonish'd ocean feels the wild uproar,
The refluent surges beat the sounding shore;
Or thick as leaves in Autumn's golden reign,
Such, and so many, moves the warrior's train.   20
In bright array they seek the work of war,
Where high unfurl'd the ensign waves in air.
Shall I to Washington their praise recite?
Enough thou know'st them in the fields of fight.
Thee, first in peace and honours,—we demand   25
The grace and glory of thy martial band.
Fam'd for thy valour, for thy virtues more,

[2]COLUMBIA: America.
[3]EOLUS: The Greek god of the winds.

Hear every tongue thy guardian aid implore!
    One century scarce perform'd its destined round,
When Gallic powers Columbia's fury found[4],   30
And so may you, whoever dares disgrace
The land of freedom's heaven-defended race!
Fix'd are the eyes of nations on the scales,
For in their hopes Columbia's arm prevails.
Anon Britannia droops the pensive head,   35
While round increase the rising hills of dead.
Ah! cruel blindness to Columbia's state!
Lament thy thirst of boundless power too late.
    Proceed, great chief, with virtue on thy side,
Thy ev'ry action let the goddess guide.   40
A crown, a mansion, and a throne that shine,
With gold unfading, WASHINGTON! be thine.

[1776]

Letter to Samson Occom[1]

Feb. 11, 1774

Reverend and honoured Sir,

I have this day received your obliging kind epistle, and am greatly satisfied with your reasons respecting the negroes, and think highly reasonable what you offer in vindication of their natural rights: Those that invade them cannot be insensible that the divine light is chasing away the thick darkness[2] which broods over the land of Africa; and the chaos which has reigned so long, is converting into beautiful order, and reveals more and more clearly the glorious dispensation of civil and religious liberty, which are so inseparably united, that there is little or no enjoyment of one without the other: Otherwise, perhaps, the Israelites had been less solicitous for their freedom from Egyptian slavery; I do not say they would have been contented without it, by no means; for in every human

---

[4]FURY FOUND: Washington had demonstrated his military abilities during the French and Indian Wars (1756–1763).
[1]SAMSON OCCOM: Samson Occom (1723–1792), a friend of the Wheatleys, was a Mohegan missionary ministering to Native Americans.
[2]THE DIVINE LIGHT IS CHASING AWAY THE THICK DARKNESS: A reference to Exodus 10:22: "And Moses stretched forth his hand toward heaven, and there was thick darkness in all the land of Egypt for three days."

breast God has implanted a principle, which we call love of freedom; it is impatient of oppression, and pants for deliverance; and by the leave of our modern Egyptians I will assert, that the same principle lives in us. God grant deliverance in his own way and time, and get him honour upon all those whose avarice impels them to countenance and help forward the calamities of their fellow creatures. This I desire not for their hurt, but to convince them of the strange absurdity of their conduct, whose words and actions are so diametrically opposite. How well the cry for liberty, and the reverse disposition for the exercise of oppressive power over others agree—I humbly think it does not require the penetration of a philosopher to determine.

[1774]

PART II

The Making of American Literature

The Age of Emerson

On August 31, 1837, Ralph Waldo Emerson presented "An Oration" to the Phi Beta Kappa Society at the First Parish Meetinghouse on Church Street in Cambridge, Massachusetts. His audience consisted of Harvard students and dignitaries from politics, business, and education, and his topic was "the American scholar," a phrase he later chose as the title when he included the address in *Nature, Addresses, and Lectures* (1849). Many in Emerson's audience, and those who read the essay soon thereafter in pamphlet form (its first printing of 500 copies sold out in a month), responded to his message enthusiastically. His fervent belief in promise, possibility, and vocation held out hope during a period of economic hardship and uncertainty.

Americans were facing the Panic of 1837, a recession that soon spiraled into a serious depression in the economy. By the early months of the year, as a result of excess spending, mounting debt, and speculation in the purchase of lands, the nation's banking system was in major crisis, unemployment was spreading, and food riots were breaking out in a number of cities. The consequences for men seeking work or maintaining their family's standard of living were severe, and the economy did not begin to turn around until the early 1840s.

Emerson's selection as speaker was something of an accident; he was invited to give the address with only two months' notice after the scheduled first choice abruptly withdrew. He began by emphasizing that the beginning of a new academic year offers hopeful prospects. It represents the possibility, and also the need, for originality, for a break from tradition and custom and for a fresh start. "In the right state," said Emerson, "the scholar" is "Man Thinking," by which he meant that each person should do his—we would now add *or her*—thinking anew, without heed to the claims and counsels of authorities. Emerson urged each hearer and reader to break free from the inclination "to become a mere thinker, or, still worse, the parrot of other men's thinking." The true identity of "Man Thinking," he insisted, could be achieved only through "self-trust," a resistance to conformity and an attainment of inner resolve, enabling the scholar "to cheer, to raise, and to guide men by showing them facts amidst appearances." "In self-trust," he concluded, "all the virtues are comprehended. Free should the scholar be, free and brave."

As the literary critic Alfred Kazin observed, Emerson in "The American Scholar" and other lectures and essays of the 1830s and 1840s celebrated and called for "freshness, discovery, openness, for all that was hopeful in his country and his century." And hopeful in persons, too: "God hid the whole world in thy heart," Emerson professed in his poem "Woodnotes II" (1847). Kazin added that this "cardinal theme" resonates for readers today, the theme of "a brave beginning," the renewed quest for the God within. Even in good economic times, Emerson's injunctions are bracing, perpetually relevant, for there is always something stirring in us that makes us feel kinship with Emerson's cultural criticism and protest in 1837—the contention that, in Kazin's words, "the actual state of society did not fit Emerson's excited discovery that the private mind had infinite possibilities."

Emerson's "Oration," recalled the poet, editor, critic, and diplomat James Russell Lowell, who was eighteen at the time, "was an event without any former parallel in our literary annals....What crowded and breathless aisles, what windows clustering with eager heads, what enthusiasm of approval, what grim silence of foregone dissent!" Oliver Wendell Holmes, a poet and essayist, and the father of the eminent jurist Oliver Wendell Holmes Jr., stated in his biography of Emerson (1885):

> This grand Oration was our intellectual Declaration of Independence. Nothing like it had been heard in the halls of Harvard since Samuel Adams supported the affirmative of the question, "Whether it be lawful to trust the chief magistrate, if the commonwealth cannot otherwise be preserved...." The young men went out from it as if a prophet had been proclaiming to them "Thus saith the Lord." No listener ever forgot that Address.

Holmes connected Emerson with the Revolutionary orator and pamphleteer Samuel Adams, and thus he accented the American dimension of Emerson's argument. This, for Holmes and others, was the literary follow-up to the Declaration of Independence of 1776: Emerson was advocating a special mission for scholars in the United States that would be in keeping with the freedom and equality embodied in their democratic society. Perhaps mindful of Emerson's training and former position as a minister, Holmes also evoked the religious and prophetic cast of the "Oration," as if, in the church where he spoke, Emerson was acting as God's mediator, perhaps even as "the Lord" himself, a man made divine.

This was Emerson's astonishing claim in the "Divinity School Address" he gave to the Harvard Senior Class in Divinity on July 15, 1838:

> Jesus Christ belonged to the true race of prophets. He saw with open eye the mystery of the soul. Drawn by its severe harmony, ravished with its beauty, he lived in it, and had his being there.

Alone in all history, he estimated the greatness of man. One man was true to what is in you and me. He saw that God incarnates himself in man, and evermore goes forth anew to take possession of his world. He said, in this jubilee of sublime emotion, "I am divine. Through me, God acts; through me, speaks. Would you see God, see me; or, see thee, when thou also thinkest as I now think."

Identifying Jesus as a man, Emerson stressed that what made Jesus unique was that he made contact with and embodied a "greatness" that exists in everyone. The words Emerson gives to Jesus are striking in their implications. Jesus proclaims he is divine: God acts and speaks through him, and if we wish to see God, we should see him, or, mirrorlike, see ourselves once we have reached the degree of insight into human possibility that he attained; any man or a woman can become God.

Because in everyday conversation we frequently use such terms as self-reliance, independent thinking, and resistance to conformity, we may not always appreciate Emerson's radicalism. In his account of the American scholar, he was inveighing against the education Harvard provided; like his father and two of his brothers, Emerson was a Harvard graduate, but here he derided the institution for its complacency, absence of genuine thinking, materialism, and shallow notion of success. Among his audience were the governor of Massachusetts, the president of Harvard, and a justice of the U.S. Supreme Court, and Emerson assailed just about everything these men had achieved and stood for.

The following year, Emerson's "Divinity School Address," according to Holmes, created "a profound sensation in religious circles…. In its simplest and broadest statement this discourse was a plea for the individual consciousness as against all historical creeds, bibles, churches; for the soul as the supreme judge in spiritual matters." The radicalism is in Emerson's articulation of his ideas, his process of thought, and we can experience it now as we read and study his work. It was there, powerfully, for his first audiences and readers, for such contemporaries as Henry David Thoreau and Walt Whitman, and for countless men and women throughout the nineteenth and twentieth centuries and into the twenty-first.

In the landmark *Cambridge History of English and American Literature* (18 vols., 1907–1921), the critic Paul Elmer More said, "It becomes more and more apparent that Emerson, judged by an international or even by a broad national standard, is the outstanding figure of American letters." This judgment is even more firmly in place now. The influential critic Harold Bloom referred (1984) to Emerson as "the inescapable theorist of virtually all subsequent American writing. From his moment to ours, American authors either are in his tradition, or else in a counter-tradition originating in opposition to him." More recently (2003), Bloom described him as:

> the dominant sage of the American imagination…. Emerson at his best was an authentic poet, but it his prose—essays, journals, lectures—that is his triumph, both as eloquence and as insight. After Shakespeare, it matches anything else in the language. He remains the central figure in American culture and informs our politics…. Emerson's mind has become the mind of America.

It is testimony to Emerson's impact that many esteemed American writers, artists, critics, musicians, and intellectuals have regarded him as central to their development, affirming that his mind crucially shaped their own and maintaining that his views, visions, and forms of expression are richly "American." The philosopher William James paid tribute (1903) to "the matchless eloquence with which Emerson proclaimed the sovereignty of the living individual"; it "electrified and emancipated his generation, and this bugle-blast will doubtless be regarded by future critics as the soul of his message." Another distinguished American philosopher, John Dewey, said (1929): "His idealism is the faith of the thinker in his thought raised to its *nth* power." The architects Louis Sullivan and Frank Lloyd Wright named Emerson as a dominant influence; so did the composer Charles Ives. Among creative writers, Walt Whitman acknowledged, "I was simmering, simmering, simmering; Emerson brought me to a boil." Citing a passage in Emerson's essay "Montaigne; or, the Skeptic," in *Representative Men* (1850), Robert Frost said (1959):

> Some of my first thinking about my own language was certainly Emersonian. "Cut these sentences and they bleed," he says. I am not submissive enough to want to be a follower, but he had me there. I never got over that.

For Whitman, Frost, and many others, Emerson was the premier advocate of personal and artistic independence, of taking chances in style and content and braving the mystified or mocking responses of authorities and defenders of the literary, cultural, and social status quo. Again, though Emerson's appeal is worldwide—the German philosopher Friedrich Nietzsche, for example, greatly admired him—most readers find something radiantly American about him. Somehow, it is felt, his message is in keeping with the principle set forth in the Declaration of Independence—that all men are created equal—to which Emerson added the astounding corollary that all persons have an equal capacity, each in his or her unique way, to be divine.

Much that is grand and glorious, and outrageously presumptuous, is contained in Emerson. His advice to us is consoling, fortifying, and, some have concluded, deeply troubling. Nathaniel Hawthorne's stories and novels can be considered as complex responses to and revisions of Emerson: Hawthorne saw the limits and dangers of self-reliance and the dark, ominous impulses that lie within the very soul that Emerson hymned as divine. Similarly, Herman Melville, in *Moby-Dick*, "Bartleby, the Scrivener," and other works, while passionate about Emerson's affirmations, explored the damage and destruction to the self and others that such claims for the self's primacy could unleash. In "Prudence," included in *Essays: First Series* (1841), Emerson wrote: "Trust men, and they will be true to you; treat them greatly, and they will show themselves great, though they make an exception in your favor to all their rules of trade." In his copy, Melville made this annotation: "God help the poor fellow who squares his life according to this."

One might be tempted to ask, Why was there no Emerson earlier? Why did it take decades for his message to appear in American culture? It is a mark of Emerson's distinction that Holmes would refer to "The American Scholar" as "our intellectual Declaration of Independence," but there were efforts prior to 1837 to initiate an independent American literature and intellectual production. During the 1770s and 1780s, a number of writers appealed for a new type of literary creation in America that would be in accord with the innovations the United States had begun to implement in its political institutions and that would, furthermore, communicate the scale and spirit of the American landscape.

In *Revolutionary Writers* (1982), the scholar Emory Elliott, surveying Timothy Dwight, Joel Barlow, Philip Freneau (included in this anthology), and others, contends that these authors of the Revolutionary period beckoned for the "Genius of America." It "would be apparent in every aspect of American life," Elliott explains:

> In the boldness and political wisdom of its leaders; in the shrewdness and courage of its soldiers; in its crafts, inventions, industry, and commerce; and in its moral purity, artistic excellence, and devotion to the Christian God who had ordained its creation.

But Freneau and the others were unable to bring into existence the new era in the arts they described. As Elliott went on to say, they "discovered that the promise of prosperity for the arts was very short-lived":

> Patriotic American poems were left unbought in the bookstores, magazines began to fold after only a few issues, and critics grew impatient and condemned American literary works as weak imitations of English or classical models or as unpolished products of the forest.

It is not entirely clear why Freneau and his contemporaries failed. Sometimes it seems the answer is painfully obvious: The members of this literary generation lacked the imagination and artistry Emerson, Hawthorne, Dickinson, and others possessed half a century later. But it was also the case that the task for writers during the Revolution was daunting. Here again, Elliott offers a cogent insight:

> The writers of the new republic were engaged in a task more difficult than they were capable of

understanding: the negotiation of an uncharted intellectual and artistic path from a dominant religious vision of America to a new nationalist ideology.

Politically, the colonies had made their break from Great Britain, but the literature American readers knew was English literature. This formidable tradition—Chaucer, Shakespeare, Milton, John Dryden, Daniel Defoe, Samuel Richardson, Alexander Pope, Samuel Johnson, and many more—could not be shunned the day after American independence was won. The United States, however tainted by slavery, was suddenly at the forefront of nations in political terms; based on the Declaration of Independence, it was the land of the future. But while there was a new nation, there was not yet a national consciousness. America was still largely a nation of English men and women and English churches, settled by Puritans in New England and by Anglicans in Virginia. For nearly two centuries, the colonists had been ministering to their souls through sermon and Scripture. When the time came to seek secular diversion and enlightenment in literature, they could turn to English authors. For stimulation and instruction, they could peruse Greek and Roman classics and the major texts of English and European history and philosophy. What intellectual service could an "American" literature perform for such readers?

By August 1837, the United States had witnessed a dozen presidential elections; American democracy (as least as it was available to white male voters) was in place, and a national consciousness had taken root in political institutions. There was a richer conception of "Americanness" for writers to work with, even as they strove to remedy the gaps and limitations in the literature and art Americans had thus far produced. This gave advocates of an

"American" literature, such as Emerson, Melville, and Whitman, a nationalist vocabulary for literary production, a budding theory and practice of American authorship through which they could challenge, explore, extend, and adapt their country's religious heritage.

Literary historians have frequently seen the work of Emerson and his contemporaries as signifying a religious movement as much as a literary one. The point is not that Emerson, Whitman, and the others were offering a Christian vision but, instead, that their arguments and artistic forms emerged within a religious context and in their own way aimed to reach readers' souls. Christianity had made readers keenly aware of their hopes and desires for salvation—for redemption from grief, despair, and the horror of eternal punishment after death. But Christianity was not providing for all the inner conviction, the spiritual power and reassurance, it had bestowed on earlier generations.

Once this point is grasped, we can perceive the relationship between the Puritans and Emerson—the Puritans who, as Janice Knight said in *Orthodoxies in Massachusetts* (1994), believed that "the surest path to salvation was by means of painful introspection." We can feel both the challenge and the appeal in Emerson's statement in his Divinity School Address that Jesus "was true to what is in you and me. He saw that God incarnates himself in man." And we can absorb the accuracy of Holmes's observation that "the young men" who heard Emerson's "Oration" the year before "went out from it as if a prophet had been proclaiming to them 'Thus saith the Lord'."

Emerson is the most influential and important writer of the period of the "American Renaissance," as the literary scholar F. O. Matthiessen (1941) characterized it. But Emerson was in the middle of a broad trend or tendency in American literature and culture, Transcendentalism.

It took root in Boston, Cambridge, and Concord, Massachusetts, but branched outward to the rest of New England, to New York City, and into the Midwest from the 1830s through the 1850s.

Transcendentalism was a literary movement, but also a movement of social protest and reform. It emerged in a period when debates over slavery and abolition were intensifying; when advocates of women's rights were pressing their cause; when increasing numbers of voters were taking part as never before in political institutions and party-building and campaigning; when Native Americans were being pushed westward through harsh treaties and military pressure; when the Second Great Awakening of the 1820s and 1830s was kindling outbreaks across the nation of religious revivalism and zeal; when public schools were expanding; when the U.S. population was growing rapidly due to immigration (700,000 immigrants arrived between 1820 and 1840) and westward expansion; when the nation's transportation system was extending its reach through networks of canals and railroads; and when new technologies and inventions (e.g., the telegraph, 1844) were boosting American industry and business. American society was energized and rapidly changing. Dynamic new economic and political structures and forces were beginning to shake social traditions and customs. The old ways felt familiar to many and were something to cling to, but it was the same old ways—in the family, the workplace, the classroom, and elsewhere—that reformers, radicals, and activists sought to dislodge and reorient.

"There is a class of persons who desire a reform in the prevailing philosophy of the day," wrote the scholar and minister George Ripley in 1840:

> These are called Transcendentalists, because they believe in an order of truths which transcends the sphere of the external senses. Their leading idea is

the supremacy of mind over matter. Hence they maintain that the truth of religion does not depend on tradition, nor historical facts, but has an unerring witness in the soul. There is a light, they believe, which enlighteneth every man that cometh into the world; there is a faculty in all — the most degraded, the most ignorant, the most obscure — to perceive spiritual truth when distinctly presented; and the ultimate appeal on all moral questions is not to a jury of scholars, a hierarchy of divines or the prescriptions of a creed, but to the common sense of the human race.

Ripley included this statement in a letter of resignation he submitted to the membership of the Purchase Street Church in Boston; like Emerson (they were cousins), who had resigned from his own ministerial position in 1832, Ripley concluded he could no longer stay in good conscience within the confines of the career and institution for which he had been trained.

In an essay in 1842, "The Transcendentalist," Emerson sketched a definition of his own:

> The Idealism of the present day acquired the name Transcendental from the use of that term by Immanuel Kant, of Konigsberg, who replied to the skeptical philosophy of Locke, which insisted that there was nothing in the intellect which was not previously in the experience of the senses, by showing that there was a very important class of ideas or imperative forms, which did not come by experience, but through which experience was acquired; that these were intuitions of the mind itself; and he denominated them Transcendental forms. The extraordinary profoundness and precision of that man's thinking have given vogue to his nomencla-

ture, in Europe and America, to that extent that whatever belongs to the class of intuitive thought is popularly called at the present day Transcendental.

German philosophy and literary theory were key sources for Emerson, the feminist critic and essayist Margaret Fuller, and the others, especially as these were articulated, interpreted (and misinterpreted) in the writings of British poet-critic Samuel Taylor Coleridge and Scottish cultural historian and essayist Thomas Carlyle. The term *transcendental* comes from Kant's *Critique of Practical Reason* (1788), where he announced: "I call all knowledge transcendental which is concerned, not with objects, but with our mode of knowing objects so far as this is possible *a priori*" (i.e., knowable without appeal to particular experience).

As they brought to the fore transcendental knowledge and the flashes of intuition through which (as they saw it) it could become known, Emerson and his associates were conducting an assault against Unitarianism, the religious practice and doctrine according to which he and most of the others in Boston and nearby were raised. Unitarianism moderated and modified the stringent tenets of Calvinism that had been at the core of New England Puritanism. It took issue with the Puritan insistence on the total depravity of humankind (the consequence of original sin) and on predestination, the belief that God had chosen some to be saved and others to be damned. Compared to Puritanism, Unitarianism was liberal, offering people the prospect for spiritual growth and inner development—for becoming good.

By the early 1830s, Emerson, for one, was finding Unitarianism cold and complacent. It had cut away the gloom and doom of Puritanism, but it had lost the intensity, the sense of immediacy and even of crisis, that Puritanism possessed. Unitarianism was a rational religion, accepting of the psychological empiricism of John Locke, author of the *Essay Concerning Human Understanding* (1690), who maintained that knowledge comes to us from the perceptions of the senses. To oversimplify the point: Locke argued that knowledge is the result of what is coming *in* from out there. What Emerson contended, as he pondered Kant, Coleridge, and Carlyle, was that the knowledge that counted came from within, from intuition, from the spark of divinity that made possible the luminous transformation of the self.

Perhaps the most liberal-minded religious leader of the period just before Emerson's ascent was William Ellery Channing, pastor of the Federal Street Church in Boston and a clergyman and author whom Emerson esteemed. In a sermon he delivered in Baltimore in May 1819, Channing touched on themes Emerson would seize upon and expand. "Our leading principle in interpreting Scripture is this," he observed:

> That the Bible is a book written for men, in the language of men, and that its meaning is to be sought in the same manner as that of other books…. The Word of God bears the stamp of the same hand, which we see in his works…. We feel it our bounden duty to exercise our reason upon it perpetually, to compare, to infer, to look beyond the letter to the spirit, to seek in the nature of the subject, and the aim of the writer, his true meaning; and, in general, to make use of what is known, for explaining what is difficult, and for discovering new truths.

Channing offered a conception of religious life that was rational, thoughtful, and decent. Calvinism, in his view, made no intellectual or spiritual sense, for it portrayed God as a cruelly harsh judge when we know he must be all-wise and immeasurably good. And "to understand a great and good being," Channing added in a sermon of 1828, "Likeness to God," "we must have the seeds of the same excellence. We must have godliness within ourselves."

This was a bold contrast to Calvinism, to the legacy of the Puritans, but for Emerson it was insufficient. What it was missing was the urgency of the soul hungering to be made new, the loftiness of the religious experience as the Puritans in seventeenth-century Boston (including Emerson's own ancestors) had understood it and as the theologian, philosopher, and preacher Jonathan Edwards had recast and expressed it in the Connecticut Valley during the First Great Awakening of the 1730s and 1740s.

Even as Channing preached and wrote and young Emerson studied, the Presbyterian minister Charles Grandison Finney in the Second Great Awakening of the 1820s and 1830s was conducting fiery religious revivals in the eastern and midwestern states. These revivals were highly emotional and intense, as Finney (whose power as a speaker Emerson recognized) and other preachers called for spiritual awakening and conversion. Everyone could be saved and participate in the "making perfect" of society—a commitment that led to a host of moral reform movements that took aim at drinking, gambling, and other vices.

Here, with something of an Emersonian ring, is a passage from one of Finney's sermons, "What a Revival of Religion Is," given in 1834 and published with other sermons in book form in 1835 (it sold 12,000 copies in three months):

> Christians will have their faith renewed. While they are in their backslidden state they are blind to the state of sinners. Their hearts are as hard as

marble. The truths of the Bible only appear like a dream. They admit it to be all true; their conscience and their judgment assent to it; but their faith does not see it standing out in bold relief, in all the burning realities of eternity. But when they enter into a revival, they no longer see men as trees walking [see Mark 8:24], but they see things in that strong light which will renew the love of God in their hearts. This will lead them to labor zealously to bring others to him. They will feel grieved that others do not love God, when they love him so much. And they will set themselves feelingly to persuade their neighbors to give him their hearts.

Emerson would not have favored the theatricality of Finney's revivals, but Finney's insistence on internalizing truth, on shedding or transforming mere externals, on changing one's vision of life—these features in his work possess a devotion and drive not far from Emerson's own.

Emerson reached back into Puritanism for religious urgency while he carried forward and elaborated the liberal insights in Channing and the Unitarians. As Phyllis Cole indicated in *Mary Moody Emerson and the Origins of Transcendentalism* (1998), this did not occur for Emerson merely on the high plane of religious debate and abstraction but rather through the complicated example of his ancestors and immediate family circle. One of the most vigorous members of this circle was Mary Moody Emerson, the younger sister of Emerson's father and a wide-ranging reader, adviser, and debater with her nephew Ralph Waldo. Emerson's family line included seven generations of ministers and scholars, and there were ample differences of opinion among them, across the span of many decades.

"Ineffable is the union of man and God in every act of the soul," affirmed Emerson in "The Over-Soul," in *Essays: First Series*: "The simplest person, who in his integrity worships God, becomes God; yet for ever and ever the influx of this better and universal self is new and unsearchable. It inspires awe and astonishment." Here we can sense, according to the literary historian Perry Miller, the richness of Emerson's inheritance and the contribution he made to American intellectual and religious history:

> The ecstasy and the vision which Calvinists knew only in the moment of vocation, the passing of which left them agonizingly aware of depravity and sin, could become the permanent joy of those who had put aside the conception of depravity, and the moments between could be filled no longer with self-accusation but with praise and wonder.

Life as Emerson conceived of it could become wondrous, indeed miraculous, a view that dramatized the grounds for his break with the Unitarians. They believed that Jesus had performed miracles through which he displayed the divine power that God had granted *him*. But for Emerson, Jesus was akin to all human beings, not essentially different from them nor in possession of capacities no other men or women could unfold. What mattered was not Jesus himself but the truths and principles he represented.

Emerson's critics saw the implications of his arguments and injunctions. One of them, Andrews Norton, a Biblical scholar and Unitarian theologian, replied directly to the "Divinity School Address." He criticized the new belief, propagated by Emerson and others of his school, that "the mind must be its own unassisted teacher," that it can "discern transcendental truths by immediate vision."

The members of this Transcendental school "announce themselves as the prophets and priests of a new future, in which all is to be changed, all old opinions done away, and all present forms of society abolished. But by what process this joyful revolution is to be effected we are not told." A year later, Norton continued the attack, noting the damage done to Christianity if Jesus' miracles were no longer believed in: "If the representation of him in the Gospels be not conformed to his real character and office, no foundation is left, on which any one can with reason pretend to regard him as an object of veneration, or to consider his teachings, whatever effect they may have had upon the world, as of any importance to himself."

Emerson taught that we know what is right not because of the authority of the state and the church, not even of the Bible itself. We know what is right because we feel it to be true. The scholar and minister Theodore Parker made just this point in Emersonian terms in his controversial sermon "The Transient and Permanent in Christianity," May 19, 1841, in Boston:

> It seems difficult to conceive any reason, why moral and religious truths should rest for their support on the personal authority of their revealer, any more than the truths of science on that of him who makes them known first or most clearly. It is hard to see why the great truths of Christianity rest on the personal authority of Jesus, more than the axioms of geometry rest on the personal authority of Euclid, or Archimedes. The authority of Jesus, as of all teachers, one would naturally think, must rest on the truth of his words, and not their truth on his authority.

Emerson and Parker counseled readers and audiences to heed the call within, to make contact with their true vocation even if it meant disputing and denying parents, teachers, and ministers. Be self-reliant: trust thyself. History, tradition, and doctrine: the lessons they teach must be right for you.

This may sound like a prescription for anarchy, but for Emerson it was not, and that is because he believed that the soul is good and is (or could become) harmoniously integrated with the divinely created currents of Nature and the cosmos: God is in them as an immanent force. His claim is that we suffer because we do not know who we are; we do not know where God is to be found. Hence we are divided from one another because we are sorely divided from our truest selves.

Emerson and Thoreau indicted folly and corruption but understood them as the products of mistaken, mismanaged, and uninspired institutions that were deforming human conduct and obstructing the possibilities for individual and social betterment. If you and I each make connection with the authentic self within, the self that has been buried behind layers of false counsels and doctrines, we will renew ourselves and reorient the world. How can it be otherwise, if the soul is intrinsically good?

Unitarianism was in particular the religion of the privileged and well-established—a fact that enables us to register the bitter, provocative force of Emerson's social criticism. The Presbyterian clergyman Lyman Beecher (his children included Harriet Beecher Stowe), pastor of Hanover Street Church in Boston, recalled about his Unitarian rivals: "All the literary men of Massachusetts were Unitarian. All the trustees and professors of Harvard College were Unitarians. All the elite of wealth and fashion crowded Unitarian churches. The judges on the bench were Unitarians." These were the people against whom Emerson directed his arguments—against what they were doing to the young and aspiring.

Raised in this Unitarian/Harvard environment but discontented by its psychological, intellectual, and spiritual cost, Emerson asserted in "New England Reformers," in *Essays: Second Series* (1844): "We are students of words. We are shut up in schools, and colleges, and recitation-rooms, for ten or fifteen years, and come out at last with a bag of wind, a memory of words, and do not know a thing." But Emerson never rested on this; he pushed toward higher possibilities, as in "Politics," also in *Essays: Second Series*: "We think our civilization near its meridian, but we are yet only at the cock-crowing and the morning star. In our barbarous society the influence of character is in its infancy." "As we are, so we do; and as we do, so it is done to us; we are the builders of our fortunes," Emerson proclaims in "Worship," in *The Conduct of Life* (1860).

The optimistic drive of Transcendentalism is both thrilling and unnerving. It has proven uplifting for many and struck others as maddeningly naïve. But one should be cautious about imputing naiveté to Emerson. It is true that he ascribed extraordinary power to the revivified self, as in this passage from "Prospects," the concluding chapter of *Nature* (1836):

> The problem of restoring to the world original and eternal beauty, is solved by the redemption of the soul. The ruin or the blank, that we see when we look at nature, is in our own eye. The axis of vision is not coincident with the axis of things, and so they appear not transparent but opaque. The reason why the world lacks unity, and lies broken and in heaps, is, because man is disunited with himself.

And a few years later, in "Circles," included in *Essays: First Series* (1841), Emerson granted to the self even more power, a thrusting desire for expansion and freedom:

The life of man is a self-evolving circle, which, from a ring imperceptibly small, rushes on all sides outwards to new and larger circles, and that without end. The extent to which this generation of circles, wheel without wheel, will go, depends on the force or truth of the individual soul. For it is the inert effort of each thought, having formed itself into a circular wave of circumstance,—as, for instance, an empire, rules of an art, a local usage, a religious rite,—to heap itself on that ridge, and to solidify and hem in the life. But if the soul is quick and strong, it bursts over that boundary on all sides, and expands another orbit on the great deep, which also runs up into a high wave, with attempt again to stop and to bind. But the heart refuses to be imprisoned; in its first and narrowest pulses, it already tends outward with a vast force, and to immense and innumerable expansions.

Yet in these passages, Emerson made his entreaty in relation to grievous disorder, to persons disunited with themselves, to forms of imprisonment. This is why the novelist Henry James was not quite accurate when he said (1883) about Emerson:

His optimism makes us wonder at times where he discovered the errors that it would seem well to set right, and what there was in his view of the world on which the spirit of criticism could feed. He had a high and noble conception of good, without having, as it would appear, a definite conception of evil.

In truth, Emerson had an acute sense of the barriers and obstacles in society to the redeemed self. He believed these could be broken through, but he recog-

nized that they were intimidating. Authorities and institutions of all kinds function to impose on persons endless
bad advice, and an essential aspect of Emerson's emphasis on "self-trust" and "self-reliance" is the extreme self-
doubt he knew afflicts many persons as a consequence: I
could never be more than I am; I wish I could, but I have
obligations to others; I cannot let down my parents and
friends; I have to do what is expected of me now—maybe
there will be time for myself later. Emerson realized how
much pain these simple-sounding words embodied.

If Emerson was an optimistic writer, he was also a
tragic writer—or maybe we should say he is a tragic optimist. He discerned suffering everywhere, unfulfilled lives
led by people who were failing to summon the courage to
believe in their abilities. From the mid-1830s to roughly
the mid-1840s, Emerson dramatized the external and
internal forces that ravage the self and professed that each
of us could engage and at least in precious flashes tran-
scend them. In a perceptive study published in 1915,
O. W. Firkins proposed: "The secret of Emerson may be
conveyed in one word, the superlative, even the superhuman, value which he found in the unit of experience, the
direct, momentary, individual act of consciousness."
True—Firkins's insight is astute. But the exorbitant
achievement of such an act of consciousness is accompanied by its almost immediate loss. The units of rapturous
experience are terribly difficult to sustain.

Beyond that, whatever we put into words about such
an act of consciousness will never do justice to it, will
never capture its essence. It will always be no more than
second best. "There is somewhat in all life untranslatable
into language," Emerson reflected (1840): "Thus what is
great usually slips through our fingers, and it seems wonderful how a life-like word ever comes to be written."

As his career progressed, Emerson became even more attentive to the limiting, oppositional forces that threaten liberation: Nature and Fate. He increasingly brooded on these terms, on their harder, more somber resonances. The ultimate issue at hand for Emerson may be this: No matter how enlightened and redeemed from a misdirected life we become, all of us will die. Death shadowed Emerson's work from the start. He explored its implications in much of his writing from the mid-1840s through the 1850s, and it is the incontrovertible fact of death that another devout reader of Emerson, Walt Whitman, examined and attempted to metamorphose in *Leaves of Grass* (1855).

The first loss Emerson experienced was the death in May 1811 of his father, age forty-two, a Harvard-educated minister in Boston. This caused financial strain for the family, but, benefiting from the mentoring and letter-writing of Mary Moody Emerson, Emerson proceeded to Boston Latin School and Harvard College, from which he graduated in 1821. Emerson taught school, attended Harvard Divinity School, and then in 1829 accepted a position as assistant to the pastor at the Second Church of Boston—the church, many decades earlier, where the eminent Puritan ministers Increase and Cotton Mather had served. He also fell in love with Ellen Tucker, whom he married in fall 1829. Her health was poor; she died in 1831, and the grief-stricken Emerson the following year submitted his resignation from his Boston ministry.

Emerson said he could not administer the rite of communion—it did not seem to him authentic, and he was not at ease in his institutional role. In a sermon to his congregation, he said about communion: "This mode of commemorating Christ is not suitable to me. That is reason enough why I should abandon it." But it may have been Ellen's death that focused for Emerson the crisis and challenge of vocation: What was the nature of the genuine work to which he should commit himself? With death as the ultimate context—its reality both certain and unknown—how should a person live?

Death preceded and coincided with much of Emerson's lecturing and writing. Besides his father and first wife, he lost three siblings who died in infancy or childhood; of those siblings who survived to adulthood, Edward died in 1834, Charles in 1836, and Bulkeley in 1852. Only his brother William, who died in 1868, lived into old age. Emerson's beloved son Waldo, age five, died in 1842 from scarlet fever, and it was this death that agonized and perplexed him most of all, figuring in the background of such later essays as "Experience" (in *Essays: Second Series*) and "Fate" and "Illusions" (both in *The Conduct of Life*). In "Experience,' he pondered the fact that the wound of his son's death had not affected him even more:

> In the death of my son, now more than two years ago, I seem to have lost a beautiful estate,—no more. I cannot get it nearer to me. If tomorrow I should be informed of the bankruptcy of my principal debtors, the loss of my property would be a great inconvenience to me, perhaps, for many years; but it would leave me as it found me—neither better nor worse. So is it with this calamity: it does not touch me: some thing which I fancied was a part of me, which could not be torn away without tearing me, nor enlarged without enriching me, falls off from me, and leaves no scar.

The urgent tasks of the American scholar, the privileges and burdens of self-reliance, the godlike properties in persons that yearn for fulfillment: the themes Emerson traces have personal as well as intellectual causes and contexts. From the outset, he was not above but in the middle of, implicated in, everything he diagnosed and decried, and from which he called for liberation.

Resigning from the ministry on December 22, 1832, three days later Emerson sailed for Europe, returning in early October 1833. He traveled in Italy, Switzerland, and France, and then England and Scotland, where he met William Wordsworth, Coleridge, and Carlyle (the two became friends, intellectual compatriots, and correspondents). Back in the United States, he did some preaching in churches, but he gave most of his time to preparing and presenting lectures for lyceums across the country—a component of his career that reminds us that much of his writing was first produced to be heard rather than read, and that this dimension of his literary work lingers even in the revised versions of his lectures that he published.

The American Lyceum movement—Lyceum was the name of the school near Athens where Aristotle taught— consisted of meetings, debates, and discussions that occurred in villages and towns as well as in the major cities. Emerson's biographer Lawrence Buell has described them as a prelude to our own schools for adult education and educational TV. For three decades, beginning in the mid- 1830s, Emerson gave a series or course of lectures for audiences in the Boston area and then in locations as far west as Iowa and Missouri. In this role, outside the formal ministry, Emerson could encourage, enlighten, preach, and prophesy as a secular minister of the mind and spirit.

Remarried, to Lydia Jackson in 1835, and settled in Concord, Emerson and others in the area formed the Transcendental Club, which met to converse about and inquire into religious and literary topics. Among its dozen or so regular members were the philosopher-educator Amos Bronson Alcott; the editor and combative essayist

Orestes Brownson; the author, lecturer, and feminist Margaret Fuller; the author, scholar, and professor F. H. Hedge; George Ripley; and Theodore Parker.

That the Transcendental Club lasted for only four years suggests one of the complications of Transcendentalism as a joint enterprise. Emerson, Thoreau, Fuller, and their colleagues shared an interest in common themes but disagreed about religion, social action, and other topics, which in a way was perfectly in keeping with the Transcendental emphasis on the self's freedom and its right to intuitions of truth. If there was a central figure in the movement, it was Emerson, and if there was for a time a principle of coherence, it lay in his early manifesto, *Nature*, published in 1836, on the day after the first meeting of the Transcendental Club. Through argument, metaphor, and aphorism, Emerson proclaimed in this text the powers of the liberated self, the correspondences between human beings and Nature, and the symbolism expressed everywhere in the natural world.

In 1837, Emerson delivered his oration on the American Scholar, and in 1838 his address at the Harvard Divinity School. Two other important books from this period are *Essays: First Series* (1841) and *Essays: Second Series* (1844). Some of his friends and associates, inspired by this body of work, developed an active interest in social reform; Theodore Parker, for instance, became an adamant abolitionist. Others undertook experiments in utopian communities. George Ripley was the pioneer in the development of the Brook Farm community in West Roxbury (near Boston), which began in 1841 (Hawthorne lived there for a time), and Amos Bronson Alcott for a few months resided with his family in a small utopian community in the town of Harvard, thirty miles west of Boston. There was also Thoreau's one-man utopia (on land owned by Emerson) at Walden

Pond in Concord from 1845 to 1847. Emerson, however, turned down an invitation to join Brook Farm, and while he was a critic of slavery, he was not a diehard public campaigner for abolitionism like Parker or like two other stalwart Bostonians, William Lloyd Garrison, editor of *The Liberator*, and Wendell Phillips, an eloquent orator.

From 1840 to 1844, Emerson and Fuller were involved with editing the Transcendentalists' journal, *The Dial*, a "Magazine for Literature, Philosophy, and Religion." But on the whole the material in the journal, and the writings by his contemporaries, disappointed Emerson. He inspired many people and encouraged them in their first efforts, but he was not often persuaded that the work of others really fulfilled their potential. Emerson made possible the careers of Thoreau, Fuller, and Whitman: they could not have become writers without his example. At first their written work excited him, and then it dismayed him—which illuminates the paradox of a mentor who promotes self-reliance and originality. The best tribute to such an empowering figure as Emerson is, finally, to move beyond him—Emersonianism without Emerson.

Emerson's later books include *Representative Men* (1850), *English Traits* (1856), and *The Conduct of Life* (1860). For fifty years he also maintained a meticulous, provocative journal of his reading and reflections, which some scholars now regard as his greatest work. But Emerson was a poet as well as a lecturer, essayist, and journal-keeper. Perhaps the most noteworthy essay in *Essays: Second Series* is the first, titled "The Poet," where he celebrates the poet as a philosopher and seer. He published a collection of his own poems in 1847, though overall they are only a mixed success, evocative and experimental in rhythm and diction but frequently awkward and abstruse.

Nevertheless, Emerson's theory and practice as a poet, linked to the vivifying images and arguments of his essays, supplied the basis for an American style, strategy, and vision in poetry, for the "American difference" in poetry, as Harold Bloom and others have defined it. Before Emerson, William Cullen Bryant (included in this anthology), known as the "American Wordsworth," had depicted nature as a soothing source of emotional and spiritual healing and sustenance, and his melancholy meditative verse on transience and mortality was widely popular. But he did not perceive the depths of possibility in English and German Romanticism that Emerson reached into and that fired his ambition.

"Adam in the garden," Emerson wrote in his journal in 1839. "I am to new name all the beasts in the field and all the gods in the sky. I am to invite men drenched in time to recover themselves and come out of time, and taste their native immortal air." Soon, in "The Poet," Emerson described the nature of the poet's identity:

> The poet is representative. He stands among partial men for the complete man, and apprises us not of his wealth, but of the common-wealth.... [The poet] sees and handles that which others dream of, traverses the whole scale of experience, and is representative of man, in virtue of being the largest power to receive and to impart.... The poet is the sayer, the namer, and represents beauty. He is a sovereign, and stands on the centre.... For it is not metres, but a metre-making argument, that makes a poem, —a thought so passionate and alive, that, like the spirit of a plant or an animal, it has an architecture of its own, and adorns nature with a new thing. The thought and the form are

equal in the order of time, but in the order of genesis the thought is prior to the form. The poet has a new thought: he has a whole new experience to unfold; he will tell us how it was with him, and all men will be the richer in his fortune.

Emerson's exalted conception of the poet, and his own uses of language as much in his prose as in his verse, equipped Whitman, Dickinson, Frost, Hart Crane, Marianne Moore, and Wallace Stevens, and he profoundly affected such poets as Allen Ginsberg, Robert Lowell, A. R. Ammons, John Ashbery, and others from the 1940s to the present. As a group, these poets are radically different from one another, yet they are united in their kinship to and descent from Emerson.

We can extend Emerson's preoccupations backward and forward in the American literary tradition, giving to it a richly complex coherence. Individualism, self-reliance, the self and its relationship to others, personal and social responsibility, the prospects for freedom, contemplation and action: these Emersonian themes return us to the Puritans, and from them we can proceed to Jonathan Edwards, Benjamin Franklin, and J. Hector St. John de Crevecoeur, and to Phillis Wheatley, Frederick Douglass, Harriet Jacobs, and other minority and women authors before, during, and after the age of Emerson who waged personal and literary campaigns for freedom and self-fulfillment. Hawthorne and Melville critically engaged Emerson's ideas and claims, as William Dean Howells and Henry James did later. In the late nineteenth and twentieth centuries, Kate Chopin, Edith Wharton, W. E. B. Du Bois, Gertrude Stein, and Willa Cather absorbed and transformed Emerson; Hemingway came to possess and project something of Emerson's contained anguish and stoic resolve; and Saul Bellow and Ralph Ellison (his full name was Ralph Waldo Ellison) studied him attentively. Emerson is the essential American writer.

He is, however, more than that, and all the more relevant for being so. Emerson's literary, intellectual, and philosophical mainstays and influences were—to name a few—Confucius, Plato, Plutarch, Plotinus, Montaigne, Shakespeare, Milton, Swedenborg, Goethe, Persian poetry, and Asian religious texts. He was an American author who inhabited a context of world literature, philosophy, biography, religion, and history. He reinforced this feature of his intellectual background and development through his lengthy visits to Europe and Great Britain in 1833, to England in 1847–1848, and to Europe and Egypt in 1872.

In an essay published in 1850, Theodore Parker declared of Emerson:

> [He] is the most American of our writers. The Idea of America, which lies at the bottom of our original institutions, appears in him with great prominence. We mean the idea of personal freedom, of the dignity and value of human nature, the superiority of a man to the accidents of a man.

Yet Emerson was multicultural and international. He belongs in the anthology of American literature you are reading even as he exceeds its boundaries. He possesses the artistic distinction he described in an essay on Plato, included in *Representative Men*: "This perpetual modernness is the measure of merit in every work of art; since the author of it was not misled by any thing short-lived or local, but abode by real and abiding traits."

This, for Emerson, was ultimately what it meant to be a transcendentalist, and it implies the nature of the intellectual experience he recommends for us—that we become expert explorers of American literature who strive to become something more. "The aim and effort of literature in the largest sense," said Emerson in a lecture in 1835, is "nothing less than *to give voice to the whole of spiritual nature* as events and ages unfold it, to record in words the whole life of the world." In another lecture several years later, he expressed a similar conviction, connecting the artist to the beholder:

> Art should exhilarate, and throw down the walls of circumstance on every side, awakening in the beholder the same sense of universal relation and power which the work evinced in the artist, and its highest effect is to make new artists.

Like circles radiating from a central point, artists function, Emerson contended, to generate new artists. Thus the highest praise one can bestow upon a writer is to say that new writers were created from the ranks of his or her readers. More than anyone, this is true of Emerson himself.

For further reading: F. O. Matthiessen, *American Renaissance: Art and Expression in the Age of Emerson and Whitman* (1941); Stephen E. Whicher, *Freedom and Fate: An Inner Life of Ralph Waldo Emerson* (1953); Lawrence Buell, *Literary Transcendentalism* (1973); Joel Porte, *Representative Man: Ralph Waldo Emerson in His Times* (1979); Leon Chai, *The Romantic Foundations of the American Renaissance* (1987); Robert D. Richardson Jr., *Emerson: The Mind on Fire* (1995); and Lawrence Buell, *Emerson* (2003).

See also *The Transcendentalists: An Anthology*, ed. Perry Miller (1950); *Selected Writings of the American Transcendentalists*, ed. George Hochfield (1966); and *Transcendentalism: A Reader*, ed. Joel Myerson (2000).

Washington Irving

(1783–1859)

*"I am always at a loss to know how much to believe of my own stories,"
Washington Irving said. The author of two of the best-known (and earliest)
American short stories—"The Legend of Sleepy Hollow," about schoolmaster Ichabod Crane's encounter with a headless horseman, and "Rip Van
Winkle," reprinted below, about a man who lapses into a twenty-year
sleep—the prolific Irving produced fictional works, essays, poems, biographies, and much else.*

*Born in New York City, Irving was the youngest in a family of
eleven children. His father, a prosperous merchant, named his son
after George Washington, and one of Irving's crowning achievements,
late in his career, was a multi-volume biography of Washington
(1855–1859). The boy's literary enthusiasms were for Shakespeare,
the English essayists Joseph Addison and Oliver Goldsmith, and the
novelist Laurence Sterne, author of the comic masterpiece* Tristram
Shandy *(1759–1767).*

*In his teens Irving prepared for a career in law, and, after traveling
in Europe for two years (1804–1806), he conducted legal and other
business as a partner in his family's hardware firm. In his twenties he
had begun writing for newspapers, journals, and magazines, and soon
he worked as a publisher and editor as well. He made his mark as a
contributor to a series of satirical essays,* Salmagundi; or, The Whim-
Whams and Opinions of Launcelot Langstaff, Esq., and Others
*(1807–1808). His first noteworthy book was a comic account of Dutch
settlement in New York,* A History of New York *(1809), purportedly
written by "Diedrich Knickerbocker." The term "Knickerbocker" came
to identify the school or group of American writers, centered in New
York City, that Irving led.*

Even more successful for Irving, however, was The Sketch Book of
Geoffrey Crayon, Gent., 1819–20 *(1819), a collection of sketches and
stories. He followed it with* Bracebridge Hall *(1822), dealing with life in
the English countryside.*

*Irving's popularity and prominence as an author and literary figure
were shadowed by the death in 1809 of the seventeen-year-old Matilda
Hoffmann, to whom he was engaged. He never married, and later told
a correspondent: "For years I could not talk on the subject of this hopeless regret; I could not even mention her name; but her image was continually before me, and I dreamt of her incessantly."*

*From 1815 to 1832 Irving lived in England, Germany, France,
and Spain. Among his books of this period are* The Life and Voyages
of Christopher Columbus *(1828),* A Chronicle of the Conquest of
Granada *(1829),* Voyages and Discoveries of the Companions of

Columbus *(1831)*, and The Legends of the Alhambra *(1832)*. *Irving made a grand return to the United States in 1832, renowned as the first American author to achieve international acclaim and fame. As he explained, "It has been a matter of marvel to my European readers that a man from the wilds of America should express himself in tolerable English. I was looked upon as something new and strange, in literature."*

Irving proceeded to tour the American West, remaining active as a writer. But by the early 1840s he was abroad again, holding an appointment as U.S. ambassador to Spain. He lived his final years on his country estate, Sunnyside, on the Hudson River near Tarrytown, New York.

Based on a German folktale, "Rip Van Winkle," included in The Sketch Book, *describes a strange happening in the life of a Dutch-American farmer in the Catskill Mountains, just before the American Revolution. After drinking an enchanted potion he falls asleep, waking twenty years later and finding that his wife is dead, his children have grown up, and his hometown has changed. Irving's tone is playfully humorous, even as he suggestively explores the themes of identity, historical change, and social transformation.*

Irving was America's first professional author and among its earliest men-of-letters, and he was, in the words of one scholar, "the father of the short story in the United States." He was a productive writer and researcher (his complete works run to twenty-one volumes) and a graceful and polished stylist who influenced Henry Wadsworth Longfellow and Nathaniel Hawthorne. He said about himself, "I have never found, in anything outside of the four walls of my study, an enjoyment equal to sitting at my writing-desk with a clean page, a new theme, and a mind awake."

For an overview: Mary Weatherspoon Bowden, Washington Irving *(1981). See also William L. Hedges,* Washington Irving: An American Study, 1802–1832 *(1965); and Jeffrey Rubin-Dorsky,* Adrift in the Old World: The Psychological Pilgrimage of Washington Irving *(1988). For critical response and interpretation:* A Century of Commentary on the Works of Washington Irving, 1860–1974, *ed. Andrew B. Myers (1976);* The Old and New World Romanticism of Washington Irving, *ed. Stanley Brodwin (1986);* Critical Essays on Washington Irving, *ed. Ralph M. Aderman (1990); and* Washington Irving: The Critical Reaction, *ed. James W. Tuttleton (1993).*

Rip Van Winkle[1]

The following Tale was found among the papers of the late Diedrich Knickerbocker,[2] an old gentleman of New York, who was very curious in the Dutch history of the province, and the manners of the descendants from its primitive settlers. His historical researches, however, did not lie so much among books as among men; for the former are lamentably scanty on his favourite topics; whereas he found the old burghers,[3] and still more their wives, rich in that legendary lore so invaluable to true history. Whenever, therefore, he happened upon a genuine Dutch family, snugly shut up in its low-roofed farmhouse, under a spreading sycamore, he looked upon it as a little clasped volume of black-letter,[4] and studied it with the zeal of a bookworm.

The result of all these researches was a history of the province during the reign of the Dutch governors, which he published some years since.[5] There have been various opinions as to the literary character of his work, and, to tell the truth, it is not a whit better than it should be. Its chief merit is its scrupulous accuracy, which indeed was a little questioned on its first appearance, but has since been completely established[6]; and it is now admitted into all historical collections as a book of unquestionable authority.

The old gentleman died shortly after the publication of his work; and now that he is dead and gone, it cannot do much harm to his memory to say that his time might have been much better employed in weightier labours. He, however, was apt to ride his hobby his own way; and though it did now and then kick up the dust a little in the eyes of his neighbours, and grieve the spirit of some friends for whom he felt the truest deference and affection; yet his errors and follies are remembered "more in sorrow than in anger,"[7] and it begins to be suspected that he never intended to injure or offend. But however his memory may be appreciated by criticks, it is still held dear by many folk whose good opinion is well worth having; particularly by certain biscuit bakers, who have

---

[1]RIP VAN WINKLE: Irving based his tale on the German folktale "Peter Klaus the Goatherd," about a goat herder who falls asleep for twenty years and awakens to find his family and friends gone.
[2]DIEDRICH KNICKERBOCKER: Irving's pseudonym.
[3]BURGHERS: Citizens; used most commonly to describe the inhabitants of Flemish and German towns.
[4]BLACK-LETTER: A gothic-style typeface used in early printed books, which, because of their great value, were often fitted with clasps and locks.
[5]SINCE: A reference to Irving's historical parody *History of New York* (1809), written also under his pseudonym, Diedrich Knickerbocker.
[6]ESTABLISHED: Irving echoes the opening comments of Miguel de Cervantes (1547–1616) in his preface to *Don Quixote* (1605).
[7]MORE IN SORROW THAN IN ANGER: A reference to the expression on the face of the ghost of Hamlet's father, *Hamlet* Act I, Scene 2, line 232.

gone so far as to imprint his likeness on their new year cakes, and have thus given him a chance for immortality, almost equal to being stamped on a Waterloo medal, or a Queen Anne's farthing.[8]

RIP VAN WINKLE

A POSTHUMOUS WRITING OF DIEDRICH KNICKERBOCKER

> *By Woden,[9] God of Saxons,*
> *From whence comes Wensday, that is Wodensday,*
> *Truth is a thing that ever I will keep*
> *Unto thylke[10] day in which I creep into*
> *My sepulchre—*
>   CARTWRIGHT[11]

Whoever has made a voyage up the Hudson must remember the Kaatskill mountains. They are a dismembered branch of the great Appalachian family, and are seen away to the west of the river swelling up to a noble height and lording it over the surrounding country. Every change of season, every change of weather, indeed, every hour of the day, produces some change in the magical hues and shapes of these mountains, and they are regarded by all the good wives far and near as perfect barometers. When the weather is fair and settled they are clothed in blue and purple, and print their bold outlines on the clear evening sky; but sometimes, when the rest of the landscape is cloudless, they will gather a hood of gray vapours about their summits, which, in the last rays of the setting sun, will glow and light up like a crown of glory.

At the foot of these fairy mountains the voyager may have descried the light smoke curling up from a village, whose shingle roofs gleam among the trees, just where the blue tints of the upland melt away into the fresh green of the nearer landscape. It is a little village of great antiquity, having been founded by some of the Dutch colonists in the early times of the province, just about the beginning of the government of the good Peter Stuyvesant,[12] (may he rest in peace!) and there were some

---

[8]WATERLOO METAL, OR A QUEEN ANNE'S FARTHING: Waterloo medals were liberally distributed following the defeat of Napoleon in 1815. Queen Anne's farthings, small coins worth about a quarter of a penny, were also widely circulated.
[9]WODEN: The Norse god of war.
[10]THYLKE: The very thing or person mentioned; the same. (Middle English)
[11]CARTWRIGHT: Quote from *The Ordinary* (1635), Act III, Scene 1, lines 1050–1054, by the British poet and playwright William Cartwright (1611–1643).
[12]PETER STUYVESANT: (c. 1611–1672), the last colonial governor of New Netherland, the Dutch colony that became New York in 1664, when it was appropriated by the English.

of the houses of the original settlers standing within a few years; built of small yellow bricks brought from Holland, having latticed windows and gable fronts, surmounted with weathercocks.

In that same village, and in one of these very houses (which, to tell the precise truth was sadly time worn and weather-beaten) there lived many years since, while the country was yet a province of Great Britain, a simple good natured fellow of the name of Rip Van Winkle. He was a descendant of the Van Winkles who figured so gallantly in the chivalrous days of Peter Stuyvesant, and accompanied him to the siege of Fort Christina.[13] He inherited, however, but little of the martial character of his ancestors. I have observed that he was a simple good natured man; he was moreover a kind neighbour, and an obedient, henpecked husband. Indeed, to the latter circumstance might be owing that meekness of spirit which gained him such universal popularity; for those men are most apt to be obsequious and conciliating abroad, who are under the discipline of shrews at home. Their tempers doubtless are rendered pliant and malleable in the fiery furnace of domestic tribulation, and a curtain lecture[14] is worth all the sermons in the world for teaching the virtues of patience and long suffering. A termagant wife may therefore in some respects be considered a tolerable blessing—and if so, Rip Van Winkle was thrice blessed.

Certain it is that he was a great favourite among all the good wives of the village, who, as usual with the amiable sex, took his part in all family squabbles, and never failed, whenever they talked those matters over in their evening gossipings, to lay all the blame on Dame Van Winkle. The children of the village too would shout with joy whenever he approached. He assisted at their sports, made their playthings, taught them to fly kites and shoot marbles, and told them long stories of ghosts, witches and Indians. Whenever he went dodging about the village he was surrounded by a troop of them hanging on his skirts, clambering on his back and playing a thousand tricks on him with impunity; and not a dog would bark at him throughout the neighbourhood.

The great error in Rip's composition was an insuperable aversion to all kinds of profitable labour. It could not be from the want of assiduity or perseverance; for he would sit on a wet rock, with a rod as long and heavy as a Tartar's lance, and fish all day without a murmur, even though he should not be encouraged by a single nibble. He would carry a fowling piece on his shoulder for hours together, trudging through woods and

---

[13]HIM TO THE SEIGE OF FORT CHRISTINA: In 1655, Stuyvesant captured the Swedish Fort Christina in Delaware.
[14]CURTAIN LECTURE: The scolding of a husband by his wife behind the curtains of their four-poster bed.

swamps and up hill and down dale, to shoot a few squirrels or wild pigeons; he would never refuse to assist a neighbour even in the roughest toil, and was a foremost man at all country frolicks for husking Indian corn, or building stone fences; the women of the village too used to employ him to run their errands and to do such little odd jobs as their less obliging husbands would not do for them—in a word Rip was ready to attend to anybody's business but his own; but as to doing family duty, and keeping his farm in order, he found it impossible.

In fact he declared it was of no use to work on his farm; it was the most pestilent little piece of ground in the whole country; everything about it went wrong and would go wrong in spite of him. His fences were continually falling to pieces; his cow would either go astray or get among the cabbages; weeds were sure to grow quicker in his fields than anywhere else; the rain always made a point of setting in just as he had some outdoor work to do. So that though his patrimonial estate had dwindled away under his management, acre by acre until there was little more left than a mere patch of Indian corn and potatoes, yet it was the worst conditioned farm in the neighbourhood.

His children too were as ragged and wild as if they belonged to nobody. His son Rip, an urchin[15] begotten in his own likeness, promised to inherit the habits with the old clothes of his father. He was generally seen trooping like a colt at his mother's heels, equipped in a pair of his father's cast-off galligaskins,[16] which he had much ado to hold up with one hand, as a fine lady does her train in bad weather.

Rip Van Winkle, however, was one of those happy mortals, of foolish, well-oiled dispositions, who take the world easy, eat white bread or brown, whichever can be got with least thought or trouble, and would rather starve on a penny than work for a pound. If left to himself, he would have whistled life away in perfect contentment, but his wife kept continually dinning in his ears about his idleness, his carelessness and the ruin he was bringing on his family. Morning noon and night, her tongue was incessantly going, and every thing he said or did was sure to produce a torrent of household eloquence. Rip had but one way of replying to all lectures of the kind, and that by frequent use had grown into a habit. He shrugged his shoulders, shook his head, cast up his eyes, but said nothing. This, however, always provoked a fresh volley from his wife, so that he was fain to draw off his forces, and take to the outside of the house—the only side which in truth belongs to a henpecked husband.

---

[15]URCHIN: Beggar child.
[16]GALLIGASKINS: Loose-fitting breeches or wide hose worn in the sixteenth and seventeenth centuries.

Rip's sole domestic adherent was his dog Wolf who was as much hen-pecked as his master, for Dame Van Winkle regarded them as companions in idleness, and even looked upon Wolf with an evil eye as the cause of his master's going so often astray. True it is, in all points of spirit befitting an honourable dog, he was as courageous an animal as ever scoured the woods—but what courage can withstand the ever during and all besetting terrors of a woman's tongue? The moment Wolf entered the house his crest fell, his tail drooped to the ground or curled between his legs, he sneaked about with a gallows air, casting many a sidelong glance at Dame Van Winkle, and at the least flourish of a broomstick or ladle he would fly to the door with yelping precipitation.

Times grew worse and worse with Rip Van Winkle as years of matrimony rolled on; a tart temper never mellows with age, and a sharp tongue is the only edged tool that grows keener with constant use. For a long while he used to console himself when driven from home, by frequenting a kind of perpetual club of the sages, philosophers and other idle personages of the village which held its sessions on a bench before a small inn, designated by a rubicund portrait of his majesty George the Third. Here they used to sit in the shade, through a long lazy summer's day, talking listlessly over village gossip, or telling endless sleepy stories about nothing. But it would have been worth any statesman's money to have heard the profound discussions that sometimes took place, when by chance an old newspaper fell into their hands from some passing traveller. How solemnly they would listen to the contents as drawled out by Derrick Van Bummel the schoolmaster, a dapper, learned little man, who was not to be daunted by the most gigantic word in the dictionary; and how sagely they would deliberate upon public events some months after they had taken place.

The opinions of this junto[17] were completely controlled by Nicholaus Vedder, a patriarch of the village, and landlord of the inn, at the door of which he took his seat from morning till night, just moving sufficiently to avoid the sun and keep in the shade of a large tree; so that the neighbours could tell the hour by his movements as accurately as by a sun dial. It is true he was rarely heard to speak, but smoked his pipe incessantly. His adherents, however (for every great man has his adherents), perfectly understood him, and knew how to gather his opinions. When any thing that was read or related displeased him, he was observed to smoke his pipe vehemently and to send forth short, frequent and angry puffs; but when pleased he would inhale the smoke slowly and tranquilly and emit

---

[17]JUNTO: A group of individuals who collect for a common purpose; a clique or club.

it in light and placid clouds, and sometimes taking the pipe from his mouth and letting the fragrant vapour curl about his nose, would gravely nod his head in token of perfect approbation.

From even this strong hold the unlucky Rip was at length routed by his termagant wife who would suddenly break in upon the tranquility of the assemblage and call the members all to naught; nor was that august personage Nicholaus Vedder himself sacred from the daring tongue of this terrible virago, who charged him outright with encouraging her husband in habits of idleness.

Poor Rip was at last reduced almost to despair; and his only alternative to escape from the labour of the farm and clamour of his wife, was to take gun in hand and stroll away into the woods. Here he would sometimes seat himself at the foot of a tree and share the contents of his wallet[18] with Wolf, with whom he sympathized as a fellow sufferer in persecution. "Poor Wolf," he would say, "thy mistress leads thee a dog's life of it; but never mind my lad, whilst I live thou shalt never want a friend to stand by thee!" Wolf would wag his tail, look wistfully in his master's face, and if dogs can feel pity I verily believe he reciprocated the sentiment with all his heart.

In a long ramble of the kind on a fine autumnal day, Rip had unconsciously scrambled to one of the highest parts of the Kaatskill mountains. He was after his favourite sport of squirrel shooting and the still solitudes had echoed and re-echoed with the reports of his gun. Panting and fatigued he threw himself, late in the afternoon, on a green knoll, covered with mountain herbage, that crowned the brow of a precipice. From an opening between the trees he could overlook all the lower country for many a mile of rich woodland. He saw at a distance the lordly Hudson, far, far below him, moving on its silent but majestic course, with the reflection of a purple cloud, or the sail of a lagging bark here and there sleeping on its glassy bosom, and at last losing itself in the blue highlands.

On the other side he looked down into a deep mountain glen, wild, lonely and shagged, the bottom filled with fragments from the impending cliffs, and scarcely lighted by the reflected rays of the setting sun. For some time Rip lay musing on this scene, evening was gradually advancing, the mountains began to throw their long blue shadows over the valleys; he saw that it would be dark, long before he could reach the village, and he heaved a heavy sigh when he thought of encountering the terrors of Dame Van Winkle.

[18]WALLET: Knapsack.

As he was about to descend he heard a voice from a distance, hallooing, "Rip Van Winkle! Rip Van Winkle!" He looked round, but could see nothing but a crow winging its solitary flight across the mountain. He thought his fancy must have deceived him and turned again to descend, when he heard the same cry ring through the still evening air: "Rip Van Winkle! Rip Van Winkle!"—at the same time Wolf bristled up his back and giving a low growl, skulked to his master's side, looking fearfully down into the glen. Rip now felt a vague apprehension stealing over him; he looked anxiously in the same direction and perceived a strange figure slowly toiling up the rocks and bending under the weight of something he carried on his back. He was surprised to see any human being in this lonely and unfrequented place, but supposing it to be some one of the neighbourhood in need of his assistance he hastened down to yield it.

On nearer approach he was still more surprised at the singularity of the stranger's appearance. He was a short, square built old fellow, with thick bushy hair and a grizzled beard. His dress was of the antique Dutch fashion, a cloth jerkin[19] strapped round the waist, several pair of breeches, the outer one of ample volume decorated with rows of buttons down the sides and bunches at the knees. He bore on his shoulder a stout keg that seemed full of liquor, and made signs for Rip to approach and assist him with the load. Though rather shy and distrustful of this new acquaintance Rip complied with his usual alacrity, and mutually relieving each other they clambered up a narrow gully, apparently the dry bed of a mountain torrent. As they ascended Rip every now and then heard long rolling peals like distant thunder, that seemed to issue out of a deep ravine or rather cleft between lofty rocks, toward which their rugged path conducted. He paused for an instant, but supposing it to be the muttering of one of those transient thunder showers which often take place in mountain heights, he proceeded. Passing through the ravine they came to a hollow like a small amphitheatre, surrounded by perpendicular precipices, over the brinks of which impending trees shot their branches, so that you only caught glimpses of the azure sky and the bright evening cloud. During the whole time Rip and his companion had laboured on in silence, for though the former marvelled greatly what could be the object of carrying a keg of liquor up this wild mountain, yet there was something strange and incomprehensible about the unknown, that inspired awe and checked familiarity.

On entering the amphitheatre new objects of wonder presented themselves. On a level spot in the centre was a company of odd looking

---

[19]JERKIN: Vest.

personages playing at ninepins.[20] They were dressed in a quaint outlandish fashion—some wore short doublets,[21] others jerkins with long
knives in their belts and most of them had enormous breeches of similar style with that of the guide's. Their visages too were peculiar. One
had a large head, broad face and small piggish eyes. The face of another
seemed to consist entirely of nose, and was surmounted by a white sug-
arloaf hat, set off with a little red cock's tail. They all had beards of various shapes and colours. There was one who seemed to be the
Commander. He was a stout old gentleman, with a weatherbeaten countenance. He wore a laced doublet, broad belt and hanger,[22] high crowned
hat and feather, red stockings and high heel'd shoes with roses in them.
The whole group reminded Rip of the figures in an old Flemish painting,[23] in the parlour of Dominie Van Schaick the village parson, and
which had been brought over from Holland at the time of the settlement.

What seemed particularly odd to Rip was, that though these folks
were evidently amusing themselves, yet they maintained the gravest faces,
the most mysterious silence, and were, withal, the most melancholy party
of pleasure he had ever witnessed. Nothing interrupted the stillness of the
scene but the noise of the balls, which, whenever they were rolled, echoed
along the mountains like rumbling peals of thunder.

As Rip and his companion approached them they suddenly desisted
from their play and stared at him with such fixed, statue like gaze, and
such strange uncouth, lack lustre countenances, that his heart turned
within him, and his knees smote together. His companion now emptied
the contents of the keg into large flagons[24] and made signs to him to wait
upon the company. He obeyed with fear and trembling; they quaffed
the liquor in profound silence and then returned to their game.

By degrees Rip's awe and apprehension subsided. He even ventured,
when no eye was fixed upon him, to taste the beverage, which he found
had much of the flavour of excellent Hollands.[25] He was naturally a
thirsty soul and was soon tempted to repeat the draught. One taste provoked another, and he reiterated his visits to the flagon so often that at
length his senses were overpowered, his eyes swam in his head—his head
gradually declined and he fell into a deep sleep.

---

[20]NINEPINS: Bowling.
[21]SHORT DOUBLETS: Close-fitting jackets, with or without sleeves, worn by men from the fourteenth to the eighteenth centuries.
[22]HANGER: A short sword hung from a belt.
[23]FLEMISH PAINTING: In the style of late Renaissance paintings from Belgium and the Netherlands.
[24]FLAGONS: Large bottles for holding wine or other liquor for use at the table, usually with a handle
and spout.
[25]HOLLANDS: Hollands gin, a grain spirit made in Holland.

On awaking he found himself on the green knoll from whence he had first seen the old man of the glen. He rubbed his eyes—it was a bright, sunny morning. The birds were hopping and twittering among the bushes, and the eagle was wheeling aloft, and breasting the pure mountain breeze. "Surely," thought Rip, "I have not slept here all night." He recalled the occurrences before he fell asleep. The strange man with a keg of liquor—the mountain ravine—the wild retreat among the rocks—the woe begone party at ninepins—the flagon—"ah! that flagon! that wicked flagon!" thought Rip—"what excuse shall I make to Dame Van Winkle?"

He looked round for his gun, but in place of the clean well oiled fowling piece, he found an old firelock lying by him, the barrel incrusted with rust; the lock falling off and the stock worm eaten. He now suspected that the grave roysters of the mountain had put a trick upon him, and having dosed him with liquor, had robbed him of his gun. Wolf too had disappeared, but he might have strayed away after a squirrel or partridge. He whistled after him and shouted his name—but all in vain; the echoes repeated his whistle and shout, but no dog was to be seen.

He determined to revisit the scene of the last evening's gambol,[26] and if he met with any of the party, to demand his dog and gun. As he rose to walk he found himself stiff in the joints and wanting in his usual activity. "These mountain beds do not agree with me," thought Rip, "and if this frolick should lay me up with a fit of rheumatism, I shall have a blessed time with Dame Van Winkle." With some difficulty he got down into the glen; he found the gully up which he and his companion had ascended the preceding evening, but to his astonishment a mountain stream was now foaming down it, leaping from rock to rock, and filling the glen with babbling murmurs. He, however, made swift to scramble up its sides working his toilsome way through thickets of birch, sassafras and witch hazel, and sometimes tripped up or entangled by the wild grape vines that twisted their coils and tendrils from tree to tree, and spread a kind of network in his path.

At length he reached to where the ravine had opened through the cliffs, to the amphitheatre—but no traces of such opening remained. The rocks presented a high impenetrable wall over which the torrent came tumbling in a sheet of feathery foam, and fell into a broad deep basin black from the shadows of the surrounding forest. Here then poor Rip was brought to a stand. He again called and whistled after his dog—he was only answered by the cawing of a flock of idle crows, sporting high in air about a dry tree that overhung a sunny precipice; and who, secure in their elevation seemed to look down and scoff at the poor man's perplexities.

[26]GAMBOL: Frolic or dance.

What was to be done? the morning was passing away and Rip felt famished for want of his breakfast. He grieved to give up his dog and gun; he dreaded to meet his wife; but it would not do to starve among the mountains. He shook his head, shouldered the rusty fire lock, and, with a heart full of trouble and anxiety, turned his steps homeward.

As he approached the village he met a number of people, but none whom he knew, which some what surprised him, for he had thought himself acquainted with every one in the country round. Their dress too was of a different fashion from that to which he was accustomed. They all stared at him with equal marks of surprise, and whenever they cast their eyes upon him, invariably stroked their chins. The constant recurrence of this gesture induced Rip involuntarily to do the same, when to his astonishment he found his beard had grown a foot long!

He had now entered the skirts of the village. A troop of strange children ran at his heels, hooting after him, and pointing at his grey beard. The dogs too, not one of which he recognized for an old acquaintance, barked at him as he passed. The very village was altered—it was larger and more populous. There were rows of houses which he had never seen before, and those which had been his familiar haunts had disappeared. Strange names were over the doors—strange faces at the windows—everything was strange. His mind now misgave him; he began to doubt whether both he and the world around him were not bewitched. Surely this was his native village which he had left but the day before. There stood the Kaatskill mountains—there ran the silver Hudson at a distance—there was every hill and dale precisely as it had always been—Rip was sorely perplexed—"That flagon last night," thought he, "has addled my poor head sadly!"

It was with some difficulty that he found the way to his own house, which he approached with silent awe, expecting every moment to hear the shrill voice of Dame Van Winkle. He found the house gone to decay—the roof fallen in, the windows shattered and the doors off the hinges. A half starved dog that looked like Wolf was skulking about it. Rip called him by name but the cur snarled, shewed his teeth and passed on. This was an unkind cut indeed—"My very dog," sighed poor Rip, "has forgotten me!"

He entered the house, which, to tell the truth, Dame Van Winkle had always kept in neat order. It was empty, forlorn and apparently abandoned. This desolateness overcame all his connubial fears—he called loudly for his wife and children—the lonely chambers rang for a moment with his voice, and then all again was silence.

He now hurried forth and hastened to his old resort, the village inn—but it too was gone. A large rickety wooden building stood in its place, with great gaping windows, some of them broken, and mended with old hats and petticoats, and over the door was printed, "The Union Hotel, by Jonathan Doolittle."[27] Instead of the great tree, that used to shelter the quiet little Dutch inn of yore, there now was reared a tall naked pole, with something on the top that looked like a red night cap,[28] and from it was fluttering a flag, on which was a singular assemblage of stars and stripes—all this was strange and incomprehensible. He recognized on the sign, however, the ruby face of King George under which he had smoked so many a peaceful pipe, but even this was singularly metamorphosed. The red coat was changed for one of blue and buff[29]; a sword was held in the hand instead of a sceptre; the head was decorated with a cocked hat, and underneath was printed in large characters GENERAL WASHINGTON.

There was as usual a crowd of folk about the door; but none that Rip recollected. The very character of the people seemed changed. There was a busy, bustling, disputatious tone about it, instead of the accustomed phlegm[30] and drowsy tranquillity. He looked in vain for the sage Nicholaus Vedder with his broad face, double chin and fair long pipe, uttering clouds of tobacco smoke instead of idle speeches. Or Van Bummell the schoolmaster doling forth the contents of an ancient newspaper. In place of these a lean bilious[31] looking fellow with his pockets full of hand bills, was haranguing vehemently about rights of citizens—elections—members of congress—liberty—Bunker's hill—heroes of seventy six—and other words which were a perfect babylonish jargon[32] to the bewildered Van Winkle.

The appearance of Rip with his long grizzled beard, his rusty fowling piece, his uncouth dress and an army of women and children at his heels, soon attracted the attention of the tavern politicians. They crowded round him eying him from head to foot, with great curiosity. The orator bustled up to him, and drawing him partly aside, enquired "On which side he voted?"—Rip stared in vacant stupidity. Another short but busy little fellow, pulled him by the arm and rising on tiptoe, enquired in his

[27]THE UNION HOTEL, BY JONATHAN DOOLITTLE: A reference to Brother Jonathan, who was the personification of American patriotism before the icon of Uncle Sam was introduced.
[28]RED NIGHT CAP: Called the cap of liberty, a limp, conical cap turned over in front. It was worn by the ancient Phrygians and, later, by American and French revolutionaries, who placed them on poles where they gathered.
[29]RED COAT WAS CHANGED FOR ONE OF BLUE AND BUFF: The red coat of the British military was exchanged for the blue and buff colors of the Revolutionary soldier.
[30]PHLEGM: Sluggishness.
[31]BILIOUS: Excitable, ill-tempered.
[32]BABYLONISH JARGON: Babel-like, confused language; gibberish. Genesis 11:1–9 recounts how God prevents the builders of the Tower of Babel from completing their sacrilegious construction by confusing their languages and thus their ability to communicate with one another.

ear, "whether he was Federal or Democrat?"[33]—Rip was equally at a loss to comprehend the question—when a knowing, self-important old gentleman, in a sharp cocked hat, made his way through the crowd, putting them to the right and left with his elbows as he passed, and planting himself before Van Winkle, with one arm akimbo,[34] the other resting on his cane, his keen eyes and sharp hat penetrating as it were into his very soul, demanded in an austere tone—"what brought him to the election with a gun on his shoulder and a mob at his heels, and whether he meant to breed a riot in the village?"—"Alas gentlemen," cried Rip, somewhat dismayed, "I am a poor quiet man, a native of the place, and a loyal subject of the King—God bless him!"

Here a general shout burst from the byestanders—"A tory! a tory! a spy! a Refugee! hustle him! away with him!"—It was with great difficulty that the self important man in the cocked hat restored order; and having assumed a ten fold austerity of brow demanded again of the unknown culprit, what he came there for and whom he was seeking. The poor man humbly assured him that he meant no harm; but merely came there in search of some of his neighbours, who used to keep about the tavern.

"—Well—who are they?—name them."

Rip bethought himself a moment and enquired, "Where's Nicholaus Vedder?"

There was a silence for a little while, when an old man replied, in a thin, piping voice, "Nicholaus Vedder! why he is dead and gone these eighteen years! There was a wooden tombstone in the church yard that used to tell all about him, but that's rotted and gone too."

"Where's Brom Dutcher?"

"Oh he went off to the army in the beginning of the war; some say he was killed at the storming of Stoney Point—others say he was drowned in a squall at the foot of Antony's Nose[35]—I don't know—he never came back again."

"Where's Van Bummel the schoolmaster?"

"He went off to the wars too—was a great militia general, and is now in Congress."

[33]FEDERAL OR DEMOCRAT: Political parties that were in heated conflict from the Revolution to around the War of 1812. Federalists (the party of John Adams and Alexander Hamilton) were willing to have an elected few represent the whole. Democrats (the party of Thomas Jefferson) opposed this view, defending the individual's right to vote.
[34]AKIMBO: With hands on hips.
[35]STONEY POINT—OTHERS SAY HE WAS DROWNED IN A SQUALL AT THE FOOT OF ANTONY'S NOSE: Stoney Point and Anthony's Nose are promontories—points of high land that jut out beyond the coastline—on the Hudson River south of West Point. Stoney Point was captured from the British by General Anthony Wayne in 1779 during the Revolution.

Rip's heart died away at hearing of these sad changes in his home and friends, and finding himself thus alone in the world—every answer puzzled him too by treating of such enormous lapses of time, and of matters which he could not understand—war—Congress—Stoney Point—he had no courage to ask after any more friends, but cried out in despair, "Does nobody here know Rip Van Winkle?"

"Oh. Rip Van Winkle!" exclaimed two or three, "oh to be sure!—that's Rip Van Winkle—yonder—leaning against the tree."

Rip looked and beheld a precise counterpart of himself, as he went up the mountain: apparently as lazy, and certainly as ragged! The poor fellow was now completely confounded. He doubted his own identity, and whether he was himself or another man. In the midst of his bewilderment, the man in the cocked hat demanded who he was,—what was his name.

"God knows," exclaimed he, at his wit's end, "I'm not myself.—I'm somebody else—that's me yonder—no—that's somebody else got into my shoes—I was myself last night; but I fell asleep on the mountain—and they've changed my gun—and everything's changed—and I'm changed—and I can't tell what's my name, or who I am!"

The byestanders began now to look at each other, nod, wink significantly and tap their fingers against their foreheads. There was a whisper also about securing the gun, and keeping the old fellow from doing mischief—at the very suggestion of which, the self-important man in the cocked hat retired with some precipitation. At this critical moment a fresh likely looking woman pressed through the throng to get a peep at the greybearded man. She had a chubby child in her arms, which frightened at his looks began to cry. "Hush, Rip," cried she, "hush, you little fool, the old man won't hurt you." The name of the child, the air of the mother, the tone of her voice, all awakened a train of recollections in his mind. "What is your name my good woman?" asked he.

"Judith Gardenier."

"And your father's name?"

"Ah, poor man, Rip Van Winkle was his name, but it's twenty years since he went away from home with his gun and never has been heard of since—his dog came home without him—but whether he shot himself, or was carried away by the Indians nobody can tell. I was then but a little girl."

Rip had but one question more to ask, but he put it with a faltering voice—

"Where's your mother?"—

Oh she too had died but a short time since—she broke a blood vessel in a fit of passion at a New England pedlar.

There was a drop of comfort at least in this intelligence. The honest man could contain himself no longer—he caught his daughter and her child in his arms—"I am your father!" cried he—"Young Rip Van Winkle once—old Rip Van Winkle now!—does nobody know poor Rip Van Winkle?"

All stood amazed, until an old woman tottering out from among the crowd put her hand to her brow and peering under it in his face for a moment exclaimed—"Sure enough!—it is Rip Van Winkle—it is himself—welcome home again old neighbour. Why, where have you been these twenty long years?"

Rip's story was soon told, for the whole twenty years had been to him but as one night. The neighbours stared when they heard it; some were seen to wink at each other and put their tongues in their cheeks, and the self important man in the cocked hat, who when the alarm was over had returned to the field, screwed down the corners of his mouth and shook his head—upon which there was a general shaking of the head throughout the assemblage.

It was determined, however, to take the opinion of old Peter Vanderdonk, who was seen slowly advancing up the road. He was a descendant of the historian of that name,[36] who wrote one of the earliest accounts of the province. Peter was the most ancient inhabitant of the village and well versed in all the wonderful events and traditions of the neighbourhood. He recollected Rip at once, and corroborated his story in the most satisfactory manner. He assured the company that it was a fact handed down from his ancestor the historian, that the Kaatskill mountains had always been haunted by strange beings. That it was affirmed that the great Hendrick Hudson,[37] the first discoverer of the river and country, kept a kind of vigil there every twenty years, with his crew of the Half Moon—being permitted in this way to revisit the scenes of his enterprize and keep a guardian eye upon the river and the great city called by his name.[38] That his father had once seen them in their old Dutch dresses playing at nine pins in a hollow of the mountain; and that he himself had heard one summer afternoon the sound of their balls, like distant peals of thunder.

---

[36]PETER VANDERDONK...DESCENDANT OF THE HISTORIAN OF THAT NAME: Adriaen Van der Donck (1620–1655), a historian and founder of present-day Yonkers ("Donckers"), New York.
[37]HENDRICK HUDSON: Henry Hudson (presumed dead c. 1611) was an English navigator who, while in the service of the Dutch East India Company, explored the New England coast of North America and the river that bears his name on his ship, the *Half Moon*.
[38]GREAT CITY CALLED BY HIS NAME: Hudson, New York, was a prosperous port city on the eastern bank of the Hudson River. In Irving's time, however, it was not a "great city," and he uses the expression somewhat ironically.

To make a long story short—the company broke up, and returned to the more important concerns of the election. Rip's daughter took him home to live with her; she had a snug, well furnished house, and a stout cheery farmer for a husband whom Rip recollected for one of the urchins that used to climb upon his back. As to Rip's son and heir, who was the ditto of himself seen leaning against the tree; he was employed to work on the farm; but evinced an hereditary disposition to attend to anything else but his business.

Rip now resumed his old walks and habits; he soon found many of his former cronies, though all rather the worse for the wear and tear of time; and preferred making friends among the rising generation, with whom he soon grew into great favour.

Having nothing to do at home, and being arrived at that happy age when a man can be idle, with impunity, he took his place once more on the bench at the inn door and was reverenced as one of the patriarchs of the village and a chronicle of the old times "before the war." It was some time before he could get into the regular track of gossip, or could be made to comprehend the strange events that had taken place during his torpor. How that there had been a revolutionary war—that the country had thrown off the yoke of Old England,—and that, instead of being a subject of his majesty George the Third, he was now a free citizen of the United States. Rip in fact was no politician; the changes of states and empires made but little impression on him; but there was one species of despotism under which he had long groaned and that was petticoat government. Happily that was at an end—he had got his neck out of the yoke of matrimony, and could go in and out whenever he pleased without dreading the tyranny of Dame Van Winkle. Whenever her name was mentioned, however, he shook his head, shrugged his shoulders and cast up his eyes; which might pass either for an expression of resignation to his fate or joy at his deliverance.

He used to tell his story to every stranger that arrived at Mr. Doolittle's Hotel. He was observed at first to vary on some points every time he told it, which was doubtless owing to his having so recently awaked. It at last settled down precisely to the tale I have related and not a man, woman, or child in the neighbourhood but knew it by heart. Some always pretended to doubt the reality of it, and insisted that Rip had been out of his head, and that this was one point on which he always remained flighty. The old Dutch inhabitants, however, almost universally gave it full credit. Even to this day they never hear a thunder storm of a summer afternoon about the Kaatskill, but they say Hendrick Hudson and his crew are at their game of nine pins; and it is a common wish of all henpecked husbands in the neighbourhood, when life hangs heavy on their hands, that they might have a quieting draught out of Rip Van Winkle's flagon.

NOTE

The foregoing tale one would suspect had been suggested to Mr. Knickerbocker by a little German superstition about the emperor Frederick *der Rothbart*,[39] and the Kypphauser Mountain; the subjoined note, however, which he had appended to the tale, shews that it is an absolute fact, narrated with his usual fidelity.—

"The story of Rip Van Winkle may seem incredible to many, but nevertheless I give it my full belief, for I know the vicinity of our old Dutch settlements to have been very subject to marvellous events and appearances. Indeed, I have heard many stranger stories than this, in the villages along the Hudson; all of which were too well authenticated to admit of a doubt. I have even talked with Rip Van Winkle myself, who when last I saw him was a very venerable old man and so perfectly rational and consistent on every other point, that I think no conscientious person could refuse to take this into the bargain—nay I have seen a certificate on the subject taken before a country justice and signed with a cross in the justice's own handwriting. The story, therefore, is beyond the possibility of doubt.

D.K."

POSTSCRIPT

The following are travelling notes from a memorandum book of Mr. Knickerbocker.

The Kaatsberg or Catskill Mountains have always been a region full of fable. The Indians considered them the abode of spirits who influenced the weather, spreading sunshine or clouds over the landscape and sending good or bad hunting seasons. They were ruled by an old squaw spirit, said to be their mother. She dwelt on the highest peak of the Catskills and had charge of the doors of day and night to open and shut them at the proper hour. She hung up the new moons in the skies and cut up the old ones into stars. In times of drought, if properly propitiated, she would

---

[39]FREDERICK DER ROTHBART: Frederick Barbarossa (c. 1121–1190), the Holy Roman Emperor from 1152 to 1190. (*Barbarossa* and *Rothbart* both mean "red beard.") Barbarossa drowned on the Third Crusade, but according to German legend, he sleeps in the Kyffhauser mountains in Thuringia and will one day awaken and bring great glory to Germany.

spin light summer clouds out of cobwebs and morning dew, and send them off, from the crest of the mountain, flake after flake, like flakes of carded cotton to float in the air: until, dissolved by the heat of the sun, they would fall in gentle showers, causing the grass to spring, the fruits to ripen and the corn to grow an inch an hour. If displeased, however, she would brew up clouds black as ink, sitting in the midst of them like a bottle bellied spider in the midst of its web; and when these clouds broke—woe betide the valleys!

In old times, say the Indian traditions, there was a kind of Manitou[40] or Spirit, who kept about the wildest recesses of the Catskill Mountains, and took a mischievous pleasure in wreaking all kinds of evils and vexations upon the red men. Sometimes he would assume the form of a bear, a panther or a deer, lead the bewildered hunter a weary chace through tangled forests and among ragged rocks; and then spring off with a loud ho! ho! leaving him aghast on the brink of a beetling precipice or raging torrent.

The favorite abode of this Manitou is still shewn. It is a great rock or cliff on the loneliest part of the mountains, and, from the flowering vines which clamber about it, and the wild flowers which abound in its neighbourhood, is known by the name of the Garden Rock. Near the foot of it is a small lake, the haunt of the solitary bittern, with water snakes basking in the sun on the leaves of the pond lilies which lie on the surface. This place was held in great awe by the Indians, insomuch that the boldest hunter would not pursue his game within its precincts. Once upon a time, however, a hunter who had lost his way, penetrated to the Garden Rock where he beheld a number of gourds placed in the crotches of trees. One of these he seized and made off with it, but in the hurry of his retreat he let it fall among the rocks, when a great stream gushed forth which washed him away and swept him down precipices, where he was dashed to pieces, and the stream made its way to the Hudson and continues to flow to the present day; being the identical stream known by the name of the Kaaters-kill.

[1819–1820]

---

[40]MANITOU: A Native American deity or spirit (of good or evil).

James Fenimore Cooper

(1789–1851)

As the scholar Donald A. Ringe noted, James Fenimore Cooper's The American Democrat, *excerpted below, is a "political essay," directed to Cooper's countrymen, on the true meaning of "democratic principles." "The fundamental issue," Ringe states, "is one that troubles social thinkers even today: how to control the leveling tendencies of a democracy to insure the protection of the intelligent and educated elite that is obviously needed to provide leadership."*

Cooper wrote The American Democrat *after a seven-year residence in Europe. While living in countries defined by class privilege and aristocracy he defended democracy, but on his return to the United States he concluded that democracy had taken disturbing forms during the era of Andrew Jackson, a popular war hero and statesman elected to the presidency in 1828 and reelected in 1832. Cooper believed the nation was rapidly growing vulgar, crude, and obnoxious, and he protested "a disposition in the majority to carry out the opinions of the system to extremes, and a disposition in the minority to abandon all to the current of the day." Presenting himself as "the voice of simple, honest, and fearless truth," Cooper sought in* The American Democrat *to describe the strengths, and even more the limits, of democracy as articulated and practiced in the United States.*

Born James Cooper in Burlington, New Jersey, the son of Quaker parents, Cooper was the twelfth of thirteen children. A year after his birth the family moved to the area of Lake Otsego, in central New York, where the boy's father established a settlement he named Cooperstown. Politically and socially ambitious, Cooper's father became a prominent judge and landowner.

Cooper was a student at Yale College from 1803 to 1805, when he was expelled for a prank he played on another student. Through his father's influence he received a commission in the U.S. Navy, and he made voyages to England and served at a post on Lake Ontario. For a time he held a position in New York City recruiting sailors, but he left the navy in 1811 to marry Susan Augusta de Lancey, of a wealthy family in Westchester, New York.

Cooper's father died in 1809, and there was much legal wrangling over his estate. As the family fell into debt, Cooper struggled to find a means of making a living. Almost by accident, he settled on a career as a writer; his daughter later said:

> *A new novel had been brought from England.... My mother was not well; she was lying on the sofa, and he was reading this newly*

*imported novel to her; it must have been very trashy; after a chapter
or two he threw it aside, exclaiming, "I could write you a better
book than that myself!" Our mother laughed at the idea, as the
height of absurdity—he who disliked writing even a letter, that he
should write a book! He persisted in his declaration, however, and
almost immediately wrote the first pages of a tale, not yet named,
the scene laid in England as a matter of course.*

This "tale" was published in 1820; titled Precaution, *it was a novel
of English upper-class society modeled on the writings of Jane Austen
and Walter Scott, which Cooper knew well. He turned next for a subject to the American Revolution, producing* The Spy: A Tale of the
Neutral Ground *(1821), and then to the founding of Cooperstown in*
The Pioneers *(1823). In the latter, Cooper introduced the heroic hunter
Natty Bumppo, nicknamed "Leatherstocking," whose exploits he went
on to depict in four more novels, known as "the Leatherstocking tales:"*
The Last of the Mohicans *(1826);* The Prairie *(1827);* The Pathfinder
(1840); and The Deerslayer *(1841). He enjoyed a wide readership
abroad as well as in America. As one critic observed, Cooper's novels,
admired by Balzac, Tolstoy, and D. H. Lawrence, "constitute a record
of American life and society and at their best present a richness, depth,
and complexity that was unsurpassed in American fiction before the
works of Hawthorne and Melville."*

Below are two excerpts from The American Democrat, *"On
American Equality" and "On American Slavery." Provocative, stimulating, and reactionary, Cooper as a social observer in this work delved
into the meaning of equality in America, a topic that possessed a special importance in the 1830s—a time when Jacksonian democracy was
challenging the old order and when the institution of slavery was
increasing in scale and power.*

For biography and context: James Grossman, James Fenimore
Cooper: A Biographical and Critical Study *(1949); Warren S. Walker,*
James Fenimore Cooper: An Introduction and Interpretation *(1962);
and Robert Emmet Long,* James Fenimore Cooper *(1990). For the
critical reception:* Fenimore Cooper: The Critical Heritage, *ed.
George Dekker and John P. McWilliams (1973). See also* James
Fenimore Cooper: New Critical Essays, *ed. Robert Clark (1985). For
critical interpretation: John P. McWilliams,* Political Justice in a
Republic: James Fenimore Cooper's America *(1972); Stephen Railton,*
Fenimore Cooper: A Study of His Life and Imagination *(1978);
Wayne Franklin,* The New World of James Fenimore Cooper *(1982);
James D. Wallace,* Early Cooper and His Audience *(1986); and
Martin Barker and Roger Sabin,* The Lasting of the Mohicans:
History of an American Myth *(1995).*

From The American Democrat

ON AMERICAN EQUALITY

The equality of the United States is no more absolute, than that of any other country. There may be less inequality in this nation than in most others, but inequality exists, and, in some respects, with stronger features than it is usual to meet with in the rest of christendom.

The rights of property being an indispensable condition of civilization, and its quiet possession every where guaranteed, equality of condition is rendered impossible. One man must labor, while another may live luxuriously on his means; one has leisure and opportunity to cultivate his tastes, to increase his information, and to refine his habits, while another is compelled to toil, that he may live. One is reduced to serve, while another commands, and, of course, there can be no equality in their social conditions.

The justice and relative advantage of these differencies, as well as their several duties, will be elsewhere considered.

By the inequality of civil and political rights that exists in certain parts of the Union, and the great equality that exists in others, we see the necessity of referring the true character of the institutions to those of the states, without a just understanding of which, it is impossible to obtain any general and accurate ideas of the real polity of the country.

The same general exceptions to civil and political equality, that are found in other free countries, exist in this, though under laws peculiar to ourselves. Women and minors are excluded from the suffrage,[1] and from maintaining suits at law, under the usual provisions, here as well as elsewhere. None but natives of the country can fill many of the higher offices, and paupers, felons and all those who have not fixed residences, are also excluded from the suffrage. In a few of the states property is made the test of political rights, and, in nearly half of them, a large portion of the inhabitants, who are of a different race from the original European occupants of the soil, are entirely excluded from all political, and from many of the civil rights, that are enjoyed by those who are deemed citizens. A slave can neither choose, nor be chosen to office, nor, in most of the states, can even a free man, unless a white man. A slave can neither sue nor be sued; he can not hold property, real

[1]SUFFRAGE: Vote.

or personal, nor can he, in many of the states be a witness in any suit, civil or criminal.

It follows from these facts, that absolute equality of condition, of political rights, or of civil rights, does not exist in the United States, though they all exist in a much greater degree in some states than in others, and in some of the states, perhaps, to as great a degree as is practicable. In what are usually called the free states of America, or those in which domestic slavery is abolished, there is to be found as much equality in every respect as comports with safety, civilization and the rights of property. This is also true, as respects the white population, in those states in which domestic slavery does exist; though the number of the bond is in a large proportion to that of the free.

As the tendency of the institutions of America is to the right, we learn in these truths, the power of facts, every question of politics being strictly a question of practice. They who fancy it possible to frame the institutions of a country, on the pure principles of abstract justice, as these principles exist in theories, know little of human nature, or of the restraints that are necessary to society. Abuses assail us in a thousand forms, and it is hopeless to aspire to any condition of humanity, approaching perfection. The very necessity of a government at all, arises from the impossibility of controlling the passions by any other means than that of force.

The celebrated proposition contained in the Declaration of Independence is not to be understood literally. All men are not 'created equal,'[2] in a physical, or even in a moral sense, unless we limit the signification to one of political rights. This much is true, since human institutions are a human invention, with which nature has had no connection. Men are not born equals, physically, since one has a good constitution, another a bad; one is handsome, another ugly; one white, another black. Neither are men born equals morally, one possessing genius, or a natural aptitude, while his brother is an idiot. As regards all human institutions men are born equal, no sophistry being able to prove that nature intended one should inherit power and wealth, another slavery and want. Still artificial inequalities are the inevitable consequences of artificial ordinances, and in founding a new governing principle for the social compact, the American legislators instituted new modes of difference.

[2]DECLARATION OF INDEPENDENCE IS NOT TO BE UNDERSTOOD LITERALLY. ALL MEN ARE NOT 'CREATED EQUAL': From the *Declaration of Independence* (1776), "We hold these truths to be self evident: that all men are created equal; that they are endowed by their Creator with inherent and inalienable rights. . ." Presidential biographer Garry Wills notes that Jefferson probably meant equal in possessing a moral sense, not that all men were equal to one another.

The very existence of government at all, infers inequality. The citizen who is preferred to office becomes the superior of those who are not, so long as he is the repository of power, and the child inherits the wealth of the parent as a controlling law of society. All that the great American proposition, therefore, can mean, is to set up new and juster notions of natural rights than those which existed previously, by asserting, in substance, that God has not instituted political inequalities, as was pretended by the advocates of the Jus Divinum,[3] and that men possessed a full and natural authority to form such social institutions as best suited their necessities.

There are numerous instances in which the social inequality of America may do violence to our notions of abstract justice, but the compromise of interests under which all civilized society must exist, renders this unavoidable. Great principles seldom escape working injustice in particular things, and this so much the more, in establishing the relations of a community, for in them many great, and frequently conflicting principles enter, to maintain the more essential features of which sacrifices of parts become necessary. If we would have civilization and the exertion indispensable to its success, we must have property; if we have property, we must have its rights; if we have the rights of property, we must take those consequences of the rights of property which are inseparable from the rights themselves.

The equality of rights in America, therefore, after allowing for the striking exception of domestic slavery, is only a greater extension of the principle than common, while there is no such thing as an equality of condition. All that can be said of the first, is that it has been carried as far as a prudent discretion will at all allow, and of the last, that the inequality is the simple result of civilization, unaided by any of those factitious plans that have been elsewhere devised in order to augment the power of the strong, and to enfeeble the weak.

Equality is no where laid down as a governing principle of the institutions of the United States, neither the word, nor any inference that can be fairly deduced from its meaning, occurring in the Constitution. As respects the states, themselves, the professions of an equality of rights are more clear, and slavery excepted, the intention in all their governments is to maintain it, as far as practicable, though equality of condition is no where mentioned, all political economists knowing that it is unattainable, if, indeed, it be desirable. Desirable in practice, it can hardly be, since the result would be to force all down to the level of the lowest.

[3]JUS DIVINUM: Divine law. (Latin)

All that a good government aims at, therefore, is to add no unnecessary and artificial aid to the force of its own unavoidable consequences, and to abstain from fortifying and accumulating social inequality as a means of increasing political inequalities.

ON AMERICAN SLAVERY

American slavery is one of the most unqualified kind, considering the slave as a chattel,[4] that is transferable at will, and in full property. The slave, however, is protected in his person to a certain extent, the power of the master to chastise and punish, amounting to no more than the parental power.

American slavery is distinguished from that of most other parts of the world, by the circumstance that the slave is a variety of the human species, and is marked by physical peculiarities so different from his master, as to render future amalgamation[5] improbable. In ancient Rome, in modern Europe generally, and in most other countries, the slave not being thus distinguished, on obtaining his freedom, was soon lost in the mass around him; but nature has made a stamp on the American slave that is likely to prevent this consummation, and which menaces much future ill to the country. The time must come when American slavery shall cease, and when that day shall arrive, (unless early and effectual means are devised to obviate it,) two races will exist in the same region, whose feelings will be embittered by inextinguishable hatred, and who carry on their faces, the respective stamps of their factions. The struggle that will follow, will necessarily be a war of extermination. The evil day may be delayed, but can scarcely be averted.

American slavery is mild, in its general features, and physical suffering cannot properly be enumerated[6] among its evils. Neither is it just to lay too heavy stress on the personal restraints of the system, as it is a question whether men feel very keenly, if at all, privations of the amount of which they know nothing. In these respects, the slavery of this country is but one modification of the restraints that are imposed on the majority, even, throughout most of Europe. It is an evil, certainly, but in a comparative sense, not as great an evil as it is usually imagined. There is scarcely a nation of Europe that does not possess institutions that inflict as gross personal privations and wrongs, as the slavery of America.

---

[4]CHATTEL: Personal goods and property, including household property and livestock.
[5]AMALGAMATION: Blending, combining.
[6]ENUMERATED: Counted, listed.

Thus the subject is compelled to bear arms in a quarrel in which he has no real concern, and to incur the risks of demoralization and death in camps and fleets, without any crime or agency of his own. From all this, the slave is exempt, as well as from the more ordinary cares of life.

Slavery in America, is an institution purely of the states, and over which the United States has no absolute control. The pretence, however, that congress has no right to entertain the subject, is unsound, and cannot be maintained. Observing the prescribed forms, slavery can be legally abolished, by amending the constitution, and congress has power, by a vote of two thirds of both houses, to propose amendments to that instrument. Now, whatever congress has power to do, it has power to discuss; by the same rule, that it is a moral innovation on the rights of the states to discuss matters in congress, on which congress has no authority to legislate. A constitutional right, and expediency, however, are very different things. Congress has full power to declare war against all the nations of the earth, but it would be madness to declare war against even one of them, without sufficient cause. It would be equal madness for congress, in the present state of the country, to attempt to propose an amendment of the Constitution, to abolish slavery altogether, as it would infallibly fail, thereby raising an irritating question without an object.

[1838]

Cherokee Memorial

Since the early 1800s, the citizens of Georgia had sought the removal of the Cherokee tribe from the state. Andrew Jackson, a former Indian fighter elected president of the United States in 1828, agreed. In his view, the Cherokees and all other tribes belonged west of the Mississippi River, far away from the expanding white population.

Many in Georgia became all the more insistent in their demands in 1828–1829, when gold was discovered in the Georgia mountains. The Cherokees now were in the way of the quest for riches that, reaching back to the Spanish expedition led by Hernando de Soto in 1540, had been rumored to exist in Georgia.

Ironically, by the 1820s, the Cherokees had become "Americanized." They had established churches (many had converted to Christianity), built roads, and erected schools. They dwelled in log cabins and worked the land as ranchers and farmers, ran a printing press, and lived under a form of representational government that included eight districts and a legislature that made laws and approved treaties. Many among the Cherokees were literate in English. Two hundred or more had intermarried with whites, and they and others followed "white" customs in clothing. A significant number owned African American slaves.

Throughout the 1820s and 1830s, the Cherokees had supporters who resisted efforts to move Indians westward. The support the Cherokees received, however, was not formidable enough to prevent the introduction in Congress of an Indian Removal Act, which many in Congress, and President Jackson, endorsed. In their newspaper, The Cherokee Phoenix, the Cherokees criticized the Act and the threatened loss of their homeland. They supplemented these articles and editorials (widely reprinted in newspapers in the East) with appeals to the courts and with letters and petitions to members of Congress and officials in the government. In March 1830, during the debate over the Removal Act, the Cherokee Council submitted twelve "memorials"—that is, petitions—from the "native citizens" of the Cherokee nation, one of which is given below.

The Removal Act was passed and signed into law soon thereafter, but it did not immediately result in the Cherokees' loss of their land. It was the expectation of many in the government that Indian tribes would choose to journey west rather than be forced there through U.S. military pressure. Concluding there was no alternative, in 1835 a few Cherokee leaders signed the Treaty of New Echota, agreeing to surrender Cherokee lands in exchange for new lands west of the Mississippi. Ralph Waldo Emerson called the treaty a "sham," and, in a public letter, he stated: "Such a dereliction of all faith and virtue, *such a denial of justice, and such deafness to screams for mercy were never heard of in times of peace and in the dealing of a nation with its own allies and wards, since the earth was made."* But once the Treaty was ratified in the U.S. Senate (and by the margin of a single vote), the Cherokees were doomed.

Among the Cherokees themselves, there was intense opposition to those who had signed the Treaty. The signers represented a minority view, and the majority favored continued resistance to the white advance on Cherokee territory. Finally, in 1838, President Martin Van Buren (who had served as Jackson's vice president) ordered military action. The first officer in command, General John Wood, resigned in protest. But General Winfield Scott, taking Wood's place, in May 1838 sent 7,000 troops into the lands of the Cherokees, as Van Buren had ordered.

The Cherokees were rounded up, confined to makeshift fortifications in bad conditions, and given little food. In June, the military began marching groups of Cherokees hundreds of miles westward to what is now the state of Oklahoma. Many lost their lives during the brutal first stages and then in the harsh winter months of 1838–1839. Of the 15,000 compelled to leave, it is estimated that 4,000 died along the route known as "The Trail of Tears," or, in a more direct rendering of the Cherokee, "The Trail Where They Cried." Others died in confinement or perished from sickness, thirst, or starvation in Georgia or, later, in Oklahoma.

Though the selection below is a written text, it is not known who the author or authors were and what kind of process was involved in its composition. It does seem clear that the Memorial draws on the Cherokees' conception of oratory and formal address. The Memorial begins deferentially, acknowledging the difference in power between the "white" and "red" populations. It tactfully but pointedly calls attention to the generosity Indians had extended to whites in the past, when Indians held greater power and enjoyed the upper hand. The Cherokees note they are presenting their appeal to Congress, having failed to gain the acceptance and understanding of the white citizens of Georgia. The painful record, they lament, is one of broken promises and violated treaties.

Jackson maintained that the policy of removal was humane. In the West, he said to the Indians, "your white brothers will not trouble you, they will have no claims to the land, and you can live upon it, you and all your children, as long as the grass grows or the water runs, in peace and plenty." In 1837, in his farewell address, he reaffirmed his commitment to the policy. "This unhappy race," he concluded, "are now placed in a situation where we may well hope that they will share in the blessings of civilization and be saved from the degradation and destruction to which they were rapidly hastening while they remained in the states." In December 1838, Van Buren declared: "It affords me *great pleasure to be able to apprise you of the entire removal of the Cherokee Nation of Indians to their new homes west of the Mississippi. The measures authorized by Congress...have had the happiest effects, and they emigrated without any apparent reluctance."*

By 1840, nearly all of the Native Americans—125,000 or more— who had lived east of the Mississippi River had been relocated to the West. During the nineteenth century, their fate seemed to the majority of Americans an unfortunate but necessary aspect of white America's manifest destiny. Today, the suffering and forced exile of the Cherokees and other Indian tribes are acknowledged as a shameful phase of American history. As the selection below attests, the Cherokees spoke and wrote forcefully on their own behalf, but their impassioned words failed to sway those determined to evict them.

For further study: The Removal of the Cherokee Nation: Manifest Destiny or National Dishonor? *ed. Louis Filler and Allen Guttmann (1962);* Cherokee Removal: Before and After, *ed. William L. Anderson (1991);* After the Trail of Tears: The Cherokees' Struggle for Sovereignty, 1839–1880; *William G. McLoughlin (1993);* The Cherokee Removal: A Brief History with Documents, *ed. Theda Perdue and Michael D. Green (1995).*

[Memorial of the Cherokee Citizens, December 18, 1829]

To the Honorable Senate and House of Representatives of the United States of America in Congress assembled:

The undersigned memorialists humbly make known to your honorable bodies, that they are free citizens of the Cherokee nation. Circumstances of late occurrence have troubled our hearts, and induced us at this time to appeal to you, knowing that you are generous and just. As weak and poor children are accustomed to look to their guardians and patrons for protection, so we would come and make our grievances known. Will you listen to us? Will you have pity upon us? You are great and renowned—the nation which you represent is like a mighty man who stands in his strength. But we are small—our name is not renowned. You are wealthy, and have need of nothing; but we are poor in life, and have not the arm and power of the rich.

By the will of our Father in Heaven, the Governor of the whole world, the red man of America has become small, and the white man great and renowned. When the ancestors of the people of these United States first came to the shores of America, they found the red man strong—though he was ignorant and savage, yet he received them kindly, and gave them dry land to rest their weary feet. They met in peace, and shook hands in token of friendship. Whatever the white man wanted and asked of the Indian, the latter willingly gave. At that time the Indian was the lord, and the white man the suppliant. But now the scene has changed. The strength of the red man has become weakness. As his neighbors increased in numbers, his power became less and less, and now, of the many and powerful tribes who once covered these United States, only a few are to be seen—a few whom a sweeping pestilence[1] has left. The Northern tribes who were once so numerous and powerful, are now nearly extinct. Thus it has happened to the red man of America. Shall we, who are remnants, share the same fate?

Brothers—we address you according to usage adopted by our forefathers, and the great and good men who have successfully directed the Councils of the nation you represent. We now make known to you our grievances. We are troubled by some of your own people. Our neighbor, the State of Georgia, is pressing hard upon us, and urging us to relinquish our possessions for her benefit. We are told, if we do not leave the country which we dearly love, and betake ourselves to the Western wilds, the laws of the State will be extended over us, and the time, 1st of June, 1830, is appointed for the execution of the edict. When we first heard of this, we were grieved, and appealed to our father the President, and begged that protection might be extended over us. But we were doubly grieved when we understood from a letter of the Secretary of War to our Delegation, dated March of the present year, that our father the President had refused us protection, and that he had decided in favor of the extension of the laws of the State over us. This decision induces us to appeal to the immediate Representatives of the American people. We love, we dearly love our country, and it is due to your honorable bodies, as well as to us, to make known why we think the country is ours, and why we wish to remain in peace where we are.

The land on which we stand we have received as an inheritance from our fathers, who possessed it from time immemorial, as a gift from our common Father in Heaven. We have already said, that, when the white man came to the shores of America, our ancestors were found in peaceable possession of this very land. They bequeathed it to us as their children, and

---

[1]PESTILENCE: This word has multiple meanings, referring to literal disease, that which is morally pestilent, or that which is fatal to the public well-being. Native American populations were severely stricken by European diseases such as measles and smallpox, for which they had no immunity. Figuratively, the word refers to the conflicts created by European settlers who stole land and goods, often without legal censure.

we have sacredly kept it, as containing the remains of our beloved men. This right of inheritance we have *never ceded*, nor ever *forfeited*. Permit us to ask, what better right can the people have to a country, than the right of *inheritance* and *immemorial peaceable possession?* We know it is said of late by the State of Georgia, and by the Executive of the United States, that we have forfeited this right—but we think this is said gratuitously. At what time have we made the forfeit? What great crime have we committed, whereby we must forever be divested of our country and rights? Was it when we were hostile to the United States, and took part with the King of Great Britain, during the struggle for Independence? If so, why was not this forfeiture declared in the first treaty of peace between the United States and our beloved men? Why was not such an article as the following inserted in the treaty: "The United States give peace to the Cherokees, but, for the part they took in the late war, declare them to be but tenants at will, to be removed, when the convenience of the States within whose chartered limits they live, shall require it." That was the proper time to assume such a possession. But it was not thought of, nor would our forefathers have agreed to any treaty, whose tendency was to deprive them of their rights and their country. All that they have conceded and relinquished are inserted in the treaties, open to the investigation of all people. We would repeat, then, the right of inheritance and peaceable possession which we claim, we have never ceded nor forfeited.

In addition to that first of all rights, the right of inheritance and peaceable possession, we have the faith and pledge of the United States, repeated over and over again, in treaties made at various times. By these treaties, our rights as a separate people are distinctly acknowledged, and guaranties given that they shall be secured and protected. So we have always understood the treaties. The conduct of the Government towards us from its organization until very lately, the talks given to our beloved men by the Presidents of the United States, and the speeches of the Agents and Commissioners, all concur to show that we are not mistaken in our interpretation. Some of our beloved men who signed the treaties are still living, and their testimony tends to the same conclusion. We have always supposed that this understanding of the treaties was in concordance with the views of the Government, nor have we ever imagined that any body would interpret them otherwise. In what light shall we view the conduct of the United States and Georgia, in their intercourse with us, in urging us to enter into treaties, and cede lands? If we were but tenants at will, why was it necessary that our consent must first be obtained, before these Governments could take lawful possession of our lands? The answer is obvious. These Governments perfectly understood our rights— our right to the country, and our right to self Government. Our understanding of the treaties is further supported by the intercourse law of the United States, which prohibits all encroachments upon our territory. The undersigned memorialists humbly represent, that if their interpretation of the treaties has been different from that of the Government, then they have ever been deceived as to how the Government regarded them, and what she has asked and promised. Moreover, they have uniformly misunderstood their own acts.

In view of the strong ground upon which their rights are founded, your memorialists solemnly protest against being considered as tenants at will, or as mere occupants of the soil, without possessing the sovereignty. We have already stated to your honorable bodies, that our forefathers were found in possession of this soil in full sovereignty, by the first European settlers; and as we have never ceded nor forfeited the occupancy of the soil, and the sovereignty over it, we do solemnly protest against being forced to leave it, either by direct or indirect measures. To the land, of which we are now in possession, we are attached. It is our fathers' gift; it contains their ashes; it is the land of our nativity, and the land of our intellectual birth. We cannot consent to abandon it for another *far inferior*, and which holds out to us no inducements. We do moreover protest against the arbitrary measures of our neighbor, the State of Georgia, in her attempt to extend her laws over us, in surveying our lands without our consent, and in direct opposition to the treaties and the intercourse law of the United States, and interfering with our municipal regulations in such a manner as to derange the regular operation of our own laws. To deliver and protect them from all these and every encroachment upon their rights, the undersigned memorialists do most earnestly pray your honorable bodies. Their existence and future happiness are at stake. Divest them of their liberty and country, and you sink them in degradation, and put a check, if not a final stop, to their present progress in the arts of civilized life, and in the knowledge of the Christian religion. Your memorialists humbly conceive, that such an act would be in the highest degree oppressive. From the people of these United States, who, perhaps, of all men under heaven, are the most religious and free, it cannot be expected. Your memorialists, therefore, cannot anticipate such a result. You represent a virtuous, intelligent, and Christian nation. To you they willingly submit their cause for your righteous decision.

[1829]

Lydia Huntley Sigourney

(1791–1865)

Born and raised in Norwich, Connecticut, Lydia Huntley Sigourney received little formal education. However, encouraged by her mother and her father's employer, she worked to educate herself and to acquire some schooling, and, in 1811, she sought on her own to establish a school for women students. This enterprise failed, but Sigourney did succeed three years later in launching a school in Hartford, and in the following year she published her first book, a collection of poems titled Moral Pieces.

Sigourney married in 1819. Her husband was far from an active supporter of her literary work—she published anonymously because he feared for his reputation if his wife were known to be an author. But in the 1820s and 1830s, in large measure because of the family's weak financial situation, Sigourney began to produce, under her own name, a wide range of books, essays, and other publications. She was prolific—nearly seventy volumes over the course of her career—and her work had popular appeal. But Sigourney was also a writer with a vision, a profound Christian sympathy for the plight of the poor and the enslaved, for women, and, especially, for Native Americans. She was sometimes referred to as a "female Milton" and a "Christian Pindar."

In the "The Indian's Welcome to the Pilgrim Fathers," below, Sigourney describes the ominous landscape the Pilgrims confronted, and, even more, an Indian chief, at first fearsome and frightening. But she immediately makes clear that though he seemed fierce, he came to speak welcome and bring words of peace. Sigourney emphasizes that the Indians' "welcome" was the word that marked their downfall. She does not say so explicitly, but she implies that perhaps the Indians would have done better not to welcome these first settlers, who at the beginning were vulnerable, exposed intruders.

The Indians and their children, Sigourney says, were "swept" from the land that belonged to them. On one level, as she knows, this is untrue, for the Indians did resist; they did not give up as easily as the word "swept" suggests. But her point is that, ultimately, the Indians had no chance once they welcomed the settlers and allowed them to remain. "Swept" captures the callousness of the white settlers and the helplessness of the Indians to defend their rights against the power that would soon overwhelm them.

For biography and context: Gordon S. Haight, Mrs. Sigourney: The Sweet Singer of Hartford (1930); Emily Stipes Watts, "Lydia Huntley Sigourney," in The Poetry of American Women from 1632 to 1945 (1977), 83–97; Mary G. De Jong, "Legacy Profile: Lydia Howard Huntley Sigourney (1791–1865)," Legacy: A Journal of American

Women Writers 5:1 (Spring 1988), 35–43; Annie Finch, "The Sentimental Poetess in the World: Metaphor and Subjectivity in Lydia Sigourney's Nature Poetry," Legacy: A Journal of American Women Writers 5:2 (Fall 1988), 3–18; and Nina Baym, "Reinventing Lydia Sigourney," American Literature 62:3 (September 1990), 385–404.

The Indian's Welcome to the Pilgrim Fathers

"On Friday, March 16th, 1622,[1] while the colonists were busied in their usual labors, they were much surprised to see a savage walk boldly towards them, and salute them with, 'much welcome, English, much welcome, Englishmen.'"

Above them spread a stranger sky
    Around, the sterile plain,
The rock-bound coast rose frowning nigh,
    Beyond,—the wrathful main:
Chill remnants of the wintry snow   5
    Still chok'd the encumber'd soil,
Yet forth these Pilgrim Fathers go,
    To mark their future toil.

'Mid yonder vale their corn must rise
    In Summer's ripening pride,   10
And there the church-spire woo the skies
    Its sister-school beside.
Perchance 'mid England's velvet green
    Some tender thought repos'd,—
Though nought upon their stoic mien.   15
    Such soft regret disclos'd.

When sudden from the forest wide
    A red-brow'd chieftain came,
With towering form, and haughty stride,
    And eye like kindling flame: 20
No wrath he breath'd, no conflict sought,
    To no dark ambush drew,

---

[1]MARCH 16, 1622: The incident actually took place on March 16, 1621, when Samoset, an Abknaki who had come to Cape Cod from southern Maine, greeted the Pilgrims in broken English he had learned from English fishermen he had met at Monchiggon (Monhegan).

But simply *to the Old World brought,*
   The welcome of the New.

That *welcome* was a blast and ban   25
   Upon thy race unborn.
Was there no seer, thou fated Man!
   Thy lavish zeal to warn?
Thou in thy fearless faith didst hail
   A weak, invading band,   30
But who shall heed thy children's wail,
   Swept from their native land?

Thou gav'st the riches of thy streams,
   The lordship o'er thy waves,
The region of thine infant dreams,   35
   And of thy fathers' graves,
But who to yon proud mansions pil'd
   With wealth of earth and sea,
Poor outcast from thy forest wild,
   Say, who shall welcome thee?   40

[1835]

William Cullen Bryant

(1794–1878)

Less widely read today than he was decades ago, William Cullen Bryant nonetheless occupies a significant place in American literary history. As the critic John Hollander pointed out:

> Bryant is our first poet of nature, recapitulating even in the earliest years of his work the movement from the passive speculations of a poetic derived from the later eighteenth-century poets of sensibility, to a meditative mode in which the mind is more actively engaged in intercourse with the natural emblems and figures of itself.

Bryant lacks the originality and depth of the British Romantic poets Samuel Taylor Coleridge and William Wordsworth, yet in his own tentative way he performed in poetry as they did, expressing and exploring the poet-observer's relationship to Nature, a relationship as much or more about the inner life of the poet than the landscape he or she described.

Bryant was born in Cummington, in western Massachusetts, and by the age of nine he was already writing poetry. As an undergraduate at Williams College he composed two of the poems for which he later became famous, "Thanatopsis" and "To a Waterfowl," but he chose at first not to publish either, focusing instead on his budding career as a lawyer in Great Barrington, Massachusetts.

"Thanatopsis" was published in September 1817; in 1821 Bryant's first book of poems appeared; and in 1824–1825 he published about two dozen poems in the United States Literary Gazette. By this point he had settled in New York City, leaving his legal career behind.

In 1829 Bryant became the editor of the New York Evening Post, a position he held for the next half-century. A strong foe of slavery, he supported the Republican Party and its leading spokesman and presidential candidate in 1860, Abraham Lincoln.

Bryant learned much from his reading of Wordsworth's poetry; he recalled that reading Lyrical Ballads caused "a thousand springs" to "gush up at once into my heart, and the face of nature, of a sudden to change into a strange freshness." He brought deep feeling and dignity to his nature poetry and evocations of the North American topography, as the poems below, "Thanatopsis" and "The Prairies," bear witness.

The critic Robert Morgan referred to Bryant as "the first American poet," explaining he merits this honor "because he is the first to have glanced at Paradise":

> His Eden is more dignified and classical than the imaginary gardens of Poe, Emerson, Thoreau, Whitman, and Dickinson, but he saw an authentic vision of vast spaces and silence in which a single waterfowl

*drifted, and forests soughed hymns to be overheard by the solitary,
and the ground was haunted and sacred with the memory of
primeval dead. Wherever he looked, in his youth, in his best poems,
there was the Eden-glimmer that was the essence of our first poetry.*

Bryant was a major nineteenth-century man-of-letters—a prominent editor, an influential voice in politics, a reformer, a distinguished
poet, an essayist, an orator (one of his final public acts was speaking
at the unveiling of a statue in New York's Central Park in 1878), a
translator of Homer's epic poems, and a literary anthologist (evident in
his excellent collection, A Library of Poetry and Song, 1871). Though a
greater poet himself, Walt Whitman appreciated Bryant's gifts:

It has always seemed to me Bryant, more than any other American,
had the power to suck in the air of spring, to put it into his song, to
breathe it forth again—never a wasted word—the last superfluity
struck off, a clear nameless beauty pervading and overarching all
the work of his pen.

For biography, background, and critical discussion, see Parke
Godwin, A Biography of William Cullen Bryant, with Extracts from his
Private Correspondence (1883; rpt. 1967); Albert F. McLean Jr.,
William Cullen Bryant, (1964); Charles H. Brown, William Cullen
Bryant (1971); Timothy Morris, "Bryant and the American Poetic
Tradition," American Transcendental Quarterly 8:1 (March 1994),
53–70; and Jules Zanger, "Poetry and Political Rhetoric: Bryant's 'The
Prairies',", in Early America Re-Explored: New Readings in Colonial,
Early National, and Antebellum Culture, ed. Klaus H. Schmidt and
Fritz Fleischmann (2000).

Thanatopsis[1]

To him who in the love of Nature holds
Communion with her visible forms, she speaks
A various language; for his gayer hours
She has a voice of gladness, and a smile
And eloquence of beauty, and she glides   5
Into his darker musings, with a mild
And healing sympathy, that steals away
Their sharpness, ere he is aware. When thoughts
Of the last bitter hour come like a blight
Over thy spirit, and sad images   10

[1]THANATOPSIS: Meditation on death. (Greek)

Of the stern agony, and shroud, and pall,
And breathless darkness, and the narrow house,
Make thee to shudder, and grow sick at heart;—
Go forth, under the open sky, and list
To Nature's teachings, while from all around—   15
Earth and her waters, and the depths of air—
Comes a still voice.²— Yet a few days, and thee
The all-beholding sun shall see no more
In all his course; nor yet in the cold ground,
Where thy pale form was laid, with many tears,   20
Nor in the embrace of ocean, shall exist
Thy image. Earth, that nourished thee, shall claim
Thy growth, to be resolved to earth again,
And, lost each human trace, surrendering up
Thine individual being, shalt thou go   25
To mix for ever with the elements,
To be a brother to th' insensible rock
And to the sluggish clod, which the rude swain³
Turns with his share,⁴ and treads upon. The oak
Shall send his roots abroad, and pierce thy mould.   30

       Yet not to thine eternal resting-place
Shalt thou retire alone, nor couldst thou wish
Couch more magnificent. Thou shalt lie down
With patriarchs of the infant world—with kings,
The powerful of the earth—the wise, the good,   35
Fair forms, and hoary seers of ages past,
All in one mighty sepulchre. The hills
Rock-ribbed and ancient as the sun,—the vales
Stretching in pensive quietness between;
The venerable woods—rivers that move   40
In majesty, and the complaining⁵ brooks
That make the meadows green; and, poured round all,
Old Ocean's gray and melancholy waste,—
Are but the solemn decorations all
Of the great tomb of man. The golden sun,   45

---

²COMES A STILL VOICE: Lines 1–17 were added in 1821, four years after the poem was originally published in the *North American Review*. Later printings show slight differences in word-choice and phrasing
³SWAIN: A rustic youth or farmhand.
⁴SHARE: The blade of a plough.
⁵COMPLAINING: Lamenting.

The planets, all the infinite host of heaven,
Are shining on the sad abodes of death,
Through the still lapse of ages. All that tread
The globe are but a handful to the tribes
That slumber in its bosom.—Take the wings   50
Of morning, pierce the Barcan[6] wilderness,
Or lose thyself in the continuous woods
Where rolls the Oregon,[7] and hears no sound,
Save his own dashings—yet the dead are there:
And millions in those solitudes, since first   55
The flight of years began, have laid them down
In their last sleep—the dead reign there alone.
So shalt thou rest, and what if thou withdraw
In silence from the living, and no friend
Take note of thy departure? All that breathe   60
Will share thy destiny. The gay will laugh
When thou art gone, the solemn brood of care
Plod on, and each one as before will chase
His favorite phantom; yet all these shall leave
Their mirth and their employments, and shall come   65
And make their bed with thee. As the long train
Of ages glide away, the sons of men,
The youth in life's green spring, and he who goes
In the full strength of years, matron and maid,
The speechless babe, and the gray-headed man—   70
Shall one by one be gathered to thy side,
By those, who in their turn shall follow them.

  So live, that when thy summons comes to join
The innumerable caravan, which moves
To that mysterious realm, where each shall take   75
His chamber in the silent halls of death,
Thou go not, like the quarry-slave at night,
Scourged to his dungeon, but, sustained and soothed
By an unfaltering trust, approach thy grave,
Like one who wraps the drapery of his couch   80
About him, and lies down to pleasant dreams.

[1817, 1821]

---

[6]BARCAN WILDERNESS: A reference to the Barcan desert in the area of Libya in Africa.
[7]OREGON: The Columbia River, which divides the states of Washington and Oregon.

The Prairies

These are the gardens of the Desert, these
The unshorn fields, boundless and beautiful,
For which the speech of England has no name[1]—
The Prairies. I behold them for the first,
And my heart swells, while the dilated sight   5
Takes in the encircling vastness. Lo! they stretch,
In airy undulations, far away,
As if the Ocean, in his gentlest swell,
Stood still, with all his rounded billows fixed,
And motionless forever.—Motionless?—   10
No—they are all unchained again. The clouds
Sweep over with their shadows, and, beneath,
The surface rolls and fluctuates to the eye;
Dark hollows seem to glide along and chase
The sunny ridges. Breezes of the South!   15
Who toss the golden and the flame-like flowers,
And pass the prairie-hawk that, poised on high,
Flaps his broad wings, yet moves not—ye have played
Among the palms of Mexico and vines
Of Texas, and have crisped the limpid brooks   20
That from the fountains of Sonora[2] glide
Into the calm Pacific—have ye fanned
A nobler or a lovelier scene than this?
Man hath no power in all this glorious work:
The hand that built the firmament hath heaved   25
And smoothed these verdant swells, and sown their slopes
With herbage, planted them with island-groves,
And hedged them round with forests. Fitting floor
For this magnificent temple of the sky—
With flowers whose glory and whose multitude   30
Rival the constellations! The great heavens
Seem to stoop down upon the scene in love,—
A nearer vault, and of a tendered blue,
Than that which bends above our Eastern hills.

---

[1]ENGLAND HAS NO NAME: *Prairie* is the French word for meadow, a landscape for which the English had no name. The word did not come into common English usage until the end of the eighteenth century. Later printings of this poem, like the previous one, often show minor variations in phrasing.
[2]SONORA: A region of northern Mexico.

As o'er the verdant waste I guide my steed,   35
Among the high rank grass that sweeps his sides
The hollow beating of his footstep seems
A sacrilegious sound. I think of those
Upon whose rest he tramples. Are they here—
The dead of other days?—and did the dust   40
Of these fair solitudes once stir with life
And burn with passion? Let the mighty mounds[3]
That overlook the rivers, or that rise
In the dim forest crowded with old oaks,
Answer. A race, that long has passed away,   45
Built them; a disciplined and populous race
Heaped, with long toil, the earth, while yet the Greek
Was hewing the Pentelicus[4] to forms
Of symmetry, and rearing on its rock
The glittering Parthenon.[5] These ample fields   50
Nourished their harvests, here their herds were fed,
When haply[6] by their stalls the bison lowed,[7]
And bowed his manéd shoulder to the yoke.
All day this desert murmured with their toils,
Till twilight blushed, and lovers walked, and wooed   55
In a forgotten language, and old tunes,
From instruments of unremembered form,
Gave the soft winds a voice. The red-man came—
The roaming hunter-tribes, warlike and fierce,
And the mound-builders vanished from the earth.   60
The solitude of centuries untold
Has settled where they dwelt. The prairie-wolf
Hunts in their meadows, and his fresh-dug den
Yawns by my path. The gopher mines the ground
Where stood their swarming cities. All is gone;   65
All—save the piles of earth that hold their bones,
The platforms where they worshipped unknown gods,
The barriers which they builded from the soil
To keep the foe at bay—till o'er the walls

[3]MIGHTY MOUNDS: The burial mounds, dating back to 4000 BCE, were built by prehistoric Native Americans.
[4]PENTELICUS: Mount Pentelicus in Greece, which supplied the marble used to construct the Parthenon (see note 5).
[5]PARTHENON: The temple to the goddess Athena in Athens.
[6]HAPLY: By chance.
[7]LOWED: Mooed; the reference is to the sound made by cattle.

The wild beleaguerers broke, and, one by one,   70
The strongholds of the plain were forced, and heaped
With corpses. The brown vultures of the wood
Flocked to those vast uncovered sepulchres,
And sat, unscared and silent, at their feast.
Haply some solitary fugitive,   75
Lurking in marsh and forest, till the sense
Of desolation and of fear became
Bitterer than death, yielded himself to die.
Man's better nature triumphed then. Kind words
Welcomed and soothed him; the rude conquerors   80
Seated the captive with their chiefs; he chose
A bride among their maidens, and at length
Seemed to forget—yet ne'er forgot—the wife
Of his first love, and her sweet little ones,
Butchered, amid their shrieks, with all his race.   85

    Thus change the forms of being. Thus arise
Races of living things, glorious in strength,
And perish, as the quickening breath of God
Fills them, or is withdrawn. The red-man, too,
Has left the blooming wilds he ranged so long,   90
And, nearer to the Rocky Mountains, sought
A wilder hunting-ground. The beaver builds
No longer by these streams, but far away,
On waters whose blue surface ne'er gave back
The white man's face—among Missouri's springs,[8]   95
And pools whose issues swell the Oregon[9]—
He rears his little Venice.[10] In these plains
The bison feeds no more. Twice twenty leagues
Beyond remotest smoke of hunter's camp,
Roams the majestic brute, in herds that shake   100
The earth with thundering steps—yet here I meet
His ancient footprints stamped beside the pool.

    Still this great solitude is quick with life.
Myriads of insects, gaudy as the flowers
They flutter over, gentle quadrupeds,   105

[8]MISSOURI'S SPRINGS: The Missouri River, which flows east to the Mississippi River.
[9]OREGON: The Columbia River, which divides the states of Washington and Oregon.
[10]VENICE: The analogy is of beaver dams and the city of Venice, Italy, whose buildings emerge from its many canals.

And birds, that scarce have learned the fear of man,
Are here, and sliding reptiles of the ground,
Startlingly beautiful. The graceful deer
Bounds to the wood at my approach. The bee,
A more adventurous colonist than man,   110
With whom he came across the eastern deep,
Fills the savannas with his murmurings,
And hides his sweets, as in the golden age,
Within the hollow oak. I listen long
To his domestic hum, and think I hear   115
The sound of that advancing multitude
Which soon shall fill these deserts. From the ground
Comes up the laugh of children, the soft voice
Of maidens, and the sweet and solemn hymn
Of Sabbath worshippers. The low of herds   120
Blends with the rustling of the heavy grain
Over the dark brown furrows. All at once
A fresher wind sweeps by, and breaks my dream,
And I am in the wilderness alone.

[1834]

William Apess

(1798–1839)

*Of mixed Pequot Indian and white (and, perhaps, African American)
ancestry, William Apess (or Apes) served, after a brutal, difficult childhood,
in the U.S. military during the War of 1812. After becoming a Methodist
minister in 1829 he worked on behalf of the Native American population
in Massachusetts. His writings include* A Son of the Forest *(1829), which
recounts the story of his life—it is the first published autobiography by a
Native American;* The Experiences of Five Christian Indians *(1833), from
which "An Indian's Looking-Glass for the White Man," below, is taken;
and "Eulogy of King Philip" (1836), about the Native American leader
who waged war against New England settlers in the seventeenth century
and from whom Apess claimed to be descended. Apess died in New York,
probably from the effects of alcoholism.*

*Apess believed Christianity should function as a force for combating
racial discrimination because, in the vision of God, all persons are
equal. In the vivid, vigorously argued selection below, Apess assails all
forms of color prejudice, in particular that imposed on Native
Americans. A powerful preacher, Apess was far ahead of his time in his
zealous exposure and exploration of racism and in his defense of the
rights of Native American people.*

For background and primary sources: On Our Own Ground: The
Complete Writings of William Apess, a Pequot, *ed. Barry O'Connell
(1992). See also the discussions in David Murray,* Forked Tongues:
Speech, Writing, and Representation in North American Indian Texts
(1991); and Cheryl Walker, Indian Nation: Native American Literature
and Nineteenth-Century Nationalisms *(1997).*

An Indian's Looking-Glass for the White Man

Having a desire to place a few things before my fellow creatures who
are travelling with me to the grave, and to that God who is the maker and
preserver both of the white man and the Indian, whose abilities are the
same, and who are to be judged by one God, who will show no favor to
outward appearances, but will judge righteousness. Now I ask if degradation has not been heaped long enough upon the Indians? And if so, can
there not be a compromise; is it right to hold and promote prejudices?
If not, why not put them all away? I mean here amongst those who are
civilized. It may be that many are ignorant of the situation of many of

my brethren within the limits of New England. Let me for a few moments turn your attention to the reservations in the different states of New England, and, with but few exceptions, we shall find them as follows: The most mean, abject, miserable race of beings in the world—a complete place of prodigality and prostitution.

Let a gentleman and lady, of integrity and respectability visit these places, and they would be surprised; as they wandered from one hut to the other they would view with the females who are left alone, children half starved, and some almost as naked as they came into the world. And it is a fact that I have seen them as much so—while the females are left without protection, and are seduced by white men, and are finally left to be common prostitutes for them, and to be destroyed by that burning, fiery curse, that has swept millions, both of red and white men, into the grave with sorrow and disgrace—Rum. One reason why they are left so is, because their most sensible and active men are absent at sea. Another reason is, because they are made to believe they are minors and have not the abilities given them from God, to take care of themselves, without it is to see to a few little articles, such as baskets and brooms. Their land is in common stock, and they have nothing to make them enterprising.

Another reason is because those men who are Agents,[1] many of them are unfaithful, and care not whether the Indians live or die; they are much imposed upon by their neighbors who have no principle. They would think it no crime to go upon Indian lands and cut and carry off their most valuable timber, or any thing else they chose; and I doubt not but they think it clear gain. Another reason is because they have no education to take care of themselves; if they had, I would risk them to take care of their property.

Now I will ask, if the Indians are not called the most ingenious people amongst us? And are they not said to be men of talents? And I would ask, could there be a more efficient way to distress and murder them by inches than the way they have taken? And there is no people in the world but who may be destroyed in the same way. Now if these people are what they are held up in our view to be, I would take the liberty to ask why they are not brought forward and pains taken to educate them? to give them all a common education, and those of the brightest and first-rate talents put forward and held up to office. Perhaps some unholy, unprincipled men would cry out, the skin was not good enough; but stop friends—I am not talking about the skin, but

---

[1]AGENTS: Federal or state government employees appointed to oversee Indian affairs.

about principles. I would ask if there cannot be as good feelings and principles under a red skin as there can be under a white? And let me ask, is it not on the account of a bad principle, that we who are red children have had to suffer so much as we have? And let me ask, did not this bad principle proceed from the whites or their forefathers? And I would ask, is it worth while to nourish it any longer? If not, then let us have a change; although some men no doubt will spout their corrupt principles against it, that are in the halls of legislation and elsewhere. But I presume this kind of talk will seem surprising and horrible. I do not see why it should so long as they (the whites) say that they think as much of us as they do of themselves.

This I have heard repeatedly, from the most respectable gentlemen and ladies—and having heard so much precept, I should now wish to see the example. And I would ask who has a better right to look for these things than the naturalist[2] himself—the candid man would say none.

I know that many say that they are willing, perhaps the majority of the people, that we should enjoy our rights and privileges as they do. If so, I would ask why are not we protected in our persons and property throughout the Union? Is it not because there reigns in the breast of many who are leaders, a most unrighteous, unbecoming and impure black principle, and as corrupt and unholy as it can be—while these very same unfeeling, self-esteemed characters pretend to take the skin as a pretext to keep us from our unalienable and lawful rights? I would ask you if you would like to be disfranchised from all your rights, merely because your skin is white, and for no other crime? I'll venture to say, these very characters who hold the skin to be such a barrier in the way, would be the first to cry out, injustice! awful injustice!

But, reader, I acknowledge that this is a confused world, and I am not seeking for office; but merely placing before you the black inconsistency that you place before me—which is ten times blacker than any skin that you will find in the Universe. And now let me exhort you to do away that principle, as it appears ten times worse in the sight of God and candid men, than skins of color—more disgraceful than all the skins that Jehovah[3] ever made. If black or red skins, or any other skin of color is disgraceful to God, it appears that he has disgraced himself a great deal—for he has made fifteen colored people to one white, and placed them here upon this earth.

[2]NATURALIST: Native American, alluding to the viewpoint that the Indians were "children of nature" or "sons of the forest".
[3]JEHOVAH: The English and common European phrasing, since the sixteenth century, for the Hebrew divine name "Yhwh"; God.

Now let me ask you, white man, if it is a disgrace for to eat, drink and sleep with the image of God, or sit, or walk and talk with them? Or have you the folly to think that the white man, being one in fifteen or sixteen, are the only beloved images of God? Assemble all nations together in your imagination, and then let the whites be seated amongst them, and then let us look for the whites, and I doubt not it would be hard finding them; for to the rest of the nations, they are still but a handful. Now suppose these skins were put together, and each skin had its national crimes written upon it—which skin do you think would have the greatest? I will ask one question more. Can you charge the Indians with robbing a nation almost of their whole Continent, and murdering their women and children, and then depriving the remainder of their lawful rights, that nature and God require them to have? And to cap the climax, rob another nation[4] to till their grounds, and welter out their days under the lash with hunger and fatigue under the scorching rays of a burning sun? I should look at all the skins, and I know that when I cast my eye upon that white skin, and if I saw those crimes written upon it, I should enter my protest against it immediately, and cleave to that which is more honorable. And I can tell you that I am satisfied with the manner of my creation, fully—whether others are or not.

But we will strive to penetrate more fully into the conduct of those who profess to have pure principles, and who tell us to follow Jesus Christ and imitate him and have his Spirit. Let us see if they come any where near him and his ancient disciples. The first thing we are to look at, are his precepts, of which we will mention a few. "Thou shalt love the Lord thy God with all thy heart, with all thy soul, with all thy mind, and with all thy strength." The second is like unto it. "Thou shalt love thy neighbor as thyself." On these two precepts hang all the law and the prophets.—Matt. xxii. 37, 38, 39, 40. "By this shall all men know that they are my disciples, if ye have love one to another"—John xiii. 35. Our Lord left this special command with his followers, that they should love one another.

Again, John in his Epistles says, "He who loveth God, loveth his brother also"—iv. 21. "Let us not love in word but in deed"—iii. 18. "Let your love be without dissimulation. See that ye love one another with a pure heart fervently"—1. Peter, viii. 22. "If any man say, I love God, and hateth his brother, he is a liar"—John iv. 20. "Whosoever hateth his brother is a murderer, and no murderer hath eternal life abiding in him."

[4]ROB ANOTHER NATION: Apess refers to the continent of Africa, from which many people were abducted and transported to America as slaves, as a "nation."

The first thing that takes our attention, is the saying of Jesus, "Thou shalt love," &c. The first question I would ask my brethren in the ministry, as well as that of the membership, What is love, or its effects? Now if they who teach are not essentially affected with pure love, the love of God, how can they teach as they ought? Again, the holy teachers of old said, "Now if any man have not the spirit of Christ, he is none of his"—Rom. viii. 9. Now my brethren in the ministry, let me ask you a few sincere questions. Did you ever hear or read of Christ teaching his disciples that they ought to despise one because his skin was different from theirs? Jesus Christ being a Jew, and those of his Apostles certainly were not whites,— and did not he who completed the plan of salvation complete it for the whites as well as for the Jews, and others? And were not the whites the most degraded people on the earth at that time and none were more so; for they sacrificed their children to dumb idols![5] And did not St. Paul labor more abundantly for building up a christian nation amongst you than any of the Apostles? And you know as well as I that you are not indebted to a principle beneath a white skin for your religious services, but to a colored one.

What then is the matter now; is not religion the same now under a colored skin as it ever was? If so I would ask why is not a man of color respected; you may say as many say, we have white men enough. But was this the spirit of Christ and his Apostles? If it had been, there would not have been one white preacher in the world—for Jesus Christ never would have imparted his grace or word to them, for he could forever have withheld it from them. But we find that Jesus Christ and his Apostles never looked at the outward appearances. Jesus in particular looked at the hearts, and his Apostles through him being discerners of the spirit, looked at their fruit without any regard to the skin, color or nation; as St. Paul himself speaks, "Where there is neither Greek nor Jew, circumcision nor uncircumcision, Barbarian nor Scythian,[6] bond nor free—but Christ is all and in all." If you can find a spirit like Jesus Christ and his Apostles prevailing now in any of the white congregations, I should like to know it. I ask, is it not the case that every body that is not white is treated with contempt and counted as barbarians? And I ask if the word of God justifies the white man in so doing? When the prophets prophesied, of whom did they speak? When they spoke of heathens, was it not the

---

[5]DUMB IDOLS: Apess may be referring to "white" groups who sacrificed children; these included various Middle Eastern polytheistic peoples, the ancient Greeks, and even "barbarian" tribes of Europe.
[6]SCYTHIAN: Of a group of ancient nomadic tribes from southeastern Europe, known for their plundering and excellent horsemanship.

whites and others who were counted Gentiles?[7] And I ask if all nations with the exception of the Jews were not counted heathens? and according to the writings of some, it could not mean the Indians, for they are counted Jews.[8] And now I would ask, why is all this distinction made among these christian societies? I would ask what is all this ado about Missionary Societies, if it be not to christianize those who are not christians? And what is it for? To degrade them worse, to bring them into society where they must welter out their days in disgrace merely because their skin is of a different complexion. What folly it is to try to make the state of human society worse than it is. How astonished some may be at this— but let me ask, is it not so? Let me refer you to the churches only. And my brethren, is there any agreement? Do brethren and sisters love one another?—Do they not rather hate one another? Outward forms and ceremonies, the lusts of the flesh, the lusts of the eye and pride of life is of more value to many professors,[9] than the love of God shed abroad in their hearts, or an attachment to his altar, to his ordinances or to his children. But you may ask who are the children of God? perhaps you may say none but white. If so, the word of the Lord is not true.

I will refer you to St. Peter's precepts—Acts 10. "God is no respecter of persons"—&c. Now if this is the case, my white brother, what better are you than God? And if no better, why do you, who profess his gospel and to have his spirit, act so contrary to it? Let me ask why the men of a different skin are so despised, why are not they educated and placed in your pulpits? I ask if his services well performed are not as good as if a white man performed them? I ask if a marriage or a funeral ceremony, or the ordinance of the Lord's house would not be as acceptable in the sight of God as though he was white? And if so, why is it not to you? I ask again, why is it not as acceptable to have men to exercise their office in one place as well as in another? Perhaps you will say that if we admit you to all of these privileges you will want more. I expect that I can guess what that is—Why, say you, there would be intermarriages. How that would be I am not able to say—and if it should be, it would be nothing strange or new to me; for I can assure you that I know a great many that have intermarried, both of the whites and the Indians—and many are their sons and daughters— and people too of the first respectability. And I could point to some in the famous city of Boston and elsewhere. You may now look at the

---

[7]GENTILES: The Jews considered the people of other nations "gentiles" and, thus, heathens.
[8]JEWS: A reference to a popular theory that Native Americans were descended from the lost tribes of Israel.
[9]PROFESSORS: Believers; those who profess the Christian faith.

disgraceful act in the statute law passed by the Legislature of Massachusetts, and behold the fifty pound fine levied upon any Clergyman or justice of the Peace that dare to encourage the laws of God and nature by a legitimate union in holy wedlock between the Indians and whites. I would ask how this looks to your law makers. I would ask if this corresponds with your sayings—that you think as much of the Indians as you do of the whites. I do not wonder that you blush many of you while you read; for many have broken the ill-fated laws made by man to hedge up the laws of God and nature. I would ask if they who have made the law have not broken it—but there is no other state in New England that has this law but Massachusetts; and I think as many of you do not, that you have done yourselves no credit.

But as I am not looking for a wife, having one of the finest cast, as you no doubt would understand while you read her experience and travail of soul in the way to heaven, you will see that it is not my object. And if I had none, I should not want any one to take my right from me and choose a wife for me; for I think that I or any of my brethren have a right to choose a wife for themselves as well as the whites—and as the whites have taken the liberty to choose my brethren, the Indians, hundreds and thousands of them as partners in life, I believe the Indians have as much right to choose their partners amongst the whites if they wish. I would ask you if you can see any thing inconsistent in your conduct and talk about the Indians? And if you do, I hope you will try to become more consistent. Now if the Lord Jesus Christ, who is counted by all to be a Jew, and it is well known that the Jews are a colored people,[10] especially those living in the East, where Christ was born—and if he should appear amongst us, would he not be shut out of doors by many, very quickly? and by those too, who profess religion?

By what you read, you may learn how deep your principles are. I should say they were skin deep. I should not wonder if some of the most selfish and ignorant would spout a charge of their principles now and then at me. But I would ask, how are you to love your neighbors as yourself? Is it to cheat them? is it to wrong them in any thing? Now to cheat them out of any of their rights is robbery. And I ask, can you deny that you are not robbing the Indians daily, and many others? But at last you may think I am what is called a hard and uncharitable man. But not so. I believe there are many who would not hesitate to advocate our cause; and those too who are men of fame and respectability—as well

---

[10]COLORED PEOPLE: Referring to the belief that the biblical Hebrews—and, by extension, Jesus himself—were people of color.

as ladies of honor and virtue. There is a Webster,[11] an Everett,[12] and a Wirt[13] and many others who are distinguished characters—besides a host of my fellow citizens, who advocate our cause daily. And how I congratulate such noble spirits—how they are to be prized and valued; for they are well calculated to promote the happiness of mankind. They well know that man was made for society, and not for hissing stocks[14] and outcasts. And when such a principle as this lies within the hearts of men, how much it is like its God—and how it honors its Maker—and how it imitates the feelings of the good Samaritan, that had his wounds bound up, who had been among thieves and robbers.

Do not get tired, ye noble-hearted—only think how many poor Indians want their wounds done up daily; the Lord will reward you, and pray you stop not till this tree of distinction shall be levelled to the earth, and the mantle of prejudice torn from every American heart—then shall peace pervade the Union.

[1833]

---

[11]WEBSTER: Daniel Webster (1782–1852), an orator and politician who served in both the House and the Senate and as secretary of state under President William Henry Harrison.
[12]EVERETT: A politician, orator, editor, and Harvard educator, Edward Everett (1794–1865) served as Massachusetts governor from 1836 to 1840 and as senator from 1853 to 1854. He also served as secretary of state when appointed by President Millard Fillmore to fill the vacancy caused by the death of Daniel Webster.
[13]WIRT: William Wirt (1772–1834), a writer, politician, and orator who served as attorney general under President James Monroe; he was a Whig party candidate for President.
[14]HISSING STOCKS: Laughingstock.

Ralph Waldo Emerson
(1803–1882)

Born in Boston, Emerson attended Boston Latin School (1812–1817) and Harvard College (1817–1821). He became a Unitarian minister (his father also was a minister, and there had been ministers in his family since the early seventeenth century) and held a position in the prestigious Second Church of Boston. But, profoundly affected by the death of his beloved wife, Ellen Tucker, in 1831 (they had been married only sixteen months), and increasingly at odds with Unitarian doctrine, Emerson resigned from the ministry in October 1832. "My business is with the living," he recorded in a journal entry. "I have sometimes thought that in order to be a good minister it was necessary to leave the ministry." He embarked on a trip to England, where he met Samuel Taylor Coleridge, William Wordsworth, and, above all, the Scottish historian, essayist, and man-of-letters Thomas Carlyle, whom Emerson esteemed.

Emerson suffered two more painful losses in the mid-1830s, the deaths of his brothers Edward (1834) and Charles (1836). In September 1835 he married Lydia Jackson, and they settled in Concord, Massachusetts. Between 1836 and 1844 they had four children, one of whom, Waldo, died in 1842, a shattering blow to his father. But in a sense Emerson had a much larger family than this—the poets, intellectuals, abolitionists, and reformers who clustered around him in Concord, Cambridge, and Boston, many of whom were involved in the Transcendentalist movement.

Transcendentalism represented an effort to break free of the heritage of Calvinism, which emphasized mankind's innate sinfulness—and, furthermore, from philosophical rationalism, which maintained that knowledge was independent of sense experience. Freedom, for the Transcendentalists, meant overcoming the tyranny of everything exterior to the self. Evolving from such prominent German thinkers as Immanuel Kant, Goethe, and the brothers August Wilhelm and Friedrich von Schlegel, and from Wordsworth, Coleridge, Carlyle, and other English writers whom the Germans influenced and energized, Transcendentalism in American accented the correspondences between each person and nature and the sheer indwelling presence of the divine in all men and women.

"God is, not was," said Emerson. "He speaketh, not spake." Transcendentalism placed special value on conscience, imagination, and personal autonomy. It called for an openness to and faith in truths that persons could intuit, and an intensive gaze outward to a nature illuminated everywhere by a higher, "transcendent" reality. It connoted breadth and limitless prospect, the possibility that persons could make contact with divinity:

*[The Transcendentalist] believes in miracle, in the perpetual open-
ness of the human mind to new influx of light and power; he believes
in inspiration, and in ecstasy. ("The Transcendentalist," 1841)*

With Margaret Fuller, Emerson launched The Dial, *the journal
(1840–1844) of Transcendentalism. It expressed and explored ideas
Emerson had articulated in a series of books and essays that included*
Nature *(1836, included here),* "The American Scholar" *(1837, also
included), and the* Divinity School Address *(1838). Among Emerson's
later works are* Essays *(1841, which contains* "Self-Reliance," *below);*
Essays: Second Series *(1844),* Poems *(1847, see below, for "Concord
Hymn" and "The Rhodora");* Nature, Addresses, and Lectures *(1849);*
Representative Men *(1850);* English Traits *(1856); and* The Conduct of
Life *(1860). From about 1820 Emerson kept a journal that includes
notes on people and current events, reflections on his reading, lengthy
entries he later adapted for use in lectures and speeches, and much
more—the scholarly edition of the* Journal *occupies sixteen volumes.*

*While many read and studied Emerson, and attended his lectures,
not all agreed with his views. Nathaniel Hawthorne, for example, had
a more ominous sense of evil, and, in New York, Herman Melville,
though an attentive reader of the* Essays, *was deeply skeptical of the
optimistic and affirmative tone of Emerson's descriptions of both Nature
and human nature. Emerson was a friend to many writers, however,
and to a significant number he was the central source of inspiration,
including Henry David Thoreau, Margaret Fuller, Louisa May Alcott,
and, outside New England, Walt Whitman. As the critic Harold Bloom
said, Emerson is "the inescapable theorist of virtually all subsequent
American writing."*

*Emerson delivered "The American Scholar" at Harvard, before the
Phi Beta Kappa Society, in 1837. He argued that America must achieve
its literary and cultural independence, breaking from the sway of
England and continental Europe. "Self-Reliance," a few years later, reit-
erates and extends this theme, as Emerson assails social and intellectual
conformity and urges his readers to allow their innate spark of divinity
to recast and revitalize their lives. The message of both works is radical,
designed to undermine the tyranny of custom and convention and liber-
ate the self. This message is itself activated in Emerson's writing, which
seeks always to provoke, challenge, destabilize; Emerson aims to be
inspirational but also mind-testing and invigorating. He expects readers
to work; he forces them to, as he articulates bracing themes and, in the
process, inquires into the powers and limits of language.*

*Emerson is eminently quotable, and the two following passages, one
from early in his career, the other from its major phase, illuminate
crucial dimensions of his mind—and the nature of his impact on so
many American writers of later generations, including Robert Frost,*

Hart Crane, and Wallace Stevens, among poets, and Edith Wharton,
Willa Cather, and Theodore Dreiser, among novelists:

> *Who is he that shall control me? Why may not I act and speak and*
> *write and think with entire freedom? What am I to the Universe, or,*
> *the Universe, what is it to me? Who hath forged the chains of wrong*
> *and right, of opinion and custom? And must I wear them? (Journal,*
> *December 1823)*

> *Let me remind the reader that I am only an experimenter. Do not*
> *set the least value on what I do, or the least discredit on what I do*
> *not, as if I pretended to settle anything as true or false. I unsettle all*
> *things. No facts are to me sacred; none are profane; I simply experi-*
> *ment, an endless seeker, with no Past at my back. ("Circles" (1841)*

For biography: Ralph L. Rusk, The Life of Ralph Waldo Emerson
(1949); Gay Wilson Allen, Waldo Emerson *(1981); and John McAleer,*
Ralph Waldo Emerson: Days of Encounter *(1984). For philosophical,*
scientific, historical, and literary contexts: Robert D. Richardson Jr.,
Emerson: The Mind on Fire *(1995). See also Len Gougeon,* Virtue's
Hero: Emerson, Antislavery, and Reform *(1990). Critical studies include*
Stephen E. Whicher, Freedom and Fate: An Inner Life of Ralph Waldo
Emerson *(1953); Jonathan Bishop,* Emerson on the Soul *(1964); and*
B. L. Packer, Emerson's Fall: A New Interpretation of the Major Essays
(1982). For a range of scholarly and critical opinion: Emerson, Prospect
and Retrospect, *ed. Joel Porte (1982); and* Critical Essays on Ralph
Waldo Emerson, *ed. Robert E. Burkholder and Joel Myerson (1983).*

Nature

Nature is but an image or imitation of wisdom, the last thing of
the soul; nature being a thing which doth only do, but not know.

PLOTINUS[1]

INTRODUCTION

Our age is retrospective. It builds the sepulchres of the fathers. It writes
biographies, histories, and criticism. The foregoing generations beheld
God and nature face to face; we, through their eyes. Why should not
we also enjoy an original relation to the universe? Why should not we
have a poetry and philosophy of insight and not of tradition, and a religion by revelation to us, and not the history of theirs? Embosomed for

---

[1]PLOTINUS: Plotinus (205–270) was a Neoplatonic philosopher. Emerson found this quote in
English theologian Ralph Cudworth's (1617–1688) *The True Intellectual System of the Universe,*
published in 1820.

a season in nature, whose floods of life stream around and through us, and invite us by the powers they supply, to action proportioned to nature, why should we grope among the dry bones of the past,[2] or put the living generation into masquerade out of its faded wardrobe? The sun shines to-day also. There is more wool and flax in the fields. There are new lands, new men, new thoughts. Let us demand our own works and laws and worship.

Undoubtedly we have no questions to ask which are unanswerable. We must trust the perfection of the creation so far, as to believe that whatever curiosity the order of things has awakened in our minds, the order of things can satisfy. Every man's condition is a solution in hieroglyphic to those inquiries he would put. He acts it as life, before he apprehends it as truth. In like manner, nature is already, in its forms and tendencies, describing its own design. Let us interrogate the great apparition, that shines so peacefully around us. Let us inquire, to what end is nature?

All science has one aim, namely, to find a theory of nature. We have theories of races and of functions, but scarcely yet a remote approximation to an idea of creation. We are now so far from the road to truth, that religious teachers dispute and hate each other, and speculative men are esteemed unsound and frivolous. But to a sound judgment, the most abstract truth is the most practical. Whenever a true theory appears, it will be its own evidence. Its test is, that it will explain all phenomena. Now many are thought not only unexplained but inexplicable; as language, sleep, dreams, beasts, sex.

Philosophically considered, the universe is composed of Nature and the Soul. Strictly speaking, therefore, all that is separate from us, all which Philosophy distinguishes as the NOT ME,[3] that is, both nature and art, all other men and my own body, must be ranked under this name, NATURE. In enumerating the values of nature and casting up their sum, I shall use the word in both senses;—in its common and in its philosophical import. In inquiries so general as our present one, the inaccuracy is not material; no confusion of thought will occur. *Nature*, in the common sense, refers to essences unchanged by man; space, the air, the river, the leaf. *Art* is applied to the mixture of his will with the same

---

[2]WHY SHOULD WE GROPE AMONG THE DRY BONES OF THE PAST: Emerson alludes to Ezekiel 37, "The hand of the LORD was upon me, and carried me out in the spirit of the LORD, and set me down in the midst of the valley which was full of bones" (37:1).
[3]NOT ME: From Scottish intellectual historian and essayist Thomas Carlyle's (1795–1881) *Sartor Resartus* (1833–1834), where it appears as a translation of the German philosophical term "*nicht-Ich,*" meaning everything but the self.

things, as in a house, a canal, a statue, a picture. But his operations taken together are so insignificant, a little chipping, baking, patching, and washing, that in an impression so grand as that of the world on the human mind, they do not vary the result.

CHAPTER I. NATURE

To go into solitude, a man needs to retire as much from his chamber as from society. I am not solitary whilst I read and write, though nobody is with me. But if a man would be alone, let him look at the stars. The rays that come from those heavenly worlds, will separate between him and vulgar things. One might think the atmosphere was made transparent with this design, to give man, in the heavenly bodies, the perpetual presence of the sublime. Seen in the streets of cities, how great they are! If the stars should appear one night in a thousand years, how would men believe and adore; and preserve for many generations the remembrance of the city of God which had been shown! But every night come out these preachers of beauty, and light the universe with their admonishing smile.

The stars awaken a certain reverence, because though always present, they are always inaccessible; but all natural objects make a kindred impression, when the mind is open to their influence. Nature never wears a mean appearance. Neither does the wisest man extort all her secret, and lose his curiosity by finding out all her perfection. Nature never became a toy to a wise spirit. The flowers, the animals, the mountains, reflected all the wisdom of his best hour, as much as they had delighted the simplicity of his childhood.

When we speak of nature in this manner, we have a distinct but most poetical sense in the mind. We mean the integrity of impression made by manifold natural objects. It is this which distinguishes the stick of timber of the wood-cutter, from the tree of the poet. The charming landscape which I saw this morning, is indubitably made up of some twenty or thirty farms. Miller owns this field, Locke that, and Manning the woodland beyond. But none of them owns the landscape. There is a property in the horizon which no man has but he whose eye can integrate all the parts, that is, the poet. This is the best part of these men's farms, yet to this their land-deeds give them no title.

To speak truly, few adult persons can see nature. Most persons do not see the sun. At least they have a very superficial seeing. The sun illuminates only the eye of the man, but shines into the eye and the heart of the child. The lover of nature is he whose inward and outward

senses are still truly adjusted to each other; who has retained the spirit of
infancy even into the era of manhood. His intercourse with heaven and
earth, becomes part of his daily food. In the presence of nature, a wild
delight runs through the man, in spite of real sorrows. Nature says,—
he is my creature, and maugre[4] all his impertinent griefs, he shall be glad
with me. Not the sun or the summer alone, but every hour and season
yields its tribute of delight; for every hour and change corresponds to and
authorizes a different state of the mind, from breathless noon to grimmest
midnight. Nature is a setting that fits equally well a comic or a mourning piece. In good health, the air is a cordial of incredible virtue. Crossing
a bare common, in snow puddles, at twilight, under a clouded sky, without having in my thoughts any occurrence of special good fortune, I have
enjoyed a perfect exhilaration. Almost I fear to think how glad I am. In
the woods too, a man casts off his years, as the snake his slough, and
at what period soever of life, is always a child. In the woods, is perpetual youth. Within these plantations of God, a decorum and sanctity reign,
a perennial festival is dressed, and the guest sees not how he should tire
of them in a thousand years. In the woods, we return to reason and
faith. There I feel that nothing can befal me in life,—no disgrace, no
calamity, (leaving me my eyes,) which nature cannot repair. Standing
on the bare ground,—my head bathed by the blithe air, and uplifted
into infinite space,—all mean egotism vanishes. I become a transparent
eye-ball.[5] I am nothing. I see all. The currents of the Universal Being
circulate through me; I am part or particle of God. The name of the nearest friend sounds then foreign and accidental. To be brothers, to be
acquaintances,—master or servant, is then a trifle and a disturbance. I
am the lover of uncontained and immortal beauty. In the wilderness, I
find something more dear and connate[6] than in streets or villages. In
the tranquil landscape, and especially in the distant line of the horizon,
man beholds somewhat as beautiful as his own nature.

The greatest delight which the fields and woods minister, is the suggestion of an occult relation between man and the vegetable. I am not alone
and unacknowledged. They nod to me and I to them. The waving of the
boughs in the storm, is new to me and old. It takes me by surprise, and
yet is not unknown. Its effect is like that of a higher thought or a better emotion coming over me, when I deemed I was thinking justly or doing right.

[4]MAUGRE: In spite of.
[5]I BECOME A TRANSPARENT EYEBALL: This statement is considered one of the most famous
phrases in the essay, often quoted as a foundation principle of transcendentalism.
[6]CONNATE: Inborn, an innate connection.

Yet it is certain that the power to produce this delight, does not reside in nature, but in man, or in a harmony of both. It is necessary to use these pleasures with great temperance. For, nature is not always tricked in holiday attire, but the same scene which yesterday breathed perfume and glittered as for the frolic of the nymphs, is overspread with melancholy today. Nature always wears the colors of the spirit. To a man laboring under calamity, the heat of his own fire hath sadness in it. Then, there is a kind of contempt of the landscape felt by him who has just lost by death a dear friend. The sky is less grand as it shuts down over less worth in the population.

CHAPTER II. COMMODITY[7]

Whoever considers the final cause[8] of the world, will discern a multitude of uses that enter as parts into that result. They all admit of being thrown into one of the following classes; Commodity; Beauty; Language; and Discipline.

Under the general name of Commodity, I rank all those advantages which our senses owe to nature. This, of course, is a benefit which is temporary and mediate, not ultimate, like its service to the soul. Yet although low, it is perfect in its kind, and is the only use of nature which all men apprehend. The misery of man appears like childish petulance, when we explore the steady and prodigal provision that has been made for his support and delight on this green ball which floats him through the heavens. What angels invented these splendid ornaments, these rich conveniences, this ocean of air above, this ocean of water beneath, this firmament of earth between? this zodiac of lights, this tent of dropping clouds, this striped coat of climates, this fourfold year? Beasts, fire, water, stones, and corn serve him. The field is at once his floor, his work-yard, his play-ground, his garden, and his bed.

"More servants wait on man
    Than he'll take notice of."——[9]

Nature, in its ministry to man, is not only the material, but is also the process and the result. All the parts incessantly work into each other's hands for the profit of man. The wind sows the seed; the sun evaporates

[7]COMMODITY: Usefulness.
[8]FINAL CAUSE: Purpose.
[9]MORE SERVANTS WAIT ON MAN/THAN HE'LL TAKE NOTICE OF: From English metaphysical poet George Herbert's (1593–1633) work, "Man."

the sea; the wind blows the vapor to the field; the ice, on the other side of the planet, condenses rain on this; the rain feeds the plant; the plant feeds the animal; and thus the endless circulations of the divine charity nourish man.

The useful arts are but reproductions or new combinations by the wit of man, of the same natural benefactors. He no longer waits for favoring gales, but by means of steam, he realizes the fable of Æolus's bag,[10] and carries the two and thirty winds in the boiler of his boat. To diminish friction, he paves the road with iron bars, and, mounting a coach with a ship-load of men, animals, and merchandise behind him, he darts through the country, from town to town, like an eagle or a swallow through the air. By the aggregate of these aids, how is the face of the world changed, from the era of Noah to that of Napoleon! The private poor man hath cities, ships, canals, bridges, built for him. He goes to the post-office, and the human race run on his errands; to the book-shop, and the human race read and write of all that happens, for him; to the court-house, and nations repair his wrongs. He sets his house upon the road, and the human race go forth every morning, and shovel out the snow, and cut a path for him.

But there is no need of specifying particulars in this class of uses. The catalogue is endless, and the examples so obvious, that I shall leave them to the reader's reflection, with the general remark, that this mercenary benefit is one which has respect to a farther good. A man is fed, not that he may be fed, but that he may work.

CHAPTER III. BEAUTY

A nobler want of man is served by nature, namely, the love of Beauty.

The ancient Greeks called the world κόσμος[11] beauty. Such is the constitution of all things, or such the plastic[12] power of the human eye, that the primary forms, as the sky, the mountain, the tree, the animal, give us a delight *in and for themselves*; a pleasure arising from outline, color, motion, and grouping. This seems partly owing to the eye itself. The eye is the best of artists. By the mutual action of its structure and of the laws of light, perspective is produced, which integrates every mass of objects,

---

[10]THE FABLE OF THE ÆOLUS'S BAG: Æolus, was the Greek god of the wind. In Homer's *The Odyssey*, Aeolus gave Odysseus a bag containing favorable winds for his sea voyage, but the crew opened the bag and accidentally released all of the winds at once, causing a terrible storm.
[11]κόσμος: Cosmos. (Greek)
[12]PLASTIC: Creative.

of what character soever, into a well colored and shaded globe, so that where the particular objects are mean and unaffecting, the landscape which they compose, is round and symmetrical. And as the eye is the best composer, so light is the first of painters. There is no object so foul that intense light will not make beautiful. And the stimulus it affords to the sense, and a sort of infinitude which it hath, like space and time, make all matter gay. Even the corpse hath its own beauty. But beside this general grace diffused over nature, almost all the individual forms are agreeable to the eye, as is proved by our endless imitations[13] of some of them, as the acorn, the grape, the pine-cone, the wheat-ear, the egg, the wings and forms of most birds, the lion's claw, the serpent, the butterfly, sea-shells, flames, clouds, buds, leaves, and the forms of many trees, as the palm.

For better consideration, we may distribute the aspects of Beauty in a threefold manner.

1. First, the simple perception of natural forms is a delight. The influence of the forms and actions in nature, is so needful to man, that, in its lowest functions, it seems to lie on the confines of commodity and beauty. To the body and mind which have been cramped by noxious work or company, nature is medicinal and restores their tone. The tradesman, the attorney comes out of the din and craft[14] of the street, and sees the sky and the woods, and is a man again. In their eternal calm, he finds himself. The health of the eye seems to demand a horizon. We are never tired, so long as we can see far enough.

But in other hours, Nature satisfies the soul purely by its loveliness, and without any mixture of corporeal benefit. I have seen the spectacle of morning from the hill-top over against my house, from day-break to sun-rise, with emotions which an angel might share. The long slender bars of cloud float like fishes in the sea of crimson light. From the earth, as a shore, I look out into that silent sea. I seem to partake its rapid transformations: the active enchantment reaches my dust, and I dilate and conspire with[15] the morning wind. How does Nature deify us with a few and cheap elements! Give me health and a day, and I will make the pomp of emperors ridiculous. The dawn is my Assyria;[16] the sun-set and moon-rise my Paphos,[17] and unimaginable realms of faerie, broad noon shall

---

[13]IMITATIONS: Emerson refers to the reproduction of natural forms in architecture and furniture design.
[14]CRAFT: Materialism.
[15]DILATE AND CONSPIRE WITH: Expand and breathe with.
[16]ASSYRIA: An ancient empire in western Asia.
[17]PAPHOS: An ancient city that served as the capital of Cyprus from the middle of the Hellenistic period until the time of the Emperor Constantine in the third century CE.

be my England of the senses and the understanding; the night shall be
my Germany of mystic philosophy and dreams.[18]

Not less excellent, except for our less susceptibility in the afternoon,
was the charm, last evening, of a January sunset. The western clouds
divided and subdivided themselves into pink flakes modulated with tints
of unspeakable softness; and the air had so much life and sweetness, that
it was a pain to come within doors. What was it that nature would say?
Was there no meaning in the live repose of the valley behind the mill,
and which Homer or Shakspeare could not re-form for me in words? The
leafless trees become spires of flame in the sunset, with the blue east
for their background, and the stars of the dead calices[19] of flowers, and
every withered stem and stubble rimed[20] with frost, contribute something to the mute music.

The inhabitants of cities suppose that the country landscape is pleasant only half the year. I please myself with observing the graces of the
winter scenery, and believe that we are as much touched by it as by the
genial[21] influences of summer. To the attentive eye, each moment of the
year has its own beauty, and in the same field, it beholds, every hour, a
picture which was never seen before, and which shall never be seen again.
The heavens change every moment, and reflect their glory or gloom on
the plains beneath. The state of the crop in the surrounding farms alters
the expression of the earth from week to week. The succession of native
plants in the pastures and roadsides, which make the silent clock by
which time tells the summer hours, will make even the divisions of the
day sensible to a keen observer. The tribes of birds and insects, like the
plants punctual to their time, follow each other, and the year has room
for all. By water-courses, the variety is greater. In July, the blue pont-
ederia or pickerel-weed blooms in large beds in the shallow parts of our
pleasant river,[22] and swarms with yellow butterflies in continual motion.
Art cannot rival this pomp of purple and gold. Indeed the river is a perpetual gala, and boasts each month a new ornament.

But this beauty of Nature which is seen and felt as beauty, is the least
part. The shows of day, the dewy morning, the rainbow, mountains,
orchards in blossom, stars, moonlight, shadows in still water, and the
like, if too eagerly hunted, become shows merely, and mock us with their

---

[18]GERMANY OF MYSTIC PHILOSOPHY AND DREAMS: Emerson contrasts the English doctrine of
common sense (utilitarianism), with German philosophical principles of post-Kant idealism.
[19]CALICES: Calyxes, the outer leaves that encase the bud of a flower.
[20]RIMED: Frost coated.
[21]GENIAL: Generative.
[22]OUR PLEASANT RIVER: The Concord River, in Massachusetts.

unreality. Go out of the house to see the moon, and 't is mere tinsel; it will not please as when its light shines upon your necessary journey. The beauty that shimmers in the yellow afternoons of October, who ever could clutch it? Go forth to find it, and it is gone: 't is only a mirage as you look from the windows of the diligence.

2. The presence of a higher, namely, of the spiritual element is essential to its perfection. The high and divine beauty which can be loved without effeminacy, is that which is found in combination with the human will, and never separate. Beauty is the mark God sets upon virtue. Every natural action is graceful. Every heroic act is also decent,[23] and causes the place and the bystanders to shine. We are taught by great actions that the universe is the property of every individual in it. Every rational creature has all nature for his dowry and estate. It is his, if he will. He may divest himself of it; he may creep into a corner, and abdicate his kingdom, as most men do, but he is entitled to the world by his constitution. In proportion to the energy of his thought and will, he takes up the world into himself. "All those things for which men plough, build, or sail, obey virtue;[24] said an ancient historian. "The winds and waves," said Gibbon,[25] "are always on the side of the ablest navigators." So are the sun and moon and all the stars of heaven. When a noble act is done,— perchance in a scene of great natural beauty; when Leonidas[26] and his three hundred martyrs consume one day in dying, and the sun and moon come each and look at them once in the steep defile of Thermopylæ; when Arnold Winkelried,[27] in the high Alps, under the shadow of the avalanche, gathers in his side a sheaf of Austrian spears to break the line for his comrades; are not these heroes entitled to add the beauty of the scene to the beauty of the deed? When the bark of Columbus[28] nears the shore of America;—before it, the beach lined with savages, fleeing out of all their huts of cane; the sea behind; and the purple mountains of the Indian Archipelago around, can we separate the man from the living picture?

[23]DECENT: Beautiful.
[24]ALL THOSE THINGS FOR WHICH MEN PLOUGH, BUILD, OR SAIL, OBEY VIRTUE: From *Bellum Catilinae* (*The Conspiracy of Catiline*) by the Roman historian, Sallust (Caius Sallustius Crispus) (86 BCE–c.34 BCE).
[25]GIBBON: Historian Edward Gibbon (1737–1794), author of *The History of the Decline and Fall of the Roman Empire* (6 vols., 1776–1788).
[26]LEONIDAS: Leonidas (d. 480 BCE) became king of Sparta around 491 BCE. When the Persians invaded Greece under Xerxes, Leonidas, with 300 Spartans soldiers, tried to defend the pass at Thermopylae. Although they were certain of defeat, the Spartans refused to flee and were all killed by the Persians.
[27]ARNOLD WINKELRIED: Arnold Winkelried was a Swiss hero who died in 1386 while defending the Swiss from an Austrian invasion at the battle of Sempach.
[28]COLUMBUS: Christopher Columbus (1451–1506).

Does not the New World clothe his form with her palm-groves and savannahs as fit drapery? Ever does natural beauty steal in like air, and envelope great actions. When Sir Harry Vane[29] was dragged up the Tower-hill, sitting on a sled, to suffer death, as the champion of the English laws, one of the multitude cried out to him, "You never sate on so glorious a seat." Charles II.,[30] to intimidate the citizens of London, caused the patriot Lord Russel[31] to be drawn in an open coach, through the principal streets of the city, on his way to the scaffold. "But," to use the simple narrative of his biographer, "the multitude imagined they saw liberty and virtue sitting by his side." In private places, among sordid objects, an act of truth or heroism seems at once to draw to itself the sky as its temple, the sun as its candle. Nature stretcheth out her arms to embrace man, only let his thoughts be of equal greatness. Willingly does she follow his steps with the rose and the violet, and bend her lines of grandeur and grace to the decoration of her darling child. Only let his thoughts be of equal scope, and the frame will suit the picture. A virtuous man, is in unison with her works, and makes the central figure of the visible sphere. Homer, Pindar, Socrates, Phocion,[32] associate themselves fitly in our memory with the whole geography and climate of Greece. The visible heavens and earth sympathize with Jesus. And in common life, whosoever has seen a person of powerful character and happy genius, will have remarked how easily he took all things along with him,—the persons, the opinions, and the day, and nature became ancillary to a man.

3. There is still another aspect under which the beauty of the world may be viewed, namely, as it becomes an object of the intellect. Beside the relation of things to virtue, they have a relation to thought. The intellect searches out the absolute order of things as they stand in the mind of God, and without the colors of affection.[33] The intellectual and the active powers seem to succeed each other in man, and the exclusive activity of the one, generates the exclusive activity of the other. There is something unfriendly in each to the other, but they are

---

[29]HARRY VANE: Sir Harry Vane (1613–1662) was colonial governor of Massachusetts in 1636. He returned to England in 1637 and was active in politics. At the Restoration in 1660, he was arrested and executed for treason by order of Charles II.

[30]CHARLES II: Charles II (1630–1685), King of England.

[31]LORD RUSSEL: Lord William Russell (1639–1683), an English statesman who was executed for conspiracy to assassinate Charles II and his brother James, duke of York (later James II).

[32]HOMER, PINDAR, SOCRATES, PHOCION: Homer (c. 850 BCE), is considered the author of the epic poems the *Iliad* and the *Odyssey*; Pindar (518?–c.438 BCE) was a Greek lyric poet; Socrates (469–399 BCE) was a Greek philosopher; and Phocion (c.402–318 BCE) was a Greek statesman and Athenian general.

[33]COLORS OF AFFECTION: Influence of emotions.

like the alternate periods of feeding and working in animals; each prepares and certainly will be followed by the other. Therefore does beauty, which, in relation to actions, as we have seen comes unsought, and comes because it is unsought, remain for the apprehension and pursuit of the intellect; and then again, in its turn, of the active power. Nothing divine dies. All good is eternally reproductive. The beauty of nature reforms itself in the mind, and not for barren contemplation, but for new creation.

All men are in some degree impressed by the face of the world. Some men even to delight. This love of beauty is Taste. Others have the same love in such excess, that, not content with admiring, they seek to embody it in new forms. The creation of beauty is Art.

The production of a work of art throws a light upon the mystery of humanity. A work of art is an abstract or epitome of the world. It is the result or expression of nature, in miniature. For although the works of nature are innumerable and all different, the result or the expression of them all is similar and single. Nature is a sea of forms radically alike and even unique. A leaf, a sun-beam, a landscape, the ocean, make an analogous impression on the mind. What is common to them all,—that perfectness and harmony, is beauty. Therefore the standard of beauty, is the entire circuit of natural forms,—the totality of nature; which the Italians expressed by defining beauty "il piu nell' uno."[34] Nothing is quite beautiful alone: nothing but is beautiful in the whole. A single object is only so far beautiful as it suggests this universal grace. The poet, the painter, the sculptor, the musician, the architect seek each to concentrate this radiance of the world on one point, and each in his several work to satisfy the love of beauty which stimulates him to produce. Thus is Art, a nature passed through the alembic[35] of man. Thus in art, does nature work through the will of a man filled with the beauty of her first works.

The world thus exists to the soul to satisfy the desire of beauty. Extend this element to the uttermost, and I call it an ultimate end. No reason can be asked or given why the soul seeks beauty. Beauty, in its largest and profoundest sense, is one expression for the universe. God is the all-fair. Truth, and goodness, and beauty, are but different faces of the same All. But beauty in nature is not ultimate. It is the herald of inward and eternal beauty, and is not alone a solid and satisfactory good. It must therefore stand as a part and not as yet the last or highest expression of the final cause of Nature.

[34]IL PIU NELL' UNO: "The many in one." (Italian)
[35]ALEMBIC: An apparatus used in distilling.

CHAPTER IV. LANGUAGE

A third use which Nature subserves to man is that of Language. Nature is the vehicle of thought, and in a simple, double, and threefold degree.

1. Words are signs of natural facts.
2. Particular natural facts are symbols of particular spiritual facts.
3. Nature is the symbol of spirit.

1. Words are signs of natural facts. The use of natural history is to give us aid in supernatural history. The use of the outer creation is to give us language for the beings and changes of the inward creation. Every word which is used to express a moral or intellectual fact, if traced to its root, is found to be borrowed from some material appearance. *Right* originally means *straight; wrong* means *twisted. Spirit* primarily means *wind; transgression*, the crossing of a *line; supercilious*, the *raising of the eye-brow.* We say the *heart* to express emotion, the *head* to denote thought; and *thought* and *emotion* are, in their turn, words borrowed from sensible things, and now appropriated to spiritual nature. Most of the process by which this transformation is made, is hidden from us in the remote time when language was framed; but the same tendency may be daily observed in children. Children and savages use only nouns or names of things, which they continually convert into verbs, and apply to analogous mental acts.

2. But this origin of all words that convey a spiritual import,—so conspicuous a fact in the history of language,—is our least debt to nature. It is not words only that are emblematic; it is things which are emblematic. Every natural fact is a symbol of some spiritual fact.[36] Every appearance in nature corresponds to some state of the mind, and that state of the mind can only be described by presenting that natural appearance as its picture. An enraged man is a lion, a cunning man is a fox, a firm man is a rock, a learned man is a torch. A lamb is innocence; a snake is subtle spite; flowers express to us the delicate affections. Light and darkness are our familiar expression for knowledge and ignorance; and heat for love. Visible distance behind and before us, is respectively our image of memory and hope.

Who looks upon a river in a meditative hour, and is not reminded of the flux of all things? Throw a stone into the stream, and the circles

[36]SYMBOL OF SOME SPIRITUAL FACT: Emerson drew much of this section from the ideas of Swedish scientist and mystic Emanuel Swedenborg (1668–1772), whom Emerson admired greatly.

that propagate themselves are the beautiful type of all influence. Man is conscious of a universal soul within or behind his individual life, wherein, as in a firmament, the natures of Justice, Truth, Love, Freedom, arise and shine. This universal soul, he calls Reason: it is not mine or thine or his, but we are its; we are its property and men. And the blue sky in which the private earth is buried, the sky with its eternal calm, and full of everlasting orbs, is the type of Reason. That which, intellectually considered, we call Reason, considered in relation to nature, we call Spirit. Spirit is the Creator. Spirit hath life in itself. And man in all ages and countries, embodies it in his language, as the FATHER.

It is easily seen that there is nothing lucky or capricious in these analogies, but that they are constant, and pervade nature. These are not the dreams of a few poets, here and there, but man is an analogist, and studies relations in all objects. He is placed in the centre of beings, and a ray of relation passes from every other being to him. And neither can man be understood without these objects, nor these objects without man. All the facts in natural history taken by themselves, have no value, but are barren like a single sex. But marry it to human history, and it is full of life. Whole Floras, all Linnæus' and Buffon's volume[37], are but dry catalogues of facts; but the most trivial of these facts, the habit of a plant, the organs, or work, or noise of an insect, applied to the illustration of a fact in intellectual philosophy, or, in any way associated to human nature, affects us in the most lively and agreeable manner. The seed of a plant,—to what affecting analogies in the nature of man, is that little fruit made use of, in all discourse, up to the voice of Paul, who calls the human corpse a seed,—"It is sown a natural body; it is raised a spiritual body."[38] The motion of the earth round its axis, and round the sun, makes the day, and the year. These are certain amounts of brute light and heat. But is there no intent of an analogy between man's life and the seasons? And do the seasons gain no grandeur or pathos from that analogy? The instincts of the ant are very unimportant considered as the ant's; but the moment a ray of relation is seen to extend from it to man, and the little drudge is seen to be a monitor, a little body with a mighty heart, then all its habits, even that said to be recently observed, that it never sleeps, become sublime.

---

[37]ALL LINNAEUS' AND BUFFON'S VOLUME: Carolus Linnaeus (1707–1778), Swedish botanist and taxonomist considered the originator of the modern scientific classification of plants and animals. Georges Louis Leclerc Buffon (1707–88), French naturalist.
[38]IT IS SOWN A NATURAL BODY; IT IS RAISED A SPIRITUAL BODY: 1 Corinthians 15:44: "It is sown a natural body; it is raised a spiritual body. There is a natural body, and there is a spiritual body."

Because of this radical correspondence[39] between visible things and human thoughts, savages, who have only what is necessary, converse in figures. As we go back in history, language becomes more picturesque, until its infancy, when it is all poetry;[40] or, all spiritual facts are represented by natural symbols. The same symbols are found to make the original elements of all languages. It has moreover been observed, that the idioms of all languages approach each other in passages of the greatest eloquence and power. And as this is the first language, so is it the last. This immediate dependence of language upon nature, this conversion of an outward phenomenon into a type of somewhat in human life, never loses its power to affect us. It is this which gives that piquancy to the conversation of a strong-natured farmer or backwoodsman, which all men relish.

Thus is nature an interpreter, by whose means man converses with his fellow men. A man's power to connect his thought with its proper symbol, and so utter it, depends on the simplicity of his character, that is, upon his love of truth and his desire to communicate it without loss. The corruption of man is followed by the corruption of language. When simplicity of character and the sovereignty of ideas is broken up by the prevalence of secondary desires, the desire of riches, the desire of pleasure, the desire of power, the desire of praise,—and duplicity and falsehood take place of simplicity and truth, the power over nature as an interpreter of the will, is in a degree lost; new imagery ceases to be created, and old words are perverted to stand for things which are not; a paper currency is employed when there is no bullion in the vaults. In due time, the fraud is manifest, and words lose all power to stimulate the understanding or the affections. Hundreds of writers may be found in every long-civilized nation, who for a short time believe, and make others believe, that they see and utter truths, who do not of themselves clothe one thought in its natural garment, but who feed unconsciously upon the language created by the primary writers of the country, those, namely, who hold primarily on nature.

But wise men pierce this rotten diction and fasten words again to visible things; so that picturesque language is at once a commanding certificate that he who employs it, is a man in alliance with truth and God. The moment our discourse rises above the ground line of familiar facts, and is inflamed with passion or exalted by thought, it clothes itself in images. A man conversing in earnest, if he watch his intellectual processes, will find that always a material image, more or less luminous,

---

[39]RADICAL CORRESPONDENCE: Inherent, a fundamental connection.
[40]UNTIL ITS INFANCY, WHEN IT IS ALL POETRY: From Percy Bysshe Shelley's (1792–1822) "A Defense of Poetry" (1821), "In the infancy of society every author is necessarily a poet."

arises in his mind, contemporaneous with every thought, which furnishes the vestment of the thought. Hence, good writing and brilliant discourse are perpetual allegories. This imagery is spontaneous. It is the blending of experience with the present action of the mind. It is proper creation. It is the working of the Original Cause through the instruments he has already made.

These facts may suggest the advantage which the country-life possesses for a powerful mind, over the artificial and curtailed life of cities. We know more from nature than we can at will communicate. Its light flows into the mind evermore, and we forget its presence. The poet, the orator, bred in the woods, whose scenes have been nourished by their fair and appeasing changes, year after year, without design and without heed,—shall not lose their lesson altogether, in the roar of cities or the broil of politics. Long hereafter, amidst agitation and terror in national councils,—in the hour of revolution,—these solemn images shall reappear in their morning lustre, as fit symbols and words of the thoughts which the passing events shall awaken. At the call of a noble sentiment, again the woods wave, the pines murmur, the river rolls and shines, and the cattle low upon the mountains, as he saw and heard them in his infancy. And with these forms, the spells of persuasion, the keys of power are put into his hands.

3. We are thus assisted by natural objects in the expression of particular meanings. But how great a language to convey such pepper-corn informations! Did it need such noble races of creatures, this profusion of forms, this host of orbs in heaven, to furnish man with the dictionary and grammar of his municipal speech? Whilst we use this grand cipher to expedite the affairs of our pot and kettle, we feel that we have not yet put it to its use, neither are able. We are like travellers using the cinders of a volcano to roast their eggs. Whilst we see that it always stands ready to clothe what we would say, we cannot avoid the question, whether the characters are not significant of themselves. Have mountains, and waves, and skies, no significance but what we consciously give them, when we employ them as emblems of our thoughts? The world is emblematic. Parts of speech are metaphors because the whole of nature is a metaphor of the human mind. The laws of moral nature answer to those of matter as face to face in a glass. "The visible world and the relation of its parts, is the dial plate of the invisible."[41] The axioms of physics translate the laws of ethics.[42] Thus, "the whole is greater than

[41]THE VISIBLE WORLD AND THE RELATION OF ITS PARTS, IS THE DIAL PLATE OF THE INVISIBLE: Emerson quotes Emanuel Swedenborg in the *New Jerusalem Magazine* (July 1832).
[42]THE AXIOMS OF PHYSICS TRANSLATE THE LAWS OF ETHICS: Adapted from French-Swiss writer Germaine de Staël's (1766–1817) *De l'Allemagne* (1810).

its part;" "reaction is equal to action;" "the smallest weight may be made to lift the greatest, the difference of weight being compensated by time;" and many the like propositions, which have an ethical as well as physical sense. These propositions have a much more extensive and universal sense when applied to human life, than when confined to technical use.

In like manner, the memorable words of history, and the proverbs of nations, consist usually of a natural fact, selected as a picture or parable of a moral truth. Thus; A rolling stone gathers no moss; A bird in the hand is worth two in the bush; A cripple in the right way, will beat a racer in the wrong; Make hay whilst the sun shines; 'T is hard to carry a full cup even; Vinegar is the son of wine; The last ounce broke the camel's back; Long-lived trees make roots first;—and the like. In their primary sense these are trivial facts, but we repeat them for the value of their analogical import. What is true of proverbs, is true of all fables, parables, and allegories.

This relation between the mind and matter is not fancied by some poet, but stands in the will of God, and so is free to be known by all men. It appears to men, or it does not appear. When in fortunate hours we ponder this miracle, the wise man doubts, if, at all other times, he is not blind and deaf;

> ———"Can these things be,
> And overcome us like a summer's cloud,
> Without our special wonder?"[43]

for the universe becomes transparent, and the light of higher laws than its own, shines through it. It is the standing problem which has exercised the wonder and the study of every fine genius since the world began; from the era of the Egyptians[44] and the Brahmins,[45] to that of Pythagoras,[46] of Plato,[47] of Bacon,[48] of Leibnitz, [49] of Swedenborg.[50] There sits the Sphinx at the road-side,[51] and from age to age, as each

---

[43]CAN THESE THINGS BE...WITHOUT OUR SPECIAL WONDER?: Slightly misquoted from Shakespeare's *Macbeth*, Act 3, Scene 4, lines 110–12. The passage should begin "Can *such* things be..."
[44]EGYPTIANS: Ancient Egypt.
[45]BRAHMINS: Ancient Hindus.
[46]PYTHAGORAS: Philosopher (582–c. 507 BCE) from ancient Greece.
[47]PLATO: Philosopher (427?–347 BCE) from ancient Greece.
[48]BACON: Francis Bacon (1561–1626), English philosopher and statesman.
[49]LEIBNITZ: Gottfried Wilhelm Leibniz (1646–1716), German philosopher.
[50]SWEDENBORG: Emanuel Swedenborg (1668-1772), Swedish scientist, religious teacher, and theologian. His religious system formed the foundation for the Church of the New Jerusalem, founded after his death.
[51]SPHINX AT THE ROAD-SIDE: In Greek mythology, the sphinx was a winged creature with the body of a lion and the head of a woman. Perched upon a rock near the city of Thebes, she challenged travelers with a riddle that they must answer correctly or die: What has four legs in the morning, two legs in the afternoon, and three legs in the evening? It remained unsolved until Oedipus gave the correct answer—man—whereupon the Sphinx killed herself.

prophet comes by, he tries his fortune at reading her riddle. There seems to be a necessity in spirit to manifest itself in material forms; and day and night, river and storm, beast and bird, acid and alkali, preëxist in necessary Ideas in the mind of God, and are what they are by virtue of preceding affections,[52] in the world of spirit. A Fact is the end or last issue of spirit. The visible creation is the terminus or the circumference of the invisible world. "Material objects," said a French philosopher,[53] "are necessarily kinds of *scoriæ* of the substantial thoughts of the Creator, which must always preserve an exact relation to their first origin; in other words, visible nature must have a spiritual and moral side."

This doctrine is abstruse, and though the images of "garment," "scoriæ,"[54] "mirror," &c., may stimulate the fancy, we must summon the aid of subtler and more vital expositors to make it plain. "Every scripture is to be interpreted by the same spirit which gave it forth,"—is the fundamental law of criticism.[55] A life in harmony with nature, the love of truth and of virtue, will purge the eyes to understand her text. By degrees we may come to know the primitive sense of the permanent objects of nature, so that the world shall be to us an open book, and every form significant of its hidden life and final cause.

A new interest surprises us, whilst, under the view now suggested, we contemplate the fearful extent and multitude of objects; since "every object rightly seen, unlocks a new faculty of the soul."[56] That which was unconscious truth, becomes, when interpreted and defined in an object, a part of the domain of knowledge,—a new amount to the magazine[57] of power.

CHAPTER V. DISCIPLINE

In view of this significance of nature, we arrive at once at a new fact, that nature is a discipline. This use of the world includes the preceding uses, as parts of itself.

Space, time, society, labor, climate, food, locomotion, the animals, the mechanical forces, give us sincerest lessons, day by day, whose meaning

---

[52]PRECEDING AFFECTIONS: Modifying emotions.
[53]A FRENCH PHILOSOPHER: Guillaume Oegger (c. 1790–1853) was a French Catholic priest who became a follower of Swedenborg's New Church around 1826. Emerson quotes Oegger's *The True Messiah* (1829), in which Elizabeth Palmer Peabody began translating into English in 1835 and published in 1842.
[54]SCORIAE: Slag that remains after smelting metal from raw ore.
[55]IS THE FUNDAMENTAL LAW OF CRITICISM: Emerson quotes English Quaker George Fox (1624–1691).
[56]EVERY OBJECT RIGHTLY SEEN, UNLOCKS A NEW FACULTY OF THE SOUL: From English poet and writer Samuel Taylor Coleridge's (1772–1834) *Aids to Reflection* (1829).
[57]MAGAZINE: Storehouse.

is unlimited. They educate both the Understanding and the Reason. Every property of matter is a school for the understanding,—its solidity or resistance, its inertia, its extension, its figure, its divisibility. The understanding adds, divides, combines, measures, and finds everlasting nutriment and room for its activity in this worthy scene. Meantime, Reason transfers all these lessons into its own world of thought, by perceiving the analogy that marries Matter and Mind.

1. Nature is a discipline of the understanding in intellectual truths. Our dealing with sensible objects is a constant exercise in the necessary lessons of difference, of likeness, of order, of being and seeming, of progressive arrangement; of ascent from particular to general; of combination to one end of manifold forces. Proportioned to the importance of the organ to be formed, is the extreme care with which its tuition[58] is provided,—a care pretermitted[59] in no single case. What tedious training, day after day, year after year, never ending, to form the common sense; what continual reproduction of annoyances, inconveniences, dilemmas; what rejoicing over us of little men; what disputing of prices, what reckonings of interest,— and all to form the Hand of the mind;—to instruct us that "good thoughts are no better than good dreams, unless they be executed!"[60]

The same good office is performed by Property and its filial systems of debt and credit. Debt, grinding debt, whose iron face the widow, the orphan, and the sons of genius fear and hate;—debt, which consumes so much time, which so cripples and disheartens a great spirit with cares that seem so base, is a preceptor whose lessons cannot be foregone, and is needed most by those who suffer from it most. Moreover, property, which has been well compared to snow,—"if it fall level to-day, it will be blown into drifts tomorrow,"—is merely the surface action of internal machinery, like the index on the face of a clock. Whilst now it is the gymnastics of the understanding, it is hiving in the foresight of the spirit, experience in profounder laws.

The whole character and fortune of the individual is affected by the least inequalities in the culture of the understanding; for example, in the perception of differences. Therefore is Space, and therefore Time, that man may know that things are not huddled and lumped, but sundered and individual. A bell and a plough have each their use, and neither

---

[58]TUITION: Guardianship.
[59]PRETERMITTED: Overlooked.
[60]GOOD THOUGHTS ARE NO BETTER THAN GOOD DREAMS, UNLESS THEY BE EXE-CUTED!: Adapted from Frances Bacon's essay "Of Great Place." "For good thoughts (though God accept them) yet towards men are little better than good dreams, except they be put in act; and that cannot be without power and place, as the vantage and commanding ground."

can do the office of the other. Water is good to drink, coal to burn, wool to wear; but wool cannot be drunk, nor water spun, nor coal eaten. The wise man shows his wisdom in separation, in gradation, and his scale of creatures and of merits, is as wide as nature. The foolish have no range in their scale, but suppose every man is as every other man. What is not good they call the worst, and what is not hateful, they call the best.

In like manner, what good heed, nature forms in us! She pardons no mistakes. Her yea is yea, and her nay, nay.

The first steps in Agriculture, Astronomy, Zoölogy, (those first steps which the farmer, the hunter, and the sailor take,) teach that nature's dice are always loaded; that in her heaps and rubbish are concealed sure and useful results.

How calmly and genially the mind apprehends one after another the laws of physics! What noble emotions dilate the mortal as he enters into the counsels of the creation, and feels by knowledge the privilege to BE! His insight refines him. The beauty of nature shines in his own breast. Man is greater that he can see this, and the universe less, because Time and Space relations vanish as laws are known.

Here again we are impressed and even daunted by the immense Universe to be explored. 'What we know, is a point to what we do not know.'[61] Open any recent journal of science, and weigh the problems suggested concerning Light, Heat, Electricity, Magnetism, Physiology, Geology, and judge whether the interest of natural science is likely to be soon exhausted.

Passing by many particulars of the discipline of nature we must not omit to specify two.

The exercise of the Will or the lesson of power is taught in every event. From the child's successive possession of his several senses up to the hour when he saith, "thy will be done!"[62] he is learning the secret, that he can reduce under his will, not only particular events, but great classes, nay the whole series of events, and so conform all facts to his character. Nature is thoroughly mediate. It is made to serve. It receives the dominion of man as meekly as the ass on which the Saviour rode.[63] It offers all its kingdoms to man as the raw material which he may mould

[61]WHAT WE KNOW, IS A POINT TO WHAT WE DO NOT KNOW: A quote ascribed to both Isaac Newton (1642–1727), English scientist and mathematician best known for his laws of light and motion, and to English bishop Joseph Butler (1692–1752).
[62]THY WILL BE DONE!: From the Lord's Prayer, Matthew 6:10, "Thy kingdom come. Thy will be done on earth, as it is in heaven."
[63]ASS ON WHICH THE SAVIOUR RODE: When Jesus entered Jerusalem, he rode upon the back of an ass, as described in Matthew 21: "Tell ye the daughter of Sion, Behold, thy King cometh unto thee, meek, and sitting upon an ass, and a colt the foal of an ass" (21:5).

into what is useful. Man is never weary of working it up. He forges the subtile and delicate air into wise and melodious words, and gives them wing as angels of persuasion and command. More and more, with every thought, does his kingdom stretch over things, until the world becomes, at last, only a realized will,—the double of the man.

2. Sensible objects conform to the premonitions of Reason and reflect the conscience. All things are moral; and in their boundless changes have an unceasing reference to spiritual nature. Therefore is nature glorious with form, color, and motion, that every globe in the remotest heaven; every chemical change from the rudest crystal up to the laws of life; every change of vegetation from the first principle of growth in the eye of a leaf, to the tropical forest and antediluvian[64] coal-mine; every animal function from the sponge up to Hercules,[65] shall hint or thunder to man the laws of right and wrong, and echo the Ten Commandments. Therefore is nature always the ally of Religion: lends all her pomp and riches to the religious sentiment. Prophet and priest, David, Isaiah, Jesus,[66] have drawn deeply from this source.

This ethical character so penetrates the bone and marrow of nature, as to seem the end for which it was made. Whatever private purpose is answered by any member or part, this is its public and universal function, and is never omitted. Nothing in nature is exhausted in its first use. When a thing has served an end to the uttermost, it is wholly new for an ulterior service. In God, every end is converted into a new means. Thus the use of Commodity, regarded by itself, is mean and squalid. But it is to the mind an education in the great doctrine of Use, namely, that a thing is good only so far as it serves; that a conspiring of parts and efforts to the production of an end, is essential to any being. The first and gross manifestation of this truth, is our inevitable and hated training in values and wants, in corn and meat.

It has already been illustrated, in treating of the significance of material things, that every natural process is but a version of a moral sentence. The moral law lies at the centre of nature and radiates to the circumference. It is the pith and marrow of every substance, every relation, and every process. All things with which we deal, preach to us. What is a farm but a mute gospel? The chaff and the wheat, weeds and plants, blight, rain,

---

[64]ANTEDILUVIAN: The period before the Great Flood described in Genesis 6–9 that destroyed all living creatures not gathered into Noah's ark.
[65]HERCULES: The hero Hercules (the Roman equivalent of Heracles), known for his great strength and courage.
[66]DAVID, ISAIAH, JESUS: Figures from the Bible. David was King of ancient Israel around 970 BCE; Isaiah was a prophet around 742 BCE, whose prophecies are collected in the Biblical book that bears his name.

insects, sun,—it is a sacred emblem from the first furrow of spring to the last stack which the snow of winter overtakes in the fields. But the sailor, the shepherd, the miner, the merchant, in their several resorts, have each an experience precisely parallel and leading to the same conclusions. Because all organizations are radically alike. Nor can it be doubted that this moral sentiment which thus scents the air, and grows in the grain, and impregnates the waters of the world, is caught by man and sinks into his soul. The moral influence of nature upon every individual is that amount of truth which it illustrates to him. Who can estimate this? Who can guess how much firmness the sea-beaten rock has taught the fisherman? how much tranquillity has been reflected to man from the azure sky, over whose unspotted deeps the winds forevermore drive flocks of stormy clouds, and leave no wrinkle or stain? how much industry and providence and affection we have caught from the pantomime of brutes? What a searching preacher of self-command is the varying phenomenon of Health!

Herein is especially apprehended the Unity of Nature,—the Unity in Variety,—which meets us everywhere. All the endless variety of things make a unique, an identical impression. Xenophanes[67] complained in his old age, that, look where he would, all things hastened back to Unity. He was weary of seeing the same entity in the tedious variety of forms. The fable of Proteus has a cordial truth. Every particular in nature, a leaf, a drop, a crystal, a moment of time is related to the whole, and partakes of the perfection of the whole. Each particle is a microcosm, and faithfully renders the likeness of the world.

Not only resemblances exist in things whose analogy is obvious, as when we detect the type of the human hand in the flipper of the fossil saurus, but also in objects wherein there is great superficial unlikeness. Thus architecture is called 'frozen music,' by De Stael and Goethe.[68] 'A Gothic church,' said Coleridge,[69] 'is a petrified religion.' Michael Angelo[70] maintained, that, to an architect, a knowledge of anatomy is essential. In Haydn's[71] oratorios, the notes present to the imagination not only motions, as, of the snake, the stag, and the elephant, but colors also; as the green grass. The granite is differenced in its laws only by the more or less of heat, from the river that wears it away. The river, as it flows,

---

[67]XENOPHANES: Pre-Socratic Greek philosopher (570–c.480 BCE) who taught the unity of all existence.
[68]DE STAEL AND GOETHE: Germaine de Staël (1766–1817) in *Corinne*; and Johann Wolfgang von Goethe (1749–1832) in *Conversations with Eckermann*.
[69]COLERIDGE: From "*Lecture on the General Character of the Gothic Mind in the Middle Ages*" (1836).
[70]MICHAEL ANGELO: Italian sculptor, painter and architect Michelangelo Buonarroti (1475–1564).
[71]HAYDN: Austrian composer Franz Joseph Haydn (1732–1809).

resembles the air that flows over it; the air resembles the light which traverses it with more subtile currents; the light resembles the heat which rides with it through Space. Each creature is only a modification of the other; the likeness in them is more than the difference, and their radical law is one and the same. Hence it is, that a rule of one art, or a law of one organization, holds true throughout nature. So intimate is this Unity, that, it is easily seen, it lies under the undermost garment of nature, and betrays its source in universal Spirit. For, it pervades Thought also. Every universal truth which we express in words, implies or supposes every other truth. *Omne verum vero consonat.*[72] It is like a great circle on a sphere, comprising all possible circles; which, however, may be drawn, and comprise it, in like manner. Every such truth is the absolute Ens[73] seen from one side. But it has innumerable sides.

The same central Unity is still more conspicuous in actions. Words are finite organs of the infinite mind. They cannot cover the dimensions of what is in truth. They break, chop, and impoverish it. An action is the perfection and publication of thought. A right action seems to fill the eye, and to be related to all nature. "The wise man, in doing one thing, does all; or, in the one thing he does rightly, he sees the likeness of all which is done rightly."

Words and actions are not the attributes of mute and brute nature. They introduce us to that singular form which predominates over all other forms. This is the human. All other organizations appear to be degradations of the human form. When this organization appears among so many that surround it, the spirit prefers it to all others. It says, 'From such as this, have I drawn joy and knowledge. In such as this, have I found and beheld myself. I will speak to it. It can speak again. It can yield me thought already formed and alive.' In fact, the eye,—the mind,—is always accompanied by these forms, male and female; and these are incomparably the richest informations[74] of the power and order that lie at the heart of things. Unfortunately, every one of them bears the marks as of some injury; is marred and superficially defective. Nevertheless, far different from the deaf and dumb nature around them, these all rest like fountain-pipes on the unfathomed sea of thought and virtue whereto they alone, of all organizations, are the entrances.

It were a pleasant inquiry to follow into detail their ministry to our education, but where would it stop? We are associated in

---

[72]OMNE VERUM VERO CONSONAT: "Every truth agrees with every other truth." (Latin)
[73]ENS: Abstract entity.
[74]INFORMATIONS: The giving of a form or character to something.

adolescent and adult life with some friends, who, like skies and waters, are coextensive with our idea; who, answering each to a certain affection of the soul, satisfy our desire on that side; whom we lack power to put at such focal distance from us, that we can mend or even analyze them. We cannot chuse but love them. When much intercourse with a friend has supplied us with a standard of excellence, and has increased our respect for the resources of God who thus sends a real person to outgo our ideal; when he has, moreover, become an object of thought, and, whilst his character retains all its unconscious effect, is converted in the mind into solid and sweet wisdom,—it is a sign to us that his office is closing, and he is commonly withdrawn from our sight in a short time.

CHAPTER VI. IDEALISM

Thus is the unspeakable but intelligible and practicable meaning of the world conveyed to man, the immortal pupil, in every object of sense. To this one end of Discipline, all parts of nature conspire.

A noble doubt perpetually suggests itself, whether this end be not the Final Cause of the Universe; and whether nature outwardly exists. It is a sufficient account of that Appearance we call the World, that God will teach a human mind, and so makes it the receiver of a certain number of congruent sensations, which we call sun and moon, man and woman, house and trade. In my utter impotence to test the authenticity of the report of my senses, to know whether the impressions they make on me correspond with outlying objects, what difference does it make, whether Orion is up there in heaven, or some god paints the image in the firmament of the soul? The relations of parts and the end of the whole remaining the same, what is the difference, whether land and sea interact, and worlds revolve and intermingle without number or end,—deep yawning under deep,[75] and galaxy balancing galaxy, throughout absolute space, or, whether, without relations of time and space, the same appearances are inscribed in the constant faith of man. Whether nature enjoy a substantial existence without, or is only in the apocalypse[76] of the mind, it is alike useful and alike venerable to me. Be it what it may, it is ideal to me, so long as I cannot try the accuracy of my senses.

[75]DEEP YAWNING UNDER DEEP: From Psalm 42:7: "Deep calleth unto deep at the noise of thy waterspouts: all thy waves and thy billows are gone over me."
[76]APOCALYPSE: A revelation.

The frivolous make themselves merry with the Ideal theory,[77] as if its consequences were burlesque; as if it affected the stability of nature. It surely does not. God never jests with us, and will not compromise the end of nature, by permitting any inconsequence in its procession. Any distrust of the permanence of laws, would paralyze the faculties of man. Their permanence is sacredly respected, and his faith therein is perfect. The wheels and springs of man are all set to the hypothesis of the permanence of nature. We are not built like a ship to be tossed, but like a house to stand. It is a natural consequence of this structure, that, so long as the active powers predominate over the reflective, we resist with indignation any hint that nature is more short-lived or mutable than spirit. The broker, the wheelwright, the carpenter, the tollman, are much displeased at the intimation.

But whilst we acquiesce entirely in the permanence of natural laws, the question of the absolute existence of nature, still remains open. It is the uniform effect of culture on the human mind, not to shake our faith in the stability of particular phenomena, as of heat, water, azote;[78] but to lead us to regard nature as a phenomenon, not a substance; to attribute necessary existence to spirit; to esteem nature as an accident and an effect.

To the senses and the unrenewed understanding, belongs a sort of instinctive belief in the absolute existence of nature. In their view, man and nature are indissolubly joined. Things are ultimates, and they never look beyond their sphere. The presence of Reason mars this faith. The first effort of thought tends to relax this despotism of the senses, which binds us to nature as if we were a part of it, and shows us nature aloof, and, as it were, afloat. Until this higher agency intervened, the animal eye sees, with wonderful accuracy, sharp outlines and colored surfaces. When the eye of Reason opens, to outline and surface are at once added, grace and expression. These proceed from imagination and affection, and abate somewhat of the angular distinctness of objects. If the Reason be stimulated to more earnest vision, outlines and surfaces become transparent, and are no longer seen; causes and spirits are seen through them. The best, the happiest moments of life, are these delicious awakenings of the higher powers, and the reverential withdrawing of nature before its God.

---

[77]IDEAL THEORY: George Berkeley (1685–1753) was an Irish philosopher and clergyman whose subjective idealism went beyond that of John Locke (1632–1704), who reasoned that qualities such as color and taste are created by the mind, while primary qualities of matter such as weight exist independent of the mind. Berkeley held all qualities are known only in the mind and that matter does not exist independent of perception (*esse est percipi*).
[78]AZOTE: Nitrogen.

Let us proceed to indicate the effects of culture. 1. Our first institution[79] in the Ideal philosophy is a hint from nature herself.

Nature is made to conspire with spirit to emancipate us. Certain mechanical changes, a small alteration in our local position apprizes us of a dualism. We are strangely affected by seeing the shore from a moving ship, from a balloon, or through the tints of an unusual sky. The least change in our point of view, gives the whole world a pictorial air. A man who seldom rides, needs only to get into a coach and traverse his own town, to turn the street into a puppet-show. The men, the women,—talking, running, bartering, fighting,—the earnest mechanic,[80] the lounger, the beggar, the boys, the dogs, are unrealized at once, or, at least, wholly detached from all relation to the observer, and seen as apparent, not substantial beings. What new thoughts are suggested by seeing a face of country quite familiar, in the rapid movement of the rail-road car! Nay, the most wonted objects, (make a very slight change in the point of vision,) please us most. In a camera obscura,[81] the butcher's cart, and the figure of one of our own family amuse us. So a portrait of a well-known face gratifies us. Turn the eyes upside down, by looking at the landscape through your legs, and how agreeable is the picture, though you have seen it any time these twenty years!

In these cases, by mechanical means, is suggested the difference between the observer and the spectacle,—between man and nature. Hence arises a pleasure mixed with awe; I may say, a low degree of the sublime is felt from the fact, probably, that man is hereby apprized, that, whilst the world is a spectacle, something in himself is stable.

2. In a higher manner, the poet communicates the same pleasure. By a few strokes he delineates, as on air, the sun, the mountain, the camp, the city, the hero, the maiden, not different from what we know them, but only lifted from the ground and float before the eye. He unfixes the land and the sea, makes them revolve around the axis of his primary thought, and disposes them anew. Possessed himself by a heroic passion, he uses matter as symbols of it. The sensual man conforms thoughts to things; the poet conforms things to his thoughts. The one esteems nature as rooted and fast; the other, as fluid, and impresses his being thereon. To him, the refractory world is ductile and flexible; he invests dusts and stones with humanity and makes them the

---

[79]INSTITUTION: Instruction, educational training.
[80]MECHANIC: A manual laborer.
[81]IN A CAMERA OBSCURA: An apparatus with a darkened compartment or box, into which light is filtered through a double convex lens, projecting an image of an external object placed at the focus of the lens onto a surface such as paper or glass.

words of the Reason. The imagination may be defined to be, the use which the Reason makes of the material world. Shakespeare possesses the power of subordinating nature for the purposes of expression, beyond all poets. His imperial muse tosses the creation like a bauble from hand to hand, to embody any capricious shade of thought that is uppermost in his mind. The remotest spaces of nature are visited, and the farthest sundered things are brought together, by a subtile spiritual connexion. We are made aware that magnitude of material things is merely relative, and all objects shrink and expand to serve the passion of the poet. Thus, in his sonnets, the lays of birds, the scents and dyes of flowers, he finds to be the *shadow* of his beloved;[82] time, which keeps her from him, is his *chest*; the suspicion she has awakened, is her *ornament*;[83]

> *The ornament of beauty is Suspect,*
> *A crow which flies in heaven's sweetest air.*[84]

His passion is not the fruit of chance; it swells, as he speaks, to a city, or a state.

> *No, it was builded far from accident;*
> *It suffers not in smiling pomp, nor falls*
> *Under the brow of thralling discontent;*
> *It fears not policy, that heretic,*
> *That works on leases of short numbered hours,*
> *But all alone stands hugely politic.*[85]

In the strength of his constancy, the Pyramids[86] seem to him recent and transitory. And the freshness of youth and love dazzles him with its resemblance to morning.

> *Take those lips away*
> *Which so sweetly were forsworn;*

[82]THE SHADOW OF HIS BELOVED: Emerson summarizes Shakespeare's Sonnet 98, "From you have I been absent in the spring / When proud-pied April, dress'd in all his trim, / Hath put a spirit of youth in every thing, / That heavy Saturn laugh'd and leap'd with him. / Yet nor the lays of birds, nor the sweet smell / Of different flowers in odour and in hue, / Could make me any summer's story tell, / Or from their proud lap pluck them where they grew: / Nor did I wonder at the lily's white, / Nor praise the deep vermilion in the rose; / They were but sweet, but figures of delight, / Drawn after you, you pattern of all those. / Yet seem'd it winter still, and you away, / As with your shadow I with these did play."

[83]IS HER ORNAMENT: Shakespeare's Sonnet 65, line 10, "Shall Time's best jewel from Time's chest lie hid?"

[84]A CROW WHICH FLIES IN HEAVEN'S SWEETEST AIR: Shakespeare's Sonnet 70, lines 3-4.

[85]BUT ALL ALONE STANDS HUGELY POLITIC: Shakespeare's Sonnet 124, lines 5-11.

[86]PYRAMIDS: Shakespeare's Sonnet 123, lines 1-4, "No, Time, thou shalt not boast that I do change / Thy pyramids built up with newer might / To me are nothing novel, nothing strange; / They are but dressings of a former sight."

> *And those eyes,—the break of day,*
> *Lights that do mislead the morn.*[87]

The wild beauty of this hyperbole, I may say, in passing, it would not be easy to match in literature.

This transfiguration which all material objects undergo through the passion of the poet,—this power which he exerts, at any moment, to magnify the small, to micrify the great,—might be illustrated by a thousand examples from his Plays. I have before me the Tempest, and will cite only these few lines.

> **PROSPERO.**   *The strong based promontory*
> *Have I made shake, and by the spurs plucked up*
> *The pine and cedar.*[88]

Prospero calls for music to sooth the frantic Alonzo, and his companions;

> *A solemn air, and the best comforter*
> *To an unsettled fancy, cure thy brains*
> *Now useless, boiled within thy skull.*[89]

Again;

> *The charm dissolves space*
> *And, as the morning steals upon the night,*
> *Melting the darkness, so their rising senses*
> *Begin to chase the ignorant fumes that mantle*
> *Their clearer reason.*[90]

> *Their understanding*
> *Begins to swell: and the approaching tide*
> *Will shortly fill the reasonable shores*
> *That now lie foul and muddy.*[91]

The perception of real affinities between events, (that is to say, of *ideal* affinities, for those only are real,) enables the poet thus to make free with the most imposing forms and phenomena of the world, and to assert the predominance of the soul.

---

[87]LIGHTS THAT DO MISLEAD THE MORN: From a song by an anonymous author featured at the beginning of Act IV, Scene I of Shakespeare's *Measure for Measure* (1604) and John Fletcher's (1579–1625) *The Bloody Brother* (1616), Act V, Scene II.
[88]THE PINE AND CEDAR: From Shakespeare's *The Tempest*, "Have I given fire and rifted Jove's stout oak / With his own bolt: the strong-bas'd promontory / Have I made shake; and by the spurs pluck'd up / The pine and cedar: graves at my command / Have wak'd their sleepers, op'd, and let them forth / By my so potent art" (Act 5, Scene I, lines 52–56).
[89]NOW USELESS, BOILED WITHIN THY SKULL: *The Tempest*, Act V, Scene I, lines 66–68.
[90]THEIR CLEARER REASON: *The Tempest*, Act V, Scene I, lines 72–76.
[91]THAT NOW LIE FOUL AND MUDDY: *The Tempest*, Act V, Scene I, 87–90.

3. Whilst thus the poet delights us by animating[92] nature like a creator, with his own thoughts, he differs from the philosopher only herein, that the one proposes Beauty as his main end; the other Truth. But, the philosopher, not less than the poet, postpones the apparent order and relations of things to the empire of thought. "The problem of philosophy," according to Plato, "is, for all that exists conditionally, to find a ground unconditioned and absolute." It proceeds on the faith that a law determines all phenomena, which being known, the phenomena can be predicted. That law, when in the mind, is an idea. Its beauty is infinite. The true philosopher and the true poet are one, and a beauty, which is truth, and a truth, which is beauty, is the aim of both. Is not the charm of one of Plato's or Aristotle's[93] definitions, strictly like that of the Antigone of Sophocles?[94] It is, in both cases, that a spiritual life has been imparted to nature; that the solid seeming block of matter has been pervaded and dissolved by a thought; that this feeble human being has penetrated the vast masses of nature with an informing soul, and recognised itself in their harmony, that is, seized their law. In physics, when this is attained, the memory disburthens itself of its cumbrous catalogues of particulars, and carries centuries of observation in a single formula.

Thus even in physics, the material is ever degraded before the spiritual. The astronomer, the geometer, rely on their irrefragable analysis, and disdain the results of observation. The sublime remark of Euler[95] on his law of arches, "This will be found contrary to all experience, yet it is true;" had already transferred nature into the mind, and left matter like an outcast corpse.

4. Intellectual science has been observed to beget invariably a doubt of the existence of matter. Turgot[96] said, "He that has never doubted the existence of matter, may be assured he has no aptitude for metaphysical inquiries." It fastens the attention upon immortal necessary uncreated natures, that is, upon Ideas; and in their beautiful and majestic presence, we feel that our outward being is a dream and a shade. Whilst we wait in this Olympus of gods, we think of nature as an appendix to the soul. We ascend into their region, and know that these are

---

[92]ANIMATING: Giving life to.
[93]ARISTOTLE: Greek philosopher (384–322 BCE), author of *De Poetica (Poetics)*.
[94]ANTIGONE OF SOPHOCLES: Greek dramatist (96–406 BCE) best known for his tragedies *Oedipus Rex* (c. 429) and *Antigone* (c. 441).
[95]SUBLIME REMARK OF EULER: Leonhard Euler (1707–1783) was a Swiss mathematician who was one of the first people to develop the methods of calculus. The quote comes from Coleridge's *Aids to Reflection* (1829).
[96]TURGOT: Anne Robert Jacques Turgot (1727–81), French economist and statesman.

the thoughts of the Supreme Being. "These are they who were set up from everlasting, from the beginning, or ever the earth was. When he prepared the heavens, they were there; when he established the clouds above, when he strengthened the fountains of the deep. Then they were by him, as one brought up with him. Of them took he counsel."[97]

Their influence is proportionate. As objects of science, they are accessible to few men. Yet all men are capable of being raised by piety or by passion, into their region. And no man touches these divine natures, without becoming, in some degree, himself divine. Like a new soul, they renew the body. We become physically nimble and lightsome; we tread on air; life is no longer irksome, and we think it will never be so. No man fears age or misfortune or death, in their serene company, for he is transported out of the district of change. Whilst we behold unveiled the nature of Justice and Truth, we learn the difference between the absolute and the conditional or relative. We apprehend the absolute. As it were, for the first time, *we exist*. We become immortal, for we learn that time and space are relations of matter; that, with a perception of truth, or a virtuous will, they have no affinity.[98]

5. Finally, religion and ethics, which may be fitly called,—the practice of ideas, or the introduction of ideas into life,—have an analogous effect with all lower culture, in degrading nature and suggesting its dependence on spirit. Ethics and religion differ herein; that the one is the system of human duties commencing from man; the other, from God. Religion includes the personality of God; Ethics does not. They are one to our present design. They both put nature under foot. The first and last lesson of religion is, "The things that are seen, are temporal; the things that are unseen are eternal." It puts an affront upon nature. It does that for the unschooled, which philosophy does for Berkeley and Viasa.[99] The uniform language that may be heard in the churches of the most ignorant sects, is,—'Contemn the unsubstantial shows of the world; they are vanities, dreams, shadows, unrealities; seek the realities of religion.' The devotee flouts nature. Some theosophists[100] have arrived at a certain hostility and indignation towards matter, as the Manichean and

---

[97]OF THEM TOOK HE COUNSEL: Proverbs 8:23–30.
[98]AFFINITY: Emerson echoes Socrates' speech in Plato's *Symposium*, in which Socrates and several other men at a banquet discuss love.
[99]VIASA: Emerson refers to Viasa as the reputed author of the Vedas, the Hindu scriptures.
[100]THEOSOPHISTS: Theosophy (Greek for "divine wisdom") is a system of belief that claims insight into the nature of God and the world through direct knowledge and philosophical speculation on humanity and nature.

Plotinus[101] They distrusted in themselves any looking back to these flesh-pots of Egypt.[102] Plotinus was ashamed of his body. In short, they might all better say of matter, what Michael Angelo said of external beauty, "it is the frail and weary weed, in which God dresses the soul, which he has called into time."[103]

It appears that motion, poetry, physical and intellectual science, and religion, all tend to affect our convictions of the reality of the external world. But I own there is something ungrateful in expanding too curiously the particulars of the general proposition, that all culture tends to imbue us with idealism. I have no hostility to nature, but a child's love to it. I expand and live in the warm day like corn and melons. Let us speak her fair. I do not wish to fling stones at my beautiful mother, nor soil my gentle nest. I only wish to indicate the true position of nature in regard to man, wherein to establish man, all right education tends; as the ground which to attain is the object of human life, that is, of man's connexion with nature. Culture inverts the vulgar views of nature, and brings the mind to call that apparent, which it uses to call real, and that real, which it uses to call visionary. Children, it is true, believe in the external world. The belief that it appears only, is an afterthought, but with culture, this faith will as surely arise on the mind as did the first.

The advantage of the ideal theory over the popular faith, is this, that it presents the world in precisely that view which is most desirable to the mind. It is, in fact, the view which Reason, both speculative and practical, that is, philosophy and virtue, take. For, seen in the light of thought, the world always is phenomenal;[104] and virtue subordinates it to the mind. Idealism sees the world in God. It beholds the whole circle of persons and things, of actions and events, of country and religion, not as painfully accumulated, atom after atom, act after act, in an aged creeping Past, but as one vast picture, which God paints on the instant eternity, for the contemplation of the soul. Therefore the soul holds itself off from a too trivial and microscopic study of the universal tablet. It respects the end too much, to immerse itself in the means. It sees something more

---

[101]MANICHEAN AND PLOTINUS: Manicheanism was a religion founded by Mani (c.216–c.276) that combined elements from several religious movements, including Gnosticism, Zoroastrianism, Christianity, Buddhism, Taoism, and other Persian religions. Plotinus (see note 1) was not so much ashamed of his body, as of the fact that his soul had to be contained in a body. He believed that unification with God could only be attained when the soul lost the restraint of the body.
[102]FLESHPOTS OF EGYPT: Exodus 16:3: "And the children of Israel said unto them, Would to God we had died by the hand of the LORD in the land of Egypt, when we sat by the flesh pots, and when we did eat bread to the full; for ye have brought us forth into this wilderness, to kill this whole assembly with hunger."
[103]WHICH HE HAS CALLED INTO TIME: From Michelangelo's Sonnet 51.
[104]PHENOMENAL: A perception.

important in Christianity, than the scandals of ecclesiastical history or the niceties of criticism; and, very incurious concerning persons or miracles, and not at all disturbed by chasms of historical evidence, it accepts from God the phenomenon, as it finds it, as the pure and awful form of religion in the world. It is not hot and passionate at the appearance of what it calls its own good or bad fortune, at the union or opposition of other persons. No man is its enemy. It accepts whatsoever befalls, as part of its lesson. It is a watcher more than a doer, and it is a doer, only that it may the better watch.

CHAPTER VII. SPIRIT

It is essential to a true theory of nature and of man, that it should contain somewhat progressive. Uses that are exhausted or that may be, and facts that end in the statement, cannot be all that is true of this brave lodging wherein man is harbored, and wherein all his faculties find appropriate and endless exercise. And all the uses of nature admit of being summed in one, which yields the activity of man an infinite scope. Through all its kingdoms, to the suburbs and outskirts of things, it is faithful to the cause whence it had its origin. It always speaks of Spirit. It suggests the absolute. It is a perpetual effect. It is a great shadow pointing always to the sun behind us.

The aspect of nature is devout. Like the figure of Jesus, she stands with bended head, and hands folded upon the breast. The happiest man is he who learns from nature the lesson of worship.

Of that ineffable essence which we call Spirit, he that thinks most, will say least. We can foresee God in the coarse and, as it were, distant phenomena of matter; but when we try to define and describe himself, both language and thought desert us, and we are as helpless as fools and savages. That essence refuses to be recorded in propositions, but when man has worshipped him intellectually, the noblest ministry of nature is to stand as the apparition of God. It is the great organ through which the universal spirit speaks to the individual, and strives to lead back the individual to it.

When we consider Spirit, we see that the views already presented do not include the whole circumference of man. We must add some related thoughts.

Three problems are put by nature to the mind; What is matter? Whence is it? and Whereto? The first of these questions only, the ideal theory answers. Idealism saith: matter is a phenomenon, not a substance. Idealism acquaints us with the total disparity between the evidence of our own being, and the evidence of the world's being. The one is perfect, the other, incapable of any assurance; the mind is a part of the nature of things; the world is a divine dream, from which we may presently awake to the glories and certainties of day. Idealism is a hypothesis to account for nature by other principles than those of carpentry and chemistry. Yet, if it only deny the existence of matter, it does not satisfy the demands of the spirit. It leaves God out of me. It leaves me in the splendid labyrinth of my perceptions, to wander without end. Then the heart resists it, because it baulks the affections in denying substantive being to men and women. Nature is so pervaded with human life, that there is something of humanity in all, and in every particular. But this theory makes nature foreign to me, and does not account for that consanguinity which we acknowledge to it.

Let it stand then, in the present state of our knowledge, merely as a useful introductory hypothesis, serving to apprize us of the eternal distinction between the soul and the world.

But when, following the invisible steps of thought, we come to inquire, Whence is matter? and Whereto? many truths arise to us out of the recesses of consciousness. We learn that the highest is present to the soul of man, that the dread universal essence, which is not wisdom, or love, or beauty, or power, but all in one, and each entirely, is that for which all things exist, and that by which they are; that spirit creates; that behind nature, throughout nature, spirit is present; that spirit is one and not compound; that spirit does not act upon us from without, that is, in space and time, but spiritually, or through ourselves. Therefore, that spirit, that is, the Supreme Being, does not build up nature around us, but puts it forth through us, as the life of the tree puts forth new branches and leaves through the pores of the old. As a plant upon the earth, so a man rests upon the bosom of God: he is nourished by unfailing fountains, and draws, at his need, inexhaustible power. Who can set bounds to the possibilities of man? Once inspire the infinite, by being admitted to behold the absolute natures of justice and truth, and we learn that man has access to the entire mind of the Creator, is himself the creator in the finite. This view, which admonishes me where the sources of wisdom and power lie, and points to virtue as to

> "The golden key
> Which opes the palace of eternity,"[105]

carries upon its face the highest certificate of truth, because it animates me to create my own world through the purification of my soul.

[105]WHICH OPES THE PALACE OF ETERNITY: From English poet John Milton's (1608–1674) masque, *Comus*, lines 13–14.

The world proceeds from the same spirit as the body of man. It is a remoter and inferior incarnation of God, a projection of God in the unconscious. But it differs from the body in one important respect. It is not, like that, now subjected to the human will. Its serene order is inviolable by us. It is therefore, to us, the present expositor of the divine mind. It is a fixed point whereby we may measure our departure. As we degenerate, the contrast between us and our house is more evident. We are as much strangers in nature, as we are aliens from God. We do not understand the notes of the birds. The fox and the deer run away from us; the bear and tiger rend us. We do not know the uses of more than a few plants, as corn and the apple, the potato and the vine. Is not the landscape, every glimpse of which hath a grandeur, a face of him? Yet this may show us what discord is between man and nature, for you cannot freely admire a noble landscape, if laborers are digging in the field hard by. The poet finds something ridiculous in his delight, until he is out of the sight of men.

CHAPTER VIII. PROSPECTS

In inquiries respecting the laws of the world and the frame of things, the highest reason is always the truest. That which seems faintly possible— it is so refined, is often faint and dim because it is deepest seated in the mind among the eternal verities. Empirical science is apt to cloud the sight, and, by the very knowledge of functions and processes, to bereave the student of the manly contemplation of the whole. The savant[106] becomes unpoetic. But the best read naturalist who lends an entire and devout attention to truth, will see that there remains much to learn of his relation to the world, and that it is not to be learned by any addition or subtraction or other comparison of known quantities, but is arrived at by untaught sallies of the spirit, by a continual self-recovery, and by entire humility. He will perceive that there are far more excellent qualities in the student than preciseness and infallibility; that a guess is often more fruitful than an indisputable affirmation, and that a dream may let us deeper into the secret of nature than a hundred concerted experiments.

For, the problems to be solved are precisely those which the physiologist and the naturalist omit to state. It is not so pertinent to man to know all the individuals of the animal kingdom, as it is to know whence and whereto is this tyrannizing unity in his constitution, which evermore

[106]SAVANT: A person engaged in learning and science.

separates and classifies things, endeavouring to reduce the most diverse to one form. When I behold a rich landscape, it is less to my purpose to recite correctly the order and super-position of the strata, than to know why all thought of multitude is lost in a tranquil sense of unity. I cannot greatly honor minuteness in details, so long as there is no hint to explain the relation between things and thoughts; no ray upon the *metaphysics* of conchology, of botany, of the arts, to show the relation of the forms of flowers, shells, animals, architecture, to the mind, and build science upon ideas. In a cabinet of natural history, we become sensible of a certain occult recognition and sympathy in regard to the most bizarre forms of beast, fish, and insect. The American who has been confined, in his own country, to the sight of buildings designed after foreign models, is surprised on entering York Minster or St. Peter's at Rome, by the feeling that these structures are imitations also,—faint copies of an invisible archetype. Nor has science sufficient humanity, so long as the naturalist overlooks that wonderful congruity which subsists between man and the world; of which he is lord, not because he is the most subtile inhabitant, but because he is its head and heart, and finds something of himself in every great and small thing, in every mountain stratum, in every new law of color, fact of astronomy, or atmospheric influence which observation or analysis lay open. A perception of this mystery inspires the muse of George Herbert, the beautiful psalmist of the seventeenth century. The following lines are part of his little poem on Man.[107]

> "Man is all symmetry,
>   Full of proportions, one limb to another,
>   And to all the world besides.
>   Each part may call the farthest, brother;
>   For head with foot hath private amity,
>   And both with moons and tides.
>
> "Nothing hath got so far
> But man hath caught and kept it as his prey;
>   His eyes dismount the highest star;
>   He is in little all the sphere.
> Herbs gladly cure our flesh, because that they
>   Find their acquaintance there.
>
> "For us, the winds do blow.
> The earth doth rest, heaven move, and fountains flow;
>   Nothing we see, but means our good,

107MAN: From "Man," stanzas 3–6, and 8.

> *"As our delight, or as our treasure;*
> *The whole is either our cupboard of food,*
>   *Or cabinet of pleasure.*
>
> *"The stars have us to bed;*
> *Night draws the curtain; which the sun withdraws.*
>   *Music and light attend our head.*
>   *All things unto our flesh are kind,*
> *In their descent and being; to our mind,*
>   *In their ascent and cause.*
>
> *"More servants wait on man*
> *Than he'll take notice of. In every path,*
>   *He treads down that which doth befriend him*
>   *When sickness makes him pale and wan.*
> *Oh mighty love! Man is one world, and hath*
>   *Another to attend him."*

The perception of this class of truths makes the eternal attraction which draws men to science, but the end is lost sight of in attention to the means. In view of this half-sight of science, we accept the sentence of Plato, that, "poetry comes nearer to vital truth than history."[108] Every surmise and vaticination[109] of the mind is entitled to a certain respect, and we learn to prefer imperfect theories, and sentences, which contain glimpses of truth, to digested systems which have no one valuable suggestion. A wise writer will feel that the ends of study and composition are best answered by announcing undiscovered regions of thought, and so communicating, through hope, new activity to the torpid spirit.

I shall therefore conclude this essay with some traditions of man and nature, which a certain poet[110] sang to me; and which, as they have always been in the world, and perhaps reappear to every bard, may be both history and prophecy.

'The foundations of man are not in matter, but in spirit. But the element of spirit is eternity. To it, therefore, the longest series of events, the oldest chronologies are young and recent. In the cycle of the universal man, from whom the known individuals proceed, centuries are points, and all history is but the epoch of one degradation.

'We distrust and deny inwardly our sympathy with nature. We own and disown our relation to it, by turns. We are, like Nebuchadnezzar,

---

[108]POETRY COMES NEARER TO VITAL TRUTH THAN HISTORY: This quote is actually not from Plato, but appears in section IX of Aristotle's *Poetics*. "Poetry, therefore, is a more philosophical and a higher thing than history: for poetry tends to express the universal, history the particular."
[109]VATICINATION: Prophecy.
[110]CERTAIN POET: The poet is really Emerson himself.

dethroned, bereft of reason, and eating grass like an ox.[111] But who can set limits to the remedial force of spirit?

'A man is a god in ruins. When men are innocent, life shall be longer, and shall pass into the immortal, as gently as we awake from dreams. Now, the world would be insane and rabid, if these disorganizations should last for hundreds of years. It is kept in check by death and infancy. Infancy is the perpetual Messiah, which comes into the arms of fallen men, and pleads with them to return to paradise.

'Man is the dwarf of himself. Once he was permeated and dissolved by spirit. He filled nature with his overflowing currents. Out from him sprang the sun and moon; from man, the sun; from woman, the moon. The laws of his mind, the periods of his actions externized themselves into day and night, into the year and the seasons. But, having made for himself this huge shell, his waters retired; he no longer fills the veins and veinlets; he is shrunk to a drop. He sees, that the structure still fits him, but fits him colossally. Say, rather, once it fitted him, now it corresponds to him from far and on high. He adores timidly his own work. Now is man the follower of the sun, and woman the follower of the moon. Yet sometimes he starts in his slumber, and wonders at himself and his house, and muses strangely at the resemblance betwixt him and it. He perceives that if his law is still paramount, if still he have elemental power, "if his word is sterling yet in nature," it is not conscious power, it is not inferior but superior to his will. It is Instinct.' Thus my Orphic poet sang.

At present, man applies to nature but half his force. He works on the world with his understanding alone. He lives in it, and masters it by a penny-wisdom; and he that works most in it, is but a half-man and whilst his arms are strong and his digestion good, his mind is imbruted and he is a selfish savage. His relation to nature, his power over it, is through the understanding; as by manure; the economic use of fire, wind, water, and the mariner's needle; steam, coal, chemical agriculture; the repairs of the human body by the dentist and the surgeon. This is such a resumption of power, as if a banished king should buy his territories inch by inch, instead of vaulting at once into his throne. Meantime, in the thick darkness, there are not wanting gleams of a better light,—occasional examples of the action of man upon nature with his entire force,—with reason as well as understanding. Such examples are:

[111]OX: A reference to Daniel 4:31–32: "While the word was in the king's mouth, there fell a voice from heaven, saying, O king Nebuchadnezzar, to thee it is spoken; The kingdom is departed from thee. / And they shall drive thee from men, and thy dwelling shall be with the beasts of the field: they shall make thee to eat grass as oxen, and seven times shall pass over thee, until thou know that the most High ruleth in the kingdom of men, and giveth it to whomsoever he will."

the traditions of miracles in the earliest antiquity of all nations; the history of Jesus Christ; the achievements of a principle, as in religious and political revolutions, and in the abolition of the Slave-trade; the miracles of enthusiasm,[112] as those reported of Swedenborg, Hohenlohe,[113] and the Shakers;[114] many obscure and yet contested facts, now arranged under the name of Animal Magnetism;[115] prayer; eloquence, self-healing; and the wisdom of children. These are examples of Reason's momentary grasp of the sceptre, the exertions of a power which exists not in time or space, but an instantaneous in-streaming causing power. The difference between the actual and the ideal force of man is happily figured by the schoolmen, in saying, that the knowledge of man is an evening knowledge, *vespertina cognitio*, but that of God is a morning knowledge, *matutina cognitio*.

The problem of restoring to the world original and eternal beauty, is solved by the redemption of the soul. The ruin or the blank, that we see when we look at nature, is in our own eye. The axis of vision is not coincident with the axis of things, and so they appear not transparent but opake. The reason why the world lacks unity, and lies broken and in heaps, is, because man is disunited with himself. He cannot be a naturalist, until he satisfies all the demands of the spirit. Love is as much its demand, as perception. Indeed, neither can be perfect without the other. In the uttermost meaning of the words, thought is devout, and devotion is thought. Deep calls unto deep.[116] But in actual life, the marriage is not celebrated. There are innocent men who worship God after the tradition of their fathers, but their sense of duty has not yet extended to the use of all their faculties. And there are patient naturalists, but they freeze their subject under the wintry light of the understanding. Is not prayer also a study of truth,—a sally of the soul into the unfound infinite? No man ever prayed heartily, without learning something. But when a faithful thinker, resolute to detach every object from personal relations, and see it in the light of thought, shall, at the same time, kindle science with the fire of the holiest affections, then will God go forth anew into the creation.

It will not need, when the mind is prepared for study, to search for objects. The invariable mark of wisdom is to see the miraculous in the

[112]ENTHUSIASM: Those under a supernatural inspiration or possession, a prophetic frenzy.
[113]HOHENLOHE: Alexander Leopold Franz Emmerich, prince of Hohenlohe (1794–1849), who had a reputation for effecting miraculous cures.
[114]SHAKERS: Originally known as the "Shaking Quakers," the Shakers (The United Society of Believers in Christ's Second Appearing) believed in miraculous cures.
[115]ANIMAL MAGNETISM: Hypnotism.
[116]DEEP CALLS UNTO DEEP: Psalm 42.7: "Deep calleth unto deep at the noise of thy waterspouts: all thy waves and thy billows are gone over me."

common. What is a day? What is a year? What is summer? What is woman? What is a child? What is sleep? To our blindness, these things seem unaffecting. We make fables to hide the baldness of the fact and conform it, as we say, to the higher law of the mind. But when the fact is seen under the light of an idea, the gaudy fable fades and shrivels. We behold the real higher law. To the wise, therefore, a fact is true poetry, and the most beautiful of fables. These wonders are brought to our own door. You also are a man. Man and woman, and their social life, poverty, labor, sleep, fear, fortune, are known to you. Learn that none of these things is superficial, but that each phenomenon hath its roots in the faculties and affections of the mind. Whilst the abstract question occupies your intellect, nature brings it in the concrete to be solved by your hands. It were a wise inquiry for the closet,[117] to compare, point by point, especially at remarkable crises in life, our daily history, with the rise and progress of ideas in the mind.

So shall we come to look at the world with new eyes. It shall answer the endless inquiry of the intellect,—What is truth? and of the affections,—What is good? by yielding itself passive to the educated Will. Then shall come to pass what my poet said; 'Nature is not fixed but fluid. Spirit alters, moulds, makes it. The immobility or bruteness of nature, is the absence of spirit; to pure spirit, it is fluid, it is volatile, it is obedient. Every spirit builds itself a house; and beyond its house, a world; and beyond its world, a heaven. Know then, that the world exists for you. For you is the phenomenon perfect. What we are, that only can we see. All that Adam had, all that Cæsar could,[118] you have and can do. Adam called his house, heaven and earth; Cæsar called his house, Rome; you perhaps call yours, a cobler's trade; a hundred acres of ploughed land; or a scholar's garret. Yet line for line and point for point, your dominion is as great as theirs, though without fine names. Build, therefore your own world. As fast as you can conform your life to the pure idea in your mind, that will unfold its great proportions. A correspondent revolution in things will attend the influx of the spirit. So fast will disagreeable appearances, swine, spiders, snakes, pests, mad-houses, prisons, enemies, vanish; they are temporary and shall be no more seen. The sordor and filths of nature, the sun shall dry up, and the wind exhale. As when the summer comes from the south, the snow-banks melt, and the face of the earth becomes green before it, so shall the advancing spirit create its ornaments

[117]CLOSET: A small, private room used for meditation and study.
[118]ADAM HAD, ALL THAT CAESAR COULD: Adam, the first man, as described in the Book of Genesis. Julius Caesar (100?–44 BCE), Roman statesman and general who became dictator of Rome.

along its path, and carry with it the beauty it visits, and the song which enchants it; it shall draw beautiful faces, and warm hearts, and wise discourse, and heroic acts, around its way, until evil is no more seen. The kingdom of man over nature, which cometh not with observation,[119] —a dominion such as now is beyond his dream of God,—he shall enter without more wonder than the blind man feels who is gradually restored to perfect sight.'

[1836]

The American Scholar

AN ORATION DELIVERED BEFORE THE PHI BETA KAPPA SOCIETY,[1] AT CAMBRIDGE, AUGUST 31, 1837

Mr. President and Gentlemen,

I greet you on the re-commencement of our literary year. Our anniversary is one of hope, and, perhaps, not enough of labor. We do not meet for games of strength or skill, for the recitation of histories, tragedies, and odes, like the ancient Greeks; for parliaments of love and poesy, like the Troubadours[2]; nor for the advancement of science, like our cotemporaries in the British and European capitals. Thus far, our holiday has been simply a friendly sign of the survival of the love of letters amongst a people too busy to give to letters any more. As such, it is precious as the sign of an indestructible instinct. Perhaps the time is already come, when it ought to be, and will be, something else; when the sluggard intellect of this continent will look from under its iron lids, and fill the postponed expectation of the world with something better than the exertions of mechanical skill. Our day of dependence, our long apprenticeship to the learning of other lands, draws to a close. The millions, that around us are rushing into life, cannot always be fed on the sere remains of foreign harvests. Events, actions arise, that must be sung, that will sing themselves. Who can doubt, that poetry will revive and lead in a new age, as the star in the constellation Harp, which now flames in our zenith, astronomers announce, shall one day be the pole-star for a thousand years?

---

[119]THE KINGDOM OF MAN OVER NATURE, WHICH COMETH NOT WITH OBSERVATION: Luke 17:20: "And when he was demanded of the Pharisees, when the kingdom of God should come, he answered them and said, The kingdom of God cometh not with observation."
[1]PHI BETA KAPPA SOCIETY: Phi Beta Kappa is the nation's oldest undergraduate honors organization.
[2]TROUBADOURS: Medieval courtly poets from southern France, especially the area of Provence.

In this hope, I accept the topic which not only usage, but the nature of our association, seem to prescribe to this day,—the AMERICAN SCHOLAR. Year by year, we come up hither to read one more chapter of his biography. Let us inquire what light new days and events have thrown on his character, and his hopes.

It is one of those fables, which, out of an unknown antiquity, convey an unlooked-for wisdom, that the gods, in the beginning, divided Man into men, that he might be more helpful to himself[3]; just as the hand was divided into fingers, the better to answer its end.

The old fable covers a doctrine ever new and sublime; that there is One Man,—present to all particular men only partially, or through one faculty; and that you must take the whole society to find the whole man. Man is not a farmer, or a professor, or an engineer, but he is all. Man is priest, and scholar, and statesman, and producer, and soldier. In the *divided* or social state, these functions are parcelled out to individuals, each of whom aims to do his stint of the joint work, whilst each other performs his. The fable implies, that the individual, to possess himself, must sometimes return from his own labor to embrace all the other laborers. But unfortunately, this original unit, this fountain of power, has been so distributed to multitudes, has been so minutely subdivided and peddled out, that it is spilled into drops, and cannot be gathered. The state of society is one in which the members have suffered amputation from the trunk, and strut about so many walking monsters,—a good finger, a neck, a stomach, an elbow, but never a man.

Man is thus metamorphosed into a thing, into many things. The planter, who is Man sent out into the field to gather food, is seldom cheered by any idea of the true dignity of his ministry. He sees his bushel and his cart, and nothing beyond, and sinks into the farmer, instead of Man on the farm. The tradesman scarcely ever gives an ideal worth to his work, but is ridden by the routine of his craft, and the soul is subject to dollars. The priest becomes a form; the attorney, a statute-book; the mechanic, a machine; the sailor, a rope of a ship.

In this distribution of functions, the scholar is the delegated intellect. In the right state, he is, *Man Thinking*. In the degenerate state, when the victim of society, he tends to become a mere thinker, or, still worse, the parrot of other men's thinking.

In this view of him, as Man Thinking, the theory of his office is contained. Him nature solicits with all her placid, all her monitory pictures; him the past instructs; him the future invites. Is not, indeed, every man

[3]THAT HE MIGHT BE MORE HELPFUL TO HIMSELF: A fable from Plato's *Symposium*.

a student, and do not all things exist for the student's behoof? And, finally, is not the true scholar the only true master? But the old oracle said, "All things have two handles: beware of the wrong one." In life, too often, the scholar errs with mankind and forfeits his privilege. Let us see him in his school, and consider him in reference to the main influences he receives.

I. The first in time and the first in importance of the influences upon the mind is that of nature. Every day, the sun; and, after sunset, night and her stars. Ever the winds blow; ever the grass grows. Every day, men and women, conversing, beholding and beholden. The scholar is he of all men whom this spectacle most engages. He must settle its value in his mind. What is nature to him? There is never a beginning, there is never an end, to the inexplicable continuity of this web of God, but always circular power returning into itself. Therein it resembles his own spirit, whose beginning, whose ending, he never can find,—so entire, so boundless. Far, too, as her splendors shine, system on system shooting like rays, upward, downward, without centre, without circumference,—in the mass and in the particle, nature hastens to render account of herself to the mind. Classification begins. To the young mind, every thing is individual, stands by itself. By and by, it finds how to join two things, and see in them one nature; then three, then three thousand; and so, tyrannized over by its own unifying instinct, it goes on tying things together, diminishing anomalies, discovering roots running under ground, whereby contrary and remote things cohere, and flower out from one stem. It presently learns, that, since the dawn of history, there has been a constant accumulation and classifying of facts. But what is classification but the perceiving that these objects are not chaotic, and are not foreign, but have a law which is also a law of the human mind? The astronomer discovers that geometry, a pure abstraction of the human mind, is the measure of planetary motion. The chemist finds proportions and intelligible method throughout matter; and science is nothing but the finding of analogy, identity, in the most remote parts. The ambitious soul sits down before each refractory fact; one after another, reduces all strange constitutions, all new powers, to their class and their law, and goes on for ever to animate the last fibre of organization, the outskirts of nature, by insight.

Thus to him, to this school-boy under the bending dome of day, is suggested, that he and it proceed from one root; one is leaf and one is flower; relation, sympathy, stirring in every vein. And what is that Root? Is not that the soul of his soul?—A thought too bold,—a dream too wild.

Yet when this spiritual light shall have revealed the law of more earthly natures,—when he has learned to worship the soul, and to see that the natural philosophy that now is, is only the first gropings of its gigantic hand, he shall look forward to an ever expanding knowledge as to a becoming creator. He shall see, that nature is the opposite of the soul, answering to it part for part. One is seal, and one is print. Its beauty is the beauty of his own mind. Its laws are the laws of his own mind. Nature then becomes to him the measure of his attainments. So much of nature as he is ignorant of, so much of his own mind does he not yet possess. And, in fine, the ancient precept, "Know thyself,"[4] and the modern precept, "Study nature," become at last one maxim.

    II. The next great influence into the spirit of the scholar, is, the mind of the Past,—in whatever form, whether of literature, of art, of institutions, that mind is inscribed. Books are the best type of the influence of the past, and perhaps we shall get at the truth,—learn the amount of this influence more conveniently,—by considering their value alone.

    The theory of books is noble. The scholar of the first age received into him the world around; brooded thereon; gave it the new arrangement of his own mind, and uttered it again. It came into him, life; it went out from him, truth. It came to him, short-lived actions; it went out from him, immortal thoughts. It came to him, business[5]; it went from him, poetry. It was dead fact; now, it is quick[6] thought. It can stand, and it can go. It now endures, it now flies, it now inspires.[7] Precisely in proportion to the depth of mind from which it issued, so high does it soar, so long does it sing.

    Or, I might say, it depends on how far the process had gone, of transmuting life into truth. In proportion to the completeness of the distillation, so will the purity and imperishableness of the product be. But none is quite perfect. As no air-pump can by any means make a perfect vacuum, so neither can any artist entirely exclude the conventional, the local, the perishable from his book, or write a book of pure thought, that shall be as efficient, in all respects, to a remote posterity, as to cotemporaries, or rather to the second age. Each age, it is found, must write its own books; or rather, each generation for the next succeeding. The books of an older period will not fit this.

<hr>

[4]KNOW THYSELF: From the inscription on the Oracle of Apollo at Delphi, Greece, 6th century BCE. The words are traditionally ascribed to Solon of Athens (c. 640–c. 558 BCE).
[5]BUSINESS: Activity.
[6]QUICK: Living.
[7]INSPIRES: Breathes.

Yet hence arises a grave mischief. The sacredness which attaches to the act of creation,—the act of thought,—is transferred to the record. The poet chanting, was felt to be a divine man: henceforth the chant is divine also. The writer was a just and wise spirit: henceforward it is settled, the book is perfect; as love of the hero corrupts into worship of his statue. Instantly, the book becomes noxious: the guide is a tyrant. The sluggish and perverted mind of the multitude, slow to open to the incursions of Reason, having once so opened, having once received this book, stands upon it, and makes an outcry, if it is disparaged. Colleges are built on it. Books are written on it by thinkers, not by Man Thinking; by men of talent, that is, who start wrong, who set out from accepted dogmas, not from their own sight of principles. Meek young men grow up in libraries, believing it their duty to accept the views, which Cicero, which Locke, which Bacon, have given, forgetful that Cicero,[8] Locke,[9] and Bacon[10] were only young men in libraries, when they wrote these books.

Hence, instead of Man Thinking, we have the bookworm. Hence, the book-learned class, who value books, as such; not as related to nature and the human constitution, but as making a sort of Third Estate[11] with the world and the soul. Hence, the restorers of readings, the emendators, the bibliomaniacs of all degrees.

Books are the best of things, well used; abused, among the worst. What is the right use? What is the one end, which all means go to effect? They are for nothing but to inspire. I had better never see a book, than to be warped by its attraction clean out of my own orbit, and made a satellite instead of a system. The one thing in the world, of value, is the active soul. This every man is entitled to; this every man contains within him, although, in almost all men, obstructed, and as yet unborn. The soul active sees absolute truth; and utters truth, or creates. In this action, it is genius; not the privilege of here and there a favorite, but the sound estate of every man. In its essence, it is progressive. The book, the college, the school of art, the institution of any kind, stop with some past utterance of genius. This is good, say they,—let us hold by this. They pin me down. They look backward and not forward. But genius looks forward: the eyes of man are set in his forehead, not in his hindhead: man

---

[8]CICERO: Marcus Tullius Cicero (106–43 BCE), a Roman philosopher and orator.
[9]LOCKE: John Locke (1632–1704), an English philosopher and founder of British empiricism, noted for his *Essay Concerning Human Understanding* (1690).
[10]BACON: Francis Bacon (1561–1626), an English scientist and philosopher.
[11]THIRD ESTATE: Emerson makes an analogy to the three-part division of estates of the traditional body politic; the first estate represented the clergy, the second estate comprised the monarchy, and the third estate encompassed commoners.

hopes: genius creates. Whatever talents may be, if the man create not, the pure efflux of the Diety is not his;—cinders and smoke there may be, but not yet flame. There are creative manners, there are creative actions, and creative words; manners, actions, words, that is, indicative of no custom or authority, but springing spontaneous from the mind's own sense of good and fair.

On the other part, instead of being its own seer, let it receive from another mind its truth, though it were in torrents of light, without periods of solitude, inquest, and self-recovery, and a fatal disservice is done. Genius is always sufficiently the enemy of genius by over influence. The literature of every nation bear me witness. The English dramatic poets have Shakspearized now for two hundred years.

Undoubtedly there is a right way of reading, so it be sternly subordinated. Man Thinking must not be subdued by his instruments. Books are for the scholar's idle times. When he can read God directly, the hour is too precious to be wasted in other men's transcripts of their readings. But when the intervals of darkness come, as come they must,—when the sun is hid, and the stars withdraw their shining,—we repair to the lamps which were kindled by their ray, to guide our steps to the East again, where the dawn is. We hear, that we may speak. The Arabian proverb says, "A fig tree, looking on a fig tree, becometh fruitful."

It is remarkable, the character of the pleasure we derive from the best books. They impress us with the conviction, that one nature wrote and the same reads. We read the verses of one of the great English poets, of Chaucer,[12] of Marvell,[13] of Dryden,[14] with the most modern joy,—with a pleasure, I mean, which is in great part caused by the abstraction of all *time* from their verses. There is some awe mixed with the joy of our surprise, when this poet, who lived in some past world, two or three hundred years ago, says that which lies close to my own soul, that which I also had wellnigh thought and said. But for the evidence thence afforded to the philosophical doctrine of the identity of all minds, we should suppose some preëstablished harmony, some foresight of souls that were to be, and some preparation of stores for their future wants, like the fact observed in insects, who lay up food before death for the young grub they shall never see.

I would not be hurried by any love of system, by any exaggeration of instincts, to underrate the Book. We all know, that, as the human

---

[12]CHAUCER: Geoffrey Chaucer (1340–1400), an English poet, considered one of the most important figures in English literature, best known for *The Canterbury Tales*.
[13]MARVELL: Andrew Marvell (1621–1678), an English metaphysical poet.
[14]DRYDEN: John Dryden (1631–1700), an English poet, dramatist, and critic.

body can be nourished on any food, though it were boiled grass and the broth of shoes, so the human mind can be fed by any knowledge. And great and heroic men have existed, who had almost no other information than by the printed page. I only would say, that it needs a strong head to bear that diet. One must be an inventor to read well. As the proverb says, "He that would bring home the wealth of the Indies, must carry out the wealth of the Indies." There is then creative reading as well as creative writing. When the mind is braced by labor and invention, the page of whatever book we read becomes luminous with manifold allusion. Every sentence is doubly significant, and the sense of our author is as broad as the world. We then see, what is always true, that, as the seer's hour of vision is short and rare among heavy days and months, so is its record, perchance, the least part of his volume. The discerning will read, in his Plato or Shakspeare, only that least part,— only the authentic utterances of the oracle;—all the rest he rejects, were it never so many times Plato's and Shakspeare's.

Of course, there is a portion of reading quite indispensable to a wise man. History and exact science he must learn by laborious reading. Colleges, in like manner, have their indispensable office,—to teach elements. But they can only highly serve us, when they aim not to drill, but to create; when they gather from far every ray of various genius to their hospitable halls, and, by the concentrated fires, set the hearts of their youth on flame. Thought and knowledge are natures in which apparatus and pretension avail nothing. Gowns, and pecuniary foundations, though of towns of gold, can never countervail the least sentence or syllable of wit. Forget this, and our American colleges will recede in their public importance, whilst they grow richer every year.

III. There goes in the world a notion, that the scholar should be a recluse, a valetudinarian,—as unfit for any handiwork or public labor, as a penknife for an axe. The so-called 'practical men' sneer at speculative men, as if, because they speculate or *see*, they could do nothing. I have heard it said that the clergy,—who are always, more universally than any other class, the scholars of their day,—are addressed as women; that the rough, spontaneous conversation of men they do not hear, but only a mincing and diluted speech. They are often virtually disfranchised; and, indeed, there are advocates for their celibacy. As far as this is true of the studious classes, it is not just and wise. Action is with the scholar subordinate, but it is essential. Without it, he is not yet man. Without it, thought can never ripen into truth. Whilst the world hangs before the eye as a cloud of beauty, we cannot even see its beauty. Inaction is cowardice, but there can be no scholar without the heroic mind. The preamble of thought, the transition through which it passes from the unconscious to the conscious, is action. Only so much do I know, as I have lived. Instantly we know whose words are loaded with life, and whose not.

The world,—this shadow of the soul, or *other me*, lies wide around. Its attractions are the keys which unlock my thoughts and make me acquainted with myself. I run eagerly into this resounding tumult. I grasp the hands of those next me, and take my place in the ring to suffer and to work, taught by an instinct, that so shall the dumb abyss be vocal with speech. I pierce its order; I dissipate its fear; I dispose of it within the circuit of my expanding life. So much only of life as I know by experience, so much of the wilderness have I vanquished and planted, or so far have I extended my being, my dominion. I do not see how any man can afford, for the sake of his nerves and his nap, to spare any action in which he can partake. It is pearls and rubies to his discourse. Drudgery, calamity, exasperation, want, are instructors in eloquence and wisdom. The true scholar grudges every opportunity of action past by, as a loss of power.

It is the raw material out of which the intellect moulds her splendid products. A strange process too, this, by which experience is converted into thought, as a mulberry leaf is converted into satin. The manufacture goes forward at all hours.

The actions and events of our childhood and youth, are now matters of calmest observation. They lie like fair pictures in the air. Not so with our recent actions,—with the business which we now have in hand. On this we are quite unable to speculate. Our affections as yet circulate through it. We no more feel or know it, than we feel the feet, or the hand, or the brain of our body. The new deed is yet a part of life,—remains for a time immersed in our unconscious life. In some contemplative hour, it detaches itself from the life like a ripe fruit, to become a thought of the mind. Instantly, it is raised, transfigured; the corruptible has put on incorruption.[15] Henceforth it is an object of beauty, however base its origin and neighborhood. Observe, too, the impossibility of antedating this act. In its grub state, it cannot fly, it cannot shine, it is a dull grub. But suddenly, without observation, the selfsame thing unfurls beautiful wings, and is an angel of wisdom. So is there no fact, no event, in our private history, which shall not, sooner or later, lose its adhesive, inert form, and astonish us by soaring from our body into the empyrean.[16] Cradle

---

[15]THE CORRUPTIBLE HAS PUT ON INCORRUPTION: From 1 Corinthians 15:53: "For this corruptible must put on incorruption, and this mortal must put on immortality."
[16]EMPYREAN: The highest sphere of heaven.

and infancy, school and playground, the fear of boys, and dogs, and ferules,[17] the love of little maids and berries, and many another fact that once filled the whole sky, are gone already; friend and relative, profession and party, town and country, nation and world, must also soar and sing.

Of course, he who has put forth his total strength in fit actions, has the richest return of wisdom. I will not shut myself out of this globe of action, and transplant an oak into a flower-pot, there to hunger and pine; nor trust the revenue of some single faculty, and exhaust one vein of thought, much like those Savoyards,[18] who, getting their livelihood by carving shepherds, shepherdesses, and smoking Dutchmen, for all Europe, went out one day to the mountain to find stock, and discovered that they had whittled up the last of their pine-trees. Authors we have, in numbers,[19] who have written out their vein, and who, moved by a commendable prudence, sail for Greece or Palestine, follow the trapper into the prairie, or ramble round Algiers, to replenish their merchantable stock.

If it were only for a vocabulary, the scholar would be covetous of action. Life is our dictionary. Years are well spent in country labors; in town,—in the insight into trades and manufactures; in frank intercourse with many men and women; in science; in art; to the one end of mastering in all their facts a language by which to illustrate and embody our perceptions. I learn immediately from any speaker how much he has already lived, through the poverty or the splendor of his speech. Life lies behind us as the quarry from whence we get tiles and copestones for the masonry of to-day. This is the way to learn grammar. Colleges and books only copy the language which the field and the work-yard made.

But the final value of action, like that of books, and better than books, is, that it is a resource. That great principle of Undulation in nature, that shows itself in the inspiring and expiring of the breath; in desire and satiety; in the ebb and flow of the sea; in day and night; in heat and cold; and as yet more deeply ingrained in every atom and every fluid, is known to us under the name of Polarity,—these "fits of easy transmission and reflection," as Newton[20] called them, are the law of nature because they are the law of spirit.

---

[17]FERULES: Rods used for punishing children.
[18]SAVOYARDS: Persons from Savoy, an area in the western Alps where France, Switzerland, and Italy meet.
[19]AUTHORS WE HAVE, IN NUMBERS: Emerson refers to literary contemporaries who would have been recognized by his audience, such as Nathaniel Parker Willis (1806–1867), James Fenimore Cooper (1789–1851), and Washington Irving (1783–1859).
[20]"FITS OF EASY TRANSMISSION AND REFLECTION," AS NEWTON CALLED THEM: Emerson quotes the *Optics*, by Sir Isaac Newton (1642–1727), English scientist and mathematician.

The mind now thinks; now acts; and each fit reproduces the other. When the artist has exhausted his materials, when the fancy no longer paints, when thoughts are no longer apprehended, and books are a weariness,—he has always the resource *to live*. Character is higher than intellect. Thinking is the function. Living is the functionary. The stream retreats to its source. A great soul will be strong to live, as well as strong to think. Does he lack organ or medium to impart his truths? He can still fall back on this elemental force of living them. This is a total act. Thinking is a partial act. Let the grandeur of justice shine in his affairs. Let the beauty of affection cheer his lowly roof. Those 'far from fame,' who dwell and act with him, will feel the force of his constitution in the doings and passages of the day better than it can be measured by any public and designed display. Time shall teach him, that the scholar loses no hour which the man lives. Herein he unfolds the sacred germ of his instinct, screened from influence. What is lost in seemliness is gained in strength. Not out of those, on whom systems of education have exhausted their culture, comes the helpful giant to destroy the old or to build the new, but out of unhandselled[21] savage nature, out of terrible Druids and Berserkirs,[22] come at last Alfred[23] and Shakspeare.

I hear therefore with joy whatever is beginning to be said of the dignity and necessity of labor to every citizen. There is virtue yet in the hoe and the spade, for learned as well as for unlearned hands. And labor is everywhere welcome; always we are invited to work; only be this limitation observed, that a man shall not for the sake of wider activity sacrifice any opinion to the popular judgments and modes of action.

I have now spoken of the education of the scholar by nature, by books, and by action. It remains to say somewhat of his duties.

They are such as become Man Thinking. They may all be comprised in self-trust. The office of the scholar is to cheer, to raise, and to guide men by showing them facts amidst appearances. He plies the slow, unhonored, and unpaid task of observation. Flamsteed and Herschel,[24] in their glazed[25] observatories, may catalogue the stars with the praise of all men, and, the results being splendid and useful, honor is sure. But he, in his

[21]UNHANDSELLED: A handsel is a lucky token or omen of good luck.
[22]DRUIDS AND BERSERKIRS: Primitive, uncivilized peoples; referring to the ancient Celts and Anglo-Saxons.
[23]ALFRED: A king (849–901) of the West Saxons who helped establish English law.
[24]FLAMSTEED AND HERSCHEL: John Flamsteed (1649–1719) and William Herschel (1732–1822), English astronomers.
[25]GLAZED: Glass-roofed.

private observatory, cataloguing obscure and nebulous stars of the human mind, which as yet no man has thought of as such,—watching days and months, sometimes, for a few facts; correcting still his old records;—must relinquish display and immediate fame. In the long period of his preparation, he must betray often an ignorance and shiftlessness in popular arts, incurring the disdain of the able who shoulder him aside. Long he must stammer in his speech; often forego the living for the dead. Worse yet, he must accept,—how often! poverty and solitude. For the ease and pleasure of treading the old road, accepting the fashions, the education, the religion of society, he takes the cross of making his own, and, of course, the self-accusation, the faint heart, the frequent uncertainty and loss of time, which are the nettles and tangling vines in the way of the self-relying and self-directed; and the state of virtual hostility in which he seems to stand to society, and especially to educated society. For all this loss and scorn, what offset? He is to find consolation in exercising the highest functions of human nature. He is one, who raises himself from private considerations, and breathes and lives on public and illustrious thoughts. He is the world's eye. He is the world's heart. He is to resist the vulgar prosperity that retrogrades ever to barbarism, by preserving and communicating heroic sentiments, noble biographies, melodious verse, and the conclusions of history. Whatsoever oracles the human heart, in all emergencies, in all solemn hours, has uttered as its commentary on the world of actions,—these he shall receive and impart. And whatsoever new verdict Reason from her inviolable seat pronounces on the passing men and events of to-day,— this he shall hear and promulgate.

These being his functions, it becomes him to feel all confidence in himself, and to defer never to the popular cry. He and he only knows the world. The world of any moment is the merest appearance. Some great decorum, some fetish of a government, some ephemeral trade, or war, or man, is cried up by half mankind and cried down by the other half, as if all depended on this particular up or down. The odds are that the whole question is not worth the poorest thought which the scholar has lost in listening to the controversy. Let him not quit his belief that a popgun is a popgun, though the ancient and honorable of the earth affirm it to be the crack of doom. In silence, in steadiness, in severe abstraction, let him hold by himself; add observation to observation, patient of neglect, patient of reproach; and bide his own time,—happy enough, if he can satisfy himself alone, that this day he has seen something truly. Success treads on every right step. For the instinct is sure, that prompts him to tell his brother what he thinks. He then learns, that in going down into the secrets of his own mind, he has descended into the secrets of all minds. He learns that he who has mastered any law in his private thoughts, is master to that extent of all men whose language he speaks, and of all into whose language his own can be translated. The poet, in utter solitude remembering his spontaneous thoughts and recording them, is found to have recorded that, which men in crowded cities find true for them also. The orator distrusts at first the fitness of his frank confessions,—his want of knowledge of the persons he addresses,—until he finds that he is the complement of his hearers;—that they drink his words because he fulfills for them their own nature; the deeper he dives into his privatest, secretest presentiment, to his wonder he finds, this is the most acceptable, most public, and universally true. The people delight in it; the better part of every man feels, This is my music; this is myself.

In self-trust, all the virtues are comprehended. Free should the scholar be,—free and brave. Free even to the definition of freedom, "without any hindrance that does not arise out of his own constitution." Brave; for fear is a thing, which a scholar by his very function puts behind him. Fear always springs from ignorance. It is a shame to him if his tranquility, amid dangerous times, arise from the presumption, that, like children and women, his is a protected class; or if he seek a temporary peace by the diversion of his thoughts from politics or vexed questions, hiding his head like an ostrich in the flowering bushes, peeping into microscopes, and turning rhymes, as a boy whistles to keep his courage up. So is the danger a danger still; so is the fear worse. Manlike let him turn and face it. Let him look into its eye and search its nature, inspect its origin,—see the whelping of this lion,—which lies no great way back; he will then find in himself a perfect comprehension of its nature and extent; he will have made his hands meet on the other side, and can henceforth defy it, and pass on superior. The world is his, who can see through its pretension. What deafness, what stone-blind custom, what overgrown error you behold, is there only by sufferance,—by your sufferance. See it to be a lie, and you have already dealt it its mortal blow.

Yes, we are the cowed,—we the trustless. It is a mischievous notion that we are come late into nature; that the world was finished a long time ago. As the world was plastic and fluid in the hands of God, so it is ever to so much of his attributes as we bring to it. To ignorance and sin, it is flint. They adapt themselves to it as they may; but in proportion as a man has any thing in him divine, the firmament flows before him and takes his signet[26] and form. Not he is great who can alter matter, but

[26]SIGNET: A seal, originally one fixed in a finger ring.

he who can alter my state of mind. They are the kings of the world who
give the color of their present thought to all nature and all art, and persuade men by the cheerful serenity of their carrying the matter, that
this thing which they do, is the apple which the ages have desired to
pluck, now at last ripe, and inviting nations to the harvest. The great man
makes the great thing. Wherever Macdonald sits, there is the head of
the table.[27] Linnæus[28] makes botany the most alluring of studies, and
wins it from the farmer and the herb-woman; Davy,[29] chemistry; and
Cuvier,[30] fossils. The day is always his, who works in it with serenity
and great aims. The unstable estimates of men crowd to him whose mind
is filled with a truth, as the heaped waves of the Atlantic follow the moon.

For this self-trust, the reason is deeper than can be fathomed,—
darker than can be enlightened. I might not carry with me the feeling
of my audience in stating my own belief. But I have already shown
the ground of my hope, in adverting to the doctrine that man is one. I
believe man has been wronged; he has wronged himself. He has almost
lost the light, that can lead him back to his prerogatives. Men are
become of no account. Men in history, men in the world of to-day are
bugs, are spawn, and are called 'the mass' and 'the herd.' In a century, in a millennium, one or two men; that is to say,—one or two
approximations to the right state of every man. All the rest behold in
the hero or the poet their own green and crude being,—ripened; yes,
and are content to be less, so *that* may attain to its full stature. What
a testimony,—full of grandeur, full of pity, is borne to the demands of
his own nature, by the poor clansman, the poor partisan, who rejoices
in the glory of his chief. The poor and the low find some amends to their
immense moral capacity, for their acquiescence in a political and social
inferiority. They are content to be brushed like flies from the path of
a great person, so that justice shall be done by him to that common
nature which it is the dearest desire of all to see enlarged and glorified. They sun themselves in the great man's light, and feel it to be their
own element. They cast the dignity of man from their downtrod selves
upon the shoulders of a hero, and will perish to add one drop of blood
to make that great heart beat, those giant sinews combat and conquer.
He lives for us, and we live in him.

[27]WHEREVER MACDONALD SITS, THERE IS THE HEAD OF THE TABLE: The traditional
proverb is "Where *Macgregor* sits, there is the head of the table."
[28]LINNAEUS: Carolus Linnaeus (1707–1778), Swedish botanist and taxonomist considered the originator of modern scientific classification of plants and animals.
[29]DAVY: Humphry Davy (1778–1829), an English chemist and physicist.
[30]CUVIER: Georges Cuvier (1769–1832), a French naturalist.

Men such as they are, very naturally seek money or power; and power because it is as good as money,—the "spoils," so called, "of office." And why not? for they aspire to the highest, and this, in their sleep-walking, they dream is highest. Wake them, and they shall quit the false good, and leap to the true, and leave governments to clerks and desks. This revolution is to be wrought by the gradual domestication of the idea of Culture. The main enterprise of the world for splendor, for extent, is the upbuilding of a man. Here are the materials strown along the ground. The private life of one man shall be a more illustrious monarchy,—more formidable to its enemy, more sweet and serene in its influence to its friend, than any kingdom in history. For a man, rightly viewed, comprehendeth the particular natures of all men. Each philosopher, each bard, each actor, has only done for me, as by a delegate, what one day I can do for myself. The books which once we valued more than the apple of the eye, we have quite exhausted. What is that but saying, that we have come up with the point of view which the universal mind took through the eyes of one scribe; we have been that man, and have passed on. First, one; then, another; we drain all cisterns, and, waxing greater by all these supplies, we crave a better and more abundant food. The man has never lived that can feed us ever. The human mind cannot be enshrined in a person, who shall set a barrier on any one side to this unbounded, unboundable empire. It is one central fire, which, flaming now out of the lips of Etna,[31] lightens the capes of Sicily; and, now out of the throat of Vesuvius,[32] illuminates the towers and vineyards of Naples. It is one light which beams out of a thousand stars. It is one soul which animates all men.

But I have dwelt perhaps tediously upon this abstraction of the Scholar. I ought not to delay longer to add what I have to say, of nearer reference to the time and to this country.

Historically, there is thought to be a difference in the ideas which predominate over successive epochs, and there are data for marking the genius of the Classic, of the Romantic, and now of the Reflective or Philosophical age.[33] With the views I have intimated of the oneness or the identity of the mind through all individuals, I do not much dwell on these differences. In fact, I believe each individual passes through all three. The boy is a Greek; the youth, romantic; the adult, reflective.

[31]ETNA: An active volcano in western Italy.
[32]VESUVIUS: An active volcano in eastern Sicily, best known for the eruption in 79 CE that buried the towns of Pompeii and Herculaneum.
[33]REFLECTIVE OR PHILOSOPHICAL AGE: Emerson calls his the "Reflective" or "Philosophical" age yet argues that it is not merely a time to reflect on the works of the past, but one of creative achievement as well.

I deny not, however, that a revolution in the leading idea may be distinctly enough traced.

Our age is bewailed as the age of Introversion. Must that needs be evil? We, it seems, are critical; we are embarrassed with second thoughts; we cannot enjoy any thing for hankering to know whereof the pleasure consists; we are lined with eyes; we see with our feet; the time is infected with Hamlet's unhappiness,—

"Sicklied o'er with the pale cast of thought."[34]

Is it so bad then? Sight is the last thing to be pitied. Would we be blind? Do we fear lest we should outsee nature and God, and drink truth dry? I look upon the discontent of the literary class, as a mere announcement of the fact, that they find themselves not in the state of mind of their fathers, and regret the coming state as untried; as a boy dreads the water before he has learned that he can swim. If there is any period one would desire to be born in,—is it not the age of Revolution; when the old and the new stand side by side, and admit of being compared; when the energies of all men are searched by fear and by hope; when the historic glories of the old, can be compensated by the rich possibilities of the new era? This time, like all times, is a very good one, if we but know what to do with it.

I read with joy some of the auspicious signs of the coming days, as they glimmer already through poetry and art, through philosophy and science, through church and state.

One of these signs is the fact, that the same movement which effected the elevation of what was called the lowest class in the state, assumed in literature a very marked and as benign an aspect. Instead of the sublime and beautiful; the near, the low, the common, was explored and poetized. That, which had been negligently trodden under foot by those who were harnessing and provisioning themselves for long journeys into far countries, is suddenly found to be richer than all foreign parts. The literature of the poor, the feelings of the child, the philosophy of the street, the meaning of household life, are the topics of the time. It is a great stride. It is a sign,—is it not? of new vigor, when the extremities are made active, when currents of warm life run into the hands and the feet. I ask not for the great, the remote, the romantic; what is doing in Italy or Arabia; what is Greek art, or Provençal[35] minstrelsy; I embrace the common, I explore and sit at the feet of the familiar, the low. Give me insight

---

[34]SICKLIED O'ER WITH THE PALE CAST OF THOUGHT: From Shakespeare's *Hamlet*, Act III, Scene 1, line 85.
[35]PROVENÇAL: Referring to the musicians of medieval southeast France.

into to-day, and you may have the antique and future worlds. What would we really know the meaning of? The meal in the firkin[36]; the milk in the pan; the ballad in the street; the news of the boat; the glance of the eye; the form and the gait of the body;—show me the ultimate reason of these matters; show me the sublime presence of the highest spiritual cause lurking, as always it does lurk, in these suburbs and extremities of nature; let me see every trifle bristling with the polarity that ranges it instantly on an eternal law; and the shop, the plough, and the leger, referred to the like cause by which light undulates and poets sing;—and the world lies no longer a dull miscellany and lumber-room,[37] but has form and order; there is no trifle; there is no puzzle; but one design unites and animates the farthest pinnacle and the lowest trench.

This idea has inspired the genius of Goldsmith,[38] Burns,[39] Cowper,[40] and, in a newer time, of Goethe,[41] Wordsworth,[42] and Carlyle.[43] This idea they have differently followed and with various success. In contrast with their writing, the style of Pope,[44] of Johnson,[45] of Gibbon,[46] looks cold and pedantic. This writing is blood-warm. Man is surprised to find that things near are not less beautiful and wondrous than things remote. The near explains the far. The drop is a small ocean. A man is related to all nature. This perception of the worth of the vulgar is fruitful in discoveries. Goethe, in this very thing the most modern of the moderns, has shown us, as none ever did, the genius of the ancients.

There is one man of genius, who has done much for this philosophy of life, whose literary value has never yet been rightly estimated;—I mean Emanuel Swedenborg.[47] The most imaginative of men, yet writing with the precision of a mathematician, he endeavored to engraft a purely philosophical Ethics on the popular Christianity of his time. Such an attempt, of course, must have difficulty, which no genius could surmount. But he saw and showed the connection between nature and the affections

---

[36]FIRKIN: Small pail.
[37]LUMBER-ROOM: Junk room.
[38]GOLDSMITH: Oliver Goldsmith (1702–1744), an Irish author of the pre-Romantic period.
[39]BURNS: Robert Burns (1759–1796), a Scottish poet.
[40]COWPER: William Cowper (1731–1800), an English poet.
[41]GOETHE: Johann Wolfgang von Goethe (1749–1832), German poet, dramatist, and novelist best known for his dramatic poem *Faust*.
[42]WORDSWORTH: William Wordsworth (1770–1850), an English poet and leader of the Romantic movement.
[43]CARLYLE: Thomas Carlyle (1795–1851), an English Romantic writer strongly influenced by Goethe.
[44]POPE: Alexander Pope (1688–1744), an English poet and satirist.
[45]JOHNSON: Samuel Johnson (1709–1784), an English author, literary scholar, and critic.
[46]GIBBON: Edward Gibbon (1737–1794), an English historian and the author of *The History of the Decline and Fall of the Roman Empire*.
[47]EMANUEL SWEDENBORG: A Swedish scientist, religious teacher, and theologian (1668–1772).

of the soul. He pierced the emblematic or spiritual character of the visible, audible, tangible world. Especially did his shade-loving muse hover over and interpret the lower parts of nature; he showed the mysterious bond that allies moral evil to the foul material forms, and has given in epical parables a theory of insanity, of beasts, of unclean and fearful things.

Another sign of our times, also marked by an analogous political movement, is, the new importance given to the single person. Every thing that tends to insulate the individual,—to surround him with barriers of natural respect, so that each man shall feel the world is his, and man shall treat with man as a sovereign state with a sovereign state;—tends to true union as well as greatness. "I learned," said the melancholy Pestalozzi,[48] "that no man in God's wide earth is either willing or able to help any other man." Help must come from the bosom alone. The scholar is that man who must take up into himself all the ability of the time, all the contributions of the past, all the hopes of the future. He must be an university of knowledges. If there be one lesson more than another, which should pierce his ear, it is, The world is nothing, the man is all; in yourself is the law of all nature, and you know not yet how a globule of sap ascends; in yourself slumbers the whole of Reason; it is for you to know all, it is for you to dare all. Mr. President and Gentlemen, this confidence in the unsearched might of man belongs, by all motives, by all prophecy, by all preparation, to the American Scholar. We have listened too long to the courtly muses of Europe. The spirit of the American freeman is already suspected to be timid, imitative, tame. Public and private avarice make the air we breathe thick and fat. The scholar is decent, indolent, complaisant. See already the tragic consequence. The mind of this country, taught to aim at low objects, eats upon itself. There is no work for any but the decorous and the complaisant. Young men of the fairest promise, who begin life upon our shores, inflated by the mountain winds, shined upon by all the stars of God, find the earth below not in unison with these,—but are hindered from action by the disgust which the principles on which business is managed inspire, and turn drudges, or die of disgust,—some of them suicides. What is the remedy? They did not yet see, and thousands of young men as hopeful now crowding to the barriers for the career, do not yet see, that, if the single man plant himself indomitably on his instincts, and there abide, the huge world will come round to him. Patience,—patience;—with the shades of all the good and great for company; and for solace, the perspective of your own infinite life; and for work, the study and the

---

[48]PESTALOZZI: Johann Heinrich Pestalozzi (1746–1827), a Swiss educational reformer. His theories influenced Emerson's friends, the American educational reformers Amos Bronson Alcott (1799–1888) and Elizabeth Palmer Peabody (1804–1894).

communication of principles, the making those instincts prevalent, the conversion of the world. Is it not the chief disgrace in the world, not to be an unit;—not to be reckoned one character;—not to yield that peculiar fruit which each man was created to bear, but to be reckoned in the gross, in the hundred, or the thousand, of the party, the section, to which we belong; and our opinion predicted geographically, as the north, or the south? Not so, brothers and friends,—please God, ours shall not be so. We will walk on our own feet; we will work with our own hands; we will speak our own minds. The study of letters shall be no longer a name for pity, for doubt, and for sensual indulgence. The dread of man and the love of man shall be a wall of defence and a wreath of joy around all. A nation of men will for the first time exist, because each believes himself inspired by the Divine Soul which also inspires all men.

[1837, 1849]

Self-Reliance

"Ne te quaesiveris extra."[1]

"Man is his own star; and the soul that can
Render an honest and a perfect man,
Commands all light, all influence, all fate;
Nothing to him falls early or too late.
Our acts our angels are, or good or ill,
Our fatal shadows that walk by us still."
——EPILOGUE TO BEAUMONT AND FLETCHER'S *HONEST MAN'S FORTUNE*[2]

Cast the bantling[3] *on the rocks,*
Suckle him with the she-wolf's teat;
Wintered with the hawk and fox,
Power and speed be hands and feet.

I read the other day some verses written by an eminent painter[4] which were original and not conventional. The soul always hears an admonition in such lines, let the subject be what it may. The sentiment they instil is of more value than any thought they may contain. To believe your own

---

[1]NE TE QUAESIVERIS EXTRA: Do not search outside yourself (Latin); that is, do not imitate.
[2]BEAUMONT AND FLETCHER'S HONEST MAN'S FORTUNE: *Honest Man's Fortune* (1613) was written by English dramatists Francis Beaumont (c. 1584–1616) and John Fletcher (1579–1625).
[3]BANTLING: Young child.
[4]EMINENT PAINTER: Emerson refers to the American painter and author Washington Allston (1799–1843).

thought, to believe that what is true for you in your private heart, is true for all men,—that is genius. Speak your latent conviction and it shall be the universal sense; for the inmost in due time becomes the outmost,— and our first thought is rendered back to us by the trumpets of the Last Judgment. Familiar as the voice of the mind is to each, the highest merit we ascribe to Moses,[5] Plato,[6] and Milton,[7] is that they set at naught books and traditions, and spoke not what men but what they thought. A man should learn to detect and watch that gleam of light which flashes across his mind from within, more than the lustre of the firmament of bards and sages. Yet he dismisses without notice his thought, because it is his. In every work of genius we recognize our own rejected thoughts: they come back to us with a certain alienated majesty. Great works of art have no more affecting lesson for us than this. They teach us to abide by our spontaneous impression with good-humored inflexibility then most when the whole cry of voices is on the other side. Else, tomorrow a stranger will say with masterly good sense precisely what we have thought and felt all the time, and we shall be forced to take with shame our own opinion from another.

There is a time in every man's education when he arrives at the conviction that envy is ignorance; that imitation is suicide; that he must take himself for better, for worse, as his portion; that though the wide universe is full of good, no kernel of nourishing corn can come to him but through his toil bestowed on that plot of ground which is given to him to till. The power which resides in him is new in nature, and none but he knows what that is which he can do, nor does he know until he has tried. Not for nothing one face, one character, one fact makes much impression on him, and another none. This sculpture in the memory is not without preëstablished harmony. The eye was placed where one ray should fall, that it might testify of that particular ray. We but half express ourselves, and are ashamed of that divine idea which each of us represents. It may be safely trusted as proportionate and of good issues, so it be faithfully imparted, but God will not have his work made manifest by cowards. A man is relieved and gay when he has put his heart into his work and done his best; but what he has said or done otherwise, shall give him no peace. It is a deliverance which does not deliver. In the attempt his genius deserts him; no muse befriends; no invention, no hope.

---

[5]MOSES: The biblical Hebrew leader who led the Israelites from slavery in Egypt to the Promised Land.
[6]PLATO: A Greek philosopher (427?–347 BCE).
[7]MILTON: John Milton (1608–1674), English poet best known for his epic work *Paradise Lost* (1667).

Trust thyself: every heart vibrates to that iron string. Accept the place the divine Providence has found for you; the society of your contemporaries, the connexion of events. Great men have always done so and confided themselves childlike to the genius of their age, betraying their perception that the absolutely trustworthy was seated at their heart, working through their hands, predominating in all their being. And we are now men, and must accept in the highest mind the same transcendent destiny; and not minors and invalids in a protected corner, not cowards fleeing before a revolution, but guides, redeemers, and benefactors, obeying the Almighty effort, and advancing on Chaos and the Dark.

What pretty oracles nature yields us on this text in the face and behavior of children, babes and even brutes. That divided and rebel mind, that distrust of a sentiment because our arithmetic has computed the strength and means opposed to our purpose, these have not. Their mind being whole, their eye is as yet unconquered, and when we look in their faces, we are disconcerted. Infancy conforms to nobody: all conform to it, so that one babe commonly makes four or five out of the adults who prattle and play to it. So God has armed youth and puberty and manhood no less with its own piquancy and charm, and made it enviable and gracious and its claims not to be put by, if it will stand by itself. Do not think the youth has no force because he cannot speak to you and me. Hark! in the next room his voice is sufficiently clear and emphatic. It seems he knows how to speak to his contemporaries. Bashful or bold, then, he will know how to make us seniors very unnecessary.

The nonchalance of boys who are sure of a dinner, and would disdain as much as a lord to do or say aught to conciliate one, is the healthy attitude of human nature. A boy is in the parlour what the pit is in the playhouse; independent, irresponsible, looking out from his corner on such people and facts as pass by, he tries and sentences them on their merits, in the swift summary way of boys, as good, bad, interesting, silly, eloquent, troublesome. He cumbers himself never about consequences, about interests: he gives an independent, genuine verdict. You must court him: he does not court you. But the man is, as it were, clapped into jail by his consciousness. As soon as he has once acted or spoken with eclat, he is a committed person, watched by the sympathy or the hatred of hundreds whose affections must now enter into his account. There is no Lethe[8] for this. Ah, that he could pass again into his neutrality! Who can thus avoid all pledges, and having observed, observe again from

---

[8]LETHE: In Greek myth, one of the rivers flowing through the underworld. Also called the River of Oblivion, its waters helped the spirits of the dead forget their past lives on earth.

the same unaffected, unbiassed, unbribable, unaffrighted innocence, must always be formidable. He would utter opinions on all passing affairs, which being seen to be not private but necessary, would sink like darts into the ear of men, and put them in fear.

These are the voices which we hear in solitude, but they grow faint and inaudible as we enter into the world. Society everywhere is in conspiracy against the manhood of every one of its members. Society is a joint-stock company in which the members agree for the better securing of his bread to each shareholder, to surrender the liberty and culture of the eater. The virtue in most request is conformity. Self-reliance is its aversion. It loves not realities and creators, but names and customs.

Whoso would be a man must be a nonconformist. He who would gather immortal palms must not be hindered by the name of goodness, but must explore if it be goodness. Nothing is at last sacred but the integrity of your own mind. Absolve you to yourself, and you shall have the suffrage of the world. I remember an answer which when quite young I was prompted to make to a valued adviser who was wont to importune me with the dear old doctrines of the church. On my saying, What have I to do with the sacredness of traditions, if I live wholly from within? my friend suggested—"But these impulses may be from below, not from above." I replied, "They do not seem to me to be such; but if I am the Devil's child, I will live then from the Devil." No law can be sacred to me but that of my nature. Good and bad are but names very readily transferable to that or this; the only right is what is after my constitution, the only wrong what is against it. A man is to carry himself in the presence of all opposition as if every thing were titular and ephemeral but he. I am ashamed to think how easily we capitulate to badges and names, to large societies and dead institutions. Every decent and well-spoken individual affects and sways me more than is right. I ought to go upright and vital, and speak the rude truth in all ways. If malice and vanity wear the coat of philanthropy, shall that pass? If an angry bigot assumes this bountiful cause of Abolition, and comes to me with his last news from Barbadoes,[9] why should I not say to him, 'Go love thy infant; love thy wood-chopper: be good-natured and modest: have that grace; and never varnish your hard, uncharitable ambition with this incredible tenderness for black folk a thousand miles off. Thy love afar is spite at home.' Rough and graceless would be such greeting, but truth is handsomer than the affectation of love. Your goodness must have some edge to it—else it is

[9]BARBADOES: Barbados, an Eastern Caribbean island that abolished slavery in 1834 and freed all its slaves by 1838.

none. The doctrine of hatred must be preached as the counteraction of the doctrine of love when that pules and whines. I shun father and mother and wife and brother, when my genius calls me. I would write on the lintels of the doorpost, *Whim*. I hope it is somewhat better than whim at last, but we cannot spend the day in explanation. Expect me not to show cause why I seek or why I exclude company. Then, again, do not tell me, as a good man did to-day, of my obligation to put all poor men in good situations. Are they *my* poor? I tell thee, thou foolish philanthropist, that I grudge the dollar, the dime, the cent I give to such men as do not belong to me and to whom I do not belong. There is a class of persons to whom by all spiritual affinity I am bought and sold; for them I will go to prison, if need be; but your miscellaneous popular charities; the education at college of fools; the building of meeting-houses to the vain end to which many now stand; alms to sots; and the thousandfold Relief Societies;—though I confess with shame I sometimes succumb and give the dollar, it is a wicked dollar which by and by I shall have the manhood to withhold.

Virtues are in the popular estimate rather the exception than the rule. There is the man *and* his virtues. Men do what is called a good action, as some piece of courage or charity, much as they would pay a fine in expiation of daily non-appearance on parade. Their works are done as an apology or extenuation of their living in the world,—as invalids and the insane pay a high board. Their virtues are penances. I do not wish to expiate, but to live. My life is for itself and not for a spectacle. I much prefer that it should be of a lower strain, so it be genuine and equal, than that it should be glittering and unsteady. I wish it to be sound and sweet, and not to need diet and bleeding.[10] I ask primary evidence that you are a man, and refuse this appeal from the man to his actions. I know that for myself it makes no difference whether I do or forbear those actions which are reckoned excellent. I cannot consent to pay for a privilege where I have intrinsic right. Few and mean as my gifts may be, I actually am, and do not need for my own assurance or the assurance of my fellows any secondary testimony.

What I must do, is all that concerns me, not what the people think. This rule, equally arduous in actual and in intellectual life, may serve for the whole distinction between greatness and meanness. It is the harder, because you will always find those who think they know what is your duty better than you know it. It is easy in the world to live after the world's opinion; it is easy in solitude to live after our own; but the great

---

[10]DIET AND BLEEDING: Medical treatments; bleeding means deliberate bloodletting.

man is he who in the midst of the crowd keeps with perfect sweetness the independence of solitude.

The objection to conforming to usages that have become dead to you, is, that it scatters your force. It loses your time and blurs the impression of your character. If you maintain a dead church, contribute to a dead Bible-Society, vote with a great party either for the Government or against it, spread your table like base housekeepers,—under all these screens, I have difficulty to detect the precise man you are. And, of course, so much force is withdrawn from your proper life. But do your work, and I shall know you. Do your work, and you shall reinforce yourself. A man must consider what a blindman's-buff is this game of conformity. If I know your sect, I anticipate your argument. I hear a preacher announce for his text and topic the expediency of one of the institutions of his church. Do I not know beforehand that not possibly can he say a new and spontaneous word? Do I not know that with all this ostentation of examining the grounds of the institution, he will do no such thing? Do I not know that he is pledged to himself not to look but at one side,—the permitted side, not as a man, but as a parish minister? He is a retained attorney, and these airs of the bench are the emptiest affectation. Well, most men have bound their eyes with one or another handkerchief, and attached themselves to some one of these communities of opinion. This conformity makes them not false in a few particulars, authors of a few lies, but false in all particulars. Their every truth is not quite true. Their two is not the real two, their four not the real four: so that every word they say chagrins us, and we know not where to begin to set them right. Meantime nature is not slow to equip us in the prison-uniform of the party to which we adhere. We come to wear one cut of face and figure, and acquire by degrees the gentlest asinine expression. There is a mortifying experience in particular which does not fail to wreak itself also in the general history; I mean "the foolish face of praise,"[11] the forced smile which we put on in company where we do not feel at ease in answer to conversation which does not interest us. The muscles, not spontaneously moved, but moved by a low usurping wilfulness, grow tight about the outline of the face with the most disagreeable sensation.

For nonconformity the world whips you with its displeasure. And therefore a man must know how to estimate a sour face. The bystanders look askance on him in the public street or in the friend's parlor. If this aversation had its origin in contempt and resistance like his own, he might well go home with a sad countenance; but the sour

---

[11]THE FOOLISH FACE OF PRAISE: A quote from Alexander Pope's "Epistle to Dr. Arbuthnot" (1735).

faces of the multitude, like their sweet faces, have no deep cause, but are put on and off as the wind blows, and a newspaper directs. Yet is the discontent of the multitude more formidable than that of the senate and the college. It is easy enough for a firm man who knows the world to brook the rage of the cultivated classes. Their rage is decorous and prudent, for they are timid as being very vulnerable themselves. But when to their feminine rage the indignation of the people is added, when the ignorant and the poor are aroused, when the unintelligent brute force that lies at the bottom of society is made to growl and mow, it needs the habit of magnanimity and religion to treat it godlike as a trifle of no concernment.

The other terror that scares us from self-trust is our consistency; a reverence for our past act or word, because the eyes of others have no other data for computing our orbit than our past acts, and we are loath to disappoint them.

But why should you keep your head over your shoulder? Why drag about this corpse of your memory, lest you contradict somewhat you have stated in this or that public place? Suppose you should contradict yourself; what then? It seems to be a rule of wisdom never to rely on your memory alone, scarcely even in acts of pure memory, but to bring the past for judgment into the thousand-eyed present, and live ever in a new day. In your metaphysics you have denied personality to the Deity; yet when the devout motions of the soul come, yield to them heart and life, though they should clothe God with shape and color. Leave your theory as Joseph his coat in the hand of the harlot, and flee.[12]

A foolish consistency is the hobgoblin of little minds, adored by little statesmen and philosophers and divines. With consistency a great soul has simply nothing to do. He may as well concern himself with his shadow on the wall. Speak what you think now in hard words, and to-morrow speak what to-morrow thinks in hard words again, though it contradict every thing you said to-day.—'Ah, so you shall be sure to be misunderstood.'—Is it so bad then to be misunderstood? Pythagoras[13] was misunderstood, and Socrates,[14] and Jesus, and Luther,[15] and

---

[12]LEAVE YOUR THEORY AS JOSEPH HIS COAT IN THE HAND OF THE HARLOT, AND FLEE: A reference to the biblical story of Joseph, who avoids the advances of Pontiphar's wife, as described in Genesis 39.
[13]PYTHAGORAS: A pre-Socratic Greek philosopher (c. 582–c. 507 BCE).
[14]SOCRATES: A Greek philosopher (469–399 BCE) who was executed for "corrupting" the youth of Athens and for religious heresy.
[15]LUTHER: Martin Luther, German leader (1483–1546) of the Protestant Reformation.

Copernicus,[16] and Galileo,[17] and Newton,[18] and every pure and wise spirit that ever took flesh. To be great is to be misunderstood.

I suppose no man can violate his nature. All the sallies of his will are rounded in by the law of his being as the inequalities of Andes and Himmaleh[19] are insignificant in the curve of the sphere. Nor does it matter how you gauge and try him. A character is like an acrostic[20] or Alexandrian stanza[21];—read it forward, backward, or across, it still spells the same thing. In this pleasing contrite wood-life which God allows me, let me record day by day my honest thought without prospect or retrospect, and, I cannot doubt, it will be found symmetrical, though I mean it not, and see it not. My book should smell of pines and resound with the hum of insects. The swallow over my window should interweave that thread or straw he carries in his bill into my web also. We pass for what we are. Character teaches above our wills. Men imagine that they communicate their virtue or vice only by overt actions and do not see that virtue or vice emit a breath every moment.

There will be an agreement in whatever variety of actions, so they be each honest and natural in their hour. For of one will, the actions will be harmonious, however unlike they seem. These varieties are lost sight of at a little distance, at a little height of thought. One tendency unites them all. The voyage of the best ship is a zigzag line of a hundred tacks. See the line from a sufficient distance, and it straightens itself to the average tendency. Your genuine action will explain itself and will explain your other genuine actions. Your conformity explains nothing. Act singly, and what you have already done singly, will justify you now. Greatness appeals to the future. If I can be firm enough to-day to do right and scorn eyes, I must have done so much right before, as to defend me now. Be it how it will, do right now. Always scorn appearances, and you always may. The force of character is cumulative. All the foregone days of virtue work their health into this. What makes the majesty of the heroes of the senate and the field, which so fills the imagination? The

---

[16]COPERNICUS: Nicholas Copernicus (1473–1543), the Polish astronomer whose radical concept it was that the sun, not the earth, is the center of the solar system.

[17]GALILEO: Galileo Galilei (1564–1642), the Italian astronomer, mathematician, and physicist who laid the foundation of modern science.

[18]NEWTON: Isaac Newton (1642–1727), the English mathematician and physicist best known for his description of the laws of gravity, motion, and light.

[19]ANDES AND HIMMALEH: Mountain ranges in South America and Asia (Himalayas).

[20]ACROSTIC: A short poem in which the first letters of each line, in order, spell a word or phrase. Sometimes the last or middle letters of the lines, or all of them, are similarly arranged to spell words. Emerson, however, is referring to a palindrome, which is a word, verse, or phrase that reads the same forward and backward.

[21]ALEXANDRIAN STANZA: Applied to a line of six or five feet or twelve syllables.

consciousness of a train of great days and victories behind. They shed an united light on the advancing actor. He is attended as by a visible escort of angels. That is it which throws thunder into Chatham's[22] voice, and dignity into Washington's[23] port, and America into Adams's[24] eye. Honor is venerable to us because it is no ephemeris. It is always ancient virtue. We worship it to-day, because it is not of to-day. We love it and pay it homage, because it is not a trap for our love and homage, but is self-dependent, self-derived, and therefore of an old immaculate pedigree, even if shown in a young person.

I hope in these days we have heard the last of conformity and consistency. Let the words be gazetted[25] and ridiculous henceforward. Instead of the gong for dinner, let us hear a whistle from the Spartan fife.[26] Let us never bow and apologize more. A great man is coming to eat at my house. I do not wish to please him: I wish that he should wish to please me. I will stand here for humanity, and though I would make it kind, I would make it true. Let us affront and reprimand the smooth mediocrity and squalid contentment of the times, and hurl in the face of custom, and trade, and office, the fact which is the upshot of all history, that there is a great responsible Thinker and Actor working wherever a man works; that a true man belongs to no other time or place, but is the centre of things. Where he is, there is nature. He measures you, and all men, and all events. Ordinarily every body in society reminds us of somewhat else or of some other person. Character, reality, reminds you of nothing else; it takes place of the whole creation. The man must be so much that he must make all circumstances indifferent. Every true man is a cause, a country, and an age; requires infinite spaces and numbers and time fully to accomplish his design;—and posterity seem to follow his steps as a train of clients. A man Cæsar is born, and for ages after, we have a Roman Empire. Christ is born, and millions of minds so grow and cleave to his genius, that he is confounded with virtue and the possible of man. An institution is the lengthened shadow of one man; as, Monachism, of the Hermit Antony[27];

---

[22]CHATHAM'S: William Pitt, Earl of Chatham (1708–1778), an English politician and orator.
[23]WASHINGTON'S PORT: George Washington (1732–1799), the first president of the United States.
[24]ADAMS'S EYE: Emerson could be referring to either Samuel Adams (1722–1803), a Revolutionary War hero from Massachusetts, John Adams (1735–1826), the second president of the United States, or John Quincy Adams (1767–1848), the sixth president of the United States.
[25]GAZETTED: Publicly announced and then forgotten.
[26]SPARTAN FIFE: Sparta was a military city-state of ancient Greece known for strict organization and discipline. A fife is a high-pitched flute often used in military marching.
[27]MONACHISM, OF THE HERMIT ANTONY: St. Antony of Egypt (c. 251–c. 350) is considered the father of Christian monasticism.

the Reformation, of Luther[28]; Quakerism, of Fox[29]; Methodism, of Wesley[30]; Abolition, of Clarkson.[31] Scipio,[32] Milton called "the height of Rome;" and all history resolves itself very easily into the biography of a few stout and earnest persons.

Let a man then know his worth, and keep things under his feet. Let him not peep or steal, or skulk up and down with the air of a charity-boy, a bastard, or an interloper, in the world which exists for him. But the man in the street finding no worth in himself which corresponds to the force which built a tower or sculptured a marble god, feels poor when he looks on these. To him a palace, a statue, or a costly book have an alien and forbidding air, much like a gay equipage, and seem to say like that, 'Who are you, sir?' Yet they all are his, suitors for his notice, petitioners to his faculties that they will come out and take possession. The picture waits for my verdict: it is not to command me, but I am to settle its claims to praise. That popular fable of the sot who was picked up dead drunk in the street, carried to the duke's house, washed and dressed and laid in the duke's bed, and, on his waking, treated with all obsequious ceremony like the duke, and assured that he had been insane, owes its popularity to the fact, that it symbolizes so well the state of man, who is in the world a sort of sot, but now and then wakes up, exercises his reason, and finds himself a true prince.

Our reading is mendicant and sycophantic. In history, our imagination plays us false. Kingdom and lordship, power and estate are a gaudier vocabulary than private John and Edward in a small house and common day's work: but the things of life are the same to both: the sum total of both is the same. Why all this deference to Alfred,[33] and Scanderbeg,[34] and Gustavus?[35] Suppose they were virtuous: did they wear out virtue? As great a stake depends on your private act to-day, as followed their public and renowned steps. When private men shall act with original views, the lustre will be transferred from the actions of kings to those of gentlemen.

---

[28]REFORMATION, OF LUTHER: See note 15.
[29]QUAKERISM, OF FOX: George Fox (1624–1691), the founder of the Society of Friends, also called the Quakers.
[30]METHODISM, OF WESLEY: John Wesley (1703–1791), the English evangelical preacher who founded Methodism.
[31]ABOLITION, OF CLARKSON: Thomas Clarkson (1760–1846), an English abolitionist.
[32]SCIPIO: Scipio Africanus Major (236–183 BCE), the Roman general who defeated the Carthaginian general Hannibal in the Second Punic War in 201 BCE.
[33]ALFRED: A king (849–901) of the West Saxons who helped establish English law.
[34]SCANDERBEG: Skanderbeg (c. 1404–1468), an Albanian hero born George Castriota or Kastrioti. As a hostage of the Turks, he was called Iskender and given the rank of Bey; Iskender Bey was eventually corrupted to Scanderbeg.
[35]GUSTAVUS: Gustavus Adolphus (1594–1632), the king of Sweden from 1611 to 1632.

The world has been instructed by its kings, who have so magnetized the eyes of nations. It has been taught by this colossal symbol the mutual reverence that is due from man to man. The joyful loyalty with which men have everywhere suffered the king, the noble, or the great proprietor to walk among them by a law of his own, make his own scale of men and things, and reverse theirs, pay for benefits not with money but with honor, and represent the Law in his person, was the hieroglyphic by which they obscurely signified their consciousness of their own right and comeliness, the right of every man.

The magnetism which all original action exerts is explained when we inquire the reason of self-trust. Who is the Trustee? What is the aboriginal Self on which a universal reliance may be grounded? What is the nature and power of that science-baffling star, without parallax,[36] without calculable elements, which shoots a ray of beauty even into trivial and impure actions, if the least mark of independence appear? The inquiry leads us to that source, at once the essence of genius, of virtue, and of life, which we call Spontaneity or Instinct. We denote this primary wisdom as Intuition, whilst all later teachings are tuitions. In that deep force, the last fact behind which analysis cannot go, all things find their common origin. For the sense of being which in calm hours rises, we know not how, in the soul, is not diverse from things, from space, from light, from time, from man, but one with them, and proceeds obviously from the same source whence their life and being also proceed. We first share the life by which things exist, and afterwards see them as appearances in nature, and forget that we have shared their cause. Here is the fountain of action and of thought. Here are the lungs of that inspiration which giveth man wisdom, and which cannot be denied without impiety and atheism. We lie in the lap of immense intelligence, which makes us receivers of its truth and organs of its activity. When we discern justice, when we discern truth, we do nothing of ourselves, but allow a passage to its beams. If we ask whence this comes, if we seek to pry into the soul that causes, all philosophy is at fault. Its presence or its absence is all we can affirm. Every man discriminates between the voluntary acts of his mind, and his involuntary perceptions, and knows that to his involuntary perceptions a perfect faith is due. He may err in the expression of them, but he knows that these things are so, like day and night, not to be disputed. My wilful actions and acquisitions are but roving;—the idlest

---

[36]PARALLAX: In astronomy, the *apparent* displacement of the position of an object, caused by a change of observation point.

reverie, the faintest native emotion, command my curiosity and respect. Thoughtless people contradict as readily the statement of perceptions as of opinions, or rather much more readily; for, they do not distinguish between perception and notion. They fancy that I choose to see this or that thing. But perception is not whimsical, but fatal. If I see a trait, my children will see it after me, and in course of time, all mankind,—although it may chance that no one has seen it before me. For my perception of it is as much a fact as the sun.

The relations of the soul to the divine spirit are so pure that it is profane to seek to interpose helps. It must be that when God speaketh, he should communicate not one thing, but all things; should fill the world with his voice; should scatter forth light, nature, time, souls, from the centre of the present thought; and new date and new create the whole. Whenever a mind is simple, and receives a divine wisdom, old things pass away,—means, teachers, texts, temples fall; it lives now and absorbs past and future into the present hour. All things are made sacred by relation to it,—one as much as another. All things are dissolved to their centre by their cause, and in the universal miracle petty and particular miracles disappear. If, therefore, a man claims to know and speak of God, and carries you backward to the phraseology of some old mouldered nation in another country, in another world, believe him not. Is the acorn better than the oak which is its fulness and completion? Is the parent better than the child into whom he has cast his ripened being? Whence then this worship of the past? The centuries are conspirators against the sanity and authority of the soul. Time and space are but physiological colors which the eye makes, but the soul is light; where it is, is day; where it was, is night; and history is an impertinence and an injury, if it be anything more than a cheerful apologue or parable of my being and becoming.

Man is timid and apologetic; he is no longer upright; he dares not say 'I think,' 'I am,' but quotes some saint or sage. He is ashamed before the blade of grass or the blowing rose. These roses under my window make no reference to former roses or to better ones; they are for what they are; they exist with God to-day. There is no time to them. There is simply the rose; it is perfect in every moment of its existence. Before a leaf-bud has burst, its whole life acts; in the full-blown flower, there is no more; in the leafless root, there is no less. Its nature is satisfied, and it satisfies nature, in all moments alike. But man postpones or remembers; he does not live in the present, but with reverted eye laments the past, or, heedless of the riches that surround him, stands on tiptoe to foresee the future. He cannot be happy and strong until he too lives with nature in the present, above time.

This should be plain enough. Yet see what strong intellects dare not yet hear God himself, unless he speak the phraseology of I know not what David, or Jeremiah, or Paul.[37] We shall not always set so great a price on a few texts, on a few lives. We are like children who repeat by rote the sentences of grandames and tutors, and, as they grow older, of the men of talents and character they chance to see,—painfully recollecting the exact words they spoke; afterwards, when they come into the point of view which those had who uttered these sayings, they understand them, and are willing to let the words go; for, at any time, they can use words as good, when occasion comes. If we live truly, we shall see truly. It is as easy for the strong man to be strong, as it is for the weak to be weak. When we have new perception, we shall gladly disburden the memory of its hoarded treasures as old rubbish. When a man lives with God, his voice shall be as sweet as the murmur of the brook and the rustle of the corn.

And now at last the highest truth on this subject remains unsaid; probably, cannot be said; for all that we say is the far off remembering of the intuition. That thought, by what I can now nearest approach to say it, is this. When good is near you, when you have life in yourself, it is not by any known or accustomed way; you shall not discern the foot-prints of any other; you shall not see the face of man; you shall not hear any name;—the way, the thought, the good shall be wholly strange and new. It shall exclude example and experience. You take the way from man, not to man. All persons that ever existed are its forgotten ministers. Fear and hope are alike beneath it. There is somewhat low even in hope. In the hour of vision, there is nothing that can be called gratitude, nor properly joy. The soul raised over passion beholds identity and eternal causation, perceives the self-existence of Truth and Right, and calms itself with knowing that all things go well. Vast spaces of nature, the Atlantic Ocean, the South Sea,—long intervals of time, years, centuries,—are of no account. This which I think and feel underlay every former state of life and circumstances, as it does underlie my present, and what is called life, and what is called death.

Life only avails, not the having lived. Power ceases in the instant of repose; it resides in the moment of transition from a past to a new state, in the shooting of the gulf, in the darting to an aim. This one fact the world hates, that the soul *becomes*; for, that forever degrades the past, turns all riches to poverty, all reputation to a shame, confounds the saint

[37]DAVID, OR JEREMIAH, OR PAUL: Religious figures credited with authorship of different parts of the Bible—David, the Book of Psalms; Jeremiah, the Book of Jeremiah; and Paul, various New Testament Epistles.

with the rogue, shoves Jesus and Judas equally aside. Why then do we prate of self-reliance? Inasmuch as the soul is present, there will be power not confident but agent. To talk of reliance, is a poor external way of speaking. Speak rather of that which relies, because it works and is. Who has more obedience than I, masters me, though he should not raise his finger. Round him I must revolve by the gravitation of spirits. We fancy it rhetoric when we speak of eminent virtue. We do not yet see that virtue is Height, and that a man or a company of men plastic and permeable to principles, by the law of nature must overpower and ride all cities, nations, kings, rich men, poets, who are not.

This is the ultimate fact which we so quickly reach on this as on every topic, the resolution of all into the ever blessed ONE. Self-existence is the attribute of the Supreme Cause, and it constitutes the measure of good by the degree in which it enters into all lower forms. All things real are so by so much virtue as they contain. Commerce, husbandry, hunting, whaling, war, eloquence, personal weight, are somewhat, and engage my respect as examples of its presence and impure action. I see the same law working in nature for conservation and growth. Power is in nature the essential measure of right. Nature suffers nothing to remain in her kingdoms which cannot help itself. The genesis and maturation of a planet, its poise and orbit, the bended tree recovering itself from the strong wind, the vital resources of every animal and vegetable, are demonstrations of the self-sufficing, and therefore self-relying soul.

Thus all concentrates; let us not rove; let us sit at home with the cause. Let us stun and astonish the intruding rabble of men and books and institutions by a simple declaration of the divine fact. Bid the invaders take the shoes from off their feet, for God is here within.[38] Let our simplicity judge them, and our docility to our own law demonstrate the poverty of nature and fortune beside our native riches.

But now we are a mob. Man does not stand in awe of man, nor is his genius admonished to stay at home, to put itself in communication with the internal ocean, but it goes abroad to beg a cup of water of the urns of other men. We must go alone. I like the silent church before the service begins, better than any preaching. How far off, how cool, how chaste the persons look, begirt each one with a precinct or sanctuary. So let us always sit. Why should we assume the faults of our friend, or wife, or father, or child, because they sit around our hearth, or are said

---

[38]BID THE INVADERS TAKE THE SHOES FROM OFF THEIR FEET, FOR GOD IS HERE WITHIN: A reference to Exodus 3:5: "And he said, Draw not nigh hither: put off thy shoes from off thy feet, for the place whereon thou standest is holy ground."

to have the same blood? All men have my blood, and I have all men's. Not for that will I adopt their petulance or folly, even to the extent of being ashamed of it. But your isolation must not be mechanical, but spiritual, that is, must be elevation. At times the whole world seems to be in conspiracy to importune you with emphatic trifles. Friend, client, child, sickness, fear, want, charity, all knock at once at thy closet door and say,—'Come out unto us.' But keep thy state; come not into their confusion. The power men possess to annoy me, I give them by a weak curiosity. No man can come near me but through my act. "What we love that we have, but by desire we bereave ourselves of the love."

If we cannot at once rise to the sanctities of obedience and faith, let us at least resist our temptations; let us enter into the state of war, and wake Thor and Woden,[39] courage and constancy, in our Saxon breasts. This is to be done in our smooth times by speaking the truth. Check this lying hospitality and lying affection. Live no longer to the expectation of these deceived and deceiving people with whom we converse. Say to them, O father, O mother, O wife, O brother, O friend, I have lived with you after appearances hitherto. Henceforward I am the truth's. Be it known unto you that henceforward I obey no law less than the eternal law. I will have no covenants but proximities. I shall endeavor to nourish my parents, to support my family, to be the chaste husband of one wife,—but these relations I must fill after a new and unprecedented way. I appeal from your customs. I must be myself. I cannot break myself any longer for you, or you. If you can love me for what I am, we shall be the happier. If you cannot, I will still seek to deserve that you should. I will not hide my tastes or aversions. I will so trust that what is deep is holy, that I will do strongly before the sun and moon whatever inly rejoices me, and the heart appoints. If you are noble, I will love you; if you are not, I will not hurt you and myself by hypocritical attentions. If you are true, but not in the same truth with me, cleave to your companions; I will seek my own. I do this not selfishly, but humbly and truly. It is alike your interest and mine and all men's, however long we have dwelt in lies, to live in truth. Does this sound harsh to-day? You will soon love what is dictated by your nature as well as mine, and if we follow the truth, it will bring us out safe at last.—But so you may give these friends pain. Yes, but I cannot sell my liberty and my power, to save their sensibility. Besides, all persons have their moments of reason when they look out into the region of absolute truth; then will they justify me and do the same thing.

[39]THOR AND WODEN: Thor is Norse god of thunder, weather, and crops; Woden (Odin) is the supreme Norse god and creator and the god of war.

The populace think that your rejection of popular standards is a rejection of all standard, and mere antinomianism[40]; and the bold sensualist will use the name of philosophy to gild his crimes. But the law of consciousness abides. There are two confessionals, in one or the other of which we must be shriven. You may fulfil your round of duties by clearing yourself in the *direct*, or, in the *reflex* way. Consider whether you have satisfied your relations to father, mother, cousin, neighbor, town, cat, and dog; whether any of these can upbraid you. But I may also neglect this reflex standard, and absolve me to myself. I have my own stern claims and perfect circle. It denies the name of duty to many offices that are called duties. But if I can discharge its debts, it enables me to dispense with the popular code. If any one imagines that this law is lax, let him keep its commandment one day.

And truly it demands something godlike in him who has cast off the common motives of humanity, and has ventured to trust himself for a taskmaster. High be his heart, faithful his will, clear his sight, that he may in good earnest be doctrine, society, law to himself, that a simple purpose may be to him as strong as iron necessity is to others.

If any man consider the present aspects of what is called by distinction *society*, he will see the need of these ethics. The sinew and heart of man seem to be drawn out, and we are become timorous desponding whimperers. We are afraid of truth, afraid of fortune, afraid of death, and afraid of each other. Our age yields no great and perfect persons. We want men and women who shall renovate life and our social state, but we see that most natures are insolvent, cannot satisfy their own wants, have an ambition out of all proportion to their practical force, and do lean and beg day and night continually. Our housekeeping is mendicant,[41] our arts, our occupations, our marriages, our religion we have not chosen, but society has chosen for us. We are parlor soldiers. We shun the rugged battle of fate, where strength is born.

If our young men miscarry in their first enterprizes, they lose all heart. If the young merchant fails, men say he is *ruined*. If the finest genius studies at one of our colleges, and is not installed in an office within one year afterwards in the cities or suburbs of Boston or New York, it seems to his friends and to himself that he is right in being disheartened and in complaining the rest of his life. A sturdy lad from New Hampshire or Vermont, who in turn tries all the professions, who *teams*

---

[40]ANTINOMIANISM: The belief that Christians are not bound by the moral law described in the Old Testament.
[41]MENDICANT: Beggarly.

it, farms it, peddles, keeps a school, preaches, edits a newspaper, goes to Congress, buys a township, and so forth, in successive years, and always, like a cat, falls on his feet, is worth a hundred of these city dolls. He walks abreast with his days, and feels no shame in not 'studying a profession,' for he does not postpone his life, but lives already. He has not one chance, but a hundred chances. Let a Stoic open the resources of man, and tell men they are not leaning willows, but can and must detach themselves; that with the exercise of self-trust, new powers shall appear; that a man is the word made flesh, born to shed healing to the nations, that he should be ashamed of our compassion, and that the moment he acts from himself, tossing the laws, the books, idolatries, and customs out of the window, we pity him no more but thank and revere him,—and that teacher shall restore the life of man to splendor, and make his name dear to all History.

It is easy to see that a greater self-reliance must work a revolution in all the offices and relations of men; in their religion; in their education; in their pursuits; their modes of living; their association; in their property; in their speculative views.

1. In what prayers do men allow themselves! That which they call a holy office, is not so much as brave and manly. Prayer looks abroad and asks for some foreign addition to come through some foreign virtue, and loses itself in endless mazes of natural and supernatural, and mediatorial and miraculous. Prayer that craves a particular commodity,—any thing less than all good,—is vicious. Prayer is the contemplation of the facts of life from the highest point of view. It is the soliloquy of a beholding and jubilant soul. It is the spirit of God pronouncing his works good. But prayer as a means to effect a private end, is meanness and theft. It supposes dualism and not unity in nature and consciousness. As soon as the man is at one with God, he will not beg. He will then see prayer in all action. The prayer of the farmer kneeling in his field to weed it, the prayer of the rower kneeling with the stroke of his oar, are true prayers heard throughout nature, though for cheap ends. Caratach, in Fletcher's Bonduca,[42] when admonished to inquire the mind of the god Audate, replies,—

> *"His hidden meaning lies in our endeavors,*
> *Our valors are our best gods."*

Another sort of false prayers are our regrets. Discontent is the want of self-reliance: it is infirmity of will. Regret calamities, if you can thereby

---

[42]FLETCHER'S BONDUCA: *Bonduca* (1614), a play by John Fletcher.

help the sufferer; if not, attend your own work, and already the evil begins to be repaired. Our sympathy is just as base. We come to them who weep foolishly, and sit down and cry for company, instead of imparting to them truth and health in rough electric shocks; putting them once more in communication with their own reason. The secret of fortune is joy in our hands. Welcome evermore to gods and men is the self-helping man. For him all doors are flung wide: him all tongues greet, all honors crown, all eyes follow with desire. Our love goes out to him and embraces him, because he did not need it. We solicitously and apologetically caress and celebrate him, because he held on his way and scorned our disapprobation. The gods love him because men hated him. "To the persevering mortal," said Zoroaster,[43] "the blessed Immortals are swift."

As men's prayers are a disease of the will, so are their creeds a disease of the intellect. They say with those foolish Israelites, 'Let not God speak to us, lest we die. Speak thou, speak any man with us, and we will obey.' Everywhere I am hindered of meeting God in my brother, because he has shut his own temple doors, and recites fables merely of his brother's, or his brother's brother's God. Every new mind is a new classification. If it prove a mind of uncommon activity and power, a Locke,[44] a Lavoisier,[45] a Hutton,[46] a Bentham,[47] a Fourier,[48] it imposes its classification on other men, and lo! a new system. In proportion to the depth of the thought, and so to the number of the objects it touches and brings within reach of the pupil, is his complacency. But chiefly is this apparent in creeds and churches, which are also classifications of some powerful mind acting on the elemental thought of Duty, and man's relation to the Highest. Such is Calvinism, Quakerism, Swedenborgianism.[49] The pupil takes the same delight in subordinating every thing to the new terminology, as a girl who has just learned botany in seeing a new earth

---

[43]ZOROASTER: The religious teacher and prophet (c. 628–c. 551 BCE) of ancient Persia who founded Zoroastrianism.

[44]LOCKE: John Locke (1632–1704), an English philosopher and founder of British empiricism, noted for his *Essay Concerning Human Understanding* (1690).

[45]LAVOISIER: Antoine Laurent Lavoisier (1743–1794), the French chemist and physicist considered the founder of modern chemistry.

[46]HUTTON: James Hutton (1726–1797), a Scottish geologist and chemist.

[47]BENTHAM: Jeremy Bentham (1748–1832), English philosopher, political theorist, and founder of utilitarianism, the theory that actions should be judged right or wrong based on their usefulness in bringing about the greatest happiness for those affected by them.

[48]FOURIER: Charles Fourier (1772–1837), a French social philosopher.

[49]CALVINISM, QUAKERISM, SWEDENBORGIANISM: Calvinism encompassed the Protestant doctrines, practices, and teachings expressed by John Calvin (1509–1564), a French Protestant theologian. Quakerism is the religious body formed under the leadership of George Fox. Swedenborgianism (the General Church of the New Jerusalem) is the religious system created by Emanuel Swedenborg (1688–1772), a Swedish scientist and theologian admired by Emerson.

and new seasons thereby. It will happen for a time, that the pupil will find his intellectual power has grown by the study of his master's mind. But in all unbalanced minds, the classification is idolized, passes for the end, and not for a speedily exhaustible means, so that the walls of the system blend to their eye in the remote horizon with the walls of the universe; the luminaries of heaven seem to them hung on the arch their master built. They cannot imagine how you aliens have any right to see,—how you can see; 'It must be somehow that you stole the light from us.' They do not yet perceive, that light, unsystematic, indomitable, will break into any cabin, even into theirs. Let them chirp awhile and call it their own. If they are honest and do well, presently their neat new pinfold will be too strait and low, will crack, will lean, will rot and vanish, and the immortal light, all young and joyful, million-orbed, million-colored, will beam over the universe as on the first morning.

2. It is for want of self-culture that the superstition of Travelling, whose idols are Italy, England, Egypt, retains its fascination for all educated Americans. They who made England, Italy, or Greece venerable in the imagination, did so by sticking fast where they were, like an axis of the earth. In manly hours, we feel that duty is our place. The soul is no traveller: the wise man stays at home, and when his necessities, his duties, on any occasion call him from his house, or into foreign lands, he is at home still, and shall make men sensible by the expression of his countenance, that he goes the missionary of wisdom and virtue, and visits cities and men like a sovereign, and not like an interloper or a valet.

I have no churlish objection to the circumnavigation of the globe, for the purposes of art, of study, and benevolence, so that the man is first domesticated, or does not go abroad with the hope of finding somewhat greater than he knows. He who travels to be amused, or to get somewhat which he does not carry, travels away from himself, and grows old even in youth among old things. In Thebes, in Palmyra, his will and mind have become old and dilapidated as they. He carries ruins to ruins.

Travelling is a fool's paradise. Our first journeys discover to us the indifference of places. At home I dream that at Naples, at Rome, I can be intoxicated with beauty, and lose my sadness. I pack my trunk, embrace my friends, embark on the sea, and at last wake up in Naples, and there beside me is the stern Fact, the sad self, unrelenting, identical, that I fled from. I seek the Vatican, and the palaces. I affect to be intoxicated with sights and suggestions, but I am not intoxicated. My giant goes with me wherever I go.

3. But the rage of travelling is a symptom of a deeper unsoundness affecting the whole intellectual action. The intellect is vagabond, and our

system of education fosters restlessness. Our minds travel when our bodies are forced to stay at home. We imitate; and what is imitation but the travelling of the mind? Our houses are built with foreign taste; our shelves are garnished with foreign ornaments; our opinions, our tastes, our faculties, lean, and follow the Past and the Distant. The soul created the arts wherever they have flourished. It was in his own mind that the artist sought his model. It was an application of his own thought to the thing to be done and the conditions to be observed. And why need we copy the Doric or the Gothic model?[50] Beauty, convenience, grandeur of thought, and quaint expression are as near to us as to any, and if the American artist will study with hope and love the precise thing to be done by him, considering the climate, the soil, the length of the day, the wants of the people, the habit and form of the government, he will create a house in which all these will find themselves fitted, and taste and sentiment will be satisfied also.

Insist on yourself; never imitate. Your own gift you can present every moment with the cumulative force of a whole life's cultivation; but of the adopted talent of another, you have only an extemporaneous, half possession. That which each can do best, none but his Maker can teach him. No man yet knows what it is, nor can, till that person has exhibited it. Where is the master who could have taught Shakspeare? Where is the master who could have instructed Franklin, or Washington, or Bacon, or Newton? Every great man is a unique. The Scipionism of Scipio[51] is precisely that part he could not borrow. Shakspeare will never be made by the study of Shakspeare. Do that which is assigned you, and you cannot hope too much or dare too much. There is at this moment for you an utterance brave and grand as that of the colossal chisel of Phidias,[52] or trowel of the Egyptians, or the pen of Moses, or Dante, but different from all these. Not possibly will the soul all rich, all eloquent, with thousand-cloven tongue, deign to repeat itself; but if you can hear what these patriarchs say, surely you can reply to them in the same pitch of voice: for the ear and the tongue are two organs of one nature. Abide in the simple and noble regions of thy life, obey thy heart, and thou shalt reproduce the Foreworld again.

4. As our Religion, our Education, our Art look abroad, so does our spirit of society. All men plume themselves on the improvement of society, and no man improves.

---

[50]DORIC OR GOTHIC MODEL: Ancient Greek or medieval European architectural styles.
[51]SCIPIONISM OF SCIPIO: Meaning the essence of a man.
[52]PHIDIAS: A sculptor (c. 500–c. 432 BCE) of ancient Greece.

Society never advances. It recedes as fast on one side as it gains on the other. It undergoes continual changes: it is barbarous, it is civilized, it is christianized, it is rich, it is scientific; but this change is not amelioration. For every thing that is given, something is taken. Society acquires new arts and loses old instincts. What a contrast between the well-clad, reading, writing, thinking American, with a watch, a pencil, and a bill of exchange in his pocket, and the naked New Zealander, whose property is a club, a spear, a mat, and an undivided twentieth of a shed to sleep under. But compare the health of the two men, and you shall see that the white man has lost his aboriginal strength. If the traveller tell us truly, strike the savage with a broad axe, and in a day or two the flesh shall unite and heal as if you struck the blow into soft pitch, and the same blow shall send the white to his grave.

The civilized man has built a coach, but has lost the use of his feet. He is supported on crutches, but lacks so much support of muscle. He has a fine Geneva watch, but he fails of the skill to tell the hour by the sun. A Greenwich nautical almanac he has, and so being sure of the information when he wants it, the man in the street does not know a star in the sky. The solstice he does not observe; the equinox he knows as little; and the whole bright calendar of the year is without a dial in his mind. His note-books impair his memory; his libraries overload his wit; the insurance office increases the number of accidents; and it may be a question whether machinery does not encumber; whether we have not lost by refinement some energy, by a christianity entrenched in establishments and forms, some vigor of wild virtue. For every stoic was a stoic[53]; but in Christendom where is the Christian?

There is no more deviation in the moral standard than in the standard of height or bulk. No greater men are now than ever were. A singular equality may be observed between the great men of the first and of the last ages; nor can all the science, art, religion and philosophy of the nineteenth century avail to educate greater men than Plutarch's[54] heroes, three or four and twenty centuries ago. Not in time is the race progressive. Phocion,[55] Socrates, Anaxagoras,[56] Diogenes,[57] are great men, but

[53]FOR EVERY STOIC WAS A STOIC: Stoicism is a school of philosophy founded by Zeno of Citium (in Cyprus) around 300 BCE. "To live consistently with nature" was one of its maxims. It taught that only by putting aside passion and approaching life's circumstances as inevitable would one find true freedom and happiness.

[54]PLUTARCH'S HEROES: Plutarch (c.46–c.120 CE) was a Greek biographer noted for his book *The Parallel Lives*, which describes the lives of famous Greeks and Romans.

[55]PHOCION: An Athenian general (402–318 BCE).

[56]ANAXAGORAS: A Greek philosopher (c. 500–428 BCE) of Clazomenae thought to be a teacher of Socrates.

[57]DIOGENES: Diogenes Laërtius was a Greek biographer who lived in the early third century CE.

they leave no class. He who is really of their class will not be called by their name, but will be his own man, and, in his turn the founder of a sect. The arts and inventions of each period are only its costume, and do not invigorate men. The harm of the improved machinery may compensate its good. Hudson[58] and Behring[59] accomplished so much in their fishing-boats, as to astonish Parry and Franklin,[60] whose equipment exhausted the resources of science and art. Galileo, with an opera-glass, discovered a more splendid series of celestial phenomena than any one since. Columbus found the New World in an undecked boat. It is curious to see the periodical disuse and perishing of means and machinery which were introduced with loud laudation, a few years or centuries before. The great genius returns to essential man. We reckoned the improvements of the art of war among the triumphs of science, and yet Napoleon conquered Europe by the Bivouac, which consisted of falling back on naked valor, and disencumbering it of all aids. The Emperor held it impossible to make a perfect army, says Las Cases,[61] "without abolishing our arms, magazines, commissaries, and carriages, until in imitation of the Roman custom, the soldier should receive his supply of corn, grind it in his hand-mill, and bake his bread himself."

Society is a wave. The wave moves onward, but the water of which it is composed, does not. The same particle does not rise from the valley to the ridge. Its unity is only phenomenal. The persons who make up a nation to-day, next year die, and their experience with them.

And so the reliance on Property, including the reliance on governments which protect it, is the want of self-reliance. Men have looked away from themselves and at things so long, that they have come to esteem the religious, learned, and civil institutions, as guards of property, and they deprecate assaults on these, because they feel them to be assaults on property. They measure their esteem of each other, by what each has, and not by what each is. But a cultivated man becomes ashamed of his property, out of new respect for his nature. Especially he hates what he has, if he see that it is accidental,—came to him by inheritance, or gift, or crime; then he feels that it is not having; it

---

[58]HUDSON: Henry Hudson (presumed dead c. 1611) was an English navigator who, while in the service of the Dutch East India Company, explored the New England coast of North America and the river that bears his name on his ship, the *Half Moon*.
[59]BEHRING: Vitus Jonassen Behing (1681–1741), the Danish explorer for whom the Bering Strait, between Alaska and Siberia, is named.
[60]PARRY AND FRANKLIN: William Edward Perry (1790–1845) and John Franklin (1786–1847) were English explorers of the Artic.
[61]LAS CASES: Emmanuel Las Cases (1766–1842), a French historian who accompanied Napoleon into exile, where he recorded a part of the ousted ruler's memoirs.

does not belong to him, has no root in him, and merely lies there, because no revolution or no robber takes it away. But that which a man is, does always by necessity acquire, and what the man acquires is living property, which does not wait the beck of rulers, or mobs, or revolutions, or fire, or storm, or bankruptcies, but perpetually renews itself wherever the man breathes. "Thy lot or portion of life," said the Caliph Ali,[62] "is seeking after thee; therefore be at rest from seeking after it." Our dependence on these foreign goods leads us to our slavish respect for numbers. The political parties meet in numerous conventions; the greater the concourse, and with each new uproar of announcement, The delegation from Essex![63] The Democrats from New Hampshire! The Whigs of Maine! the young patriot feels himself stronger than before by a new thousand of eyes and arms. In like manner the reformers summon conventions, and vote and resolve in multitude. Not so, O friends! will the God deign to enter and inhabit you, but by a method precisely the reverse. It is only as a man puts off all foreign support, and stands alone, that I see him to be strong and to prevail. He is weaker by every recruit to his banner. Is not a man better than a town? Ask nothing of men, and in the endless mutation, thou only firm column must presently appear the upholder of all that surrounds thee. He who knows that power is inborn, that he is weak because he has looked for good out of him and elsewhere, and so perceiving, throws himself unhesitatingly on his thought, instantly rights himself, stands in the erect position, commands his limbs, works miracles; just as a man who stands on his feet is stronger than a man who stands on his head.

So use all that is called Fortune. Most men gamble with her, and gain all, and lose all, as her wheel rolls. But do thou leave as unlawful these winnings, and deal with Cause and Effect, the chancellors of God. In the Will work and acquire, and thou hast chained the wheel of Chance, and shalt sit hereafter out of fear from her rotations. A political victory, a rise of rents, the recovery of your sick, or the return of your absent friend, or some other favorable event, raises your spirits, and you think good days are preparing for you. Do not believe it. Nothing can bring you peace but yourself. Nothing can bring you peace but the triumph of principles.

[1841, 1847]

---

[62]CALIPH ALI: Caliph Ali (598?–661 CE) was the fourth caliph (656–661 CE) of Islam.
[63]DELEGATION FROM ESSEX: Essex County, in northeastern Massachusetts.

Concord Hymn

SUNG AT THE COMPLETION OF THE BATTLE MONUMENT,[1]
JULY 4, 1837

By the rude bridge that arched the flood,
   Their flag to April's breeze unfurled,
Here once the embattled farmers stood
   And fired the shot heard round the world.

The foe long since in silence slept;   5
   Alike the conqueror silent sleeps;
And Time the ruined bridge has swept
   Down the dark stream which seaward creeps.

On this green bank, by this soft stream,
   We set to-day a votive stone;   10
That memory may their deed redeem,
   When, like our sires, our sons are gone.

Spirit, that made those heroes dare
   To die, and leave their children free,
Bid Time and Nature gently spare   15
   The shaft we raise to them and thee.

[1837, 1847]

The Rhodora[1]

ON BEING ASKED, WHENCE IS THE FLOWER?

In May, when sea-winds pierced our solitudes,
I found the fresh Rhodora in the woods,
Spreading its leafless blooms in a damp nook,
To please the desert and the sluggish brook.
The purple petals, fallen in the pool,   5
Made the black water with their beauty gay;

---

[1]BATTLE MONUMENT: Emerson composed this poem for the dedication ceremony of the Battle
Monument, a memorial to the battle of Lexington and Concord, April 19, 1775, the first battle of the
American Revolution.
[1]RHODORA: An azalea of northeastern North America.

Here might the red-bird come his plumes to cool,
And court the flower that cheapens his array.
Rhodora! if the sages ask thee why
This charm is wasted on the earth and sky,   10
Tell them, dear, that if eyes were made for seeing,
Then Beauty is its own excuse for being:
Why thou wert there, O rival of the rose!
I never thought to ask, I never knew:
But, in my simple ignorance, suppose   15
The self-same Power that brought me there brought you.

[1839]

Nathaniel Hawthorne

(1804–1864)

The scholar Edward H. Davidson has stated, "In the life history of Nathaniel Hawthorne are no high surges of drama and excitement....His life was commonplace, even dull." Hawthorne's contemporaries often made the same point. The poet John Greenleaf Whittier, for example, recalled, "He never seemed to be doing anything, and yet he did not like to be disturbed at it." But as his novels and stories testify, Hawthorne was an extraordinarily passionate writer. Behind the appearance of a man living uneventfully was an imagination acutely sensitive to ecstasy and pain. He observed, reflected, brooded. "I am slow to feel," he acknowledged, "slow, I suppose, to comprehend and, like the anaconda, I need to lubricate any object a great deal before I can swallow it and actually make it my own."

Hawthorne was born in Salem, Massachusetts, fourteen miles northeast of Boston. His father was a sea captain, a descendant of John Hathorne (Hawthorne himself later added the "w" to his surname), one of the judges at the Salem witch trials of the 1690s. Hawthorne's father died of yellow fever in Dutch Guiana when the boy was four, and Hawthorne and the rest of the family then went to live in the home of the Mannings, his mother's relatives, in Raymond, Maine. He attended Bowdoin College (1821–1824) in Maine, where his friends included Franklin Pierce, who would become the nation's fourteenth president, and the future poet Henry Wadsworth Longfellow. At age seventeen Hawthorne wondered to his mother in a letter, "What do you think of my becoming an author, and relying for support upon my pen?"

During the 1820s (the Hawthorne family had moved back to Salem in summer 1822) and the 1830s Hawthorne worked as a writer and contributed short stories to magazines. His first novel, Fanshawe, *was published in 1828, anonymously and at his own expense, but soon he disavowed the book and destroyed every copy he could find. He continued, through the 1830s and early 1840s, to compose tales, stories, sketches, and books for children. After an unsatisfying period of living at Brook Farm, a utopian community in West Roxbury, Massachusetts, Hawthorne married Sophia Peabody and settled with her at the Old Manse in Concord, Massachusetts, becoming friends there with Ralph Waldo Emerson (the Old Manse was an ancestral home of the Emerson family), Henry David Thoreau, and Amos Bronson Alcott and his wife and children (one of whom was Louisa May Alcott, later the author of* Little Women). *Many of Hawthorne's stories were collected in* Twice-Told Tales *(1837; enlarged, 1842) and* Mosses from an Old Manse *(1846).*

In 1846 Hawthorne received an appointment as surveyor of the port of Salem, and he and his family moved there. Because of a change in political administrations, he lost the job in June 1849, whereupon he relocated to Lenox, Massachusetts, in the Berkshire Mountains, and in the summer of 1850 he and Herman Melville began an intense friendship—Melville loved Hawthorne and dedicated Moby-Dick *(1851) to him. But early in 1853, thanks to Franklin Pierce, now president, Hawthorne was awarded an overseas appointment as U.S. consul, and he and his family for the next seven years lived in Liverpool, England, and, at the end of the decade, in Italy. Upon his return to the United States, Hawthorne lived in Concord. He died in Plymouth, New Hampshire, while on a trip with Pierce.*

Hawthorne's novels, which include The Scarlet Letter *(1850),* The House of the Seven Gables *(1851),* The Blithedale Romance *(1852), and* The Marble Faun *(1860), especially the first and third of these, are among the best in all of American literature. Hawthorne wrote with profound psychological insight and with a deep (and disturbed) feeling for the burdens of history—the history of settlement and colonization in New England, the history of Puritanism, with its stark, anguished conception of evil and sin, and, perhaps above all, the history of the human heart, in its desperate longing and deep suffering. In his creation of memorable characters—Hester Prynne, Arthur Dimmesdale, and Roger Chillingworth in* The Scarlet Letter *(below) immediately leap to mind—Hawthorne has few rivals in the nineteenth century. At his best, in his handling of imagery, symbol, and allegory he is intricately suggestive from sentence to sentence and compelling across the span of the plot as a whole.*

Hawthorne is equally a master of the short story and tale, where he demonstrates the special gift Henry James described thus: "He combined in a singular degree the spontaneity of the imagination with a haunting care for moral problems." Below are three of Hawthorne's piercing shorter works: "Young Goodman Brown," "The May-Pole of Merry Mount," and "The Minister's Black Veil."

Hawthorne's power in these three stories and as a writer of fiction in general was expressed authoritatively by Melville in a review-essay, published in 1850, on Mosses from an Old Manse. *Concerned that many had been misled by their impression of Hawthorne the man, and concerned, too, that the expertly crafted surface of Hawthorne's prose might lead to another kind of over-simple impression, Melville offered this portrait:*

> *Where Hawthorne is known, he seems to be deemed a pleasant writer, with a pleasant style—a sequestered, harmless man, from whom any deep and weighty thing would hardly be anticipated:—a man who means no meanings.... For spite of all the Indian-summer sunlight on the hither side of Hawthorne's soul, the other side—like the dark half of the physical sphere—is shrouded in a blackness, ten times black....*

This power of blackness in him derives its force from its appeals to that Calvinistic sense of Innate Depravity and Original Sin, from whose visitations, in some shape or other, no deeply thinking mind is always and wholly free. For, in certain moods, no man can weigh this world, without throwing in something, somehow like Original Sin, to strike the uneven balance. At all events, perhaps no writer has ever wielded this terrific thought with greater terror than this same harmless Hawthorne. Still more: this black conceit pervades him, through and through. You may be witched by his sunlight, transported by the bright gildings in the skies he builds over you; but there is the blackness of darkness beyond; and even his bright gildings but fringe, and play upon the edges of thunder-clouds.—In one word, the world is mistaken in this Nathaniel Hawthorne.

Biographies include Arlin Turner, Nathaniel Hawthorne: A Biography *(1980); James R. Mellow,* Nathaniel Hawthorne in His Times *(1980); Edwin Haviland Miller,* Salem Is My Dwelling Place: A Life of Nathaniel Hawthorne *(1991); and Brenda Wineapple,* Hawthorne: A Life *(2003). On the short stories: Lea Bertani Vozar Newman,* A Reader's Guide to the Short Stories of Nathaniel Hawthorne *(1979);* Critical Essays on Hawthorne's Short Stories, *ed. Albert J. Von Frank (1991); and* New Essays on Hawthorne's Major Tales, *ed. Millicent Bell (1993). See also Robert L. Gale,* A Nathaniel Hawthorne Encyclopedia *(1991); and* A Historical Guide to Nathaniel Hawthorne, *ed. Larry J. Reynolds (2001).*

Young Goodman Brown

Young Goodman[1] Brown came forth, at sunset, into the street of Salem village, but put his head back, after crossing the threshold, to exchange a parting kiss with his young wife. And Faith, as the wife was aptly named, thrust her own pretty head into the street, letting the wind play with the pink ribbons of her cap, while she called to Goodman Brown.

"Dearest heart," whispered she, softly and rather sadly, when her lips were close to his ear, "pr'y thee, put off your journey until sunrise, and sleep in your own bed to-night. A lone woman is troubled with such dreams and such thoughts, that she's afeard of herself, sometimes. Pray, tarry with me this night, dear husband, of all nights in the year!"

"My love and my Faith," replied young Goodman Brown, "of all nights in the year, this one night must I tarry away from thee. My journey, as thou callest it, forth and back again, must needs be done 'twixt

[1]GOODMAN: Polite term of address for a man of humble standing.

now and sunrise. What, my sweet, pretty wife, dost thou doubt me already, and we but three months married!"

"Then, God bless you!" said Faith, with the pink ribbons, "and may you find all well when you come back."

"Amen!" cried Goodman Brown. "Say thy prayers, dear Faith, and go to bed at dusk, and no harm will come to thee."

So they parted; and the young man pursued his way, until, being about to turn the corner by the meeting-house, he looked back, and saw the head of Faith still peeping after him, with a melancholy air, in spite of her pink ribbons.

"Poor little Faith!" thought he, for his heart smote him. "What a wretch am I, to leave her on such an errand! She talks of dreams, too. Methought, as she spoke, there was trouble in her face, as if a dream had warned her what work is to be done to-night. But, no, no! 'twould kill her to think it. Well; she's a blessed angel on earth; and after this one night, I'll cling to her skirts and follow her to Heaven."

With this excellent resolve for the future, Goodman Brown felt himself justified in making more haste on his present evil purpose. He had taken a dreary road, darkened by all the gloomiest trees of the forest, which barely stood aside to let the narrow path creep through, and closed immediately behind. It was all as lonely as could be; and there is this peculiarity in such a solitude, that the traveller knows not who may be concealed by the innumerable trunks and the thick boughs overhead; so that, with lonely footsteps, he may yet be passing through an unseen multitude.

"There may be a devilish Indian behind every tree," said Goodman Brown, to himself; and he glanced fearfully behind him, as he added, "What if the devil himself should be at my very elbow!"

His head being turned back, he passed a crook of the road, and looking forward again, beheld the figure of a man, in grave and decent attire, seated at the foot of an old tree. He arose, at Goodman Brown's approach, and walked onward, side by side with him.

"You are late, Goodman Brown," said he. "The clock of the Old South was striking as I came through Boston; and that is full fifteen minutes agone."

"Faith kept me back awhile," replied the young man, with a tremor in his voice, caused by the sudden appearance of his companion, though not wholly unexpected.

It was now deep dusk in the forest, and deepest in that part of it where these two were journeying. As nearly as could be discerned, the second traveller was about fifty years old, apparently in the same rank of life as Goodman Brown, and bearing a considerable resemblance to him, though perhaps more in expression than features. Still, they might have been taken for father and son. And yet, though the elder person was as simply clad as the younger, and as simple in manner too, he had an indescribable air of one who knew the world, and would not have felt abashed at the governor's dinner-table, or in King William's court, were it possible that his affairs should call him thither. But the only thing about him, that could be fixed upon as remarkable, was his staff, which bore the likeness of a great black snake, so curiously wrought, that it might almost be seen to twist and wriggle itself, like a living serpent. This, of course, must have been an ocular deception, assisted by the uncertain light.

"Come, Goodman Brown!" cried his fellow-traveller, "this is a dull pace for the beginning of a journey. Take my staff, if you are so soon weary."

"Friend," said the other, exchanging his slow pace for a full stop, "having kept covenant by meeting thee here, it is my purpose now to return whence I came. I have scruples, touching the matter thou wot'st[2] of."

"Sayest thou so?" replied he of the serpent, smiling apart. "Let us walk on, nevertheless, reasoning as we go, and if I convince thee not, thou shalt turn back. We are but a little way in the forest, yet."

"Too far, too far!" exclaimed the goodman, unconsciously resuming his walk. "My father never went into the woods on such an errand, nor his father before him. We have been a race of honest men and good Christians, since the days of the martyrs. And shall I be the first of the name of Brown, that ever took this path, and kept—"

"Such company, thou wouldst say," observed the elder person, interpreting his pause. "Well said, Goodman Brown! I have been as well acquainted with your family as with ever a one among the Puritans; and that's no trifle to say. I helped your grandfather, the constable, when he lashed the Quaker woman so smartly through the streets of Salem. And it was I that brought your father a pitch-pine knot, kindled at my own hearth, to set fire to an Indian village, in King Philip's war.[3] They were my good friends, both; and many a pleasant walk have we had along this path, and returned merrily after midnight. I would fain be friends with you, for their sake."

"If it be as thou sayest," replied Goodman Brown, I marvel they never spoke of these matters. Or, verily, I marvel not, seeing that the least rumor of the sort would have driven them from New-England. We are a people of prayer, and good works, to boot, and abide no such wickedness."

---

[2]WOT'ST: Knowest.
[3]KING PHILIP'S WAR: War waged by the colonists (1675–1676) against the Wampanoag Indian leader Metcom (or Metacom), known as King Philip.

"Wickedness or not," said the traveller with the twisted staff, "I have a very general acquaintance here in New-England. The deacons of many a church have drunk the communion wine with me; the selectmen, of divers towns, make me their chairman; and a majority of the Great and General Court are firm supporters of my interest. The governor and I, too—but these are state-secrets."

"Can this be so!" cried Goodman Brown, with a stare of amazement at his undisturbed companion. "Howbeit, I have nothing to do with the governor and council; they have their own ways, and are no rule for a simple husbandman,[4] like me. But, were I to go on with thee, how should I meet the eye of that good old man, our minister, at Salem village? Oh, his voice would make me tremble, both Sabbath-day and lecture-day!"

Thus far, the elder traveller had listened with due gravity, but now burst into a fit of irrepressible mirth, shaking himself so violently, that his snake-like staff actually seemed to wriggle in sympathy.

"Ha! ha! ha!" shouted he, again and again; then composing himself, "Well, go on, Goodman Brown, go on; but pr'y thee, don't kill me with laughing!"

"Well, then, to end the matter at once," said Goodman Brown, considerably nettled, "there is my wife, Faith. It would break her dear little heart; and I'd rather break my own!"

"Nay, if that be the case," answered the other, "e'en go thy ways, Goodman Brown. I would not, for twenty old women like the one hobbling before us, that Faith should come to any harm."

As he spoke, he pointed his staff at a female figure on the path, in whom Goodman Brown recognized a very pious and exemplary dame, who had taught him his catechism, in youth, and was still his moral and spiritual adviser, jointly with the minister and Deacon Gookin.

"A marvel, truly, that Goody[5] Cloyse should be so far in the wilderness, at night-fall!" said he. "But, with your leave, friend, I shall take a cut through the woods, until we have left this Christian woman behind. Being a stranger to you, she might ask whom I was consorting with, and whither I was going."

"Be it so," said his fellow-traveller. "Betake you to the woods, and let me keep the path."

Accordingly, the young man turned aside, but took care to watch his companion, who advanced softly along the road, until he had come within a staff's length of the old dame. She, meanwhile, was making the best of her way, with singular speed for so aged a woman, and mum-

---

[4]HUSBANDMAN: Farmer; more generally, any man of humble standing.
[5]GOODY: Contraction of Goodwife, a polite term of address for a married woman of humble standing.

bling some indistinct words, a prayer, doubtless, as she went. The traveller put forth his staff, and touched her withered neck with what seemed
the serpent's tail.

"The devil!" screamed the pious old lady.

"Then Goody Cloyse knows her old friend?" observed the traveller,
confronting her, and leaning on his writhing stick.

"Ah, forsooth, and is it your worship, indeed?" cried the good dame.
"Yea, truly is it, and in the very image of my old gossip, Goodman Brown,
the grandfather of the silly fellow that now is. But—would your worship
believe it?—my broomstick hath strangely disappeared, stolen, as I suspect, by that unhanged witch, Goody Cory, and that, too, when I was all
anointed with the juice of smallage and cinque-foil and wolf's-bane—"

"Mingled with fine wheat and the fat of a new-born babe," said the
shape of old Goodman Brown.

"Ah, your worship knows the receipt," cried the old lady, cackling
aloud. "So, as I was saying, being all ready for the meeting, and no horse
to ride on, I made up my mind to foot it; for they tell me, there is a nice
young man to be taken into communion to-night. But now your good worship will lend me your arm, and we shall be there in a twinkling."

"That can hardly be," answered her friend. I may not spare you my
arm, Goody Cloyse, but here is my staff, if you will."

So saying, he threw it down at her feet, where, perhaps, it assumed life,
being one of the rods which its owner had formerly lent to the Egyptian
Magi.[6] Of this fact, however, Goodman Brown could not take cognizance.
He had cast up his eyes in astonishment, and looking down again, beheld
neither Goody Cloyse nor the serpentine staff, but his fellow-traveller alone,
who waited for him as calmly as if nothing had happened.

"That old woman taught me my catechism!" said the young man; and
there was a world of meaning in this simple comment.

They continued to walk onward, while the elder traveller exhorted his
companion to make good speed and persevere in the path, discoursing so
aptly, that his arguments seemed rather to spring up in the bosom of his
auditor, than to be suggested by himself. As they went, he plucked a branch
of maple, to serve for a walking-stick, and began to strip it of the twigs
and little boughs, which were wet with evening dew. The moment his fingers touched them, they became strangely withered and dried up, as with
a week's sunshine. Thus the pair proceeded, at a good free pace, until suddenly, in a gloomy hollow of the road, Goodman Brown sat himself down
on the stump of a tree, and refused to go any farther.

[6]EGYPTIAN MAGI: See Exodus 7:11–12, where the magicians of Egypt turn rods into serpents.

"Friend," said he, stubbornly, "my mind is made up. Not another step will I budge on this errand. What if a wretched old woman do choose to go to the devil, when I thought she was going to Heaven! Is that any reason why I should quit my dear Faith, and go after her?"

"You will think better of this, by-and-by," said his acquaintance, composedly. "Sit here and rest yourself awhile; and when you feel like moving again, there is my staff to help you along."

Without more words, he threw his companion the maple stick, and was as speedily out of sight, as if he had vanished into the deepening gloom. The young man sat a few moments, by the road-side, applauding himself greatly, and thinking with how clear a conscience he should meet the minister, in his morning-walk, nor shrink from the eye of good old Deacon Gookin. And what calm sleep would be his, that very night, which was to have been spent so wickedly, but purely and sweetly now, in the arms of Faith! Amidst these pleasant and praiseworthy meditations, Goodman Brown heard the tramp of horses along the road, and deemed it advisable to conceal himself within the verge of the forest, conscious of the guilty purpose that had brought him thither, though now so happily turned from it.

On came the hoof-tramps and the voices of the riders, two grave old voices, conversing soberly as they drew near. These mingled sounds appeared to pass along the road, within a few yards of the young man's hiding-place; but owing, doubtless, to the depth of the gloom, at that particular spot, neither the travellers nor their steeds were visible. Though their figures brushed the small boughs by the way-side, it could not be seen that they intercepted, even for a moment, the faint gleam from the strip of bright sky, athwart which they must have passed. Goodman Brown alternately crouched and stood on tip-toe, pulling aside the branches, and thrusting forth his head as far as he durst, without discerning so much as a shadow. It vexed him the more, because he could have sworn, were such a thing possible, that he recognized the voices of the minister and Deacon Gookin, jogging along quietly, as they were wont to do, when bound to some ordination or ecclesiastical council. While yet within hearing, one of the riders stopped to pluck a switch.

"Of the two, reverend Sir," said the voice like the deacon's, "I had rather miss an ordination-dinner than to-night's meeting. They tell me that some of our community are to be here from Falmouth and beyond, and others from Connecticut and Rhode-Island; besides several of the Indian powows, who, after their fashion, know almost as much deviltry as the best of us. Moreover, there is a goodly young woman to be taken into communion."

"Mighty well, Deacon Gookin!" replied the solemn old tones of the minister. "Spur up, or we shall be late. Nothing can be done, you know, until I get on the ground."

The hoofs clattered again, and the voices, talking so strangely in the empty air, passed on through the forest, where no church had ever been gathered, nor solitary Christian prayed. Whither, then, could these holy men be journeying, so deep into the heathen wilderness? Young Goodman Brown caught hold of a tree, for support, being ready to sink down on the ground, faint and overburthened with the heavy sickness of his heart. He looked up to the sky, doubting whether there really was a Heaven above him. Yet, there was the blue arch, and the stars brightening in it.

"With Heaven above, and Faith below, I will yet stand firm against the devil!" cried Goodman Brown.

While he still gazed upward, into the deep arch of the firmament, and had lifted his hands to pray, a cloud, though no wind was stirring, hurried across the zenith, and hid the brightening stars. The blue sky was still visible, except directly overhead, where this black mass of cloud was sweeping swiftly northward. Aloft in the air, as if from the depths of the cloud, came a confused and doubtful sound of voices. Once, the listener fancied that he could distinguish the accents of town's-people of his own, men and women, both pious and ungodly, many of whom he had met at the communion-table, and had seen others rioting at the tavern. The next moment, so indistinct were the sounds, he doubted whether he had heard aught but the murmur of the old forest, whispering without a wind. Then came a stronger swell of those familiar tones, heard daily in the sunshine, at Salem village, but never, until now, from a cloud of night. There was one voice, of a young woman, uttering lamentations, yet with an uncertain sorrow, and entreating for some favor, which, perhaps, it would grieve her to obtain. And all the unseen multitude, both saints and sinners, seemed to encourage her onward.

"Faith!" shouted Goodman Brown, in a voice of agony and desperation; and the echoes of the forest mocked him, crying—"Faith! Faith!" as if bewildered wretches were seeking her, all through the wilderness.

The cry of grief, rage, and terror, was yet piercing the night, when the unhappy husband held his breath for a response. There was a scream, drowned immediately in a louder murmur of voices, fading into far-off laughter, as the dark cloud swept away, leaving the clear and silent sky above Goodman Brown. But something fluttered lightly down through the air, and caught on the branch of a tree. The young man seized it, and beheld a pink ribbon.

"My Faith is gone!" cried he, after one stupefied moment. "There is no good on earth; and sin is but a name. Come, devil! for to thee is this world given."

And maddened with despair, so that he laughed loud and long, did Goodman Brown grasp his staff and set forth again, at such a rate, that he seemed to fly along the forest-path, rather than to walk or run. The road grew wilder and drearier, and more faintly traced, and vanished at length, leaving him in the heart of the dark wilderness, still rushing onward, with the instinct that guides mortal man to evil. The whole forest was peopled with frightful sounds; the creaking of the trees, the howling of wild beasts, and the yell of Indians; while, sometimes, the wind tolled like a distant church-bell, and sometimes gave a broad roar around the traveller, as if all Nature were laughing him to scorn. But he was himself the chief horror of the scene, and shrank not from its other horrors.

"Ha! ha! ha!" roared Goodman Brown, when the wind laughed at him. "Let us hear which will laugh loudest! Think not to frighten me with your deviltry! Come witch, come wizard, come Indian powow,[7] come devil himself! and here comes Goodman Brown. You may as well fear him as he fear you!"

In truth, all through the haunted forest, there could be nothing more frightful than the figure of Goodman Brown. On he flew, among the black pines, brandishing his staff with frenzied gestures, now giving vent to an inspiration of horrid blasphemy, and now shouting forth such laughter, as set all the echoes of the forest laughing like demons around him. The fiend in his own shape is less hideous, than when he rages in the breast of man. Thus sped the demoniac on his course, until, quivering among the trees, he saw a red light before him, as when the felled trunks and branches of a clearing have been set on fire, and throw up their lurid blaze against the sky, at the hour of midnight. He paused, in a lull of the tempest that had driven him onward, and heard the swell of what seemed a hymn, rolling solemnly from a distance, with the weight of many voices. He knew the tune; it was a familiar one in the choir of the village meeting-house. The verse died heavily away, and was lengthened by a chorus, not of human voices, but of all the sounds of the benighted wilderness, pealing in awful harmony together. Goodman Brown cried out; and his cry was lost to his own ear, by its unison with the cry of the desert.

In the interval of silence, he stole forward, until the light glared full upon his eyes. At one extremity of an open space, hemmed in by the dark wall of the forest, arose a rock, bearing some rude, natural resemblance

---

[7] INDIAN POWOW: An Indian medicine man.

either to an altar or a pulpit, and surrounded by four blazing pines, their tops aflame, their stems untouched, like candles at an evening meeting. The mass of foliage, that had overgrown the summit of the rock, was all on fire, blazing high into the night, and fitfully illuminating the whole field. Each pendent twig and leafy festoon was in a blaze. As the red light arose and fell, a numerous congregation alternately shone forth, then disappeared in shadow, and again grew, as it were, out of the darkness, peopling the heart of the solitary woods at once.

"A grave and dark-clad company!" quoth Goodman Brown.

In truth, they were such. Among them, quivering to-and-fro, between gloom and splendor, appeared faces that would be seen, next day, at the council-board of the province, and others which, Sabbath after Sabbath, looked devoutly heavenward, and benignantly over the crowded pews, from the holiest pulpits in the land. Some affirm, that the lady of the governor was there. At least, there were high dames well known to her, and wives of honored husbands, and widows, a great multitude, and ancient maidens, all of excellent repute, and fair young girls, who trembled, lest their mothers should espy them. Either the sudden gleams of light, flashing over the obscure field, bedazzled Goodman Brown, or he recognized a score of the churchmembers of Salem village, famous for their especial sanctity. Good old Deacon Gookin had arrived, and waited at the skirts of that venerable saint, his revered pastor. But, irreverently consorting with these grave, reputable, and pious people, these elders of the church, these chaste dames and dewy virgins, there were men of dissolute lives and women of spotted fame, wretches given over to all mean and filthy vice, and suspected even of horrid crimes. It was strange to see, that the good shrank not from the wicked, nor were the sinners abashed by the saints. Scattered, also, among their pale-faced enemies, were the Indian priests, or powows, who had often scared their native forest with more hideous incantations than any known to English witchcraft.

"But, where is Faith?" thought Goodman Brown; and, as hope came into his heart, he trembled.

Another verse of the hymn arose, a slow and mournful strain, such as the pious love, but joined to words which expressed all that our nature can conceive of sin, and darkly hinted at far more. Unfathomable to mere mortals is the lore of fiends. Verse after verse was sung, and still the chorus of the desert swelled between, like the deepest tone of a mighty organ. And, with the final peal of that dreadful anthem, there came a sound, as if the roaring wind, the rushing streams, the howling beasts, and every other voice of the unconverted wilderness, were mingling and according with the voice of guilty man, in homage to the prince of all.

The four blazing pines threw up a loftier flame, and obscurely discovered shapes and visages of horror on the smoke-wreaths, above the impious assembly. At the same moment, the fire on the rock shot redly forth, and formed a glowing arch above its base, where now appeared a figure. With reverence be it spoken, the figure bore no slight similitude, both in garb and manner, to some grave divine of the New-England churches.

"Bring forth the converts!" cried a voice, that echoed through the field and rolled into the forest.

At the word, Goodman Brown stept forth from the shadow of the trees, and approached the congregation, with whom he felt a loathful brotherhood, by the sympathy of all that was wicked in his heart. He could have well nigh sworn, that the shape of his own dead father beckoned him to advance, looking downward from a smoke-wreath, while a woman, with dim features of despair, threw out her hand to warn him back. Was it his mother? But he had no power to retreat one step, nor to resist, even in thought, when the minister and good old Deacon Gookin seized his arms, and led him to the blazing rock. Thither came also the slender form of a veiled female, led between Goody Cloyse, that pious teacher of the catechism, and Martha Carrier, who had received the devil's promise to be queen of hell. A rampant hag was she! And there stood the proselytes, beneath the canopy of fire.

"Welcome, my children," said the dark figure, "to the communion of your race! Ye have found, thus young, your nature and your destiny. My children, look behind you!"

They turned; and flashing forth, as it were, in a sheet of flame, the fiend-worshippers were seen; the smile of welcome gleamed darkly on every visage.

"There," resumed the sable form, "are all whom ye have reverenced from youth. Ye deemed them holier than yourselves, and shrank from your own sin, contrasting it with their lives of righteousness, and prayerful aspirations heavenward. Yet, here are they all, in my worshipping assembly! This night it shall be granted you to know their secret deeds; how hoary-bearded elders of the church have whispered wanton words to the young maids of their households; how many a woman, eager for widow's weeds, has given her husband a drink at bedtime, and let him sleep his last sleep in her bosom; how beardless youths have made haste to inherit their fathers' wealth; and how fair damsels—blush not, sweet ones!—have dug little graves in the garden, and bidden me, the sole guest, to an infant's funeral. By the sympathy of your human hearts for sin, ye shall scent out all the places—whether in church, bed-chamber, street, field, or forest—where crime has been committed, and shall exult to behold the whole earth one stain of guilt, one mighty blood-spot. Far more than this! It shall be yours to penetrate, in every bosom, the deep mystery of sin, the fountain of all wicked arts, and which inexhaustibly supplies more evil impulses than human power—than my power, at its utmost!—can make manifest in deeds. And now, my children, look upon each other."

They did so; and, by the blaze of the hell-kindled torches, the wretched man beheld his Faith, and the wife her husband, trembling before that unhallowed altar.

"Lo! there ye stand, my children," said the figure, in a deep and solemn tone, almost sad, with its despairing awfulness, as if his once angelic nature could yet mourn for our miserable race. "Depending upon one another's hearts, ye had still hoped, that virtue were not all a dream. Now are ye undeceived! Evil is the nature of mankind. Evil must be your only happiness. Welcome, again, my children, to the communion of your race!"

"Welcome!" repeated the fiend-worshippers, in one cry of despair and triumph.

And there they stood, the only pair, as it seemed, who were yet hesitating on the verge of wickedness, in this dark world. A basin was hollowed, naturally, in the rock. Did it contain water, reddened by the lurid light? or was it blood? or, perchance, a liquid flame? Herein did the Shape of Evil dip his hand, and prepare to lay the mark of baptism upon their foreheads, that they might be partakers of the mystery of sin, more conscious of the secret guilt of others, both in deed and thought, than they could now be of their own. The husband cast one look at his pale wife, and Faith at him. What polluted wretches would the next glance shew them to each other, shuddering alike at what they disclosed and what they saw!

"Faith! Faith!" cried the husband. "Look up to Heaven, and resist the Wicked One!"

Whether Faith obeyed, he knew not. Hardly had he spoken, when he found himself amid calm night and solitude, listening to a roar of the wind, which died heavily away through the forest. He staggered against the rock and felt it chill and damp, while a hanging twig, that had been all on fire, besprinkled his cheek with the coldest dew.

The next morning, young Goodman Brown came slowly into the street of Salem village, staring around him like a bewildered man. The good old minister was taking a walk along the grave-yard, to get an appetite for breakfast and meditate his sermon, and bestowed a blessing, as he passed, on Goodman Brown. He shrank from the venerable saint, as if to avoid an anathema. Old Deacon Gookin was at domestic worship, and the holy words of his prayer were heard through the open window. "What God doth the wizard pray to?" quoth Goodman Brown. Goody Cloyse, that excellent old Christian, stood in the early sunshine, at her own lattice, catechising a little girl, who had brought her a pint of morning's milk. Goodman Brown snatched away the child, as from the grasp of the fiend himself. Turning the corner by the meeting-house, he spied the head of Faith, with the pink ribbons, gazing anxiously forth, and bursting into such joy at sight of him, that she skipt along the street, and almost kissed her husband before the whole village. But, Goodman Brown looked sternly and sadly into her face, and passed on without a greeting.

Had Goodman Brown fallen asleep in the forest, and only dreamed a wild dream of a witch-meeting?

Be it so, if you will. But, alas! it was a dream of evil omen for young Goodman Brown. A stern, a sad, a darkly meditative, a distrustful, if not a desperate man, did he become, from the night of that fearful dream. On the Sabbath-day, when the congregation were singing a holy psalm, he could not listen, because an anthem of sin rushed loudly upon his ear, and drowned all the blessed strain. When the minister spoke from the pulpit, with power and fervid eloquence, and, with his hand on the open Bible, of the sacred truths of our religion, and of saint-like lives and triumphant deaths, and of future bliss or misery unutterable, then did Goodman Brown turn pale, dreading, lest the roof should thunder down upon the gray blasphemer and his hearers. Often, awakening suddenly at midnight, he shrank from the bosom of Faith, and at morning or even-tide, when the family knelt down at prayer, he scowled, and muttered to himself, and gazed sternly at his wife, and turned away. And when he had lived long, and was borne to his grave, a hoary corpse, followed by Faith, an aged woman, and children and grand-children, a goodly procession, besides neighbors, not a few, they carved no hopeful verse upon his tomb-stone; for his dying hour was gloom.

[1835]

The May-Pole of Merry Mount

There is an admirable foundation for a philosophic romance, in the curious history of the early settlement of Mount

Wollaston,[1] or Merry Mount. In the slight sketch here attempted, the facts, recorded on the grave pages of our New England annalists, have wrought themselves, almost spontaneously, into a sort of allegory. The masques, mummeries, and festive customs, described in the text, are in accordance with the manners of the age. Authority on these points may be found in Strutt's Book of English Sports and Pastimes.[2]

Bright were the days at Merry Mount, when the May-Pole was the banner-staff of that gay colony! They who reared it, should their banner be triumphant, were to pour sunshine over New England's rugged hills, and scatter flower-seeds throughout the soil. Jollity and gloom were contending for an empire. Midsummer eve[3] had come, bring deep verdure to the forest, and roses in her lap, of a more vivid hue than the tender buds of Spring. But May, or her mirthful spirit, dwelt all the year round at Merry Mount, sporting with the Summer months, and reveling with Autumn, and basking in the glow of Winter's fireside. Through a world of toil and care, she flitted with a dreamlike smile, and came hither to find a home among the lightsome hearts of Merry Mount.

Never had the May-Pole been so gaily decked as at sunset on midsummer eve. This venerated emblem was a pine tree, which had preserved the slender grace of youth, while it equalled the loftiest height of the old wood monarchs. From its top streamed a silken banner, colored like the rainbow. Down nearly to the ground, the pole was dressed with birchen boughs, and others of the liveliest green, and some with silvery leaves, fastened by ribbons that fluttered in fantastic knots of twenty different colors, but no sad ones. Garden flowers, and blossoms of the wilderness, laughed gladly forth amid the verdure, so fresh and dewy, that they must have grown by magic on that happy pine tree. Where this green and flower splendor terminated, the shaft of the May-Pole was stained with the seven brilliant hues of the banner at its top. On the lowest green bough hung an abundant wreath of roses, some that had

---

[1]MOUNT WOLLASTON: An English settlement in the area of Braintree, Massachusetts, founded by Captain Wollaston in 1625. A year later, Thomas Morton (d. 1645) assumed the leadership of the colony and renamed it Mere Mount, or Merry Mount. Morton, who was not a Puritan, and the men at Merry Mount shocked the Pilgrims in nearby Plymouth when they erected a maypole and danced with local Indian women. In 1627, the scandalized Pilgrims dispatched Miles Standish to arrest Morton and sent him back to England.
[2]STRUTT'S BOOK OF ENGLISH SPORTS AND PASTIMES: Joseph Strutt (1749–1802), *The Sports and Pastimes of the People of England* (1801).
[3]MIDSUMMER EVE: June 23, the eve of the feast day of St. John the Baptist on June 24. It falls near the summer solstice (21 or 22 June).

been gathered in the sunniest spots of the forest, and others, of still richer blush, which the colonists had reared from English seed. Oh, people of the Golden Age, the chief of your husbandry, was to raise flowers!

But what was the wild throng that stood hand in hand about the May-Pole? It could not be, that the Fauns and Nymphs, when driven from their classic groves and homes of ancient fable, had sought refuge, as all the persecuted did, in the fresh woods of the West. These were Gothic monsters, though perhaps of Grecian ancestry. On the shoulders of a comely youth, uprose the head and branching antlers of a stag; a second, human in all other points, had the grim visage of a wolf; a third, still with the trunk and limbs of a mortal man, showed the beard and horns of a venerable he-goat. There was the likeness of a bear erect, brute in all but his hind legs, which were adorned with pink silk stockings. And there again, almost as wondrous, stood a real bear of the dark forest, lending each of his fore paws to the grasp of a human hand, and as ready for the dance as any in that circle. His inferior nature rose half-way, to meet his companions as they stooped. Other faces wore the similitude of a man or women, but distorted or extravagant, with red noses pendulous before their mouths, which seemed of awful depth, and stretched from ear to ear in an eternal fit of laughter. Here might be seen the Salvage Man,[4] well known in heraldry, hairy as a baboon, and girdled with green leaves. By his side, a nobler figure, but still a counterfeit, appeared an Indian hunter, with feathery crest and wampum belt. Many of this strange company wore fools-caps, and had little bells appended to their garments, tinkling with a silvery sound, responsive to the inaudible music of their gleesome spirits. Some youths and maidens were of soberer garb, yet well maintained their places in the irregular throng, by the expression of wild revelry upon their features. Such were the colonists of Merry Mount, as they stood in the broad smile of sunset, round their venerated May-Pole.

Had a wanderer, bewildered in the melancholy forest, heard their mirth, and stolen a half-affrighted glance, he might have fancied them the crew of Comus,[5] some already transformed to brutes, some midway between man and beast, and the others rioting in the flow of tipsey jollity that foreran the change. But a band of Puritans, who watched the scene, invisible themselves, compared the masques to those devils and ruined souls, with whom their supersitition peopled the black wilderness.

[4]SALVAGE MAN: The salvage man was a character depicted in medieval and Renaissance heraldry and pageants as a man wearing foliage or rough animal skins.
[5]COMUS: *Comus* (1634), a masque written by the English poet John Milton (1608–1674), whose title character turns people into creatures with human bodies and the heads of animals.

Within the ring of monsters, appeared the two airiest forms, that had ever trodden on any more solid footing than a purple and golden cloud. One was a youth, in glistening apparel, with a scarf of the rainbow pattern crosswise on his breast. His right hand held a gilded staff, the ensign[6] of high dignity among the revellers, and his left grasped the slender fingers of a fair maiden, not less gaily decorated than himself. Bright roses glowed in contrast with the dark and glossy curls of each, and were scattered round their feet, or had sprung up spontaneously there. Behind this lightsome couple, so close to the May-Pole that its boughs shaded his jovial face, stood the figure of an English priest, canonically dressed, yet decked with flowers, in heathen fashion, and wearing a chaplet of the native vine leaves. By the riot of his rolling eye, and the pagan decorations of his holy garb, he seemed the wildest monster there, and the very Comus of the crew.

"Votaries of the May-Pole," cried the flower-decked priest, "merrily, all day long, have the woods echoed to your mirth. But be this your merriest hour, my hearts! Lo, here stand the Lord and Lady of the May, whom I, a clerk of Oxford, and high priest of Merry Mount, am presently to join in holy matrimony. Up with your nimble spirits, ye morrice-dancers,[7] green-men,[8] and glee-maidens,[9] bears and wolves, and horned gentlemen! Come; a chorus now, rich with the old mirth of Merry England, and the wilder glee of this fresh forest; and then a dance, to show the youthful pair what life is made of, and how airily they should go through it! All ye that love the May-Pole, lend your voices to the nuptial song of the Lord and Lady of the May!"

This wedlock was more serious than most affairs of Merry Mount, where jest and delusion, trick and fantasy, kept up a continued carnival. The Lord and Lady of the May, though their titles must be laid down at sunset, were really and truly to be partners for the dance of life, beginning the measure that same bright eve. The wreath of roses, that hung from the lowest green bough of the May-Pole, had been twined for them, and would be thrown over both their heads, in symbol of their flowery union. When the priest had spoken, therefore, a riotous uproar burst from the rout of monstrous figures.

"Begin you the stave,[10] reverend Sire," cried they all; "and never did the woods ring to such a merry peal, as we of the May-Pole shall send up!"

---

[6]ENSIGN: A lay minister of the Anglican Church (Church of England).
[7]MORRICE-DANCERS: Dressed in bells and ribbons, morrice dancers performed as a group to lively music, carrying sticks and handkerchiefs to emphasize the movement.
[8]GREEN-MEN: Men dressed up in greenery and foliage to represent wild men of the woods.
[9]GLEE-MAIDENS: Girl singers.
[10]STAVE: Stanza.

Immediately a prelude of pipe, cittern,[11] and viol, touched with practised minstrelsy, began to play from a neighboring thicket, in such a
mirthful cadence, that the bough of the May-Pole quivered to the sound.
But the May Lord, he of the gilded staff, chancing to look into his Lady's
eyes, was wonderstruck at the almost pensive glance that met his own.

"Edith, sweet Lady of the May," whispered he, reproachfully, "is
yon wreath of roses a garland to hang above our graves, that you look
so sad? Oh, Edith, this is our golden time! Tarnish it not by any pensive shadow of the mind; for it may be, that nothing of futurity will be
brighter than the mere remembrance of what is now passing."

"That was the very thought that saddened me! How came it in your
mind too?" said Edith, in a still lower tone than he; for it was high treason to be sad at Merry Mount. "Therefore do I sigh amid this festive
music. And besides, dear Edgar, I struggle as with a dream, and fancy
that these shapes of our jovial friends are visionary, and their mirth
unreal, and that we are no true Lord and Lady of the May. What is the
mystery in my heart?"

Just then, as if a spell had loosened them, down came a little shower
of withering rose leaves from the May-Pole. Alas, for the young lovers! No
sooner had their hearts glowed with real passion, than they were sensible of something vague and unsubstantial in their former pleasures, and
felt a dreary presentiment of inevitable change. From the moment that
they truly loved, they had subjected themselves to earth's doom of care,
and sorrow, and troubled joy, and had no more a home at Merry Mount.
That was Edith's mystery. Now leave we the priest to marry them, and the
masquers to sport round the May-Pole, till the last sunbeam be withdrawn
from its summit, and the shadows of the forest mingle gloomily in the
dance. Meanwhile, we may discover who these gay people were.

Two hundred years ago, and more, the old world and its inhabitants became mutually weary of each other. Men voyaged by thousands
to the West; some to barter glass beads, and such like jewels, for the furs
of the Indian hunter; some to conquer virgin empires; and one stern band
to pray. But none of these motives had much weight with the colonists
of Merry Mount. Their leaders were men who had sported so long with
life, that when Thought and Wisdom came, even these unwelcome guests
were led astray, by the crowd of vanities which they should have put
to flight. Erring Thought and perverted Wisdom were made to put on
masques, and play the fool. The men of whom we speak after losing
the heart's fresh gaiety, imagined a wild philosophy of pleasure, and

[11]CITTERN: A Renaissance guitar with a wide, pear-shaped body, played with a quill.

came hither to act out their latest day-dream. They gathered followers from all that giddy tribe, whose whole life is like the festal days of soberer men. In their train were minstrels, not unknown in London streets; wandering players, whose theatres had been the halls of noblemen; mummers, rope-dancers, and mountebanks,[12] who would long be missed at wakes, church-ales, and fairs; in a word, mirth-makers of every sort, such as abounded in that age, but now began to be discountenanced by the rapid growth of Puritanism. Light had their footsteps been on land, and as lightly they came across the sea. Many had been maddened by their previous troubles into a gay despair; others were as madly gay in the flush of youth, like the May Lord and his Lady; but whatever might be the quality of their mirth, old and young were gay at Merry Mount. The young deemed themselves happy. The elder spirits, if they knew that mirth was but the counterfeit of happiness, yet followed the false shadow wilfully, because at least her garments glittered brightest. Sworn triflers of a lifetime, they would not venture among the sober truths of life, not even to be truly blest.

All the hereditary pastimes of Old England were transplanted hither. The King of Christmas was duly crowned, and the Lord of Misrule[13] bore potent sway. On the eve of Saint John,[14] they felled whole acres of the forest to make bonfires, and danced by the blaze all night, crowned with garlands, and throwing flowers into the flame. At harvest time, though their crop was of the smallest, they made an image with the sheaves of Indian corn, and wreathed it with autumnal garlands, and bore it home triumphantly. But what chiefly characterized the colonists of Merry Mount, was their veneration for the May-Pole. It has made their true history a poet's tale. Spring decked the hallowed emblem with young blossoms and fresh green boughs; Summer brought roses of the deepest blush, and the perfected foliage of the forest; Autumn enriched it with that red and yellow gorgeousness, which converts each wild-wood leaf into a painted flower; and Winter silvered it with sleet, and hung it round with icicles, till it flashed in the cold sunshine, itself a frozen sunbeam. Thus each alternate season did homage to the May-Pole, and paid it a tribute of its own richest splendor. Its votaries danced round it, once, at least, in every month; sometimes they called it their religion, or their altar; but always, it was the banner-staff of Merry Mount.

[12]MUMMERS, ROPE-DANCERS, AND MOUNTEBANKS: Charlatans who sold "medical" potions and remedies using various entertainments to attract a crowd of potential customers. Mummeries were masked actors, and rope-dancers performed tightrope walking routines.
[13]LORD OF MISRULE: The traditional master of Christmas revels.
[14]THE EVE OF SAINT JOHN: Midsummer's Eve (see note 3).

Unfortunately, there were men in the new world, of a sterner faith than these May-Pole worshippers. Not far from Merry Mount was a settlement of Puritans, most dismal wretches, who said their prayers before daylight, and then wrought in the forest or the cornfield, till evening made it prayer time again. Their weapons were always at hand, to shoot down the straggling savage. When they met in conclave, it was never to keep up the old English mirth, but to hear sermons three hours long, or to proclaim bounties on the heads of wolves and the scalps of Indians. Their festivals were fast-days, and their chief pastime the singing of psalms. Woe to the youth or maiden, who did but dream of a dance! The selectman nodded to the constable; and there sat the light-heeled reprobate in the stocks; or if he danced, it was round the whipping-post, which might be termed the Puritan May-Pole.

A party of these grim Puritans, toiling through the difficult woods, each with a horse-load of iron armor to burthen his footsteps, would sometimes draw near the sunny precincts of Merry Mount. There were the silken colonists, sporting round their May-Pole; perhaps teaching a bear to dance, or striving to communicate their mirth to the grave Indian; or masquerading in the skins of deer and wolves, which they had hunted for that especial purpose. Often, the whole colony were playing at blindman's buff, magistrates and all with their eyes bandaged, except a single scape-goat, whom the blinded sinners pursued by the tinkling of the bells at his garments. Once, it is said, they were seen following a flower-decked corpse, with merriment and festive music, to his grave. But did the dead man laugh? In their quietest times, they sang ballads and told tales, for the edification of their pious visiters; or perplexed them with juggling tricks; or grinned at them through horse-collars; and when sport itself grew wearisome, they made game of their own stupidity, and began a yawning match. At the very least of these enormities, the men of iron shook their heads and frowned so darkly, that the revellers looked up, imagining that a momentary cloud had overcast the sunshine, which was to be perpetual there. On the other hand, the Puritans affirmed, that, when a psalm was pealing from their place of worship, the echo, which the forest sent them back, seemed often like the chorus of a jolly catch, closing with a roar of laughter. Who but the fiend and his bond-slaves, the crew of Merry Mount, had thus disturbed them! In due time, a feud arose, stern and bitter on one side, and as serious on the other as any thing could be, among such light spirits as had sworn allegiance to the May-Pole. The future complexion of New England was involved in this important quarrel. Should the grisly saints establish their jurisdiction over the gay sinners, then would their spirits darken all the clime, and make it a land of clouded visages, of hard toil, of sermon and psalm, forever. But should the banner-staff of Merry Mount be fortunate, sunshine would break upon the hills, and flowers would beautify the forest, and late posterity do homage to the May-Pole!

After these authentic passages from history, we return to the nuptials of the Lord and Lady of the May. Alas! we have delayed too long, and must darken our tale too suddenly. As we glance again at the May-Pole, a solitary sunbeam is fading from the summit, and leaves only a faint golden tinge, blended with the hues of the rainbow banner. Even that dim light is now withdrawn, relinquishing the whole domain of Merry Mount to the evening gloom, which has rushed so instantaneously from the black surrounding woods. But some of these black shadows have rushed forth in human shape.

Yes: with the setting sun, the last day of mirth had passed from Merry Mount. The ring of gay masquers was disordered and broken; the stag lowered his antlers in dismay; the wolf grew weaker than a lamb; the bells of the morrice-dancers tinkled with tremulous affright. The Puritans had played a characteristic part in the May-Pole mummeries. Their darksome figures were intermixed with the wild shapes of their foes, and made the scene a picture of the moment, when waking thoughts start up amid the scattered fantasies of a dream. The leader of the hostile party stood in the center of the circle, while the rout of monsters cowered around him, like evil spirits in the presence of a dread magician. No fantastic foolery could look him in the face. So stern was the energy of his aspect, that the whole man, visage, frame, and soul, seemed wrought of iron, gifted with life and thought, yet all of one substance with his head-piece and breast-plate. It was the Puritan of Puritans; it was Endicott[15] himself!

"Stand off, priest of Baal!"[16] said he, with a grim frown, and laying no reverent hand upon the surplice. "I know thee, Blackstone![17] Thou art the man, who couldst not abide the rule even of thine own corrupted church, and hast come hither to preach iniquity, and to give example of

---

[15]ENDICOTT: John Endicott (1588–1665), one of the Puritan founders of Massachusetts Bay Colony and the first governor (1629–1630) of the colony at Salem. A stern and devout Puritan, he was a zealous persecutor of the Quakers.
[16]BAAL: The name of the chief deity of Canaan, a pagan fertility god condemned in the Old Testament.
[17]BLACKSTONE: "Did Governor Endicott speak less positively, we should suspect a mistake here. The Rev. Mr. Blackstone, though an eccentric, is not known to have been an immoral man. We rather doubt his identity with the priest of Merry Mount." (Hawthorne's note) William Blackstone (1595–1675) was an Anglican clergyman who lived near Merry Mount in the 1620s.

it in thy life. But now shall it be seen that the Lord hath sanctified this wilderness for his peculiar people. Woe unto them that would defile it! And first for this flower-decked abomination, the altar of thy worship!"

And with his keen sword, Endicott assaulted the hallowed May-Pole. Nor long did it resist his arm. It groaned with a dismal sound; it showered leaves and rose-buds upon the remorseless enthusiast; and finally, with all its green boughs, and ribbons, and flowers, symbolic of departed pleasures, down fell the banner-staff of Merry Mount. As it sank, tradition says, the evening sky grew darker, and the woods threw forth a more sombre shadow.

"There," cried Endicott, looking triumphantly on his work, "there lies the only May-Pole in New England! The thought is strong within me, that, by its fall, is shadowed forth the fate of light and idle mirth-makers, amongst us and our posterity. Amen, saith John Endicott!"

"Amen!" echoed his followers.

But the votaries of the May-Pole gave one groan for their idol. At the sound, the Puritan leader glanced at the crew of Comus, each a figure of broad mirth, yet, at this moment, strangely expressive of sorrow and dismay.

"Valiant captain," quoth Peter Palfrey, the Ancient[18] of the band, "what order shall be taken with the prisoners?"

"I thought not to repent me of cutting down a May-Pole," replied Endicott, "yet now I could find in my heart to plant it again, and give each of these bestial pagans one other dance round their idol. It would have served rarely for a whipping-post!"

"But there are pine trees enow," suggested the lieutenant.

"True, good Ancient," said the leader. "Wherefore, bind the heathen crew, and bestow on them a small matter of stripes apiece, as earnest of our future justice. Set some of the rogues in the stocks to rest themselves, so soon as Providence shall bring us to one of our own well-ordered settlements, where such accommodations may be found. Further penalties, such as branding and cropping of ears, shall be thought of hereafter."

"How many stripes for the priest?" inquired Ancient Palfrey.

"None as yet," answered Endicott, bending his iron frown upon the culprit. "It must be fore Great and General Court[19] to determine, whether

---

[18]PETER PALFREY, THE ANCIENT: An early resident (1605–1663) of Salem. An *ancient* is a lieutenant or flagbearer in a military unit.
[19]GREAT AND GENERAL COURT: The Massachusetts legislature.

stripes and long imprisonment, and other grievous penalty, may atone for his transgressions. Let him look to himself! For such as violate our civil order, it may be permitted us to show mercy. But woe to the wretch that troubleth our religion!"

"And this dancing bear," resumed the officer. "ust he share the stripes of his fellows?"

"Shoot him through the head!" said the energetic Puritan. "I suspect witchcraft in the beast."

"Here be a couple of shining ones," continued Peter Palfrey, pointing his weapon at the Lord and Lady of the May. "They seem to be of high station among these mis-doers. Methinks their dignity will not be fitted with less than a double share of stripes."

Endicott rested on his sword, and closely surveyed the dress and aspect of the hapless pair. There they stood, pale, downcast, and apprehensive. Yet there was an air of mutual support, and of pure affection, seeking aid and giving it, that showed them to be man and wife, with the sanction of a priest upon their love. The youth, in the peril of the moment, had dropped his gilded staff, and thrown his arm about the Lady of the May, who leaned against his breast, too lightly to burthen him, but with weight enough to express that their destinies were linked together, for good or evil. They looked first at each other, and then into the grim captain's face. There they stood, in the first hour of wedlock, while the idle pleasures, of which their companions were the emblems, had given place to the sternest cares of life, personified by the dark Puritans. But never had their youthful beauty seemed so pure and high, as when its glow was chastened by adversity.

"Youth," said Endicott, "ye stand in an evil case, thou and thy maiden wife. Make ready presently; for I am minded that ye shall both have a token to remember your wedding-day!"

"Stern man," cried the May Lord, "how can I move thee? Were the means at hand, I would resist to the death. Being powerless, I entreat! Do with me as thou wilt; but let Edith go untouched!"

"Not so," replied the immitigable zealot. "We are not wont to show an idle courtesy to that sex, which requireth the stricter discipline. What sayest thou maid? Shall thy silken bridegroom suffer thy share of the penalty, beside his own?"

"Be it death," said Edith, "and lay it all on me!"

Truly, as Endicott had said, the poor lovers stood in a woeful case. Their foes were triumphant, their friends captive and abased, their home desolate, the benighted wilderness around them, and a rigorous destiny, in the shape of the Puritan leader, their only guide. Yet the deepening twilight could not altogether conceal, that the iron man was softened; he smiled, at the fair spectacle of early love; he almost sighed, for the inevitable blight of early hopes.

"The troubles of life have come hastily on this young couple," observed Endicott. "We will see how they comport themselves under their present trials, ere we burthen them with greater. If, among the spoil, there be any garments of a more decent fashion, let them be put upon this May Lord and his Lady, instead of their glistening vanities. Look to it, some of you."

"And shall not the youth's hair be cut?" asked Peter Palfrey, looking with abhorrence at the love-lock and long glossy curls of the young man.

"Crop it forthwith, and that in the true pumpkin-shell fashion,"[20] answered the captain. "Then bring them along with us, but more gently than their fellows. There be qualities in the youth, which may make him valiant to fight, and sober to toil, and pious to pray; and in the maiden, that may fit her to become a mother in our Israel,[21] bring up babes in better nurture than her own hath been. Nor think ye, young ones, that they are the happiest, even in our lifetime of a moment, who misspend it in dancing round a May-Pole!"

And Endicott, the severest Puritan of all who laid the rock-foundation of New England, lifted the wreath of roses from the ruin of the May-Pole, and threw it, with his own gauntleted hand, over the heads of the Lord and Lady of the May. It was a deed of prophecy. As the moral gloom of the world overpowers all systematic gaiety, even so was their home of wild mirth made desolate amid the sad forest. They returned to it no more. But, as their flowery garland was wreathed of the brightest roses that had grown there, so, in the tie that united them, were intertwined all the purest and best of their early joys. They went heavenward, supporting each other along the difficult path which it was their lot to tread, and never wasted one regretful thought on the vanities of Merry Mount.

[1835]

---

[20]TRUE PUMPKIN-SHELL FASHION: A close-cropped Puritan hairstyle, also known as the "round-head" style.
[21]ISRAEL: New England Puritans thought of themselves as God's new "Chosen People," thus comparing themselves to the Israelites.

The Minister's Black Veil

A PARABLE[1]

The sexton stood in the porch of Milford meeting-house, pulling lustily at the bell-rope. The old people of the village came stooping along the street. Children, with bright faces, tript merrily beside their parents, or mimicked a graver gait, in the conscious dignity of their Sunday clothes. Spruce bachelors looked sidelong at the pretty maidens, and fancied that the Sabbath sunshine made them prettier than on weekdays. When the throng had mostly streamed into the porch, the sexton began to toll the bell, keeping his eye on the Reverend Mr. Hooper's door. The first glimpse of the clergyman's figure was the signal for the bell to cease its summons.

"But what has good Parson Hooper got upon his face?" cried the sexton in astonishment.

All within hearing immediately turned about, and beheld the semblance of Mr. Hooper, pacing slowly his meditative way towards the meeting-house. With one accord they started, expressing more wonder than if some strange minister were coming to dust the cushions of Mr. Hooper's pulpit.

"Are you sure it is our parson?" inquired Goodman Gray of the sexton.

"Of a certainty it is good Mr. Hooper," replied the sexton. "He was to have exchanged pulpits with Parson Shute of Westbury; but Parson Shute sent to excuse himself yesterday, being to preach a funeral sermon."

The cause of so much amazement may appear sufficiently slight. Mr. Hooper, a gentlemanly person of about thirty, though still a bachelor, was dressed with due clerical neatness, as if a careful wife had starched his band, and brushed the weekly dust from his Sunday's garb. There was but one thing remarkable in his appearance. Swathed about his forehead, and hanging down over his face, so low as to be shaken by his breath, Mr. Hooper had on a black veil. On a nearer view, it seemed to consist of two folds of crape, which entirely concealed his features, except the mouth and chin, but probably did not intercept his sight, farther than to give a darkened aspect to all living and inanimate things. With this gloomy shade before him, good Mr. Hooper walked onward, at a slow and

---

[1] A PARABLE: Of this story, Hawthorne writes, "Another clergyman in New England, Mr. Joseph Moody, of York, Maine, who died about eighty years since, made himself remarkable by the same eccentricity that is here related of the Reverend Mr. Hooper. In his case, however, the symbol had a different import. In early life, he had accidentally killed a beloved friend; and from that day till the hour of his own death, he hid his face from men." Joseph "Handkerchief" Moody, a graduate of Harvard, was a minister in Maine in the early 1700s.

quiet pace, stooping somewhat and looking on the ground, as is customary with abstracted men, yet nodding kindly to those of his parishioners who still waited on the meeting-house steps. But so wonder-struck were they, that his greeting hardly met with a return.

"I can't really feel as if good Mr. Hooper's face was behind that piece of crape," said the sexton.

"I don't like it," muttered an old woman, as she hobbled into the meeting-house. "He has changed himself into something awful, only by hiding his face."

"Our parson has gone mad!" cried Goodman Gray, following him across the threshold.

A rumor of some unaccountable phenomenon had preceded Mr. Hooper into the meeting-house, and set all the congregation astir. Few could refrain from twisting their heads towards the door; many stood upright, and turned directly about; while several little boys clambered upon the seats, and came down again with a terrible racket. There was a general bustle, a rustling of the women's gowns and shuffling of the men's feet, greatly at variance with that hushed repose which should attend the entrance of the minister. But Mr. Hooper appeared not to notice the perturbation of his people. He entered with an almost noiseless step, bent his head mildly to the pews on each side, and bowed as he passed his oldest parishioner, a white-haired great-grandsire, who occupied an arm-chair in the centre of the aisle. It was strange to observe, how slowly this venerable man became conscious of something singular in the appearance of his pastor. He seemed not fully to partake of the prevailing wonder, till Mr. Hooper had ascended the stairs, and showed himself in the pulpit, face to face with his congregation, except for the black veil. That mysterious emblem was never once withdrawn. It shook with his measured breath as he gave out the psalm; it threw its obscurity between him and the holy page, as he read the Scriptures; and while he prayed, the veil lay heavily on his uplifted countenance. Did he seek to hide it from the dread Being whom he was addressing?

Such was the effect of this simple piece of crape, that more than one woman of delicate nerves was forced to leave the meeting-house. Yet perhaps the pale-faced congregation was almost as fearful a sight to the minister, as his black veil to them.

Mr. Hooper had the reputation of a good preacher, but not an energetic one: he strove to win his people heavenward, by mild persuasive influences, rather than to drive them thither, by the thunders of the Word. The sermon which he now delivered, was marked by the same characteristics of style and manner, as the general series of his pulpit oratory.

But there was something, either in the sentiment of the discourse itself, or in the imagination of the auditors, which made it greatly the most powerful effort that they had ever heard from their pastor's lips. It was tinged, rather more darkly than usual, with the gentle gloom of Mr. Hooper's temperament. The subject had reference to secret sin, and those sad mysteries which we hide from our nearest and dearest, and would fain conceal from our own consciousness, even forgetting that the Omniscient can detect them. A subtle power was breathed into his words. Each member of the congregation, the most innocent girl, and the man of hardened breast, felt as if the preacher had crept upon them, behind his awful veil, and discovered their boarded iniquity of deed or thought. Many spread their clasped hands on their bosoms. There was nothing terrible in what Mr. Hooper said; at least, no violence; and yet, with every tremor of his melancholy voice, the hearers quaked. An unsought pathos came hand in hand with awe. So sensible were the audience of some unwonted attribute in their minister, that they longed for a breath of wind to blow aside the veil, almost believing that a stranger's visage would be discovered; though the form, gesture, and voice were those of Mr. Hooper.

At the close of the services, the people hurried out with indecorous confusion, eager to communicate their pent-up amazement, and conscious of lighter spirits, the moment they lost sight of the black veil. Some gathered in little circles, huddled closely together, with their mouths all whispering in the centre; some went homeward alone, wrapt in silent meditation; some talked loudly, and profaned the Sabbath-day with ostentatious laughter. A few shook their sagacious heads, intimating that they could penetrate the mystery; while one or two affirmed that there was no mystery at all, but only that Mr. Hooper's eyes were so weakened by the midnight lamp, as to require a shade. After a brief interval, forth came good Mr. Hooper also, in the rear of his flock. Turning his veiled face from one group to another, he paid due reverence to the hoary heads, saluted the middle-aged with kind dignity, as their friend and spiritual guide, greeted the young with mingled authority and love, and laid his hands on the little children's heads to bless them. Such was always his custom on the Sabbath-day. Strange and bewildered looks repaid him for his courtesy. None, as on former occasions, aspired to the honor of walking by their pastor's side. Old Squire Saunders, doubtless by an accidental lapse of memory, neglected to invite Mr. Hooper to his table, where the good clergyman had been wont to bless the food, almost every Sunday since his settlement. He returned, therefore, to the parsonage, and, at the moment of closing the door, was observed to look back upon the people, all of whom had their eyes fixed upon the minister. A sad smile gleamed faintly from beneath the black veil, and flickered about his mouth, glimmering as he disappeared.

"How strange," said a lady, "that a simple black veil, such as any woman might wear on her bonnet, should become such a terrible thing on Mr. Hooper's face!"

"Something must surely be amiss with Mr. Hooper's intellects," observed her husband, the physician of the village. "But the strangest part of the affair is the effect of this vagary, even on a sober-minded man like myself. The black veil, though it covers only our pastor's face, throws its influence over his whole person, and makes him ghost-like from head to foot. Do you not feel it so?"

"Truly do I," replied the lady; "and I would not be alone with him for the world. I wonder he is not afraid to be alone with himself!"

"Men sometimes are so," said her husband.

The afternoon service was attended with similar circumstances. At its conclusion, the bell tolled for the funeral of a young lady. The relatives and friends were assembled in the house, and the more distant acquaintances stood about the door, speaking of the good qualities of the deceased, when their talk was interrupted by the appearance of Mr. Hooper, still covered with his black veil. It was now an appropriate emblem. The clergyman stepped into the room where the corpse was laid, and bent over the coffin, to take a last farewell of his deceased parishioner. As he stooped, the veil hung straight down from his forehead, so that, if her eye-lids had not been closed for ever, the dead maiden might have seen his face. Could Mr. Hooper be fearful of her glance, that he so hastily caught back the black veil? A person, who watched the interview between the dead and living, scrupled not to affirm, that, at the instant when the clergyman's features were disclosed, the corpse had slightly shuddered, rustling the shroud and muslin cap, though the countenance retained the composure of death. A superstitious old woman was the only witness of this prodigy. From the coffin, Mr. Hooper passed into the chamber of the mourners, and thence to the head of the staircase, to make the funeral prayer. It was a tender and heart-dissolving prayer, full of sorrow, yet so imbued with celestial hopes, that the music of a heavenly harp, swept by the fingers of the dead, seemed faintly to be heard among the saddest accents of the minister. The people trembled, though they but darkly understood him, when he prayed that they, and himself, and all of mortal race, might be ready, as he trusted this young maiden had been, for the dreadful hour that should snatch the veil from their faces. The bearers went heavily forth, and the mourners followed, saddening all the street, with the dead before them, and Mr. Hooper in his black veil behind.

"Why do you look back?" said one in the procession to his partner.

"I had a fancy," replied she, "that the minister and the maiden's spirit were walking hand in hand."

"And so had I, at the same moment," said the other.

That night, the handsomest couple in Milford village were to be joined in wedlock. Though reckoned a melancholy man, Mr. Hooper had a placid cheerfulness for such occasions, which often excited a sympathetic smile, where livelier merriment would have been thrown away. There was no quality of his disposition which made him more beloved than this. The company at the wedding awaited his arrival with impatience, trusting that the strange awe, which had gathered over him throughout the day, would now be dispelled. But such was not the result. When Mr. Hooper came, the first thing that their eyes rested on was the same horrible black veil, which had added deeper gloom to the funeral, and could portend nothing but evil to the wedding. Such was its immediate effect on the guests, that a cloud seemed to have rolled duskily from beneath the black crape, and dimmed the light of the candles. The bridal pair stood up before the minister. But the bride's cold fingers quivered in the tremulous hand of the bridegroom, and her deathlike paleness caused a whisper, that the maiden who had been buried a few hours before, was come from her grave to be married. If ever another wedding were so dismal, it was that famous one, where they tolled the wedding-knell.[2] After performing the ceremony, Mr. Hooper raised a glass of wine to his lips, wishing happiness to the new-married couple, in a strain of mild pleasantry that ought to have brightened the features of the guests, like a cheerful gleam from the hearth. At that instant, catching a glimpse of his figure in the looking-glass, the black veil involved his own spirit in the horror with which it overwhelmed all others. His frame shuddered—his lips grew white—he spilt the untasted wine upon the carpet—and rushed forth into the darkness. For the Earth, too, had on her Black Veil.

The next day, the whole village of Milford talked of little else than Parson Hooper's black veil. That, and the mystery concealed behind it, supplied a topic for discussion between acquaintances meeting in the street, and good women gossiping at their open windows. It was the first item of news that the tavern-keeper told to his guests. The

[2]WEDDING-KNELL: Hawthorne alludes to his short story "The Wedding-Knell," published in the same collection, *The Token* (1836).

children babbled of it on their way to school. One imitative little imp covered his face with an old black handkerchief, thereby so affrighting his playmates, that the panic seized himself, and he well nigh lost his wits by his own waggery.[3]

It was remarkable, that, of all the busy-bodies and impertinent people in the parish, not one ventured to put the plain question to Mr. Hooper, wherefore he did this thing. Hitherto, whenever there appeared the slightest call for such interference, he had never lacked advisers, nor shown himself averse to be guided by their judgment. If he erred at all, it was by so painful a degree of self-distrust, that even the mildest censure would lead him to consider an indifferent action as a crime. Yet, though so well acquainted with this amiable weakness, no individual among his parishioners chose to make the black veil a subject of friendly remonstrance. There was a feeling of dread, neither plainly confessed nor carefully concealed, which caused each to shift the responsibility upon another, till at length it was found expedient to send a deputation of the church, in order to deal with Mr. Hooper about the mystery, before it should grow into a scandal. Never did an embassy so ill discharge its duties. The minister received them with friendly courtesy, but became silent, after they were seated, leaving to his visiters the whole burthen of introducing their important business. The topic, it might be supposed, was obvious enough. There was the black veil, swathed round Mr. Hooper's forehead, and concealing every feature above his placid mouth, on which, at times, they could perceive the glimmering of a melancholy smile. But that piece of crape, to their imagination, seemed to hang down before his heart, the symbol of a fearful secret between him and them. Were the veil but cast aside, they might speak freely of it, but not, till then. Thus they sat a considerable time, speechless, confused, and shrinking uneasily from Mr. Hooper's eye, which they felt to be fixed upon them with an invisible glance. Finally, the deputies returned abashed to their constituents, pronouncing the matter too weighty to be handled, except by a council of the churches, if, indeed, it might not require a general synod.

But there was one person in the village, unappalled by the awe with which the black veil had impressed all beside herself. When the deputies returned without an explanation, or even venturing to demand one, she, with the calm energy of her character, determined to chase away the strange cloud that appeared to be settling round Mr. Hooper, every moment more darkly than before. As his plighted wife, it should be her

---

[3]WAGGERY: Mischievous joking.

privilege to know what the black veil concealed. At the minister's first visit, therefore, she entered upon the subject, with a direct simplicity, which made the task easier both for him and her. After he had seated himself, she fixed her eyes steadfastly upon the veil, but could discern nothing of the dreadful gloom that had so overawed the multitude: it was but a double fold of crape, hanging down from his forehead to his mouth, and slightly stirring with his breath.

"No," said she aloud, and smiling, "there is nothing terrible in this piece of crape, except that it hides a face which I am always glad to look upon. Come, good sir, let the sun shine from behind the cloud. First lay aside your black veil: then tell me why you put it on."

Mr. Hooper's smile glimmered faintly.

"There is an hour to come," said he, "when all of us shall cast aside our veils. Take it not amiss, beloved friend, if I wear this piece of crape till then."

"Your words are a mystery too," returned the young lady. "Take away the veil from them, at least."

"Elizabeth, I will," said he, "so far as my vow may suffer me. Know, then, this veil is a type[4] and a symbol, and I am bound to wear it ever, both in light and darkness, in solitude and before the gaze of multitudes, and as with strangers, so with my familiar friends. No mortal eye will see it withdrawn. This dismal shade must separate me from the world: even you, Elizabeth, can never come behind it!"

"What grievous affliction hath befallen you," she earnestly inquired, "that you should thus darken your eyes for ever?"

"If it be a sign of mourning," replied Mr. Hooper, "I, perhaps, like most other mortals, have sorrows dark enough to be typified by a black veil."

"But what if the world will not believe that it is the type of an innocent sorrow?" urged Elizabeth. "Beloved and respected as you are, there may be whispers, that you hide your face under the consciousness of secret sin. For the sake of your holy office, do away this scandal!"

The color rose into her cheeks, as she intimated the nature of the rumors that were already abroad in the village. But Mr. Hooper's mildness did not forsake him. He even smiled again—that same sad smile, which always appeared like a faint glimmering of light, proceeding from the obscurity beneath the veil.

"If I hide my face for sorrow, there is cause enough," he merely replied; "and if I cover it for secret sin, what mortal might not do the same?"

---

[4]TYPE: Distinguishing mark; a sign.

And with this gentle, but unconquerable obstinacy, did he resist all her entreaties. At length Elizabeth sat silent. For a few moments she appeared lost in thought, considering, probably, what new methods might be tried, to withdraw her lover from so dark a fantasy, which, if it had no other meaning, was perhaps a symptom of mental disease. Though of a firmer character than his own, the tears rolled down her cheeks. But, in an instant, as it were, a new feeling took the place of sorrow: her eyes were fixed insensibly on the black veil, when, like a sudden twilight in the air, its terrors fell around her. She arose, and stood trembling before him.

"And do you feel it then at last?" said he mournfully.

She made no reply, but covered her eyes with her hand, and turned to leave the room. He rushed forward and caught her arm.

"Have patience with me, Elizabeth!" cried he passionately. "Do not desert me, though this veil must be between us here on earth. Be mine, and hereafter there shall be no veil over my face, no darkness between our souls! It is but a mortal veil—it is not for eternity! Oh! you know not how lonely I am, and how frightened to be alone behind my black veil. Do not leave me in this miserable obscurity for ever!"

"Lift the veil but once, and look me in the face," said she.

"Never! It cannot be!" replied Mr. Hooper.

"Then, farewell!" said Elizabeth.

She withdrew her arm from his grasp, and slowly departed, pausing at the door, to give one long, shuddering gaze, that seemed almost to penetrate the mystery of the black veil. But, even amid his grief, Mr. Hooper smiled to think that only a material emblem had separated him from happiness, though the horrors which it shadowed forth, must be drawn darkly between the fondest of lovers.

From that time no attempts were made to remove Mr. Hooper's black veil, or, by a direct appeal, to discover the secret which it was supposed to hide. By persons who claimed a superiority to popular prejudice, it was reckoned merely an eccentric whim, such as often mingles with the sober actions of men otherwise rational, and tinges them all with its own semblance of insanity. But with the multitude, good Mr. Hooper was irreparably a bugbear. He could not walk the streets with any peace of mind, so conscious was he that the gentle and timid would turn aside to avoid him, and that others would make it a point of hardihood to throw themselves in his way. The impertinence of the latter class compelled him to give up his customary walk, at sunset, to the burial ground; for when he leaned pensively over the gate, there would always be faces behind the grave-stones, peeping at his black veil. A fable went the rounds, that the stare of the dead people drove him thence. It grieved him, to the very depth of his kind heart, to observe how the children fled from his approach, breaking up their merriest sports, while his melancholy figure was yet afar off. Their instinctive dread caused him to feel, more strongly than aught else, that a preternatural horror was interwoven with the threads of the black crape. In truth, his own antipathy to the veil was known to be so great, that he never willingly passed before a mirror, nor stooped to drink at a still fountain, lest, in its peaceful bosom, he should be affrighted by himself. This was what gave plausibility to the whispers, that Mr. Hooper's conscience tortured him for some great crime, too horrible to be entirely concealed, or otherwise than so obscurely intimated. Thus, from beneath the black veil, there rolled a cloud into the sunshine, an ambiguity of sin or sorrow, which enveloped the poor minister, so that love or sympathy could never reach him. It was said, that ghost and fiend consorted with him there. With self-shudderings and outward terrors, he walked continually in its shadow, groping darkly within his own soul, or gazing through a medium that saddened the whole world. Even the lawless wind, it was believed, respected his dreadful secret, and never blew aside the veil. But still good Mr. Hooper sadly smiled, at the pale visages of the worldly throng as he passed by.

Among all its bad influences, the black veil had the one desirable effect, of making its wearer a very efficient clergyman. By the aid of his mysterious emblem—for there was no other apparent cause—he became a man of awful power, over souls that were in agony for sin. His converts always regarded him with a dread peculiar to themselves, affirming, though but figuratively, that, before he brought them to celestial light, they had been with him behind the black veil. Its gloom, indeed, enabled him to sympathize with all dark affections. Dying sinners cried aloud for Mr. Hooper, and would not yield their breath till he appeared; though ever, as he stooped to whisper consolation, they shuddered at the veiled face so near their own. Such were the terrors of the black veil, even when Death had bared his visage! Strangers came long distances to attend service at his church, with the mere idle purpose of gazing at his figure, because it was forbidden them to behold his face. But many were made to quake ere they departed! Once, during Governor Belcher's[5] administration, Mr. Hooper was appointed to preach the election sermon.[6] Covered with his black veil, he stood before the chief magistrate, the council, and the representatives, and wrought so deep an impression, that the

[5]GOVERNOR BELCHER: Jonathan Belcher (1681–1757), governor of Massachusetts and New Hampshire from 1730 to 1741.
[6]THE ELECTION SERMON: It was a tradition for a minister of repute to give a sermon at the installation of a new or the renewal of a current governor.

legislative measures of that year, were characterized by all the gloom and piety of our earliest ancestral sway.

In this manner Mr. Hooper spent a long life, irreproachable in outward act, yet shrouded in dismal suspicions; kind and loving, though unloved, and dimly feared; a man apart from men, shunned in their health and joy, but ever summoned to their aid in mortal anguish. As years wore on, shedding their snows above his sable veil, he acquired a name throughout the New-England churches, and they called him Father Hooper. Nearly all his parishioners, who were of mature age when he was settled, had been borne away by many a funeral: he had one congregation in the church, and a more crowded one in the church-yard; and having wrought so late into the evening, and done his work so well, it was now good Father Hooper's turn to rest.

Several persons were visible by the shaded candlelight, in the death-chamber of the old clergyman. Natural connections he had none. But there was the decorously grave, though unmoved physician, seeking only to mitigate the last pangs of the patient whom he could not save. There were the deacons, and other eminently pious members of his church. There, also, was the Reverend Mr. Clark, of Westbury, a young and zealous divine, who had ridden in haste to pray by the bed-side of the expiring minister. There was the nurse, no hired handmaiden of death, but one whose calm affection had endured thus long, in secresy, in solitude, amid the chill of age, and would not perish, even at the dying hour. Who, but Elizabeth! And there lay the hoary head of good Father Hooper upon the death-pillow, with the black veil still swathed about his brow and reaching down over his face, so that each more difficult gasp of his faint breath caused it to stir. All through life that piece of crape had hung between him and the world: it had separated him from cheerful brotherhood and woman's love, and kept him in that saddest of all prisons, his own heart; and still it lay upon his face, as if to deepen the gloom of his darksome chamber, and shade him from the sunshine of eternity.

For some time previous, his mind had been confused, wavering doubtfully between the past and the present, and hovering forward, as it were, at intervals, into the indistinctness of the world to come. There had been feverish turns, which tossed him from side to side, and wore away what little strength he had. But in his most convulsive struggles, and in the wildest vagaries of his intellect, when no other thought retained its sober influence, he still showed an awful solicitude lest the black veil should slip aside. Even if his bewildered soul could have forgotten, there was a faithful woman at his pillow, who, with averted eyes, would have covered that aged face, which she had last beheld in the comeliness of manhood. At length the death-stricken old man lay quietly in the torpor of mental and bodily exhaustion, with an imperceptible pulse, and breath that grew fainter and fainter, except when a long, deep, and irregular inspiration seemed to prelude the flight of his spirit.

The minister of Westbury approached the bedside.

"Venerable Father Hooper," said he, "the moment of your release is at hand. Are you ready for the lifting of the veil, that shuts in time from eternity?"

Father Hooper at first replied merely by a feeble motion of his head; then, apprehensive, perhaps, that his meaning might be doubtful, he exerted himself to speak.

"Yea," said he, in faint accents, "my soul hath a patient weariness until that veil be lifted."

"And is it fitting," resumed the Reverend Mr. Clark, "that a man so given to prayer, of such a blameless example, holy in deed and thought, so far as mortal judgment may pronounce; is it fitting that a father in the church should leave a shadow on his memory, that may seem to blacken a life so pure? I pray you, my venerable brother, let not this thing be! Suffer us to be gladdened by your triumphant aspect, as you go to your reward. Before the veil of eternity be lifted, let me cast aside this black veil from your face!"

And thus speaking, the Reverend Mr. Clark bent forward to reveal the mystery of so many years. But, exerting a sudden energy, that made all the beholders stand aghast, Father Hooper snatched both his hands from beneath the bed-clothes, and pressed them strongly on the black veil, resolute to struggle, if the minister of Westbury would contend with a dying man.

"Never!" cried the veiled clergyman. "On earth, never!"

"Dark old man!" exclaimed the affrighted minister, "with what horrible crime upon your soul are you now passing to the judgment?"

Father Hooper's breath heaved; it rattled in his throat; but, with a mighty effort, grasping forward with his hands, he caught hold of life, and held it back till he should speak. He even raised himself in bed; and there he sat, shivering with the arms of death around him, while the black veil hung down, awful, at that last moment, in the gathered terrors of a life-time. And yet the faint, sad smile, so often there, now seemed to glimmer from its obscurity, and linger on Father Hooper's lips.

"Why do you tremble at me alone?" cried he, turning his veiled face round the circle of pale spectators. "Tremble also at each other! Have men avoided me, and women shown no pity, and children screamed and fled, only for my black veil? What, but the mystery which it obscurely typifies, has made this piece of crape so awful? When the friend shows his inmost heart to his friend; the lover to his best-beloved; when man does not vainly shrink from the eye of his Creator, loathsomely treasuring up the secret of his sin; then deem me a monster, for the symbol beneath which I have lived, and die! I look around me, and, lo! on every visage a Black Veil!"

While his auditors shrank from one another, in mutual affright, Father Hooper fell back upon his pillow, a veiled corpse, with a faint smile lingering on the lips. Still veiled, they laid him in his coffin, and a veiled corpse they bore him to the grave. The grass of many years has sprung up and withered on that grave, the burial-stone is moss-grown, and good Mr. Hooper's face is dust; but awful is still the thought, that it mouldered beneath the Black Veil!

[1836]

The Scarlet Letter

SALEM, *March 30, 1850.*

THE CUSTOM-HOUSE

INTRODUCTORY TO *THE SCARLET LETTER*

It is a little remarkable, that—though disinclined to talk overmuch of myself and my affairs at the fireside, and to my personal friends—an autobiographical impulse should twice in my life have taken possession of me, in addressing the public. The first time was three or four years since, when I favored the reader—inexcusably, and for no earthly reason, that either the indulgent reader or the intrusive author could imagine— with a description of my way of life in the deep quietude of an Old Manse.[1] And now—because, beyond my deserts, I was happy enough to find a listener or two on the former occasion—I again seize the public by the button, and talk of my three years' experience in a Custom-House.[2] The example of the famous "P.P., Clerk of this Parish,"[3] was never more faithfully followed. The truth seems to be, however, that,

---

[1] OLD MANSE: A reference to Hawthorne's introduction to *Mosses from an Old Manse* (1846).
[2] CUSTOM-HOUSE: The government office at which customs levied on imported or exported goods are collected; usually found at seaports.
[3] P.P., CLERK OF THIS PARISH: An anonymous eighteenth-century parody of the rather egocentric *History of My Own Time* (1724), by the Scottish bishop Gilbert Burnet (1643–1715).

when he casts his leaves forth upon the wind, the author addresses, not the many who will fling aside his volume, or never take it up, but the few who will understand him, better than most of his schoolmates or life-mates. Some authors, indeed, do far more than this, and indulge themselves in such confidential depths of revelation as could fittingly be addressed, only and exclusively, to the one heart and mind of perfect sympathy; as if the printed book, thrown at large on the wide world, were certain to find out the divided segment of the writer's own nature, and complete his circle of existence by bringing him into communion with it. It is scarcely decorous,[4] however, to speak all, even where we speak impersonally. But—as thoughts are frozen and utterance benumbed, unless the speaker stand in some true relation with his audience—it may be pardonable to imagine that a friend, a kind and apprehensive, though not the closest friend, is listening to our talk; and then, a native reserve being thawed by this genial consciousness, we may prate[5] of the circumstances that lie around us, and even of ourself, but still keep the inmost Me behind its veil. To this extent and within these limits, an author, methinks, may be autobiographical, without violating either the reader's rights or his own.

It will be seen, likewise, that this Custom-House sketch has a certain propriety, of a kind always recognized in literature, as explaining how a large portion of the following pages came into my possession, and as offering proofs of the authenticity of a narrative therein contained. This, in fact,—a desire to put myself in my true position as editor, or very little more, of the most prolix[6] among the tales that make up my volume,—this, and no other, is my true reason for assuming a personal relation with the public. In accomplishing the main purpose, it has appeared allowable, by a few extra touches, to give a faint representation of a mode of life not heretofore described, together with some of the characters that move in it, among whom the author happened to make one.

In my native town of Salem,[7] at the head of what, half a century ago, in the days of old King Derby, was a bustling wharf,—but which is now burdened with decayed wooden warehouses, and exhibits few or no symptoms of commercial life; except, perhaps, a bark or brig, half-way down its melancholy length, discharging hides; or, nearer at hand, a Nova Scotia schooner, pitching out her cargo of firewood,—at the head, I say,

[4]DECOROUS: Appropriate.
[5]PRATE: Talk.
[6]PROLIX: Lengthy.
[7]SALEM: Salem, Massachusetts, a seaport town about thirty miles north of Boston.

of this dilapidated wharf, which the tide often overflows, and along which, at the base and in the rear of the row of buildings, the track of many languid years is seen in a border of unthrifty grass,—here, with a view from its front windows adown this not very enlivening prospect, and thence across the harbour, stands a spacious edifice of brick. From the loftiest point of its roof, during precisely three and a half hours of each forenoon, floats or droops, in breeze or calm, the banner of the republic; but with the thirteen stripes turned vertically, instead of horizontally, and thus indicating that a civil, and not a military post of Uncle Sam's government, is here established. Its front is ornamented with a portico of half a dozen wooden pillars, supporting a balcony, beneath which a flight of wide granite steps descends towards the street. Over the entrance hovers an enormous specimen of the American eagle, with outspread wings, a shield before her breast, and, if I recollect aright, a bunch of intermingled thunderbolts and barbed arrows in each claw. With the customary infirmity of temper that characterizes this unhappy fowl, she appears, by the fierceness of her beak and eye and the general truculency[8] of her attitude, to threaten mischief to the inoffensive community; and especially to warn all citizens, careful of their safety, against intruding on the premises which she overshadows with her wings. Nevertheless, vixenly[9] as she looks, many people are seeking, at this very moment, to shelter themselves under the wing of the federal eagle; imagining, I presume, that her bosom has all the softness and snugness of an eider-down pillow. But she has no great tenderness, even in her best of moods, and, sooner or later,—oftener soon than late,—is apt to fling off her nestlings with a scratch of her claw, a dab of her beak, or a rankling wound from her barbed arrows.

The pavement round about the above-described edifice—which we may as well name at once as the Custom-House of the port—has grass enough growing in its chinks to show that it has not, of late days, been worn by any multitudinous resort of business. In some months of the year, however, there often chances a forenoon when affairs move onward with a livelier tread. Such occasions might remind the elderly citizen of that period, before the last war with England,[10] when Salem was a port by itself; not scorned, as she is now, by her own merchants and ship-owners, who permit her wharves to crumble to ruin, while their ventures go to swell, needlessly and imperceptibly, the mighty flood of commerce at

---

[8]TRUCULENCY: Ferocity.
[9]VIXENLY: Ill-tempered, usually applied to a woman.
[10]BEFORE THE LAST WAR WITH ENGLAND: The War of 1812.

New York or Boston. On some such morning, when three or four vessels happen to have arrived at once,—usually from Africa or South America,—or to be on the verge of their departure thitherward, there is a sound of frequent feet, passing briskly up and down the granite steps. Here, before his own wife has greeted him, you may greet the sea-flushed ship-master, just in port, with his vessel's papers under his arm in a tarnished tin box. Here, too, comes his owner, cheerful or sombre, gracious or in the sulks, accordingly as his scheme of the now accomplished voyage has been realized in merchandise that will readily be turned to gold, or has buried him under a bulk of incommodities, such as nobody will care to rid him of. Here, likewise,—the germ of the wrinkle-browed, grizzly-bearded, careworn merchant,—we have the smart young clerk, who gets the taste of traffic as a wolf-cub does of blood, and already sends adventures in his master's ships, when he had better be sailing mimic boats upon a mill-pond. Another figure in the scene is the outward-bound sailor, in quest of a protection[11]; or the recently arrived one, pale and feeble, seeking a passport to the hospital. Nor must we forget the captains of the rusty little schooners that bring firewood from the British provinces; a rough-looking set of tarpaulins, without the alertness of the Yankee aspect, but contributing an item of no slight importance to our decaying trade.

Cluster all these individuals together, as they sometimes were, with other miscellaneous ones to diversify the group, and, for the time being, it made the Custom-House a stirring scene. More frequently, however, on ascending the steps, you would discern—in the entry, if it were summer time, or in their appropriate rooms, if wintry or inclement weather—a row of venerable figures, sitting in old-fashioned chairs, which were tipped on their hind legs back against the wall. Oftentimes they were asleep, but occasionally might be heard talking together, in voices between speech and a snore, and with that lack of energy that distinguishes the occupants of alms-houses, and all other human beings who depend for subsistence on charity, on monopolized labor, or any thing else but their own independent exertions. These old gentlemen—seated, like Matthew,[12] at the receipt of custom, but not very liable to be summoned thence, like him, for apostolic errands—were Custom-House officers.

Furthermore, on the left hand as you enter the front door, is a certain room or office, about fifteen feet square, and of a lofty height; with

[11]IN QUEST OF A PROTECTION: In search of a passport.
[12]SEATED, LIKE MATTHEW: A reference to Matthew 9:9: "And as Jesus passed forth from thence, he saw a man, named Matthew, sitting at the receipt of custom: and he saith unto him, Follow me. And he arose, and followed him."

two of its arched windows commanding a view of the aforesaid dilapidated wharf, and the third looking across a narrow lane, and along a portion of Derby Street. All three give glimpses of the shops of grocers, block-makers,[13] slop-sellers,[14] and ship-chandlers[15]; around the doors of which are generally to be seen, laughing and gossiping, clusters of old salts, and such other wharf-rats as haunt the Wapping[16] of a seaport. The room itself is cobwebbed, and dingy with old paint; its floor is strewn with gray sand, in a fashion that has elsewhere fallen into long disuse; and it is easy to conclude, from the general slovenliness of the place, that this is a sanctuary into which womankind, with her tools of magic, the broom and mop, has very infrequent access. In the way of furniture, there is a stove with a voluminous funnel; an old pine desk, with a three-legged stool beside it; two or three wooden-bottom chairs, exceedingly decrepit and infirm; and,—not to forget the library,—on some shelves, a score or two of volumes of the Acts of Congress, and a bulky Digest of the Revenue Laws. A tin pipe ascends through the ceiling, and forms a medium of vocal communication with other parts of the edifice. And here, some six months ago,—pacing from corner to corner, or lounging on the long-legged stool, with his elbow on the desk, and his eyes wandering up and down the columns of the morning newspaper,—you might have recognized, honored reader, the same individual who welcomed you into his cheery little study, where the sunshine glimmered so pleasantly through the willow branches, on the western side of the Old Manse. But now, should you go thither to seek him, you would inquire in vain for the Locofoco Surveyor.[17] The besom[18] of reform hath swept him out of office; and a worthier successor wears his dignity and pockets his emoluments.[19]

This old town of Salem—my native place, though I have dwelt much away from it, both in boyhood and maturer years—possesses, or did possess, a hold on my affections, the force of which I have never realized during my seasons of actual residence here. Indeed, so far as its physical aspect is concerned, with its flat, unvaried surface, covered chiefly with wooden houses, few or none of which pretend to architectural

---

[13]BLOCK-MAKERS: Pulley-makers.
[14]SLOP-SELLERS: Clothiers who sold cheap ready-made clothing to seamen from the ship's stores.
[15]SHIP-CHANDLERS: Merchants who sold general provisions to ships.
[16]WAPPING: A rundown area of a seaport community.
[17]LOCOFOCO SURVEYOR: "Loco-foco" was the Whig party term of ridicule for a Democrat, although it properly applied to the radical section of the Democratic party. A surveyor is a supervisor.
[18]BESOM: Twig broom.
[19]EMOLUMENTS: Profit or gain arising from station, office, or employment; dues; reward, remuneration, salary.

beauty,—its irregularity, which is neither picturesque nor quaint, but only tame,—its long and lazy street, lounging wearisomely through the whole extent of the peninsula, with Gallows Hill and New Guinea at one end, and a view of the alms-house at the other,—such being the features of my native town, it would be quite as reasonable to form a sentimental attachment to a disarranged checkerboard. And yet, though invariably happiest elsewhere, there is within me a feeling for old Salem, which, in lack of a better phrase, I must be content to call affection. The sentiment is probably assignable to the deep and aged roots which my family has struck into the soil. It is now nearly two centuries and a quarter since the original Briton, the earliest emigrant of my name,[20] made his appearance in the wild and forest-bordered settlement, which has since become a city. And here his descendants have been born and died, and have mingled their earthy substance with the soil; until no small portion of it must necessarily be akin to the mortal frame wherewith, for a little while, I walk the streets. In part, therefore, the attachment which I speak of is the mere sensuous sympathy of dust for dust. Few of my countrymen can know what it is; nor, as frequent transplantation is perhaps better for the stock, need they consider it desirable to know.

But the sentiment has likewise its moral quality. The figure of that first ancestor, invested by family tradition with a dim and dusky grandeur, was present to my boyish imagination, as far back as I can remember. It still haunts me, and induces a sort of home-feeling with the past, which I scarcely claim in reference to the present phase of the town. I seem to have a stronger claim to a residence here on account of this grave, bearded, sable-cloaked, and steeple-crowned progenitor,—who came so early, with his Bible and his sword, and trode the unworn street with such a stately port, and made so large a figure, as a man of war and peace,—a stronger claim than for myself, whose name is seldom heard and my face hardly known. He was a soldier, legislator, judge; he was a ruler in the Church; he had all the Puritanic traits, both good and evil. He was likewise a bitter persecutor; as witness the Quakers,[21] who have remembered him in their histories, and relate an incident of his hard severity towards a woman of their sect, which will last longer, it is to be feared, than any record of

[20]THE EARLIEST EMIGRANT OF MY NAME: Major William Hathorne (1606–1681), who emigrated from England in 1630 and settled in Salem around 1636. Hawthorne refers to his great-great-great-grandfather in several other short stories, including "Main Street" and "Young Goodman Brown."
[21]BITTER PERSECUTOR; AS WITNESS THE QUAKERS: Hawthorne notes that his ancestor was a "a bitter persecutor" of Quakers and was remembered for ordering the whipping of Ann Coleman. After King Charles II prohibited the execution of Quakers, the Puritans passed the Cart and Whip Act in 1662, which allowed Quakers to be dragged behind a cart through the towns and whipped through the streets until they came to the outskirts of the province, where they were thrown out.

his better deeds, although these were many. His son, too, inherited the persecuting spirit, and made himself so conspicuous in the martyrdom of the witches, that their blood may fairly be said to have left a stain upon him.[22] So deep a stain, indeed, that his old dry bones, in the Charter Street burial-ground, must still retain it, if they have not crumbled utterly to dust! I know not whether these ancestors of mine bethought themselves to repent, and ask pardon of Heaven for their cruelties; or whether they are now groaning under the heavy consequences of them, in another state of being. At all events, I, the present writer, as their representative, hereby take shame upon myself for their sakes, and pray that any curse incurred by them—as I have heard, and as the dreary and unprosperous condition of the race, for many a long year back, would argue to exist—may be now and henceforth removed.

Doubtless, however, either of these stern and black-browed Puritans would have thought it quite a sufficient retribution for his sins, that, after so long a lapse of years, the old trunk of the family tree, with so much venerable moss upon it, should have borne, as its topmost bough, an idler like myself. No aim, that I have ever cherished, would they recognize as laudable; no success of mine—if my life, beyond its domestic scope, had ever been brightened by success—would they deem otherwise than worthless, if not positively disgraceful. "What is he?" murmurs one gray shadow of my forefathers to the other. "A writer of story-books! What kind of a business in life,—what mode of glorifying God, or being serviceable to mankind in his day and generation,—may that be? Why, the degenerate fellow might as well have been a fiddler!" Such are the compliments bandied between my great-grandsires and myself, across the gulf of time! And yet, let them scorn me as they will, strong traits of their nature have intertwined themselves with mine.

Planted deep, in the town's earliest infancy and childhood, by these two earnest and energetic men, the race has ever since subsisted here; always, too, in respectability; never, so far as I have known, disgraced by a single unworthy member; but seldom or never, on the other hand, after the first two generations, performing any memorable deed, or so much as putting forward a claim to public notice. Gradually, they have sunk almost out of sight; as old houses, here and there about the streets, get covered half-way to the eaves by the accumulation of new soil. From

[22]TO HAVE LEFT A STAIN UPON HIM: Justice John Hathorne (son of Major William Hathorne, 1641–1717), best known for his role as chief interrogator of the accused witches in the Salem witchcraft hysteria of 1692. It has been suggested that Hawthorne added the *w* to his name in his early twenties to distance himself from this relative.

father to son, for above a hundred years, they followed the sea; a gray-headed shipmaster, in each generation, retiring from the quarter-deck to the homestead, while a boy of fourteen took the hereditary place before the mast, confronting the salt spray and the gale, which had blustered against his sire and grandsire. The boy, also, in due time, passed from the forecastle to the cabin,[23] spent a tempestuous manhood, and returned from his world-wanderings, to grow old, and die, and mingle his dust with the natal earth. This long connection of a family with one spot, as its place of birth and burial, creates a kindred between the human being and the locality, quite independent of any charm in the scenery or moral circumstances that surround him. It is not love, but instinct. The new inhabitant—who came himself from a foreign land, or whose father or grandfather came—has little claim to be called a Salemite; he has no conception of the oyster-like tenacity with which an old settler, over whom his third century is creeping, clings to the spot where his successive generations have been imbedded. It is no matter that the place is joyless for him; that he is weary of the old wooden houses, the mud and dust, the dead level of site and sentiment, the chill east wind, and the chillest of social atmospheres;—all these, and whatever faults besides he may see or imagine, are nothing to the purpose. The spell survives, and just as powerfully as if the natal spot were an earthly paradise. So has it been in my case. I felt it almost as a destiny to make Salem my home; so that the mould of features and cast of character which had all along been familiar here—ever, as one representative of the race lay down in his grave, another assuming, as it were, his sentry-march along the Main Street—might still in my little day be seen and recognized in the old town. Nevertheless, this very sentiment is an evidence that the connection, which has become an unhealthy one, should at last be severed. Human nature will not flourish, any more than a potato, if it be planted and replanted, for too long a series of generations, in the same worn-out soil. My children have had other birthplaces, and, so far as their fortunes may be within my control, shall strike their roots into unaccustomed earth.

On emerging from the Old Manse, it was chiefly this strange, indolent, unjoyous attachment for my native town, that brought me to fill a place in Uncle Sam's brick edifice,[24] when I might as well, or better, have gone somewhere else. My doom was on me. It was not the first time, nor the second, that I had gone away,—as it seemed, permanently,—but yet

---

[23]PASSED FROM THE FORECASTLE TO THE CABIN: Moved up through the ranks from ordinary seaman to captain.
[24]UNCLE SAM'S BRICK EDIFICE: The custom house.

returned, like the bad half-penny; or as if Salem were for me the inevitable centre of the universe. So, one fine morning, I ascended the flight of granite steps, with the President's commission in my pocket, and was introduced to the corps of gentlemen who were to aid me in my weighty responsibility, as chief executive officer of the Custom-House.

I doubt greatly—or rather, I do not doubt at all—whether any public functionary of the United States, either in the civil or military line, has ever had such a patriarchal body of veterans under his orders as myself. The whereabouts of the Oldest Inhabitant was at once settled, when I looked at them. For upwards of twenty years before this epoch, the independent position of the Collector had kept the Salem Custom-House out of the whirlpool of political vicissitude,[25] which makes the tenure of office generally so fragile. A soldier,—New England's most distinguished soldier,[26]—he stood firmly on the pedestal of his gallant services; and, himself secure in the wise liberality of the successive administrations through which he had held office, he had been the safety of his subordinates in many an hour of danger and heart-quake. General Miller was radically conservative; a man over whose kindly nature habit had no slight influence; attaching himself strongly to familiar faces, and with difficulty moved to change, even when change might have brought unquestionable improvement. Thus, on taking charge of my department, I found few but aged men. They were ancient sea-captains, for the most part, who, after being tost on every sea, and standing up sturdily against life's tempestuous blast, had finally drifted into this quiet nook; where, with little to disturb them, except the periodical terrors of a Presidential election, they one and all acquired a new lease of existence. Though by no means less liable than their fellow-men to age and infirmity, they had evidently some talisman or other that kept death at bay. Two or three of their number, as I was assured, being gouty and rheumatic, or perhaps bed-ridden, never dreamed of making their appearance at the Custom-House, during a large part of the year; but, after a torpid winter, would creep out into the warm sunshine of May or June, go lazily about what they termed duty, and, at their own leisure and convenience, betake themselves to bed again. I must plead guilty to the charge of abbreviating the official breath of more than one of these venerable servants of the republic. They were allowed, on my representation, to rest from their arduous labors, and soon

---

[25]VICISSITUDE: Change.
[26]NEW ENGLAND'S MOST DISTINGUISHED SOLDIER: General James F. Miller (1776–1851) was a hero of the War of 1812 and is reputed to have said to General Winfield Scott, "I'll try, Sir!" when told to capture a British position at Lundy's Lane in Ontario, near Niagara Falls. He served as Salem's Collector of the Port from 1825 to 1849.

afterwards—as if their sole principle of life had been zeal for their country's service; as I verily believe it was—withdrew to a better world. It is a pious consolation to me, that, through my interference, a sufficient space was allowed them for repentance of the evil and corrupt practices, into which, as a matter of course, every Custom-House officer must be supposed to fall. Neither the front nor the back entrance of the Custom-House opens on the road to Paradise.

The greater part of my officers were Whigs.[27] It was well for their venerable brotherhood, that the new Surveyor was not a politician, and, though a faithful Democrat in principle, neither received nor held his office with any reference to political services. Had it been otherwise,—had an active politician been put into this influential post, to assume the easy task of making head against a Whig Collector, whose infirmities withheld him from the personal administration of his office,—hardly a man of the old corps would have drawn the breath of official life, within a month after the exterminating angel had come up the Custom-House steps. According to the received code in such matters, it would have been nothing short of duty, in a politician, to bring every one of those white heads under the axe of the guillotine. It was plain enough to discern, that the old fellows dreaded some such discourtesy at my hands. It pained, and at the same time amused me, to behold the terrors that attended my advent; to see a furrowed cheek, weather-beaten by half a century of storm, turn ashy pale at the glance of so harmless an individual as myself; to detect, as one or another addressed me, the tremor of a voice, which, in long-past days, had been wont to bellow through a speaking-trumpet, hoarsely enough to frighten Boreas[28] himself to silence. They knew, these excellent old persons, that, by all established rule,—and, as regarded some of them, weighed by their own lack of efficiency for business,—they ought to have given place to younger men, more orthodox in politics, and altogether fitter than themselves to serve our common Uncle. I knew it too, but could never quite find in my heart to act upon the knowledge. Much and deservedly to my own discredit, therefore, and considerably to the detriment of my official conscience, they continued, during my incumbency, to creep about the wharves, and loiter up and down the Custom-House steps. They spent a good deal of time, also, asleep in their accustomed corners, with their chairs tilted back against the wall; awaking, however,

---

[27]WHIGS: In the early 1830s, the Whigs were the political party that opposed the Democrats. They supported a protective tariff and a strong central federal government. They were succeeded in 1856 by the Republican party.
[28]BOREAS: In Greek myth, the god of the north wind.

once or twice in a forenoon, to bore one another with the several thousandth repetition of old sea-stories, and mouldy jokes, that had grown to be pass-words and countersigns among them.

The discovery was soon made, I imagine, that the new Surveyor had no great harm in him. So, with lightsome hearts, and the happy consciousness of being usefully employed,—in their own behalf, at least, if not for our beloved country,—these good old gentlemen went through the various formalities of office. Sagaciously, under their spectacles, did they peep into the holds of vessels! Mighty was their fuss about little matters, and marvellous, sometimes, the obtuseness that allowed greater ones to slip between their fingers! Whenever such a mischance occurred,—when a wagon-load of valuable merchandise had been smuggled ashore, at noonday, perhaps, and directly beneath their unsuspicious noses,—nothing could exceed the vigilance and alacrity with which they proceeded to lock, and double-lock, and secure with tape and sealing-wax, all the avenues of the delinquent vessel. Instead of a reprimand for their previous negligence, the case seemed rather to require an eulogium on their praiseworthy caution, after the mischief had happened; a grateful recognition of the promptitude of their zeal, the moment that there was no longer any remedy!

Unless people are more than commonly disagreeable, it is my foolish habit to contract a kindness for them. The better part of my companion's character, if it have a better part, is that which usually comes uppermost in my regard, and forms the type whereby I recognize the man. As most of these old Custom-House officers had good traits, and as my position in reference to them, being paternal and protective, was favorable to the growth of friendly sentiments, I soon grew to like them all. It was pleasant, in the summer forenoons,—when the fervent heat, that almost liquefied the rest of the human family, merely communicated a genial warmth to their half-torpid systems,—it was pleasant to hear them chatting in the back entry, a row of them all tipped against the wall, as usual; while the frozen witticisms of past generations were thawed out, and came bubbling with laughter from their lips. Externally, the jollity of aged men has much in common with the mirth of children; the intellect, any more than a deep sense of humor, has little to do with the matter; it is, with both, a gleam that plays upon the surface, and imparts a sunny and cheery aspect alike to the green branch, and gray, mouldering trunk. In one case, however, it is real sunshine; in the other, it more resembles the phosphorescent glow of decaying wood.

It would be sad injustice, the reader must understand, to represent all my excellent old friends as in their dotage. In the first place, my coadjutors were not invariably old; there were men among them in their strength and prime, of marked ability and energy, and altogether superior to the sluggish and dependent mode of life on which their evil stars had cast them. Then, moreover, the white locks of age were sometimes found to be the thatch of an intellectual tenement in good repair. But, as respects the majority of my corps of veterans, there will be no wrong done, if I characterize them generally as a set of wearisome old souls, who had gathered nothing worth preservation from their varied experience of life. They seemed to have flung away all the golden grain of practical wisdom, which they had enjoyed so many opportunities of harvesting, and most carefully to have stored their memories with the husks. They spoke with far more interest and unction of their morning's breakfast, or yesterday's, to-day's, or to-morrow's dinner, than of the shipwreck of forty or fifty years ago, and all the world's wonders which they had witnessed with their youthful eyes.

The father of the Custom-House—the patriarch, not only of this little squad of officials, but, I am bold to say, of the respectable body of tide-waiters[29] all over the United States—was a certain permanent Inspector.[30] He might truly be termed a legitimate son of the revenue system, dyed in the wool, or rather, born in the purple; since his sire, a Revolutionary colonel, and formerly collector of the port, had created an office for him, and appointed him to fill it, at a period of the early ages which few living men can now remember. This Inspector, when I first knew him, was a man of fourscore years, or thereabouts, and certainly one of the most wonderful specimens of winter-green that you would be likely to discover in a lifetime's search. With his florid cheek, his compact figure, smartly arrayed in a bright-buttoned blue coat, his brisk and vigorous step, and his hale and hearty aspect, altogether, he seemed—not young, indeed—but a kind of new contrivance of Mother Nature in the shape of man, whom age and infirmity had no business to touch. His voice and laugh, which perpetually reëchoed through the Custom-House, had nothing of the tremulous quaver and cackle of an old man's utterance; they came strutting out of his lungs, like the crow of a cock, or the blast of a clarion.[31] Looking at him merely as an animal,—and there was very little else to look at,—he was a most satisfactory object, from the thorough healthfulness and wholesomeness of his system, and

[29]TIDE-WAITERS: Customs officers who awaited the arrival of ships as they came in with the tide and boarded them to ensure all duties were appropriately paid.
[30]A CERTAIN PERMANENT INSPECTOR: William Lee, appointed 1814.
[31]CLARION: A trumpet with a narrow tube, originally sounded as a signal of war.

his capacity, at that extreme age, to enjoy all, or nearly all, the delights which he had ever aimed at, or conceived of. The careless security of his life in the Custom-House, on a regular income, and with but slight and infrequent apprehensions of removal, had no doubt contributed to make time pass lightly over him. The original and more potent causes, however, lay in the rare perfection of his animal nature, the moderate proportion of intellect, and the very trifling admixture of moral and spiritual ingredients; these latter qualities, indeed, being in barely enough measure to keep the old gentleman from walking on all-fours. He possessed no power of thought, no depth of feeling, no troublesome sensibilities; nothing, in short, but a few commonplace instincts, which, aided by the cheerful temper that grew inevitably out of his physical well-being, did duty very respectably, and to general acceptance, in lieu of a heart. He had been the husband of three wives, all long since dead; the father of twenty children, most of whom, at every age of childhood or maturity, had likewise returned to dust. Here, one would suppose, might have been sorrow enough to imbue the sunniest disposition, through and through, with a sable tinge. Not so with our old Inspector! One brief sigh sufficed to carry off the entire burden of these dismal reminiscences. The next moment, he was as ready for sport as any unbreeched infant: far readier than the Collector's junior clerk, who, at nineteen years, was much the elder and graver man of the two.

I used to watch and study this patriarchal personage with, I think, livelier curiosity than any other form of humanity there presented to my notice. He was, in truth, a rare phenomenon; so perfect in one point of view; so shallow, so delusive, so impalpable, such an absolute nonentity, in every other. My conclusion was that he had no soul, no heart, no mind; nothing, as I have already said, but instincts; and yet, withal, so cunningly had the few materials of his character been put together, that there was no painful perception of deficiency, but, on my part, an entire contentment with what I found in him. It might be difficult—and it was so—to conceive how he should exist hereafter, so earthy and sensuous did he seem; but surely his existence here, admitting that it was to terminate with his last breath, had been not unkindly given; with no higher moral responsibilities than the beasts of the field, but with a larger scope of enjoyment than theirs, and with all their blessed immunity from the dreariness and duskiness of age.

One point, in which he had vastly the advantage over his four-footed brethren, was his ability to recollect the good dinners which it had made no small portion of the happiness of his life to eat. His gourmandism was a highly agreeable trait; and to hear him talk of roast-meat was as appetizing as a pickle or an oyster. As he possessed no higher attribute, and neither sacrificed nor vitiated any spiritual endowment by devoting all his energies and ingenuities to subserve the delight and profit of his maw, it always pleased and satisfied me to hear him expatiate on fish, poultry, and butcher's meat, and the most eligible methods of preparing them for the table. His reminiscences of good cheer, however ancient the date of the actual banquet, seemed to bring the savor of pig or turkey under one's very nostrils. There were flavors on his palate, that had lingered there not less than sixty or seventy years, and were still apparently as fresh as that of the mutton-chop which he had just devoured for his breakfast. I have heard him smack his lips over dinners, every guest at which, except himself, had long been food for worms. It was marvellous to observe how the ghosts of bygone meals were continually rising up before him; not in anger or retribution, but as if grateful for his former appreciation, and seeking to repudiate an endless series of enjoyment, at once shadowy and sensual. A tenderloin of beef, a hind-quarter of veal, a spare-rib of pork, a particular chicken, or a remarkably praiseworthy turkey, which had perhaps adorned his board in the days of the elder Adams,[32] would be remembered; while all the subsequent experience of our race, and all the events that brightened or darkened his individual career, had gone over him with as little permanent effect as the passing breeze. The chief tragic event of the old man's life, so far as I could judge, was his mishap with a certain goose, which lived and died some twenty or forty years ago; a goose of most promising figure, but which, at table, proved so inveterately tough that the carving-knife would make no impression on its carcase; and it could only be divided with an axe and handsaw.

But it is time to quit this sketch; on which, however, I should be glad to dwell at considerably more length, because, of all men whom I have ever known, this individual was fittest to be a Custom-House officer. Most persons, owing to causes which I may not have space to hint at, suffer moral detriment from this peculiar mode of life. The old Inspector was incapable of it, and, were he to continue in office to the end of time, would be just as good as he was then, and sit down to dinner with just as good an appetite.

There is one likeness, without which my gallery of Custom-House portraits would be strangely incomplete; but which my comparatively few opportunities for observation enable me to sketch only in the merest outline. It is that of the Collector, our gallant old General, who,

[32]ELDER ADAMS: During the presidential term of John Adams (1735–1826), from 1797 to 1801.

after his brilliant military service, subsequently to which he had ruled over a wild Western territory,[33] had come hither, twenty years before, to spend the decline of his varied and honorable life. The brave soldier had already numbered, nearly or quite, his threescore years and ten, and was pursuing the remainder of his earthly march, burdened with infirmities which even the martial music of his own spirit-stirring recollections could do little towards lightening. The step was palsied now, that had been foremost in the charge. It was only with the assistance of a servant, and by leaning his hand heavily on the iron balustrade, that he could slowly and painfully ascend the Custom-House steps, and, with a toilsome progress across the floor, attain his customary chair beside the fireplace. There he used to sit, gazing with a somewhat dim serenity of aspect at the figures that came and went; amid the rustle of papers, the administering of oaths, the discussion of business, and the casual talk of the office; all which sounds and circumstances seemed but indistinctly to impress his senses, and hardly to make their way into his inner sphere of contemplation. His countenance, in this repose, was mild and kindly. If his notice was sought, an expression of courtesy and interest gleamed out upon his features; proving that there was light within him, and that it was only the outward medium of the intellectual lamp that obstructed the rays in their passage. The closer you penetrated to the substance of his mind, the sounder it appeared. When no longer called upon to speak, or listen, either of which operations cost him an evident effort, his face would briefly subside into its former not uncheerful quietude. It was not painful to behold this look; for, though dim, it had not the imbecility of decaying age. The framework of his nature, originally strong and massive, was not yet crumbled into ruin.

To observe and define his character, however, under such disadvantages, was as difficult a task as to trace out and build up anew, in imagination, an old fortress, like Ticonderoga,[34] from a view of its gray and broken ruins. Here and there, perchance, the walls may remain almost complete; but elsewhere may be only a shapeless mound, cumbrous with its very strength, and overgrown, through long years of peace and neglect, with grass and alien weeds.

Nevertheless, looking at the old warrior with affection,—for, slight as was the communication between us, my feeling towards him, like that of all

---

[33]HE HAD RULED OVER A WILD WESTERN TERRITORY: Before serving as Salem's Collector of the Port, Miller was governor of the Arkansas territory from 1819 to 1825.
[34]TICONDEROGA: A fort captured from the British in 1775.

bipeds and quadrupeds who knew him, might not improperly be termed so,—I could discern the main points of his portrait. It was marked with the noble and heroic qualities which showed it to be not a mere accident, but of good right, that he had won a distinguished name. His spirit could never, I conceive, have been characterized by an uneasy activity; it must, at any period of his life, have required an impulse to set him in motion; but, once stirred up, with obstacles to overcome, and an adequate object to be attained, it was not in the man to give out or fail. The heat that had formerly pervaded his nature, and which was not yet extinct, was never of the kind that flashes and flickers in a blaze, but, rather, a deep, red glow, as of iron in a furnace. Weight, solidity, firmness; this was the expression of his repose, even in such decay as had crept untimely over him, at the period of which I speak. But I could imagine, even then, that, under some excitement which should go deeply into his consciousness,—roused by a trumpet-peal, loud enough to awaken all of his energies that were not dead, but only slumbering,—he was yet capable of flinging off his infirmities like a sick man's gown, dropping the staff of age to seize a battle-sword, and starting up once more a warrior. And, in so intense a moment, his demeanour would have still been calm. Such an exhibition, however, was but to be pictured in fancy; not to be anticipated, nor desired. What I saw in him—as evidently as the indestructible ramparts of Old Ticonderoga, already cited as the most appropriate simile—were the features of stubborn and ponderous endurance, which might well have amounted to obstinacy in his earlier days; of integrity, that, like most of his other endowments, lay in a somewhat heavy mass, and was just as unmalleable or unmanageable as a ton of iron ore; and of benevolence, which, fiercely as he led the bayonets on at Chippewa or Fort Erie,[35] I take to be of quite as genuine a stamp as what actuates any or all the polemical philanthropists of the age. He had slain men with his own hand, for aught I know;—certainly, they had fallen, like blades of grass at the sweep of the scythe, before the charge to which his spirit imparted its triumphant energy;—but, be that as it might, there was never in his heart so much cruelty as would have brushed the down off a butterfly's wing. I have not known the man, to whose innate kindliness I would more confidently make an appeal.

Many characteristics—and those, too, which contribute not the least forcibly to impart resemblance in a sketch—must have vanished, or been obscured, before I met the General. All merely graceful attributes are

[35]CHIPPEWA OR FORT ERIE: Chippewa and Fort Erie as well as Fort Ticonderoga were battle-grounds on the Niagara front of the War of 1812.

usually the most evanescent; nor does Nature adorn the human ruin with blossoms of new beauty, that have their roots and proper nutriment only in the chinks and crevices of decay, as she sows wall-flowers over the ruined fortress of Ticonderoga. Still, even in respect of grace and beauty, there were points well worth noting. A ray of humor, now and then, would make its way through the veil of dim obstruction, and glimmer pleasantly upon our faces. A trait of native elegance, seldom seen in the masculine character after childhood or early youth, was shown in the General's fondness for the sight and fragrance of flowers. An old soldier might be supposed to prize only the bloody laurel on his brow; but here was one, who seemed to have a young girl's appreciation of the floral tribe.

There, beside the fireplace, the brave old General used to sit; while the Surveyor—though seldom, when it could be avoided, taking upon himself the difficult task of engaging him in conversation—was fond of standing at a distance, and watching his quiet and almost slumberous countenance. He seemed away from us, although we saw him but a few yards off; remote, though we passed close beside his chair; unattainable, though we might have stretched forth our hands and touched his own. It might be, that he lived a more real life within his thoughts, than amid the unappropriate environment of the Collector's office. The evolutions of the parade; the tumult of the battle; the flourish of old, heroic music, heard thirty years before;—such scenes and sounds, perhaps, were all alive before his intellectual sense. Meanwhile, the merchants and shipmasters, the spruce clerks, and uncouth sailors, entered and departed; the bustle of this commercial and Custom-House life kept up its little murmur roundabout him; and neither with the men nor their affairs did the General appear to sustain the most distant relation. He was as much out of place as an old sword—now rusty, but which had flashed once in the battle's front, and showed still a bright gleam along its blade—would have been, among the inkstands, paper-folders, and mahogany rulers, on the Deputy Collector's desk.

There was one thing that much aided me in renewing and re-creating the stalwart soldier of the Niagara frontier,—the man of true and simple energy. It was the recollection of those memorable words of his,—"I'll try, Sir!"—spoken on the very verge of a desperate and heroic enterprise, and breathing the soul and spirit of New England hardihood, comprehending all perils, and encountering all. If, in our country, valor were rewarded by heraldic honor, this phrase—which it seems so easy to speak, but which only he, with such a task of danger and glory before him, has ever spoken—would be the best and fittest of all mottoes for the General's shield of arms.

It contributes greatly towards a man's moral and intellectual health, to be brought into habits of companionship with individuals unlike himself, who care little for his pursuits, and whose sphere and abilities he must go out of himself to appreciate. The accidents of my life have often afforded me this advantage, but never with more fulness and variety than during my continuance in office. There was one man,[36] especially, the observation of whose character gave me a new idea of talent. His gifts were emphatically those of a man of business; prompt, acute, clearminded; with an eye that saw through all perplexities, and a faculty of arrangement that made them vanish, as by the waving of an enchanter's wand. Bred up from boyhood in the Custom-House, it was his proper field of activity; and the many intricacies of business, so harassing to the interloper, presented themselves before him with the regularity of a perfectly comprehended system. In my contemplation, he stood as the ideal of his class. He was, indeed, the Custom-House in himself; or, at all events, the main-spring that kept its variously revolving wheels in motion; for, in an institution like this, where its officers are appointed to subserve their own profit and convenience, and seldom with a leading reference to their fitness for the duty to be performed, they must perforce seek elsewhere the dexterity which is not in them. Thus, by an inevitable necessity, as a magnet attracts steel-filings, so did our man of business draw to himself the difficulties which everybody met with. With an easy condescension, and kind forbearance towards our stupidity,—which, to his order of mind, must have seemed little short of crime,—would he forthwith, by the merest touch of his finger, make the incomprehensible as clear as daylight. The merchants valued him not less than we, his esoteric friends. His integrity was perfect; it was a law of nature with him, rather than a choice or a principle; nor can it be otherwise than the main condition of an intellect so remarkably clear and accurate as his, to be honest and regular in the administration of affairs. A stain on his conscience, as to any thing that came within the range of his vocation, would trouble such a man very much in the same way, though to a far greater degree, than an error in the balance of an account, or an ink-blot on the fair page of a book of record. Here, in a word,— and it is a rare instance in my life,—I had met with a person thoroughly adapted to the situation which he held.

Such were some of the people with whom I now found myself connected. I took it in good part at the hands of Providence,[37] that I was thrown

---

[36]ONE MAN: Hawthorne's friend Zachariah Burchmore (1809–1894).
[37]PROVIDENCE: God.

into a position so little akin to my past habits; and set myself seriously to gather from it whatever profit was to be had. After my fellowship of toil and impracticable schemes, with the dreamy brethren of Brook Farm[38]; after living for three years within the subtile influence of an intellect like Emerson's[39]; after those wild, free days on the Assabeth,[40] indulging fantastic speculations beside our fire of fallen boughs, with Ellery Channing[41]; after talking with Thoreau[42] about pine-trees and Indian relics, in his hermitage at Walden[43]; after growing fastidious by sympathy with the classic refinement of Hillard's[44] culture; after becoming imbued with poetic sentiment at Longfellow's[45] hearth-stone;—it was time, at length, that I should exercise other faculties of my nature, and nourish myself with food for which I had hitherto had little appetite. Even the old Inspector was desirable, as a change of diet, to a man who had known Alcott.[46] I looked upon it as an evidence, in some measure, of a system naturally well balanced, and lacking no essential part of a thorough organization, that, with such associates to remember, I could mingle at once with men of altogether different qualities, and never murmur at the change.

Literature, its exertions and objects, were now of little moment in my regard. I cared not, at this period, for books; they were apart from me. Nature,—except it were human nature,—the nature that is developed in earth and sky, was, in one sense, hidden from me; and all the imaginative delight, wherewith it had been spiritualized, passed away out of my mind. A gift, a faculty, if it had not been departed, was suspended and inanimate within me. There would have something sad, unutterably dreary, in all this, had I not been conscious that it lay at my own option to recall whatever was valuable in the past. It might be true,

[38]BROOK FARM: A utopian agricultural commune near Boston where Hawthorne briefly lived.

[39]EMERSON'S: Ralph Waldo Emerson (1803–1882), an American poet and essayist and a leader of the Transcendental movement.

[40]ASSABETH: A river that joins the Concord River in Massachusetts.

[41]ELLERY CHANNING: William Ellery Channing (1818–1901), poet, essayist, and biographer.

[42]THOREAU: Henry David Thoreau (1817–1862), American author best known for his work *Walden* (1854).

[43]WALDEN: In 1845, Thoreau built and lived in a small cabin on Walden Pond near Concord, Massachusetts, seeking to commune with nature and "living deep and sucking out all the marrow of life." His journal of his observations and thoughts from this two-year experience formed the basis of his masterpiece *Walden*.

[44]HILLARD'S: George Stillman Hillard (1808–1879), a Boston lawyer and philanthropist who was a friend of Hawthorne.

[45]LONGFELLOW'S: Henry Wadsworth Longfellow (1807–1882), an American poet and friend of Hawthorne.

[46]ALCOTT: Amos Bronson Alcott (1799–1888), an American advocate of educational and social reform and a nonresident member of Brook Farm.

indeed, that this was a life which could not, with impunity, be lived too long; else, it might make me permanently other than I had been, without transforming me into any shape which it would be worth my while to take. But I never considered it as other than a transitory life. There was always a prophetic instinct, a low whisper in my ear, that, within no long period, and whenever a new change of custom should be essential to my good, a change would come.

Meanwhile, there I was, a Surveyor of the Revenue, and, so far as I have been able to understand, as good a Surveyor as need be. A man of thought, fancy, and sensibility, (had he ten times the Surveyor's proportion of those qualities,) may, at any time, be a man of affairs, if he will only choose to give himself the trouble. My fellow-officers, and the merchants and sea-captains with whom my official duties brought me into any manner of connection, viewed me in no other light, and probably knew me in no other character. None of them, I presume, had ever read a page of my inditing, or would have cared a fig the more for me, if they had read them all; nor would it have mended the matter, in the least, had those same unprofitable pages been written with a pen like that of Burns[47] or of Chaucer,[48] each of whom was a Custom-House officer in his day, as well as I. It is a good lesson—though it may often be a hard one—for a man who has dreamed of literary fame, and of making for himself a rank among the world's dignitaries by such means, to step aside out of the narrow circle in which his claims are recognized, and to find how utterly devoid of significance, beyond that circle, is all that he achieves, and all he aims at. I know not that I especially needed the lesson, either in the way of warning or rebuke; but, at any rate, I learned it thoroughly; nor, it gives me pleasure to reflect, did the truth, as it came home to my perception, ever cost me a pang, or require to be thrown off in a sigh. In the way of literary talk, it is true, the Naval Officer—an excellent fellow, who came into office with me, and went out only a little later—would often engage me in a discussion about one or the other of his favorite topics, Napoleon[49] or Shakespeare.[50] The Collector's junior clerk, too,—a young gentleman who, it was whispered, occasionally covered a sheet of Uncle Sam's letter-paper with what, (at the distance of a few yards,) looked very much like poetry,—used now and then to speak

[47]BURNS: Robert Burns (1759–1796), a Scottish poet who was a collector of excise taxes in Dumfries, Scotland.
[48]CHAUCER: Geoffrey Chaucer (c. 1340–1400), the English poet who wrote *The Canterbury Tales*.
[49]NAPOLEON: Napoleon Bonaparte (1769–1821), the great military leader who became the emperor of France.
[50]SHAKESPEARE: William Shakespeare (1564–1616), the English dramatist and poet considered the greatest playwright of English literature.

to me of books, as matters with which I might possibly be conversant. This was my all of lettered intercourse; and it was quite sufficient for my necessities.

No longer seeking nor caring that my name should be blazoned abroad on title-pages, I smiled to think that it had now another kind of vogue. The Custom-House marker imprinted it, with a stencil and black paint, on pepper-bags, and baskets of anatto,[51] and cigar-boxes, and bales of all kinds of dutiable merchandise, in testimony that these commodities had paid the impost,[52] and gone regularly through the office. Borne on such queer vehicle of fame, a knowledge of my existence, so far as a name conveys it, was carried where it had never been before, and, I hope, will never go again.

But the past was not dead. Once in a great while, the thoughts, that had seemed so vital and so active, yet had been put to rest so quietly, revived again. One of the most remarkable occasions, when the habit of bygone days awoke in me, was that which brings it within the law of literary propriety to offer the public the sketch which I am now writing.

In the second story of the Custom-House, there is a large room, in which the brick-work and naked rafters have never been covered with panelling and plaster. The edifice—originally projected on a scale adapted to the old commercial enterprise of the port, and with an idea of subsequent prosperity destined never to be realized—contains far more space than its occupants know what to do with. This airy hall, therefore, over the Collector's apartments, remains unfinished to this day, and, in spite of the aged cobwebs that festoon its dusky beams, appears still to await the labor of the carpenter and mason. At one end of the room, in a recess, were a number of barrels, piled one upon another, containing bundles of official documents. Large quantities of similar rubbish lay lumbering[53] the floor. It was sorrowful to think how many days, and weeks, and months, and years of toil, had been wasted on these musty papers, which were now only an encumbrance on earth, and were hidden away in this forgotten corner, never more to be glanced at by human eyes. But, then, what reams of other manuscripts—filled, not with the dulness of official formalities, but with the thought of inventive brains and the rich effusion of deep hearts—had gone equally to oblivion; and

---

[51]ANATTO: An orange-red dye from the waxy pulp surrounding the seeds of the *Bixa orellana* tree, found in Central America.
[52]IN TESTIMONY THAT THESE COMMODITIES HAD PAID THE IMPOST: In his official capacity as surveyor, Hawthorne's name was stenciled on boxes of trade goods.
[53]LUMBERING: Littering.

that, moreover, without serving a purpose in their day, as these heaped-up papers had, and—saddest of all—without purchasing for their writers the comfortable livelihood which the clerks of the Custom-House had gained by these worthless scratchings of the pen! Yet not altogether worthless, perhaps, as materials of local history. Here, no doubt, statistics of the former commerce of Salem might be discovered, and memorials of her princely merchants,—old King Derby,—old Billy Gray,[54]—old Simon Forrester,[55]—and many another magnate in his day; whose powdered head, however, was scarcely in the tomb, before his mountain-pile of wealth began to dwindle. The founders of the greater part of the families which now compose the aristocracy of Salem might here be traced, from the petty and obscure beginnings of their traffic, at periods generally much posterior to the Revolution, upward to what their children look upon as long-established rank.

Prior to the Revolution, there is a dearth of records; the earlier documents and archives of the Custom-House having, probably, been carried off to Halifax, when all the King's officials accompanied the British army in its flight from Boston.[56] It has often been a matter of regret with me; for, going back, perhaps, to the days of the Protectorate,[57] those papers must have contained many references to forgotten or remembered men, and to antique customs, which would have affected me with the same pleasure as when I used to pick up Indian arrow-heads in the field near the Old Manse.

But, one idle and rainy day, it was my fortune to make a discovery of some little interest. Poking and burrowing into the heaped-up rubbish in the corner; unfolding one and another document, and reading the names of vessels that had long ago foundered at sea or rotted at the wharves, and those of merchants, never heard of now on 'Change,[58] nor very readily decipherable on their mossy tombstones; glancing at such matters with the saddened, weary, half-reluctant interest which we bestow on the corpse of dead activity,—and exerting my fancy, sluggish with little use, to raise up from these dry bones an image of the old town's brighter aspect, when India was a new region, and only Salem knew the way thither,—I chanced to lay my hand on a small package, carefully done up in a piece of ancient

[54]OLD BILLY GRAY: William Gray (1750–1825), a lieutenant governor of Massachusetts.
[55]OLD SIMON FORRESTER: Captain Simon Forrester (1776–1851), a wealthy relative of Hawthorne's.
[56]BRITISH ARMY IN ITS FLIGHT FROM BOSTON: The British general William Howe (1729–1814) evacuated his troops to Halifax, Nova Scotia, after George Washington took Boston in 1776.
[57]PROTECTORATE: A reference to the years 1653–1660, when Oliver Cromwell (1599–1658) served as Lord Protector of England during the period called The Commonwealth.
[58] 'CHANGE: Exchange, where trade was conducted.

yellow parchment. This envelope had the air of an official record of some period long past, when clerks engrossed their stiff and formal chirography on more substantial materials than at present. There was something about it that quickened an instinctive curiosity, and made me undo the faded red tape, that tied up the package, with the sense that a treasure would here be brought to light. Unbending the rigid folds of the parchment cover, I found it to be a commission, under the hand and seal of Governor Shirley,[59] in favor of one Jonathan Pue,[60] as Surveyor of his Majesty's Customs for the port of Salem, in the Province of Massachusetts Bay. I remembered to have read (probably in Felt's Annals) a notice of the decease of Mr. Surveyor Pue, about fourscore years ago; and likewise, in a newspaper of recent times, an account of the digging up of his remains in the little grave-yard of St. Peter's Church,[61] during the renewal of that edifice. Nothing, if I rightly call to mind, was left of my respected predecessor, save an imperfect skeleton, and some fragments of apparel, and a wig of majestic frizzle; which, unlike the head that it once adorned, was in very satisfactory preservation. But, on examining the papers which the parchment commission served to envelop, I found more traces of Mr. Pue's mental part, and the internal operations of his head, than the frizzled wig had contained of the venerable skull itself.

They were documents, in short, not official, but of a private nature, or, at least, written in his private capacity, and apparently with his own hand. I could account for their being included in the heap of Custom-House lumber only by the fact, that Mr. Pue's death had happened suddenly; and that these papers, which he probably kept in his official desk, had never come to the knowledge of his heirs, or were supposed to relate to the business of the revenue. On the transfer of the archives to Halifax, this package, proving to be of no public concern, was left behind, and had remained ever since unopened.

The ancient Surveyor—being little molested, I suppose, at that early day, with business pertaining to his office—seems to have devoted some of his many leisure hours to researches as a local antiquarian, and other inquisitions of a similar nature. These supplied material for petty activity to a mind that would otherwise have been eaten up with rust.

---

[59]GOVERNOR SHIRLEY: William Shirley (1694–1771), a colonial governor of Massachusetts (1741–1749, 1753–1756).
[60]JONATHAN PUE: Hawthorne found the name of Jonathan Pue in a book of Salem history, *Annals of Salem*, by Joseph P. Felt, which reports that Pue died March 24, 1760. Pue's gravestone can still be found in the graveyard of St. Peter's Church (see note 61). Hawthorne's story about Pue, however, is fictitious. There was no scarlet letter, and Hawthorne never discovered one nor gave it to the Essex Historical Society.
[61]ST. PETER'S CHURCH: The first Anglican Church in Salem.

   A portion of his facts, by the by, did me good service in the preparation of the article entitled "MAIN STREET," included in the present volume.[62] The remainder may perhaps be applied to purposes equally valuable, hereafter; or not impossibly may be worked up, so far as they go, into a regular history of Salem, should my veneration for the natal soil ever impel me to so pious a task. Meanwhile, they shall be at the command of any gentleman, inclined, and competent, to take the unprofitable labor off my hands. As a final disposition, I contemplate depositing them with the Essex Historical Society.[63]

But the object that most drew my attention, in the mysterious package, was a certain affair of fine red cloth, much worn and faded. There were traces about it of gold embroidery, which, however, was greatly frayed and defaced; so that none, or very little, of the glitter was left. It had been wrought, as was easy to perceive, with wonderful skill of needlework; and the stitch (as I am assured by ladies conversant with such mysteries) gives evidence of a now forgotten art, not to be recovered even by the process of picking out the threads. This rag of scarlet cloth,—for time, and wear, and a sacrilegious moth, had reduced it to little other than a rag,—on careful examination, assumed the shape of a letter. It was the capital letter A. By an accurate measurement, each limb proved to be precisely three inches and a quarter in length. It had been intended, there could be no doubt, as an ornamental article of dress; but how it was to be worn, or what rank, honor, and dignity, in by-past times, were signified by it, was a riddle which (so evanescent are the fashions of the world in these particulars) I saw little hope of solving. And yet it strangely interested me. My eyes fastened themselves upon the old scarlet letter, and would not be turned aside. Certainly, there was some deep meaning in it, most worthy of interpretation, and which, as it were, streamed forth from the mystic symbol, subtly communicating itself to my sensibilities, but evading the analysis of my mind.

   While thus perplexed,—and cogitating, among other hypotheses, whether the letter might not have been one of those decorations which the white men used to contrive, in order to take the eyes of Indians,—I happened to place it on my breast. It seemed to me,—the reader may smile, but must not doubt my word,—it seemed to me, then, that I experienced a sensation not altogether physical, yet almost so, as of burning

---

[62]"MAIN STREET," INCLUDED IN THE PRESENT VOLUME: Hawthorne refers to a short story he intended to publish with *The Scarlet Letter*.
[63]ESSEX HISTORICAL SOCIETY: Now called the Essex Institute (John Tucker Daland House), an institution in Salem, Massachusetts, that is now part of the Peabody Essex Museum.

heat; and as if the letter were not of red cloth, but red-hot iron. I shuddered, and involuntarily let it fall upon the floor.

In the absorbing contemplation of the scarlet letter, I had hitherto neglected to examine a small roll of dingy paper, around which it had been twisted. This I now opened, and had the satisfaction to find, recorded by the old Surveyor's pen, a reasonably complete explanation of the whole affair. There were several foolscap sheets,[64] containing many particulars respecting the life and conversation of one Hester Prynne, who appeared to have been rather a noteworthy personage in the view of our ancestors. She had flourished during a period between the early days of Massachusetts and the close of the seventeenth century. Aged persons, alive in the time of Mr. Surveyor Pue, and from whose oral testimony he had made up his narrative, remembered her, in their youth, as a very old, but not decrepit woman, of a stately and solemn aspect. It had been her habit, from an almost immemorial date, to go about the country as a kind of voluntary nurse, and doing whatever miscellaneous good she might; taking upon herself, likewise, to give advice in all matters, especially those of the heart; by which means, as a person of such propensities inevitably must, she gained from many people the reverence due to an angel, but, I should imagine, was looked upon by others as an intruder and a nuisance. Prying farther into the manuscript, I found the record of other doings and sufferings of this singular woman, for most of which the reader is referred to the story[65] entitled "THE SCARLET LETTER"; and it should be borne carefully in mind, that the main facts of that story are authorized and authenticated by the document of Mr. Surveyor Pue. The original papers, together with the scarlet letter itself,—a most curious relic,—are still in my possession, and shall be freely exhibited to whomsoever, induced by the great interest of the narrative, may desire a sight of them. I must not be understood affirming, that, in the dressing up of the tale, and imagining the motives and modes of passion that influenced the characters who figure in it, I have invariably confined myself within the limits of the old Surveyor's half a dozen sheets of foolscap. On the contrary, I have allowed myself, as to such points, nearly or altogether as much license as if the facts had been entirely of my own invention. What I contend for is the authenticity of the outline.

[64]SEVERAL FOOLSCAP SHEETS: Long folio sheets of writing or printing paper, usually 13 by 16 inches, which are folded.
[65]THE READER IS REFERRED TO THE STORY: This essay was written before Hawthorne had finished *The Scarlet Letter* as a novel and not a shorter story.

This incident recalled my mind, in some degree, to its old track. There seemed to be here the groundwork of a tale. It impressed me as if the ancient Surveyor, in his garb of a hundred years gone by, and wearing his immortal wig,—which was buried with him, but did not perish in the grave,—had met me in the deserted chamber of the Custom-House. In his port was the dignity of one who had borne his Majesty's commission, and who was therefore illuminated by a ray of the splendor that shone so dazzlingly about the throne. How unlike, alas! the hang-dog look of a republican official, who, as the servant of the people, feels himself less than the least, and below the lowest, of his masters. With his own ghostly hand, the obscurely seen, but majestic, figure had imparted to me the scarlet symbol, and the little roll of explanatory manuscript. With his own ghostly voice, he had exhorted me, on the sacred consideration of my filial duty and reverence towards him,—who might reasonably regard himself as my official ancestor,—to bring his mouldy and moth-eaten lucubrations[66] before the public. "Do this," said the ghost of Mr. Surveyor Pue, emphatically nodding the head that looked so imposing within its memorable wig, "do this, and the profit shall be all your own! You will shortly need it; for it is not in your days as it was in mine, when a man's office was a life-lease, and oftentimes an heirloom. But, I charge you, in this matter of old Mistress Prynne, give to your predecessor's memory the credit which will be rightfully its due!" And I said to the ghost of Mr. Surveyor Pue,—"I will!"

On Hester Prynne's story, therefore, I bestowed much thought. It was the subject of my meditations for many an hour, while pacing to and fro across my room, or traversing, with a hundredfold repetition, the long extent from the front-door of the Custom-House to the side-entrance, and back again. Great were the weariness and annoyance of the old Inspector and the Weighers and Gaugers, whose slumbers were disturbed by the unmercifully lengthened tramp of my passing and returning footsteps. Remembering their own former habits, they used to say that the Surveyor was walking the quarter-deck. They probably fancied that my sole object—and, indeed, the sole object for which a sane man could ever put himself into voluntary motion—was, to get an appetite for dinner. And to say the truth, an appetite, sharpened by the east-wind that generally blew along the passage, was the only valuable result of so much indefatigable exercise. So little adapted is the atmosphere of a Custom-House to the delicate harvest of fancy and sensibility, that, had I remained

[66]LUCUBRATIONS: Work done by candlelight.

there through ten Presidencies yet to come, I doubt whether the tale of "The Scarlet Letter" would ever have been brought before the public eye. My imagination was a tarnished mirror. It would not reflect, or only with miserable dimness, the figures with which I did my best to people it. The characters of the narrative would not be warmed and rendered malleable, by any heat that I could kindle at my intellectual forge. They would take neither the glow of passion nor the tenderness of sentiment, but retained all the rigidity of dead corpses, and stared me in the face with a fixed and ghastly grin of contemptuous defiance. "What have you to do with us?" that expression seemed to say. "The little power you might once have possessed over the tribe of unrealities is gone! You have bartered it for a pittance of the public gold. Go, then, and earn your wages!" In short, the almost torpid creatures of my own fancy twitted me with imbecility, and not without fair occasion.

It was not merely during the three hours and a half which Uncle Sam claimed as his share of my daily life, that this wretched numbness held possession of me. It went with me on my sea-shore walks and rambles into the country, whenever—which was seldom and reluctantly—I bestirred myself to seek that invigorating charm of Nature, which used to give me such freshness and activity of thought, the moment that I stepped across the threshold of the Old Manse. The same torpor, as regarded the capacity for intellectual effort, accompanied me home, and weighed upon me, in the chamber which I most absurdly termed my study. Nor did it quit me when, late at night, I sat in the deserted parlour, lighted only by the glimmering coal-fire and the moon, striving to picture forth imaginary scenes, which, the next day, might flow out on the brightening page in many-hued description.

If the imaginative faculty refused to act at such an hour, it might well be deemed a hopeless case. Moonlight, in a familiar room, falling so white upon the carpet, and showing all its figures so distinctly,—making every object so minutely visible, yet so unlike a morning or noontide visibility,—is a medium the most suitable for a romance-writer to get acquainted with his illusive guests. There is the little domestic scenery of the well-known apartment; the chairs, with each its separate individuality; the centre-table, sustaining a work-basket, a volume or two, and an extinguished lamp; the sofa; the bookcase; the picture on the wall;—all these details, so completely seen, are so spiritualized by the unusual light, that they seem to lose their actual substance, and become things of intellect. Nothing is too small or too trifling to undergo this change, and acquire dignity thereby. A child's shoe; the doll, seated in her little wicker carriage; the hobby-horse:—whatever, in a word, has been used or played with, during the day, is now invested with a quality of strangeness and remoteness, though still almost as vividly present as by daylight. Thus, therefore, the floor of our familiar room has become a neutral territory, somewhere between the real world and fairy-land, where the Actual and the Imaginary may meet, and each imbue itself with the nature of the other. Ghosts might enter here, without affrighting us. It would be too much in keeping with the scene to excite surprise, were we to look about us and discover a form, beloved, but gone hence, now sitting quietly in a streak of this magic moonshine, with an aspect that would make us doubt whether it had returned from afar, or had never once stirred from our fireside.

The somewhat dim coal-fire has an essential influence in producing the effect which I would describe. It throws its unobtrusive tinge throughout the room, with a faint ruddiness upon the walls and ceiling, and a reflected gleam from the polish of the furniture. This warmer light mingles itself with the cold spirituality of the moonbeams, and communicates, as it were, a heart and sensibilities of human tenderness to the forms which fancy summons up. It converts them from snow-images into men and women. Glancing at the looking-glass, we behold—deep within its haunted verge—the smouldering glow of the half-extinguished anthracite, the white moonbeams on the floor, and a repetition of all the gleam and shadow of the picture, with one remove farther from the actual, and nearer to the imaginative. Then, at such an hour, and with this scene before him, if a man, sitting all alone, cannot dream strange things, and make them look like truth, he need never try to write romances.

But, for myself, during the whole of my Custom-House experience, moonlight and sunshine, and the glow of fire-light, were just alike in my regard; and neither of them was of one whit more avail than the twinkle of a tallow-candle. An entire class of susceptibilities, and a gift connected with them,—of no great richness or value, but the best I had,—was gone from me.

It is my belief, however, that, had I attempted a different order of composition, my faculties would not have been found so pointless and inefficacious. I might, for instance, have contented myself with writing out the narratives of a veteran shipmaster, one of the Inspectors, whom I should be most ungrateful not to mention; since scarcely a day passed that he did not stir me to laughter and admiration by his marvellous gifts as a story-teller. Could I have preserved the picturesque force of his style, and the humorous coloring which nature taught him how to throw over his descriptions, the result, I honestly believe, would have been something new in literature. Or I might readily have found a more serious task. It was a folly, with the materiality of this daily life pressing so intrusively upon me, to attempt to fling myself back into another age; or to insist on creating the semblance of a world out of airy matter, when, at every moment, the impalpable beauty of my soap-bubble was broken by the rude contact of some actual circumstance. The wiser effort would have been, to diffuse thought and imagination through the opaque substance of to-day, and thus to make it a bright transparency; to spiritualize the burden that began to weigh so heavily; to seek, resolutely, the true and indestructible value that lay hidden in the petty and wearisome incidents, and ordinary characters, with which I was now conversant. The fault was mine. The page of life that was spread out before me seemed dull and commonplace, only because I had not fathomed its deeper import. A better book than I shall ever write was there; leaf after leaf presenting itself to me, just as it was written out by the reality of the flitting hour, and vanishing as fast as written, only because my brain wanted the insight and my hand the cunning to transcribe it. At some future day, it may be, I shall remember a few scattered fragments and broken paragraphs, and write them down, and find the letters turn to gold upon the page.

These perceptions have come too late. At the instant, I was only conscious that what would have been a pleasure once was now a hopeless toil. There was no occasion to make much moan about this state of affairs. I had ceased to be a writer of tolerably poor tales and essays, and had become a tolerably good Surveyor of the Customs. That was all. But, nevertheless, it is any thing but agreeable to be haunted by a suspicion that one's intellect is dwindling away; or exhaling, without your consciousness, like ether out of a phial; so that, at every glance, you find a smaller and less volatile residuum. Of the fact, there could be no doubt; and, examining myself and others, I was led to conclusions in reference to the effect of public office on the character, not very favorable to the mode of life in question. In some other form, perhaps, I may hereafter develop these effects. Suffice it here to say, that a Custom-House officer, of long continuance, can hardly be a very praiseworthy or respectable personage, for many reasons; one of them, the tenure by which he holds his situation, and another, the very nature of his business, which—though, I trust, an honest one—is of such a sort that he does not share in the united effort of mankind.

An effect—which I believe to be observable, more or less, in every individual who has occupied the position—is, that, while he leans on the mighty arm of the Republic, his own proper strength departs from him. He loses, in an extent proportioned to the weakness or force of his original nature, the capability of self-support. If he possess an unusual share of native energy, or the enervating magic of place do not operate too long upon him, his forfeited powers may be redeemable. The ejected officer—fortunate in the unkindly shove that sends him forth betimes, to struggle amid a struggling world—may return to himself, and become all that he has ever been. But this seldom happens. He usually keeps his ground just long enough for his own ruin, and is then thrust out, with sinews all unstrung, to totter along the difficult footpath of life as he best may. Conscious of his own infirmity,—that his tempered steel and elasticity are lost,—he for ever afterwards looks wistfully about him in quest of support external to himself. His pervading and continual hope—a hallucination, which, in the face of all discouragement, and making light of impossibilities, haunts him while he lives, and, I fancy, like the convulsive throes of the cholera, torments him for a brief space after death— is, that, finally, and in no long time, by some happy coincidence of circumstances, he shall be restored to office. This faith, more than any thing else, steals the pith and availability out of whatever enterprise he may dream of undertaking. Why should he toil and moil, and be at so much trouble to pick himself up out of the mud, when, in a little while hence, the strong arm of his Uncle will raise and support him? Why should he work for his living here, or go to dig gold in California,[67] when he is so soon to be made happy, at monthly intervals, with a little pile of glittering coin out of his Uncle's pocket? It is sadly curious to observe how slight a taste of office suffices to infect a poor fellow with this singular disease. Uncle Sam's gold—meaning no disrespect to the worthy old gentleman—has, in this respect, a quality of enchantment like that of the Devil's wages. Whoever touches it should look well to himself, or he may find the bargain to go hard against him, involving, if not his soul, yet many of its better attributes; its sturdy force, its courage and constancy, its truth, its self-reliance, and all that gives the emphasis to manly character.

Here was a fine prospect in the distance! Not that the Surveyor brought the lesson home to himself, or admitted that he could be so utterly undone, either by continuance in office, or ejectment. Yet my reflections were not the most comfortable. I began to grow melancholy and restless; continually prying into my mind, to discover which of its poor properties were gone, and what degree of detriment had already accrued to the remainder. I endeavoured to calculate how much longer I could stay

[67]DIG GOLD IN CALIFORNIA: Hawthorne wrote this essay in 1849, the year of the California gold rush.

in the Custom-House, and yet go forth a man. To confess the truth, it was my greatest apprehension,—as it would never be a measure of policy to turn out so quiet an individual as myself, and it being hardly in the nature of a public officer to resign,—it was my chief trouble, therefore, that I was likely to grow gray and decrepit in the Surveyorship, and become much such another animal as the old Inspector. Might it not, in the tedious lapse of official life that lay before me, finally be with me as it was with this venerable friend,—to make the dinner-hour the nucleus of the day, and to spend the rest of it, as an old dog spends it, asleep in the sunshine or the shade? A dreary look-forward this, for a man who felt it to be the best definition of happiness to live throughout the whole range of his faculties and sensibilities! But, all this while, I was giving myself very unnecessary alarm. Providence had meditated better things for me than I could possibly imagine for myself.

A remarkable event of the third year of my Surveyorship—to adopt the tone of "P.P."—was the election of General Taylor to the Presidency.[68] It is essential, in order to form a complete estimate of the advantages of official life, to view the incumbent at the incoming of a hostile administration. His position is then one of the most singularly irksome, and, in every contingency, disagreeable, that a wretched mortal can possibly occupy; with seldom an alternative of good, on either hand, although what presents itself to him as the worst event may very probably be the best. But it is a strange experience, to a man of pride and sensibility, to know that his interests are within the control of individuals who neither love nor understand him, and by whom, since one or the other must needs happen, he would rather be injured than obliged. Strange, too, for one who has kept his calmness throughout the contest, to observe the bloodthirstiness that is developed in the hour of triumph, and to be conscious that he is himself among its objects! There are few uglier traits of human nature than this tendency—which I now witnessed in men no worse than their neighbours—to grow cruel, merely because they possessed the power of inflicting harm. If the guillotine, as applied to office-holders, were a literal fact, instead of one of the most apt of metaphors, it is my sincere belief, that the active members of the victorious party were sufficiently excited to have chopped off all our heads, and have thanked Heaven for the opportunity! It appears to me—who have been a calm and curious observer, as well in victory as defeat—that this fierce

---

[68]GENERAL TAYLOR TO THE PRESIDENCY: Zachary Taylor (1784–1850), the twelfth president of the United States, was of the Whig Party. His election led to political reappointments in the custom house and, in turn, Hawthorne's dismissal.

and bitter spirit of malice and revenge has never distinguished the many triumphs of my own party as it now did that of the Whigs. The Democrats take the offices, as a general rule, because they need them, and because the practice of many years has made it the law of political warfare, which, unless a different system be proclaimed, it was weakness and cowardice to murmur at. But the long habit of victory has made them generous. They know how to spare, when they see occasion; and when they strike, the axe may be sharp, indeed, but its edge is seldom poisoned with ill-will; nor is it their custom ignominiously to kick the head which they have just struck off.

In short, unpleasant as was my predicament, at best, I saw much reason to congratulate myself that I was on the losing side, rather than the triumphant one. If, heretofore, I had been none of the warmest of partisans, I began now, at this season of peril and adversity, to be pretty acutely sensible with which party my predilections lay; nor was it without something like regret and shame, that, according to a reasonable calculation of chances, I saw my own prospect of retaining office to be better than those of my Democratic brethren. But who can see an inch into futurity, beyond his nose? My own head was the first that fell!

The moment when a man's head drops off is seldom or never, I am inclined to think, precisely the most agreeable of his life. Nevertheless, like the greater part of our misfortunes, even so serious a contingency brings its remedy and consolation with it, if the sufferer will but make the best, rather than the worst, of the accident which has befallen him. In my particular case, the consolatory topics were close at hand, and, indeed, had suggested themselves to my meditations a considerable time before it was requisite to use them. In view of my previous weariness of office, and vague thoughts of resignation, my fortune somewhat resembled that of a person who should entertain an idea of committing suicide, and, altogether beyond his hopes, meet with the good hap to be murdered. In the Custom-House, as before in the Old Manse, I had spent three years; a term long enough to rest a weary brain; long enough to break off old intellectual habits, and make room for new ones; long enough, and too long, to have lived in an unnatural state, doing what was really of no advantage nor delight to any human being, and withholding myself from toil that would, at least, have stilled an unquiet impulse in me. Then, moreover, as regarded his unceremonious ejectment, the late Surveyor was not altogether ill-pleased to be recognized by the Whigs as an enemy; since his inactivity in political affairs,—his tendency to roam, at will, in that broad and quiet field where all mankind may meet, rather than confine himself to those narrow paths where brethren of the same household must diverge from one another,—had sometimes made it questionable with his brother Democrats whether he was a friend. Now, after he had won the crown of martyrdom, (though with no longer a head to wear it on,) the point might be looked upon as settled. Finally, little heroic as he was, it seemed more decorous to be overthrown in the downfall of the party with which he had been content to stand, than to remain a forlorn survivor, when so many worthier men were falling; and, at last, after subsisting for four years on the mercy of a hostile administration, to be compelled then to define his position anew, and claim the yet more humiliating mercy of a friendly one.

Meanwhile, the press had taken up my affair, and kept me, for a week or two, careering through the public prints, in my decapitated state, like Irving's Headless Horseman[69]; ghastly and grim, and longing to be buried, as a political dead man ought. So much for my figurative self. The real human being, all this time, with his head safely on his shoulders, had brought himself to the comfortable conclusion, that every thing was for the best; and, making an investment in ink, paper, and steel-pens, had opened his long-disused writing-desk, and was again a literary man.

Now it was, that the lucubrations of my ancient predecessor, Mr. Surveyor Pue, came into play. Rusty through long idleness, some little space was requisite before my intellectual machinery could be brought to work upon the tale, with an effect in any degree satisfactory. Even yet, though my thoughts were ultimately much absorbed in the task, it wears, to my eye, a stern and sombre aspect; too much ungladdened by genial sunshine; too little relieved by the tender and familiar influences which soften almost every scene of nature and real life, and, undoubtedly, should soften every picture of them. This uncaptivating effect is perhaps due to the period of hardly accomplished revolution, and still seething turmoil, in which the story shaped itself. It is no indication, however, of a lack of cheerfulness in the writer's mind; for he was happier, while straying through the gloom of these sunless fantasies, than at any time since he had quitted the Old Manse. Some of the briefer articles, which contribute to make up the volume, have likewise been written since my involuntary withdrawal from the toils and honors of public life, and the remainder are gleaned from annuals and magazines, of such antique date that they have gone round the circle, and come back to novelty again.[70] Keeping up the

---

[69]IRVING'S HEADLESS HORSEMAN: A reference to the short story, "The Legend of Sleepy Hollow," by Washington Irving (1783–1859).
[70]COME BACK TO NOVELTY AGAIN: Hawthorne notes, "At the time of writing this article, the author intended to publish, along with *The Scarlet Letter*, several shorter tales and sketches. These it has been thought advisable to defer."

metaphor of the political guillotine, the whole may be considered as the POSTHUMOUS PAPERS OF A DECAPITATED SURVEYOR; and the sketch which I am now bringing to a close, if too autobiographical for a modest person to publish in his lifetime, will readily be excused in a gentleman who writes from beyond the grave. Peace be with all the world! My blessing on my friends! My forgiveness to my enemies! For I am in the realm of quiet!

The life of the Custom-House lies like a dream behind me. The old Inspector,—who, by the by, I regret to say, was overthrown and killed by a horse, some time ago; else he would certainly have lived for ever,—he, and all those other venerable personages who sat with him at the receipt of custom, are but shadows in my view; white-headed and wrinkled images, which my fancy used to sport with, and has now flung aside for ever. The merchants,—Pingree, Phillips, Shepard, Upton, Kimball, Bertram, Hunt,—these, and many other names, which had such a classic familiarity for my ear six months ago,—these men of traffic, who seemed to occupy so important a position in the world,—how little time has it required to disconnect me from them all, not merely in act, but recollection! It is with an effort that I recall the figures and appellations of these few. Soon, likewise, my old native town will loom upon me through the haze of memory, a mist brooding over and around it; as if it were no portion of the real earth, but an overgrown village in cloud-land, with only imaginary inhabitants to people its wooden houses, and walk its homely lanes, and the unpicturesque prolixity of its main street. Henceforth, it ceases to be a reality of my life. I am a citizen of somewhere else. My good townspeople will not much regret me; for—though it has been as dear an object as any, in my literary efforts, to be of some importance in their eyes, and to win myself a pleasant memory in this abode and burial-place of so many of my forefathers—there has never been, for me, the genial atmosphere which a literary man requires, in order to ripen the best harvest of his mind. I shall do better amongst other faces; and these familiar ones, it need hardly be said, will do just as well without me.

It may be, however,—O, transporting and triumphant thought!—that the great-grandchildren of the present race may sometimes think kindly of the scribbler of bygone days, when the antiquary of days to come, among the sites memorable in the town's history, shall point out the locality of THE TOWN-PUMP![71]

---

[71]THE TOWN PUMP: A reference to another story by Hawthorne, "A Rill from the Town-Pump."

I. THE PRISON-DOOR

A throng of bearded men, in sad-colored garments and gray, steeple-crowned hats, intermixed with women, some wearing hoods, and others bareheaded, was assembled in front of a wooden edifice, the door of which was heavily timbered with oak, and studded with iron spikes.

The founders of a new colony, whatever Utopia of human virtue and happiness they might originally project, have invariably recognized it among their earliest practical necessities to allot a portion of the virgin soil as a cemetery, and another portion as the site of a prison. In accordance with this rule, it may safely be assumed that the forefathers of Boston had built the first prison-house, somewhere in the vicinity of Cornhill,[1] almost as seasonably as they marked out the first burial-ground, on Isaac Johnson's[2] lot, and round about his grave, which subsequently became the nucleus of all the congregated sepulchres in the old church-yard of King's Chapel.[3] Certain it is, that, some fifteen or twenty years after the settlement of the town, the wooden jail was already marked with weather-stains and other indications of age, which gave a yet darker aspect to its beetle-browed and gloomy front. The rust on the ponderous iron-work of its oaken door looked more antique than any thing else in the new world. Like all that pertains to crime, it seemed never to have known a youthful era. Before this ugly edifice, and between it and the wheel-track of the street, was a grass-plot, much overgrown with burdock, pig-weed, apple-peru, and such unsightly vegetation, which evidently found something congenial in the soil that had so early borne the black flower of civilized society, a prison. But, on one side of the portal, and rooted almost at the threshold, was a wild rose-bush, covered, in this month of June, with its delicate gems, which might be imagined to offer their fragrance and fragile beauty to the prisoner as he went in, and to the condemned criminal as he came forth to his doom, in token that the deep heart of Nature could pity and be kind to him.

This rose-bush, by a strange chance, has been kept alive in history; but whether it had merely survived out of the stern old wilderness, so long after the fall of the gigantic pines and oaks that originally overshadowed it,—or whether, as there is fair authority for believing, it had sprung

---

[1]CORNHILL: According to the Boston Historical Society, most of the Boston's early residents settled along Cornhill (now Washington Street) and what is now State Street. The area was close to both the harbor and a fresh water spring on what is still referred to as Spring Street.
[2]ISAAC JOHNSON: Isaac Johnson (1601–1630), who died the year after the Puritans formed the settlement of Boston. His land went to public use.
[3]KING'S CHAPEL: The first Anglican Church in Boston, built in 1688.

up under the footsteps of the sainted Ann Hutchinson,[4] as she entered the prison-door,—we shall not take upon us to determine. Finding it so directly on the threshold of our narrative, which is now about to issue from that inauspicious portal, we could hardly do otherwise than pluck one of its flowers and present it to the reader. It may serve, let us hope, to symbolize some sweet moral blossom, that may be found along the track, or relieve the darkening close of a tale of human frailty and sorrow.

II. THE MARKET-PLACE

The grass-plot before the jail, in Prison Lane, on a certain summer morning, not less than two centuries ago, was occupied by a pretty large number of the inhabitants of Boston; all with their eyes intently fastened on the iron-clamped oaken door. Amongst any other population, or at a later period in the history of New England, the grim rigidity that petrified the bearded physiognomies[5] of these good people would have augured some awful business in hand. It could have betokened nothing short of the anticipated execution of some noted culprit, on whom the sentence of a legal tribunal had but confirmed the verdict of public sentiment. But, in that early severity of the Puritan character, an inference of this kind could not so indubitably be drawn. It might be that a sluggish bond-servant, or an undutiful child, whom his parents had given over to the civil authority, was to be corrected at the whipping-post. It might be, that an Antinomian,[6] a Quaker,[7] or other heterodox religionist,[8] was to be scourged out of the town, or an idle and vagrant Indian, whom the white man's fire-water[9] had made riotous about the streets, was to be driven with stripes into the shadow of the forest. It might be, too, that a witch, like old Mistress Hibbins,[10]

---

[4]ANN HUTCHINSON: Anne Hutchinson (1591–1643) was a religious leader in New England who was tried as a heretic for antinomianism. (In truth, Hutchinson taught the covenant of grace as opposed to the covenant of works; that faith alone was necessary to salvation, which is not antinomianism.) She was tried by the General Court and banished from Massachusetts Bay Colony for "traducing the ministers." She resettled in Rhode Island, and later in the area of modern New York City, where she and her family were killed by Native Americans.
[5]PHYSIOGNOMIES: Facial expressions.
[6]ANTINOMIAN: Antinomians were deemed heretics in Puritan New England. They believed that Christians were not bound by moral law, particularly that of the Old Testament. Anne Hutchinson was persecuted for supposed antinomianism (see note 4).
[7]QUAKER: A member of the Society of Friends, a religious body formed under the leadership of George Fox (1624–1691). Four Quakers were executed for refusing to leave Massachusetts Bay Colony between 1659 and 1661 (see note 21 of the Custom House sketch).
[8]HETERODOX RELIGIONIST: Not in keeping with established doctrines or opinions of the dominant religion—in this case, Puritan doctrine.
[9]FIRE-WATER: Alcohol.
[10]OLD MISTRESS HIBBINS: Ann Hibbins, who was tried for witchcraft in 1655 and executed in 1656.

the bitter-tempered widow of the magistrate, was to die upon the gallows. In either case, there was very much the same solemnity of demeanour on the part of the spectators; as befitted a people amongst whom religion and law were almost identical, and in whose character both were so thoroughly interfused, that the mildest and the severest acts of public discipline were alike made venerable and awful. Meagre, indeed, and cold, was the sympathy that a transgressor might look for, from such bystanders at the scaffold. On the other hand, a penalty which, in our days, would infer a degree of mocking infamy and ridicule, might then be invested with almost as stern a dignity as the punishment of death itself.

It was a circumstance to be noted, on the summer morning when our story begins its course, that the women, of whom there were several in the crowd, appeared to take a peculiar interest in whatever penal infliction might be expected to ensue. The age had not so much refinement, that any sense of impropriety restrained the wearers of petticoat and farthingale[11] from stepping forth into the public ways, and wedging their not unsubstantial persons, if occasion were, into the throng nearest to the scaffold at an execution. Morally, as well as materially, there was a coarser fibre in those wives and maidens of old English birth and breeding, than in their fair descendants, separated from them by a series of six or seven generations; for, throughout that chain of ancestry, every successive mother had transmitted to her child a fainter bloom, a more delicate and briefer beauty, and a slighter physical frame, if not a character of less force and solidity, than her own. The women, who were now standing about the prison-door, stood within less than half a century of the period when the man-like Elizabeth[12] had been the not altogether unsuitable representative of the sex. They were her countrywomen; and the beef and ale of their native land, with a moral diet not a whit more refined, entered largely into their composition. The bright morning sun, therefore, shone on broad shoulders and well-developed busts, and on round and ruddy cheeks, that had ripened in the far-off island, and had hardly yet grown paler or thinner in the atmosphere of New England. There was, moreover, a boldness and rotundity of speech among these matrons, as most of them seemed to be, that would startle us at the present day, whether in respect to its purport or its volume of tone.

---

[11]FARTHINGALE: Hooped petticoat.
[12]MAN-LIKE ELIZABETH: Queen Elizabeth I (1533–1603) of England, who ruled in her own right and never married. She made a famous speech to her navy before their battle with the Spanish Armada in 1588 in which she said, "I know I have but the body of a weak and feeble woman; but I have the heart of a king, and of a king of England, too."

"Goodwives," said a hard-featured dame of fifty, "I'll tell ye a piece of my mind. It would be greatly for the public behoof, if we women, being of mature age and church-members in good repute, should have the handling of such malefactresses[13] as this Hester Prynne. What think ye, gossips? If the hussy stood up for judgment before us five, that are now here in a knot together, would she come off with such a sentence as the worshipful magistrates have awarded? Marry, I trow not!"

"People say," said another, "that the Reverend Master Dimmesdale, her godly pastor, takes it very grievously to heart that such a scandal should have come upon his congregation."

"The magistrates are God-fearing gentlemen, but merciful over-much,—that is a truth," added a third autumnal matron. "At the very least, they should have put the brand of a hot iron on Hester Prynne's forehead. Madame Hester would have winced at that, I warrant me. But she,—the naughty baggage,—little will she care what they put upon the bodice of her gown! Why, look you, she may cover it with a brooch, or such like, heathenish adornment, and so walk the streets as brave as ever!"

"Ah, but," interposed, more softly, a young wife, holding a child by the hand, "let her cover the mark as she will, the pang of it will be always in her heart."

"What do we talk of marks and brands, whether on the bodice of her gown, or the flesh of her forehead?" cried another female, the ugliest as well as the most pitiless of these self-constituted judges. "This woman has brought shame upon us all, and ought to die. Is there not law for it? Truly there is, both in the Scripture and the statute-book.[14] Then let the magistrates, who have made it of no effect, thank themselves if their own wives and daughters go astray!"

"Mercy on us, goodwife," exclaimed a man in the crowd, "is there no virtue in woman, save what springs from a wholesome fear of the gallows? That is the hardest word yet! Hush, now, gossips; for the lock is turning in the prison-door, and here comes Mistress Prynne herself."

The door of the jail being flung open from within, there appeared, in the first place, like a black shadow emerging into sunshine, the grim and grisly presence of the town-beadle, with a sword by his side and his staff of office in his hand. This personage prefigured and represented in his aspect the whole dismal severity of the Puritanic code of law, which

---

[13]MALEFACTRESSES: Women guilty of scandalous offenses against the law.
[14]STATUTE-BOOK: The woman refers to Exodus 20:14: "Thou shalt not commit adultery"; and Leviticus 20:10: "If a man commits adultery with the wife of his neighbor, both the adulterer and the adulteress shall be put to death." A 1641 Boston law (as recorded in the statute-book) cited death as the punishment for adultery.

it was his business to administer in its final and closest application to the offender. Stretching forth the official staff in his left hand, he laid his right upon the shoulder of a young woman, whom he thus drew forward until, on the threshold of the prison-door, she repelled him, by an action marked with natural dignity and force of character, and stepped into the open air, as if by her own free-will. She bore in her arms a child, a baby of some three months old, who winked and turned aside its little face from the too vivid light of day; because its existence, heretofore, had brought it acquainted only with the gray twilight of a dungeon, or other darksome apartment of the prison.

When the young woman—the mother of this child—stood fully revealed before the crowd, it seemed to be her first impulse to clasp the infant closely to her bosom; not so much by an impulse of motherly affection, as that she might thereby conceal a certain token, which was wrought or fastened into her dress. In a moment, however, wisely judging that one token of her shame would but poorly serve to hide another, she took the baby on her arm, and, with a burning blush, and yet a haughty smile, and a glance that would not be abashed, looked around at her townspeople and neighbours. On the breast of her gown, in fine red cloth, surrounded with an elaborate embroidery and fantastic flourishes of gold thread, appeared the letter A. It was so artistically done, and with so much fertility and gorgeous luxuriance of fancy, that it had all the effect of a last and fitting decoration to the apparel which she wore; and which was of a splendor in accordance with the taste of the age, but greatly beyond what was allowed by the sumptuary regulations[15] of the colony.

The young woman was tall, with a figure of perfect elegance, on a large scale. She had dark and abundant hair, so glossy that it threw off the sunshine with a gleam, and a face which, besides being beautiful from regularity of feature and richness of complexion, had the impressiveness belonging to a marked brow and deep black eyes. She was lady-like, too, after the manner of the feminine gentility of those days; characterized by a certain state and dignity, rather than by the delicate, evanescent, and indescribable grace, which is now recognized as its indication. And never had Hester Prynne appeared more lady-like, in the antique interpretation of the term, than as she issued from the prison. Those who had before known her, and had expected to behold her dimmed and obscured by a disastrous cloud, were astonished, and even startled, to perceive how her beauty shone out, and made a halo of the misfortune and ignominy in

---

[15]SUMPTUARY REGULATIONS: Sumptuary laws restricted excessive spending on clothing, food, and equipage in order to preserve religious decorum and class distinctions.

which she was enveloped. It may be true, that, to a sensitive observer, there was something exquisitely painful in it. Her attire, which, indeed, she had wrought for the occasion, in prison, and had modelled much after her own fancy, seemed to express the attitude of her spirit, the desperate reck-lessness of her mood, by its wild and picturesque peculiarity. But the point which drew all eyes, and, as it were, transfigured the wearer,—so that both men and women, who had been familiarly acquainted with Hester Prynne, were now impressed as if they beheld her for the first time,—was that SCARLET LETTER, so fantastically embroidered and illuminated upon her bosom. It had the effect of a spell, taking her out of the ordinary rela-tions with humanity, and inclosing her in a sphere by herself.

"She hath good skill at her needle, that's certain," remarked one of the female spectators; "but did ever a woman, before this brazen hussy, contrive such a way of showing it! Why, gossips, what is it but to laugh in the faces of our godly magistrates, and make a pride out of what they, worthy gentlemen, meant for a punishment?"

"It were well," muttered the most iron-visaged of the old dames, "if we stripped Madam Hester's rich gown off her dainty shoulders; and as for the red letter, which she hath stitched so curiously, I'll bestow a rag of mine own rheumatic flannel, to make a fitter one!"

"O, peace, neighbours, peace!" whispered their youngest companion. "Do not let her hear you! Not a stitch in that embroidered letter, but she has felt it in her heart."

The grim beadle now made a gesture with his staff.

"Make way, good people, make way, in the King's name," cried he. "Open a passage; and, I promise ye, Mistress Prynne shall be set where man, woman, and child may have a fair sight of her brave apparel, from this time till an hour past meridian. A blessing on the righteous Colony of the Massachusetts, where iniquity is dragged out into the sunshine! Come along, Madam Hester, and show your scarlet letter in the market-place!"

A lane was forthwith opened through the crowd of spectators. Preceded by the beadle, and attended by an irregular procession of stern-browed men and unkindly-visaged women, Hester Prynne set forth towards the place appointed for her punishment. A crowd of eager and curious schoolboys, understanding little of the matter in hand, except that it gave them a half-holiday, ran before her progress, turning their heads continually to stare into her face, and at the winking baby in her arms, and at the ignominious[16] letter on her breast. It was no great distance, in those days, from the prison-door to the market-place. Measured by the

[16]IGNOMINIOUS: Shameful or disgraceful.

prisoner's experience, however, it might be reckoned a journey of some length; for, haughty as her demeanour was, she perchance underwent an agony from every footstep of those that thronged to see her, as if her heart had been flung into the street for them all to spurn and trample upon. In our nature, however, there is a provision, alike marvellous and merciful, that the sufferer should never know the intensity of what he endures by its present torture, but chiefly by the pang that rankles after it. With almost a serene deportment, therefore, Hester Prynne passed through this portion of her ordeal, and came to a sort of scaffold, at the western extremity of the market-place. It stood nearly beneath the eaves of Boston's earliest church, and appeared to be a fixture there.

In fact, this scaffold constituted a portion of a penal machine, which now, for two or three generations past, has been merely historical and traditionary among us, but was held, in the old time, to be as effectual an agent in the promotion of good citizenship, as ever was the guillotine among the terrorists of France.[17] It was, in short, the platform of the pillory; and above it rose the framework of that instrument of discipline, so fashioned as to confine the human head in its tight grasp, and thus hold it up to the public gaze. The very ideal of ignominy was embodied and made manifest in this contrivance of wood and iron. There can be no outrage, methinks, against our common nature,—whatever be the delinquencies of the individual,—no outrage more flagrant than to forbid the culprit to hide his face for shame; as it was the essence of this punishment to do. In Hester Prynne's instance, however, as not unfrequently in other cases, her sentence bore, that she should stand a certain time upon the platform, but without undergoing that gripe about the neck and confinement of the head, the proneness to which was the most devilish characteristic of this ugly engine. Knowing well her part, she ascended a flight of wooden steps, and was thus displayed to the surrounding multitude, at about the height of a man's shoulders above the street.

Had there been a Papist[18] among the crowd of Puritans, he might have seen in this beautiful woman, so picturesque in her attire and mien,[19] and with the infant at her bosom, an object to remind him of the image of Divine Maternity,[20] which so many illustrious painters have vied with one another to represent; something which should remind him, indeed, but only by contrast, of that sacred image of sinless motherhood, whose

[17]GUILLOTINE AMONG THE TERRORISTS OF FRANCE: A reference to the Reign of Terror (1793–1794) during the French Revolution.
[18]PAPIST: Roman Catholic.
[19]MIEN: Carriage and demeanor; air of character.
[20]DIVINE MATERNITY: The image of the Madonna and child—that is, Mary and the infant Jesus.

infant was to redeem the world. Here, there was the taint of deepest sin in the most sacred quality of human life, working such effect, that the world was only the darker for this woman's beauty, and the more lost for the infant that she had borne.

The scene was not without a mixture of awe, such as must always invest the spectacle of guilt and shame in a fellow-creature, before society shall have grown corrupt enough to smile, instead of shuddering, at it. The witnesses of Hester Prynne's disgrace had not yet passed beyond their simplicity. They were stern enough to look upon her death, had that been the sentence, without a murmur at its severity, but had none of the heartlessness of another social state, which would find only a theme for jest in an exhibition like the present. Even had there been a disposition to turn the matter into ridicule, it must have been repressed and overpowered by the solemn presence of men no less dignified than the Governor, and several of his counsellors, a judge, a general, and the ministers of the town; all of whom sat or stood in a balcony of the meeting-house, looking down upon the platform. When such personages could constitute a part of the spectacle, without risking the majesty or reverence of rank and office, it was safely to be inferred that the infliction of a legal sentence would have an earnest and effectual meaning. Accordingly, the crowd was sombre and grave. The unhappy culprit sustained herself as best a woman might, under the heavy weight of a thousand unrelenting eyes, all fastened upon her, and concentrated at her bosom. It was almost intolerable to be borne. Of an impulsive and passionate nature, she had fortified herself to encounter the stings and venomous stabs of public contumely,[21] wreaking itself in every variety of insult; but there was a quality so much more terrible in the solemn mood of the popular mind, that she longed rather to behold all those rigid countenances contorted with scornful merriment, and herself the object. Had a roar of laughter burst from the multitude,—each man, each woman, each little shrill-voiced child, contributing their individual parts,—Hester Prynne might have repaid them all with a bitter and disdainful smile. But, under the leaden infliction which it was her doom to endure, she felt, at moments, as if she must needs shriek out with the full power of her lungs, and cast herself from the scaffold down upon the ground, or else go mad at once.

Yet there were intervals when the whole scene, in which she was the most conspicuous object, seemed to vanish from her eyes, or, at least,

---

[21]CONTUMELY: Humiliation.

glimmered indistinctly before them, like a mass of imperfectly shaped and spectral images. Her mind, and especially her memory, was preternaturally active, and kept bringing up other scenes than this roughly hewn street of a little town, on the edge of the Western wilderness; other faces than were lowering upon her from beneath the brims of those steeple-crowned hats. Reminiscences, the most trifling and immaterial, passages of infancy and school-days, sports, childish quarrels, and the little domestic traits of her maiden years, came swarming back upon her, intermingled with recollections of whatever was gravest in her subsequent life; one picture precisely as vivid as another; as if all were of similar importance, or all alike a play. Possibly, it was an instinctive device of her spirit to relieve itself, by the exhibition of these phantasmagoric forms, from the cruel weight and hardness of the reality.

Be that as it might, the scaffold of the pillory[22] was a point of view that revealed to Hester Prynne the entire track along which she had been treading, since her happy infancy. Standing on that miserable eminence, she saw again her native village, in Old England, and her paternal home; a decayed house of gray stone, with a poverty-stricken aspect, but retaining a half-obliterated shield of arms over the portal, in token of antique gentility. She saw her father's face, with its bold brow, and reverend white beard, that flowed over the old-fashioned Elizabethan ruff[23]; her mother's, too, with the look of heedful and anxious love which it always wore in her remembrance, and which, even since her death, had so often laid the impediment of a gentle remonstrance in her daughter's pathway. She saw her own face, glowing with girlish beauty, and illuminating all the interior of the dusky mirror in which she had been wont to gaze at it. There she beheld another countenance, of a man well stricken in years, a pale, thin, scholar-like visage, with eyes dim and bleared by the lamp-light that had served them to pore over many ponderous books. Yet those same bleared optics had a strange, penetrating power, when it was their owner's purpose to read the human soul. This figure of the study and the cloister, as Hester Prynne's womanly fancy failed not to recall, was slightly deformed, with the left shoulder a trifle higher than the right. Next rose before her, in memory's picture-gallery, the intricate and narrow thoroughfares, the tall, gray houses, the huge cathedrals, and the public edifices, ancient in date and quaint in architecture, of a

---

[22]PILLORY: Hester stands on a wooden platform used for public punishment. The pillory itself was a stocks made of two movable boards with holes for the head and arms; it closed around an offender, restraining him while exposing his head and hands to public ridicule and insult.
[23]ELIZABETHAN RUFF: An elaborate, wide, stiff collar worn by the wealthier classes and nobility during the sixteenth and seventeenth centuries.

Continental city[24]; where a new life had awaited her, still in connection with the misshapen scholar; a new life, but feeding itself on time-worn materials, like a tuft of green moss on a crumbling wall. Lastly, in lieu of these shifting scenes, came back the rude market-place of the Puritan settlement, with all the townspeople assembled and levelling their stern regards at Hester Prynne,—yes, at herself,—who stood on the scaffold of the pillory, an infant on her arm, and the letter A, in scarlet, fantastically embroidered with gold thread, upon her bosom!

Could it be true? She clutched the child so fiercely to her breast, that it sent forth a cry; she turned her eyes downward at the scarlet letter, and even touched it with her finger, to assure herself that the infant and the shame were real. Yes!—these were her realities,—all else had vanished!

III. THE RECOGNITION

From this intense consciousness of being the object of severe and universal observation, the wearer of the scarlet letter was at length relieved by discerning, on the outskirts of the crowd, a figure which irresistibly took possession of her thoughts. An Indian, in his native garb, was standing there; but the red men were not so infrequent visitors of the English settlements, that one of them would have attracted any notice from Hester Prynne, at such a time; much less would he have excluded all other objects and ideas from her mind. By the Indian's side, and evidently sustaining a companionship with him, stood a white man, clad in a strange disarray of civilized and savage costume.

He was small in stature, with a furrowed visage, which, as yet, could hardly be termed aged. There was a remarkable intelligence in his features, as of a person who had so cultivated his mental part that it could not fail to mould the physical to itself, and become manifest by unmistakable tokens. Although, by a seemingly careless arrangement of his heterogeneous garb, he had endeavoured to conceal or abate the peculiarity, it was sufficiently evident to Hester Prynne, that one of this man's shoulders rose higher than the other. Again, at the first instant of perceiving that thin visage, and the slight deformity of the figure, she pressed her infant to her bosom, with so convulsive a force that the poor babe uttered another cry of pain. But the mother did not seem to hear it.

At his arrival in the market-place, and some time before she saw him, the stranger had bent his eyes on Hester Prynne. It was carelessly, at first,

[24]CONTINENTAL CITY: Amsterdam.

like a man chiefly accustomed to look inward, and to whom external matters are of little value and import, unless they bear relation to something within his mind. Very soon, however, his look became keen and penetrative. A writhing horror twisted itself across his features, like a snake gliding swiftly over them, and making one little pause, with all its wreathed intervolutions in open sight. His face darkened with some powerful emotion, which, nevertheless, he so instantaneously controlled by an effort of his will, that, save at a single moment, its expression might have passed for calmness. After a brief space, the convulsion grew almost imperceptible, and finally subsided into the depths of his nature. When he found the eyes of Hester Prynne fastened on his own, and saw that she appeared to recognize him, he slowly and calmly raised his finger, made a gesture with it in the air, and laid it on his lips.

Then, touching the shoulder of a townsman who stood near to him, he addressed him in a formal and courteous manner.

"I pray you, good Sir," said he, "who is this woman?—and wherefore is she here set up to public shame?"

"You must needs be a stranger in this region, friend," answered the townsman, looking curiously at the questioner and his savage companion; "else you would surely have heard of Mistress Hester Prynne, and her evil doings. She hath raised a great scandal, I promise you, in godly Master Dimmesdale's church."

"You say truly," replied the other. "I am a stranger, and have been a wanderer, sorely against my will. I have met with grievous mishaps by sea and land, and have been long held in bonds among the heathen-folk, to the southward; and am now brought hither by this Indian, to be redeemed out of my captivity. Will it please you, therefore, to tell me of Hester Prynne's,—have I her name rightly?—of this woman's offences, and what has brought her to yonder scaffold?"

"Truly, friend, and methinks it must gladden your heart, after your troubles and sojourn in the wilderness," said the townsman, "to find yourself, at length, in a land where iniquity is searched out, and punished in the sight of rulers and people; as here in our godly New England. Yonder woman, Sir, you must know, was the wife of a certain learned man, English by birth, but who had long dwelt in Amsterdam, whence, some good time agone, he was minded to cross over and cast in his lot with us of the Massachusetts. To this purpose, he sent his wife before him, remaining himself to look after some necessary affairs. Marry, good Sir, in some two years, or less, that the woman has been a dweller here in Boston, no tidings have come of this learned gentleman, Master Prynne; and his young wife, look you, being left to her own misguidance—"

"Ah!—aha!—I conceive you,"[25] said the stranger with a bitter smile. "So learned a man as you speak of should have learned this too in his books. And who, by your favor, Sir, may be the father of yonder babe— it is some three or four months old, I should judge—which Mistress Prynne is holding in her arms?"

"Of a truth, friend, that matter remaineth a riddle; and the Daniel who shall expound it is yet a-wanting,"[26] answered the townsman. "Madam Hester absolutely refuseth to speak, and the magistrates have laid their heads together in vain. Peradventure the guilty one stands looking on at this sad spectacle, unknown of man, and forgetting that God sees him."

"The learned man," observed the stranger, with another smile, "should come himself to look into the mystery."

"It behooves him well, if he be still in life," responded the towns-man. "Now, good Sir, our Massachusetts magistracy, bethinking them-selves that this woman is youthful and fair, and doubtless was strongly tempted to her fall;—and that, moreover, as is most likely, her husband may be at the bottom of the sea;—they have not been bold to put in force the extremity of our righteous law against her. The penalty thereof is death. But, in their great mercy and tenderness of heart, they have doomed Mistress Prynne to stand only a space of three hours on the plat-form of the pillory, and then and thereafter, for the remainder of her nat-ural life, to wear a mark of shame upon her bosom."

"A wise sentence," remarked the stranger, gravely bowing his head. "Thus she will be a living sermon against sin, until the ignominious let-ter be engraved upon her tombstone. It irks me, nevertheless, that the partner of her iniquity should not, at least, stand on the scaffold by her side. But he will be known!—he will be known!—he will be known!"

He bowed courteously to the communicative townsman, and, whis-pering a few words to his Indian attendant, they both made their way through the crowd.

While this passed, Hester Prynne had been standing on her pedestal, still with a fixed gaze towards the stranger; so fixed a gaze, that, at moments of intense absorption, all other objects in the visible world seemed to vanish, leaving only him and her. Such an interview, perhaps, would have been more terrible than even to meet him as she now did, with the hot, mid-day sun burning down upon her face, and lighting up its shame; with the scarlet token of infamy on her breast; with the sin-born

---

[25]I CONCEIVE YOU: I understand you.
[26]THE DANIEL WHO SHALL EXPOUND IT IS YET A-WANTING: A reference to the biblical prophet Daniel, who interpreted the mysterious handwriting on the wall during the great feast at Belshazzar's palace, as described in Daniel 5.

infant in her arms; with a whole people, drawn forth as to a festival, staring at the features that should have been seen only in the quiet gleam of the fireside, in the happy shadow of a home, or beneath a matronly veil, at church. Dreadful as it was, she was conscious of a shelter in the presence of these thousand witnesses. It was better to stand thus, with so many betwixt him and her, than to greet him, face to face, they two alone. She fled for refuge, as it were, to the public exposure, and dreaded the moment when its protection should be withdrawn from her. Involved in these thoughts, she scarcely heard a voice behind her, until it had repeated her name more than once, in a loud and solemn tone, audible to the whole multitude.

"Hearken unto me, Hester Prynne!" said the voice.

It has already been noticed, that directly over the platform on which Hester Prynne stood was a kind of balcony, or open gallery, appended to the meeting-house. It was the place whence proclamations were wont to be made, amidst an assemblage of the magistracy, with all the ceremonial that attended such public observances in those days. Here, to witness the scene which we are describing, sat Governor Bellingham[27] himself, with four sergeants about his chair, bearing halberds,[28] as a guard of honor. He wore a dark feather in his hat, a border of embroidery on his cloak, and a black velvet tunic beneath; a gentleman advanced in years, and with a hard experience written in his wrinkles. He was not ill fitted to be the head and representative of a community, which owed its origin and progress, and its present state of development, not to the impulses of youth, but to the stern and tempered energies of manhood, and the sombre sagacity of age; accomplishing so much, precisely because it imagined and hoped so little. The other eminent characters, by whom the chief ruler was surrounded, were distinguished by a dignity of mien, belonging to a period when the forms of authority were felt to possess the sacredness of divine institutions. They were, doubtless, good men, just, and sage. But, out of the whole human family, it would not have been easy to select the same number of wise and virtuous persons, who should be less capable of sitting in judgment on an erring woman's heart, and disentangling its mesh of good and evil, than the sages of rigid aspect towards whom Hester Prynne now turned her face. She seemed conscious, indeed, that whatever sympathy she might expect lay in the larger and warmer heart of

---

27GOVERNOR BELLINGHAM: Richard Bellingham (1592–1672), the governor of Massachusetts Bay Colony in 1641, 1654, and 1665–1672.
28HALBERDS: A military weapon used in the fifteenth and sixteenth centuries; it resembled a combination spear and battleaxe and was mounted on a handle five to seven feet long.

the multitude; for, as she lifted her eyes towards the balcony, the unhappy woman grew pale and trembled.

The voice which had called her attention was that of the reverend and famous John Wilson,[29] the eldest clergyman of Boston, a great scholar, like most of his contemporaries in the profession, and withal a man of kind and genial spirit. This last attribute, however, had been less carefully developed than his intellectual gifts, and was, in truth, rather a matter of shame than self-congratulation with him. There he stood, with a border of grizzled locks beneath his skull-cap; while his gray eyes, accustomed to the shaded light of his study, were winking, like those of Hester's infant, in the unadulterated sunshine. He looked like the darkly engraved portraits which we see prefixed to old volumes of sermons; and had no more right than one of those portraits would have, to step forth, as he now did, and meddle with a question of human guilt, passion, and anguish.

"Hester Prynne," said the clergyman, "I have striven with my young brother here, under whose preaching of the word you have been privileged to sit,"—here Mr. Wilson laid his hand on the shoulder of a pale young man beside him,—"I have sought, I say, to persuade this godly youth, that he should deal with you, here in the face of Heaven, and before these wise and upright rulers, and in hearing of all the people, as touching the vileness and blackness of your sin. Knowing your natural temper better than I, he could the better judge what arguments to use, whether of tenderness or terror, such as might prevail over your hardness and obstinacy; insomuch that you should no longer hide the name of him who tempted you to this grievous fall. But he opposes to me, (with a young man's oversoftness, albeit wise beyond his years,) that it were wronging the very nature of woman to force her to lay open her heart's secrets in such broad daylight, and in presence of so great a multitude. Truly, as I sought to convince him, the shame lay in the commission of the sin, and not in the showing of it forth. What say you to it, once again, brother Dimmesdale? Must it be thou or I that shall deal with this poor sinner's soul?"

There was a murmur among the dignified and reverend occupants of the balcony; and Governor Bellingham gave expression to its purport, speaking in an authoritative voice, although tempered with respect towards the youthful clergyman whom he addressed.

"Good Master Dimmesdale," said he, "the responsibility of this woman's soul lies greatly with you. It behooves you, therefore, to exhort her to repentance, and to confession, as a proof and consequence thereof."

---

[29]JOHN WILSON: A Congregational minister (1591–1667) who settled in Boston in the 1630s.

The directness of this appeal drew the eyes of the whole crowd upon the Reverend Mr. Dimmesdale; a young clergyman, who had come from one of the great English universities, bringing all the learning of the age into our wild forest-land. His eloquence and religious fervor had already given the earnest of high eminence in his profession. He was a person of very striking aspect, with a white, lofty, and impending brow, large, brown, melancholy eyes, and a mouth which, unless when he forcibly compressed it, was apt to be tremulous, expressing both nervous sensibility and a vast power of self-restraint. Notwithstanding his high native gifts and scholar-like attainments, there was an air about this young minister,—an apprehensive, a startled, a half-frightened look,—as of a being who felt himself quite astray and at a loss in the pathway of human existence, and could only be at ease in some seclusion of his own. Therefore, so far as his duties would permit, he trode in the shadowy by-paths, and thus kept himself simple and childlike; coming forth, when occasion was, with a freshness, and fragrance, and dewy purity of thought, which, as many people said, affected them like the speech of an angel.

Such was the young man whom the Reverend Mr. Wilson and the Governor had introduced so openly to the public notice, bidding him speak, in the hearing of all men, to that mystery of a woman's soul, so sacred even in its pollution. The trying nature of his position drove the blood from his cheek, and made his lips tremulous.

"Speak to the woman, my brother," said Mr. Wilson. "It is of moment to her soul, and therefore, as the worshipful Governor says, momentous to thine own, in whose charge hers is. Exhort her to confess the truth!"

The Reverend Mr. Dimmesdale bent his head, in silent prayer, as it seemed, and then came forward.

"Hester Prynne," said he, leaning over the balcony, and looking down stedfastly into her eyes, "thou hearest what this good man says, and seest the accountability under which I labor. If thou feelest it to be for thy soul's peace, and that thy earthly punishment will thereby be made more effectual to salvation, I charge thee to speak out the name of thy fellow-sinner and fellow-sufferer! Be not silent from any mistaken pity and tenderness for him; for, believe me, Hester, though he were to step down from a high place, and stand there beside thee, on thy pedestal of shame, yet better were it so, than to hide a guilty heart through life. What can thy silence do for him, except it tempt him—yea, compel him, as it were—to add hypocrisy to sin? Heaven hath granted thee an open ignominy, that thereby thou mayest work out an open triumph over the evil within thee, and the sorrow without. Take heed how thou deniest to him—who, perchance, hath not the courage to grasp it for himself—the bitter, but wholesome, cup that is now presented to thy lips!"

The young pastor's voice was tremulously sweet, rich, deep, and broken. The feeling that it so evidently manifested, rather than the direct purport of the words, caused it to vibrate within all hearts, and brought the listeners into one accord of sympathy. Even the poor baby, at Hester's bosom, was affected by the same influence; for it directed its hitherto vacant gaze towards Mr. Dimmesdale, and held up its little arms, with a half pleased, half plaintive murmur. So powerful seemed the minister's appeal, that the people could not believe but that Hester Prynne would speak out the guilty name; or else that the guilty one himself, in whatever high or lowly place he stood, would be drawn forth by an inward and inevitable necessity, and compelled to ascend the scaffold.

Hester shook her head.

"Woman, transgress not beyond the limits of Heaven's mercy!" cried the Reverend Mr. Wilson, more harshly than before. "That little babe hath been gifted with a voice, to second and confirm the counsel which thou hast heard. Speak out the name! That, and thy repentance, may avail to take the scarlet letter off thy breast."

"Never!" replied Hester Prynne, looking, not at Mr. Wilson, but into the deep and troubled eyes of the younger clergyman. "It is too deeply branded. Ye cannot take it off. And would that I might endure his agony, as well as mine!"

"Speak, woman!" said another voice, coldly and sternly, proceeding from the crowd about the scaffold. "Speak; and give your child a father!"

"I will not speak!" answered Hester, turning pale as death, but responding to this voice, which she too surely recognized. "And my child must seek a heavenly Father; she shall never know an earthly one!"

"She will not speak!" murmured Mr. Dimmesdale, who, leaning over the balcony, with his hand upon his heart, had awaited the result of his appeal. He now drew back, with a long respiration. "Wondrous strength and generosity of a woman's heart! She will not speak!"

Discerning the impracticable state of the poor culprit's mind, the elder clergyman, who had carefully prepared himself for the occasion, addressed to the multitude a discourse on sin, in all its branches, but with continual reference to the ignominious letter. So forcibly did he dwell upon this symbol, for the hour or more during which his periods were rolling over the people's heads, that it assumed new terrors in their imagination, and seemed to derive its scarlet hue from the flames of the infernal pit. Hester Prynne, meanwhile, kept her place upon the pedestal of shame, with glazed eyes, and an air of weary indifference. She had borne, that morning, all that nature could endure; and as her temperament was not of the order that escapes from too intense suffering by a swoon, her spirit could only shelter itself beneath a stony crust of insensibility, while the faculties of animal life remained entire. In this state, the voice of the preacher thundered remorselessly, but unavailingly, upon her ears. The infant, during the latter portion of her ordeal, pierced the air with its wailings and screams; she strove to hush it, mechanically, but seemed scarcely to sympathize with its trouble. With the same hard demeanour, she was led back to prison, and vanished from the public gaze within its iron-clamped portal. It was whispered, by those who peered after her, that the scarlet letter threw a lurid gleam along the dark passage-way of the interior.

IV. The Interview

After her return to the prison, Hester Prynne was found to be in a state of nervous excitement that demanded constant watchfulness, lest she should perpetrate violence on herself, or do some half-frenzied mischief to the poor babe. As night approached, it proving impossible to quell her insubordination by rebuke or threats of punishment, Master Brackett, the jailer, thought fit to introduce a physician. He described him as a man of skill in all Christian modes of physical science, and likewise familiar with whatever the savage people could teach, in respect to medicinal herbs and roots that grew in the forest. To say the truth, there was much need of professional assistance, not merely for Hester herself, but still more urgently for the child; who, drawing its sustenance from the maternal bosom, seemed to have drank in with it all the turmoil, the anguish, and despair, which pervaded the mother's system. It now writhed in convulsions of pain, and was a forcible type, in its little frame, of the moral agony which Hester Prynne had borne throughout the day.

Closely following the jailer into the dismal apartment, appeared that individual, of singular aspect, whose presence in the crowd had been of such deep interest to the wearer of the scarlet letter. He was lodged in the prison, not as suspected of any offence, but as the most convenient and suitable mode of disposing of him, until the magistrates should have conferred with the Indian sagamores[30] respecting his ransom. His name was announced as Roger Chillingworth. The jailer, after ushering him into the room, remained a moment, marvelling at the comparative quiet that

[30]SAGAMORES: Chiefs.

followed his entrance; for Hester Prynne had immediately become as still as death, although the child continued to moan.

"Prithee, friend, leave me alone with my patient," said the practitioner. "Trust me, good jailer, you shall briefly have peace in your house; and, I promise you, Mistress Prynne shall hereafter be more amenable to just authority than you may have found her heretofore."

"Nay, if your worship can accomplish that," answered Master Brackett, "I shall own you for a man of skill indeed! Verily, the woman hath been like a possessed one; and there lacks little, that I should take in hand to drive Satan out of her with stripes."[31]

The stranger had entered the room with the characteristic quietude of the profession to which he announced himself as belonging. Nor did his demeanour change, when the withdrawal of the prison-keeper left him face to face with the woman, whose absorbed notice of him, in the crowd, had intimated so close a relation between himself and her. His first care was given to the child; whose cries, indeed, as she lay writhing on the trundle-bed, made it of peremptory necessity to postpone all other business to the task of soothing her. He examined the infant carefully, and then proceeded to unclasp a leathern case, which he took from beneath his dress. It appeared to contain certain medical preparations, one of which he mingled with a cup of water.

"My old studies in alchemy,"[32] observed he, "and my sojourn, for above a year past, among a people well versed in the kindly properties of simples, have made a better physician of me than many that claim the medical degree. Here, woman! The child is yours,—she is none of mine,—neither will she recognize my voice or aspect as a father's. Administer this draught,[33] therefore, with thine own hand."

Hester repelled the offered medicine, at the same time gazing with strongly marked apprehension into his face.

"Wouldst thou avenge thyself on the innocent babe?" whispered she.

"Foolish woman!" responded the physician, half coldly, half soothingly. "What should ail me to harm this misbegotten and miserable babe? The medicine is potent for good; and were it my child,—yea, mine own, as well as thine!—I could do no better for it."

As she still hesitated, being, in fact, in no reasonable state of mind, he took the infant in his arms, and himself administered the draught. It soon proved its efficacy, and redeemed the leech's[34] pledge. The moans

---

[31]STRIPES: Welts raised by a whip, usually across the back.
[32]ALCHEMY: The chemistry applied to the pursuit of the tranforming base metals such as lead into gold.
[33]DRAUGHT: A dose of liquid medicine.
[34]LEECH'S: A slang term for a physician, referring to the old practice of bloodletting to treat illness.

of the little patient subsided; its convulsive tossings gradually ceased; and in a few moments, as is the custom of young children after relief from pain, it sank into a profound and dewy slumber. The physician, as he had a fair right to be termed, next bestowed his attention on the mother. With calm and intent scrutiny, he felt her pulse, looked into her eyes,—a gaze that made her heart shrink and shudder, because so familiar, and yet so strange and cold,—and, finally, satisfied with his investigation, proceeded to mingle another draught.

"I know not Lethe[35] nor Nepenthe,"[36] remarked he; "but I have learned many new secrets in the wilderness, and here is one of them,—a recipe that an Indian taught me, in requital of some lessons of my own, that were as old as Paracelsus.[37] Drink it! It may be less soothing than a sinless conscience. That I cannot give thee. But it will calm the swell and heaving of thy passion, like oil thrown on the waves of a tempestuous sea."

He presented the cup to Hester, who received it with a slow, earnest look into his face; not precisely a look of fear, yet full of doubt and questioning, as to what his purposes might be. She looked also at her slumbering child.

"I have thought of death," said she,—"have wished for it,—would even have prayed for it, were it fit that such as I should pray for any thing. Yet, if death be in this cup, I bid thee think again, ere thou beholdest me quaff[38] it. See! it is even now at my lips."

"Drink, then," replied he, still with the same cold composure. "Dost thou know me so little, Hester Prynne? Are my purposes wont to be so shallow? Even if I imagine a scheme of vengeance, what could I do better for my object than to let thee live,—than to give thee medicines against all harm and peril of life,—so that this burning shame may still blaze upon thy bosom?"—As he spoke, he laid his long forefinger on the scarlet letter, which forthwith seemed to scorch into Hester's breast, as if it had been red-hot. He noticed her involuntary gesture, and smiled.—"Live, therefore, and bear about thy doom with thee, in the eyes of men and women,—in the eyes of him whom thou didst call thy husband,—in the eyes of yonder child! And, that thou mayest live, take off this draught."

Without further expostulation[39] or delay, Hester Prynne drained the cup, and, at the motion of the man of skill, seated herself on the bed

---

[35]LETHE: In Greek myth, one of the rivers flowing through the underworld. Also called the River of Oblivion, its waters helped the spirits of the dead forget their past lives on earth.
[36]NEPENTHE: An ancient sedative drink (perhaps opium) used to bring forgetfulness of trouble or grief, or to dull pain.
[37]PARACELSUS: Philippus Aureolus Paracelsus (c. 1493–1541), a Swiss physician and alchemist.
[38]QUAFF: Drink deeply; gulp.
[39]EXPOSTULATION: Argument.

where the child was sleeping; while he drew the only chair which the room afforded, and took his own seat beside her. She could not but tremble at these preparations; for she felt that—having now done all that humanity, or principle, or, if so it were, a refined cruelty, impelled him to do, for the relief of physical suffering—he was next to treat with her as the man whom she had most deeply and irreparably injured.

"Hester," said he, "I ask not wherefore, nor how, thou hast fallen into the pit, or say rather, thou hast ascended to the pedestal of infamy, on which I found thee. The reason is not far to seek. It was my folly, and thy weakness. I,—a man of thought,—the book-worm of great libraries,—a man already in decay, having given my best years to feed the hungry dream of knowledge,—what had I to do with youth and beauty like thine own! Misshapen from my birth-hour, how could I delude myself with the idea that intellectual gifts might veil physical deformity in a young girl's fantasy! Men call me wise. If sages were ever wise in their own behoof, I might have foreseen all this. I might have known that, as I came out of the vast and dismal forest, and entered this settlement of Christian men, the very first object to meet my eyes would be thyself, Hester Prynne, standing up, a statue of ignominy, before the people. Nay, from the moment when we came down the old church-steps together, a married pair, I might have beheld the bale-fire of that scarlet letter blazing at the end of our path!"

"Thou knowest," said Hester,—for, depressed as she was, she could not endure this last quiet stab at the token of her shame,—"thou knowest that I was frank with thee. I felt no love, nor feigned any."

"True!" replied he. "It was my folly! I have said it. But, up to that epoch of my life, I had lived in vain. The world had been so cheerless! My heart was a habitation large enough for many guests, but lonely and chill, and without a household fire. I longed to kindle one! It seemed not so wild a dream,—old as I was, and sombre as I was, and misshapen as I was,—that the simple bliss, which is scattered far and wide, for all mankind to gather up, might yet be mine. And so, Hester, I drew thee into my heart, into its innermost chamber, and sought to warm thee by the warmth which thy presence made there!"

"I have greatly wronged thee," murmured Hester.

"We have wronged each other," answered he. "Mine was the first wrong, when I betrayed thy budding youth into a false and unnatural relation with my decay. Therefore, as a man who has not thought and philosophized in vain, I seek no vengeance, plot no evil against thee. Between thee and me, the scale hangs fairly balanced. But, Hester, the man lives who has wronged us both! Who is he?"

"Ask me not!" replied Hester Prynne, looking firmly into his face. "That thou shalt never know!"

"Never, sayest thou?" rejoined he, with a smile of dark and self-relying intelligence. "Never know him! Believe me, Hester, there are few things,—whether in the outward world, or, to a certain depth, in the invisible sphere of thought,—few things hidden from the man, who devotes himself earnestly and unreservedly to the solution of a mystery. Thou mayest cover up thy secret from the prying multitude. Thou mayest conceal it, too, from the ministers and magistrates, even as thou didst this day, when they sought to wrench the name out of thy heart, and give thee a partner on thy pedestal. But, as for me, I come to the inquest with other senses than they possess. I shall seek this man, as I have sought truth in books; as I have sought gold in alchemy. There is a sympathy that will make me conscious of him. I shall see him tremble. I shall feel myself shudder, suddenly and unawares. Sooner or later, he must needs be mine!"

The eyes of the wrinkled scholar glowed so intensely upon her, that Hester Prynne clasped her hands over her heart, dreading lest he should read the secret there at once.

"Thou wilt not reveal his name? Not the less he is mine," resumed he, with a look of confidence, as if destiny were at one with him. "He bears no letter of infamy wrought into his garment, as thou dost; but I shall read it on his heart. Yet fear not for him! Think not that I shall interfere with Heaven's own method of retribution, or, to my own loss, betray him to the gripe of human law. Neither do thou imagine that I shall contrive aught against his life; no, nor against his fame, if, as I judge, he be a man of fair repute. Let him live! Let him hide himself in outward honor, if he may! Not the less he shall be mine!"

"Thy acts are like mercy," said Hester, bewildered and appalled. "But thy words interpret thee as a terror!"

"One thing, thou that wast my wife, I would enjoin upon thee," continued the scholar. "Thou hast kept the secret of thy paramour.[40] Keep, likewise, mine! There are none in this land that know me. Breathe not, to any human soul, that thou didst ever call me husband! Here, on this wild outskirt of the earth, I shall pitch my tent; for, elsewhere a wanderer, and isolated from human interests, I find here a woman, a man, a child, amongst whom and myself there exist the closest ligaments. No matter whether of love or hate; no matter whether of right or wrong! Thou and thine, Hester Prynne, belong to me. My home is where thou art, and where he is. But betray me not!"

[40]PARAMOUR: Lover.

"Wherefore dost thou desire it?" inquired Hester, shrinking, she hardly knew why, from this secret bond. "Why not announce thyself openly, and cast me off at once?"

"It may be," he replied, "because I will not encounter the dishonor that besmirches the husband of a faithless woman. It may be for other reasons. Enough, it is my purpose to live and die unknown. Let, therefore, thy husband be to the world as one already dead, and of whom no tidings shall ever come. Recognize me not, by word, by sign, by look! Breathe not the secret, above all, to the man thou wottest[41] of. Shouldst thou fail me in this, beware! His fame, his position, his life, will be in my hands. Beware!"

"I will keep thy secret, as I have his," said Hester.

"Swear it!" rejoined he.

And she took the oath.

"And now, Mistress Prynne," said old Roger Chillingworth, as he was hereafter to be named, "I leave thee alone; alone with thy infant, and the scarlet letter! How is it, Hester? Doth thy sentence bind thee to wear the token in thy sleep? Art thou not afraid of nightmares and hideous dreams?"

"Why dost thou smile so at me?" inquired Hester, troubled at the expression of his eyes. "Art thou like the Black Man that haunts the forest[42] round about us? Hast thou enticed me into a bond that will prove the ruin of my soul?"

"Not thy soul," he answered, with another smile. "No, not thine!"

V. Hester at Her Needle

Hester Prynne's term of confinement was now at an end. Her prison-door was thrown open, and she came forth into the sunshine, which, falling on all alike, seemed, to her sick and morbid heart, as if meant for no other purpose than to reveal the scarlet letter on her breast. Perhaps there was a more real torture in her first unattended footsteps from the threshold of the prison, than even in the procession and spectacle that have been described, where she was made the common infamy, at which all mankind was summoned to point its finger. Then, she was supported by an unnatural tension of the nerves, and by all the combative energy of her character, which enabled her to convert the scene into a kind of lurid triumph. It was, moreover, a separate and insulated event, to occur

[41]WOTTEST: Knowest.
[42]ART THOU LIKE THE BLACK MAN THAT HAUNTS THE FOREST: The Puritans often referred to the Devil as a "Black Man" who roamed the forest with a great book in which converts to sin signed their names. See Hawthorne's "Young Goodman Brown" for details.

but once in her lifetime, and to meet which, therefore, reckless of economy, she might call up the vital strength that would have sufficed for many quiet years. The very law that condemned her—a giant of stern features, but with vigor to support, as well as to annihilate, in his iron arm—had held her up, through the terrible ordeal of her ignominy. But now, with this unattended walk from her prison-door, began the daily custom, and she must either sustain and carry it forward by the ordinary resources of her nature, or sink beneath it. She could no longer borrow from the future, to help her through the present grief. To-morrow would bring its own trial with it; so would the next day, and so would the next; each its own trial, and yet the very same that was now so unutterably grievous to be borne. The days of the far-off future would toil onward, still with the same burden for her to take up, and bear along with her, but never to fling down; for the accumulating days, and added years, would pile up their misery upon the heap of shame. Throughout them all, giving up her individuality, she would become the general symbol at which the preacher and moralist might point, and in which they might vivify and embody their images of woman's frailty and sinful passion. Thus the young and pure would be taught to look at her, with the scarlet letter flaming on her breast,—at her, the child of honorable parents,—at her, the mother of a babe, that would hereafter be a woman,— at her, who had once been innocent,—as the figure, the body, the reality of sin. And over her grave, the infamy that she must carry thither would be her only monument.

It may seem marvellous, that, with the world before her,—kept by no restrictive clause of her condemnation within the limits of the Puritan settlement, so remote and so obscure,—free to return to her birthplace, or to any other European land, and there hide her character and identity under a new exterior, as completely as if emerging into another state of being,—and having also the passes of the dark, inscrutable forest open to her, where the wildness of her nature might assimilate itself with a people whose customs and life were alien from the law that had condemned her,—it may seem marvellous, that this woman should still call that place her home, where, and where only, she must needs be the type of shame. But there is a fatality, a feeling so irresistible and inevitable that it has the force of doom, which almost invariably compels human beings to linger around and haunt, ghost-like, the spot where some great and marked event has given the color to their lifetime; and still the more irresistibly, the darker the tinge that saddens it. Her sin, her ignominy, were the roots which she had struck into the soil. It was as if a new birth, with stronger assimilations than the first, had converted the forest-land, still so uncongenial to every other pilgrim and wanderer, into Hester Prynne's wild and dreary, but life-long home. All other scenes of earth—even that village of rural England, where happy infancy and stainless maidenhood seemed yet to be in her mother's keeping, like garments put off long ago—were foreign to her, in comparison. The chain that bound her here was of iron links, and galling to her inmost soul, but could never be broken.

It might be, too,—doubtless it was so, although she hid the secret from herself, and grew pale whenever it struggled out of her heart, like a serpent from its hole,—it might be that another feeling kept her within the scene and pathway that had been so fatal. There dwelt, there trode the feet of one with whom she deemed herself connected in a union, that, unrecognized on earth, would bring them together before the bar of final judgment, and make that their marriage-altar, for a joint futurity of endless retribution. Over and over again, the tempter of souls had thrust this idea upon Hester's contemplation, and laughed at the passionate and desperate joy with which she seized, and then strove to cast it from her. She barely looked the idea in the face, and hastened to bar it in its dungeon. What she compelled herself to believe,—what, finally, she reasoned upon, as her motive for continuing a resident of New England,—was half a truth, and half a self-delusion. Here, she said to herself, had been the scene of her guilt, and here should be the scene of her earthly punishment; and so, perchance, the torture of her daily shame would at length purge her soul, and work out another purity than that which she had lost; more saint-like, because the result of martyrdom.

Hester Prynne, therefore, did not flee. On the outskirts of the town, within the verge of the peninsula, but not in close vicinity to any other habitation, there was a small thatched cottage. It had been built by an earlier settler, and abandoned, because the soil about it was too sterile for cultivation, while its comparative remoteness put it out of the sphere of that social activity which already marked the habits of the emigrants. It stood on the shore, looking across a basin of the sea at the forest-covered hills, towards the west. A clump of scrubby trees, such as alone grew on the peninsula, did not so much conceal the cottage from view, as seem to denote that here was some object which would fain have been, or at least ought to be, concealed. In this little, lonesome dwelling, with some slender means that she possessed, and by the license of the magistrates, who still kept an inquisitorial watch over her, Hester established herself, with her infant child. A mystic shadow of suspicion immediately attached itself to the spot. Children, too young to comprehend wherefore this woman should be shut out from the sphere of human charities, would creep nigh enough to behold her plying her needle at the cottage-window, or standing in the door-way, or laboring in her little garden, or coming forth along the pathway that led townward; and, discerning the scarlet letter on her breast, would scamper off, with a strange, contagious fear.

Lonely as was Hester's situation, and without a friend on earth who dared to show himself, she, however, incurred no risk of want. She possessed an art that sufficed, even in a land that afforded comparatively little scope for its exercise, to supply food for her thriving infant and herself. It was the art—then, as now, almost the only one within a woman's grasp—of needle-work. She bore on her breast, in the curiously embroidered letter, a specimen of her delicate and imaginative skill, of which the dames of a court might gladly have availed themselves, to add the richer and more spiritual adornment of human ingenuity to their fabrics of silk and gold. Here, indeed, in the sable simplicity that generally characterized the Puritanic modes of dress, there might be an infrequent call for the finer productions of her handiwork. Yet the taste of the age, demanding whatever was elaborate in compositions of this kind, did not fail to extend its influence over our stern progenitors,[43] who had cast behind them so many fashions which it might seem harder to dispense with. Public ceremonies, such as ordinations, the installation of magistrates, and all that could give majesty to the forms in which a new government manifested itself to the people, were, as a matter of policy, marked by a stately and well-conducted ceremonial, and a sombre, but yet a studied magnificence. Deep ruffs, painfully wrought bands, and gorgeously embroidered gloves, were all deemed necessary to the official state of men assuming the reins of power; and were readily allowed to individuals dignified by rank or wealth, even while sumptuary laws forbade these and similar extravagances to the plebeian[44] order. In the array of funerals, too,—whether for the apparel of the dead body, or to typify, by manifold emblematic devices of sable cloth and snowy lawn, the sorrow of the survivors,—there was a frequent and characteristic demand for such labor as Hester Prynne could supply. Baby-linen—for babies then wore robes of state—afforded still another possibility of toil and emolument.[45]

By degrees, nor very slowly, her handiwork became what would now be termed the fashion. Whether from commiseration for a woman of so miserable a destiny; or from the morbid curiosity that gives a fictitious

---

[43]PROGENITORS: Ancestors.
[44]PLEBEIAN: Common folk.
[45]EMOLUMENT: Payment for employment.

value even to common or worthless things; or by whatever other intangible circumstance was then, as now, sufficient to bestow, on some persons, what others might seek in vain; or because Hester really filled a gap which must otherwise have remained vacant; it is certain that she had ready and fairly equited employment for as many hours as she saw fit to occupy with her needle. Vanity, it may be, chose to mortify itself, by putting on, for ceremonials of pomp and state, the garments that had been wrought by her sinful hands. Her needle-work was seen on the ruff of the Governor; military men wore it on their scarfs, and the minister on his band; it decked the baby's little cap; it was shut up, to be mildewed and moulder away, in the coffins of the dead. But it is not recorded that, in a single instance, her skill was called in aid to embroider the white veil which was to cover the pure blushes of a bride. The exception indicated the ever relentless vigor with which society frowned upon her sin.

Hester sought not to acquire any thing beyond a subsistence, of the plainest and most ascetic[46] description, for herself, and a simple abundance for her child. Her own dress was of the coarsest materials and the most sombre hue; with only that one ornament,—the scarlet letter,—which it was her doom to wear. The child's attire, on the other hand, was distinguished by a fanciful, or, we may rather say, a fantastic ingenuity, which served, indeed, to heighten the airy charm that early began to develop itself in the little girl, but which appeared to have also a deeper meaning. We may speak further of it hereafter. Except for that small expenditure in the decoration of her infant, Hester bestowed all her superfluous means in charity, on wretches less miserable than herself, and who not unfrequently insulted the hand that fed them. Much of the time, which she might readily have applied to the better efforts of her art, she employed in making coarse garments for the poor. It is probable that there was an idea of penance in this mode of occupation, and that she offered up a real sacrifice of enjoyment, in devoting so many hours to such rude handiwork. She had in her nature a rich, voluptuous, Oriental characteristic,[47]—a taste for the gorgeously beautiful, which, save in the exquisite productions of her needle, found nothing else, in all the possibilities of her life, to exercise itself upon. Women derive a pleasure, incomprehensible to the other sex, from the delicate toil of the needle. To Hester Prynne it might have been a mode of expressing, and therefore soothing, the passion of her life. Like all other joys, she rejected it as sin. This morbid meddling of conscience with an immaterial matter betokened, it

[46]ASCETIC: Severely abstinent.
[47]ORIENTAL CHARACTERISTIC: Exotic.

652 • *Nathaniel Hawthorne*

is to be feared, no genuine and stedfast penitence, but something doubtful, something that might be deeply wrong beneath.

In this matter, Hester Prynne came to have a part to perform in the world. With her native energy of character, and rare capacity, it could not entirely cast her off, although it had set a mark upon her, more intolerable to a woman's heart than that which branded the brow of Cain.[48] In all her intercourse with society, however, there was nothing that made her feel as if she belonged to it. Every gesture, every word, and even the silence of those with whom she came in contact, implied, and often expressed, that she was banished, and as much alone as if she inhabited another sphere, or communicated with the common nature by other organs and senses than the rest of human kind. She stood apart from mortal interests, yet close beside them, like a ghost that revisits the familiar fireside, and can no longer make itself seen or felt; no more smile with the household joy, nor mourn with the kindred sorrow; or, should it succeed in manifesting its forbidden sympathy, awakening only terror and horrible repugnance. These emotions, in fact, and its bitterest scorn besides, seemed to be the sole portion that she retained in the universal heart. It was not an age of delicacy; and her position, although she understood it well, and was in little danger of forgetting it, was often brought before her vivid self-perception, like a new anguish, by the rudest touch upon the tenderest spot. The poor, as we have already said, whom she sought out to be the objects of her bounty, often reviled the hand that was stretched forth to succor them. Dames of elevated rank, likewise, whose doors she entered in the way of her occupation, were accustomed to distil drops of bitterness into her heart; sometimes through that alchemy of quiet malice, by which women can concoct a subtile poison from ordinary trifles; and sometimes, also, by a coarser expression, that fell upon the sufferer's defenceless breast like a rough blow upon an ulcerated wound. Hester had schooled herself long and well; she never responded to these attacks, save by a flush of crimson that rose irrepressibly over her pale cheek, and again subsided into the depths of her bosom. She was patient,—a martyr, indeed,—but she forebore to pray for enemies; lest, in spite of her forgiving aspirations, the words of the blessing should stubbornly twist themselves into a curse.

Continually, and in a thousand other ways, did she feel the innumerable throbs of anguish that had been so cunningly contrived for her by the undying, the ever-active sentence of the Puritan tribunal.

---

[48]CAIN: A reference to Genesis 4:15: "And the Lord set a mark upon Cain, lest any finding him should kill him."

Clergymen paused in the street to address words of exhortation, that brought a crowd, with its mingled grin and frown, around the poor, sinful woman. If she entered a church, trusting to share the Sabbath smile of the Universal Father, it was often her mishap to find herself the text of the discourse. She grew to have a dread of children; for they had imbibed from their parents a vague idea of something horrible in this dreary woman, gliding silently through the town, with never any companion but one only child. Therefore, first allowing her to pass, they pursued her at a distance with shrill cries, and the utterance of a word that had no distinct purport to their own minds, but was none the less terrible to her, as proceeding from lips that babbled it unconsciously. It seemed to argue so wide a diffusion of her shame, that all nature knew of it; it could have caused her no deeper pang, had the leaves of the trees whispered the dark story among themselves,—had the summer breeze murmured about it,—had the wintry blast shrieked it aloud! Another peculiar torture was felt in the gaze of a new eye. When strangers looked curiously at the scarlet letter,—and none ever failed to do so,—they branded it afresh into Hester's soul; so that, oftentimes, she could scarcely refrain, yet always did refrain, from covering the symbol with her hand. But then, again, an accustomed eye had likewise its own anguish to inflict. Its cool stare of familiarity was intolerable. From first to last, in short, Hester Prynne had always this dreadful agony in feeling a human eye upon the token; the spot never grew callous; it seemed, on the contrary, to grow more sensitive with daily torture.

But sometimes, once in many days, or perchance in many months, she felt an eye—a human eye—upon the ignominious brand, that seemed to give a momentary relief, as if half of her agony were shared. The next instant, back it all rushed again, with still a deeper throb of pain; for, in that brief interval, she had sinned anew. Had Hester sinned alone?

Her imagination was somewhat affected, and, had she been of a softer moral and intellectual fibre, would have been still more so, by the strange and solitary anguish of her life. Walking to and fro, with those lonely footsteps, in the little world with which she was outwardly connected, it now and then appeared to Hester,—if altogether fancy, it was nevertheless too potent to be resisted,—she felt or fancied, then, that the scarlet letter had endowed her with a new sense. She shuddered to believe, yet could not help believing, that it gave her a sympathetic knowledge of the hidden sin in other hearts. She was terror-stricken by the revelations that were thus made. What were they? Could they be other than the insidious whispers of the bad angel, who would fain have persuaded the struggling woman, as yet only half his victim, that the outward guise of purity was but a lie, and that, if truth were everywhere to be shown, a scarlet letter would blaze forth on many a bosom besides Hester Prynne's? Or, must she receive those intimations—so obscure, yet so distinct—as truth? In all her miserable experience, there was nothing else so awful and so loathsome as this sense. It perplexed, as well as shocked her, by the irreverent inopportuneness of the occasions that brought it into vivid action. Sometimes, the red infamy upon her breast would give a sympathetic throb, as she passed near a venerable minister or magistrate, the model of piety and justice, to whom that age of antique reverence looked up, as to a mortal man in fellowship with angels. "What evil thing is at hand?" would Hester say to herself. Lifting her reluctant eyes, there would be nothing human within the scope of view, save the form of this earthly saint! Again, a mystic sisterhood would contumaciously[49] assert itself, as she met the sanctified frown of some matron, who, according to the rumor of all tongues, had kept cold snow within her bosom throughout life. That unsunned snow in the matron's bosom, and the burning shame on Hester Prynne's,—what had the two in common? Or, once more, the electric thrill would give her warning,—"Behold, Hester, here is a companion!"—and, looking up, she would detect the eyes of a young maiden glancing at the scarlet letter, shyly and aside, and quickly averted, with a faint, chill crimson in her cheeks; as if her purity were somewhat sullied by that momentary glance. O Fiend, whose talisman[50] was that fatal symbol, wouldst thou leave nothing, whether in youth or age, for this poor sinner to revere?—Such loss of faith is ever one of the saddest results of sin. Be it accepted as a proof that all was not corrupt in this poor victim of her own frailty, and man's hard law, that Hester Prynne yet struggled to believe that no fellow-mortal was guilty like herself.

The vulgar, who, in those dreary old times, were always contributing a grotesque horror to what interested their imaginations, had a story about the scarlet letter which we might readily work up into a terrific legend. They averred, that the symbol was not mere scarlet cloth, tinged in an earthly dye-pot, but was red-hot with infernal fire, and could be seen glowing all alight, whenever Hester Prynne walked abroad in the night-time. And we must needs say, it seared Hester's bosom so deeply, that perhaps there was more truth in the rumor than our modern incredulity may be inclined to admit.

[49]CONTUMACIOUSLY: Rebelliously.
[50]TALISMAN: A charm with occult powers.

VI. PEARL

We have as yet hardly spoken of the infant; that little creature, whose innocent life had sprung, by the inscrutable decree of Providence, a lovely and immortal flower, out of the rank luxuriance of a guilty passion. How strange it seemed to the sad woman, as she watched the growth, and the beauty that became every day more brilliant, and the intelligence that threw its quivering sunshine over the tiny features of this child! Her Pearl!—For so had Hester called her; not as a name expressive of her aspect, which had nothing of the calm, white, unimpassioned lustre that would be indicated by the comparison. But she named the infant "Pearl," as being of great price,[51]—purchased with all she had,—her mother's only treasure! How strange, indeed! Man had marked this woman's sin by a scarlet letter, which had such potent and disastrous efficacy that no human sympathy could reach her, save it were sinful like herself. God, as a direct consequence of the sin which man thus punished, had given her a lovely child, whose place was on that same dishonored bosom, to connect her parent for ever with the race and descent of mortals, and to be finally a blessed soul in heaven! Yet these thoughts affected Hester Prynne less with hope than apprehension. She knew that her deed had been evil; she could have no faith, therefore, that its result would be for good. Day after day, she looked fearfully into the child's expanding nature; ever dreading to detect some dark and wild peculiarity, that should correspond with the guiltiness to which she owed her being.

Certainly, there was no physical defect. By its perfect shape, its vigor, and its natural dexterity in the use of all its untried limbs, the infant was worthy to have been brought forth in Eden[52]; worthy to have been left there, to be the plaything of the angels, after the world's first parents were driven out. The child had a native grace which does not invariably coexist with faultless beauty; its attire, however simple, always impressed the beholder as if it were the very garb that precisely became it best. But little Pearl was not clad in rustic weeds.[53] Her mother, with a morbid purpose that may be better understood hereafter, had bought the richest tissues that could be procured, and allowed her imaginative faculty its full play in the arrangement and decoration of the dresses

---

[51]AS BEING OF GREAT PRICE: A reference to Matthew 13:45–46: "Again, the kingdom of heaven is like unto a merchant man, seeking goodly pearls: / Who, when he had found one pearl of great price, went and sold all that he had, and bought it."
[52]EDEN: The Garden of Eden, the home of Adam and Eve before the fall; Paradise.
[53]RUSTIC WEEDS: Rough clothing.

which the child wore, before the public eye. So magnificent was the small figure, when thus arrayed, and such was the splendor of Pearl's own proper beauty, shining through the gorgeous robes which might have extinguished a paler loveliness, that there was an absolute circle of radiance around her, on the darksome cottage-floor. And yet a russet gown, torn and soiled with the child's rude play, made a picture of her just as perfect. Pearl's aspect was imbued with a spell of infinite variety; in this one child there were many children, comprehending the full scope between the wild-flower prettiness of a peasant-baby, and the pomp, in little, of an infant princess. Throughout all, however, there was a trait of passion, a certain depth of hue, which she never lost; and if, in any of her changes, she had grown fainter or paler, she would have ceased to be herself;—it would have been no longer Pearl!

This outward mutability indicated, and did not more than fairly express, the various properties of her inner life. Her nature appeared to possess depth, too, as well as variety; but—or else Hester's fears deceived her—it lacked reference and adaptation to the world into which she was born. The child could not be made amenable to rules. In giving her existence, a great law had been broken; and the result was a being, whose elements were perhaps beautiful and brilliant, but all in disorder; or with an order peculiar to themselves, amidst which the point of variety and arrangement was difficult or impossible to be discovered. Hester could only account for the child's character—and even then, most vaguely and imperfectly—by recalling what she herself had been, during that momentous period while Pearl was imbibing her soul from the spiritual world, and her bodily frame from its material of earth. The mother's impassioned state had been the medium through which were transmitted to the unborn infant the rays of its moral life; and, however white and clear originally, they had taken the deep stains of crimson and gold, the fiery lustre, the black shadow, and the untempered light, of the intervening substance. Above all, the warfare of Hester's spirit, at that epoch, was perpetuated in Pearl. She could recognize her wild, desperate, defiant mood, the flightiness of her temper, and even some of the very cloud-shapes of gloom and despondency that had brooded in her heart. They were now illuminated by the morning radiance of a young child's disposition, but, later in the day of earthly existence, might be prolific of the storm and whirlwind.

The discipline of the family, in those days, was of a far more rigid kind than now. The frown, the harsh rebuke, the frequent application of the rod, enjoined by Scriptural authority,[54] were used, not merely in the

---

[54]ENJOINED BY SCRIPTURAL AUTHORITY: Proverbs 13:24: "He that spareth his rod hateth his son: but he that loveth him chasteneth him betimes."

way of punishment for actual offences, but as a wholesome regimen for the growth and promotion of all childish virtues. Hester Prynne, nevertheless, the lonely mother of this one child, ran little risk of erring on the side of undue severity. Mindful, however, of her own errors and misfortunes, she early sought to impose a tender, but strict, control over the infant immortality that was committed to her charge. But the task was beyond her skill. After testing both smiles and frowns, and proving that neither mode of treatment possessed any calculable influence, Hester was ultimately compelled to stand aside, and permit the child to be swayed by her own impulses. Physical compulsion or restraint was effectual, of course, while it lasted. As to any other kind of discipline, whether addressed to her mind or heart, little Pearl might or might not be within its reach, in accordance with the caprice that ruled the moment. Her mother, while Pearl was yet an infant, grew acquainted with a certain peculiar look, that warned her when it would be labor thrown away to insist, persuade or plead. It was a look so intelligent, yet so inexplicable, perverse, sometimes so malicious, but generally accompanied by a wild flow of spirits, that Hester could not help questioning, at such moments, whether Pearl was a human child. She seemed rather an airy sprite, which, after playing its fantastic sports for a little while upon the cottage-floor, would flit away with a mocking smile. Whenever that look appeared in her wild, bright, deeply black eyes, it invested her with a strange remoteness and intangibility; it was as if she were hovering in the air and might vanish, like a glimmering light that comes we know not whence, and goes we know not whither. Beholding it, Hester was constrained to rush towards the child,—to pursue the little elf in the flight which she invariably began,—to snatch her to her bosom, with a close pressure and earnest kisses,—not so much from overflowing love, as to assure herself that Pearl was flesh and blood, and not utterly delusive. But Pearl's laugh, when she was caught, though full of merriment and music, made her mother more doubtful than before.

Heart-smitten at this bewildering and baffling spell, that so often came between herself and her sole treasure, whom she had bought so dear, and who was all her world, Hester sometimes burst into passionate tears. Then, perhaps,—for there was no foreseeing how it might affect her,—Pearl would frown, and clench her little fist, and harden her small features into a stern, unsympathizing look of discontent. Not seldom, she would laugh anew, and louder than before, like a thing incapable and unintelligent of human sorrow. Or—but this more rarely happened— she would be convulsed with a rage of grief, and sob out her love for her mother, in broken words, and seem intent on proving that she had a heart, by breaking it. Yet Hester was hardly safe in confiding herself to that gusty tenderness; it passed, as suddenly as it came. Brooding over all these matters, the mother felt like one who has evoked a spirit, but, by some irregularity in the process of conjuration, has failed to win the master-word that should control this new and incomprehensible intelligence. Her only real comfort was when the child lay in the placidity of sleep. Then she was sure of her, and tasted hours of quiet, sad, delicious happiness; until—perhaps with that perverse expression glimmering from beneath her opening lids—little Pearl awoke!

How soon—with what strange rapidity, indeed!—did Pearl arrive at an age that was capable of social intercourse beyond the mother's ever-ready smile and nonsense-words! And then what a happiness would it have been, could Hester Prynne have heard her clear, bird-like voice mingling with the uproar of other childish voices, and have distinguished and unravelled her own darling's tones, amid all the entangled outcry of a group of sportive children! But this could never be. Pearl was a born outcast of the infantile world. An imp of evil, emblem and product of sin, she had no right among christened infants. Nothing was more remarkable than the instinct, as it seemed, with which the child comprehended her loneliness; the destiny that had drawn an inviolable circle round about her; the whole peculiarity, in short, of her position in respect to other children. Never, since her release from prison, had Hester met the public gaze without her. In all her walks about the town, Pearl, too, was there; first as the babe in arms, and afterwards as the little girl, small companion of her mother, holding a forefinger with her whole grasp, and tripping along at the rate of three or four footsteps to one of Hester's. She saw the children of the settlement, on the grassy margin of the street, or at the domestic thresholds, disporting themselves in such grim fashion as the Puritanic nurture would permit; playing at going to church, perchance; or at scourging[55] Quakers; or taking scalps in a sham-fight with the Indians; or scaring one another with freaks of imitative witchcraft. Pearl saw, and gazed intently, but never sought to make acquaintance. If spoken to, she would not speak again. If the children gathered about her, as they sometimes did, Pearl would grow positively terrible in her puny wrath, snatching up stones to fling at them, with shrill, incoherent exclamations that made her mother tremble, because they had so much the sound of a witch's anathemas[56] in some unknown tongue.

[55]SCOURGING: Whipping.
[56]ANATHEMAS: Curses.

The truth was, that the little Puritans, being of the most intolerant brood that ever lived, had got a vague idea of something outlandish, unearthly, or at variance with ordinary fashions, in the mother and child; and therefore scorned them in their hearts, and not unfrequently reviled them with their tongues. Pearl felt the sentiment, and requited it with the bitterest hatred that can be supposed to rankle in a childish bosom. These outbreaks of a fierce temper had a kind of value, and even comfort, for her mother; because there was at least an intelligible earnestness in the mood, instead of the fitful caprice that so often thwarted her in the child's manifestations. It appalled her, nevertheless, to discern here, again, a shadowy reflection of the evil that had existed in herself. All this enmity and passion had Pearl inherited, by inalienable right, out of Hester's heart. Mother and daughter stood together in the same circle of seclusion from human society; and in the nature of the child seemed to be perpetuated those unquiet elements that had distracted Hester Prynne before Pearl's birth, but had since begun to be soothed away by the softening influences of maternity.

At home, within and around her mother's cottage, Pearl wanted not a wide and various circle of acquaintance. The spell of life went forth from her ever creative spirit, and communicated itself to a thousand objects, as a torch kindles a flame wherever it may be applied. The unlikeliest materials, a stick, a bunch of rags, a flower, were the puppets of Pearl's witchcraft, and, without undergoing any outward change, became spiritually adapted to whatever drama occupied the stage of her inner world. Her one baby-voice served a multitude of imaginary personages, old and young, to talk withal. The pine-trees, aged, black, and solemn, and flinging groans and other melancholy utterances on the breeze, needed little transformation to figure as Puritan elders; the ugliest weeds of the garden were their children, whom Pearl smote down and uprooted, most unmercifully. It was wonderful, the vast variety of forms into which she threw her intellect, with no continuity, indeed, but darting up and dancing, always in a state of preternatural activity,—soon sinking down, as if exhausted by so rapid and feverish a tide of life,— and succeeded by other shapes of a similar wild energy. It was like nothing so much as the phantasmagoric play of the northern lights. In the mere exercise of the fancy, however, and the sportiveness of a growing mind, there might be a little more than was observable in other children of bright faculties; except as Pearl, in the dearth of human playmates, was thrown more upon the visionary throng which she created. The singularity lay in the hostile feelings with which the child regarded all these offsprings of her own heart and mind. She never created a friend, but seemed always to be sowing broadcast the dragon's teeth,[57] whence sprung a harvest of armed enemies, against whom she rushed to battle. It was inexpressibly sad—then what depth of sorrow to a mother, who felt in her own heart the cause!—to observe, in one so young, this constant recognition of an adverse world, and so fierce a training of the energies that were to make good her cause, in the contest that must ensue.

Gazing at Pearl, Hester Prynne often dropped her work upon her knees, and cried out, with an agony which she would fain have hidden, but which made utterance for itself, betwixt speech and a groan,—"O Father in Heaven,—if Thou art still my Father,—what is this being which I have brought into the world?" And Pearl, overhearing the ejaculation, or aware, through some more subtle channel, of those throbs of anguish, would turn her vivid and beautiful little face upon her mother, smile with sprite-like intelligence, and resume her play.

One peculiarity of the child's deportment remains yet to be told. The very first thing which she had noticed, in her life, was—what?—not the mother's smile, responding to it, as other babies do, by that faint, embryo smile of the little mouth, remembered so doubtfully afterwards, and with such fond discussion whether it were indeed a smile. By no means! But that first object of which Pearl seemed to become aware was—shall we say it?—the scarlet letter on Hester's bosom! One day, as her mother stooped over the cradle, the infant's eyes had been caught by the glimmering of the gold embroidery about the letter; and, putting up her little hand, she grasped at it, smiling, not doubtfully, but with a decided gleam that gave her face the look of a much older child. Then, gasping for breath, did Hester Prynne clutch the fatal token, instinctively endeavouring to tear it away; so infinite was the torture inflicted by the intelligent touch of Pearl's baby-hand. Again, as if her mother's agonized gesture were meant only to make sport for her, did little Pearl look into her eyes, and smile! From that epoch, except when the child was asleep, Hester had never felt a moment's safety; not a moment's calm enjoyment of her. Weeks, it is true, would sometimes elapse, during which Pearl's gaze might never once be fixed upon the scarlet letter; but then, again, it would come at unawares, like the stroke of sudden death, and always with that peculiar smile, and odd expression of the eyes.

[57]SOWING BROADCAST THE DRAGON'S TEETH: Greek mythology relates how Cadmus killed a serpent and was told by the goddess Athena to sow its teeth in the earth. When he did so, armed soldiers sprang up from the teeth; these fought each other until only five were left. The five survivors became the ancestors of the noble house of Thebes.

Once, this freakish, elfish cast came into the child's eyes, while Hester was looking at her own image in them, as mothers are fond of doing; and, suddenly,—for women in solitude, and with troubled hearts, are pestered with unaccountable delusions,—she fancied that she beheld, not her own miniature portrait, but another face in the small black mirror of Pearl's eye. It was a face, fiend-like, full of smiling malice, yet bearing the semblance of features that she had known full well, though seldom with a smile, and never with malice, in them. It was as if an evil spirit possessed the child, and had just then peeped forth in mockery. Many a time afterwards had Hester been tortured, though less vividly, by the same illusion.

In the afternoon of a certain summer's day, after Pearl grew big enough to run about, she amused herself with gathering handfuls of wild-flowers, and flinging them, one by one, at her mother's bosom; dancing up and down, like a little elf, whenever she hit the scarlet letter. Hester's first motion had been to cover her bosom with her clasped hands. But, whether from pride or resignation, or a feeling that her penance might best be wrought out by this unutterable pain, she resisted the impulse, and sat erect, pale as death, looking sadly into little Pearl's wild eyes. Still came the battery of flowers, almost invariably hitting the mark, and covering the mother's breast with hurts for which she could find no balm in this world, nor knew how to seek it in another. At last, her shot being all expended, the child stood still and gazed at Hester, with that little, laughing image of a fiend peeping out—or, whether it peeped or not, her mother so imagined it—from the unsearchable abyss of her black eyes.

"Child, what art thou?" cried the mother.

"O, I am your little Pearl!" answered the child.

But, while she said it, Pearl laughed and began to dance up and down, with the humorsome gesticulation of a little imp, whose next freak might be to fly up the chimney.

"Art thou my child, in very truth?" asked Hester.

Nor did she put the question altogether idly, but, for the moment, with a portion of genuine earnestness; for, such was Pearl's wonderful intelligence, that her mother half doubted whether she were not acquainted with the secret spell of her existence, and might not now reveal herself.

"Yes; I am little Pearl!" repeated the child, continuing her antics.

"Thou art not my child! Thou art no Pearl of mine!" said the mother, half playfully; for it was often the case that a sportive impulse came over her, in the midst of her deepest suffering. "Tell me, then, what thou art, and who sent thee hither?"

"Tell me, mother!" said the child, seriously, coming up to Hester, and pressing herself close to her knees. "Do thou tell me!"

"Thy Heavenly Father sent thee!" answered Hester Prynne.

But she said it with a hesitation that did not escape the acuteness of the child. Whether moved only by her ordinary freakishness, or because an evil spirit prompted her, she put up her small forefinger, and touched the scarlet letter.

"He did not send me!" cried she, positively. "I have no Heavenly Father!"

"Hush, Pearl, hush! Thou must not talk so!" answered the mother, suppressing a groan. "He sent us all into the world. He sent even me, thy mother. Then, much more, thee! Or, if not, thou strange and elfish child, whence didst thou come?"

"Tell me! Tell me!" repeated Pearl, no longer seriously, but laughing, and capering about the floor. "It is thou that must tell me!"

But Hester could not resolve the query, using herself in a dismal labyrinth of doubt. She remembered—betwixt a smile and a shudder— the talk of the neighbouring townspeople; who, seeking vainly elsewhere for the child's paternity, and observing some of her odd attributes, had given out that poor little Pearl was a demon offspring; such as, ever since old Catholic times, had occasionally been seen on earth, through the agency of their mothers' sin, and to promote some foul and wicked purpose. Luther,[58] according to the scandal of his monkish enemies, was a brat of that hellish breed; nor was Pearl the only child to whom this inauspicious origin was assigned, among the New England Puritans.

VII. THE GOVERNOR'S HALL

Hester Prynne went, one day, to the mansion of Governor Bellingham, with a pair of gloves, which she had fringed and embroidered to his order, and which were to be worn on some great occasion of state; for, though the chances of a popular election had caused this former ruler to descend a step or two from the highest rank, he still held an honorable and influential place among the colonial magistracy.

Another and far more important reason than the delivery of a pair of embroidered gloves impelled Hester, at this time, to seek an interview with a personage of so much power and activity in the affairs of the settlement. It had reached her ears, that there was a design on the part of some of the leading inhabitants, cherishing the more rigid order of principles in religion and government, to deprive her of her child. On

---

[58]LUTHER: Martin Luther (1483–1546), German leader of the Protestant Reformation.

the supposition that Pearl, as already hinted, was of demon origin, these good people not unreasonably argued that a Christian interest in the mother's soul required them to remove such a stumbling-block from her path. If the child, on the other hand, were really capable of moral and religious growth, and possessed the elements of ultimate salvation, then, surely, it would enjoy all the fairer prospect of these advantages by being transferred to wiser and better guardianship than Hester Prynne's. Among those who promoted the design, Governor Bellingham was said to be one of the most busy. It may appear singular, and, indeed, not a little ludicrous, that an affair of this kind, which, in later days, would have been referred to no higher jurisdiction than that of the selectmen of the town, should then have been a question publicly discussed, and on which statesmen of eminence took sides. At that epoch of pristine simplicity, however, matters of even slighter public interest, and of far less intrinsic weight than the welfare of Hester and her child, were strangely mixed up with the deliberations of legislators and acts of state. The period was hardly, if at all, earlier than that of our story, when a dispute concerning the right of property in a pig, not only caused a fierce and bitter contest in the legislative body of the colony, but resulted in an important modification of the framework itself of the legislature.[59]

Full of concern, therefore,—but so conscious of her own right, that it seemed scarcely an unequal match between the public, on the one side, and a lonely woman, backed by the sympathies of nature, on the other,— Hester Prynne set forth from her solitary cottage. Little Pearl, of course, was her companion. She was now of an age to run lightly along by her mother's side, and, constantly in motion from morn till sunset, could have accomplished a much longer journey than that before her. Often, nevertheless, more from caprice than necessity, she demanded to be taken up in arms, but was soon as imperious to be set down again, and frisked onward before Hester the grassy pathway, with many a harmless trip and tumble. We have spoken of Pearl's rich and luxuriant beauty; a beauty that shone with deep and vivid tints; a bright complexion, eyes possessing intensity both of depth and glow, and hair already of a deep, glossy brown, and which, in after years, would be nearly akin to black. There

[59]FRAMEWORK ITSELF OF THE LEGISLATURE: Hawthorne is referring to the "Sow Case" of *Shearman* v. *Keayne* that led to the legislature's dividing into two houses in 1644. In 1642, a minor neighborhood spat turned into a political crisis when Goodwife Shearman charged Captain Keayne with pig stealing. Keayne had run afoul of the law before. The Deputies of the General Court supported the Shearman, while Governor Bellingham and his appointed members, known as the Assistants, took Keayne's side. They formally split over the issue, and 1644 the Assistants formed a Senate as a higher legislative body, and the lower Deputies of the General Court became independent.

was fire in her and throughout her; she seemed the unpremeditated off-shoot of a passionate moment. Her mother, in contriving the child's garb, had allowed the gorgeous tendencies of her imagination their full play; arraying her in a crimson velvet tunic, of a peculiar cut, abundantly embroidered in fantasies and flourishes of gold thread. So much strength of coloring, which must have given a wan and pallid aspect to cheeks of a fainter bloom, was admirably adapted to Pearl's beauty, and made her the very brightest little jet of flame that ever danced upon the earth.

But it was a remarkable attribute of this garb, and, indeed, of the child's whole appearance, that it irresistibly and inevitably reminded the beholder of the token which Hester Prynne was doomed to wear upon her bosom. It was the scarlet letter in another form; the scarlet letter endowed with life! The mother herself—as if the red ignominy were so deeply scorched into her brain, that all her conceptions assumed its form—had carefully wrought out the similitude[60]; lavishing many hours of morbid ingenuity, to create an analogy between the object of her affection, and the emblem of her guilt and torture. But, in truth, Pearl was the one, as well as the other; and only in consequence of that identity had Hester contrived so perfectly to represent the scarlet letter in her appearance.

As the two wayfarers came within the precincts of the town, the children of the Puritans looked up from their play,—or what passed for play with those sombre little urchins,—and spoke gravely one to another:—

"Behold, verily, there is the woman of the scarlet letter; and, of a truth, moreover, there is the likeness of the scarlet letter running along by her side! Come, therefore, and let us fling mud at them!"

But Pearl, who was a dauntless child, after frowning, stamping her foot, and shaking her little hand with a variety of threatening gestures, suddenly made a rush at the knot of her enemies, and put them all to flight. She resembled, in her fierce pursuit of them, an infant pestilence,—the scarlet fever, or some such half-fledged angel of judgment,—whose mission was to punish the sins of the rising generation. She screamed and shouted, too, with a terrific volume of sound, which doubtless caused the hearts of the fugitives to quake within them. The victory accomplished, Pearl returned quietly to her mother, and looked up smiling into her face.

Without further adventure, they reached the dwelling of Governor Bellingham. This was a large wooden house, built in a fashion of which there are specimens still extant in the streets of our elder towns; now moss-grown, crumbling to decay, and melancholy at heart with the many

---

[60]SIMILITUDE: A person or thing that resembles some other person or thing.

sorrowful or joyful occurrences, remembered or forgotten, that have happened, and passed away, within their dusky chambers. Then, however, there was the freshness of the passing year on its exterior, and the cheerfulness, gleaming forth from the sunny windows, of a human habitation into which death had never entered. It had indeed a very cheery aspect; the walls being overspread with a kind of stucco, in which fragments of broken glass were plentifully intermixed; so that, when the sunshine fell aslant-wise over the front of the edifice, it glittered and sparkled as if diamonds had been flung against it by the double handful. The brilliancy might have befitted Aladdin's palace,[61] rather than the mansion of a grave old Puritan ruler. It was further decorated with strange and seemingly cabalistic[62] figures and diagrams, suitable to the quaint taste of the age, which had been drawn in the stucco when newly laid on, and had now grown hard and durable, for the admiration of after times.

Pearl, looking at this bright wonder of a house, began to caper and dance, and imperatively required that the whole breadth of sunshine should be stripped off its front, and given her to play with.

"No, my little Pearl!" said her mother. "Thou must gather thine own sunshine. I have none to give thee!"

They approached the door; which was of an arched form, and flanked on each side by a narrow tower or projection of the edifice, in both of which were lattice-windows, with wooden shutters to close over them at need. Lifting the iron hammer that hung at the portal, Hester Prynne gave a summons, which was answered by one of the Governor's bond-servants; a free-born Englishman, but now a seven years' slave.[63] During that term he was to be the property of his master, and as much a commodity of bargain and sale as an ox, or a joint-stool. The serf wore the blue coat, which was the customary garb of serving-men at that period, and long before, in the old hereditary halls of England.

"Is the worshipful Governor Bellingham within?" inquired Hester.

"Yea, forsooth," replied the bond-servant, staring with wide-open eyes at the scarlet letter, which, being a new-comer in the country, he had never before seen. "Yea, his honorable worship is within. But he hath a godly minister or two with him, and likewise a leech. Ye may not see his worship now."

---

[61]ALADDIN'S PALACE: From *The Arabian Nights* (c.1450), an opulent treasure palace.
[62]CABALISTIC: Occult.
[63]SEVEN YEARS' SLAVE: An indentured or "bond" servant signed a contract to work for a period of years, usually seven, in return for passage to America, clothing, room, and board. The term *indenture* refers to the practice of tearing, or "indenting," the contract in half, with each party keeping a portion of the signed copy.

"Nevertheless, I will enter," answered Hester Prynne; and the bond-servant, perhaps judging from the decision of her air and the glittering symbol in her bosom, that she was a great lady in the land, offered no opposition.

So the mother and little Pearl were admitted into the hall of entrance. With many variations, suggested by the nature of his building-materials, diversity of climate, and a different mode of social life, Governor Bellingham had planned his new habitation after the residences of gentlemen of fair estate in his native land. Here, then, was a wide and reasonably lofty hall, extending through the whole depth of the house, and forming a medium of general communication, more or less directly, with all the other apartments. At one extremity, this spacious room was lighted by the windows of the two towers, which formed a small recess on either side of the portal. At the other end, though partly muffled by a curtain, it was more powerfully illuminated by one of those embowed hall-windows which we read of in old books, and which was provided with a deep and cushioned seat. Here, on the cushion, lay a folio tome,[64] probably of the Chronicles of England,[65] or other such substantial literature; even as, in our own days, we scatter gilded volumes on the centre-table, to be turned over by the casual guest. The furniture of the hall consisted of some ponderous chairs, the backs of which were elaborately carved with wreaths of oaken flowers; and likewise a table in the same taste; the whole being of the Elizabethan age, or perhaps earlier, and heirlooms, transferred hither from the Governor's paternal home. On the table—in token that the sentiment of old English hospitality had not been left behind—stood a large pewter tankard,[66] at the bottom of which, had Hester or Pearl peeped into it, they might have seen the frothy remnant of a recent draught of ale.

On the wall hung a row of portraits, representing the forefathers of the Bellingham lineage, some with armour on their breasts, and others with stately ruffs and robes of peace. All were characterized by the sternness and severity which old portraits so invariably put on; as if they were the ghosts, rather than the pictures, of departed worthies, and were gazing with harsh and intolerant criticism at the pursuits and enjoyments of living men.

---

[64]FOLIO TOME: Large volume.
[65]CHRONICLES OF ENGLAND: *Chronicles of England, Scotland, and Ireland* (1577), by English historian Raphael Holinshed (d.1580).
[66]TANKARD: Drinking vessel, with a lid, used for beer.

At about the centre of the oaken panels, that lined the hall, was suspended a suit of mail, not, like the pictures, an ancestral relic, but of the most modern date; for it had been manufactured by a skilful armorer in London, the same year in which Governor Bellingham came over to New England. There was a steel head-piece, a cuirass,[67] a gorget,[68] and greaves,[69] with a pair of gauntlets[70] and a sword hanging beneath; all, and especially the helmet and breastplate, so highly burnished as to glow with white radiance, and scatter an illumination everywhere about upon the floor. This bright panoply[71] was not meant for mere idle show, but had been worn by the Governor on many a solemn muster and training field, and had glittered, moreover, at the head of a regiment in the Pequod war.[72] For, though bred a lawyer, and accustomed to speak of Bacon, Coke, Noye, and Finch,[73] as his professional associates, the exigencies of this new country had transformed Governor Bellingham into a soldier, as well as a statesman and ruler.

Little Pearl—who was as greatly pleased with the gleaming armour as she had been with the glittering frontispiece of the house—spent some time looking into the polished mirror of the breastplate.

"Mother," cried she, "I see you here. Look! Look!"

Hester looked, by way of humoring the child; and she saw that, owing to the peculiar effect of this convex mirror, the scarlet letter was represented in exaggerated and gigantic proportions, so as to be greatly the most prominent feature of her appearance. In truth, she seemed absolutely hidden behind it. Pearl pointed upward, also, at a similar picture in the head-piece; smiling at her mother, with the elfish intelligence that was so familiar an expression on her small physiognomy. That look of naughty merriment was likewise reflected in the mirror, with so much breadth and intensity of effect, that it made Hester Prynne feel

---

[67]CUIRASS: Breastplate.
[68]GORGET: Armored collar.
[69]GREAVES: Shin protectors.
[70]GAUNTLETS: Gloves laced with steel, worn as part of armor.
[71]PANOPLY: Suit of armor.
[72]PEQUOD WAR: In 1637, Puritans from Massachusetts Bay Colony and Connecticut Colony, along with some Mohegan and Narragansett allies, surrounded a fortified Pequot village near Mystic, Connecticut, killing between 400 and 700 tribe members, including women and children. Captain John Underhill, one of the Puritan commanders, noted of the attack, "It may be demanded... Should not Christians have more mercy and compassion? Sometimes the Scripture declareth women and children must perish with their parents. Sometimes the case alters, but we will not dispute it now. We had sufficient light from the word of God for our proceedings."
[73]BACON, COKE, NOYE, AND FINCH: English legal authorities of the period: Francis Bacon (1561–1626), lord chancellor of England; Sir Edward Coke (1552–1634), lord chief justice; William Noye (1577–1634), attorney general; and Sir John Finch (1584–1660), speaker of the House of Commons and chief justice.

as if it could not be the image of her own child, but of an imp who was seeking to mould itself into Pearl's shape.

"Come along, Pearl," said she, drawing her away. "Come and look into this fair garden. It may be, we shall see flowers there; more beautiful ones than we find in the woods."

Pearl, accordingly, ran to the bow-window, at the farther end of the hall, and looked along the vista of a garden-walk, carpeted with closely shaven grass, and bordered with some rude and immature attempt at shrubbery. But the proprietor appeared already to have relinquished, as hopeless, the effort to perpetuate on this side of the Atlantic, in a hard soil and amid the close struggle for subsistence, the native English taste for ornamental gardening. Cabbages grew in plain sight; and a pumpkin vine, rooted at some distance, had run across the intervening space, and deposited one of its gigantic products directly beneath the hall-window; as if to warn the Governor that this great lump of vegetable gold was as rich an ornament as New England earth would offer him. There were a few rose-bushes, however, and a number of apple-trees, probably the descendants of those planted by the Reverend Mr. Blackstone,[74] the first settler of the peninsula; that half mythological personage who rides through our early annals, seated on the back of a bull.

Pearl, seeing the rose-bushes, began to cry for a red rose, and would not be pacified.

"Hush, child, hush!" said her mother earnestly. "Do not cry, dear little Pearl! I hear voices in the garden. The Governor is coming, and gentlemen along with him!"

In fact, adown the vista of the garden-avenue, a number of persons were seen approaching towards the house. Pearl, in utter scorn of her mother's attempt to quiet her, gave an eldritch[75] scream, and then became silent; not from any notion of obedience, but because the quick and mobile curiosity of her disposition was excited by the appearance of those new personages.

---

[74]REVEREND MR. BLACKSTONE: William Blackstone (1595–1675) was an Anglican clergyman who had settled and extensively planted the area of Boston near present-day Beacon Hill. When the original Puritan colony failed to thrive in Charlestown, partly due to a lack of drinking water, Blackstone invited the group to live near him. Despite his kindness to them, the Puritans did not care for the Anglican Blackstone, accusing him of trying to bring the established Church of England to the new country. The Puritan court ordered his house burned down, and he left the area for Rhode Island soon after.
[75]ELDRITCH: Haunting; unnatural.

VIII. THE ELF-CHILD AND THE MINISTER

Governor Bellingham, in a loose gown and easy cap,—such as elderly gentlemen loved to indue themselves with, in their domestic privacy,— walked foremost, and appeared to be showing off his estate, and expatiating on his projected improvements. The wide circumference of an elaborate ruff, beneath his gray beard, in the antiquated fashion of King James's reign,[76] caused his head to look not a little like that of John the Baptist in a charger.[77] The impression made by his aspect, so rigid and severe, and frost-bitten with more than autumnal age, was hardly in keeping with the appliances of worldly enjoyment wherewith he had evidently done his utmost to surround himself. But it is an error to suppose that our great forefathers—though accustomed to speak and think of human existence as a state merely of trial and warfare, and though unfeignedly prepared to sacrifice goods and life at the behest of duty— made it a matter of conscience to reject such means of comfort, or even luxury, as lay fairly within their grasp. This creed was never taught, for instance, by the venerable pastor, John Wilson, whose beard, white as a snow-drift, was seen over Governor Bellingham's shoulders; while its wearer suggested that pears and peaches might yet be naturalized in the New England climate, and that purple grapes might possibly be compelled to flourish, against the sunny garden-wall. The old clergyman, nurtured at the rich bosom of the English Church, had a long established and legitimate taste for all good and comfortable things; and however stern he might show himself in the pulpit, or in his public reproof of such transgressions as that of Hester Prynne, still, the genial benevolence of his private life had won him warmer affection than was accorded to any of his professional contemporaries.

Behind the Governor and Mr. Wilson came two other guests; one, the Reverend Arthur Dimmesdale, whom the reader may remember, as having taken a brief and reluctant part in the scene of Hester Prynne's disgrace; and, in close companionship with him, old Roger Chillingworth, a person of great skill in physic, who, for two or three years, past had

---

[76]KING JAMES'S REIGN: King James I of England (1566–1625), who reigned from 1603 to 1625.
[77]JOHN THE BAPTIST IN A CHARGER: A head on a plate. Referring to the biblical story of Salomé and John the Baptist (Mark 6:17–28). Princess Salomé was the daughter of Queen Herodias, who was married to King Herod. John the Baptist had publicly denounced the Queen's marriage to Herod and was imprisoned for his opposition. After watching Salomé dance, Herod promised to grant her anything she wished. At her mother's urging, Salomé requested that the head of John the Baptist be delivered to her on a platter.

been settled in the town. It was understood that this learned man was the physician as well as friend of the young minister, whose health had severely suffered, of late, by his too unreserved self-sacrifice to the labors and duties of the pastoral relation.

The Governor, in advance of his visitors, ascended one or two steps, and, throwing open the leaves of the great hall-window, found himself close to little Pearl. The shadow of the curtain fell on Hester Prynne, and partially concealed her.

"What have we here?" said Governor Bellingham, looking with surprise at the scarlet little figure before him. "I profess, I have never seen the like, since my days of vanity, in old King James's time, when I was wont to esteem it a high favor to be admitted to a court mask! There used to be a swarm of these small apparitions, in holiday-time; and we called them children of the Lord of Misrule.[78] But how gat such a guest into my hall?"

"Ay, indeed!" cried good old Mr. Wilson. "What little bird of scarlet plumage may this be? Methinks I have seen just such figures, when the sun has been shining through a richly painted window, and tracing out the golden and crimson images across the floor. But that was in the old land. Prithee, young one, who art thou, and what has ailed thy mother to bedizen thee in this strange fashion? Art thou a Christian child,—ha? Dost know thy catechism?[79] Or art thou one of those naughty elfs or fairies, whom we thought to have left behind us, with other relics of Papistry,[80] in merry old England?"

"I am mother's child," answered the scarlet vision, "and my name is Pearl!"

"Pearl?—Ruby, rather!—or Coral!—or Red Rose, at the very least, judging from thy hue!" responded the old minister, putting forth his hand in a vain attempt to pat little Pearl on the cheek. "But where is this mother of thine? Ah! I see," he added; and, turning to Governor Bellingham, whispered,—"This is the selfsame child of whom we have held speech together; and behold here the unhappy woman, Hester Prynne, her mother!"

"Sayest thou so?" cried the Governor. "Nay, we might have judged that such a child's mother must needs be a scarlet woman, and a worthy type

---

[78]LORD OF MISRULE: The traditional master of Christmas revels.
[79]CATECHISM: Elementary instruction in the rules of Christian religions.
[80]PAPISTRY: Roman Catholicism.

of her of Babylon![81] But she comes at a good time; and we will look into this matter forthwith."

Governor Bellingham stepped through the window into the hall, followed by his three guests.

"Hester Prynne," said he, fixing his naturally stern regard on the wearer of the scarlet letter, 'there hath been much question concerning thee, of late. The point hath been weightily discussed, whether we, that are of authority and influence, do well discharge our consciences by trusting an immortal soul, such as there is in yonder child, to the guidance of one who hath stumbled and fallen, amid the pitfalls of this world. Speak thou, the child's own mother! Were it not, thinkest thou, for thy little one's temporal and eternal welfare, that she be taken out of thy charge, and clad soberly, and disciplined strictly, and instructed in the truths of heaven and earth? What canst thou do for the child, in this kind?"

"I can teach my little Pearl what I have learned from this!" answered Hester Prynne, laying her finger on the red token.

"Woman, it is thy badge of shame!" replied the stern magistrate. "It is because of the stain which that letter indicates, that we would transfer thy child to other hands."

"Nevertheless," said the mother calmly, though growing more pale, "this badge hath taught me,—it daily teaches me,—it is teaching me at this moment,—lessons whereof my child may be the wiser and better, albeit they can profit nothing to myself."

"We will judge warily," said Bellingham, "and look well what we are about to do. Good Master Wilson, I pray you, examine this Pearl,—since that is her name,—and see whether she hath had such Christian nurture as befits a child of her age."

The old minister seated himself in an arm-chair, and made an effort to draw Pearl betwixt his knees. But the child, unaccustomed to the touch or familiarity of any but her mother, escaped through the open window and stood on the upper step, looking like a wild, tropical bird, of rich plumage, ready to take flight into the upper air. Mr. Wilson, not a little astonished at this outbreak,—for he was a grandfatherly sort of personage, and

---

[81]BABYLON: A reference to Revelation 17:3–5: "So he carried me away in the spirit into the wilderness: and I saw a woman sit upon a scarlet coloured beast, full of names of blasphemy, having seven heads and ten horns. / And the woman was arrayed in purple and scarlet colour, and decked with gold and precious stones and pearls, having a golden cup in her hand full of abominations and filthiness of her fornication: / And upon her forehead was a name written, MYSTERY, BABYLON THE GREAT, THE MOTHER OF HARLOTS AND ABOMINATIONS OF THE EARTH."

usually a vast favorite with children,—essayed, however, to proceed with the examination.

"Pearl," said he, with great solemnity, "thou must take heed to instruction, that so, in due season, thou mayest wear in thy bosom the pearl of great price. Canst thou tell me, my child, who made thee?"

Now Pearl knew well enough who made her; for Hester Prynne, the daughter of a pious home, very soon after her talk with the child about her Heavenly Father, had begun to inform her of those truths which the human spirit, at whatever stage of immaturity, imbibes with such eager interest. Pearl, therefore, so large were the attainments of her three years' lifetime, could have borne a fair examination in the New England Primer,[82] or the first column of the Westminster Catechism,[83] although unacquainted with the outward form of either of those celebrated works. But that perversity, which all children have more or less of, and of which little Pearl had a tenfold portion, now, at the most inopportune moment, took thorough possession of her, and closed her lips, or impelled her to speak words amiss. After putting her finger in her mouth, with many ungracious refusals to answer good Mr. Wilson's question, the child finally announced that she had not been made at all, but had been plucked by her mother off the bush of wild roses, that grew by the prison-door.

This fantasy was probably suggested by the near proximity of the Governor's red roses, as Pearl stood outside of the window; together with her recollection of the prison rose-bush, which she had passed in coming hither.

Old Roger Chillingworth, with a smile on his face, whispered something in the young clergyman's ear. Hester Prynne looked at the man of skill, and even then, with her fate hanging in the balance, was startled to perceive what a change had come over his features,—how much uglier they were,—how his dark complexion seemed to have grown duskier, and his figure more misshapen,—since the days when she had familiarly known him. She met his eyes for an instant, but was immediately constrained to give all her attention to the scene now going forward.

"This is awful!" cried the Governor, slowly recovering from the astonishment into which Pearl's response had thrown him. "Here is a child of three years old, and she cannot tell who made her! Without question,

---

[82]NEW ENGLAND PRIMER: A small book that taught the alphabet with moralizing verses, such as "A: In Adam's fall we sinned all."
[83]WESTMINSTER CATECHISM: A compendium of Calvinistic doctrine adopted in 1648 by Presbyterians and Congregationalists.

she is equally in the dark as to her soul, its present depravity, and future destiny! Methinks, gentlemen, we need inquire no further."

Hester caught hold of Pearl, and drew her forcibly into her arms, confronting the old Puritan magistrate with almost a fierce expression. Alone in the world, cast off by it, and with this sole treasure to keep her heart alive, she felt that she possessed indefeasible rights against the world, and was ready to defend them to the death.

"God gave me the child!" cried she. "He gave her, in requital of all things else, which ye had taken from me. She is my happiness!—she is my torture, none the less! Pearl keeps me here in life! Pearl punishes me, too! See ye not, she is the scarlet letter, only capable of being loved, and so endowed with a million-fold the power of retribution for my sin? Ye shall not take her! I will die first!"

"My poor woman," said the not unkind old minister, "the child shall be well cared for!—far better than thou canst do it."

"God gave her into my keeping," repeated Hester Prynne, raising her voice almost to a shriek. "I will not give her up!"—And here, by a sudden impulse, she turned to the young clergyman, Mr. Dimmesdale, at whom, up to this moment, she had seemed hardly so much as once to direct her eyes.—"Speak thou for me!" cried she. "Thou wast my pastor, and hadst charge of my soul, and knowest me better than these men can. I will not lose the child! Speak for me! Thou knowest,—for thou hast sympathies which these men lack!—thou knowest what is in my heart, and what are a mother's rights, and how much the stronger they are, when that mother has but her child and the scarlet letter! Look thou to it! I will not lose the child! Look to it!"

At this wild and singular appeal, which indicated that Hester Prynne's situation had provoked her to little less than madness, the young minister at once came forward, pale, and holding his hand over his heart, as was his custom whenever his peculiarly nervous temperament was thrown into agitation. He looked now more careworn and emaciated than as we described him at the scene of Hester's public ignominy; and whether it were his failing health, or whatever the cause might be, his large dark eyes had a world of pain in their troubled and melancholy depth.

"There is truth in what she says," began the minister, with a voice sweet, tremulous, but powerful, insomuch that the hall reëchoed, and the hollow armour rang with it,—"truth in what Hester says, and in the feeling which inspires her! God gave her the child, and gave her, too, an instinctive knowledge of its nature and requirements,—both seemingly so peculiar,—which no other mortal being can possess. And, moreover, is there not a quality of awful sacredness in the relation between this mother and this child?"

"Ay!—how is that, good Master Dimmesdale?" interrupted the Governor. "Make that plain, I pray you!"

"It must be even so," resumed the minister. "For, if we deem it otherwise, do we not thereby say that the Heavenly Father, the Creator of all flesh, hath lightly recognized a deed of sin, and made of no account the distinction between unhallowed lust and holy love? This child of its father's guilt and its mother's shame has come from the hand of God, to work in many ways upon her heart, who pleads so earnestly, and with such bitterness of spirit, the right to keep her. It was meant for a blessing; for the one blessing of her life! It was meant, doubtless, as the mother herself hath told us, for a retribution too; a torture, to be felt at many an unthought of moment; a pang, a sting, an ever-recurring agony, in the midst of a troubled joy! Hath she not expressed this thought in the garb of the poor child, so forcibly reminding us of that red symbol which sears her bosom?"

"Well said, again!" cried good Mr. Wilson. "I feared the woman had no better thought than to make a mountebank[84] of her child!"

"O, not so!—not so!" continued Mr. Dimmesdale. "She recognizes, believe me, the solemn miracle which God hath wrought, in the existence of that child. And may she feel, too,—what, methinks, is the very truth,— that this boon[85] was meant, above all things else, to keep the mother's soul alive, and to preserve her from blacker depths of sin into which Satan might else have sought to plunge her! Therefore it is good for this poor, sinful woman that she hath an infant immortality, a being capable of eternal joy or sorrow, confided to her care,—to be trained up by her to righteousness,—to remind her, at every moment, of her fall,— but yet to teach her, as it were by the Creator's sacred pledge, that, if she bring the child to heaven, the child also will bring its parent thither! Herein is the sinful mother happier than the sinful father. For Hester Prynne's sake, then, and no less for the poor child's sake, let us leave them as Providence hath seen fit to place them!"

"You speak, my friend, with a strange earnestness," said old Roger Chillingworth, smiling at him.

"And there is weighty import in what my young brother hath spoken," added the Reverend Mr. Wilson. "What say you, worshipful Master Bellingham? Hath he not pleaded well for the poor woman?"

[84]MOUNTEBANK: Charlatans who sold "medical" potions and remedies, using entertainment to attract a crowd of potential customers.
[85]BOON: Benefit, favor, blessing.

"Indeed hath he," answered the magistrate, "and hath adduced such arguments, that we will even leave the matter as it now stands; so long, at least, as there shall be no further scandal in the woman. Care must be had, nevertheless, to put the child to due and stated examination in the catechism at thy hands or Master Dimmesdale's. Moreover, at a proper season, the tithing-men[86] must take heed that she go both to school and to meeting."

The young minister, on ceasing to speak, had withdrawn a few steps from the group, and stood with his face partially concealed in the heavy folds of the window-curtain; while the shadow of his figure, which the sunlight cast upon the floor, was tremulous with the vehemence of his appeal. Pearl, that wild and flighty little elf, stole softly towards him, and, taking his hand in the grasp of both her own, laid her cheek against it; a caress so tender, and withal so unobtrusive, that her mother, who was looking on, asked herself,—"Is that my Pearl?" Yet she knew that there was love in the child's heart, although it mostly revealed itself in passion, and hardly twice in her lifetime had been softened by such gentleness as now. The minister,—for, save the long-sought regards of woman, nothing is sweeter than these marks of childish preference, accorded spontaneously by a spiritual instinct, and therefore seeming to imply in us something truly worthy to be loved,—the minister looked round, laid his hand on the child's head, hesitated an instant, and then kissed her brow. Little Pearl's unwonted mood of sentiment lasted no longer; she laughed, and went capering down the hall, so airily, that old Mr. Wilson raised a question whether even her tiptoes touched the floor.

"The little baggage hath witchcraft in her, I profess," said he to Mr. Dimmesdale. "She needs no old woman's broomstick to fly withal!"

"A strange child!" remarked old Roger Chillingworth. "It is easy to see the mother's part in her. Would it be beyond a philosopher's research, think ye, gentlemen, to analyze that child's nature, and, from its make and mould, to give a shrewd guess at the father?"

"Nay; it would be sinful, in such a question, to follow the clew of profane philosophy," said Mr. Wilson. "Better to fast and pray upon it; and still better, it may be, to leave the mystery as we find it, unless Providence reveal it of its own accord. Thereby, every good Christian man hath a title to show a father's kindness towards the poor, deserted babe."

The affair being so satisfactorily concluded, Hester Prynne, with Pearl, departed from the house. As they descended the steps, it is averred

---

[86]TITHING-MEN: Parish officers.

that the lattice of a chamber-window was thrown open, and forth into the sunny day was thrust the face of Mistress Hibbins, Governor Bellingham's bitter-tempered sister, and the same who, a few years later, was executed as a witch.

"Hist, hist!" said she, while her ill-omened physiognomy seemed to cast a shadow over the cheerful newness of the house. "Wilt thou go with us to-night? There will be a merry company in the forest; and I well-nigh promised the Black Man that comely Hester Prynne should make one."

"Make my excuse to him, so please you!" answered Hester, with a triumphant smile. "I must tarry at home, and keep watch over my little Pearl. Had they taken her from me, I would willingly have gone with thee into the forest, and signed my name in the Black Man's book too, and that with mine own blood!"

"We shall have thee there anon!" said the witch-lady, frowning, as she drew back her head.

But here—if we suppose this interview betwixt Mistress Hibbins and Hester Prynne to be authentic, and not a parable—was already an illustration of the young minister's argument against sundering the relation of a fallen mother to the offspring of her frailty. Even thus early had the child saved her from Satan's snare.

IX. THE LEECH

Under the appellation of Roger Chillingworth, the reader will remember, was hidden another name, which its former wearer had resolved should never more be spoken. It has been related, how, in the crowd that witnessed Hester Prynne's ignominious exposure, stood a man, elderly, travel-worn, who, just emerging from the perilous wilderness, beheld the woman, in whom he hoped to find embodied the warmth and cheerfulness of home, set up as a type of sin before the people. Her matronly fame was trodden under all men's feet. Infamy was babbling around her in the public market-place. For her kindred, should the tidings ever reach them, and for the companions of her unspotted life, there remained nothing but the contagion of her dishonor; which would not fail to be distributed in strict accordance and proportion with the intimacy and sacredness of their previous relationship. Then why—since the choice was with himself—should the individual, whose connection with the fallen woman had been the most intimate and sacred of them all, come forward to vindicate his claim to an inheritance so little desirable? He resolved not to be pilloried beside her on her pedestal of shame. Unknown to all but Hester Prynne, and possessing the lock and key of her silence, he chose to withdraw his name from the roll of mankind, and, as regarded his former ties and interest, to vanish out of life as completely as if he indeed lay at the bottom of the ocean, whither rumor had long ago consigned him. This purpose once effected, new interests would immediately spring up, and likewise a new purpose; dark, it is true, if not guilty, but of force enough to engage the full strength of his faculties.

In pursuance of this resolve, he took up his residence in the Puritan town, as Roger Chillingworth, without other introduction than the learning and intelligence of which he possessed more than a common measure. As his studies, at a previous period of his life, had made him extensively acquainted with the medical science of the day, it was as a physician that he presented himself, and as such was cordially received. Skilful men, of the medical and chirurgical[87] profession, were of rare occurrence in the colony. They seldom, it would appear, partook of the religious zeal that brought other emigrants across the Atlantic. In their researches into the human frame, it may be that the higher and more subtile faculties of such men were materialized, and that they lost the spiritual view of existence amid the intricacies of that wondrous mechanism, which seemed to involve art enough to comprise all of life within itself. At all events, the health of the good town of Boston, so far as medicine had aught to do with it, had hitherto lain in the guardianship of an aged deacon and apothecary,[88] whose piety and godly deportment were stronger testimonials in his favor, than any that he could have produced in the shape of a diploma. The only surgeon was one who combined the occasional exercise of that noble art with the daily and habitual flourish of a razor. To such a professional body Roger Chillingworth was a brilliant acquisition. He soon manifested his familiarity with the ponderous and imposing machinery of antique physic; in which every remedy contained a multitude of far-fetched and heterogeneous ingredients, as elaborately compounded as if the proposed result had been the Elixir of Life.[89] In his Indian captivity, moreover, he had gained much knowledge of the properties of native herbs and roots; nor did he conceal from his patients, that these simple medicines, Nature's boon to the untutored savage, had quite as large a share of his own confidence as the European pharmacopoeia,[90] which so many learned doctors had spent centuries in elaborating.

---

[87]CHIRURGICAL: Surgical.
[88]APOTHECARY: An individual who prepares and sells drugs for medicinal purposes.
[89]ELIXIR OF LIFE: A legendary substance that could indefinitely prolong life. Along with the philosopher's stone, which was reputed to turn lead into gold, it was the object of alchemy.
[90]PHARMACOPOEIA: A collection of drugs; the arsenal of available drugs.

This learned stranger was exemplary, as regarded at least the outward forms of a religious life, and, early after his arrival, had chosen for his spiritual guide the Reverend Mr. Dimmesdale. The young divine, whose scholar-like renown still lived in Oxford, was considered by his more fervent admirers as little less than a heavenly-ordained apostle, destined, should he live and labor for the ordinary term of life, to do as great deeds for the now feeble New England Church, as the early Fathers had achieved for the infancy of the Christian faith. About this period, however, the health of Mr. Dimmesdale had evidently begun to fail. By those best acquainted with his habits, the paleness of the young minister's cheek was accounted for by his too earnest devotion to study, his scrupulous fulfilment of parochial duty, and more than all, to the fasts and vigils of which he made a frequent practice, in order to keep the grossness of this earthly state from clogging and obscuring his spiritual lamp. Some declared, that, if Mr. Dimmesdale were really going to die, it was cause enough, that the world was not worthy to be any longer trodden by his feet. He himself, on the other hand, with characteristic humility, avowed his belief, that, if Providence should see fit to remove him, it would be because of his own unworthiness to perform its humblest mission here on earth. With all this difference of opinion as to the cause of his decline, there could be no question of the fact. His form grew emaciated; his voice, though still rich and sweet, had a certain melancholy prophecy of decay in it; he was often observed, on any slight alarm or other sudden accident, to put his hand over his heart, with first a flush and then a paleness, indicative of pain.

Such was the young clergyman's condition, and so imminent the prospect that his dawning light would be extinguished, all untimely, when Roger Chillingworth made his advent to the town. His first entry on the scene, few people could tell whence, dropping down, as it were, out of the sky, or starting from the nether earth, had an aspect of mystery, which was easily heightened to the miraculous. He was now known to be a man of skill; it was observed that he gathered herbs, and the blossoms of wild-flowers, and dug up roots and plucked off twigs from the forest-trees, like one acquainted with hidden virtues in what was valueless to common eyes. He was heard to speak of Sir Kenelm Digby,[91] and other famous men,—whose scientific attainments were esteemed hardly less than supernatural,—as having been his correspondents or associates. Why,

---

[91]SIR KENELM DIGBY: An English politician and writer (1603–1665). He is best known for advancing the theory of the "powder of sympathy," which was purported to heal wounds without direct application. The powder was applied to the weapon that had caused a wound, thus supposedly curing or healing the injury.

with such rank in the learned world, had he come hither? What could he, whose sphere was in great cities, be seeking in the wilderness? In answer to this query, a rumor gained ground,—and, however absurd, was entertained by some very sensible people—that Heaven had wrought an absolute miracle, by transporting an eminent Doctor of Physic, from a German university, bodily through the air, and setting him down at the door of Mr. Dimmesdale's study! Individuals of wiser faith, indeed, who knew that Heaven promotes its purposes without aiming at the stage-effect of what is called miraculous interposition, were inclined to see a providential hand in Roger Chillingworth's so opportune arrival.

This idea was countenanced by the strong interest which the physician ever manifested in the young clergyman; he attached himself to him as a parishioner, and sought to win a friendly regard and confidence from his naturally reserved sensibility. He expressed great alarm at his pastor's state of health, but was anxious to attempt the cure, and, if early undertaken, seemed not despondent of a favorable result. The elders, the deacons, the motherly dames, and the young and fair maidens, of Mr. Dimmesdale's flock, were alike importunate that he should make trial of the physician's frankly offered skill. Mr. Dimmesdale gently repelled their entreaties.

"I need no medicine," said he.

But how could the young minister say so, when, with every successive Sabbath, his cheek was paler and thinner, and his voice more tremulous than before,—when it had now become a constant habit, rather than a casual gesture, to press his hand over his heart? Was he weary of his labors? Did he wish to die? These questions were solemnly propounded to Mr. Dimmesdale by the elder ministers of Boston and the deacons of his church, who, to use their own phrase, "dealt with him," on the sin of rejecting the aid which Providence so manifestly held out. He listened in silence, and finally promised to confer with the physician.

"Were it God's will," said the Reverend Mr. Dimmesdale, when, in fulfilment of this pledge, he requested old Roger Chillingworth's professional advice, "I could be well content, that my labors, and my sorrows, and my sins, and my pains, should shortly end with me, and what is earthly of them be buried in my grave, and the spiritual go with me to my eternal state, rather than that you should put your skill to the proof in my behalf."

"Ah," replied Roger Chillingworth, with that quietness which, whether imposed or natural, marked all his deportment, "it is thus that a young clergyman is apt to speak. Youthful men, not having taken a deep root, give up their hold of life so easily! And saintly men, who walk with God on earth, would fain be away, to walk with him on the golden pavements of the New Jerusalem."[92]

"Nay," rejoined the young minister, putting his hand to his heart, with a flush of pain flitting over his brow, "were I worthier to walk there, I could be better content to toil here."

"Good men ever interpret themselves too meanly," said the physician.

In this manner, the mysterious old Roger Chillingworth became the medical adviser of the Reverend Mr. Dimmesdale. As not only the disease interested the physician, but he was strongly moved to look into the character and qualities of the patient, these two men, so different in age, came gradually to spend much time together. For the sake of the minister's health, and to enable the leech to gather plants with healing balm in them, they took long walks on the sea-shore, or in the forest; mingling various talk with the plash and murmur of the waves, and the solemn wind-anthem among the tree-tops. Often, likewise, one was the guest of the other, in his place of study and retirement. There was a fascination for the minister in the company of the man of science, in whom he recognized an intellectual cultivation of no moderate depth or scope; together with a range and freedom of ideas, that he would have vainly looked for among the members of his own profession. In truth, he was startled, if not shocked, to find this attribute in the physician. Mr. Dimmesdale was a true priest, a true religionist, with the reverential sentiment largely developed, and an order of mind that impelled itself powerfully along the track of a creed, and wore its passage continually deeper with the lapse of time. In no state of society would he have been what is called a man of liberal views; it would always be essential to his peace to feel the pressure of a faith about him, supporting, while it confined him within its iron framework. Not the less, however, though with a tremulous enjoyment, did he feel the occasional relief of looking at the universe through the medium of another kind of intellect than those with which he habitually held converse. It was as if a window were thrown open, admitting a freer atmosphere into the close and stifled study, where his life was wasting itself away, amid lamp-light, or obstructed day-beams, and the musty fragrance, be it sensual or moral, that exhales from books. But the air was too fresh and chill to be long breathed, with comfort. So the minister, and the physician with him, withdrew again within the limits of what their church defined as orthodox.

---

[92]NEW JERUSALEM: A reference to Revelation 21:2: "And I John saw the holy city, new Jerusalem, coming down from God out of heaven, prepared as a bride adorned for her husband."

Thus Roger Chillingworth scrutinized his patient carefully, both as he saw him in his ordinary life, keeping an accustomed pathway in the range of thoughts familiar to him, and as he appeared when thrown amidst other moral scenery, the novelty of which might call out something new to the surface of his character. He deemed it essential, it would seem, to know the man, before attempting to do him good. Wherever there is a heart and an intellect, the diseases of the physical frame are tinged with the peculiarities of these. In Arthur Dimmesdale, thought and imagination were so active, and sensibility so intense, that the bodily infirmity would be likely to have its groundwork there. So Roger Chillingworth—the man of skill, the kind and friendly physician—strove to go deep into his patient's bosom, delving among his principles, prying into his recollections, and probing every thing with a cautious touch, like a treasure-seeker in a dark cavern. Few secrets can escape an investigator, who has opportunity and license to undertake such a quest, and skill to follow it up. A man burdened with a secret should especially avoid the intimacy of his physician. If the latter possess native sagacity, and a nameless something more,—let us call it intuition; if he show no intrusive egotism, nor disagreeably prominent characteristics of his own; if he have the power, which must be born with him, to bring his mind into such affinity with his patient's, that this last shall unawares have spoken what he imagines himself only to have thought; if such revelations be received without tumult, and acknowledged not so often by an uttered sympathy, as by silence, an inarticulate breath, and here and there a word, to indicate that all is understood; if, to these qualifications of a confidant be joined the advantages afforded by his recognized character as a physician;—then, at some inevitable moment, will the soul of the sufferer be dissolved, and flow forth in a dark, but transparent stream, bringing all its mysteries into the daylight.

Roger Chillingworth possessed all, or most, of the attributes above enumerated. Nevertheless, time went on; a kind of intimacy, as we have said, grew up between these two cultivated minds, which had as wide a field as the whole sphere of human thought and study, to meet upon; they discussed every topic of ethics and religion, of public affairs, and private character; they talked much, on both sides, of matters that seemed personal to themselves; and yet no secret, such as the physician fancied must exist there, ever stole out of the minister's consciousness into his companion's ear. The latter had his suspicions, indeed, that even the nature of Mr. Dimmesdale's bodily disease had never fairly been revealed to him. It was a strange reserve!

After a time, at a hint from Roger Chillingworth, the friends of Mr. Dimmesdale effected an arrangement by which the two were lodged in the same house; so that every ebb and flow of the minister's life-tide might pass under the eye of his anxious and attached physician. There was much joy throughout the town, when this greatly desirable object was attained. It was held to be the best possible measure for the young clergyman's welfare; unless, indeed, as often urged by such as felt authorized to do so, he had selected some one of the many blooming damsels, spiritually devoted to him, to become his devoted wife. This latter step, however, there was no present prospect that Arthur Dimmesdale would be prevailed upon to take; he rejected all suggestions of the kind, as if priestly celibacy were one of his articles of church-discipline. Doomed by his own choice, therefore, as Mr. Dimmesdale so evidently was, to eat his unsavory morsel always at another's board, and endure the life-long chill which must be his lot who seeks to warm himself only at another's fireside, it truly seemed that this sagacious, experienced, benevolent, old physician, with his concord of paternal and reverential love for the young pastor, was the very man, of all mankind, to be constantly within reach of his voice.

The new abode of the two friends was with a pious widow, of good social rank, who dwelt in a house covering pretty nearly the site on which the venerable structure of King's Chapel has since been built. It had the grave-yard, originally Isaac Johnson's home-field, on one side, and so was well adapted to call up serious reflections, suited to their respective employments, in both minister and man of physic. The motherly care of the good widow assigned to Mr. Dimmesdale a front apartment, with a sunny exposure, and heavy window-curtains to create a noontide shadow, when desirable. The walls were hung round with tapestry, said to be from the Gobelin looms,[93] and, at all events, representing the Scriptural story of David and Bathsheba, and Nathan the Prophet,[94] in colors still unfaded, but which made the fair woman of the scene almost as grimly picturesque as the woe-denouncing seer. Here, the pale clergyman piled up his library, rich with parchment-bound folios of the Fathers,[95] and the lore of Rabbis, and monkish erudition, of which the Protestant divines, even while they vilified and decried that class of

---

[93]GOBELIN LOOMS: The Gobelin tapestry factory opened in 1601; its products were expensive but reputed to be the finest French tapestry.
[94]SCRIPTURAL STORY OF DAVID AND BATHSHEBA, AND NATHAN THE PROPHET: 2 Samuel 11–12 tells the story of King David's adultery with Bathsheba and the prophet Nathan's denunciation of the affair.
[95]FOLIOS OF THE FATHERS: Works of the early Christians who wrote down the doctrines, beliefs, and practices of the developing church.

writers, were yet constrained often to avail themselves. On the other side of the house, old Roger Chillingworth arranged his study and laboratory; not such as a modern man of science would reckon even tolerably complete, but provided with a distilling apparatus, and the means of compounding drugs and chemicals, which the practised alchemist knew well how to turn to purpose. With such commodiousness of situation, these two learned persons sat themselves down, each in his own domain, yet familiarly passing from one apartment to the other, and bestowing a mutual and not incurious inspection into one another's business.

And the Reverend Arthur Dimmesdale's best discerning friends, as we have intimated, very reasonably imagined that the hand of Providence had done all this, for the purpose—besought in so many public, and domestic, and secret prayers—of restoring the young minister to health. But—it must now be said—another portion of the community had latterly begun to take its own view of the relation betwixt Mr. Dimmesdale and the mysterious old physician. When an uninstructed multitude attempts to see with its eyes, it is exceedingly apt to be deceived. When, however, it forms its judgment, as it usually does, on the intuitions of its great and warm heart, the conclusions thus attained are often so profound and so unerring, as to possess the character of truths supernaturally revealed. The people, in the case of which we speak, could justify its prejudice against Roger Chillingworth by no fact or argument worthy of serious refutation. There was an aged handicraftsman, it is true, who had been a citizen of London at the period of Sir Thomas Overbury's murder,[96] now some thirty years agone; he testified to having seen the physician, under some other name, which the narrator of the story had now forgotten, in company with Doctor Forman,[97] the famous old conjurer, who was implicated in the affair of Overbury. Two or three individuals hinted, that the man of skill, during his Indian captivity, had enlarged his medical attainments by joining in the incantations of the savage priests; who were universally acknowledged to be powerful enchanters, often performing seemingly miraculous cures by their skill in the black art. A large number—and many of these were persons of such sober sense and practical observation, that their opinions would have

---

[96]SIR THOMAS OVERBURY'S MURDER: Sir Thomas Overbury (1581–1613) was an English author and a friend to Robert Carr (1587?–1645), the favorite of King James I of England. Overbury was imprisoned in the Tower of London after he objected to Carr's marriage to Frances Howard, the divorced wife of the earl of Essex. While there, he was poisoned by Ann Turner at the request of Howard. Both women were found guilty of murder, but James I spared Howard's life; Turner was hanged.
[97]DOCTOR FORMAN: Dr. Simon Forman (1552–1611), an alchemist, assisted Frances Howard and Ann Turner in plotting the death of Sir Thomas Overbury. Subtle, the main character in *The Alchemist* (1610), by the English playwright Ben Jonson (1572–1637), is based on Forman.

been valuable, in other matters—affirmed that Roger Chillingworth's aspect had undergone a remarkable change while he had dwelt in town, and especially since his abode with Mr. Dimmesdale. At first, his expression had been calm, meditative, scholar-like. Now, there was something ugly and evil in his face, which they had not previously noticed, and which grew still the more obvious to sight, the oftener they looked upon him. According to the vulgar idea, the fire in his laboratory had been brought from the lower regions, and was fed with infernal fuel; and so, as might be expected, his visage was getting sooty with the smoke.

To sum up the matter, it grew to be a widely diffused opinion, that the Reverend Arthur Dimmesdale, like many other personages of especial sanctity, in all ages of the Christian world, was haunted either by Satan himself, or Satan's emissary, in the guise of old Roger Chillingworth. This diabolical agent had the Divine permission, for a season, to burrow into the clergyman's intimacy, and plot against his soul. No sensible man, it was confessed, could doubt on which side the victory would turn. The people looked, with an unshaken hope, to see the minister come forth out of the conflict, transfigured with the glory which he would unquestionably win. Meanwhile, nevertheless, it was sad to think of the perchance mortal agony through which he must struggle towards his triumph.

Alas, to judge from the gloom and terror in the depths of the poor minister's eyes, the battle was a sore one, and the victory any thing but secure!

X. THE LEECH AND HIS PATIENT

Old Roger Chillingworth, throughout life, had been calm in temperament, kindly, though not of warm affections, but ever, and in all his relations with the world, a pure and upright man. He had begun an investigation, as he imagined, with the severe and equal integrity of a judge, desirous only of truth, even as if the question involved no more than the air-drawn lines and figures of a geometrical problem, instead of human passions, and wrongs inflicted on himself. But, as he proceeded, a terrible fascination, a kind of fierce, though still calm, necessity seized the old man within its gripe, and never set him free again, until he had done all its bidding. He now dug into the poor clergyman's heart, like a miner searching for gold; or, rather, like a sexton[98] delving into a grave, possibly in quest of a jewel that had been buried on the dead man's bosom, but likely to find nothing save mortality and corruption. Alas for his own soul, if these were what he sought!

---

[98]SEXTON: A church employee responsible for maintenance, bell-ringing, and gravedigging.

Sometimes, a light glimmered out of the physician's eyes, burning blue and ominous, like the reflection of a furnace, or, let us say, like one of those gleams of ghastly fire that darted from Bunyan's[99] awful doorway in the hill-side, and quivered on the pilgrim's face. The soil where this dark miner was working had perchance shown indications that encouraged him.

"This man," said he, at one such moment, to himself, "pure as they deem him,—all spiritual as he seems,—hath inherited a strong animal nature from his father or his mother. Let us dig a little farther in the direction of this vein!"

Then, after long search into the minister's dim interior, and turning over many precious materials, in the shape of high aspirations for the welfare of his race, warm love of souls, pure sentiments, natural piety, strengthened by thought and study, and illuminated by revelation,—all of which invaluable gold was perhaps no better than rubbish to the seeker,—he would turn back, discouraged, and begin his quest towards another point. He groped along as stealthily, with as cautious a tread, and as wary an outlook, as a thief entering a chamber where a man lies only half asleep,—or, it may be, broad awake,—with purpose to steal the very treasure which this man guards as the apple of his eye. In spite of his premeditated carefulness, the floor would now and then creak; his garments would rustle; the shadow of his presence, in a forbidden proximity, would be thrown across his victim. In other words, Mr. Dimmesdale, whose sensibility of nerve often produced the effect of spiritual intuition, would become vaguely aware that something inimical to his peace had thrust itself into relation with him. But Old Roger Chillingworth, too, had perceptions that were almost intuitive; and when the minister threw his startled eyes towards him, there the physician sat; his kind, watchful, sympathizing, but never intrusive friend.

Yet Mr. Dimmesdale would perhaps have seen this individual's character more perfectly, if a certain morbidness, to which sick hearts are liable, had not rendered him suspicious of all mankind. Trusting no man as his friend, he could not recognize his enemy when the latter actually appeared. He therefore still kept up a familiar intercourse with him, daily receiving the old physician in his study; or visiting the laboratory, and,

[99]BUNYAN'S: From *Pilgrim's Progress* (1678), by John Bunyan (1628–1688): "Then I saw in my dream, that the Shepherds had them to another place, in a bottom, where was a door in the side of a hill, and they opened the door, and bid them look in. They looked in, therefore, and saw that within it was very dark and smoky; they also thought that they heard there a rumbling noise as of fire, and a cry of some tormented, and that they smelt the scent of brimstone. Then said Christian, What means this? The Shepherds told them, This is a by-way to hell, a way that hypocrites go in at."

for recreation's sake, watching the processes by which weeds were converted into drugs of potency.

One day, leaning his forehead on his hand, and his elbow on the sill of the open window, that looked towards the grave-yard, he talked with Roger Chillingworth, while the old man was examining a bundle of unsightly plants.

"Where," asked he, with a look askance at them,—for it was the clergyman's peculiarity that he seldom, now-a-days, looked straightforth at any object, whether human or inanimate,—"where, my kind doctor, did you gather those herbs, with such a dark, flabby leaf?"

"Even in the grave-yard here at hand," answered the physician, continuing his employment. "They are new to me. I found them growing on a grave, which bore no tombstone, no other memorial of the dead man, save these ugly weeds that have taken upon themselves to keep him in remembrance. They grew out of his heart, and typify, it may be, some hideous secret that was buried with him, and which he had done better to confess during his lifetime."

"Perchance," said Mr. Dimmesdale, "he earnestly desired it, but could not."

"And wherefore?" rejoined the physician. "Wherefore not; since all the powers of nature call so earnestly for the confession of sin, that these black weeds have sprung up out of a buried heart to make manifest, an outspoken crime?"

"That, good Sir, is but a fantasy of yours," replied the minister. "There can be, if I forbode aright, no power, short of the Divine mercy, to disclose, whether by uttered words, or by type or emblem, the secrets that may be buried with a human heart. The heart, making itself guilty of such secrets, must perforce hold them, until the day when all hidden things shall be revealed. Nor have I so read or interpreted Holy Writ,[100] as to understand that the disclosure of human thoughts and deeds, then to be made, is intended as a part of the retribution. That, surely, were a shallow view of it. No; these revelations, unless I greatly err, are meant merely to promote the intellectual satisfaction of all intelligent beings, who will stand waiting, on that day, to see the dark problem of this life made plain. A knowledge of men's hearts will be needful to the completest solution of that problem. And I conceive, moreover, that the hearts holding such miserable secrets as you speak of will yield them up, at that last day,[101] not with reluctance, but with a joy unutterable."

---

[100]HOLY WRIT: Holy writings, especially from the Bible or Holy Scriptures, or from texts addressing sacred subjects.
[101]THAT LAST DAY: Judgment Day .

"Then why not reveal them here?" asked Roger Chillingworth, glancing quietly aside at the minister. "Why should not the guilty ones sooner avail themselves of this unutterable solace?"

"They mostly do," said the clergyman, griping hard at his breast, as if afflicted with an importunate throb of pain. "Many, many a poor soul hath given its confidence to me, not only on the death-bed, but while strong in life, and fair in reputation. And ever, after such an outpouring, O, what a relief have I witnessed in those sinful brethren! even as in one who at last draws free air, after long stifling with his own polluted breath. How can it be otherwise? Why should a wretched man, guilty, we will say, of murder, prefer to keep the dead corpse buried in his own heart, rather than fling it forth at once, and let the universe take care of it!"

"Yet some men bury their secrets thus," observed the calm physician.

"True; there are such men," answered Mr. Dimmesdale. "But, not to suggest more obvious reasons, it may be that they are kept silent by the very constitution of their nature. Or,—can we not suppose it?—guilty as they may be, retaining, nevertheless, a zeal for God's glory and man's welfare, they shrink from displaying themselves black and filthy in the view of men; because, thenceforward, no good can be achieved by them; no evil of the past be redeemed by better service. So, to their own unutterable torment, they go about among their fellow-creatures, looking pure as new-fallen snow; while their hearts are all speckled and spotted with iniquity of which they cannot rid themselves."

"These men deceive themselves," said Roger Chillingworth, with somewhat more emphasis than usual, and making a slight gesture with his forefinger. "They fear to take up the shame that rightfully belongs to them. Their love for man, their zeal for God's service,—these holy impulses may or may not coexist in their hearts with the evil inmates to which their guilt has unbarred the door, and which must needs propagate a hellish breed within them. But, if they seek to glorify God, let them not lift heavenward their unclean hands! If they would serve their fellow-men, let them do it by making manifest the power and reality of conscience, in constraining them to penitential self-abasement! Wouldst thou have me to believe, O wise and pious friend, that a false show can be better—can be more for God's glory, or man's welfare—than God's own truth? Trust me, such men deceive themselves!"

"It may be so," said the young clergyman indifferently, as waiving a discussion that he considered irrelevant or unseasonable. He had a ready faculty, indeed, of escaping from any topic that agitated his too sensitive and nervous temperament.—"But, now, I would ask of my well-skilled physician, whether, in good sooth, he deems me to have profited by his kindly care of this weak frame of mine?"

Before Roger Chillingworth could answer, they heard the clear, wild laughter of a young child's voice, proceeding from the adjacent burial-ground. Looking instinctively from the open window,—for it was summer-time,—the minister beheld Hester Prynne and little Pearl passing along the footpath that traversed the inclosure. Pearl looked as beautiful as the day, but was in one of those moods of perverse merriment which, whenever they occurred, seemed to remove her entirely out of the sphere of sympathy or human contact. She now skipped irreverently from one grave to another; until, coming to the broad, flat, armorial tombstone of a departed worthy,—perhaps of Isaac Johnson himself,—she began to dance upon it. In reply to her mother's command and entreaty that she would behave more decorously, little Pearl paused gather the prickly burrs from a tall burdock, which grew beside the tomb. Taking a handful of these, she arranged them along the lines of the scarlet letter that decorated the maternal bosom, to which the burrs, as their nature was, tenaciously adhered. Hester did not pluck them off.

Roger Chillingworth had by this time approached the window, and smiled grimly down.

"There is no law, nor reverence for authority, no regard for human ordinances or opinions, right or wrong, mixed up with that child's composition," remarked he, as much to himself as to his companion. "I saw her, the other day, bespatter the Governor himself with water, at the cattle-trough in Spring Lane. What, in Heaven's name, is she? Is the imp altogether evil? Hath she affections? Hath she any discoverable principle of being?"

"None,—save the freedom of a broken law," answered Mr. Dimmesdale, in a quiet way, as if he had been discussing the point within himself. "Whether capable of good, I know not."

The child probably overheard their voices; for, looking up to the window, with a bright, but naughty smile of mirth and intelligence, she threw one of the prickly burrs at the Reverend Mr. Dimmesdale. The sensitive clergyman shrank, with nervous dread, from the light missile. Detecting his emotion, Pearl clapped her little hands in the most extravagant ecstasy. Hester Prynne, likewise, had involuntarily looked up; and all these four persons, old and young, regarded one another in silence, till the child laughed aloud, and shouted,—"Come away, mother! Come away, or yonder old Black Man will catch you! He hath got hold of the minister already. Come away, mother, or he will catch you! But he cannot catch little Pearl!"

So she drew her mother away, skipping, dancing, and frisking fantastically among the hillocks of the dead people, like a creature that had nothing in common with a bygone and buried generation, nor owned herself akin to it. It was as if she had been made afresh, out of new elements, and must perforce be permitted to live her own life, and be a law unto herself, without her eccentricities being reckoned to her for a crime.

"There goes a woman," resumed Roger Chillingworth, after a pause, "who, be her demerits what they may, hath none of that mystery of hidden sinfulness which you deem so grievous to be borne. Is Hester Prynne the less miserable, think you, for that scarlet letter on her breast?"

"I do verily believe it," answered the clergyman. "Nevertheless, I cannot answer for her. There was a look of pain in her face, which I would gladly have been spared the sight of. But still, methinks, it must needs be better for the sufferer to be free to show his pain, as this poor woman Hester is, than to cover it all up in his heart."

There was another pause; and the physician began anew to examine and arrange the plants which he had gathered.

"You inquired of me, a little time agone," said he, at length, "my judgment as touching your health."

"I did," answered the clergyman, "and would gladly learn it. Speak frankly, I pray you, be it for life or death."

"Freely, then, and plainly," said the physician, still busy with his plants, but keeping a wary eye on Mr. Dimmesdale, "the disorder is a strange one; not so much in itself, nor as outwardly manifested,—in so far, at least, as the symptoms have been laid open to my observation. Looking daily at you, my good Sir, and watching the tokens of your aspect, now for months gone by, I should deem you a man sore sick, it may be, yet not so sick but that an instructed and watchful physician might well hope to cure you. But—I know not what to say—the disease is what I seem to know, yet know it not."

"You speak in riddles, learned Sir," said the pale minister, glancing aside out of the window.

"Then, to speak more plainly," continued the physician, "and I crave pardon, Sir,—should it seem to require pardon,—for this needful plainness of my speech. Let me ask,—as your friend,—as one having charge, under Providence, of your life and physical well-being,—hath all the operations of this disorder been fairly laid open and recounted to me?"

"How can you question it?" asked the minister. "Surely, it were child's play to call in a physician, and then hide the sore!"

"You would tell me, then, that I know all?" said Roger Chillingworth, deliberately, and fixing an eye, bright with intense and concentrated intelligence, on the minister's face. "Be it so! But, again! He to whom only the outward and physical evil is laid open knoweth, oftentimes, but half the evil which he is called upon to cure. A bodily disease, which we look upon as whole and entire within itself, may, after all, be but a symptom of some ailment in the spiritual part. Your pardon, once again, good Sir, if my speech give the shadow of offence. You, Sir, of all men whom I have known, are he whose body is the closest conjoined, and imbued, and identified, so to speak, with the spirit whereof it is the instrument."

"Then I need ask no further," said the clergyman, somewhat hastily rising from his chair. "You deal not, I take it, in medicine for the soul!"

"Thus, a sickness," continued Roger Chillingworth, going on, in an unaltered tone, without heeding the interruption,—but standing up, and confronting the emaciated and white-cheeked minister with his low, dark, and misshapen figure,—"a sickness, a sore place, if we may so call it, in your spirit, hath immediately its appropriate manifestation in your bodily frame. Would you, therefore, that your physician heal the bodily evil? How may this be, unless you first lay open to him the wound or trouble in your soul?"

"No!—not to thee!—not to an earthly physician!" cried Mr. Dimmesdale, passionately, and turning his eyes, full and bright, and with a kind of fierceness, on old Roger Chillingworth. "Not to thee! But, if it be the soul's disease, then do I commit myself to the one Physician of the soul! He, if it stand with his good pleasure, can cure; or he can kill! Let him do with me as, in his justice and wisdom, he shall see good. But who art thou, that meddlest in this matter?—that dares thrust himself between the sufferer and his God?"

With a frantic gesture, he rushed out of the room.

"It is as well to have made this step," said Roger Chillingworth to himself, looking after the minister with a grave smile. "There is nothing lost. We shall be friends again anon. But see, now, how passion takes hold upon this man, and hurrieth him out of himself! As with one passion, so with another! He hath done a wild thing ere now, this pious Master Dimmesdale, in the hot passion of his heart!"

It proved not difficult to reëstablish the intimacy of the two companions, on the same footing and in the same degree as heretofore. The young clergyman, after a few hours of privacy, was sensible that the disorder of his nerves had hurried him into an unseemly outbreak of temper, which there had been nothing in the physician's words to excuse or palliate.[102] He marvelled, indeed, at the violence with which he had thrust back the kind old man, when merely proffering the advice which it was his duty to bestow, and which the minister himself had

---

[102]PALLIATE: Alleviate suffering.

expressly sought. With these remorseful feelings, he lost no time in making the amplest apologies, and besought his friend still to continue the care, which, if not successful in restoring him to health, had, in all probability, been the means of prolonging his feeble existence to that hour. Roger Chillingworth readily assented, and went on with his medical supervision of the minister; doing his best for him, in all good faith, but always quitting the patient's apartment, at the close of the professional interview, with a mysterious and puzzled smile upon his lips. This expression was invisible in Mr. Dimmesdale's presence, but grew strongly evident as the physician crossed the threshold.

"A rare case!" he muttered. "I must needs look deeper into it. A strange sympathy betwixt soul and body! Were it only for the art's sake, I must search this matter to the bottom!"

It came to pass, not long after the scene above recorded, that the Reverend Mr. Dimmesdale, at noonday, and entirely unawares, fell into a deep, deep slumber, sitting in his chair, with a large black-letter[103] volume open before him on the table. It must have been a work of vast ability in the somniferous school of literature. The profound depth of the minister's repose was the more remarkable; inasmuch as he was one of those persons whose sleep, ordinarily, is as light, as fitful, and as easily scared away, as a small bird hopping on a twig. To such an unwonted remoteness, however, had his spirit now withdrawn into itself, that he stirred not in his chair, when old Roger Chillingworth, without any extraordinary precaution, came into the room. The physician advanced directly in front of his patient, laid his hand upon his bosom, and thrust aside the vestment, that, hitherto, had always covered it even from the professional eye.

Then, indeed, Mr. Dimmesdale shuddered, and slightly stirred.

After a brief pause, the physician turned away.

But with what a wild look of wonder, joy, and honor! With what a ghastly rapture, as it were, too mighty to be expressed only by the eye and features, and therefore bursting forth through the whole ugliness of his figure, and making itself even riotously manifest by the extravagant gestures with which he threw up his arms towards the ceiling, and stamped his foot upon the floor! Had a man seen old Roger Chillingworth, at that moment of his ecstasy, he would have had no need to ask how Satan comports himself, when a precious human soul is lost to heaven, and won into his kingdom.

But what distinguished the physician's ecstasy from Satan's was the trait of wonder in it!

---

[103]BLACK-LETTER: A gothic-style typeface used in early printed books.

XI. THE INTERIOR OF A HEART

After the incident last described, the intercourse between the clergyman and the physician, though externally the same, was really of
another character than it had previously been. The intellect of Roger
Chillingworth had now a sufficiently plain path before it. It was not,
indeed, precisely that which he had laid out for himself to tread. Calm,
gentle, passionless, as he appeared, there was yet, we fear, a quiet
depth of malice, hitherto latent, but active now, in this unfortunate old
man, which led him to imagine a more intimate revenge than any mortal had ever wreaked upon an enemy. To make himself the one trusted
friend, to whom should be confided all the fear, the remorse, the agony,
the ineffectual repentance, the backward rush of sinful thoughts,
expelled in vain! All that guilty sorrow, hidden from the world, whose
great heart would have pitied and forgiven, to be revealed to him, the
Pitiless, to him, the Unforgiving! All that dark treasure to be lavished
on the very man, to whom nothing else could so adequately pay the
debt of vengeance!

The clergyman's shy and sensitive reserve had balked this scheme.
Roger Chillingworth, however, was inclined to be hardly, if at all, less
satisfied with the aspect of affairs, which Providence—using the
avenger and his victim for its own purposes, and, perchance, pardon-
ing, where it seemed most to punish—had substituted for his black
devices. A revelation, he could almost say, had been granted to him.
It mattered little, for his object, whether celestial, or from what other
region. By its aid, in all the subsequent relations betwixt him and Mr.
Dimmesdale, not merely the external presence, but the very inmost soul
of the latter seemed to be brought out before his eyes, so that he could
see and comprehend its every movement. He became, thenceforth,
not a spectator only, but a chief actor, in the poor minister's interior
world. He could play upon him as he chose. Would he arouse him
with a throb of agony? The victim was for ever on the rack; it needed
only to know the spring that controlled the engine;—and the physician
knew it well! Would he startle him with sudden fear? As at the waving of a magician's wand, uprose a grisly phantom,—uprose a thousand phantoms,—in many shapes, of death, or more awful shame, all
flocking roundabout the clergyman, and pointing with their fingers
at his breast!

All this was accomplished with a subtlety so perfect, that the minister, though he had constantly a dim perception of some evil influence
watching over him, could never gain a knowledge of its actual nature.

True, he looked doubtfully, fearfully,—even, at times, with horror and the bitterness of hatred,—at the deformed figure of the old physician. His gestures, his gait, his grizzled beard, his slightest and most indifferent acts, the very fashion of his garments, were odious in the clergyman's sight; a token, implicitly to be relied on, of a deeper antipathy in the breast of the latter than he was willing to acknowledge to himself. For, as it was impossible to assign a reason for such distrust and abhorrence, so Mr. Dimmesdale, conscious that the poison of one morbid spot was infecting his heart's entire substance, attributed all his presentiments to no other cause. He took himself to task for his bad sympathies in reference to Roger Chillingworth, disregarded the lesson that he should have drawn from them, and did his best to root them out. Unable to accomplish this, he nevertheless, as a matter of principle, continued his habits of social familiarity with the old man, and thus gave him constant opportunities for perfecting the purpose to which— poor, forlorn creature that he was, and more wretched than his victim— the avenger had devoted himself.

While thus suffering under bodily disease, and gnawed and tortured by some black trouble of the soul, and given over to the machinations of his deadliest enemy, the Reverend Mr. Dimmesdale had achieved a brilliant popularity in his sacred office. He won it, indeed, in great part, by his sorrows. His intellectual gifts, his moral perceptions, his power of experiencing and communicating emotion, were kept in a state of preternatural activity by the prick and anguish of his daily life. His fame, though still on its upward slope, already overshadowed the soberer reputations of his fellow-clergymen, eminent as several of them were. There are scholars among them, who had spent more years in acquiring abstruse lore, connected with the divine profession, than Mr. Dimmesdale had lived; and who might well, therefore, be more profoundly versed in such solid and valuable attainments than their youthful brother. There were men, too, of a sturdier texture of mind than his, and endowed with a far greater share of shrewd, hard, iron or granite understanding; which, duly mingled with a fair proportion of doctrinal ingredient, constitutes a highly respectable, efficacious, and unamiable variety of the clerical species. There were others, again, true saintly fathers, whose faculties had been elaborated by weary toil among their books, and by patient thought, and etherealized, moreover, by spiritual communications with the better world, into which their purity of life had almost introduced these holy personages, with their garments of mortality still clinging to them. All that they lacked was the gift that descended upon the chosen disciples, at

Pentecost, in tongues of flame;[104] symbolizing, it would seem, not the power of speech in foreign and unknown languages, but that of addressing the whole human brotherhood in the heart's native language. These fathers, otherwise so apostolic, lacked Heaven's last and rarest attestation of their office, the Tongue of Flame. They would have vainly sought—had they ever dreamed of seeking—to express the highest truths through the humblest medium of familiar words and images. Their voices came down, afar and indistinctly, from the upper heights where they habitually dwelt.

Not improbably, it was to this latter class of men that Mr. Dimmesdale, by many of his traits of character, naturally belonged. To their high mountain-peaks of faith and sanctity he would have climbed, had not the tendency been thwarted by the burden, whatever it might be, of crime or anguish, beneath which it was his doom to totter. It kept him down, on a level with the lowest; him, the man of ethereal attributes, whose voice the angels might else have listened to and answered! But this very burden it was, that gave him sympathies so intimate with the sinful brotherhood of mankind; so that his heart vibrated in unison with theirs, and received their pain into itself, and sent its own throb of pain through a thousand other hearts, in gushes of sad, persuasive eloquence. Oftenest persuasive, but sometimes terrible! The people knew not the power that moved them thus. They deemed the young clergyman a miracle of holiness. They fancied him the mouth-piece of Heaven's messages of wisdom, and rebuke, and love. In their eyes, the very ground on which he trod was sanctified. The virgins of his church grew pale around him, victims of a passion so imbued with religious sentiment that they imagined it to be all religion, and brought it openly, in their white bosoms, as their most acceptable sacrifice before the altar. The aged members of his flock, beholding Mr. Dimmesdale's frame so feeble, while they were themselves so rugged in their infirmity, believed that he would go heavenward before them, and enjoined it upon their children, that their old bones should be buried close to their young pastor's holy grave. And, all this time, perchance, when poor Mr. Dimmesdale was thinking of his grave, he questioned with himself whether the grass would ever grow on it, because an accursed thing must there be buried!

It is inconceivable, the agony with which this public veneration tortured him! It was his genuine impulse to adore the truth, and to reckon

[104]PENTECOST, IN TONGUES OF FLAME: A reference to Acts 2:1–4: "And when the day of Pentecost was fully come, they were all with one accord in one place. / And suddenly there came a sound from heaven as of a rushing mighty wind, and it filled all the house where they were sitting. / And there appeared unto them cloven tongues like as of fire, and it sat upon each of them. / And they were all filled with the Holy Ghost, and began to speak with other tongues, as the Spirit gave them utterance."

all things shadow-like, and utterly devoid of weight or value, that had not its divine essence as the life within their life. Then, what was he?— a substance?—or the dimmest of all shadows? He longed to speak out, from his own pulpit, at the full height of his voice, and tell the people what he was. "I, whom you behold in these black garments of the priest-hood,—I, who ascend the sacred desk, and turn my pale face heaven-ward, taking upon myself to hold communion, in your behalf, with the Most High Omniscience,—I, in whose daily life you discern the sanctity of Enoch,[105]—I, whose footsteps, as you suppose, leave a gleam along my earthly track, whereby the pilgrims that shall come after me may be guided to the regions of the blest,—I, who have laid the hand of bap-tism upon your children,—I, who have breathed the parting prayer over your dying friends, to whom the Amen sounded faintly from a world which they had quitted,—I, your pastor, whom you so reverence and trust, am utterly a pollution and a lie!"

More than once, Mr. Dimmesdale had gone into the pulpit, with a pur-pose never to come down its steps, until he should have spoken words like the above. More than once, he had cleared his throat, and drawn in the long, deep, and tremulous breath, which, when sent forth again, would come burdened with the black secret of his soul. More than once—nay, more than a hundred times—he had actually spoken! Spoken! But how? He had told his hearers that he was altogether vile, a viler companion of the vilest, the worst of sinners, an abomination, a thing of unimag-inable iniquity; and that the only wonder was, that they did not see his wretched body shrivelled up before their eyes, by the burning wrath of the Almighty! Could there be plainer speech than this? Would not the peo-ple start up in their seats, by a simultaneous impulse, and tear him down out of the pulpit which he defiled? Not so, indeed! They heard it all, and did but reverence him the more. They little guessed what deadly pur-port lurked in those self-condemning words. "The godly youth!" said they among themselves. "The saint on earth! Alas, if he discern such sin-fulness in his own white soul, what horrid spectacle would he behold in thine or mine!" The minister well knew—subtle, but remorseful hypocrite that he was!—the light in which his vague confession would be viewed. He had striven to put a cheat upon himself[106] by making the avowal of a guilty conscience, but had gained only one other sin, and a self-acknowl-edged shame, without the momentary relief of being self-deceived. He had

---

[105]ENOCH: In Genesis 5:21–24, Enoch "walked with God," which the Apostle Paul in Hebrews inter-preted to mean that Enoch did not physically die but was "translated" to heaven.
[106]HE HAD STRIVEN TO PUT A CHEAT UPON HIMSELF: Meaning Dimmesdale is deluding him-self into believing he has made a full confession.

spoken the very truth, and transformed it into the veriest falsehood. And yet, by the constitution of his nature, he loved the truth, and loathed the lie, as few men ever did. Therefore, above all things else, he loathed his miserable self!

His inward trouble drove him to practices, more in accordance with the old, corrupted faith of Rome,[107] than with the better light of the church in which he had been born and bred. In Mr. Dimmesdale's secret closet, under lock and key, there was a bloody scourge.[108] Oftentimes, this Protestant and Puritan divine had plied it on his own shoulders; laughing bitterly at himself the while, and smiting so much the more pitilessly, because of that bitter laugh. It was his custom, too, as it has been that of many other pious Puritans, to fast,—not, however, like them, in order to purify the body and render it the fitter medium of celestial illumination,—but rigorously, and until his knees trembled beneath him, as an act of penance. He kept vigils, likewise, night after night, sometimes in utter darkness; sometimes with a glimmering lamp; and sometimes, viewing his own face in a looking-glass, by the most powerful light which he could throw upon it. He thus typified the constant introspection wherewith he tortured, but could not purify, himself. In these lengthened vigils, his brain often reeled, and visions seemed to flit before him; perhaps seen doubtfully, and by a faint light of their own, in the remote dimness of the chamber, or more vividly, and close beside him, within the looking-glass. Now it was a herd of diabolic shapes, that grinned and mocked at the pale minister, and beckoned him away with them; now a group of shining angels, who flew upward heavily, as sorrow-laden, but grew more ethereal as they rose. Now came the dead friends of his youth, and his white-bearded father, with a saint-like frown, and his mother, turning her face away as she passed by. Ghost of a mother,—thinnest fantasy of a mother,—methinks she might yet have thrown a pitying glance towards her son! And now, through the chamber which these spectral thoughts had made so ghastly, glided Hester Prynne, leading along little Pearl, in her scarlet garb, and pointing her forefinger, first, at the scarlet letter on her bosom, and then at the clergyman's own breast.

None of these visions ever quite deluded him. At any moment, by an effort of his will, he could discern substances through their misty lack of substance, and convince himself that they were not solid in their nature, like yonder table of carved oak, or that big, square, leather-bound and brazen-clasped volume of divinity. But, for all that, they were, in one

[107]OLD, CORRUPTED FAITH OF ROME: The Roman Catholic Church.
[108]BLOODY SCOURGE: Whip or lash.

sense, the truest and most substantial things which the poor minister now dealt with. It is the unspeakable misery of a life so false as his, that it steals the pith and substance out of whatever realities there are around us, and which were meant by Heaven to be the spirit's joy and nutriment. To the untrue man, the whole universe is false,—it is impalpable,—it shrinks to nothing within his grasp. And he himself, in so far as he shows himself in a false light, becomes a shadow, or, indeed, ceases to exist. The only truth, that continued to give Mr. Dimmesdale a real existence on this earth, was the anguish in his inmost soul, and the undissembled expression of it in his aspect. Had he once found power to smile, and wear a face of gayety, there would have been no such man!

On one of those ugly nights, which we have faintly hinted at, but forborne to picture forth, the minister started from his chair. A new thought had struck him. There might be a moment's peace in it. Attiring himself with as much care as if it had been for public worship, and precisely in the same manner, he stole softly down the staircase, undid the door, and issued forth.

XII. THE MINISTER'S VIGIL

Walking in the shadow of a dream, as it were, and perhaps actually under the influence of a species of somnambulism, Mr. Dimmesdale reached the spot, where, now so long since, Hester Prynne had lived through her first hour of public ignominy. The same platform or scaffold, black and weather-stained with the storm or sunshine of seven long years, and foot-worn, too, with the tread of many culprits who had since ascended it, remained standing beneath the balcony of the meeting-house. The minister went up the steps.

It was an obscure night of early May. An unvaried pall of cloud muffled the whole expanse of sky from zenith to horizon. If the same multitude which had stood as eyewitnesses while Hester Prynne sustained her punishment could now have been summoned forth, they would have discerned no face above the platform, nor hardly the outline of a human shape, in the dark gray of the midnight. But the town was all asleep. There was no peril of discovery. The minister might stand there, if it so pleased him, until morning should redden in the east, without other risk than that the dank and chill night-air would creep into his frame, and stiffen his joints with rheumatism, and clog his throat with catarrh[109] and cough; thereby defrauding the expectant audience of to-morrow's prayer

---

[109]CATARRH: The mucus discharge from the nose and eyes that generally accompanies a cold or flu.

and sermon. No eye could see him, save that ever-wakeful one which had seen him in his closet, wielding the bloody scourge. Why, then, had he come hither? Was it but the mockery of penitence? A mockery, indeed, but in which his soul trifled with itself! A mockery at which angels blushed and wept, while fiends rejoiced, with jeering laughter! He had been driven hither by the impulse of that Remorse which dogged him everywhere, and whose own sister and closely linked companion was that Cowardice which invariably drew him back, with her tremulous gripe, just when the other impulse had hurried him to the verge of a disclosure. Poor, miserable man! what right had infirmity like his to burden itself with crime? Crime is for the iron-nerved, who have their choice either to endure it, or, if it press too hard, to exert their fierce and savage strength for a good purpose, and fling it off at once! This feeble and most sensitive of spirits could do neither, yet continually did one thing or another, which intertwined, in the same inextricable knot, the agony of heaven-defying guilt and vain repentance.

And thus, while standing on the scaffold, in this vain show of expiation, Mr. Dimmesdale was overcome with a great horror of mind, as if the universe were gazing at a scarlet token on his naked breast, right over his heart. On that spot, in very truth, there was, and there had long been, the gnawing and poisonous tooth of bodily pain. Without any effort of his will, or power to restrain himself, he shrieked aloud; an outcry that went pealing through the night, and was beaten back from one house to another, and reverberated from the hills in the background; as if a company of devils, detecting so much misery and terror in it, had made a plaything of the sound, and were bandying it to and fro.

"It is done!" muttered the minister, covering his face with his hands. "The whole town will awake, and hurry forth, and find me here!"

But it was not so. The shriek had perhaps sounded with a far greater power, to his own startled ears, than it actually possessed. The town did not awake; or, if it did, the drowsy slumberers mistook the cry either for something frightful in a dream, or for the noise of witches; whose voices, at that period, were often heard to pass over the settlements or lonely cottages, as they rode with Satan through the air. The clergyman, therefore, hearing no symptoms of disturbance, uncovered his eyes and looked about him. At one of the chamber-windows of Governor Bellingham's mansion, which stood at some distance, on the line of another street, he beheld the appearance of the old magistrate himself, with a lamp in his hand, a white night-cap on his head, and a long white gown enveloping his figure. He looked like a ghost, evoked unseasonably from the grave. The cry had evidently startled him. At another window of the same house, moreover, appeared old Mistress Hibbins, the Governor's sister, also with a lamp, which, even thus far off, revealed the expression of her sour and discontented face. She thrust forth her head from the lattice, and looked anxiously upward. Beyond the shadow of a doubt, this venerable witch-lady had heard Mr. Dimmesdale's outcry, and interpreted it, with its multitudinous echoes and reverberations, as the clamor of the fiends and night-hags, with whom she was well known to make excursions into the forest.

Detecting the gleam of Governor Bellingham's lamp, the old lady quickly extinguished her own, and vanished. Possibly, she went up among the clouds. The minister saw nothing further of her motions. The magistrate, after a wary observation of the darkness—into which, nevertheless, he could see but little farther than he might into a mill-stone—retired from the window.

The minister grew comparatively calm. His eyes, however, were soon greeted by a little, glimmering light, which, at first a long way off, was approaching up the street. It threw a gleam of recognition on here a post, and there a garden-fence, and here a latticed window-pane, and there a pump, with its full trough of water, and here, again, an arched door of oak, with an iron knocker, and a rough log for the door-step. The Reverend Mr. Dimmesdale noted all these minute particulars, even while firmly convinced that the doom of his existence was stealing onward, in the footsteps which he now heard; and that the gleam of the lantern would fall upon him, in a few moments more, and reveal his long-hidden secret. As the light drew nearer, he beheld, within its illuminated circle, his brother clergyman,—or, to speak more accurately, his professional father, as well as highly valued friend,—the Reverend Mr. Wilson; who, as Mr. Dimmesdale now conjectured, had been praying at the bedside of some dying man. And so he had. The good old minister came freshly from the death-chamber of Governor Winthrop,[110] who had passed from earth to heaven within that very hour. And now, surrounded, like the saint-like personages of olden times, with a radiant halo, that glorified him amid this gloomy night of sin,—as if the departed Governor had left him an inheritance of his glory, or as if he had caught upon himself the distant shine of the celestial city, while looking thitherward to see the triumphant pilgrim pass within its gates,—now, in short, good Father Wilson was moving homeward, aiding his footsteps with a lighted lantern! The glimmer of this luminary suggested the above conceits to

---

[110]DEATH-CHAMBER OF GOVERNOR WINTHROP: John Winthrop (1588–1649), a revered governor of Massachusetts Bay Colony, who died in March 1649, not May.

Mr. Dimmesdale, who smiled,—nay, almost laughed at them,—and then wondered if he were going mad.

As the Reverend Mr. Wilson passed beside the scaffold, closely muffling his Geneva cloak[111] about him with one arm, and holding the lantern before his breast with the other, the minister could hardly restrain himself from speaking.

"A good evening to you, venerable Father Wilson! Come up hither, I pray you, and pass a pleasant hour with me!"

Good Heavens! Had Mr. Dimmesdale actually spoken? For one instant, he believed that these words had passed his lips. But they were uttered only within his imagination. The venerable Father Wilson continued to step slowly onward, looking carefully at the muddy pathway before his feet, and never once turning his head towards the guilty platform. When the light of the glimmering lantern had faded quite away, the minister discovered, by the faintness which came over him, that the last few moments had been a crisis of terrible anxiety; although his mind had made an involuntary effort to relieve itself by a kind of lurid playfulness.

Shortly afterwards, the like grisly sense of the humorous again stole in among the solemn phantoms of his thought. He felt his limbs growing stiff with the unaccustomed chilliness of the night, and doubted whether he should be able to descend the steps of the scaffold. Morning would break, and find him there. The neighbourhood would begin to rouse itself. The earliest riser, coming forth in the dim twilight, would perceive a vaguely defined figure aloft on the place of shame; and, half crazed betwixt alarm and curiosity, would go, knocking from door to door, summoning all the people to behold the ghost—as he needs must think it—of some defunct transgressor. A dusky tumult would flap its wings from one house to another. Then—the morning light still waxing stronger—old patriarchs would rise up in great haste, each in his flannel gown, and matronly dames, without pausing to put off their nightgear. The whole tribe of decorous personages, who had never heretofore been seen with a single hair of their heads awry, would start into public view, with the disorder of a nightmare in their aspects. Old Governor Bellingham would come grimly forth, with his King James's ruff fastened askew; and Mistress Hibbins, with some twigs of the forest clinging to her skirts, and looking sourer than ever, as having hardly got a wink of sleep after her night ride; and good Father Wilson, too, after spending half the night at a death-bed, and liking ill to be disturbed, thus early, out of his dreams about the glorified saints. Hither, likewise, would come the

---

[111]GENEVA CLOAK: A long, black ministerial cloak.

elders and deacons of Mr. Dimmesdale's church, and the young virgins who so idolized their minister, and had made a shrine for him in their white bosoms; which, now, by the by, in their hurry and confusion, they would scantly have given themselves time to cover with their kerchiefs. All people, in a word, would come stumbling over their thresholds, and turning up their amazed and horror-stricken visages around the scaffold. Whom would they discern there, with the red eastern light upon his brow? Whom, but the Reverend Arthur Dimmesdale, half frozen to death, overwhelmed with shame, and standing where Hester Prynne had stood!

Carried away by the grotesque horror of this picture, the minister, unawares, and to his own infinite alarm, burst into a great peal of laughter. It was immediately responded to by a light, airy, childish laugh, in which, with a thrill of the heart,—but he knew not whether of exquisite pain, or pleasure as acute,—he recognized the tones of little Pearl.

"Pearl! Little Pearl!" cried he, after a moment's pause; then, suppressing his voice,—"Hester! Hester Prynne! Are you there?"

"Yes; it is Hester Prynne!" she replied, in a tone of surprise; and the minister heard her footsteps approaching from the sidewalk, along which she had been passing.—"It is I, and my little Pearl."

"Whence come you, Hester?" asked the minister. "What sent you hither?"

"I have been watching at a death-bed," answered Hester Prynne;—"at Governor Winthrop's death-bed, and have taken his measure for a robe, and am now going homeward to my dwelling."

"Come up hither, Hester, thou and little Pearl," said the Reverend Mr. Dimmesdale. "Ye have both been here before, but I was not with you. Come up hither once again, and we will stand all three together!"

She silently ascended the steps, and stood on the platform, holding little Pearl by the hand. The minister felt for the child's other hand, and took it. The moment that he did so, there came what seemed a tumultuous rush of new life, other life than his own, pouring like a torrent into his heart, and hurrying through all his veins, as if the mother and the child were communicating their vital warmth to his half-torpid system. The three formed an electric chain.

"Minister!" whispered little Pearl.

"What wouldst thou say, child?" asked Mr. Dimmesdale.

"Wilt thou stand here with mother and me, to-morrow noontide?" inquired Pearl.

"Nay; not so, my little Pearl!" answered the minister; for, with the new energy of the moment, all the dread of public exposure, that had so long been the anguish of his life, had returned upon him; and he was already trembling at the conjunction in which—with a strange joy, nevertheless—he now found himself. "Not so, my child. I shall, indeed, stand with thy mother and thee one other day, but not to-morrow!"

Pearl laughed, and attempted to pull away her hand. But the minister held it fast.

"A moment longer, my child!" said he.

"But wilt thou promise," asked Pearl, "to take my hand, and mother's hand, to-morrow noontide?"

"Not then, Pearl," said the minister, "but another time!"

"And what other time?" persisted the child.

"At the great judgment day!" whispered the minister,—and, strangely enough, the sense that he was a professional teacher of the truth impelled him to answer the child so. "Then, and there, before the judgment-seat, thy mother, and thou, and I, must stand together! But the daylight of this world shall not see our meeting!"

Pearl laughed again.

But, before Mr. Dimmesdale had done speaking, a light gleamed far and wide over all the muffled sky. It was doubtless caused by one of those meteors, which the night-watcher may so often observe burning out to waste, in the vacant regions of the atmosphere. So powerful was its radiance, that it thoroughly illuminated the dense medium of cloud betwixt the sky and earth. The great vault brightened, like the dome of an immense lamp. It showed the familiar scene of the street, with the distinctness of mid-day, but also with the awfulness that is always imparted to familiar objects by an unaccustomed light. The wooden houses, with their jutting stories and quaint gable-peaks; the doorsteps and thresholds, with the early grass springing up about them; the gardenplots, black with freshly turned earth; the wheel-track, little worn, and, even in the market-place, margined with green on either side;—all were visible, but with a singularity of aspect that seemed to give another moral interpretation to the things of this world than they had ever borne before. And there stood the minister, with his hand over his heart; and Hester Prynne, with the embroidered letter glimmering on her bosom; and little Pearl, herself a symbol, and the connecting link between those two. They stood in the noon of that strange and solemn splendor, as if it were the light that is to reveal all secrets, and the daybreak that shall unite all who belong to one another.

There was witchcraft in little Pearl's eyes; and her face, as she glanced upward at the minister, wore that naughty smile which made its expression frequently so elvish. She withdrew her hand from Mr. Dimmesdale's, and pointed across the street. But he clasped both his hands over his breast, and cast his eyes towards the zenith.

Nothing was more common, in those days, than to interpret all meteoric appearances, and other natural phenomena, that occurred with less regularity than the rise and set of sun and moon, as so many revelations from a supernatural source. Thus, a blazing spear, a sword of flame, a bow, or a sheaf of arrows, seen in the midnight sky, prefigured Indian warfare. Pestilence was known to have been foreboded by a shower of crimson light. We doubt whether any marked event, for good or evil, ever befell New England, from its settlement down to Revolutionary times, of which the inhabitants had not been previously warned by some spectacle of this nature. Not seldom, it had been seen by multitudes. Oftener, however, its credibility rested on the faith of some lonely eyewitness, who beheld the wonder through the colored, magnifying, and distorting medium of his imagination, and shaped it more distinctly in his afterthought. It was, indeed, a majestic idea, that the destiny of nations should be revealed, in these awful hieroglyphics, on the cope[112] of heaven. A scroll so wide might not be deemed too expansive for Providence to write a people's doom upon. The belief was a favorite one with our forefathers, as betokening that their infant commonwealth was under a celestial guardianship of peculiar intimacy and strictness. But what shall we say, when an individual discovers a revelation, addressed to himself alone, on the same vast sheet of record! In such a case, it could only be the symptom of a highly disordered mental state, when a man, rendered morbidly self-contemplative by long, intense, and secret pain, had extended his egotism over the whole expanse of nature, until the firmament itself should appear no more than a fitting page for his soul's history and fate.

We impute it, therefore, solely to the disease in his own eye and heart, that the minister, looking upward to the zenith, beheld there the appearance of an immense letter,—the letter A,—marked out in lines of dull red light. Not but the meteor may have shown itself at that point, burning duskily through a veil of cloud; but with no such shape as his guilty imagination gave it; or, at least, with so little definiteness, that another's guilt might have seen another symbol in it.

There was a singular circumstance that characterized Mr. Dimmesdale's psychological state, at this moment. All the time that he gazed upward to the zenith, he was, nevertheless, perfectly aware that little Pearl was pointing her finger towards old Roger Chillingworth, who stood at no great distance from the scaffold. The minister appeared to see him, with the same glance that discerned the miraculous letter. To his features, as to all other objects, the meteoric light imparted a new

---

[112]COPE: Canopy.

expression; or it might well be that the physician was not careful then, as at all other times, to hide the malevolence with which he looked upon his victim. Certainly, if the meteor kindled up the sky, and disclosed the earth, with an awfulness that admonished Hester Prynne and the clergyman of the day of judgment, then might Roger Chillingworth have passed with them for the arch-fiend, standing there, with a smile and scowl, to claim his own. So vivid was the expression, or so intense the minister's perception of it, that it seemed still to remain painted on the darkness, after the meteor had vanished, with an effect as if the street and all things else were at once annihilated.

"Who is that man, Hester?" gasped Mr. Dimmesdale, overcome with terror. "I shiver at him! Dost thou know the man? I hate him, Hester!"

She remembered her oath, and was silent.

"I tell thee, my soul shivers at him," muttered the minister again. "Who is he? Who is he? Canst thou do nothing for me? I have a name-less horror of the man."

"Minister," said little Pearl, "I can tell thee who he is!"

"Quickly, then, child!" said the minister, bending his ear close to her lips. "Quickly!—and as low as thou canst whisper."

Pearl mumbled something into his ear, that sounded, indeed, like human language, but was only such gibberish as children may be heard amusing themselves with, by the hour together. At all events, if it involved any secret information in regard to old Roger Chillingworth, it was in a tongue unknown to the erudite clergyman, and did but increase the bewilderment of his mind. The elfish child then laughed aloud.

"Dost thou mock me now?" said the minister.

"Thou was not bold!—thou was not true!" answered the child. "Thou wouldst not promise to take my hand, and mother's hand, to-morrow noontide!"

"Worthy Sir," said the physician, who had now advanced to the foot of the platform. "Pious Master Dimmesdale! can this be you? Well, well, indeed! We men of study, whose heads are in our books, have need to be straitly looked after! We dream in our waking moments, and walk in our sleep. Come, good Sir, and my dear friend, I pray you, let me lead you home!"

"How knewest thou that I was here?" asked the minister, fearfully.

"Verily, and in good faith," answered Roger Chillingworth, "I knew nothing of the matter. I had spent the better part of the night at the bedside of the worshipful Governor Winthrop, doing what my poor skill might to give him ease. He going home to a better world, I, likewise, was on my way homeward, when this strange light shone out. Come with me, I beseech you, Reverend Sir; else you will be poorly able to do Sabbath duty tomorrow. Aha! see now, how they trouble the brain,—these books!—these books! You should study less, good Sir, and take a little pastime; or these night-whimseys will grow upon you!"

"I will go home with you," said Mr. Dimmesdale.

With a chill despondency, like one awaking, all nerveless, from an ugly dream, he yielded himself to the physician, and was led away.

The next day, however, being the Sabbath, he preached a discourse which was held to be the richest and most powerful, and the most replete with heavenly influences, that had ever proceeded from his lips. Souls, it is said, more souls than one, were brought to the truth by the efficacy of that sermon, and vowed within themselves to cherish a holy gratitude towards Mr. Dimmesdale throughout the long hereafter. But, as he came down the pulpit-steps, the gray-bearded sexton met him, holding up a black glove, which the minister recognized as his own.

"It was found," said the sexton, "this morning, on the scaffold, where evil-doers are set up to public shame. Satan dropped it there, I take it, intending a scurrilous jest against your reverence. But, indeed, he was blind and foolish, as he ever and always is. A pure hand needs no glove to cover it!"

"Thank you, my good friend," said the minister gravely, but startled at heart; for, so confused was his remembrance, that he had almost brought himself to look at the events of the past night as visionary. "Yes, it seems to be my glove, indeed!"

"And, since Satan saw fit to steal it, your reverence must needs handle him without gloves, henceforward," remarked the old sexton, grimly smiling. "But did your reverence hear of the portent that was seen last night? a great red letter in the sky,—the letter A,—which we interpret to stand for Angel. For, as our good Governor Winthrop was made an angel this past night, it was doubtless held fit that there should be some notice thereof!"

"No," answered the minister; "I had not heard of it."

XIII. ANOTHER VIEW OF HESTER

In her late singular interview with Mr. Dimmesdale, Hester Prynne was shocked at the condition to which she found the clergyman reduced. His nerve seemed absolutely destroyed. His moral force was abased into more than childish weakness. It grovelled helpless on the ground, even while his intellectual faculties retained their pristine strength, or had perhaps acquired a morbid energy, which disease only could have given them. With her knowledge of a train of circumstances hidden from all others, she could readily infer, that, besides the legitimate action of his own conscience, a terrible machinery had been brought to bear, and was still operating, on Mr. Dimmesdale's well-being and repose. Knowing what this poor, fallen man had once been, her whole soul was moved by the shuddering terror with which he had appealed to her,—the outcast woman,—for support against his instinctively discovered enemy. She decided, moreover, that he had a right to her utmost aid. Little accustomed, in her long seclusion from society, to measure her ideas of right and wrong by any standard external to herself, Hester saw—or seemed to see—that there lay a responsibility upon her, in reference to the clergyman, which she owned to no other, nor to the whole world besides. The links that united her to the rest of human kind—links of flowers, or silk, or gold, or whatever the material—had all been broken. Here was the iron link of mutual crime, which neither he nor she could break. Like all other ties, it brought along with it its obligations.

Hester Prynne did not now occupy precisely the same position in which we beheld her during the earlier periods of her ignominy. Years had come, and gone. Pearl was now seven years old. Her mother, with the scarlet letter on her breast, glittering in its fantastic embroidery, had long been a familiar object to the townspeople. As is apt to be the case when a person stands out in any prominence before the community, and, at the same time, interferes neither with public nor individual interests and convenience, a species of general regard had ultimately grown up in reference to Hester Prynne. It is to the credit of human nature, that, except where its selfishness is brought into play, it loves more readily than it hates. Hatred, by a gradual and quiet process, will even be transformed to love, unless the change be impeded by a continually new irritation of the original feeling of hostility. In this matter of Hester Prynne, there was neither irritation nor irksomeness. She never battled with the public, but submitted uncomplainingly to its worst usage; she made no claim upon it, in requital for what she suffered; she did not weigh upon its sympathies. Then, also, the blameless purity of her life, during all these years in which she had been set apart to infamy, was reckoned largely in her favor. With nothing now to lose, in the sight of mankind, and with no hope, and seemingly no wish, of gaining any thing, it could only be a genuine regard for virtue that had brought back the poor wanderer to its paths.

It was perceived, too, that, while Hester never put forward even the humblest title to share in the world's privileges,—farther than to breathe the common air, and earn daily bread for little Pearl and herself by the faithful labor of her hands,—she was quick to acknowledge her sisterhood with the race of man, whenever benefits were to be conferred. None so ready as she to give of her little substance to every demand of poverty; even though the bitter-hearted pauper threw back a gibe in requital of the food brought regularly to his door, or the garments wrought for him by the fingers that could have embroidered a monarch's robe. None so self-devoted as Hester, when pestilence stalked through the town. In all seasons of calamity, indeed, whether general or of individuals, the outcast of society at once found her place. She came, not as a guest, but as a rightful inmate, into the household that was darkened by trouble; as if its gloomy twilight were a medium in which she was entitled to hold intercourse with her fellow-creatures. There glimmered the embroidered letter, with comfort in its unearthly ray. Elsewhere the token of sin, it was the taper of the sick-chamber. It had even thrown its gleam, in the sufferer's hard extremity, across the verge of time. It had shown him where to set his foot, while the light of earth was fast becoming dim, and ere the light of futurity[113] could reach him. In such emergencies, Hester's nature showed itself warm and rich; a well-spring of human tenderness, unfailing to every real demand, and inexhaustible by the largest. Her breast, with its badge of shame, was but the softer pillow for the head that needed one. She was self-ordained a Sister of Mercy; or, we may rather say, the world's heavy hand had so ordained her, when neither the world nor she looked forward to this result. The letter was the symbol of her calling. Such helpfulness was found in her,—so much power to do, and power to sympathize,—that many people refused to interpret the scarlet A by its original signification. They said that it meant Able; so strong was Hester Prynne, with a woman's strength.

It was only the darkened house that could contain her. When sunshine came again, she was not there. Her shadow had faded across the threshold. The helpful inmate had departed, without one backward glance to gather up the meed[114] of gratitude, if any were in the hearts of those whom she had served so zealously. Meeting them in the street, she never raised her head to receive their greeting. If they were resolute to accost her, she laid her finger on the scarlet letter, and passed on. This might be pride, but was so like humility, that it produced all the softening influence of the latter quality on the public mind. The public is despotic in its temper; it is capable of denying common justice, when too strenuously demanded as a right; but quite as frequently it awards more than justice, when the appeal is made, as despots love to have it made,

---

[113]FUTURITY: A future time.
[114]MEED: Reward.

entirely to its generosity. Interpreting Hester Prynne's deportment as an appeal of this nature, society was inclined to show its former victim a more benign countenance than she cared to be favored with, or, perchance, than she deserved.

The rulers, and the wise and learned men of the community, were longer in acknowledging the influence of Hester's good qualities than the people. The prejudices which they shared in common with the latter were fortified in themselves by an iron framework of reasoning, that made it a far tougher labor to expel them. Day by day, nevertheless, their sour and rigid wrinkles were relaxing into something which, in the due course of years, might grow to be an expression of almost benevolence. Thus it was with the men of rank, on whom their eminent position imposed the guardianship of the public morals. Individuals in private life, meanwhile, had quite forgiven Hester Prynne for her frailty; nay, more, they had begun to look upon the scarlet letter as the token, not of that one sin, for which she had borne so long and dreary a penance, but of her many good deeds since. "Do you see that woman with the embroidered badge?" they would say to strangers. "It is our Hester,—the town's own Hester,—who is so kind to the poor, so helpful to the sick, so comfortable to the afflicted!" Then, it is true, the propensity of human nature to tell the very worst of itself, when embodied in the person of another, would constrain them to whisper the black scandal of bygone years. It was none the less a fact, however, that, in the eyes of the very men who spoke thus, the scarlet letter had the effect of the cross on a nun's bosom. It imparted to the wearer a kind of sacredness, which enabled her to walk securely amid all peril. Had she fallen among thieves, it would have kept her safe. It was reported, and believed by many, that an Indian had drawn his arrow against the badge, and that the missile struck it, but fell harmless to the ground.

The effect of the symbol—or rather, of the position in respect to society that was indicated by it—on the mind of Hester Prynne herself, was powerful and peculiar. All the light and graceful foliage of her character had been withered up by this red-hot brand, and had long ago fallen away, leaving a bare and harsh outline, which might have been repulsive, had she possessed friends or companions to be repelled by it. Even the attractiveness of her person had undergone a similar change. It might be partly owing to the studied austerity of her dress, and partly to the lack of demonstration in her manners. It was a sad transformation, too, that her rich and luxuriant hair had either been cut off, or was so completely hidden by a cap, that not a shining lock of it ever once gushed into the sunshine. It was due in part to all these causes, but still more to something else, that there seemed to be no longer any thing in Hester's face for Love to dwell upon; nothing in Hester's form, though majestic and statue-like, that Passion would ever dream of clasping in its embrace; nothing in Hester's bosom, to make it ever again the pillow of Affection. Some attribute had departed from her, the permanence of which had been essential to keep her a woman. Such is frequently the fate, and such the stern development, of the feminine character and person, when the woman has encountered, and lived through, an experience of peculiar severity. If she be all tenderness, she will die. If she survive, the tenderness will either be crushed out of her, or—and the outward semblance is the same—crushed so deeply into her heart that it can never show itself more. The latter is perhaps the truest theory. She who has once been woman, and ceased to be so, might at any moment become a woman again, if there were only the magic touch to effect the transformation. We shall see whether Hester Prynne were ever afterwards so touched, and so transfigured.

Much of the marble coldness of Hester's impression was to be attributed to the circumstance that her life had turned, in a great measure, from passion and feeling, to thought. Standing alone in the world,—alone, as to any dependence on society, and with little Pearl to be guided and protected,—alone, and hopeless of retrieving her position, even had she not scorned to consider it desirable,—she cast away the fragment of a broken chain. The world's law was no law for her mind. It was an age in which the human intellect, newly emancipated, had taken a more active and a wider range than for many centuries before. Men of the sword had overthrown nobles and kings. Men bolder than these had overthrown and rearranged—not actually, but within the sphere of theory, which was their most real abode—the whole system of ancient prejudice, wherewith was linked much of ancient principle. Hester Prynne imbibed this spirit. She assumed a freedom of speculation, then common enough on the other side of the Atlantic, but which our forefathers, had they known of it, would have held to be a deadlier crime than that stigmatized by the scarlet letter. In her lonesome cottage, by the sea-shore, thoughts visited her, such as dared to enter no other dwelling in New England; shadowy guests, that would have been as perilous as demons to their entertainer, could they have been seen so much as knocking at her door.

It is remarkable, that persons who speculate the most boldly often conform with the most perfect quietude to the external regulations of society. The thought suffices them, without investing itself in the flesh and blood of action. So it seemed to be with Hester. Yet, had little Pearl never come to her from the spiritual world, it might have been far otherwise. Then, she might have come down to us in history, hand in hand with Ann Hutchinson, as the foundress of a religious sect. She might, in one of her phases, have been a prophetess. She might, and not improbably would, have suffered death from the stern tribunals of the period, for attempting to undermine the foundations of the Puritan establishment. But, in the education of her child, the mother's enthusiasm of thought had something to wreak itself upon. Providence, in the person of this little girl, had assigned to Hester's charge the germ and blossom of womanhood, to be cherished and developed amid a host of difficulties. Every thing was against her. The world was hostile. The child's own nature had something wrong in it, which continually betokened that she had been born amiss,—the effluence of her mother's lawless passion,—and often impelled Hester to ask, in bitterness of heart, whether it were for ill or good that the poor little creature had been born at all.

Indeed, the same dark question often rose into her mind, with reference to the whole race of womanhood. Was existence worth accepting even to the happiest among them? As concerned her own individual existence, she had long ago decided in the negative, and dismissed the point as settled. A tendency to speculation, though it may keep woman quiet, as it does man, yet makes her sad. She discerns, it may be, such a hopeless task before her. As a first step, the whole system of society is to be torn down, and built up anew. Then, the very nature of the opposite sex, or its long hereditary habit, which has become like nature, is to be essentially modified, before woman can be allowed to assume what seems a fair and suitable position. Finally, all other difficulties being obviated,[115] woman cannot take advantage of these preliminary reforms, until she herself shall have undergone a still mightier change; in which, perhaps, the ethereal essence, wherein she has her truest life, will be found to have evaporated. A woman never overcomes these problems by any exercise of thought. They are not to be solved, or only in one way. If her heart chance to come uppermost, they vanish. Thus, Hester Prynne, whose heart had lost its regular and healthy throb, wandered without a clew in the dark labyrinth of mind; now turned aside by an insurmountable precipice; now starting back from a deep chasm. There was wild and ghastly scenery all around her, and a home and comfort nowhere. At times, a fearful doubt strove to possess her soul, whether

[115]OBVIATED: Cleared out of the way.

it were not better to send Pearl at once to heaven, and go herself to such futurity as Eternal Justice should provide.

The scarlet letter had not done its office.

Now, however, her interview with the Reverend Mr. Dimmesdale, on the night of his vigil, had given her a new theme of reflection, and held up to her an object that appeared worthy of any exertion and sacrifice for its attainment. She had witnessed the intense misery beneath which the minister struggled, or, to speak more accurately, had ceased to struggle. She saw that he stood on the verge of lunacy, if he had not already stepped across it. It was impossible to doubt, that, whatever painful efficacy there might be in the secret sting of remorse, a deadlier venom had been infused into it by the hand that proffered relief. A secret enemy had been continually by his side, under the semblance of a friend and helper, and had availed himself of the opportunities thus afforded for tampering with the delicate springs of Mr. Dimmesdale's nature. Hester could not but ask herself, whether there had not originally been a defect of truth, courage, and loyalty, on her own part, in allowing the minister to be thrown into a position where so much evil was to be foreboded, and nothing auspicious to be hoped. Her only justification lay in the fact, that she had been able to discern no method of rescuing him from a blacker ruin than had overwhelmed herself, except by acquiescing in Roger Chillingworth's scheme of disguise. Under that impulse, she had made her choice, and had chosen, as it now appeared, the more wretched alternative of the two. She determined to redeem her error, so far as it might yet be possible. Strengthened by years of hard and solemn trial, she felt herself no longer so inadequate to cope with Roger Chillingworth as on that night, abased by sin, and half maddened by the ignominy that was still new, when they had talked together in the prison-chamber. She had climbed her way, since then, to a higher point. The old man, on the other hand, had brought himself nearer to her level, or perhaps below it, by the revenge which he had stooped for.

In fine,[116] Hester Prynne resolved to meet her former husband, and do what might be in her power for the rescue of the victim on whom he had so evidently set his gripe. The occasion was not long to seek. One afternoon, walking with Pearl in a retired part of the peninsula, she beheld the old physician, with a basket, on one arm and a staff in the other hand, stooping along the ground, in quest of roots and herbs to concoct his medicines withal.

[116]IN FINE: In conclusion.

XIV. HESTER AND THE PHYSICIAN

Hester bade little Pearl run down to the margin of the water, and play with the shells and tangled sea-weed, until she should have talked awhile with yonder gatherer of herbs. So the child flew away like a bird, and, making bare her small white feet, went pattering along the moist margin of the sea. Here and there, she came to a full stop, and peeped curiously into a pool, left by the retiring tide as a mirror for Pearl to see her face in. Forth peeped at her, out of the pool, with dark, glistening curls around her head, and an elf-smile in her eyes, the image of a little maid, whom Pearl, having no other playmate, invited to take her hand and run a race with her. But the visionary little maid, on her part, beckoned likewise, as if to say,—"This is a better place! Come thou into the pool!" And Pearl, stepping in, mid-leg deep, beheld her own white feet at the bottom; while, out of a still lower depth, came the gleam of a kind of fragmentary smile, floating to and fro in the agitated water.

Meanwhile her mother had accosted the physician.

"I would speak a word with you," said she,—"a word that concerns us much."

"Aha! And is it Mistress Hester that has a word for old Roger Chillingworth?" answered he, raising himself from his stooping posture. "With all my heart! Why, Mistress, I hear good tidings of you on all hands! No longer ago than yester-eve, a magistrate, a wise and godly man, was discoursing of your affairs, Mistress Hester, and whispered me that there had been question concerning you in the council. It was debated whether or no, with safety to the common weal,[117] yonder scarlet letter might be taken off your bosom. On my life, Hester, I made my entreaty to the worshipful magistrate that it might be done forthwith!"

"It lies not in the pleasure of the magistrates to take off this badge," calmly replied Hester. "Were I worthy to be quit of it, it would fall away of its own nature, or be transformed into something that should speak a different purport."

"Nay, then, wear it, if it suit you better," rejoined he, "A woman must needs follow her own fancy, touching the adornment of her person. The letter is gayly embroidered, and shows right bravely on your bosom!"

All this while, Hester had been looking steadily at the old man, and was shocked, as well as wonder-smitten, to discern what a change had been wrought upon him within the past seven years. It was not so much that he had grown older; for though the traces of advancing life were

[117]WEAL: Welfare.

visible, he bore his age well, and seemed to retain a wiry vigor and alertness. But the former aspect of an intellectual and studious man, calm and quiet, which was what she best remembered in him, had altogether vanished, and been succeeded by an eager, searching, almost fierce, yet carefully guarded look. It seemed to be his wish and purpose to mask this expression with a smile; but the latter played him false, and flickered over his visage so derisively that the spectator could see his blackness all the better for it. Ever and anon,[118] too, there came a glare of red light out of his eyes; as if the old man's soul were on fire, and kept on smouldering duskily within his breast, until, by some casual puff of passion, it was blown into a momentary flame. This he repressed as speedily as possible, and strove to look as if nothing of the kind had happened.

In a word, old Roger Chillingworth was a striking evidence of man's faculty of transforming himself into a devil, if he will only, for a reasonable space of time, undertake a devil's office. This unhappy person had effected such a transformation by devoting himself, for seven years, to the constant analysis of a heart full of torture, and deriving his enjoyment thence, and adding fuel to those fiery tortures which he analyzed and gloated over.

The scarlet letter burned on Hester Prynne's bosom. Here was another ruin, the responsibility of which came partly home to her.

"What see you in my face," asked the physician, "that you look at it so earnestly?"

"Something that would make me weep, if there were any tears bitter enough for it," answered she. "But let it pass! It is of yonder miserable man that I would speak."

"And what of him?" cried Roger Chillingworth eagerly, as if he loved the topic, and were glad of an opportunity to discuss it with the only person of whom he could make a confidant. "Not to hide the truth, Mistress Hester, my thoughts happen just now to be busy with the gentleman. So speak freely; and I will make answer."

"When we last spake together," said Hester, "now seven years ago, it was your pleasure to extort a promise of secrecy, as touching the former relation betwixt yourself and me. As the life and good fame of yonder man were in your hands, there seemed no choice to me, save to be silent, in accordance with your behest. Yet it was not without heavy misgivings that I thus bound myself; for, having cast off all duty towards other human beings, there remained a duty towards him; and something whispered me that I was betraying it, in pledging myself to keep

---

[118]EVER AND ANON: Every now and then.

your counsel. Since that day, no man is so near to him as you. You tread behind his every footstep. You are beside him, sleeping and waking. You search his thoughts. You burrow and rankle in his heart! Your clutch is on his life, and you cause him to die daily a living death; and still he knows you not. In permitting this, I have surely acted a false part by the only man to whom the power was left me to be true!"

"What choice had you?" asked Roger Chillingworth. "My finger, pointed at this man, would have hurled him from his pulpit into a dungeon,—thence, peradventure, to the gallows!"

"It had been better so!" said Hester Prynne.

"What evil have I done the man?" asked Roger Chillingworth again. "I tell thee, Hester Prynne, the richest fee that ever physician earned from monarch could not have bought such care as I have wasted on this miserable priest! But for my aid, his life would have burned away in torments, within the first two years after the perpetration of his crime and thine. For, Hester, his spirit lacked the strength that could have borne up, as thine has, beneath a burden like thy scarlet letter. O, I could reveal a goodly secret! But enough! What art can do, I have exhausted on him. That he now breathes, and creeps about on earth, is owing all to me!"

"Better he had died at once!" said Hester Prynne.

"Yea, woman, thou sayest truly!" cried old Roger Chillingworth, letting the lurid fire of his heart blaze out before her eyes. "Better had he died at once! Never did mortal suffer what this man has suffered. And all, all, in the sight of his worst enemy! He has been conscious of me. He has felt an influence dwelling always upon him like a curse. He knew, by some spiritual sense,—for the Creator never made another being so sensitive as this,—he knew that no friendly hand was pulling at his heart-strings, and that an eye was looking curiously into him, which sought only evil, and found it. But he knew not that the eye and hand were mine! With the superstition common to his brotherhood, he fancied himself given over to a fiend, to be tortured with frightful dreams, and desperate thoughts, the sting of remorse, and despair of pardon; as a foretaste of what awaits him beyond the grave. But it was the constant shadow of my presence!—the closest propinquity[119] of the man whom he had most vilely wronged!—and who had grown to exist only by this perpetual poison of the direst revenge! Yea, indeed!—he did not err!—there was a fiend at his elbow! A mortal man, with once a human heart, has become a fiend for his especial torment!"

[119]PROPINQUITY: Proximity.

The unfortunate physician, while uttering these words, lifted his hands with a look of horror, as if he had beheld some frightful shape, which he could not recognize, usurping the place of his own image in a glass. It was one of those moments—which sometimes occur only at the interval of years—when a man's moral aspect is faithfully revealed to his mind's eye. Not improbably, he had never before viewed himself as he did now.

"Hast thou not tortured him enough?" said Hester, noticing the old man's look. "Has he not paid thee all?"

"No!—no!—He has but increased the debt!" answered the physician; and, as he proceeded, his manner lost its fiercer characteristics, and subsided into gloom. "Dost thou remember me, Hester, as I was nine years agone? Even then, I was in the autumn of my days, nor was it the early autumn. But all my life had been made up of earnest, studious, thoughtful, quiet years, bestowed faithfully for the increase of mine own knowledge, and faithfully, too, though this latter object was but casual to the other,—faithfully for the advancement of human welfare. No life had been more peaceful and innocent than mine; few lives so rich with benefits conferred. Dost thou remember me? Was I not, though you might deem me cold, nevertheless a man thoughtful for others, craving little for himself,—kind, true, just, and of constant, if not warm affections? Was I not all this?"

"All this, and more," said Hester.

"And what am I now?" demanded he, looking into her face, and permitting the whole evil within him to be written on his features. "I have already told thee what I am! A fiend! Who made me so?"

"It was myself!" cried Hester, shuddering. "It was I, not less than he. Why hast thou not avenged thyself on me?"

"I have left thee to the scarlet letter," replied Roger Chillingworth. "If that have not avenged me, I can do no more!"

He laid his finger on it, with a smile.

"It has avenged thee!" answered Hester Prynne.

"I judged no less," said the physician. "And now, what wouldst thou with me touching this man?"

"I must reveal the secret," answered Hester, firmly. "He must discern thee in thy true character. What may be the result, I know not. But this long debt of confidence, due from me to him, whose bane and ruin I have been, shall at length be paid. So far as concerns the overthrow or preservation of his fair fame and his earthly state, and perchance his life, he is in thy hands. Nor do I,—whom the scarlet letter has disciplined to truth, though it be the truth of red-hot iron, entering into the soul,— nor do I perceive such advantage in his living any longer a life of ghastly emptiness, that I shall stoop to implore thy mercy. Do with him as thou wilt! There is no good for him,—no good for me,—no good for thee! There is no good for little Pearl! There is no path to guide us out of this dismal maze!"

"Woman, I could wellnigh pity thee!" said Roger Chillingworth, unable to restrain a thrill of admiration too; for there was a quality almost majestic in the despair which she expressed. "Thou hadst great elements. Peradventure, hadst thou met earlier with a better love than mine, this evil had not been. I pity thee, for the good that has been wasted in thy nature!"

"And I thee," answered Hester Prynne, "for the hatred that has transformed a wise and just man to a fiend! Wilt thou yet purge it out of thee, and be once more human? If not for his sake, then doubly for thine own! Forgive, and leave his further retribution to the Power that claims it! I said, but now, that there could be no good event for him, or thee, or me, who are here wandering together in this gloomy maze of evil, and stumbling at every step, over the guilt wherewith we have strewn our path. It is not so! There might be good for thee, and thee alone, since thou hast been deeply wronged, and hast it at thy will to pardon. Wilt thou give up that only privilege? Wilt thou reject that priceless benefit?"

"Peace, Hester, peace!" replied the old man, with gloomy sternness. "It is not granted me to pardon. I have no such power as thou tellest me of. My old faith, long forgotten, comes back to me, and explains all that we do, and all we suffer. By thy first step awry, thou didst plant the germ of evil; but, since that moment, it has all been a dark necessity. Ye that have wronged me are not sinful, save in a kind of typical illusion; neither am I fiend-like, who have snatched a fiend's office from his hands. It is our fate. Let the black flower blossom as it may! Now go thy ways, and deal as thou wilt with yonder man."

He waved his hand, and betook himself again to his employment of gathering herbs.

XV. HESTER AND PEARL

So Roger Chillingworth—a deformed old figure, with a face that haunted men's memories longer than they liked—took leave of Hester Prynne, and went stooping away along the earth. He gathered here and there an herb, or grubbed up a root, and put it into the basket on his arm. His gray beard almost touched the ground, as he crept onward. Hester gazed after him a little while, looking with a half-fantastic curiosity to see whether the tender grass of early spring would not be blighted beneath him, and show the wavering track of his footsteps, sere and brown, across its cheerful verdure. She wondered what sort of herbs they were, which the old man was so sedulous[120] to gather. Would not the earth, quickened to an evil purpose by the sympathy of his eye, greet him with poisonous shrubs, of species hitherto unknown, that would start up under his fingers? Or might it suffice him, that every wholesome growth should be converted into something deleterious and malignant at his touch? Did the sun, which shone so brightly everywhere else, really fall upon him? Or was there, as it rather seemed, a circle of ominous shadow moving along with his deformity, whichever way he turned himself? And whither was he now going? Would he not suddenly sink into the earth, leaving a barren and blasted spot, where, in due course of time, would be seen deadly nightshade, dogwood, henbane,[121] and whatever else of vegetable wickedness the climate could produce, all flourishing with hideous luxuriance? Or would he spread bat's wings and flee away, looking so much the uglier, the higher he rose towards heaven?

"Be it sin or no," said Hester Prynne bitterly, as she still gazed after him, "I hate the man!"

She upbraided herself for the sentiment, but could not overcome or lessen it. Attempting to do so, she thought of those long-past days, in a distant land, when he used to emerge at eventide from the seclusion of his study, and sit down in the fire-light of their home, and in the light of her nuptial smile. He needed to bask himself in that smile, he said, in order that the chill of so many lonely hours among his books might be taken off the scholar's heart. Such scenes had once appeared not otherwise than happy, but now, as viewed through the dismal medium of her subsequent life, they classed themselves among her ugliest remembrances. She marvelled how such scenes could have been! She marvelled how she could ever have been wrought upon to marry him! She deemed in her crime most to be repented of, that she had ever endured, and reciprocated, the lukewarm grasp of his hand, and had suffered the smile of her lips and eyes to mingle and melt into his own. And it seemed a fouler offence committed by Roger Chillingworth, than any which had since been done him, that, in the time when her heart knew no better, he had persuaded her to fancy herself happy by his side.

---

[120]SEDULOUS: Diligent.
[121]NIGHTSHADE, DOGWOOD, HENBANE: Poisonous plants that, while having medicinal properties, are also associated with witchcraft.

"Yes, I hate him!" repeated Hester, more bitterly than before. "He betrayed me! He has done me worse wrong than I did him!"

Let men tremble to win the hand of woman, unless they win along with it the utmost passion of her heart! Else it may be their miserable fortune, as it was Roger Chillingworth's, when some mightier touch than their own may have awakened all her sensibilities, to be reproached even for the calm content, the marble image of happiness, which they will have imposed upon her as the warm reality. But Hester ought long ago to have done with this injustice. What did it betoken? Had seven long years, under the torture of the scarlet letter, inflicted so much of misery, and wrought out no repentance?

The emotions of that brief space, while she stood gazing after the crooked figure of old Roger Chillingworth, threw a dark light on Hester's state of mind, revealing much that she might not otherwise have acknowledged to herself.

He being gone, she summoned back her child.

"Pearl! Little Pearl! Where are you?"

Pearl, whose activity of spirit never flagged, had been at no loss for amusement while her mother talked with the old gatherer of herbs. At first, as already told, she had flirted fancifully with her own image in a pool of water, beckoning the phantom forth, and—as it declined to venture—seeking a passage for herself into its sphere of impalpable earth and unattainable sky. Soon finding, however, that either she or the image was unreal, she turned elsewhere for better pastime. She made little boats out of birch-bark, and freighted them with snail-shells, and sent out more ventures on the mighty deep than any merchant in New England; but the larger part of them foundered near the shore. She seized a live horseshoe[122] by the tail, and made prize of several five-fingers,[123] and laid out a jelly-fish to melt in the warm sun. Then she took up the white foam, that streaked the line of the advancing tide, and threw it upon the breeze, scampering after it with winged footsteps, to catch the great snow-flakes ere they fell. Perceiving a flock of beach-birds, that fed and fluttered along the shore, the naughty child picked up her apron full of pebbles, and, creeping from rock to rock after these small sea-fowl, displayed remarkable dexterity in pelting them. One little gray bird, with a white breast, Pearl was almost sure, had been hit by a pebble, and fluttered away with a broken wing. But then the elf-child sighed, and gave up

[122]HORSESHOE: A horseshoe crab.
[123]FIVE-FINGERS: Starfish.

her sport; because it grieved her to have done harm to a little being that was as wild as the sea-breeze, or as wild as Pearl herself.

Her final employment was to gather sea-weed, of various kinds, and make herself a scarf, or mantle, and a head-dress, and thus assume the aspect of a little mermaid. She inherited her mother's gift for devising drapery and costume. As the last touch to her mermaid's garb, Pearl took some eel-grass, and imitated, as best she could, on her own bosom, the decoration with which she was so familiar on her mother's. A letter,—the letter A,—but freshly green, instead of scarlet! The child bent her chin upon her breast, and contemplated this device with strange interest; even as if the one only thing for which she had been sent into the world was to make out its hidden import.

"I wonder if mother will ask me what it means!" thought Pearl.

Just then, she heard her mother's voice, and, flitting along as lightly as one of the little sea-birds, appeared before Hester Prynne, dancing, laughing, and pointing her finger to the ornament upon her bosom.

"My little Pearl," said Hester, after a moment's silence, "the green letter, and on thy childish bosom, has no purport. But dost thou know, my child, what this letter means which thy mother is doomed to wear?"

"Yes mother," said the child. "It is the great letter A. Thou hast taught it me in the horn-book."[124]

Hester looked steadily into her little face; but, though there was that singular expression which she had so often remarked in her black eyes, she could not satisfy herself whether Pearl really attached any meaning to the symbol. She felt a morbid desire to ascertain the point.

"Dost thou know, child, wherefore thy mother wears this letter?"

"Truly do I!" answered Pearl, looking brightly into her mother's face. "It is for the same reason that the minister keeps his hand over his heart!"

"And what reason is that?" asked Hester, half smiling at the absurd incongruity of the child's observation; but on second thoughts turning pale. "What has the letter to do with any heart, save mine?"

"Nay, mother, I have told all I know," said Pearl, more seriously than she was wont to speak. "Ask yonder old man whom thou hast been talking with! It may be he can tell. But in good earnest now, mother dear, what does this scarlet letter mean?—and why dost thou wear it on thy bosom?—and why does the minister keep his hand over his heart?"

[124]HORN-BOOK: A child's first textbook, made of a leaf of paper printed with the alphabet, vowels, first ten Arabic numerals, and the Lord's Prayer, protected by a thin sheet of translucent horn usually mounted on a piece of wood resembling a paddle.

She took her mother's hand in both her own, and gazed into her eyes with an earnestness that was seldom seen in her wild and capricious character. The thought occurred to Hester, that the child might really be seeking to approach her with childlike confidence, and doing what she could, and as intelligently as she knew how, to establish a meeting-point of sympathy. It showed Pearl in an unwonted aspect. Heretofore, the mother, while loving her child with the intensity of a sole affection, had schooled herself to hope for little other return than the waywardness of an April breeze; which spends its time in airy sport, and has its gusts of inexplicable passion, and is petulant in its best of moods, and chills oftener than caresses you, when you take it to your bosom; in requital of which misdemeanours it will sometimes, of its own vague purpose, kiss your cheek with a kind of doubtful tenderness, and play gently with your hair, and then begone about its other idle business, leaving a dreamy pleasure at your heart. And this, moreover, was a mother's estimate of the child's disposition. Any other observer might have seen few but unamiable traits, and have given them a far darker coloring. But now the idea came strongly into Hester's mind, that Pearl, with her remarkable precocity and acuteness, might already have approached the age when she could be made a friend, and intrusted with as much of her mother's sorrows as could be imparted, without irreverence either to the parent or the child. In the little chaos of Pearl's character, there might be seen emerging—and could have been, from the very first—the stedfast principles of an unflinching courage,—an uncontrollable will,—a sturdy pride, which might be disciplined into self-respect,—and a bitter scorn of many things, which, when examined, might be found to have the taint of falsehood in them. She possessed affections, too, though hitherto acrid and disagreeable, as are the richest flavors of unripe fruit. With all these sterling attributes, thought Hester, the evil which she inherited from her mother must be great indeed, if a noble woman do not grow out of this elfish child.

Pearl's inevitable tendency to hover about the enigma of the scarlet letter seemed an innate quality of her being. From the earliest epoch of her conscious life, she had entered upon this as her appointed mission. Hester had often fancied that Providence had a design of justice and retribution, in endowing the child with this marked propensity; but never, until now, had she bethought herself to ask, whether, linked with that design, there might not likewise be a purpose of mercy and beneficence. If little Pearl were entertained with faith and trust, as a spirit-messenger no less than an earthly child, might it not be her errand to soothe away the sorrow that lay cold in her mother's heart, and converted it into a tomb?—and to help her to overcome the passion, once so wild, and even yet neither dead nor asleep, but only imprisoned within the same tomb-like heart?

Such were some of the thoughts that now stirred in Hester's mind, with as much vivacity of impression as if they had actually been whispered into her ear. And there was little Pearl, all this while, holding her mother's hand in both her own, and turning her face upward, while she put these searching questions, once, and again, and still a third time.

"What does the letter mean, mother?—and why dost thou wear it?—and why does the minister keep his hand over his heart?"

"What shall I say?" thought Hester to herself.—"No! if this be the price of the child's sympathy, I cannot pay it!"

Then she spoke aloud.

"Silly Pearl," said she, "what questions are these? There are many things in this world that a child must not ask about. What know I of the minister's heart? And as for the scarlet letter, I wear it for the sake of its gold thread!"

In all the seven bygone years, Hester Prynne had never before been false to the symbol on her bosom. It may be that it was the talisman of a stern and severe, but yet a guardian spirit, who now forsook her; as recognizing that, in spite of his strict watch over her heart, some new evil had crept into it, or some old one had never been expelled. As for little Pearl, the earnestness soon passed out of her face.

But the child did not see fit to let the matter drop. Two or three times, as her mother and she went homeward, and as often at supper-time, and while Hester was putting her to bed, and once after she seemed to be fairly asleep, Pearl looked up, with mischief gleaming in her black eyes.

"Mother," said she, "what does the scarlet letter mean?"

And the next morning, the first indication the child gave of being awake was by popping up her head from the pillow, and making that other inquiry, which she had so unaccountably connected with her investigations about the scarlet letter:—

"Mother!—Mother!—Why does the minister keep his hand over his heart?"

"Hold thy tongue, naughty child!" answered her mother, with an asperity that she had never permitted to herself before. "Do not tease me; else I shall put thee into the dark closet!"

XVI. A FOREST WALK

Hester Prynne remained constant in her resolve to make known to Mr. Dimmesdale, at whatever risk of present pain or ulterior consequences, the true character of the man who had crept into his intimacy. For several days, however, she vainly sought an opportunity of addressing him in some of the meditative walks which she knew him to be in the habit of taking, along the shores of the peninsula, or on the wooded hills of the neighbouring country. There would have been no scandal, indeed, nor peril to the holy whiteness of the clergyman's good fame, had she visited him in his own study; where many a penitent, ere now, had confessed sins of perhaps as deep a dye as the one betokened by the scarlet letter. But, partly that she dreaded the secret or undisguised interference of old Roger Chillingworth, and partly that her conscious heart imparted suspicion where none could have been felt, and partly that both the minister and she would need the whole wide world to breathe in, while they talked together,—for all these reasons, Hester never thought of meeting him in any narrower privacy than beneath the open sky.

At last, while attending in a sick-chamber, whither the Reverend Mr. Dimmesdale had been summoned to make a prayer, she learnt that he had gone, the day before, to visit the Apostle Eliot,[125] among his Indian converts. He would probably return, by a certain hour, in the afternoon of the morrow. Betimes, therefore, the next day, Hester took little Pearl,—who was necessarily the companion of all her mother's expeditions, however inconvenient her presence,—and set forth.

The road, after the two wayfarers had crossed from the peninsula to the mainland, was no other than a footpath. It straggled onward into the mystery of the primeval forest. This hemmed it in so narrowly, and stood so black and dense on either side, and disclosed such imperfect glimpses of the sky above, that, to Hester's mind, it imaged not amiss the moral wilderness in which she had so long been wandering. The day was chill and sombre. Overhead was a gray expanse of cloud, slightly stirred, however, by a breeze; so that a gleam of flickering sunshine might now and then be seen at its solitary play along the path. This flitting cheerfulness was always at the farther extremity of some long vista through the forest. The sportive sunlight—feebly sportive, at best, in the predominant pensiveness of the day and scene—withdrew itself as they came nigh, and left the spots where it had danced the drearier, because they had hoped to find them bright.

---

[125]APOSTLE ELIOT: John Eliot (1604–1690), a missionary to the local Native American tribes, called "the Apostle to the Indians."

"Mother," said little Pearl, "the sunshine does not love you. It runs away and hides itself, because it is afraid of something on your bosom. Now, see! There it is, playing, a good way off. Stand you here, and let me run and catch it. I am but a child. It will not flee from me; for I wear nothing on my bosom yet!"

"Nor ever will, my child, I hope," said Hester.

"And why not, mother?" asked Pearl, stopping short, just at the beginning of her race. "Will not it come of its own accord, when I am a woman grown?"

"Run away, child," answered her mother, "and catch the sunshine! It will soon be gone."

Pearl set forth, at a great pace, and, as Hester smiled to perceive, did actually catch the sunshine, and stood laughing in the midst of it, all brightened by its splendor, and scintillating with the vivacity excited by rapid motion. The light lingered about the lonely child, as if glad of such a playmate, until her mother had drawn almost nigh enough to step into the magic circle too.

"It will go now!" said Pearl, shaking her head.

"See!" answered Hester, smiling. "Now I can stretch out my hand, and grasp some of it."

As she attempted to do so, the sunshine vanished; or, to judge from the bright expression that was dancing on Pearl's features, her mother could have fancied that the child had absorbed it into herself, and would give it forth again, with a gleam about her path, as they should plunge into some gloomier shade. There was no other attribute that so much impressed her with a sense of new and untransmitted vigor in Pearl's nature, as this never-failing vivacity of spirits; she had not the disease of sadness, which almost all children, in these latter days, inherit, with the scrofula,[126] from the troubles of their ancestors. Perhaps this too was a disease, and but the reflex of the wild energy with which Hester had fought against her sorrows, before Pearl's birth. It was certainly a doubtful charm, imparting a hard, metallic lustre to the child's character. She wanted—what some people want throughout life—a grief that should deeply touch her, and thus humanize and make her capable of sympathy. But there was time enough yet for little Pearl!

"Come, my child!" said Hester, looking about her, from the spot where Pearl had stood still in the sunshine. "We will sit down a little way within the wood, and rest ourselves."

---

[126]SCROFULA: A tubercular disease usually affecting the young and spread via the unpasteurized milk of infected cows.

"I am not aweary, mother," replied the little girl. "But you may sit down, if you will tell me a story meanwhile."

"A story, child!" said Hester. "And about what?"

"O, a story about the Black Man!" answered Pearl, taking hold of her mother's gown, and looking up, half earnestly, half mischievously, into her face. "How he haunts this forest, and carries a book with him,—a big, heavy book, with iron clasps; and how this ugly Black Man offers his book and an iron pen to every body that meets him here among the trees; and they are to write their names with their own blood. And then he sets his mark on their bosoms! Didst thou ever meet the Black Man, mother?"

"And who told you this story, Pearl?" asked her mother, recognizing a common superstition of the period.

"It was the old dame in the chimney-corner, at the house where you watched last night," said the child. "But she fancied me asleep while she was talking of it. She said that a thousand and a thousand people had met him here, and had written in his book, and have his mark on them. And that ugly-tempered lady, old Mistress Hibbins, was one. And, mother, the old dame said that this scarlet letter was the Black Man's mark on thee, and that it glows like a red flame when thou meetest him at midnight, here in the dark wood. Is it true, mother? And dost thou go to meet him in the night-time?"

"Didst thou ever awake, and find thy mother gone?" asked Hester.

"Not that I remember," said the child. "If thou fearest to leave me in our cottage, thou mightest take me along with thee. I would very gladly go! But, mother, tell me now! Is there such a Black Man? And didst thou ever meet him? And is this his mark?"

"Wilt thou let me be at peace, if I once tell thee?" asked her mother.

"Yes, if thou tellest me all," answered Pearl.

"Once in my life I met the Black Man!" said her mother. "This scarlet letter is his mark!"

Thus conversing, they entered sufficiently deep into the wood to secure themselves from the observation of any casual passenger along the forest-track. Here they sat down on a luxuriant heap of moss; which, at some epoch of the preceding century, had been a gigantic pine, with its roots and trunk in the darksome shade, and its head aloft in the upper atmosphere. It was a little dell where they had seated themselves, with a leafstrewn bank rising gently on either side, and a brook flowing through the midst, over a bed of fallen and drowned leaves. The trees impending over it had flung down great branches, from time to time, which choked up the current, and compelled it to form eddies and black depths at some points; while, in its swifter and livelier passages, there appeared a channel-way of pebbles, and brown, sparkling sand. Letting the eyes follow along the course of the stream, they could catch the reflected light from its water, at some short distance within the forest, but soon lost all traces of it amid the bewilderment of tree-trunks and underbrush, and here and there a huge rock, covered over with gray lichens. All these giant trees and boulders of granite seemed intent on making a mystery of the course of this small brook; fearing, perhaps, that, with its never-ceasing loquacity, it should whisper tales out of the heart of the old forest whence it flowed, or mirror its revelations on the smooth surface of a pool. Continually, indeed, as it stole onward, the streamlet kept up a babble, kind, quiet, soothing, but melancholy, like the voice of a young child that was spending its infancy without playfulness, and knew not how to be merry among sad acquaintance and events of sombre hue.

"O, brook! O, foolish and tiresome little brook!" cried Pearl, after listening awhile to its talk. "Why art thou so sad? Pluck up a spirit, and do not be all the time sighing and murmuring!"

But the brook, in the course of its little lifetime among the forest-trees, had gone through so solemn an experience that it could not help talking about it, and seemed to have nothing else to say. Pearl resembled the brook, inasmuch as the current of her life gushed from a well-spring as mysterious, and had flowed through scenes shadowed as heavily with gloom. But, unlike the little stream, she danced and sparkled, and prattled airily along her course.

"What does this sad little brook say, mother?" inquired she.

"If thou hadst a sorrow of thine own, the brook might tell thee of it," answered her mother, "even as it is telling me of mine! But now, Pearl, I hear a footstep along the path, and the noise of one putting aside the branches. I would have thee betake thyself to play, and leave me to speak with him that comes yonder."

"Is it the Black Man?" asked Pearl.

"Wilt thou go and play, child?" repeated her mother. "But do not stray far into the wood. And take heed that thou come at my first call."

"Yes, mother," answered Pearl. "But, if it be the Black Man, wilt thou not let me stay a moment, and look at him, with his big book under his arm?"

"Go, silly child!" said her mother, impatiently. "It is no Black Man! Thou canst see him now through the trees. It is the minister!"

"And so it is!" said the child. "And, mother, he has his hand over his heart! Is it because, when the minister wrote his name in the book, the Black Man set his mark in that place? But why does he not wear it outside his bosom, as thou dost, mother?"

"Go now, child, and thou shalt tease me as thou wilt another time!" cried Hester Prynne. "But do not stray far. Keep where thou canst hear the babble of the brook."

The child went singing away, following up the current of the brook, and striving to mingle a more lightsome cadence with its melancholy voice. But the little stream would not be comforted, and still kept telling its unintelligible secret of some very mournful mystery that had happened—or making a prophetic lamentation about something that was yet to happen—within the verge of the dismal forest. So Pearl, who had enough of shadow in her own little life, chose to break off all acquaintance with this repining brook. She set herself, therefore, to gathering violets and wood-anemones,[127] and some scarlet columbines[128] that she found growing in the crevices of a high rock.

When her elf-child had departed, Hester Prynne made a step or two towards the track that led through the forest, but still remained under the deep shadow of the trees. She beheld the minister advancing along the path, entirely alone, and leaning on a staff which he had cut by the way-side. He looked haggard and feeble, and betrayed a nerveless despondency in his air, which had never so remarkably characterized him in his walks about the settlement, nor in any other situation where he deemed himself liable to notice. Here it was wofully visible, in this intense seclusion of the forest, which of itself would have been a heavy trial to the spirits. There was a listlessness in his gait; as if he saw no reason for taking one step farther, nor felt any desire to do so, but would have been glad, could he be glad of any thing, to fling himself down at the root of the nearest tree, and lie there passive for evermore. The leaves might bestrew him, and the soil gradually accumulate and form a little hillock over his frame, no matter whether there were life in it or no. Death was too definite an object to be wished for, or avoided.

To Hester's eye, the Reverend Mr. Dimmesdale exhibited no symptom of positive and vivacious suffering, except that, as little Pearl had remarked, he kept his hand over his heart.

---

[127]WOOD-ANEMONES: Pastel flowers that grow in dark, wooded regions.
[128]COLUMBINES: Inverted flowers that grow in rocky soil.

XVII. THE PASTOR AND HIS PARISHIONER

Slowly as the minister walked, he had almost gone by, before Hester Prynne could gather voice enough to attract his observation. At length, she succeeded.

"Arthur Dimmesdale!" she said, faintly at first; then louder, but hoarsely. "Arthur Dimmesdale!"

"Who speaks?" answered the minister.

Gathering himself quickly up, he stood more erect, like a man taken by surprise in a mood to which he was reluctant to have witnesses. Throwing his eyes anxiously in the direction of the voice, he indistinctly beheld a form under the trees, clad in garments so sombre, and so little relieved from the gray twilight into which the clouded sky and the heavy foliage had darkened the noontide, that he knew not whether it were a woman or a shadow. It may be, that his pathway through life was haunted thus, by a spectre that had stolen out from among his thoughts.

He made a step nigher, and discovered the scarlet letter.

"Hester! Hester Prynne!" said he. "Is it thou? Art thou in life?"

"Even so!" she answered. "In such life as has been mine these seven years past! And thou, Arthur Dimmesdale, dost thou yet live?"

It was no wonder that they thus questioned one another's actual and bodily existence, and even doubted of their own. So strangely did they meet, in the dim wood, that it was like the first encounter, in the world beyond the grave, of two spirits who had been intimately connected in their former life, but now stood coldly shuddering, in mutual dread; as not yet familiar with their state, nor wonted to the companionship of disembodied beings. Each a ghost, and awe-stricken at the other ghost! They were awe-stricken likewise at themselves; because the crisis flung back to them their consciousness, and revealed to each heart its history and experience, as life never does, except at such breathless epochs. The soul beheld its features in the mirror of the passing moment. It was with fear, and tremulously, and, as it were, by a slow, reluctant necessity, that Arthur Dimmesdale put forth his hand, chill as death, and touched the chill hand of Hester Prynne. The grasp, cold as it was, took away what was dreariest in the interview. They now felt themselves, at least, inhabitants of the same sphere.

Without a word more spoken,—neither he nor she assuming the guidance, but with an unexpressed consent,—they glided back into the shadow of the woods, whence Hester had emerged, and sat down on the heap of moss where she and Pearl had before been sitting. When they found voice to speak, it was, at first, only to utter remarks and inquiries such as any two acquaintance might have made, about the gloomy sky, the threatening storm, and, next, the health of each. Thus they went onward, not boldly, but step by step, into the themes that were brooding deepest in their hearts. So long estranged by fate and circumstances, they needed something slight and casual to run before, and throw open the doors of intercourse, so that their real thoughts might be led across the threshold.

After a while, the minister fixed his eyes on Hester Prynne's.

"Hester," said he, "hast thou found peace?"

She smiled drearily, looking down upon her bosom.

"Hast thou?" she asked.

"None!—nothing but despair!" he answered. "What else could I look for, being what I am, and leading such a life as mine? Were I an atheist,—a man devoid of conscience,—a wretch with coarse and brutal instincts,—I might have found peace long, ere now. Nay, I never should have lost it! But, as matters stand with my soul, whatever of good capacity there originally was in me, all of God's gifts that were the choicest have become the ministers of spiritual torment. Hester, I am most miserable!"

"The people reverence thee," said Hester. "And surely thou workest good among them! Doth this bring thee no comfort?"

"More misery, Hester!—Only the more misery!" answered the clergyman, with a bitter smile. "As concerns the good which I may appear to do, I have no faith in it. It must needs be a delusion. What can a ruined soul, like mine, effect towards the redemption of other souls?—or a polluted soul, towards their purification? And as for the people's reverence, would that it were turned to scorn and hatred! Canst thou deem it, Hester, a consolation, that I must stand up in my pulpit, and meet so many eyes turned upward to my face, as if the light of heaven were beaming from it!—must see my flock hungry for the truth, and listening to my words as if a tongue of Pentecost were speaking!—and then look inward, and discern the black reality of what they idolize? I have laughed, in bitterness and agony of heart, at the contrast between what I seem and what I am! And Satan laughs at it!"

"You wrong yourself in this," said Hester gently. "You have deeply and sorely repented. Your sin is left behind you, in the days long past. Your present life is not less holy, in very truth, than it seems in people's eyes. Is there no reality in the penitence thus sealed and witnessed by good works? And wherefore should it not bring you peace?"

"No, Hester, no!" replied the clergyman. "There is no substance in it! It is cold and dead, and can do nothing for me! Of penance I have had enough! Of penitence there has been none! Else, I should long ago have thrown off these garments of mock holiness, and have shown myself to mankind as they will see me at the judgment-seat. Happy are you, Hester, that wear the scarlet letter openly upon your bosom! Mine burns in secret! Thou little knowest what a relief it is, after the torment of a seven years' cheat, to look into an eye that recognizes me for what I am! Had I one friend,—or were it my worst enemy!—to whom, when sickened with the praises of all other men, I could daily betake myself, and be known as the vilest of all sinners, methinks my soul might keep itself alive thereby. Even thus much of truth would save me! But, now, it is all falsehood!—all emptiness!—all death!"

Hester Prynne looked into his face, but hesitated to speak. Yet, uttering his long-restrained emotions so vehemently as he did, his words here offered her the very point of circumstances in which to interpose what she came to say. She conquered her fears, and spoke.

"Such a friend as thou hast even now wished for," said she, "with whom to weep over thy sin, thou hast in me, the partner of it!"—Again she hesitated, but brought out the words with an effort.—"Thou hast long had such an enemy, and dwellest with him under the same roof!"

The minister started to his feet, gasping for breath, and clutching at his heart as if he would have torn it out of his bosom.

"Ha! What sayest thou?" cried he. "An enemy! And under mine own roof! What mean you?"

Hester Prynne was now fully sensible of the deep injury for which she was responsible to this unhappy man, in permitting him to lie for so many years, or, indeed, for a single moment, at the mercy of one, whose purposes could not be other than malevolent. The very contiguity of his enemy, beneath whatever mask the latter might conceal himself, was enough to disturb the magnetic sphere of a being so sensitive as Arthur Dimmesdale. There had been a period when Hester was less alive to this consideration; or, perhaps, in the misanthropy of her own trouble, she left the minister to bear what she might picture to herself as a more tolerable doom. But of late, since the night of his vigil, all her sympathies towards him had been both softened and invigorated. She now read his heart more accurately. She doubted not, that the continual presence of Roger Chillingworth,—the secret poison of his malignity, infecting all the air about him,—and his authorized interference, as a physician, with the minister's physical and spiritual infirmities,—that these bad opportunities had been turned to a cruel purpose. By means of them, the sufferer's conscience had been kept in an irritated state, the tendency of which was, not to cure by wholesome pain, but to disorganize and corrupt his spiritual being.

Its result, on earth, could hardly fail to be insanity, and hereafter, that eternal alienation from the Good and True, of which madness is perhaps the earthly type.

Such was the ruin to which she had brought the man, once,—nay, why should we not speak it?—still so passionately loved! Hester felt that the sacrifice of the clergyman's good name, and death itself, as she had already told Roger Chillingworth, would have been infinitely preferable to the alternative which she had taken upon herself to choose. And now, rather than have had this grievous wrong to confess, she would gladly have lain down on the forest-leaves, and died there, at Arthur Dimmesdale's feet.

"O Arthur," cried she, "forgive me! In all things else, I have striven to be true! Truth was the one virtue which I might have held fast, and did hold fast through all extremity; save when thy good,—thy life,—thy fame,—were put in question! Then I consented to a deception. But a lie is never good, even though death threaten on the other side! Dost thou not see what I would say? That old man!—the physician!—he whom they call Roger Chillingworth!—he was my husband!"

The minister looked at her, for an instant, with all that violence of passion, which—intermixed, in more shapes than one, with his higher, purer, softer qualities—was, in fact, the portion of him which the Devil claimed, and through which he sought to win the rest. Never was there a blacker or a fiercer frown, than Hester now encountered. For the brief space that it lasted, it was a dark transfiguration. But his character had been so much enfeebled by suffering, that even its lower energies were incapable of more than a temporary struggle. He sank down on the ground, and buried his face in his hands.

"I might have known it!" murmured he." I did know it! Was not the secret told me in the natural recoil of my heart, at the first sight of him, and as often as I have seen him since? Why did I not understand? O Hester Prynne, thou little, little knowest all the horror of this thing! And the shame!—the indelicacy!—the horrible ugliness of this exposure of a sick and guilty heart to the very eye that would gloat over it! Woman, woman, thou art accountable for this! I cannot forgive thee!"

"Thou shalt forgive me!" cried Hester, flinging herself on the fallen leaves beside him. "Let God punish! Thou shalt forgive!"

With sudden and desperate tenderness, she threw her arms around him, and pressed his head against her bosom; little caring though his cheek rested on the scarlet letter. He would have released himself, but strove in vain to do so. Hester would not set him free, lest he should look her sternly in the face. All the world had frowned on her,—for seven long years had it frowned upon this lonely woman,—and still she bore it all, nor ever once turned away her firm, sad eyes. Heaven, likewise, had frowned upon her, and she had not died. But the frown of this pale, weak, sinful, and sorrow-stricken man was what Hester could not bear, and live!

"Wilt thou yet forgive me?" she repeated, over and over again. "Wilt thou not frown? Wilt thou forgive?"

"I do forgive you, Hester," replied the minister, at length, with a deep utterance out of an abyss of sadness, but no anger. "I freely forgive you now. May God forgive us both! We are not, Hester, the worst sinners in the world. There is one worse than even the polluted priest! That old man's revenge has been blacker than my sin. He has violated, in cold blood, the sanctity of a human heart. Thou and I, Hester, never did so!"

"Never, never!" whispered she. "What we did had a consecration of its own. We felt it so! We said so to each other! Hast thou forgotten it?"

"Hush, Hester!" said Arthur Dimmesdale, rising from the ground. "No; I have not forgotten!"

They sat down again, side by side, and hand clasped in hand, on the mossy trunk of the fallen tree. Life had never brought them a gloomier hour; it was the point whither their pathway had so long been tending, and darkening ever, as it stole along;—and yet it inclosed a charm that made them linger upon it, and claim another, and another, and, after all, another moment. The forest was obscure around them, and creaked with a blast that was passing through it. The boughs were tossing heavily above their heads; while one solemn old tree groaned dolefully to another, as if telling the sad story of the pair that sat beneath, or constrained to forbode evil to come.

And yet they lingered. How dreary looked the forest-track that led backward to the settlement, where Hester Prynne must take up again the burden of her ignominy, and the minister the hollow mockery of his good name! So they lingered an instant longer. No golden light had ever been so precious as the gloom of this dark forest. Here, seen only by his eyes, the scarlet letter need not burn into the bosom of the fallen woman! Here, seen only by her eyes, Arthur Dimmesdale, false to God and man, might be, for one moment, true!

He started at a thought that suddenly occurred to him.

"Hester," cried he, "here is a new horror! Roger Chillingworth knows your purpose to reveal his true character. Will he continue, then, to keep our secret? What will now be the course of his revenge?"

"There is a strange secrecy in his nature," replied Hester, thoughtfully; "and it has grown upon him by the hidden practices of his revenge. I deem it not likely that he will betray the secret. He will doubtless seek other means of satiating his dark passion."

"And I!—how am I to live longer, breathing the same air with this deadly enemy?" exclaimed Arthur Dimmesdale, shrinking within himself, and pressing his hand nervously against his heart,—a gesture that had grown involuntary with him. "Think for me, Hester! Thou art strong. Resolve for me!"

"Thou must dwell no longer with this man," said Hester, slowly and firmly. "Thy heart must be no longer under his evil eye!"

"It were far worse than death!" replied the minister. "But how to avoid it? What choice remains to me? Shall I lie down again on these withered leaves, where I cast myself when thou didst tell me what he was? Must I sink down there, and die at once?"

"Alas, what a ruin has befallen thee!" said Hester, with the tears gushing into her eyes. "Wilt thou die for very weakness? There is no other cause!"

"The judgment of God is on me," answered the conscience-stricken priest. "It is too mighty for me to struggle with!"

"Heaven would show mercy," rejoined Hester, "hadst thou but the strength to take advantage of it."

"Be thou strong for me!" answered he. "Advise me what to do."

"Is the world then so narrow?" exclaimed Hester Prynne, fixing her deep eyes on the minister's, and instinctively exercising a magnetic power over a spirit so shattered and subdued, that it could hardly hold itself erect. "Doth the universe lie within the compass of yonder town, which only a little time ago was but a leaf-strewn desert, as lonely as this around us? Whither leads yonder forest-track? Backward to the settlement, thou sayest! Yes; but onward, too! Deeper it goes, and deeper, into the wilderness, less plainly to be seen at every step; until, some few miles hence, the yellow leaves will show no vestige of the white man's tread. There thou art free! So brief a journey would bring thee from a world where thou hast been most wretched, to one where thou mayest still be happy! Is there not shade enough in all this boundless forest to hide thy heart from the gaze of Roger Chillingworth?"

"Yes, Hester; but only under the fallen leaves!" replied the minister, with a sad smile.

"Then there is the broad pathway of the sea!" continued Hester. "It brought thee hither. If thou so choose, it will bear thee back again. In our native land, whether in some remote rural village or in vast London,—or, surely, in Germany, in France, in pleasant Italy,—thou wouldst be beyond his power and knowledge! And what hast thou to do with all these iron men, and their opinions? They have kept thy better part in bondage too long already!"

"It cannot be!" answered the minister, listening as if he were called upon to realize a dream. "I am powerless to go. Wretched and sinful as I am, I have had no other thought than to drag on my earthly existence in the sphere where Providence hath placed me. Lost as my own soul is, I would still do what I may for other human souls! I dare not quit my post, though an unfaithful sentinel, whose sure reward is death and dishonor, when his dreary watch shall come to an end!"

"Thou art crushed under this seven years' weight of misery," replied Hester, fervently resolved to buoy him up with her own energy. "But thou shalt leave it all behind thee! It shall not cumber thy steps, as thou treadest along the forest-path; neither shalt thou freight the ship with it, if thou prefer to cross the sea. Leave this wreck and ruin here where it hath happened! Meddle no more with it! Begin all anew! Hast thou exhausted possibility in the failure of this one trial? Not so! The future is yet full of trial and success. There is happiness to be enjoyed! There is good to be done! Exchange this false life of thine for a true one. Be, if thy spirit summon thee to such a mission, the teacher and apostle of the red men. Or,—as is more thy nature,—be a scholar and a sage among the wisest and the most renowned of the cultivated world. Preach! Write! Act! Do any thing, save to lie down and die! Give up this name of Arthur Dimmesdale, and make thyself another, and a high one, such as thou canst wear without fear or shame. Why shouldst thou tarry so much as one other day in the torments that have so gnawed into thy life!—that have made thee feeble to will and to do!—that will leave thee powerless even to repent! Up, and away!"

"O Hester!" cried Arthur Dimmesdale, in whose eyes a fitful light, kindled by her enthusiasm, flashed up and died away, "thou tellest of running a race to a man whose knees are tottering beneath him! I must die here. There is not the strength or courage left me to venture into the wide, strange, difficult world, alone!"

It was the last expression of the despondency of a broken spirit. He lacked energy to grasp the better fortune that seemed within his reach.

He repeated the word.

"Alone, Hester!"

"Thou shall not go alone!" answered she, in a deep whisper.

Then, all was spoken!

XVIII. *A Flood of Sunshine*

Arthur Dimmesdale gazed into Hester's face with a look in which hope and joy shone out, indeed, but with fear betwixt them, and a kind of horror at her boldness, who had spoken what he vaguely hinted at, but dared not speak.

But Hester Prynne, with a mind of native courage and activity, and for so long a period not merely estranged, but outlawed, from society, had habituated herself to such latitude of speculation as was altogether foreign to the clergyman. She had wandered, without rule or guidance, in a moral wilderness; as vast, as intricate and shadowy, as the untamed forest, amid the gloom of which they were now holding a colloquy that was to decide their fate. Her intellect and heart had their home, as it were, in desert places, where she roamed as freely as the wild Indian in his woods. For years past she had looked from this estranged point of view at human institutions, and whatever priests or legislators had established; criticizing all with hardly more reverence than the Indian would feel for the clerical band, the judicial robe, the pillory, the gallows, the fireside, or the church. The tendency of her fate and fortunes had been to set her free. The scarlet letter was her passport into regions where other women dared not tread. Shame, Despair, Solitude! These had been her teachers,—stern and wild ones,—and they had made her strong, but taught her much amiss.

The minister, on the other hand, had never gone through an experience calculated to lead him beyond the scope of generally received laws; although, in a single instance, he had so fearfully transgressed one of the most sacred of them. But this had been a sin of passion, not of principle, nor even purpose. Since that wretched epoch, he had watched, with morbid zeal and minuteness, not his acts,—for those it was easy to arrange,—but each breath of emotion, and his every thought. At the head of the social system, as the clergymen of that day stood, he was only the more trammelled by its regulations, its principles, and even its prejudices. As a priest, the framework of his order inevitably hemmed him in. As a man who had once sinned, but who kept his conscience all alive and painfully sensitive by the fretting of an unhealed wound, he might have been supposed safer within the line of virtue, than if he had never sinned at all.

Thus, we seem to see that, as regarded Hester Prynne, the whole seven years of outlaw and ignominy had been little other than a preparation for this very hour. But Arthur Dimmesdale! Were such a man once more to fall, what plea could be urged in extenuation of his crime? None; unless it avail him somewhat, that he was broken down by long and exquisite suffering; that his mind was darkened and confused by the very remorse which harrowed it; that, between fleeing as an avowed criminal, and remaining as a hypocrite, conscience might find it hard to strike the balance; that it was human to avoid the peril of death and infamy, and the inscrutable machinations of an enemy; that, finally, to this poor pilgrim, on his dreary and desert path, faint, sick, miserable, there appeared a glimpse of human affection and sympathy, a new life, and a true one, in exchange for the heavy doom which he was now expiating. And be the stern and sad truth spoken, that the breach which guilt has once made into the human soul is never, in this mortal state, repaired. It may be watched and guarded; so that the enemy shall not force his way again into the citadel, and might even, in his subsequent assaults, select some other avenue, in preference to that where he had formerly succeeded. But there is still the ruined wall, and, near it, the stealthy tread of the foe that would win over again his unforgotten triumph.

The struggle, if there were one, need not be described. Let it suffice, that the clergyman resolved to flee, and not alone.

"If, in all these past seven years," thought he, "I could recall one instant of peace or hope, I would yet endure, for the sake of that earnest of Heaven's mercy. But now,—since I am irrevocably doomed,—wherefore should I not snatch the solace allowed to the condemned culprit before his execution? Or, if this be the path to a better life, as Hester would persuade me, I surely give up no fairer prospect by pursuing it! Neither can I any longer live without her companionship; so powerful is she to sustain,—so tender to soothe! O Thou to whom I dare not lift mine eyes, wilt Thou yet pardon me!"

"Thou wilt go!" said Hester calmly, as he met her glance.

The decision once made, a glow of strange enjoyment threw its flickering brightness over the trouble of his breast. It was the exhilarating effect—upon a prisoner just escaped from the dungeon of his own heart—of breathing the wild, free atmosphere of an unredeemed, unchristianized, lawless region. His spirit rose, as it were, with a bound, and attained a nearer prospect of the sky, than throughout all the misery which had kept him grovelling on the earth. Of a deeply religious temperament, there was inevitably a tinge of the devotional in his mood.

"Do I feel joy again?" cried he, wondering at himself. "Methought the germ of it was dead in me! O Hester, thou art my better angel! I seem to have flung myself—sick, sin-stained, and sorrow-blackened—down upon these forest-leaves, and to have risen up all made anew, and with new powers to glorify Him that hath been merciful! This is already the better life! Why did we not find it sooner?"

"Let us not look back," answered Hester Prynne. "The past is gone! Wherefore should we linger upon it now? See! With this symbol, I undo it all, and make it as if it had never been!"

So speaking, she undid the clasp that fastened the scarlet letter, and, taking it from her bosom, threw it to a distance among the withered leaves. The mystic token alighted on the hither verge of the stream. With a hand's breadth farther flight it would have fallen into the water, and have given the little brook another woe to carry onward, besides the unintelligible tale which it still kept murmuring about. But there lay the embroidered letter, glittering like a lost jewel, which some ill-fated wanderer might pick up, and thenceforth be haunted by strange phantoms of guilt, sinkings of the heart, and unaccountable misfortune.

The stigma gone, Hester heaved a long, deep sigh, in which the burden of shame and anguish departed from her spirit. O exquisite relief! She had not known the weight, until she felt the freedom! By another impulse, she took off the formal cap that confined her hair; and down it fell upon her shoulders, dark and rich, with at once a shadow and a light in its abundance, and imparting the charm of softness to her features. There played around her mouth, and beamed out of her eyes, a radiant and tender smile, that seemed gushing from the very heart of womanhood. A crimson flush was glowing on her cheek, that had been long so pale. Her sex, her youth, and the whole richness of her beauty, came back from what men call the irrevocable past, and clustered themselves, with her maiden hope, and a happiness before unknown, within the magic circle of this hour. And, as if the gloom of the earth and sky had been but the effluence of these two mortal hearts, it vanished with their sorrow. All at once, as with a sudden smile of heaven, forth burst the sunshine, pouring a very flood into the obscure forest, gladdening each green leaf, transmuting the yellow fallen ones to gold, and gleaming adown the gray trunks of the solemn trees. The objects that had made a shadow hitherto, embodied the brightness now. The course of the little brook might be traced by its merry gleam afar into the wood's heart of mystery, which had become a mystery of joy.

Such was the sympathy of Nature—that wild, heathen Nature of the forest, never subjugated by human law, nor illumined by higher truth—with the bliss of these two spirits! Love, whether newly born, or aroused from a deathlike slumber, must always create a sunshine, filling the heart so full of radiance, that it overflows upon the outward world. Had the forest still kept its gloom, it would have been bright in Hester's eyes, and bright in Arthur Dimmesdale's!

Hester looked at him with the thrill of another joy.

"Thou must know Pearl!" said she. "Our little Pearl! Thou hast seen her,—yes, I know it!—but thou wilt see her now with other eyes. She is a strange child! I hardly comprehend her! But thou wilt love her dearly, as I do, and wilt advise me how to deal with her."

"Dost thou think the child will be glad to know me?" asked the minister, somewhat uneasily. "I have long shrunk from children, because they often show a distrust,—a backwardness to be familiar with me. I have even been afraid of little Pearl!"

"Ah, that was sad!" answered the mother. "But she will love thee dearly, and thou her. She is not far off. I will call her! Pearl! Pearl!"

"I see the child," observed the minister. "Yonder she is, standing in a streak of sunshine, a good way off, on the other side of the brook. So thou thinkest the child will love me?"

Hester smiled, and again called to Pearl, who was visible, at some distance, as the minister had described her, like a bright-apparelled vision, in a sunbeam, which fell down upon her through an arch of boughs. The ray quivered to and fro, making her figure dim or distinct,—now like a real child, now like a child's spirit,—as the splendor went and came again. She heard her mother's voice, and approached slowly through the forest.

Pearl had not found the hour pass wearisomely, while her mother sat talking with the clergyman. The great black forest—stern as it showed itself to those who brought the guilt and troubles of the world into its bosom—became the playmate of the lonely infant, as well as it knew how. Sombre as it was, it put on the kindest of its moods to welcome her. It offered her the partridge-berries, the growth of the preceding autumn, but ripening only in the spring, and now red as drops of blood upon the withered leaves. These Pearl gathered, and was pleased with their wild flavor. The small denizens of the wilderness hardly took pains to move out of her path. A partridge, indeed, with a brood of ten behind her, ran forward threateningly, but soon repented of her fierceness, and clucked to her young ones not to be afraid. A pigeon, alone on a low branch, allowed Pearl to come beneath, and uttered a sound as much of greeting as alarm. A squirrel, from the lofty depths of his domestic tree, chattered either in anger or merriment,—for a squirrel is such a choleric and humorous little personage that it is hard to distinguish between his moods,—so he chattered at the child, and flung down a nut upon her head. It was a last year's nut, and already gnawed by his sharp tooth.

A fox, startled from his sleep by her light footstep on the leaves, looked inquisitively at Pearl, as doubting whether it were better to steal off, or renew his nap on the same spot. A wolf, it is said,—but here the tale has surely lapsed into the improbable,—came up, and smelt of Pearl's robe, and offered his savage head to be patted by her hand. The truth seems to be, however, that the mother-forest, and these wild things which it nourished, all recognized a kindred wildness in the human child.

And she was gentler here than in the grassy-margined streets of the settlement, or in her mother's cottage. The flowers appeared to know it; and one and another whispered, as she passed, "Adorn thyself with me, thou beautiful child, adorn thyself with me!"—and, to please them, Pearl gathered the violets, and anemones, and columbines, and some twigs of the freshest green, which the old trees held down before her eyes. With these she decorated her hair, and her young waist, and became a nymph-child, or an infant dryad,[129] or whatever else was in closest sympathy with the antique wood. In such guise had Pearl adorned herself, when she heard her mother's voice, and came slowly back.

Slowly; for she saw the clergyman!

XIX. *The Child at the Brook-Side*

"Thou wilt love her dearly," repeated Hester Prynne, as she and the minister sat watching little Pearl. "Dost thou not think her beautiful? And see with what natural skill she has made those simple flowers adorn her! Had she gathered pearls, and diamonds, and rubies, in the wood, they could not have become her better. She is a splendid child! But I know whose brow she has!"

"Dost thou know, Hester," said Arthur Dimmesdale, with an unquiet smile, "that this dear child, tripping about always at thy side, hath caused me many an alarm? Methought—O Hester, what a thought is that, and how terrible to dread it!—that my own features were partly repeated in her face, and so strikingly that the world might see them! But she is mostly thine!"

"No, no! Not mostly!" answered the mother with a tender smile. "A little longer, and thou needest not to be afraid to trace whose child she is. But how strangely beautiful she looks, with those wild flowers in her hair! It is as if one of the fairies, whom we left in dear old England, had decked her out to meet us."

[129]DRYAD: Wood nymph.

It was with a feeling which neither of them had ever before experienced, that they sat and watched Pearl's slow advance. In her was visible the tie that united them. She had been offered to the world, these seven past years, as the living hieroglyphic, in which was revealed the secret they so darkly sought to hide,—all written in this symbol,—all plainly manifest,—had there been a prophet or magician skilled to read the character of flame! And Pearl was the oneness of their being. Be the foregone evil what it might, how could they doubt that their earthly lives and future destinies were conjoined, when they beheld at once the material union, and the spiritual idea, in whom they met, and were to dwell immortally together? Thoughts like these—and perhaps other thoughts, which they did not acknowledge or define—threw an awe about the child, as she came onward.

"Let her see nothing strange—no passion or eagerness—in thy way of accosting her," whispered Hester. "Our Pearl is a fitful and fantastic little elf, sometimes. Especially, she is seldom tolerant of emotion, when she does not fully comprehend the why and wherefore. But the child hath strong affections! She loves me, and will love thee!"

"Thou canst not think," said the minister, glancing aside at Hester Prynne, "how my heart dreads this interview, and yearns for it! But, in truth, as I already told thee, children are not readily won to be familiar with me. They will not climb my knee, nor prattle in my ear, nor answer to my smile; but stand apart, and eye me strangely. Even little babes, when I take them in my arms, weep bitterly. Yet Pearl, twice in her little lifetime, hath been kind to me! The first time,—thou knowest it well! The last was when thou ledst her with thee to the house of yonder stern old Governor."

"And thou didst plead so bravely in her behalf and mine!" answered the mother. "I remember it; and so shall little Pearl. Fear nothing! She may be strange and shy at first, but will soon learn to love thee!"

By this time Pearl had reached the margin of the brook, and stood on the farther side, gazing silently at Hester and the clergyman, who still sat together on the mossy tree-trunk, waiting to receive her. Just where she had paused the brook chanced to form a pool, so smooth and quiet that it reflected a perfect image of her little figure, with all the brilliant picturesqueness of her beauty, in its adornment of flowers and wreathed foliage, but more refined and spiritualized than the reality. This image, so nearly identical with the living Pearl, seemed to communicate somewhat of its own shadowy and intangible quality to the child herself. It was strange, the way in which Pearl stood, looking so stedfastly at them through the dim medium of the forest-gloom; herself, meanwhile, all glorified with a ray of sunshine, that was attracted thitherward as by a certain sympathy. In the brook beneath stood another child,—another and the same,—with likewise its ray of golden light. Hester felt herself, in some indistinct and tantalizing manner, estranged from Pearl; as if the child, in her lonely ramble through the forest, had strayed out of the sphere in which she and her mother dwelt together, and was now vainly seeking to return to it.

There were both truth and error in the impression; the child and mother were estranged, but through Hester's fault, not Pearl's. Since the latter rambled from her side, another inmate had been admitted within the circle of the mother's feelings, and so modified the aspect of them all, that Pearl, the returning wanderer, could not find her wonted place, and hardly knew where she was.

"I have a strange fancy," observed the sensitive minister, "that this brook is the boundary between two worlds, and that thou canst never meet thy Pearl again. Or is she an elfish spirit, who, as the legends of our childhood taught us, is forbidden to cross a running stream? Pray hasten her; for this delay has already imparted a tremor to my nerves."

"Come, dearest child!" said Hester encouragingly, and stretching out both her arms. "How slow thou art! When hast thou been so sluggish before now? Here is a friend of mine, who must be thy friend also. Thou wilt have twice as much love, henceforward, as thy mother alone could give thee! Leap across the brook and come to us. Thou canst leap like a young deer!"

Pearl, without responding in any manner to these honey-sweet expressions, remained on the other side of the brook. Now she fixed her bright, wild eyes on her mother, now on the minister, and now included them both in the same glance; as if to detect and explain to herself the relation which they bore to one another. For some unaccountable reason, as Arthur Dimmesdale felt the child's eyes upon himself, his hand—with that gesture so habitual as to have become involuntary—stole over his heart. At length, assuming a singular air of authority, Pearl stretched out her hand, with the small forefinger extended, and pointing evidently towards her mother's breast. And beneath, in the mirror of the brook, there was the flower-girdled and sunny image of little Pearl, pointing her small forefinger too.

"Thou strange child, why dost thou not come to me?" exclaimed Hester.

Pearl still pointed with her forefinger; and a frown gathered on her brow; the more impressive from the childish, the almost baby-like aspect of the features that conveyed it. As her mother still kept beckoning to her, and arraying her face in a holiday suit of unaccustomed smiles, the child stamped her foot with a yet more imperious look and gesture. In the brook, again, was the fantastic beauty of the image, with its reflected frown, its pointed finger, and imperious gesture, giving emphasis to the aspect of little Pearl.

"Hasten, Pearl; or I shall be angry with thee!" cried Hester Prynne, who, however inured to such behaviour on the elf-child's part at other seasons, was naturally anxious for a more seemly deportment now. "Leap across the brook, naughty child, and run hither! Else I must come to thee!"

But Pearl, not a whit startled at her mother's threats, any more than mollified by her entreaties, now suddenly burst into a fit of passion, gesticulating violently, and throwing her small figure into the most extravagant contortions. She accompanied this wild outbreak with piercing shrieks, which the woods reverberated on all sides; so that, alone as she was in her childish and unreasonable wrath, it seemed as if a hidden multitude were lending her their sympathy and encouragement. Seen in the brook, once more, was the shadowy wrath of Pearl's image, crowned and girdled with flowers, but stamping its foot, wildly gesticulating, and, in the midst of all, still pointing its small forefinger at Hester's bosom!

"I see what ails the child," whispered Hester to the clergyman, and turning pale in spite of a strong effort to conceal her trouble and annoyance. "Children will not abide any, the slightest, change in the accustomed aspect of things that are daily before their eyes. Pearl misses something which she has always seen me wear!"

"I pray you," answered the minister, "if thou hast any means of pacifying the child, do it forthwith! Save it were the cankered wrath of an old witch, like Mistress Hibbins," added he, attempting to smile, "I know nothing that I would not sooner encounter than this passion in a child. In Pearl's young beauty, as in the wrinkled witch, it has a preternatural effect. Pacify her, if thou lovest me!"

Hester turned again towards Pearl, with a crimson blush upon her cheek, a conscious glance aside at the clergyman, and then a heavy sigh; while, even before she had time to speak, the blush yielded to a deadly pallor.

"Pearl," said she, sadly, "look down at thy feet! There!—before thee!—on the hither side of the brook!"

The child turned her eyes to the point indicated; and there lay the scarlet letter, so close upon the margin of the stream, that the gold embroidery was reflected in it.

"Bring it hither!" said Hester.

"Come thou and take it up!" answered Pearl.

"Was ever such a child!" observed Hester aside to the minister. "O, I have much to tell thee about her. But, in very truth, she is right as regards this hateful token. I must bear its torture yet a little longer,— only a few days longer,—until we shall have left this region, and look back hither as to a land which we have dreamed of. The forest cannot hide it! The mid-ocean shall take it from my hand, and swallow it up for ever!"

With these words, she advanced to the margin of the brook, took up the scarlet letter, and fastened it again into her bosom. Hopefully, but a moment ago, as Hester had spoken of drowning it in the deep sea, there was a sense of inevitable doom upon her, as she thus received back this deadly symbol from the hand of fate. She had flung it into infinite space!—she had drawn an hour's free breath!—and here again was the scarlet misery, glittering on the old spot! So it ever is, whether thus typified or no, that an evil deed invests itself with the character of doom. Hester next gathered up the heavy tresses of her hair, and confined them beneath her cap. As if there were a withering spell in the sad letter, her beauty, the warmth and richness of her womanhood, departed, like fading sunshine; and a gray shadow seemed to fall across her.

When the dreary change was wrought, she extended her hand to Pearl.

"Dost thou know thy mother now, child?" asked she, reproachfully, but with a subdued tone. "Wilt thou come across the brook, and own thy mother, now that she has her shame upon her,—now that she is sad?"

"Yes; now I will!" answered the child, bounding across the brook, and clasping Hester in her arms. "Now thou art my mother indeed! And I am thy little Pearl!"

In a mood of tenderness that was not usual with her, she drew down her mother's head, and kissed her brow and both her cheeks. But then— by a kind of necessity that always impelled this child to alloy whatever comfort she might chance to give with a throb of anguish—Pearl put up her mouth, and kissed the scarlet letter, too!

"That was not kind!" said Hester. "When thou hast shown me a little love, thou mockest me!"

"Why doth the minister sit yonder?" asked Pearl.

"He waits to welcome thee," replied her mother. "Come thou, and entreat his blessing! He loves thee, my little Pearl, and loves thy mother too. Wilt thou not love him? Come! he longs to greet thee!"

"Doth he love us?" said Pearl, looking up with acute intelligence into her mother's face. "Will he go back with us, hand in hand, we three together, into the town?"

"Not now, dear child," answered Hester. "But in days to come he will walk hand in hand with us. We will have a home and fireside of our own; and thou shalt sit upon his knee; and he will teach thee many things, and love thee dearly. Thou wilt love him; wilt thou not?"

"And will he always keep his hand over his heart?" inquired Pearl.

"Foolish child, what a question is that!" exclaimed her mother. "Come and ask his blessing!"

But, whether influenced by the jealousy that seems instinctive with every petted child towards a dangerous rival, or from whatever caprice of her freakish nature, Pearl would show no favor to the clergyman. It was only by an exertion of force that her mother brought her up to him, hanging back, and manifesting her reluctance by odd grimaces; of which, ever since her babyhood, she had possessed a singular variety, and could transform her mobile physiognomy into a series of different aspects, with a new mischief in them, each and all. The minister—painfully embarrassed, but hoping that a kiss might prove a talisman to admit him into the child's kindlier regards—bent forward, and impressed one on her brow. Hereupon, Pearl broke away from her mother, and, running to the brook, stooped over it, and bathed her forehead, until the unwelcome kiss was quite washed off, and diffused through a long lapse of the gliding water. She then remained apart, silently watching Hester and the clergyman; while they talked together, and made such arrangements as were suggested by their new position, and the purposes soon to be fulfilled.

And now this fateful interview had come to a close. The dell was to be left in solitude among its dark, old trees, which, with their multitudinous tongues, would whisper long of what had passed there, and no mortal be the wiser. And the melancholy brook would add this other tale to the mystery with which its little heart was already overburdened, and whereof it still kept up a murmuring babble, with not a whit more cheerfulness of tone than for ages heretofore.

XX. THE MINISTER IN A MAZE

As the minister departed, in advance of Hester Prynne and little Pearl, he threw a backward glance; half expecting that he should discover only some faintly traced features or outline of the mother and the child, slowly fading into the twilight of the woods. So great a vicissitude in his life could not at once be received as real. But there was Hester, clad in her gray robe, still standing beside the tree-trunk, which some blast had overthrown a long antiquity ago, and which time had ever since been covering with moss, so that these two fated ones, with earth's heaviest burden on them, might there sit down together, and find a single hour's rest and solace. And there was Pearl, too, lightly dancing from the margin of the brook,—now that the intrusive third person was gone,—and taking her old place by her mother's side. So the minister had not fallen asleep, and dreamed!

In order to free his mind from this indistinctness and duplicity of impression, which vexed it with a strange disquietude, he recalled and more thoroughly defined the plans which Hester and himself had sketched for their departure. It had been determined between them, that the Old World, with its crowds and cities, offered them a more eligible shelter and concealment than the wilds of New England, or all America, with its alternatives of an Indian wigwam,[130] or the few settlements of Europeans, scattered thinly along the sea-board. Not to speak of the clergyman's health, so inadequate to sustain the hardships of a forest life, his native gifts, his culture, and his entire development would secure him a home only in the midst of civilization and refinement; the higher the state, the more delicately adapted to it the man. In furtherance of this choice, it so happened that a ship lay in the harbour; one of those unquestionable cruisers, frequent at that day, which, without being absolutely outlaws of the deep, yet roamed over its surface with a remarkable irresponsibility of character. This vessel had recently arrived from the Spanish Main, and, within three days' time, would sail for Bristol.[131] Hester Prynne—whose vocation, as a self-enlisted Sister of Charity, had brought her acquainted with the captain and crew—could take upon herself to secure the passage of two individuals and a child, with all the secrecy which circumstances rendered more than desirable.

The minister had inquired of Hester, with no little interest, the precise time at which the vessel might be expected to depart. It would probably be on the fourth day from the present. "This is most fortunate!" he had then said to himself. Now, why the Reverend Mr. Dimmesdale considered it so very fortunate, we hesitate to reveal. Nevertheless,—to hold nothing back from the reader,—it was because, on the third day from the present, he was to preach the Election Sermon[132]; and, as such an occasion formed an honorable epoch in the life of a New England clergyman, he

[130]WIGWAM: A tent or hut used for shelter by Native Americans east of the Great Lakes.
[131]BRISTOL: A seaport in western England.
[132]ELECTION SERMON: Traditionally, a minister of high reputation gave a sermon at the installation of a new or the renewal of a current governor.

could not have chanced upon a more suitable mode and time of terminating his professional career. "At least, they shall say of me," thought this exemplary man, "that I leave no public duty unperformed, nor ill performed!" Sad, indeed, that an introspection so profound and acute as this poor minister's should be so miserably deceived! We have had, and may still have, worse things to tell of him; but none, we apprehend, so pitiably weak; no evidence, at once so slight and irrefragable,[133] of a subtle disease, that had long since begun to eat into the real substance of his character. No man, for any considerable period, can wear one face to himself, and another to the multitude, without finally getting bewildered as to which may be the true.

The excitement of Mr. Dimmesdale's feelings, as he returned from his interview with Hester, lent him unaccustomed physical energy, and hurried him townward at a rapid pace. The pathway among the woods seemed wilder, more uncouth with its rude natural obstacles, and less trodden by the foot of man, than he remembered it on his outward journey. But he leaped across the plashy places, thrust himself through the clinging underbrush, climbed the ascent, plunged into the hollow, and overcame, in short, all the difficulties of the track, with an unweariable activity that astonished him. He could not but recall how feebly, and with what frequent pauses for breath, he had toiled over the same ground only two days before. As he drew near the town, he took an impression of change from the series of familiar objects that presented themselves. It seemed not yesterday, not one, nor two, but many days, or even years ago, since he had quitted them. There, indeed, was each former trace of the street, as he remembered it, and all the peculiarities of the houses, with the due multitude of gable-peaks, and a weathercock at every point where his memory suggested one. Not the less, however, came this importunately obtrusive sense of change. The same was true as regarded the acquaintances whom he met, and all the well-known shapes of human life, about the little town. They looked neither older nor younger, now; the beards of the aged were no whiter, nor could the creeping babe of yesterday walk on his feet to-day; it was impossible to describe in what respect they differed from the individuals on whom he had so recently bestowed a parting glance; and yet the minister's deepest sense seemed to inform him of their mutability. A similar impression struck him most remarkably, as he passed under the walls of his own church. The edifice had so very strange, and yet so familiar, an aspect, that Mr. Dimmesdale's mind vibrated between two

[133]IRREFRAGABLE: Indisputable, undeniable.

ideas; either that he had seen it only in a dream hitherto, or that he was merely dreaming about it now.

This phenomenon, in the various shapes which it assumed, indicated no external change, but so sudden and important a change in the spectator of the familiar scene, that the intervening space of a single day had operated on his consciousness like the lapse of years. The minister's own will, and Hester's will, and the fate that grew between them, had wrought this transformation. It was the same town as heretofore; but the same minister returned not from the forest. He might have said to the friends who greeted him,—"I am not the man for whom you take me! I left him yonder in the forest, withdrawn into a secret dell, by a mossy tree-trunk, and near a melancholy brook! Go, seek your minister, and see if his emaciated figure, his thin cheek, his white, heavy, pain-wrinkled brow, be not flung down there like a cast-off garment!" His friends, no doubt, would still have insisted with him,—"Thou art thyself the man!"—but the error would have been their own, not his.

Before Mr. Dimmesdale reached home, his inner man gave him other evidences of a revolution in the sphere of thought and feeling. In truth, nothing short of a total change of dynasty and moral code, in that interior kingdom, was adequate to account for the impulses now communicated to the unfortunate and startled minister. At every step he was incited to do some strange, wild, wicked thing or other, with a sense that it would be at once involuntary and intentional; in spite of himself, yet growing out of a profounder self than that which opposed the impulse. For instance, he met one of his own deacons. The good old man addressed him with the paternal affection and patriarchal privilege, which his venerable age, his upright and holy character, and his station in the Church, entitled him to use; and, conjoined with this, the deep, almost worshipping respect, which the minister's professional and private claims alike demanded. Never was there a more beautiful example of how the majesty of age and wisdom may comport with the obeisance and respect enjoined upon it, as from a lower social rank and inferior order of endowment, towards a higher. Now, during a conversation of some two or three moments between the Reverend Mr. Dimmesdale and this excellent and hoary-bearded deacon, it was only by the most careful self-control that the former could refrain from uttering certain blasphemous suggestions that rose into his mind, respecting the communion-supper. He absolutely trembled and turned pale as ashes, lest his tongue should wag itself, in utterance of these horrible matters, and plead his own consent for so doing, without his having fairly given it. And, even with this terror in his heart, he could hardly avoid laughing to imagine how the sanctified old patriarchal deacon would have been petrified by his minister's impiety!

Again, another incident of the same nature. Hurrying along the street, the Reverend Mr. Dimmesdale encountered the eldest female member of his church; a most pious and exemplary old dame; poor, widowed, lonely, and with a heart as full of reminiscences about her dead husband and children, and her dead friends of long ago, as a burial-ground is full of storied grave-stones. Yet all this, which would else have been such heavy sorrow, was made almost a solemn joy to her devout old soul by religious consolations and the truths of Scripture, wherewith she had fed herself continually for more than thirty years. And, since Mr. Dimmesdale had taken her in charge, the good grandam's chief earthly comfort—which, unless it had been likewise a heavenly comfort, could have been none at all—was to meet her pastor, whether casually, or of set purpose, and be refreshed with a word of warm, fragrant, heaven-breathing Gospel truth from his beloved lips into her dulled, but rapturously attentive ear. But, on this occasion, up to the moment of putting his lips to the old woman's ear, Mr. Dimmesdale, as the great enemy of souls would have it, could recall no text of Scripture, nor aught else, except a brief, pithy, and, as it then appeared to him, unanswerable argument against the immortality of the human soul. The instilment thereof into her mind would probably have caused this aged sister to drop down dead, at once, as by the effect of an intensely poisonous infusion. What he really did whisper, the minister could never afterwards recollect. There was, perhaps, a fortunate disorder in his utterance, which failed to impart any distinct idea to the good widow's comprehension, or which Providence interpreted after a method of its own. Assuredly, as the minister looked back, he beheld an expression of divine gratitude and ecstasy that seemed like the shine of the celestial city on her face, so wrinkled and ashy pale.

Again, a third instance. After parting from the old churchmember, he met the youngest sister of them all. It was a maiden newly won—and won by the Reverend Mr. Dimmesdale's own sermon, on the Sabbath after his vigil—to barter the transitory pleasures of the world for the heavenly hope, that was to assume brighter substance as life grew dark around her, and which would gild the utter gloom with final glory. She was fair and pure as a lily that had bloomed in Paradise. The minister knew well that he was himself enshrined within the stainless sanctity of her heart, which hung its snowy curtains about his image, imparting to religion the warmth of love, and to love a religious purity. Satan, that afternoon, had surely led the poor young girl away from her mother's side, and thrown her into the pathway of this sorely tempted, or—shall we not rather say?—this lost and desperate man. As she drew nigh, the arch-fiend whispered him to condense into small compass and drop into her tender bosom a germ of evil that would be sure to blossom darkly soon, and bear black fruit betimes. Such was his sense of power over this virgin soul, trusting him as she did, that the minister felt potent to blight all the field of innocence with but one wicked look, and develop all its opposite with but a word. So—with a mightier struggle than he had yet sustained—he held his Geneva cloak before his face, and hurried onward, making no sign of recognition, and leaving the young sister to digest his rudeness as she might. She ransacked her conscience,—which was full of harmless little matters, like her pocket or her work-bag,—and took herself to task, poor thing, for a thousand imaginary faults; and went about her household duties with swollen eyelids the next morning.

Before the minister had time to celebrate his victory over this last temptation, he was conscious of another impulse, more ludicrous, and almost as horrible. It was,—we blush to tell it,—it was to stop short in the road, and teach some very wicked words to a knot of little Puritan children who were playing there, and had but just begun to talk. Denying himself this freak, as unworthy of his cloth, he met a drunken seaman, one of the ship's crew from the Spanish Main. And, here, since he had so valiantly forborne all other wickedness, poor Mr. Dimmesdale longed, at least, to shake hands with the tarry blackguard,[134] and recreate himself with a few improper jests, such as dissolute sailors so abound with, and a volley of good, round, solid, satisfactory, and heaven-defying oaths! It was not so much a better principle, as partly his natural good taste, and still more his buckramed[135] habit of clerical decorum, that carried him safely through the latter crisis.

"What is it that haunts and tempts me thus?" cried the minister to himself, at length, pausing in the street, and striking his hand against his forehead. "Am I mad? or am I given over utterly to the fiend? Did I make a contract with him in the forest, and sign it with my blood? And does he now summon me to its fulfilment, by suggesting the performance of every wickedness which his most foul imagination can conceive?"

At the moment when the Reverend Mr. Dimmesdale thus communed with himself, and struck his forehead with his hand, old Mistress Hibbins, the reputed witch-lady, is said to have been passing by. She made a very grand appearance; having on a high head-dress, a rich gown of velvet, and

[134]TARRY BLACKGUARD: A dark and rough character of ill repute.
[135]BUCKRAMED: In a stiff manner.

a ruff done up with the famous yellow starch, of which Anne Turner,[136] her especial friend, had taught her the secret, before this last good lady had been hanged for Sir Thomas Overbury's murder. Whether the witch had read the minister's thoughts, or no, she came to a full stop, looked shrewdly into his face, smiled craftily, and—though little given to converse with clergymen—began a conversation.

"So, reverend Sir, you have made a visit into the forest," observed the witch-lady, nodding her high head-dress at him. "The next time, I pray you to allow me only a fair warning, and I shall be proud to bear you company. Without taking overmuch upon myself, my good word will go far towards gaining any strange gentleman a fair reception from yonder potentate you wot of!"

"I profess, madam," answered the clergyman, with a grave obeisance, such as the lady's rank demanded, and his own good-breeding made imperative,—"I profess, on my conscience and character, that I am utterly bewildered as touching the purport of your words! I went not into the forest to seek a potentate, neither do I, at any future time, design a visit thither, with a view to gaining the favor of such personage. My one sufficient object was to greet that pious friend of mine, the Apostle Eliot, and rejoice with him over the many precious souls he hath won from heathendom!"

"Ha, ha, ha!" cackled the old witch-lady, still nodding her high head-dress at the minister. "Well, well, we must needs talk thus in the daytime! You carry it off like an old hand! But at midnight, and in the forest, we shall have other talk together!"

She passed on with her aged stateliness, but often turning back her head and smiling at him, like one willing to recognize a secret intimacy of connection.

"Have I then sold myself," thought the minister, "to the fiend whom, if men say true, this yellow-starched and velveted old hag has chosen for her prince and master!"

The wretched minister! He had made a bargain very like it! Tempted by a dream of happiness, he had yielded himself with deliberate choice, as he had never done before, to what he knew was deadly sin. And the infectious poison of that sin had been thus rapidly diffused throughout his moral system. It had stupefied all blessed impulses, and awakened into vivid life the whole brotherhood of bad ones. Scorn, bitterness,

[136]ANNE TURNER: Ann Turner, a good friend of Frances Howard (Lady Essex), was hanged for poisoning Sir Thomas Overbury while he was imprisoned in the Tower of London. She was the court dressmaker for King James I. She introduced from France a yellow starch for ruffs and sleeves that became fashionable at court. Financially profiting from the popular starch, she kept its ingredients a closely guarded secret, which made her disliked by many high-ranking people. At her trial in 1615 for Overbury's murder, Sir Edward Coke, the Lord Chief Justice, stipulated that Ann be hanged wearing one of her yellow ruffs.

unprovoked malignity, gratuitous desire of ill, ridicule of whatever was good and holy, all awoke, to tempt, even while they frightened him. And his encounter with old Mistress Hibbins, if it were a real incident, did but show its sympathy and fellowship with wicked mortals and the world of perverted spirits.

He had by this time reached his dwelling, on the edge of the burial-ground, and, hastening up the stairs, took refuge in his study. The minister was glad to have reached this shelter, without first betraying himself to the world by any of those strange and wicked eccentricities to which he had been continually impelled while passing through the streets. He entered the accustomed room, and looked around him on its books, its windows, its fireplace, and the tapestried comfort of the walls, with the same perception of strangeness that had haunted him throughout his walk from the forest-dell into the town, and thitherward. Here he had studied and written; here, gone through fast and vigil, and come forth half alive; here, striven to pray; here, borne a hundred thousand agonies! There was the Bible, in its rich old Hebrew, with Moses and the Prophets speaking to him, and God's voice through all! There, on the table, with the inky pen beside it, was an unfinished sermon, with a sentence broken in the midst, where his thoughts had ceased to gush out upon the page two days before. He knew that it was himself, the thin and white-cheeked minister, who had done and suffered these things, and written thus far into the Election Sermon! But he seemed to stand apart, and eye this former self with scornful pitying, but half-envious curiosity. That self was gone! Another man had returned out of the forest; a wiser one; with a knowledge of hidden mysteries which the simplicity of the former never could have reached. A bitter kind of knowledge that!

While occupied with these reflections, a knock came at the door of the study, and the minister said, "Come in!"—not wholly devoid of an idea that he might behold an evil spirit. And so he did! It was old Roger Chillingworth that entered. The minister stood, white and speechless, with one hand on the Hebrew Scriptures, and the other spread upon his breast.

"Welcome home, reverend Sir!" said the physician. "And how found you that godly man, the Apostle Eliot? But methinks, dear Sir, you look pale; as if the travel through the wilderness had been too sore for you. Will not my aid be requisite to put you in heart and strength to preach your Election Sermon?"

"Nay, I think not so," rejoined the Reverend Mr. Dimmesdale. "My journey, and the sight of the holy Apostle yonder, and the free air which I have breathed, have done me good, after so long confinement in my study. I think to need no more of your drugs, my kind physician, good though they be, and administered by a friendly hand."

All this time, Roger Chillingworth was looking at the minister with the grave and intent regard of a physician towards his patient. But, in spite of this outward show, the latter was almost convinced of the old man's knowledge, or, at least, his confident suspicion, with respect to his own interview with Hester Prynne. The physician knew, then, that, in the minister's regard, he was no longer a trusted friend, but his bitterest enemy. So much being known, it would appear natural that a part of it should be expressed. It is singular, however, how long a time often passes before words embody things; and with what security two persons, who choose to avoid a certain subject, may approach its very verge, and retire without disturbing it. Thus, the minister felt no apprehension that Roger Chillingworth would touch, in express words, upon the real position which they sustained towards one another. Yet did the physician, in his dark way, creep frightfully near the secret.

"Were it not better," said he, "that you use my poor skill to-night? Verily, dear Sir, we must take pains to make you strong and vigorous for this occasion of the Election discourse. The people look for great things from you; apprehending that another year may come about, and find their pastor gone."

"Yea, to another world," replied the minister, with pious resignation. "Heaven grant it be a better one; for, in good sooth, I hardly think to tarry with my flock through the flitting seasons of another year! But, touching your medicine, kind Sir, in my present frame of body I need it not."

"I joy to hear it," answered the physician. "It may be that my remedies, so long administered in vain, begin now to take due effect. Happy man were I, and well deserving of New England's gratitude, could I achieve this cure!"

"I thank you from my heart, most watchful friend," said the Reverend Mr. Dimmesdale, with a solemn smile. "I thank you, and can but requite your good deeds with my prayers."

"A good man's prayers are golden recompense!" rejoined old Roger Chillingworth, as he took his leave. "Yea, they are the current gold coin of the New Jerusalem, with the King's own mint-mark on them!"

Left alone, the minister summoned a servant of the house, and requested food, which, being set before him, he ate with ravenous appetite. Then, flinging the already written pages of the Election Sermon into the fire, he forthwith began another, which he wrote with such an impulsive flow of thought and emotion, that he fancied himself inspired; and only wondered that Heaven should see fit to transmit the grand and solemn music of its oracles through so foul an organ-pipe as he. However, leaving that mystery to solve itself, or go unsolved for ever, he drove his task onward, with earnest haste and ecstasy. Thus the night fled away, as if it were a winged steed, and he careering on it; morning came, and peeped blushing through the curtains; and at last sunrise threw a golden beam into the study, and laid it right across the minister's bedazzled eyes. There he was, with the pen still between his fingers, and a vast, immeasurable tract of written space behind him!

XXI. THE NEW ENGLAND HOLIDAY

Betimes[137] in the morning of the day on which the new Governor was to receive his office at the hands of the people, Hester Prynne and little Pearl came into the market-place. It was already thronged with the craftsmen and other plebeian inhabitants of the town, in considerable numbers; among whom, likewise, were many rough figures, whose attire of deer-skins marked them as belonging to some of the forest settlements, which surrounded the little metropolis of the colony.

On this public holiday, as on all other occasions, for seven years past, Hester was clad in a garment of coarse gray cloth. Not more by its hue than by some indescribable peculiarity in its fashion, it had the effect of making her fade personally out of sight and outline; while, again, the scarlet letter brought her back from this twilight indistinctness, and revealed her under the moral aspect of its own illumination. Her face, so long familiar to the townspeople, showed the marble quietude which they were accustomed to behold there. It was like a mask; or rather, like the frozen calmness of a dead woman's features; owing this dreary resemblance to the fact that Hester was actually dead, in respect to any claim of sympathy, and had departed out of the world with which she still seemed to mingle.

It might be, on this one day, that there was an expression unseen before, nor, indeed, vivid enough to be detected now; unless some preternaturally gifted observer should have first read the heart, and have afterwards sought a corresponding development in the countenance and mien. Such a spiritual seer might have conceived, that, after sustaining the gaze of the multitude through seven miserable years as a necessity, a penance, and something which it was a stern religion to endure, she now, for one last time more, encountered it freely and voluntarily, in order to convert what had so long been agony into a kind

---

[137]BETIMES: Early.

of triumph. "Look your last on the scarlet letter and its wearer!"—the people's victim and life-long bond-slave, as they fancied her, might say to them. "Yet a little while, and she will be beyond your reach! A few hours longer, and the deep, mysterious ocean will quench and hide for ever the symbol which ye have caused to burn on her bosom!" Nor were it an inconsistency too improbable to be assigned to human nature, should we suppose a feeling of regret in Hester's mind, at the moment when she was about to win her freedom from the pain which had been thus deeply incorporated with her being. Might there not be an irresistible desire to quaff a last, long, breathless draught of the cup of wormwood and aloes, with which nearly all her years of womanhood had been perpetually flavored? The wine of life, henceforth to be presented to her lips, must be indeed rich, delicious, and exhilarating, in its chased and golden beaker; or else leave an inevitable and weary languor, after the lees of bitterness wherewith she had been drugged, as with a cordial of intensest potency.

Pearl was decked out with airy gaiety. It would have been impossible to guess that this bright and sunny apparition owed its existence to the shape of gloomy gray; or that a fancy, at once so gorgeous and so delicate as must have been requisite to contrive the child's apparel, was the same that had achieved a task perhaps more difficult, in imparting so distinct a peculiarity to Hester's simple robe. The dress, so proper was it to little Pearl, seemed an effluence, or inevitable development and outward manifestation of her character, no more to be separated from her than the many-hued brilliancy from a butterfly's wing, or the painted glory from the leaf of a bright flower. As with these, so with the child; her garb was all of one idea with her nature. On this eventful day, moreover, there was a certain singular inquietude and excitement in her mood, resembling nothing so much as the shimmer of a diamond, that sparkles and flashes with the varied throbbings of the breast on which it is displayed. Children have always a sympathy in the agitations of those connected with them; always, especially, a sense of any trouble or impending revolution, of whatever kind, in domestic circumstances; and therefore Pearl, who was the gem on her mother's unquiet bosom, betrayed, by the very dance of her spirits, the emotions which none could detect in the marble passiveness of Hester's brow.

This effervescence made her flit with a bird-like movement, rather than walk by her mother's side. She broke continually into shouts of a wild, inarticulate, and sometimes piercing music. When they reached the market-place, she became still more restless, on perceiving the stir and bustle that enlivened the spot; for it was usually more like the broad and lonesome green before a village meeting-house, than the centre of a town's business.

"Why, what is this, mother?" cried she. "Wherefore have all the people left their work to-day? Is it a play-day for the whole world? See, there is the blacksmith! He has washed his sooty face, and put on his Sabbath-day clothes, and looks as if he would gladly be merry, if any kind body would only teach him how! And there is Master Brackett, the old jailer, nodding and smiling at me. Why does he do so, mother?"

"He remembers thee a little babe, my child," answered Hester.

"He should not nod and smile at me, for all that,—the black, grim, ugly-eyed old man!" said Pearl. "He may nod at thee if he will; for thou art clad in gray, and wearest the scarlet letter. But see, mother, how many faces of strange people, and Indians among them, and sailors! What have they all come to do here in the market-place?"

"They wait to see the procession pass," said Hester. "For the Governor and the magistrates are to go by, and the ministers, and all the great people and good people, with the music, and the soldiers marching before them."

"And will the minister be there?" asked Pearl. "And will he hold out both his hands to me, as when thou ledst me to him from the brook-side?"

"He will be there, child," answered her mother. "But he will not greet thee to-day; nor must thou greet him."

"What a strange, sad man is he!" said the child, as if speaking partly to herself. "In the dark night-time, he calls us to him, and holds thy hand and mine, as when we stood with him on the scaffold yonder! And in the deep forest, where only the old trees can hear, and the strip of sky see it, he talks with thee, sitting on a heap of moss! And he kisses my forehead, too, so that the little brook would hardly wash it off! But here in the sunny day, and among all the people, he knows us not; nor must we know him! A strange, sad man is he, with his hand always over his heart!"

"Be quiet, Pearl! Thou understandest not these things," said her mother. "Think not now of the minister, but look about thee, and see how cheery is every body's face to-day. The children have come from their schools, and the grown people from their workshops and their fields, on purpose to be happy. For, to-day, a new man is beginning to rule over them; and so—as has been the custom of mankind ever since a nation was first gathered—they make merry and rejoice; as if a good and golden year were at length to pass over the poor old world!"

It was as Hester said, in regard to the unwonted jollity that brightened the faces of the people. Into this festal season of the year—as it already was, and continued to be during the greater part of two centuries—the Puritans compressed whatever mirth and public joy they deemed allowable to human infirmity; thereby so far dispelling the customary cloud, that, for the space of a single holiday, they appeared scarcely more grave than most other communities at a period of general affliction.

But we perhaps exaggerate the gray or sable tinge, which undoubtedly characterized the mood and manners of the age. The persons now in the market-place of Boston had not been born to an inheritance of Puritanic gloom. They were native Englishmen, whose fathers had lived in the sunny richness of the Elizabethan epoch; a time when the life of England, viewed as one great mass, would appear to have been as stately, magnificent, and joyous, as the world has ever witnessed. Had they followed their hereditary taste, the New England settlers would have illustrated all events of public importance by bonfires, banquets, pageantries, and processions. Nor would it have been impracticable, in the observance of majestic ceremonies, to combine mirthful recreation with solemnity, and give, as it were, a grotesque and brilliant embroidery to the great robe of state, which a nation, at such festivals, puts on. There was some shadow of an attempt of this kind in the mode of celebrating the day on which the political year of the colony commenced. The dim reflection of a remembered splendor, a colorless and manifold diluted repetition of what they had beheld in proud old London,—we will not say at a royal coronation, but at a Lord Mayor's show,[138]—might be traced in the customs which our forefathers instituted, with reference to the annual installation of magistrates. The fathers and founders of the commonwealth—the statesman, the priest, and the soldier—seemed it a duty then to assume the outward state and majesty, which, in accordance with antique style, was looked upon as the proper garb of public and social eminence. All came forth, to move in procession before the people's eye, and thus impart a needed dignity to the simple framework of a government so newly constructed.

Then, too, the people were countenanced, if not encouraged, in relaxing the severe and close application to their various modes of rugged industry, which, at all other times, seemed of the same piece and material with their religion. Here, it is true, were none of the appliances which popular merriment would so readily have found in the England of Elizabeth's time, or that of James[139];—no rude shows of a theatrical kind;

[138]A LORD MAYOR'S SHOW: The procession, held on November 9, during which the Lord Mayor of London, with the aldermen and other city dignitaries, participates in a great parade to Westminster, where he is formally told by the Lord Chancellor of the Crown's assent to his election.
[139]ELIZABETH'S TIME, OR THAT OF JAMES: Queen Elizabeth I; King James I.

no minstrel with his harp and legendary ballad, nor gleeman, with an ape dancing to his music; no juggler, with his tricks of mimic witchcraft; no Merry Andrew,[140] to stir up the multitude with jests, perhaps hundreds of years old, but still effective, by their appeals to the very broadest sources of mirthful sympathy. All such professors of the several branches of jocularity would have been sternly repressed, not only by the rigid discipline of law, but by the general sentiment which gives law its vitality. Not the less, however, the great, honest face of the people smiled, grimly, perhaps, but widely too. Nor were sports wanting, such as the colonists had witnessed, and shared in, long ago, at the country fairs and on the village-greens of England; and which it was thought well to keep alive on this new soil, for the sake of the courage and manliness that were essential in them. Wrestling-matches, in the differing fashions of Cornwall and Devonshire, were seen here and there about the market-place; in one corner, there was a friendly bout at quarterstaff[141]; and—what attracted most interest of all—on the platform of the pillory, already so noted in our pages, two masters of defence were commencing an exhibition with the buckler and broadsword.[142] But, much to the disappointment of the crowd, this latter business was broken off by the interposition of the town beadle,[143] who had no idea of permitting the majesty of the law to be violated by such an abuse of one of its consecrated places.

It may not be too much to affirm, on the whole, (the people being then in the first stages of joyless deportment, and the offspring of sires who had known how to be merry, in their day,) that they would compare favorably, in point of holiday keeping, with their descendants, even at so long an interval as ourselves. Their immediate posterity, the generation next to the early emigrants, wore the blackest shade of Puritanism, and so darkened the national visage with it, that all the subsequent years have not sufficed to clear it up. We have yet to learn again the forgotten art of gayety.

The picture of human life in the market-place, though its general tint was the sad gray, brown, or black of the English emigrants, was yet enlivened by some diversity of hue. A party of Indians—in their savage finery of curiously embroidered deer-skin robes, wampum-belts,[144]

---

[140]MERRY ANDREW: A clown.
[141]BOUT AT QUARTERSTAFF: A fighting contest with staffs six to eight feet long, used as weapons by the English peasantry.
[142]BUCKLER AND BROADSWORD: A buckler is a small round shield worn on the arm. A broadsword is a sword with a broad, flat blade.
[143]BEADLE: Crier.
[144]WAMPUM-BELTS: Belts decorated with cylindrical beads made from the polished insides of seashells, threaded on strings.

red and yellow ochre, and feathers, and armed with the bow and arrow and stone-headed spear—stood apart, with countenances of inflexible gravity, beyond what even the Puritan aspect could attain. Nor, wild as were these painted barbarians, were they the wildest feature of the scene. This distinction could more justly be claimed by some mariners,—a part of the crew of the vessel from the Spanish Main,—who had come ashore to see the humors of Election Day. They were rough-looking desperadoes, with sun-blackened faces, and an immensity of beard; their wide short trousers were confined about the waist by belts, often clasped with a rough plate of gold, and sustaining always a long knife, and, in some instances, a sword. From beneath their broad-brimmed hats of palm-leaf, gleamed eyes which, even in good nature and merriment, had a kind of animal ferocity. They transgressed, without fear or scruple, the rules of behaviour that were binding on all others; smoking tobacco under the beadle's very nose, although each whiff would have cost a townsman a shilling; and quaffing, at their pleasure, draughts of wine or aqua-vitæ[145] from pocket-flasks, which they freely tendered to the gaping crowd around them. It remarkably characterized the incomplete morality of the age, rigid as we call it, that a license was allowed the seafaring class, not merely for their freaks on shore, but for far more desperate deeds on their proper element. The sailor of that day would go near to be arraigned as a pirate in our own. There could be little doubt, for instance, that this very ship's crew, though no unfavorable specimens of the nautical brotherhood, had been guilty, as we should phrase it, of depredations on the Spanish commerce, such as would have perilled all their necks in a modern court of justice.

But the sea, in those old times, heaved, swelled, and foamed very much at its own will, or subject only to the tempestuous wind, with hardly any attempts at regulation by human law. The buccaneer on the wave might relinquish his calling, and become at once, if he chose, a man of probity and piety on land; nor, even in the full career of his reckless life, was he regarded as a personage with whom it was disreputable to traffic, or casually associate. Thus, the Puritan elders, in their black cloaks, starched bands, and steeple-crowned hats, smiled not unbenignantly at the clamor and rude deportment of these jolly seafaring men; and it excited neither surprise nor animadversion when so reputable a citizen as old Roger Chillingworth, the physician, was seen to enter the market-place, in close and familiar talk with the commander of the questionable vessel.

[145]AQUA-VITAE: Brandy.

The latter was by far the most showy and gallant figure, so far as apparel went, anywhere to be seen among the multitude. He wore a profusion of ribbons on his garment, and gold lace on his hat, which was also encircled by a gold chain, and surmounted with a feather. There was a sword at his side, and a sword-cut on his forehead, which, by the arrangement of his hair, he seemed anxious rather to display than hide. A landsman could hardly have worn this garb and shown this face, and worn and shown them both with such a galliard air,[146] without undergoing stern question before a magistrate, and probably incurring a fine or imprisonment, or perhaps an exhibition in the stocks. As regarded the shipmaster, however, all was looked upon as pertaining to the character, as to a fish his glistening scales.

After parting from the physician, the commander of the Bristol ship strolled idly through the market-place; until, happening to approach the spot where Hester Prynne was standing, he appeared to recognize, and did not hesitate to address her. As was usually the case wherever Hester stood, a small, vacant area—a sort of magic circle—had formed itself about her, into which, though the people were elbowing one another at a little distance, none ventured, or felt disposed to intrude. It was a forcible type of the moral solitude in which the scarlet letter enveloped its fated wearer; partly by her own reserve, and partly by the instinctive, though no longer so unkindly, withdrawal of her fellow-creatures. Now, if never before, it answered a good purpose, by enabling Hester and the seaman to speak together without risk of being overheard; and so changed was Hester Prynne's repute before the public, that the matron in town most eminent for rigid morality could not have held such intercourse with less result of scandal than herself.

"So, mistress," said the mariner, "I must bid the steward make ready one more berth than you bargained for! No fear of scurvy or ship-fever, this voyage! What with the ship's surgeon and this other doctor, our only danger will be from drug or pill; more by token, as there is a lot of apothecary's stuff aboard, which I traded for with a Spanish vessel."

"What mean you?" inquired Hester, startled more than she permitted to appear. "Have you another passenger?"

"Why, know you not," cried the shipmaster, "that this physician here—Chillingworth, he calls himself—is minded to try my cabin-fare with you? Ay, ay, you must have known it; for he tells me he is of your party, and a close friend to the gentleman you spoke of,—he that is in peril from these sour old Puritan rulers!"

[146]GALLIARD AIR: Lively and in high spirits.

"They know each other well, indeed," replied Hester, with a mien of calmness, though in the utmost consternation. "They have long dwelt together."

Nothing further passed between the mariner and Hester Prynne. But, at that instant, she beheld old Roger Chillingworth himself, standing in the remotest corner of the market-place, and smiling on her; a smile which—across the wide and bustling square, and through all the talk and laughter, and various thoughts, moods, and interests of the crowd—conveyed secret and fearful meaning.

XXII. THE PROCESSION

Before Hester Prynne could call together her thoughts, and consider what was practicable to be done in this new and startling aspect of affairs, the sound of military music was heard approaching along a contiguous street. It denoted the advance of the procession of magistrates and citizens, on its way towards the meeting-house; where, in compliance with a custom thus early established, and ever since observed, the Reverend Mr. Dimmesdale was to deliver an Election Sermon.

Soon the head of the procession showed itself, with a slow and stately march, turning a corner, and making its way across the market-place. First came the music. It comprised a variety of instruments, perhaps imperfectly adapted to one another, and played with no great skill, but yet attaining the great object for which the harmony of drum and clarion addresses itself to the multitude,—that of imparting a higher and more heroic air to the scene of life that passes before the eye. Little Pearl at first clapped her hands, but then lost, for an instant, the restless agitation that had kept her in a continual effervescence throughout the morning; she gazed silently, and seemed to be borne upward, like a floating sea-bird, on the long heaves and swells of sound. But she was brought back to her former mood by the shimmer of the sunshine on the weapons and bright armour of the military company, which followed after the music, and formed the honorary escort of the procession. This body of soldiery[147]—which still sustains a corporate existence, and marches down from past ages with an ancient and honorable fame—was composed of no mercenary materials. Its ranks were filled with gentlemen, who felt the stirrings of martial impulse, and sought to establish a kind of College of Arms,[148] where, as in an association of

[147]THIS BODY OF SOLDIERY: The Military Company of Massachusetts. It still exists as the "Ancient and Honorable Artillery Company of Massachusetts" and marches on ceremonial occasions.
[148]COLLEGE OF ARMS: The College of Arms records the titles, pedigrees, and coats of arms of the English aristocracy.

Knights Templars,[149] they might learn the science, and, so far as peaceful exercise would teach them, the practices of war. The high estimation then placed upon the military character might be seen in the lofty port of each individual member of the company. Some of them, indeed, by their services in the Low Countries[150] and on other fields of European warfare, had fairly won their title to assume the name and pomp of soldiership. The entire array, moreover, clad in burnished steel, and with plumage nodding over their bright morions,[151] had a brilliancy of effect which no modern display can aspire to equal.

And yet the men of civil eminence, who came immediately behind the military escort, were better worth a thoughtful observer's eye. Even in outward demeanour they showed a stamp of majesty that made the warrior's haughty stride look vulgar, if not absurd. It was an age when what we call talent had far less consideration than now, but the massive materials which produce stability and dignity of character a great deal more. The people possessed, by hereditary right, the quality of reverence; which, in their descendants, if it survive at all, exists in smaller proportion, and with a vastly diminished force in the selection and estimate of public men. The change may be for good or ill, and is partly, perhaps, for both. In that old day, the English settler on these rude shores,—having left king, nobles, and all degrees of awful rank behind, while still the faculty and necessity of reverence were strong in him,—bestowed it on the white hair and venerable brow of age; on long-tried integrity; on solid wisdom and sad-colored experience; on endowments of that grave and weighty order, which gives the idea of permanence, and comes under the general definition of respectability. These primitive statesmen, therefore,—Bradstreet, Endicott, Dudley, Bellingham,[152] and their compeers,—who were elevated to power by the early choice of the people, seem to have been not often brilliant, but distinguished by a ponderous sobriety, rather than activity of intellect. They had fortitude and self-reliance, and, in time of difficulty or peril, stood up for the welfare of the state like a line of cliffs against a tempestuous tide. The traits of character here indicated were well represented in the square cast of countenance and large physical development of the new colonial magistrates. So far as a demeanour of

---

[149]KNIGHTS TEMPLARS: An order of knights founded around 1118. Hawthorne could also be alluding to Freemasons or members of a Masonic order.
[150]LOW COUNTRIES: An area known as Flanders during the seventeenth century, it comprised modern Belgium, the Netherlands, and Luxembourg.
[151]BRIGHT MORIONS: Crested helmets with curved beaks at the front and back.
[152]BRADSTREET, ENDICOTT, DUDLEY, BELLINGHAM: Early governors of New England colonies: Simon Bradstreet (1603–1697); John Endicott (1588–1665); Thomas Dudley (1576–1653); Richard Bellingham (1592–1672).

natural authority was concerned, the mother country need not have been ashamed to see these foremost men of an actual democracy adopted into the House of Peers,[153] or make the Privy Council[154] of the sovereign.

Next in order to the magistrates came the young and eminently distinguished divine, from whose lips the religious discourse of the anniversary was expected. His was the profession, at that era, in which intellectual ability displayed itself far more than in political life; for— leaving a higher motive out of the question—it offered inducements powerful enough, in the almost worshipping respect of the community, to win the most aspiring ambition into its service. Even political power—as in the case of Increase Mather[155]—was within the grasp of a successful priest.

It was the observation of those who beheld him now, that never, since Mr. Dimmesdale first set his foot on the New England shore, had he exhibited such energy as was seen in the gait and air with which he kept his pace in the procession. There was no feebleness of step, as at other times; his frame was not bent; nor did his hand rest ominously upon his heart. Yet, if the clergyman were rightly viewed, his strength seemed not of the body. It might be spiritual, and imparted to him by angelic ministrations. It might be the exhilaration of that potent cordial, which is distilled only in the furnace-glow of earnest and long-continued thought. Or, perchance, his sensitive temperament was invigorated by the loud and piercing music, that swelled heavenward, and uplifted him on its ascending wave. Nevertheless, so abstracted was his look, it might be questioned whether Mr. Dimmesdale ever heard the music. There was his body, moving onward, and with an unaccustomed force. But where was his mind? Far and deep in its own region, busying itself, with preternatural activity, to marshal a procession of stately thoughts that were soon to issue thence; and so he saw nothing, heard nothing, knew nothing, of what was around him; but the spiritual element took up the feeble frame, and carried it along, unconscious of the burden, and converting it to spirit like itself. Men of uncommon intellect, who have grown morbid, possess this occasional power of mighty effort, into which they throw the life of many days, and then are lifeless for as many more.

---

[153]HOUSE OF PEERS: The House of Lords, the upper house of the British parliament.
[154]PRIVY COUNCIL: The council chosen by the monarch to administer public affairs.
[155]INCREASE MATHER: A Puritan clergyman (1639–1723), who had great influence over Massachusetts politics. He was one of the inquisitors of the Salem witchcraft trials of 1692, and a year later, published *Cases of Conscience Concerning Evil Spirits* (1693), which denounced the "spectral evidence" that had condemned many individuals during the trials.

Hester Prynne, gazing stedfastly at the clergyman, felt a dreary influence come over her, but wherefore or whence she knew not; unless that he seemed so remote from her own sphere, and utterly beyond her reach. One glance of recognition, she had imagined, must needs pass between them. She thought of the dim forest, with its little dell of solitude, and love, and anguish, and the mossy tree-trunk, where, sitting hand in hand, they had mingled their sad and passionate talk with the melancholy murmur of the brook. How deeply had they known each other then! And was this the man? She hardly knew him now! He, moving proudly past, enveloped, as it were, in the rich music, with the procession of majestic and venerable fathers; he, so unattainable in his worldly position, and still more so in that far vista of his unsympathizing thoughts, through which she now beheld him! Her spirit sank with the idea that all must have been a delusion, and that, vividly as she had dreamed it, there could be no real bond betwixt the clergyman and herself. And thus much of woman was there in Hester, that she could scarcely forgive him,—least of all now, when the heavy footstep of their approaching Fate might be heard, nearer, nearer, nearer!—for being able so completely to withdraw himself from their mutual world; while she groped darkly, and stretched forth her cold hands, and found him not.

Pearl either saw and responded to her mother's feelings, or herself felt the remoteness and intangibility that had fallen around the minister. While the procession passed, the child was uneasy, fluttering up and down, like a bird on the point of taking flight. When the whole had gone by, she looked up into Hester's face.

"Mother," said she, "was that the same minister that kissed me by the brook?"

"Hold thy peace, dear little Pearl!" whispered her mother. "We must not always talk in the market-place of what happens to us in the forest."

"I could not be sure that it was he; so strange he looked," continued the child. "Else I would have run to him, and bid him kiss me now, before all the people; even as he did yonder among the dark old trees. What would the minister have said, mother? Would he have clapped his hand over his heart, and scowled on me, and bid me begone?"

"What should he say, Pearl," answered Hester, "save that it was no time to kiss, and that kisses are not to be given in the market-place? Well for thee, foolish child, that thou didst not speak to him!"

Another shade of the same sentiment, in reference to Mr. Dimmesdale, was expressed by a person whose eccentricities—or insanity, as we should term it—led her to do what few of the townspeople would have ventured on; to begin a conversation with the wearer of the scarlet letter,

Mistress Hibbins, who, arrayed in great magnificence, in public. I~~ff,~~ a broidered stomacher,[156] a gown of rich velvet, and with a tri~~cane,~~ had come forth to see the procession. As this ancient a gold-~~renown~~ (which subsequently cost her no less a price than lady ~~being~~ a principal actor in all the works of necromancy that her ~~annually~~ going forward, the crowd gave way before her, and ~~fear~~ the touch of her garment, as if it carried the plague among ~~ous~~ folds. Seen in conjunction with Hester Prynne,—kindly as ~~y~~ now felt towards the latter,—the dread inspired by Mistress ~~ns~~ had doubled, and caused a general movement from that part ~~e~~ market-place in which the two women stood.

"Now, what mortal imagination could conceive it!" whispered the ~~lady~~ confidentially to Hester. "Yonder divine man! That saint on earth, as the people uphold him to be, and as—I must needs say—he really looks! Who, now, that saw him pass in the procession, would think how little while it is since he went forth out of his study,—chewing a Hebrew text of Scripture in his mouth, I warrant,—to take an airing in the forest! Aha! we know what that means, Hester Prynne! But, truly, I find it hard to believe him the same man. Many a church-member saw I, walking behind the music, that has danced in the same measure with me, when Somebody was fiddler, and, it might be, an Indian powwow or a Lapland wizard changing hands with us! That is but a trifle, when a woman knows the world. But this minister! Couldst thou surely tell, Hester, whether he was the same man that encoun-tered thee on the forest-path!"

"Madam, I know not of what you speak," answered Hester Prynne, feeling Mistress Hibbins to be of infirm mind; yet strangely startled and awe-stricken by the confidence with which she affirmed a personal con-nection between so many persons (herself among them) and the Evil One. "It is not for me to talk lightly of a learned and pious minister of the Word, like the Reverend Mr. Dimmesdale!"

"Fie, woman, fie!" cried the old lady, shaking her finger at Hester. "Dost thou think I have been to the forest so many times, and have yet no skill to judge who else has been there? Yea; though no leaf of the wild garlands, which they wore while they danced, be left in their hair! I know thee, Hester; for I behold the token. We may all see it in the sun-shine; and it glows like a red flame in the dark. Thou wearest it openly; so there need be no question about that. But this minister! Let me tell

[156]BROIDERED STOMACHER: An embroidered covering for the chest worn under the lacing of a woman's bodice.

thee in thine ear! When the Black Man sees one of his servants, signed and sealed, so shy of owning to the bond as is the Mr. Dimmesdale, he hath a way of ordering matters so that the and Mr. be disclosed in open daylight to the eyes of all the world! Whall that the minister seeks to hide, with his hand always over his hea. Hester Prynne!"

"What is it, good Mistress Hibbins?" eagerly asked little Pearl. "I thou seen it?"

"No matter, darling!" responded Mistress Hibbins, making Pearl profound reverence. "Thou thyself wilt see it, one time or another. They say, child, thou art of the lineage of the Prince of Air![157] Wilt thou ride with me, some fine night, to see thy father? Then thou shalt know wherefore the minister keeps his hand over his heart!"

Laughing so shrilly that all the market-place could hear her, the weird old gentlewoman took her departure.

By this time the preliminary prayer had been offered in the meeting-house, and the accents of the Reverend Mr. Dimmesdale were heard commencing his discourse. An irresistible feeling kept Hester near the spot. As the sacred edifice was too much thronged to admit another auditor, she took up her position close beside the scaffold of the pillory. It was in sufficient proximity to bring the whole sermon to her ears, in the shape of an indistinct, but varied, murmur and flow of the minister's very peculiar voice.

This vocal organ was in itself a rich endowment; insomuch that a listener, comprehending nothing of the language in which the preacher spoke, might still have been swayed to and fro by the mere tone and cadence. Like all other music, it breathed passion and pathos, and emotions high or tender, in a tongue native to the human heart, wherever educated. Muffled as the sound was by its passage through the church-walls, Hester Prynne listened with such intentness, and sympathized so intimately, that the sermon had throughout a meaning for her, entirely apart from its indistinguishable words. These, perhaps, if more distinctly heard, might have been only a grosser medium, and have clogged the spiritual sense. Now she caught the low undertone, as of the wind sinking down to repose itself; then ascended with it, as it rose through progressive gradations of sweetness and power, until its volume seemed to envelop her with an atmosphere of awe and solemn grandeur. And yet, majestic as

[157]PRINCE OF AIR: Satan. Hibbins references Ephesians 2:2: "Wherein in time past ye walked according to the course of this world, according to the prince of the power of the air, the spirit that now worketh in the children of disobedience."

the voice sometimes became, there was for ever in it an essential character of plaintiveness. A loud or low expression of anguish,—the whisper, or the shriek, as it might be conceived, of suffering humanity, that touched a sensibility in every bosom! At times this deep strain of pathos was all that could be heard, and scarcely heard, sighing amid a desolate silence. But even when the minister's voice grew high and commanding,—when it gushed irrepressibly upward,—when it assumed its utmost breadth and power, so overfilling the church as to burst its way through the solid walls, and diffuse itself in the open air,—still, if the auditor listened intently, and for the purpose, he could detect the same cry of pain. What was it? The complaint of a human heart, sorrow-laden, perchance guilty, telling its secret, whether of guilt or sorrow, to the great heart of mankind; beseeching its sympathy or forgiveness,—at every moment,—in each accent,—and never in vain! It was this profound and continual undertone that gave the clergyman his most appropriate power.

During all this time Hester stood, statue-like, at the foot of the scaffold. If the minister's voice had not kept her there, there would nevertheless have been an inevitable magnetism in that spot, whence she dated the first hour of her life of ignominy. There was a sense within her,— too ill-defined to be made a thought, but weighing heavily on her mind,— that her whole orb of life, both before and after, was connected with this spot, as with the one point that gave it unity.

Little Pearl, meanwhile, had quitted her mother's side, and was playing at her own will about the market-place. She made the sombre crowd cheerful by her erratic and glistening ray; even as a bird of bright plumage illuminates a whole tree of dusky foliage by darting to and fro, half seen and half concealed, amid the twilight of the clustering leaves. She had an undulating, but, oftentimes, a sharp and irregular movement. It indicated the restless vivacity of her spirit, which to-day was doubly indefatigable in its tip-toe dance, because it was played upon and vibrated with her mother's disquietude. Whenever Pearl saw any thing to excite her ever active and wandering curiosity, she flew thitherward, and, as we might say, seized upon that man or thing as her own property, so far as she desired it; but without yielding the minutest degree of control over her motions in requital. The Puritans looked on, and, if they smiled, were none the less inclined to pronounce the child a demon off-spring, from the indescribable charm of beauty and eccentricity that shone through her little figure, and sparkled with its activity. She ran and looked the wild Indian in the face; and he grew conscious of a nature wilder than his own. Thence, with native audacity, but still with a reserve as characteristic, she flew into the midst of a group of mariners, the swarthy-cheeked wild men of the ocean, as the Indians were of the land; and they gazed wonderingly and admiringly at Pearl, as if a flake of the sea-foam had taken the shape of a little maid, and were gifted with a soul of the sea-fire, that flashes beneath the prow in the night-time.

One of these seafaring men—the shipmaster, indeed, who had spoken to Hester Prynne—was so smitten with Pearl's aspect, that he attempted to lay hands upon her, with purpose to snatch a kiss. Finding it as impossible to touch her as to catch a humming-bird in the air, he took from his hat the gold chain that was twisted about it, and threw it to the child. Pearl immediately twined it around her neck and waist, with such happy skill, that, once seen there, it became a part of her, and it was difficult to imagine her without it.

"Thy mother is yonder woman with the scarlet letter," said the seaman. "Wilt thou carry her a message from me?"

"If the message pleases me I will," answered Pearl.

"Then tell her," rejoined he, "that I spake again with the black-a-visaged, hump-shouldered old doctor, and he engages to bring his friend, the gentleman she wots[158] of, aboard with him. So let thy mother take no thought, save for herself and thee. Wilt thou tell her this, thou witch-baby?"

"Mistress Hibbins says my father is the Prince of the Air!" cried Pearl, with her naughty smile. "If thou callest me that ill name; I shall tell him of thee; and he will chase thy ship with a tempest!"

Pursuing a zigzag course across the market-place, the child returned to her mother, and communicated what the mariner had said. Hester's strong, calm, stedfastly enduring spirit almost sank, at last, on beholding this dark and grim countenance of an inevitable doom, which—at the moment when a passage seemed to open for the minister and herself out of their labyrinth of misery—showed itself, with an unrelenting smile, right in the midst of their path.

With her mind harassed by the terrible perplexity in which the shipmaster's intelligence involved her, she was also subjected to another trial. There were many people present, from the country roundabout, who had often heard of the scarlet letter, and to whom it had been made terrific by a hundred false or exaggerated rumors, but who had never beheld it with their own bodily eyes. These, after exhausting other modes of amusement, now thronged about Hester Prynne with rude and boorish intrusiveness. Unscrupulous as it was, however, it could not bring them nearer than a circuit of several yards. At that distance they accordingly stood, fixed

---

[158]WOTS: Knows.

there by the centrifugal force of the repugnance which the mystic symbol inspired. The whole gang of sailors, likewise, observing the press of spectators, and learning the purport of the scarlet letter, came and thrust their sunburnt and desperado-looking faces into the ring. Even the Indians were affected by a sort of cold shadow of the white man's curiosity, and, gliding through the crowd, fastened their snake-like black eyes on Hester's bosom; conceiving, perhaps, that the wearer of this brilliantly embroidered badge must needs be a personage of high dignity among her people. Lastly, the inhabitants of the town (their own interest in this worn-out subject languidly reviving itself, by sympathy with what they saw others feel) lounged idly to the same quarter, and tormented Hester Prynne, perhaps more than all the rest, with their cool, well-acquainted gaze at her familiar shame. Hester saw and recognized the self-same faces of that group of matrons, who had awaited her forthcoming from the prison-door, seven years ago; all save one, the youngest and only compassionate among them, whose burial-robe she had since made. At the final hour, when she was so soon to fling aside the burning letter, it had strangely become the centre of more remark and excitement, and was thus made to sear her breast more painfully, than at any time since the first day she put it on.

While Hester stood in that magic circle of ignominy, where the cunning cruelty of her sentence seemed to have fixed her for ever, the admirable preacher was looking down from the sacred pulpit upon an audience, whose very inmost spirits had yielded to his control. The sainted minister in the church! The woman of the scarlet letter in the market-place! What imagination would have been irreverent enough to surmise that the same scorching stigma was on them both?

XXIII. THE REVELATION OF THE SCARLET LETTER

The eloquent voice, on which the souls of the listening audience had been borne aloft, as on the swelling waves of the sea, at length came to a pause. There was a momentary silence, profound as what should follow the utterance of oracles. Then ensued a murmur and half-hushed tumult; as if the auditors, released from the high spell that had transported them into the region of another's mind, were returning into themselves, with all their awe and wonder still heavy on them. In a moment more, the crowd began to gush forth from the doors of the church. Now that there was an end, they needed more breath, more fit to support the gross and earthly life into which they relapsed, than that atmosphere which the preacher had converted into words of flame, and had burdened with the rich fragrance of his thought.

In the open air their rapture broke into speech. The street and the market-place absolutely babbled, from side to side, with applauses of the minister. His hearers could not rest until they had told one another of what each knew better than he could tell or hear. According to their united testimony, never had man spoken in so wise, so high, and so holy a spirit, as he that spake this day; nor had inspiration ever breathed through mortal lips more evidently than it did through his. Its influence could be seen, as it were, descending upon him, and possessing him, and continually lifting him out of the written discourse that lay before him, and filling him with ideas that must have been as marvellous to himself as to his audience. His subject, it appeared, had been the relation between the Deity and the communities of mankind, with a special reference to the New England which they were here planting in the wilderness. And, as he drew towards the close, a spirit as of prophecy had come upon him, constraining him to its purpose as mightily as the old prophets of Israel were constrained; only with this difference, that, whereas the Jewish seers had denounced judgments and ruin on their country, it was his mission to foretell a high and glorious destiny for the newly gathered people of the Lord. But, throughout it all, and through the whole discourse, there had been a certain deep, sad undertone of pathos, which could not be interpreted otherwise than as the natural regret of one soon to pass away. Yes; their minister whom they so loved—and who so loved them all, that he could not depart heavenward without a sigh—had the foreboding of untimely death upon him, and would soon leave them in their tears! This idea of his transitory stay on earth gave the last emphasis to the effect which the preacher had produced; it was as if an angel, in his passage to the skies, had shaken his bright wings over the people for an instant,—at once a shadow and a splendor,—and had shed down a shower of golden truths upon them.

Thus, there had come to the Reverend Mr. Dimmesdale—as to most men, in their various spheres, though seldom recognized until they see it far behind them—an epoch of life more brilliant and full of triumph than any previous one, or than any which could hereafter be. He stood, at this moment, on the very proudest eminence of superiority, to which the gifts of intellect, rich lore, prevailing eloquence, and a reputation of whitest sanctity, could exalt a clergyman in New England's earliest days, when the professional character was of itself a lofty pedestal. Such was the position which the minister occupied, as he bowed his head forward on the cushions of the pulpit at the close of his Election Sermon. Meanwhile, Hester Prynne was standing beside the scaffold of the pillory, with the scarlet letter still burning on her breast!

Now was heard again the clangor of the music, and the measured tramp of the military escort, issuing from the church-door. The procession was to be marshalled thence to the town-hall, where a solemn banquet would complete the ceremonies of the day.

Once more, therefore, the train of venerable and majestic fathers was seen moving through a broad pathway of the people, who drew back reverently, on either side, as the Governor and magistrates, the old and wise men, the holy ministers, and all that were eminent and renowned, advanced into the midst of them. When they were fairly in the market-place, their presence was greeted by a shout. This—though doubtless it might acquire additional force and volume from the child-like loyalty which the age awarded to its rulers—was felt to be an irrepressible outburst of the enthusiasm kindled in the auditors by that high strain of eloquence which was yet reverberating in their ears. Each felt the impulse in himself, and, in the same breath, caught it from his neighbour. Within the church, it had hardly been kept down; beneath the sky, it pealed upward to the zenith. There were human beings enough, and enough of highly wrought and symphonious feeling, to produce that more impressive sound than the organ-tones of the blast, or the thunder, or the roar of the sea; even that mighty swell of many voices, blended into one great voice by the universal impulse which makes likewise one vast heart out of the many. Never, from the soil of New England, had gone up such a shout! Never, on New England soil, had stood the man so honored by his mortal brethren as the preacher!

How fared it with him then? Were there not the brilliant particles of a halo in the air about his head? So etherealized by spirit as he was, and so apotheosized by worshipping admirers, did his footsteps in the procession really tread upon the dust of earth?

As the ranks of military men and civil fathers moved onward, all eyes were turned towards the point where the minister was seen to approach among them. The shout died into a murmur, as one portion of the crowd after another obtained a glimpse of him. How feeble and pale he looked amid all his triumph! The energy—or say, rather, the inspiration which had held him up, until he should have delivered the sacred message that brought its own strength along with it from heaven—was withdrawn, now that it had so faithfully performed its office. The glow, which they had just before beheld burning on his cheek, was extinguished, like a flame that sinks down hopelessly among the late-decaying embers. It seemed hardly the face of a man alive, with such a deathlike hue; it was hardly a man with life in him, that tottered on his path so nervelessly, yet tottered, and did not fall!

One of his clerical brethren,—it was the venerable John Wilson,— observing the state in which Mr. Dimmesdale was left by the retiring wave of intellect and sensibility, stepped forward hastily to offer his support. The minister tremulously, but decidedly, repelled the old man's arm. He still walked onward, if that movement could be so described, which rather resembled the wavering effort of an infant, with its mother's arms in view, outstretched to tempt him forward. And now, almost imperceptible as were the latter steps of his progress, he had come opposite the well-remembered and weather-darkened scaffold, where, long since, with all that dreary lapse of time between, Hester Prynne had encountered the world's ignominious stare. There stood Hester, holding little Pearl by the hand! And there was the scarlet letter on her breast! The minister here made a pause; although the music still played the stately and rejoicing march to which the procession moved. It summoned him onward,— onward to the festival!—but here he made a pause.

Bellingham, for the last few moments, had kept an anxious eye upon him. He now left his own place in the procession, and advanced to give assistance; judging from Mr. Dimmesdale's aspect that he must otherwise inevitably fall. But there was something in the latter's expression that warned back the magistrate, although a man not readily obeying the vague intimations that pass from one spirit to another. The crowd, meanwhile, looked on with awe and wonder. This earthly faintness was, in their view, only another phase of the minister's celestial strength; nor would it have seemed a miracle too high to be wrought for one so holy, had he ascended before their eyes, waxing dimmer and brighter, and fading at last into the light of heaven!

He turned towards the scaffold, and stretched forth his arms.

"Hester," said he, "come hither! Come, my little Pearl!"

It was a ghastly look with which he regarded them; but there was something at once tender and strangely triumphant in it. The child, with the bird-like motion which was one of her characteristics, flew to him, and clasped her arms about his knees. Hester Prynne—slowly, as if impelled by inevitable fate, and against her strongest will—likewise drew near, but paused before she reached him. At this instant old Roger Chillingworth thrust himself through the crowd,—or, perhaps, so dark, disturbed, and evil was his look, he rose up out of some nether region,— to snatch back his victim from what he sought to do! Be that as it might, the old man rushed forward and caught the minister by the arm.

"Madman, hold! What is your purpose?" whispered he. "Wave back that woman! Cast off this child! All shall be well! Do not blacken your fame, and perish in dishonor! I can yet save you! Would you bring infamy on your sacred profession?"

"Ha, tempter! Methinks thou art too late!" answered the minister, encountering his eye, fearfully, but firmly. "Thy power is not what it was! With God's help, I shall escape thee now!"

He again extended his hand to the woman of the scarlet letter.

"Hester Prynne," cried he, with a piercing earnestness, "in the name of Him, so terrible and so merciful, who gives me grace, at this last moment, to do what—for my own heavy sin and miserable agony—I withheld myself from doing seven years ago, come hither now, and twine thy strength about me! Thy strength, Hester; but let it be guided by the will which God hath granted me! This wretched and wronged old man is opposing it with all his might!—with all his own might and the fiend's! Come, Hester, come! Support me up yonder scaffold!"

The crowd was in a tumult. The men of rank and dignity, who stood more immediately around the clergyman, were so taken by surprise, and so perplexed as to the purport of what they saw,—unable to receive the explanation which most readily presented itself, or to imagine any other,—that they remained silent and inactive spectators of the judgment which Providence seemed about to work. They beheld the minister, leaning on Hester's shoulder and supported by her arm around him, approach the scaffold, and ascend its steps; while still the little hand of the sin-born child was clasped in his. Old Roger Chillingworth followed, as one intimately connected with the drama of guilt and sorrow in which they had all been actors, and well entitled, therefore, to be present at its closing scene.

"Hadst thou sought the whole earth over," said he, looking darkly at the clergyman, "there was no one place so secret,—no high place nor lowly place, where thou couldst have escaped me,—save on this very scaffold!"

"Thanks be to Him who hath led me hither!" answered the minister.

Yet he trembled, and turned to Hester with an expression of doubt and anxiety in his eyes, not the less evidently betrayed, that there was a feeble smile upon his lips.

"Is not this better," murmured he, "than what we dreamed of in the forest?"

"I know not! I know not!" she hurriedly replied. "Better? Yea; so we may both die, and little Pearl die with us!"

"For thee and Pearl, be it as God shall order," said the minister; "and God is merciful! Let me now do the will which he hath made plain before my sight. For, Hester, I am a dying man. So let me make haste to take my shame upon me."

Partly supported by Hester Prynne, and holding one hand of little Pearl's, the Reverend Mr. Dimmesdale turned to the dignified and venerable rulers; to the holy ministers, who were his brethren; to the people, whose great heart was thoroughly appalled, yet overflowing with tearful sympathy, as knowing that some deep life-matter—which, if full of sin, was full of anguish and repentance likewise—was now to be laid open to them. The sun, but little past its meridian, shone down upon the clergyman, and gave a distinctness to his figure, as he stood out from all the earth to put in his plea of guilty at the bar of Eternal Justice.

"People of New England!" cried he, with a voice that rose over them, high, solemn, and majestic,—yet had always a tremor through it, and sometimes a shriek, struggling up out of a fathomless depth of remorse and woe,—"ye, that have loved me!—ye, that have deemed me holy!—behold me here, the one sinner of the world! At last!—at last!—I stand upon the spot where, seven years since, I should have stood; here, with this woman, whose arm, more than the little strength wherewith I have crept hitherward, sustains me, at this dreadful moment, from grovelling down upon my face! Lo, the scarlet letter which Hester wears! Ye have all shuddered at it! Wherever her walk hath been,—wherever, so miserably burdened, she may have hoped to find repose,—it hath cast a lurid gleam of awe and horrible repugnance roundabout her. But there stood one in the midst of you, at whose brand of sin and infamy ye have not shuddered!"

It seemed, at this point, as if the minister must leave the remainder of his secret undisclosed. But he fought back the bodily weakness,—and, still more, the faintness of heart,—that was striving for the mastery with him. He threw off all assistance, and stepped passionately forward a pace before the woman and the child.

"It was on him!" he continued, with a kind of fierceness; so determined was he to speak out the whole. "God's eye beheld it! The angels were for ever pointing at it! The Devil knew it well, and fretted it continually with the touch of his burning finger! But he hid it cunningly from men, and walked among you with the mien of a spirit, mournful, because so pure in a sinful world!—and sad, because he missed his heavenly kindred! Now, at the death-hour, he stands up before you! He bids you look again at Hester's scarlet letter! He tells you, that, with all its mysterious horror, it is but the shadow of what he bears on his own breast, and that even this, his own red stigma, is no more than the type of what has seared his inmost heart! Stand any here that question God's judgment on a sinner? Behold! Behold a dreadful witness of it!"

With a convulsive motion he tore away the ministerial band from before his breast. It was revealed! But it were irreverent to describe that revelation. For an instant the gaze of the horror-stricken multitude was concentred on the ghastly miracle; while the minister stood with a flush of triumph in his face, as one who, in the crisis of acutest pain, had won a victory. Then, down he sank upon the scaffold! Hester partly raised him, and supported his head against her bosom. Old Roger Chillingworth knelt down beside him, with a blank, dull countenance, out of which the life seemed to have departed.

"Thou hast escaped me!" he repeated more than once. "Thou hast escaped me!"

"May God forgive thee!" said the minister. "Thou, too, hast deeply sinned!"

He withdrew his dying eyes from the old man, and fixed them on the woman and the child.

"My little Pearl," said he feebly,—and there was a sweet and gentle smile over his face, as of a spirit sinking into deep repose; nay, now that the burden was removed, it seemed almost as if he would be sportive with the child,—"dear little Pearl, wilt thou kiss me now? Thou wouldst not yonder, in the forest! But now thou wilt?"

Pearl kissed his lips. A spell was broken. The great scene of grief, in which the wild infant bore a part, had developed all her sympathies; and as her tears fell upon her father's cheek, they were the pledge that she would grow up amid human joy and sorrow, nor for ever do battle with the world, but be a woman in it. Towards her mother, too, Pearl's errand as a messenger of anguish was fulfilled.

"Hester," said the clergyman, "farewell!"

"Shall we not meet again?" whispered she, bending her face down close to his. "Shall we not spend our immortal life together? Surely, surely, we have ransomed one another, with all this woe! Thou lookest far into eternity, with those bright dying eyes! Then tell me what thou seest?"

"Hush, Hester, hush!" said he, with tremulous solemnity. "The law we broke!—the sin here so awfully revealed!—let these alone be in thy thoughts! I fear! I fear! It may be, that, when we forgot our God,—when we violated our reverence each for the other's soul,—it was thenceforth vain to hope that we could meet hereafter, in an everlasting and pure reunion. God knows; and He is merciful! He hath proved his mercy, most of all, in my afflictions. By giving me this burning torture to bear upon my breast! By sending yonder dark and terrible old man, to keep the torture always at red-heat! By bringing me hither, to die this death of triumphant ignominy before the people! Had either of these agonies been wanting, I had been lost for ever! Praised be his name! His will be done! Farewell!"

That final word came forth with the minister's expiring breath. The multitude, silent till then, broke out in a strange, deep voice of awe and wonder, which could not as yet find utterance, save in this murmur that rolled so heavily after the departed spirit.

XXIV. CONCLUSION

After many days, when time sufficed for the people to arrange their thoughts in reference to the foregoing scene, there was more than one account of what had been witnessed on the scaffold.

Most of the spectators testified to having seen, on the breast of the unhappy minister, a SCARLET LETTER—the very semblance of that worn by Hester Prynne—imprinted in the flesh. As regarded its origin, there were various explanations, all of which must necessarily have been conjectural. Some affirmed that the Reverend Mr. Dimmesdale, on the very day when Hester Prynne first wore her ignominious badge, had begun a course of penance,—which he afterwards, in so many futile methods, followed out,—by inflicting a hideous torture on himself. Others contended that the stigma had not been produced until a long time subsequent, when old Roger Chillingworth, being a potent necromancer,[159] had caused it to appear, through the agency of magic and poisonous drugs. Others, again,—and those best able to appreciate the minister's peculiar sensibility, and the wonderful operation of his spirit upon the body,— whispered their belief, that the awful symbol was the effect of the ever active tooth of remorse, gnawing from the inmost heart outwardly, and at last manifesting Heaven's dreadful judgment by the visible presence of the letter. The reader may choose among these theories. We have thrown all the light we could acquire upon the portent, and would gladly, now that it has done its office, erase its deep print out of our own brain, where long meditation has fixed it in very undesirable distinctness.

It is singular, nevertheless, that certain persons, who were spectators of the whole scene, and professed never once to have removed their eyes from the Reverend Mr. Dimmesdale, denied that there was any mark whatever on his breast, more than on a newborn infant's. Neither, by their report, had his dying words acknowledged, nor even remotely implied, any, the slightest connection, on his part, with the guilt for which Hester

---

[159]NECROMANCER: Wizard; one who practices black magic.

Prynne had so long worn the scarlet letter. According to these highly respectable witnesses, the minister, conscious that he was dying,—conscious, also, that the reverence of the multitude placed him already among saints and angels,—had desired, by yielding up his breath in the arms of that fallen woman, to express to the world how utterly nugatory is the choicest of man's own righteousness. After exhausting life in his efforts for mankind's spiritual good, he had made the manner of his death a parable, in order to impress on his admirers the mighty and mournful lesson, that, in the view of Infinite Purity, we are sinners all alike. It was to teach them, that the holiest amongst us has but attained so far above his fellows as to discern more clearly the Mercy which looks down, and repudiate more utterly the phantom of human merit, which would look aspiringly upward. Without disputing a truth so momentous, we must be allowed to consider this version of Mr. Dimmesdale's story as only an instance of that stubborn fidelity with which a man's friends—and especially a clergyman's—will sometimes uphold his character; when proofs, clear as the mid-day sunshine on the scarlet letter, establish him a false and sin-stained creature of the dust.

The authority which we have chiefly followed—a manuscript of old date, drawn up from the verbal testimony of individuals, some of whom had known Hester Prynne, while others had heard the tale from contemporary witnesses—fully confirms the view taken in the foregoing pages. Among many morals which press upon us from the poor minister's miserable experience, we put only this into a sentence:—"Be true! Be true! Be true! Show freely to the world, if not your worst, yet some trait whereby the worst may be inferred!"

Nothing was more remarkable than the change which took place, almost immediately after Mr. Dimmesdale's death, in the appearance and demeanour of the old man known as Roger Chillingworth. All his strength and energy—all his vital and intellectual force—seemed at once to desert him; insomuch that he positively withered up, shrivelled away, and almost vanished from mortal sight, like an uprooted weed that lies wilting in the sun. This unhappy man had made the very principle of his life to consist in the pursuit and systematic exercise of revenge; and when, by its completest triumph and consummation, that evil principle was left with no further material to support it,—when, in short, there was no more devil's work on earth for him to do, it only remained for the unhumanized mortal to betake himself whither his Master would find him tasks enough, and pay him his wages duly. But, to all these shadowy beings, so long our near acquaintances,—as well Roger Chillingworth as his companions,—we would fain be merciful. It is a curious subject of observation and inquiry, whether hatred and love be not the same thing at bottom. Each, in its utmost development, supposes a high degree of intimacy and heart-knowledge; each renders one individual dependent for the food of his affections and spiritual life upon another; each leaves the passionate lover, or the no less passionate hater, forlorn and desolate by the withdrawal of his object. Philosophically considered, therefore, the two passions seem essentially the same, except that one happens to be seen in a celestial radiance, and the other in a dusky and lurid glow. In the spiritual world, the old physician and the minister—mutual victims as they have been—may, unawares, have found their earthly stock of hatred and antipathy transmuted into golden love.

Leaving this discussion apart, we have a matter of business to communicate to the reader. At old Roger Chillingworth's decease (which took place within the year), and by his last will and testament, of which Governor Bellingham and the Reverend Mr. Wilson were executors, he bequeathed a very considerable amount of property, both here and in England, to little Pearl, the daughter of Hester Prynne.

So Pearl—the elf-child,—the demon offspring, as some people, up to that epoch, persisted in considering her—became the richest heiress of her day, in the New World. Not improbably, this circumstance wrought a very material change in the public estimation; and, had the mother and child remained here, little Pearl, at a marriageable period of life, might have mingled her wild blood with the lineage of the devoutest Puritan among them all. But, in no long time after the physician's death, the wearer of the scarlet letter disappeared, and Pearl along with her. For many years, though a vague report would now and then find its way across the sea,—like a shapeless piece of driftwood tost ashore, with the initials of a name upon it,—yet no tidings of them unquestionably authentic were received. The story of the scarlet letter grew into a legend. Its spell, however, was still potent, and kept the scaffold awful where the poor minister had died, and likewise the cottage by the sea-shore, where Hester Prynne had dwelt. Near this latter spot, one afternoon, some children were at play, when they beheld a tall woman, in a gray robe, approach the cottage-door. In all those years it had never once been opened; but either she unlocked it, or the decaying wood and iron yielded to her hand, or she glided shadow-like through these impediments,—and, at all events, went in.

On the threshold she paused,—turned partly round,—for, perchance, the idea of entering, all alone, and all so changed, the home of so intense a former life, was more dreary and desolate than even she could bear. But her hesitation was only for an instant, though long enough to display a scarlet letter on her breast.

And Hester Prynne had returned, and taken up her long-forsaken shame. But where was little Pearl? If still alive, she must now have been in the flush and bloom of early womanhood. None knew—nor ever learned, with the fulness of perfect certainty—whether the elf-child had gone thus untimely to a maiden grave; or whether her wild, rich nature had been softened and subdued, and made capable of a woman's gentle happiness. But, through the remainder of Hester's life, there were indications that the recluse of the scarlet letter was the object of love and interest with some inhabitant of another land. Letters came, with armorial seals[160] upon them, though of bearings unknown to English heraldry. In the cottage there were articles of comfort and luxury, such as Hester never cared to use, but which only wealth could have purchased, and affection have imagined for her. There were trifles, too, little ornaments, beautiful tokens of a continual remembrance, that must have been wrought by delicate fingers, at the impulse of a fond heart. And, once, Hester was seen embroidering a baby-garment, with such a lavish richness of golden fancy as would have raised a public tumult, had any infant, thus apparelled, been shown to our sombre-hued community.

In fine, the gossips of that day believed,—and Mr. Surveyor Pue, who made investigations a century later, believed,—and one of his recent successors in office, moreover, faithfully believes,—that Pearl was not only alive, but married, and happy, and mindful of her mother; and that she would most joyfully have entertained that sad and lonely mother at her fireside.

But there was a more real life for Hester Prynne, here, in New England, that in that unknown region where Pearl had found a home. Here had been her sin; here, her sorrow; and here was yet to be her penitence. She had returned, therefore, and resumed,—of her own free will, for not the sternest magistrate of that iron period would have imposed it,—resumed the symbol of which we have related so dark a tale. Never afterwards did it quit her bosom. But, in the lapse of the toilsome, thoughtful, and self-devoted years that made up Hester's life, the scarlet letter ceased to be a stigma which attracted the world's scorn and bitterness, and became a type of something to be sorrowed over, and looked upon with awe, yet with reverence too. And, as Hester Prynne had no selfish ends, nor lived in any measure for her own profit and enjoyment, people brought all their sorrows and perplexities, and besought her counsel, as one who had herself gone through a mighty trouble. Women, more especially,—in the continually recurring trials of wounded, wasted,

[160]ARMORIAL SEALS: Coat of arms.

wronged, misplaced, or erring and sinful passion,—or with the dreary burden of a heart unyielded, because unvalued and unsought,—came to Hester's cottage, demanding why they were so wretched, and what the remedy! Hester comforted and counselled them, as best she might. She assured them, too, of her firm belief, that, at some brighter period, when the world should have grown ripe for it, in Heaven's own time, a new truth would be revealed, in order to establish the whole relation between man and woman on a surer ground of mutual happiness. Earlier in life, Hester had vainly imagined that she herself might be the destined prophetess, but had long since recognized the impossibility that any mission of divine and mysterious truth should be confided to a woman stained with sin, bowed down with shame, or even burdened with a life-long sorrow. The angel and apostle of the coming revelation must be a woman, indeed, but lofty, pure, and beautiful; and wise; moreover, not through dusky grief, but the ethereal medium of joy; and showing how sacred love should make us happy, by the truest test of a life successful to such an end!

So said Hester Prynne, and glanced her sad eyes downward at the scarlet letter. And, after many, many years, a new grave was delved, near an old and sunken one, in that burial-ground beside which King's Chapel has since been built. It was near that old and sunken grave, yet with a space between, as if the dust of the two sleepers had no right to mingle. Yet one tombstone served for both. All around, there were monuments carved with armorial bearings; and on this simple slab of slate—as the curious investigator may still discern, and perplex himself with the purport—there appeared the semblance of an engraved escutcheon. It bore a device, a herald's wording of which might serve for a motto and brief description of our now concluded legend; so sombre is it, and relieved only by one ever-glowing point of light gloomier than the shadow:—

"On a field, sable, the letter A, gules"[161]

THE END

[1850]

---

[161]"ON A FIELD, SABLE, THE LETTER A, GULES: That is, on a black shield, the letter *A* in red.

Henry Wadsworth Longfellow

(1807–1882)

The most popular American poet of the nineteenth century and the poet most widely read and taught in grammar schools and high schools during much of the twentieth century, Henry Wadsworth Longfellow has faded from view. His poems, beloved for many decades, are not as well known as they once were, and literary historians devote little attention to him. Compared to Walt Whitman and Emily Dickinson, Longfellow lacks originality and thematic power, and his favorite subjects—youth, age, the passing of time—and long verse narratives feel distant from the direct engagement of Ralph Waldo Emerson, Frederick Douglass, and Henry David Thoreau with the social and political crises of the early to mid-nineteenth century. One critic summed him up this way: "Longfellow was clear, decent, patriotic, uncritical, retrospective, sentimental, cozy, and—above all else—moralistic."

Yet, as a highly accomplished man of letters as well as a poet, Longfellow should not be overlooked. He had genuine talent as a lyric poet (and, in his own way, as a political poet, in his verse attacking slavery), and he had extraordinary skills as a linguist and master of prosody and genre. Many of his songs, ballads, sonnets, and lyric poems, including the two below, "The Jewish Cemetery at Newport" and "My Lost Youth," are haunting performances, stranger than they appear at first, and unforgettable. In his best poetry he is neither preachy nor pious but, rather, brooding, grieving, captivating. As another critic, more generously, said: "At the very least, Longfellow is probably nineteenth-century America's most versatile poet, one whose oeuvre is wide-ranging and ingenious and possesses great aesthetic and cultural interest."

Born in Portland, Maine, Longfellow as a young man was drawn to literature, but, at his father's insistence, he first explored careers in law, medicine, and the ministry. Through a stroke of good fortune, however, Longfellow was offered a professorship in foreign languages at Bowdoin College (from which he graduated in 1825), a career path his father found acceptable.

To extend and deepen his knowledge of foreign languages and cultures before taking up this academic post, Longfellow was granted a three-year period (1826–1829) of study in Europe, where he mastered German, French, Italian, and Spanish. He returned to Europe in 1835 and 1836 for further travel and research, which included work on Scandinavian languages, and he made additional trips abroad later in his career.

Beginning in 1836 Longfellow held a professorship at Harvard University. He was a notable scholar and, throughout his life, a gifted translator (one of his major achievements was a blank verse translation, 1865–1867, of Dante's Divine Comedy).

On the whole Longfellow lived simply; he once remarked to a friend, "Most of the time am alone; smoke a great deal; wear a broad-brimmed black hat, black frock-coat, a black cane. Molest no one. Dine out frequently. In winter go much into Boston society." But Longfellow suffered terrible losses that can be felt in the undertones of his poetry. His first wife died, in 1835, from an infection after suffering a miscarriage, and his second wife was killed in a horrific accident, in 1861, when the summer dress she was wearing caught fire—Longfellow himself was so badly burned trying to save her that he was unable to attend the funeral.

In his own day and afterward Longfellow was indeed popular, not only in the United States but in Great Britain as well, where his books sold more copies than did those by Robert Browning and Alfred, Lord Tennyson. One of his longer poems, The Song of Hiawatha *(1855) sold 30,000 copies in its first six months, and another,* The Courtship of Miles Standish *(1858), sold 15,000 copies on the first day it went on sale. By 1900 there were hundreds of editions of Longfellow's writings, and translations of them in twenty languages.*

"The Jewish Cemetery at Newport" developed from a visit Longfellow made in July 1852 to the Jewish cemetery in this Rhode Island town; Jewish settlers had begun to arrive in Newport in the mid-seventeenth century, and soon the Jewish community there was one of the largest in the nation. "My Lost Youth," written in early 1855, is about Longfellow's boyhood in Portland.

For biography and interpretation: Newton Arvin, Longfellow: His Life and Work *(1963); and Edward Wagenknecht,* Henry Wadsworth Longfellow: His Poetry and Prose *(1986).*

The Jewish Cemetery at Newport[1]

How strange it seems! These Hebrews in their graves,
    Close by the street of this fair seaport town,
Silent beside the never-silent waves,
    At rest in all this moving up and down!

The trees are white with dust, that o'er their sleep   5
    Wave their broad curtains in the south-wind's breath,

---

[1]NEWPORT: Newport, Rhode Island. In his diary (July 9, 1852), Longfellow wrote of the Jewish Cemetery: "Went this morning into the Jewish burying-ground with a polite old gentleman who keeps the key. There are a few graves; nearly all are low tombstones of marble, with Hebrew inscriptions, and a few words added in English or Portuguese." During the colonial period, Jews, encouraged by the relative religious tolerance afforded them in Rhode Island, settled in the area of Newport, which is also home to the oldest continually operating synagogue in the United States.

While underneath these leafy tents they keep
    The long, mysterious Exodus[2] of Death.

And these sepulchral stones, so old and brown,
    That pave with level flags their burial-place,   10
Seem like the tablets of the Law,[3] thrown down
    And broken by Moses[4] at the mountain's base.

The very names recorded here are strange,
    Of foreign accent, and of different climes;
Alvares and Rivera[5] interchange   15
    With Abraham and Jacob[6] of old times.

"Blessed be God! for he created Death!"
    The mourners said, "and Death is rest and peace";
Then added, in the certainty of faith,
    "And giveth Life that nevermore shall cease."   20

Closed are the portals of their Synagogue,
    No Psalms of David[7] now the silence break,
No Rabbi reads the ancient Decalogue[8]
    In the grand dialect the Prophets spake.

Gone are the living, but the dead remain,   25
    And not neglected; for a hand unseen,
Scattering its bounty, like a summer rain,
    Still keeps their graves and their remembrance green.

How came they here? What burst of Christian hate,
    What persecution, merciless and blind,   30
Drove o'er the sea—that desert desolate—
    These Ishmaels and Hagars[9] of mankind?

---

[2]EXODUS: The second book of the Bible, which begins with the Hebrews' bondage in Egypt and details their liberation from slavery under the leadership of Moses. The last portion of the book includes the Ten Commandments and the codes of conduct Jews are to follow as part of their covenant with God.
[3]TABLETS OF THE LAW: The Ten Commandments, which Moses casts down in anger. "Moses' anger waxed hot, and he cast the tables out of his hands, and brake them beneath the mount" (Exodus 32:19).
[4]MOSES: The leader of the Hebrews who led them from slavery in Egypt to the Promised Land.
[5]ALVARES AND RIVERA: Portuguese surnames; a reference to the Sephardic Jews from Spain and Portugal who settled in the Newport area.
[6]ABRAHAM AND JACOB: Biblical patriarchs.
[7]PSALMS OF DAVID: The 150 hymnic pieces ascribed to David, a king of ancient Israel.
[8]DECALOGUE: The Ten Commandments.
[9]ISHMAELS AND HAGARS: Outcasts. Ishmael was the son of Hagar, the patriarch Abraham's concubine. They were driven out of Abraham's tent when his wife, Sarah, bore their son, Isaac (Genesis 16, 17, 25).

They lived in narrow streets and lanes obscure,
    Ghetto and Judenstrass,[10] in mirk and mire;
Taught in the school of patience to endure   35
    The life of anguish and the death of fire.

All their lives long, with the unleavened bread
    And bitter herbs of exile[11] and its fears,
The wasting famine of the heart they fed,
    And slaked its thirst with marah[12] of their tears.   40

Anathema maranatha![13] was the cry
    That rang from town to town, from street to street;
At every gate the accursed Mordecai[14]
    Was mocked and jeered, and spurned by Christian feet.

Pride and humiliation hand in hand   45
    Walked with them through the world where'er they went;
Trampled and beaten were they as the sand,
    And yet unshaken as the continent.

For in the background figures vague and vast
    Of patriarchs and of prophets rose sublime,   50
And all the great traditions of the Past
    They saw reflected in the coming time.

And thus forever with reverted look
    The mystic volume of the world they read,
Spelling it backward,[15] like a Hebrew book,   55
    Till life became a Legend of the Dead.

But ah! what once has been shall be no more!
    The groaning earth in travail and in pain

---

[10]GHETTO AND JUDENSTRASS: *Judenstraas* means "Street of the Jews" in German. In many European cities, Jews were forced to live in restricted areas, called ghettos.
[11]BITTER HERBS OF EXILE: Foods eaten during Passover in memory of the biblical exodus in which the Hebrews, led by Moses, fled slavery in Egypt.
[12]MARAH: A reference to Exodus 15: 22–23: "So Moses brought Israel from the Red Sea, and they went out into the wilderness of Shur; and they went three days in the wilderness, and found no water. / And when they came to Marah, they could not drink of the waters of Marah, for they were bitter: therefore the name of it was called Marah."
[13]ANATHEMA MARANTHA: Cursed or damned. 1 Corinthians 16:22: "If any man love not the Lord Jesus Christ, let him be Anathema Maranatha."
[14]MORDECAI: In the biblical book of Esther, Mordecai was the guardian and cousin of Esther, the Jewish wife and queen of the Persian King Ahasuerus (Xerxes I or II).
[15]SPELLING IT BACKWARD: Hebrew is read from right to left.

Brings forth its races, but does not restore,
　　And the dead nations never rise again.　　　　　　60

[1854]

My Lost Youth

Often I think of the beautiful town[1]
　　That is seated by the sea;
Often in thought go up and down
The pleasant streets of that dear old town,
　　　　And my youth comes back to me.　　　　　　5
　　　　　　And a verse of a Lapland[2] song
　　　　　　Is haunting my memory still:
"A boy's will is the wind's will,
And the thoughts of youth are long, long thoughts."

I can see the shadowy lines of its trees,　　　　　　10
　　And catch, in sudden gleams,
The sheen of the far-surrounding seas,
And islands that were the Hesperides[3]
　　　　Of all my boyish dreams.
　　　　　　And the burden of that old song,　　　　　　15
　　　　　　It murmurs and whispers still:
"A boy's will is the wind's will,
And the thoughts of youth are long, long thoughts."

I remember the black wharves and the slips,
　　And the sea-tides tossing free;　　　　　　20
And Spanish sailors with bearded lips,
And the beauty and mystery of the ships,
　　　　And the magic of the sea.
　　　　　　And the voice of that wayward song
　　　　　　Is singing and saying still:　　　　　　25

---

[1]BEAUTIFUL TOWN: Longfellow's hometown of Portland, Maine.
[2]LAPLAND: Longfellow derived the refrain for this poem from lines in John Scheffer's *The History of Lapland* (1674): "A Youth's desire is the desire of the wind, / All his essaies [endeavors] / Are long delaies [delays], / No issue [outlet] can they find." Lapland is a region in the northernmost part of Scandinavia.
[3]HESPERIDES: In Greek myth, islands where golden apples were fabled to grow.

"A boy's will is the wind's will,
And the thoughts of youth are long, long thoughts."

I remember the bulwarks[4] by the shore,
    And the fort upon the hill;
The sunrise gun, with its hollow roar,   30
The drum-beat repeated o'er and o'er,
    And the bugle wild and shrill.
        And the music of that old song
        Throbs in my memory still:
  "A boy's will is the wind's will,   35
And the thoughts of youth are long, long thoughts."

I remember the sea-fight far away,
    How it thundered o'er the tide!
And the dead captains,[5] as they lay
In their graves, o'erlooking the tranquil bay,   40
    Where they in battle died.
        And the sound of that mournful song
        Goes through me with a thrill:
"A boy's will is the wind's will,
And the thoughts of youth are long, long thoughts."   45

I can see the breezy domes of groves,
    The shadows of Deering's Woods;
And the friendships old and the early loves
Come back with a Sabbath sound, as of doves
    In quiet neighborhoods.   50
        And the verse of that sweet old song,
        It flutters and murmurs still:
"A boy's will is the wind's will,
And the thoughts of youth are long, long thoughts."

I remember the gleams and glooms that dart   55
    Across the school-boy's brain;
The song and the silence in the heart,
That in part are prophecies, and in part
    Are longings wild and vain.
        And the voice of that fitful song   60

---

[4]BULWARKS: Defensive constructions; fortifications.
[5]DEAD CAPTAINS: A reference to the captains of the USS *Enterprise* and the HMS *Boxer*, who died
in a naval battle near Portland during the War of 1812.

Sings on, and is never still:
"A boy's will is the wind's will,
And the thoughts of youth are long, long thoughts."

There are things of which I may not speak;
 There are dreams that cannot die;
There are thoughts that make the strong heart weak, 65
And bring a pallor into the cheek,
 And a mist before the eye.
  And the words of that fatal song
  Come over me like a chill: 70
"A boy's will is the wind's will,
And the thoughts of youth are long, long thoughts."

Strange to me now are the forms I meet
 When I visit the dear old town;
But the native air is pure and sweet, 75
And the trees that o'ershadow each well-known street,
 As they balance up and down,
  Are singing the beautiful song,
  Are sighing and whispering still:
"A boy's will is the wind's will, 80
And the thoughts of youth are long, long thoughts."

And Deering's Woods are fresh and fair,
 And with joy that is almost pain
My heart goes back to wander there,
And among the dreams of the days that were, 85
 I find my lost youth again.
  And the strange and beautiful song,
  The groves are repeating it still:
"A boy's will is the wind's will,
And the thoughts of youth are long, long thoughts." 90

[1855]

Edgar Allan Poe

(1809–1849)

Edgar Allan Poe is one of the curiosities of American literature. His poetry, literary theory and criticism, and short stories have been avidly read and studied, not only in the United States but also in many countries around the world—in Germany and France in particular, where Poe has been as influential (perhaps more so) than any other American writer. Yet from his own time to the present, there has been much skepticism about Poe's merit.

Impatient with Poe's fondness for rhyme, assonance, and alliteration, Ralph Waldo Emerson termed him "the jingle man." Henry James added, "To take him with more than a certain degree of seriousness is to lack seriousness oneself." T. S. Eliot remarked, "The forms which his lively curiosity takes are those in which a pre-adolescent mentality delights: wonders of nature and of mechanics and of the supernatural, cryptograms and ciphers, puzzles and labyrinths, mechanical chess-players and wild flights of speculation." More recently, the critic Harold Bloom observed, "I can think of no other American writer, down to this moment, at once so inescapable and so dubious."

Born in Boston, Poe was the son of an actor and actress. Orphaned at an early age—his father deserted the family the year after Poe was born, and the boy's mother died a year later—he was raised in the home of John Allan, a merchant in Richmond, Virginia. He lived with the Allans in England from 1815 to 1820, attending school there. Later, after returning to the United States, and as his relationship with John Allan became tense and embittered, Poe spent a year at the University of Virginia, falling into gambling and debt. His first book, Tamerlane and Other Poems *(1827), was published anonymously, after which Poe enlisted in the U.S. Army under the name of Edgar A. Perry.*

Poe published a second volume of verse, Al Aaraaf, Tamerlane, and Other Minor Poems *(1829), and in 1830 he entered West Point for military training as an officer. He was dishonorably discharged in 1831 for failure to perform his duties. He settled in New York City, published another book,* Poems by Edgar A. Poe *(1831), and then looked to literature and journalism for a career.*

Poe lived with an aunt, Maria Clemm, in Baltimore, Maryland, marrying her thirteen-year-old daughter (his cousin), Virginia, in 1836. He held a position as an editor and writer for The Southern Literary Messenger *and contributed short stories to various magazines. He published an adventure novel,* The Narrative of A. Gordon Pym *(1838), and his first collection of stories,* Tales of the Arabesque and Grotesque *(1840); it includes several of his best-known stories, "William Wilson," "The Fall of the House of Usher," and "Ligeia."*

With the appearance of the poem "The Raven" in a New York newspaper in 1845, Poe's fame spread. But he and his wife struggled amid poverty, and his health was poor. After the death of his wife from tuberculosis in 1847 Poe's own condition worsened, largely from the effects of alcohol and drugs. His end came in Baltimore, in strange circumstances: He was found delirious near a saloon, and died a few days later.

Much of Poe's work was first-rate, the product of impressive technical skill and craftsmanship and of a tormented and vivid imagination. Among his distinguished stories are "The Masque of the Red Death" (1842); "The Black Cat" (1843); and "The Cask of Amontillado" (1846). But much, too, that Poe produced was mediocre, done in a rush, while he was harrassed by debt or distracted by one of his many literary quarrels and feuds.

Is Poe a great writer? Not in the view of Emerson, James, Eliot, and Bloom. But others strongly believe he is, including the French poet-critics Charles Baudelaire, Stéphane Mallarmé, and Paul Valéry; the Irish poet and dramatist William Butler Yeats; Robert Louis Stevenson and Jules Verne, two eminent writers of mystery, scientific romance, and adventure; the short-story writer Ambrose Bierce; and the poet Hart Crane. Poe is also honored as a pioneer (and perhaps the inventor) of the detective story, praised highly for such tales as "The Murders in the Rue Morgue" (1841) and "The Gold-Bug" (1843).

Poe, in addition, enjoys a significant place in American poetic theory for his essays "The Philosophy of Composition" (1846; see below) and "The Poetic Principle" (1850). He stressed the importance of a unified effect in verse and the creation of an emotional aura and atmosphere, which in his view took precedence over plot and character. For him, the "most poetical topic in the world" was the death of a beautiful woman. Sound pattern, rhythm, brevity: these were the elements Poe highlighted and through which he maintained a poet could achieve "an elevating excitement of the Soul."

Below are three poems: "To Helen," an evocation of pure and elusive beauty; "The Raven," a revelation (in the words of the critic Edward H. Davidson) of the "inner workings of a disturbed consciousness"; and "Annabel Lee," about a woman's burial and death and the speaker's enduring love for her. Next are three stories: "The Fall of the House of Usher," a grotesque and gripping account of love, death, and madness, rendered in a gloomy, fantastical atmosphere; "The Tell-Tale Heart," a nameless narrator's murderous monologue; and "The Purloined Letter," which features the brilliant detective skills of C. Auguste Dupin. Lastly, there is "The Philosophy of Composition," a detailed account of the writing of "The Raven" that Poe intends to counter the Romantic theory of ecstatic and frenzied literary creation.

For biography: Kenneth Silverman, Edgar A. Poe: Mournful and Never-Ending Remembrance *(1991). For critical analysis: J. Gerald Kennedy,* Poe, Death, and the Life of Writing *(1987); and* The American Face of Edgar Allan Poe, *ed. Shawn Rosenheim and Stephen Rachman (1995). Helpful resources: J. R. Hammond,* An Edgar Allan Poe Companion: A Guide to the Short Stories, Romances, and Essays *(1981);* Critical Essays on Edgar Allan Poe *(1987) and* A Companion to Poe Studies, *ed. Eric W. Carlson (1996);* A Historical Guide to Edgar Allan Poe, *ed. J. Gerald Kennedy (2001); and* The Cambridge Companion to Edgar Allan Poe, *ed. Kevin J. Hayes (2002).*

To Helen

Helen, thy beauty is to me
    Like those Nicéan barks of yore,[1]
That gently, o'er a perfumed sea,
    The weary, way-worn wanderer bore
    To his own native shore.   5

On desperate seas long wont to roam,
    Thy hyacinth hair,[2] thy classic face,
Thy Naiad[3] airs have brought me home
    To the glory that was Greece,
    And the grandeur that was Rome.   10

Lo! in yon brilliant window-niche
    How statue-like I see thee stand,
The agate lamp[4] within thy hand!
    Ah, Psyche,[5] from the regions which
    Are Holy-Land!   15

[1831]

---

[1]NICÉAN BARKS OF YORE: Perhaps referring to vessels from the Greek island of Nysa, or to the Greek goddess of victory, Nike—thus, victorious boats.
[2]HYACINTH HAIR: A hyacinth is a spring flower with rows of curled blossoms. Poe uses the metaphor to invoke the image of the tightly curled hair on Greek statues.
[3]NAIAD: Sea nymph.
[4]AGATE LAMP: Agate is a stone often featuring bands, stripes, or swirls of muted color due to the infiltration of other minerals throughout the rock.
[5]PSYCHE: In Greek mythology, Psyche is the goddess of the soul.

The Raven

Once upon a midnight dreary, while I pondered, weak and weary,
Over many a quaint and curious volume of forgotten lore—
While I nodded, nearly napping, suddenly there came a tapping,
As of some one gently rapping, rapping at my chamber door—
"'Tis some visiter," I muttered, "tapping at my chamber door—   5
          Only this and nothing more."

Ah, distinctly I remember it was in the bleak December;
And each separate dying ember wrought its ghost upon the floor.
Eagerly I wished the morrow;—vainly I had sought to borrow
From my books surcease of sorrow—sorrow for the lost Lenore—   10
For the rare and radiant maiden whom the angels name Lenore—
          Nameless *here* for evermore.

And the silken, sad, uncertain rustling of each purple curtain
Thrilled me—filled me with fantastic terrors never felt before;
So that now, to still the beating of my heart, I stood repeating   15
"'Tis some visiter entreating entrance at my chamber door—
Some late visiter entreating entrance at my chamber door;—
          This it is and nothing more."

Presently my soul grew stronger; hesitating then no longer,
"Sir," said I, "or Madam, truly your forgiveness I implore;   20
But the fact is I was napping, and so gently you came rapping,
And so faintly you came tapping, tapping at my chamber door,
That I scarce was sure I heard you"—here I opened wide the door;—
          Darkness there and nothing more.

Deep into that darkness peering, long I stood there wondering, fearing, 25
Doubting, dreaming dreams no mortal ever dared to dream before;
But the silence was unbroken, and the stillness gave no token,
And the only word there spoken was the whispered word, "Lenore?"
This I whispered, and an echo murmured back the word "Lenore!"
          Merely this and nothing more.   30

Back into the chamber turning, all my soul within me burning,
Soon again I heard a tapping somewhat louder than before.
"Surely," said I, "surely that is something at my window lattice;
Let me see, then, what thereat is, and this mystery explore—
Let my heart be still a moment and this mystery explore;—   35
          'Tis the wind and nothing more!

Open here I flung the shutter, when, with many a flirt and flutter
In there stepped a stately Raven of the saintly days of yore;
Not the least obeisance[1] made he; not a minute stopped or stayed he;
But, with mien[2] of lord or lady, perched above my chamber door— 40
Perched upon a bust of Pallas[3] just above my chamber door—
                  Perched, and sat, and nothing more.

Then this ebony bird beguiling my sad fancy into smiling,
By the grave and stern decorum of the countenance it wore,
"Though thy crest be shorn and shaven, thou," I said, "art sure no
    craven,[4]   45
Ghastly grim and ancient Raven wandering from the Nightly shore—
Tell me what thy lordly name is on the Night's Plutonian[5] shore!"
                  Quoth the Raven, "Nevermore."

Much I marvelled this ungainly fowl to hear discourse so plainly,
Though its answer little meaning—little relevancy bore;   50
For we cannot help agreeing that no living human being[6]
Ever yet was blessed with seeing bird above his chamber door—
Bird or beast upon the sculptured bust above his chamber door,
                  With such name as "Nevermore."

But the Raven, sitting lonely on the placid bust, spoke only   55
That one word, as if his soul in that one word he did outpour.
Nothing farther then he uttered—not a feather then he fluttered—
Till I scarcely more than muttered "Other friends have flown before—
On the morrow *he* will leave me, as my hopes have flown before."
                  Then the bird said "Nevermore." 60

Startled at the stillness broken by reply so aptly spoken,
"Doubtless," said I, "what it utters is its only stock and store
Caught from some unhappy master whom unmerciful Disaster
Followed fast and followed faster till his songs one burden bore—
Till the dirges of his Hope that melancholy burden bore   65
                  Of 'Never—nevermore.'"

But the Raven still beguiling all my fancy into smiling,
Straight I wheeled a cushioned seat in front of bird, and bust and door;

---

[1]OBEISANCE: Bow; act of deference.
[2]MIEN: Bearing.
[3]PALLAS: Athena, the Greek goddess of wisdom and war.
[4]CRAVEN: Coward.
[5]PLUTONIAN: Suggestive of the infernal regions inhabited by Pluto, the Roman god of the underworld.
[6]LIVING HUMAN: Some printings of the poem here use the word "sublunary." There are many such
variations among the available texts.

Then, upon the velvet sinking, I betook myself to linking
Fancy unto fancy, thinking what this ominous bird of yore—   70
What this grim, ungainly, ghastly, gaunt, and ominous bird of yore
        Meant in croaking "Nevermore."

This I sat engaged in guessing, but no syllable expressing
To the fowl whose fiery eyes now burned into my bosom's core;
This and more I sat divining, with my head at ease reclining   75
On the cushion's velvet lining that the lamp-light gloated[7] o'er,
But whose velvet-violet lining with the lamp-light gloating o'er,
        She shall press, ah, nevermore!

Then, methought, the air grew denser, perfumed from an unseen censer
Swung by Seraphim[8] whose foot-falls tinkled on the tufted floor.   80
"Wretch," I cried, "thy God hath lent thee—by these angels he hath
    sent thee
Respite—respite and nepenthe[9] from thy memories of Lenore;
Quaff,[10] oh quaff this kind nepenthe and forget this lost Lenore!
        Quoth the Raven "Nevermore."

"Prophet!"[11] said I, "thing of evil! prophet still, if bird or devil!—   85
Whether Tempter sent, or whether tempest tossed thee here ashore,
Desolate yet all undaunted, on this desert land enchanted—
On this home by Horror haunted—tell me truly, I implore—
Is there—*is* there balm in Gilead?[12]—tell me—tell me, I implore!"
        Quoth the Raven "Nevermore."   90

"Prophet!" said I, "thing of evil!—prophet still, if bird or devil!
By that Heaven that bends above us—by that God we both adore—
Tell this soul with sorrow laden if, within the distant Aidenn,[13]
It shall clasp a sainted maiden whom the angels name Lenore—
Clasp a rare and radiant maiden whom the angels name Lenore."   95
        Quoth the Raven "Nevermore."

[7]GLOATED: Referring to reflected or refracted light.
[8]SERAPHIM: The highest order of angels, described in a vision of the prophet Isaiah as hovering above the throne of God.
[9]NEPENTHE: A drugged drink mentioned in the *Odyssey* as capable of banishing grief and emotional pain.
[10]QUAFF: Drink deeply.
[11]PROPHET: In Greek mythology, Corvus, depicted as a crow or raven, was a servant and messenger for Apollo. It was through the raven that Apollo related his prophecies.
[12]BALM IN GILEAD: A reference to Jeremiah 8:22: "Is there no balm in Gilead; is there no physician there?" Gilead is a mountainous area east of the Jordan River between the Sea of Galilee and the Dead Sea. Evergreen trees in this area were a source of many medicinal preparations, including an antiseptic called Balm of Gilead, named after the biblical reference in Jeremiah.
[13]AIDENN: Eden, paradise.

"Be that word our sign of parting, bird or fiend!" I shrieked,
 upstarting—
"Get thee back into the tempest and the Night's Plutonian shore!
Leave no black plume as a token of that lie thy soul hath spoken!
Leave my loneliness unbroken!—quit the bust above my door!   100
Take thy beak from out my heart, and take thy form from off my door!"
        Quoth the Raven "Nevermore."

And the Raven, never flitting, still is sitting, *still* is sitting
On the pallid bust of Pallas just above my chamber door;
And his eyes have all the seeming of a demon's that is dreaming, 105
And the lamp-light o'er him streaming throws his shadow on the floor;
And my soul from out that shadow that lies floating on the floor
        Shall be lifted—nevermore!

[1845]

Annabel Lee

It was many and many a year ago,
 In a kingdom by the sea,
That a maiden there lived whom you may know
 By the name of Annabel Lee;—
And this maiden she lived with no other thought   5
 Than to love and be loved by me.

I was a child and *she* was a child,
 In this kingdom by the sea;
But we loved with a love that was more than love—
 I and my Annabel Lee—   10
With a love that the wingéd seraphs[1] of heaven
 Coveted her and me.

And this was the reason that, long ago,
 In this kingdom by the sea,
A wind blew out of a cloud, chilling   15
 My beautiful Annabel Lee;
So that her high-born kinsmen came
 And bore her away from me,

---

[1]SERAPHS: Seraphim, the highest order of angels, described in a vision by the prophet Isaiah as hovering above the throne of God.

To shut her up in a sepulchre,[2]
   In this kingdom by the sea.   20

The angels, not half so happy in Heaven,
   Went envying her and me—
Yes!—that was the reason (as all men know,
   In this kingdom by the sea)
That the wind came out of the cloud by night,   25
   Chilling and killing my Annabel Lee.

But our love it was stronger by far than the love
   Of those who were older than we—
   Of many far wiser than we—
And neither the angels in Heaven above,   30
   Nor the demons down under the sea,
Can ever dissever my soul from the soul
   Of the beautiful Annabel Lee:—

For the moon never beams, without bringing me dreams
   Of the beautiful Annabel Lee;   35
And the stars never rise, but I feel the bright eyes
   Of the beautiful Annabel Lee:—
And so, all the night-tide, I lie down by the side
Of my darling—my darling—my life and my bride,
   In the sepulchre there by the sea—   40
   In her tomb by the sounding sea.

[1849]

The Fall of the House of Usher

Son coeur est un luth suspendu;
Sitôt qu'on le touche il résonne.

—DE BÉRANGER[1]

During the whole of a dull, dark, and soundless day in the autumn of
the year, when the clouds hung oppressively low in the heavens, I had

[2]SEPULCHRE: A building or vault, usually for a tomb.
[1]SON COEUR…DE BÉRANGER: From "Le Refus," by Pierre-Jean de Béranger (1780–1857),
French poet. The lines may be translated thus: "His heart is a lute, tightly strung. / The instant one
touches it, it resounds."

been passing alone, on horseback, through a singularly dreary tract of country, and at length found myself, as the shades of the evening drew on, within view of the melancholy House of Usher. I know not how it was—but, with the first glimpse of the building, a sense of insufferable gloom pervaded my spirit. I say insufferable; for the feeling was unrelieved by any of that half-pleasurable, because poetic, sentiment, with which the mind usually receives even the sternest natural images of the desolate or terrible. I looked upon the scene before me—upon the mere house, and the simple landscape features of the domain—upon the bleak walls—upon the vacant eye-like windows—upon a few rank sedges—and upon a few white trunks of decayed trees—with an utter depression of soul which I can compare to no earthly sensation more properly than to the after-dream of the reveller upon opium—the bitter lapse into every-day life—the hideous dropping off of the veil. There was an iciness, a sinking, a sickening of the heart—an unredeemed dreariness of thought which no goading of the imagination could torture into aught of the sublime. What was it—I paused to think—what was it that so unnerved me in the contemplation of the House of Usher? It was a mystery all insoluble; nor could I grapple with the shadowy fancies that crowded upon me as I pondered. I was forced to fall back upon the unsatisfactory conclusion, that while, beyond doubt, there *are* combinations of very simple natural objects which have the power of thus affecting us, still the analysis of this power lies among considerations beyond our depth. It was possible, I reflected, that a mere different arrangement of the particulars of the scene, of the details of the picture, would be sufficient to modify, or perhaps to annihilate its capacity for sorrowful impression; and, acting upon this idea, I reined my horse to the precipitous brink of a black and lurid tarn[2] that lay in unruffled lustre by the dwelling, and gazed down—but with a shudder even more thrilling than before—upon the remodelled and inverted images of the gray sedge, and the ghastly tree-stems, and the vacant and eye-like windows.

Nevertheless, in this mansion of gloom I now proposed to myself a sojourn of some weeks. Its proprietor, Roderick Usher, had been one of my boon companions in boyhood; but many years had elapsed since our last meeting. A letter, however, had lately reached me in a distant part of the country—a letter from him—which, in its wildly importunate nature, had admitted of no other than a personal reply. The MS. gave evidence of nervous agitation. The writer spoke of acute

[2]TARN: Small mountain lake.

bodily illness—of a mental disorder[3] which oppressed him—and of an earnest desire to see me, as his best, and indeed his only personal friend, with a view of attempting, by the cheerfulness of my society, some alleviation of his malady. It was the manner in which all this, and much more, was said—it was the apparent *heart* that went with his request—which allowed me no room for hesitation; and I accordingly obeyed forthwith what I still considered a very singular summons.

Although, as boys, we had been even intimate associates, yet I really knew little of my friend. His reserve had been always excessive and habitual. I was aware, however, that his very ancient family had been noted, time out of mind, for a peculiar sensibility of temperament, displaying itself, through long ages, in many works of exalted art, and manifested, of late, in repeated deeds of munificent yet unobtrusive charity, as well as in a passionate devotion to the intricacies, perhaps even more than to the orthodox and easily recognizable beauties, of musical science. I had learned, too, the very remarkable fact, that the stem of the Usher race, all time-honoured as it was, had put forth, at no period, any enduring branch; in other words, that the entire family lay in the direct line of descent, and had always, with very trifling and very temporary variation, so lain. It was this deficiency, I considered, while running over in thought the perfect keeping of the character of the premises with the accredited character of the people, and while speculating upon the possible influence which the one, in the long lapse of centuries, might have exercised upon the other—it was this deficiency, perhaps of collateral issue, and the consequent undeviating transmission, from sire to son, of the patrimony with the name, which had, at length, so identified the two as to merge the original title of the estate in the quaint and equivocal appellation of the "House of Usher"—an appellation which seemed to include, in the minds of the peasantry who used it, both the family and the family mansion.

I have said that the sole effect of my somewhat childish experiment—that of looking down within the tarn—had been to deepen the first singular impression. There can be no doubt that the consciousness of the rapid increase of my superstition—for why should I not so term it?—served mainly to accelerate the increase itself. Such, I have long known, is the paradoxical law of all sentiments having terror as a basis. And it might have been for this reason only, that, when I again uplifted my eyes to the house itself, from its image in the pool, there grew in my mind a strange fancy—a fancy so ridiculous, indeed, that I but mention it to show the vivid force of the sensations which oppressed me. I had so

[3]MENTAL DISORDER: Other printings give "pitiable mental idiosyncrasy." Poe's stories have been printed with many such variations.

worked upon my imagination as really to believe that about the whole mansion and domain there hung an atmosphere peculiar to themselves and their immediate vicinity—an atmosphere which had no affinity with the air of heaven, but which had reeked up from the decayed trees, and the gray wall, and the silent tarn—a pestilent and mystic vapour, dull, sluggish, faintly discernible, and leaden-hued.

Shaking off from my spirit what *must* have been a dream, I scanned more narrowly the real aspect of the building. Its principal feature seemed to be that of an excessive antiquity. The discoloration of ages had been great. Minute fungi overspread the whole exterior, hanging in a fine tangled web-work from the eaves. Yet all this was apart from an extraordinary dilapidation. No portion of the masonry had fallen; and there appeared to be a wild inconsistency between its still perfect adaptation of parts, and the crumbling condition of the individual stones. In this there was much that reminded me of the specious totality of old woodwork which has rotted for long years in some neglected vault, with no disturbance from the breath of the external air. Beyond this indication of extensive decay, however, the fabric gave little token of instability. Perhaps the eye of a scrutinizing observer might have discovered a barely perceptible fissure, which, extending from the roof of the building in front, made its way down the wall in a zigzag direction, until it became lost in the sullen waters of the tarn.

Noticing these things, I rode over a short causeway to the house. A servant in waiting took my horse, and I entered the Gothic archway of the hall. A valet, of stealthy step, thence conducted me, in silence, through many dark and intricate passages in my progress to the *studio* of his master. Much that I encountered on the way contributed, I know not how, to heighten the vague sentiments of which I have already spoken. While the objects around me—while the carvings of the ceilings, the sombre tapestries of the walls, the ebon blackness of the floors, and the phantasmagoric armorial trophies which rattled as I strode, were but matters to which, or to such as which, I had been accustomed from my infancy—while I hesitated not to acknowledge how familiar was all this—I still wondered to find how unfamiliar were the fancies which ordinary images were stirring up. On one of the staircases, I met the physician of the family. His countenance, I thought, wore a mingled expression of low cunning and perplexity. He accosted me with trepidation and passed on. The valet now threw open a door and ushered me into the presence of his master.

The room in which I found myself was very large and lofty. The windows were long, narrow, and pointed, and at so vast a distance from the black oaken floor as to be altogether inaccessible from within. Feeble gleams of encrimsoned light made their way through the trellissed panes, and served to render sufficiently distinct the more prominent objects around; the eye, however, struggled in vain to reach the remoter angles of the chamber, or the recesses of the vaulted and fretted ceiling. Dark draperies hung upon the walls. The general furniture was profuse, comfortless, antique, and tattered. Many books and musical instruments lay scattered about, but failed to give any vitality to the scene. I felt that I breathed an atmosphere of sorrow. An air of stern, deep, and irredeemable gloom hung over and pervaded all.

Upon my entrance, Usher arose from a sofa on which he had been lying at full length, and greeted me with a vivacious warmth which had much in it, I at first thought of an overdone cordiality—of the constrained effort of the *ennuyé*[4] man of the world. A glance, however, at his countenance convinced me of his perfect sincerity. We sat down; and for some moments, while he spoke not, I gazed upon him with a feeling half of pity, half of awe. Surely, man had never before so terribly altered, in so brief a period, as had Roderick Usher! It was with difficulty that I could bring myself to admit the identity of the wan being before me with the companion of my early boyhood. Yet the character of his face had been at all times remarkable. A cadaverousness of complexion; an eye large, liquid, and luminous beyond comparison; lips somewhat thin and very pallid, but of a surpassingly beautiful curve; a nose of a delicate Hebrew model, but with a breadth of nostril unusual in similar formations; a finely moulded chin, speaking, in its want of prominence, of a want of moral energy; hair of a more than web-like softness and tenuity; these features, with an inordinate expansion above the regions of the temple, made up altogether a countenance not easily to be forgotten. And now in the mere exaggeration of the prevailing character of these features, and of the expression they were wont to convey, lay so much of change that I doubted to whom I spoke. The now ghastly pallor of the skin, and the now miraculous lustre of the eye, above all things startled and even awed me. The silken hair, too, had been suffered to grow all unheeded, and as, in its wild gossamer texture, it floated rather than fell about the face, I could not, even with effort, connect its Arabesque[5] expression with any idea of simple humanity.

In the manner of my friend I was at once struck with an incoherence—an inconsistency; and I soon found this to arise from a series of feeble and futile struggles to overcome an habitual trepidancy—an excessive nervous agitation. For something of this nature I had indeed been prepared, no less by his letter, than by reminiscences of certain boyish traits, and by conclusions deducted from his peculiar physical conformation and

[4]ENNUYÉ: Bored.
[5]ARABESQUE: Intricate.

temperament. His action was alternately vivacious and sullen. His voice varied rapidly from a tremulous indecision (when the animal spirits seemed utterly in abeyance) to that species of energetic concision—that abrupt, weighty, unhurried, and hollow-sounding enunciation—that leaden, self-balanced, and perfectly modulated guttural utterance, which may be observed in the lost drunkard, or the irreclaimable eater of opium, during the periods of his most intense excitement.

It was thus that he spoke of the object of my visit, of his earnest desire to see me, and of the solace he expected me to afford him. He entered, at some length, into what he conceived to be the nature of his malady. It was, he said, a constitutional and a family evil, and one for which he despaired to find a remedy—a mere nervous affection, he immediately added, which would undoubtedly soon pass off. It displayed itself in a host of unnatural sensations. Some of these, as he detailed them, interested and bewildered me; although, perhaps, the terms and the general manner of their narration had their weight. He suffered much from a morbid acuteness of the senses; the most insipid food was alone endurable; he could wear only garments of certain texture; the odours of all flowers were oppressive; his eyes were tortured by even a faint light; and there were but peculiar sounds, and these from stringed instruments, which did not inspire him with horror.

To an anomalous species of terror I found him a bounden slave. "I shall perish," said he, "I *must* perish in this deplorable folly. Thus, thus, and not otherwise, shall I be lost. I dread the events of the future, not in themselves, but in their results. I shudder at the thought of any, even the most trivial, incident, which may operate upon this intolerable agitation of soul. I have, indeed, no abhorrence of danger, except in its absolute effect—in terror. In this unnerved—in this pitiable condition—I feel that the period will sooner or later arrive when I must abandon life and reason together, in some struggle with the grim phantasm, FEAR."

I learned, moreover, at intervals, and through broken and equivocal hints, another singular feature of his mental condition. He was enchained by certain superstitious impressions in regard to the dwelling which he tenanted, and whence, for many years, he had never ventured forth—in regard to an influence whose supposititious force was conveyed in terms too shadowy here to be re-stated—an influence which some peculiarities in the mere form and substance of his family mansion had, by dint of long sufferance, he said, obtained over his spirit—an effect which the *physique* of the gray wall and turrets, and of the dim tarn into which they all looked down, had, at length, brought about upon the *morale* of his existence.

He admitted, however, although with hesitation, that much of the peculiar gloom which thus afflicted him could be traced to a more natural and far more palpable origin—to the severe and long-continued illness—indeed to the evidently approaching dissolution—of a tenderly beloved sister, his sole companion for long years, his last and only relative on earth. "Her decease," he said, with a bitterness which I can never forget, "would leave him (him the hopeless and the frail) the last of the ancient race of the Ushers." While he spoke, the lady Madeline (for so was she called) passed slowly through a remote portion of the apartment, and, without having noticed my presence, disappeared. I regarded her with an utter astonishment not unmingled with dread—and yet I found it impossible to account for such feelings. A sensation of stupor oppressed me, as my eyes followed her retreating steps. When a door, at length, closed upon her, my glance sought instinctively and eagerly the countenance of the brother—but he had buried his face in his hands, and I could only perceive that a far more than ordinary wanness had overspread the emaciated fingers through which trickled many passionate tears.

The disease of the lady Madeline had long baffled the skill of her physicians. A settled apathy, a gradual wasting away of the person, and frequent although transient affections of a partially cataleptical character were the unusual diagnosis. Hitherto she had steadily borne up against the pressure of her malady, and had not betaken herself finally to bed; but on the closing in of the evening of my arrival at the house, she succumbed (as her brother told me at night with inexpressible agitation) to the prostrating power of the destroyer; and I learned that the glimpse I had obtained of her person would thus probably be the last I should obtain—that the lady, at least while living, would be seen by me no more.

For several days ensuing, her name was unmentioned by either Usher or myself: and during this period I was busied in earnest endeavours to alleviate the melancholy of my friend. We painted and read together, or I listened, as if in a dream, to the wild improvisations of his speaking guitar. And thus, as a closer and still closer intimacy admitted me more unreservedly into the recesses of his spirit, the more bitterly did I perceive the futility of all attempt at cheering a mind from which darkness, as if an inherent positive quality, poured forth upon all objects of the moral and physical universe in one unceasing radiation of gloom.

I shall ever bear about me a memory of the many solemn hours I thus spent alone with the master of the House of Usher. Yet I should fail in any attempt to convey an idea of the exact character of the studies, or of the occupations, in which he involved me, or led me the way. An excited and highly distempered ideality threw a sulphureous lustre over all. His long improvised dirges will ring forever in my ears. Among other things, I hold painfully in mind a certain singular perversion and amplification of the wild air of the last waltz of Von Weber.[6] From the paintings over which his elaborate fancy brooded, and which grew, touch by touch, into vagueness at which I shuddered the more thrillingly, because I shuddered knowing not why;—from these paintings (vivid as their images now are before me) I would in vain endeavour to educe more than a small portion which should lie within the compass of merely written words. By the utter simplicity, by the nakedness of his designs, he arrested and overawed attention. If ever mortal painted an idea, that mortal was Roderick Usher. For me at least—in the circumstances then surrounding me—there arose out of the pure abstractions which the hypochondriac contrived to throw upon his canvas, an intensity of intolerable awe, no shadow of which I felt ever yet in the contemplation of the certainly glowing yet too concrete reveries of Fuseli.[7]

One of the phantasmagoric conceptions of my friend, partaking not so rigidly of the spirit of abstraction, may be shadowed forth, although feebly, in words. A small picture presented the interior of an immensely long and rectangular vault or tunnel, with low walls, smooth, white, and without interruption or device. Certain accessory points of the design served well to convey the idea that this excavation lay at an exceeding depth below the surface of the earth. No outlet was observed in any portion of its vast extent, and no torch or other artificial source of light was discernible; yet a flood of intense rays rolled throughout, and bathed the whole in a ghastly and inappropriate splendour.

I have just spoken of that morbid condition of the auditory nerve which rendered all music intolerable to the sufferer, with the exception of certain effects of stringed instruments. It was, perhaps, the narrow limits to which he thus confined himself upon the guitar, which gave birth, in great measure, to the fantastic character of his performances. But the fervid *facility* of his *impromptus* could not be so accounted for. They must have been, and were, in the notes, as well as in the words of his wild fantasias (for he not unfrequently accompanied himself with rhymed verbal improvisations), the result of that intense mental collectedness and concentration to which I have previously alluded as observable only in particular moments of the highest artificial excitement. The words of one of these rhapsodies I have easily remembered. I was, perhaps, the more forcibly impressed with it, as he gave it, because, in the under or mystic current of its meaning, I fancied that I perceived, and for the first time, a full consciousness on the part of Usher, of the tottering of his lofty

---

[6]VON WEBER: Karl Gottlieb Reissiger (1758–1859) composed "The Last Waltz of Von Weber"; Karl Maria Von Weber (1786–1826), German composer and pianist.
[7]FUSELI: Henry Fuseli (1741–1825), Swiss-born British painter and art critic.

reason upon her throne. The verses, which were entitled "The Haunted Palace," ran very nearly, if not accurately, thus:

I

In the greenest of our valleys,
By good angels tenanted,
Once a fair and stately palace—
Radiant palace—reared its head.
In the monarch Thought's dominion—
It stood there!
Never seraph spread a pinion
Over fabric half so fair.

II

Banners yellow, glorious, golden,
On its roof did float and flow;
(This—all this—was in the olden
Time long ago)
And every gentle air that dallied,
In that sweet day,
Along the ramparts plumed and pallid,
A winged odour went away.

III

Wanderers in that happy valley
Through two luminous windows saw
Spirits moving musically
To a lute's well-tunèd law,
Round about a throne, where sitting
(Porphyrogene!⁸)
In state his glory well befitting,
The ruler of the realm was seen,

IV

And all with pearl and ruby glowing
Was the fair palace door,
Through which came flowing, flowing, flowing
And sparkling evermore,
A troop of Echoes whose sweet duty
Was but to sing,
In voices of surpassing beauty,
The wit and wisdom of their king.

---

⁸PORPHYROGENE: Born to the purple—that is, royal.

V

> But evil things, in robes of sorrow,
> >   Assailed the monarch's high estate;
> (Ah, let us mourn, for never morrow
> >   Shall dawn upon him, desolate!)
> And, round about his home, the glory
> >   That blushed and bloomed
> Is but a dim-remembered story
> >   Of the old time entombed.

VI

> And travellers now within that valley,
> >   Through the red-litten windows see
> Vast forms that move fantastically
> >   To a discordant melody;
> While, like a rapid ghastly river,
> >   Through the pale door,
> A hideous throng rush out forever,
> >   And laugh—but smile no more.

I well remember that suggestions arising from this ballad, led us into a train of thought, wherein there became manifest an opinion of Usher's which I mention not so much on account of its novelty, (for other men have thought thus,) as on account of the pertinacity with which he maintained it. This opinion, in its general form, was that of the sentience of all vegetable things. But, in his disordered fancy, the idea had assumed a more daring character, and trespassed, under certain conditions, upon the kingdom of inorganization. I lack words to express the full extent, or the earnest *abandon* of his persuasion. The belief, however, was connected (as I have previously hinted) with the gray stones of the home of his forefathers. The conditions of the sentience had been here, he imagined, fulfilled in the method of collocation of these stones—in the order of their arrangement, as well as in that of the many *fungi* which overspread them, and of the decayed trees which stood around—above all, in the long undisturbed endurance of this arrangement, and in its reduplication in the still waters of the tarn. Its evidence—the evidence of the sentience—was to be seen, he said (and I here started as he spoke), in the gradual yet certain condensation of an atmosphere of their own about the waters and the walls. The result was discoverable, he added, in that silent yet importunate and terrible influence which for centuries had moulded the destinies of his family, and which made *him* what I now saw him— what he was. Such opinions need no comment, and I will make none.

Our books—the books which, for years, had formed no small portion of the mental existence of the invalid—were, as might be supposed, in strict keeping with his character of phantasm. We pored together over such works[9] as the Ververt et Chartreuse of Gresset; the Belphegor of Machiavelli; the Heaven and Hell of Swedenborg; the Subterranean Voyage of Nicholas Klimm of Holberg; the Chiromancy of Robert Flud, of Jean D'Indaginé, and of De la Chambre; the Journey into the Blue Distance of Tieck; and the City of the Sun of Campanella. One favourite volume was a small octavo edition of the *Directorium Inquisitorum*, by the Dominican Eymeric de Gironne; and there were passages in Pomponius Mela, about the old African Satyrs and Ægipans, over which Usher would sit dreaming for hours. His chief delight, however, was found in the perusal of an exceedingly rare and curious book in quarto Gothic—the manual of a forgotten church—the *Vigiliæ Mortuorum secundum Chorum Ecclesiæ Maguntinæ.*

I could not help thinking of the wild ritual of this work, and of its probable influence upon the hypochondriac, when, one evening, having informed me abruptly that the lady Madeline was no more, he stated his intention of preserving her corpse for a fortnight, (previously to its final interment,) in one of the numerous vaults within the main walls of the building. The worldly reason, however, assigned for this singular proceeding, was one which I did not feel at liberty to dispute. The brother had been led to his resolution (so he told me) by consideration of the unusual character of the malady of the deceased, of certain obtrusive and eager inquiries on the part of her medical men, and of the remote and exposed situation of the burial-ground of the family. I will not deny that when I called to mind the sinister countenance of the person whom I met upon the staircase, on the day of my arrival at the house, I had no desire to oppose what I regarded as at best but a harmless, and by no means an unnatural, precaution.

At the request of Usher, I personally aided him in the arrangements for the temporary entombment. The body having been encoffined, we two alone bore it to its rest. The vault in which we placed it (and which had been so long unopened that our torches, half smothered in its oppressive atmosphere, gave us little opportunity for investigation) was small, damp, and entirely without means of admission for light; lying, at great depth, immediately beneath that portion of the building in which was my own sleeping apartment. It had been used, apparently, in remote feudal times, for the worst purposes of a donjon-keep, and, in later days, as a place of deposit for powder, or some other highly combustible substance,

[9]WORKS: What follows is an array of texts dealing with science, mysticism, demonology, and related esoterica and fantastical subjects. The list concludes by referencing *The Vigils of the Dead, According to the Church-Choir of Mayence* (c. 1500).

as a portion of its floor, and the whole interior of a long archway through which we reached it, were carefully sheathed with copper. The door, of massive iron, had been, also, similarly protected. Its immense weight caused an unusually sharp grating sound, as it moved upon its hinges.

Having deposited our mournful burden upon tressels within this region of horror, we partially turned aside the yet unscrewed lid of the coffin, and looked upon the face of the tenant. A striking similitude between the brother and sister now first arrested my attention; and Usher, divining, perhaps, my thoughts, murmured out some few words from which I learned that the deceased and himself had been twins, and that sympathies of a scarcely intelligible nature had always existed between them. Our glances, however, rested not long upon the dead—for we could not regard her unawed. The disease which had thus entombed the lady in the maturity of youth, had left, as usual in all maladies of a strictly cataleptical character, the mockery of a faint blush upon the bosom and the face, and that suspiciously lingering smile upon the lip which is so terrible in death. We replaced and screwed down the lid, and, having secured the door of iron, made our way, with toil, into the scarcely less gloomy apartments of the upper portion of the house.

And now, some days of bitter grief having elapsed, an observable change came over the features of the mental disorder of my friend. His ordinary manner had vanished. His ordinary occupations were neglected or forgotten. He roamed from chamber to chamber with hurried, unequal, and objectless step. The pallor of his countenance had assumed, if possible, a more ghastly hue—but the luminousness of his eye had utterly gone out. The once occasional huskiness of his tone was heard no more; and a tremulous quaver, as if of extreme terror, habitually characterized his utterance. There were times, indeed, when I thought his unceasingly agitated mind was labouring with some oppressive secret, to divulge which he struggled for the necessary courage. At times, again, I was obliged to resolve all into the mere inexplicable vagaries of madness, for I beheld him gazing upon vacancy for long hours, in an attitude of the profoundest attention, as if listening to some imaginary sound. It was no wonder that his condition terrified—that it infected me. I felt creeping upon me, by slow yet certain degrees, the wild influences of his own fantastic yet impressive superstitions.

It was, especially, upon retiring to bed late in the night of the seventh or eighth day after the placing of the lady Madeline within the donjon, that I experienced the full power of such feelings. Sleep came not near my couch—while the hours waned and waned away. I struggled to reason off the nervousness which had dominion over me. I endeavoured to believe that much, if not all of what I felt, was due to the bewildering influence of the gloomy furniture of the room—of the dark and tattered draperies, which, tortured into motion by the breath of a rising tempest, swayed fitfully to and fro upon the walls, and rustled uneasily about the decorations of the bed. But my efforts were fruitless. An irrepressible tremour gradually pervaded my frame; and, at length, there sat upon my very heart an incubus[10] of utterly causeless alarm. Shaking this off with a gasp and a struggle, I uplifted myself upon the pillows, and, peering earnestly within the intense darkness of the chamber, hearkened—I know not why, except that an instinctive spirit prompted me—to certain low and indefinite sounds which came, through the pauses of the storm, at long intervals, I knew not whence. Overpowered by an intense sentiment of horror, unaccountable yet unendurable, I threw on my clothes with haste, (for I felt that I should sleep no more during the night) and endeavoured to arouse myself from the pitiable condition into which I had fallen, by pacing rapidly to and fro through the apartment.

I had taken but few turns in this manner, when a light step on an adjoining staircase arrested my attention. I presently recognised it as that of Usher. In an instant afterward he rapped, with a gentle touch, at my door, and entered, bearing a lamp. His countenance was, as usual, cadaverously wan—but, moreover, there was a species of mad hilarity in his eyes—an evidently restrained *hysteria* in his whole demeanour. His air appalled me—but anything was preferable to the solitude which I had so long endured, and I even welcomed his presence as a relief.

"And you have not seen it?" he said abruptly, after having stared about him for some moments in silence—"you have not then seen it?—but, stay! you shall." Thus speaking, and having carefully shaded his lamp, he hurried to one of the casements, and threw it freely open to the storm.

The impetuous fury of the entering gust nearly lifted us from our feet. It was, indeed, a tempestuous yet sternly beautiful night, and one wildly singular in its terror and its beauty. A whirlwind had apparently collected its force in our vicinity; for there were frequent and violent alterations in the direction of the wind; and the exceeding density of the clouds (which hung so low as to press upon the turrets of the house) did not prevent our perceiving the life-like velocity with which they flew careering from all points against each other, without passing away into the distance. I say that even their exceeding density did not prevent our perceiving this—yet we had no glimpse of the moon or stars—nor was there any flashing forth of the lightning. But the under surfaces of the huge masses of agitated vapour, as well as all terrestrial objects immediately around us, were glowing in the unnatural light of a faintly luminous and distinctly visible gaseous exhalation which hung about and enshrouded the mansion.

---

[10]INCUBUS: An evil spirit that lies on persons while they are sleeping.

"You must not—you shall not behold this!" said I, shudderingly, to Usher, as I led him, with a gentlè violence, from the window to a seat. "These appearances, which bewilder you, are merely electrical phenomena not uncommon—or it may be that they have their ghastly origin in the rank miasma of the tarn. Let us close this casement;—the air is chilling and dangerous to your frame. Here is one of your favourite romances. I will read, and you shall listen;—and so we will pass away this terrible night together."

The antique volume which I had taken up was the "Mad Trist"[11] of Sir Launcelot Canning, but I had called it a favourite of Usher's more in sad jest than in earnest; for, in truth, there is little in its uncouth and unimaginative prolixity which could have had interest for the lofty and spiritual ideality of my friend. It was, however, the only book immediately at hand; and I indulged a vague hope that the excitement which now agitated the hypochondriac, might find relief (for the history of mental disorder is full of similar anomalies) even in the extremeness of the folly which I could read. Could I have judged, indeed, by the wild overstrained air of vivacity with which he hearkened, or apparently hearkened, to the words of the tale, I might well have congratulated myself upon the success of my design.

I had arrived at that well-known portion of the story where Ethelred, the hero of the Trist, having sought in vain for peaceable admission into the dwelling of the hermit, proceeds to make good an entrance by force. Here, it will be remembered, the words of the narrative run thus:

"And Ethelred, who was by nature of a doughty heart, and who was now mighty withal, on account of the powerfulness of the wine which he had drunken, waited no longer to hold parley with the hermit, who, in sooth, was of an obstinate and maliceful turn, but, feeling the rain upon his shoulders, and fearing the rising of the tempest, uplifted his mace outright, and, with blows, made quickly room in the plankings of the door for his gauntleted hand; and now pulling therewith sturdily, he so cracked, and ripped, and tore all asunder, that the noise of the dry and hollow-sounding wood alarmed and reverberated throughout the forest."

At the termination of this sentence I started and, for a moment, paused; for it appeared to me (although I at once concluded that my excited fancy had deceived me)—it appeared to me that, from some very remote portion of the mansion, there came, indistinctly, to my ears, what might have been, in its exact similarity of character, the echo (but

[11]MAD TRIST: Poe invented this story.

a stifled and dull one certainly) of the very cracking and ripping sound which Sir Launcelot had so particularly described. It was, beyond doubt, the coincidence alone which had arrested my attention; for, amid the rattling of the sashes of the casements, and the ordinary commingled noises of the still increasing storm, the sound, in itself, had nothing, surely, which should have interested or disturbed me. I continued the story:

"But the good champion Ethelred, now entering within the door, was sore enraged and amazed to perceive no signal of the maliceful hermit; but, in the stead thereof, a dragon of a scaly and prodigious demeanour, and of a fiery tongue, which sate in guard before a palace of gold, with a floor of silver; and upon the wall there hung a shield of shining brass with this legend enwritten—

> *Who entereth herein, a conqueror hath bin;*
> *Who slayeth the dragon, the shield he shall win.*

And Ethelred uplifted his mace, and struck upon the head of the dragon, which fell before him, and gave up his pesty breath, with a shriek so horrid and harsh, and withal so piercing, that Ethelred had fain to close his ears with his hands against the dreadful noise of it, the like whereof was never before heard."

Here again I paused abruptly, and now with a feeling of wild amazement—for there could be no doubt whatever that, in this instance, I did actually *hear* (although from what direction it proceeded I found it impossible to say) a low and apparently distant, but harsh, protracted, and most unusual screaming or grating sound—the exact counterpart of what my fancy had already conjured up for the dragon's unnatural shriek as described by the romancer.

Oppressed, as I certainly was, upon the occurrence of the second and most extraordinary coincidence, by a thousand conflicting sensations, in which wonder and extreme terror were predominant, I still retained sufficient presence of mind to avoid exciting, by any observation, the sensitive nervousness of my companion. I was by no means certain that he had noticed the sounds in question; although, assuredly, a strange alteration had, during the last few minutes, taken place in his demeanour. From a position fronting my own, he had gradually brought round his chair, so as to sit with his face to the door of the chamber; and thus I could but partially perceive his features, although I saw that his lips trembled as if he were murmuring inaudibly. His head had dropped upon his breast—yet I knew that he was not asleep, from the wide and rigid opening of the eye as I caught a glance of it in profile. The motion of his body, too, was at variance with this idea—for he rocked from side to side with a gentle yet constant and uniform sway. Having rapidly taken notice of all this, I resumed the narrative of Sir Launcelot, which thus proceeded:

"And now, the champion, having escaped from the terrible fury of the dragon, bethinking himself of the brazen shield, and of the breaking up of the enchantment which was upon it, removed the carcass from out of the way before him, and approached valorously over the silver pavement of the castle to where the shield was upon the wall; which in sooth tarried not for his full coming, but fell down at his feet upon the silver floor, with a mighty great and terrible ringing sound."

No sooner had these syllables passed my lips, than—as if a shield of brass had indeed, at the moment, fallen heavily upon a floor of silver—I became aware of a distinct, hollow, metallic, and clangorous, yet apparently muffled reverberation. Completely unnerved, I leaped to my feet; but the measured rocking movement of Usher was undisturbed. I rushed to the chair in which he sat. His eyes were bent fixedly before him, and throughout his whole countenance there reigned a stony rigidity. But, as I placed my hand upon his shoulder, there came a strong shudder over his whole person; a sickly smile quivered about his lips; and I saw that he spoke in a low, hurried, and gibbering murmur, as if unconscious of my presence. Bending closely over him, I at length drank in the hideous import of his words.

"Not hear it?—yes, I hear it, and *have* heard it. Long—long—long—many minutes, many hours, many days, have I heard it—yet I dared not—oh, pity me, miserable wretch that I am!—I dared not—I *dared* not speak! *We have put her living in the tomb!* Said I not that my senses were acute? I *now* tell you that I heard her first feeble movements in the hollow coffin. I heard them—many, many days ago—yet I dared not—I *dared not speak*! And now—to-night—Ethelred—ha! ha!—the breaking of the hermit's door, and the death-cry of the dragon, and the clangour of the shield!—say, rather, the rending of her coffin, and the grating of the iron hinges of her prison, and her struggles within the coppered archway of the vault! Oh whither shall I fly? Will she not be here anon? Is she not hurrying to upbraid me for my haste? Have I not heard her footsteps on the stair? Do I not distinguish that heavy and horrible beating of her heart? MADMAN!"—here he sprang furiously to his feet, and shrieked out his syllables, as if in the effort he were giving up his soul—"MADMAN! I TELL YOU THAT SHE NOW STANDS WITHOUT THE DOOR!"

As if in the superhuman energy of his utterance there had been found the potency of a spell—the huge antique panels to which the speaker pointed threw slowly back, upon the instant, their ponderous and ebony jaws. It was the work of the rushing gust—but then without those doors there DID stand the lofty and enshrouded figure of the lady Madeline of Usher. There was blood upon her white robes, and the evidence of some bitter struggle upon every portion of her emaciated frame. For a moment she remained trembling and reeling to and fro upon the threshold, then, with a low moaning cry, fell heavily inward upon the person of her brother, and in her violent and now final death-agonies, bore him to the floor a corpse, and a victim to the terrors he had anticipated.

From that chamber, and from that mansion, I fled aghast. The storm was still abroad in all its wrath as I found myself crossing the old causeway. Suddenly there shot along the path a wild light, and I turned to see whence a gleam so unusual could have issued; for the vast house and its shadows were alone behind me. The radiance was that of the full, setting, and blood-red moon, which now shone vividly through that once barely discernible fissure, of which I have before spoken as extending from the roof of the building, in a zigzag direction, to the base. While I gazed, this fissure rapidly widened—there came a fierce breath of the whirlwind—the entire orb of the satellite burst at once upon my sight— my brain reeled as I saw the mighty walls rushing asunder—there was a long tumultuous shouting sound like the voice of a thousand waters— and the deep and dank tarn at my feet closed sullenly and silently over the fragments of the "HOUSE OF USHER."

[1839]

The Tell-Tale Heart

True!—nervous—very, very dreadfully nervous I had been and am; but why *will* you say that I am mad? The disease had sharpened my senses— not destroyed—not dulled them. Above all was the sense of hearing acute. I heard all things in the heaven and in the earth. I heard many things in hell. How, then, am I mad? Hearken! and observe how healthily—how calmly I can tell you the whole story.

It is impossible to say how first the idea entered my brain; but once conceived, it haunted me day and night. Object there was none. Passion there was none. I loved the old man. He had never wronged me. He had never given me insult. For his gold I had no desire. I think it was his eye! yes, it was this! He had the eye of a vulture—a pale blue eye, with a film over it. Whenever it fell upon me, my blood ran cold; and so by degrees—very gradually—I made up my mind to take the life of the old man, and thus rid myself of the eye forever.

Now this is the point. You fancy me mad. Madmen know nothing. But you should have seen *me*. You should have seen how wisely I proceeded—with what caution—with what foresight—with what dissimulation[1] I went to work! I was never kinder to the old man than during the whole week before I killed him. And every night, about midnight, I turned the latch of his door and opened it—oh so gently! And then, when I had made an opening sufficient for my head, I put in a dark lantern,[2] all closed, closed, so that no light shone out, and then I thrust in my head. Oh, you would have laughed to see how cunningly I thrust it in! I moved it slowly—very, very slowly, so that I might not disturb the old man's sleep. It took me an hour to place my whole head within the opening so far that I could see him as he lay upon his bed. Ha!—would a madman have been so wise as this? And then, when my head was well in the room, I undid the lantern cautiously—oh, so cautiously—cautiously (for the hinges creaked)—I undid it just so much that a single thin ray fell upon the vulture eye. And this I did for seven long nights—every night just at midnight—but I found the eye always closed; and so it was impossible to do the work; for it was not the old man who vexed me, but his Evil Eye.[3] And every morning, when the day broke, I went boldly into the chamber, and spoke courageously to him, calling him by name in a hearty tone and inquiring how he had passed the night. So you see he would have been a very profound old man, indeed, to suspect that every night, just at twelve, I looked in upon him while he slept.

Upon the eighth night I was more than usually cautious in opening the door. A watch's minute hand moves more quickly than did mine. Never, before that night, had I *felt* the extent of my own powers—of my sagacity. I could scarcely contain my feelings of triumph. To think that there I was, opening the door, little by little, and he not even to dream of my secret deeds or thoughts. I fairly chuckled at the idea; and perhaps he heard me; for he moved on the bed suddenly, as if startled. Now you may think that I drew back—but no. His room was as black as pitch with the thick darkness, (for the shutters were close fastened, through fear of robbers,) and so I knew that he could not see the opening of the door, and I kept pushing it on steadily, steadily.

I had my head in, and was about to open the lantern, when my thumb slipped upon the tin fastening, and the old man sprang up in bed, crying out—"Who's there?"

[1]DISSIMULATION: Deception.
[2]DARK LANTERN: A lantern with a slide that can conceal the light within.
[3]EVIL EYE: An eye or a glance capable of inflicting harm.

I kept quite still and said nothing. For a whole hour I did not move a muscle, and in the meantime I did not hear him lie down. He was still sitting up in the bed listening;—just as I have done, night after night, hearkening to the death watches[4] in the wall.

Presently I heard a slight groan, and I knew it was the groan of mortal terror. It was not a groan of pain or of grief—oh, no!—it was the low stifled sound that arises from the bottom of the soul when overcharged with awe. I knew the sound well. Many a night, just at midnight, when all the world slept, it had welled up from my own bosom, deepening, with its dreadful echo, the terrors that distracted me. I say I knew it well. I knew what the old man felt, and pitied him, although I chuckled at heart. I knew that he had been lying awake ever since the first slight noise, when he had turned in the bed. His fears had been ever since growing upon him. He had been trying to fancy them causeless, but could not. He had been saying to himself—"It is nothing but the wind in the chimney—it is only a mouse crossing the floor," or "it is merely a cricket which has made a single chirp." Yes, he had been trying to comfort himself with these suppositions: but he had found all in vain. *All in vain*; because Death, in approaching him, had stalked with his black shadow before him, and enveloped the victim. And it was the mournful influence of the perceived shadow that caused him to feel—although he neither saw nor heard me—to *feel* the presence of my head within the room.

When I had waited a long time, very patiently, without hearing him lie down, I resolved to open a little—a very, very little crevice in the lantern. So I opened it—you cannot imagine how stealthily, stealthily—until, at length, a simple dim ray, like the thread of the spider, shot from out the crevice and fell full upon the vulture eye.

It was open—wide, wide open—and I grew furious as I gazed upon it. I saw it with perfect distinctness—all a dull blue, with a hideous veil over it that chilled the very marrow in my bones; but I could see nothing else of the old man's face or person: for I had directed the ray as if by instinct, precisely upon the damned spot.

And have I not told you that what you mistake for madness is but over acuteness of the senses?—now, I say, there came to my ears a low, dull quick sound, such as a watch makes when enveloped in cotton. I knew *that* sound well, too. It was the beating of the old man's heart. It increased my fury, as the beating of a drum stimulates the soldier into courage.

---

[4]DEATH WATCHES: Beetles that make noises similar to a watch ticking, which the superstitious believed foretold death.

But even yet I refrained and kept still. I scarcely breathed. I held the lantern motionless. I tried how steadily I could maintain the ray upon the eye. Meantime the hellish tattoo[5] of the heart increased. It grew quicker and quicker, and louder and louder every instant. The old man's terror *must* have been extreme! It grew louder, I say, louder every moment!—do you mark me well? I have told you that I am nervous: so I am. And now at the dead hour of the night, amid the dreadful silence of that old house, so strange a noise as this excited me to uncontrollable terror. Yet, for some minutes longer I refrained and stood still. But the beating grew louder, louder! I thought the heart must burst. And now a new anxiety seized me—the sound would be heard by a neighbour! The old man's hour had come! With a loud yell, I threw open the lantern and leaped into the room. He shrieked once—once only. In an instant I dragged him to the floor, and pulled the heavy bed over him. I then smiled gaily,[6] to find the deed so far done. But, for many minutes, the heart beat on with a muffled sound. This, however, did not vex me; it would not be heard through the wall. At length it ceased. The old man was dead. I removed the bed and examined the corpse. Yes, he was stone, stone dead. I placed my hand upon the heart and held it there many minutes. There was no pulsation. He was stone dead. His eye would trouble me no more.

If still you think me mad, you will think so no longer when I describe the wise precautions I took for the concealment of the body. The night waned, and I worked hastily, but in silence. First of all I dismembered the corpse. I cut off the head and the arms and the legs.

I then took up three planks from the flooring of the chamber, and deposited all between the scantlings.[7] I then replaced the boards so cleverly, so cunningly, that no human eye—not even *his*—could have detected anything wrong. There was nothing to wash out—no stain of any kind—no blood-spot whatever. I had been too wary for that. A tub had caught all—ha! ha!

When I had made an end of these labors, it was four o'clock—still dark as midnight. As the bell sounded the hour, there came a knocking at the street door. I went down to open it with a light heart,—for what had I *now* to fear? There entered three men, who introduced themselves, with perfect suavity, as officers of the police. A shriek had been heard by a neighbour during the night; suspicion of foul play had been aroused; information had been lodged at the police office, and they (the officers) had been deputed to search the premises.

[5]TATTOO: Drumbeat.
[6]GAILY: Cheerfully, joyfully.
[7]SCANTLINGS: Wood beams.

I smiled,—for *what* had I to fear? I bade the gentlemen welcome. The shriek, I said, was my own in a dream. The old man, I mentioned, was absent in the country. I took my visitors all over the house. I bade them search—search *well*. I led them, at length, to *his* chamber. I showed them his treasures, secure, undisturbed. In the enthusiasm of my confidence, I brought chairs into the room and desired them *here* to rest from their fatigues, while I myself, in the wild audacity of my perfect triumph, placed my own seat upon the very spot beneath which reposed the corpse of the victim.

The officers were satisfied. My *manner* had convinced them. I was singularly at ease. They sat, and while I answered cheerily, they chatted of familiar things. But, ere long, I felt myself getting pale and wished them gone. My head ached, and I fancied a ringing in my ears: but still they sat and still chatted. The ringing became more distinct:—it continued and became more distinct: I talked more freely to get rid of the feeling: but it continued and gained definiteness—until, at length, I found that the noise was *not* within my ears.

No doubt I now grew *very* pale;—but I talked more fluently, and with a heightened voice. Yet the sound increased—and what could I do? It was *a low, dull, quick sound—much such a sound as a watch makes when enveloped in cotton.* I gasped for breath—and yet the officers heard it not. I talked more quickly—more vehemently; but the noise steadily increased. I arose and argued about trifles, in a high key and with violent gesticulations; but the noise steadily increased. Why *would* they not be gone? I paced the floor to and fro with heavy strides, as if excited to fury by the observations of the men—but the noise steadily increased. Oh God! what *could* I do? I foamed—I raved—I swore! I swung the chair upon which I had been sitting, and grated it upon the boards, but the noise arose over all and continually increased. It grew louder—louder—*louder!* And still the men chatted pleasantly, and smiled. Was it possible they heard not? Almighty God!—no, no! They heard!—they suspected!—they *knew!*—they were making a mockery of my horror!— this I thought, and this I think. But anything was better than this agony! Anything was more tolerable than this derision! I could bear those hypocritical smiles no longer! I felt that I must scream or die! and now— again!—hark! louder! louder! louder! *louder!*

"Villains!" I shrieked, "dissemble[8] no more! I admit the deed!—tear up the planks! here, here!—it is the beating of his hideous heart!"

[1843]

[8]DISSEMBLE: Pretend.

The Purloined[1] Letter

Nil sapientiae odiosius acumine nimio.[2]

—SENECA[3]

At Paris, just after dark one gusty evening in the autumn of 18—, I was enjoying the twofold luxury of meditation and a meerschaum,[4] in company with my friend C. Auguste Dupin, in his little back library, or bookcloset, *au troisième,*[5] *No. 33, Rue Dunôt, Faubourg St. Germain.* For one hour at least we had maintained a profound silence; while each, to any casual observer, might have seemed intently and exclusively occupied with the curling eddies of smoke that oppressed the atmosphere of the chamber. For myself, however, I was mentally discussing certain topics which had formed matter for conversation between us at an earlier period of the evening; I mean the affair of the Rue Morgue, and the mystery attending the murder of Marie Rogêt.[6] I looked upon it, therefore, as something of a coincidence, when the door of our apartment was thrown open and admitted our old acquaintance, Monsieur G——, the Prefect[7] of the Parisian police.

We gave him a hearty welcome; for there was nearly half as much of the entertaining as of the contemptible about the man, and we had not seen him for several years. We had been sitting in the dark, and Dupin now arose for the purpose of lighting a lamp, but sat down again, without doing so, upon G.'s saying that he had called to consult us, or rather to ask the opinion of my friend, about some official business which had occasioned a great deal of trouble.

"If it is any point requiring reflection," observed Dupin, as he forbore to enkindle the wick, "we shall examine it to better purpose in the dark."

"That is another of your odd notions," said the Prefect, who had a fashion of calling every thing "odd" that was beyond his comprehension, and thus lived amid an absolute legion of "oddities."

"Very true," said Dupin, as he supplied his visiter with a pipe, and rolled towards him a comfortable chair.

[1]PURLOINED: Stolen.
[2]NIL SAPIENTIAE ODIOSIUS ACUMINE NIMIO: "Nothing is more hateful to wisdom than too much cunning." (Latin)
[3]SENECA: Seneca the Younger (c. 3 BCE–65 CE), Roman philosopher and statesman. The epigraph, however, does not appear among Seneca's writings.
[4]MEERSCHAUM: A meerschaum pipe; a tobacco pipe.
[5]AU TROISIÈME: The third floor above the ground floor.
[6]MARIE ROGÊT: Poe refers to two previously published detective stories featuring Dupin, *The Murders in the Rue Morgue* (1841) and *The Mystery of Marie Rogêt* (1842).
[7]PREFECT: Chief.

"And what is the difficulty now?" I asked. "Nothing more in the assassination way, I hope?"

"Oh no; nothing of that nature. The fact is, the business is very simple indeed, and I make no doubt that we can manage it sufficiently well ourselves; but then I thought Dupin would like to hear the details of it, because it is so excessively *odd*."

"Simple and odd," said Dupin.

"Why, yes; and not exactly that, either. The fact is, we have all been a good deal puzzled because the affair *is* so simple, and yet baffles us altogether."

"Perhaps it is the very simplicity of the thing which puts you at fault," said my friend.

"What nonsense you *do* talk!" replied the Prefect, laughing heartily.

"Perhaps the mystery is a little *too* plain," said Dupin.

"Oh, good heavens! who ever heard of such an idea?"

"A little *too* self-evident."

"Ha! ha! ha!—ha! ha! ha!—ho! ho! ho!"—roared our visiter, profoundly amused, "oh, Dupin, you will be the death of me yet!"

"And what, after all, *is* the matter on hand?" I asked.

"Why, I will tell you," replied the Prefect, as he gave a long, steady, and contemplative puff, and settled himself in his chair. "I will tell you in a few words; but, before I begin, let me caution you that this is an affair demanding the greatest secrecy, and that I should most probably lose the position I now hold, were it known that I confided it to any one."

"Proceed," said I.

"Or not," said Dupin.

"Well, then; I have received personal information, from a very high quarter, that a certain document of the last importance, has been purloined from the royal apartments. The individual who purloined it is known; this beyond a doubt; he was seen to take it. It is known, also, that it still remains in his possession."

"How is this known?" asked Dupin.

"It is clearly inferred," replied the Prefect, "from the nature of the document, and from the nonappearance of certain results which would at once arise from its passing *out* of the robber's possession;—that is to say, from his employing it as he must design in the end to employ it."

"Be a little more explicit," I said.

"Well, I may venture so far as to say that the paper gives its holder a certain power in a certain quarter where such power is immensely valuable." The Prefect was fond of the cant[8] of diplomacy.

---

[8]CANT: Language, especially jargon or overly conventional forms of speech.

"Still I do not quite understand," said Dupin.

"No? Well; the disclosure of the document to a third person, who shall be nameless, would bring in question the honor of a personage of most exalted station; and this fact gives the holder of the document an ascendancy over the illustrious personage whose honor and peace are so jeopardized."

"But this ascendancy," I interposed, "would depend upon the robber's knowledge of the loser's knowledge of the robber. Who would dare—"

"The thief," said G., "is the Minister D——, who dares all things, those unbecoming as well as those becoming a man. The method of the theft was not less ingenious than bold. The document in question—a letter, to be frank—has been received by the personage robbed while alone in the royal *boudoir*.[9] During its perusal she was suddenly interrupted by the entrance of the other exalted personage from whom especially it was her wish to conceal it. After a hurried and vain endeavor to thrust it in a drawer, she was forced to place it, open as it was, upon a table. The address, however, was uppermost, and, the contents thus unexposed, the letter escaped notice. At this juncture enters the Minister D——. His lynx eye immediately perceives the paper, recognises the handwriting of the address, observes the confusion of the personage addressed, and fathoms her secret. After some business transactions, hurried through in his ordinary manner, he produces a letter somewhat similar to the one in question, opens it, pretends to read it, and then places it in close juxtaposition to the other. Again he converses, for some fifteen minutes, upon the public affairs. At length, in taking leave, he takes also from the table the letter to which he had no claim. Its rightful owner saw, but, of course, dared not call attention to the act, in the presence of the third personage who stood at her elbow. The minister decamped; leaving his own letter—one of no importance—upon the table."

"Here, then," said Dupin to me, "you have precisely what you demand to make the ascendancy complete—the robber's knowledge of the loser's knowledge of the robber."

"Yes," replied the Prefect; "and the power thus attained has, for some months past, been wielded, for political purposes, to a very dangerous extent. The personage robbed is more thoroughly convinced, every day, of the necessity of reclaiming her letter. But this, of course, cannot be done openly. In fine, driven to despair, she has committed the matter to me."

"Than whom," said Dupin, amid a perfect whirlwind of smoke, "no more sagacious agent could, I suppose, be desired, or even imagined."

[9]BOUDOIR: Private dressing room.

"You flatter me," replied the Prefect; "but it is possible that some such opinion may have been entertained."

"It is clear," said I, "as you observe, that the letter is still in possession of the minister; since it is this possession, and not any employment of the letter, which bestows the power. With the employment the power departs."

"True," said G.; "and upon this conviction I proceeded. My first care was to make thorough search of the minister's hotel[10]; and here my chief embarrassment lay in the necessity of searching without his knowledge. Beyond all things, I have been warned of the danger which would result from giving him reason to suspect our design."

"But," said I, "you are quite *au fait*[11] in these investigations. The Parisian police have done this thing often before."

"O yes; and for this reason I did not despair. The habits of the minister gave me, too, a great advantage. He is frequently absent from home all night. His servants are by no means numerous. They sleep at a distance from their master's apartment, and, being chiefly Neapolitans, are readily made drunk. I have keys, as you know, with which I can open any chamber or cabinet in Paris. For three months a night has not passed, during the greater part of which I have not been engaged, personally, in ransacking the D—— Hôtel. My honor is interested, and, to mention a great secret, the reward is enormous. So I did not abandon the search until I had become fully satisfied that the thief is a more astute man than myself. I fancy that I have investigated every nook and corner of the premises in which it is possible that the paper can be concealed."

"But is it not possible," I suggested, "that although the letter may be in possession of the minister, as it unquestionably is, he may have concealed it elsewhere than upon his own premises?"

"This is barely possible," said Dupin. "The present peculiar condition of affairs at court, and especially of those intrigues in which D—— is known to be involved, would render the instant availability of the document—its susceptibility of being produced at a moment's notice—a point of nearly equal importance with its possession."

"Its susceptibility of being produced?" said I.

"That is to say, of being *destroyed*," said Dupin.

"True," I observed; "the paper is clearly then upon the premises. As for its being upon the person of the minister, we may consider that as out of the question."

---

[10]HOTEL: A large private residence or town mansion.
[11]AU FAIT: Expert, up to date. (French)

"Entirely," said the Prefect. "He has been twice waylaid, as if by foot-pads,[12] and his person rigorously searched under my own inspection."

"You might have spared yourself this trouble," said Dupin. "D——, I presume, is not altogether a fool, and, if not, must have anticipated these waylayings, as a matter of course."

"Not *altogether* a fool," said G., "but then he's a poet, which I take to be only one remove from a fool."

"True," said Dupin, after a long and thoughtful whiff from his meer-schaum, "although I have been guilty of certain doggerel[13] myself."

"Suppose you detail," said I, "the particulars of your search."

"Why the fact is, we took our time, and we searched *every where*. I have had long experience in these affairs. I took the entire building, room by room; devoting the nights of a whole week to each. We examined, first, the furniture of each apartment. We opened every possible drawer; and I presume you know that, to a properly trained police agent, such a thing as a *secret* drawer is impossible. Any man is a dolt who permits a 'secret' drawer to escape him in a search of this kind. The thing is *so* plain. There is a certain amount of bulk—of space—to be accounted for in every cabinet. Then we have accurate rules. The fiftieth part of a line could not escape us. After the cabinets we took the chairs. The cushions we probed with the fine long needles you have seen me employ. From the tables we removed the tops."

"Why so?"

"Sometimes the top of a table, or other similarly arranged piece of fur-niture, is removed by the person wishing to conceal an article; then the leg is excavated, the article deposited within the cavity, and the top replaced. The bottoms and tops of bed-posts are employed in the same way."

"But could not the cavity be detected by sounding?" I asked.

"By no means, if, when the article is deposited, a sufficient wadding of cotton be placed around it. Besides, in our case, we were obliged to proceed without noise."

"But you could not have removed—you could not have taken to pieces *all* articles of furniture in which it would have been possible to make a deposit in the manner you mention. A letter may be compressed into a thin spiral roll, not differing much in shape or bulk from a large knitting-needle, and in this form it might be inserted into the rung of a chair, for example. You did not take to pieces all the chairs?"

"Certainly not; but we did better—we examined the rungs of every chair in the hotel, and, indeed, the jointings of every description of furniture,

---

[12]FOOTPADS: Robbers of pedestrians.
[13]DOGGEREL: Poor or tasteless poetry.

by the aid of a most powerful microscope. Had there been any traces of recent disturbance we should not have failed to detect it instantly. A single grain of gimlet-dust,[14] for example, would have been as obvious as an apple. Any disorder in the glueing—any unusual gaping in the joints—would have sufficed to insure detection."

"I presume you looked to the mirrors, between the boards and the plates, and you probed the beds and the bed-clothes, as well as the curtains and carpets."

"That of course; and when we had absolutely completed every particle of the furniture in this way, then we examined the house itself. We divided its entire surface into compartments, which we numbered, so that none might be missed; then we scrutinized each individual square inch throughout the premises, including the two houses immediately adjoining, with the microscope, as before."

"The two houses adjoining!" I exclaimed; "you must have had a great deal of trouble."

"We had; but the reward offered is prodigious."

"You include the *grounds* about the houses?"

"All the grounds are paved with brick. They gave us comparatively little trouble. We examined the moss between the bricks, and found it undisturbed."

"You looked among D——'s papers, of course, and into the books of the library?"

"Certainly; we opened every package and parcel; we not only opened every book, but we turned over every leaf in each volume, not contenting ourselves with a mere shake, according to the fashion of some of our police officers. We also measured the thickness of every book-*cover*, with the most accurate admeasurement, and applied to each the most jealous scrutiny of the microscope. Had any of the bindings been recently meddled with, it would have been utterly impossible that the fact should have escaped observation. Some five or six volumes, just from the hands of the binder, we carefully probed, longitudinally, with the needles."

"You explored the floors beneath the carpets?"

"Beyond doubt. We removed every carpet, and examined the boards with the microscope."

"And the paper on the walls?"

"Yes."

"You looked into the cellars?"

"We did."

---

[14]GIMLET-DUST: Sawdust left by a gimlet, a small drilling tool.

"Then," I said, "you have been making a miscalculation, and the letter is *not* upon the premises, as you suppose."

"I fear you are right there," said the Prefect. "And now, Dupin, what would you advise me to do?"

"To make a thorough re-search of the premises."

"That is absolutely needless," replied G——. "I am not more sure that I breathe than I am that the letter is not at the Hôtel."

"I have no better advice to give you," said Dupin. "You have, of course, an accurate description of the letter?"

"Oh, yes!"—And here the Prefect, producing a memorandum-book, proceeded to read aloud a minute account of the internal, and especially of the external appearance of the missing document. Soon after finishing the perusal of this description, he took his departure, more entirely depressed in spirits than I had ever known the good gentleman before.

In about a month afterwards he paid us another visit, and found us occupied very nearly as before. He took a pipe and a chair and entered into some ordinary conversation. At length I said,—

"Well, but G——, what of the purloined letter? I presume you have at last made up your mind that there is no such thing as overreaching the Minister?"

"Confound him, say I—yes; I made the reexamination, however, as Dupin suggested—but it was all labor lost, as I knew it would be."

"How much was the reward offered, did you say?" asked Dupin.

"Why, a very great deal—a *very* liberal reward—I don't like to say how much, precisely; but one thing I *will* say, that I would n't mind giving my individual check for fifty thousand francs to any one who could obtain me that letter. The fact is, it is becoming of more and more importance every day; and the reward has been lately doubled. If it were trebled, however, I could do no more than I have done."

"Why, yes," said Dupin, drawlingly, between the whiffs of his meerschaum, "I really—think, G——, you have not exerted yourself—to the utmost in this matter. You might—do a little more, I think, eh?"

"How?—in what way?"

"Why—puff, puff—you might—puff, puff—employ counsel in the matter, eh?—puff, puff, puff. Do you remember the story they tell of Abernethy?"[15]

"No; hang Abernethy!"

"To be sure! hang him and welcome. But, once upon a time, a certain rich miser conceived the design of spunging upon this Abernethy for a

[15]ABERNETHY: John Abernethy (1764–1831), British surgeon, professor, and lecturer known for his eccentric behavior.

medical opinion. Getting up, for this purpose, an ordinary conversation in a private company, he insinuated his case to the physician, as that of an imaginary individual.

"'We will suppose,' said the miser, 'that his symptoms are such and such; now, doctor, what would *you* have directed him to take?'

"'Take!' said Abernethy, 'why, take *advice*, to be sure.'"

"But," said the Prefect, a little discomposed, "I am *perfectly* willing to take advice, and to pay for it. I would *really* give fifty thousand francs to any one who would aid me in the matter."

"In that case," replied Dupin, opening a drawer, and producing a check-book, "you may as well fill me up a check for the amount mentioned. When you have signed it, I will hand you the letter."

I was astounded. The Prefect appeared absolutely thunder-stricken. For some minutes he remained speechless and motionless, looking incredulously at my friend with open mouth, and eyes that seemed starting from their sockets; then, apparently recovering himself in some measure, he seized a pen, and after several pauses and vacant stares, finally filled up and signed a check for fifty thousand francs, and handed it across the table to Dupin. The latter examined it carefully and deposited it in his pocket-book; then, unlocking an *escritoire*,[16] took thence a letter and gave it to the Prefect. This functionary grasped it in a perfect agony of joy, opened it with a trembling hand, cast a rapid glance at its contents, and then, scrambling and struggling to the door, rushed at length unceremoniously from the room and from the house, without having uttered a syllable since Dupin had requested him to fill up the check.

When he had gone, my friend entered into some explanations.

"The Parisian police," he said, "are exceedingly able in their way. They are persevering, ingenious, cunning, and thoroughly versed in the knowledge which their duties seem chiefly to demand. Thus, when G—— detailed to us his mode of searching the premises at the Hôtel D——, I felt entire confidence in his having made a satisfactory investigation—so far as his labors extended."

"So far as his labors extended?" said I.

"Yes," said Dupin. "The measures adopted were not only the best of their kind, but carried out to absolute perfection. Had the letter been deposited within the range of their search, these fellows would, beyond a question, have found it."

I merely laughed—but he seemed quite serious in all that he said.

[16]ESCRITOIRE: Writing desk.

"The measures, then," he continued, "were good in their kind, and well executed; their defect lay in their being inapplicable to the case, and to the man. A certain set of highly ingenious resources are, with the Prefect, a sort of Procrustean bed,[17] to which he forcibly adapts his designs. But he perpetually errs by being too deep or too shallow, for the matter in hand; and many a schoolboy is a better reasoner than he. I knew one about eight years of age, whose success at guessing in the game of 'even and odd' attracted universal admiration. This game is simple, and is played with marbles. One player holds in his hand a number of these toys, and demands of another whether that number is even or odd. If the guess is right, the guesser wins one; if wrong, he loses one. The boy to whom I allude won all the marbles of the school. Of course he had some principle of guessing; and this lay in mere observation and admeasurement of the astuteness of his opponents. For example, an arrant simpleton is his opponent, and, holding up his closed hand, asks, 'are they even or odd?' Our schoolboy replies, 'odd,' and loses; but upon the second trial he wins, for he then says to himself, 'the simpleton had them even upon the first trial, and his amount of cunning is just sufficient to make him have them odd upon the second; I will therefore guess odd;'—he guesses odd, and wins. Now, with a simpleton a degree above the first, he would have reasoned thus: 'This fellow finds that in the first instance I guessed odd, and, in the second, he will propose to himself upon the first impulse, a simple variation from even to odd, as did the first simpleton; but then a second thought will suggest that this is too simple a variation, and finally he will decide upon putting it even as before. I will therefore guess even;'—he guesses even, and wins. Now this mode of reasoning in the schoolboy, whom his fellows termed 'lucky,'—what, in its last analysis, is it?"

"It is merely," I said, "an identification of the reasoner's intellect with that of his opponent."

"It is," said Dupin; "and, upon inquiring of the boy by what means he effected the *thorough* identification in which his success consisted, I received answer as follows: 'When I wish to find out how wise, or how stupid, or how good, or how wicked is any one, or what are his thoughts at the moment, I fashion the expression of my face, as accurately as possible, in accordance with the expression of his, and then wait to see what thoughts or sentiments arise in my mind or heart, as if to match

---

[17]PROCRUSTEAN BED: Procrustes was a legendary thief from Attica who placed his victims on an iron bed. If they were too tall for it, he cut off their legs; if they were too short, he stretched their bodies until they fit. Hence, a Procrustean bed refers to a way of thinking in which facts are forcibly made to fit an idea or hypothesis.

or correspond with the expression.' This response of the schoolboy lies at the bottom of all the spurious profundity which has been attributed to Rochefoucauld, to La Bruyère, to Machiavelli, and to Campanella."[18]

"And the identification," I said, "of the reasoner's intellect with that of his opponent, depends, if I understand you aright, upon the accuracy with which the opponent's intellect is admeasured."

"For its practical value it depends upon this," replied Dupin; "and the Prefect and his cohort fail so frequently, first, by default of this identification, and, secondly, by ill-admeasurement, or rather through non-admeasurement, of the intellect with which they are engaged. They consider only their *own* ideas of ingenuity; and, in searching for anything hidden, advert only to the modes in which *they* would have hidden it. They are right in this much—that their own ingenuity is a faithful representative of that of *the mass;* but when the cunning of the individual felon is diverse in character from their own, the felon foils them, of course. This always happens when it is above their own, and very usually when it is below. They have no variation of principle in their investigations; at best, when urged by some unusual emergency—by some extraordinary reward—they extend or exaggerate their old modes of *practice*, without touching their principles. What, for example, in this case of D——, has been done to vary the principle of action? What is all this boring, and probing, and sounding, and scrutinizing with the microscope, and dividing the surface of the building into registered square inches— what is it all but an exaggeration *of the application* of the one principle or set of principles of search, which are based upon the one set of notions regarding human ingenuity, to which the Prefect, in the long routine of his duty, has been accustomed? Do you not see he has taken it for granted that all men proceed to conceal a letter,—not exactly in a gimlet-hole bored in a chair-leg—but, at least, in *some* out-of-the-way hole or corner suggested by the same tenor of thought which would urge a man to secrete a letter in a gimlet-hole bored in a chair-leg? And do you not see also, that such *recherchés*[18] nooks for concealment are adapted only for ordinary occasions, and would be adopted only by ordinary intellects; for, in all cases of concealment, a disposal of the article concealed—a disposal of it in this *recherché* manner,—is, in the very first instance, presumable and presumed; and thus its discovery depends, not at all upon the acumen, but altogether upon the mere care, patience, and determination of the

[18]ROCHEFOUCAULD . . . CAMPANELLA: A disparate group of moralists and politcal philosophers.
[19]RECHERCHÉS: Out of the ordinary. (French)

seekers; and where the case is of importance—or, what amounts to the same thing in the policial eyes, when the reward is of magnitude,—the qualities in question have *never* been known to fail. You will now understand what I meant in suggesting that, had the purloined letter been hidden any where within the limits of the Prefect's examination—in other words, had the principle of its concealment been comprehended within the principles of the Prefect—its discovery would have been a matter altogether beyond question. This functionary, however, has been thoroughly mystified; and the remote source of his defeat lies in the supposition that the Minister is a fool, because he has acquired renown as a poet. All fools are poets; this the Prefect *feels;* and he is merely guilty of a *non distributio medii*[20] in thence inferring that all poets are fools."

"But is this really the poet?" I asked. "There are two brothers, I know; and both have attained reputation in letters. The Minister I believe has written learnedly on the Differential Calculus. He is a mathematician, and no poet."

"You are mistaken; I know him well; he is both. As poet *and* mathematician, he would reason well; as mere mathematician, he could not have reasoned at all, and thus would have been at the mercy of the Prefect."

"You surprise me," I said, "by these opinions, which have been contradicted by the voice of the world. You do not mean to set at naught the well-digested idea of centuries. The mathematical reason has long been regarded as *the* reason *par excellence*."

"'*Il y a à parier,*'" replied Dupin, quoting from Chamfort,[21] "'*que toute idée publique, toute convention reçue, est une sottise, car elle a convenu au plus grand nombre.*'[22] The mathematicians, I grant you, have done their best to promulgate the popular error to which you allude, and which is none the less an error for its promulgation as truth. With an art worthy a better cause, for example, they have insinuated the term 'analysis' into application to algebra. The French are the originators of this particular deception; but if a term is of any importance—if words derive any value from applicability—then 'analysis' conveys 'algebra' about as much as, in Latin, '*ambitus*' implies 'ambition,' '*religio*' 'religion,' or '*homines honesti,*' a set of *honorable* men."

[20]NON DISTRIBUTIO MEDII: A fallacy in logic due to a faulty syllogism in which the premise fails to share a middle term that leads to a true conclusion. In this case, Dupin means that the Prefect does not allow for the possibility that some poets are *not* fools.
[21]CHAMFORT: Sebastian Roch Nicolas Chamfort (1740–1794), a French writer best known for *Maximes et Pensées*, a book of maxims and epigrams.
[22]IL Y A À PARIER...QUE TOUTE IDÉE PUBLIQUE...PLUS GRAND NOMBRE: "Odds are that all popular ideas, all received wisdom, is stupid because it suits the greatest number." (French)

"You have a quarrel on hand, I see," said I, "with some of the algebraists of Paris; but proceed."

"I dispute the availability, and thus the value, of that reason which is cultivated in any especial form other than the abstractly logical. I dispute, in particular, the reason educed by mathematical study. The mathematics are the science of form and quantity; mathematical reasoning is merely logic applied to observation upon form and quantity. The great error lies in supposing that even the truths of what is called *pure* algebra, are abstract or general truths. And this error is so egregious that I am confounded at the universality with which it has been received. Mathematical axioms are *not* axioms of general truth. What is true of *relation*—of form and quantity—is often grossly false in regard to morals, for example. In this latter science it is very usually *un*true that the aggregated parts are equal to the whole. In chemistry also the axiom fails. In the consideration of motive it fails; for two motives, each of a given value, have not, necessarily, a value when united, equal to the sum of their values apart. There are numerous other mathematical truths which are only truths within the limits of *relation*. But the mathematician argues, from his *finite truths*, through habit, as if they were of an absolutely general applicability—as the world indeed imagines them to be. Bryant,[23] in his very learned 'Mythology,' mentions an analogous source of error, when he says that 'although the Pagan fables are not believed, yet we forget ourselves continually, and make inferences from them as existing realities.' With the algebraists, however, who are Pagans themselves, the 'Pagan fables' *are* believed, and the inferences are made, not so much through lapse of memory, as through an unaccountable addling of the brains. In short, I never yet encountered the mere mathematician who could be trusted out of equal roots, or one who did not clandestinely hold it as a point of his faith that $x^2 + px$ was absolutely and unconditionally equal to q. Say to one of these gentlemen, by way of experiment, if you please, that you believe occasions may occur where $x^2 + px$ is *not* altogether equal to q, and, having made him understand what you mean, get out of his reach as speedily as convenient, for, beyond doubt, he will endeavor to knock you down.

"I mean to say," continued Dupin, while I merely laughed at his last observations, "that if the Minister had been no more than a mathematician, the Prefect would have been under no necessity of giving me this check. I knew him, however, as both mathematician and poet, and my

[23]BRYANT: Jacob Bryant (1715–1804), English mythologist who wrote *A New System, or an Analysis of Antient Mythology* (1774).

measures were adapted to his capacity, with reference to the circumstances by which he was surrounded. I knew him as a courtier, too, and as a bold *intriguant*.[24] Such a man, I considered, could not fail to be aware of the ordinary policial modes of action. He could not have failed to anticipate—and events have proved that he did not fail to anticipate—the waylayings to which he was subjected. He must have foreseen, I reflected, the secret investigations of his premises. His frequent absences from home at night, which were hailed by the Prefect as certain aids to his success, I regarded only as *ruses*, to afford opportunity for thorough search to the police, and thus the sooner to impress them with the conviction to which G——, in fact, did finally arrive—the conviction that the letter was not upon the premises. I felt, also, that the whole train of thought, which I was at some pains in detailing to you just now, concerning the invariable principle of policial action in searches for articles concealed—I felt that this whole train of thought would necessarily pass through the mind of the Minister. It would imperatively lead him to despise all the ordinary *nooks* of concealment. *He* could not, I reflected, be so weak as not to see that the most intricate and remote recess of his hotel would be as open as his commonest closets to the eyes, to the probes, to the gimlets, and to the microscopes of the Prefect. I saw, in fine, that he would be driven, as a matter of course, to *simplicity*, if not deliberately induced to it as a matter of choice. You will remember, perhaps, how desperately the Prefect laughed when I suggested, upon our first interview, that it was just possible this mystery troubled him so much on account of its being so *very* self-evident."

"Yes," said I, "I remember his merriment well. I really thought he would have fallen into convulsions."

"The material world," continued Dupin, "abounds with very strict analogies to the immaterial; and thus some color of truth has been given to the rhetorical dogma, that metaphor, or simile, may be made to strengthen an argument, as well as to embellish a description. The principle of the *vis inertiae*,[25] for example, seems to be identical in physics and metaphysics. It is not more true in the former, that a large body is with more difficulty set in motion than a smaller one, and that its subsequent *momentum* is commensurate with this difficulty, than it is, in the latter, that intellects of the vaster capacity, while more forcible, more constant, and more eventful in their movements than those of inferior grade, are yet the less readily moved, and more embarrassed and full

[24]INTRIGUANT: Schemer, plotter.
[25]VIS INERTIAE: "The power of inertia" (Latin); the resistance offered by matter to any force that tries to alter its state at rest or in motion.

of hesitation in the first few steps of their progress. Again: have you ever noticed which of the street signs, over the shop doors, are the most attractive of attention?"

"I have never given the matter a thought," I said.

"There is a game of puzzles," he resumed, "which is played upon a map. One party playing requires another to find a given word—the name of town, river, state or empire—any word, in short, upon the motley and perplexed surface of the chart. A novice in the game generally seeks to embarrass his opponents by giving them the most minutely lettered names; but the adept selects such words as stretch, in large characters, from one end of the chart to the other. These, like the over-largely lettered signs and placards of the street, escape observation by dint of being excessively obvious; and here the physical oversight is precisely analogous with the moral inapprehension by which the intellect suffers to pass unnoticed those considerations which are too obtrusively and too palpably self-evident. But this is a point, it appears, somewhat above or beneath the understanding of the Prefect. He never once thought it probable, or possible, that the Minister had deposited the letter immediately beneath the nose of the whole world, by way of best preventing any portion of that world from perceiving it.

"But the more I reflected upon the daring, dashing, and discriminating ingenuity of D——; upon the fact that the document must always have been *at hand*, if he intended to use it to good purpose; and upon the decisive evidence, obtained by the Prefect, that it was not hidden within the limits of that dignitary's ordinary search—the more satisfied I became that, to conceal this letter, the Minister had resorted to the comprehensive and sagacious expedient of not attempting to conceal it at all.

"Full of these ideas, I prepared myself with a pair of green spectacles, and called one fine morning, quite by accident, at the Ministerial hotel. I found D—— at home, yawning, lounging, and dawdling, as usual, and pretending to be in the last extremity of *ennui*.[26] He is, perhaps, the most really energetic human being now alive—but that is only when nobody sees him.

"To be even with him, I complained of my weak eyes, and lamented the necessity of the spectacles, under cover of which I cautiously and thoroughly surveyed the apartment, while seemingly intent only upon the conversation of my host.

"I paid special attention to a large writing-table near which he sat, and upon which lay confusedly, some miscellaneous letters and other papers, with one or two musical instruments and a few books. Here,

[26]ENNUI: Boredom. (French)

however, after a long and very deliberate scrutiny, I saw nothing to excite particular suspicion.

"At length my eyes, in going the circuit of the room, fell upon a trumpery[27] fillagree card-rack of pasteboard, that hung dangling by a dirty blue ribbon, from a little brass knob just beneath the middle of the mantelpiece. In this rack, which had three or four compartments, were five or six visiting cards and a solitary letter. This last was much soiled and crumpled. It was torn nearly in two, across the middle—as if a design, in the first instance, to tear it entirely up as worthless, had been altered, or stayed, in the second. It had a large black seal, bearing the D—— cipher *very* conspicuously, and was addressed, in a diminutive female hand, to D——, the minister, himself. It was thrust carelessly, and even, as it seemed, contemptuously, into one of the upper divisions of the rack.

"No sooner had I glanced at this letter, than I concluded it to be that of which I was in search. To be sure, it was, to all appearance, radically different from the one of which the Prefect had read us so minute a description. Here the seal was large and black, with the D—— cipher; there it was small and red, with the ducal arms of the S—— family. Here, the address, to the Minister, was diminutive and feminine; there the superscription, to a certain royal personage, was markedly bold and decided; the size alone formed a point of correspondence. But, then, the *radicalness* of these differences, which was excessive; the dirt; the soiled and torn condition of the paper, so inconsistent with the *true* methodical habits of D——, and so suggestive of a design to delude the beholder into an idea of the worthlessness of the document; these things, together with the hyperobtrusive situation of this document, full in the view of every visitor, and thus exactly in accordance with the conclusions to which I had previously arrived; these things, I say, were strongly corroborative of suspicion, in one who came with the intention to suspect.

"I protracted my visit as long as possible, and, while I maintained a most animated discussion with the Minister, on a topic which I knew well had never failed to interest and excite him, I kept my attention really riveted upon the letter. In this examination, I committed to memory its external appearance and arrangement in the rack; and also fell, at length, upon a discovery which set at rest whatever trivial doubt I might have entertained. In scrutinizing the edges of the paper, I observed them to be more *chafed* than seemed necessary. They presented the *broken* appearance which is manifested when a stiff paper, having been

---

[27]TRUMPERY: Showy and cheap; worthless.

once folded and pressed with a folder, is refolded in a reversed direction, in the same creases or edges which had formed the original fold. This discovery was sufficient. It was clear to me that the letter had been turned, as a glove, inside out, re-directed, and re-sealed. I bade the Minister good morning, and took my departure at once, leaving a gold snuff-box upon the table.

"The next morning I called for the snuff-box, when we resumed, quite eagerly, the conversation of the preceding day. While thus engaged, however, a loud report, as if of a pistol, was heard immediately beneath the windows of the hotel, and was succeeded by a series of fearful screams, and the shoutings of a mob. D—— rushed to a casement, threw it open, and looked out. In the meantime, I stepped to the card-rack, took the letter, put it in my pocket, and replaced it by a *fac-simile*, (so far as regards externals,) which I had carefully prepared at my lodgings; imitating the D—— cipher, very readily, by means of a seal formed of bread.

"The disturbance in the street had been occasioned by the frantic behavior of a man with a musket. He had fired it among a crowd of women and children. It proved, however, to have been without ball, and the fellow was suffered to go his way as a lunatic or a drunkard. When he had gone, D—— came from the window, whither I had followed him immediately upon securing the object in view. Soon afterwards I bade him farewell. The pretended lunatic was a man in my own pay."

"But what purpose had you," I asked, "in replacing the letter by a *fac-simile?* Would it not have been better, at the first visit, to have seized it openly, and departed?"

"D——," replied Dupin, "is a desperate man, and a man of nerve. His hotel, too, is not without attendants devoted to his interests. Had I made the wild attempt you suggest, I might never have left the Ministerial presence alive. The good people of Paris might have heard of me no more. But I had an object apart from these considerations. You know my political prepossessions. In this matter, I act as a partisan of the lady concerned. For eighteen months the Minister has had her in his power. She has now him in hers; since, being unaware that the letter is not in his possession, he will proceed with his exactions as if it was. Thus will he inevitably commit himself, at once, to his political destruction. His downfall, too, will not be more precipitate[28] than awkward. It is all very well to talk about the *facilis descensus Averni*[29]; but in all kinds of climbing, as Catalani[30] said of singing, it is far more easy to get up than to come down. In the present instance I have no sympathy—at least no

[28]PRECIPITATE: Ruinous; of a sudden fall from a high position.
[29]FACILIS DESCENSUS AVERNI: "The decent to Hell is easy." (Virgil's *Aeneid*)
[30]CATALANI: Italian soprano Angelica Catalani (1779–1849).

pity—for him who descends. He is that *monstrum horrendum*,[31] an unprincipled man of genius. I confess, however, that I should like very well to know the precise character of his thoughts, when, being defied by her whom the Prefect terms 'a certain personage,' he is reduced to opening the letter which I left for him in the card-rack.

"How? did you put any thing particular in it?"

"Why—it did not seem altogether right to leave the interior blank—that would have been insulting. D——, at Vienna once, did me an evil turn, which I told him, quite good-humoredly, that I should remember. So, as I knew he would feel some curiosity in regard to the identity of the person who had outwitted him, I thought it a pity not to give him a clue. He is well acquainted with my MS., and I just copied into the middle of the blank sheet the words—

——*Un dessein si funeste,*
S'il n'est digne d'Atrée, est digne de Thyeste.[32]

They are to be found in Crébillon's 'Atrée.'"[33]

[1844]

The Philosophy of Composition

Charles Dickens,[1] in a note[2] now lying before me, alluding to an examination I once made of the mechanism of "Barnaby Rudge," says—"By the way, are you aware that Godwin wrote his 'Caleb Williams'[3] backwards?

---

[31]MONSTRUM HORRENDUM: Dreadful monstrosity. (Latin)
[32]UN DESSEIN SI FUNESTE, S'IL N'EST DIGNE ATRÉE, EST DIGNE DE THYESTE: "A scheme so deadly, if not worthy of Atreus, is worthy of Thyestes." (French)
[32]THEY ARE TO BE FOUND IN CRÉBILLON'S ATRÉE: Prosper Jolyot de Crébillon (1674–1762), a French dramatist who wrote *Atrée et Thyeste* (1707), based on the Greek story of the rival brothers Atreus and Thyestes, in which Atreus, in retaliation for his brother's seduction of his wife and theft of the throne of Mycenae, murders Thyestes's sons and serves them to him at a feast.
[1]CHARLES DICKENS: Prolific English novelist Charles Dickens (1812–1870), whose published works at the time Poe writes included *Oliver Twist* (1838), *Nicholas Nickleby* (1839), and *A Christmas Carol* (1843).
[2]NOTE: Dated March 6, 1842, printed in Dickens's *Letters* 3.106–107.
[3]GODWIN WROTE HIS 'CALEB WILLIAMS' BACKWARDS: William Godwin (1756–1836) was an English writer and political philosopher who wrote his novel, *Adventures of Caleb Williams* (1794) backwards—that is, he completed the third volume before the first. "I formed a conception of a book of fictitious adventure, that should in some way be distinguished by a very powerful interest. Pursuing this idea, I invented first the third volume of my tale, then the second, and last of all the first" (Preface to *Caleb Williams*, 1832).

He first involved his hero in a web of difficulties, forming the second volume, and then, for the first, cast about him for some mode of accounting for what had been done."

I cannot think this the *precise* mode of procedure on the part of Godwin—and indeed what he himself acknowledges, is not altogether in accordance with Mr. Dickens' idea—but the author of "Caleb Williams" was too good an artist not to perceive the advantage derivable from at least a somewhat similar process. Nothing is more clear than that every plot, worth the name, must be elaborated to its *dénouement*[4] before any thing be attempted with the pen. It is only with the *dénouement* constantly in view that we can give a plot its indispensable air of consequence, or causation, by making the incidents, and especially the tone at all points, tend to the development of the intention.

There is a radical error, I think, in the usual mode of constructing a story. Either history affords a thesis—or one is suggested by an incident of the day—or, at best, the author sets himself to work in the combination of striking events to form merely the basis of his narrative—designing, generally, to fill in with description, dialogue, or autorial comment, whatever crevices of fact, or action, may, from page to page, render themselves apparent.

I prefer commencing with the consideration of an *effect*. Keeping originality *always* in view—for he is false to himself who ventures to dispense with so obvious and so easily attainable a source of interest—I say to myself, in the first place, "Of the innumerable effects, or impressions, of which the heart, the intellect, or (more generally) the soul is susceptible, what one shall I, on the present occasion, select?" Having chosen a novel, first, and secondly a vivid effect, I consider whether it can best be wrought by incident or tone—whether by ordinary incidents and peculiar tone, or the converse, or by peculiarity both of incident and tone—afterward looking about me (or rather within) for such combinations of event, or tone, as shall best aid me in the construction of the effect.

I have often thought how interesting a magazine paper might be written by any author who would—that is to say, who could—detail, step by step, the processes by which any one of his compositions attained its ultimate point of completion. Why such a paper has never been given to the world, I am much at a loss to say—but, perhaps, the autorial vanity has had more to do with the omission than any one other cause. Most writers—poets in especial—prefer having it understood that they compose

[4]DÉNOUEMENT: The final unraveling of the complications of the plot in a dramatic work.

by a species of fine frenzy[5]—an ecstatic intuition—and would positively shudder at letting the public take a peep behind the scenes, at the elaborate and vacillating crudities of thought—at the true purposes seized only at the last moment—at the innumerable glimpses of idea that arrived not at the maturity of full view—at the fully matured fancies discarded in despair as unmanageable—at the cautious selections and rejections—at the painful erasures and interpolations—in a word, at the wheels and pinions—the tackle for scene-shifting—the step-ladders and demon-traps—the cock's feathers, the red paint and the black patches, which, in ninety-nine cases out of the hundred, constitute the properties of the literary *histrio*.[6]

I am aware, on the other hand, that the case is by no means common, in which an author is at all in condition to retrace the steps by which his conclusions have been attained. In general, suggestions, having arisen pell-mell,[7] are pursued and forgotten in a similar manner.

For my own part, I have neither sympathy with the repugnance alluded to, nor, at any time, the least difficulty in recalling to mind the progressive steps of any of my compositions; and, since the interest of an analysis, or reconstruction, such as I have considered a *desideratum*,[8] is quite independent of any real or fancied interest in the thing analyzed, it will not be regarded as a breach of decorum on my part to show the *modus operandi*[9] by which some one of my own works was put together. I select "The Raven," as the most generally known. It is my design to render it manifest that no one point in its composition is referrible either to accident or intuition—that the work proceeded, step by step, to its completion with the precision and rigid consequence of a mathematical problem.

Let us dismiss, as irrelevant to the poem *per se*, the circumstance—or say the necessity—which, in the first place, gave rise to the intention of composing *a* poem that should suit at once the popular and the critical taste.

We commence, then, with this intention.

The initial consideration was that of extent. If any literary work is too long to be read at one sitting, we must be content to dispense with

---

[5]FINE FRENZY: A reference to Theseus's description of a poet in Shakespeare's *Midsummer Night's Dream*: "The poet's eye, in a fine frenzy rolling, / Doth glance from heaven to earth, from earth to heaven / And as imagination bodies forth / The forms of things unknown, the poet's pen / Turns them to shapes and gives to airy nothing / A local habitation and a name" (Act 5, Scene 1).
[6]HISTRIO: Artist. (Latin)
[7]PELL-MELL: A confused mingling; without order or method.
[8]DESIDERATUM: Something desired or longed for. (Latin)
[9]MODUS OPERANDI: Method of procedure. (Latin)

the immensely important effect derivable from unity of impression—for, if two sittings be required, the affairs of the world interfere, and every thing like totality is at once destroyed. But since, *ceteris paribus*,[10] no poet can afford to dispense with *any thing* that may advance his design, it but remains to be seen whether there is, in extent, any advantage to counterbalance the loss of unity which attends it. Here I say no, at once. What we term a long poem is, in fact, merely a succession of brief ones— that is to say, of brief poetical effects. It is needless to demonstrate that a poem is such, only inasmuch as it intensely excites, by elevating, the soul; and all intense excitements are, through a psychal necessity, brief. For this reason, at least one half of the "Paradise Lost"[11] is essentially prose—a succession of poetical excitements interspersed, *inevitably*, with corresponding depressions—the whole being deprived, through the extremeness of its length, of the vastly important artistic element, total- ity, or unity, of effect.

It appears evident, then, that there is a distinct limit, as regards length, to all works of literary art—the limit of a single sitting—and that, although in certain classes of prose composition, such as "Robinson Crusoe,"[12] (demanding no unity,) this limit may be advantageously over- passed, it can never properly be overpassed in a poem. Within this limit, the extent of a poem may be made to bear mathematical relation to its merit—in other words, to the excitement or elevation—again in other words, to the degree of the true poetical effect which it is capable of inducing; for it is clear that the brevity must be in direct ratio of the inten- sity of the intended effect:—this, with one proviso—that a certain degree of duration is absolutely requisite for the production of any effect at all.

Holding in view these considerations, as well as that degree of excitement which I deemed not above the popular, while not below the critical, taste, I reached at once what I conceived the proper *length* for my intended poem—a length of about one hundred lines. It is, in fact, a hundred and eight.

My next thought concerned the choice of an impression, or effect, to be conveyed: and here I may as well observe that, throughout the con- struction, I kept steadily in view the design of rendering the work *universally* appreciable. I should be carried too far out of my immediate

---

[10]CETERIS PARIBUS: Other things being equal. (Latin)
[11]PARADISE LOST: The epic work first published in 1667 and published in twelve books in 1674 by English poet John Milton (1608–1674).
[12]ROBINSON CRUSOE: A novel published in 1719 by the English author Daniel Defoe (1660?–1731). The title character, Robinson Crusoe, is an English sailor who is shipwrecked on a deserted island. He survives on the island for 28 years before he is rescued.

topic were I to demonstrate a point upon which I have repeatedly insisted, and which, with the poetical, stands not in the slightest need of demonstration—the point, I mean, that Beauty is the sole legitimate province of the poem. A few words, however, in elucidation of my real meaning, which some of my friends have evinced a disposition to misrepresent. That pleasure which is at once the most intense, the most elevating, and the most pure, is, I believe, found in the contemplation of the beautiful. When, indeed, men speak of Beauty, they mean, precisely, not a quality, as is supposed, but an effect—they refer, in short, just to that intense and pure elevation of *soul*—*not* of intellect, or of heart—upon which I have commented, and which is experienced in consequence of contemplating "the beautiful." Now I designate Beauty as the province of the poem, merely because it is an obvious rule of Art that effects should be made to spring from direct causes—that objects should be attained through means best adapted for their attainment—no one as yet having been weak enough to deny that the peculiar elevation alluded to, is *most readily* attained in the poem. Now the object, Truth, or the satisfaction of the intellect, and the object, Passion, or the excitement of the heart, are, although attainable, to a certain extent, in poetry, far more readily attainable in prose. Truth, in fact, demands a precision, and Passion, a *homeliness* (the truly passionate will comprehend me) which are absolutely antagonistic to that Beauty which, I maintain, is the excitement, or pleasurable elevation, of the soul. It by no means follows from any thing here said, that passion, or even truth, may not be introduced, and even profitably introduced, into a poem—for they may serve in elucidation, or aid the general effect, as do discords in music, by contrast—but the true artist will always contrive, first, to tone them into proper subservience to the predominant aim, and, secondly, to enveil them, as far as possible, in that Beauty which is the atmosphere and the essence of the poem.

Regarding, then, Beauty as my province, my next question referred to the *tone* of its highest manifestation—and all experience has shown that this tone is one of *sadness*. Beauty of whatever kind, in its supreme development, invariably excites the sensitive soul to tears. Melancholy is thus the most legitimate of all the poetical tones.

The length, the province, and the tone, being thus determined, I betook myself to ordinary induction, with the view of obtaining some artistic piquancy which might serve me as a key-note in the construction of the poem—some pivot upon which the whole structure might turn. In carefully thinking over all the usual artistic effects—or more properly *points*, in the theatrical sense—I did not fail to perceive immediately that no one had been so universally employed as that of the *refrain*. The universality of its employment sufficed to assure me of its intrinsic value, and spared me the necessity of submitting it to analysis. I considered it, however, with regard to its susceptibility of improvement, and soon saw it to be in a primitive condition. As commonly used, the *refrain*, or burden, not only is limited to lyric verse, but depends for its impression upon the force of monotone—both in sound and thought. The pleasure is deduced solely from the sense of identity—of repetition. I resolved to diversify, and so vastly heighten, the effect, by adhering, in general, to the monotone of sound, while I continually varied that of thought; that is to say, I determined to produce continuously novel effects, by the variation *of the application* of the *refrain*—the *refrain* itself remaining, for the most part, unvaried.

These points being settled, I next bethought me of the *nature* of my *refrain*. Since its application was to be repeatedly varied, it was clear that the *refrain* itself must be brief, for there would have been an insurmountable difficulty in frequent variations of application in any sentence of length. In proportion to the brevity of the sentence, would, of course, be the facility of the variation. This led me at once to a single word as the best *refrain*.

The question now arose as to the *character* of the word. Having made up my mind to a *refrain*, the division of the poem into stanzas was, of course, a corollary: the *refrain* forming the close to each stanza. That such a close, to have force, must be sonorous and susceptible of protracted emphasis, admitted no doubt: and these considerations inevitably led me to the long *o* as the most sonorous vowel, in connection with *r* as the most producible consonant.

The sound of the *refrain* being thus determined, it became necessary to select a word embodying this sound, and at the same time in the fullest possible keeping with that melancholy which I had predetermined as the tone of the poem. In such a search it would have been absolutely impossible to overlook the word "Nevermore." In fact, it was the very first which presented itself.

The next *desideratum* was a pretext for the continuous use of the one word "nevermore." In observing the difficulty which I at once found in inventing a sufficiently plausible reason for its continuous repetition, I did not fail to perceive that this difficulty arose solely from the preassumption that the word was to be so continuously or monotonously spoken by *a human* being—I did not fail to perceive, in short, that the difficulty lay in the reconciliation of this monotony with the exercise of reason on the part of the creature repeating the word. Here, then, immediately arose the idea of a *non*-reasoning creature capable of speech; and, very naturally, a parrot, in the first instance, suggested itself, but was superseded forthwith by a Raven, as equally capable of speech, and infinitely more in keeping with the intended *tone*.

I had now gone so far as the conception of a Raven—the bird of ill omen—monotonously repeating the one word, "Nevermore," at the conclusion of each stanza, in a poem of melancholy tone, and in length about one hundred lines. Now, never losing sight of the object *supremeness*, or perfection, at all points, I asked myself—"Of all melancholy topics, what, according to the *universal* understanding of mankind, is the *most* melancholy?" Death—was the obvious reply. "And when," I said, "is this most melancholy of topics most poetical?" From what I have already explained at some length, the answer, here also, is obvious—"When it most closely allies itself to *Beauty*: the death, then, of a beautiful woman is, unquestionably, the most poetical topic in the world—and equally is it beyond doubt that the lips best suited for such topic are those of a bereaved lover."

I had now to combine the two ideas, of a lover lamenting his deceased mistress and a Raven continuously repeating the word "Nevermore"—I had to combine these, bearing in mind my design of varying, at every turn, the *application* of the word repeated; but the only intelligible model of such combination is that of imagining the Raven employing the word in answer to the queries of the lover. And here it was that I saw at once the opportunity afforded for the effect on which I had been depending—that is to say, the effect of the *variation of application*. I saw that I could make the first query propounded by the lover—the first query to which the Raven should reply "Nevermore"—that I could make this first query a commonplace one—the second less so—the third still less, and so on—until at length the lover, startled from his original *nonchalance* by the melancholy character of the word itself—by its frequent repetition—and by a consideration of the ominous reputation of the fowl that uttered it—is at length excited to superstition, and wildly propounds queries of a far different character—queries whose solution he has passionately at heart—propounds them half in superstition and half in that species of despair which delights in self-torture—propounds them not altogether because he believes in the prophetic or demoniac character of the bird (which, reason assures him, is merely repeating a lesson learned by rote) but because he experiences a phrenzied pleasure in so modeling his questions as to receive from the *expected* "Nevermore" the most delicious because the most intolerable of sorrow. Perceiving the opportunity thus afforded me—or, more strictly, thus forced upon me in the progress of the construction—I first established in mind the climax, or concluding query—that to which "Nevermore" should be in the last place an answer—that in reply to which this word "Nevermore" should involve the utmost conceivable amount of sorrow and despair.

Here then the poem may be said to have its beginning—at the end, where all works of art should begin—for it was here, at this point of my preconsiderations, that I first put pen to paper in the composition of the stanza:

> *"Prophet," said I, "thing of evil! prophet still if bird or devil!*
> *By that heaven that bends above us—by that God we both adore,*
> *Tell this soul with sorrow laden, if within the distant Aidenn,*
> *It shall clasp a sainted maiden whom the angels name Lenore—*
> *Clasp a rare and radiant maiden whom the angels name Lenore."*
>   *Quoth the raven "Nevermore."*

I composed this stanza, at this point, first that, by establishing the climax, I might the better vary and graduate, as regards seriousness and importance, the preceding queries of the lover—and, secondly, that I might definitely settle the rhythm, the metre, and the length and general arrangement of the stanza—as well as graduate the stanzas which were to precede, so that none of them might surpass this in rhythmical effect. Had I been able, in the subsequent composition, to construct more vigorous stanzas, I should, without scruple, have purposely enfeebled them, so as not to interfere with the climacteric effect.

And here I may as well say a few words of the versification. My first object (as usual) was originality. The extent to which this has been neglected, in versification, is one of the most unaccountable things in the world. Admitting that there is little possibility of variety in mere *rhythm*, it is still clear that the possible varieties of metre and stanza are absolutely infinite—and yet, *for centuries, no man, in verse, has ever done, or ever seemed to think of doing, an original thing.* The fact is, originality (unless in minds of very unusual force) is by no means a matter, as some suppose, of impulse or intuition. In general, to be found, it must be elaborately sought, and although a positive merit of the highest class, demands in its attainment less of invention than negation.

Of course, I pretend to no originality in either the rhythm or metre of the "Raven." The former is trochaic—the latter is octameter acatalectic, alternating with heptameter catalectic repeated in the *refrain* of the fifth verse, and terminating with tetrameter catalectic. Less pedantically—the feet employed throughout (trochees) consist of a long syllable followed by a short: the first line of the stanza consists of eight of these feet—the second of seven and a half (in effect two-thirds)—the third of eight—the fourth of seven and a half—the fifth the same—the sixth three and a half. Now, each of these lines, taken individually, has been employed before, and what originality the "Raven" has, is in their *combination into stanza*; nothing even remotely approaching this combination has ever been attempted. The effect of this originality of combination is aided by other unusual, and some altogether novel effects, arising from an extension of the application of the principles of rhyme and alliteration.

The next point to be considered was the mode of bringing together the lover and the Raven—and the first branch of this consideration was the *locale*. For this the most natural suggestion might seem to be a forest, or the fields—but it has always appeared to me that a close *circumscription of space* is absolutely necessary to the effect of insulated incident:—it has the force of a frame to a picture. It has an indisputable moral power in keeping concentrated the attention, and, of course, must not be confounded with mere unity of place.

I determined, then, to place the lover in his chamber—in a chamber rendered sacred to him by memories of her who had frequented it. The room is represented as richly furnished—this in mere pursuance of the ideas I have already explained on the subject of Beauty, as the sole true poetical thesis.

The *locale* being thus determined, I had now to introduce the bird— and the thought of introducing him through the window, was inevitable. The idea of making the lover suppose, in the first instance, that the flapping of the wings of the bird against the shutter, is a "tapping" at the door, originated in a wish to increase, by prolonging, the reader's curiosity, and in a desire to admit the incidental effect arising from the lover's throwing open the door, finding all dark, and thence adopting the half-fancy that it was the spirit of his mistress that knocked.

I made the night tempestuous, first, to account for the Raven's seeking admission, and secondly, for the effect of contrast with the (physical) serenity within the chamber.

I made the bird alight on the bust of Pallas,[13] also for the effect of contrast between the marble and the plumage—it being understood that the bust was absolutely *suggested* by the bird—the bust of *Pallas* being chosen, first, as most in keeping with the scholarship of the lover, and, secondly, for the sonorousness of the word, Pallas, itself.

About the middle of the poem, also, I have availed myself of the force of contrast, with a view of deepening the ultimate impression. For

[13]PALLAS: Athena, the Greek goddess of wisdom and war.

example, an air of the fantastic—approaching as nearly to the ludicrous as was admissible—is given to the Raven's entrance. He comes in "with many a flirt and flutter."

> *Not the* least obeisance made he—*not a moment stopped or stayed he,*
> But with mien of lord or lady, *perched above my chamber door.*

In the two stanzas which follow, the design is more obviously carried out:—

> *Then this ebony bird beguiling my sad fancy into smiling*
> *By the* grave and stern decorum of the countenance it wore,
> *"Though thy* crest be shorn and shaven *thou,"* I said, *"art sure no craven,*
> *Ghastly grim and ancient Raven wandering from the nightly shore—*
> *Tell me what thy lordly name is on the Night's Plutonian shore!"*
> Quoth the Raven *"Nevermore."*

> *Much I marvelled* this ungainly fowl *to hear discourse so plainly,*
> *Though its answer little meaning—little relevancy bore;*
> *For we cannot help agreeing that no living human being*
> Ever yet was blessed with seeing bird above his chamber door—
> Bird or beast upon the sculptured bust above his chamber door,
> *With such name as "Nevermore."*

The effect of the *dénouement* being thus provided for, I immediately drop the fantastic for a tone of the most profound seriousness:—this tone commencing in the stanza directly following the one last quoted, with the line,

But the Raven, sitting lonely on that placid bust, spoke only, etc.

From this epoch the lover no longer jests—no longer sees any thing even of the fantastic in the Raven's demeanor. He speaks of him as a "grim, ungainly, ghastly, gaunt, and ominous bird of yore," and feels the "fiery eyes" burning into his "bosom's core." This revolution of thought, or fancy, on the lover's part, is intended to induce a similar one on the part of the reader—to bring the mind into a proper frame for the *dénouement*—which is now brought about as rapidly and as *directly* as possible.

With the *dénouement* proper—with the Raven's reply, "Nevermore," to the lover's final demand if he shall meet his mistress in another world—the poem, in its obvious phase, that of a simple narrative, may be said to have its completion. So far, every thing is within the limits of the accountable—of the real. A raven, having learned by rote the single word

"Nevermore," and having escaped from the custody of its owner, is driven, at midnight, through the violence of a storm, to seek admission at a window from which a light still gleams—the chamber-window of a student, occupied half in poring over a volume, half in dreaming of a beloved mistress deceased. The casement being thrown open at the fluttering of the bird's wings, the bird itself perches on the most convenient seat out of the immediate reach of the student, who, amused by the incident and the oddity of the visiter's demeanor, demands of it, in jest and without looking for a reply, its name. The raven addressed, answers with its customary word, "Nevermore"—a word which finds immediate echo in the melancholy heart of the student, who, giving utterance aloud to certain thoughts suggested by the occasion, is again startled by the fowl's repetition of "Nevermore." The student now guesses the state of the case, but is impelled, as I have before explained, by the human thirst for self-torture, and in part by superstition, to propound such queries to the bird as will bring him, the lover, the most of the luxury of sorrow, through the anticipated answer "Nevermore." With the indulgence, to the utmost extreme, of this self-torture, the narration, in what I have termed its first or obvious phase, has a natural termination, and so far there has been no overstepping of the limits of the real.

But in subjects so handled, however skilfully, or with however vivid an array of incident, there is always a certain hardness or nakedness, which repels the artistical eye. Two things are invariably required—first, some amount of complexity, or more properly, adaptation; and, secondly, some amount of suggestiveness—some under current, however indefinite of meaning. It is this latter, in especial, which imparts to a work of art so much of that *richness* (to borrow from colloquy a forcible term) which we are too fond of confounding with *the ideal*. It is the *excess* of the suggested meaning—it is the rendering this the upper instead of the under current of the theme—which turns into prose (and that of the very flattest kind) the so called poetry of the so called transcendentalists.

Holding these opinions, I added the two concluding stanzas of the poem—their suggestiveness being thus made to pervade all the narrative which has preceded them. The under-current of meaning is rendered first apparent in the lines—

> *"Take thy beak from out* my heart, *and take thy form from off my door!"*
>
> Quoth the Raven "Nevermore!"

It will be observed that the words, "from out my heart," involve the first metaphorical expression in the poem. They, with the answer,

"Nevermore," dispose the mind to seek a moral in all that has been previously narrated. The reader begins now to regard the Raven as emblematical—but it is not until the very last line of the very last stanza, that the intention of making him emblematical of *Mournful and Never-ending Remembrance* is permitted distinctly to be seen:

> *And the Raven, never flitting, still is sitting, still is sitting,*
> *On the pallid bust of Pallas just above my chamber door;*
> *And his eyes have all the seeming of a demon's that is dreaming,*
> *And the lamplight o'er him streaming throws his shadow on the*
>   *floor;*
> *And my soul* from out that shadow *that lies floating on the floor*
>   *Shall be lifted—nevermore.*

[1846]

PART III

American Literature in a Divided Nation

Slavery in America

When Abraham Lincoln accepted the Republican Party's nomination for U.S. senator from the state of Illinois, June 16, 1858, he maintained: "A house divided against itself cannot stand. I believe this government cannot endure permanently, half-slave and half-free." This has become one of Lincoln's best-known utterances, but his point was not a new one. For decades, abolitionists had warned that violence and war would erupt if slavery continued. The Boston editor, reformer, and abolitionist William Lloyd Garrison, for example, had been making this argument since the 1830s and had amplified it during the 1840s and 1850s. The American Union could not contain freedom *and* slavery; the house must not, could not, be divided, he emphasized.

Garrison's phrase derived from Jesus' words warning against sin and Satan (see Mark 3:25; Matthew 12:25–28; Luke 11:16–20). As Garrison stated in a resolution he introduced at the May 1855 meeting in New York City of the American Anti-Slavery Society: "A Church or Government which accords the same rights and privileges to Slavery as to Liberty, is a house divided against itself, which cannot stand." Two years later, he declared that no Union could reconcile "elements which are eternally hostile. God has never made it possible for Liberty and Slavery to live together in partnership."

When the war Garrison feared finally came in April 1861, it proved immensely damaging. Its overall cost was 20 billion dollars—five times the total expenditure of the federal government from the 1780s to 1861. Far worse were the numbers of wounded and dead. Between 700,000 and 800,000 men served in the Confederate armies, and about 2.3 million in the Union armies. The number of casualties was 1 million in a country whose population was 31 million. The death toll was 618,000: 360,000 North, 258,000 South. This exceeds the number of deaths in all of America's other wars combined.

Slavery had taken root in North America during the early to mid-seventeenth century. The first Africans sold into bondage were the twenty conveyed by a Dutch merchant to the Jamestown, Virginia, settlement in August 1619—though, strictly speaking, they were probably sold as indentured servants rather than slaves. By 1860 slavery was so firmly established as a Southern—indeed, as an American—institution that its abolition required terrible bloodshed. The moral appeal Garrison favored and practiced was forceful, forthright, and ultimately inadequate. The inevitability of war was also the tormented insight Lincoln expressed in his Second Inaugural Address, March 4, 1865—that slavery "was, somehow, the cause of the war" and that the lives sacrificed in battle were the price God had decreed the nation must pay for it.

With the defeat of the Confederacy and the adoption of the Thirteenth Amendment, slavery in the United States was abolished. But the tragic legacies of slavery deeply affected American history and literature throughout the nineteenth and twentieth centuries, and remain with us today in the national debate and discussion of such issues as affirmative action, multicultural and multiethnic education, and reparation payments to the descendants of slaves. Some of the greatest, most widely read and studied authors of American literature, including Frederick Douglass, Herman Melville, Mark Twain, William Faulkner, Ralph Ellison, and Toni Morrison, have explored through autobiography, fiction, and essay the terrible irony of human bondage in a nation based on the principles of freedom and quality. They and countless others have described, too, the dehumanizing horrors of racism and racial violence. James Baldwin, Ellison, and Morrison have even proposed that slavery and race have shaped and resonate within American literary works that refer rarely, or not even at all, to slavery and race. All of American literature, Morrison said, has an "African presence" on some level. Though at first this seems an overstatement, it carries the ring of truth. Is it possible to read Emerson's affirmations of self-reliance in the 1840s, for example, and Whitman's tributes to the democratic self in the 1850s, without being mindful of the huge fact of American slavery?

Students find the historical reality of slavery, and its importance as a context for the study of American literature, both provocative and puzzling. How had this state of affairs arisen? Why had slavery not ended with the Revolution? What was the evolving nature of this institution that abolitionists such as Garrison and Douglass set themselves against? Everyone today knows that slavery is wrong. How, then, could it have happened here? As the Philadelphia-born African American reformer James Forten stated in 1813, "It seems almost incredible that the advocates of liberty should conceive of the idea of selling a fellow creature to slavery."

Sometimes we forget that slavery was a national institution before it became a sectional one that divided the North from the South. Slavery existed in Boston as early as the late 1630s, and, more generally, the New England colonies, not those in the South, had been at the forefront of the Atlantic slave trade. When revolution simmered in the 1760s and early 1770s, slavery was legal in every one of the thirteen colonies. In 1763 there were 5,200 black slaves in Massachusetts, working as seamen, farmhands, lumberjacks, craftsmen, and domestic servants. As the historian Jack P. Greene has shown, in the early 1770s "slavery was an expanding institution in all of Britain's continental American colonies except Nova Scotia, New Hampshire, and Canada." As another historian, Edgar J. McManus, noted, slavery significantly benefited the North, making a "vital contribution" to the economy of settlements and colonies there—so much so that slave trading was considered as "honorable" as other types of commerce.

America's leading statesmen of the Revolutionary era lived in the midst of slavery. When the Declaration of Independence was published in 1776, one in every six Americans was a slave, and seventeen members of the Constitutional Convention in 1787 (including George Washington and James Madison) were slave-owners holding a total of 1,400 slaves. Few at the time, however, thought slavery would endure and expand as it did later. It seemed to many that the Revolution would make a moral and, eventually, a political and economic difference and that slavery would, somehow, fade away.

This did happen in the North, where black and white resistance and state abolition societies, inspired by the ideals of the Revolution, dealt slavery a fatal blow, as antislavery argument and activism dovetailed with the system's ebbing profitability. In 1787 the Northwest Ordinance prohibited slavery in the Ohio Valley. It was abolished by the constitutions of Vermont (1777), Ohio (1802), Illinois (1818), and Indiana (1816); by judicial decision and by the state bill of rights in Massachusetts (1783); by gradual abolition acts in Pennsylvania (1780), Rhode Island (1784), Connecticut (1784, 1797), New York (1799, 1817), and New Jersey (1804, 1820); and by constitutional interpretation in New Hampshire (1792).

There were encouraging trends on the national scene as well. In 1794, U.S. law prohibited "American ships or foreign ships clearing American ports from carrying on the slave trade between foreign ports," and in 1808 the Atlantic slave trade (the importation of slaves) was abolished. Both of these changes met with resistance. The slave trade in Rhode Island had reached its height *after* the Revolution, and the merchants there "did everything they could to save it," fighting abolition, agitating Congress, and breaking laws, as the scholar Jay Coughtry has demonstrated. As early as 1785, in "The Slave Trade and Slavery," the antislavery Congregational minister Samuel Hopkins observed that "trade in human species has been the first wheel of commerce in Newport [Rhode Island], on which every movement in business has chiefly depended."

While ending the slave trade was significant, this was, as the historian James H. Broussard has indicated, "the aspect of slavery most easily dispensed with, for it did not touch the heart of the system at all, and there were strong economic arguments against a large influx of new slaves." Many might detest the overseas slave trade yet not agree that slavery should cease where it was central to the economy. Maintaining fewer slaves, if anything, kept their value high, and eliminating the overseas trade induced the development of a well-paying trade — "Negro speculation" — within and between states. As the writer and reformer Lydia Maria Child said in 1833, "the breeding of negro cattle for the foreign markets of Louisiana, Georgia, Alabama, Arkansas, and Missouri, is a very lucrative branch of business."

The first U.S. Census in 1790 counted nearly 700,000 slaves. Two decades later, and even with the foreign slave trade having been banned for two years, the census count of slaves had jumped to 1.2 million.

Between 1790 and 1860, over 800,000 African Americans were, state the historians Ira Berlin and Philip D. Morgan, "forcibly transferred from seaboard to interior states." Fortunes were made from this trading of slaves. For example, during the period from the 1810s to the 1840s, a Tennessee man named Isaac Franklin became wealthy from slave trading and investing his profits in land. He presided over Fairvue, the finest estate in Tennessee, and he had extensive holdings in Louisiana and Texas. From 1828 to 1835, Franklin and his partner, John Armfield, sold an average of 1,200 slaves per year. It was not until the mid-1830s that Franklin retired from trafficking in the slave trade. At his death, he owned 600 slaves.

Thomas Jefferson and other Southern patriots like George Mason and Richard Henry Lee condemned slave trading for profit and inveighed against the evils of slavery. But whatever their hopes for abolition in the long run, they could not readily envision slavery's actual demise, given its importance for the economy; they engaged in the practices they castigated and excluded slavery from national political discussion and debate. Neither they nor anyone else could imagine how the two races could live together *free* without falling into miscegenation and hurtling the South into race war. By 1850, 92 percent of the black American population was concentrated in the South, and of this group approximately 95 percent were slaves.

A number of the early abolitionists were Southerners (e.g., the Grimké sisters of Charleston, South Carolina, and James Birney of Danville, Kentucky), but on the whole antislavery sentiment in the South declined as Southern agriculture expanded and crop production grew, as planters took advantage of the cotton gin (invented by Eli Whitney in 1793) to increase yield, and as Southern plantations fed the textile industries of Great Britain and New England.

The Revolution did spur a number of owners to manumit (free) their slaves, and the number of voluntary manumissions rose in its immediate aftermath. The Manumission Act of 1782 in Virginia led to freedom for 10,000 slaves over the next ten years. In 1805, however, a change in the law allowed owners to free slaves only if Negroes then left the state—which was a return to an earlier law of 1691 that had permitted freedom for slaves only if they were transported from the colony within six months. Freed slaves meant a free black population, and this alarmed nearly everybody; no state or territory wanted free Negroes. Manumissions lapsed; slavery thrived.

The Revolution was an educational experience for many slaves. They traveled widely with their masters, who were serving in the army, the Continental Congress, or state governments, and many of them seized opportunities for escape. Some, in addition, learned directly from their masters what the revolution was about—that it was about resistance to tyranny and oppression. Some slaves were aware of the Declaration of Independence as an expression of basic human rights, and this soon triggered petitions by slaves for their own freedom.

Still, it is important to remember that in large areas of the South, the Revolution had little or no effect on slaveowners. In Georgia, for example, which the scholar Betty Wood has studied, "nothing happened during or as a result of the American Revolution to dispel the pervasive white belief in the comparative profitability of enslaved labor in the context of plantation agriculture." Slavery meant profit; slavery was required for racial order and control. It was unimaginable that it be given up.

Slaves, after all, were precious property. The value of slave property in 1790 was about $140 million—twice the entire Revolutionary War debt. Within two years of the invention of the cotton gin, the price of slaves had doubled. A field hand priced at $500 in 1794 cost three times as much in 1825. During the antebellum period, the cotton that slaves raised was the nation's most important commercial crop and major export, amounting to 50 to 60 percent of America's total exports. Slave labor was crucial, too, for rice, sugar, corn, and tobacco. The more slavery was practiced, the more necessary it was reckoned on economic grounds; and the larger the slave population, the more imperative that blacks be defined and restrained by slavery.

In the thirty years from 1780 to 1810, almost as many Africans were shipped to the United States as in the previous 160 years (1620 to 1780). The slave population expanded by 33 percent between 1800 and 1810, and by another 29 percent between 1810 and 1820. Despite the Atlantic slave trade's termination in 1808, the American slave population soared, boosted by illegal trading (approximately 1,000 per year brought in illegally), slave breeding, and interstate slave trading. Between 1808 and 1860, the slave population tripled, and the profit from investment in slaves averaged an impressive 10 percent during the 1840s and 1850s. In Virginia alone, 300,000 slaves were sold out of state between 1830 and 1860. As Toni Morrison reflected in an interview (*Time*, May 22, 1989), trading and selling slaves, evil yet addictive, "was like cocaine is now….Imagine getting $1,000 for a human being. That's a lot of money. There are fortunes in this country that were made that way."

"The initial capital outlay for a slave was great," the scholar Christine Daniels acknowledges, but "depreciated over his or her working life, the cost per year for a slave was less than that for any other type of laborer." Slaves brought a return equal to or exceeding other kinds of investments, and by the 1850s, slaveowners in the East were shipping and selling 25,000 slaves to the West each year. "Slaves," comments R. H. Kilbourne Jr., "represented a huge store of highly liquid wealth that ensured the financial stability and viability of planting operations even after a succession of bad harvests, years of low prices, or both."

Between 1770 and 1860, then, slavery simultaneously diminished and grew, dying out in the North and West and expanding in the South and consequently in the body politic. Four million slaves lived in the South when the Civil War began, compared to 500,000 at the outset of the Revolution in 1775–1776; approximately 384,000 whites owned slaves; and more than 46,000 slaveowners were planters—meaning that they owned twenty or more slaves. In the states of Louisiana, Mississippi, Alabama, Georgia, and South Carolina, by 1860 the value of slaves amounted to 60 percent of all agricultural wealth. By 1850–1860, slavery was "flourishing as never before" (C. Vann Woodward) in the South, and thus the United States, the "land of liberty," was "the largest slaveholding country in the world," with plantation agriculture "more profitable" and slaveowners "more prosperous" (James McPherson) than had ever been the case.

The facts and statistics that I have highlighted, and that I bring to the attention of my students, attest to the magnitude of slavery in the United States. Antislavery agitators such as William Lloyd Garrison and Frederick Douglass repeatedly called attention to its horrors. They sought to give slavery a human face by making vivid the intellectual and emotional, personal and familial price paid by human beings held in bondage. Not only the innumerable articles in Garrison's paper, *The Liberator*, and other antislavery periodicals but also books, pamphlets, and slave narratives depicted the inhumanity of slavery—its murders, tortures, and everyday brutalities, its separation of families, sexual outrages, denial of literacy, and restrictions on religious practices. Graphic antislavery works include Theodore Weld's *American Slavery As It Is: Testimony of a Thousand Witnesses* (1839), Douglass's *Narrative* (1845) and *My Bondage and My Freedom* (1855), Massachusetts senator Charles Sumner's antislavery orations, "The Crime Against Kansas" (1856) and "The Barbarism of Slavery" (1860), first delivered in the U.S. Senate and widely distributed in pamphlet form, and Harriet Jacobs's *Incidents in the Life of a Slave Girl* (1861).

John Greenleaf Whittier, Henry Wadsworth Longfellow, and others wrote evocative antislavery poems. Another noteworthy figure is the African American Frances Ellen Watkins Harper, author of a volume of poems and essays, *Poems and Miscellaneous Subjects* (1855; 2nd ed., with an Introduction by Garrison, Boston, 1857). But most important of all was Harriet Beecher Stowe's *Uncle Tom's Cabin*, which appeared first in a serialized version in the abolitionist journal *The National Era* (June 1851 to April 1852) and then was published as a book. The 5,000 copies of the first edition of the novel sold out in forty-eight hours, and for the next two years the presses never caught up with the demand; 300,000 copies were sold in 1852 alone.

In reply to these antislavery publications, Southern slaveholders, statesmen, clergymen, professors, and men of letters produced an enormous body of passionate, detailed, perversely complicated proslavery literature. Their position was a hard one to defend, for it was opposed to the ideas of enlightenment and progress and equality on which the new nation had been built—and it was at odds with the abolitionism undertaken by England and France that succeeded in their Caribbean colonies by the 1830s.

Nonetheless, in countless speeches, essays, monographs, and in two mammoth multi-author collections, *Pro-Slavery Arguments as Maintained by the Most Distinguished Writers of the Southern States* (1852) and *Cotton Is King, and Pro-Slavery Arguments* (1860), many talented, well-educated Southerners labored to prove the rightness of slavery. Religion, the social and natural sciences, literature, economics, philosophy, classical studies, political theory—every discipline of knowledge and branch of culture was drawn on and deployed to confirm the rewards of the institution and the necessity for locating black people (an "inferior," "dependent" race) within it.

By the late 1850s, as Garrison and Lincoln recognized, the United States had become a "house divided." The Republican Party, under Lincoln's leadership, stood against the extension of slavery into new territories. Unlike Garrison and Douglass, most of the key Republican leaders did not insist on the abolition of slavery where it already existed in the South; they believed that, over time, slavery in the Southern states would end on its own and that its termination would occur more quickly there if slavery were prevented from moving west and southwest into other parts of the country. The Republicans were not abolitionists; they feared that calls for abolition (that is, ending slavery everywhere, now or in the near future) would bring about the dissolution of the Union. No *extension* of slavery into new states and territories—this was the line that Lincoln and his supporters insisted upon.

The Republicans' policy allowed Southerners to keep what they had. But to the South, such a policy imperiled slavery, the institution that for economic and racial reasons they depended on. The South did not believe Lincoln's assurances to the contrary. Furthermore, and even more fundamentally, Southerners claimed that such a policy infringed on a slaveowner's right to use his property (that is, his human chattel) and transport it wherever he wanted to. It became common for Southerners to invoke the Declaration of Independence to dramatize the grievances they believe they suffered and the principles they espoused. Thus, when Lincoln was elected in 1860, eleven slaveholding states, in a second American revolution taken in defense of white rights and black bondage, withdrew from the Union and formed the Confederate States of America.

To many Americans today, the Civil War and, especially, slavery seem very distant. For a long time, I felt this way myself. But through my own reading and research, and through my work over the years in the classroom, I have come to feel the painful reality that Ellison and Morrison, among others, have described — that slavery is present in American literature, even when it is not immediately visible, and that its effects linger. It is part of the American past but also part of the present, and it will be part of the future as we continue to struggle with race and ethnicity and the nature of the union that does and does not exist in the United States.

Bibliographical note: Important studies of slavery include Kenneth M. Stampp, *The Peculiar Institution: Slavery in the Antebellum South* (1956); Eugene D. Genovese, *Roll, Jordan, Roll: The World the Slaves Made* (1974); Herbert G. Gutman, *The Black Family in Slavery and Freedom, 1750–1925* (1976); Jacqueline Jones, *Labor of Love, Labor of Sorrow: Black Women, Work, and the Family from Slavery to the Present* (1985); Elizabeth Fox-Genovese, *Within the Plantation Household: Black and White Women of the Old South* (1988); and Peter Kolchin, *American Slavery, 1619–1877* (1993). See also Henry Louis Gates Jr. and Charles T. Davis, eds., *The Slave's Narrative: Texts and Contexts* (1984). On the proslavery argument, see *The Ideology of Slavery: Proslavery Thought in the Antebellum South, 1830–1860*, ed. Drew Gilpin Faust (1981); and Larry E. Tise, *Proslavery: A History of the Defense of Slavery in America, 1701–1840* (1987).

Abraham Lincoln

(1809–1865)

Abraham Lincoln is not only one of the nation's greatest presidents but also one of its greatest writers, ranking alongside such masters of nineteenth-century American prose as Ralph Waldo Emerson and Frederick Douglass.

Born of humble origins in a cabin in Hardin County, Kentucky, Lincoln received little formal schooling. He did not know many authors and books, but those he knew—the Bible, Shakespeare, Aesop's Fables, Bunyan's Pilgrim's Progress—he knew well, and they entered into the rhythm and structure of his speeches, public letters, proclamations, and other documents. As a young man in Illinois, Lincoln worked as a storekeeper and then as a surveyor, postmaster, and storekeeper again. After a brief period of service in the Black Hawk War of 1832, when the Illinois militia battled Native American tribes, Lincoln served several terms in the state legislature. He was admitted to the state bar in 1836 and then settled in Springfield, Illinois, starting a law practice and marrying Mary Todd, who came from a prominent family in the area.

A successful lawyer, Lincoln was a member for a term of the U. S. Congress in the mid-1840s, but he did not run for reelection. It seemed his political career had come to a premature end. But as the crisis over slavery intensified, and as the Republican Party emerged and grew during the early 1850s, Lincoln became active once more in politics. In 1858, as his state's Republican nominee for the U. S. Senate, he engaged in a series of memorable debates with Stephen Douglas. Lincoln lost, but his reputation as a national leader was established, and in 1860 he was elected to the presidency.

When Lincoln began his term of office, he emphasized that while he was opposed to the extension of slavery into new territories and states, he was not committed to attacking slavery where it already existed. Lincoln's hope was to preserve the Union and avoid war, but his reassurances did not satisfy the South, which viewed him as deeply hostile to their interests.

During the years of the Civil War (1861–1865), Lincoln directed the federal government and the Northern side with extraordinary skill, showing depths of insight and compassion that no president before or since (with the possible exception of Franklin D. Roosevelt during the Great Depression and World War II) has rivaled. Perhaps his boldest decision, made with an uncanny sense of timing, was the Emancipation Proclamation, issued on January 1, 1863, declaring that all slaves in states or in parts of states in rebellion against the United States "are and henceforward shall be free." Lincoln thereby connected the prosecution of the war—that is, the defeat of the

Confederacy—to the abolition of slavery. This meant a revolutionary change in the nature of American society that few, when the conflict erupted, could have imagined possible.

The first text below is the Gettysburg Address, which Lincoln presented at the dedication of the Gettysburg battlefield cemetery, November 19, 1863. The other speaker that day was Edward Everett, a statesman from Massachusetts, whose address took two hours. Later, Everett wrote to Lincoln, "I should be glad if I could flatter myself that I came as near to the central idea of the occasion in two hours as you did in two minutes." As the literary scholar Andrew Delbanco has observed, a striking feature of the address is that nowhere does Lincoln mention the enemy.

The Second Inaugural Address, March 4, 1865, is sublime as well. "In his excruciating sense of responsibility for the nation, for the future," the critic Alfred Kazin remarked, "Lincoln had come through a terrible experience to submit to a power higher and greater than anything he had felt it necessary in his political ambition to acknowledge before." A few weeks later, on the night of April 15, in Ford's Theatre in Washington, D.C., Lincoln was assassinated.

Of Lincoln, Emerson said, "His heart was as great as the world, but there was no room in it to hold a memory of a wrong." He was, said Walt Whitman, "the grandest figure on the crowded canvas of the drama of the nineteenth century." "Mr. Lincoln," recalled Frederick Douglass, "was not only a great President, but a GREAT MAN—too great to be small in anything. In his company I was never in any way reminded of my humble origin, or of my unpopular color." Lincoln was a majestic and inspirational yet utterly direct and focused writer and speaker, the possessor of an unequalled, and profoundly American, eloquence.

For biography: David Herbert Donald, Lincoln (1995); and William E. Gienapp, Abraham Lincoln and Civil War America: A Biography (2002). See also Garry Wills, Lincoln at Gettysburg: The Words That Remade America (1992); Mark E. Neely Jr., The Last Best Hope of Earth: Abraham Lincoln and the Promise of America (1993); and Harry V. Jaffa, A New Birth of Freedom: Abraham Lincoln and the Coming of the Civil War (2000). An excellent resource: Mark E. Neely Jr., The Abraham Lincoln Encyclopedia (1982).

Address Delivered at the Dedication of the Cemetery at Gettysburg

NOVEMBER 19, 1863

Four score[1] and seven years ago our fathers brought forth on this continent, a new nation, conceived in Liberty, and dedicated to the proposition that all men are created equal.

Now we are engaged in a great civil war, testing whether that nation, or any nation so conceived and so dedicated, can long endure. We are met on a great battlefield of that war. We have come to dedicate a portion of that field as a final resting-place for those who here gave their lives that that nation might live. It is altogether fitting and proper that we should do this.

But, in a larger sense, we cannot dedicate—we cannot consecrate—we cannot hallow—this ground. The brave men, living and dead, who struggled here have consecrated it, far above our poor power to add or detract. The world will little note, nor long remember, what we say here, but it can never forget what they did here. It is for us the living, rather, to be dedicated here to the unfinished work which they who fought here have thus far so nobly advanced. It is rather for us to be here dedicated to the great task remaining before us—that from these honored dead we take increased devotion—to that cause for which they gave the last full measure of devotion; that we here highly resolve that these dead shall not have died in vain—that this nation, under God, shall have a new birth of freedom—and that government of the people, by the people, for the people, shall not perish from the earth.

---

[1]SCORE: A score equals twenty years; thus, Lincoln is referring to eighty-seven years prior—that is, 1776.

Second Inaugural Address

MARCH 4, 1865

At this second appearing to take the oath of the presidential office, there is less occasion for an extended address than there was at the first. Then a statement, somewhat in detail, of a course to be pursued, seemed fitting and proper. Now, at the expiration of four years, during which public declarations have been constantly called forth on every point and phase of the great contest which still absorbs the attention, and engrosses the energies of the nation, little that is new could be presented. The progress of our arms,[1] upon which all else chiefly depends, is as well known to the public as to myself; and it is, I trust, reasonably satisfactory and encouraging to all. With high hope for the future, no prediction in regard to it is ventured.

On the occasion corresponding to this four years ago, all thoughts were anxiously directed to an impending civil war.[2] All dreaded it—all sought to avert it. While the inaugural address was being delivered from this place, devoted altogether to *saving* the Union without war, insurgent agents were in the city seeking to *destroy* it without war—seeking to dissolve the Union, and divide effects, by negotiation. Both parties deprecated war; but one of them would *make* war rather than let the nation survive; and the other would *accept* war rather than let it perish. And the war came.

One eighth of the whole population were colored slaves, not distributed generally over the Union, but localized in the Southern part of it. These slaves constituted a peculiar and powerful interest. All knew that this interest was, somehow, the cause of the war. To strengthen, perpetuate, and extend this interest was the object for which the insurgents[3] would rend the Union, even by war; while the government claimed no right to do more than to restrict the territorial enlargement of it. Neither party expected for the war, the magnitude, or the duration, which it has already attained. Neither anticipated that the *cause* of the conflict might cease with, or even before, the conflict itself should cease. Each looked for an easier triumph, and a result less fundamental and astounding. Both

---

[1]THE PROGRESS OF OUR ARMS: The accomplishments and movements of the Union Army fighting the Civil War. The War would officially end on April 9, 1865.
[2]CIVIL WAR: The conflict (1861–1865) between the Northern states (the Union) and the Southern states (the Confederacy) that seceded from the Union. It is also called the War Between the States.
[3]INSURGENTS: Those who rise in revolt.

read the same Bible, and pray to the same God; and each invokes His aid against the other. It may seem strange that any men should dare to ask a just God's assistance in wringing their bread from the sweat of other men's faces; but let us judge not that we be not judged. The prayers of both could not be answered; that of neither has been answered fully. The Almighty has his own purposes. "Woe unto the world because of offences! for it must needs be that offences come; but woe to that man by whom the offence cometh!" If we shall suppose that American Slavery is one of those offences which, in the providence of God, must needs come, but which, having continued through His appointed time, He now wills to remove, and that He gives to both North and South, this terrible war, as the woe due to those by whom the offence came, shall we discern therein any departure from those divine attributes which the believers in a Living God always ascribe to Him? Fondly do we hope—fervently do we pray—that this mighty scourge of war may speedily pass away. Yet, if God wills that it continue, until all the wealth piled by the bond-man's[4] two hundred and fifty years of unrequited toil shall be sunk, and until every drop of blood drawn with the lash, shall be paid by another drawn with the sword, as was said three thousand years ago, so still it must be said "the judgments of the Lord, are true and righteous altogether."

With malice toward none; with charity for all; with firmness in the right, as God gives us to see the right, let us strive on to finish the work we are in; to bind up the nation's wounds; to care for him who shall have borne the battle, and for his widow, and his orphan—to do all which may achieve and cherish a just and lasting peace, among ourselves, and with all nations.

---

[4]BOND-MAN'S: A man in bondage—that is, a slave.

Margaret Fuller

(1810–1850)

Timothy Fuller, Margaret's father, was a lawyer trained at Harvard and a political figure of some prominence who served in the Massachusetts legislature and the U.S. Congress. In an era when few women received much education, he gave Latin lessons to his little girl, listening to her each evening, after he returned from work, recite translations from Ovid, Virgil, and Horace and report on other studies in literature, philosophy, and history she had done. When she was ten, her father wrote to her: "To excel in all things should be your constant aim; mediocrity is obscurity."

Born in Cambridgeport (now part of Cambridge, Massachusetts), Fuller briefly attended (1823–1824), a school for girls in Groton, Massachusetts, returning home to pursue her education on her own. Her father died in 1835, and she was then obliged to help her mother with the care and support of the seven other children in the family.

Fuller worked for a time as a schoolteacher, but she made a greater impact as the leader of "Conversations"—seminars with topics in literature, culture, and ethics—for elite women (later, men took part as well) in the Boston and Cambridge area. She was a passionate intellectual, an admirer of the formidable German author Goethe, and a translator herself of German poetry and prose. One of her friends, and her mentor, was Ralph Waldo Emerson, and she was well known to and respected by Emerson's circle of intellectuals and reformers. Emerson stated about Fuller, "We are taught by her how lifeless and outward we were, what poor Laplanders burrowing under the snows of prudence and pedantry."

Some, it is true, disliked Fuller's manner and personality, judging her self-absorbed and pretentious; and she did speak highly of herself, as when she observed, "I now know all the people worth knowing in America, and I find no intellect comparable to my own." Emerson, too, was often ambivalent, noting in his Journal: "Strange, cold-warm, attractive-repelling conversation with Margaret, whom I always admire, and sometimes love; yet whom I freeze and who freezes me to silence when we promise to come nearest." But such comments and opinions may say less about Fuller than they do about the uneasy attitude toward female aspiration and intellectual display so common at this time.

Fuller edited the Transcendentalist quarterly journal, The Dial, from 1840 to 1842. She also served as a literary critic and writer for the New York Tribune, a newspaper edited by the reform-minded Horace Greeley, where she treated a diverse group of topics in art, literature, culture, and social reform.

In August 1846 Fuller traveled to England and mainland Europe and became a strong supporter of the Italian revolutionary cause. She became romantically involved with a young Italian nobleman, Marchese Giovanni Angelo Ossoli, and gave birth to their son. After the defeat of the Roman republic, the family journeyed to the United States but died tragically in a shipwreck off the coast of Fire Island, New York.

Fuller was the author of a travel narrative about the Midwest, Summer on the Lakes *(1844); a collection,* Papers on Literature and Art *(1846); and many essays, reviews, and journalistic pieces, in particular a series of reports she sent to the* New York Tribune *while she was abroad. But her most important work was "The Great Lawsuit: Man Versus Men, Woman Versus Women," published in* The Dial *in 1843 and later republished in an expanded form as* Woman in the Nineteenth Century *(1845). "The Great Lawsuit" is a vigorous, learned critique of gender roles and an argument on behalf of female self-development and women's rights, and a central text (the first printing sold out in two weeks) for women activists of the period.*

Shortly after Fuller's death, Emerson and two of her close friends, James Freeman Clarke and W. H. Channing, prepared and published Memoirs of Margaret Fuller Ossoli *(2 vols., 1852), a publication that praised her even as it as slighted her literary work, made changes in letters and other texts she had written, and downplayed her activities as a reformer. Popular and often reprinted in the nineteenth century (1,000 copies were sold on the first day of publication, and later reprints exceeded a dozen), the* Memoirs *reveal yet again that even Emerson harbored ambivalent feelings toward this high-powered female intellectual. Only in the mid- to late twentieth century did biographers and scholars succeed in giving a richer, more accurate account of Fuller's life and career.*

The excerpt below is taken from "The Great Lawsuit." Fuller emphasizes the connection between the anti-slavery movement and the campaign for women's rights, calls for the opening of all opportunities for women, and suggests the benefits to both sexes once the barriers to female development are removed.

For biography: Paula Blanchard, Margaret Fuller: From Transcendentalism to Revolution *(1979); Madeleine B. Stern,* The Life of Margaret Fuller *(2nd ed., 1991); Charles Capper,* Margaret Fuller: An American Romantic Life *(1992); and Joan Von Mehren,* Minerva and the Muse: A Life of Margaret Fuller *(1994). For critical response and interpretation:* Critical Essays on Margaret Fuller, *ed. Joel Myerson (1980); Marie Mitchell Olesen Urbanski,* Margaret Fuller's Woman in the Nineteenth Century: *A Literary Study of Form and Content, of Sources and Influence (1980); Belle Gale Chevigny,* The Woman and the Myth: Margaret Fuller's Life and Writing *(rev. ed., 1997); and*

Jeffrey Steele, Transfiguring America: Myth, Ideology, and Mourning in Margaret Fuller's Writing *(2001).*

From The Great Lawsuit

Of all its banners, none has been more steadily upheld, and under none has more valor and willingness for real sacrifices been shown, than that of the champions of the enslaved African. And this band it is, which, partly in consequence of a natural following out of principles, partly because many women have been prominent in that cause, makes, just now, the warmest appeal in behalf of woman.

Though there has been a growing liberality on this point, yet society at large is not so prepared for the demands of this party, but that they are, and will be for some time, coldly regarded as the Jacobins[1] of their day.

"Is it not enough," cries the sorrowful trader, "that you have done all you could to break up the national Union, and thus destroy the prosperity of our country, but now you must be trying to break up family union, to take my wife away from the cradle, and the kitchen hearth, to vote at polls, and preach from a pulpit? Of course, if she does such things, she cannot attend to those of her own sphere. She is happy enough as she is. She has more leisure than I have, every means of improvement, every indulgence."

"Have you asked her whether she was satisfied with these indulgences?"

"No, but I know she is. She is too amiable to wish what would make me unhappy, and too judicious to wish to step beyond the sphere of her sex. I will never consent to have our peace disturbed by any such discussions."

"'Consent'—you? it is not consent from you that is in question, it is assent from your wife."

"Am I not the head of my house?"

"You are not the head of your wife. God has given her a mind of her own."

"I am the head and she the heart."

"God grant you play true to one another then. If the head represses no natural pulse of the heart, there can be no question as to your giv-

---

[1]JACOBINS: Members of a French political group, established in 1789 near the church of Saint-Jacques in Paris, who sought to propagate the principles of extreme democracy and absolute equality; political radicals of the extreme left.

ing your consent. Both will be of one accord, and there needs but to present any question to get a full and true answer. There is no need of precaution, of indulgence, or consent. But our doubt is whether the heart consents with the head, or only acquiesces in its decree; and it is to ascertain the truth on this point, that we propose some liberating measures."

Thus vaguely are these questions proposed and discussed at present. But their being proposed at all implies much thought, and suggests more. Many women are considering within themselves what they need that they have not, and what they can have, if they find they need it. Many men are considering whether women are capable of being and having more than they are and have, and whether, if they are, it will be best to consent to improvement in their condition.

The numerous party, whose opinions are already labelled and adjusted too much to their mind to admit of any new light, strive, by lectures on some model-women of bridal-like beauty and gentleness, by writing or lending little treatises, to mark out with due precision the limits of woman's sphere, and woman's mission, and to prevent other than the rightful shepherd from climbing the wall, or the flock from using any chance gap to run astray.

Without enrolling ourselves at once on either side, let us look upon the subject from that point of view which to-day offers. No better, it is to be feared, than a high house-top. A high hill-top, or at least a cathedral spire, would be desirable.

It is not surprising that it should be the Anti-Slavery party that pleads for woman, when we consider merely that she does not hold property on equal terms with men; so that, if a husband dies without a will, the wife, instead of stepping at once into his place as head of the family, inherits only a part of his fortune, as if she were a child, or ward only, not an equal partner.

We will not speak of the innumerable instances, in which profligate or idle men live upon the earnings of industrious wives; or if the wives leave them and take with them the children, to perform the double duty of mother and father, follow from place to place, and threaten to rob them of the children, if deprived of the rights of a husband, as they call them, planting themselves in their poor lodgings, frightening them into paying tribute by taking from them the children, running into debt at the expense of these otherwise so overtasked helots.[2]

---

[2]HELOTS: The Helots were serfs in the ancient Greek city of Sparta; their status was between that of owned slaves and free citizens. Fuller describes the legal situation of women, who, while not complete slaves, do not share the rights of full citizens.

Though such instances abound, the public opinion of his own sex is against the man, and when cases of extreme tyranny are made known, there is private action in the wife's favor. But if woman be, indeed, the weaker party, she ought to have legal protection, which would make such oppression impossible.

And knowing that there exists, in the world of men, a tone of feeling towards women as towards slaves, such as is expressed in the common phrase, "Tell that to women and children;" that the infinite soul can only work through them in already ascertained limits; that the prerogative of reason, man's highest portion, is allotted to them in a much lower degree; that it is better for them to be engaged in active labor, which is to be furnished and directed by those better able to think, &c. &c.; we need not go further, for who can review the experience of last week, without recalling words which imply, whether in jest or earnest, these views, and views like these? Knowing this, can we wonder that many reformers think that measures are not likely to be taken in behalf of women, unless their wishes could be publicly represented by women?

That can never be necessary, cry the other side. All men are privately influenced by women; each has his wife, sister, or female friends, and is too much biased by these relations to fail of representing their interests. And if this is not enough, let them propose and enforce their wishes with the pen. The beauty of home would be destroyed, the delicacy of the sex be violated, the dignity of halls of legislation destroyed, by an attempt to introduce them there. Such duties are inconsistent with those of a mother; and then we have ludicrous pictures of ladies in hysterics at the polls, and senate chambers filled with cradles.

But if, in reply, we admit as truth that woman seems destined by nature rather to the inner circle, we must add that the arrangements of civilized life have not been as yet such as to secure it to her. Her circle, if the duller, is not the quieter. If kept from excitement, she is not from drudgery. Not only the Indian carries the burdens of the camp, but the favorites of Louis the Fourteenth[3] accompany him in his journeys, and the washerwoman stands at her tub and carries home her work at all seasons, and in all states of health.[4]

As to the use of the pen, there was quite as much opposition to woman's possessing herself of that help to free-agency as there is now

---

[3]LOUIS THE FOURTEENTH: King of France (1638–1715). Because of the opulence of his court, Louis XIV was called the Sun King.
[4]HEALTH: Fuller states that French courtesans and washerwomen were equally enslaved, as they are both at the beck and call of men.

to her seizing on the rostrum or the desk; and she is likely to draw, from a permission to plead her cause that way, opposite inferences to what might be wished by those who now grant it.

As to the possibility of her filling, with grace and dignity, any such position, we should think those who had seen the great actresses, and heard the Quaker preachers of modern times, would not doubt, that woman can express publicly the fulness of thought and emotion, without losing any of the peculiar beauty of her sex.

As to her home, she is not likely to leave it more than she now does for balls, theatres, meetings for promoting missions, revival meetings, and others to which she flies, in hope of an animation for her existence, commensurate with what she sees enjoyed by men. Governors of Ladies' Fairs are no less engrossed by such a charge, than the Governor of the State by his; presidents of Washingtonian societies,[5] no less away from home than presidents of conventions. If men look straitly to it, they will find that, unless their own lives are domestic, those of the women will not be. The female Greek, of our day, is as much in the street as the male, to cry, What news? We doubt not it was the same in Athens of old. The women, shut out from the market-place, made up for it at the religious festivals. For human beings are not so constituted, that they can live without expansion; and if they do not get it one way, must another, or perish.

And, as to men's representing women fairly, at present, while we hear from men who owe to their wives not only all that is comfortable and graceful, but all that is wise in the arrangement of their lives, the frequent remark, "You cannot reason with a woman," when from those of delicacy, nobleness, and poetic culture, the contemptuous phrase, "Women and children," and that in no light sally of the hour, but in works intended to give a permanent statement of the best experiences, when not one man in the million, shall I say, no, not in the hundred million, can rise above the view that woman was made *for man*, when such traits as these are daily forced upon the attention, can we feel that man will always do justice to the interests of woman? Can we think that he takes a sufficiently discerning and religious view of her office and destiny, ever to do her justice, except when prompted by sentiment; accidentally or transiently, that is, for his sentiment will vary according to the relations in which he is placed. The lover, the poet, the artist, are likely to view her nobly. The father and the philosopher have some chance of liberality; the man of the world, the legislator for expediency, none.

[5]WASHINGTONIAN SOCIETIES: Women's social clubs similar in function and political purpose to the modern Daughters of the American Revolution.

Under these circumstances, without attaching importance in themselves to the changes demanded by the champions of woman, we hail them as signs of the times. We would have every arbitrary barrier thrown down. We would have every path laid open to woman as freely as to man. Were this done, and a slight temporary fermentation allowed to subside, we believe that the Divine would ascend into nature to a height unknown in the history of past ages, and nature, thus instructed, would regulate the spheres not only so as to avoid collision, but to bring forth ravishing harmony.

Yet then, and only then, will human beings be ripe for this, when inward and outward freedom for woman, as much as for man, shall be acknowledged as a right, not yielded as a concession. As the friend of the negro assumes that one man cannot, by right, hold another in bondage, should the friend of woman assume that man cannot, by right, lay even well-meant restrictions on woman. If the negro be a soul, if the woman be a soul, apparelled in flesh, to one master only are they accountable. There is but one law for all souls, and, if there is to be an interpreter of it, he comes not as man, or son of man, but as Son of God.

Were thought and feeling once so far elevated than man should esteem himself the brother and friend, but nowise the lord and tutor of woman, were he really bound with her in equal worship, arrangements as to function and employment would be of no consequence. What woman needs is not as a woman to act or rule, but as a nature to grow, as an intellect to discern, as a soul to live freely, and unimpeded to unfold such powers as were given her when we left our common home. If fewer talents were given her, yet, if allowed the free and full employment of these, so that she may render back to the giver his own with usury, she will not complain, nay, I dare to say she will bless and rejoice in her earthly birthplace, her earthly lot.

[1843]

Harriet Beecher Stowe

(1811–1896)

Harriet Beecher Stowe's antislavery novel Uncle Tom's Cabin *appeared first in a serialized version in the abolitionist journal* The National Era *from June 1851 to April 1852 and then was published as a book. The 5,000 copies of the first edition sold out in forty-eight hours. Total sales in the United States reached a million in the next seven years and were about the same in England. So momentous was the novel's impact that when President Lincoln met Stowe with the Civil War underway, he is reported to have said to her, "So this is the little lady who wrote the book that made this great war."*

Born in Litchfield, Connecticut, Stowe was the daughter of Lyman Beecher, an influential Presbyterian minister and a commanding preacher. Stowe's mother died when the little girl was five, and thus she and her ten brothers and sisters came all the more under the influence of her father, who strongly advocated Christianity as a power for individual reformation and social betterment. One of her brothers was Henry Ward Beecher, who became an esteemed minister and orator in Brooklyn, New York; one of her sisters was Catherine Beecher, a prominent educator and writer; and another was Isabella Beecher, who played a role in the campaign for women's suffrage.

Stowe attended Hartford Female Seminary (established by her sister Catherine) and then served as a teacher there. In 1832 the family relocated to Cincinnati, Ohio, where Lyman Beecher had been appointed president of Lane Theological Seminary. One of the faculty was Calvin Stowe, whom Harriet married; they had seven children, whom she cared for and raised even as she began her career as an author, taking part in literary societies and publishing articles and stories in magazines.

While living in Cincinnati, Stowe gained some first-hand knowledge of the horrors of slavery, for the city was just across the river from Kentucky, a slave state. Most of Uncle Tom's Cabin *was written, however, in Brunswick, Maine, where the Stowe family moved after Calvin Stowe became a member of the faculty of Bowdoin College.*

Two events in particular inspired Stowe's work on her book. The first was the death in 1849 of Stowe's son Charlie, who contracted cholera when he was eighteen months old. This grievous loss gave Stowe an even more acute responsiveness to the plight of America's slave families, which so often were torn apart by slaveholders and auctioneers. What must a slave mother feel, Stowe asked, when her son or daughter is taken from her? The second was the passage of the

Fugitive Slave Law in 1850, requiring Northerners to assist in the recapture of fugitive slaves and the return of them to their masters in the South. For Stowe and many others, this law was an outrageous violation of the rights of free Northerners that forced them into supporting the slavery system.

During her half century as a writer, Stowe produced many books. Among them are: Dred: A Tale of the Great Dismal Swamp *(1856), a second anti-slavery novel;* The Minister's Wooing *(1859), a novel that explores slavery, Protestant theology, and gender in an eighteenth-century Newport, Rhode Island setting; and* Old Town Folks *(1869), about life in a New England village in the years following the Revolutionary War. But it is* Uncle Tom's Cabin *for which she will above all be remembered.*

Sometimes criticized for being "sentimental," Uncle Tom's Cabin *is sentimental in a strong sense of the word, a novel that seeks, to great effect, to make connection through its characters and incidents with the feelings of its readers, awakening them to the gross injustices and barbarities of slavery. Stowe confessed, "I no more thought of style or literary excellence than the mother who rushes into the street and cries for help to save her children from a burning house, thinks of the teachings of the rhetorician or the elocutionist." But she under-rated the power of her narrative, and the extraordinary impact of the characters—Tom above all, but the others as well—that her impassioned style created. One is inclined to agree with a comment she made in a letter, after completing the final chapter: "I feel as if I had written some of it almost with my heart's blood."*

The chapters below focus on Tom's death at the hands of the brutal Simon Legree. Though "Uncle Tom" is now a phrase that connotes submissiveness and undue deference, from Stowe's point of view, the devout Christian who resists temptation even at the cost of his life is, in truth, exemplary in his resolve, courage, and strength.

The first of these chapters refers to Cassy, a slave woman, and Emmeline, a young mulatto; George Shelby, in the second chapter, is the son of the man who sold Tom at the beginning of the story, separating him from his family. The scenes depicted here are deeply moving today, and of course they were even more so in the 1850s, when everyone could perceive the bond that Stowe was evoking between the martyrdom of Tom and the redemptive death of Jesus on the cross, and when every women in America, as the critic Alfred Kazin has noted, had as a "prime belief" the "Christian sacredness of the family."

Southerners criticized, mocked, and ridiculed Stowe, denouncing her on all sides, as did many supporters of slavery in the North. But

*their hostility dramatized the power of her work, and the contribution
to the anti-slavery cause and to American literature that she made.
Whatever the criticisms directed at it, "there is no denying," as the literary scholar Constance Rourke has observed, that* Uncle Tom's Cabin
*possesses an epic scope and mythic dimension, presenting "an elemen-
tary human condition with all its stark humiliations and compulsions."*

For biography: Joan D. Hedrick, Harriet Beecher Stowe: A Life
(1994). For a cogent study of the novel: Josephine Donovan, Uncle
Tom's Cabin: *Evil, Affliction, and Redemptive Love (1991). Critical
reception and analysis:* Critical Essays on Harriet Beecher Stowe, *ed.
Elizabeth Ammons (1980); Thomas F. Gossett,* Uncle Tom's Cabin *and
American Culture (1985);* New Essays on *Uncle Tom's Cabin, ed. Eric
J. Sundquist (1986); and* The Stowe Debate: Rhetorical Strategies in
Uncle Tom's Cabin, *ed. Mason I. Lowance Jr., Ellen E. Westbrook, and
R. C. De Prospo (1994).*

From *Uncle Tom's Cabin*

XL. THE MARTYR

*"Deem not the just by Heaven forgot!
    Though life its common gifts deny,—
Though, with a crushed and bleeding heart,
    And spurned of man, he goes to die!
For God hath marked each sorrowing day,
    And numbered every bitter tear;
And heaven's long years of bliss shall pay
    For all his children suffer here."*

—*BRYANT*[1]

The longest way must have its close,—the gloomiest night will wear
on to a morning. An eternal, inexorable lapse of moments is ever hurrying the day of the evil to an eternal night, and the night of the just
to an eternal day. We have walked with our humble friend thus far in
the valley of slavery; first through flowery fields of ease and indulgence,
then through heart-breaking separations from all that man holds dear.
Again, we have waited with him in a sunny island, where generous
hands concealed his chains with flowers; and, lastly, we have followed

---

[1]BRYANT: This poem is of unknown origin. It does not appear in the collected works of William
Cullen Bryant or the works of his brother, John Howard Bryant.

him when the last ray of earthly hope went out in night, and seen how, in the blackness of earthly darkness, the firmament of the unseen has blazed with stars of new and significant lustre.

The morning-star now stands over the tops of the mountains, and gales and breezes, not of earth, show that the gates of day are unclosing.

The escape of Cassy and Emmeline irritated the before surly temper of Legree to the last degree; and his fury, as was to be expected, fell upon the defenceless head of Tom. When he hurriedly announced the tidings among his hands, there was a sudden light in Tom's eye, a sudden upraising of his hands, that did not escape him. He saw that he did not join the muster of the pursuers. He thought of forcing him to do it; but, having had, of old, experience of his inflexibility when commanded to take part in any deed of inhumanity, he would not, in his hurry, stop to enter into any conflict with him.

Tom, therefore, remained behind, with a few who had learned of him to pray, and offered up prayers for the escape of the fugitives.

When Legree returned, baffled and disappointed, all the long-working hatred of his soul towards his slave began to gather in a deadly and desperate form. Had not this man braved him,—steadily, powerfully, resistlessly,—ever since he bought him? Was there not a spirit in him which, silent as it was, burned on him like the fires of perdition?

"I *hate* him!" said Legree, that night, as he sat up in his bed; "I *hate* him! And isn't he MINE? Can't I do what I like with him? Who's to hinder, I wonder?" And Legree clenched his fist, and shook it, as if he had something in his hands that he could rend in pieces.

But, then, Tom was a faithful, valuable servant; and, although Legree hated him the more for that, yet the consideration was still somewhat of a restraint to him.

The next morning, he determined to say nothing, as yet; to assemble a party, from some neighboring plantations, with dogs and guns; to surround the swamp, and go about the hunt systematically. If it succeeded, well and good; if not, he would summon Tom before him, and—his teeth clenched and his blood boiled—*then* he would break that fellow down, or—there was a dire inward whisper, to which his soul assented.

Ye say that the *interest* of the master is a sufficient safeguard for the slave. In the fury of man's mad will, he will wittingly, and with open eye, sell his own soul to the devil to gain his ends; and will he be more careful of his neighbor's body?

"Well," said Cassy, the next day, from the garret, as she reconnoitred through the knot-hole, "the hunt's going to begin again, to-day!"

Three or four mounted horsemen were curvetting about, on the space front of the house; and one or two leashes of strange dogs were struggling with the negroes who held them, baying and barking at each other.

The men are, two of them, overseers of plantations in the vicinity; and others were some of Legree's associates at the tavern-bar of a neighboring city, who had come for the interest of the sport. A more hard-favored set, perhaps, could not be imagined. Legree was serving brandy, profusely, round among them, as also among the negroes, who had been detailed from the various plantations for this service; for it was an object to make every service of this kind, among the negroes, as much of a holiday as possible.

Cassy placed her ear at the knot-hole; and, as the morning air blew directly towards the house, she could overhear a good deal of the conversation. A grave sneer overcast the dark, severe gravity of her face, as she listened, and heard them divide out the ground, discuss the rival merits of the dogs, give orders about firing, and the treatment of each, in case of capture.

Cassy drew back; and, clasping her hands, looked upward, and said, "O, great Almighty God! we are *all* sinners; but what have *we* done, more than all the rest of the world, that we should be treated so?"

There was a terrible earnestness in her face and voice, as she spoke.

"If it wasn't for *you*, child," she said, looking at Emmeline, "I'd *go* out to them; and I'd thank any one of them that *would* shoot me down; for what use will freedom be to me? Can it give me back my children, or make me what I used to be?"

Emmeline, in her child-like simplicity, was half afraid of the dark moods of Cassy. She looked perplexed, but made no answer. She only took her hand, with a gentle, caressing movement.

"Don't!" said Cassy, trying to draw it away; "you'll get me to loving you; and I never mean to love anything, again!"

"Poor Cassy!" said Emmeline, "don't feel so! If the Lord gives us liberty, perhaps he'll give you back your daughter; at any rate, I'll be like a daughter to you. I know I'll never see my poor old mother again! I shall love you, Cassy, whether you love me or not!"

The gentle, child-like spirit conquered. Cassy sat down by her, put her arm round her neck, stroked her soft, brown hair; and Emmeline then wondered at the beauty of her magnificent eyes, now soft with tears.

"O, Em!" said Cassy, "I've hungered for my children, and thirsted for them, and my eyes fail with longing for them! Here! here!" she said, striking her breast, "it's all desolate, all empty! If God would give me back my children, then I could pray."

"You must trust him, Cassy," said Emmeline; "he is our Father!"

"His wrath is upon us," said Cassy; "he has turned away in anger."

"No, Cassy! He will be good to us! Let us hope in Him," said Emmeline,—"I always have had hope."

The hunt was long, animated, and thorough, but unsuccessful; and, with grave, ironic exultation, Cassy looked down on Legree, as, weary and dispirited, he alighted from his horse.

"Now, Quimbo," said Legree, as he stretched himself down in the sitting-room, "you jest go and walk that Tom up here, right away! The old cuss is at the bottom of this yer whole matter; and I'll have it out of his old black hide, or I'll know the reason why!"

Sambo and Quimbo, both, though hating each other, were joined in one mind by a no less cordial hatred of Tom. Legree had told them, at first, that he had bought him for a general overseer,[2] in his absence; and this had begun an ill will, on their part, which had increased, in their debased and servile natures, as they saw him becoming obnoxious to their master's displeasure. Quimbo, therefore, departed, with a will, to execute his orders.

Tom heard the message with a forewarning heart; for he knew all the plan of the fugitives' escape, and the place of their present concealment;—he knew the deadly character of the man he had to deal with, and his despotic[3] power. But he felt strong in God to meet death, rather than betray the helpless.

He sat his basket down by the row, and, looking up, said, "Into thy hands I commend my spirit! Thou hast redeemed me, oh Lord God of truth!" and then quietly yielded himself to the rough, brutal grasp with which Quimbo seized him.

"Ay, ay!" said the giant, as he dragged him along; "ye'll cotch it, now! I'll boun' Mas'r's back 's up *high!* No sneaking out, now! Tell ye, ye'll get it, and no mistake! See how ye'll look, now, helpin' Mas'r's niggers to run away! See what ye'll get!"

The savage words none of them reached that ear!—a higher voice there was saying, "Fear not them that kill the body, and, after that, have no more that they can do." Nerve and bone of that poor man's body vibrated to those words, as if touched by the finger of God; and he felt the strength of a thousand souls in one. As he passed along,

---

[2]GENERAL OVERSEER: Supervisor.
[3]DESPOTIC: Tyrannical.

the trees and bushes, the huts of his servitude, the whole scene of his degradation, seemed to whirl by him as the landscape by the rushing car. His soul throbbed,—his home was in sight,—and the hour of release seemed at hand.

"Well, Tom!" said Legree, walking up, and seizing him grimly by the collar of his coat, and speaking through his teeth, in a paroxysm of determined rage, "do you know I've made up my mind to KILL you?"

"It's very likely, Mas'r," said Tom, calmly.

"I *have*," said Legree, with grim, terrible calmness, "*done—just—that— thing*, Tom, unless you'll tell me what you know about these yer gals!"

Tom stood silent.

"D'ye hear?" said Legree, stamping, with a roar like that of an incensed lion. "Speak!"

"*I han't got nothing to tell, Mas'r*," said Tom, with a slow, firm, deliberate utterance.

"Do you dare to tell me, ye old black Christian, ye don't *know*?" said Legree.

Tom was silent.

"Speak!" thundered Legree, striking him furiously. "Do you know anything?"

"I know, Mas'r; but I can't tell anything. *I can die!*"

Legree drew in a long breath; and, suppressing his rage, took Tom by the arm, and, approaching his face almost to his, said, in a terrible voice, "Hark'e, Tom!—ye think, 'cause I've let you off before, I don't mean what I say; but, this time, I've *made up my mind*, and counted the cost. You've always stood it out agin' me: now, I'll *conquer ye; or kill ye!*—one or t' other. I'll count every drop of blood there is in you, and take 'em, one by one, till ye give up!"

Tom looked up to his master, and answered, "Mas'r, if you was sick, or in trouble, or dying, and I could save ye, I'd *give* ye my heart's blood; and, if taking every drop of blood in this poor old body would save your precious soul, I'd give 'em freely, as the Lord gave his for me. O, Mas'r! don't bring this great sin on your soul! It will hurt you more than 't will me! Do the worst you can, my troubles 'll be over soon; but, if ye don't repent, yours won't *never* end!"

Like a strange snatch of heavenly music, heard in the lull of a tempest, this burst of feeling made a moment's blank pause. Legree stood aghast, and looked at Tom; and there was such a silence, that the tick of the old clock could be heard, measuring, with silent touch, the last moments of mercy and probation to that hardened heart.

It was but a moment. There was one hesitating pause,—one irresolute, relenting thrill,—and the spirit of evil came back, with seven-fold vehemence; and Legree, foaming with rage, smote his victim to the ground.

Scenes of blood and cruelty are shocking to our ear and heart. What man has nerve to do, man has not nerve to hear. What brother-man and brother-Christian must suffer, cannot be told us, even in our secret chamber, it so harrows up the soul! And yet, oh my country! these things are done under the shadow of thy laws! O, Christ! thy church sees them, almost in silence!

But, of old, there was One whose suffering changed an instrument of torture, degradation and shame, into a symbol of glory, honor, and immortal life; and, where His spirit is, neither degrading stripes, nor blood, nor insults, can make the Christian's last struggle less than glorious.

Was he alone, that long night, whose brave, loving spirit was bearing up, in that old shed, against buffeting and brutal stripes?

Nay! There stood by him ONE,—seen by him alone,—"like unto the Son of God."

The tempter stood by him, too,—blinded by furious, despotic will,—every moment pressing him to shun that agony by the betrayal of the innocent. But the brave, true heart was firm on the Eternal Rock. Like his Master, he knew that, if he saved others, himself he could not save; nor could utmost extremity wring from him words, save of prayer and holy trust.

"He's most gone, Mas'r," said Sambo, touched, in spite of himself, by the patience of his victim.

"Pay away, till he gives up! Give it to him!—give it to him!" shouted Legree. "I'll take every drop of blood he has, unless he confesses!"

Tom opened his eyes, and looked upon his master. "Ye poor miserable critter!" he said, "there an't no more ye can do! I forgive ye, with all my soul!" and he fainted entirely away.

"I b'lieve, my soul, he's done for, finally," said Legree, stepping forward, to look at him. "Yes, he is! Well, his mouth's shut up, at last,—that's one comfort!"

Yes, Legree; but who shall shut up that voice in thy soul? that soul, past repentance, past prayer, past hope, in whom the fire that never shall be quenched is already burning!

Yet Tom was not quite gone. His wondrous words and pious prayers had struck upon the hearts of the imbruted blacks, who had been the instruments of cruelty upon him; and, the instant Legree withdrew, they took him down, and, in their ignorance, sought to call him back to life,—as if *that* were any favor to him.

"Sartin, we's been doin' a drefful wicked thing!" said Sambo; "hopes Mas'r 'll have to 'count for it, and not we."

They washed his wounds,—they provided a rude bed, of some refuse cotton, for him to lie down on; and one of them, stealing up to the house, begged a drink of brandy of Legree, pretending that he was tired, and wanted it for himself. He brought it back, and poured it down Tom's throat.

"O, Tom!" said Quimbo, "we's been awful wicked to ye!"

"I forgive ye, with all my heart!" said Tom, faintly.

"O, Tom! do tell us who is *Jesus*, anyhow?" said Sambo;—"Jesus, that's been a standin' by you so, all this night!—Who is he?"

The word roused the failing, fainting spirit. He poured forth a few energetic sentences of that wondrous One,—his life, his death, his ever-lasting presence, and power to save.

They wept,—both the two savage men.

"Why didn't I never hear this before?" said Sambo; "but I do believe!—I can't help it! Lord Jesus, have mercy on us!"

"Poor critters!" said Tom, "I'd be willing to bar' all I have, if it'll only bring ye to Christ! O, Lord! give me these two more souls, I pray!"

That prayer was answered!

XLI. The Young Master

Two days after, a young man drove a light wagon up through the avenue of china-trees,[4] and, throwing the reins hastily on the horses' neck, sprang out and inquired for the owner of the place.

It was George Shelby; and, to show how he came to be there, we must go back in our story.

The letter of Miss Ophelia to Mrs. Shelby had, by some unfortunate accident, been detained, for a month or two, at some remote post-office, before it reached its destination; and, of course, before it was received, Tom was already lost to view among the distant swamps of the Red river.

Mrs. Shelby read the intelligence with the deepest concern; but any immediate action upon it was an impossibility. She was then in attendance on the sick-bed of her husband who lay delirious in the crisis of a fever.

---

[4]CHINA-TREES: Tall trees (*Melia Azedarach*) with fragrant lilac-colored flowers, native to the East Indies.

Master George Shelby, who, in the interval, had changed from a boy to a tall young man, was her constant and faithful assistant, and her only reliance in superintending his father's affairs. Miss Ophelia had taken the precaution to send them the name of the lawyer who did business for the St. Clares; and the most that, in the emergency, could be done, was to address a letter of inquiry to him. The sudden death of Mr. Shelby, a few days after, brought, of course, an absorbing pressure of other interests, for a season.

Mr. Shelby showed his confidence in his wife's ability, by appointing her sole executrix upon his estates; and thus immediately a large and complicated amount of business was brought upon her hands.

Mrs. Shelby, with characteristic energy, applied herself to the work of straightening the entangled web of affairs; and she and George were for some time occupied with collecting and examining accounts, selling property and settling debts; for Mrs. Shelby was determined that everything should be brought into tangible and recognizable shape, let the consequences to her prove what they might. In the mean time, they received a letter from the lawyer to whom Miss Ophelia had referred them, saying that he knew nothing of the matter; that the man was sold at a public auction, and that, beyond receiving the money, he knew nothing of the affair.

Neither George nor Mrs. Shelby could be easy at this result; and, accordingly, some six months after, the latter, having business for his mother, down the river, resolved to visit New Orleans, in person, and push his inquiries, in hopes of discovering Tom's whereabouts, and restoring him.

After some months of unsuccessful search, by the merest accident, George fell in with a man, in New Orleans, who happened to be possessed of the desired information; and with his money in his pocket, our hero took steamboat for Red river, resolving to find out and repurchase his old friend.

He was soon introduced into the house, where he found Legree in the sitting-room.

Legree received the stranger with a kind of surly hospitality.

"I understand," said the young man, "that you bought, in New Orleans, a boy, named Tom. He used to be on my father's place, and I came to see if I couldn't buy him back."

Legree's brow grew dark, and he broke out, passionately: "Yes, I did buy such a fellow,—and a h—l of a bargain I had of it, too! The most rebellious, saucy, impudent dog! Set up my niggers to run away; got off two gals, worth eight hundred or a thousand dollars apiece. He owned to that, and, when I bid him tell me where they was, he up and said he knew, but he wouldn't tell; and stood to it, though I gave him the cussedest flogging I ever gave nigger yet. I b'lieve he's trying to die; but I don't know as he'll make it out."

"Where is he?" said George, impetuously. "Let me see him." The cheeks of the young man were crimson, and his eyes flashed fire; but he prudently said nothing, as yet.

"He's in dat ar shed," said a little fellow, who stood holding George's horse.

Legree kicked the boy, and swore at him; but George, without saying another word, turned and strode to the spot.

Tom had been lying two days since the fatal night; not suffering, for every nerve of suffering was blunted and destroyed. He lay, for the most part, in a quiet stupor; for the laws of a powerful and well-knit frame would not at once release the imprisoned spirit. By stealth, there had been there, in the darkness of the night, poor desolated creatures, who stole from their scanty hours' rest, that they might repay to him some of those ministrations of love in which he had always been so abundant. Truly, those poor disciples had little to give,—only the cup of cold water; but it was given with full hearts.

Tears had fallen on that honest, insensible face,—tears of late repentance in the poor, ignorant heathen, whom his dying love and patience had awakened to repentance, and bitter prayers, breathed over him to a late-found Saviour, of whom they scarce knew more than the name, but whom the yearning ignorant heart of man never implores in vain.

Cassy, who had glided out of her place of concealment, and, by overhearing, learned the sacrifice that had been made for her and Emmeline, had been there, the night before, defying the danger of detection; and, moved by the few last words which the affectionate soul had yet strength to breathe, the long winter of despair, the ice of years, had given way, and the dark, despairing woman had wept and prayed.

When George entered the shed, he felt his head giddy and his heart sick. "Is it possible,—is it possible?" said he, kneeling down by him. "Uncle Tom, my poor, poor old friend!"

Something in the voice penetrated to the ear of the dying. He moved his head gently, smiled, and said,

> *"Jesus can make a dying-bed*
> *Feel soft as downy pillows are."*

Tears which did honor to his manly heart fell from the young man's eyes, as he bent over his poor friend.

"O, dear Uncle Tom! do wake,—do speak once more! Look up! Here's Mas'r George,—your own little Mas'r George. Don't you know me?"

"Mas'r George!" said Tom, opening his eyes, and speaking in a feeble voice; "Mas'r George!" He looked bewildered.

Slowly the idea seemed to fill his soul; and the vacant eye became fixed and brightened, the whole face lighted up, the hard hands clasped, and tears ran down the cheeks.

"Bless the Lord! it is,—it is,—it's all I wanted! They haven't forgot me. It warms my soul; it does my heart good! Now I shall die content! Bless the Lord, on my soul!"

"You shan't die! you mustn't die, nor think of it! I've come to buy you, and take you home," said George, with impetuous vehemence.

"O, Mas'r George, ye're too late. The Lord's bought me, and is going to take me home,—and I long to go. Heaven is better than Kintuck."

"O, don't die! It'll kill me!—it'll break my heart to think what you've suffered,—and lying in this old shed, here! Poor, poor fellow!"

"Don't call me poor fellow!" said Tom, solemnly, "I have been poor fellow; but that's all past and gone, now. I'm right in the door, going into glory! O, Mas'r George! Heaven has come! I've got the victory!—the Lord Jesus has given it to me! Glory be to His name!"

George was awe-struck at the force, the vehemence, the power, with which these broken sentences were uttered. He sat gazing in silence.

Tom grasped his hand, and continued,—"Ye mustn't, now, tell Chloe, poor soul! how ye found me;—'t would be so dreadful to her. Only tell her ye found me going into glory; and that I couldn't stay for no one. And tell her the Lord's stood by me everywhere and al'ays, and made everything light and easy. And oh, the poor chil'en, and the baby;—my old heart's been most broke for 'em, time and agin! Tell 'em all to follow me—follow me! Give my love to Mas'r, and dear good Missis, and everybody in the place! Ye don't know! 'Pears like I loves 'em all! I loves every creature everywhar!—it's nothing but love! O, Mas'r George! what a thing 't is to be a Christian!"

At this moment, Legree sauntered up to the door of the shed, looked in, with a dogged air of affected carelessness, and turned away.

"The old satan!" said George, in his indignation. "It's a comfort to think the devil will pay him for this, some of these days!"

"O, don't!,—oh, ye mustn't!" said Tom, grasping his hand; "he's a poor mis'able critter! it's awful to think on 't! Oh, if he only could repent, the Lord would forgive him now; but I'm 'feared he never will!"

"I hope he won't!" said George; "I never want to see him in heaven!"

"Hush, Mas'r George!—it worries me! Don't feel so! He an't done me no real harm,—only opened the gate of the kingdom for me; that's all!"

At this moment, the sudden flush of strength which the joy of meeting his young master had infused into the dying man gave way. A sudden sinking fell upon him; he closed his eyes; and that mysterious and sublime change passed over his face, that told the approach of other worlds.

He began to draw his breath with long, deep inspirations; and his broad chest rose and fell, heavily. The expression of his face was that of a conqueror.

"Who,—who,—who shall separate us from the love of Christ?" he said, in a voice that contended with mortal weakness; and, with a smile, he fell asleep.

George sat fixed with solemn awe. It seemed to him that the place was holy; and, as he closed the lifeless eyes, and rose up from the dead, only one thought possessed him,—that expressed by his simple old friend,— "What a thing it is to be a Christian!"

He turned: Legree was standing, sullenly, behind him.

Something in that dying scene had checked the natural fierceness of youthful passion. The presence of the man was simply loathsome to George; and he felt only an impulse to get away from him, with as few words as possible.

Fixing his keen dark eyes on Legree, he simply said, pointing to the dead, "You have got all you ever can of him. What shall I pay you for the body? I will take it away, and bury it decently."

"I don't sell dead niggers," said Legree, doggedly. "You are welcome to bury him where and when you like."

"Boys," said George, in an authoritative tone, to two or three negroes, who were looking at the body, "help me lift him up, and carry him to my wagon; and get me a spade."

One of them ran for a spade; the other two assisted George to carry the body to the wagon.

George neither spoke to nor looked at Legree, who did not countermand his orders, but stood, whistling, with an air of forced unconcern. He sulkily followed them to where the wagon stood at the door.

George spread his cloak in the wagon, and had the body carefully disposed of in it,—moving the seat, so as to give it room. Then he turned, fixed his eyes on Legree, and said, with forced composure,

"I have not, as yet, said to you what I think of this most atrocious affair;—this is not the time and place. But, sir, this innocent blood shall have justice. I will proclaim this murder. I will go to the very first magistrate, and expose you."

"Do!" said Legree, snapping his fingers, scornfully. "I'd like to see you doing it. Where you going to get witnesses?—how you going to prove it?—Come, now!"

George saw, at once, the force of this defiance. There was not a white person on the place; and, in all southern courts, the testimony of colored blood is nothing. He felt, at that moment, as if he could have rent the heavens with his heart's indignant cry for justice; but in vain.

"After all, what a fuss, for a dead nigger!" said Legree.

The word was as a spark to a powder magazine. Prudence was never a cardinal virtue of the Kentucky boy. George turned, and, with one indignant blow, knocked Legree flat upon his face; and, as he stood over him, blazing with wrath and defiance, he would have formed no bad personification of his great namesake triumphing over the dragon.[5]

Some men, however, are decidedly bettered by being knocked down. If a man lays them fairly flat in the dust, they seem immediately to conceive a respect for him; and Legree was one of this sort. As he rose, therefore, and brushed the dust from his clothes, he eyed the slowly-retreating wagon with some evident consideration; nor did he open his mouth till it was out of sight.

Beyond the boundaries of the plantation, George had noticed a dry, sandy knoll, shaded by a few trees: there they made the grave.

"Shall we take off the cloak, Mas'r?" said the negroes, when the grave was ready.

"No, no,—bury it with him! It's all I can give you, now, poor Tom, and you shall have it."

They laid him in; and the men shovelled away, silently. They banked it up, and laid green turf over it.

"You may go, boys," said George, slipping a quarter into the hand of each. They lingered about, however.

"If young Mas'r would please buy us—" said one.

"We'd serve him so faithful!" said the other.

"Hard times here, Mas'r!" said the first. "Do, Mas'r, buy us, please!"

"I can't!—I can't!" said George, with difficulty, motioning them off; "it's impossible!"

The poor fellows looked dejected, and walked off in silence.

---

[5]TRIUMPHING OVER THE DRAGON: A reference to Saint George, the patron saint of England, who, according to legend, killed a huge dragon.

"Witness, eternal God!" said George, kneeling on the grave of his poor friend; "oh, witness, that, from this hour, I will do *what one man can* to drive out this curse of slavery from my land!"

There is no monument to mark the last resting-place of our friend. He needs none! His Lord knows where he lies, and will raise him up, immortal, to appear with him when he shall appear in his glory.

Pity him not! Such a life and death is not for pity! Not in the riches of omnipotence is the chief glory of God; but in self-denying, suffering love! And blessed are the men whom he calls to fellowship with him, bearing their cross after him with patience. Of such it is written, "Blessed are they that mourn, for they shall be comforted."[6]

[1852]

---

[6]BLESSED ARE THEY THAT MOURN, FOR THEY SHALL BE COMFORTED: Matthew 5:4.

Harriet Jacobs

(1813–1897)

*Born a slave in Edenton, North Carolina, Harriet Jacobs lost both of her
parents (they were owned by different masters) when she was still a child;
her mother died when Jacobs was six, and her father died when she was
twelve. Jacobs grew up in the home of her mistress and then went to live
with the Norcom family, where in her early teens she fell prey to the sexual harassment of Dr. James Norcom. To forestall his advances, Jacobs
entered into a relationship with Samuel Tredwell Sawyer, an unmarried
white neighbor and lawyer, with whom she had a son (b. 1829) and a
daughter (b. 1833).*

*Norcom persisted, however, and Jacobs was forced to seek refuge
from him. For seven years she hid in the attic (9 by 7 feet, and 3 feet
high) of her grandmother's house in town, where she studied the Bible,
sewed clothes, and as best she could kept watch over her children. She
escaped to New York in 1842, and eventually she was reunited there
with her children—though as a fugitive slave, Jacobs remained under
threat of recapture and forced return to North Carolina. Her own freedom was secured—she was age forty—when a sympathetic Northern
friend bought her from the Norcom family (Norcom himself had died in
1850) and immediately freed her.*

*Jacobs was active in antislavery activity and agitation, and in the
1850s she started on the composition of her own life-story—a process
she detailed in a series of letters to Amy Post, a Quaker abolitionist
friend, and others. The manuscript was completed in 1858, but at first
Jacobs could not find a publisher for it.* Incidents in the Life of a Slave
Girl, *with a preface by the noted reformer and author Lydia Maria
Child, was privately printed and published early in 1861, just as the
Civil War began. During the war, and later, Jacobs worked on behalf of
African Americans in Washington, D.C., Virginia, and Georgia. She
spent the final decades of her life in Cambridge, Massachusetts, and
Washington, D.C.*

Incidents, *excerpted below, was Jacobs's only book, and for
decades after her death it was neglected, or mischaracterized as a
novel, or attributed to a white author who had produced a work of fiction in the persona of a slave woman. Finally, in the 1980s, through
the biographical research of Jean Fagan Yellin, scholars and students
came to value and study* Incidents *as an autobiographical narrative.
Yellin showed that Child played a role as editor but that Jacobs was
the author of* Incidents *and, furthermore, that she always regarded the
book as her work.*

At the outset of Incidents *Jacobs makes clear her intention: "I do
earnestly desire to arouse the women of the North to a realizing sense*

of the condition of two millions of women at the South, still in bondage, suffering what I suffered, and most of them far worse." But these words, directed to Northern white women and designed to rally them to the antislavery side, barely suggest the shocking nature of the account Jacobs gives, which takes readers into the intimate sexual details of her day-to-day experiences. Depicting Norcom as *"Dr. Flint"* and Sawyer as *"Mr. Sands,"* Jacobs presents herself as *"Linda Brent"* an effort to veil her identity, with its harrowing sexual history. Jacobs's own name did not appear on the book's title-page.

Jacobs demonstrates and dramatizes her abiding love for her children, and her heroism in this role linked her to the high ideal of motherhood prevalent in her era—and also connected her story with Harriet Beecher Stowe's account of brave, loving mothers in Uncle Tom's Cabin *(1852)*. But Jacobs portrays her maternal care and loyalty in the context of her own sexual victimization, as a woman compelled to enter one sexual relationship in order to protect herself from another. In its focus on sexual exploitation and resistance, family life, and domestic anguish, Incidents *effectively complements Frederick Douglass's* Narrative *(1845) and* My Bondage and My Freedom *(1855), the other great slave narratives of the period. Douglass, too, decries sexual attacks on black women by their white masters, but he does so from the outside, not from the perspective of the women themselves. The first and best female slave narrative,* Incidents in the Life of a Slave Girl *is now acknowledged as a landmark in African American and American literary histories.*

For biography, see Jean Fagan Yellin's introduction to Harriet A. Jacobs, Incidents in the Life of a Slave Girl: Written by Herself *(rev. ed., 2000). For additional texts and contexts:* Incidents in the Life of a Slave Girl, *ed. Nellie Y. McKay and Frances Smith Foster (2001). Also stimulating: William L. Andrews,* To Tell a Free Story: The First Century of Afro-American Autobiography, 1760–1865 *(1986); Karen Sánchez-Eppler,* Touching Liberty: Abolition, Feminism, and the Politics of the Body *(1993); and Harriet Jacobs and* Incidents in the Life of a Slave Girl: New Critical Essays, *ed. Deborah M. Garfield and Rafia Zafar (1996).*

From Incidents in the Life of a Slave Girl: Written by Herself

PREFACE BY THE AUTHOR

Reader, be assured this narrative is no fiction. I am aware that some of my adventures may seem incredible; but they are, nevertheless, strictly true. I have not exaggerated the wrongs inflicted by Slavery; on the contrary, my descriptions fall far short of the facts. I have concealed the names of places, and given persons fictitious names. I had no motive for secrecy on my own account, but I deemed it kind and considerate towards others to pursue this course.

I wish I were more competent to the task I have undertaken. But I trust my readers will excuse deficiencies in consideration of circumstances. I was born and reared in Slavery; and I remained in a Slave State twenty-seven years. Since I have been at the North, it has been necessary for me to work diligently for my own support, and the education of my children. This has not left me much leisure to make up for the loss of early opportunities to improve myself; and it has compelled me to write these pages at irregular intervals, whenever I could snatch an hour from household duties.

When I first arrived in Philadelphia, Bishop Paine[1] advised me to publish a sketch of my life, but I told him I was altogether incompetent to such an undertaking. Though I have improved my mind somewhat since that time, I still remain of the same opinion; but I trust my motives will excuse what might otherwise seem presumptuous. I have not written my experiences in order to attract attention to myself; on the contrary, it would have been more pleasant to me to have been silent about my own history. Neither do I care to excite sympathy for my own sufferings. But I do earnestly desire to arouse the women of the North to a realizing sense of the condition of two millions of women at the South, still in bondage, suffering what I suffered, and most of them far worse. I want to add my testimony to that of abler pens to convince the people of the Free States what Slavery really is. Only by experience can any one realize how

---

[1]BISHOP PAINE: Daniel A. Payne (1811–1893) was the child of free African Americans living in South Carolina. He moved north to attend Gettysburg Seminary in Pennsylvania and later became the sixth bishop of the African Methodist Episcopal Church. He was president of Wilberforce University in Ohio from 1863 to 1876.

deep, and dark, and foul is that pit of abominations. May the blessing of God rest on this imperfect effort in behalf of my persecuted people!

Linda Brent[2]

INTRODUCTION BY THE EDITOR

The author of the following autobiography is personally known to me, and her conversation and manners inspire me with confidence. During the last seventeen years, she has lived the greater part of the time with a distinguished family in New York, and has so deported herself as to be highly esteemed by them. This fact is sufficient, without further credentials of her character. I believe those who know her will not be disposed to doubt her veracity, though some incidents in her story are more romantic than fiction.

At her request, I have revised her manuscript; but such changes as I have made have been mainly for purposes of condensation and orderly arrangement. I have not added any thing to the incidents, or changed the import of her very pertinent remarks. With trifling exceptions, both the ideas and the language are her own. I pruned excrescences a little, but otherwise I had no reason for changing her lively and dramatic way of telling her own story. The names of both persons and places are known to me; but for good reasons I suppress them.

It will naturally excite surprise that a woman reared in Slavery should be able to write so well. But circumstances will explain this. In the first place, nature endowed her with quick perceptions. Secondly, the mistress, with whom she lived till she was twelve years old, was a kind, considerate friend, who taught her to read and spell. Thirdly, she was placed in favorable circumstances after she came to the North; having frequent intercourse with intelligent persons, who felt a friendly interest in her welfare, and were disposed to give her opportunities for self-improvement.

I am well aware that many will accuse me of indecorum for presenting these pages to the public; for the experiences of this intelligent and much-injured woman belong to a class which some call delicate subjects, and others indelicate. This peculiar phase of Slavery has generally been kept veiled; but the public ought to be made acquainted with its monstrous features, and I willingly take the responsibility of presenting them with the veil withdrawn. I do this for the sake of my sisters in bondage, who are suffering wrongs so foul, that our ears are too delicate to listen

[2]LINDA BRENT: The pseudonym under which Jacobs wrote and published her book.

to them. I do it with the hope of arousing conscientious and reflecting women at the North to a sense of their duty in the exertion of moral influence on the question of Slavery, on all possible occasions. I do it with the hope that every man who reads this narrative will swear solemnly before God that, so far as he has power to prevent it, no fugitive from Slavery shall ever be sent back to suffer in that loathsome den of corruption and cruelty.

    L. Maria Child[3]

I. CHILDHOOD

I was born a slave; but I never knew it till six years of happy childhood had passed away. My father was a carpenter, and considered so intelligent and skilful in his trade, that, when buildings out of the common line were to be erected, he was sent for from long distances, to be head workman. On condition of paying his mistress two hundred dollars a year, and supporting himself, he was allowed to work at his trade, and manage his own affairs. His strongest wish was to purchase his children; but, though he several times offered his hard earnings for that purpose, he never succeeded. In complexion my parents were a light shade of brownish yellow, and were termed mulattoes. They lived together in a comfortable home; and, though we were all slaves, I was so fondly shielded that I never dreamed I was a piece of merchandise, trusted to them for safe keeping, and liable to be demanded of them at any moment. I had one brother, William, who was two years younger than myself—a bright, affectionate child. I had also a great treasure in my maternal grandmother, who was a remarkable woman in many respects. She was the daughter of a planter in South Carolina, who, at his death, left her mother and his three children free, with money to go to St. Augustine,[4] where they had relatives. It was during the Revolutionary War; and they were captured on their passage, carried back, and sold to different purchasers. Such was the story my grandmother used to tell me; but I do not remember all the particulars. She was a little girl when she was captured and sold to the keeper of a large hotel.[5] I have often heard her tell how hard she fared during childhood. But as she grew older she evinced so much

[3]L. MARIA CHILD: Lydia Maria Child (1802–1880) was an American author and abolitionist from Massachusetts.
[4]ST. AUGUSTINE: During the Revolutionary War, St. Augustine, Florida, was a British port.
[5]KEEPER OF A LARGE HOTEL: Jacobs's grandmother, Molly Horniblow (c. 1771–1853), was purchased by John Horniblow, the innkeeper of the King's Arms hotel in Edenton, North Carolina. Slaves were often given the surname of their owner.

intelligence, and was so faithful, that her master and mistress could not help seeing it was for their interest to take care of such a valuable piece of property. She became an indispensable personage in the household, officiating in all capacities, from cook and wet nurse to seamstress. She was much praised for her cooking; and her nice crackers became so famous in the neighborhood that many people were desirous of obtaining them. In consequence of numerous requests of this kind, she asked permission of her mistress to bake crackers at night, after all the household work was done; and she obtained leave to do it, provided she would clothe herself and her children from the profits. Upon these terms, after working hard all day for her mistress, she began her midnight bakings, assisted by her two oldest children. The business proved profitable; and each year she laid by a little, which was saved for a fund to purchase her children. Her master died, and the property was divided among his heirs. The widow had her dower[6] in the hotel, which she continued to keep open. My grandmother remained in her service as a slave; but her children were divided among her master's children. As she had five, Benjamin, the youngest one, was sold, in order that each heir might have an equal portion of dollars and cents. There was so little difference in our ages that he seemed more like my brother than my uncle. He was a bright, handsome lad, nearly white; for he inherited the complexion my grandmother had derived from Anglo-Saxon ancestors. Though only ten years old, seven hundred and twenty dollars were paid for him. His sale was a terrible blow to my grandmother; but she was naturally hopeful, and she went to work with renewed energy, trusting in time to be able to purchase some of her children. She had laid up three hundred dollars, which her mistress one day begged as a loan, promising to pay her soon. The reader probably knows that no promise or writing given to a slave is legally binding; for, according to Southern laws, a slave, *being* property, can *hold* no property. When my grandmother lent her hard earnings to her mistress, she trusted solely to her honor. The honor of a slaveholder to a slave!

To this good grandmother I was indebted for many comforts. My brother Willie and I often received portions of the crackers, cakes, and preserves, she made to sell; and after we ceased to be children we were indebted to her for many more important services.

Such were the unusually fortunate circumstances of my early childhood. When I was six years old, my mother died; and then, for the first

---

[6]WIDOW HAD HER DOWER: A portion of a deceased husband's estate granted to his widow for her lifetime.

time, I learned, by the talk around me, that I was a slave. My mother's mistress was the daughter of my grandmother's mistress. She was the foster sister of my mother; they were both nourished at my grandmother's breast. In fact, my mother had been weaned at three months old, that the babe of the mistress might obtain sufficient food. They played together as children; and, when they became women, my mother was a most faithful servant to her whiter foster sister. On her death-bed her mistress promised that her children should never suffer for any thing; and during her lifetime she kept her word. They all spoke kindly of my dead mother, who had been a slave merely in name, but in nature was noble and womanly. I grieved for her, and my young mind was troubled with the thought who would now take care of me and my little brother. I was told that my home was now to be with her mistress; and I found it a happy one. No toilsome or disagreeable duties were imposed upon me. My mistress was so kind to me that I was always glad to do her bidding, and proud to labor for her as much as my young years would permit. I would sit by her side for hours, sewing diligently, with a heart as free from care as that of any free-born white child. When she thought I was tired, she would send me out to run and jump; and away I bounded, to gather berries or flowers to decorate her room. Those were happy days—too happy to last. The slave child had no thought for the morrow; but there came that blight, which too surely waits on every human being born to be a chattel.

When I was nearly twelve years old, my kind mistress sickened and died. As I saw the cheek grow paler, and the eye more glassy, how earnestly I prayed in my heart that she might live! I loved her; for she had been almost like a mother to me. My prayers were not answered. She died, and they buried her in the little churchyard, where, day after day, my tears fell upon her grave.

I was sent to spend a week with my grandmother. I was now old enough to begin to think of the future; and again and again I asked myself what they would do with me. I felt sure I should never find another mistress so kind as the one who was gone. She had promised my dying mother that her children should never suffer for any thing; and when I remembered that, and recalled her many proofs of attachment to me, I could not help having some hopes that she had left me free. My friends were almost certain it would be so. They thought she would be sure to do it, on account of my mother's love and faithful service. But, alas! we all know that the memory of a faithful slave does not avail much to save her children from the auction block.

After a brief period of suspense, the will of my mistress was read, and we learned that she had bequeathed me to her sister's daughter, a child of five years old. So vanished our hopes. My mistress had taught me the precepts of God's Word: "Thou shalt love thy neighbor as thyself."[7] "Whatsoever ye would that men should do unto you, do ye even so unto them."[8] But I was her slave, and I suppose she did not recognize me as her neighbor. I would give much to blot out from my memory that one great wrong. As a child, I loved my mistress; and, looking back on the happy days I spent with her, I try to think with less bitterness of this act of injustice. While I was with her, she taught me to read and spell; and for this privilege, which so rarely falls to the lot of a slave, I bless her memory.

She possessed but few slaves; and at her death those were all distributed among her relatives. Five of them were my grandmother's children, and had shared the same milk that nourished her mother's children. Notwithstanding my grandmother's long and faithful service to her owners, not one of her children escaped the auction block. These God-breathing machines are no more, in the sight of their masters, than the cotton they plant, or the horses they tend.

II. *The New Master and Mistress*

Dr. Flint,[9] a physician in the neighborhood, had married the sister of my mistress, and I was now the property of their little daughter. It was not without murmuring that I prepared for my new home; and what added to my unhappiness, was the fact that my brother William was purchased by the same family. My father, by his nature, as well as by the habit of transacting business as a skilful mechanic, had more of the feelings of a freeman than is common among slaves. My brother was a spirited boy; and being brought up under such influences, he early detested the name of master and mistress. One day, when his father and his mistress both happened to call him at the same time, he hesitated between the two; being perplexed to know which had the strongest claim upon his obedience. He finally concluded to go to his mistress. When my father reproved him for it, he said, "You both called me, and I didn't know which I ought to go to first."

"You are *my* child," replied our father, "and when I call you, you should come immediately, if you have to pass through fire and water."

[7]THOU SHALT LOVE THY NEIGHBOR AS THYSELF: Mark: 12:31.
[8]WHATSOEVER YE WOULD THAT MEN SHOULD DO UNTO YOU, DO YE EVEN SO UNTO THEM: Matthew 7:12.
[9]DR. FLINT: Dr. James Norcom.

Poor Willie! He was now to learn his first lesson of obedience to a master. Grandmother tried to cheer us with hopeful words, and they found an echo in the credulous hearts of youth.

When we entered our new home we encountered cold looks, cold words, and cold treatment. We were glad when the night came. On my narrow bed I moaned and wept, I felt so desolate and alone.

I had been there nearly a year, when a dear little friend of mine was buried. I heard her mother sob, as the clods fell on the coffin of her only child, and I turned away from the grave, feeling thankful that I still had something left to love. I met my grandmother, who said, "Come with me, Linda;" and from her tone I knew that something sad had happened. She led me apart from the people, and then said, "My child, your father is dead." Dead! How could I believe it? He had died so suddenly I had not even heard that he was sick. I went home with my grandmother. My heart rebelled against God, who had taken from me mother, father, mistress, and friend. The good grandmother tried to comfort me. "Who knows the ways of God?" said she. "Perhaps they have been kindly taken from the evil days to come." Years afterwards I often thought of this. She promised to be a mother to her grandchildren, so far as she might be permitted to do so; and strengthened by her love, I returned to my master's. I thought I should be allowed to go to my father's house the next morning; but I was ordered to go for flowers, that my mistress's house might be decorated for an evening party. I spent the day gathering flowers and weaving them into festoons, while the dead body of my father was lying within a mile of me. What cared my owners for that? he was merely a piece of property. Moreover, they thought he had spoiled his children, by teaching them to feel that they were human beings. This was blasphemous doctrine for a slave to teach; presumptuous in him, and dangerous to the masters.

The next day I followed his remains to a humble grave beside that of my dear mother. There were those who knew my father's worth, and respected his memory.

My home now seemed more dreary than ever. The laugh of the little slave-children sounded harsh and cruel. It was selfish to feel so about the joy of others. My brother moved about with a very grave face. I tried to comfort him, by saying, "Take courage, Willie; brighter days will come by and by."

"You don't know any thing about it, Linda," he replied. "We shall have to stay here all our days; we shall never be free."

I argued that we were growing older and stronger, and that perhaps we might, before long, be allowed to hire our own time, and then we could earn money to buy our freedom. William declared this was much easier to say than to do; moreover, he did not intend to *buy* his freedom. We held daily controversies upon this subject.

Little attention was paid to the slaves' meals in Dr. Flint's house. If they could catch a bit of food while it was going, well and good. I gave myself no trouble on that score, for on my various errands I passed my grandmother's house, where there was always something to spare for me. I was frequently threatened with punishment if I stopped there; and my grandmother, to avoid detaining me, often stood at the gate with something for my breakfast or dinner. I was indebted to *her* for all my comforts, spiritual or temporal. It was *her* labor that supplied my scanty wardrobe. I have a vivid recollection of the linsey-woolsey[10] dress given me every winter by Mrs. Flint. How I hated it! It was one of the badges of slavery.

While my grandmother was thus helping to support me from her hard earnings, the three hundred dollars she had lent her mistress were never repaid. When her mistress died, her son-in-law, Dr. Flint, was appointed executor. When grandmother applied to him for payment, he said the estate was insolvent, and the law prohibited payment. It did not, however, prohibit him from retaining the silver candelabra, which had been purchased with that money. I presume they will be handed down in the family, from generation to generation.

My grandmother's mistress had always promised her that, at her death, she should be free; and it was said that in her will she made good the promise. But when the estate was settled, Dr. Flint told the faithful old servant that, under existing circumstances, it was necessary she should be sold.

On the appointed day, the customary advertisement was posted up, proclaiming that there would be a "public sale of negroes, horses, &c." Dr. Flint called to tell my grandmother that he was unwilling to wound her feelings by putting her up at auction, and that he would prefer to dispose of her at private sale. My grandmother saw through his hypocrisy; she understood very well that he was ashamed of the job. She was a very spirited woman, and if he was base enough to sell her, when her mistress intended she should be free, she was determined the public should know it. She had for a long time supplied many families with crackers and preserves; consequently, "Aunt Marthy," as she was called, was generally known, and every body who knew her respected her intelligence and good character. Her long and faithful service in the family was also well known, and the intention of her

---

[10]LINSEY-WOOLSEY: A dress material of coarse, inferior wool.

mistress to leave her free. When the day of sale came, she took her place among the chattels, and at the first call she sprang upon the auction-block. Many voices called out, "Shame! Shame! Who is going to sell *you*, aunt Marthy? Don't stand there! That is no place for *you*." Without saying a word, she quietly awaited her fate. No one bid for her. At last, a feeble voice said, "Fifty dollars." It came from a maiden lady, seventy years old, the sister of my grandmother's deceased mistress. She had lived forty years under the same roof with my grandmother; she knew how faithfully she had served her owners, and how cruelly she had been defrauded of her rights; and she resolved to protect her. The auctioneer waited for a higher bid; but her wishes were respected; no one bid above her. She could neither read nor write; and when the bill of sale was made out, she signed it with a cross. But what consequence was that, when she had a big heart overflowing with human kindness? She gave the old servant her freedom.

At that time, my grandmother was just fifty years old. Laborious years had passed since then; and now my brother and I were slaves to the man who had defrauded her of her money, and tried to defraud her of her freedom. One of my mother's sisters, called Aunt Nancy, was also a slave in his family. She was a kind, good aunt to me; and supplied the place of both housekeeper and waiting maid to her mistress. She was, in fact, at the beginning and end of every thing.

Mrs. Flint, like many southern women, was totally deficient in energy. She had not strength to superintend her household affairs; but her nerves were so strong, that she could sit in her easy chair and see a woman whipped, till the blood trickled from every stroke of the lash. She was a member of the church; but partaking of the Lord's supper did not seem to put her in a Christian frame of mind. If dinner was not served at the exact time on that particular Sunday, she would station herself in the kitchen, and wait till it was dished, and then spit in all the kettles and pans that had been used for cooking. She did this to prevent the cook and her children from eking out their meagre fare with the remains of the gravy and other scrapings. The slaves could get nothing to eat except what she chose to give them. Provisions were weighed out by the pound and ounce, three times a day. I can assure you she gave them no chance to eat wheat bread from her flour barrel. She knew how many biscuits a quart of flour would make, and exactly what size they ought to be.

Dr. Flint was an epicure.[11] The cook never sent a dinner to his table without fear and trembling; for if there happened to be a dish not to his liking, be would either order her to be whipped, or compel her to

[11]EPICURE: A person who cultivates a refined taste in food and drink.

eat every mouthful of it in his presence. The poor, hungry creature might not have objected to eating it; but she did object to having her master cram it down her throat till she choked.

They had a pet dog, that was a nuisance in the house. The cook was ordered to make some Indian mush[12] for him. He refused to eat, and when his head was held over it, the froth flowed from his mouth into the basin. He died a few minutes after. When Dr. Flint came in, he said the mush had not been well cooked, and that was the reason the animal would not eat it. He sent for the cook, and compelled her to eat it. He thought that the woman's stomach was stronger than the dog's; but her sufferings afterwards proved that he was mistaken. This poor woman endured many cruelties from her master and mistress; sometimes she was locked up, away from her nursing baby, for a whole day and night.

When I had been in the family a few weeks, one of the plantation slaves was brought to town, by order of his master. It was near night when he arrived, and Dr. Flint ordered him to be taken to the work house, and tied up to the joist,[13] so that his feet would just escape the ground. In that situation he was to wait till the doctor had taken his tea. I shall never forget that night. Never before, in my life, had I heard hundreds of blows fall, in succession, on a human being. His piteous groans, and his "O, pray don't, massa," rang in my ear for months afterwards. There were many conjectures as to the cause of this terrible punishment. Some said master accused him of stealing corn; others said the slave had quarrelled with his wife, in presence of the overseer, and had accused his master of being the father of her child. They were both black, and the child was very fair.

I went into the work house next morning, and saw the cowhide still wet with blood, and the boards all covered with gore. The poor man lived, and continued to quarrel with his wife. A few months afterwards Dr. Flint handed them both over to a slave-trader. The guilty man put their value into his pocket, and had the satisfaction of knowing that they were out of sight and hearing. When the mother was delivered into the trader's hands, she said, "You *promised* to treat me well." To which he replied, "You have let your tongue run too far; damn you!" She had forgotten that it was a crime for a slave to tell who was the father of her child.

From others than the master persecution also comes in such cases. I once saw a young slave girl dying soon after the birth of a child nearly white. In her agony she cried out, "O Lord, come and take me!" Her

---

[12]INDIAN MUSH: A thick porridge made of cornmeal.
[13]JOIST: A crossbeam to which the boards of a floor or ceiling are nailed.

mistress stood by, and mocked at her like an incarnate fiend. "You suffer, do you?" she exclaimed. "I am glad of it. You deserve it all, and more too."

The girl's mother said, "The baby is dead, thank God; and I hope my poor child will soon be in heaven, too."

"Heaven!" retorted the mistress. "There is no such place for the like of her and her bastard."

The poor mother turned away, sobbing. Her dying daughter called her, feebly, and as she bent over her, I heard her say, "Don't grieve so, mother; God knows all about it; and HE will have mercy upon me."

Her sufferings, afterwards, became so intense, that her mistress felt unable to stay; but when she left the room, the scornful smile was still on her lips. Seven children called her mother. The poor black woman had but the one child, whose eyes she saw closing in death, while she thanked God for taking her away from the greater bitterness of life.

III. THE SLAVES' NEW YEAR'S DAY

Dr. Flint owned a fine residence in town, several farms, and about fifty slaves, besides hiring a number by the year.

Hiring-day at the south takes place on the 1st of January. On the 2d, the slaves are expected to go to their new masters. On a farm, they work until the corn and cotton are laid. They then have two holidays. Some masters give them a good dinner under the trees. This over, they work until Christmas eve. If no heavy charges are meantime brought against them, they are given four or five holidays, whichever the master or overseer may think proper. Then comes New Year's eve; and they gather together their little alls, or more properly speaking, their little nothings, and wait anxiously for the dawning of day. At the appointed hour the grounds are thronged with men, women, and children, waiting, like criminals, to hear their doom pronounced. The slave is sure to know who is the most humane, or cruel master, within forty miles of him.

It is easy to find out, on that day, who clothes and feeds his slaves well; for he is surrounded by a crowd, begging, "Please, massa, hire me this year. I will work *very* hard, massa."

If a slave is unwilling to go with his new master, he is whipped, or locked up in jail, until he consents to go, and promises not to run away during the year. Should he chance to change his mind, thinking it justifiable to violate an extorted promise, woe unto him if he is caught! The whip is used till the blood flows at his feet; and his stiffened limbs are put in chains, to be dragged in the field for days and days!

If he lives until the next year, perhaps the same man will hire him again, without even giving him an opportunity of going to the hiring-ground. After those for hire are disposed of, those for sale are called up.

O, you happy free women, contrast *your* New Year's day with that of the poor bond-woman! With you it is a pleasant season, and the light of the day is blessed. Friendly wishes meet you every where, and gifts are showered upon you. Even hearts that have been estranged from you soften at this season, and lips that have been silent echo back, "I wish you a happy New Year." Children bring their little offerings, and raise their rosy lips for a caress. They are your own, and no hand but that of death can take them from you.

But to the slave mother New Year's day comes laden with peculiar sorrows. She sits on her cold cabin floor, watching the children who may all be torn from her the next morning; and often does she wish that she and they might die before the day dawns. She may be an ignorant creature, degraded by the system that has brutalized her from childhood; but she has a mother's instincts, and is capable of feeling a mother's agonies.

On one of these sale days, I saw a mother lead seven children to the auction-block. She knew that *some* of them would be taken from her; but they took *all*. The children were sold to a slave-trader, and their mother was bought by a man in her own town. Before night her children were all far away. She begged the trader to tell her where he intended to take them; this he refused to do. How *could* he, when he knew he would sell them, one by one, wherever he could command the highest price? I met that mother in the street, and her wild, haggard face lives to-day in my mind. She wrung her hands in anguish, and exclaimed, "Gone! All gone! Why *dont* God kill me?" I had no words wherewith to comfort her. Instances of this kind are of daily, yea, of hourly occurrence.

Slaveholders have a method, peculiar to their institution, of getting rid of *old* slaves, whose lives have been worn out in their service. I knew an old woman, who for seventy years faithfully served her master. She had become almost helpless, from hard labor and disease. Her owners moved to Alabama, and the old black woman was left to be sold to any body who would give twenty dollars for her.

V. *The Trials of Girlhood*

During the first years of my service in Dr. Flint's family, I was accustomed to share some indulgences with the children of my mistress. Though this seemed to me no more than right, I was grateful for it, and tried to merit the kindness by the faithful discharge of my duties. But I now entered on my fifteenth year—a sad epoch in the life of a slave girl. My master began to whisper foul words in my ear. Young as I was, I could not remain ignorant of their import. I tried to treat them with indifference or contempt. The master's age, my extreme youth, and the fear that his conduct would be reported to my grandmother, made him bear this treatment for many months. He was a crafty man, and resorted to many means to accomplish his purposes. Sometimes he had stormy, terrific ways, that made his victims tremble; sometimes he assumed a gentleness that he thought must surely subdue. Of the two, I preferred his stormy moods, although they left me trembling. He tried his utmost to corrupt the pure principles my grandmother had instilled. He peopled my young mind with unclean images, such as only a vile monster could think of. I turned from him with disgust and hatred. But he was my master. I was compelled to live under the same roof with him—where I saw a man forty years my senior daily violating the most sacred commandments of nature. He told me I was his property; that I must be subject to his will in all things. My soul revolted against the mean tyranny. But where could I turn for protection? No matter whether the slave girl be as black as ebony or as fair as her mistress. In either case, there is no shadow of law to protect her from insult, from violence, or even from death; all these are inflicted by fiends who bear the shape of men. The mistress, who ought to protect the helpless victim, has no other feelings towards her but those of jealousy and rage. The degradation, the wrongs, the vices, that grow out of slavery, are more than I can describe. They are greater than you would willingly believe. Surely, if you credited one half the truths that are told you concerning the helpless millions suffering in this cruel bondage, you at the north would not help to tighten the yoke. You surely would refuse to do for the master, on your own soil, the mean and cruel work which trained bloodhounds and the lowest class of whites do for him at the south.[14]

Every where the years bring to all enough of sin and sorrow; but in slavery the very dawn of life is darkened by these shadows. Even the little child, who is accustomed to wait on her mistress and her children, will learn, before she is twelve years old, why it is that her mistress hates such and such a one among the slaves. Perhaps the child's own mother

---

[14]YOU SURELY WOULD REFUSE...THE LOWEST CLASS OF WHITES DO FOR HIM AT THE SOUTH: The Fugitive Slave Law, passed as part of the Compromise of 1850, mandated that citizens of northern (nonslave) states had to aid and assist federal authorities in the return of fugitive slaves. Heavy penalties were to be imposed on anyone who assisted a slave's escape. The law incensed many northerners who had been previously uninvolved in issues connected to slavery. The act was repealed by Congress on June 28, 1864.

is among those hated ones. She listens to violent outbreaks of jealous passion, and cannot help understanding what is the cause. She will become prematurely knowing in evil things. Soon she will learn to tremble when she hears her master's footfall. She will be compelled to realize that she is no longer a child. If God has bestowed beauty upon her, it will prove her greatest curse. That which commands admiration in the white woman only hastens the degradation of the female slave. I know that some are too much brutalized by slavery to feel the humiliation of their position; but many slaves feel it most acutely, and shrink from the memory of it. I cannot tell how much I suffered in the presence of these wrongs, nor how I am still pained by the retrospect. My master met me at every turn, reminding me that I belonged to him, and swearing by heaven and earth that he would compel me to submit to him. If I went out for a breath of fresh air, after a day of unwearied toil, his footsteps dogged me. If I knelt by my mother's grave, his dark shadow fell on me even there. The light heart which nature had given me became heavy with sad forebodings. The other slaves in my master's house noticed the change. Many of them pitied me; but none dared to ask the cause. They had no need to inquire. They knew too well the guilty practices under that roof; and they were aware that to speak of them was an offence that never went unpunished.

I longed for some one to confide in. I would have given the world to have laid my head on my grandmother's faithful bosom, and told her all my troubles. But Dr. Flint swore he would kill me, if I was not as silent as the grave. Then, although my grandmother was all in all to me, I feared her as well as loved her. I had been accustomed to look up to her with a respect bordering upon awe. I was very young, and felt shamefaced about telling her such impure things, especially as I knew her to be very strict on such subjects. Moreover, she was a woman of a high spirit. She was usually very quiet in her demeanor; but if her indignation was once roused, it was not very easily quelled. I had been told that she once chased a white gentleman with a loaded pistol, because he insulted one of her daughters. I dreaded the consequences of a violent outbreak; and both pride and fear kept me silent. But though I did not confide in my grandmother, and even evaded her vigilant watchfulness and inquiry, her presence in the neighborhood was some protection to me. Though she had been a slave, Dr. Flint was afraid of her. He dreaded her scorching rebukes. Moreover, she was known and patronized by many people; and he did not wish to have his villainy made public. It was lucky for me that I did not live on a distant plantation, but in a town not so large that the inhabitants were ignorant of each other's affairs. Bad as are the laws and customs in a slaveholding community, the doctor, as a professional man, deemed it prudent to keep up some outward show of decency.

O, what days and nights of fear and sorrow that man caused me! Reader, it is not to awaken sympathy for myself that I am telling you truthfully what I suffered in slavery. I do it to kindle a flame of compassion in your hearts for my sisters who are still in bondage, suffering as I once suffered.

I once saw two beautiful children playing together. One was a fair white child; the other was her slave, and also her sister. When I saw them embracing each other, and heard their joyous laughter, I turned sadly away from the lovely sight. I foresaw the inevitable blight that would fall on the little slave's heart. I knew how soon her laughter would be changed to sighs. The fair child grew up to be a still fairer woman. From childhood to womanhood her pathway was blooming with flowers, and overarched by a sunny sky. Scarcely one day of her life had been clouded when the sun rose on her happy bridal morning.

How had those years dealt with her slave sister, the little playmate of her childhood? She, also, was very beautiful; but the flowers and sunshine of love were not for her. She drank the cup of sin, and shame, and misery, whereof her persecuted race are compelled to drink.

In view of these things, why are ye silent, ye free men and women of the north? Why do your tongues falter in maintenance of the right? Would that I had more ability! But my heart is so full, and my pen is so weak! There are noble men and women who plead for us, striving to help those who cannot help themselves. God bless them! God give them strength and courage to go on! God bless those, every where, who are laboring to advance the cause of humanity!

VI. THE JEALOUS MISTRESS

I would ten thousand times rather that my children should be the half-starved paupers of Ireland[15] than to be the most pampered among the slaves of America. I would rather drudge out my life on a cotton plantation, till the grave opened to give me rest, than to live with an unprincipled master and a jealous mistress. The felon's home in a penitentiary is preferable. He may repent, and turn from the error of his ways, and so find peace; but it is not so with a favorite slave. She is not allowed

---

[15]HALF-STARVED PAUPERS OF IRELAND: Jacobs is referring to victims of the Great Potato Famine (1845–1849) in Ireland, when the potato crop failed due to blight. Hundreds of thousands of people died from hunger and disease. The argument was often made by proslavery advocates that slaves were better off than the impoverished lower classes of England, Ireland, and continental Europe.

to have any pride of character. It is deemed a crime in her to wish to be virtuous.

Mrs. Flint possessed the key to her husband's character before I was born. She might have used this knowledge to counsel and to screen the young and the innocent among her slaves; but for them she had no sympathy. They were the objects of her constant suspicion and malevolence. She watched her husband with unceasing vigilance; but he was well practised in means to evade it. What he could not find opportunity to say in words he manifested in signs. He invented more than were ever thought of in a deaf and dumb asylum. I let them pass, as if I did not understand what he meant; and many were the curses and threats bestowed on me for my stupidity. One day he caught me teaching myself to write. He frowned, as if he was not well pleased; but I suppose be came to the conclusion that such an accomplishment might help to advance his favorite scheme. Before long, notes were often slipped into my hand. I would return them, saying, "I can't read them, sir." "Can't you?" he replied; "then I must read them to you." He always finished the reading by asking, "Do you understand?" Sometimes he would complain of the heat of the tea room, and order his supper to be placed on a small table in the piazza. He would seat himself there with a well-satisfied smile, and tell me to stand by and brush away the flies. He would eat very slowly, pausing between the mouthfuls. These intervals were employed in describing the happiness I was so foolishly throwing away, and in threatening me with the penalty that finally awaited my stubborn disobedience. He boasted much of the forbearance he had exercised towards me, and reminded me that there was a limit to his patience. When I succeeded in avoiding opportunities for him to talk to me at home, I was ordered to come to his office, to do some errand. When there, I was obliged to stand and listen to such language as he saw fit to address to me. Sometimes I so openly expressed my contempt for him that he would become violently enraged, and I wondered why he did not strike me. Circumstanced as he was, he probably thought it was better policy to be forbearing. But the state of things grew worse and worse daily. In desperation I told him that I must and would apply to my grandmother for protection. He threatened me with death, and worse than death, if I made any complaint to her. Strange to say, I did not despair. I was naturally of a buoyant disposition, and always I had a hope of somehow getting out of his clutches. Like many a poor, simple slave before me, I trusted that some threads of joy would yet be woven into my dark destiny.

I had entered my sixteenth year, and every day it became more apparent that my presence was intolerable to Mrs. Flint. Angry words frequently passed between her and her husband. He had never punished me himself, and he would not allow any body else to punish me. In that respect, she was never satisfied; but, in her angry moods, no terms were too vile for her to bestow upon me. Yet I, whom she detested so bitterly, had far more pity for her than he had, whose duty it was to make her life happy. I never wronged her, or wished to wrong her; and one word of kindness from her would have brought me to her feet.

After repeated quarrels between the doctor and his wife, he announced his intention to take his youngest daughter, then four years old, to sleep in his apartment. It was necessary that a servant should sleep in the same room, to be on hand if the child stirred. I was selected for that office, and informed for what purpose that arrangement had been made. By managing to keep within sight of people, as much as possible, during the day time, I had hitherto succeeded in eluding my master, though a razor was often held to my throat to force me to change this line of policy. At night I slept by the side of my great aunt, where I felt safe. He was too prudent to come into her room. She was an old woman, and had been in the family many years. Moreover, as a married man, and a professional man, he deemed it necessary to save appearances in some degree. But he resolved to remove the obstacle in the way of his scheme; and he thought he had planned it so that he should evade suspicion. He was well aware how much I prized my refuge by the side of my old aunt, and he determined to dispossess me of it. The first night the doctor had the little child in his room alone. The next morning, I was ordered to take my station as nurse the following night. A kind Providence interposed in my favor. During the day Mrs. Flint heard of this new arrangement, and a storm followed. I rejoiced to hear it rage.

After a while my mistress sent for me to come to her room. Her first question was, "Did you know you were to sleep in the doctor's room?"

"Yes, ma'am."

"Who told you?"

"My master."

"Will you answer truly all the questions I ask?"

"Yes, ma'am."

"Tell me, then, as you hope to be forgiven, are you innocent of what I have accused you?"

"I am."

She handed me a Bible, and said, "Lay your hand on your heart, kiss this holy book, and swear before God that you tell me the truth."

I took the oath she required, and I did it with a clear conscience.

"You have taken God's holy word to testify your innocence," said she. "If you have deceived me, beware! Now take this stool, sit down, look me directly in the face, and tell me all that has passed between your master and you."

I did as she ordered. As I went on with my account her color changed frequently, she wept, and sometimes groaned. She spoke in tones so sad, that I was touched by her grief. The tears came to my eyes; but I was soon convinced that her emotions arose from anger and wounded pride. She felt that her marriage vows were desecrated, her dignity insulted; but she had no compassion for the poor victim of her husband's perfidy. She pitied herself as a martyr; but she was incapable of feeling for the condition of shame and misery in which her unfortunate, helpless slave was placed.

Yet perhaps she had some touch of feeling for me; for when the conference was ended, she spoke kindly, and promised to protect me. I should have been much comforted by this assurance if I could have had confidence in it; but my experiences in slavery had filled me with distrust. She was not a very refined woman, and had not much control over her passions. I was an object of her jealousy, and, consequently, of her hatred; and I knew I could not expect kindness or confidence from her under the circumstances in which I was placed. I could not blame her. Slaveholders' wives feel as other women would under similar circumstances. The fire of her temper kindled from small sparks, and now the flame became so intense that the doctor was obliged to give up his intended arrangement.

I knew I had ignited the torch, and I expected to suffer for it afterwards; but I felt too thankful to my mistress for the timely aid she rendered me to care much about that. She now took me to sleep in a room adjoining her own. There I was an object of her especial care, though not of her especial comfort, for she spent many a sleepless night to watch over me. Sometimes I woke up, and found her bending over me. At other times she whispered in my ear, as though it was her husband who was speaking to me, and listened to hear what I would answer. If she startled me, on such occasions, she would glide stealthily away; and the next morning she would tell me I had been talking in my sleep, and ask who I was talking to. At last, I began to be fearful for my life. It had been often threatened; and you can imagine, better than I can describe, what an unpleasant sensation it must produce to wake up in the dead of night and find a jealous woman bending over you. Terrible as this experience was, I had fears that it would give place to one more terrible.

My mistress grew weary of her vigils; they did not prove satisfactory. She changed her tactics. She now tried the trick of accusing my master of crime, in my presence, and gave my name as the author of the accusation. To my utter astonishment, he replied, "I don't believe it; but if she did acknowledge it, you tortured her into exposing me." Tortured into exposing him! Truly, Satan had no difficulty in distinguishing the color of his soul! I understood his object in making this false representation. It was to show me that I gained nothing by seeking the protection of my mistress; that the power was still all in his own hands. I pitied Mrs. Flint. She was a second wife, many years the junior of her husband; and the hoary-headed miscreant was enough to try the patience of a wiser and better woman. She was completely foiled, and knew not how to proceed. She would gladly have had me flogged for my supposed false oath; but, as I have already stated, the doctor never allowed any one to whip me. The old sinner was politic. The application of the lash might have led to remarks that would have exposed him in the eyes of his children and grandchildren. How often did I rejoice that I lived in a town where all the inhabitants knew each other! If I had been on a remote plantation, or lost among the multitude of a crowded city, I should not be a living woman at this day.

The secrets of slavery are concealed like those of the Inquisition.[16] My master was, to my knowledge, the father of eleven slaves. But did the mothers dare to tell who was the father of their children? Did the other slaves dare to allude to it, except in whispers among themselves? No, indeed! They knew too well the terrible consequences.

My grandmother could not avoid seeing things which excited her suspicions. She was uneasy about me, and tried various ways to buy me; but the never-changing answer was always repeated: "Linda does not belong to *me*. She is my daughter's property, and I have no legal right to sell her." The conscientious man! He was too scrupulous to *sell* me; but he had no scruples whatever about committing a much greater wrong against the helpless young girl placed under his guardianship, as his daughter's property. Sometimes my persecutor would ask me whether I would like to be sold. I told him I would rather be sold to any body than to lead such a life as I did. On such occasions he would assume the air of a very injured individual, and reproach me for my ingratitude. "Did I not take you into the house, and make you the companion of my own children?" he would say. "Have I ever treated you like a negro? I have never allowed you to be punished, not even to please your mistress. And this is the recompense I get, you ungrateful girl!" I answered that he had reasons

---

[16]INQUISITION: A court of the Roman Catholic Church, established to investigate heresy, with a reputation for secrecy and intrigue. It was abolished in 1834.

of his own for screening me from punishment, and that the course he pursued made my mistress hate me and persecute me. If I wept, he would say, "Poor child! Don't cry! don't cry! I will make peace for you with your mistress. Only let me arrange matters in my own way. Poor, foolish girl! you don't know what is for your own good. I would cherish you. I would make a lady of you. Now go, and think of all I have promised you."

I did think of it.

Reader, I draw no imaginary pictures of southern homes. I am telling you the plain truth. Yet when victims make their escape from this wild beast of Slavery, northerners consent to act the part of bloodhounds, and hunt the poor fugitive back into his den, "full of dead men's bones, and all uncleanness."[17] Nay, more, they are not only willing, but proud, to give their daughters in marriage to slaveholders. The poor girls have romantic notions of a sunny clime, and of the flowering vines that all the year round shade a happy home. To what disappointments are they destined! The young wife soon learns that the husband in whose hands she has placed her happiness pays no regard to his marriage vows. Children of every shade of complexion play with her own fair babies, and too well she knows that they are born unto him of his own household. Jealousy and hatred enter the flowery home, and it is ravaged of its loveliness.

Southern women often marry a man knowing that he is the father of many little slaves. They do not trouble themselves about it. They regard such children as property, as marketable as the pigs on the plantation; and it is seldom that they do not make them aware of this by passing them into the slave-trader's hands as soon as possible, and thus getting them out of their sight. I am glad to say there are some honorable exceptions.

I have myself known two southern wives who exhorted their husbands to free those slaves towards whom they stood in a "parental relation;" and their request was granted. These husbands blushed before the superior nobleness of their wives' natures. Though they had only counselled them to do that which it was their duty to do, it commanded their respect, and rendered their conduct more exemplary. Concealment was at an end, and confidence took the place of distrust.

Though this bad institution deadens the moral sense, even in white women, to a fearful extent, it is not altogether extinct. I have heard southern ladies say of Mr. Such a one, "He not only thinks it no disgrace to

---

[17]FULL OF DEAD MEN'S BONES, AND ALL UNCLEANESS: Matthew 23:27: "Woe unto you, scribes and Pharisees, hypocrites! for ye are like unto whited sepulchres, which indeed appear beautiful outward, but are within full of dead men's bones, and of all uncleanness."

be the father of those little niggers, but he is not ashamed to call himself their master. I declare, such things ought not to be tolerated in any decent society!"

VII. THE LOVER

Why does the slave ever love? Why allow the tendrils of the heart to twine around objects which may at any moment be wrenched away by the hand of violence? When separations come by the hand of death, the pious soul can bow in resignation, and say, "Not my will, but thine be done, O Lord!"[18] But when the ruthless hand of man strikes the blow, regardless of the misery he causes, it is hard to be submissive. I did not reason thus when I was a young girl. Youth will be youth. I loved, and I indulged the hope that the dark clouds around me would turn out a bright lining. I forgot that in the land of my birth the shadows are too dense for light to penetrate. A land

> *"Where laughter is not mirth; nor thought the mind;*
> *Nor words a language; nor e'en men mankind.*
> *Where cries reply to curses, shrieks to blows,*
> *And each is tortured in his separate hell."*[19]

There was in the neighborhood a young colored carpenter; a free born man. We had been well acquainted in childhood, and frequently met together afterwards. We became mutually attached, and he proposed to marry me. I loved him with all the ardor of a young girl's first love. But when I reflected that I was a slave, and that the laws gave no sanction to the marriage of such, my heart sank within me. My lover wanted to buy me; but I knew that Dr. Flint was too wilful and arbitrary a man to consent to that arrangement. From him, I was sure of experiencing all sorts of opposition, and I had nothing to hope from my mistress. She would have been delighted to have got rid of me, but not in that way. It would have relieved her mind of a burden if she could have seen me sold to some distant state, but if I was married near home I should be just as much in her husband's power as I had previously been,—for the husband of a slave has no power to protect her. Moreover, my mistress, like many others, seemed to think that slaves had no right to any family ties

[18]NOT MY WILL, BUT THINE BE DONE, O LORD: Words spoken by Jesus in the olive garden of Gethsemane before his arrest, which led to his crucifixion. Matthew 26:39: "And he went a little further, and fell on his face, and prayed, saying, O my Father, if it be possible, let this cup pass from me: nevertheless not as I will, but as thou wilt."
[19]AND EACH IS TORTURED IN HIS SEPARATE HELL: From "The Lament of Tasso," by George Gordon, Lord Byron (1788–1824).

of their own; that they were created merely to wait upon the family of the mistress. I once heard her abuse a young slave girl, who told her that a colored man wanted to make her his wife. "I will have you peeled and pickled,[20] my lady," said she, "if I ever hear you mention that subject again. Do you suppose that I will have you tending *my* children with the children of that nigger?" The girl to whom she said this had a mulatto child, of course not acknowledged by its father. The poor black man who loved her would have been proud to acknowledge his helpless offspring.

Many and anxious were the thoughts I revolved in my mind. I was at a loss what to do. Above all things, I was desirous to spare my lover the insults that had cut so deeply into my own soul. I talked with my grandmother about it, and partly told her my fears. I did not dare to tell her the worst. She had long suspected all was not right, and if I confirmed her suspicions I knew a storm would rise that would prove the overthrow of all my hopes.

This love-dream had been my support through many trials; and I could not bear to run the risk of having it suddenly dissipated. There was a lady in the neighborhood, a particular friend of Dr. Flint's, who often visited the house. I had a great respect for her, and she had always manifested a friendly interest in me. Grandmother thought she would have great influence with the doctor. I went to this lady, and told her my story. I told her I was aware that my lover's being a free-born man would prove a great objection; but he wanted to buy me; and if Dr. Flint would consent to that arrangement, I felt sure he would be willing to pay any reasonable price. She knew that Mrs. Flint disliked me; therefore, I ventured to suggest that perhaps my mistress would approve of my being sold, as that would rid her of me. The lady listened with kindly sympathy, and promised to do her utmost to promote my wishes. She had an interview with the doctor, and I believe she pleaded my cause earnestly; but it was all to no purpose.

How I dreaded my master now! Every minute I expected to be summoned to his presence; but the day passed, and I heard nothing from him. The next morning, a message was brought to me: "Master wants you in his study." I found the door ajar, and I stood a moment gazing at the hateful man who claimed a right to rule me, body and soul. I entered, and tried to appear calm. I did not want him to know how my heart was bleeding. He looked fixedly at me, with an expression which seemed to say, "I have half a mind to kill you on the spot." At last he broke the silence, and that was a relief to both of us.

[20]PEELED AND PICKED: Whipped and then doused with brine or saltwater.

"So you want to be married, do you?" said he, "and to a free nigger."

"Yes, sir."

"Well, I'll soon convince you whether I am your master, or the nigger fellow you honor so highly. If you *must* have a husband, you may take up with one of my slaves."

What a situation I should be in, as the wife of one of *his* slaves, even if my heart had been interested!

I replied, "Don't you suppose, sir, that a slave can have some preference about marrying? Do you suppose that all men are alike to her?"

"Do you love this nigger?" said he, abruptly.

"Yes, sir."

"How dare you tell me so!" he exclaimed, in great wrath. After a slight pause, he added, "I supposed you thought more of yourself; that you felt above the insults of such puppies."

I replied, "If he is a puppy I am a puppy, for we are both of the negro race. It is right and honorable for us to love each other. The man you call a puppy never insulted me, sir: and he would not love me if he did not believe me to be a virtuous woman."

He sprang upon me like a tiger, and gave me a stunning blow. It was the first time he had ever struck me; and fear did not enable me to control my anger. When I had recovered a little from the effects, I exclaimed, "You have struck me for answering you honestly. How I despise you!"

There was silence for some minutes. Perhaps he was deciding what should be my punishment; or, perhaps, he wanted to give me time to reflect on what I had said, and to whom I had said it. Finally, he asked, "Do you know what you have said?"

"Yes, sir; but your treatment drove me to it."

"Do you know that I have a right to do as I like with you,—that I can kill you, if I please?"

"You have tried to kill me, and I wish you had; but you have no right to do as you like with me."

"Silence!" he exclaimed, in a thundering voice. "By heavens, girl, you forget yourself too far! Are you mad? If you are, I will soon bring you to your senses. Do you think any other master would bear what I have borne from you this morning? Many masters would have killed you on the spot. How would you like to be sent to jail for your insolence?"

"I know I have been disrespectful, sir," I replied; "but you drove me to it; I couldn't help it. As for the jail, there would be more peace for me there than there is here."

"You deserve to go there," said he, "and to be under such treatment, that you would forget the meaning of the word *peace*. It would do you good. It would take some of your high notions out of you. But I am not ready to send you there yet, notwithstanding your ingratitude for all my kindness and forbearance. You have been the plague of my life. I have wanted to make you happy, and I have been repaid with the basest ingratitude; but though you have proved yourself incapable of appreciating my kindness, I will be lenient towards you, Linda. I will give you one more chance to redeem your character. If you behave yourself and do as I require, I will forgive you and treat you as I always have done; but if you disobey me, I will punish you as I would the meanest slave on my plantation. Never let me hear that fellow's name mentioned again. If I ever know of your speaking to him, I will cowhide you both; and if I catch him lurking about my premises, I will shoot him as soon as I would a dog. Do you hear what I say? I'll teach you a lesson about marriage and free niggers! Now go, and let this be the last time I have occasion to speak to you on this subject."

Reader, did you ever hate? I hope not. I never did but once; and I trust I never shall again. Somebody has called it "the atmosphere of hell;" and I believe it is so.

For a fortnight the doctor did not speak to me. He thought to mortify me; to make me feel that I had disgraced myself by receiving the honorable addresses of a respectable colored man, in preference to the base proposals of a white man. But though his lips disdained to address me, his eyes were very loquacious. No animal ever watched its prey more narrowly than he watched me. He knew that I could write, though he had failed to make me read his letters; and he was now troubled lest I should exchange letters with another man. After a while he became weary of silence; and I was sorry for it. One morning, as he passed through the hall, to leave the house, he contrived to thrust a note into my hand. I thought I had better read it, and spare myself the vexation of having him read it to me. It expressed regret for the blow he had given me, and reminded me that I myself was wholly to blame for it. He hoped I had become convinced of the injury I was doing myself by incurring his displeasure. He wrote that he had made up his mind to go to Louisiana; that he should take several slaves with him, and intended I should be one of the number. My mistress would remain where she was; therefore I should have nothing to fear from that quarter. If I merited kindness from him, he assured me that it would be lavishly bestowed. He begged me to think over the matter, and answer the following day.

The next morning I was called to carry a pair of scissors to his room. I laid them on the table, with the letter beside them. He thought it was my answer, and did not call me back. I went as usual to attend my young mistress to and from school. He met me in the street, and ordered me to stop at his office on my way back. When I entered, he showed me his letter, and asked me why I had not answered it. I replied, "I am your daughter's property, and it is in your power to send me, or take me, wherever you please." He said he was very glad to find me so willing to go, and that we should start early in the autumn. He had a large practice in the town, and I rather thought he had made up the story merely to frighten me. However that might be, I was determined that I would never go to Louisiana with him.

Summer passed away, and early in the autumn Dr. Flint's eldest son was sent to Louisiana to examine the country, with a view to emigrating. That news did not disturb me. I knew very well that I should not be sent with *him*. That I had not been taken to the plantation before this time, was owing to the fact that his son was there. He was jealous of his son; and jealousy of the overseer had kept him from punishing me by sending me into the fields to work. Is it strange that I was not proud of these protectors? As for the overseer, he was a man for whom I had less respect than I had for a bloodhound.

Young Mr. Flint did not bring back a favorable report of Louisiana, and I heard no more of that scheme. Soon after this, my lover met me at the corner of the street, and I stopped to speak to him. Looking up, I saw my master watching us from his window. I hurried home, trembling with fear. I was sent for, immediately, to go to his room. He met me with a blow. "When is mistress to be married?" said he, in a sneering tone. A shower of oaths and imprecations followed. How thankful I was that my lover was a free man! that my tyrant had no power to flog him for speaking to me in the street!

Again and again I revolved in my mind how all this would end. There was no hope that the doctor would consent to sell me on any terms. He had an iron will, and was determined to keep me, and to conquer me. My lover was an intelligent and religious man. Even if he could have obtained permission to marry me while I was a slave, the marriage would give him no power to protect me from my master. It would have made him miserable to witness the insults I should have been subjected to. And then, if we had children, I knew they must "follow the condition of the mother."[21] What a terrible blight that would be on the heart of a free, intelligent father! For *his* sake, I felt that I ought not to link his fate with

[21]FOLLOW THE CONDITION OF THE MOTHER: Children were designated as free-born or slave based on the legal status of their mothers. Because Jacobs is a slave, her children will be slaves also, regardless of the status of their father.

my own unhappy destiny. He was going to Savannah to see about a little property left him by an uncle; and hard as it was to bring my feelings to it, I earnestly entreated him not to come back. I advised him to go to the Free States, where his tongue would not be tied, and where his intelligence would be of more avail to him. He left me, still hoping the day would come when I could be bought. With me the lamp of hope had gone out. The dream of my girlhood was over. I felt lonely and desolate.

Still I was not stripped of all. I still had my good grandmother, and my affectionate brother. When he put his arms round my neck, and looked into my eyes, as if to read there the troubles I dared not tell, I felt that I still had something to love. But even that pleasant emotion was chilled by the reflection that he might be torn from me at any moment, by some sudden freak of my master. If he had known how we loved each other, I think he would have exulted in separating us. We often planned together how we could get to the north. But, as William remarked, such things are easier said than done. My movements were very closely watched, and we had no means of getting any money to defray our expenses. As for grandmother, she was strongly opposed to her children's undertaking any such project. She had not forgotten poor Benjamin's sufferings, and she was afraid that if another child tried to escape, he would have a similar or a worse fate. To me, nothing seemed more dreadful than my present life. I said to myself, "William *must* be free. He shall go to the north, and I will follow him." Many a slave sister has formed the same plans.

VIII. WHAT SLAVES ARE TAUGHT TO THINK OF THE NORTH

Slaveholders pride themselves upon being honorable men; but if you were to hear the enormous lies they tell their slaves, you would have small respect for their veracity. I have spoken plain English. Pardon me. I cannot use a milder term. When they visit the north, and return home, they tell their slaves of the runaways they have seen, and describe them to be in the most deplorable condition. A slaveholder once told me that he had seen a runaway friend of mine in New York, and that she besought him to take her back to her master, for she was literally dying of starvation; that many days she had only one cold potato to eat, and at other times could get nothing at all. He said he refused to take her, because he knew her master would not thank him for bringing such a miserable wretch to his house. He ended by saying to me, "This is the punishment she brought on herself for running away from a kind master."

This whole story was false. I afterwards staid with that friend in New York, and found her in comfortable circumstances. She had never thought of such a thing as wishing to go back to slavery. Many of the slaves believe such stories, and think it is not worth while to exchange slavery for such a hard kind of freedom. It is difficult to persuade such that freedom could make them useful men, and enable them to protect their wives and children. If those heathen in our Christian land had as much teaching as some Hindoos,[22] they would think otherwise. They would know that liberty is more valuable than life. They would begin to understand their own capabilities, and exert themselves to become men and women.

But while the Free States sustain a law which hurls fugitives back into slavery, how can the slaves resolve to become men? There are some who strive to protect wives and daughters from the insults of their masters; but those who have such sentiments have had advantages above the general mass of slaves. They have been partially civilized and Christianized by favorable circumstances. Some are bold enough to *utter* such sentiments to their masters. O, that there were more of them!

Some poor creatures have been so brutalized by the lash that they will sneak out of the way to give their masters free access to their wives and daughters. Do you think this proves the black man to belong to an inferior order of beings? What would you be, if you had been born and brought up a slave, with generations of slaves for ancestors? I admit that the black man is inferior. But what is it that makes him so? It is the ignorance in which white men compel him to live; it is the torturing whip that lashes manhood out of him; it is the fierce bloodhounds of the South, and the scarcely less cruel human bloodhounds of the north, who enforce the Fugitive Slave Law.[23] *They* do the work.

Southern gentlemen indulge in the most contemptuous expressions about the Yankees, while they, on their part, consent to do the vilest work for them, such as the ferocious bloodhounds and the despised negro-hunters are employed to do at home. When southerners go to the north, they are proud to do them honor; but the northern man is not welcome south of Mason and Dixon's line,[24] unless he suppresses every thought and feeling at variance with their "peculiar institution." Nor is it enough to be silent. The masters are not pleased, unless they obtain a greater degree of subservience than that; and they are generally accomodated.

---

[22]HINDOOS: Practioners of Hinduism, the Western term for the dominant religion of India. Its beliefs include the doctrine of *karma*, in which individuals must balance good and bad actions through a series of lifetimes, and *moksha*, the liberation from suffering and cyclic rebirth achieved by union with the divine essence.

[23]FUGITIVE SLAVE LAW: See note 14.

[24]MASON AND DIXON'S LINE: The division between slave and free states, with Pennsylvania to the north and Delaware and Maryland to the south.

Do they respect the northerner for this? I trow not. Even the slaves despise "a northern man with southern principles;" and that is the class they generally see. When northerners go to the south to reside, they prove very apt scholars. They soon imbibe the sentiments and disposition of their neighbors, and generally go beyond their teachers. Of the two, they are proverbially the hardest masters.

They seem to satisfy their consciences with the doctrine that God created the Africans to be slaves. What a libel upon the heavenly Father, who "made of one blood all nations of men!"[25] And then who *are* Africans? Who can measure the amount of Anglo-Saxon blood coursing in the veins of American slaves?

I have spoken of the pains slaveholders take to give their slaves a bad opinion of the north; but, notwithstanding this, intelligent slaves are aware that they have many friends in the Free States. Even the most ignorant have some confused notions about it. They knew that I could read; and I was often asked if I had seen any thing in the newspapers about white folks over in the big north, who were trying to get their freedom for them. Some believe that the abolitionists have already made them free, and that it is established by law, but that their masters prevent the law from going into effect. One woman begged me to get a newspaper and read it over. She said her husband told her that the black people had sent word to the queen of 'Merica that they were all slaves; that she didn't believe it, and went to Washington city to see the president about it. They quarrelled; she drew her sword upon him, and swore that he should help her to make them all free.

That poor, ignorant woman thought that America was governed by a Queen, to whom the President was subordinate. I wish the President was subordinate to Queen Justice.

X. A PERILOUS PASSAGE IN THE SLAVE GIRL'S LIFE

After my lover went away, Dr. Flint contrived a new plan. He seemed to have an idea that my fear of my mistress was his greatest obstacle. In the blandest tones, he told me that he was going to build a small house for me, in a secluded place, four miles away from the town. I shuddered; but I was constrained to listen, while he talked of his intention to give me a home of my own, and to make a lady of me. Hitherto, I had escaped

---

[25]MADE OF ONE BLOOD ALL NATIONS OF MEN: Acts 17:26: "And hath made of one blood all nations of men for to dwell on all the face of the earth, and hath determined the times before appointed, and the bounds of their habitation."

my dreaded fate, by being in the midst of people. My grandmother had already had high words with my master about me. She had told him pretty plainly what she thought of his character, and there was considerable gossip in the neighborhood about our affairs, to which the open-mouthed jealousy of Mrs. Flint contributed not a little. When my master said he was going to build a house for me, and that he could do it with little trouble and expense, I was in hopes something would happen to frustrate his scheme; but I soon heard that the house was actually begun. I vowed before my Maker that I would never enter it. I had rather toil on the plantation from dawn till dark; I had rather live and die in jail, than drag on, from day to day, through such a living death. I was determined that the master, whom I so hated and loathed, who had blighted the prospects of my youth, and made my life a desert, should not, after my long struggle with him, succeed at last in trampling his victim under his feet. I would do any thing, every thing, for the sake of defeating him. What *could* I do? I thought and thought, till I became desperate, and made a plunge into the abyss.

And now, reader, I come to a period in my unhappy life, which I would gladly forget if I could. The remembrance fills me with sorrow and shame. It pains me to tell you of it; but I have promised to tell you the truth, and I will do it honestly, let it cost me what it may. I will not try to screen myself behind the plea of compulsion from a master; for it was not so. Neither can I plead ignorance or thoughtlessness. For years, my master had done his utmost to pollute my mind with foul images, and to destroy the pure principles inculcated by my grandmother, and the good mistress of my childhood. The influences of slavery had had the same effect on me that they had on other young girls; they had made me prematurely knowing, concerning the evil ways of the world. I knew what I did, and I did it with deliberate calculation.

But, O, ye happy women, whose purity has been sheltered from childhood, who have been free to choose the objects of your affection, whose homes are protected by law, do not judge the poor desolate slave girl too severely! If slavery had been abolished, I, also, could have married the man of my choice; I could have had a home shielded by the laws; and I should have been spared the painful task of confessing what I am now about to relate; but all my prospects had been blighted by slavery. I wanted to keep myself pure; and, under the most adverse circumstances, I tried hard to preserve my self-respect; but I was struggling alone in the powerful grasp of the demon Slavery; and the monster proved too strong for me. I felt as if I was forsaken by God and man; as if all my efforts must be frustrated; and I became reckless in my despair.

I have told you that Dr. Flint's persecutions and his wife's jealousy had given rise to some gossip in the neighborhood. Among others, it chanced that a white unmarried gentleman had obtained some knowledge of the circumstances in which I was placed. He knew my grandmother, and often spoke to me in the street. He became interested for me, and asked questions about my master, which I answered in part. He expressed a great deal of sympathy, and a wish to aid me. He constantly sought opportunities to see me, and wrote to me frequently. I was a poor slave girl, only fifteen years old.

So much attention from a superior person was, of course, flattering; for human nature is the same in all. I also felt grateful for his sympathy, and encouraged by his kind words. It seemed to me a great thing to have such a friend. By degrees, a more tender feeling crept into my heart. He was an educated and eloquent gentleman; too eloquent, alas, for the poor slave girl who trusted in him. Of course I saw whither all this was tending. I knew the impassable gulf between us; but to be an object of interest to a man who is not married, and who is not her master, is agreeable to the pride and feelings of a slave, if her miserable situation has left her any pride or sentiment. It seems less degrading to give one's self, than to submit to compulsion. There is something akin to freedom in having a lover who has no control over you, except that which he gains by kindness and attachment. A master may treat you as rudely as he pleases, and you dare not speak; moreover, the wrong does not seem so great with an unmarried man, as with one who has a wife to be made unhappy. There may be sophistry in all this; but the condition of a slave confuses all principles of morality, and, in fact, renders the practice of them impossible.

When I found that my master had actually begun to build the lonely cottage, other feelings mixed with those I have described. Revenge, and calculations of interest, were added to flattered vanity and sincere gratitude for kindness. I knew nothing would enrage Dr. Flint so much as to know that I favored another; and it was something to triumph over my tyrant even in that small way. I thought he would revenge himself by selling me, and I was sure my friend, Mr. Sands, would buy me. He was a man of more generosity and feeling than my master, and I thought my freedom could be easily obtained from him. The crisis of my fate now came so near that I was desperate. I shuddered to think of being the mother of children that should be owned by my old tyrant. I knew that as soon as a new fancy took him, his victims were sold far off to get rid of them; especially if they had children. I had seen several women sold, with his babies at the breast. He never allowed his offspring by slaves to remain long in sight of himself and his wife. Of a man who was not my master I could ask to have my children well supported; and in this case, I felt confident I should obtain the boon.[26] I also felt quite sure that they would be made free. With all these thoughts revolving in my mind, and seeing no other way of escaping the doom I so much dreaded, I made a headlong plunge. Pity me, and pardon me, O virtuous reader! You never knew what it is to be a slave; to be entirely unprotected by law or custom; to have the laws reduce you to the condition of a chattel, entirely subject to the will of another. You never exhausted your ingenuity in avoiding the snares, and eluding the power of a hated tyrant; you never shuddered at the sound of his footsteps, and trembled within hearing of his voice. I know I did wrong. No one can feel it more sensibly than I do. The painful and humiliating memory will haunt me to my dying day. Still, in looking back, calmly, on the events of my life, I feel that the slave woman ought not to be judged by the same standard as others.

The months passed on. I had many unhappy hours. I secretly mourned over the sorrow I was bringing on my grandmother, who had so tried to shield me from harm. I knew that I was the greatest comfort of her old age, and that it was a source of pride to her that I had not degraded myself, like most of the slaves. I wanted to confess to her that I was no longer worthy of her love; but I could not utter the dreaded words.

As for Dr. Flint, I had a feeling of satisfaction and triumph in the thought of telling *him*. From time to time he told me of his intended arrangements, and I was silent. At last, he came and told me the cottage was completed, and ordered me to go to it. I told him I would never enter it. He said, "I have heard enough of such talk as that. You shall go, if you are carried by force; and you shall remain there."

I replied, "I will never go there. In a few months I shall be a mother."

He stood and looked at me in dumb[27] amazement, and left the house without a word. I thought I should be happy in my triumph over him. But now that the truth was out, and my relatives would hear of it, I felt wretched. Humble as were their circumstances, they had pride in my good character. Now, how could I look them in the face? My self-respect was gone! I had resolved that I would be virtuous, though I was a slave. I had said, "Let the storm beat! I will brave it till I die." And now, how humiliated I felt!

I went to my grandmother. My lips moved to make confession, but the words stuck in my throat. I sat down in the shade of a tree at her door

[26]BOON: Favor.
[27]DUMB: Silent.

and began to sew. I think she saw something unusual was the matter with me. The mother of slaves is very watchful. She knows there is no security for her children. After they have entered their teens she lives in daily expectation of trouble. This leads to many questions. If the girl is of a sensitive nature, timidity keeps her from answering truthfully, and this well-meant course has a tendency to drive her from maternal counsels. Presently, in came my mistress, like a mad woman, and accused me concerning her husband. My grandmother, whose suspicions had been previously awakened, believed what she said. She exclaimed, "O Linda! has it come to this? I had rather see you dead than to see you as you now are. You are a disgrace to your dead mother." She tore from my fingers my mother's wedding ring and her silver thimble. "Go away!" she exclaimed, "and never come to my house, again." Her reproaches fell so hot and heavy, that they left me no chance to answer. Bitter tears, such as the eyes never shed but once, were my only answer. I rose from my seat, but fell back again, sobbing. She did not speak to me; but the tears were running down her furrowed cheeks, and they scorched me like fire. She had always been so kind to me! So kind! How I longed to throw myself at her feet, and tell her all the truth! But she had ordered me to go, and never to come there again. After a few minutes, I mustered strength, and started to obey her. With what feelings did I now close that little gate, which I used to open with such an eager hand in my childhood! It closed upon me with a sound I never heard before.

Where could I go? I was afraid to return to my master's. I walked on recklessly, not caring where I went, or what would become of me. When I had gone four or five miles, fatigue compelled me to stop. I sat down on the stump of an old tree. The stars were shining through the boughs above me. How they mocked me, with their bright, calm light! The hours passed by, and as I sat there alone a chilliness and deadly sickness came over me. I sank on the ground. My mind was full of horrid thoughts. I prayed to die; but the prayer was not answered. At last, with great effort I roused myself, and walked some distance further, to the house of a woman who had been a friend of my mother. When I told her why I was there, she spoke soothingly to me; but I could not be comforted. I thought I could bear my shame if I could only be reconciled to my grandmother. I longed to open my heart to her. I thought if she could know the real state of the case, and all I had been bearing for years, she would perhaps judge me less harshly. My friend advised me to send for her. I did so; but days of agonizing suspense passed before she came. Had she utterly forsaken me? No. She came at last. I knelt before her, and told her the things that had poisoned my life; how long I had been persecuted;

that I saw no way of escape; and in an hour of extremity I had become desperate. She listened in silence. I told her I would bear any thing and do any thing, if in time I had hopes of obtaining her forgiveness. I begged of her to pity me, for my dead mother's sake. And she did pity me. She did not say, "I forgive you;" but she looked at me lovingly, with her eyes full of tears. She laid her old hand gently on my head, and murmured, "Poor child! Poor child!"

XII. FEAR OF INSURRECTION

Not far from this time Nat Turner's insurrection[28] broke out; and the news threw our town into great commotion. Strange that they should be alarmed, when their slaves were so "contented and happy"! But so it was.

It was always the custom to have a muster[29] every year. On that occasion every white man shouldered his musket. The citizens and the so-called country gentlemen wore military uniforms. The poor whites took their places in the ranks in every-day dress, some without shoes, some without hats. This grand occasion had already passed; and when the slaves were told there was to be another muster, they were surprised and rejoiced. Poor creatures! They thought it was going to be a holiday. I was informed of the true state of affairs, and imparted it to the few I could trust. Most gladly would I have proclaimed it to every slave; but I dared not. All could not be relied on. Mighty is the power of the torturing lash.

By sunrise, people were pouring in from every quarter within twenty miles of the town. I knew the houses were to be searched; and I expected it would be done by country bullies and the poor whites. I knew nothing annoyed them so much as to see colored people living in comfort and respectability; so I made arrangements for them with especial care. I arranged every thing in my grandmother's house as neatly as possible. I put white quilts on the beds, and decorated some of the rooms with flowers. When all was arranged, I sat down at the window to watch. Far as my eye could reach, it rested on a motley crowd of soldiers. Drums and fifes were discoursing martial music. The men were divided into companies of sixteen, each headed by a captain. Orders were given, and the wild scouts rushed in every direction, wherever a colored face was to be found.

---

[28]NAT TURNER'S INSURRECTION: Jacobs refers to Nat Turner's Rebellion (Southampton Insurrection) of 1831. Nat Turner (1800–1831) was an American slave from Virginia. With approximately sixty slaves and free blacks, he plotted a revolt in which fifty-five white people were killed. The rebellion was quickly put down, and sixteen people were hanged for their involvement in the uprising. The revolt led to more restrictive slave laws in the South.
[29]MUSTER: An assembly for inspection.

It was a grand opportunity for the low whites, who had no negroes of their own to scourge. They exulted in such a chance to exercise a little brief authority, and show their subserviency to the slaveholders; not reflecting that the power which trampled on the colored people also kept themselves in poverty, ignorance, and moral degradation. Those who never witnessed such scenes can hardly believe what I know was inflicted at this time on innocent men, women, and children, against whom there was not the slightest ground for suspicion. Colored people and slaves who lived in remote parts of the town suffered in an especial manner. In some cases the searchers scattered powder and shot among their clothes, and then sent other parties to find them, and bring them forward as proof that they were plotting insurrection. Every where men, women, and children were whipped till the blood stood in puddles at their feet. Some received five hundred lashes; others were tied hands and feet, and tortured with a bucking paddle, which blisters the skin terribly. The dwellings of the colored people, unless they happened to be protected by some influential white person, who was nigh at hand, were robbed of clothing and every thing else the marauders thought worth carrying away. All day long these unfeeling wretches went round, like a troop of demons, terrifying and tormenting the helpless. At night, they formed themselves into patrol bands, and went wherever they chose among the colored people, acting out their brutal will. Many women hid themselves in woods and swamps, to keep out of their way. If any of the husbands or fathers told of these outrages, they were tied up to the public whipping post, and cruelly scourged for telling lies about white men. The consternation was universal. No two people that had the slightest tinge of color in their faces dared to be seen talking together.

I entertained no positive fears about our household, because we were in the midst of white families who would protect us. We were ready to receive the soldiers whenever they came. It was not long before we heard the tramp of feet and the sound of voices. The door was rudely pushed open; and in they tumbled, like a pack of hungry wolves. They snatched at every thing within their reach. Every box, trunk, closet, and corner underwent a thorough examination. A box in one of the drawers containing some silver change was eagerly pounced upon. When I stepped forward to take it from them, one of the soldiers turned and said angrily, "What d'ye foller us fur? D'ye s'pose white folks is come to steal?"

I replied, "You have come to search; but you have searched that box, and I will take it, if you please."

At that moment I saw a white gentleman who was friendly to us; and I called to him, and asked him to have the goodness to come in and stay till the search was over. He readily complied. His entrance into the house brought in the captain of the company, whose business it was to guard the outside of the house, and see that none of the inmates left it. This officer was Mr. Litch, the wealthy slaveholder whom I mentioned, in the account of neighboring planters, as being notorious for his cruelty. He felt above soiling his hands with the search. He merely gave orders; and, if a bit of writing was discovered, it was carried to him by his ignorant followers, who were unable to read.

My grandmother had a large trunk of bedding and table cloths. When that was opened, there was a great shout of surprise; and one exclaimed, "Where'd the damned niggers git all dis sheet an' table clarf?"

My grandmother, emboldened by the presence of our white protector, said, "You may be sure we didn't pilfer 'em from *your* houses."

"Look here, mammy," said a grim-looking fellow without any coat, "you seem to feel mighty gran' 'cause you got all them 'ere fixens. White folks oughter have 'em all."

His remarks were interrupted by a chorus of voices shouting, "We's got 'em! We's got 'em! Dis 'ere yaller gal's got letters!"

There was a general rush for the supposed letter, which, upon examination, proved to be some verses written to me by a friend. In packing away my things, I had overlooked them. When their captain informed them of their contents, they seemed much disappointed. He inquired of me who wrote them. I told him it was one of my friends. "Can you read them?" he asked. When I told him I could, he swore, and raved, and tore the paper into bits. "Bring me all your letters!" said he, in a commanding tone. I told him I had none. "Don't be afraid," he continued, in an insinuating way. "Bring them all to me. Nobody shall do you any harm." Seeing I did not move to obey him, his pleasant tone changed to oaths and threats, "Who writes to you? half free niggers?" inquired he. I replied, "O, no; most of my letters are from white people. Some request me to burn them after they are read, and some I destroy without reading."

An exclamation of surprise from some of the company put a stop to our conversation. Some silver spoons which ornamented an old-fashioned buffet had just been discovered. My grandmother was in the habit of preserving fruit for many ladies in the town, and of preparing suppers for parties; consequently she had many jars of preserves. The closet that contained these was next invaded, and the contents tasted. One of them, who was helping himself freely, tapped his neighbor on the shoulder, and said, "Wal done! Don't wonder de niggers want to kill all de white folks, when dey live on 'sarves" [meaning preserves].

I stretched out my hand to take the jar, saying, "You were not sent here to search for sweetmeats."[30]

"And what *were* we sent for?" said the captain, bristling up to me. I evaded the question.

The search of the house was completed, and nothing found to condemn us. They next proceeded to the garden, and knocked about every bush and vine, with no better success. The captain called his men together, and, after a short consultation, the order to march was given. As they passed out of the gate, the captain turned back, and pronounced a malediction on the house. He said it ought to be burned to the ground, and each of its inmates receive thirty-nine lashes. We came out of this affair very fortunately; not losing any thing except some wearing apparel.

Towards evening the turbulence increased. The soldiers, stimulated by drink, committed still greater cruelties. Shrieks and shouts continually rent the air. Not daring to go to the door, I peeped under the window curtain. I saw a mob dragging along a number of colored people, each white man, with his musket upraised, threatening instant death if they did not stop their shrieks. Among the prisoners was a respectable old colored minister. They had found a few parcels of shot in his house, which his wife had for years used to balance her scales. For this they were going to shoot him on Court House Green. What a spectacle was that for a civilized country! A rabble, staggering under intoxication, assuming to be the administrators of justice!

The better class of the community exerted their influence to save the innocent, persecuted people; and in several instances they succeeded, by keeping them shut up in jail till the excitement abated. At last the white citizens found that their own property was not safe from the lawless rabble they had summoned to protect them. They rallied the drunken swarm, drove them back into the country, and set a guard over the town.

The next day, the town patrols were commissioned to search colored people that lived out of the city; and the most shocking outrages committed with perfect impunity. Every day for a fortnight, if I looked out, I saw horsemen with some poor panting negro tied to their saddles, and compelled by the lash to keep up with their speed, till they arrived at the jail yard. Those who had been whipped too unmercifully to walk were washed with brine, tossed into a cart, and carried to jail. One black man, who had not fortitude to endure scourging, promised to give information about the conspiracy. But it turned out that he knew nothing at all. He had not even heard the name of Nat Turner. The poor fellow had,

---

[30]SWEETMEATS: Sweet foods, such as candied or sugared fruits.

however, made up a story, which augmented his own sufferings and those of the colored people.

The day patrol continued for some weeks, and at sundown a night guard was substituted. Nothing at all was proved against the colored people, bond or free. The wrath of the slaveholders was somewhat appeased by the capture of Nat Turner. The imprisoned were released. The slaves were sent to their masters, and the free were permitted to return to their ravaged homes. Visiting was strictly forbidden on the plantations. The slaves begged the privilege of again meeting at their little church in the woods, with their burying ground around it. It was built by the colored people, and they had no higher happiness than to meet there and sing hymns together, and pour out their hearts in spontaneous prayer. Their request was denied, and the church was demolished. They were permitted to attend the white churches, a certain portion of the galleries being appropriated to their use. There, when every body else had partaken of the communion, and the benediction had been pronounced, the minister said, "Come down, now, my colored friends." They obeyed the summons, and partook of the bread and wine, in commemoration of the meek and lowly Jesus, who said, "God is your Father, and all ye are brethren."[31]

XVII. THE FLIGHT

Mr. Flint was hard pushed for house servants, and rather than lose me he had restrained his malice. I did my work faithfully, though not, of course, with a willing mind. They were evidently afraid I should leave them. Mr. Flint wished that I should sleep in the great house instead of the servants' quarters. His wife agreed to the proposition, but said I mustn't bring my bed into the house, because it would scatter feathers on her carpet. I knew when I went there that they would never think of such a thing as furnishing a bed of any kind for me and my little one. I therefore carried my own bed, and now I was forbidden to use it. I did as I was ordered. But now that I was certain my children were to be put in their power, in order to give them a stronger hold on me, I resolved to leave them that night. I remembered the grief this step would bring upon my dear old grandmother; and nothing less than the freedom of my children would have induced me to disregard her advice. I went about my evening work with trembling steps. Mr. Flint twice called from his chamber door to inquire why the house was not locked up. I replied that I

[31]GOD IS YOUR FATHER, AND ALL YE ARE BRETHREN: Matthew 23:8: "But be not ye called Rabbi: for one is your Master, even Christ; and all ye are brethren."

had not done my work. "You have had time enough to do it," said he. "Take care how you answer me!"

I shut all the windows, locked all the doors, and went up to the third story, to wait till midnight. How long those hours seemed, and how fervently I prayed that God would not forsake me in this hour of utmost need! I was about to risk every thing on the throw of a die; and if I failed, O what would become of me and my poor children? They would be made to suffer for my fault.

At half past twelve I stole softly down stairs. I stopped on the second floor, thinking I heard a noise. I felt my way down into the parlor, and looked out of the window. The night was so intensely dark that I could see nothing. I raised the window very softly and jumped out. Large drops of rain were falling, and the darkness bewildered me. I dropped on my knees, and breathed a short prayer to God for guidance and protection. I groped my way to the road, and rushed towards the town with almost lightning speed. I arrived at my grandmother's house, but dared not see her. She would say, "Linda, you are killing me;" and I knew that would unnerve me. I tapped softly at the window of a room, occupied by a woman, who had lived in the house several years. I knew she was a faithful friend, and could be trusted with my secret. I tapped several times before she heard me. At last she raised the window, and I whispered, "Sally, I have run away. Let me in, quick." She opened the door softly, and said in low tones, "For God's sake, don't. Your grandmother is trying to buy you and de chillern. Mr. Sands was here last week. He tole her he was going away on business, but he wanted her to go ahead about buying you and de chillern, and he would help her all he could. Don't run away, Linda. Your grandmother is all bowed down wid trouble now."

I replied, "Sally, they are going to carry my children to the plantation to-morrow; and they will never sell them to any body so long as they have me in their power. Now, would you advise me to go back?"

"No, chile, no," answered she. "When dey finds you is gone, dey won't want de plague ob de chillern; but where is you going to hide? Dey knows ebery inch ob dis house."

I told her I had a hiding-place, and that was all it was best for her to know. I asked her to go into my room as soon as it was light, and take all my clothes out of my trunk, and pack them in hers; for I knew Mr. Flint and the constable would be there early to search my room. I feared the sight of my children would be too much for my full heart; but I could not go out into the uncertain future without one last look. I bent over the bed where lay my little Benny and baby Ellen. Poor little ones! fatherless and motherless! Memories of their father came over me. He wanted to be kind to them; but they were not all to him, as they were to my womanly heart. I knelt and prayed for the innocent little sleepers. I kissed them lightly, and turned away.

As I was about to open the street door, Sally laid her hand on my shoulder, and said, "Linda, is you gwine all alone? Let me call your uncle."

"No, Sally," I replied, "I want no one to be brought into trouble on my account."

I went forth into the darkness and rain. I ran on till I came to the house of the friend who was to conceal me.

Early the next morning Mr. Flint was at my grandmother's inquiring for me. She told him she had not seen me, and supposed I was at the plantation. He watched her face narrowly, and said, "Don't you know any thing about her running off?" She assured him that she did not. He went on to say, "Last night she ran off without the least provocation. We had treated her very kindly. My wife liked her. She will soon be found and brought back. Are her children with you?" When told that they were, he said, "I am very glad to hear that. If they are here, she cannot be far off. If I find out that any of my niggers have had any thing to do with this damned business, I'll give 'em five hundred lashes." As he started to go to his father's, he turned round and added, persuasively, "Let her be brought back, and she shall have her children to live with her."

The tidings made the old doctor rave and storm at a furious rate. It was a busy day for them. My grandmother's house was searched from top to bottom. As my trunk was empty, they concluded I had taken my clothes with me. Before ten o'clock every vessel northward bound was thoroughly examined, and the law against harboring fugitives was read to all on board. At night a watch was set over the town. Knowing how distressed my grandmother would be, I wanted to send her a message; but it could not be done. Every one who went in or out of her house was closely watched. The doctor said he would take my children, unless she became responsible for them; which of course she willingly did. The next day was spent in searching. Before night, the following advertisement was posted at every corner, and in every public place for miles round:—

"$300 REWARD! Ran away from the subscriber, an intelligent, bright, mulatto girl, named Linda, 21 years of age. Five feet four inches high. Dark eyes, and black hair inclined to curl; but it can be made straight. Has a decayed spot on a front tooth. She can read and write, and in all probability will try to get to the Free

States. All persons are forbidden, under penalty of the law, to harbor or employ said slave. $150 will be given to whoever takes her in the state, and $300 if taken out of the state and delivered to me, or lodged in jail.

Dr. Flint."

XXI. THE LOOPHOLE OF RETREAT[32]

A small shed had been added to my grandmother's house years ago. Some boards were laid across the joists at the top, and between these boards and the roof was a very small garret, never occupied by any thing but rats and mice. It was a pent roof, covered with nothing but shingles, according to the southern custom for such buildings. The garret was only nine feet long and seven wide. The highest part was three feet high, and sloped down abruptly to the loose board floor. There was no admission for either light or air. My uncle Phillip, who was a carpenter, had very skilfully made a concealed trap-door, which communicated with the storeroom. He had been doing this while I was waiting in the swamp. The storeroom opened upon a piazza.[33] To this hole I was conveyed as soon as I entered the house. The air was stifling; the darkness total. A bed had been spread on the floor. I could sleep quite comfortably on one side; but the slope was so sudden that I could not turn on the other without hitting the roof. The rats and mice ran over my bed; but I was weary, and I slept such sleep as the wretched may, when a tempest has passed over them. Morning came. I knew it only by the noises I heard; for in my small den day and night were all the same. I suffered for air even more than for light. But I was not comfortless. I heard the voices of my children. There was joy and there was sadness in the sound. It made my tears flow. How I longed to speak to them! I was eager to look on their faces; but there was no hole, no crack, through which I could peep. This continued darkness was oppressive. It seemed horrible to sit or lie in a cramped position day after day, without one gleam of light. Yet I would have chosen this, rather than my lot as a slave, though white people considered it an easy one; and it was so compared with the fate of others. I was never cruelly overworked; I was never lacerated with the whip from head to foot; I was never so beaten and bruised that I could not turn from one side to the other; I never had my heel-strings cut to prevent my running away;

---

[32]RETREAT: Jacobs borrows her title for this chapter from the poem "The Task" (Book 4, lines 89–90), by William Cowper (1731–1800): "Tis pleasant through the loop-holes of retreat / To peep at such a world."
[33]PIAZZA: Patio.

I was never chained to a log and forced to drag it about, while I toiled in the fields from morning till night; I was never branded with hot iron, or torn by bloodhounds. On the contrary, I had always been kindly treated, and tenderly cared for, until I came into the hands of Dr. Flint. I had never wished for freedom till then. But though my life in slavery was comparatively devoid of hardships, God pity the woman who is compelled to lead such a life!

My food was passed up to me through the trap-door my uncle had contrived; and my grandmother, my uncle Phillip, and aunt Nancy would seize such opportunities as they could, to mount up there and chat with me at the opening. But of course this was not safe in the daytime. It must all be done in darkness. It was impossible for me to move in an erect position, but I crawled about my den for exercise. One day I hit my head against something, and found it was a gimlet.[34] My uncle had left it sticking there when he made the trap-door. I was as rejoiced as Robinson Crusoe[35] could have been at finding such a treasure. It put a lucky thought into my head. I said to myself, "Now I will have some light. Now I will see my children." I did not dare to begin my work during the daytime, for fear of attracting attention. But I groped round; and having found the side next the street, where I could frequently see my children, I stuck the gimlet in and waited for evening. I bored three rows of holes, one above another; then I bored out the interstices between. I thus succeeded in making one hole about an inch long and an inch broad. I sat by it till late into the night, to enjoy the little whiff of air that floated in. In the morning I watched for my children. The first person I saw in the street was Dr. Flint. I had a shuddering, superstitious feeling that it was a bad omen. Several familiar faces passed by. At last I heard the merry laugh of children, and presently two sweet little faces were looking up at me, as though they knew I was there, and were conscious of the joy they imparted. How I longed to *tell* them I was there!

My condition was now a little improved. But for weeks I was tormented by hundreds of little red insects, fine as a needle's point, that pierced through my skin, and produced an intolerable burning. The good grandmother gave me herb teas and cooling medicines, and finally I got rid of them. The heat of my den was intense, for nothing but thin shingles protected me from the scorching summer's sun. But I had my consolations. Through my peeping-hole I could watch the children, and when they were near enough, I could hear their talk. Aunt Nancy brought me

---

[34]GIMLET: Small tool for boring holes.
[35]ROBINSON CRUSOE: A novel (1719) by the English author Daniel Defoe (1660?–1731). The title character is an English sailor who is shipwrecked on a deserted island, where he survives for twenty-eight years before being rescued.

all the news she could hear at Dr. Flint's. From her I learned that the doctor had written to New York to a colored woman, who had been born and raised in our neighborhood, and had breathed his contaminating atmosphere. He offered her a reward if she could find out any thing about me. I know not what was the nature of her reply; but he soon after started for New York in haste, saying to his family that he had business of importance to transact. I peeped at him as he passed on his way to the steamboat. It was a satisfaction to have miles of land and water between us, even for a little while; and it was a still greater satisfaction to know that he believed me to be in the Free States. My little den seemed less dreary than it had done. He returned, as he did from his former journey to New York, without obtaining any satisfactory information. When he passed our house next morning, Benny was standing at the gate. He had heard them say that he had gone to find me, and he called out, "Dr. Flint, did you bring my mother home? I want to see her." The doctor stamped his foot at him in a rage, and exclaimed, "Get out of the way, you little damned rascal! If you don't, I'll cut off your head."

Benny ran terrified into the house, saying, "You can't put me in jail again. I don't belong to you now." It was well that the wind carried the words away from the doctor's ear. I told my grandmother of it, when we had our next conference at the trap-door; and begged of her not to allow the children to be impertinent to the irascible old man.

Autumn came, with a pleasant abatement of heat. My eyes had become accustomed to the dim light, and by holding my book or work in a certain position near the aperture I contrived to read and sew. That was a great relief to the tedious monotony of my life. But when winter came, the cold penetrated through the thin shingle roof, and I was dreadfully chilled. The winters there are not so long, or so severe, as in northern latitudes; but the houses are not built to shelter from cold, and my little den was peculiarly comfortless. The kind grandmother brought me bedclothes and warm drinks. Often I was obliged to lie in bed all day to keep comfortable; but with all my precautions, my shoulders and feet were frostbitten. O, those long, gloomy days, with no object for my eye to rest upon, and no thoughts to occupy my mind, except the dreary past and the uncertain future! I was thankful when there came a day sufficiently mild for me to wrap myself up and sit at the loophole to watch the passers by. Southerners have the habit of stopping and talking in the streets, and I heard many conversations not intended to meet my ears. I heard slavehunters planning how to catch some poor fugitive. Several times I heard allusions to Dr. Flint, myself, and the history of my children, who, perhaps, were playing near the gate. One would say, "I wouldn't move my little finger to catch her, as old Flint's property." Another would say, "I'll catch *any* nigger for the reward. A man ought to have what belongs to him, if he *is* a damned brute." The opinion was often expressed that I was in the Free States. Very rarely did any one suggest that I might be in the vicinity. Had the least suspicion rested on my grandmother's house, it would have been burned to the ground. But it was the last place they thought of. Yet there was no place, where slavery existed, that could have afforded me so good a place of concealment.

Dr. Flint and his family repeatedly tried to coax and bribe my children to tell something they had heard said about me. One day the doctor took them into a shop, and offered them some bright little silver pieces and gay handkerchiefs if they would tell where their mother was. Ellen shrank away from him, and would not speak; but Benny spoke up, and said, "Dr. Flint, I don't know where my mother is. I guess she's in New York; and when you go there again, I wish you'd ask her to come home, for I want to see her; but if you put her in jail, or tell her you'll cut her head off, I'll tell her to go right back."

XXIX. Preparations for Escape

I hardly expect that the reader will credit me, when I affirm that I lived in that little dismal hole, almost deprived of light and air, and with no space to move my limbs, for nearly seven years. But it is a fact; and to me a sad one, even now; for my body still suffers from the effects of that long imprisonment, to say nothing of my soul. Members of my family, now living in New York and Boston, can testify to the truth of what I say.

Countless were the nights that I sat late at the little loophole scarcely large enough to give me a glimpse of one twinkling star. There, I heard the patrols and slave-hunters conferring together about the capture of runaways, well knowing how rejoiced they would be to catch me.

Season after season, year after year, I peeped at my children's faces, and heard their sweet voices, with a heart yearning all the while to say, "Your mother is here." Sometimes it appeared to me as if ages had rolled away since I entered upon that gloomy, monotonous existence. At times, I was stupefied and listless; at other times I became very impatient to know when these dark years would end, and I should again be allowed to feel the sunshine, and breathe the pure air.

After Ellen left us, this feeling increased. Mr. Sands had agreed that Benny might go to the north whenever his uncle Phillip could go with him; and I was anxious to be there also, to watch over my children, and protect them so far as I was able. Moreover, I was likely to be drowned out of my den, if I remained much longer; for the slight roof was getting badly out of repair, and uncle Phillip was afraid to remove the shingles, lest some one should get a glimpse of me. When storms occurred in the night, they spread mats and bits of carpet, which in the morning appeared to have been laid out to dry; but to cover the roof in the daytime might have attracted attention. Consequently, my clothes and bedding were often drenched; a process by which the pains and aches in my cramped and stiffened limbs were greatly increased. I revolved various plans of escape in my mind, which I sometimes imparted to my grandmother, when she came to whisper with me at the trap-door. The kind-hearted old woman had an intense sympathy for runaways. She had known too much of the cruelties inflicted on those who were captured. Her memory always flew back at once to the sufferings of her bright and handsome son, Benjamin, the youngest and dearest of her flock. So, whenever I alluded to the subject, she would groan out, "O, don't think of it, child. You'll break my heart." I had no good old aunt Nancy now to encourage me; but my brother William and my children were continually beckoning me to the north.

And now I must go back a few months in my story. I have stated that the first of January was the time for selling slaves, or leasing them out to new masters. If time were counted by heart-throbs, the poor slaves might reckon years of suffering during that festival so joyous to the free. On the New Year's day preceding my aunt's death, one of my friends, named Fanny, was to be sold at auction, to pay her master's debts. My thoughts were with her during all the day, and at night I anxiously inquired what had been her fate. I was told that she had been sold to one master, and her four little girls to another master, far distant; that she had escaped from her purchaser, and was not to be found. Her mother was the old Aggie I have spoken of. She lived in a small tenement belonging to my grandmother, and built on the same lot with her own house. Her dwelling was searched and watched, and that brought the patrols so near me that I was obliged to keep very close in my den. The hunters were somehow eluded; and not long afterwards Benny accidentally caught sight of Fanny in her mother's hut. He told his grandmother, who charged him never to speak of it, explaining to him the frightful consequences; and he never betrayed the trust. Aggie little dreamed that my grandmother knew where her daughter was concealed, and that the stooping form of her old neighbor was bending under a similar burden of anxiety and fear; but these dangerous secrets deepened the sympathy between the two old persecuted mothers.

My friend Fanny and I remained many weeks hidden within call of each other; but she was unconscious of the fact. I longed to have her share my den, which seemed a more secure retreat than her own; but I had brought so much trouble on my grandmother, that it seemed wrong to ask her to incur greater risks. My restlessness increased. I had lived too long in bodily pain and anguish of spirit. Always I was in dread that by some accident, or some contrivance, slavery would succeed in snatching my children from me. This thought drove me nearly frantic, and I determined to steer for the North Star at all hazards. At this crisis, Providence opened an unexpected way for me to escape. My friend Peter came one evening, and asked to speak with me. "Your day has come, Linda," said he. "I have found a chance for you to go to the Free States. You have a fortnight to decide." The news seemed too good to be true; but Peter explained his arrangements, and told me all that was necessary was for me to say I would go. I was going to answer him with a joyful yes, when the thought of Benny came to my mind. I told him the temptation was exceedingly strong, but I was terribly afraid of Dr. Flint's alleged power over my child, and that I could not go and leave him behind. Peter remonstrated earnestly. He said such a good chance might never occur again; that Benny was free, and could be sent to me; and that for the sake of my children's welfare I ought not to hesitate a moment. I told him I would consult with uncle Phillip. My uncle rejoiced in the plan, and bade me go by all means. He promised, if his life was spared, that he would either bring or send my son to me as soon as I reached a place of safety. I resolved to go, but thought nothing had better be said to my grandmother till very near the time of departure. But my uncle thought she would feel it more keenly if I left her so suddenly. "I will reason with her," said he, "and convince her how necessary it is, not only for your sake, but for hers also. You cannot be blind to the fact that she is sinking under her burdens." I was not blind to it. I knew that my concealment was an ever-present source of anxiety, and that the older she grew the more nervously fearful she was of discovery. My uncle talked with her, and finally succeeded in persuading her that it was absolutely necessary for me to seize the chance so unexpectedly offered.

The anticipation of being a free woman proved almost too much for my weak frame. The excitement stimulated me, and at the same time bewildered me. I made busy preparations for my journey, and for my son to follow me. I resolved to have an interview with him before I went, that I might give him cautions and advice, and tell him how anxiously I should be waiting for him at the north. Grandmother stole up to me as often as possible to whisper words of counsel. She insisted upon my writing to Dr. Flint, as soon as I arrived in the Free States, and asking him to sell me to her. She said she would sacrifice her house, and all she had in the world, for the sake of having me safe with my children in any part of the world. If she could only live to know *that* she could die in peace. I promised the dear old faithful friend that I would write to her as soon as I arrived, and put the letter in a safe way to reach her; but in my own mind I resolved that not another cent of her hard earnings should be spent to pay rapacious slaveholders for what they called their property. And even if I had not been unwilling to buy what I had already a right to possess, common humanity would have prevented me from accepting the generous offer, at the expense of turning my aged relative out of house and home, when she was trembling on the brink of the grave.

I was to escape in a vessel; but I forbear to mention any further particulars. I was in readiness, but the vessel was unexpectedly detained several days. Meantime, news came to town of a most horrible murder committed on a fugitive slave, named James. Charity, the mother of this unfortunate young man, had been an old acquaintance of ours. I have told the shocking particulars of his death, in my description of some of the neighboring slaveholders. My grandmother, always nervously sensitive about runaways, was terribly frightened. She felt sure that a similar fate awaited me, if I did not desist from my enterprise. She sobbed, and groaned, and entreated me not to go. Her excessive fear was somewhat contagious, and my heart was not proof against her extreme agony. I was grievously disappointed, but I promised to relinquish my project.

When my friend Peter was apprised of this, he was both disappointed and vexed. He said, that judging from our past experience, it would be a long time before I had such another chance to throw away. I told him it need not be thrown away; that I had a friend concealed near by, who would be glad enough to take the place that had been provided for me. I told him about poor Fanny, and the kind-hearted, noble fellow, who never turned his back upon any body in distress, white or black, expressed his readiness to help her. Aggie was much surprised when she found that we knew her secret. She was rejoiced to hear of such a chance for Fanny, and arrangements were made for her to go on board the vessel the next night. They both supposed that I had long been at the north, therefore my name was not mentioned in the transaction. Fanny was carried on board at the appointed time, and stowed away in a very small cabin. This accommodation had been purchased at a price that would pay for a voyage to England. But when one proposes to go to fine old England, they stop to calculate whether they can afford the cost of the pleasure; while in making a bargain to escape from slavery, the trembling victim is ready to say, "Take all I have, only don't betray me!"

The next morning I peeped through my loophole, and saw that it was dark and cloudy. At night I received news that the wind was ahead, and the vessel had not sailed. I was exceedingly anxious about Fanny, and Peter too, who was running a tremendous risk at my instigation. Next day the wind and weather remained the same. Poor Fanny had been half dead with fright when they carried her on board, and I could readily imagine how she must be suffering now. Grandmother came often to my den, to say how thankful she was I did not go. On the third morning she rapped for me to come down to the storeroom. The poor old sufferer was breaking down under her weight of trouble. She was easily flurried now. I found her in a nervous, excited state, but I was not aware that she had forgotten to lock the door behind her, as usual. She was exceedingly worried about the detention of the vessel. She was afraid all would be discovered, and then Fanny, and Peter, and I, would all be tortured to death, and Phillip would be utterly ruined, and her house would be torn down. Poor Peter! If he should die such a horrible death as the poor slave James had lately done, and all for his kindness in trying to help me, how dreadful it would be for us all! Alas, the thought was familiar to me, and had sent many a sharp pang through my heart. I tried to suppress my own anxiety, and speak soothingly to her. She brought in some allusion to aunt Nancy, the dear daughter she had recently buried, and then she lost all control of herself. As she stood there, trembling and sobbing, a voice from the piazza called out, "Whar is you, aunt Marthy?" Grandmother was startled, and in her agitation opened the door, without thinking of me. In stepped Jenny, the mischievous housemaid, who had tried to enter my room, when I was concealed in the house of my white benefactress. "I's bin huntin ebery whar for you, aunt Marthy," said she. "My missis wants you to send her some crackers." I had slunk down behind a barrel, which entirely screened me, but I imagined that Jenny was looking directly at the spot, and my heart beat violently. My grandmother immediately thought what she had done, and went out quickly with Jenny to count the crackers locking the door after her. She returned to me, in a few minutes, the perfect picture of despair. "Poor child!" she exclaimed, "my carelessness has ruined you. The boat ain't gone yet. Get ready immediately, and go with Fanny. I ain't got another word to say against it now; for there's no telling what may happen this day."

Uncle Phillip was sent for, and he agreed with his mother in thinking that Jenny would inform Dr. Flint in less than twenty-four hours.

He advised getting me on board the boat, if possible; if not, I had better keep very still in my den, where they could not find me without tearing the house down. He said it would not do for him to move in the matter, because suspicion would be immediately excited; but he promised to communicate with Peter. I felt reluctant to apply to him again, having implicated him too much already; but there seemed to be no alternative. Vexed as Peter had been by my indecision, he was true to his generous nature, and said at once that he would do his best to help me, trusting I should show myself a stronger woman this time.

He immediately proceeded to the wharf, and found that the wind had shifted, and the vessel was slowly beating down stream. On some pretext of urgent necessity, he offered two boatmen a dollar apiece to catch up with her. He was of lighter complexion than the boatmen he hired, and when the captain saw them coming so rapidly, he thought officers were pursuing his vessel in search of the runaway slave he had on board. They hoisted sails, but the boat gained upon them, and the indefatigable Peter sprang on board.

The captain at once recognized him. Peter asked him to go below, to speak about a bad bill he had given him. When he told his errand, the captain replied, "Why, the woman's here already; and I've put her where you or the devil would have a tough job to find her."

"But it is another woman I want to bring," said Peter. "*She* is in great distress, too, and you shall be paid any thing within reason, if you'll stop and take her."

"What's her name?" inquired the captain.

"Linda," he replied.

"That's the name of the woman already here," rejoined the captain. "By George! I believe you mean to betray me."

"O!" exclaimed Peter, "God knows I wouldn't harm a hair of your head. I am too grateful to you. But there really *is* another woman in great danger. Do have the humanity to stop and take her!"

After a while they came to an understanding. Fanny, not dreaming I was any where about in that region, had assumed my name, though she called herself Johnson. "Linda is a common name," said Peter, "and the woman I want to bring is Linda Brent."

The captain agreed to wait at a certain place till evening, being handsomely paid for his detention.

Of course, the day was an anxious one for us all. But we concluded that if Jenny had seen me, she would be too wise to let her mistress know of it; and that she probably would not get a chance to see Dr. Flint's family till evening, for I knew very well what were the rules in that household.

I afterwards believed that she did not see me; for nothing ever came of it, and she was one of those base characters that would have jumped to betray a suffering fellow being for the sake of thirty pieces of silver.[36]

I made all my arrangements to go on board as soon as it was dusk. The intervening time I resolved to spend with my son. I had not spoken to him for seven years, though I had been under the same roof, and seen him every day, when I was well enough to sit at the loophole. I did not dare to venture beyond the storeroom; so they brought him there, and locked us up together, in a place concealed from the piazza door. It was an agitating interview for both of us. After we had talked and wept together for a little while, he said, "Mother, I'm glad you're going away. I wish I could go with you. I knew you was here; and I have been *so* afraid they would come and catch you!"

I was greatly surprised, and asked him how he had found it out.

He replied, "I was standing under the eaves, one day, before Ellen went away, and I heard somebody cough up over the wood shed. I don't know what made me think it was you, but I did think so. I missed Ellen, the night before she went away; and grandmother brought her back into the room in the night; and I thought maybe she'd been to see *you,* before she went, for I heard grandmother whisper to her, 'Now go to sleep; and remember never to tell.'"

I asked him if he ever mentioned his suspicions to his sister. He said he never did; but after he heard the cough, if he saw her playing with other children on that side of the house, he always tried to coax her round to the other side, for fear they would hear me cough, too. He said he had kept a close lookout for Dr. Flint, and if he saw him speak to a constable, or a patrol, he always told grandmother. I now recollected that I had seen him manifest uneasiness, when people were on that side of the house, and I had at the time been puzzled to conjecture a motive for his actions. Such prudence may seem extraordinary in a boy of twelve years, but slaves, being surrounded by mysteries, deceptions, and dangers, early learn to be suspicious and watchful, and prematurely cautious and cunning. He had never asked a question of grandmother, or uncle Phillip, and I had often heard him chime in with other children, when they spoke of my being at the north.

I told him I was now really going to the Free States, and if he was a good, honest boy, and a loving child to his dear old grandmother, the Lord would bless him, and bring him to me, and we and Ellen would live

[36]SHE WAS ONE OF THOSE BASE CHARACTERS...FOR THE SAKE OF THIRTY PIECES OF SILVER: A reference to Judas Iscariot, who betrayed Jesus for thirty pieces of silver (Matthew 26:14–15).

together. He began to tell me that grandmother had not eaten any thing all day. While he was speaking, the door was unlocked, and she came in with a small bag of money, which she wanted me to take. I begged her to keep a part of it, at least, to pay for Benny's being sent to the north; but she insisted, while her tears were falling fast, that I should take the whole. "You may be sick among strangers," she said, "and they would send you to the poorhouse to die." Ah, that good grandmother!

For the last time I went up to my nook. Its desolate appearance no longer chilled me, for the light of hope had risen in my soul. Yet, even with the blessed prospect of freedom before me, I felt very sad at leaving forever that old homestead, where I had been sheltered so long by the dear old grandmother; where I had dreamed my first young dream of love; and where, after that had faded away, my children came to twine themselves so closely round my desolate heart. As the hour approached for me to leave, I again descended to the storeroom. My grandmother and Benny were there. She took me by the hand, and said, "Linda, let us pray." We knelt down together, with my child pressed to my heart, and my other arm round the faithful, loving old friend I was about to leave forever. On no other occasion has it ever been my lot to listen to so fervent a supplication for mercy and protection. It thrilled through my heart, and inspired me with trust in God.

Peter was waiting for me in the street. I was soon by his side, faint in body, but strong of purpose. I did not look back upon the old place, though I felt that I should never see it again.

XXXV. Prejudice against Color

It was a relief to my mind to see preparations for leaving the city.[37] We went to Albany in the steamboat Knickerbocker. When the gong sounded for tea, Mrs. Bruce said, "Linda, it is late, and you and baby had better come to the table with me." I replied, "I know it is time baby had her supper, but I had rather not go with you, if you please. I am afraid of being insulted." "O no, not if you are with *me*," she said. I saw several white nurses go with their ladies, and I ventured to do the same. We were at the extreme end of the table. I was no sooner seated, than a gruff voice said, "Get up! You know you are not allowed to sit here." I looked up, and, to my astonishment and indignation, saw that the speaker was a colored man. If his office required him to enforce the by-laws of the boat, he might, at least, have done it politely. I replied, "I shall not get up, unless the captain comes and

---

[37]THE CITY: After her escape to the North, Jacobs worked as a nursemaid in New York City, caring for the daughter of the editor and writer Nathaniel Parker Willis (Mr. Bruce) and Mary Stace Willis (Mrs. Bruce).

takes me up." No cup of tea was offered me, but Mrs. Bruce handed me hers and called for another. I looked to see whether the other nurses were treated in a similar manner. They were all properly waited on.

Next morning, when we stopped at Troy for breakfast, every body was making a rush for the table. Mrs. Bruce said, "Take my arm, Linda, and we'll go in together." The landlord heard her, and said, "Madam, will you allow your nurse and baby to take breakfast with my family?" I knew this was to be attributed to my complexion; but he spoke courteously, and therefore I did not mind it.

At Saratoga we found the United States Hotel[38] crowded, and Mr. Bruce took one of the cottages belonging to the hotel. I had thought, with gladness, of going to the quiet of the country, where I should meet few people, but here I found myself in the midst of a swarm of Southerners. I looked round me with fear and trembling, dreading to see some one who would recognize me. I was rejoiced to find that we were to stay but a short time.

We soon returned to New York, to make arrangements for spending the remainder of the summer at Rockaway.[39] While the laundress was putting the clothes in order, I took an opportunity to go over to Brooklyn to see Ellen. I met her going to a grocery store, and the first words she said, were, "O, mother, don't go to Mrs. Hobbs's. Her brother, Mr. Thorne, has come from the south, and may be he'll tell where you are." I accepted the warning. I told her I was going away with Mrs. Bruce the next day, and would try to see her when I came back.

Being in servitude to the Anglo-Saxon race, I was not put into a "Jim Crow car,"[40] on our way to Rockaway, neither was I invited to ride through the streets on the top of trunks in a truck; but every where I found the same manifestations of that cruel prejudice, which so dis-courages the feelings, and represses the energies of the colored people. We reached Rockaway before dark, and put up at the Pavilion—a large hotel, beautifully situated by the sea-side—a great resort of the fashionable world. Thirty or forty nurses were there, of a great variety of nations. Some of the ladies had colored waiting-maids and coachmen, but I was the only nurse tinged with the blood of Africa. When the tea bell rang, I took little Mary and followed the other nurses. Supper was served in a long hall. A young man, who had the ordering of things, took the circuit of the table two or three times, and finally pointed me

[38]UNITED STATES HOTEL: In Saratoga Springs, New York.
[39]ROCKAWAY: The Marine Pavilion at Rockaway, Queens, New York.
[40]JIM CROW CAR: A car reserved for African Americans on a racially segregated passenger train. Jim Crow, whose name became attached to such segregationist laws and customs, was a minstrel show character who wore blackface makeup.

to a seat at the lower end of it. As there was but one chair, I sat down and took the child in my lap. Whereupon the young man came to me and said, in the blandest manner possible, "Will you please to seat the little girl in the chair, and stand behind it and feed her? After they have done, you will be shown to the kitchen, where you will have a good supper."

This was the climax! I found it hard to preserve my self-control, when I looked round, and saw women who were nurses, as I was, and only one shade lighter in complexion, eyeing me with a defiant look, as if my presence were a contamination. However, I said nothing. I quietly took the child in my arms, went to our room, and refused to go to the table again. Mr. Bruce ordered meals to be sent to the room for little Mary and I. This answered for a few days; but the waiters of the establishment were white, and they soon began to complain, saying they were not hired to wait on negroes. The landlord requested Mr. Bruce to send me down to my meals, because his servants rebelled against bringing them up, and the colored servants of other boarders were dissatisfied because all were not treated alike.

My answer was that the colored servants ought to be dissatisfied with *themselves*, for not having too much self-respect to submit to such treatment; that there was no difference in the price of board for colored and white servants, and there was no justification for difference of treatment. I staid a month after this, and finding I was resolved to stand up for my rights, they concluded to treat me well. Let every colored man and woman do this, and eventually we shall cease to be trampled under foot by our oppressors.

XXXVIII. RENEWED INVITATIONS TO GO SOUTH

We had a tedious winter passage, and from the distance spectres seemed to rise up on the shores of the United States.[41] It is a sad feeling to be afraid of one's native country. We arrived in New York safely, and I hastened to Boston to look after my children. I found Ellen well, and improving at her school; but Benny was not there to welcome me. He had been left at a good place to learn a trade, and for several months every thing worked well. He was liked by the master, and was a favorite with his fellow-apprentices; but one day they accidentally discovered a fact they had never before suspected—that he was colored! This at once transformed him into a different being. Some of the apprentices were Americans, others American-born Irish; and it was offensive to their dignity to have a "nigger" among them, after they had been told that he *was* a "nigger." They began by treating him with silent scorn, and finding that he returned the same, they resorted to insults and abuse. He was too spirited a boy to stand that, and he went off. Being desirous to do something to support himself, and having no one to advise him, he shipped for a whaling voyage. When I received these tidings I shed many tears, and bitterly reproached myself for having left him so long. But I had done it for the best, and now all I could do was to pray to the heavenly Father to guide and protect him.

Not long after my return, I received the following letter from Miss Emily Flint, now Mrs. Dodge:—

"In this you will recognized the hand of your friend and mistress. Having heard that you had gone with a family to Europe, I have waited to hear of your return to write to you. I should have answered the letter you wrote to me long since, but as I could not then act independently of my father, I knew there could be nothing done satisfactory to you. There were persons here who were willing to buy you and run the risk of getting you. To this I would not consent. I have always been attached to you, and would not like to see you the slave of another, or have unkind treatment. I am married now, and can protect you. My husband expects to move to Virginia this spring, where we think of settling. I am very anxious that you should come and live with me. If you are not willing to come, you may purchase yourself; but I should prefer having you live with me. If you come, you may, if you like, spend a month with your grandmother and friends, then come to me in Norfolk, Virginia. Think this over, and write as soon as possible, and let me know the conclusion. Hoping that your children are well, I remain you friend and mistress."

Of course I did not write to return thanks for this cordial invitation. I felt insulted to be thought stupid enough to be caught by such professions.

"'Come up into my parlor,' said the spider to the fly;
'Tis the prettiest little parlor that ever you did spy.'"[42]

It was plain that Dr. Flint's family were apprised of my movements, since they knew of my voyage to Europe. I expected to have further trouble from them; but having eluded them thus far, I hoped to be as successful in future. The money I had earned, I was desirous to devote to the

[42]COME UP INTO MY PARLOR...THAT EVER YOU DID SPY: From the children's poem "The Spider and the Fly" (1844), by Mary Howitt (1800–1888).

education of my children, and to secure a home for them. It seemed not
only hard, but unjust, to pay for myself. I could not possibly regard
myself as a piece of property. Moreover, I had worked many years without wages, and during that time had been obliged to depend on my
grandmother for many comforts in food and clothing. My children certainly belonged to me; but though Dr. Flint had incurred no expense
for their support, he had received a large sum of money for them. I knew
the law would decide that I was his property, and would probably still
give his daughter a claim to my children; but I regarded such laws as
the regulations of robbers, who had no rights that I was bound to respect.

The Fugitive Slave Law had not then passed. The judges of
Massachusetts had not then stooped under chains to enter her courts
of justice, so called. I knew my old master was rather skittish of
Massachusetts. I relied on her love of freedom, and felt safe on her soil.
I am now aware that I honored the old Commonwealth beyond her
deserts.

XXXIX. The Confession

For two years my daughter and I supported ourselves comfortably in
Boston. At the end of that time, my brother William offered to send Ellen
to a boarding school. It required a great effort for me to consent to part
with her, for I had few near ties, and it was her presence that made my
two little rooms seem home-like. But my judgment prevailed over my selfish feelings. I made preparations for her departure. During the two years
we had lived together I had often resolved to tell her something about her
father; but I had never been able to muster sufficient courage. I had a
shrinking dread of diminishing my child's love. I knew she must have
curiosity on the subject, but she had never asked a question. She was
always very careful not to say any thing to remind me of my troubles.
Now that she was going from me, I thought if I should die before she
returned, she might hear my story from some one who did not understand the palliating circumstances; and that if she were entirely ignorant on the subject, her sensitive nature might receive a rude shock.

When we retired for the night, she said, "Mother, it is very hard to
leave you alone. I am almost sorry I am going, though I do want to
improve myself. But you will write to me often; won't you, mother?"

I did not throw my arms round her. I did not answer her. But in a
calm, solemn way, for it cost me great effort, I said, "Listen to me, Ellen;
I have something to tell you!" I recounted my early sufferings in slavery, and told her how nearly they had crushed me. I began to tell her how

they had driven me into a great sin, when she clasped me in her arms, and exclaimed, "O, don't, mother! Please don't tell me any more."

I said, "But, my child, I want you to know about your father."

"I know all about it, mother," she replied; "I am nothing to my father and he is nothing to me. All my love is for you. I was with him five months in Washington, and he never cared for me. He never spoke to me as he did to his little Fanny. I knew all the time he was my father, for Fanny's nurse told me so; but she said I must never tell any body, and I never did. I used to wish he would take me in his arms and kiss me, as he did Fanny; or that he would sometimes smile at me, as he did at her. I thought if he was my own father, he ought to love me. I was a little girl then, and didn't know any better. But now I never think any thing about my father. All my love is for you." She hugged me closer as she spoke, and I thanked God that the knowledge I had so much dreaded to impart had not diminished the affection of my child. I had not the slightest idea she knew that portion of my history. If I had, I should have spoken to her long before; for my pent-up feelings had often longed to pour themselves out to some one I could trust. But I loved the dear girl better for the delicacy she had manifested towards her unfortunate mother.

The next morning, she and her uncle started on their journey to the village in New York, where she was to be placed at school. It seemed as if all the sunshine had gone away. My little room was dreadfully lonely. I was thankful when a message came from a lady, accustomed to employ me, requesting me to come and sew in her family for several weeks. On my return, I found a letter from brother William. He thought of opening an anti-slavery reading room in Rochester, and combining with it the sale of some books and stationery; and he wanted me to unite with him. We tried it, but it was not successful. We found warm anti-slavery friends there, but the feeling was not general enough to support such an establishment. I passed nearly a year in the family of Isaac and Amy Post,[43] practical believers in the Christian doctrine of human brotherhood. They measured a man's worth by his character, not by his complexion. The memory of those beloved and honored friends will remain with me to my latest hour.

XL. The Fugitive Slave Law

My brother, being disappointed in his project, concluded to go to California; and it was agreed that Benjamin should go with him. Ellen

---

[43]ISAAC AND AMY POST: Isaac (1798–1872) and Amy (1802–1889) Post were Quaker abolitionists.

liked her school, and was a great favorite there. They did not know her history, and she did not tell it, because she had no desire to make capital out of their sympathy. But when it was accidentally discovered that her mother was a fugitive slave, every method was used to increase her advantages and diminish her expenses.

I was alone again. It was necessary for me to be earning money, and I preferred that it should be among those who knew me. On my return from Rochester, I called at the house of Mr. Bruce, to see Mary, the darling little babe that had thawed my heart, when it was freezing into a cheerless distrust of all my fellow-beings. She was growing a tall girl now, but I loved her always. Mr. Bruce had married again, and it was proposed that I should become nurse to a new infant. I had but one hesitation, and that was my feeling of insecurity in New York, now greatly increased by the passage of the Fugitive Slave Law. However, I resolved to try the experiment. I was again fortunate in my employer. The new Mrs. Bruce was an American, brought up under aristocratic influences; and still living in the midst of them; but if she had any prejudice against color, I was never made aware of it; and as for the system of slavery, she had a most hearty dislike of it. No sophistry of Southerners could blind her to its enormity. She was a person of excellent principles and a noble heart. To me, from that hour to the present, she has been a true and sympathizing friend. Blessings be with her and hers!

About the time that I reëntered the Bruce family an event occurred of disastrous import to the colored people. The slave Hamlin,[44] the first fugitive that came under the new law, was given up by the bloodhounds of the north to the bloodhounds of the south. It was the beginning of a reign of terror to the colored population. The great city rushed on in its whirl of excitement, taking no note of the "short and simple annals of the poor."[45] But while fashionables were listening to the thrilling voice of Jenny Lind in Metropolitan Hall,[46] the thrilling voices of poor hunted colored people went up, in an agony of supplication, to the Lord, from Zion's church.[47] Many families, who had lived in the city for twenty years, fled from it now. Many a poor washerwoman, who, by hard labor, had made herself a comfortable home, was obliged to sacrifice her furniture, bid

[44]HAMLIN: James Hamlin is reputed to be the first slave recaptured in New York under the new fugitive slave law of the Compromise of 1850.
[45]SHORT AND SIMPLE ANNALS OF THE POOR: From the poem "Elegy Written in a Country Churchyard" (1751), by the English poet Thomas Gray (1716–1771).
[46]JENNY LIND IN METROPOLITAN HALL: Jenny Lind (1820–1887) was a Swedish soprano. Metropolitan Hall was built for her American debut. She toured in the United States from 1850 to 1852 under the management of the famed circus showman and promoter P.T. Barnum.
[47]ZION'S CHURCH: Zion Chapel Street Church, the site of an October 1, 1850, gathering to protest James Hamlin's recapture.

a hurried farewell to friends, and seek her fortune among strangers in Canada. Many a wife discovered a secret she had never known before— that her husband was a fugitive, and must leave her to insure his own safety. Worse still, many a husband discovered that his wife had fled from slavery years ago, and as "the child follows the condition of its mother," the children of his love were liable to be seized and carried into slavery. Every where, in those humble homes, there was consternation and anguish. But what cared the legislators of the "dominant race" for the blood they were crushing out of trampled hearts?

When my brother William spent his last evening with me, before he went to California, we talked nearly all the time of the distress brought on our oppressed people by the passage of this iniquitous law; and never had I seen him manifest such bitterness of spirit, such stern hostility to our oppressors. He was himself free from the operation of the law; for he did not run from any Slaveholding State, being brought into the Free States by his master. But I was subject to it; and so were hundreds of intelligent and industrious people all around us. I seldom ventured into the streets; and when it was necessary to do an errand for Mrs. Bruce, or any of the family, I went as much as possible through back streets and by-ways. What a disgrace to a city calling itself free, that inhabitants, guiltless of offence, and seeking to perform their duties conscientiously, should be condemned to live in such incessant fear, and have nowhere to turn for protection! This state of things, of course, gave rise to many impromptu vigilance committees. Every colored person, and every friend of their persecuted race, kept their eyes wide open. Every evening I examined the newspapers carefully, to see what Southerners had put up at the hotels. I did this for my own sake, thinking my young mistress and her husband might be among the list; I wished also to give information to others, if necessary; for if many were "running to and fro," I resolved that "knowledge should be increased."[48]

This brings up one of my Southern reminiscences, which I will here briefly relate. I was somewhat acquainted with a slave named Luke, who belonged to a wealthy man in our vicinity. His master died, leaving a son and daughter heirs to his large fortune. In the division of the slaves, Luke was included in the son's portion. This young man became a prey to the vices growing out of the "patriarchal institution," and when he went to the north, to complete his education, he carried his vices with him. He was brought home, deprived of the use of

---

[48]KNOWLEDGE SHOULD BE INCREASED: Daniel 12:4: "But thou, O Daniel, shut up the words, and seal the book, even to the time of the end: many shall run to and fro, and knowledge shall be increased."

his limbs, by excessive dissipation. Luke was appointed to wait upon his bed-ridden master, whose despotic habits were greatly increased by exasperation at his own helplessness. He kept a cowhide beside him, and, for the most trivial occurrence, he would order his attendant to bare his back, and kneel beside the couch, while he whipped him till his strength was exhausted. Some days he was not allowed to wear any thing but his shirt, in order to be in readiness to be flogged. A day seldom passed without his receiving more or less blows. If the slightest resistance was offered, the town constable was sent for to execute the punishment, and Luke learned from experience how much more the constable's strong arm was to be dreaded than the comparatively feeble one of his master. The arm of his tyrant grew weaker, and was finally palsied; and then the constable's services were in constant requisition. The fact that he was entirely dependent on Luke's care, and was obliged to be tended like an infant, instead of inspiring any gratitude or compassion towards his poor slave, seemed only to increase his irritability and cruelty. As he lay there on his bed, a mere degraded wreck of manhood, he took into his head the strangest freaks of despotism; and if Luke hesitated to submit to his orders, the constable was immediately sent for. Some of these freaks were of a nature too filthy to be repeated. When I fled from the house of bondage, I left poor Luke still chained to the bedside of this cruel and disgusting wretch.

One day, when I had been requested to do an errand for Mrs. Bruce, I was hurrying through back streets, as usual, when I saw a young man approaching, whose face was familiar to me. As he came nearer, I recognized Luke. I always rejoiced to see or hear of any one who had escaped from the black pit; but, remembering this poor fellow's extreme hardships, I was peculiarly glad to see him on Northern soil, though I no longer called it *free* soil. I well remembered what a desolate feeling it was to be alone among strangers, and I went up to him and greeted him cordially. At first, he did not know me; but when I mentioned my name, he remembered all about me. I told him of the Fugitive Slave Law, and asked him if he did not know that New York was a city of kidnappers.

He replied, "De risk ain't so bad for me, as 'tis fur you. 'Cause I runned away from de speculator, and you runned away from de massa. Dem speculators vont spen dar money to come here fur a runaway, if dey ain't sartin sure to put dar hans right on him. An I tell you I's tuk good car 'bout dat. I had too hard times down dar, to let 'em ketch dis nigger."

He then told me of the advice he had received, and the plans he had laid. I asked if he had money enough to take him to Canada. "'Pend upon it, I hab," he replied. "I tuk car fur dat. I'd bin workin all my days fur

dem cussed whites, an got no pay but kicks and cuffs. So I tought dis nigger had a right to money nuff to bring him to de Free States. Massa Henry
he lib till ebery body vish him dead; an ven he did die, I knowed de
debbil would hab him, an vouldn't vant him to bring his money 'long too.
So I tuk some of his bills, and put 'em in de pocket of his ole trousers.
An ven he was buried, dis nigger ask fur dem ole trousers, an dey gub
'em to me." With a low, chuckling laugh, he added, "You see I didn't *steal*
it; dey *gub* it to me. I tell you, I had mighty hard time to keep de speculator from findin it; but he didn't git it."

This is a fair specimen of how the moral sense is educated by slavery. When a man has his wages stolen from him, year after year, and
the laws sanction and enforce the theft, how can he be expected to have
more regard to honesty than has the man who robs him? I have become
somewhat enlightened, but I confess that I agree with poor, ignorant,
much-abused Luke, in thinking he had a *right* to that money, as a portion of his unpaid wages. He went to Canada forthwith, and I have not
since heard from him.

All that winter I lived in a state of anxiety. When I took the children out to breathe the air, I closely observed the countenances of all
I met. I dreaded the approach of summer, when snakes and slaveholders make their appearance. I was, in fact, a slave in New York, as subject to slave laws as I had been in a Slave State. Strange incongruity
in a State called free!

Spring returned, and I received warning from the south that Dr. Flint
knew of my return to my old place, and was making preparations to have
me caught. I learned afterwards that my dress, and that of Mrs. Bruce's
children, had been described to him by some of the Northern tools, which
slaveholders employ for their base purposes, and then indulge in sneers
at their cupidity and mean servility.

I immediately informed Mrs. Bruce of my danger, and she took
prompt measures for my safety. My place as nurse could not be supplied immediately, and this generous, sympathizing lady proposed that
I should carry her baby away. It was a comfort to me to have the child
with me; for the heart is reluctant to be torn away from every object it
loves. But how few mothers would have consented to have one of their
own babes become a fugitive, for the sake of a poor, hunted nurse, on
whom the legislators of the country had let loose the bloodhounds! When
I spoke of the sacrifice she was making, in depriving herself of her dear
baby, she replied, "It is better for you to have baby with you, Linda;
for if they get on your track, they will be obliged to bring the child to me;
and then, if there is a possibility of saving you, you shall be saved."

This lady had a very wealthy relative, a benevolent gentleman in many respects, but aristocratic and proslavery. He remonstrated with her for harboring a fugitive slave; told her she was violating the laws of her country; and asked her if she was aware of the penalty. She replied, "I am very well aware of it. It is imprisonment and one thousand dollars fine. Shame on my country that it *is* so! I am ready to incur the penalty. I will go to the state's prison, rather than have any poor victim torn from *my* house, to be carried back to slavery."

The noble heart! The brave heart! The tears are in my eyes while I write of her. May the God of the helpless reward her for her sympathy with my persecuted people!

I was sent into New England, where I was sheltered by the wife of a senator, whom I shall always hold in grateful remembrance. This honorable gentleman would not have voted for the Fugitive Slave Law, as did the senator in "Uncle Tom's Cabin;"[49] on the contrary, he was strongly opposed to it; but he was enough under its influence to be afraid of having me remain in his house many hours. So I was sent into the country, where I remained a month with the baby. When it was supposed that Dr. Flint's emissaries had lost track of me, and given up the pursuit for the present, I returned to New York.

XLI. FREE AT LAST

Mrs. Bruce, and every member of her family, were exceedingly kind to me. I was thankful for the blessings of my lot, yet I could not always wear a cheerful countenance. I was doing harm to no one; on the contrary, I was doing all the good I could in my small way; yet I could never go out to breathe God's free air without trepidation at my heart. This seemed hard; and I could not think it was a right state of things in any civilized country.

From time to time I received news from my good old grandmother. She could not write; but she employed others to write for her. The following is an extract from one of her last letters:—

"Dear Daughter: I cannot hope to see you again on earth; but I pray to God to unite us above, where pain will no more rack this feeble body of mine; where sorrow and parting from my children will be no more. God has promised these things if we are faithful unto the end. My age and feeble health deprive me of going

[49]UNCLE TOM'S CABIN: Antislavery novel first published serially from 1851 to 1852 in the abolitionist newspaper, *The National Era*, by American writer Harriet Beecher Stowe (1811–1896). The New England "senator" was not a U. S. senator, but Joseph Grinnell, a member of the U. S. House of Representatives from 1843 to 1851.

to church now; but God is with me here at home. Thank your brother for his kindness. Give much love to him, and tell him to remember the Creator in the days of his youth,[50] and strive to meet me in the Father's kingdom. Love to Ellen and Benjamin. Don't neglect him. Tell him for me, to be a good boy. Strive, my child, to train them for God's children. May he protect and provide for you, is the prayer of your loving old mother."

These letters both cheered saddened me. I was always glad to have tidings from the kind, faithful old friend of my unhappy youth; but her messages of love made my heart yearn to see her before she died, and I mourned over the fact that it was impossible. Some months after I returned from my flight to New England, I received a letter from her, in which she wrote, "Dr. Flint is dead. He has left a distressed family. Poor old man! I hope he made his peace with God."

I remembered how he had defrauded my grandmother of the hard earnings she had loaned; how he had tried to cheat her out of the freedom her mistress had promised her, and how he had persecuted her children; and I thought to myself that she was a better Christian than I was, if she could entirely forgive him. I cannot say, with truth, that the news of my old master's death softened my feelings towards him. There are wrongs which even the grave does not bury. The man was odious to me while he lived, and his memory is odious now.

His departure from this world did not diminish my danger. He had threatened my grandmother that his heirs should hold me in slavery after he was gone; that I never should be free so long as a child of his survived. As for Mrs. Flint, I had seen her in deeper afflictions than I supposed the loss of her husband would be, for she had buried several children; yet I never saw any signs of softening in her heart. The doctor had died in embarrassed circumstances, and had little to will to his heirs, except such property as he was unable to grasp. I was well aware what I had to expect from the family of Flints; and my fears were confirmed by a letter from the south, warning me to be on my guard, because Mrs. Flint openly declared that her daughter could not afford to lose so valuable a slave as I was.

I kept close watch of the newspapers for arrivals; but one Saturday night, being much occupied, I forgot to examine the Evening Express as usual. I went down into the parlor for it, early in the morning, and found the boy about to kindle a fire with it. I took it from him and examined the list of arrivals. Reader, if you have never been a slave, you cannot

---

[50]CREATOR IN THE DAYS OF HIS YOUTH: Ecclesiates 12:1: "Remember now thy Creator in the days of thy youth, while the evil days come not, nor the years draw nigh, when thou shalt say, I have no pleasure in them."

imagine the acute sensation of suffering at my heart, when I read the names of Mr. and Mrs. Dodge, at a hotel in Courtland Street. It was a third-rate hotel, and that circumstance convinced me of the truth of what I had heard, that they were short of funds and had need of my value, as *they* valued me; and that was by dollars and cents. I hastened with the paper to Mrs. Bruce. Her heart and hand were always open to every one in distress, and she always warmly sympathized with mine. It was impossible to tell how near the enemy was. He might have passed and repassed the house while we were sleeping. He might at that moment be waiting to pounce upon me if I ventured out of doors. I had never seen the husband of my young mistress, and therefore I could not distinguish him from any other stranger. A carriage was hastily ordered; and, closely veiled, I followed Mrs. Bruce, taking the baby again with me into exile. After various turnings and crossings, and returnings, the carriage stopped at the house of one of Mrs. Bruce's friends, where I was kindly received. Mrs. Bruce returned immediately, to instruct the domestics what to say if any one came to inquire for me.

It was lucky for me that the evening paper was not burned up before I had a chance to examine the list of arrivals. It was not long after Mrs. Bruce's return to her house, before several people came to inquire for me. One inquired for me, another asked for my daughter Ellen, and another said he had a letter from my grandmother, which he was requested to deliver in person.

They were told, "She *has* lived here, but she has left."

"How long ago?"

"I don't know, sir."

"Do you know where she went?"

"I do not, sir." And the door was closed.

This Mr. Dodge, who claimed me as his property, was originally a Yankee pedler in the south; then he became a merchant, and finally a slaveholder. He managed to get introduced into what was called the first society, and married Miss Emily Flint. A quarrel arose between him and her brother, and the brother cowhided him. This led to a family feud, and he proposed to remove to Virginia. Dr. Flint left him no property, and his own means had become circumscribed, while a wife and children depended upon him for support. Under these circumstances, it was very natural that he should make an effort to put me into his pocket.

I had a colored friend, a man from my native place, in whom I had the most implicit confidence. I sent for him, and told him that Mr. and Mrs. Dodge had arrived in New York. I proposed that he should call upon them to make inquiries about his friends at the south, with whom Dr. Flint's family were well acquainted. He thought there was no impropriety in his doing so, and he consented. He went to the hotel, and knocked at the door of Mr. Dodge's room, which was opened by the gentleman himself, who gruffly inquired, "What brought you here? How came you to know I was in the city?"

"Your arrival was published in the evening papers, sir; and I called to ask Mrs. Dodge about my friends at home. I didn't suppose it would give any offence."

"Where's that negro girl, that belongs to my wife?"

"What girl, sir?"

"You know well enough. I mean Linda, that ran away from Dr. Flint's plantation, some years ago. I dare say you've seen her, and know where she is."

"Yes, sir, I've seen her, and know where she is. She is out of your reach, sir."

"Tell me where she is, or bring her to me, and I will give her a chance to buy her freedom."

"I don't think it would be of any use, sir. I have heard her say she would go to the ends of the earth, rather than pay any man or woman for her freedom, because she thinks she has a right to it. Besides, she couldn't do it, if she would, for she has spent her earnings to educate her children."

This made Mr. Dodge very angry, and some high words passed between them. My friend was afraid to come where I was; but in the course of the day I received a note from him. I supposed they had not come from the south, in the winter, for a pleasure excursion; and now the nature of their business was very plain.

Mrs. Bruce came to me and entreated me to leave the city the next morning. She said her house was watched, and it was possible that some clew to me might be obtained. I refused to take her advice. She pleaded with an earnest tenderness, that ought to have moved me; but I was in a bitter, disheartened mood. I was weary of flying from pillar to post. I had been chased during half my life, and it seemed as if the chase was never to end. There I sat, in that great city, guiltless of crime, yet not daring to worship God in any of the churches. I heard the bells ringing for afternoon service, and, with contemptuous sarcasm, I said, "Will the preachers take for their text, 'Proclaim liberty to the captive, and the opening of prison doors to them that are bound'?[51] or will they preach from the text, 'Do unto others as ye

[51]PROCLAIM LIBERTY TO THE CAPTIVE, AND THE OPENING OF PRISON DOORS TO THEM THAT ARE BOUND: Isaiah 61:1: "The Spirit of the Lord God is upon me; because the Lord hath anointed me to preach good tidings unto the meek; he hath sent me to bind up the brokenhearted, to proclaim liberty to the captives, and the opening of the prison to them that are bound."

would they should do unto you'?"[52] Oppressed Poles and Hungarians could find a safe refuge in that city; John Mitchell[53] was free to proclaim in the City Hall his desire for "a plantation well stocked with slaves;" but there I sat, an oppressed American, not daring to show my face. God forgive the black and bitter thoughts I indulged on that Sabbath day! The Scripture says, "Oppression makes even a wise man mad;"[54] and I was not wise.

I had been told that Mr. Dodge said his wife had never signed away her right to my children, and if he could not get me, he would take them. This it was, more than any thing else, that roused such a tempest in my soul. Benjamin was with his uncle William in California, but my innocent young daughter had come to spend a vacation with me. I thought of what I had suffered in slavery at her age, and my heart was like a tiger's when a hunter tries to seize her young.

Dear Mrs. Bruce! I seem to see the expression of her face, as she turned away discouraged by my obstinate mood. Finding her expostulations unavailing, she sent Ellen to entreat me. When ten o'clock in the evening arrived and Ellen had not returned, this watchful and unwearied friend became anxious. She came to us in a carriage, bringing a well-filled trunk for my journey—trusting that by this time I would listen to reason. I yielded to her, as I ought to have done before.

The next day, baby and I set out in a heavy snow storm, bound for New England again. I received letters from the City of Iniquity, addressed to me under an assumed name. In a few days one came from Mrs. Bruce, informing me that my new master was still searching for me, and that she intended to put an end to this persecution by buying my freedom. I felt grateful for the kindness that prompted this offer, but the idea was not so pleasant to me as might have been expected. The more my mind had become enlightened, the more difficult it was for me to consider myself an article of property; and to pay money to those who had so grievously oppressed me seemed like taking from my sufferings the glory of triumph. I wrote to Mrs. Bruce, thanking her, but saying that being sold from one owner to another seemed too much like slavery; that such a great obligation could not be easily cancelled; and that I preferred to go to my brother in California.

---

[52]DO UNTO OTHERS AS YE WOULD THEY SHOULD DO UNTO YOU: Matthew 7:12: "Therefore all things whatsoever ye would that men should do to you, do ye even so to them: for this is the law and the prophets."
[53]JOHN MITCHELL: An Irish revolutionary and journalist (1815–1875) who in 1853 came to the United States, where he edited a proslavery newspaper, *The Citizen* (1854–1855) in New York City.
[54]OPPRESSION MAKES EVEN A WISE MAN MAD: Ecclesiastes 7:7: "Surely oppression maketh a wise man mad; and a gift destroyeth the heart."

Without my knowledge, Mrs. Bruce employed a gentleman in New York to enter into negotiations with Mr. Dodge. He proposed to pay three hundred dollars down, if Mr. Dodge would sell me, and enter into obligations to relinquish all claim to me or my children forever after. He who called himself my master said he scorned so small an offer for such a valuable servant. The gentleman replied, "You can do as you choose, sir. If you reject this offer you will never get any thing; for the woman has friends who will convey her and her children out of the country."

Mr. Dodge concluded that "half a loaf was better than no bread," and he agreed to the proffered terms. By the next mail I received this brief letter from Mrs. Bruce: "I am rejoiced to tell you that the money for your freedom has been paid to Mr. Dodge. Come home to-morrow. I long to see you and my sweet babe."

My brain reeled as I read these lines. A gentleman near me said, "It's true; I have seen the bill of sale." "The bill of sale!" Those words struck me like a blow. So I was *sold* at last! A human being *sold* in the free city of New York! The bill of sale is on record, and future generations will learn from it that women were articles of traffic in New York, late in the nineteenth century of the Christian religion. It may hereafter prove a useful document to antiquaries, who are seeking to measure the progress of civilization in the United States. I well know the value of that bit of paper; but much as I love freedom, I do not like to look upon it. I am deeply grateful to the generous friend who procured it, but I despise the miscreant who demanded payment for what never rightfully belonged to him or his.

I had objected to having my freedom bought, yet I must confess that when it was done I felt as if a heavy load had been lifted from my weary shoulders. When I rode home in the cars I was no longer afraid to unveil my face and look at people as they passed. I should have been glad to have met Daniel Dodge himself; to have had him seen me and known me, that he might have mourned over the untoward circumstances which compelled him to sell me for three hundred dollars.

When I reached home, the arms of my benefactress were thrown round me, and our tears mingled. As soon as she could speak, she said, "O Linda, I'm so glad it's all over! You wrote to me as if you thought you were going to be transferred from one owner to another. But I did not buy you for your services. I should have done just the same, if you had been going to sail for California to-morrow. I should, at least, have the satisfaction of knowing that you left me a free woman."

My heart was exceedingly full. I remembered how my poor father had tried to buy me, when I was a small child, and how he had been disappointed. I hoped his spirit was rejoicing over me now. I remembered how my good old grandmother had laid up her earnings to purchase me in later years, and how often her plans had been frustrated. How that faithful, loving old heart would leap for joy, if she could look on me and my children now that we were free! My relatives had been foiled in all their efforts, but God had raised me up a friend among strangers, who had bestowed on me the precious, long-desired boon. Friend! It is a common word, often lightly used. Like other good and beautiful things, it may be tarnished by careless handling; but when I speak of Mrs. Bruce as my friend, the word is sacred.

My grandmother lived to rejoice in my freedom; but not long after, a letter came with a black seal. She had gone "where the wicked cease from troubling, and the weary are at rest."[55]

Time passed on, and a paper came to me from the south, containing an obituary notice of my uncle Phillip. It was the only case I ever knew of such an honor conferred upon a colored person. It was written by one of his friends, and contained these words: "Now that death has laid him low, they call him a good man and a useful citizen; but what are eulogies to the black man, when the world has faded from his vision? It does not require man's praise to obtain rest in God's kingdom." So they called a colored man a *citizen*! Strange words to be uttered in that region!

Reader, my story ends with freedom; not in the usual way, with marriage. I and my children are now free! We are as free from the power of slaveholders as are the white people of the north; and though that, according to my ideas, is not saying a great deal, it is a vast improvement in *my* condition. The dream of my life is not yet realized. I do not sit with my children in a home of my own. I still long for a hearthstone of my own, however humble. I wish it for my children's sake far more than for my own. But God so orders circumstances as to keep me with my friend Mrs. Bruce. Love, duty, gratitude, also bind me to her side. It is a privilege to serve her who pities my oppressed people, and who has bestowed the inestimable boon of freedom on me and my children.

It has been painful to me, in many ways, to recall the dreary years I passed in bondage. I would gladly forget them if I could. Yet the retrospection is not altogether without solace; for with those gloomy recollections come tender memories of my good old grandmother, like light, fleecy clouds floating over a dark and troubled sea.

[1861]

[55]WHERE THE WICKED CEASE FROM TROUBLING, AND THE WEARY ARE AT REST: Job 3:17–19: "There the wicked cease from troubling; and there the weary be at rest. / There the prisoners rest together; they hear not the voice of the oppressor. / The small and great are there; and the servant is free from his master."

Henry David Thoreau
(1817–1862)

Born in Concord, Massachusetts, Henry David Thoreau graduated from Harvard in 1837 and soon thereafter became close friends with Ralph Waldo Emerson, who was the major influence on Thoreau's intellectual development. From July 1845 to September 1847, Thoreau resided in a small cabin near Walden Pond in Concord, an experience he describes in Walden; or, Life in the Woods *(1854). His other important works include* A Week on the Concord and Merrimack Rivers *(1849); several provocative essays, written in 1859–1860, on the militant abolitionist John Brown; and a long, immensely detailed Journal spanning his entire life and rich with meticulous observations about Nature.*

Thoreau began building his cabin near Walden Pond in March 1845. The idea was not new; in the summer of 1837, he had spent a six-week period sharing a shanty with Charles Stearns Wheeler, a friend from Harvard, which Wheeler had erected near Flint's Pond in Lincoln, bordering Concord. Named after the English town of Saffron Walden, forty miles from London, Walden Pond is, in Thoreau's words, "a clear and deep well, half a mile long and a mile and three quarters in circumference, and contains about sixty-one and a half acres; a perennial spring in the midst of pine and oak woods, without any visible inlet or outlet except by the clouds and evaporation." Thoreau's site was about a mile and a half south of town, on land (a pasture and woodlot of about fifteen acres) that Emerson had purchased in September 1844.

The subtitle of the book Thoreau later wrote about his experiences is "Life in the Woods," and we tend to associate him with forests near a pond and paths between tall trees. But the woods where Thoreau resided, as the cultural historians Paul Brooks and David R. Foster have noted, were one of the few forest areas remaining in the Concord environs. Most people made their living from cleared land. By the first decades of the nineteenth century, some 60 percent or more of New England was open fields, and by the 1840s, only about one-tenth of the Concord landscape was wooded. Thoreau was fortunate in being able to find and settle on a good woodland site.

Thoreau did not build from scratch but instead bought an existing hut that he took apart and then reassembled. It was fifteen feet long, ten feet wide, and sited to allow the morning sun to shine into the doorway. He moved in on the Fourth of July—a fitting date for his declaration of independence, though he says it was simply "by accident."

The cabin contained three chairs, a table, a desk, a small mirror, and a few other items, and it was not until the fall that Thoreau constructed the fireplace and chimney. In May and June, before moving in, he cleared two and a half acres of land and planted beans, corn, and potatoes so these crops would be growing when he arrived.

The dwelling was simple and sturdy because Thoreau wanted it that way; it was the right choice for the nature of the new life he had in mind. But his choice may also have derived from a "mountain house" he had seen and admired on a trip the previous summer to the Catskills in upstate New York—and, more broadly, as the critic W. Barksdale Maynard showed, from ideas about the reform of domestic architecture and the benefits of the humble English cottage that a number of English and American authors had outlined. Thoreau was a bookish radical; his thoughts and actions took shape from what he saw around him but as much or more from what he read.

Thoreau's experiment was an act of protest and social criticism. By 1860, 40 percent of America's working population worked for wages—a rise from 12 percent in 1800. Many employees were women, toiling either in mills and factories or as "outworkers" in the home (making hats or dresses, for instance). Already by 1840, two-thirds of the workers in manufacturing in Massachusetts were women. People everywhere in the state were working harder and more intensively, as if there were no other choice, and this is why Thoreau emphasized an unhurried, contemplative pace. He addressed his readers in an irritated, mocking tone intended to destabilize the numbing way of life to which many were becoming habituated.

Walden's point of view is highly individualized, not only in relation to Thoreau himself but also in relation to his reader; this author is speaking to you, and it is your life he tells you must be changed. Thoreau believes that social structures that impair the self must be confronted and resisted, yet he repeatedly suggests that, ultimately, these structures do not matter because we have the capacity to change our lives wherever and however we are situated. Society is an enemy, not an excuse.

Thoreau resided at Walden for twenty-six months. However, perhaps to relieve the pressure of his acts of writing, he took frequent breaks, and even when he was in his cabin, his life was not a solitary one. Often he walked to town or to the family home a short distance away; he collected specimens for the Swiss naturalist Louis Agassiz, who was in Boston as the guest of the U.S. government and Harvard University; he entertained friends (Emerson, for example) and family, including his mother and sisters, who brought treats to him on weekends. Thoreau's friend F. B. Sanborn even said that Thoreau "really lived at home, where he went every day" while he "bivouacked" at his cabin.

Thoreau also spent a night in jail, the result of his arrest in July 1846 for failing to pay his poll tax—a tax, Thoreau argued, that meant giving support to the Mexican War. In his antiwar sentiments he was in the minority, for most Americans supported the war and viewed it as a romantic military adventure that would extend America's democratic ideals. Abolitionists, believing that the real goal was the expansion of slavery south and west, criticized the Mexican War and later condemned the peace treaty, signed in 1848, which gave the United States 500,000 miles of new territory. Thoreau agreed with them; he refused to pay his tax and thought no more about it.

Then, one day in late July, on a trip into Concord to have a shoe repaired, Thoreau was stopped by Sam Staples, the town constable. Staples told Thoreau it was time to pay the tax, which was overdue. When Thoreau balked, Staples offered to loan him the money. When Thoreau said no to that too, the constable led him to jail. Someone, probably Thoreau's Aunt Maria, paid the tax as soon as the family learned what had happened. Thoreau should have been released, but Staples by then was at home and did not want to go back to the jail.

Thoreau was not the first to break this law; his friend Amos Bronson Alcott (the father of Louis May Alcott, the author of Little Women*) had been arrested for the same reason in January 1843. What made Thoreau special, Staples later said, was that he did not want to leave jail; he was "mad as the devil" that someone had interfered with his gesture by paying the tax for him.*

Thoreau left Walden in September 1847, and for the next ten months he lived again with the Emerson family, helping out while Emerson traveled in Europe. On January 26, 1848, he lectured at the Concord Lyceum on "the relation of the individual to the State," which with the title "Resistance to Civil Government" was published in 1849 in the volume Aesthetic Papers, *edited by Elizabeth Peabody, an educator, reformer, and Hawthorne's sister-in-law. When it was reprinted after Thoreau's death, the essay was given the title "Civil Disobedience," by which it is familiarly known.*

With the possible exception of Walt Whitman, Thoreau has been the American author most beloved by reformers and dissenters. The Indian religious and political leader Mohandas K. Gandhi read and translated Thoreau's writings, including "Civil Disobedience," when he campaigned in the 1900s and 1910s for Indian civil rights in South Africa, and he returned to these texts in subsequent decades when he called for Indian independence from the British. Martin Luther King Jr., read the essay in college in the 1940s and remembered it in 1955 in the midst of the bus boycott in Montgomery, Alabama: "I became convinced that what we were preparing to do in Montgomery was related to what Thoreau had expressed. We were simply saying to the white community, 'We can no longer lend our cooperation to an evil system.'"

Sometimes it is said that Thoreau's political principles are impractical and utopian, but one could argue to the contrary that the end of British imperial rule in India and the dismantling of segregation in the American South resulted from the practical application of precisely these principles.

The most important literary event for Thoreau of the 1850s was the publication on August 9, 1854, of Walden; or, Life in the Woods. *Thoreau had finished a draft of the book while he was still living at Walden, and a note included in* A Week on the Concord and Merrimack Rivers *indicated that* Walden *would be published "soon." But the poor sales of* A Week *made the publisher unwilling to proceed with the second book—a misfortune for Thoreau, to be sure, but also a stroke of literary good luck, as it allowed him to revise and expand the* Walden *manuscript and to test this material on lecture audiences.*

Thoreau worked on Walden *from 1846 to 1849, with an intense period from the middle of 1848 through 1849 when he produced most of the pages that went into the first seven chapters. At some point he inserted at the top of the first page of the first version: "Walden or Life in / the Woods by Henry Thoreau / Addressed to my Townsmen." Apparently he pretty much set the manuscript aside from late 1849 to late 1851 or early 1852, though he did weave into it passages from Hindu and Chinese texts. In the first months of 1852 and thereafter, Thoreau added the material that became chapters 8 through 18.*

Thoreau inlaid chapter titles and reworked and linked chapters to draw special notice to the cycle of the seasons. The cyclical rhythm was crucial because it unified a book that was pieced together, assembled, and built up over a first draft and six revisions, plus the final copy for the printer, during seven years of work.

The text as experienced may feel like the flow of a river but, as far as its composition is concerned, Thoreau constructed the book piece by piece like a mosaic; it is the product of countless acts of revision, large and small. As Thoreau later stated in his journal on March 11, 1859, his main literary principle was to identify "as soon as possible what are the best things in your composition, and then shape the rest to fit them. The former will be the midrib and the veins of the leaf." The best-known sentence in the book, "The mass of men lead lives of quiet desperation" (in the chapter entitled "Economy") first appears in a draft of A Week on the Concord and Merrimack Rivers; *after being cut from that text, and after much reworking of context, Thoreau placed it in* Walden.

For this book about his Walden experiences of the mid-1840s, Thoreau even included, according to J. Lyndon Shanley, material from his journals for the 1830s and early 1840s. When, for instance, he describes playing his flute in his boat ("The Ponds"), he is drawing on a journal entry for May 27, 1841. A piece of his account of the growth of new life ("Spring") comes from an entry dated September 29, 1843, that Thoreau wrote while he was working for a few months as a tutor on Staten Island. And the first paragraph of "Conclusion" takes shape from a journal entry for March 21, 1840.

Walden *hence is a work of art; in the best sense, it is highly artificial. It is not the story of Thoreau's life but a story that represents that story, recreating it for emblematic and symbolic purposes.*

The selections by Thoreau included below are "Resistance to Civil Government"; the second chapter of Walden, *"Where I Lived, and What I Lived for"; and "Life Without Principle," published a year after his death, an essay that brings into sharp focus the exhilarating, tough-minded individualism that characterizes this author's life and work.*

For biography: Walter Harding, The Days of Henry Thoreau: A Biography *(1965; 2nd ed., 1982); and Robert D. Richardson Jr.,* Henry Thoreau: A Life of the Mind *(1986). For context and background: Robert A. Gross, "Culture and Cultivation: Agriculture and Society in Thoreau's Concord,"* Journal of American History *69 (June 1982): 42–61; Paul Brooks,* The People of Concord: One Year in the Flowering of New England *(1990); David R. Foster,* Thoreau's Country: Journey Through a Transformed Landscape *(1999); and W. Barksdale Maynard, "Thoreau's House at Walden,"* Art Bulletin *81, no. 2 (June 1999): 303–325.*

On the composition of Walden: *J. Lyndon Shanley,* The Making of Walden, *with the Text of the First Version (1957). For literary and philosophical analysis: Sherman Paul,* The Shores of America: Thoreau's Inward Exploration; *and Stanley Cavell,* The Senses of Walden: An Expanded Edition *(1981). See also, on the life and writings: Michael Meyer,* Several More Lives to Live: Thoreau's Political Reputation in America *(1977); and* A Historical Guide to Henry David Thoreau, *ed. William E. Cain (2000).*

Resistance to Civil Government

I heartily accept the motto, "That government is best which governs least[1];" and I should like to see it acted up to more rapidly and systematically. Carried out, it finally amounts to this, which also I believe,— "That government is best which governs not at all;" and when men are prepared for it, that will be the kind of government which they will have. Government is at best but an expedient; but most governments are usually, and all governments are sometimes, inexpedient. The objections which have been brought against a standing army, and they are many and weighty, and deserve to prevail, may also at last be brought against

---

[1]THAT GOVERNMENT IS BEST WHICH GOVERNS LEAST: A quote attributed to Thomas Jefferson, the words appeared on the masthead of *The Democratic Review*, a New York magazine.

a standing government. The standing army is only an arm of the stand-ing government. The government itself, which is only the mode which the people have chosen to execute their will, is equally liable to be abused and perverted before the people can act through it. Witness the present Mexican war,[2] the work of comparatively a few individuals using the standing government as their tool; for, in the outset, the people would not have consented to this measure.

This American government,—what is it but a tradition, though a recent one, endeavoring to transmit itself unimpaired to posterity, but each instant losing some of its integrity? It has not the vitality and force of a single living man; for a single man can bend it to his will. It is a sort of wooden gun to the people themselves. But it is not the less nec-essary for this; for the people must have some complicated machinery or other, and hear its din, to satisfy that idea of government which they have. Governments show thus how successfully men can be imposed on, even impose on themselves, for their own advantage. It is excellent, we must all allow. Yet this government never of itself furthered any enter-prise, but by the alacrity with which it got out of its way. *It* does not keep the country free. *It* does not settle the West. *It* does not educate. The char-acter inherent in the American people has done all that has been accom-plished; and it would have done somewhat more, if the government had not sometimes got in its way. For government is an expedient by which men would fain succeed in letting one another alone; and, as has been said, when it is most expedient, the governed are most let alone by it. Trade and commerce, if they were not made of india-rubber, would never manage to bounce over the obstacles which legislators are continually putting in their way; and, if one were to judge these men wholly by the effects of their actions and not partly by their intentions, they would deserve to be classed and punished with those mischievous persons who put obstructions on the railroads.

But, to speak practically and as a citizen, unlike those who call them-selves no-government men, I ask for, not at once no government, but *at once* a better government. Let every man make known what kind of government would command his respect, and that will be one step toward obtaining it.

After all, the practical reason why, when the power is once in the hands of the people, a majority are permitted, and for a long period

---

[2]MEXICAN WAR: An armed conflict (1846–1848) between the United States and Mexico. It was opposed by some members of Congress who viewed it as an unjust war that was intended to increase U. S. territory available for slavery. The war ended just after Thoreau delivered this essay as a lecture.

continue, to rule is not because they are most likely to be in the right, nor because this seems fairest to the minority, but because they are physically the strongest. But a government in which the majority rule in all cases cannot be based on justice, even as far as men understand it. Can there not be a government in which majorities do not virtually decide right and wrong, but conscience?—in which majorities decide only those questions to which the rule of expediency is applicable? Must the citizen ever for a moment, or in the least degree, resign his conscience to the legislator? Why has every man a conscience, then? I think that we should be men first, and subjects afterward. It is not desirable to cultivate a respect for the law, so much as for the right. The only obligation which I have a right to assume is to do at any time what I think right. It is truly enough said that a corporation has no conscience; but a corporation of conscientious men is a corporation *with* a conscience. Law never made men a whit more just; and, by means of their respect for it, even the well-disposed are daily made the agents of injustice. A common and natural result of an undue respect for law is, that you may see a file of soldiers, colonel, captain, corporal, privates, powder-monkeys, and all, marching in admirable order over hill and dale to the wars, against their wills, ay, against their common sense and consciences, which makes it very steep marching indeed, and produces a palpitation of the heart. They have no doubt that it is a damnable business in which they are concerned; they are all peaceably inclined. Now, what are they? Men at all? or small movable forts and magazines, at the service of some unscrupulous man in power? Visit the Navy-Yard, and behold a marine, such a man as an American government can make, or such as it can make a man with its black arts,—a mere shadow and reminiscence of humanity, a man laid out alive and standing, and already, as one may say, buried under arms with funeral accompaniments, though it may be,—

> "Not a drum was heard, not a funeral note,
>   As his corse to the rampart we hurried;
> Not a soldier discharged his farewell shot
>   O'er the grave where our hero we buried."[3]

The mass of men serve the state thus, not as men mainly, but as machines, with their bodies. They are the standing army, and the militia, jailers, constables, *posse comitatus*,[4] etc. In most cases there is no free

---

[3]"NOT A DRUM WAS HEARD...O'ER THE GRAVE WHERE OUR HERO WE BURIED": Thoreau quotes the song "Burial of Sir John Moore at Corunna" (1817), by Charles Wolfe (1791–1823).
[4]POSSE COMITATUS: The force of the county (Latin); a body of men whom the sheriff may summon in cases of civil emergency.

exercise whatever of the judgment or of the moral sense; but they put themselves on a level with wood and earth and stones; and wooden men can perhaps be manufactured that will serve the purpose as well. Such command no more respect than men of straw or a lump of dirt. They have the same sort of worth only as horses and dogs. Yet such as these even are commonly esteemed good citizens. Others—as most legislators, politicians, lawyers, ministers, and office-holders—serve the state chiefly with their heads; and, as they rarely make any moral distinctions, they are as likely to serve the devil, without *intending* it, as God. A very few— as heroes, patriots, martyrs, reformers in the great sense, and *men*—serve the state with their consciences also, and so necessarily resist it for the most part; and they are commonly treated as enemies by it. A wise man will only be useful as a man, and will not submit to be "clay," and "stop a hole to keep the wind away,"[5] but leave that office to his dust at least:—

> *"I am too high-born to be propertied,*
> *To be a secondary at control,*
> *Or useful serving-man and instrument*
> *To any sovereign state throughout the world."[6]*

He who gives himself entirely to his fellow-men appears to them useless and selfish; but he who gives himself partially to them is pronounced a benefactor and philanthropist.

How does it become a man to behave toward this American government today? I answer, that he cannot without disgrace be associated with it. I cannot for an instant recognize that political organization as *my* government which is the *slave's* government also.

All men recognize the right of revolution; that is, the right to refuse allegiance to, and to resist, the government, when its tyranny or its inefficiency are great and unendurable. But almost all say that such is not the case now. But such was the case, they think, in the Revolution of '75.[7] If one were to tell me that this was a bad government because it taxed certain foreign commodities brought to its ports, it is most probable that I should not make an ado about it, for I can do without them. All machines have their friction; and possibly this does enough good to counterbalance the evil. At any rate, it is a great evil to make a stir about it. But when the friction comes to have its machine, and oppression and rob-

[5]STOP A HOLE TO KEEP THE WIND AWAY: From Shakespeare's *Hamlet*, Act 5, Scene 1, lines 236–237.
[6]I AM TOO HIGH-BORN TO BE PROPERTIED...TO ANY SOVEREIGN STATE THROUGHOUT THE WORLD: From Shakespeare's *King John*, Act V, Scene 1, lines 79–82.
[7]REVOLUTION OF '75: The American Revolution.

bery are organized, I say, let us not have such a machine any longer. In other words, when a sixth of the population of a nation which has undertaken to be the refuge of liberty are slaves, and a whole country is unjustly overrun and conquered by a foreign army, and subjected to military law, I think that it is not too soon for honest men to rebel and revolutionize. What makes this duty the more urgent is the fact that the country so overrun is not our own, but ours is the invading army.

Paley,[8] a common authority with many on moral questions, in his chapter on the "Duty of Submission to Civil Government," resolves all civil obligation into expediency; and he proceeds to say that "so long as the interest of the whole society requires it, that is, so long as the established government cannot be resisted or changed without public inconveniency, it is the will of God...that the established government be obeyed,—and no longer. This principle being admitted, the justice of every particular case of resistance is reduced to a computation of the quantity of the danger and grievance on the one side, and of the probability and expense of redressing it on the other." Of this, he says, every man shall judge for himself. But Paley appears never to have contemplated those cases to which the rule of expediency does not apply, in which a people, as well as an individual, must do justice, cost what it may. If I have unjustly wrested a plank from a drowning man, I must restore it to him though I drown myself. This, according to Paley, would be inconvenient. But he that would save his life, in such a case, shall lose it.[9] This people must cease to hold slaves, and to make war on Mexico,[10] though it cost them their existence as a people.

In their practice, nations agree with Paley; but does any one think that Massachusetts does exactly what is right at the present crisis?

> *"A drab of state, a cloth-o'-silver slut,*
> *To have her train borne up, and her soul trail in the dirt."*[11]

Practically speaking, the opponents to a reform in Massachusetts are not a hundred thousand politicians at the South, but a hundred thousand merchants and farmers here,[12] who are more interested in commerce and

---

[8]PALEY: William Paley (1743–1805), English theologian and moralist who wrote *Principles of Moral and Political Philosophy* (1785).
[9]BUT HE THAT WOULD SAVE HIS LIFE, IN SUCH A CASE, SHALL LOSE IT: Matthew 10:39: "He that findeth his life shall lose it: and he that loseth his life for my sake shall find it."
[10]WAR ON MEXICO: See note 2.
[11]A DRAB OF STATE...TRAIL IN THE DIRT: From *The Revenger's Tragedy* (1607), by English dramatist Cyril Tourneur (1575?–1626).
[12]A HUNDRED THOUSAND MERCHANTS AND FARMERS HERE: Thoreau alludes to the trade alliance between Southern (slaveholding) cotton growers and Northern merchants.

agriculture than they are in humanity, and are not prepared to do justice to the slave and to Mexico, *cost what it may.* I quarrel not with far-off foes, but with those who, near at home, coöperate with, and do the bidding of, those far away, and without whom the latter would be harmless. We are accustomed to say, that the mass of men are unprepared; but improvement is slow, because the few are not materially wiser or better than the many. It is not so important that many should be as good as you, as that there be some absolute goodness somewhere; for that will leaven the whole lump.[13] There are thousands who are *in opinion* opposed to slavery and to the war, who yet in effect do nothing to put an end to them; who, esteeming themselves children of Washington and Franklin,[14] sit down with their hands in their pockets, and say that they know not what to do, and do nothing; who even postpone the question of freedom to the question of free trade, and quietly read the prices-current along with the latest advices from Mexico, after dinner, and, it may be, fall asleep over them both. What is the price-current of an honest man and patriot to-day? They hesitate, and they regret, and sometimes they petition; but they do nothing in earnest and with effect. They will wait, well disposed, for others to remedy the evil, that they may no longer have it to regret. At most, they give only a cheap vote, and a feeble countenance and God-speed, to the right, as it goes by them. There are nine hundred and ninety-nine patrons of virtue to one virtuous man. But it is easier to deal with the real possessor of a thing than with the temporary guardian of it.

All voting is a sort of gaming, like checkers or backgammon, with a slight moral tinge to it, a playing with right and wrong, with moral questions; and betting naturally accompanies it. The character of the voters is not staked. I cast my vote, perchance, as I think right; but I am not vitally concerned that that right should prevail. I am willing to leave it to the majority. Its obligation, therefore, never exceeds that of expediency. Even voting *for the right* is *doing* nothing for it. It is only expressing to men feebly your desire that it should prevail. A wise man will not leave the right to the mercy of chance, nor wish it to prevail through the power of the majority. There is but little virtue in the action of masses of men. When the majority shall at length vote for the abolition of slavery, it will be because they are indifferent to slavery, or because there is but little slavery left to be abolished by their vote. *They* will then be the

---

[13]FOR THAT WILL LEAVEN THE WHOLE LUMP: 1 Corinthians 5:6: "Your glorying is not good. Know ye not that a little leaven leaveneth the whole lump?"

[14]WASHINGTON AND FRANKLIN: George Washington and Benjamin Franklin, meaning the generation following and inspired by the spirit of the American Revolution.

only slaves. Only *his* vote can hasten the abolition of slavery who asserts his own freedom by his vote.

I hear of a convention to be held at Baltimore, or elsewhere, for the selection of a candidate for the Presidency, made up chiefly of editors, and men who are politicians by profession; but I think, what is it to any independent, intelligent, and respectable man what decision they may come to? Shall we not have the advantage of his wisdom and honesty, nevertheless? Can we not count upon some independent votes? Are there not many individuals in the country who do not attend conventions? But no: I find that the respectable man, so called, has immediately drifted from his position, and despairs of his country, when his country has more reason to despair of him. He forthwith adopts one of the candidates thus selected as the only *available* one, thus proving that he is himself *available* for any purposes of the demagogue. His vote is of no more worth than that of any unprincipled foreigner or hireling native, who may have been bought. O for a man who is a *man*, and, as my neighbor says, has a bone in his back which you cannot pass your hand through! Our statistics are at fault: the population has been returned too large. How many *men* are there to a square thousand miles in this country? Hardly one. Does not America offer any inducement for men to settle here? The American has dwindled into an Odd Fellow,[15]—one who may be known by the development of his organ of gregariousness, and a manifest lack of intellect and cheerful self-reliance; whose first and chief concern, on coming into the world, is to see that the almshouses are in good repair; and, before yet he has lawfully donned the virile garb,[16] to collect a fund for the support of the widows and orphans that may be; who, in short, ventures to live only by the aid of the mutual insurance company, which has promised to bury him decently.

It is not a man's duty, as a matter of course, to devote himself to the eradication of any, even the most enormous, wrong; he may still properly have other concerns to engage him; but it is his duty, at least, to wash his hands of it, and, if he gives it no thought longer, not to give it practically his support. If I devote myself to other pursuits and contemplations, I must first see, at least, that I do not pursue them sitting upon another man's shoulders. I must get off him first, that he may pursue his contemplations too. See what gross inconsistency is tolerated. I have heard some of my townsmen say, "I should like to have them order me out to help put down an insurrection of the slaves, or to march to

[15]ODD FELLOW: The Odd Fellows are a secret fraternal society.
[16]VIRILE GARB: The adult clothing assumed by a Roman boy at the age of fourteen.

Mexico;—see if I would go;" and yet these very men have each, directly by their allegiance, and so indirectly, at least, by their money, furnished a substitute. The soldier is applauded who refuses to serve in an unjust war by those who do not refuse to sustain the unjust government which makes the war; is applauded by those whose own act and authority he disregards and sets at naught; as if the state were penitent to that degree that it hired one to scourge it while it sinned, but not to that degree that it left off sinning for a moment. Thus, under the name of order and civil government, we are all made at last to pay homage to and support our own meanness. After the first blush of sin comes its indifference; and from immoral it becomes, as it were, *un*moral, and not quite unnecessary to that life which we have made.

The broadest and most prevalent error requires the most disinterested virtue to sustain it. The slight reproach to which the virtue of patriotism is commonly liable, the noble are most likely to incur. Those who, while they disapprove of the character and measures of a government, yield to it their allegiance and support are undoubtedly its most conscientious supporters, and so frequently the most serious obstacles to reform. Some are petitioning the State to dissolve the Union, to disregard the requisitions of the President. Why do they not dissolve it themselves,—the union between themselves and the State,—and refuse to pay their quota into its treasury? Do not they stand in the same relation to the State that the State does to the Union? And have not the same reasons prevented the State from resisting the Union which have prevented them from resisting the State?

How can a man be satisfied to entertain an opinion merely, and enjoy *it*? Is there any enjoyment in it, if his opinion is that he is aggrieved? If you are cheated out of a single dollar by your neighbor, you do not rest satisfied with knowing that you are cheated, or with saying that you are cheated, or even with petitioning him to pay you your due; but you take effectual steps at once to obtain the full amount, and see that you are never cheated again. Action from principle, the perception and the performance of right, changes things and relations; it is essentially revolutionary, and does not consist wholly with anything which was. It not only divides States and churches, it divides families; ay, it divides the *individual*, separating the diabolical in him from the divine.

Unjust laws exist: shall we be content to obey them, or shall we endeavor to amend them, and obey them until we have succeeded, or shall we transgress them at once? Men generally, under such a government as this, think that they ought to wait until they have persuaded the majority to alter them. They think that, if they should resist, the remedy would be worse than the evil. But it is the fault of the government itself that the remedy *is* worse than the evil. *It* makes it worse. Why is it not more apt to anticipate and provide for reform? Why does it not cherish its wise minority? Why does it cry and resist before it is hurt? Why does it not encourage its citizens to be on the alert to point out its faults, and *do* better than it would have them? Why does it always crucify Christ, and excommunicate Copernicus[17] and Luther,[18] and pronounce Washington and Franklin rebels?

One would think, that a deliberate and practical denial of its authority was the only offence never contemplated by government; else, why has it not assigned its definite, its suitable and proportionate, penalty? If a man who has no property refuses but once to earn nine shillings for the State,[19] he is put in prison for a period unlimited by any law that I know, and determined only by the discretion of those who placed him there; but if he should steal ninety times nine shillings from the State, he is soon permitted to go at large again.

If the injustice is part of the necessary friction of the machine of government, let it go, let it go: perchance it will wear smooth,—certainly the machine will wear out. If the injustice has a spring, or a pulley, or a rope, or a crank, exclusively for itself, then perhaps you may consider whether the remedy will not be worse than the evil; but if it is of such a nature that it requires you to be the agent of injustice to another, then, I say, break the law. Let your life be a counter-friction to stop the machine. What I have to do is to see, at any rate, that I do not lend myself to the wrong which I condemn.

As for adopting the ways which the State has provided for remedying the evil, I know not of such ways. They take too much time, and a man's life will be gone. I have other affairs to attend to. I came into this world, not chiefly to make this a good place to live in, but to live in it, be it good or bad. A man has not everything to do, but something; and

---

[17]COPERNICUS: Nicholas Copernicus (1473–1543), Polish astronomer who published his unorthodox views of a new system of astronomy in *De revolutionibus orbium coelestiu* (1543), considered the foundation for modern astronomy. Copernicus was not excommunicated, but his contemporary, Galileo Galilei (1564–1642), was tried for heresy by the Catholic Church for confirming Copernicus' theories.
[18]LUTHER: Martin Luther (1483–1546), German leader of the Protestant Reformation who was excommunicated in 1521 from the Catholic Church for renouncing papal authority.
[19]NINE SHILLINGS FOR THE STATE: The amount of the poll tax Thoreau refused to pay, for which he was imprisoned for one night.

because he cannot do *everything*, it is not necessary that he should do *something* wrong. It is not my business to be petitioning the Governor or the Legislature any more than it is theirs to petition me; and if they should not hear my petition, what should I do then? But in this case the State has provided no way: its very Constitution is the evil. This may seem to be harsh and stubborn and unconciliatory; but it is to treat with the utmost kindness and consideration the only spirit that can appreciate or deserves it. So is all change for the better, like birth and death, which convulse the body.

I do not hesitate to say, that those who call themselves Abolitionists should at once effectually withdraw their support, both in person and property, from the government of Massachusetts, and not wait till they constitute a majority of one, before they suffer the right to prevail through them. I think that it is enough if they have God on their side, without waiting for that other one. Moreover, any man more right than his neighbors constitutes a majority of one already.

I meet this American government, or its representative, the State government, directly, and face to face, once a year—no more—in the person of its tax-gatherer; this is the only mode in which a man situated as I am necessarily meets it; and it then says distinctly, Recognize me; and the simplest, the most effectual, and, in the present posture of affairs, the indispensablest mode of treating with it on this head, of expressing your little satisfaction with and love for it, is to deny it then. My civil neighbor, the tax-gatherer,[20] is the very man I have to deal with,—for it is, after all, with men and not with parchment that I quarrel,—and he has voluntarily chosen to be an agent of the government. How shall he ever know well what he is and does as an officer of the government, or as a man, until he is obliged to consider whether he shall treat me, his neighbor, for whom he has respect, as a neighbor and well-disposed man, or as a maniac and disturber of the peace, and see if he can get over this obstruction to his neighborliness without a ruder and more impetuous thought or speech corresponding with his action. I know this well, that if one thousand, if one hundred, if ten men whom I could name,—if ten *honest* men only,—ay, if *one* HONEST man, in this State of Massachusetts, *ceasing to hold slaves*, were actually to withdraw from this copartnership, and be locked up in the county jail therefor, it would be the abolition of slavery in America. For it matters not how small the beginning may seem to be: what is once well done is done forever. But we love better to talk about it:

---

[20]TAX-GATHERER: Sam Staples, Thoreau's friend and the town constable and tax collector of Concord, Massachusetts.

that we say is our mission. Reform keeps many scores of newspapers in its service, but not one man. If my esteemed neighbor,[21] the State's ambassador, who will devote his days to the settlement of the question of human rights in the Council Chamber, instead of being threatened with the prisons of Carolina, were to sit down the prisoner of Massachusetts, that State which is so anxious to foist the sin of slavery upon her sister,—though at present she can discover only an act of inhospitality to be the ground of a quarrel with her,—the Legislature would not wholly waive the subject the following winter.

Under a government which imprisons any unjustly, the true place for a just man is also a prison. The proper place to-day, the only place which Massachusetts has provided for her freer and less desponding spirits, is in her prisons, to be put out and locked out of the State by her own act, as they have already put themselves out by their principles. It is there that the fugitive slave, and the Mexican prisoner on parole, and the Indian come to plead the wrongs of his race should find them; on that separate, but more free and honorable ground, where the State places those who are not *with* her, but *against* her,—the only house in a slave State in which a free man can abide with honor. If any think that their influence would be lost there, and their voices no longer afflict the ear of the State, that they would not be as an enemy within its walls, they do not know by how much truth is stronger than error, nor how much more eloquently and effectively he can combat injustice who has experienced a little in his own person. Cast your whole vote, not a strip of paper merely, but your whole influence. A minority is powerless while it conforms to the majority; it is not even a minority then; but it is irresistible when it clogs by its whole weight. If the alternative is to keep all just men in prison, or give up war and slavery, the State will not hesitate which to choose. If a thousand men were not to pay their tax-bills this year, that would not be a violent and bloody measure, as it would be to pay them, and enable the State to commit violence and shed innocent blood. This is, in fact, the definition of a peaceable revolution, if any such is possible. If the tax-gatherer, or any other public officer, asks me, as one has done, "But what shall I do?" my answer is, "If you really wish to do anything, resign your office." When the subject has refused allegiance, and the officer has resigned his office, then the revolution is accomplished. But even suppose blood should flow. Is there not a sort of blood shed when the conscience is wounded? Through this wound a

[21]IF MY ESTEEMED NEIGHBOR: Samuel Hoar (1778–1856) of Concord, Massachusetts, a politician who had been expelled from Charleston, South Carolina, while protesting on behalf of the Massachusetts legislature the impoundment (capture and impressment into service) of free black sailors from Massachusetts.

man's real manhood and immortality flow out, and he bleeds to an ever-lasting death. I see this blood flowing now.

I have contemplated the imprisonment of the offender, rather than the seizure of his goods,—though both will serve the same purpose,—because they who assert the purest right, and consequently are most dangerous to a corrupt State, commonly have not spent much time in accumulating property. To such the State renders comparatively small service, and a slight tax is wont to appear exorbitant, particularly if they are obliged to earn it by special labor with their hands. If there were one who lived wholly without the use of money, the State itself would hesitate to demand it of him. But the rich man—not to make any invidious comparison—is always sold to the institution which makes him rich. Absolutely speaking, the more money, the less virtue; for money comes between a man and his objects, and obtains them for him; and it was certainly no great virtue to obtain it. It puts to rest many questions which he would otherwise be taxed to answer; while the only new question which it puts is the hard but superfluous one, how to spend it. Thus his moral ground is taken from under his feet. The opportunities of living are diminished in proportion as what are called the "means" are increased. The best thing a man can do for his culture when he is rich is to endeavour to carry out those schemes which he entertained when he was poor. Christ answered the Herodians according to their condition. "Show me the tribute-money," said he;—and one took a penny out of his pocket;—if you use money which has the image of Cæsar on it, and which he has made current and valuable, that is, *if you are men of the State*, and gladly enjoy the advantages of Cæsar's government, then pay him back some of his own when he demands it. "Render therefore to Cæsar that which is Cæsar's, and to God those things which are God's,"[22]—leaving them no wiser than before as to which was which; for they did not wish to know.

When I converse with the freest of my neighbors, I perceive that, whatever they may say about the magnitude and seriousness of the question, and their regard for the public tranquillity, the long and the short of the matter is, that they cannot spare the protection of the existing government, and they dread the consequences to their property and families of disobedience to it. For my own part, I should not like to think that I ever rely on the protection of the State. But, if I deny the authority of the State when it presents its tax-bill, it will soon take and waste all my property, and so harass me and my children without end. This

[22]RENDER THEREFORE TO CAESAR THAT WHICH IS CAESAR'S, AND TO GOD THOSE THINGS WHICH ARE GOD'S: Luke 20:25.

is hard. This makes it impossible for a man to live honestly, and at the same time comfortably, in outward respects. It will not be worth the while to accumulate property; that would be sure to go again. You must hire or squat somewhere, and raise but a small crop, and eat that soon. You must live within yourself, and depend upon yourself always tucked up and ready for a start, and not have many affairs. A man may grow rich in Turkey even, if he will be in all respects a good subject of the Turkish government. Confucius[23] said: "If a state is governed by the principles of reason, poverty and misery are subjects of shame; if a state is not governed by the principles of reason, riches and honors are the subjects of shame." No: until I want the protection of Massachusetts to be extended to me in some distant Southern port, where my liberty is endangered, or until I am bent solely on building up an estate at home by peaceful enterprise, I can afford to refuse allegiance to Massachusetts, and her right to my property and life. It costs me less in every sense to incur the penalty of disobedience to the State than it would to obey. I should feel as if I were worth less in that case.

Some years ago, the State met me in behalf of the Church, and commanded me to pay a certain sum toward the support of a clergyman whose preaching my father attended, but never I myself. "Pay" it said, "or be locked up in the jail." I declined to pay. But, unfortunately, another man saw fit to pay it. I did not see why the schoolmaster should be taxed to support the priest, and not the priest the schoolmaster; for I was not the State's schoolmaster, but I supported myself by voluntary subscription. I did not see why the lyceum[24] should not present its tax-bill, and have the State to back its demand, as well as the Church. However, at the request of the selectmen, I condescended to make some such statement as this in writing:—"Know all men by these presents, that I, Henry Thoreau, do not wish to be regarded as a member of any incorporated society which I have not joined." This I gave to the town clerk; and he has it. The State, having thus learned that I did not wish to be regarded as a member of that church, has never made a like demand on me since; though it said that it must adhere to its original presumption that time. If I had known how to name them, I should then have signed off in detail from all the societies which I never signed on to; but I did not know where to find a complete list.

I have paid no poll-tax for six years. I was put into a jail once on this account, for one night; and, as I stood considering the walls of solid

---

[23]CONFUCIUS: (c. 551–479 BCE), Chinese philosopher credited with the sayings and dialogs recorded in the *Analects*, from which Thoreau quotes 8.13.
[24]LYCEUM: Place of education.

stone, two or three feet thick, the door of wood and iron, a foot thick, and the iron grating which strained the light, I could not help being struck with the foolishness of that institution which treated me as if I were mere flesh and blood and bones, to be locked up. I wondered that it should have concluded at length that this was the best use it could put me to, and had never thought to avail itself of my services in some way. I saw that, if there was a wall of stone between me and my townsmen, there was a still more difficult one to climb or break through before they could get to be as free as I was. I did not for a moment feel confined, and the walls seemed a great waste of stone and mortar. I felt as if I alone of all my townsmen had paid my tax. They plainly did not know how to treat me, but behaved like persons who are underbred. In every threat and in every compliment there was a blunder; for they thought that my chief desire was to stand the other side of that stone wall. I could not but smile to see how industriously they locked the door on my meditations, which followed them out again without let or hindrance, and *they* were really all that was dangerous. As they could not reach me, they had resolved to punish my body; just as boys, if they cannot come at some person against whom they have a spite, will abuse his dog. I saw that the State was half-witted, that it was timid as a lone woman with her silver spoons, and that it did not know its friends from its foes, and I lost all my remaining respect for it, and pitied it.

Thus the State never intentionally confronts a man's sense, intellectual or moral, but only his body, his senses. It is not armed with superior wit or honesty, but with superior physical strength. I was not born to be forced. I will breathe after my own fashion. Let us see who is the strongest. What force has a multitude? They only can force me who obey a higher law than I. They force me to become like themselves. I do not hear of *men* being *forced* to live this way or that by masses of men. What sort of life were that to live? When I meet a government which says to me, "Your money or your life,"[25] why should I be in haste to give it my money? It may be in a great strait, and not know what to do: I cannot help that. It must help itself; do as I do. It is not worth the while to snivel about it. I am not responsible for the successful working of the machinery of society. I am not the son of the engineer. I perceive that, when an acorn and a chestnut fall side by side, the one does not remain inert to make way for the other, but both obey their own laws, and spring and grow and flourish as best they can, till one, perchance, overshadows and destroys the other. If a plant cannot live according to its nature, it dies; and so a man.

[25]YOUR MONEY OR YOUR LIFE: A statement made by a robber to his victim.

The night in prison was novel and interesting enough. The prisoners in their shirt-sleeves were enjoying a chat and the evening air in the doorway, when I entered. But the jailer said, "Come, boys, it is time to lock up;" and so they dispersed, and I heard the sound of their steps returning into the hollow apartments. My roommate was introduced to me by the jailer, as "a first-rate fellow and a clever man." When the door was locked, he showed me where to hang my hat, and how he managed matters there. The rooms were whitewashed once a month; and this one, at least, was the whitest, most simply furnished, and probably the neatest apartment in the town. He naturally wanted to know where I came from, and what brought me there; and, when I had told him, I asked him in turn how he came there, presuming him to be an honest man of course; and, as the world goes, I believe he was. "Why," said he, "they accused me of burning a barn; but I never did it." As near as I could discover, he had probably gone to bed in a barn when drunk, and smoked his pipe there; and so a barn was burnt. He had the reputation of being a clever man, had been there some three months waiting for his trial to come on, and would have to wait as much longer; but he was quite domesticated and contented, since he got his board for nothing, and thought that he was well treated.

He occupied one window, and I the other; and I saw that if one stayed there long, his principal business would be to look out the window. I had soon read all the tracts that were left there, and examined where former prisoners had broken out, and where a grate had been sawed off, and heard the history of the various occupants of that room; for I found that even here there was a history and a gossip which never circulated beyond the walls of the jail. Probably this is the only house in the town where verses are composed, which are afterward printed in a circular form, but not published. I was shown quite a long list of verses which were composed by some young men who had been detected in an attempt to escape, who avenged themselves by singing them.

I pumped my fellow-prisoner as dry as I could, for fear I should never see him again; but at length he showed me which was my bed, and left me to blow out the lamp.

It was like traveling into a far country, such as I had never expected to behold, to lie there for one night. It seemed to me that I never had heard the town clock strike before, nor the evening sounds of the village; for we slept with the windows open, which were inside the grating. It was to see my native village in the light of the Middle Ages, and our Concord was turned into a Rhine stream,[26] and visions of knights and

---

[26]RHINE STREAM: The chief river that runs through Germany.

castles passed before me. They were the voices of old burghers that I heard in the streets. I was an involuntary spectator and auditor of whatever was done and said in the kitchen of the adjacent village inn,—a wholly new and rare experience to me. It was a closer view of my native town. I was fairly inside of it. I never had seen its institutions before. This is one of its peculiar institutions; for it is a shire town. I began to comprehend what its inhabitants were about.

In the morning, our breakfasts were put through the hole in the door, in small oblong-square tin pans, made to fit, and holding a pint of chocolate, with brown bread, and an iron spoon. When they called for the vessels again, I was green enough to return what bread I had left; but my comrade seized it, and said that I should lay that up for lunch or dinner. Soon after he was let out to work at haying in a neighboring field, whither he went every day, and would not be back till noon; so he bade me good-day, saying that he doubted if he should see me again.

When I came out of prison,—for some one interfered, and paid that tax,—I did not perceive that great changes had taken place on the common, such as he observed who went in a youth and emerged a tottering and gray-headed man; and yet a change had to my eyes come over the scene,—the town, and State, and country,—greater than any that mere time could effect. I saw yet more distinctly the State in which I lived. I saw to what extent the people among whom I lived could be trusted as good neighbors and friends; that their friendship was for summer weather only; that they did not greatly purpose to do right; that they were a distinct race from me by their prejudices and superstitions, as the Chinamen and Malays are; that in their sacrifices to humanity they ran no risks, not even to their property; that after all they were not so noble but they treated the thief as he had treated them, and hoped, by a certain outward observance and a few prayers, and by walking in a particular straight though useless path from time to time, to save their souls. This may be to judge my neighbors harshly; for I believe that many of them are not aware that they have such an institution as the jail in their village.

It was formerly the custom in our village, when a poor debtor came out of jail, for his acquaintances to salute him, looking through their fingers, which were crossed to represent the grating of a jail window, "How do ye do?" My neighbors did not thus salute me, but first looked at me, and then at one another, as if I had returned from a long journey. I was put into jail as I was going to the shoemaker's to get a shoe which was mended. When I was let out the next morning, I proceeded to finish my errand, and, having put on my mended shoe, joined a huckleberry party, who were impatient to put themselves under my conduct; and in half an hour,—for the horse was soon tackled,[27]—was in the midst of a huckleberry field, on one of our highest hills, two miles off, and then the State was nowhere to be seen.

This is the whole history of "My Prisons."

I have never declined paying the highway tax, because I am as desirous of being a good neighbor as I am of being a bad subject; and as for supporting schools, I am doing my part to educate my fellow-countrymen now. It is for no particular item in the tax-bill that I refuse to pay it. I simply wish to refuse allegiance to the State, to withdraw and stand aloof from it effectually. I do not care to trace the course of my dollar, if I could, till it buys a man or a musket to shoot one with,—the dollar is innocent,—but I am concerned to trace the effects of my allegiance. In fact, I quietly declare war with the State, after my fashion, though I will still make what use and get what advantage of her I can, as is usual in such cases.

If others pay the tax which is demanded of me, from a sympathy with the State, they do but what they have already done in their own case, or rather they abet injustice to a greater extent than the State requires. If they pay the tax from a mistaken interest in the individual taxed, to save his property, or prevent his going to jail, it is because they have not considered wisely how far they let their private feelings interfere with the public good.

This, then, is my position at present. But one cannot be too much on his guard in such a case, lest his action be biased by obstinacy or an undue regard for the opinions of men. Let him see that he does only what belongs to himself and to the hour.

I think sometimes, Why, this people mean well, they are only ignorant; they would do better if they knew how: why give your neighbors this pain to treat you as they are not inclined to? But I think, again, This is no reason why I should do as they do, or permit others to suffer much greater pain of a different kind. Again, I sometimes say to myself, When many millions of men, without heat, without ill will, without personal feeling of any kind, demand of you a few shillings only, without the possibility, such is their constitution, of retracting or altering their present demand, and without the possibility, on your side, of appeal to any other millions, why expose yourself to this overwhelming brute force? You do not resist cold and hunger, the winds and the waves, thus obstinately; you quietly submit to a thousand similar necessities. You do not put your head

[27]TACKLED: Harnessed.

into the fire. But just in proportion as I regard this as not wholly a brute force, but partly a human force, and consider that I have relations to those millions as to so many millions of men, and not of mere brute or inanimate things, I see that appeal is possible, first and instantaneously, from them to the Maker of them, and, secondly, from them to themselves. But if I put my head deliberately into the fire, there is no appeal to fire or to the Maker of fire, and I have only myself to blame. If I could convince myself that I have any right to be satisfied with men as they are, and to treat them accordingly, and not according, in some respects, to my requisitions and expectations of what they and I ought to be, then, like a good Mussulman[28] and fatalist, I should endeavor to be satisfied with things as they are, and say it is the will of God. And, above all, there is this difference between resisting this and a purely brute or natural force, that I can resist this with some effect; but I cannot expect, like Orpheus,[29] to change the nature of the rocks and trees and beasts.

I do not wish to quarrel with any man or nation. I do not wish to split hairs, to make fine distinctions, or set myself up as better than my neighbors. I seek rather, I may say, even an excuse for conforming to the laws of the land. I am but too ready to conform to them. Indeed I have reason to suspect myself on this head; and each year, as the tax-gatherer comes round, I find myself disposed to review the acts and position of the general and State governments, and the spirit of the people, to discover a pretext for conformity.

> "We must affect our country as our parents,
> And if at any time we alienate
> Our love or industry from doing it honor,
> We must respect effects and teach the soul
> Matter of conscience and religion,
> And not desire of rule or benefit."[30]

I believe that the State will soon be able to take all my work of this sort out of my hands, and then I shall be no better a patriot than my fellow-countrymen. Seen from a lower point of view, the Constitution, with all its faults, is very good; the law and the courts are very respectable; even this State and this American government are, in many respects, very admirable and rare things, to be thankful for, such as a great many have described them; but seen from a point of view a little

[28]MUSSULMAN: Muslim.
[29]ORPHEUS: In Greek myth, the son of the Muse Calliope. Orpheus had the gift of music, and his lyre (harp) could charm wild beasts and make rocks and trees sway.
[30]"WE MUST AFFECT OUR COUNTRY AS OUR PARENTS...AND NOT DESIRE OF RULE OR BENEFIT": From the play *The Battle of Alcazar* (1594), by English playwright George Peele (c. 1558–1605).

higher, they are what I have described them; seen from a higher still, and the highest, who shall say what they are, or that they are worth looking at or thinking of at all?

However, the government does not concern me much, and I shall bestow the fewest possible thoughts on it. It is not many moments that I live under a government, even in this world. If a man is thought-free, fancy-free, imagination-free, that which *is not* never for a long time appearing *to be* to him, unwise rulers or reformers cannot fatally interrupt him.

I know that most men think differently from myself; but those whose lives are by profession devoted to the study of these or kindred subjects content me as little as any. Statesmen and legislators, standing so completely within the institution, never distinctly and nakedly behold it. They speak of moving society, but have no resting-place without it. They may be men of a certain experience and discrimination, and have no doubt invented ingenious and even useful systems, for which we sincerely thank them; but all their wit and usefulness lie within certain not very wide limits. They are wont to forget that the world is not governed by policy and expediency. Webster[31] never goes behind government, and so cannot speak with authority about it. His words are wisdom to those legislators who contemplate no essential reform in the existing government; but for thinkers, and those who legislate for all time, he never once glances at the subject. I know of those whose serene and wise speculations on this theme would soon reveal the limits of his mind's range and hospitality. Yet, compared with the cheap professions of most reformers, and the still cheaper wisdom and eloquence of politicians in general, his are almost the only sensible and valuable words, and we thank Heaven for him. Comparatively, he is always strong, original, and, above all, practical. Still, his quality is not wisdom, but prudence. The lawyer's truth is not Truth, but consistency or a consistent expediency. Truth is always in harmony with herself, and is not concerned chiefly to reveal the justice that may consist with wrong-doing. He well deserves to be called, as he has been called, the Defender of the Constitution. There are really no blows to be given by him but defensive ones. He is not a leader, but a follower. His leaders are the men of '87.[32] "I have never made an effort," he says, "and never propose to make an effort; I have never countenanced an effort, and never mean

[31]WEBSTER: Daniel Webster (1782–1852), an orator and prominent politician who served in both the House and the Senate and who advocated the preservation of the Union during the crisis with the South over the issue of slavery. In 1850 he supported the Fugitive Slave Bill, which required federal authorities in the northern states to return runaway slaves caught in their territory.
[32]HIS LEADERS ARE THE MEN OF '87: The framers of the U.S. Constitution, who convened in Philadelphia in 1787.

to countenance an effort, to disturb the arrangement as originally made, by which the various States came into the Union."[33] Still thinking of the sanction which the Constitution gives to slavery, he says, "Because it was a part of the original compact,—let it stand." Notwithstanding his special acuteness and ability, he is unable to take a fact out of its merely political relations, and behold it as it lies absolutely to be disposed of by the intellect,—what, for instance, it behooves a man to do here in America to-day with regard to slavery,—but ventures, or is driven, to make some such desperate answer as the following, while professing to speak absolutely, and as a private man,—from which what new and singular code of social duties might be inferred? "The manner," says he, "in which the governments of those States where slavery exists are to regulate it is for their own consideration, under their responsibility to their constituents, to the general laws of propriety, humanity, and justice, and to God. Associations formed elsewhere, springing from a feeling of humanity, or any other cause, have nothing whatever to do with it. They have never received any encouragement from me, and they never will."[34]

They who know of no purer sources of truth, who have traced up its stream no higher, stand, and wisely stand, by the Bible and the Constitution, and drink at it there with reverence and humility; but they who behold where it comes trickling into this lake or that pool, gird up their loins once more, and continue their pilgrimage toward its fountain-head.

No man with a genius for legislation has appeared in America. They are rare in the history of the world. There are orators, politicians, and eloquent men, by the thousand; but the speaker has not yet opened his mouth to speak who is capable of settling the much-vexed questions of the day. We love eloquence for its own sake, and not for any truth which it may utter, or any heroism it may inspire. Our legislators have not yet learned the comparative value of free trade and of freedom, of union, and of rectitude, to a nation. They have no genius or talent for comparatively humble questions of taxation and finance, commerce and manufactures and agriculture. If we were left solely to the wordy wit of legislators in Congress for our guidance, uncorrected by the seasonable experience and the effectual complaints of the people, America would not long retain her rank among the nations. For eighteen hundred years, though perchance I have no right to say it, the New Testament has been written; yet where is the legislator who has wisdom and practical talent enough to avail himself of the light which it sheds on the science of legislation?

[33]STATES CAME INTO THE UNION: From a speech that Daniel Webster delivered on December 22, 1845, on the admission of Texas to the Union.
[34]THEY HAVE NEVER RECEIVED ANY ENCOURAGEMENT FROM ME, AND THEY NEVER WILL: Of this line, Thoreau noted, "These extracts have been inserted since the Lecture was read."

The authority of government, even such as I am willing to submit to,—for I will cheerfully obey those who know and can do better than I, and in many things even those who neither know nor can do so well,—is still an impure one: to be strictly just, it must have the sanction and consent of the governed. It can have no pure right over my person and property but what I concede to it. The progress from an absolute to a limited monarchy, from a limited monarchy to a democracy, is a progress toward a true respect for the individual. Is a democracy, such as we know it, the last improvement possible in government? Is it not possible to take a step further towards recognizing and organizing the rights of man? There will never be a really free and enlightened State until the State comes to recognize the individual as a higher and independent power, from which all its own power and authority are derived, and treats him accordingly. I please myself with imagining a State at last which can afford to be just to all men, and to treat the individual with respect as a neighbor; which even would not think it inconsistent with its own repose if a few were to live aloof from it, not meddling with it, nor embraced by it, who fulfilled all the duties of neighbors and fellow-men. A State which bore this kind of fruit, and suffered it to drop off as fast as it ripened, would prepare the way for a still more perfect and glorious State, which also I have imagined, but not yet anywhere seen.

[1849]

From *Walden;* Chapter 2: Where I Lived, and What I Lived For

At a certain season of our life we are accustomed to consider every spot as the possible site of a house. I have thus surveyed the country on every side within a dozen miles of where I live. In imagination I have bought all the farms in succession, for all were to be bought and I knew their price. I walked over each farmer's premises, tasted his wild apples, discoursed on husbandry with him, took his farm at his price, at any price, mortgaging it to him in my mind; even put a higher price on it,—took every thing but a deed of it,—took his word for his deed, for I dearly love to talk,—cultivated it, and him too to some extent, I trust, and withdrew when I had enjoyed it long enough, leaving him to carry it on. This experience entitled me to be regarded as a sort of real-estate broker by my friends. Wherever I sat, there I might live, and the landscape radiated from me accordingly. What is a house but a *sedes*, a seat?—better if a country seat. I discovered many a site for a house not likely to be soon improved, which some might have thought too far from the village, but to my eyes the village was too far from it. Well, there I might live, I said; and there I did live, for an hour, a summer and a winter life; saw how I could let the years run off, buffet the winter through, and see the spring come in. The future inhabitants of this region, wherever they may place their houses, may be sure that they have been anticipated. An afternoon sufficed to lay out the land into orchard woodlot and pasture, and to decide what fine oaks or pines should be left to stand before the door, and whence each blasted tree could be seen to the best advantage; and then I let it lie, fallow perchance, for a man is rich in proportion to the number of things which he can afford to let alone.

My imagination carried me so far that I even had the refusal of several farms,—the refusal was all I wanted,—but I never got my fingers burned by actual possession. The nearest that I came to actual possession was when I bought the Hollowell Place, and had begun to sort my seeds, and collected materials with which to make a wheelbarrow to carry it on or off with; but before the owner gave me a deed of it, his wife—every man has such a wife—changed her mind and wished to keep it, and he offered me ten dollars to release him. Now, to speak the truth, I had but ten cents in the world, and it surpassed my arithmetic to tell, if I was that man who had ten cents, or who had a farm, or ten dollars, or all together. However, I let him keep the ten dollars and the farm too, for I had carried it far enough; or rather, to be generous, I sold him the farm for just what I gave for it, and, as he was not a rich man, made him a present of ten dollars, and still had my ten cents, and seeds, and materials for a wheelbarrow left. I found thus that I had been a rich man without any damage to my poverty. But I retained the landscape, and I have since annually carried off what it yielded without a wheelbarrow. With respect to landscapes,—

> "I am monarch of all I *survey*,
> My right there is none to dispute."[1]

I have frequently seen a poet withdraw, having enjoyed the most valuable part of a farm, while the crusty farmer supposed that he had got a few wild apples only. Why, the owner does not know it for many years

[1] I AM MONARCH OF ALL I SURVEY, MY RIGHT THERE IS NONE TO DISPUTE: From *Verses Supposed to be Written by Alexander Selkirk*, by the English poet William Cowper (1731–1800). Selkirk (1676–1721) was the shipwrecked Scottish sailor who served as the model for Robinson Crusoe in the novel (1719) of that name by Daniel Defoe (1660–1731).

when a poet has put his farm in rhyme, the most admirable kind of invisible fence, has fairly impounded it, milked it, skimmed it, and got all the cream, and left the farmer only the skimmed milk.

The real attractions of the Hollowell farm, to me, were: its complete retirement, being about two miles from the village, half a mile from the nearest neighbor, and separated from the highway by a broad field; its bounding on the river, which the owner said protected it by its fogs from frosts in the spring, though that was nothing to me; the gray color and ruinous state of the house and barn, and the dilapidated fences, which put such an interval between me and the last occupant; the hollow and lichen-covered apple trees, gnawed by rabbits, showing what kind of neighbors I should have; but above all, the recollection I had of it from my earliest voyages up the river, when the house was concealed behind a dense grove of red maples, through which I heard the house-dog bark. I was in haste to buy it, before the proprietor finished getting out some rocks, cutting down the hollow apple trees, and grubbing up some young birches which had sprung up in the pasture, or, in short, had made any more of his improvements. To enjoy these advantages I was ready to carry it on; like Atlas,[2] to take the world on my shoulders,—I never heard what compensation he received for that,—and do all those things which had no other motive or excuse but that I might pay for it and be unmolested in my possession of it; for I knew all the while that it would yield the most abundant crop of the kind I wanted if I could only afford to let it alone. But it turned out as I have said.

All that I could say, then, with respect to farming on a large scale, (I have always cultivated a garden,) was, that I had had my seeds ready. Many think that seeds improve with age. I have no doubt that time discriminates between the good and the bad; and when at last I shall plant, I shall be less likely to be disappointed. But I would say to my fellows, once for all, As long as possible live free and uncommitted. It makes but little difference whether you are committed to a farm or the county jail.

Old Cato,[3] whose "De Re Rusticâ" is my "Cultivator," says, and the only translation I have seen makes sheer nonsense of the passage, "When you think of getting a farm, turn it thus in your mind, not to buy greedily; nor spare your pains to look at it, and do not think it enough to go round it once. The oftener you go there the more it will please you, if it is good."[4] I think I shall not buy greedily, but go round

[2]ATLAS: In Greek myth, Atlas was a descendant of the giants called Titans. He participated in the revolt of the Titans against the gods of Olympus; his punishment, devised by Zeus, was to forever bear the heavens on his shoulders.
[3]OLD CATO: *De re rustica* ("On Farming"), by Marcus Porcius Cato (234–149 BCE), described agricultural methods and country life in ancient Rome.

and round it as long as I live, and be buried in it first, that it may please me the more at last.

The present was my next experiment of this kind, which I purpose to describe more at length; for convenience, putting the experience of two years into one. As I have said, I do not propose to write an ode to dejection, but to brag as lustily as chanticleer in the morning, standing on his roost, if only to wake my neighbors up.

When first I took up my abode in the woods, that is, began to spend my nights as well as days there, which, by accident, was on Independence Day, or the fourth of July, 1845, my house was not finished for winter, but was merely a defence against the rain, without plastering or chimney, the walls being of rough weather-stained boards, with wide chinks, which made it cool at night. The upright white hewn studs and freshly planed door and window casings gave it a clean and airy look, especially in the morning, when its timbers were saturated with dew, so that I fancied that by noon some sweet gum would exude from them. To my imagination it retained throughout the day more or less of this auroral character, reminding me of a certain house on a mountain which I had visited the year before. This was an airy and unplastered cabin, fit to entertain a travelling god, and where a goddess might trail her garments. The winds which passed over my dwelling were such as sweep over the ridges of mountains, bearing the broken strains, or celestial parts only, of terrestrial music. The morning wind forever blows, the poem of creation is uninterrupted; but few are the ears that hear it. Olympus is but the outside of the earth every where.

The only house I had been the owner of before, if I except a boat, was a tent, which I used occasionally when making excursions in the summer, and this is still rolled up in my garret; but the boat, after passing from hand to hand, has gone down the stream of time. With this more substantial shelter about me, I had made some progress toward settling in the world. This frame, so slightly clad, was a sort of crystallization around me, and reacted on the builder. It was suggestive somewhat as a picture in outlines. I did not need to go out doors to take the air, for the atmosphere within had lost none of its freshness. It was not so much within doors as behind a door where I sat, even in the rainiest weather. The Harivansa[5] says, "An abode without birds is like a meat without seasoning." Such was not my abode, for I found myself suddenly neighbor to the birds; not by

[4]IF IT IS GOOD: *De re rustica* 1.1 (see note 3).
[5]HARIVANSA: The title of a Hindu epic poem.

having imprisoned one, but having caged myself near them. I was not only nearer to some of those which commonly frequent the garden and the orchard, but to those wilder and more thrilling songsters of the forest which never, or rarely, serenade a villager,—the wood-thrush, the veery, the scarlet tanager, the field-sparrow, the whippoorwill, and many others.

I was seated by the shore of a small pond, about a mile and a half south of the village of Concord and somewhat higher than it, in the midst of an extensive wood between that town and Lincoln, and about two miles south of that our only field known to fame, Concord Battle Ground[6]; but I was so low in the woods that the opposite shore, half a mile off, like the rest, covered with wood, was my most distant horizon. For the first week, whenever I looked out on the pond it impressed me like a tarn high up on the side of a mountain, its bottom far above the surface of other lakes, and, as the sun arose, I saw it throwing off its nightly clothing of mist, and here and there, by degrees, its soft ripples or its smooth reflecting surface was revealed, while the mists, like ghosts, were stealthily withdrawing in every direction into the woods, as at the breaking up of some nocturnal conventicle. The very dew seemed to hang upon the trees later into the day than usual, as on the sides of mountains.

This small lake was of most value as a neighbor in the intervals of a gentle rain storm in August, when, both air and water being perfectly still, but the sky overcast, mid-afternoon had all the serenity of evening, and the wood-thrush sang around, and was heard from shore to shore. A lake like this is never smoother than at such a time; and the clear portion of the air above it being shallow and darkened by clouds, the water, full of light and reflections, becomes a lower heaven itself so much the more important. From a hill top near by, where the wood had been recently cut off, there was a pleasing vista southward across the pond, through a wide indentation in the hills which form the shore there, where their opposite sides sloping toward each other suggested a stream flowing out in that direction through a wooded valley, but stream there was none. That way I looked between and over the near green hills to some distant and higher ones in the horizon, tinged with blue. Indeed, by standing on tiptoe I could catch a glimpse of some of the peaks of the still bluer and more distant mountain ranges in the north-west, those true-blue coins from heaven's own mint, and also of some portion of the village. But in other directions, even from this point, I could not see over or beyond the woods which surrounded me. It is well to have some water in your neighborhood, to give buoyancy to and

[6]CONCORD BATTLE GROUND: The site of the first battle of the American Revolution, which took place on April 19, 1775.

float the earth. One value even of the smallest well is, that when you look into it you see that earth is not continent but insular. This is as important as that it keeps butter cool. When I looked across the pond from this peak toward the Sudbury meadows, which in time of flood I distinguished elevated perhaps by a mirage in their seething valley, like a coin in a basin, all the earth beyond the pond appeared like a thin crust insulated and floated even by this small sheet of intervening water, and I was reminded that this on which I dwelt was but *dry land*.

Though the view from my door was still more contracted, I did not feel crowded or confined in the least. There was pasture enough for my imagination. The low shrub-oak plateau to which the opposite shore arose, stretched away toward the prairies of the West and the steppes of Tartary, affording ample room for all the roving families of men. "There are none happy in the world but beings who enjoy freely a vast horizon,"—said Damodara,[7] when his herds required new and larger pastures.

Both place and time were changed, and I dwelt nearer to those parts of the universe and to those eras in history which had most attracted me. Where I lived was as far off as many a region viewed nightly by astronomers. We are wont to imagine rare and delectable places in some remote and more celestial corner of the system, behind the constellation of Cassiopeia's Chair, far from noise and disturbance. I discovered that my house actually had its site in such a withdrawn, but forever new and unprofaned, part of the universe. If it were worth the while to settle in those parts near to the Pleiades or the Hyades, to Aldebaran or Altair,[8] then I was really there, or at an equal remoteness from the life which I had left behind, dwindled and twinkling with as fine a ray to my nearest neighbor, and to be seen only in moonless nights by him. Such was that part of creation where I had squatted;—

> "There was a shepherd that did live,
> And held his thoughts as high
> As were the mounts whereon his flocks
> Did hourly feed him by."[9]

What should we think of the shepherd's life if his flocks always wandered to higher pastures than his thoughts?

Every morning was a cheerful invitation to make my life of equal simplicity, and I may say innocence, with Nature herself. I have been

---

[7]DAMODARA: Another name for Krishna, a Hindu deity.
[8]PLEIADES OR THE HYADES, TO ALDEBARAN OR ALTAIR: The Pleiades and the Hyades are neighboring groups of stars in the constellation Taurus. Aldebaran is the brightest star of the Hyades. Altair is a star in the constellation Aquila.
[9]DID HOURLY FEED HIM BY: A line from an anonymous seventeenth-century poem.

as sincere a worshipper of Aurora as the Greeks. I got up early and bathed in the pond; that was a religious exercise, and one of the best things which I did. They say that characters were engraven on the bathing tub of king Tching-thang to this effect: "Renew thyself completely each day; do it again, and again, and forever again."[10] I can understand that. Morning brings back the heroic ages. I was as much affected by the faint hum of a mosquito making its invisible and unimaginable tour through my apartment at earliest dawn, when I was sitting with door and windows open, as I could be by any trumpet that ever sang of fame. It was Homer's requiem; itself an Iliad and Odyssey in the air, singing its own wrath and wanderings. There was something cosmical about it; a standing advertisement, till forbidden,[11] of the everlasting vigor and fertility of the world. The morning, which is the most memorable season of the day, is the awakening hour. Then there is least somnolence in us; and for an hour, at least, some part of us awakes which slumbers all the rest of the day and night. Little is to be expected of that day, if it can be called a day, to which we are not awakened by our Genius, but by the mechanical nudgings of some servitor, are not awakened by our own newly-acquired force and aspirations from within, accompanied by the undulations of celestial music, instead of factory bells, and a fragrance filling the air—to a higher life than we fell asleep from; and thus the darkness bear its fruit, and prove itself to be good, no less than the light. That man who does not believe that each day contains an earlier, more sacred, and auroral hour than he has yet profaned, has despaired of life, and is pursuing a descending and darkening way. After a partial cessation of his sensuous life, the soul of man, or its organs rather, are reinvigorated each day, and his Genius tries again what noble life it can make. All memorable events, I should say, transpire in morning time and in a morning atmosphere. The Vedas[12] say, "All intelligences awake with the morning." Poetry and art, and the fairest and most memorable of the actions of men, date from such an hour. All poets and heroes, like Memnon,[13] are the children of Aurora, and emit their

---

[10]RENEW THYSELF COMPLETELY EACH DAY; DO IT AGAIN, AND AGAIN, AND FOREVER AGAIN: From *Ta Hsüeh*, based in the teachings of Confucius (c. 551–479 BCE).
[11]TILL FORBIDDEN: In nineteenth-century newspaper advertisements, "TF" alerted the typesetters to repeat the ad daily "till forbidden."
[12]VEDAS: The Hindu scriptures.
[13]MEMNON: Aurora was the Roman goddess of the dawn, equivalent to Eos in Greek mythology. Memnon was her son with Tithonus, the brother of King Priam of Troy. Memnon was mortally wounded by Achilles during the Trojan war but granted immortality by Zeus.

music at sunrise. To him whose elastic and vigorous thought keeps pace with the sun, the day is a perpetual morning. It matters not what the clocks say or the attitudes and labors of men. Morning is when I am awake and there is a dawn in me. Moral reform is the effort to throw off sleep. Why is it that men give so poor an account of their day if they have not been slumbering? They are not such poor calculators. If they had not been overcome with drowsiness they would have performed something. The millions are awake enough for physical labor; but only one in a million is awake enough for effective intellectual exertion, only one in a hundred millions to a poetic or divine life. To be awake is to be alive. I have never yet met a man who was quite awake. How could I have looked him in the face?

We must learn to reawaken and keep ourselves awake, not by mechanical aids, but by an infinite expectation of the dawn, which does not forsake us in our soundest sleep. I know of no more encouraging fact than the unquestionable ability of man to elevate his life by a conscious endeavor. It is something to be able to paint a particular picture, or to carve a statue, and so to make a few objects beautiful; but it is far more glorious to carve and paint the very atmosphere and medium through which we look, which morally we can do. To affect the quality of the day, that is the highest of arts. Every man is tasked to make his life, even in its details, worthy of the contemplation of his most elevated and critical hour. If we refused, or rather used up, such paltry information as we get, the oracles would distinctly inform us how this might be done.

I went to the woods because I wished to live deliberately, to front only the essential facts of life, and see if I could not learn what it had to teach, and not, when I came to die, discover that I had not lived. I did not wish to live what was not life, living is so dear; nor did I wish to practise resignation, unless it was quite necessary. I wanted to live deep and suck out all the marrow of life, to live so sturdily and Spartan-like[14] as to put to rout all that was not life, to cut a broad swath and shave close, to drive life into a corner, and reduce it to its lowest terms, and, if it proved to be mean, why then to get the whole and genuine meanness of it, and publish its meanness to the world; or if it were sublime, to know it by experience, and be able to give a true account of it in my next excursion. For most men, it appears to me, are in a strange uncertainty about it, whether it is of the devil or of God, and have

---

[14]SPARTAN-LIKE: Sparta was a nation in ancient Greece whose citizens lived a simple, militaristic lifestyle.

somewhat hastily concluded that it is the chief end of man here to "glorify God and enjoy him forever."[15]

Still we live meanly, like ants; though the fable tells us that we were long ago changed into men[16]; like pygmies we fight with cranes; it is error upon error, and clout upon clout, and our best virtue has for its occasion a superfluous and evitable wretchedness. Our life is frittered away by detail. An honest man has hardly need to count more than his ten fingers, or in extreme cases he may add his ten toes, and lump the rest. Simplicity, simplicity, simplicity! I say, let your affairs be as two or three, and not a hundred or a thousand; instead of a million count half a dozen, and keep your accounts on your thumb nail. In the midst of this chopping sea of civilized life, such are the clouds and storms and quicksands and thousand-and-one items to be allowed for, that a man has to live, if he would not founder and go to the bottom and not make his port at all, by dead reckoning, and he must be a great calculator indeed who succeeds. Simplify, simplify. Instead of three meals a day, if it be necessary eat but one; instead of a hundred dishes, five; and reduce other things in proportion. Our life is like a German Confederacy,[17] made up of petty states, with its boundary forever fluctuating, so that even a German cannot tell you how it is bounded at any moment. The nation itself, with all its so called internal improvements, which, by the way, are all external and superficial, is just such an unwieldy and overgrown establishment, cluttered with furniture and tripped up by its own traps, ruined by luxury and heedless expense, by want of calculation and a worthy aim, as the million households in the land; and the only cure for it as for them is in a rigid economy, a stern and more than Spartan simplicity of life and elevation of purpose. It lives too fast. Men think that it is essential that the *Nation* have commerce, and export ice, and talk through a telegraph, and ride thirty miles an hour, without a doubt, whether *they* do or not; but whether we should live like baboons or like men, is a little uncertain. If we do not get out sleepers,[18] and forge rails, and devote days and nights to the work, but go to tinkering upon

[15]GLORIFY GOD AND ENJOY HIM FOREVER: The first two questions of the Shorter Catechism from the *New England Primer*, a Sunday School reader published in the late seventeenth century. "Q. 1. What is the chief end of man? A. Man's chief end is to glorify God, and to enjoy him forever. Q. 2. What rule hath God given to direct us how we may glorify and enjoy him? A. The word of God, which is contained in the Scriptures of the Old and New Testaments, is the only rule to direct us how we may glorify and enjoy him."
[16]CHANGED INTO MEN: In Greek mythology, Aeacus, a son of Zeus, was the king of the island of Aegina. When he lost most of his subjects to the plague, Zeus repopulated the island by changing ants into people; they were called Myrmidons ("ant-people").
[17]GERMAN CONFEDERACY: Germany comprised many small principalities, later unified under Otto von Bismarck (1815–1898), who became chancellor of the German Empire.
[18]IF WE DO NOT GET OUT SLEEPERS: Railroad ties.

our *lives* to improve *them*, who will build railroads? And if railroads are not built, how shall we get to heaven in season? But if we stay at home and mind our business, who will want railroads? We do not ride on the railroad; it rides upon us. Did you ever think what those sleepers are that underlie the railroad? Each one is a man, an Irish-man, or a Yankee man. The rails are laid on them, and they are covered with sand, and the cars run smoothly over them. They are sound sleepers, I assure you. And every few years a new lot is laid down and run over; so that, if some have the pleasure of riding on a rail, others have the misfortune to be ridden upon. And when they run over a man that is walking in his sleep, a supernumerary sleeper in the wrong position, and wake him up, they suddenly stop the cars, and make a hue and cry about it, as if this were an exception. I am glad to know that it takes a gang of men for every five miles to keep the sleepers down and level in their beds as it is, for this is a sign that they may sometime get up again.

Why should we live with such hurry and waste of life? We are determined to be starved before we are hungry. Men say that a stitch in time saves nine, and so they take a thousand stitches to-day to save nine to-morrow. As for *work*, we haven't any of any consequence. We have the Saint Vitus' dance,[19] and cannot possibly keep our heads still. If I should only give a few pulls at the parish bell-rope,[20] as for a fire, that is, without setting the bell, there is hardly a man on his farm in the outskirts of Concord, notwithstanding that press of engagements which was his excuse so many times this morning, nor a boy, nor a woman, I might almost say, but would forsake all and follow that sound, not mainly to save property from the flames, but, if we will confess the truth, much more to see it burn, since burn it must, and we, be it known, did not set it on fire,—or to see it put out, and have a hand in it, if that is done as handsomely; yes, even if it were the parish church itself. Hardly a man takes a half hour's nap after dinner, but when he wakes he holds up his head and asks, "What's the news?" as if the rest of mankind had stood his sentinels. Some give directions to be waked every half hour, doubtless for no other purpose; and then, to pay for it, they tell what they have dreamed. After a night's sleep the news is as indispensable as the breakfast. "Pray tell me any thing new that has happened to a man any where on this globe",—and he reads it over his coffee and rolls, that a man had had his eyes gouged out this morning on the

---

[19]SAINT VITUS' DANCE: Chorea, a convulsive disorder characterized by involuntary muscle contractions, especially of the arms and legs, causing jerky motions.
[20]PARISH BELL-ROPE: Before civic fire departments were instituted, towns used the church bell to call for volunteer aid in the case of a fire.

Wachito River[21]; never dreaming the while that he lives in the dark unfathomed mammoth cave of this world, and has but the rudiment of an eye himself.

For my part, I could easily do without the post-office. I think that there are very few important communications made through it. To speak critically, I never received more than one or two letters in my life—I wrote this some years ago—that were worth the postage. The penny-post is, commonly, an institution through which you seriously offer a man that penny for his thoughts which is so often safely offered in jest. And I am sure that I never read any memorable news in a newspaper. If we read of one man robbed, or murdered, or killed by accident, or one house burned, or one vessel wrecked, or one steamboat blown up, or one cow run over on the Western Railroad, or one mad dog killed, or one lot of grasshoppers in the winter,—we never need read of another. One is enough. If you are acquainted with the principle, what do you care for a myriad instances and applications? To a philosopher all *news*, as it is called, is gossip, and they who edit and read it are old women over their tea. Yet not a few are greedy after this gossip. There was such a rush, as I hear, the other day at one of the offices to learn the foreign news by the last arrival, that several large squares of plate glass belonging to the establishment were broken by the pressure,—news which I seriously think a ready wit might write a twelvemonth or twelve years beforehand with sufficient accuracy. As for Spain, for instance, if you know how to throw in Don Carlos and the Infanta, and Don Pedro and Seville and Granada, from time to time in the right proportions,—they may have changed the names a little since I saw the papers,—and serve up a bull-fight when other entertainments fail, it will be true to the letter, and give us as good an idea of the exact state or ruin of things in Spain as the most succinct and lucid reports under this head in the newspapers: and as for England, almost the last significant scrap of news from that quarter was the revolution of 1649[22]; and if you have learned the history of her crops for an average year, you never need attend to that thing again, unless your speculations are of a merely pecuniary character. If one may judge who rarely looks into the newspapers, nothing new does ever happen in foreign parts, a French revolution not excepted.

What news! how much more important to know what that is which was never old! "Kieou-pe-yu (great dignitary of the state of Wei) sent a man to Khoung-tseu to know his news. Khoung-tseu caused the messenger to

---

[21]WACHITO RIVER: The Ouachita (or Wachita) River, in Oklahoma and Texas.
[22]REVOLUTION OF 1649: The year the English Commonwealth, under the direction of Oliver Cromwell (1599–1658), Lord Protector of England, abolished the monarchy and executed Charles I (1600–1649).

be seated near him, and questioned him in these terms: What is your master doing? The messenger answered with respect: My master desires to diminish the number of his faults, but he cannot accomplish it. The messenger being gone, the philosopher remarked: What a worthy messenger! What a worthy messenger!"[23] The preacher, instead of vexing the ears of drowsy farmers on their day of rest at the end of the week,—for Sunday is the fit conclusion of an ill-spent week, and not the fresh and brave beginning of a new one,—with this one other draggle-tail of a sermon, should shout with thundering voice,—"Pause! Avast! Why so seeming fast, but deadly slow?"[24]

Shams and delusions are esteemed for soundest truths, while reality is fabulous. If men would steadily observe realities only, and not allow themselves to be deluded, life, to compare it with such things as we know, would be like a fairy tale and the Arabian Nights' Entertainments. If we respected only what is inevitable and has a right to be, music and poetry would resound along the streets. When we are unhurried and wise, we perceive that only great and worthy things have any permanent and absolute existence,—that petty fears and petty pleasures are but the shadow of the reality. This is always exhilarating and sublime. By closing the eyes and slumbering, and consenting to be deceived by shows, men establish and confirm their daily life of routine and habit every where, which still is built on purely illusory foundations. Children, who play life, discern its true law and relations more clearly than men, who fail to live it worthily, but who think that they are wiser by experience, that is, by failure. I have read in a Hindoo[25] book, that "there was a king's son, who, being expelled in infancy from his native city, was brought up by a forester, and, growing up to maturity in that state, imagined himself to belong to the barbarous race with which he lived. One of his father's ministers having discovered him, revealed to him what he was, and the misconception of his character was removed, and he knew himself to be a prince. So soul," continues the Hindoo philosopher, "from the circumstances in which it is placed, mistakes its own character, until the truth is revealed to it by some holy teacher, and then it knows itself to be *Brahme*."[26] I perceive that we inhabitants of New England live this mean life that we do because our vision does not penetrate the surface of things.

[23]WHAT A WORTHY MESSENGER: A story from Confucius's *Analects* (Book XIV).
[24]WHY SO SEEMING FAST, BUT DEADLY SLOW: A possible reference to the Methodist minister Edward Thompson "Father" Taylor (1793–1871), the missionary in charge of the Seaman's Bethel in Boston; he was known for the nautical phrasing in his sermons and served as the model for Father Mapple in Herman Melville's *Moby-Dick* (1851).
[25]HINDOO: Hindu.
[26]BRAHME: In Hinduism, Brahme, or Brahma, is the creator of the world and the teacher of the gods.

We think that that *is* which *appears* to be. If a man should walk through this town and see only the reality, where, think you, would the "Mill-dam"[27] go to? If he should give us an account of the realities he beheld there, we should not recognize the place in his description. Look at a meeting-house, or a court-house, or a jail, or a shop, or a dwelling-house, and say what that thing really is before a true gaze, and they would all go to pieces in your account of them. Men esteem truth remote, in the outskirts of the system, behind the farthest star, before Adam and after the last man. In eternity there is indeed something true and sublime. But all these times and places and occasions are now and here. God himself culminates in the present moment, and will never be more divine in the lapse of all the ages. And we are enabled to apprehend at all what is sublime and noble only by the perpetual instilling and drenching of the reality which surrounds us. The universe constantly and obediently answers to our conceptions; whether we travel fast or slow, the track is laid for us. Let us spend our lives in conceiving them. The poet or the artist never yet had so fair and noble a design but some of his posterity at least could accomplish it.

Let us spend one day as deliberately as Nature, and not be thrown off the track by every nutshell and mosquito's wing that falls on the rails. Let us rise early and fast, or break fast, gently and without perturbation; let company come and let company go, let the bells ring and the children cry,—determined to make a day of it. Why should we knock under and go with the stream? Let us not be upset and overwhelmed in that terrible rapid and whirlpool called a dinner, situated in the meridian shallows. Weather this danger and you are safe, for the rest of the way is down hill. With unrelaxed nerves, with morning vigor, sail by it, looking another way, tied to the mast like Ulysses.[28] If the engine whistles, let it whistle till it is hoarse for its pains. If the bell rings, why should we run? We will consider what kind of music they are like. Let us settle ourselves, and work and wedge our feet downward through the mud and slush of opinion, and prejudice, and tradition, and delusion, and appearance, that alluvion[29] which covers the globe, through Paris and London, through New York and Boston and Concord, through church and state, through poetry and philosophy and religion, till we come to a hard bottom and rocks in place, which we can call *reality*, and say, This is, and no mistake; and then begin, having

[27]MILL-DAM: The business center of Concord, Massachusetts.
[28]TIED TO THE MAST LIKE ULYSSES: In Homer's epic poem the *Odyssey*, Ulysses has himself tied to the mast of his ship so he can hear the Sirens' (sea nymphs) deadly song but not succumb to their call.
[29]ALLUVION: Sediment deposited along the shore or bank of a stream or river.

a *point d'appui*,[30] below freshet and frost and fire, a place where you might found a wall or a state, or set a lamp-post safely, or perhaps a gauge, not a Nilometer, but a Realometer,[31] that future ages might know how deep a freshet of shams and appearances had gathered from time to time. If you stand right fronting and face to face to a fact, you will see the sun glimmer on both its surfaces, as if it were a cimeter,[32] and feel its sweet edge dividing you through the heart and marrow, and so you will happily conclude your mortal career. Be it life or death, we crave only reality. If we are really dying, let us hear the rattle in our throats and feel cold in the extremities; if we are alive, let us go about our business.

Time is but the stream I go a-fishing in. I drink at it; but while I drink I see the sandy bottom and detect how shallow it is. Its thin current slides away, but eternity remains. I would drink deeper; fish in the sky, whose bottom is pebbly with stars. I cannot count one. I know not the first letter of the alphabet. I have always been regretting that I was not as wise as the day I was born. The intellect is a cleaver; it discerns and rifts its way into the secret of things. I do not wish to be any more busy with my hands than is necessary. My head is hands and feet. I feel all my best faculties concentrated in it. My instinct tells me that my head is an organ for burrowing, as some creatures use their snout and fore-paws, and with it I would mine and burrow my way through these hills. I think that the richest vein is somewhere hereabouts; so by the divining rod and thin rising vapors I judge; and here I will begin to mine.

[1854]

Life Without Principle

At a lyceum, not long since, I felt that the lecturer had chosen a theme too foreign to himself, and so failed to interest me as much as he might have done. He described things not in or near to his heart, but toward his extremities and superficies. There was, in this sense, no truly central or centralizing thought in the lecture. I would have had him deal with his privatest experience, as the poet does. The greatest compliment that was ever paid me was when one asked me what *I thought*, and attended to

---

[30]POINT D'APPUI: Point of support; fulcrum. (French)
[31]NILOMETER, BUT A REALOMETER: Thoreau makes a joke. A nilometer was a gauge used in the ancient Egyptian city of Memphis to measure the rise of the Nile River.
[32]CIMETER: Scimitar, a sword with a curved blade.

my answer. I am surprised, as well as delighted, when this happens, it is such a rare use he would make of me, as if he were acquainted with the tool. Commonly, if men want anything of me, it is only to know how many acres I make of their land,—since I am a surveyor,—or, at most, what trivial news I have burdened myself with. They never will go to law for my meat; they prefer the shell. A man once came a considerable distance to ask me to lecture on Slavery; but on conversing with him, I found that he and his clique expected seven eighths of the lecture to be theirs, and only one eighth mine; so I declined. I take it for granted, when I am invited to lecture anywhere,—for I have had a little experience in that business,—that there is a desire to hear what *I think* on some subject, though I may be the greatest fool in the country,—and not that I should say pleasant things merely, or such as the audience will assent to; and I resolve, accordingly, that I will give them a strong dose of myself. They have sent for me, and engaged to pay for me, and I am determined that they shall have me, though I bore them beyond all precedent.

So now I would say something similar to you, my readers. Since *you* are my readers, and I have not been much of a traveler, I will not talk about people a thousand miles off, but come as near home as I can. As the time is short, I will leave out all the flattery, and retain all the criticism.

Let us consider the way in which we spend our lives.

This world is a place of business. What an infinite bustle! I am awaked almost every night by the panting of the locomotive. It interrupts my dreams. There is no sabbath.[1] It would be glorious to see mankind at leisure for once. It is nothing but work, work, work. I cannot easily buy a blank-book to write thoughts in; they are commonly ruled for dollars and cents. An Irishman, seeing me making a minute[2] in the fields, took it for granted that I was calculating my wages. If a man was tossed out of a window when an infant, and so made a cripple for life, or scared out of his wits by the Indians, it is regretted chiefly because he was thus incapacitated for—business! I think that there is nothing, not even crime, more opposed to poetry, to philosophy, ay, to life itself, than this incessant business.

There is a coarse and boisterous money-making fellow in the outskirts of our town, who is going to build a bank-wall under the hill along the edge of his meadow. The powers have put this into his head to keep him out of mischief, and he wishes me to spend three weeks digging there with him. The result will be that he will perhaps get some more money to

---

[1]SABBATH: Sunday as a day for rest and religious reflection.
[2]MAKING A MINUTE: Taking a note.

hoard, and leave for his heirs to spend foolishly. If I do this, most will commend me as an industrious and hard-working man; but if I choose to devote myself to certain labors which yield more real profit, though but little money, they may be inclined to look on me as an idler. Nevertheless, as I do not need the police of meaningless labor to regulate me, and do not see anything absolutely praiseworthy in this fellow's undertaking any more than in many an enterprise of our own or foreign governments, however amusing it may be to him or them, I prefer to finish my education at a different school.

If a man walk in the woods for love of them half of each day, he is in danger of being regarded as a loafer; but if he spends his whole day as a speculator, shearing off those woods and making earth bald before her time, he is esteemed an industrious and enterprising citizen. As if a town had no interest in its forests but to cut them down!

Most men would feel insulted if it were proposed to employ them in throwing stones over a wall, and then in throwing them back, merely that they might earn their wages. But many are no more worthily employed now. For instance: just after sunrise, one summer morning, I noticed one of my neighbors walking beside his team, which was slowly drawing a heavy hewn stone swung under the axle, surrounded by an atmosphere of industry,—his day's work begun,—his brow commenced to sweat,—a reproach to all sluggards and idlers,—pausing abreast the shoulders of his oxen, and half turning round with a flourish of his merciful whip, while they gained their length on him. And I thought, Such is the labor which the American Congress exists to protect,—honest, manly toil,—honest as the day is long,—that makes his bread taste sweet, and keeps society sweet,—which all men respect and have consecrated; one of the sacred band, doing the needful but irksome drudgery. Indeed, I felt a slight reproach, because I observed this from a window, and was not abroad and stirring about a similar business. The day went by, and at evening I passed the yard of another neighbor, who keeps many servants, and spends much money foolishly, while he adds nothing to the common stock, and there I saw the stone of the morning lying beside a whimsical structure intended to adorn this Lord Timothy Dexter's[3] premises, and the dignity forthwith departed from the teamster's labor, in my eyes. In my opinion, the sun was made to light worthier toil than this. I may add that his employer has since run off, in debt to a good part

[3]LORD TIMOTHY DEXTER: An American merchant and admitted eccentric (1747–1806) from Massachusetts. He decorated the gardens of his "palace" with life-size painted statues of famous people, including presidents Washington, Adams, and Jefferson. His friends dubbed him "Lord Timothy Dexter," a title he accepted.

of the town, and, after passing through Chancery,[4] has settled somewhere else, there to become once more a patron of the arts.

The ways by which you may get money almost without exception lead downward. To have done anything by which you earned money *merely* is to have been truly idle or worse. If the laborer gets no more than the wages which his employer pays him, he is cheated, he cheats himself. If you would get money as a writer or lecturer, you must be popular, which is to go down perpendicularly. Those services which the community will most readily pay for, it is most disagreeable to render. You are paid for being something less than a man. The state does not commonly reward a genius any more wisely. Even the poet laureate would rather not have to celebrate the accidents of royalty. He must be bribed with a pipe of wine[5]; and perhaps another poet is called away from his muse to gauge that very pipe. As for my own business, even that kind of surveying which I could do with most satisfaction my employers do not want. They would prefer that I should do my work coarsely and not too well, ay, not well enough. When I observe that there are different ways of surveying, my employer commonly asks which will give him the most land, not which is most correct. I once invented a rule for measuring cord-wood, and tried to introduce it in Boston; but the measurer there told me that the sellers did not wish to have their wood measured correctly,—that he was already too accurate for them, and therefore they commonly got their wood measured in Charlestown before crossing the bridge.

The aim of the laborer should be, not to get his living, to get "a good job," but to perform well a certain work; and, even in a pecuniary sense, it would be economy for a town to pay its laborers so well that they would not feel that they were working for low ends, as for a livelihood merely, but for scientific, or even moral ends. Do not hire a man who does your work for money, but him who does it for love of it.

It is remarkable that there are few men so well employed, so much to their minds, but that a little money or fame would commonly buy them off from their present pursuit. I see advertisements for *active* young men, as if activity were the whole of a young man's capital. Yet I have been surprised when one has with confidence proposed to me, a grown man, to embark in some enterprise of his, as if I had absolutely nothing to do, my life having been a complete failure hitherto. What a doubtful compliment this to pay me! As if he had met me half-way across the ocean beating up against the wind, but bound nowhere, and

---

[4]CHANCERY: Bankruptcy court.
[5]PIPE OF WINE: Cask of wine containing about 105 imperial (British) gallons.

proposed to me to go along with him! If I did, what do you think the underwriters would say? No, no! I am not without employment at this stage of the voyage. To tell the truth, I saw an advertisement for able-bodied seamen, when I was a boy, sauntering in my native port, and as soon as I came of age I embarked.

The community has no bribe that will tempt a wise man. You may raise money enough to tunnel a mountain, but you cannot raise money enough to hire a man who is minding *his own* business. An efficient and valuable man does what he can, whether the community pay him for it or not. The inefficient offer their inefficiency to the highest bidder, and are forever expecting to be put into office. One would suppose that they were rarely disappointed.

Perhaps I am more than usually jealous with respect to my freedom. I feel that my connection with and obligation to society are still very slight and transient. Those slight labors which afford me a livelihood, and by which it is allowed that I am to some extent serviceable to my contemporaries, are as yet commonly a pleasure to me, and I am not often reminded that they are a necessity. So far I am successful. But I foresee that if my wants should be much increased, the labor required to supply them would become a drudgery. If I should sell both my forenoons and afternoons to society, as most appear to do, I am sure that for me there would be nothing left worth living for. I trust that I shall never thus sell my birthright for a mess of pottage.[6] I wish to suggest that a man may be very industrious, and yet not spend his time well. There is no more fatal blunderer than he who consumes the greater part of his life getting his living. All great enterprises are self-supporting. The poet, for instance, must sustain his body by his poetry, as a steam planing-mill feeds its boilers with the shavings it makes. You must get your living by loving. But as it is said of the merchants that ninety-seven in a hundred fail, so the life of men generally, tried by this standard, is a failure, and bankruptcy may be surely prophesied.

Merely to come into the world the heir of a fortune is not to be born, but to be still-born, rather. To be supported by the charity of friends, or a government pension,—provided you continue to breathe,—by whatever fine synonyms you describe these relations, is to go into the almshouse.

[6]SELL MY BIRTHRIGHT FOR A MESS OF POTTAGE: Genesis 25:30–34: "And Esau said to Jacob, Feed me, I pray thee, with that same red pottage; for I am faint: therefore was his name called Edom. / And Jacob said, Sell me this day thy birthright. / And Esau said, Behold, I am at the point to die: and what profit shall this birthright do to me? / And Jacob said, Swear to me this day; and he sware unto him: and he sold his birthright unto Jacob. / Then Jacob gave Esau bread and pottage of lentiles; and he did eat and drink, and rose up, and went his way: thus Esau despised his birthright."

On Sundays the poor debtor goes to church to take an account of stock, and finds, of course, that his outgoes have been greater than his income. In the Catholic Church, especially, they go into chancery, make a clean confession, give up all, and think to start again. Thus men will lie on their backs, talking about the fall of man, and never make an effort to get up.

As for the comparative demand which men make on life, it is an important difference between two, that the one is satisfied with a level success, that his marks can all be hit by point-blank shots, but the other, however low and unsuccessful his life may be, constantly elevates his aim, though at a very slight angle to the horizon. I should much rather be the last man,—though, as the Orientals[7] say, "Greatness doth not approach him who is forever looking down; and all those who are looking high are growing poor."

It is remarkable that there is little or nothing to be remembered written on the subject of getting a living; how to make getting a living not merely honest and honorable, but altogether inviting and glorious; for if *getting* a living is not so, then living is not. One would think, from looking at literature, that this question had never disturbed a solitary individual's musings. Is it that men are too much disgusted with their experience to speak of it? The lesson of value which money teaches, which the Author of the Universe has taken so much pains to teach us, we are inclined to skip altogether. As for the means of living, it is wonderful how indifferent men of all classes are about it, even reformers, so called,—whether they inherit, or earn, or steal it. I think that Society has done nothing for us in this respect, or at least has undone what she has done. Cold and hunger seem more friendly to my nature than those methods which men have adopted and advise to ward them off.

The title *wise* is, for the most part, falsely applied. How can one be a wise man, if he does not know any better how to live than other men?— if he is only more cunning and intellectually subtle? Does Wisdom work in a tread-mill? or does she teach how to succeed *by her example*? Is there any such thing as wisdom not applied to life? Is she merely the miller who grinds the finest logic? It is pertinent to ask if Plato got his *living* in a better way or more successfully than his contemporaries,—or did he succumb to the difficulties of life like other men? Did he seem to prevail over some of them merely by indifference, or by assuming grand airs? or find it easier to live, because his aunt remembered him in her will? The ways in which most men get their living, that is, live, are mere makeshifts, and

[7]ORIENTALS: People of Asian or Middle Eastern origin.

a shirking of the real business of life,—chiefly because they do not know, but partly because they do not mean, any better.

The rush to California,[8] for instance, and the attitude, not merely of merchants, but of philosophers and prophets, so called, in relation to it, reflect the greatest disgrace on mankind. That so many are ready to live by luck, and so get the means of commanding the labor of others less lucky, without contributing any value to society! And that is called enterprise! I know of no more startling development of the immorality of trade, and all the common modes of getting a living. The philosophy and poetry and religion of such a mankind are not worth the dust of a puffball. The hog that gets his living by rooting, stirring up the soil so, would be ashamed of such company. If I could command the wealth of all the worlds by lifting my finger, I would not pay *such* a price for it. Even Mahomet[9] knew that God did not make this world in jest. It makes God to be a moneyed gentleman who scatters a handful of pennies in order to see mankind scramble for them. The world's raffle! A subsistence in the domains of Nature a thing to be raffled for! What a comment, what a satire, on our institutions! The conclusion will be, that mankind will hang itself upon a tree. And have all the precepts in all the Bibles taught men only this? and is the last and most admirable invention of the human race only an improved muck-rake? Is this the ground on which Orientals and Occidentals[10] meet? Did God direct us so to get our living, digging where we never planted,—and He would, perchance, reward us with lumps of gold?

God gave the righteous man a certificate entitling him to food and raiment, but the unrighteous man found a facsimile of the same in God's coffers, and appropriated it, and obtained food and raiment like the former. It is one of the most extensive systems of counterfeiting that the world has seen. I did not know that mankind was suffering for want of gold. I have seen a little of it. I know that it is very malleable, but not so malleable as wit. A grain of gold will gild a great surface, but not so much as a grain of wisdom.

The gold-digger in the ravines of the mountains is as much a gambler as his fellow in the saloons of San Francisco. What difference does it make whether you shake dirt or shake dice? If you win, society is the loser. The gold-digger is the enemy of the honest laborer, whatever checks and

---

[8]CALIFORNIA: The gold rush that began at Sutter's Mill early in 1848 brought more than 40,000 fortune seekers to California within two years.
[9]MAHOMET: Mohammed (570?–632), the Prophet of Islam. From the Quran, 21.16, and 44.38: "And We did not create the heaven and the earth and what is between them for sport."
[10]OCCIDENTALS: Of European or Western origin, including America and the Western Hemisphere.

compensations there may be. It is not enough to tell me that you worked hard to get your gold. So does the Devil work hard. The way of transgressors may be hard in many respects. The humblest observer who goes to the mines sees and says that gold-digging is of the character of a lottery; the gold thus obtained is not the same thing with the wages of honest toil. But, practically, he forgets what he has seen, for he has seen only the fact, not the principle, and goes into trade there, that is, buys a ticket in what commonly proves another lottery, where the fact is not so obvious.

After reading Howitt's account[11] of the Australian gold-diggings one evening, I had in my mind's eye, all night, the numerous valleys, with their streams, all cut up with foul pits, from ten to one hundred feet deep, and half a dozen feet across, as close as they can be dug, and partly filled with water,—the locality to which men furiously rush to probe for their fortunes,—uncertain where they shall break ground,—not knowing but the gold is under their camp itself,—sometimes digging one hundred and sixty feet before they strike the vein, or then missing it by a foot,—turned into demons, and regardless of each others' rights, in their thirst for riches,—whole valleys, for thirty miles, suddenly honeycombed by the pits of the miners, so that even hundreds are drowned in them,—standing in water, and covered with mud and clay, they work night and day, dying of exposure and disease. Having read this, and partly forgotten it, I was thinking, accidentally, of my own unsatisfactory life, doing as others do; and with that vision of the diggings still before me, I asked myself why *I* might not be washing some gold daily, though it were only the finest particles,—why *I* might not sink a shaft down to the gold within me, and work that mine. *There* is a Ballarat, a Bendigo[12] for you,— what though it were a sulky-gully?[13] At any rate, I might pursue some path, however solitary and narrow and crooked, in which I could walk with love and reverence. Wherever a man separates from the multitude, and goes his own way in this mood, there indeed is a fork in the road, though ordinary travelers may see only a gap in the paling.[14] His solitary path across lots will turn out the *higher way* of the two.

Men rush to California and Australia as if the true gold were to be found in that direction; but that is to go to the very opposite extreme

[11]HOWITT'S ACCOUNT: William Howitt (1830–1908) was the author of *Land, Labour, and Gold, or, Two Years in Victoria* (1855).
[12]BALLARAT, A BENDIGO: Australian gold rush towns.
[13]SULKY-GULLY: Many of the surface mines during the Australian gold rush of the 1850s had the word *gully* in their name, such as Peg Leg Gully and Eagle Hawk Gully. A sulky (obstinate) gully would be hard to mine. On October 19, 1855, Thoreau noted in his journal, "Hear some of the names of the places where they dig: "Jackass Flat," "Sheep's-Head Gully," "Sulky Gully," "Murderer's Bar." He rephrased the passage for this essay.
[14]PALING: The pales or pickets of a fence.

to where it lies. They go prospecting farther and farther away from the true lead, and are most unfortunate when they think themselves most successful. Is not our *native* soil auriferous?[15] Does not a stream from the golden mountains flow through our native valley? and has not this for more than geologic ages been bringing down the shining particles and forming the nuggets for us? Yet, strange to tell, if a digger steal away, prospecting for this true gold, into the unexplored solitudes around us, there is no danger that any will dog his steps, and endeavor to supplant him. He may claim and undermine the whole valley even, both the cultivated and the uncultivated portions, his whole life long in peace, for no one will ever dispute his claim. They will not mind his cradles or his toms. He is not confined to a claim twelve feet square, as at Ballarat, but may mine anywhere, and wash the whole wide world in his tom.

Howitt says of the man who found the great nugget which weighed twenty-eight pounds, at the Bendigo diggings in Australia: "He soon began to drink; got a horse, and rode all about, generally at full gallop, and, when he met people, called out to inquire if they knew who he was, and then kindly informed them that he was 'the bloody wretch that had found the nugget.' At last he rode full speed against a tree, and nearly knocked his brains out." I think, however, there was no danger of that, for he had already knocked his brains out against the nugget. Howitt adds, "He is a hopelessly ruined man." But he is a type of the class. They are all fast men. Hear some of the names of the places where they dig: "Jackass Flat,"—"Sheep's-Head Gully,"—"Murderer's Bar," etc. Is there no satire in these names? Let them carry their ill-gotten wealth where they will, I am thinking it will still be "Jackass Flat," if not "Murderer's Bar," where they live.

The last resource of our energy has been the robbing of graveyards on the Isthmus of Darien,[16] an enterprise which appears to be but in its infancy; for, according to late accounts, an act has passed its second reading in the legislature of New Granada,[17] regulating this kind of mining; and a correspondent of the "Tribune"[18] writes: "In the dry season, when the weather will permit of the country being properly prospected, no doubt other rich *guacas* [that is, graveyards] will be found." To emigrants he says: "Do not come before December; take the Isthmus route in preference to the Boca del Toro one; bring no useless baggage, and do not

---

[15]AURIFEROUS: Yielding or containing gold.
[16]ISTHMUS OF DARIEN: Panama.
[17]NEW GRANADA: Colombia.
[18]TRIBUNE: The *New York Tribune*, a daily newspaper founded in 1841 by Horace Greeley (1811–1872).

cumber yourself with a tent; but a good pair of blankets will be necessary; a pick, shovel, and axe of good material will be almost all that is required:" advice which might have been taken from the "Burker's Guide."[19] And he concludes with this line in Italics and small capitals: "*If you are doing well at home,* STAY THERE," which may fairly be interpreted to mean, "If you are getting a good living by robbing graveyards at home, stay there."

But why go to California for a text? She is the child of New England, bred at her own school and church.

It is remarkable that among all the preachers there are so few moral teachers. The prophets are employed in excusing the ways of men. Most reverend seniors, the *illuminati*[20] of the age, tell me, with a gracious, reminiscent smile, betwixt an aspiration and a shudder, not to be too tender about these things,—to lump all that, that is, make a lump of gold of it. The highest advice I have heard on these subjects was groveling. The burden of it was,—It is not worth your while to undertake to reform the world in this particular. Do not ask how your bread is buttered; it will make you sick, if you do,—and the like. A man had better starve at once than lose his innocence in the process of getting his bread. If within the sophisticated man there is not an unsophisticated one, then he is but one of the devil's angels. As we grow old, we live more coarsely, we relax a little in our disciplines, and, to some extent, cease to obey our finest instincts. But we should be fastidious to the extreme of sanity, disregarding the gibes of those who are more unfortunate than ourselves.

In our science and philosophy, even, there is commonly no true and absolute account of things. The spirit of sect and bigotry has planted its hoof amid the stars. You have only to discuss the problem, whether the stars are inhabited or not, in order to discover it. Why must we daub the heavens as well as the earth? It was an unfortunate discovery that Dr. Kane was a Mason,[21] and that Sir John Franklin was another.[22] But it was a more cruel suggestion that possibly that was the reason why the former went in search of the latter. There is not a popular magazine in

[19]BURKER'S GUIDE: A reference to the body snatcher William Burke (1792–1829), who robbed graves to supply bodies to medical schools for dissection but soon resorted to murder to keep up the supply. After his execution for murder in Edinburgh, Scotland, his own body was dissected.
[20]ILLUMINATI: Persons who claim to have exceptional knowledge or insight on any subject; the term is often used sarcastically.
[21]DR. KANE WAS A MASON: Elisha Kent Kane (1820–1857), an American physician, explorer of Greenland, and a member of the fraternity of Freemasons.
[22]SIR JOHN FRANKLIN WAS ANOTHER: Sir John Franklin (1786–1847) was a British explorer whose disappearance with 129 others in the area of Point Victory inspired an extensive search of the Arctic, including Elisha Kent Kane's second expedition.

this country that would dare to print a child's thought on important subjects without comment. It must be submitted to the D.D.'s. I would it were the chickadee-dees.[23]

You come from attending the funeral of mankind to attend to a natural phenomenon. A little thought is sexton[24] to all the world.

I hardly know an *intellectual* man, even, who is so broad and truly liberal that you can think aloud in his society. Most with whom you endeavor to talk soon come to a stand against some institution in which they appear to hold stock,—that is, some particular, not universal, way of viewing things. They will continually thrust their own low roof, with its narrow skylight, between you and the sky, when it is the unobstructed heavens you would view. Get out of the way with your cobwebs; wash your windows, I say! In some lyceums they tell me that they have voted to exclude the subject of religion. But how do I know what their religion is, and when I am near to or far from it? I have walked into such an arena and done my best to make a clean breast of what religion I have experienced, and the audience never suspected what I was about. The lecture was as harmless as moonshine to them. Whereas, if I had read to them the biography of the greatest scamps in history, they might have thought that I had written the lives of the deacons of their church. Ordinarily, the inquiry is, Where did you come from? or, Where are you going? That was a more pertinent question which I overheard one of my auditors put to another once,—"What does he lecture for?" It made me quake in my shoes.

To speak impartially, the best men that I know are not serene, a world in themselves. For the most part, they dwell in forms, and flatter and study effect only more finely than the rest. We select granite for the underpinning of our houses and barns; we build fences of stone; but we do not ourselves rest on an underpinning of granitic truth, the lowest primitive rock. Our sills are rotten. What stuff is the man made of who is not coexistent in our thought with the purest and subtilest truth? I often accuse my finest acquaintances of an immense frivolity; for, while there are manners and compliments we do not meet, we do not teach one another the lessons of honesty and sincerity that the brutes do, or of steadiness and solidity that the rocks do. The fault is commonly mutual, however; for we do not habitually demand any more of each other.

[23]CHICKADEE-DEES: A pun on the Doctors of Divinity (D.D.s) who imposed an unofficial form of literary censorship on Victorian society.
[24]SEXTON: Church employee responsible for digging graves.

That excitement about Kossuth,[25] consider how characteristic, but superficial, it was!—only another kind of politics or dancing. Men were making speeches to him all over the country, but each expressed only the thought, or the want of thought, of the multitude. No man stood on truth. They were merely banded together, as usual one leaning on another, and all together on nothing; as the Hindoos made the world rest on an elephant, the elephant on a tortoise, and the tortoise on a serpent, and had nothing to put under the serpent. For all fruit of that stir we have the Kossuth hat.

Just so hollow and ineffectual, for the most part, is our ordinary conversation. Surface meets surface. When our life ceases to be inward and private, conversation degenerates into mere gossip. We rarely meet a man who can tell us any news which he has not read in a newspaper, or been told by his neighbor; and, for the most part, the only difference between us and our fellow is that he has seen the newspaper, or been out to tea, and we have not. In proportion as our inward life fails, we go more constantly and desperately to the post-office. You may depend on it, that the poor fellow who walks away with the greatest number of letters, proud of his extensive correspondence, has not heard from himself this long while.

I do not know but it is too much to read one newspaper a week. I have tried it recently, and for so long it seems to me that I have not dwelt in my native region. The sun, the clouds, the snow, the trees say not so much to me. You cannot serve two masters. It requires more than a day's devotion to know and to possess the wealth of a day.

We may well be ashamed to tell what things we have read or heard in our day. I do not know why my news should be so trivial,—considering what one's dreams and expectations are, why the developments should be so paltry. The news we hear, for the most part, is not news to our genius. It is the stalest repetition. You are often tempted to ask why such stress is laid on a particular experience which you have had,—that, after twenty-five years, you should meet Hobbins, Registrar of Deeds, again on the sidewalk. Have you not budged an inch, then? Such is the daily news. Its facts appear to float in the atmosphere, insignificant as the sporules of fungi, and impinge on some neglected *thallus*,[26] or surface of our minds, which affords a basis for them, and hence a parasitic growth. We should wash ourselves clean of such news. Of what

---

[25]KOSSUTH: Lajos Kossuth (1802–1894), a Hungarian revolutionary hero. He was welcomed in the United States during a 1851 visit as a great champion of liberty. His slouch hat became a fashion fad in the United States.
[26]THALLUS: A stemless, rootless, leafless plant body characteristic of plants such as algae and certain types of fungi.

consequence, though our planet explode, if there is no character involved in the explosion? In health we have not the least curiosity about such events. We do not live for idle amusement. I would not run round a corner to see the world blow up.

All summer, and far into the autumn, perchance, you unconsciously went by the newspapers and the news, and now you find it was because the morning and the evening were full of news to you. Your walks were full of incidents. You attended, not to the affairs of Europe, but to your own affairs in Massachusetts fields. If you chance to live and move and have your being in that thin stratum[27] in which the events that make the news transpire,—thinner than the paper on which it is printed,—then these things will fill the world for you; but if you soar above or dive below that plane, you cannot remember nor be reminded of them. Really to see the sun rise or go down every day, so to relate ourselves to a universal fact, would preserve us sane forever. Nations! What are nations? Tartars, and Huns, and Chinamen! Like insects, they swarm. The historian strives in vain to make them memorable. It is for want of a man that there are so many men. It is individuals that populate the world. Any man thinking may say with the Spirit of Lodin,[28]—

> *"I look down from my height on nations,*
> *And they become ashes before me;—*
> *Calm is my dwelling in the clouds;*
> *Pleasant are the great fields of my rest."[29]*

Pray, let us live without being drawn by dogs, Esquimaux-fashion, tearing over hill and dale, and biting each other's ears.

Not without a slight shudder at the danger, I often perceive how near I had come to admitting into my mind the details of some trivial affair,— the news of the street; and I am astonished to observe how willing men are to lumber their minds with such rubbish,—to permit idle rumors and incidents of the most insignificant kind to intrude on ground which should be sacred to thought. Shall the mind be a public arena, where the affairs of the street and the gossip of the tea-table chiefly are discussed? Or shall it be a quarter of heaven itself,—an hypæthral[30] temple, consecrated to the service of the gods? I find it so difficult to dispose of

[27]IF YOU CHANCE TO LIVE AND MOVE AND HAVE YOUR BEING IN THAT STRATUM: Acts 17:28: "For in him we live, and move, and have our being; as certain also of your own poets have said, For we are also his offspring."
[28]SPIRIT OF LODIN: The Spirit of Loda from the poem "Carric-Thura," by the Scottish author James Macpherson (1736–1796), appearing in *The Works of Ossian* (1765).
[29]I LOOK DOWN FROM MY HEIGHT ON NATIONS...PLEASANT ARE THE GREAT FIELDS OF MY REST: The Spirit of Loda's speech to the hero Fingal in the poem "Carric-Thura" (see note 27).
[30]HYPÆTHRAL TEMPLE: A roofless, open-air temple.

the few facts which to me are significant, that I hesitate to burden my attention with those which are insignificant, which only a divine mind could illustrate. Such is, for the most part, the news in newspapers and conversation. It is important to preserve the mind's chastity in this respect. Think of admitting the details of a single case of the criminal court into our thoughts, to stalk profanely through their very *sanctum sanctorum*[31] for an hour, ay, for many hours! to make a very barroom of the mind's inmost apartment, as if for so long the dust of the street had occupied us,—the very street itself, with all its travel, its bustle, and filth, had passed through our thoughts' shrine! Would it not be an intellectual and moral suicide? When I have been compelled to sit spectator and auditor in a court-room for some hours, and have seen my neighbors, who were not compelled, stealing in from time to time, and tiptoeing about with washed hands and faces, it has appeared to my mind's eye, that, when they took off their hats, their ears suddenly expanded into vast hoppers for sound, between which even their narrow heads were crowded. Like the vanes of windmills, they caught the broad but shallow stream of sound, which, after a few titillating gyrations in their coggy brains, passed out the other side. I wondered if, when they got home, they were as careful to wash their ears as before their hands and faces. It has seemed to me, at such a time, that the auditors and the witnesses, the jury and the counsel, the judge and the criminal at the bar,—if I may presume him guilty before he is convicted,—were all equally criminal, and a thunderbolt might be expected to descend and consume them all together.

By all kinds of traps and signboards, threatening the extreme penalty of the divine law, exclude such trespassers from the only ground which can be sacred to you. It is so hard to forget what it is worse than useless to remember! If I am to be a thoroughfare, I prefer that it be of the mountain brooks, the Parnassian streams,[32] and not the town sewers. There is inspiration, that gossip which comes to the ear of the attentive mind from the courts of heaven. There is the profane and stale revelation of the barroom and the police court. The same ear is fitted to receive both communications. Only the character of the hearer determines to which it shall be open, and to which closed. I believe that the mind can be permanently profaned by the habit of attending to trivial things, so that all our thoughts shall be tinged with triviality. Our very intellect shall

---

[31]SANCTUM SANCTORUM: Literally, the Holy of Holies (Latin) of the Jewish temple in Jerusalem—that is, the most sacred place.
[32]PARNASSIAN STREAMS: In Greek myth, Mount Parnassus, in central Greece, was considered sacred to the Muses (goddesses of artistic inspiration).

be macadamized,[33] as it were,—its foundation broken into fragments for the wheels of travel to roll over; and if you would know what will make the most durable pavement, surpassing rolled stones, spruce blocks, and asphaltum, you have only to look into some of our minds which have been subjected to this treatment so long.

If we have thus desecrated ourselves,—as who has not?—the remedy will be by wariness and devotion to reconsecrate ourselves, and make once more a fane[34] of the mind. We should treat our minds, that is, ourselves, as innocent and ingenuous children, whose guardians we are, and be careful what objects and what subjects we thrust on their attention. Read not the Times. Read the Eternities. Conventionalities are at length as bad as impurities. Even the facts of science may dust the mind by their dryness, unless they are in a sense effaced each morning, or rather rendered fertile by the dews of fresh and living truth. Knowledge does not come to us by details, but in flashes of light from heaven. Yes, every thought that passes through the mind helps to wear and tear it, and to deepen the ruts, which, as in the streets of Pompeii, evince how much it has been used. How many things there are concerning which we might well deliberate whether we had better know them,—had better let their peddling-carts be driven, even at the slowest trot or walk, over that bridge of glorious span by which we trust to pass at last from the farthest brink of time to the nearest shore of eternity! Have we no culture, no refinement,—but skill only to live coarsely and serve the Devil?—to acquire a little worldly wealth, or fame, or liberty, and make a false show with it, as if we were all husk and shell, with no tender and living kernel to us? Shall our institutions be like those chestnut burs which contain abortive nuts, perfect only to prick the fingers?

America is said to be the arena on which the battle of freedom is to be fought; but surely it cannot be freedom in a merely political sense that is meant. Even if we grant that the American has freed himself from a political tyrant, he is still the slave of an economical and moral tyrant. Now that the republic—the *res-publica*—has been settled, it is time to look after the *res-privata*,—the private state,—to see, as the Roman senate charged its consuls, *"ne quid res-*PRIVATA *detrimenti caparet,"* that the *private* state receive no detriment.

Do we call this the land of the free? What is it to be free from King George[35] and continue the slaves of King Prejudice? What is it to be born

---

[33]MACADAMIZED: Referring to John Loudon McAdam (1736–1836), the Scottish engineer who pioneered modern road building.
[34]FANE: Temple.
[35]KING GEORGE: George III (1738–1820), the king of England against whom the American colonists rebelled.

free and not to live free? What is the value of any political freedom, but as a means to moral freedom? Is it a freedom to be slaves, or a freedom to be free, of which we boast? We are a nation of politicians, concerned about the outmost defenses only of freedom. It is our children's children who may perchance be really free. We tax ourselves unjustly. There is a part of us which is not represented. It is taxation without representation. We quarter troops, we quarter fools and cattle of all sorts upon ourselves. We quarter our gross bodies on our poor souls, till the former eat up all the latter's substance.

With respect to a true culture and manhood, we are essentially provincial still, not metropolitan,—mere Jonathans.[36] We are provincial, because we do not find at home our standards; because we do not worship truth, but the reflection of truth; because we are warped and narrowed by an exclusive devotion to trade and commerce and manufactures and agriculture and the like, which are but means, and not the end.

So is the English Parliament provincial. Mere country bumpkins, they betray themselves, when any more important question arises for them to settle, the Irish question, for instance,—the English question why did I not say? Their natures are subdued to what they work in. Their "good breeding" respects only secondary objects. The finest manners in the world are awkwardness and fatuity when contrasted with a finer intelligence. They appear but as the fashions of past days,—mere courtliness, knee-buckles and small-clothes, out of date. It is the vice, but not the excellence of manners, that they are continually being deserted by the character; they are cast-off clothes or shells, claiming the respect which belonged to the living creature. You are presented with the shells instead of the meat, and it is no excuse generally, that, in the case of some fishes, the shells are of more worth than the meat. The man who thrusts his manners upon me does as if he were to insist on introducing me to his cabinet of curiosities, when I wished to see himself. It was not in this sense that the poet Decker[37] called Christ "the first true gentleman that ever breathed." I repeat that in this sense the most splendid court in Christendom is provincial, having authority to consult about Transalpine interests only, and not the affairs of Rome.[38] A prætor[39] or proconsul

---

[36]JONATHANS: Brother Jonathan; a generic name for a patriotic American, popular before the advent of the icon of Uncle Sam.
[37]DECKER: Thomas Dekker (c.1570–1632), an English playwright. The quotation is from *The Honest Whore* (1604), Act 1.12, by Dekker and the English dramatist John Middleton (1580–1627).
[38]TRANSALPINE INTERESTS ONLY, AND NOT THE AFFAIRS OF ROME: Referring to the papal court in Rome, which ironically had more power beyond the Alps of Italy than it did in its home city of Rome.
[39]PRÆTOR: Mayor or civil magistrate in Italy.

would suffice to settle the questions which absorb the attention of the English Parliament and the American Congress.

Government and legislation! these I thought were respectable professions. We have heard of heaven-born Numas, Lycurguses, and Solons,[40] in the history of the world, whose *names* at least may stand for ideal legislators; but think of legislating to *regulate* the breeding of slaves, or the exportation of tobacco! What have divine legislators to do with the exportation or the importation of tobacco? what humane ones with the breeding of slaves? Suppose you were to submit the question to any son of God,—and has He no children in the Nineteenth Century? is it a family which is extinct?—in what condition would you get it again? What shall a State like Virginia say for itself at the last day, in which these have been the principal, the staple productions? What ground is there for patriotism in such a State? I derive my facts from statistical tables which the States themselves have published.

A commerce that whitens[41] every sea in quest of nuts and raisins, and makes slaves of its sailors for this purpose! I saw, the other day, a vessel which had been wrecked, and many lives lost, and her cargo of rags, juniper berries, and bitter almonds were strewn along the shore. It seemed hardly worth the while to tempt the dangers of the sea between Leghorn and New York for the sake of a cargo of juniper berries and bitter almonds. America sending to the Old World for her bitters! Is not the sea-brine, is not shipwreck, bitter enough to make the cup of life go down here? Yet such, to a great extent, is our boasted commerce; and there are those who style themselves statesmen and philosophers who are so blind as to think that progress and civilization depend on precisely this kind of interchange and activity,—the activity of flies about a molasses-hogshead. Very well, observes one, if men were oysters. And very well, answer I, if men were mosquitoes.

Lieutenant Herndon,[42] whom our government sent to explore the Amazon, and, it is said, to extend the area of slavery, observed that there was wanting there "an industrious and active population, who know what the comforts of life are, and who have artificial wants to draw out the great resources of the country." But what are the "artificial wants" to be encouraged? Not the love of luxuries, like the tobacco and slaves of, I believe,

[40]NUMAS, LYCURGUSES, AND SOLONS: Numa Pompilius, semi-mythical king of Rome credited with founding Roman ceremonial law; Lycurgus, the legendary author of the Spartan constitution; and Solon (c.639–c.559 BCE), Athenian statesman and legal reformer.
[41]A COMMERCE THAT WHITENS: Referring to the white sails of ships.
[42]LIEUTENANT HERNDON: William Lewis Herndon (1813–1857), coauthor (with Lardner Gibbon) of *Exploration of the Valley of the Amazon.*

his native Virginia, nor the ice and granite and other material wealth of our native New England; nor are "the great resources of a country" that fertility or barrenness of soil which produces these. The chief want, in every State that I have been into, was a high and earnest purpose in its inhabitants. This alone draws out "the great resources" of Nature, and at last taxes her beyond her resources; for man naturally dies out of her. When we want culture more than potatoes, and illumination more than sugar-plums, then the great resources of a world are taxed and drawn out, and the result, or staple production, is, not slaves, nor operatives,[43] but men,—those rare fruits called heroes, saints, poets, philosophers, and redeemers.

In short, as a snow-drift is formed where there is a lull in the wind, so, one would say, where there is a lull of truth, an institution springs up. But the truth blows right on over it, nevertheless, and at length blows it down.

What is called politics is comparatively something so superficial and inhuman, that practically I have never fairly recognized that it concerns me at all. The newspapers, I perceive, devote some of their columns specially to politics or government without charge; and this, one would say, is all that saves it; but as I love literature and to some extent the truth also, I never read those columns at any rate. I do not wish to blunt my sense of right so much. I have not got to answer for having read a single President's Message. A strange age of the world this, when empires, kingdoms, and republics come a-begging to a private man's door, and utter their complaints at his elbow! I cannot take up a newspaper but I find that some wretched government or other, hard pushed and on its last legs, is interceding with me, the reader, to vote for it,—more importunate than an Italian beggar; and if I have a mind to look at its certificate, made, perchance, by some benevolent merchant's clerk, or the skipper that brought it over, for it cannot speak a word of English itself, I shall probably read of the eruption of some Vesuvius,[44] or the overflowing of some Po,[45] true or forged, which brought it into this condition. I do not hesitate, in such a case, to suggest work, or the almshouse; or why not keep its castle in silence, as I do commonly? The poor President,[46] what with preserving his popularity and doing his duty, is completely bewildered. The newspapers are the ruling power. Any other government is reduced to a few marines at Fort Independence.[47] If a man neglects to

[43]OPERATIVES: Factory workers.
[44]VESUVIUS: Active volcano on the eastern shore of the Bay of Naples in Italy, best known for the eruption that buried the towns of Pompeii and Herculaneum in 79 CE.
[45]PO: The Po River of Italy.
[46]THE POOR PRESIDENT: Franklin Pierce (1804–1869), fourteenth president of the United States.
[47]FORT INDEPENDENCE: A fort located in Boston Harbor.

read the Daily Times, government will go down on its knees to him, for this is the only treason in these days.

Those things which now most engage the attention of men, as politics and the daily routine, are, it is true, vital functions of human society, but should be unconsciously performed, like the corresponding functions of the physical body. They are *infra*[48]-human, a kind of vegetation. I sometimes awake to a half-consciousness of them going on about me, as a man may become conscious of some of the processes of digestion in a morbid state, and so have the dyspepsia, as it is called. It is as if a thinker submitted himself to be rasped by the great gizzard of creation. Politics is, as it were, the gizzard of society, full of grit and gravel, and the two political parties are its two opposite halves,—sometimes split into quarters, it may be, which grind on each other. Not only individuals, but states, have thus a confirmed dyspepsia, which expresses itself, you can imagine by what sort of eloquence. Thus our life is not altogether a forgetting, but also, alas! to a great extent, a remembering, of that which we should never have been conscious of, certainly not in our waking hours. Why should we not meet, not always as dyspeptics, to tell our bad dreams, but sometimes as *eu*peptics,[49] to congratulate each other on the ever-glorious morning? I do not make an exorbitant demand, surely.

[1863]

---

[48]INFRA: Below, under. (Latin)
[49]EUPEPTICS: Individuals in a state of vibrant health attributed to good digestion.

Frederick Douglass

(1818–1895)

Frederick Douglass was born on a plantation on the Eastern Shore of Maryland in February 1818. His mother was a slave, Harriet Bailey, and his father was a white man whose identity is unknown. Denied schooling, but aided by a white woman who soon regretted her actions, Douglass learned to read and write. At the age of sixteen, he fought back triumphantly against Edward Covey, a brutal breaker of slaves, as described in chapter 10 of his Narrative of the Life of Frederick Douglass, an American Slave, Written by Himself *(1845), one of the classic texts of African American, American, and world literatures.*

In September 1838, Douglass escaped from slavery, traveling in disguise by train from Baltimore to New York City. He settled with his wife, Anna Murray, in New Bedford, Massachusetts, and soon became involved in the radical abolitionist movement led by William Lloyd Garrison, the fiery editor of The Liberator.

For nearly half a century, Douglass was a dedicated, determined, and eloquent advocate for African Americans, lecturing widely, writing many essays, editing The North Star *and other papers, and revising and expanding his autobiography in* My Bondage and My Freedom *(1855) and* The Life and Times of Frederick Douglass *(1881, 1892).*

The Narrative *presents in written form the story of his life as a slave that Douglass had been describing for four years in antislavery lectures and addresses. He gives a detailed, vivid account of slavery as a system and an ideology, showing its horrific impact on black persons but also depicting its damaging effects on the white population in the South. As a result of wielding unlimited power over their black slaves, white masters and mistresses have distorted and disfigured themselves, Douglass contends, violating the best instincts and impulses of their human nature.*

In this respect, Douglass demonstrates to his readers that slavery is a Southern nightmare and, even more, a national tragedy. The North has cooperated with the South to secure the existence of slavery and extend its reach, and many in the North have done so not simply because of indifference toward the fate of enslaved persons but because of their contempt for black people and hostility toward a truly fair and equal biracial society. He touches on this position toward the end of the Narrative *and even more explicitly in later speeches and writings that denounced cruel forms of bigotry and segregation common in the North.*

The Narrative *is a work of art. It is the story of Douglass's life, but we should remember that it is the result of a process of selection and construction, as Douglass makes choices about which aspects of* his life he wishes to emphasize, downplay, or exclude. As the scholar Eric J. Sundquist observed, "The rhetorical reshaping of his experience that Douglass perfected as an abolitionist speaker is everywhere evident in the written texts." Douglass is writing with a purpose: he aims to compel readers in the North—few in the slaveholding South would read such an incendiary text—to face the shocking day-to-day realities of slavery: the destruction of families, the sexual exploitation of women, the constant assault on the hearts and minds, the souls and bodies, of its victims.

This intention helps clarify why the Narrative is, paradoxically, an intensely personal yet somewhat impersonal literary work. Douglass depicts with great depth and drama his own privations, his relationships with masters and overseers, his poignant feeling of fellowship with other slaves, and much more, but he is deliberately silent or vague about other matters. He says almost nothing, for example, about his wife, and many readers today wonder why he does not offer information about her and the nature of their lives together. But in Douglass's view, this dimension of his life is not pertinent to the public purpose his autobiography is meant to serve.

Nor does Douglass disclose to the reader anything about the composition of the Narrative itself. Did he discuss the work with anyone while it was in progress? Did he show the final manuscript to friends and associates for comments and suggestions before it was published? What was he thinking and feeling while he was writing? On these and other questions, Douglass is silent.

Douglass's story is his story, but also is meant to be a representative account. Few slaves managed to write their autobiographies, and only a fortunate minority succeeded in making their way to the North. Douglass was a successful fugitive who by the mid-1840s had become a prominent abolitionist and orator. The year after the Narrative appeared, he became legally free when British antislavery friends purchased him for $711—an action that, however practical and pragmatic it was for Douglass, some abolitionists decried, saying it gave legitimacy to a transaction that was profoundly illegitimate and evil.

Douglass was distinctive and, some would say, unique. But while the Narrative does make clear his array of virtues—his piercing intelligence and sensitivity, his resourcefulness, resilience, and courage—it functions also to describe slavery as a system, an institution that brutalizes and dehumanizes an entire race of people. What happened to Douglass, what he witnessed: he works with the facts of his own experiences on behalf of all his fellow slaves, representing them through the account he presents of his own life.

Douglass began the Narrative sometime in 1844, and he completed it in the spring of 1845. Priced at fifty cents, the 125-page book was *published by the Anti-Slavery Office in Boston in June 1845. Aided by publicity given it by the antislavery press, it sold 4,500 copies within the next several months. Soon, the* Narrative *was published abroad as well, and it created such a stir both in the United States and overseas that many readers, including some who were sympathetic to abolition, maintained that it could not have been written by a slave. Surely, they said, the* Narrative *had been ghostwritten by a white author.*

This was a common charge hurled against slave narratives and autobiographies, and on his title page Douglass tries to counter it in advance. This, he announces, is the "Narrative of the Life of Frederick Douglass, An American Slave, Written by Himself." Here he dramatizes the irony of slavery in the United States, a country founded on the affirmation in the Declaration of Independence that all men are created equal. He resolutely declares that he, an American and a slave, authored this book "himself."

So important is this fact, and so likely was it that some readers would believe otherwise, that Douglass next provided introductory statements—testimonials—by the white abolitionists William Lloyd Garrison and Wendell Phillips. In his later autobiographies, he deleted these sections, but here, in this first telling of his life, he judged he needed them to authenticate both the story itself and the fact that he had crafted it on his own. As an African American and thus presumed to be inferior to whites, Douglass at this juncture and throughout his life frequently encountered disbelief, denial, and rejection; the more forceful and forthright he was as a speaker and writer, the more some readers and audiences asserted he was not the person he claimed to be.

For most of the twentieth century, Douglass's Narrative *was absent from literary histories and scholarly and critical studies. Like African American literature in general, it was neglected or marginalized. It was not perceived to belong in the American literary tradition but, instead, was viewed as a form of social history, political writing, or antislavery propaganda that lacked enduring literary merit.*

Scholars in the 1960s, 1970s, and later, seeking to expand the literary canon and articulate the contributions to it by women and minorities, called attention to Douglass as one of the premier literary figures of his own era. They noted the striking affinity between Douglass's emphasis on African American initiative and self-discovery and Ralph Waldo Emerson's insistence on self-reliance and opposition to authority and convention. As Douglass's biographer William S. McFeely pointed out, Douglass and his Narrative *also make for a potent comparison and contrast with the life and work of Henry David Thoreau, whose stay by the shores of Walden Pond began the month after Douglass's book was published. Like* Walden, *published in 1854, the* Narrative, *says McFeely, delivers "a message of radical repudiation of corrupt society."*

Douglass is, furthermore, an author whose insights into human nature, power, and race are perpetually relevant and provocative. He resembles Emerson and Thoreau, and Nathaniel Hawthorne, Herman Melville, and Emily Dickinson, in being a writer who dwells both inside and outside a specific historical context. His books and essays have in particular inspired and empowered countless African Americans across many generations. Every African American author must acknowledge, absorb, and perhaps alter or adjust the meanings of Douglass's example and record of achievement.

In the words of the literary critic William L. Andrews, "Douglass's artistry invested his model of selfhood with a moral and political authority that subsequent aspirants to the role of African American culture hero— from the conservative Booker T. Washington to the radical W. E. B. Du Bois—would seek to appropriate for their own autobiographical portraits." One could extend Andrews's insight to include Douglass's contemporary Harriet Jacobs (included in this anthology) and such twentieth-century African American writers as Richard Wright, Ralph Ellison, Maya Angelou, and Toni Morrison. Like Emerson, Douglass is essential and inescapable— for African American and indeed for all *American readers.*

Below is the complete text of Douglass's Narrative, *preceded by one additional selection: Douglass's impassioned letter to his former master, Thomas Auld, which was published in both* The North Star, *September 8, 1848, and* The Liberator, *September 22, 1848.*

For further study, see Benjamin Quarles, Frederick Douglass *(1948); Dickson J. Preston,* Young Frederick Douglass: The Maryland Years *(1980);* Frederick Douglass: New Literary and Historical Essays *(1990), ed. Eric J. Sundquist; and William S. McFeely,* Frederick Douglass *(1991). Also illuminating: Waldo E. Martin Jr.,* The Mind of Frederick Douglass *(1984); and David W. Blight,* Frederick Douglass' Civil War: Keeping Faith in Jubilee *(1989).*

Narrative of the Life of Frederick Douglass, an American Slave, Written by Himself

PREFACE[1]

In the month of August, 1841, I attended an anti-slavery convention in Nantucket, at which it was my happiness to become acquainted with

---

[1]PREFACE: Written by William Lloyd Garrison (1805–1879), editor and abolitionist.

FREDERICK DOUGLASS, the writer of the following Narrative. He was a stranger to nearly every member of that body; but, having recently made his escape from the southern prisonhouse of bondage, and feeling his curiosity excited to ascertain the principles and measures of the abolitionists,—of whom he had heard a somewhat vague description while he was a slave,—he was induced to give his attendance, on the occasion alluded to, though at that time a resident in New Bedford.[2]

Fortunate, most fortunate occurrence!—fortunate for the millions of his manacled brethren, yet panting for deliverance from their awful thraldom!—fortunate for the cause of negro emancipation, and of universal liberty!—fortunate for the land of his birth, which he has already done so much to save and bless!—fortunate for a large circle of friends and acquaintances, whose sympathy and affection he has strongly secured by the many sufferings he has endured, by his virtuous traits of character, by his ever-abiding remembrance of those who are in bonds, as being bound with them!—fortunate for the multitudes, in various parts of our republic, whose minds he has enlightened on the subject of slavery, and who have been melted to tears by his pathos, or roused to virtuous indignation by his stirring eloquence against the enslavers of men!—fortunate for himself, as it at once brought him into the field of public usefulness, "gave the world assurance of a man,"[3] quickened the slumbering energies of his soul, and consecrated him to the great work of breaking the rod of the oppressor, and letting the oppressed go free!

I shall never forget his first speech at the convention—the extraordinary emotion it excited in my own mind—the powerful impression it created upon a crowded auditory, completely taken by surprise—the applause which followed from the beginning to the end of his felicitous remarks. I think I never hated slavery so intensely as at that moment; certainly, my perception of the enormous outrage which is inflicted by it, on the godlike nature of its victims, was rendered far more clear than ever. There stood one, in physical proportion and stature commanding and exact—in intellect richly endowed—in natural eloquence a prodigy—in soul manifestly "created but a little lower than the angels"[4]—yet a slave, ay, a fugitive slave,—trembling for his safety, hardly daring to believe that on the American soil, a single white person could be found who would befriend him at all hazards, for the love of God and humanity! Capable of high attainments as an intellectual and moral being—needing nothing but a comparatively small amount of cultivation to make him an ornament to society and a blessing to his race—by the law of the land, by

2NEW BEDFORD: New Bedford, Massachusetts.
3GAVE THE WORLD ASSURANCE OF A MAN: From Shakespeare's *Hamlet*, Act 3, Scene 4, line 62.
4CREATED BUT A LITTLE LOWER THAN THE ANGELS: Psalms 8:5.

the voice of the people, by the terms of the slave code, he was only a piece of property, a beast of burden, a chattel personal, nevertheless!

A beloved friend from New Bedford[5] prevailed on MR. DOUGLASS to address the convention: He came forward to the platform with a hesitancy and embarrassment, necessarily the attendants of a sensitive mind in such a novel position. After apologizing for his ignorance, and reminding the audience that slavery was a poor school for the human intellect and heart, he proceeded to narrate some of the facts in his own history as a slave, and in the course of his speech gave utterance to many noble thoughts and thrilling reflections. As soon as he had taken his seat, filled with hope and admiration, I rose, and declared that PATRICK HENRY,[6] of revolutionary fame, never made a speech more eloquent in the cause of liberty, than the one we had just listened to from the lips of that hunted fugitive. So I believed at that time—such is my belief now. I reminded the audience of the peril which surrounded this self-emancipated young man at the North,—even in Massachusetts, on the soil of the Pilgrim Fathers, among the descendants of revolutionary sires; and I appealed to them, whether they would ever allow him to be carried back into slavery,—law or no law, constitution or no constitution. The response was unanimous and in thundertones—"NO!" "Will you succor and protect him as a brother-man—a resident of the old Bay State."[7] "YES!" shouted the whole mass, with an energy so startling, that the ruthless tyrants south of Mason and Dixon's line[8] might almost have heard the mighty burst of feeling, and recognized it as the pledge of an invincible determination, on the part of those who gave it, never to betray him that wanders, but to hide the outcast, and firmly to abide the consequences.

It was at once deeply impressed upon my mind, that, if Mr. DOUGLASS could be persuaded to consecrate his time and talents to the promotion of the anti-slavery enterprise, a powerful impetus would be given to it, and a stunning blow at the same time inflicted on northern prejudice against a colored complexion. I therefore endeavored to instill hope and courage into his mind, in order that he might dare to engage in a vocation so anomalous and responsible for a person in his situation; and I was seconded in this effort by warm-hearted friends, especially by the late General Agent of the Massachusetts Anti-Slavery

---

[5]A BELOVED FRIEND FROM NEW BEDFORD: William C. Coffin, a Quaker abolitionist from New Bedford, Massachusetts.
[6]PATRICK HENRY: A political leader (1736–1799) of the American Revolution, most famous for his "liberty or death" speech to the Virginia House of Delegates in 1775. The speech was often quoted in antislavery writings.
[7]BAY STATE: Massachusetts.
[8]MASON AND DIXON'S LINE: The border between slave and free states, with Pennsylvania to the North and Delaware and Maryland to the South.

Society, Mr. JOHN A. COLLINS,[9] whose judgment in this instance entirely coincided with my own. At first, he could give no encouragement; with unfeigned diffidence, he expressed his conviction that he was not adequate to the performance of so great a task; the path marked out was wholly an untrodden one; he was sincerely apprehensive that he should do more harm than good. After much deliberation, however, he consented to make a trial; and ever since that period, he has acted as a lecturing agent, under the auspices either of the American or the Massachusetts Anti-Slavery Society. In labors he has been most abundant; and his success in combating prejudice, in gaining proselytes, in agitating the public mind, has far surpassed the most sanguine expectations that were raised at the commencement of his brilliant career. He has borne himself with gentleness and meekness, yet with true manliness of character. As a public speaker, he excels in pathos, wit, comparison, imitation, strength of reasoning, and fluency of language. There is in him that union of head and heart, which is indispensable to an enlightenment of the heads and a winning of the hearts of others. May his strength continue to be equal to his day! May he continue to "grow in grace, and in the knowledge of God,"[10] that he may be increasingly serviceable in the cause of bleeding humanity, whether at home or abroad!

It is certainly a very remarkable fact, that one of the most efficient advocates of the slave population, now before the public, is a fugitive slave, in the person of FREDERICK DOUGLASS; and that the free colored population of the United States are as ably represented by one of their own number, in the person of CHARLES LENOX REMOND,[11] whose eloquent appeals have extorted the highest applause of multitudes on both sides of the Atlantic. Let the calumniators of the colored race despise themselves for their baseness and illiberality of spirit, and henceforth cease to talk of the natural inferiority of those who require nothing but time and opportunity to attain to the highest point of human excellence.

It may, perhaps, be fairly questioned, whether any other portion of the population of the earth could have endured the privations, sufferings and horrors of slavery, without having become more degraded in the scale of humanity than the slaves of African descent. Nothing has been left undone to cripple their intellects, darken their minds, debase their

[9]MR. JOHN A. COLLINS: A general agent (1810–1879) of the Massachusetts Anti-Slavery Society.
[10]GROW IN GRACE, AND IN THE KNOWLEDGE OF GOD: 2 Peter 3:17–18: "Ye therefore, beloved, seeing ye know these things before, beware lest ye also, being led away with the error of the wicked, fall from your own stedfastness. / But grow in grace, and in the knowledge of our Lord and Saviour Jesus Christ."
[11]CHARLES LENOX REMOND: A free-born African American abolitionist (1810–1873) from Massachusetts who was known for his powerful and compelling speeches against slavery.

moral nature, obliterate all traces of their relationship to mankind; and yet how wonderfully they have sustained the mighty load of a most frightful bondage, under which they have been groaning for centuries! To illustrate the effect of slavery on the white man,—to show that he has no powers of endurance, in such a condition, superior to those of his black brother,—DANIEL O'CONNELL,[12] the distinguished advocate of universal emancipation, and the mightiest champion of prostrate but not conquered Ireland, relates the following anecdote in a speech delivered by him in the Conciliation Hall, Dublin, before the Loyal National Repeal Association,[13] March 31, 1845. "No matter," said Mr. O'CONNELL, "under what specious term it may disguise itself, slavery is still hideous. *It has a natural, an inevitable tendency to brutalize every noble faculty of man.* An American sailor, who was cast away on the shore of Africa, where he was kept in slavery for three years, was at the expiration of that period, found to be imbruted and stultified—he had lost all reasoning power; and having forgotten his native language, could only utter some savage gibberish between Arabic and English, which nobody could understand, and which even he himself found difficulty in pronouncing. So much for the humanizing influence of THE DOMESTIC INSTITUTION!" Admitting this to have been an extraordinary case of mental deterioration, it proves at least that the white slave can sink as low in the scale of humanity as the black one.

Mr. DOUGLASS has very properly chosen to write his own Narrative, in his own style, and according to the best of his ability, rather than to employ some one else. It is, therefore, entirely his own production; and, considering how long and dark was the career he had to run as a slave,—how few have been his opportunities to improve his mind since he broke his iron fetters,—it is, in my judgment, highly creditable to his head and heart. He who can peruse it without a tearful eye, a heaving breast, an afflicted spirit,—without being filled with an unutterable abhorrence of slavery and all its abettors, and animated with a determination to seek the immediate overthrow of that execrable system,—without trembling for the fate of this country in the hands of a righteous God,[14] who is ever on the side of the oppressed, and whose arm is not shortened that

---

[12]DANIEL O'CONNELL: An Irish Catholic political leader and abolitionist (1775–1847) sometimes called "the Liberator."
[13]LOYAL NATIONAL REPEAL ASSOCIATION: An organization, formed in 1840 by Daniel O'Connell, that advocated an independent Irish parliament.
[14]A RIGHTEOUS GOD: A reference to Thomas Jefferson's statement in *Notes on the State of Virginia* (1782, 1784) on the moral consequences of slavery: "I tremble for my country when I reflect that God is just."

it cannot save,[15]—must have a flinty heart, and be qualified to act the part of a trafficker "in slaves and the souls of men."[16] I am confident that it is essentially true in all its statements; that nothing has been set down in malice, nothing exaggerated, nothing drawn from the imagination; that it comes short of the reality, rather than overstates a single fact in regard to SLAVERY AS IT IS. The experience of FREDERICK DOUGLASS, as a slave, was not a peculiar one; his lot was not especially a hard one; his case may be regarded as a very fair specimen of the treatment of slaves in Maryland, in which State it is conceded that they are better fed and less cruelly treated than in Georgia, Alabama, or Louisiana. Many have suffered incomparably more, while very few on the plantations have suffered less, than himself. Yet how deplorable was his situation! what terrible chastisements were inflicted upon his person! what still more shocking outrages were perpetrated upon his mind! with all his noble powers and sublime aspirations, how like a brute was he treated, even by those professing to have the same mind in them that was in Christ Jesus! to what dreadful liabilities was he continually subjected! how destitute of friendly counsel and aid, even in his greatest extremities! how heavy was the midnight of woe which shrouded in blackness the last ray of hope, and filled the future with terror and gloom! what longings after freedom took possession of his breast, and how his misery augmented, in proportion as he grew reflective and intelligent,—thus demonstrating that a happy slave is an extinct man! how he thought, reasoned, felt, under the lash of the driver, with the chains upon his limbs! what perils he encountered in his endeavors to escape from his horrible doom! and how signal have been his deliverance and preservation in the midst of a nation of pitiless enemies!

This Narrative contains many affecting incidents, many passages of great eloquence and power; but I think the most thrilling one of them all is the description DOUGLASS gives of his feelings, as he stood soliloquizing respecting his fate, and the chances of his one day being a freeman, on the banks of the Chesapeake Bay—viewing the receding vessels as they flew with their white wings before the breeze, and apostrophizing them as animated by the living spirit of freedom. Who can read that passage,

---

[15]THAT IT CANNOT SAVE: Isaiah 50:2: "Wherefore, when I came, was there no man? when I called, was there none to answer? Is my hand shortened at all, that it cannot redeem? or have I no power to deliver? behold, at my rebuke I dry up the sea, I make the rivers a wilderness: their fish stinketh, because there is no water, and dieth for thirst."
[16]IN SLAVES AND THE SOULS OF MEN: Revelation 18:10–13: "Standing afar off for the fear of her torment, saying, Alas, alas, that great city Babylon, that mighty city! for in one hour is thy judgment come. / And the merchants of the earth shall weep and mourn over her; for no man buyeth their merchandise any more: / ...And cinnamon, and odours, and ointments, and frankincense, and wine, and oil, and fine flour, and wheat, and beasts, and sheep, and horses, and chariots, and slaves, and souls of men."

and be insensible to its pathos and sublimity? Compressed into it is a whole Alexandrian library[17] of thought, feeling, and sentiment—all that can, all that need be urged, in the form of expostulation, entreaty, rebuke, against that crime of crimes,—making man the property of his fellow-man! O, how accursed is that system, which entombs the godlike mind of man, defaces the divine image, reduces those who by creation were crowned with glory and honor to a level with four-footed beasts, and exalts the dealer in human flesh above all that is called God! Why should its existence be prolonged one hour? Is it not evil, only evil, and that continually? What does its presence imply but the absence of all fear of God, all regard for man, on the part of the people of the United States! Heaven speed its eternal overthrow!

So profoundly ignorant of the nature of slavery are many persons, that they are stubbornly incredulous whenever they read or listen to any recital of the cruelties which are daily inflicted on its victims. They do not deny that the slaves are held as property; but that terrible fact seems to convey to their minds no idea of injustice, exposure to outrage, or savage barbarity. Tell them of cruel scourgings, of mutilations and brandings, of scenes of pollution and blood, of the banishment of all light and knowledge, and they affect to be greatly indignant at such enormous exaggerations, such wholesale misstatements, such abominable libels on the character of the southern planters! As if all these direful outrages were not the natural results of slavery! As if it were less cruel to reduce a human being to the condition of a thing, than to give him a severe flagellation, or to deprive him of necessary food and clothing! As if whips, chains, thumb-screws, paddles, bloodhounds, overseers, drivers, patrols, were not all indispensable to keep the slaves down, and to give protection to their ruthless oppressors! As if, when the marriage institution is abolished, concubinage, adultery, and incest, must not necessary abound; when all the rights of humanity are annihilated, any barrier remains to protect the victim from the fury of the spoiler; when absolute power is assumed over life and liberty, it will not be wielded with destructive sway! Skeptics of this character abound in society. In some few instances, their incredulity arises from a want of reflection; but, generally, it indicates a hatred of the light, a desire to shield slavery from the assaults of its foes, a contempt of the colored race, whether bond or free. Such will try to discredit the shocking tales of slaveholding cruelty which are recorded in this truthful Narrative, but they will labor in vain. Mr. Douglass has frankly disclosed the place of his birth, the names of those who claimed ownership in his body and soul, and the names also of those

[17]ALEXANDRIAN LIBRARY: The great library at Alexandria, in Egypt.

who committed the crimes which he has alleged against them. His statements, therefore, may easily be disproved, if they are untrue.

In the course of his Narrative, he relates two instances of murderous cruelty,—in one of which a planter deliberately shot a slave belonging to a neighboring plantation, who had unintentionally gotten within his lordly domain in quest of fish; and in the other, an overseer blew out the brains of a slave who had fled to a stream of water to escape a bloody scourging. Mr. DOUGLASS states that in neither of these instances was any thing done by way of legal arrest or judicial investigation. The Baltimore American, of March 17, 1845, relates a similar case of atrocity, perpetrated with similar impunity—as follows:—*"Shooting a Slave.—* We learn, upon the authority of a letter from Charles county, Maryland, received by a gentleman of this city, that a young man, named Matthews, a nephew of General Matthews, and whose father, it is believed, holds an office at Washington, killed one of the slaves upon his father's farm by shooting him. The letter states that young Matthews had been left in charge of the farm; that he gave an order to the servant, which was disobeyed, when he proceeded to the house, *obtained a gun, and, returning, shot the servant.* He immediately, the letter continues, fled to his father's residence, where he still remains unmolested."—Let it never be forgotten, that no slaveholder or overseer can be convicted of any outrage perpetrated on the person of a slave, however diabolical it may be, on the testimony of colored witnesses, whether bond or free. By the slave code, they are adjudged to be as incompetent to testify against a white man, as though they were indeed a part of the brute creation. Hence, there is no legal protection in fact, whatever there may be in form, for the slave population; and any amount of cruelty may be inflicted on them with impunity. Is it possible for the human mind to conceive of a more horrible state of society?

The effect of a religious profession on the conduct of southern masters is vividly described in the following Narrative, and shown to be any thing but salutary. In the nature of the case, it must be in the highest degree pernicious. The testimony of Mr. DOUGLASS, on this point, is sustained by a cloud of witnesses, whose veracity is unimpeachable. "A slaveholder's profession of Christianity is a palpable imposture. He is a felon of the highest grade. He is a man-stealer. It is of no importance what you put in the other scale."

Reader! are you with the man-stealers in sympathy and purpose, or on the side of their down-trodden victims? If with the former, then are you the foe of God and man. If with the latter, what are you prepared to do and dare in their behalf? Be faithful, be vigilant, be untiring in your efforts to break every yoke, and let the oppressed go free. Come what may—cost what it may—inscribe on the banner which you unfurl to the breeze, as your religious and political motto—

"NO COMPROMISE WITH SLAVERY! NO UNION WITH SLAVEHOLDERS!"
Wm. Lloyd Garrison
Boston, May *1, 1845.*

LETTER FROM WENDELL PHILLIPS, ESQ.[18]

Boston, April 22, 1845.
My Dear Friend:
You remember the old fable of "The Man and the Lion," where the lion complained that he should not be so misrepresented "when the lions wrote history."

I am glad the time has come when the "lions write history." We have been left long enough to gather the character of slavery from the involuntary evidence of the masters. One might, indeed, rest sufficiently satisfied with what, it is evident, must be, in general, the results of such a relation, without seeking farther to find whether they have followed in every instance. Indeed, those who stare at the half-peck of corn a week, and love to count the lashes on the slave's back, are seldom the "stuff" out of which reformers and abolitionists are to be made. I remember that, in 1838, many were waiting for the results of the West India experiment,[19] before they could come into our ranks. Those "results" have come long ago; but, alas! few of that number have come with them, as converts. A man must be disposed to judge of emancipation by other tests than whether it has increased the produce of sugar,—and to have slavery for other reasons than because it starves men and whips women,—before he is ready to lay the first stone of his anti-slavery life.

I was glad to learn, in your story, how early the most neglected of God's children waken to a sense of their rights, and of the injustice done them. Experience is a keen teacher; and long before you had mastered your A B C, or knew where the "white sails" of the Chesapeake were bound, you began, I see, to gauge the wretchedness of the slave, not by his hunger and want, not by his lashes and toil, but by the cruel and blighting death which gathers over his soul.

[18]WENDELL PHILLIPS, ESQ.: An American reformer and orator (1811–1884) who frequently contributed to Garrison's newspaper *The Liberator*. He served as a delegate to the World Anti-Slavery Convention in London in 1840.
[19]THE WEST INDIA EXPERIMENT: The Abolition Act of August 28, 1833, emancipated slaves in the West Indies. The island of Barbados abolished slavery in 1834 and freed all slaves by 1838.

In connection with this, there is one circumstance which makes your recollections peculiarly valuable, and renders your early insight the more remarkable. You come from that part of the country where we are told slavery appears with its fairest features. Let us hear, then, what it is at its best estate—gaze on its bright side, if it has one; and then imagination may task her powers to add dark lines to the picture, as she travels southward to that (for the colored man) Valley of the Shadow of Death, where the Mississippi sweeps along.

Again, we have known you long, and can put the most entire confidence in your truth, candor, and sincerity. Every one who has heard you speak has felt, and, I am confident, every one who reads your book will feel, persuaded that you give them a fair specimen of the whole truth. No one-sided portrait,—no wholesale complaints,—but a strict justice done, whenever individual kindliness has neutralized, for a moment, the deadly system with which it was strangely allied. You have been with us, too, some years, and can fairly compare the twilight of rights, which your race enjoy at the North, with that "noon of night" under which they labor south of Mason and Dixon's line. Tell us whether, after all, the half-free colored man of Massachusetts is worse off than the pampered slave of the rice swamps!

In reading your life, no one can say that we have unfairly picked out some rare specimens of cruelty. We know that the bitter drops, which even you have drained from the cup, are no incidental aggravations, no individual ills, but such as must mingle always and necessarily in the lot of every slave. They are the essential ingredients, not the occasional results, of the system.

After all, I shall read your book with trembling for you. Some years ago, when you were beginning to tell me your real name and birthplace, you may remember I stopped you, and preferred to remain ignorant of all. With the exception of a vague description, so I continued, till the other day, when you read me your memoirs. I hardly knew, at the time, whether to thank you or not for the sight of them, when I reflected that it was still dangeorus, in Massachusetts, for honest men to tell their names! They say the fathers, in 1776, signed the Declaration of Independence with the halter about their necks. You, too, publish your declaration of freedom with danger compassing you around. In all the broad lands which the Constitution of the United States overshadows, there is no single spot,—however narrow or desolate,—where a fugitive slave can plant himself and say, "I am safe." The whole armory of Northern Law has no shield for you. I am free to say that, in your place, I should throw the MS. into the fire.

You, perhaps, may tell your story in safety, endeared as you are to so many warm hearts by rare gifts, and a still rare devotion of them to the service of others. But it will be owing only to your labors, and the fearless efforts of those who, trampling the laws and Constitution of the country under their feet, are determined that they will "hide the outcast,"[20] and that their hearts shall be, spite of the law, an asylum for the oppressed, if, some time or other, the humblest may stand in our streets, and bear witness in safety against the cruelties of which he has been the victim.

Yet it is sad to think, that these very throbbing hearts which welcome your story, and form your best safeguard in telling it, are all beating contrary to the "statute in such case made and provided." Go on, my dear friend, till you, and those who, like you, have been saved, so as by fire, from the dark prisonhouse, shall stereotype these free, illegal pulses into statutes; and New England, cutting loose from a blood-stained Union, shall glory in being the house of refuge for the oppressed;—till we no longer merely "hide the outcast," or make a merit of standing idly by while he is hunted in our midst; but, consecrating anew the soil of the Pilgrims as an asylum for the oppressed, proclaim our welcome to the slave so loudly, that the tones shall reach every hut in the Carolinas, and make the broken-hearted bondman leap up at the thought of old Massachusetts.

God speed the day!

Till then, and ever,
Yours truly,
Wendell Phillips

Chapter I

I was born in Tuckahoe, near Hillsborough, and about twelve miles from Easton, in Talbot county, Maryland. I have no accurate knowledge of my age, never having seen any authentic record containing it. By far the larger part of the slaves know as little of their ages as horses know of theirs, and it is the wish of most masters within my knowledge to keep their slaves thus ignorant. I do not remember to have ever met a slave who could tell of his birthday. They seldom come nearer to it than planting-time, harvest-time, cherry-time, spring-time, or fall-time. A want of information concerning my own was a source of unhappiness to me even during childhood. The white children could tell their ages. I could not tell why I ought to be deprived of the same privilege. I was not allowed to make any inquiries of my master concerning it. He deemed all such inquiries on the part of a slave improper and impertinent, and evidence of a restless

---

[20]HIDE THE OUTCAST: Isaiah 16:3: "Take counsel, execute judgment; make thy shadow as the night in the midst of the noonday; hide the outcasts; betray not him that wandereth."

spirit. The nearest estimate I can give makes me now between twenty-seven and twenty-eight years of age. I come to this, from hearing my master say, some time during 1835, I was about seventeen years old.

My mother was named Harriet Bailey. She was the daughter of Isaac and Betsey Bailey, both colored, and quite dark. My mother was of a darker complexion than either my grandmother or grandfather.

My father was a white man. He was admitted to be such by all I ever heard speak of my parentage. The opinion was also whispered that my master was my father; but of the correctness of this opinion, I know nothing; the means of knowing was withheld from me. My mother and I were separated when I was but an infant—before I knew her as my mother. It is a common custom, in the part of Maryland from which I ran away, to part children from their mothers at a very early age. Frequently, before the child has reached its twelfth month, its mother is taken from it, and hired out on some farm a considerable distance off, and the child is placed under the care of an old woman, too old for field labor. For what this separation is done, I do not know, unless it be to hinder the development of the child's affection toward its mother, and to blunt and destroy the natural affection of the mother for the child. This is the inevitable result.

I never saw my mother, to know her as such, more than four or five times in my life; and each of these times was very short in duration, and at night. She was hired by a Mr. Stewart, who lived about twelve miles from my home. She made her journeys to see me in the night, travelling the whole distance on foot, after the performance of her day's work. She was a field hand, and a whipping is the penalty of not being in the field at sunrise, unless a slave has special permission from his or her master to the contrary—a permission which they seldom get, and one that gives to him that gives it the proud name of being a kind master. I do not recollect of ever seeing my mother by the light of day. She was with me in the night. She would lie down with me, and get me to sleep, but long before I waked she was gone. Very little communication ever took place between us. Death soon ended what little we could have while she lived, and with it her hardships and suffering. She died when I was about seven years old, on one of my master's farms, near Lee's Mill. I was not allowed to be present during her illness, at her death, or burial. She was gone long before I knew anything about it. Never having enjoyed, to any considerable extent, her soothing presence, her tender and watchful care, I received the tidings of her death with much the same emotions I should have probably felt at the death of a stranger.

Called thus suddenly away, she left me without the slightest intimation of who my father was. The whisper that my master was my father, may or may not be true; and, true or false, it is of but little consequence to my purpose whilst the fact remains, in all its glaring odiousness, that slaveholders have ordained, and by law established, that the children of slave women shall in all cases follow the condition of their mothers; and this is done too obviously to administer to their own lusts, and make a gratification of their wicked desires profitable as well as pleasurable; for by this cunning arrangement, the slaveholder, in cases not a few, sustains to his slaves the double relation of master and father.

I know of such cases; and it is worthy of remark that such slaves invariably suffer greater hardships, and have more to contend with, than others. They are, in the first place, a constant offence to their mistress. She is ever disposed to find fault with them; they can seldom do anything to please her; she is never better pleased than when she sees them under the lash, especially when she suspects her husband of showing to his mulatto children favors which he withholds from his black slaves. The master is frequently compelled to sell this class of his slaves, out of deference to the feelings of his white wife; and, cruel as the deed may strike any one to be, for a man to sell his own children to human flesh-mongers, it is often the dictate of humanity for him to do so; for, unless he does this, he must not only whip them himself, but must stand by and see one white son tie up his brother, of but few shades darker complexion than himself, and ply the gory lash to his naked back; and if he lisp one word of disapproval, it is set down to his parental partiality, and only makes a bad matter worse, both for himself and the slave whom he would protect and defend.

Every year brings with it multitudes of this class of slaves. It was doubtless in consequence of a knowledge of this fact, that one great statesman of the south predicted the downfall of slavery by the inevitable laws of population. Whether this prophecy is ever fulfilled or not, it is nevertheless plain that a very different-looking class of people are springing up at the south, and are now held in slavery, from those originally brought to this country from Africa; and if their increase will do no other good, it will do away the force of the argument, that God cursed Ham,[21] and therefore American slavery is right. If the lineal descendants of Ham are alone to be scripturally enslaved, it is certain that slavery at the south must soon become unscriptural;

[21]GOD CURSED HAM: A reference to Genesis 9:20–27. "Canaan's curse" was used by some slavery advocates to justify the enslavement of Africans and individuals of African descent. Ham accidentally sees his father, Noah, in a state of "nakedness." Ham's brothers, Shem and Japheth, put a cloak on their shoulders and walk into Noah's tent backward to avoid also seeing him, and cover their father. When Noah awakens, he curses Ham's son, Canaan, for his father's transgression. "And he said, Cursed be Canaan; a servant of servants shall he be unto his brethren. / And he said, Blessed be the LORD God of Shem; and Canaan shall be his servant. / God shall enlarge Japheth, and he shall dwell in the tents of Shem; and Canaan shall be his servant."

for thousands are ushered into the world, annually, who, like myself, owe their existence to white fathers, and those fathers most frequently their own masters.

I have had two masters. My first master's name was Anthony. I do not remember his first name. He was generally called Captain Anthony—a title which, I presume, he acquired by sailing a craft on the Chesapeake Bay. He was not considered a rich slaveholder. He owned two or three farms, and about thirty slaves. His farms and slaves were under the care of an overseer. The overseer's name was Plummer. Mr. Plummer was a miserable drunkard, a profane swearer, and a savage monster. He always went armed with a cowskin[22] and a heavy cudgel. I have known him to cut and slash the women's heads so horribly, that even master would be enraged at his cruelty, and would threaten to whip him if he did not mind himself. Master, however, was not a humane slaveholder. It required extraordinary barbarity on the part of an overseer to affect him. He was a cruel man, hardened by a long life of slaveholding. He would at times seem to take great pleasure in whipping a slave. I have often been awakened at the dawn of day by the most heartrending shrieks of an old aunt of mine, whom he used to tie up to a joist, and whip upon her naked back till she was literally covered with blood. No words, no tears, no prayers, from his gory victim, seemed to move his iron heart from its bloody purpose. The louder she screamed, the harder he whipped; and where the blood ran fastest, there he whipped longest. He would whip her to make her scream, and whip her to make her hush; and not until overcome by fatigue, would he cease to swing the blood-clotted cowskin. I remember the first time I ever witnessed this horrible exhibition. I was quite a child, but I well remember it. I never shall forget it whilst I remember any thing. It was the first of a long series of such outrages, of which I was doomed to be a witness and a participant. It struck me with awful force. It was the bloodstained gate, the entrance to the hell of slavery, through which I was about to pass. It was a most terrible spectacle. I wish I could commit to paper the feelings with which I beheld it.

This occurence took place very soon after I went to live with my old master, and under the following circumstances. Aunt Hester went out one night,—where or for what I do not know,—and happened to be absent when my master desired her presence. He had ordered her not to go out evenings, and warned her that she must never let him catch her in company with a young man, who was paying attention to her belonging to Colonel Lloyd. The young man's named was Ned Roberts, generally

[22]COWSKIN: A whip of cowhide.

called Lloyd's Ned. Why master was so careful of her, may be safely left to conjecture. She was a woman of noble form, and of graceful proportions, having very few equals, and fewer superiors, in personal appearance, among the colored or white women of our neighborhood.

Aunt Hester had not only disobeyed his orders in going out, but had been found in company with Lloyd's Ned; which circumstance, I found, from what he said while whipping her, was the chief offence. Had he been a man of pure morals himself, he might have been thought interested in protecting the innocence of my aunt; but those who knew him will not suspect him of any such virtue. Before he commenced whipping Aunt Hester, he took her into the kitchen, and stripped her from neck to waist, leaving her neck, shoulders, and back, entirely naked. He then told her to cross her hands, calling her at the same time a d—d b—h. After crossing her hands, he tied them with a strong rope, and led her to a stool under a large hook in the joist, put in for the purpose. He made her get upon the stool, and tied her hands to the hook. She now stood fair for his infernal purpose. Her arms were stretched up at their full length, so that she stood upon the ends of her toes. He then said to her, "Now, you d—d b—h, I'll learn you how to disobey my orders!" and after rolling up his sleeves, he commenced to lay on the heavy cowskin, and soon the warm, red blood (amid heart-rending shrieks from her, and horrid oaths from him) came dripping to the floor. I was so terrified and horror-stricken at the sight, that I hid myself in a closet, and dared not venture out till long after the bloody transaction was over. I expected it would be my turn next. It was all new to me. I had never seen any thing like it before. I had always lived with my grandmother on the outskirts of the plantation, where she was put to raise the children of the younger women. I had therefore been, until now, out of the way of the bloody scenes that often occurred on the plantation.

Chapter II

My master's family consisted of two sons, Andrew and Richard; one daughter, Lucretia, and her husband, Captain Thomas Auld. They lived in one house, upon the home plantation of Colonel Edward Lloyd. My master was Colonel Lloyd's clerk and superintendent. He was what might be called the overseer of the overseers. I spent two years of childhood on this plantation in my old master's family. It was here that I witnessed the bloody transaction recorded in the first chapter; and as I received my first impressions of slavery on this plantation, I will give some description of it, and of slavery as it there existed. The plantation is about twelve miles north of Easton, in Talbot county, and is situated on the border of Miles River. The principal products raised upon it were tobacco, corn, and wheat. These were raised in great abundance; so that, with the products of this and the other farms belonging to him, he was able to keep in almost constant employment a large sloop, in carrying them to market at Baltimore. This sloop was named Sally Lloyd, in honor of one of the colonel's daughters. My master's son-in-law, Captain Auld, was master of the vessel; she was otherwise manned by the colonel's own slaves. Their names were Peter, Isaac, Rich, and Jake. These were esteemed very highly by the other slaves, and looked upon as the privileged ones of the plantation; for it was no small affair, in the eyes of the slaves, to be allowed to see Baltimore.

Colonel Lloyd kept from three to four hundred slaves on his home plantation, and owned a large number more on the neighboring farms belonging to him. The names of the farms nearest to the home plantation were Wye Town and New Design. "Wye Town" was under the overseership of a man named Noah Willis. New Design was under the overseership of a Mr. Townsend. The overseers of these, and all the rest of the farms, numbering over twenty, received advice and direction from the managers of the home plantation. This was the great business place. It was the seat of government for the whole twenty farms. All disputes among the overseers were settled here. If a slave was convicted of any high misdemeanor, became unmanageable, or evinced a determination to run away, he was brought immediately here, severely whipped, put on board the sloop, carried to Baltimore, and sold to Austin Woolfolk, or some other slave-trader, as a warning to the slaves remaining.

Here, too, the slaves of all the other farms received their monthly allowance of food, and their yearly clothing. The men and women slaves received, as their monthly allowance of food, eight pounds of pork, or its equivalent in fish, and one bushel of corn meal. Their yearly clothing consisted of two coarse linen shirts, one pair of linen trousers, like the shirts, one jacket, one pair of trousers for winter, made of coarse negro cloth, one pair of stockings, and one pair of shoes; the whole of which could not have cost more than seven dollars. The allowance of the slave children was given to their mothers, or the old women having the care of them. The children unable to work in the field had neither shoes, stockings, jackets, nor trousers, given to them; their clothing consisted of two coarse linen shirts per year. When these failed them, they went naked until the next allowance-day. Children from seven to ten years old, of both sexes, almost naked, might be seen at all seasons of the year.

There were no beds given the slaves, unless one coarse blanket be considered such, and none but the men and women had these. This, however, is not considered a very great privation. They find less difficulty from the want of beds, than from the want of time to sleep; for when their day's work in the field is done, the most of them having their washing, mending, and cooking to do, and having few or none of the ordinary facilities for doing either of these, very many of their sleeping hours are consumed in preparing for the field the coming day; and when this is done, old and young, male and female, married and single, drop down side by side, on one common bed,—the cold, damp floor,—each covering himself or herself with their miserable blankets; and here they sleep till they are summoned to the field by the driver's horn. At the sound of this, all must rise, and be off to the field. There must be no halting; every one must be at his or her post; and woe betides them who hear not this morning summons to the field; for if they are not awakened by the sense of hearing, they are by the sense of feeling: no age nor sex finds any favor. Mr. Severe, the overseer, used to stand by the door of the quarter, armed with a large hickory stick and heavy cowskin, ready to whip any one who was so unfortunate as not to hear, or, from any other cause, was prevented from being ready to start for the field at the sound of the horn.

Mr. Severe was rightly named: he was a cruel man. I have seen him whip a woman, causing the blood to run half an hour at the time; and this, too, in the midst of her crying children, pleading for their mother's release. He seemed to take pleasure in manifesting his fiendish barbarity. Added to his cruelty, he was a profane swearer. It was enough to chill the blood and stiffen the hair of an ordinary man to hear him talk. Scarce a sentence escaped him but that was commenced or concluded by some horrid oath. The field was the place to witness his cruelty and profanity. His presence made it both the field of blood and of blasphemy. From the rising till the going down of the sun, he was cursing, raving, cutting, and slashing among the slaves of the field, in the most frightful manner. His career was short. He died very soon after I went to Colonel Lloyd's; and he died as he lived, uttering, with his dying groans, bitter curses and horrid oaths. His death was regarded by the slaves as the result of a merciful providence.

Mr. Severe's place was filled by a Mr. Hopkins. He was a very different man. He was less cruel, less profane, and made less noise, than Mr. Severe. His course was characterized by no extraordinary demonstrations of cruelty. He whipped, but seemed to take no pleasure in it. He was called by the slaves a good overseer.

The home plantation of Colonel Lloyd wore the appearance of a country village. All the mechanical operations for all the farms were performed here. The shoemaking and mending, the black-smithing, cartwrighting, coopering, weaving, and grain-grinding, were all performed by the slaves on the home plantation. The whole place wore a business-like aspect very unlike the neighboring farms. The number of houses, too, conspired to give it advantage over the neighboring farms. It was called by the slaves the *Great House Farm.* Few privileges were esteemed higher, by the slaves of the out-farms, than that of being selected to do errands at the Great House Farm. It was associated in their minds with greatness. A representative could not be prouder of his election to a seat in the American Congress, than a slave on one of the out-farms would be of his election to do errands at the Great House Farm. They regarded it as evidence of great confidence reposed in them by their overseers; and it was on this account, as well as a constant desire to be out of the field from under the driver's lash, that they esteemed it a high privilege, one worth careful living for. He was called the smartest and most trusty fellow, who had this honor conferred upon him the most frequently. The competitors for this office sought as diligently to please their overseers, as the office-seekers in the political parties seek to please and deceive the people. The same traits of character might be seen in Colonel Lloyd's slaves, as are seen in the slaves of the political parties.

The slaves selected to go to the Great House Farm, for the monthly allowance for themselves and their fellow-slaves, were peculiarly enthusiastic. While on their way, they would make the dense old woods, for miles around, reverberate with their wild songs, revealing at once the highest joy and the deepest sadness. They would compose and sing as they went along, consulting neither time nor tune. The thought that came up, came out—if not in the word, in the sound;—and as frequently in the one as in the other. They would sometimes sing the most pathetic sentiment in the most rapturous tone, and the most rapturous sentiment in the most pathetic tone. Into all of their songs they would manage to weave something of the Great House Farm. Especially would they do this, when leaving home. They would then sing most exultingly the following words:—

> "*I am going away to the Great House Farm!*
> *O, yea! O, yea! O!*"

This they would sing, as a chorus, to words which to many would seem unmeaning jargon, but which, nevertheless, were full of meaning to themselves. I have sometimes thought that the mere hearing of those songs would do more to impress some minds with the horrible character of slavery, than the reading of whole volumes of philosophy on the subject could do.

I did not, when a slave, understand the deep meaning of those rude and apparently incoherent songs. I was myself within the circle; so that I neither saw nor heard as those without might see and hear. They told a tale of woe which was then altogether beyond my feeble comprehension; they were tones loud, long, and deep; they breathed the prayer and complaint of souls boiling over with the bitterest anguish. Every tone was a testimony against slavery, and a prayer to God for deliverance from chains. The hearing of those wild notes always depressed my spirit, and filled me with ineffable sadness. I have frequently found myself in tears while hearing them. The mere recurrence to those songs, even now, afflicts me; and while I am writing these lines, an expression of feeling has already found its way down my cheek. To those songs I trace my first glimmering conception of the dehumanizing character of slavery. I can never get rid of that conception. Those songs still follow me, to deepen my hatred of slavery, and quicken my sympathies for my brethren in bonds. If any one wishes to be impressed with the soul-killing effects of slavery, let him go to Colonel Lloyd's plantation, and, on allowance-day, place himself in the deep pine woods, and there let him, in silence analyze the sounds that shall pass through the chambers of his soul,—and if he is not thus impressed, it will only be because "there is no flesh in his obdurate heart."[23]

I have often been utterly astonished, since I came to the north, to find persons who could speak of the singing, among slaves, as evidence of their contentment and happiness. It is impossible to conceive of a greater mistake. Slaves sing most when they are most unhappy. The songs of the slave represent the sorrows of his heart; and he is relieved by them, only as an aching heart is relieved by its tears. At least, such is my experience. I have often sung to drown my sorrow, but seldom to express my happiness. Crying for joy, and singing for joy, were alike uncommon to me while in the jaws of slavery. The singing of a man cast away upon a desolate island might be as appropriately considered as evidence of contentment and happiness, as the singing of a slave; the songs of the one and of the other are prompted by the same emotion.

CHAPTER III

Colonel Lloyd kept a large and finely cultivated garden, which afforded almost constant employment for four men, besides the chief gardener (Mr. M'Durmond). This garden was probably the greatest attraction of

[23]THERE IS NO FLESH IN HIS OBDURATE HEART: From "The Time-Piece," Book II of *The Task* (1785), a poem by William Cowper (1731–1800).

the place. During the summer months, people came from far and near—from Baltimore, Easton, and Annapolis—to see it. It abounded in fruits of almost every description, from the hardy apple of the north to the delicate orange of the south. This garden was not the least source of trouble on the plantation. Its excellent fruit was quite a temptation to the hungry swarms of boys, as well as the older slaves, belonging to the colonel, few of whom had the virtue or the vice to resist it. Scarcely a day passed, during the summer, but that some slave had to take the lash for stealing fruit. The colonel had to resort to all kinds of strategems to keep his slaves out of the garden. The last and most successful one was that of tarring his fence all around, after which, if a slave was caught with any tar upon his person, it was deemed sufficient proof that he had either been into the garden, or had tried to get in. In either case, he was severely whipped by the chief gardener. This plan worked well; the slaves became as fearful of tar as of the lash. They seemed to realize the impossiblity of touching *tar* without being defiled.

The colonel also kept a splendid riding equipage. His stable and carriage-house presented the appearance of some of our large city livery establishments. His horses were of the finest form and noblest blood. His carriage-house contained three splendid coaches, three or four gigs, besides dearborns and barouches[24] of the most fashionable style.

This establishment was under the care of two slaves—old Barney and young Barney—father and son. To attend to this establishment was their sole work. But it was by no means an easy employment; for in nothing was Colonel Lloyd more particular than in the management of his horses. The slightest inattention to these was unpardonable, and was visited upon those, under whose care they were placed, with the severest punishment; no excuse could shield them, if the colonel only suspected any want of attention to his horses—a supposition which he frequently indulged, and one which, of course, made the office of old and young Barney a very trying one. They never knew when they were safe from punishment. They were frequently whipped when least deserving, and escaped whipping when most deserving it. Every thing depended upon the looks of the horses, and the state of Colonel Lloyd's own mind when his horses were brought to him for use. If a horse did not move fast enough, or hold his head high enough, it was owing to some fault of his keepers. It was painful to stand near the stabledoor, and hear the various complaints against the keepers when a horse was taken out for use. "This horse has not had proper attention. He has not been sufficiently rubbed and curried, or he has not been properly fed; his food was too wet or too dry; he got it too

[24]GIGS, BESIDES DEARBORNS AND BAROUCHES: Types of horse-drawn carriages.

soon or too late; he was too hot or too cold; he had too much hay, and not enough of grain; or he had too much grain, and not enough of hay; instead of old Barney's attending to the horse, he had very improperly left it to his son." To all these complaints, no matter how unjust, the slave must answer never a word. Colonel Lloyd could not brook any contradiction from a slave. When he spoke, a slave must stand, listen, and tremble; and such was literally the case. I have seen Colonel Lloyd make old Barney, a man between fifty and sixty years of age, uncover his bald head, kneel down upon the cold, damp ground, and receive upon his naked and toil-worn shoulders more than thirty lashes at the time. Colonel Lloyd had three sons—Edward, Murray, and Daniel,—and three sons-in-law, Mr. Winder, Mr. Nicholson, and Mr. Lowndes. All of these lived at the Great House Farm, and enjoyed the luxury of whipping the servants when they pleased, from old Barney down to William Wilkes, the coach-driver. I have seen Winder make one of the house-servants stand off from him a suitable distance to be touched with the end of his whip, and at every stroke raise great ridges upon his back.

To describe the wealth of Colonel Lloyd would be almost equal to describing the riches of Job.[25] He kept from ten to fifteen house-servants. He was said to own a thousand slaves, and I think this estimate quite within the truth. Colonel Lloyd owned so many that he did not know them when he saw them; nor did all the slaves of the out-farms know him. It is reported of him, that, while riding along the road one day, he met a colored man, and addressed him in the usual manner of speaking to colored people on the public highways of the south: "Well, boy, whom do you belong to?" "To Colonel Lloyd," replied the slave. "Well, does the colonel treat you well?" "No, sir," was the ready reply. "What, does he work you too hard?" "Yes, sir." "Well, don't he give you enough to eat?" "Yes, sir, he gives me enough, such as it is."

The colonel, after ascertaining where the slave belonged, rode on; the man also went on about his business, not dreaming that he had been conversing with his master. He thought, said, and heard nothing more of the matter, until two or three weeks afterwards. The poor man was then informed by his overseer that, for having found fault with his master, he was now to be sold to a Georgia trader. He was immediately chained and handcuffed; and thus, without a moment's warning, he was snatched away, and forever sundered, from his family and friends, by a hand more unrelenting than death. This is the penalty of telling the truth, of telling the simple truth, in answer to a series of plain questions.

25JOB: The biblical Job is a wealthy man whose righteousness is tested by God when everything he owns is taken from him.

It is partly in consequence of such facts, that slaves, when inquired of as to their condition and the character of their masters, almost universally say they are contented, and that their masters are kind. The slaveholders have been known to send in spies among their slaves, to ascertain their views and feelings in regard to their condition. The frequency of this has had the effect to establish among the slaves the maxim, that a still tongue makes a wise head. They suppress the truth rather than take the consequences of telling it, and in so doing prove themselves a part of the human family. If they have any thing to say of their masters, it is generally in their masters' favor, especially when speaking to an untried man. I have been frequently asked, when a slave, if I had a kind master, and do not remember ever to have given a negative answer; nor did I, in pursuing this course, consider myself as uttering what was absolutely false; for I always measured the kindness of my master by the standard of kindness set up among slaveholders around us. Moreover, slaves are like other people, and imbibe prejudices quite common to others. They think their own better than that of others. Many, under the influence of this prejudice, think their own masters are better than the masters of other slaves; and this, too, in some cases, when the very reverse is true. Indeed, it is not uncommon for slaves even to fall out and quarrel among themselves about the relative goodness of their masters, each contending for the superior goodness of his own over that of the others. At the very same time, they mutually execrate their masters when viewed separately. It was so on our plantation. When Colonel Lloyd's slaves met the slaves of Jacob Jepson, they seldom parted without a quarrel about their masters; Colonel Lloyd's slaves contending that he was the richest, and Mr. Jepson's slaves that he was the smartest, and most of a man. Colonel Lloyd's slaves would boast his ability to buy and sell Jacob Jepson. Mr. Jepson's slaves would boast his ability to whip Colonel Lloyd. These quarrels would almost always end in a fight between the parties, and those that whipped were supposed to have gained the point at issue. They seemed to think that the greatness of their masters was transferable to themselves. It was considered as being bad enough to be a slave; but to be a poor man's slave was deemed a disgrace indeed!

CHAPTER IV

Mr. Hopkins remained but a short time in the office of overseer. Why his career was so short, I do not know, but suppose he lacked the necessary severity to suit Colonel Lloyd. Mr. Hopkins was succeeded by Mr. Austin Gore, a man possessing, in an eminent degree, all those traits of character indispensable to what is called a first-rate overseer. Mr. Gore had served Colonel Lloyd, in the capacity of overseer, upon one of the out-farms, and had shown himself worthy of the high station of overseer upon the home or Great House Farm.

Mr. Gore was proud, ambitious, and persevering. He was artful, cruel, and obdurate. He was just the man for such a place, and it was just the place for such a man. It afforded scope for the full exercise of all his powers, and he seemed to be perfectly at home in it. He was one of those who could torture the slightest look, word, or gesture, on the part of the slave, into impudence, and would treat it accordingly. There must be no answering back to him; no explanation was allowed a slave, showing himself to have been wrongfully accused. Mr. Gore acted fully up to the maxim laid down by slaveholders,—"It is better that a dozen slaves suffer under the lash, than that the overseer should be convicted, in the presence of the slaves, of having been at fault." No matter how innocent a slave might be—it availed him nothing, when accused by Mr. Gore of any misdemeanor. To be accused was to be convicted, and to be convicted was to be punished; the one always following the other with immutable certainty. To escape punishment was to escape accusation; and few slaves had the fortune to do either, under the overseership of Mr. Gore. He was just proud enough to demand the most debasing homage of the slave, and quite servile enough to crouch, himself, at the feet of the master. He was ambitious enough to be contented with nothing short of the highest rank of overseers, and persevering enough to reach the height of his ambition. He was cruel enough to inflict the severest punishment, artful enough to descend to the lowest trickery, and obdurate enough to be insensible to the voice of a reproving conscience. He was, of all the overseers, the most dreaded by the slaves. His presence was painful; his eye flashed confusion; and seldom was his sharp, shrill voice heard, without producing horror and trembling in their ranks.

Mr. Gore was a grave man, and though a young man, he indulged in no jokes, said no funny words, seldom smiled. His words were in perfect keeping with his looks, and his looks were in perfect keeping with his words. Overseers will sometimes indulge in a witty word, even with the slaves; not so with Mr. Gore. He spoke but to command, and commanded but to be obeyed; he dealt sparingly with his words, and bountifully with his whip, never using the former where the latter would answer as well. When he whipped, he seemed to do so from a sense of duty, and feared no consequences. He did nothing reluctantly, no matter how disagreeable; always at his post, never inconsistent. He never promised but to fulfil. He was, in a word, a man of the most inflexible firmness and stone-like coolness.

His savage barbarity was equalled only by the consummate coolness with which he committed the grossest and most savage deeds upon the slaves under his charge. Mr. Gore once undertook to whip one of Colonel Lloyd's slaves, by the name of Demby. He had given Demby but few stripes, when, to get rid of the scourging, he ran and plunged himself into a creek, and stood there at the depth of his shoulders, refusing to come out. Mr. Gore told him that he would give him three calls, and that, if he did not come out at the third call, he would shoot him. The first call was given. Demby made no response, but stood his ground. The second and third calls were given with the same result. Mr. Gore then, without consultation or deliberation with any one, not even giving Demby an additional call, raised his musket to his face, taking deadly aim at his standing victim, and in an instant poor Demby was no more. His mangled body sank out of sight, and blood and brains marked the water where he had stood.

A thrill of horror flashed though every soul upon the plantation, excepting Mr. Gore. He alone seemed cool and collected. He was asked by Colonel Lloyd and my old master, why he resorted to this extraordinary expedient. His reply was, (as well as I can remember,) that Demby had become unmanageable. He was setting a dangerous example to the other slaves,—one which, if suffered to pass without some such demonstration on his part, would finally lead to the total subversion of all rule and order upon the plantation. He argued that if one slave refused to be corrected, and escaped with his life, the other slaves would soon copy the example; the result of which would be, the freedom of the slaves, and the enslavement of the whites. Mr. Gore's defence was satisfactory. He was continued in his station as overseer upon the home plantation. His fame as an overseer went abroad. His horrid crime was not even submitted to judicial investigation. It was committed in the presence of slaves, and they of course could neither institute a suit, nor testify against him; and thus the guilty perpetrator of one of the bloodiest and most foul murders goes unwhipped of justice, and uncensured by the community in which he lives. Mr. Gore lived in St. Michael's, Talbot county, Maryland, when I left there; and if he is still alive, he very probably lives there now; and if so, he is now, as he was then, as highly esteemed and as much respected as though his guilty soul had not been stained with his brother's blood.

I speak advisedly when I say this,—that killing a slave, or any colored person, in Talbot county, Maryland, is not treated as a crime, either by the courts or the community. Mr. Thomas Lanman, of St. Michael's, killed two slaves, one of whom he killed with a hatchet, by knocking his brains out. He used to boast of the commission of the awful and bloody deed. I have heard him do so laughingly, saying, among other things, that he was the only benefactor of his country in the company, and that when others would do as much as he had done, we should be relieved of "the d—d niggers."

The wife of Mr. Giles Hicks, living but a short distance from where I used to live, murdered my wife's cousin, a young girl between fifteen and sixteen years of age, mangling her person in the most horrible manner, breaking her nose and breastbone with a stick, so that the poor girl expired in a few hours afterward. She was immediately buried, but had not been in her untimely grave but a few hours before she was taken up and examined by the coroner, who decided that she had come to her death by severe beating. The offence for which this girl was thus murdered was this:—She had been set that night to mind Mrs. Hicks's baby, and during the night she fell asleep, and the baby cried. She, having lost her rest for several night previous, did not hear the crying. They were both in the room with Mrs. Hicks. Mrs. Hicks, finding the girl slow to move, jumped from her bed, seized an oak stick of wood by the fireplace, and with it broke the girl's nose and breastbone, and thus ended her life. I will not say that this most horrid murder produced no sensation in the community. It did produce sensation, but not enough to bring the murderess to punishment. There was a warrant issued for her arrest, but it was never served. Thus she escaped not only punishment, but even the pain of being arraigned before a court for her horrid crime.

Whilst I am detailing bloody deeds which took place during my stay on Colonel Lloyd's plantation, I will briefly narrate another, which occurred about the same time as the murder of Demby by Mr. Gore.

Colonel Lloyd's slaves were in the habit of spending a part of their nights and Sundays in fishing for oysters, and in this way made up the deficiency of their scanty allowance. An old man belonging to Colonel Lloyd, while thus engaged, happened to get beyond the limits of Colonel Lloyd's, and on the premises of Mr. Beal Bondly. At this trespass, Mr. Bondly took offense, and with his musket came down to the shore, and blew its deadly contents into the poor old man.

Mr. Bondly came over to see Colonel Lloyd the next day, whether to pay him for his property, or to justify himself in what he had done, I know not. At any rate, this whole fiendish transaction was soon hushed up. There was very little said about it at all, and nothing done. It was a common saying, even among little white boys, that it was worth a half-cent to kill a "nigger," and a half-cent to bury one.

CHAPTER V

As to my own treatment while I lived on Colonel Lloyd's plantation, it was very similar to that of the other slave children. I was not old enough to work in the field, and there being little else than field work to do, I had a great deal of leisure time. The most I had to do was to drive up the cows at evening, keep the fowls out of the garden, keep the front yard clean, and run of errands for my old master's daughter, Mrs. Lucretia Auld. The most of my leisure time I spent in helping Master Daniel Lloyd in finding his birds, after he had shot them. My connection with Master Daniel was of some advantage to me. He became quite attached to me, and was a sort of protector of me. He would not allow the older boys to impose upon me, and would divide his cakes with me.

I was seldom whipped by my old master, and suffered little from any thing else than hunger and cold. I suffered much from hunger, but much more from cold. In hottest summer and coldest winter, I was kept almost naked—no shoes, no stockings, no jacket, no trousers, nothing on but a coarse tow linen shirt, reaching only to my knees. I had no bed. I must have perished with cold, but that, the coldest nights, I used to steal a bag which was used for carrying corn to the mill. I would crawl into this bag, and there sleep on the cold, damp, clay floor, with my head in and feet out. My feet have been so cracked with the frost, that the pen with which I am writing might be laid in the gashes.

We were not regularly allowanced. Our food was coarse corn meal boiled. This was called *mush*. It was put into a large wooden tray or trough, and set down upon the ground. The children were then called, like so many pigs, and like so many pigs they would come and devour the mush; some with oyster-shells, others with pieces of shingle, some with naked hands, and none with spoons. He that ate fastest got most; he that was strongest secured the best place; and few left the trough satisfied.

I was probably between seven and eight years old when I left Colonel Lloyd's plantation. I left it with joy. I shall never forget the ecstasy with which I received the intelligence that my old master (Anthony) had determined to let me go to Baltimore, to live with Mr. Hugh Auld, brother to my old master's son-in-law, Captain Thomas Auld. I received this information about three days before my departure. They were three of the happiest days I ever enjoyed. I spent the most part of all these three days in the creek, washing off the plantation scurf,[26] and preparing myself for my departure.

---

[26]SCURF: Foul flakes or scales.

The pride of appearance which this would indicate was not my own. I spent the time in washing, not so much because I wished to, but because Mrs. Lucretia had told me I must get all the dead skin off my feet and knees before I could go to Baltimore; for the people in Baltimore were very cleanly, and would laugh at me if I looked dirty. Besides, she was going to give me a pair of trousers, which I should not put on unless I got all the dirt off me. The thought of owning a pair of trousers was great indeed! It was almost a sufficient motive, not only to make me take off what would be called by pigdrovers the mange, but the skin itself. I went at it in good earnest, working for the first time with the hope of reward.

The ties that ordinarily bind children to their homes were all suspended in my case. I found no severe trial in my departure. My home was charmless; it was not home to me; on parting from it, I could not feel that I was leaving any thing which I could have enjoyed by staying. My mother was dead, my grandmother lived far off, so that I seldom saw her. I had two sisters and one brother, that lived in the same house with me; but the early separation of us from our mother had well nigh blotted the fact of our relationship from our memories. I looked for home elsewhere, and was confident of finding none which I should relish less than the one which I was leaving. If, however, I found in my new home hardship, hunger, whipping, and nakedness, I had the consolation that I should not have escaped any one of them by staying. Having already had more than a taste of them in the house of my old master, and having endured them there, I very naturally inferred my ability to endure them elsewhere, and especially at Baltimore; for I had something of the feeling about Baltimore that is expressed in the proverb, that "being hanged in England is preferable to dying a natural death in Ireland." I had the strongest desire to see Baltimore. Cousin Tom, though not fluent in speech, had inspired me with that desire by his eloquent description of the place. I could never point out any thing at the Great House, no matter how beautiful or powerful, but that he had seen something at Baltimore far exceeding, both in beauty and strength, the object which I pointed out to him. Even the Great House itself, with all its pictures, was far inferior to many buildings in Baltimore. So strong was my desire, that I thought a gratification of it would fully compensate for whatever loss of comforts I should sustain by the exchange. I left without a regret, and with the highest hopes of future happiness.

We sailed out of Miles River for Baltimore on a Saturday morning. I remember only the day of the week, for at that time I had no knowledge of the days of the month, nor the months of the year. On setting sail, I walked aft, and gave to Colonel Lloyd's plantation what I hoped would be the last look. I then placed myself in the bows of the sloop, and there spent the remainder of the day in looking ahead, interesting myself in what was in the distance rather than in things near by or behind.

In the afternoon of that day, we reached Annapolis, the capital of the State. We stopped but a few moments, so that I had no time to go on shore. It was the first large town that I had ever seen, and though it would look small compared with some of our New England factory villages, I thought it a wonderful place for its size—more imposing even than the Great House Farm!

We arrived at Baltimore early on Sunday morning, landing at Smith's Wharf, not far from Bowley's Wharf. We had on board the sloop a large flock of sheep; and after aiding in driving them to the slaughterhouse of Mr. Curtis on Louden Slater's Hill, I was conducted by Rich, one of the hands belonging on board of the sloop to my new home in Alliciana Street, near Mr. Gardner's ship-yard, on Fells Point.

Mr. and Mrs. Auld were both at home, and met me at the door with their little son Thomas, to take care of whom I had been given. And here I saw what I had never seen before; it was a white face beaming with the most kindly emotions; it was the face of my new mistress, Sophia Auld. I wish I could describe the rapture that flashed through my soul as I beheld it. It was a new and strange sight to me, brightening up my pathway with the light of happiness. Little Thomas was told, there was his Freddy,—and I was told to take care of little Thomas; and thus I entered upon the duties of my new home with the most cheering prospect ahead.

I looked upon my departure from Colonel Lloyd's plantation as one of the most interesting events of my life. It is possible, and even quite probable, that but for the mere circumstance of being removed from that plantation to Baltimore, I should have to-day, instead of being here seated by my own table, in the enjoyment of freedom and the happiness of home, writing this Narrative, been confined in the galling chains of slavery. Going to live at Baltimore laid the foundation, and opened the gateway, to all my subsequent prosperity. I have ever regarded it as the first plain manifestation of that kind providence which has ever since attended me, and marked my life with so many favors. I regarded the selection of myself as being somewhat remarkable. There were a number of slave children that might have been sent from the plantation to Baltimore. There were those younger, those older, and those of the same age. I was chosen from among them all, and was the first, last, and only choice.

I may be deemed superstitious, and even egotistical, in regarding this event as a special interposition of divine Providence in my favor.

But I should be false to the earliest sentiments of my soul, if I suppressed the opinion. I prefer to be true to myself, even at the hazard of incurring the ridicule of others, rather than to be false, and incur my own abhorrence. From my earliest recollection, I date the entertainment of a deep conviction that slavery would not always be able to hold me within its foul embrace; and in the darkest hours of my career in slavery, this living word of faith and spirit of hope departed not from me, but remained like ministering angels to cheer me through the gloom. This good spirit was from God, and to him I offer thanksgiving and praise.

CHAPTER VI

My new mistress proved to be all she appeared when I first met her at the door,—a woman of the kindest heart and finest feelings. She had never had a slave under her control previously to myself, and prior to her marriage she had been dependent upon her own industry for a living. She was by trade a weaver; and by constant application to her business, she had been in a good degree preserved from the blighting and dehumanizing effects of slavery. I was utterly astonished at her goodness. I scarcely knew how to behave towards her. She was entirely unlike any other white woman I had ever seen. I could not approach her as I was accustomed to approach other white ladies. My early instruction was all out of place. The crouching servility, usually so acceptable a quality in a slave, did not answer when manifested toward her. Her favor was not gained by it; she seemed to be disturbed by it. She did not deem it impudent or unmannerly for a slave to look her in the face. The meanest slave was put fully at ease in her presence, and none left without feeling better for having seen her. Her face was made of heavenly smiles, and her voice of tranquil music.

But, alas! this kind heart had but a short time to remain such. The fatal poison of irresponsible power was already in her hands, and soon commenced its infernal work. That cheerful eye, under the influence of slavery, soon became red with rage; that voice, made all of sweet accord, changed to one of harsh and horrid discord; and that angelic face gave place to that of a demon.

Very soon after I went to live with Mr. and Mrs. Auld, she kindly commenced to teach me the A, B, C. After I had learned this, she assisted me in learning to spell words of three or four letters. Just at this point of my progress, Mr. Auld found out what was going on, and at once forbade Mrs. Auld to instruct me further, telling her, among other things, that it was unlawful, as well as unsafe, to teach a slave to read. To use his own words further, he said, "If you give a nigger an inch, he will take an ell.[27] A nigger should know nothing but to obey his master—to do as he is told to do. Learning would *spoil* the best nigger in the world. Now," said he, "if you teach that nigger (speaking of myself) how to read, there would be no keeping him. It would forever unfit him to be a slave. He would at once become unmanageable, and of no value to his master. As to himself, it could do him no good, but a great deal of harm. It would make him discontented and unhappy." These words sank deep into my heart, stirred up sentiments within that lay slumbering, and called into existence an entirely new train of thought. It was a new and special revelation, explaining dark and mysterious things, with which my youthful understanding had struggled, but struggled in vain. I now understood what had been to me a most perplexing difficulty—to wit, the white man's power to enslave the black man. It was a grand achievement, and I prized it highly. From that moment, I understood the pathway from slavery to freedom. It was just what I wanted, and I got it at a time when I the least expected it. Whilst I was saddened by the thought of losing the aid of my kind mistress, I was gladdened by the invaluable instruction which, by the merest accident, I had gained from my master. Though conscious of the difficulty of learning without a teacher, I set out with high hope, and a fixed purpose, at whatever cost of trouble, to learn how to read. The very decided manner with which he spoke, and strove to impress his wife with the evil consequences of giving me instruction, served to convince me that he was deeply sensible of the truths he was uttering. It gave me the best assurance that I might rely with the utmost confidence on the results which, he said, would flow from teaching me to read. What he most dreaded, that I most desired. What he most loved, that I most hated. That which to him was a great evil, to be carefully shunned, was to me a great good, to be diligently sought; and the argument which he so warmly urged, against my learning to read, only served to inspire me with a desire and determination to learn. In learning to read, I owe almost as much to the bitter opposition of my master, as to the kindly aid of my mistress. I acknowledge the benefit of both.

I had resided but a short time in Baltimore before I observed a marked difference, in the treatment of slaves, from that which I had witnessed in the country. A city slave is almost a freeman, compared with a slave on the plantation. He is much better fed and clothed, and enjoys privileges

---

[27]ELL: An obsolete measure of length that varied in different countries. (An English ell was 45 inches, and a Scottish ell was about 37 inches). The phrase means undue advantages will be taken when the smallest concessions are granted.

altogether unknown to the slave on the plantation. There is a vestige of decency, a sense of shame, that does much to curb and check those outbreaks of atrocious cruelty so commonly enacted upon the plantation. He is a desperate slaveholder, who will shock the humanity of his non-slaveholding neighbors with the cries of his lacerated slave. Few are willing to incur the odium attaching to the reputation of being a cruel master; and above all things, they would not be known as not giving a slave enough to eat. Every city slaveholder is anxious to have it known of him, that he feeds his slaves well; and it is due to them to say, that most of them do give their slaves enough to eat. There are, however, some painful exceptions to this rule. Directly opposite to us, on Philpot Street, lived Mr. Thomas Hamilton. He owned two slaves. Their names were Henrietta and Mary. Henrietta was about twenty-two years of age, Mary was about fourteen; and of all the mangled and emaciated creatures I ever looked upon, these two were the most so. His heart must be harder than stone, that could look upon these unmoved. The head, neck, and shoulders of Mary were literally cut to pieces. I have frequently felt her head, and found it nearly covered with festering sores, caused by the lash of her cruel mistress. I do not know that her master ever whipped her, but I have been an eye-witness to the cruelty of Mrs. Hamilton. I used to be in Mr. Hamilton's house nearly every day. Mrs. Hamilton used to sit in a large chair in the middle of the room, with a heavy cowskin always by her side, and scarce an hour passed during the day but was marked by the blood of one of these slaves. The girls seldom passed her without her saying, "Move faster, you *black gip!*"[28] at the same time giving them a blow with the cowskin over the head or shoulders, often drawing the blood. She would then say, "Take that, you *black gip!*"—continuing, "If you don't move faster, I'll move you!" Added to the cruel lashings to which these slaves were subjected, they were kept nearly half-starved. They seldom knew what it was to eat a full meal. I have seen Mary contending with the pigs for the offal[29] thrown into the street. So much was Mary kicked and cut to pieces, that she was oftener called "*pecked*" than by her name.

CHAPTER VII

I lived in Master Hugh's family about seven years. During this time, I succeeded in learning to read and write. In accomplishing this, I was compelled to resort to various stratagems. I had no regular teacher. My

---

[28]GIP: A term that expresses anger, impatience, contempt.
[29]OFFAL: By-products, waste; something thrown away as worthless.

mistress, who had kindly commenced to instruct me, had, in compliance with the advice and direction of her husband, not only ceased to instruct, but had set her face against my being instructed by any one else. It is due, however, to my mistress to say of her, that she did not adopt this course of treatment immediately. She at first lacked the depravity indispensable to shutting me up in mental darkness. It was at least necessary for her to have some training in the exercise of irresponsible power, to make her equal to the task of treating me as though I were a brute.

My mistress was, as I have said, a kind and tender-hearted woman; and in the simplicity of her soul she commenced, when I first went to live with her, to treat me as she supposed one human being ought to treat another. In entering upon the duties of a slaveholder, she did not seem to perceive that I sustained to her the relation of a mere chattel, and that for her to treat me as a human being was not only wrong, but dangerously so. Slavery proved as injurious to her as it did to me. When I went there, she was a pious, warm, and tender-hearted woman. There was no sorrow or suffering for which she had not a tear. She had bread for the hungry, clothes for the naked, and comfort for every mourner that came within her reach. Slavery soon proved its ability to divest her of these heavenly qualities. Under its influence, the tender heart became stone, and the lamblike disposition gave way to one of tiger-like fierceness. The first step in her downward course was in her ceasing to instruct me. She now commenced to practise her husband's precepts. She finally became even more violent in her opposition than her husband himself. She was not satisfied with simply doing as well as he had commanded; she seemed anxious to do better. Nothing seemed to make her more angry than to see me with a newspaper. She seemed to think that here lay the danger. I have had her rush at me with a face made all up of fury, and snatch from me a newspaper, in a manner that fully revealed her apprehension. She was an apt woman; and a little experience soon demonstrated, to her satisfaction, that education and slavery were incompatible with each other.

From this time I was most narrowly watched. If I was in a separate room any considerable length of time, I was sure to be suspected of having a book, and was at once called to give an account of myself. All this, however, was too late. The first step had been taken. Mistress, in teaching me the alphabet, had given me the *inch*, and no precaution could prevent me from taking the *ell*.

The plan which I adopted, and the one by which I was most successful, was that of making friends of all the little white boys whom I met in the street. As many of these as I could, I converted into teachers. With their kindly aid, obtained at different times and in different places, I finally succeeded in learning to read. When I was sent of errands, I always took my book with me, and by going one part of my errand quickly, I found time to get a lesson before my return. I used also to carry bread with me, enough of which was always in the house, and to which I was always welcome; for I was much better off in this regard than many of the poor white children in our neighborhood. This bread I used to bestow upon the hungry little urchins, who, in return, would give me that more valuable bread of knowledge. I am strongly tempted to give the names of two or three of those little boys, as a testimonial of the gratitude and affection I bear them; but prudence forbids;—not that it would injure me, but it might embarrass them; for it is almost an unpardonable offence to teach slaves to read in this Christian country. It is enough to say of the dear little fellows, that they lived on Philpot Street, very near Durgin and Bailey's ship-yard. I used to talk this matter of slavery over with them. I would sometimes say to them, I wished I could be as free as they would be when they got to be men. "You will be free as soon as you are twenty-one, *but I am a slave for life*! Have not I as good a right to be free as you have?" These words used to trouble them; they would express for me the liveliest sympathy, and console me with the hope that something would occur by which I might be free.

I was now about twelve years old, and the thought of being *a slave for life* began to bear heavily upon my heart. Just about this time, I got hold of a book entitled "The Columbian Orator."[30] Every opportunity I got, I used to read this book. Among much of other interesting matter, I found in it a dialogue between a master and his slave. The slave was represented as having run away from his master three times. The dialogue represented the conversation which took place between them, when the slave was retaken the third time. In this dialogue, the whole argument in behalf of slavery was brought forward by the master, all of which was disposed of by the slave. The slave was made to say some very smart as well as impressive things in reply to his master—things which had the desired though unexpected effect; for the conversation resulted in the voluntary emancipation of the slave on the part of the master.

In the same book, I met with one of Sheridan's[31] mighty speeches on and in behalf of Catholic emancipation. These were choice documents to me. I read them over and over again with unabated interest. They gave tongue to interesting thoughts of my own soul, which had frequently

[30]THE COLUMBIAN ORATOR: A 1797 book by Caleb Bingham (1757–1817) that expressed anti-slavery sympathies.
[31]SHERIDAN'S: The Irish dramatist Richard Brinsley Sheridan (1751–1816), who argued for Catholic emancipation from the British parliament.

flashed through my mind, and died away for want of utterance. The moral which I gained from the dialogue was the power of truth over the conscience of even a slaveholder. What I got from Sheridan was a bold denunciation of slavery, and a powerful vindication of human rights. The reading of these documents enabled me to utter my thoughts, and to meet the arguments brought forward to sustain slavery; but while they relieved me of one difficulty, they brought on another even more painful than the one of which I was relieved. The more I read, the more I was led to abhor and detest my enslavers. I could regard them in no other light than a band of unsuccessful robbers, who had left their homes, and gone to Africa, and stolen us from our homes, and in a strange land reduced us to slavery. I loathed them as being the meanest as well as the most wicked of men. As I read and contemplated the subject, behold! that very discontentment which Master Hugh had predicted would follow my learning to read had already come, to torment and sting my soul to unutterable anguish. As I writhed under it, I would at times feel that learning to read had been a curse rather than a blessing. It had given me a view of my wretched condition, without the remedy. It opened my eyes to the horrible pit, but to no ladder upon which to get out. In moments of agony, I envied my fellow-slaves for their stupidity. I have often wished myself a beast. I preferred the condition of the meanest reptile to my own. Any thing, no matter what, to get rid of thinking! It was this everlasting thinking of my condition that tormented me. There was no getting rid of it. It was pressed upon me by every object within sight of hearing, animate or inanimate. The silver trump of freedom had roused my soul to eternal wakefulness. Freedom now appeared, to disappear no more forever. It was heard in every sound, and seen in every thing. It was ever present to torment me with a sense of my wretched condition. I saw nothing without seeing it, I heard nothing without hearing it, and felt nothing without feeling it. It looked from every star, it smiled in every calm, breathed in every wind, and moved in every storm.

I often found myself regretting my own existence, and wishing myself dead; and but for the hope of being free, I have no doubt but that I should have killed myself, or done something for which I should have been killed. While in this state of mind, I was eager to hear any one speak of slavery. I was a ready listener. Every little while, I could hear something about the abolitionists. It was some time before I found what the word meant. It was always used in such connections as to make it an interesting word to me. If a slave ran away, and succeeded in getting clear, or if a slave killed his master, set fire to a barn, or did any thing very wrong in the mind of a slaveholder, it was spoken of as the fruit of *abolition.* Hearing the word in this connection very often, I set about learning what it meant. The dictionary afforded me little or no help. I found it was "the act of abolishing;" but then I did not know what was to be abolished. Here I was perplexed. I did not dare to ask any one about its meaning, for I was satisfied that it was something they wanted me to know very little about. After a patient waiting, I got one of our city papers, containing an account of the number of petitions from the north, praying for the abolition of slavery in the District of Columbia, and of the slave trade between the States. From this time I understood the words *abolition* and *abolitionist,* and always drew near when that word was spoken, expecting to hear something of importance to myself and fellow-slaves. The light broke in upon me by degrees. I went one day down on the wharf of Mr. Waters; and seeing two Irishmen unloading a scow[32] of stone, I went, unasked, and helped them. When we had finished, one of them came to me and asked me if I were a slave. I told him I was. He asked, "Are ye a slave for life?" I told him that I was. The good Irishman seemed to be deeply affected by the statement. He said to the other that it was a pity so fine a little fellow as myself should be a slave for life. He said it was a shame to hold me. They both advised me to run away to the north; that I should find friends there, and that I should be free. I pretended not to be interested in what they said, and treated them as if I did not understand them; for I feared they might be treacherous. White men have been known to encourage slaves to escape, and then, to get the reward, catch them and return them to their masters. I was afraid that these seemingly good men might use me so; but I nevertheless remembered their advice, and from that time I resolved to run away. I looked forward to a time at which it would be safe for me to escape. I was too young to think of doing so immediately; besides, I wished to learn how to write, as I might have occasion to write my own pass. I consoled myself with the hope that I should one day find a good chance. Meanwhile, I would learn to write.

The idea as to how I might learn to write was suggested to me by being in Durgin and Bailey's ship-yard, and frequently seeing the ship carpenters, after hewing, and getting a piece of timber ready for use, write on the timber the name of that part of the ship for which it was intended. When a piece of timber was intended for the larboard side, it would be marked—"L." When a piece was for the starboard side, it would be marked thus—"S." A piece for the larboard side forward, would be marked thus—"L.F." When a piece was for starboard side

---

[32]SCOW: A large, flat-bottomed boat.

forward, it would be marked thus—"S.F." For larboard aft, it would be marked thus—"L.A." For starboard aft, it would be marked thus—"S.A." I soon learned the names of these letters, and for what they were intended when placed upon a piece of timber in the ship-yard. I immediately commenced copying them, and in a short time was able to make the four letters named. After that, when I met with any boy who I knew could write, I would tell him I could write as well as he. The next word would be, "I don't believe you. Let me see you try it." I would then make the letters which I had been so fortunate as to learn, and ask him to beat that. In this way I got a good many lessons in writing, which it is quite possible I should never have gotten in any other way. During this time, my copy-book was the board fence, brick way, and pavement; my pen and ink was a lump of chalk. With these, I learned mainly how to write. I then commenced and continued copying the Italics in Webster's Spelling Book,[33] until I could make them all without looking on the book. By this time, my little Master Thomas had gone to school, and learned how to write, and had written over a number of copy-books. These had been brought home, and shown to some of our near neighbors, and then laid aside. My mistress used to go to class meeting at the Wilk Street meetinghouse every Monday afternoon, and leave me to take care of the house. When left thus, I used to spend the time in writing in the spaces left in Master Thomas's copy-book, copying what he had written. I continued to do this until I could write a hand very similar to that of Master Thomas. Thus, after a long, tedious effort for years, I finally succeeded in learning how to write.

CHAPTER VIII

In a very short time after I went to live at Baltimore, my old master's youngest son Richard died; and in about three years and six months after his death, my old master, Captain Anthony, died, leaving only his son, Andrew, and daughter, Lucretia, to share his estate. He died while on a visit to see his daughter at Hillsborough. Cut off thus unexpectedly, he left no will as to the disposal of his property. It was therefore necessary to have a valuation of the property, that it might be equally divided between Mrs. Lucretia and Master Andrew. I was immediately sent for, to be valued with the other property. Here again my feelings rose up in detestation of slavery. I had now a new conception of my degraded

[33]WEBSTER'S SPELLING BOOK: A popular nineteenth-century schoolbook written by Noah Webster (1758–1843).

condition. Prior to this, I had become, if not insensible to my lot, at least partly so. I left Baltimore with a young heart overborne with sadness, and a soul full of apprehension. I took passage with Captain Rowe, in the schooner Wild Cat, and, after a sail of about twenty-four hours, I found myself near the place of my birth. I had now been absent from it almost, if not quite, five years. I, however, remembered the place very well. I was only about five years old when I left it, to go and live with my old master on Colonel Lloyd's plantation; so that I was now between ten and eleven years old.

We were all ranked together at the valuation. Men and women, old and young, married and single, were ranked with horses, sheep and swine. There were horses and men, cattle and women, pigs and children, all holding the same rank in the scale of being, and were all subjected to the same narrow examination. Silvery-headed age and sprightly youth, maids and matrons, had to undergo the same indelicate inspection. At this moment, I saw more clearly than ever the brutalizing effects of slavery upon both slave and slaveholder.

After the valuation, then came the division. I have no language to express the high excitement and deep anxiety which were felt among us poor slaves during this time. Our fate for life was now to be decided. We had no more voice in that decision than the brutes among whom we were ranked. A single word from the white men was enough—against all our wishes, prayers, and entreaties—to sunder forever the dearest friends, dearest kindred, and strongest ties known to human beings. In addition to the pain of separation, there was the horrid dread of falling into the hands of Master Andrew. He was known to us all as being a most cruel wretch,—a common drunkard who had, by his reckless mismanagement and profligate dissipation, already wasted a large portion of his father's property. We all felt that we might as well be sold at once to the Georgia traders, as to pass into his hands; for we knew that that would be our inevitable condition,—a condition held by us all in the utmost horror and dread.

I suffered more anxiety than most of my fellow-slaves. I had known what it was to be kindly treated; they had known nothing of the kind. They had seen little or nothing of the world. They were in very deed men and women of sorrow, and acquainted with grief. Their backs had been made familiar with the bloody lash, so that they had become callous; mine was yet tender; for while at Baltimore I got few whippings, and few slaves could boast of a kinder master and mistress than myself; and the thought of passing out of their hands into those of Master Andrew—a man who, but a few days before, to give me a sample of his bloody disposition, took my little brother by the throat, threw him on the ground, and with the heel of his boot stamped upon his head till the blood gushed from his nose and ears—was well calculated to make me anxious as to my fate. After he had committed this savage outrage upon my brother, he turned to me, and said that was the way he meant to serve me one of these days,—meaning, I suppose, when I came into his possession.

Thanks to a kind Providence, I fell to the portion of Mrs. Lucretia, and was sent immediately back to Baltimore, to live again in the family of Master Hugh. Their joy at my return equalled their sorrow at my departure. It was a glad day to me. I had escaped a fate worse than lion's jaws. I was absent from Baltimore, for the purpose of valuation and division, just about one month, and it seemed to have been six.

Very soon after my return to Baltimore, my mistress, Lucretia, died, leaving her husband and one child, Amanda; and in a very short time after her death, Master Andrew died. Now all the property of my old master, slaves included, was in the hands of strangers,—strangers who had had nothing to do with accumulating it. Not a slave was left free. All remained slaves, from the youngest to the oldest. If any one thing in my experience, more than another, served to deepen my conviction of the infernal character of slavery, and to fill me with unutterable loathing of slaveholders, it was their base ingratitude to my poor old grandmother. She had served my old master faithfully from youth to old age. She had been the source of all his wealth; she had peopled his plantation with slaves; she had become a great grandmother in his service. She had rocked him in infancy, attended him in childhood, served him through life, and at his death wiped from his icy brow the cold death-sweat, and closed his eyes forever. She was nevertheless left a slave—a slave for life—a slave in the hands of strangers; and in their hands she saw her children, her grandchildren, and her great-grandchildren, divided, like so many sheep, without being gratified with the small privilege of a single word, as to their or her own destiny. And, to cap the climax of their base ingratitude and fiendish barbarity, my grandmother, who was now very old, having outlived my old master and all his children, having seen the beginning and end of all of them, and her present owners finding she was of but little value, her frame already racked with the pains of old age, and complete helplessness fast stealing over her once active limbs, they took her to the woods, built her a little hut, put up a little mud-chimney, and then made her welcome to the privilege of supporting herself there in perfect loneliness; thus virtually turning her out to die! If my poor old grandmother now lives, she lives to suffer in utter loneliness; she lives to remember and mourn over the loss of children, the loss of grandchildren, and the loss of great-grandchildren. "They are, in the language of the slave's poet, Whittier,[34]—

> "Gone, gone, sold and gone
> To the rice swamp dank and lone,
> Where the slave-whip ceaseless swings,
> Where the noisome insect stings,
> Where the fever-demon strews
> Poison with the falling dews,
> Where the sickly sunbeams glare
> Through the hot and misty air:—
>   Gone, gone, sold and gone
> To the rice swamp dank and lone,
> From Virginia hills and waters—
> Woe is me, my stolen daughters!"[35]

The hearth is desolate. The children, the unconscious children, who once sang and danced in her presence, are gone. She gropes her way, in the darkness of age, for a drink of water. Instead of the voices of her children, she hears by day the moans of the dove, and by night the screams of the hideous owl. All is gloom. The grave is at the door. And now, when weighed down by the pains and aches of old age, when the head inclines to the feet, when the beginning and ending of human existence meet, and helpless infancy and painful old age combine together—at this time, this most needful time, the time for the exercise of that tenderness and affection which children only can exercise toward a declining parent—my poor old grandmother, the devoted mother of twelve children, is left all alone, in yonder little hut, before a few dim embers. She stands—she sits—she staggers—she falls—she groans—she dies—and there are none of her children or grandchildren present, to wipe from her wrinkled brow the cold sweat of death, or to place beneath the sod her fallen remains. Will not a righteous God visit for these things?

In about two years after the death of Mrs. Lucretia, Master Thomas married his second wife. Her name was Rowena Hamilton. She was the eldest daughter of Mr. William Hamilton. Master now lived in St. Michael's. Not long after his marriage, a misunderstanding took place between himself and Master Hugh; and as a means of punishing his brother, he took me from him to live with himself at St. Michael's. Here I under-

---

[34]WHITTIER: The Quaker abolitionist John Greenleaf Whittier (1807–1892).
[35]GONE, GONE . . . WOE IS ME, MY STOLEN DAUGHTERS: From John Greenleaf Whittier's poem "The Farewell of a Virginia Slave Mother to Her Daughters Sold into Southern Bondage" (1838).

went another most painful separation. It, however, was not so severe as the one I dreaded at the division of property; for, during this interval, a great change had taken place in Master Hugh and his once kind and affectionate wife. The influence of brandy upon him, and of slavery upon her, had effected a disastrous change in the characters of both; so that, as far as they were concerned, I thought I had little to lose by the change. But it was not to them that I was attached. It was to those little Baltimore boys that I felt the strongest attachment. I had received many good lessons from them, and was still receiving them, and the thought of leaving them was painful indeed. I was leaving, too, without the hope of ever being allowed to return. Master Thomas had said he would never let me return again. The barrier betwixt himself and brother he considered impassable.

I then had to regret that I did not at least make the attempt to carry out my resolution to run away; for the chances of success are tenfold greater from the city than from the country.

I sailed from Baltimore for St. Michael's in the sloop Amanda, Captain Edward Dodson. On my passage, I paid particular attention to the direction which the steamboats took to go to Philadelphia. I found, instead of going down, on reaching North Point they went up the bay, in a northeasterly direction. I deemed this knowledge of the utmost importance. My determination to run away was again revived. I resolved to wait only so long as the offering of a favorable opportunity. When that came, I was determined to be off.

CHAPTER IX

I have now reached a period of my life when I can give dates. I left Baltimore, and went to live with Master Thomas Auld, at St. Michael's, in March, 1832. It was now more than seven years since I lived with him in the family of my old master, on Colonel Lloyd's plantation. We of course were now almost entire strangers to each other. He was to me a new master, and I to him a new slave. I was ignorant of his temper and disposition; he was equally so of mine. A very short time, however, brought us into full acquaintance with each other. I was made acquainted with his wife not less than with himself. They were well matched, being equally mean and cruel. I was now, for the first time during a space of more than seven years, made to feel the painful gnawings of hunger—a something which I had not experienced before since I left Colonel Lloyd's plantation. It went hard enough with me then, when I could look back at no period at which I had enjoyed a sufficiency. It was tenfold harder after living in Master Hugh's family, where I had always had enough to eat, and of that which was good. I have said Master Thomas was a mean man. He was so. Not to give a slave enough to eat, is regarded as the most aggravated development of meanness even among slaveholders. The rule is, no matter how coarse the food, only let there be enough of it. This is the theory; and in the part of Maryland from which I came, it is the general practice,—though there are many exceptions. Master Thomas gave us enough of neither coarse nor fine food. There were four slaves of us in the kitchen—my sister Eliza, my aunt Priscilla, Henny, and myself; and we were allowed less than half of a bushel of cornmeal per week, and very little else, either in the shape of meat or vegetables. It was not enough for us to subsist upon. We were therefore reduced to the wretched necessity of living at the expense of our neighbors. This we did by begging and stealing, whichever came handy in the time of need, the one being considered as legitimate as the other. A great many times have we poor creatures been nearly perishing with hunger, when food in abundance lay mouldering in the safe and smoke-house,[36] and our pious mistress was aware of the fact; and yet that mistress and her husband would kneel every morning, and pray that God would bless them in basket and store!

Bad as slaveholders are, we seldom meet one destitute of every element of character commanding respect. My master was one of this rare sort. I do not know of one single noble act ever performed by him. The leading trait in his character was meanness; and if there were any other element in his nature, it was made subject to this. He was mean; and, like most other mean men, he lacked the ability to conceal his meanness. Captan Auld was not born a slaveholder. He had been a poor man, master only of a Bay craft. He came into possession of all his slaves by marriage; and of all men, adopted slaveholders are the worst. He was cruel, but cowardly. He commanded without firmness. In the enforcement of his rules, he was at times rigid, and at times lax. At times, he spoke to his slaves with the firmness of Napoleon[37] and the fury of a demon; at other times, he might well be mistaken for an inquirer who had lost his way. He did nothing of himself. He might have passed for a lion, but for his ears. In all things noble which he attempted, his own meanness shone most conspicuous. His airs, words, and actions, were the airs, words, and actions of born slaveholders, and, being assumed, were awkward enough. He was not even a good imitator. He possessed

---

[36]SMOKE-HOUSE: Where meat and fish were cured by exposure to smoke and thereby preserved. The cured meat was then housed in a meat safe for long-term storage.
[37]NAPOLEON: Napoleon Bonaparte (1769–1821), French emperor.

all the disposition to deceive, but wanted the power. Having no resources within himself, he was compelled to be the copyist of many, and being such, he was forever the victim of inconsistency; and of consequence he was an object of contempt, and was held as such even by his slaves. The luxury of having slaves of his own to wait upon him was something new and unprepared for. He was a slaveholder without the ability to hold slaves. He found himself incapable of managing his slaves either by force, fear, or fraud. We seldom called him "master," we generally called him "Captain Auld," and were hardly disposed to title him at all. I doubt not that our conduct had much to do with making him appear awkward, and of consequence fretful. Our want of reverence for him must have perplexed him greatly. He wished to have us call him master, but lacked the firmness necessary to command us to do so. His wife used to insist upon our calling him so, but to no purpose. In August, 1832, my master attended a Methodist camp-meeting held in the Bay-side, Talbot county, and there experienced religion. I indulged a faint hope that his conversion would lead him to emancipate his slaves, and that, if he did not do this, it would at any rate, make him more kind and humane. I was disappointed in both these respects. It neither made him to be humane to his slaves, nor to emancipate them. If it had any effect on his character, it made him more cruel and hateful in all his ways; for I believe him to have been a much worse man after his conversion than before. Prior to his conversion, he relied upon his own depravity to shield and sustain him in his savage barbarity; but after his conversion, he found religious sanction and support for his slaveholding cruelty. He made the greatest pretensions to piety. His house was the house of prayer. He prayed morning, noon, and night. He very soon distinguished himself among his brethren, and was soon made a class-leader and exhorter. His activity in revivals was great, and he proved himself an instrument in the hands of the church in converting many souls. His house was the preachers' home. They used to take great pleasure in coming there to put up; for while he starved us, he stuffed them. We have had three or four preachers there at a time. The names of those who used to come most frequently while I lived there, were Mr. Storks, Mr. Ewery, Mr. Humphry, and Mr. Hickey. I have also seen Mr. George Cookman at our house. We slaves loved Mr. Cookman. We believed him to be a good man. We thought him instrumental in getting Mr. Samuel Harrison, a very rich slaveholder, to emancipate his slaves; and by some means got the impression that he was laboring to effect the emancipation of all the slaves. When he was at our house, we were sure to be called in to prayers. When the others were there, we were sometimes called in and sometimes not. Mr. Cookman took more notice of us than either of the other ministers. He could not come among us without betraying his sympathy for us, and, stupid as we were, we had the sagacity to see it.

While I lived with my master in St. Michael's, there was a white young man, a Mr. Wilson, who proposed to keep a Sabbath school for the instruction of such slaves as might be disposed to learn to read the New Testament. We met but three times, when Mr. West and Mr. Fairbanks, both class-leaders, with many others, came upon us with sticks and other missiles, drove us off, and forbade us to meet again. Thus ended our little Sabbath school in the pious town of St. Michael's.

I have said my master found religious sanction for his cruelty. As an example, I will state one of many facts going to prove the charge. I have seen him tie up a lame young woman, and whip her with a heavy cowskin upon her naked shoulders, causing the warm red blood to drip; and, in justification of the bloody deed, he would quote this passage of Scripture—"He that knoweth his master's will, and doeth it not, shall be beaten with many stripes."[38]

Master would keep this lacerated young woman tied up in this horrid situation four or five hours at a time. I have known him to tie her up early in the morning, and whip her before breakfast; leave her, go to his store, return at dinner, and whip her again, cutting her in the places already made raw with his cruel lash. The secret of master's cruelty toward "Henny" is found in the fact of her being almost helpless. When quite a child, she fell into the fire, and burned herself horribly. Her hands were so burnt that she never got the use of them. She could do very little but bear heavy burdens. She was to master a bill of expense; and as he was a mean man, she was a constant offence to him. He seemed desirous of getting the poor girl out of existence. He gave her away once to his sister; but, being a poor gift, she was not disposed to keep her. Finally, my benevolent master, to use his own words, "set her adrift to take care of herself." Here was a recently-converted man, holding on upon the mother, and at the same time turning out her helpless child, to starve and die! Master Thomas was one of the many pious slaveholders who hold slaves for the very charitable purpose of taking care of them.

[38]HE THAT KNOWETH HIS MASTER'S WILL, AND DOETH IT NOT, SHALL BE BEATEN WITH MANY STRIPES: Luke 12:47: "And that servant, which knew his lord's will, and prepared not himself, neither did according to his will, shall be beaten with many stripes." In other words, only those servants with enduring faith will be saved.

My master and myself had quite a number of differences. He found me unsuitable to his purpose. My city life, he said, had had a very pernicious effect upon me. It had almost ruined me for every good purpose, and fitted me for every thing which was bad. One of my greatest faults was that of letting his horse run away, and go down to his father-in-law's farm, which was about five miles from St. Michael's. I would then have to go after it. My reason for this kind of carelessness, or carefulness, was, that I could always get something to eat when I went there. Master William Hamilton, my master's father-in-law, always gave his slaves enough to eat. I never left there hungry, no matter how great the need of my speedy return. Master Thomas at length said he would stand it no longer. I had lived with him nine months, during which time he had given me a number of severe whippings, all to no good purpose. He resolved to put me out, as he said, to be broken; and, for this purpose, he let me for one year to a man named Edward Covey. Mr. Covey was a poor man, a farm-renter. He rented the place upon which he lived, as also the hands with which he tilled it. Mr. Covey had acquired a very high reputation for breaking young slaves, and this reputation was of immense value to him. It enabled him to get his farm tilled with much less expense to himself than he could have had it done without such a reputation. Some slaveholders thought it not much loss to allow Mr. Covey to have their slaves one year, for the sake of the training to which they were subjected, without any other compensation. He could hire young help with great ease, in consequence of this reputation. Added to the natural good qualities of Mr. Covey, he was a professor of religion—a pious soul—a member and a class-leader in the Methodist church. All of this added weight to his reputation as a "nigger-breaker." I was aware of all the facts, having been made acquainted with them by a young man who had lived there. I nevertheless made the change gladly; for I was sure of getting enough to eat, which is not the smallest consideration to a hungry man.

CHAPTER X

I left Master Thomas's house, and went to live with Mr. Covey, on the 1st of January, 1833. I was now, for the first time in my life, a field hand. In my new employment, I found myself even more awkward than a country boy appeared to be in a large city. I had been at my new home but one week before Mr. Covey gave me a very severe whipping, cutting my back, causing the blood to run, and raising ridges on my flesh as large as my little finger. The details of this affair are as follows: Mr. Covey sent me, very early in the morning of one of our coldest days in the month of January, to the woods, to get a load of wood. He gave me a team of unbroken oxen. He told me which was the in-hand ox,[39] and which the off-hand one. He then tied the end of a large rope around the horns of the in-hand ox, and gave me the other end of it, and told me, if the oxen started to run, that I must hold on upon the rope. I had never driven oxen before, and of course I was very awkward. I, however, succeeded in getting to the edge of the woods with little difficulty; but I had got a very few rods into the woods, when the oxen took fright, and started full tilt, carrying the cart against trees, and over stumps, in the most frightful manner. I expected every moment that my brains would be dashed out against the trees. After running thus for a considerable distance, they finally upset the cart, dashing it with great force against a tree, and threw themselves into a dense thicket. How I escaped death, I do not know. There I was, entirely alone, in a thick wood, in a place new to me. My cart was upset and shattered, my oxen were entangled among the young trees, and there was none to help me. After a long spell of effort, I succeeded in getting my cart righted, my oxen disentangled and again yoked to the cart. I now proceeded with my team to the place where I had, the day before, been chopping wood, and loaded my cart pretty heavily, thinking in this way to tame my oxen. I then proceeded on my way home. I had now consumed one half of the day. I got out of the woods safely, and now felt out of danger. I stopped my oxen to open the woods gate; and just as I did so, before I could get hold of my ox-rope, the oxen again started, rushed through the gate, catching it between the wheel and the body of the cart, tearing it to pieces, and coming within a few inches of crushing me against the gate-post. Thus twice, in one short day, I escaped death by the merest chance. On my return, I told Mr. Covey what had happened, and how it happened. He ordered me to return to the woods again immediately. I did so, and he followed on after me. Just as I got into the woods, he came up and told me to stop my cart, and that he would teach me how to trifle away my time, and break gates. He then went to a large gum-tree, and with his axe cut three large switches, and, after trimming them up neatly with his pocketknife, he ordered me to take off my clothes. I made him no answer, but stood with my clothes on. He repeated his order. I still made him no answer, nor did I move to strip myself. Upon this he rushed at me with the fierceness of a tiger, tore off my clothes, and lashed me till he had worn out his switches, cutting me so savagely as to leave the marks visible for a long time after. This whipping was the first of a number just like it, and for similar offences.

---

[39]IN-HAND OX: Of a team of oxen, the in-hand ox was to the left, the off-hand ox to the right.

I lived with Mr. Covey one year. During the first six months, of that year, scarce a week passed without his whipping me. I was seldom free from a sore back. My awkwardness was almost always his excuse for whipping me. We were worked fully up to the point of endurance. Long before day we were up, our horses fed, and by the first approach of day we were off to the field with our hoes and ploughing teams. Mr. Covey gave us enough to eat, but scarce time to eat it. We were often less than five minutes taking our meals. We were often in the field from the first approach of day till its last lingering ray had left us; and at saving-fodder time, midnight often caught us in the field binding blades.[40]

Covey would be out with us. The way he used to stand it, was this. He would spend the most of his afternoons in bed. He would then come out fresh in the evening, ready to urge us on with his words, example, and frequently with the whip. Mr. Covey was one of the few slaveholders who could and did work with his hands. He was a hard-working man. He knew by himself just what a man or a boy could do. There was no deceiving him. His work went on in his absence almost as well as in his presence; and he had the faculty of making us feel that he was ever present with us. This he did by surprising us. He seldom approached the spot where we were at work openly, if he could do it secretly. He always aimed at taking us by surprise. Such was his cunning, that we used to call him, among ourselves, "the snake." When we were at work in the cornfield, he would sometimes crawl on his hands and knees to avoid detection, and all at once he would rise nearly in our midst, and scream out, "Ha, ha! Come, come! Dash on, dash on!" This being his mode of attack, it was never safe to stop a single minute. His comings were like a thief in the night. He appeared to us as being ever at hand. He was under every tree, behind every stump, in every bush, and at every window, on the plantation. He would sometimes mount his horse, as if bound to St. Michael's, a distance of seven miles, and in half an hour afterwards you would see him coiled up in the corner of the wood-fence, watching every motion of the slaves. He would, for this purpose, leave his horse tied up in the woods. Again, he would sometimes walk up to us, and give us orders as though he was upon the point of starting on a long journey, turn his back upon us, and make as though he was going to the house to get ready; and, before he would get half way thither, he would turn short and crawl into a fence-corner, or behind some tree, and there watch us till the going down of the sun.

Mr. Covey's *forte* consisted in his power to deceive. His life was devoted to planning and perpetrating the grossest deceptions. Every thing he possessed in the shape of learning or religion, he made conform to his

---

[40]BINDING BLADES: Binding sheaves (stalks) of cut grain at harvest time.

disposition to deceive. He seemed to think himself equal to deceiving the Almighty. He would make a short prayer in the morning, and a long prayer at night; and, strange as it may seem, few men would at times appear more devotional than he. The exercises of his family devotions were always commenced with singing; and, as he was a very poor singer himself, the duty of raising the hymn generally came upon me. He would read his hymn, and nod at me to commence. I would at times do so; at others, I would not. My non-compliance would almost always produce much confusion. To show himself independent of me, he would start and stagger through with his hymn in the most discordant manner. In this state of mind, he prayed with more than ordinary spirit. Poor man! such was his disposition, and success at deceiving. I do verily believe that he sometimes deceived himself into the solemn belief, that he was a sincere worshipper of the most high God; and this, too, at a time when he may be said to have been guilty of compelling his woman slave to commit the sin of adultery. The facts in the case are these: Mr. Covey was a poor man; he was just commencing in life; he was only able to buy one slave; and, shocking as is the fact, he bought her, as he said, for a *breeder*. This woman was named Caroline. Mr. Covey bought her from Mr. Thomas Lowe, about six miles from St. Michael's. She was a large, able-bodied woman, about twenty years old. She had already given birth to one child, which proved her to be just what he wanted. After buying her, he hired a married man of Mr. Samuel Harrison, to live with him one year; and him he used to fasten up with her every night! The result was, that, at the end of the year, the miserable woman gave birth to twins. At this result Mr. Covey seemed to be highly pleased, both with the man and the wretched woman. Such was his joy, and that of his wife, that nothing they could do for Caroline during her confinement was too good, or too hard to be done. The children were regarded as being quite an addition to his wealth.

If at any one time of my life more than another, I was made to drink the bitterest dregs of slavery, that time was during the first six months of my stay with Mr. Covey. We were worked in all weathers. It was never too hot or too cold; it could never rain, blow, hail, or snow, too hard for us to work in the field. Work, work, work, was scarcely more the order of the day than of the night. The longest days were too short for him, and the shortest nights too long for him. I was somewhat unmanageable when I first went there, but a few months of this discipline tamed me. Mr. Covey succeeded in breaking me. I was broken in body, soul, and spirit. My natural elasticity was crushed, my intellect languished, the disposition to read departed, the cheerful spark that lingered about my eye died; the dark night of slavery closed in upon me, and behold a man transformed into a brute!

Sunday was my only leisure time. I spent this in a sort of beastlike stupor, between sleep and wake, under some large tree. At times I would rise up, a flash of energetic freedom would dart through my soul, accompanied with a faint beam of hope, that flickered for a moment, and then vanished. I sank down again, mourning over my wretched condition. I was sometimes prompted to take my life, and that of Covey, but was prevented by a combination of hope and fear. My sufferings on this plantation seem now like a dream rather than a stern reality.

Our house stood within a few rods of the Chesapeake Bay, whose broad bosom was ever white with sails from every quarter of the habitable globe. Those beautiful vessels, robed in purest white, so delightful to the eye of freemen, were to me so many shrouded ghosts, to terrify and torment me with thoughts of my wretched condition. I have often, in the deep stillness of a summer's Sabbath, stood all alone upon the lofty banks of that noble bay, and traced, with saddened heart and tearful eye, the countless number of sails moving off to the mighty ocean. The sight of these always affected me powerfully. My thoughts would compel utterance; and there, with no audience but the Almighty, I would pour out my soul's complaint, in my rude way, with an apostrophe to the moving multitude of ships:—

"You are loosed from your moorings, and are free; I am fast in my chains, and am a slave! You move merrily before the gentle gale, and I sadly before the bloody whip! You are freedom's swift-winged angels, that fly round the world; I am confined in bands of iron! O that I were free! Oh, that I were on one of your gallant decks, and under your protecting wing! Alas! betwixt me and you, the turbid waters roll. Go on, go on. O that I could also go! Could I but swim! If I could fly! O, why was I born a man, of whom to make a brute! The glad ship is gone; she hides in the dim distance. I am left in the hottest hell of unending slavery. O God, save me! God, deliver me! Let me be free! Is there any God? Why am I a slave? I will run away. I will not stand it. Get caught, or get clear, I'll try it. I had as well die with ague[41] as the fever. I have only one life to lose. I had as well be killed running as die standing. Only think of it; one hundred miles straight north, and I am free! Try it? Yes! God helping me, I will. It cannot be that I shall live and die a slave. I will take to the water. This very bay shall yet bear me into freedom. The steamboats steered in a north-east course from North Point. I will do the same; and when I get to the head of the bay, I will turn my canoe adrift, and walk straight through Delaware into Pennsylvania. When I get there, I shall not be

---

[41]AGUE: A malarial fever marked by paroxysms of chills and sweating.

required to have a pass; I can travel without being disturbed. Let but the first opportunity offer, and, come what will, I am off. Meanwhile, I will try to bear up under the yoke. I am not the only slave in the world. Why should I fret? I can bear as much as any of them. Besides, I am but a boy, and all boys are bound to some one. It may be that my misery in slavery will only increase my happiness when I get free. There is a better day coming."

Thus I used to think, and thus I used to speak to myself; goaded almost to madness at one moment, and at the next reconciling myself to my wretched lot.

I have already intimated that my condition was much worse, during the first six months of my stay at Mr. Covey's, than in the last six. The circumstances leading to the change in Mr. Covey's course toward me form an epoch in my humble history. You have seen how a man was made a slave; you shall see how a slave was made a man. On one of the hottest days of the month of August, 1833, Bill Smith, William Hughes, a slave named Eli, and myself, were engaged in fanning wheat.[42] Hughes was clearing the fanned wheat from before the fan. Eli was turning, Smith was feeding, and I was carrying wheat to the fan. The work was simple, requiring strength rather than intellect; yet, to one entirely unused to such work, it came very hard. About three o'clock of that day, I broke down; my strength failed me; I was seized with a violent aching of the head, attended with extreme dizziness; I trembled in every limb. Finding what was coming, I nerved myself up, feeling it would never do to stop work. I stood as long as I could stagger to the hopper with grain. When I could stand no longer, I fell, and felt as if held down by an immense weight. The fan of course stopped; every one had his own work to do; and no one could do the work of the other, and have his own go on at the same time.

Mr. Covey was at the house, about one hundred yards from the treading-yard where we were fanning. On hearing the fan stop, he left immediately, and came to the spot where we were. He hastily inquired what the matter was. Bill answered that I was sick, and there was no one to bring wheat to the fan. I had by this time crawled away under the side of the post and rail-fence by which the yard was enclosed, hoping to find relief by getting out of the sun. He then asked where I was. He was told by one of the hands. He came to the spot, and, after looking at me awhile, asked me what was the matter. I told him as well as I could, for I scarce had strength to speak. He then gave me a savage kick in the side, and told me to get up. I tried to do so, but fell back in the attempt. He

[42]FANNING WHEAT: Separating wheat from chaff.

gave me another kick, and again told me to rise. I again tried, and succeeded in gaining my feet; but, stooping to get the tub with which I was feeding the fan, I again staggered and fell. While down in this situation, Mr. Covey took up the hickory slat with which Hughes had been striking off the half-bushel measure, and with it gave me a heavy blow upon the head, making a large wound, and the blood ran freely; and with this again told me to get up. I made no effort to comply, having now made up my mind to let him do his worst. In a short time after receiving this blow, my head grew better. Mr. Covey had now left me to my fate. At this moment I resolved, for the first time, to go to my master, enter a complaint, and ask his protection. In order to do this, I must that afternoon walk seven miles; and this, under the circumstances, was truly a severe undertaking. I was exceedingly feeble; made so as much by the kicks and blows which I received, as by the severe fit of sickness to which I had been subjected. I, however, watched my chance, while Covey was looking in an opposite direction, and started for St. Michael's. I succeeded in getting a considerable distance on my way to the woods, when Covey discovered me, and called after me to come back, threatening what he would do if I did not come. I disregarded both his calls and his threats, and made my way to the woods as fast as my feeble state would allow; and thinking I might be overhauled by him if I kept the road, I walked through the woods, keeping far enough from the road to avoid detection, and near enough to prevent losing my way. I had not gone far before my little strength again failed me. I could go no farther. I fell down, and lay for a considerable time. The blood was yet oozing from the wound on my head. For a time I thought I should bleed to death; and think now that I should have done so, but that the blood so matted my hair as to stop the wound. After lying there about three quarters of an hour, I nerved myself up again, and started on my way, through bogs and briers, barefooted and bareheaded, tearing my feet sometimes at nearly every step; and after a journey of about seven miles, occupying some five hours to perform it, I arrived at master's store. I then presented an appearance enough to affect any but a heart of iron. From the crown of my head to my feet, I was covered with blood. My hair was all clotted with dust and blood; my shirt was stiff with blood. My legs and feet were torn in sundry places with briers and thorns, and were also covered with blood. I suppose I looked like a man who had escaped a den of wild beasts, and barely escaped them. In this state I appeared before my master, humbly entreating him to interpose his authority for my protection. I told him all the circumstances as well as I could, and it seemed, as I spoke, at times to affect him. He would then walk the floor, and seek to justify Covey by saying he expected I deserved it. He asked me what I wanted. I told him, to let me get a new home; that as sure as I lived with Mr. Covey again, I should live with but to die with him; that Covey would surely kill me; he was in a fair way for it. Master Thomas ridiculed the idea that there was any danger of Mr. Covey's killing me, and said that he knew Mr. Covey; that he was a good man, and that he could not think of taking me from him; that, should he do so, he would lose the whole year's wages; that I belonged to Mr. Covey for one year, and that I must go back to him, come what might; and that I must not trouble him with any more stories, or that he would himself *get hold of me.* After threatening me thus, he gave me a very large dose of salts, telling me that I might remain in St. Michael's that night, (it being quite late,) but that I must be off back to Mr. Covey's early in the morning; and that if I did not, he would *get hold of me*, which meant that he would whip me. I remained all night, and, according to his orders, I started off to Covey's in the morning, (Saturday morning), wearied in body and broken in spirit. I got no supper that night, or breakfast that morning. I reached Covey's about nine o'-clock; and just as I was getting over the fence that divided Mrs. Kemp's fields from ours, out ran Covey with his cowskin, to give me another whipping. Before he could reach me, I succeeded in getting to the cornfield; and as the corn was very high, it afforded me the means of hiding. He seemed very angry, and searched for me a long time. My behavior was altogether unaccountable. He finally gave up the chase, thinking, I suppose, that I must come home for something to eat; he would give himself no further trouble in looking for me. I spent that day mostly in the woods, having the alternative before me,—to go home and be whipped to death, or stay in the woods and be starved to death. That night, I fell in with Sandy Jenkins, a slave with whom I was somewhat acquainted. Sandy had a free wife[43] who lived about four miles from Mr. Covey's; and it being Saturday, he was on his way to see her. I told him my circumstances, and he very kindly invited me to go home with him. I went home with him, and talked this whole matter over, and got his advice as to what course it was best for me to pursue. I found Sandy an old adviser. He told me, with great solemnity, I must go back to Covey; but that before I went, I must go with him into another part of the woods, where there was a certain *root*, which, if I would take some of it with me, carrying it *always on my right side*, would render it impossible for Mr. Covey, or any other white man, to whip me. He said he had carried it for years; and since he had done so, he had never received a blow, and never expected to while he carried it. I

---

[43]FREE WIFE: A free African American woman; in other words, she was not a slave.

at first rejected the idea, that the simple carrying of a root in my pocket would have any such effect as he had said, and was not disposed to take it; but Sandy impressed the necessity with much earnestness, telling me it could do no harm, if it did no good. To please him, I at length took the root, and, according to his direction, carried it upon my right side. This was Sunday morning. I immediately started for home; and upon entering the yard gate, out came Mr. Covey on his way to meeting. He spoke to me very kindly, bade me drive the pigs from a lot near by, and passed on towards the church. Now, this singular conduct of Mr. Covey really made me begin to think that there was something in the *root* which Sandy had given me; and had it been on any other day than Sunday, I could have attributed the conduct to no other cause than the influence of that root; and as it was, I was half inclined to think the *root* to be something more than I at first had taken it to be. All went well till Monday morning. On this morning, the virtue of the *root* was fully tested. Long before daylight, I was called to go and rub, curry, and feed, the horses. I obeyed, and was glad to obey. But whilst thus engaged, whilst in the act of throwing down some blades from the loft, Mr. Covey entered the stable with a long rope; and just as I was half out of the loft, he caught hold of my legs, and was about tying me. As soon as I found what he was up to, I gave a sudden spring, and as I did so, he holding to my legs, I was brought sprawling on the stable floor. Mr. Covey seemed now to think he had me, and could do what he pleased; but at this moment— from whence came the spirit I don't know—I resolved to fight; and, suiting my action to the resolution, I seized Covey hard by the throat; and as I did so, I rose. He held on to me, and I to him. My resistance was so entirely unexpected, that Covey seemed taken all aback. He trembled like a leaf. This gave me assurance, and I held him uneasy, causing the blood to run where I touched him with the ends of my fingers. Mr. Covey soon called out to Hughes for help. Hughes came, and, while Covey held me, attempted to tie my right hand. While he was in the act of doing so, I watched my chance, and gave him a heavy kick close under the ribs. This kick fairly sickened Hughes, so that he left me in the hands of Mr. Covey. This kick had the effect of not only weakening Hughes, but Covey also. When he saw Hughes bending over with pain, his courage quailed. He asked me if I meant to persist in my resistance. I told him I did, come what might; that he had used me like a brute for six months, and that I was determined to be used so no longer. With that, he strove to drag me to a stick that was lying just out of the stable door. He meant to knock me down. But just as he was leaning over to get the stick, I seized him with both hands by his collar, and brought him by a sudden snatch to the ground. By this time, Bill came. Covey called upon him for assistance. Bill wanted to know what he could do. Covey said, "Take hold of him, take hold of him!" Bill said his master hired him out to work, and not to help to whip me; so he left Covey and myself to fight our own battle out. We were at it for nearly two hours. Covey at length let me go, puffing and blowing at a great rate, saying that if I had not resisted, he would not have whipped me half so much. The truth was, that he had not whipped me at all. I considered him as getting entirely the worst end of the bargain; for he had drawn no blood from me, but I had from him. The whole six months afterwards, that I spent with Mr. Covey, he never laid the weight of his finger upon me in anger. He would occasionally say, he didn't want to get hold of me again. "No," thought I, "you need not; for you will come off worse than you did before."

This battle with Mr. Covey was the turning-point in my career as a slave. It rekindled the few expiring embers of freedom, and revived within me a sense of my own manhood. It recalled the departed self-confidence, and inspired me again with a determination to be free. The gratification afforded by the triumph was a full compensation for whatever else might follow, even death itself. He only can understand the deep satisfaction which I experienced, who has himself repelled by force the bloody arm of slavery. I felt as I never felt before. It was a glorious resurrection, from the tomb of slavery, to the heaven of freedom. My long-crushed spirit rose, cowardice departed, bold defiance took its place; and I now resolved that, however long I might remain a slave in form, the day had passed forever when I could be a slave in fact. I did not hesitate to let it be known of me, that the white man who expected to succeed in whipping, must also succeed in killing me.

From this time I was never again what might be called fairly whipped, though I remained a slave four years afterwards. I had several fights, but was never whipped.

It was for a long time a matter of surprise to me why Mr. Covey did not immediately have me taken by the constable to the whipping-post, and there regularly whipped for the crime of raising my hand against a white man in defence of myself. And the only explanation I can now think of does not entirely satisfy me; but such as it is, I will give it. Mr. Covey enjoyed the most unbounded reputation for being a first-rate overseer and negro-breaker. It was of considerable importance to him. That reputation was at stake; and had he sent me—a boy about sixteen years old—to the public whipping-post, his reputation would have been lost; so, to save his reputation, he suffered me to go unpunished.

My term of actual service to Mr. Edward Covey ended on Christmas day, 1833. The days between Christmas and New Year's day are allowed as holidays; and, accordingly, we were not required to perform any labor, more than to feed and take care of the stock. This time we regarded as our own, by the grace of our masters; and we therefore used or abused it nearly as we pleased. Those of us who had families at a distance, were generally allowed to spend the whole six days in their society. This time, however, was spent in various ways. The staid, sober, thinking and industrious ones of our number would employ themselves in making corn-brooms, mats, horse-collars, and baskets; and another class of us would spend the time hunting opossums, hares, and coons. But by far the larger part engaged in such sports and merriments as playing ball, wrestling, running foot-races, fiddling, dancing, and drinking whisky; and this latter mode of spending the time was by far the most agreeable to the feelings of our master. A slave who would work during the holidays was considered by our masters as scarcely deserving them. He was regarded as one who rejected the favor of his master. It was deemed a disgrace not to get drunk at Christmas; and he was regarded as lazy indeed, who had not provided himself with the necessary means, during the year, to get whisky enough to last him through Christmas.

From what I know of the effect of these holidays upon the slave, I believe them to be among the most effective means in the hands of the slaveholder in keeping down the spirit of insurrection. Were the slaveholders at once to abandon this practice, I have not the slightest doubt it would lead to an immediate insurrection among the slaves. These holidays serve as conductors, or safety-valves, to carry off the rebellious spirit of enslaved humanity. But for these, the slave would be forced up to the wildest desperation; and woe betide the slaveholder, the day he ventures to remove or hinder the operation of those conductors! I warn him that, in such an event, a spirit will go forth in their midst, more to be dreaded than the most appalling earthquake.

The holidays are part and parcel of the gross fraud, wrong, and inhumanity of slavery. They are professedly a custom established by the benevolence of the slaveholders; but I undertake to say, it is the result of selfishness, and one of the grossest frauds committed upon the down-trodden slave. They do not give the slaves this time because they would not like to have their work during its continuance, but because they know it would be unsafe to deprive them of it. This will be seen by the fact, that the slaveholders like to have their slaves spend those days just in such a manner as to make them as glad of their ending as of their beginning.

Their object seems to be, to disgust their slaves with freedom, by plunging them into the lowest depths of dissipation. For instance, the slaveholders not only like to see the slave drink of his own accord, but will adopt various plans to make him drunk. One plan is, to make bets on their slaves, as to who can drink the most whisky without getting drunk; and in this way they succeed in getting whole multitudes to drink to excess. Thus, when the slave asks for virtuous freedom, the cunning slaveholder, knowing his ignorance, cheats him with a dose of vicious dissipation, artfully labelled with the name of liberty. The most of us used to drink it down, and the result was just what might be supposed: many of us were led to think that there was little to choose between liberty and slavery. We felt, and very properly too, that we had almost as well be slaves to man as to rum. So, when the holidays ended, we staggered up from the filth of our wallowing, took a long breath, and marched to the field,—feeling, upon the whole, rather glad to go, from what our master had deceived us into a belief was freedom, back to the arms of slavery.

I have said that this mode of treatment is a part of the whole system of fraud and inhumanity of slavery. It is so. The mode here adopted to disgust the slave with freedom, by allowing him to see only the abuse of it, is carried out in other things. For instance, a slave loves molasses; he steals some. His master, in many cases, goes off to town, and buys a large quantity; he returns, takes his whip, and commands the slave to eat the molasses, until the poor fellow is made sick at the very mention of it. The same mode is sometimes adopted to make the slaves refrain from asking for more food than their regular allowance. A slave runs through his allowance, and applies for more. His master is enraged at him; but, not willing to send him off without food, gives him more than is necessary, and compels him to eat it within a given time. Then, if he complains that he cannot eat it, he is said to be satisfied neither full nor fasting, and is whipped for being hard to please! I have an abundance of such illustrations of the same principle, drawn from my own observation, but think the cases I have cited sufficient. The practice is a very common one.

On the first of January, 1834, I left Mr. Covey, and went to live with Mr. William Freeland, who lived about three miles from St. Michael's. I soon found Mr. Freeland a very different man from Mr. Covey. Though not rich, he was what would be called an educated southern gentleman. Mr. Covey, as I have shown, was a well-trained negro-breaker and slave-driver. The former (slaveholder though he was) seemed to possess some regard for honor, some reverence for justice, and some respect for humanity. The latter seemed totally insensible to all such sentiments. Mr. Freeland had many of the faults peculiar to slaveholders, such as being very passionate and fretful; but I must do him the justice to say, that he was exceedingly free from those degrading vices to which Mr. Covey was constantly addicted. The one was open and frank, and we always knew where to find him. The other was a most artful deceiver, and could be understood only by such as were skilful enough to detect his cunningly-devised frauds. Another advantage I gained in my new master was, he made no pretensions to, or profession of, religion; and this, in my opinion, was truly a great advantage. I assert most unhesitatingly, that the religion of the south is a mere covering for the most horrid crimes,—a justifier of the most appalling barbarity,—a sanctifier of the most hateful frauds,—and a dark shelter under, which the darkest, foulest, grossest, and most infernal deeds of slaveholders find the strongest protection. Were I to be again reduced to the chains of slavery, next to that enslavement, I should regard being the slave of a religious master the greatest calamity that could befall me. For of all slaveholders with whom I have ever met, religious slaveholders are the worst. I have ever found them the meanest and basest, the most cruel and cowardly, of all others. It was my unhappy lot not only to belong to a religious slaveholder, but to live in a community of such religionists. Very near Mr. Freeland lived the Rev. Daniel Weeden, and in the same neighborhood lived the Rev. Rigby Hopkins. These were members and ministers in the Reformed Methodist Church. Mr. Weeden owned, among others, a woman slave, whose name I have forgotten. This woman's back, for weeks, was kept literally raw, made so by the lash of this merciless, *religious* wretch. He used to hire hands. His maxim was, Behave well or behave ill, it is the duty of a master occasionally to whip a slave, to remind him of his master's authority. Such was his theory, and such his practice.

Mr. Hopkins was even worse than Mr. Weeden. His chief boast was his ability to manage slaves. The peculiar feature of his government was that of whipping slaves in advance of deserving it. He always managed to have one or more of his slaves to whip every Monday morning. He did this to alarm their fears, and strike terror into those who escaped. His plan was to whip for the smallest offences, to prevent the commission of large ones. Mr. Hopkins could always find some excuse for whipping a slave. It would astonish one, unaccustomed to a slave-holding life, to see with what wonderful ease a slave-holder can find things, of which to make occasion to whip a slave. A mere look, word, or motion,—a mistake, accident, or want of power,—are all matters for which a slave may be whipped at any time. Does a slave look dissatisfied? It is said, he has the devil in him, and it must be whipped out.

Does he speak loudly when spoken to by his master? Then he is wanting in reverence, and should be whipped for it. Does he ever venture to vindicate his conduct, when censured for it? Then he is guilty of impudence,—one of the greatest crimes of which a slave can be guilty. Does he ever venture to suggest a different mode of doing things from that pointed out by his master? He is indeed presumptuous, and getting above himself; and nothing less than a flogging will do for him. Does he, while ploughing, break a plough,—or, while hoeing, break a hoe? It is owing to his carelessness, and for it a slave must always be whipped. Mr. Hopkins could always find something of this sort to justify the use of the lash, and he seldom failed to embrace such opportunities. There was not a man in the whole county, with whom the slaves who had the getting their own home, would not prefer to live, rather than with this Rev. Mr. Hopkins. And yet there was not a man any where round, who made higher professions of religion, or was more active in revivals,—more attentive to the class, love-feast, prayer and preaching meetings, or more devotional in his family,—that prayed earlier, later, louder, and longer,—than this same reverend slave-driver, Rigby Hopkins.

But to return to Mr. Freeland, and to my experience while in his employment. He, like Mr. Covey, gave us enough to eat; but, unlike Mr. Covey, he also gave us sufficient time to take our meals. He worked us hard, but always between sunrise and sunset. He required a good deal of work to be done, but gave us good tools with which to work. His farm was large, but he employed hands enough to work it, and with ease, compared with many of his neighbors. My treatment, while in his employment, was heavenly, compared with what I experienced at the hands of Mr. Edward Covey.

Mr. Freeland was himself the owner of but two slaves. Their names were Henry Harris and John Harris. The rest of his hands he hired. These consisted of myself, Sandy Jenkins,[44] and Handy Caldwell. Henry and John were quite intelligent, and in a very little while after I went there, I succeeded in creating in them a strong desire to learn how to read. This desire soon sprang up in the others also. They very soon mustered up some old spelling-books, and nothing would do but that I must keep a Sabbath school. I agreed to do so, and accordingly devoted my Sundays to teaching these my loved fellow-slaves how to read. Neither of them knew his

[44]SANDY JENKINS: Of Jenkins, Douglass notes, "This is the same man who gave the roots to prevent my being whipped by Mr. Covey. He was a 'clever soul.' We used frequently to talk about the fight with Covey, and as often as we did so, he would claim my success as the results of the roots which he gave me. This superstition is very common among the more ignorant slaves. A slave seldom dies but that his death is attributed to trickery."

letters when I went there. Some of the slaves of the neighboring farms found what was going on, and also availed themselves of this little opportunity to learn to read. It was understood, among all who came, that there must be as little display about it as possible. It was necessary to keep our religious masters at St. Michael's unacquainted with the fact, that, instead of spending the Sabbath in wrestling, boxing, and drinking whisky, we were trying to learn how to read the will of God; for they had much rather see us engaged in those degrading sports, than to see us behaving like intellectual, moral, and accountable beings. My blood boils as I think of the bloody manner in which Messrs. Wright Fairbanks and Garrison West, both class-leaders, in connection with many others, rushed in upon us with sticks and stones, and broke up our virtuous little Sabbath school, at St. Michael's—all calling themselves Christians! humble followers of the Lord Jesus Christ! But I am again digressing.

I held my Sabbath school at the house of a free colored man, whose name I deem it imprudent to mention; for should it be known, it might embarrass him greatly, though the crime of holding the school was committed ten years ago. I had at one time over forty scholars, and those of the right sort, ardently desiring to learn. They were of all ages, though mostly men and women. I look back to those Sundays with an amount of pleasure not to be expressed. They were great days to my soul. The work of instructing my dear fellow-slaves was the sweetest engagement with which I was ever blessed. We loved each other, and to leave them at the close of the Sabbath was a severe cross indeed. When I think that these precious souls are to-day shut up in the prison-house of slavery, my feelings overcome me, and I am almost ready to ask, "Does a righteous God govern the universe? and for what does he hold the thunders in his right hand, if not to smite the oppressor, and deliver the spoiled out of the hand of the spoiler?" These dear souls came not to Sabbath school because it was popular to do so, nor did I teach them because it was reputable to be thus engaged. Every moment they spent in that school, they were liable to be taken up, and given thirty-nine lashes. They came because they wished to learn. Their minds had been starved by their cruel masters. They had been shut up in mental darkness. I taught them, because it was the delight of my soul to be doing something that looked like bettering the condition of my race. I kept up my school nearly the whole year I lived with Mr. Freeland; and, beside my Sabbath school, I devoted three evenings in the week, during the winter, to teaching the slaves at home. And I have the happiness to know, that several of those who came to Sabbath school learned how to read; and that one, at least, is now free through my agency.

The year passed off smoothly. It seemed only about half as long as the year which preceded it. I went through it without receiving a single blow. I will give Mr. Freeland the credit of being the best master I ever had, *till I became my own master.* For the ease with which I passed the year, I was, however, somewhat indebted to the society of my fellow-slaves. They were noble souls; they not only possessed loving hearts, but brave ones. We were linked and interlinked with each other. I loved them with a love stronger than any thing I have experienced since. It is sometimes said that we slaves do not love and confide in each other. In answer to this assertion, I can say, I never loved any or confided in any people more than my fellow-slaves, and especially those with whom I lived at Mr. Freeland's. I believe we would have died for each other. We never undertook to do any thing, of any importance, without a mutual consultation. We never moved separately. We were one; and as much so by our tempers and dispositions, as by the mutual hardships to which we were necessarily subjected by our condition as slaves.

At the close of the year 1834, Mr. Freeland again hired me of my master, for the year 1835. But, by this time, I began to want to live *upon free land* as well as *with Freeland*; and I was no longer content, therefore, to live with him or any other slave-holder. I began, with the commencement of the year, to prepare myself for a final struggle, which should decide my fate one way or the other. My tendency was upward. I was fast approaching manhood, and year after year had passed, and I was still a slave. These thoughts roused me—I must do something. I therefore resolved that 1835 should not pass without witnessing an attempt, on my part, to secure my liberty. But I was not willing to cherish this determination alone. My fellow-slaves were dear to me. I was anxious to have them participate with me in this, my life-giving determination. I therefore, though with great prudence, commenced early to ascertain their views and feelings in regard to their condition, and to imbue their minds with thoughts of freedom. I bent myself to devising ways and means for our escape, and meanwhile strove, on all fitting occasions, to impress them with the gross fraud and inhumanity of slavery. I went first to Henry, next to John, then to the others. I found, in them all, warm hearts and noble spirits. They were ready to hear, and ready to act when a feasible plan should be proposed. This was what I wanted. I talked to them of our want of manhood, if we submitted to our enslavement without at least one noble effort to be free. We met often, and consulted frequently, and told our hopes and fears, recounted the difficulties, real and imagined, which we should be called on to meet. At times we were almost disposed to give up and try to content ourselves with our wretched lot; at others, we were firm and unbending in our determination to go. Whenever we sugggested any plan, there was shrinking—the odds were fearful. Our path was beset with the greatest obstacles; and if we succeeded in gaining the end of it, our right to be free was yet questionable—we were yet liable to be returned to bondage. We could see no spot, this side of the ocean, where we could be free. We knew nothing about Canada. Our knowledge of the north did not extend farther than New York; and to go there, and be forever harassed with the frightful liability of being returned to slavery—with the certainty of being treated tenfold worse than before—the thought was truly a horrible one, and one which it was not easy to overcome. The case sometimes stood thus: At every gate through which we were to pass, we saw a watchman—at every ferry a guard—on every bridge a sentinel—and in every wood a patrol. We were hemmed in upon every side. Here were the difficulties, real or imagined—the good to be sought, and the evil to be shunned. On the one hand, there stood slavery, a stern reality, glaring frightfully upon us,— its robes already crimsoned with the blood of millions, and even now feasting itself greedily upon our own flesh. On the other hand, away back in the dim distance, under the flickering light of the north star, behind some craggy hill or snow-covered mountain, stood a doubtful freedom—half frozen—beckoning us to come and share its hospitality. This in itself was sometimes enough to stagger us; but when we permitted ourselves to survey the road, we were frequently appalled. Upon either side we saw grim death, assuming the most horrid shapes. Now it was starvation, causing us to eat our own flesh;—now we were contending with the waves, and were drowned;—now we were overtaken, and torn to pieces by the fangs of the terrible bloodhound. We were stung by scorpions, chased by wild beasts, bitten by snakes, and finally, after having nearly reached the desired spot,—after swimming rivers, encountering wild beasts, sleeping in the woods, suffering hunger and nakedness,—we were overtaken by our pursuers, and in our resistance, we were shot dead upon the spot! I say, this picture sometimes appalled us, and made us

> *"rather bear those ills we had,*
> *Than fly to others, that we knew not of."*[45]

In coming to a fixed determination to run away, we did more than Patrick Henry,[46] when he resolved upon liberty or death. With us it was a doubtful liberty at most, and almost certain death if we failed. For my part, I should prefer death to hopeless bondage.

---

[45]RATHER BEAR THOSE ILLS WE HAD, THAN FLY TO OTHERS/THAT WE KNEW NOT OF: From Shakespeare's *Hamlet*, Act 3, Scene 1, lines 80–81.
[46]PATRICK HENRY: American Revolutionary leader (1736–1799), who declared in the Virginia Assembly in 1775, "Give me liberty or give me death!"

Sandy, one of our number, gave up the notion, but still encouraged us. Our company then consisted of Henry Harris, John Harris, Henry Bailey, Charles Roberts, and myself. Henry Bailey was my uncle, and belonged to my master. Charles married my aunt: he belonged to my master's father-in-law, Mr. William Hamilton.

The plan we finally concluded upon was, to get a large canoe belonging to Mr. Hamilton, and upon the Saturday night previous to Easter holidays, paddle directly up the Chesapeake Bay. On our arrival at the head of the bay, a distance of seventy or eighty miles from where we lived, it was our purpose to turn our canoe adrift, and follow the guidance of the north star till we got beyond the limits of Maryland. Our reason for taking the water route was, that we were less liable to be suspected as runaways; we hoped to be regarded as fishermen; whereas, if we should take the land route, we should be subjected to interruptions of almost every kind. Any one having a white face, and being so disposed, could stop us, and subject us to examination.

The week before our intended start, I wrote several protections, one for each of us. As well as I can remember they were in the following words, to wit:—

"This is to certify that I, the undersigned, have given the bearer, my servant, full liberty to go to Baltimore, and spend the Easter holidays. Written with mine own hand &c., 1835.

> "William Hamilton,
> "Near St. Michael's, in Talbot county, Maryland."

We were not going to Baltimore; but, in going up the bay, we went toward Baltimore; and these protections were only intended to protect us while on the bay.

As the time drew near for our departure, our anxiety became more and more intense. It was truly a matter of life and death with us. The strength of our determination was about to be fully tested. At this time, I was very active in explaining every difficulty, removing every doubt, dispelling every fear, and inspiring all with the firmness indispensable to success in our undertaking; assuring them that half was gained the instant we made the move; we had talked long enough; we were now ready to move; if not now, we never should be; and if we did not intend to move now, we had as well fold our arms, sit down, and acknowledge ourselves fit only to be slaves. This, none of us were prepared to acknowledge. Every man stood firm; and at our last meeting, we pledged ourselves afresh, in the most solemn manner, that at the time appointed, we would certainly start in pursuit of freedom. This was in the middle of the week, at the end of which we were to be off. We went, as usual, to our several fields of labor, but with bosoms highly agitated with thoughts of our truly hazardous undertaking. We tried to conceal our feelings as much as possible; and I think we succeeded very well.

After a painful waiting, the Saturday morning, whose night was to witness our departure, came. I hailed it with joy, bring what of sadness it might. Friday night was a sleepless one for me. I probably felt more anxious than the rest, because I was, by common consent, at the head of the whole affair. The responsibility of success or failure lay heavily upon me. The glory of the one, and the confusion of the other, were alike mine. The first two hours of that morning were such as I never experienced before, and hope never to again. Early in the morning, we went, as usual, to the field. We were spreading manure; and all at once, while thus engaged, I was overwhelmed with an indescribable feeling, in the fulness of which I turned to Sandy, who was near by, and said, "We are betrayed!" "Well," said he, "that thought has this moment struck me." We said no more. I was never more certain of any thing.

The horn was blown as usual, and we went up from the field to the house for breakfast. I went for the form, more than for want of any thing to eat that morning. Just as I got to the house, in looking out at the lane gate, I saw four white men, with two colored men. The white men were on horseback, and the colored ones were walking behind, as if tied. I watched them a few moments till they got up to our lane gate. Here they halted, and tied the colored men to the gate-post. I was not yet certain as to what the matter was. In a few moments, in rode Mr. Hamilton, with a speed betokening great excitement. He came to the door, and inquired if Master William was in. He was told he was at the barn. Mr. Hamilton, without dismounting, rode up to the barn with extraordinary speed. In a few moments, he and Mr. Freeland returned to the house. By this time, the three constables rode up, and in great haste dismounted, tied their horses, and met Master William and Mr. Hamilton returning from the barn; and after talking awhile, they all walked up to the kitchen door. There was no one in the kitchen but myself and John. Henry and Sandy were up at the barn. Mr. Freeland put his head in at the door, and called me by name, saying, there were some gentlemen at the door who wished to see me. I stepped to the door, and inquired what they wanted. They at once seized me, and, without giving me any satisfaction, tied me—lashing my hands closely together. I insisted upon knowing what the matter was. They at length said, that they had learned I had been in a "scrape," and that I was to be examined before my master; and if their information proved false, I should not be hurt.

In a few moments, they succeeded in tying John. They then turned to Henry, who had by this time returned, and commanded him to cross his hands. "I won't!" said Henry, in a firm tone, indicating his readiness to meet the consequences of his refusal. "Won't you?" said Tom Graham, the constable. "No, I won't!" said Henry, in a still stronger tone. With this, two of the constables pulled out their shining pistols, and swore, by their Creator, that they would make him cross his hands or kill him. Each cocked his pistol, and, with fingers on the trigger, walked up to Henry, saying, at the same time, if he did not cross his hands, they would blow his damned heart out. "Shoot me, shoot me!" said Henry; "you can't kill me but once. Shoot, shoot,—and be damned! *I won't be tied!*" This he said in a tone of loud defiance; and at the same time, with a motion as quick as lightning, he with one single stroke dashed the pistols from the hand of each constable. As he did this, all hands fell upon him, and, after beating him some time, they finally overpowered him, and got him tied.

During the scuffle, I managed, I know not how, to get my pass out, and, without being discovered, put it into the fire. We were all now tied; and just as we were to leave for Easton jail, Betsy Freeland, mother of William Freeland, came to the door with her hands full of biscuits, and divided them between Henry and John. She then delivered herself of a speech, to the following effect:—addressing herself to me, she said, *"You devil! You yellow devil!* It was you that put it into the heads of Henry and John to run away. But for you, you long-legged mulatto devil! Henry nor John would never have thought of such a thing." I made no reply, and was immediately hurried off towards St. Michael's. Just a moment previous to the scuffle with Henry, Mr. Hamilton suggested the propriety of making a search for the protections which he had understood Frederick had written for himself and the rest. But, just at the moment he was about carrying his proposal into effect, his aid was needed in helping to tie Henry; and the excitement attending the scuffle caused them either to forget, or to deem it unsafe, under the circumstances, to search. So we were not yet convicted of the intention to run away.

When we got about halfway to St. Michael's, while the constables having us in charge were looking ahead, Henry inquired of me what he should do with his pass. I told him to eat it with his biscuit, and own nothing; and we passed the word around, *"Own nothing;"* and *"Own nothing!"* said we all. Our confidence in each other was unshaken. We were resolved to succeed or fail together, after the calamity had befallen us as much as before. We were now prepared for any thing.

We were to be dragged that morning fifteen miles behind horses, and then to be placed in the Easton jail. When we reached St. Michael's, we underwent a sort of examination. We all denied that we ever intended to run away. We did this more to bring out the evidence against us, than from any hope of getting clear of being sold; for, as I have said, we were ready for that. The fact was, we cared but little where we went, so we went together. Our greatest concern was about separation. We dreaded that more than any thing this side of death. We found the evidence against us to be the testimony of one person; our master would not tell who it was; but we came to a unanimous decision among ourselves as to who their informant was. We were sent off to the jail at Easton. When we got there, we were delivered up to the sheriff, Mr. Joseph Graham, and by him placed in jail. Henry, John, and myself, were placed in one room together—Charles, and Henry Bailey, in another. Their object in separating us was to hinder concert.

We had been in jail scarcely twenty minutes, when a swarm of slave traders, and agents for slave traders, flocked into jail to look at us, and to ascertain if we were for sale. Such a set of beings I never saw before! I felt myself surrounded by so many fiends from perdition. A band of pirates never looked more like their father, the devil. They laughed and grinned over us, saying, "Ah, my boys! we have got you, haven't we?" And after taunting us in various ways, they one by one went into an examination of us, with intent to ascertain our value. They would impudently ask us if we would not like to have them for our masters. We would make them no answer, and leave them to find out as best they could. Then they would curse and swear at us, telling us that they could take the devil out of us in a very little while, if we were only in their hands.

While in jail, we found ourselves in much more confortable quarters than we expected when we went there. We did not get much to eat, nor that which was very good; but we had a good clean room, from the windows of which we could see what was going on in the street, which was very much better than though we had been placed in one of the dark, damp cells. Upon the whole, we got along very well, so far as the jail and its keeper were concerned. Immediately after the holidays were over, contrary to all our expectations, Mr. Hamilton and Mr. Freeland came up to Easton, and took Charles, the two Henrys, and John, out of jail, and carried them home, leaving me alone. I regarded this separation as a final one. It caused me more pain than any thing else in the whole transaction. I was ready for any thing rather than separation. I supposed that they had consulted together, and had decided that, as I was the whole cause of the intention of the others to run away, it was hard to make the innocent suffer with the guilty; and that they had, therefore, concluded to take the others home, and sell me, as a warning to the others that remained. It is due to the noble Henry to say, he seemed almost as reluctant at leaving the prison as at leaving home to come to the prison. But we knew we should, in all probability, be separated, if we were sold; and since he was in their hands, he concluded to go peaceably home.

I was now left to my fate. I was all alone, and within the walls of a stone prison. But a few days before, and I was full of hope. I expected to have been safe in a land of freedom; but now I was covered with gloom, sunk down to the utmost despair. I thought the possibility of freedom was gone. I was kept in this way about one week, at the end of which, Captain Auld, my master, to my surprise and utter astonishment, came up, and took me out, with the intention of sending me, with a gentleman of his acquaintance, into Alabama. But, from some cause or other, he did not send me to Alabama, but concluded to send me back to Baltimore, to live again with his brother Hugh, and to learn a trade.

Thus, after an absence of three years and one month, I was once more permitted to return to my old home at Baltimore. My master sent me away, because there existed against me a very great prejudice in the community, and he feared I might be killed.

In a few weeks after I went to Baltimore, Master Hugh hired me to Mr. William Gardner, an extensive ship-builder, on Fell's Point. I was put there to learn how to calk. It, however, proved a very unfavorable place for the accomplishment of this object. Mr. Gardner was engaged that spring in building two large man-of-war brigs, professedly for the Mexican government. The vessels were to be launched in the July of that year, and in failure thereof, Mr. Gardner was to lose a considerable sum; so that when I entered, all was hurry. There was no time to learn any thing. Every man had to do that which he knew how to do. In entering the shipyard, my orders from Mr. Gardner were, to do whatever the carpenters commanded me to do. This was placing me at the beck and call of about seventy-five men. I was to regard all these as masters. Their word was to be my law. My situation was a most trying one. At times I needed a dozen pair of hands. I was called a dozen ways in the space of a single minute. Three or four voices would strike my ear at the same moment. It was—"Fred., come help me to cant this timber here."—"Fred., come carry this timber yonder."—"Fred., hold on the end of this fall."[47]—"Fred., go to the blacksmith's shop, and get a new punch."[48]—"Hurra, Fred.! run and bring me a cold

---

[47]FALL: A system of ropes; the end of a cable.
[48]PUNCH: A tool, in the form of a short rod made of iron or steel.

chisel."—"I say, Fred., bear a hand, and get up a fire as quick as lightning under that steambox."—"Halloo, nigger! come, turn this grindstone."—"Come, come! move, move! and *bowse*[49] this timber forward."—"I say, darky, blast your eyes, why don't you heat up some pitch?"—"Halloo! halloo! halloo!" (Three voices at the same time.) "Come here!—Go there!—Hold on where you are! Damn you, if you move, I'll knock your brains out!"

This was my school for eight months; and I might have remained there longer, but for a most horrid fight I had with four of the white apprentices, in which my left eye was nearly knocked out and I was horribly mangled in other respects. The facts in the case were these: Until a very little while after I went there, white and black ship-carpenters worked side by side, and no one seemed to see any impropriety in it. All hands seemed to be very well satisfied. Many of the black carpenters were freemen. Things seemed to be going on very well. All at once, the white carpenters knocked off, and said they would not work with free colored workmen. Their reason for this, as alleged, was, that if free colored carpenters were encouraged, they would soon take the trade into their own hands, and poor white men would be thrown out of employment. They therefore felt called upon at once to put a stop to it. And, taking advantage of Mr. Gardner's necessities, they broke off, swearing they would work no longer, unless he would discharge his black carpenters. Now, though this did not extend to me in form, it did reach me in fact. My fellow-apprentices very soon began to feel it degrading to them to work with me. They began to put on airs, and talk about the "niggers" taking the country, saying we all ought to be killed; and, being encouraged by the journeymen, they commenced making my condition as hard as they could, by hectoring me around, and sometimes striking me. I, of course, kept the vow I made after the fight with Mr. Covey, and struck back again, regardless of consequences; and while I kept them from combining, I succeeded very well; for I could whip the whole of them, taking them separately. They, however, at length combined, and came upon me, armed with sticks, stones, and heavy handspikes. One came in front with a half brick. There was one at each side of me, and one behind me. While I was attending to those in front, and on either side, the one behind ran up with the handspike, and struck me a heavy blow upon the head. It stunned me. I fell, and with this they all ran upon me, and fell to beating me with their fists. I let them lay on for a while, gathering strength. In an instant, I gave a sudden surge, and rose to my hands and knees. Just as I did that,

---

[49]BOWSE: Haul.

one of their number gave me, with his heavy boot, a powerful kick in the left eye. My eyeball seemed to have burst. When they saw my eye closed, and badly swollen, they left me. With this I seized the handspike, and for a time pursued them. But here the carpenters interfered, and I thought I might as well give it up. It was impossible to stand my hand against so many. All this took place in sight of not less than fifty white ship-carpenters, and not one interposed a friendly word; but some cried, "Kill the damned nigger! Kill him! kill him! He struck a white person." I found my only chance for life was in flight. I succeeded in getting away without an additional blow, and barely so, for to strike a white man is death by Lynch law,[50]—and that was the law in Mr. Gardner's ship-yard; nor is there much of any other out of Mr. Gardner's ship-yard.

I went directly home, and told the story of my wrongs to Master Hugh; and I am happy to say of him irreligious as he was, his conduct was heavenly, compared with that of his brother Thomas under similar circumstances. He listened attentively to my narration of the circumstances leading to the savage outrage, and gave many proofs of his strong indignation at it. The heart of my once overkind mistress was again melted into pity. My puffed-out eye and blood-covered face moved her to tears. She took a chair by me, washed the blood from my face, and, with a mother's tenderness, bound up my head, covering the wounded eye with a lean piece of fresh beef. It was almost compensation for my suffering to witness, once more, a manifestation of kindness from this, my once affectionate old mistress. Master Hugh was very much enraged. He gave expression to his feelings by pouring out curses upon the heads of those who did the deed. As soon as I got a little the better of my bruises, he took me with him to Esquire Watson's, on Bond Street, to see what could be done about the matter. Mr. Watson inquired who saw the assault committed. Master Hugh told him it was done in Mr. Gardner's ship-yard, at midday, where there were a large company of men at work. "As to that," he said, "the deed was done, and there was no question as to who did it." His answer was, he could do nothing in the case, unless some white man would come forward and testify. He could issue no warrant on my word. If I had been killed in the presence of a thousand colored people, their testimony combined would have been insufficient to have arrested one of the murderers. Master Hugh, for once, was compelled to say this state of things was too bad. Of course, it was impossible to get any white man to volunteer his testimony in my behalf, and against the white young men. Even those who may have sympathized with me were not prepared to do this. It required a degree of

---

[50]LYNCH LAW: Lynching, without legal proceedings or protections.

courage unknown to them to do so; for just at that time, the slightest manifestation of humanity toward a colored person was denounced as abolitionism, and that name subjected its bearer to frightful liabilities. The
watchwords of the bloody-minded in that region, and in those days, were,
"Damn the abolitionists!" and "Damn the niggers!" There was nothing
done, and probably nothing would have been done if I had been killed. Such
was, and such remains, the state of things in the Christian city of Baltimore.

Master Hugh, finding he could get no redress, refused to let me go back
again to Mr. Gardner. He kept me himself, and his wife dressed my wound
till I was again restored to health. He then took me into the ship-yard of
which he was foreman, in the employment of Mr. Walter Price. There I
was immediately set to calking, and very soon learned the art of using
my mallet and irons. In the course of one year from the time I left Mr.
Gardner's, I was able to command the highest wages given to the most
experienced calkers. I was now of some importance to my master. I was
bringing him from six to seven dollars per week. I sometimes brought him
nine dollars per week: my wages were a dollar and a half a day. After
learning how to calk, I sought my own employment, made my own contracts, and collected the money which I earned. My pathway became much
more smooth than before; my condition was now much more comfortable.
When I could get no calking to do, I did nothing. During these leisure
times, those old notions about freedom would steal over me again. When
in Mr. Gardner's employment, I was kept in such a perpetual whirl of
excitement, I could think of nothing, scarcely, but my life; and in thinking of my life, I almost forgot my liberty. I have observed this in my experience of slavery,—that whenever my condition was improved, instead
of its increasing my contentment, it only increased my desire to be free,
and set me to thinking of plans to gain my freedom. I have found that,
to make a contented slave, it is necesary to make a thoughtless one. It is
necessary to darken his moral and mental vision, and, as far as possible, to annihilate the power of reason. He must be able to detect no inconsistencies in slavery; he must be made to feel that slavery is right; and
he can be brought to that only when he ceases to be a man.

I was now getting, as I have said, one dollar and fifty cents per day.
I contracted for it; I earned it; it was paid to me; it was rightfully my own;
yet, upon each returning Saturday night, I was compelled to deliver every
cent of that money to Master Hugh. And why? Not because he earned
it,—not because he had any hand in earning it,—not because I owed it
to him,—nor because he possessed the slightest shadow of a right to it;
but solely because he had the power to compel me to give it up. The right
of the grim-visaged pirate upon the high seas is exactly the same.

CHAPTER XI

I now come to that part of my life during which I planned, and finally succeeded in making, my escape from slavery. But before narrating any of the
peculiar circumstances, I deem it proper to make known my intention not
to state all the facts connected with the transaction. My reasons for pursuing this course may be understood from the following: First, were I to
give a minute statement of all the facts, it is not only possible but quite
probable, that others would thereby be involved in the most embarrassing difficulties. Secondly, such a statement would most undoubtedly
induce greater vigilance on the part of slaveholders than has existed
heretofore among them; which would, of course, be the means of guarding a door whereby some dear brother bondman might escape his galling
chains. I deeply regret the necessity that impels me to suppress any thing
of importance connected with my experience in slavery. It would afford
me great pleasure indeed, as well as materially add to the interest of my
narrative, were I at liberty to gratify a curiosity, which I know exists in the
minds of many, by an accurate statement of all the facts pertaining to
my most fortunate escape. But I must deprive myself of this pleasure,
and the curious of the gratification which such a statement would afford.
I would allow myself to suffer under the greatest imputations which evil-
minded men might suggest, rather than exculpate myself, and thereby run
the hazard of closing the slightest avenue by which a brother slave might
clear himself of the chains and fetters of slavery.

I have never approved of the very public manner in which some of our
western friends have conducted what they call the *underground railroad*,
but which I think, by their open declarations, has been made most emphatically the *upperground railroad*. I honor those good men and women for
their noble daring, and applaud them for willingly subjecting themselves
to bloody persecution, by openly avowing their participation in the escape
of slaves. I, however, can see very little good resulting from such a course,
either to themselves or the slaves escaping; while, upon the other hand, I see
and feel assured that those open declarations are a positive evil to the slaves
remaining, who are seeking to escape. They do nothing towards enlightening the slave, whilst they do much towards enlightening the master. They
stimulate him to greater watchfulness, and enhance his power to capture
his slave. We owe something to the slave south of the line as well as to
those north of it; and in aiding the latter on their way to freedom, we should
be careful to do nothing which would be likely to hinder the former from
escaping from slavery. I would keep the merciless slaveholder profoundly
ignorant of the means of flight adopted by the slave. I would leave him to
imagine himself surrounded by myriads of invisible tormentors, ever ready

to snatch from his infernal grasp his trembling prey. Let him be left to feel his way in the dark; let darkness commensurate with his crime hover over him; and let him feel that at every step he takes, in pursuit of the flying bondman, he is running the frightful risk of having his hot brains dashed out by an invisible agency. Let us render the tyrant no aid; let us not hold the light by which he can trace the footprints of our flying brother. But enough of this. I will not proceed to the statement of those facts, connected with my escape, for which I am alone responsible, and for which no one can be made to suffer but myself.

In the early part of the year 1838, I became quite restless. I could see no reason why I should, at the end of each week, pour the reward of my toil into the purse of my master. When I carried to him my weekly wages, he would, after counting the money, look me in the face with a robber-like fierceness, and say, "Is this all?" He was satisfied with nothing less than the last cent. He would, however, when I made him six dollars, sometimes give me six cents, to encourage me. It had the opposite effect. I regarded it as a sort of admission of my right to the whole. The fact that he gave me any part of my wages was proof, to my mind, that he believed me entitled to the whole of them. I always felt worse for having received any thing; for I feared that the giving me a few cents would ease his conscience, and make him feel himself to be a pretty honorable sort of robber. My discontent grew upon me. I was ever on the look-out for means of escape; and, finding no direct means, I determined to try to hire my time, with a view of getting money with which to make my escape. In the spring of 1838, when Master Thomas came to Baltimore to purchase his spring goods, I got an opportunity, and applied to him to allow me to hire my time. He unhesitatingly refused my request, and told me this was another strategem by which to escape. He told me I could go nowhere but that he could get me; and that, in the event of my running away, he should spare no pains in his efforts to catch me. He exhorted me to content myself, and be obedient. He told me, if I would be happy, I must lay out no plans for the future. He said, if I behaved myself properly, he would take care of me. Indeed, he advised me to complete thoughtlessness of the future, and taught me to depend solely upon him for happiness. He seemed to see fully the pressing necessity of setting aside my intellectual nature, in order to insure contentment in slavery. But in spite of him, and even in spite of myself, I continued to think, and to think about the injustice of my enslavement, and the means of escape.

About two months after this, I applied to Master Hugh for the privilege of hiring my time. He was not acquainted with the fact that I had applied to Master Thomas, and had been refused. He too, at first, seemed disposed to refuse; but, after some reflection, he granted me the privilege, and proposed the following terms: I was to be allowed all my time, make all contracts with those for whom I worked, and find my own employment; and, in return for this liberty, I was to pay him three dollars at the end of each week; find myself in calking tools, and in board and clothing. My board was two dollars and a half per week. This, with the wear and tear of clothing and calking tools, made my regular expenses about six dollars per week. This amount I was compelled to make up, or relinquish the privilege of hiring my time. Rain or shine, work or no work, at the end of each week the money must be forthcoming, or I must give up my privilege. This arrangement, it will be perceived, was decidedly in my master's favor. It relieved him of all need of looking after me. His money was sure. He received all the benefits of slaveholding without its evils; while I endured all the evils of a slave, and suffered all the care and anxiety of a freeman. I found it a hard bargain. But, hard as it was I thought it better than the old mode of getting along. It was a step towards freedom to be allowed to bear the responsibilities of a freeman, and I was determined to hold on upon it. I bent myself to the work of making money. I was ready to work at night as well as day, and by the most untiring perservance and industry, I made enough to meet my expenses, and lay up a little money every week. I went on thus from May till August. Master Hugh then refused to allow me to hire my time longer. The ground for his refusal was a failure on my part, one Saturday night, to pay him for my week's time. This failure was occasioned by my attending a camp meeting about ten miles from Baltimore. During the week, I had entered into an engagement with a number of young friends to start from Baltimore to the camp ground early Saturday evening; and being detained by my employer, I was unable to get down to Master Hugh's without disappointing the company. I knew that Master Hugh was in no special need of the money that night. I therefore decided to go to the camp meeting, and upon my return pay him the three dollars. I staid at the camp meeting one day longer than I intended when I left. But as soon as I returned, I called upon him to pay him what he considered his due. I found him very angry; he could scarce restrain his wrath. He said he had a great mind to give me a severe whipping. He wished to know how I dared go out of the city without asking his permission. I told him I hired my time, and while I paid him the price which he asked for it, I did not know that I was bound to ask him when and where I should go. This reply troubled him; and, after reflecting a few moments, he turned to me, and said I should hire my time no longer; that the next thing he should know of, I would be running away. Upon the same plea, he told me to bring my tools and clothing home forthwith. I did so; but instead of seeking work, as I had been accustomed to do previously to hiring my time, I spent the whole week without the performance of a single stroke of work. I did this in retaliation.

Saturday night, he called upon me as usual for my week's wages. I told him I had no wages; I had done no work that week. Here we were upon the point of coming to blows. He raved, and swore his determination to get hold of me. I did not allow myself a single word; but was resolved, if he laid the weight of his hand upon me, it should be blow for blow. He did not strike me, but told me that he would find me in constant employment in future. I thought the matter over during the next day, Sunday, and finally resolved upon the third day of September, as the day upon which I would make a second attempt to secure my freedom. I now had three weeks during which to prepare for my journey. Early on Monday morning, before Master Hugh had time to make any engagement for me, I went out and got employment of Mr. Butler, at his ship-yard near the drawbridge, upon what is called the City Block, thus making it unnecessary for him to seek employment for me. At the end of the week, I brought him between eight and nine dollars. He seemed very well pleased, and asked why I did not do the same the week before. He little knew what my plans were. My object in working steadily was to remove any suspicion he might entertain of my intent to run away; and in this I succeeded admirably. I suppose he thought I was never better satisfied with my condition than at the very time during which I was planning my escape. The second week passed, and again I carried him my full wages; and so well pleased was he, that he gave me twenty-five cents, (quite a large sum for a slaveholder to give a slave), and bade me to make a good use of it. I told him I would.

Things went on without very smoothly indeed, but within there was trouble. It is impossible for me to describe my feelings as the time of my contemplated start drew near. I had a number of warm-hearted friends in Baltimore,—friends that I loved almost as I did my life,—and the thought of being separated from them forever was painful beyond expression. It is my opinion that thousands would escape from slavery, who now remain, but for the strong cords of affection that bind them to their friends. The thought of leaving my friends was decidedly the most painful thought with which I had to contend. The love of them was my tender point, and shook my decision more than all things else. Besides the pain of separation, the dread and apprehension of a failure exceeded what I had experienced at my first attempt. The appalling defeat I then sustained returned to torment me. I felt assured that, if I failed in this attempt, my case would be a hopeless one—it would seal my fate as a slave forever. I could not hope to get off with any thing less than the severest punishment, and being placed beyond the means of escape. It required no very vivid imagination to depict the most frightful scenes through which I should have to pass, in case I failed. The wretchedness of slavery, and the blessedness of freedom, were perpetually before me. It was life and death with me. But

I remained firm, and, according to my resolution, on the third day of September, 1838, I left my chains, and succeeded in reaching New York without the slightest interruption of any kind. How I did so,—what means I adopted,—what direction I travelled, and by what mode of conveyance,—I must leave unexplained, for the reasons before mentioned.

I have been frequently asked how I felt when I found myself in a free State. I have never been able to answer the question with any satisfaction to myself. It was a moment of the highest excitement I ever experienced. I suppose I felt as one may imagine the unarmed mariner to feel when he is rescued by a friendly man-of-war from the pursuit of a pirate. In writing to a dear friend, immediately after my arrival at New York, I said I felt like one who had escaped a den of hungry lions. This state of mind, however, very soon subsided; and I was again seized by a feeling of great insecurity and loneliness. I was yet liable to be taken back, and subjected to all the tortures of slavery. This in itself was enough to damp the ardor of my enthusiasm. But the loneliness overcame me. There I was in the midst of thousands, and yet a perfect stranger; without home and without friends, in the midst of thousands of my own brethren—children of a common Father, and yet I dared not to unfold to any one of them my sad condition. I was afraid to speak to any one for fear of speaking to the wrong one, and thereby falling into the hands of money-loving kidnappers, whose business it was to lie in wait for the panting fugitive, as the ferocious beasts of the forest lie in wait for their prey. The motto which I adopted when I started from slavery was this—"Trust no man!" I saw in every white man an enemy, and in almost every colored man cause for distrust. It was a most painful situation; and, to understand it, one must needs experience it, or imagine himself in similar circumstances. Let him be a fugitive slave in a strange land—a land given up to be the hunting-ground for slaveholders—whose inhabitants are legalized kidnappers—where he is every moment subjected to the terrible liability of being seized upon by his fellowmen, as the hideous crocodile seizes upon his prey!—I say, let him place himself in my situation—without home or friends—without money or credit—wanting shelter, and no one to give it—wanting bread, and no money to buy it,—and at the same time let him feel that he is pursued by merciless men-hunters, and in total darkness as to what to do, where to go, or where to stay,—perfectly helpless both as to the means of defence and means of escape,—in the midst of plenty, yet suffering the terrible gnawings of hunger,—in the midst of houses, yet having no home,—among fellowmen, yet feeling as if in the midst of wild beasts, whose greediness to swallow up the trembling and half-famished fugitive is only equalled by that with which the monsters of the deep swallow up the helpless fish upon which they subsist,—I say, let him be placed in this most trying situation,—the situation in which I was placed,—then, and not till then, will he fully appreciate the hardships of, and know how to sympathize with, the toil-worn and whip-scarred fugitive slave.

Thank Heaven, I remained but a short time in this distressed situation. I was relieved from it by the humane hand of Mr. DAVID RUGGLES,[51] whose vigilance, kindness, and perseverance, I shall never forget. I am glad of an opportunity to express, as far as words can, the love and gratitude I bear him. Mr. Ruggles is now afflicted with blindness, and is himself in need of the same kind offices which he was once so forward in the performance of toward others. I had been in New York but a few days, when Mr. Ruggles sought me out, and very kindly took me to his boarding-house at the corner of Church and Lespenard Streets. Mr. Ruggles was then very deeply engaged in the memorable *Darg* case,[52] as well as attending to a number of other fugitive slaves; devising ways and means for their successful escape; and, though watched and hemmed in on almost every side, he seemed to be more than a match for his enemies.

Very soon after I went to Mr. Ruggles, he wished to know of me where I wanted to go; as he deemed it unsafe for me to remain in New York. I told him I was a calker, and should like to go where I could get work. I thought of going to Canada; but he decided against it, and in favor of my going to New Bedford, thinking I should be able to get work there at my trade. At this time, Anna,[53] my intended wife, came on; for I wrote to her immediately after my arrival at New York, (notwithstanding my homeless, houseless, and helpless condition,) informing her of my successful flight, and wishing her to come on forthwith. In a few days after her arrival, Mr. Ruggles called in the Rev. J.W.C. Pennington,[54] who, in the presence of Mr. Ruggles, Mrs. Michaels, and two or three others, performed the marriage ceremony, and gave us a certificate, of which the following is an exact copy:—

"This may certify, that I joined together in holy matrimony Frederick Johnson[55] and Anna Murray, as man and wife, in the presence of Mr. David Ruggles and Mrs. Michaels.

"James W.C. Pennington
New York, Sept. 15, 1838."

[51]MR. DAVID RUGGLES: An abolitionist (1810–1849) who aided in Douglass's escape and housed him on his way to New Bedford.
[52]DARG CASE: John P. Darg (1771–1852) was a slaveowner who charged David Ruggles with harboring his fugitive slave, Thomas Hughes. The charges were eventually dropped.
[53]ANNA: Douglass notes, "She was free." Anna Murray Douglass (1813–1882) was the daughter of free parents, who resided in Caroline County, on the eastern shore of Maryland.
[54]REV. J.W.C. PENNINGTON: An escaped slave (1807–1870) who fled Maryland around 1830 and became an influential African American abolitionist.
[55]FREDERICK JOHNSON: Douglass notes, "I had changed my name from Frederick Bailey to that of Johnson."

Upon receiving this certificate, and a five-dollar bill from Mr. Ruggles, I shouldered one part of our baggage, and Anna took up the other, and we set out forthwith to take passage on board of the steamboat John W. Richmond for Newport, on our way to New Bedford. Mr. Ruggles gave me a letter to a Mr. Shaw in Newport, and told me, in case my money did not serve me to New Bedford, to stop in Newport and obtain further assistance; but upon our arrival at Newport, we were so anxious to get to a place of safety, that, notwithstanding we lacked the necessary money to pay our fare, we decided to take seats in the stage, and promise to pay when we got to New Bedford. We were encouraged to do this by two excellent gentlemen, residents of New Bedford, whose names I afterward ascertained to be Joseph Ricketson and William C. Taber. They seemed at once to understand our circumstances, and gave us such assurance of their friendliness as put us fully at ease in their presence. It was good indeed to meet with such friends, at such a time. Upon reaching New Bedford, we were directed to the house of Mr. Nathan Johnson, by whom we were kindly received, and hospitably provided for. Both Mr. and Mrs. Johnson took a deep and lively interest in our welfare.[56] They proved themselves quite worthy of the name of abolitionists. When the stage-driver found us unable to pay our fare, he held on upon our baggage as security for the debt. I had but to mention the fact to Mr. Johnson, and he forthwith advanced the money.

We now began to feel a degree of safety, and to prepare ourselves for the duties and responsibilities of a life of freedom. On the morning after our arrival at New Bedford, while at the breakfast-table, the question arose as to what name I should be called by. The name given me by my mother was, "Frederick Augustus Washington Bailey." I, however, had dispensed with the two middle names long before I left Maryland so that I was generally known by the name of "Frederick Bailey." I started from Baltimore bearing the name of "Stanley." When I got to New York I again changed my name to "Frederick Johnson," and thought that would be the last change. But when I got to New Bedford, I found it necessary again to change my name. The reason of this necessity was, that there were so many Johnsons in New Bedford, it was already quite difficult to distinguish between them. I gave Mr. Johnson the privilege of choosing me a name, but told him he must not take from me the name of "Frederick." I must hold on to that, to preserve a sense of my identity. Mr. Johnson had

---

[56]MR. AND MRS. JOHNSON TOOK A DEEP AND LIVELY INTEREST IN OUR WELFARE: Mary and Nathan Johnson were a free African American couple.

just been reading the "Lady of the Lake,"[57] and at once suggested that my name be "Douglass." From that time until now I have been called "Frederick Douglass"; and as I am more widely known by that name than by either of the others, I shall continue to use it as my own.

I was quite disappointed at the general appearance of things in New Bedford. The impression which I had received respecting the character and condition of the people of the north, I found to be singularly erroneous. I had very strangely supposed, while in slavery, that few of the comforts, and scarcely any of the luxuries, of life were enjoyed at the north, compared with what were enjoyed by the slaveholders of the south. I probably came to this conclusion from the fact that northern people owned no slaves. I supposed that they were about upon a level with the non-slaveholding population of the south. I knew *they* were exceedingly poor, and I had been accustomed to regard their poverty as the necessary consequence of their being non-slaveholders. I had somehow imbibed the opinion that, in the absence of slaves, there could be no wealth, and very little refinement. And upon coming to the north, I expected to meet with a rough, hard-handed, and uncultivated population, living in the most Spartanlike simplicity, knowing nothing of the ease, luxury, pomp, and grandeur of southern slaveholders. Such being my conjectures, any one acquainted with the appearance of New Bedford may very readily infer how palpably I must have seen my mistake.

In the afternoon of the day when I reached New Bedford, I visited the wharves, to take a view of the shipping. Here I found myself surrounded with the strongest proofs of wealth. Lying at the wharves, and riding in the stream, I saw many ships of the finest model, in the best order, and of the largest size. Upon the right and left, I was walled in by granite warehouses of the widest dimensions, stowed to their utmost capacity with the necessaries and comforts of life. Added to this, almost every body seemed to be at work, but noiselessly so, compared with what I had been accustomed to in Baltimore. There were no loud songs heard from those engaged in loading and unloading ships. I heard no deep oaths or horrid curses on the laborer. I saw no whipping of men; but all seemed to go smoothly on. Every man appeared to understand his work, and went at it with a sober, yet cheerful earnestness, which betokened the deep interest which he felt in what he was doing, as well as a sense of his own dignity as man. To me this looked exceedingly strange. From the

[57]LADY OF THE LAKE: The poem "The Lady of the Lake" (1810), by Sir Walter Scott (1771–1832), is a historical romance set in the Scottish highlands during the sixteenth century. The poem's main character is James of Douglass.

wharves I strolled around and over the town, gazing with wonder and admiration at the splendid churches, beautiful dwellings, and finely-cultivated gardens; evincing an amount of wealth, comfort, taste, and refinement, such as I had never seen in any part of slaveholding Maryland.

Every thing looked clean, new, and beautiful. I saw few or no dilapidated houses, with poverty-stricken inmates; no half-naked children and barefooted women, such as I had been accustomed to see in Hillsborough, Easton, St. Michael's, and Baltimore. The people looked more able, stronger, healthier, and happier than those of Maryland. I was for once made glad by a view of extreme wealth, without being saddened by seeing extreme poverty. But the most astonishing as well as the most interesting thing to me was the condition of the colored people, a great many of whom, like myself, had escaped thither as a refuge from the hunters of men. I found many, who had not been seven years out of their chains, living in finer houses, and evidently enjoying more of the comforts of life, than the average of slaveholders in Maryland. I will venture to assert, that my friend Mr. Nathan Johnson (of whom I can say with a grateful heart, "I was hungry, and he gave me meat; I was thirsty, and he gave me drink; I was a stranger, and he took me in"[58]) lived in a neater house; dined at a better table; took, paid for, and read, more newspapers; better understood the moral, religious, and political character of the nation,—than nine tenths of the slaveholders in Talbot county Maryland. Yet Mr. Johnson was a working man. His hands were hardened by toil, and not his alone, but those also of Mrs. Johnson. I found the colored people much more spirited than I had supposed they would be. I found among them a determination to protect each other from the blood-thirsty kidnapper, at all hazards. Soon after my arrival, I was told a circumstance which illustrated their spirit. A colored man and a fugitive slave were on unfriendly terms. The former was heard to threaten the latter with informing his master of his whereabouts. Straightway a meeting was called among the colored people, under the stereotyped notice, "Business of importance!" The betrayer was invited to attend. The people came at the appointed hour, and organized the meeting by appointing a very religious old gentleman as president, who, I believe, made a prayer, after which he addressed the meeting as follows: *"Friends, we have got him here, and I would recommend that you young men just take him outside the door, and kill him!"* With this, a number of them bolted at him; but they were

---

[58] I WAS A STRANGER, AND HE TOOK ME IN: Matthew 25:37–40: "Then shall the righteous answer him, saying, Lord, when saw we thee an hungred, and fed thee? or thirsty, and gave thee drink? / When saw we thee a stranger, and took thee in? or naked, and clothed thee? / Or when saw we thee sick, or in prison, and came unto thee? / And the King shall answer and say unto them, Verily I say unto you, Inasmuch as ye have done it unto one of the least of these my brethren, ye have done it unto me."

intercepted by some more timid than themselves, and the betrayer escaped their vengeance, and has not been seen in New Bedford since. I believe there have been no more such threats, and should there be hereafter, I doubt not that death would be the consequence.

I found employment, the third day after my arrival, in stowing a sloop with a load of oil. It was new, dirty, and hard work for me; but I went at it with a glad heart and a willing hand. I was now my own master. It was a happy moment, the rapture of which can be understood only by those who have been slaves. It was the first work, the reward of which was to be entirely my own. There was no Master Hugh standing ready, the moment I earned the money, to rob me of it. I worked that day with a pleasure I had never before experienced. I was at work for myself and newly-married wife. It was to me the starting point of a new existence. When I got through with that job, I went in pursuit of a job of calking; but such was the strength of prejudice against color, among the white calkers, that they refused to work with me, and of course I could get no employment.[59] Finding my trade of no immediate benefit, I threw off my calking habiliments, and prepared myself to do any kind of work I could get to do. Mr. Johnson kindly let me have his wood-horse and saw, and I very soon found myself a plenty of work. There was no work too hard— none too dirty. I was ready to saw wood, shovel coal, carry wood, sweep the chimney, or roll oil casks,—all of which I did for nearly three years in New Bedford, before I became known to the anti-slavery world.

In about four months after I went to New Bedford, there came a young man to me, and inquired if I did not wish to take the "Liberator."[60] I told him I did; but, just having made my escape from slavery, I remarked that I was unable to pay for it then. I, however, finally became a subscriber to it. The paper came, and I read it from week to week with such feelings as it would be quite idle for me to attempt to describe. The paper became my meat and my drink. My soul was set all on fire. Its sympathy for my brethren in bonds—its scathing denunciations of slaveholders—its faithful exposures of slavery—and its powerful attacks upon the upholders of the institution—sent a thrill of joy through my soul, such as I had never felt before!

I had not long been a reader of the "Liberator," before I got a pretty correct idea of the principles, measures and spirit of the anti-slavery reform. I took right hold of the cause. I could do but little; but what I could, I did with a joyful heart, and never felt happier than when in an

[59]I COULD GET NO EMPLOYMENT: Douglass notes, "I am told that colored persons can now get employment at calking in New Bedford—a result of anti-slavery effort."
[60]LIBERATOR: An abolitionist newspaper (1831–1865) published weekly by William Lloyd Garrison.

1090 • *Frederick Douglass*

anti-slavery meeting. I seldom had much to say at the meetings, because what I wanted to say was said so much better by others. But, while attending an anti-slavery convention at Nantucket, on the 11th of August, 1841, I felt strongly moved to speak, and was at the same time much urged to do so by Mr. William C. Coffin, a gentleman who had heard me speak in the colored people's meeting at New Bedford. It was a severe cross, and I took it up reluctantly. The truth was, I felt myself a slave, and the idea of speaking to white people weighed me down. I spoke but a few moments, when I felt a degree of freedom, and said what I desired with considerable ease. From that time until now, I have been engaged in pleading the cause of my brethren—with what success, and with what devotion, I leave those acquainted with my labors to decide.

APPENDIX

I find, since reading over the foregoing Narrative, that I have, in several instances, spoken in such a tone and manner, respecting religion, as may possibly lead those unacquainted with my religious views to suppose me an opponent of all religion. To remove the liability of such misapprehensions, I deem it proper to append the following brief explanation. What I have said respecting and against religion, I mean strictly to apply to the *slaveholding religion* of this land, and with no possible reference to Christianity proper; for, between the Christianity of this land, and the Christianity of Christ, I recognize the widest possible difference—so wide, that to receive the one as good, pure, and holy, is of necessity to reject the other as bad, corrupt, and wicked. To be the friend of the one, is of necessity to be the enemy of the other. I love the pure, peaceable, and impartial Christianity of Christ: I therefore hate the corrupt, slaveholding, women-whipping, cradle-plundering, partial and hypocritical Christianity of this land. Indeed, I can see no reason, but the most deceitful one, for calling the religion of this land Christianity. I look upon it as the climax of all misnomers, the boldest of all frauds, and the grossest of all libels. Never was there a clearer case of "stealing the livery of the court of heaven to serve the devil in."[61] I am filled with unutterable loathing when I contemplate the religious pomp and show, together with the horrible inconsistencies, which every where surrounded me. We have men-stealers for ministers, women-whippers for missionaries, and cradle-plunderers for church members. The man who wields the blood-clotted cowskin during the week fills the pulpit on Sunday, and claims to be a minister of the meek and lowly Jesus. The

[61]STEALING THE LIVERY OF THE COURT OF HEAVEN TO SERVE THE DEVIL IN: A paraphrase of lines from "The Course of Time," by Reverend Robert Pollok (1798–1827), a Scottish poet.

man who robs me of my earnings at the end of each week meets me as a class-leader on Sunday morning, to show me the way of life, and the path of salvation. He who sells my sister, for purposes of prostitution, stands forth as the pious advocate of purity. He who proclaims it a religious duty to read the Bible denies me the right of learning to read the name of the God who made me. He who is the religious advocate of marriage robs whole millions of its sacred influence, and leaves them to the ravages of wholesale pollution. The warm defender of the sacredness of the family relation is the same that scatters whole families,—sundering husbands and wives, parents and children, sisters and brothers,—leaving the hut vacant, and the hearth desolate. We see the thief preaching against theft, and the adulterer against adultery. We have men sold to build churches, women sold to support the gospel, and babes sold to purchase Bibles for the *poor heathen! all for the glory of God and the good of souls!* The slave auctioneer's bell and the church-going bell chime in with each other, and the bitter cries of the heart-broken slave are drowned in the religious shouts of his pious master. Revivals of religion and revivals in the slave-trade go hand in hand together. The slave prison and the church stand near each other. The clanking of fetters and the rattling of chains in the prison, and the pious psalm and solemn prayer in the church, may be heard at the same time. The dealers in the bodies and souls of men erect their stand in the presence of the pulpit, and they mutually help each other. The dealer gives his blood-stained gold to support the pulpit, and the pulpit, in return, covers his infernal business with the garb of Christianity. Here we have religion and robbery the allies of each other—devils dressed in angels' robes, and hell presenting the semblance of paradise.

> "*Just God! and these are they,*
> *Who minister at thine altar, God of right!*[62]
> *Men who their hands, with prayer and blessing, lay*
> *On Israel's ark of light.*

> "*What! preach, and kidnap men?*
> *Give thanks, and rob thy own afflicted poor?*
> *Talk of thy glorious liberty, and then*
> *Bolt hard the captive's door?*

> "*What! servants of thy own*
> *Merciful Son, who came to seek and save*
> *The homeless and the outcast, fettering down*
> *The tasked and plundered slave!*

---

[62]JUST GOD! AND THESE ARE THEY, WHO MINISTER AT THINE ALTAR, GOD OF RIGHT: From the antislavery poem, "Clerical Oppressors" (1836), by John Greenleaf Whittier.

> "Pilate and Herod friends
>   Chief priests and rulers, as of old, combine!
> Just God and holy! is that church which lends
>   Strength to the spoiler thine?"

The Christianity of America is a Christianity, of whose votaries it may be as truly said, as it was of the ancient scribes and Pharisees,[63] "They bind heavy burdens, and grievous to be borne, and lay them on men's shoulders, but they themselves will not move them with one of their fingers. All their works they do for to be seen of men.—They love the uppermost rooms at feasts, and the chief seats in the synagogues,...and to be called of men, Rabbi, Rabbi.— But woe unto you, scribes and Pharisees, hypocrites! for ye shut up the kingdom of heaven against men; for ye neither go in yourselves, neither suffer ye them that are entering to go in. Ye devour widows' houses, and for a pretence make long prayers; therefore ye shall receive the greater damnation. Ye compass sea and land to make one proselyte, and when he is made, ye make him twofold more the child of hell than yourselves.—Woe unto you, scribes and Pharisees, hypocrites! for ye pay tithe of mint, and anise, and cumin,[64] and have omitted the weightier matters of the law, judgment, mercy, and faith; these ought ye to have done, and not to leave the other undone. Ye blind guides! which strain at a gnat, and swallow a camel. Woe unto you, scribes and Pharisees, hypocrites! for ye make clean the outside of the cup and of the platter; but within, they are full of extortion and excess.—Woe unto you, scribes and Pharisees, hypocrites! for ye are like unto whited sepulchres, which indeed appear beautiful outward, but are within full of dead men's bones, and of all uncleanness. Even so ye also outwardly appear righteous unto men, but within ye are full of hypocrisy and iniquity."

Dark and terrible as is this picture, I hold it to be strictly true of the overwhelming mass of professed Christians in America. They strain at a gnat, and swallow a camel. Could any thing be more true of our churches? They would be shocked at the proposition of fellowshipping a *sheep*-stealer; and at the same time they hug to their communion a *man*-stealer, and brand me with being an infidel, if I find fault with them for it. They attend with Pharisaical strictness to the outward forms of religion, and at the same time neglect the weightier matters of the law, judgment, mercy, and faith. They are always ready to sacrifice, but seldom to show mercy. They are they who are represented as professing to love God whom they have not seen, whilst they hate their brother

---

[63]PHARISEES: The Pharisees were a powerful Jewish sect that enforced strict observance of oral and written religious laws (see Matthew 23).
[64]ANISE, AND CUMIN: Anise, an aromatic herb; cumin, an aromatic plant used for flavoring.

whom they have seen. They love the heathen on the other side of the globe. They can pray for him, pay money to have the Bible put into his hand, and missionaries to instruct him; while they despise and totally neglect the heathen at their own doors.

Such is, very briefly, my view of the religion of this land; and to avoid any misunderstanding, growing out of the use of general terms, I mean, by the religion of this land, that which is revealed in the words, deeds, and actions, of those bodies, north and south, calling themselves Christian churches, and yet in union with slaveholders. It is against religion, as presented by these bodies, that I have felt it my duty to testify.

I conclude these remarks by copying the following portrait of the religion of the south, (which is, by communion and fellowship, the religion of the north,) which I soberly affirm is "true to the life," and without caricature or the slightest exaggeration. It is said to have been drawn, several years before the present anti-slavery agitation began, by a northern Methodist preacher, who, while residing at the south, had an opportunity to see slaveholding morals, manners, and piety, with his own eyes. "Shall I not visit for these things? saith the Lord. Shall not my soul be avenged on such a nation as this?"[65]

A PARODY[66]

"Come, saints and sinners, hear me tell
How pious priests whip Jack and Nell,
And women buy and children sell,
And preach all sinners down to hell,
    And sing of heavenly union.

"They'll bleat and baa, dona like goats,
Gorge down black sheep, and strain at motes,
Array their backs in fine black coats,
Then seize their negroes by their throats,
    And choke, for heavenly union.

"They'll church you if you sip a dram,
And damn you if you steal a lamb;
Yet rob old Tony, Doll, and Sam,
Of human rights, and bread and ham;
    Kidnapper's heavenly union.

[65]SHALL I NOT VISIT FOR THESE THINGS? SAITH THE LORD. SHALL NOT MY SOUL BE AVENGED ON SUCH A NATION AS THIS?: Jeremiah 5:9.
[66]A PARODY: Douglass's parody is based on a popular Southern hymn, "Heavenly Union." The first stanza begins, "Come, saints and sinners, hear me tell / The wonders of Emmanuel, / Who saved me from a burning hell, / And brought my soul with Christ to dwell, / And gave me heav'nly union."

"They'll loudly talk of Christ's reward,
And bind his image with a cord
And scold, and swing the lash abhorred,
And sell their brother in the Lord
    To handcuffed heavenly union.

"They'll read and sing a sacred song,
And make a prayer both loud and long,
And teach the right and do the wrong,
Hailing the brother, sister throng,
    With words of heavenly union.

"We wonder how such saints can sing,
Or praise the Lord upon the wing,
Who roar, and scold, and whip, and sting,
And to their slaves and mammon cling,
    In guilty conscience union.

"They'll raise tobacco, corn, and rye,
And drive, and thieve, and cheat, and lie,
And lay up treasures in the sky,
By making switch and cowskin fly,
    In hope of heavenly union.

"They'll crack old Tony on the skull,
And preach and roar like Bashan[67] *bull,*
Or braying ass, of mischief full,
Then seize old Jacob by the wool,
    And pull for heavenly union.

"A roaring, ranting, sleek man-thief,
Who lived on mutton, veal, and beef,
Yet never would afford relief
To needy, sable sons of grief,
    Was big with heavenly union.

"'Love not the world,' the preacher said,
And winked his eye, and shook his head;
He seized on Tom, and Dick, and Ned,
Cut short their meat, and clothes, and bread,
    Yet still loved heavenly union.

"Another preacher whining spoke
Of One whose heart for sinners broke:

[67]BASHAN: Ancient country, eastern Palestine.

He tied old Nanny to an oak,
  And drew the blood at every stroke,
    And prayed for heavenly union.

"Two others oped their iron jaws,
  And waved their children-stealing paws;
  There sat their children in gewgaws;
  By stinting negroes' blacks and maws,
    They kept up heavenly union.

"All good from Jack another takes,
  And entertains their flirts and rakes,
  Who dress as sleek as glossy snakes,
  And cram their mouths with sweetened cakes;
    And this goes down for union."

Sincerely and earnestly hoping that this little book may do something toward throwing light on the American slave system, and hastening the glad day of deliverance to the millions of my brethren in bonds—faithfully relying upon the power of truth, love, and justice, for success in my humble efforts—and solemnly pledging my self anew to the sacred cause,—I subscribe myself,

FREDERICK DOUGLASS
Lynn, Mass., April 28, 1845.

[1845]

[Letter to His Former Master]

Sir—
    The long and intimate, though by no means friendly relation which unhappily subsisted between you and myself, leads me to hope that you will easily account for the great liberty which I now take in addressing you in this open and public manner. The same fact may possibly remove any disagreeable surprise which you may experience on again finding your name coupled with mine, in any other way than in an advertisement, accurately describing my person, and offering a large sum for my arrest. In thus dragging you again before the public, I am aware that I shall subject myself to no inconsiderable amount of censure. I shall probably be charged with

an unwarrantable, if not a wanton and reckless disregard of the rights and proprieties of private life. There are those North as well as South who entertain a much higher respect for rights which are merely conventional, than they do for rights which are personal and essential. Not a few there are in our country, who, while they have no scruples against robbing the laborer of the hard earned results of his patient industry, will be shocked by the extremely indelicate manner of bringing your name before the public. Believing this to be the case, and wishing to meet every reasonable or plausible objection to my conduct, I will frankly state the ground upon which I justify myself in this instance, as well as on former occasions when I have thought proper to mention your name in public. All will agree that a man guilty of theft, robbery, or murder, has forfeited the right to concealment and private life; that the community have a right to subject such persons to the most complete exposure. However much they may desire retirement, and aim to conceal themselves and their movements from the popular gaze, the public have a right to ferret them out, and bring their conduct before the proper tribunals of the country for investigation. Sir, you will undoubtedly make the proper application of these generally admitted principles, and will easily see the light in which you are regarded by me. I will not therefore manifest ill temper, by calling you hard names. I know you to be a man of some intelligence, and can readily determine the precise estimate which I entertain of your character. I may therefore indulge in language which may seem to others indirect and ambiguous, and yet be quite well understood by yourself.

I have selected this day on which to address you, because it is the anniversary of my emancipation[1]; and knowing of no better way, I am led to this as the best mode of celebrating that truly important event. Just ten years ago this beautiful September morning, yon bright sun beheld me a slave—a poor, degraded chattel—trembling at the sound of your voice, lamenting that I was a man, and wishing myself a brute. The hopes which I had treasured up for weeks of a safe and successful escape from your grasp, were powerfully confronted at this last hour by dark clouds of doubt and fear, making my person shake and my bosom to heave with the heavy contest between hope and fear. I have no words to describe to you the deep agony of soul which I experienced on that never to be forgotten morning—(for I left by daylight). I was making a leap in the dark. The probabilities, so far as I could by reason determine them, were stoutly against the undertaking. The preliminaries and precautions I had adopted

---

[1] EMANCIPATION: Douglass wrote this letter on September 3, 1848, the tenth anniversary of his escape from slavery.

previously, all worked badly. I was like one going to war without weapons—ten chances of defeat to one of victory. One in whom I had confided, and one who had promised me assistance, appalled by fear at the trial hour, deserted me, thus leaving the responsibility of success or failure solely with myself. You, sir, can never know my feelings. As I look back to them, I can scarcely realize that I have passed through a scene so trying. Trying however as they were, and gloomy as was the prospect, thanks be to the Most High, who is ever the God of the oppressed, at the moment which was to determine my whole earthly career. His grace was sufficient, my mind was made up. I embraced the golden opportunity, took the morning tide at the flood, and a free man, young, active and strong, is the result.

I have often thought I should like to explain to you the grounds upon which I have justified myself in running away from you. I am almost ashamed to do so now, for by this time you may have discovered them yourself. I will, however, glance at them. When yet but a child about six years old, I imbibed the determination to run away. The very first mental effort that I now remember on my part, was an attempt to solve the mystery, Why am I a slave? and with this question my youthful mind was troubled for many days, pressing upon me more heavily at times than others. When I saw the slave-driver whip a slave woman, cut the blood out of her neck, and heard her piteous cries, I went away into the corner of the fence, wept and pondered over the mystery. I had, through some medium, I know not what, got some idea of God, the Creator of all mankind, the black and the white, and that he had made the blacks to serve the whites as slaves. How he could do this and be *good*, I could not tell. I was not satisfied with this theory, which made God responsible for slavery, for it pained me greatly, and I have wept over it long and often. At one time, your first wife, Mrs. Lucretia, heard me singing and saw me shedding tears, and asked of me the matter, but I was afraid to tell her. I was puzzled with this question, till one night, while sitting in the kitchen, I heard some of the old slaves talking of their parents having been stolen from Africa by white men, and were sold here as slaves. The whole mystery was solved at once. Very soon after this my aunt Jinny and uncle Noah ran away, and the great noise made about it by your father-in-law, made me for the first time acquainted with the fact, that there were free States as well as slave States. From that time, I resolved that I would some day run away. The morality of the act, I dispose as follows: I am myself; you are yourself; we are two distinct persons, equal persons. What you are, I am. You are a man, and so am I. God created both, and made us separate beings. I am not by nature bound to you, or you to me. Nature does not make your existence depend upon me, or mine to depend upon yours. I cannot walk upon your legs, or you upon mine. I cannot breathe for you, or you for me; I must breathe for myself, and you for yourself. We are distinct persons, and are each equally provided with faculties necessary to our individual existence. In leaving you, I took nothing but what belonged to me, and in no way lessened your means for obtaining an *honest* living. Your faculties remained yours, and mine became useful to their rightful owner. I therefore see no wrong in any part of the transaction. It is true, I went off secretly, but that was more your fault than mine. Had I let you into the secret, you would have defeated the enterprise entirely; but for this, I should have been really glad to have made you acquainted with my intentions to leave.

You may perhaps want to know how I like my present condition. I am free to say, I greatly prefer it to that which I occupied in Maryland. I am, however, by no means prejudiced against the State as such. Its geography, climate, fertility and products, are such as to make it a very desirable abode for any man; and but for the existence of slavery there, it is not impossible that I might again take up my abode in that State. It is not that I love Maryland less, but freedom more. You will be surprised to learn that people at the North labor under the strange delusion that if the slaves were emancipated at the South, they would flock to the North. So far from this being the case, in that event, you would see many old and familiar faces back again to the South. The fact is, there are few here who would not return to the South in the event of emancipation. We want to live in the land of our birth, and to lay our bones by the side of our fathers'; and nothing short of an intense love of personal freedom keeps us from the South. For the sake of this, most of us would live on a crust of bread and a cup of cold water.

Since I left you, I have had a rich experience. I have occupied stations which I never dreamed of when a slave. Three out of the ten years since I left you, I spent as a common laborer on the wharves of New Bedford, Massachusetts. It was there I earned my first free dollar. It was mine. I could spend it as I pleased. I could buy hams or herring with it, without asking any odds of any body. That was a precious dollar to me. You remember when I used to make seven or eight, or even nine dollars a week in Baltimore, you would take every cent of it from me every Saturday night, saying that I belonged to you, and my earnings also. I never liked this conduct on your part—to say the best, I thought it a little mean. I would not have served you so. But let that pass. I was a little awkward about counting money in New England fashion when I first landed in New Bedford. I like to have betrayed myself several times.

I caught myself saying phip, for fourpence; and at one time a man actually charged me with being a runaway, whereupon I was silly enough to become one by running away from him, for I was greatly afraid he might adopt measures to get me again into slavery, a condition I then dreaded more than death.

I soon, however, learned to count money, as well as to make it, and got on swimmingly. I married soon after leaving you: in fact, I was engaged to be married before I left you; and instead of finding my companion a burden, she was truly a helpmeet. She went to live at service,[2] and I to work on the wharf, and though we toiled hard the first winter, we never lived more happily. After remaining in New Bedford for three years, I met with Wm. Lloyd Garrison,[3] a person of whom you have *possibly* heard, as he is pretty generally known among slaveholders. He put it into my head that I might make myself serviceable to the cause of the slave by devoting a portion of my time to telling my own sorrows, and those of other slaves which had come under my observation. This was the commencement of a higher state of existence than any to which I had ever aspired. I was thrown into society the most pure, enlightened and benevolent that the country affords. Among these I have never forgotten you, but have invariably made you the topic of conversation—thus giving you all the notoriety I could do. I need not tell you that the opinion formed of you in these circles, is far from being favorable. They have little respect for your honesty, and less for your religion.

But I was going on to relate to you something of my interesting experience. I had not long enjoyed the excellent society to which I have referred, before the light of its excellence exerted a beneficial influence on my mind and heart. Much of my early dislike of white persons was removed, and their manners, habits and customs, so entirely unlike what I had been used to in the kitchen-quarters on the plantations of the South, fairly charmed me, and gave me a strong disrelish for the coarse and degrading customs of my former condition. I therefore made an effort so to improve my mind and deportment, as to be somewhat fitted to the station to which I seemed almost providentially called. The transition from degradation to respectability was indeed great, and to get from one to the other without carrying some marks of one's former condition, is truly a difficult matter. I would not have

---

[2]AT SERVICE: As a domestic servant.
[3]WM. LLOYD GARRISON: An American abolitionist (1805–1879) from Massachusetts. In 1831, he began publishing an antislavery newspaper, *The Liberator*, in Boston, and in 1832 he helped to form the New England Anti-Slavery Society. He continued to issue the paper for thirty-five years, until the Thirteenth Amendment abolishing slavery was adopted by Congress.

you think that I am now entirely clear of all plantation peculiarities, but my friends here, while they entertain the strongest dislike to them, regard me with that charity to which my past life somewhat entitles me, so that my condition in this respect is exceedingly pleasant. So far as my domestic affairs are concerned, I can boast of as comfortable a dwelling as your own. I have an industrious and neat companion, and four dear children—the oldest a girl of nine years, and three fine boys, the oldest eight, the next six, and the youngest four years old. The three oldest are now going regularly to school—two can read and write, and the other can spell with tolerable correctness words of two sylla-bles: Dear fellows! they are all in comfortable beds, and are sound asleep, perfectly secure under my own roof. There are no slavehold-ers here to rend my heart by snatching them from my arms, or blast a mother's dearest hopes by tearing them from her bosom. These dear children are ours—not to work up into rice, sugar and tobacco, but to watch over, regard, and protect, and to rear them up in the nur-ture and admonition of the gospel—to train them up in the paths of wisdom and virtue, and, as far as we can to make them useful to the world and to themselves. Oh! sir, a slaveholder never appears to me so completely an agent of hell, as when I think of and look upon my dear children. It is then that my feelings rise above my control. I meant to have said more with respect to my own prosperity and happiness, but thoughts and feelings which this recital has quickened unfits me to proceed further in that direction. The grim horrors of slavery rise in all their ghastly terror before me, the wails of millions pierce my heart, and chill my blood. I remember the chain, the gag, the bloody whip, the death-like gloom overshadowing the broken spirit of the fettered bondman, the appalling liability of his being torn away from wife and children, and sold like a beast in the market. Say not that that this is a picture of fancy. You well know that I wear stripes on my back inflicted by your direction; and that you, while we were brothers in the same church, caused this right hand, with which I am now penning this letter, to be closely tied to my left, and my person dragged at the pis-tol's mouth, fifteen miles, from the Bay side to Easton to be sold like a beast in the market, for the alleged crime of intending to escape from your possession. All this and more you remember, and know to be per-fectly true, not only of yourself, but of nearly all of the slaveholders around you.

At this moment, you are probably the guilty holder of at least three of my own dear sisters, and my only brother in bondage. These you regard as your property. They are recorded on your ledger, or perhaps have been sold to human flesh mongers, with a view to filling your own ever-hungry purse. Sir, I desire to know how and where these dear sisters are. Have you sold them? or are they still in your possession? What has become of them? are they living or dead? And my dear old grandmother, whom you turned out like an old horse, to die in the woods—is she still alive? Write and let me know all about them. If my grandmother be still alive, she is of no service to you, for by this time she must be nearly eighty years old—too old to be cared for by one to whom she has ceased to be of service, send her to me at Rochester, or bring her to Philadelphia, and it shall be the crowning happiness of my life to take care of her in her old age. Oh! she was to me a mother, and a father, so far as hard toil for my comfort could make her such. Send me my grandmother! that I may watch over and take care of her in her old age. And my sisters, let me know all about them. I would write to them, and learn all I want to know of them, without disturbing you in any way, but that, through your unrighteous conduct, they have been entirely deprived of the power to read and write. You have kept them in utter ignorance, and have therefore robbed them of the sweet enjoyments of writing or receiving letters from absent friends and relatives. Your wickedness and cruelty committed in this respect on your fellow-creatures, are greater than all the stripes you have laid upon my back, or theirs. It is an outrage upon the soul—a war upon the immortal spirit, and one for which you must give account at the bar of our common Father and Creator.

The responsibility which you have assumed in this regard is truly awful—and how you could stagger under it these many years is marvellous. Your mind must have become darkened, your heart hardened, your conscience seared and petrified, or you would have long since thrown off the accursed load and sought relief at the hands of a sin-forgiving God. How, let me ask, would you look upon me, were I some dark night in company with a band of hardened villains, to enter the precincts of your elegant dwelling and seize the person of your own lovely daughter Amanda, and carry her off from your family, friends and all the loved ones of her youth—make her my slave—compel her to work, and I take her wages— place her name on my ledger as property—disregard her personal rights— fetter the powers of her immortal soul by denying her the right and privilege of learning to read and write—feed her coarsely—clothe her scantily, and whip her on the naked back occasionally; more and still more horrible, leave her unprotected—a degraded victim to the brutal lust of fiendish overseers, who would pollute, blight, and blast her fair soul—rob her of all dignity—destroy her virtue, and annihilate all in her person the graces that adorn the character of virtuous womanhood? I ask how would you regard me, if such were my conduct? Oh! the vocabulary of the damned would not afford a word sufficiently infernal, to express your idea of my God-provoking wickedness. Yet sir, your treatment of my beloved sisters is in all essential points, precisely like the case I have now supposed. Damning as would be such a deed on my part, it would be no more so than that which you have committed against me and my sisters.

I will now bring this letter to a close, you shall hear from me again unless you let me hear from you. I intend to make use of you as a weapon with which to assail the system of slavery—as a means of concentrating public attention on the system, and deepening their horror of trafficking in the souls and bodies of men. I shall make use of you as a means of exposing the character of the American church and clergy—and as a means of bringing this guilty nation with yourself to repentance. In doing this I entertain no malice towards you personally. There is no roof under which you would be more safe than mine, and there is nothing in my house which you might need for your comfort, which I would not readily grant. Indeed, I should esteem it a privilege, to set you an example as to how mankind ought to treat each other.

I am your fellow man, but not your slave,

Frederick Douglass

[1848]

Herman Melville

(1819–1891)

Herman Melville was born in New York City, a descendant of eminent Dutch and English colonial families. His father died when the boy was twelve, leading to a period of financial hardship for Melville's mother and her children.

Melville left school when he was fifteen, and, after a series of odd jobs and efforts at various occupations, he went to sea in 1839 as a cabin boy on a ship bound for Liverpool, England. In January 1841, he took to the sea again, this time on a whaler traveling to the South Seas. He relished the grueling, exhilarating, adventurous life of a seaman and made other voyages on a whaling ship and a frigate.

Back in the United States, Melville entered the literary circles of Boston and New York City and soon wrote two novels, Typee *(1846) and* Omoo *(1847), based on his experiences at sea. Both were successful, Melville's name became widely known, and his next works were eagerly anticipated.*

Melville's third novel, Mardi *(1849), was a failure, however. A long allegorical romance packed with learning, lore, and metaphysical speculation, it baffled readers, and even today only the most dedicated Melville scholars peruse it. The emerging problem for Melville was that his ambition as a writer was at odds with the desires and demands of the literary marketplace. Readers wanted him to supply more novels like* Typee, *whereas he sought greater imaginative challenges and innovations; he did not wish to repeat himself, becoming financially secure but artistically unfulfilled.*

Melville's next novels, Redburn *(1849), describing the experiences of a young man journeying to Liverpool and back, and* White-Jacket *(1850), depicting another young man's life during his service on a naval frigate, proved familiar enough in their storylines to regain for their author the favorable notice of readers. The positive responses convinced him that he had come to understand the interests of a general audience of readers; he could satisfy them through engaging characters and plots even as he pushed himself to accomplish something more profound for a select group of intellectually curious readers willing to be unsettled and provoked. Determined to achieve both financial security and literary renown, in the spring of 1850 Melville started to compose the book about whaling that eventually became* Moby-Dick.

Living in Pittsfield, in western Massachusetts, in 1850–1851, and with the new novel underway, Melville became friends with Nathaniel Hawthorne, whose novels and tales inspired and energized him. Melville believed Hawthorne was a kindred spirit; his example (as Melville interpreted it) demonstrated the artistic craft and thematic intensity and depth that an American writer could display. Melville also was avidly reading King Lear, Hamlet, *and Shakespeare's other major tragedies during this period; an American Shakespeare was for him a genuine possibility, and he aspired to that identity himself.*

In order to understand Melville and to rise to the level of response Moby-Dick *requires, we need to feel the epic scale and scope of this writer's aspirations, the largeness of what he was aiming for in his story of the crazed, blasphemous Captain Ahab's relentless pursuit of the white whale that sheared away his leg. Ahab is horrifying, cruel, and destructive. Even so, he is capable of tenderness, imprisoned by his obsession, committed to his vengeful goal, and hence he is charismatic, compelling, and, for many readers, sympathetic despite his terrible flaws. For Melville, Ahab represents the essential human drive to know the absolute meaning of life, to get to the center of the cosmos's mystery, the innermost truth (if there is one) of Nature, God, and the Universe.*

Moby-Dick, *published in 1851, was dedicated to Hawthorne. Melville's important essay "Hawthorne and His Mosses," excerpted below, offers compelling insights into Hawthorne's achievement and, even more, illuminates the workings of Melville's own literary imagination. It is a prelude to, and a companion piece for,* Moby-Dick.

Dense and difficult, Moby-Dick *proved less successful with the reading public than Melville had hoped. Considering its unprecedented form and style, and the immensity of its vision, the reviews were fairly good. Some, to be sure, contained harsh criticisms. A reviewer in New York, for instance, said that the characterization of Ahab "has been grievously spoiled, nay altogether ruined, by a vile overdaubing with a coat of book-learning and mysticism; there is no method in his madness; and we must needs pronounce the chief feature of the volume a perfect failure, and the work itself inartistic." Yet this reviewer acknowledged the intricacy of Melville's account of whaling and the striking array of other characters. Another reviewer praised "this wildly imaginative and truly thrilling story. We think it the best production which has yet come from that seething brain." But overall both the critical responses and the sales figures disappointed Melville, and his next novel, the weird and wrenching* Pierre *(1852), was very poorly received. One newspaper account of it carried the headline "HERMAN MELVILLE CRAZY."*

Melville understood his dilemma, explaining it in a June 1851 letter to Hawthorne as he was finishing Moby-Dick: *"What I feel most moved to write, that is banned,—it will not pay. Yet, altogether, write the other way I cannot. So the product is a final hash, and all my books are botches."*

Deeply in debt, and with a family to support, Melville then turned to the writing of short stories, expecting to make money by selling them to magazines. Between late 1853 and mid-1856 he published thirteen stories, seven of them in Putnam's Monthly Magazine *in New York City.*

In May 1856, five of the seven, including the two reprinted below, "Bartleby, the Scrivener" and "Benito Cereno," were published in a collection, The Piazza Tales.

"Bartleby, the Scrivener," a disquieting inquiry into the perilous isolation to which self-reliant individualism may lead, and "Benito Cereno," a mesmerizing account of rebellion on a Spanish slave ship, are brilliant pieces of writing. The reviews of The Piazza Tales were mostly positive, and Melville followed it with a stinging satiric novel, The Confidence-Man, published in 1857. But Melville's hopes for an income through his art came to nothing. Hardly anyone, it seems, read The Confidence-Man; Melville did not earn anything from it. And the publisher of The Piazza Tales went out of business in 1857; Melville received no money for this publication, either.

Except for the short novel Billy Budd, which was found among Melville's papers after his death, he produced no fiction after 1860, focusing instead on lyric poems—a number of which he published in Battle Pieces and Aspects of the Civil War (1866)—and on a long narrative in verse, Clarel (1876), which took shape from a trip that Melville made to the Holy Land. During the final decades of his life, Melville held a job as a customs inspector in New York City. His death in 1891 was almost entirely unnoticed by literary journals and newspapers; the obituary in the New York Times misidentified him as Henry Melville.

Melville was slow to gain recognition as one of the classic authors of American literature. Like Ralph Waldo Emerson, Emily Dickinson, and Henry James, he is not easy of access, but in a way this amounts to a tribute to the originality of his work in Moby-Dick and in the best of his stories. As the critic Richard Chase observed, Melville's "idea of art" was "Promethean": "He thought of a work of art as something never finished, something that remained living, organic, and emergent."

The selections below begin with the excerpt from "Hawthorne and His Mosses." Next is "Bartleby, the Scrivener," and then the long, complex, brooding story "Benito Cereno." The final selections are two Civil War poems: "The Portent," keyed to the execution of the radical abolitionist John Brown, and "The March into Virginia," dealing with a battle early in the war.

Both "Bartleby, the Scrivener" and "Benito Cereno," as the critic Willard Thorp has stated, are "mystery" tales. Who is this eccentric, passive, unresponsive young man, Bartleby, and what is to be done about him? What is the truth of the situation aboard the slave ship that Captain Amasa Delano visits, with its agitated Spanish captain Benito Cereno and his seemingly obedient and faithful black attendant, Babo? While different in character and setting, both of these stories show Melville exploring the relationship between fact and fiction, reality and appearance. Both, furthermore, dramatize failures of knowledge— knowledge of the self and of others. The persons we encounter and their *actions are time and again inscrutable; when we think we know the truth about them, that is when we may be most deluded.*

Melville and Hawthorne had a final meeting in November 1856, when Melville, on his way to the Mediterranean, made a stop in Liverpool, where Hawthorne was serving as American Consul. In an entry in his journal, Hawthorne captured the painful grandeur of his extraordinary, isolated friend, who had by this point produced some of the greatest work in American literary history yet whose career as a successful writer had already come to an end:

> *Melville, as he always does, began to reason of Providence and futurity, and of everything that lies beyond human ken, and informed me that he had "pretty much made up his mind to be annihilated"; but still he does not seem to rest in that anticipation; and, I think, will never rest until he gets hold of a definite belief. It is strange how he persists—and has persisted ever since I knew him, and probably long before—in wandering to and fro over these deserts, as dismal and monotonous as the sand hills amid we were sitting. He can neither believe, nor be comfortable in his unbelief; and he is too honest and courageous not to try to do one or the other. If he were a religious man, he would be one of the most truly religious and reverential; he has a very high and noble nature, and better worth immortality than most of us.*

For biography: Laurie Robertson-Lorant, Melville: A Biography *(1996); and Hershel Parker*, Herman Melville: A Biography *(2 vols., 1996–2002). Older but still valuable studies include Newton Arvin,* Herman Melville *(1950); Lawrance Thompson,* Melville's Quarrel with God *(1952); and Warner Berthoff,* The Example of Melville *(1962). Among more recent commentaries, the following are recommended: Richard H. Brodhead,* Hawthorne, Melville, and the Novel *(1976); and Neal L. Tolchin,* Mourning, Gender, and Creativity in the Art of Herman Melville *(1988). A helpful resource is* A Companion to Melville Studies, *ed. John Bryant (1986)*

For analyses of Melville's stories: William B. Dillingham, Melville's Short Fiction, 1853–1856 *(1977);* Bartleby the Inscrutable: A Collection of Commentary on Herman Melville's tale "Bartleby, the Scrivener", *ed. M. Thomas Inge (1979); and* Critical Essays on Herman Melville's "Benito Cereno", *ed. Robert E. Burkholder (1992).*

From Hawthorne and His Mosses

BY A VIRGINIAN SPENDING JULY IN VERMONT[1]

But it is the least part of genius that attracts admiration. Where Hawthorne is known, he seems to be deemed a pleasant writer, with a pleasant style,— a sequestered, harmless man, from whom any deep and weighty thing would hardly be anticipated:—a man who means no meanings. But there is no man, in whom humor and love, like mountain peaks, soar to such a rapt height, as to receive the irradiations of the upper skies;—there is no man in whom humor and love are developed in that high form called genius; no such man can exist without also possessing, as the indispensable complement of these, a great, deep intellect, which drops down into the universe like a plummet. Or, love and humor are only the eyes, through which such an intellect views this world. The great beauty in such a mind is but the product of its strength. What, to all readers, can be more charming than the piece entitled "Monsieur du Miroir"; and to a reader at all capable of fully fathoming it, what, at the same time, can possess more mystical depth of meaning?—Yes, there he sits, and looks at me,—this "shape of mystery," this "identical Monsieur du Miroir."—"Methinks I should tremble now, were his wizard power of gliding through all impediments in search of me, to place him suddenly before my eyes."

How profound, nay appalling, is the moral evolved by the "Earth's Holocaust"; where—beginning with the hollow follies and affectations of the world,—all vanities and empty theories and forms, are, one after another, and by an admirably graduated, growing comprehensiveness, thrown into the allegorical fire, till, at length, nothing is left but the all-engendering heart of man; which remaining still unconsumed, the great conflagration is nought.

Of a piece with this, is the "Intelligence Office," a wondrous symbolizing of the secret workings in men's souls. There are other sketches, still more charged with ponderous import.

"The Christmas Banquet," and "The Bosom Serpent" would be fine subjects for a curious and elaborate analysis, touching the conjectural parts of the mind that produced them. For spite of all the Indian-summer sunlight on the hither side of Hawthorne's soul, the other side—like the dark half

---

[1]IN VERMONT: Melville used this pseudonym for his essay, published in mid-August 1850. He had met Hawthorne earlier in the month, in the Berkshires in western Massachusetts.

of the physical sphere—is shrouded in a blackness, ten times black. But this darkness but gives more effect to the ever-moving dawn, that forever advances through it, and circumnavigates his world. Whether Hawthorne has simply availed himself of this mystical blackness as a means to the wondrous effects he makes it to produce in his lights and shades; or whether there really lurks in him, perhaps unknown to himself, a touch of Puritanic gloom,—this, I cannot altogether tell. Certain it is, however, that this great power of blackness in him derives its force from its appeals to that Calvinistic[2] sense of Innate Depravity and Original Sin, from whose visitations, in some shape or other, no deeply thinking mind is always and wholly free. For, in certain moods, no man can weigh this world, without throwing in something, somehow like Original Sin, to strike the uneven balance. At all events, perhaps no writer has ever wielded this terrific thought with greater terror than this same harmless Hawthorne. Still more: this black conceit pervades him, through and through. You may be witched by his sunlight,—transported by the bright gildings in the skies he builds over you;—but there is the blackness of darkness beyond; and even his bright gildings but fringe, and play upon the edges of thunder-clouds.—In one word, the world is mistaken in this Nathaniel Hawthorne. He himself must often have smiled at its absurd misconception of him. He is immeasurably deeper than the plummet of the mere critic. For it is not the brain that can test such a man; it is only the heart. You cannot come to know greatness by inspecting it; there is no glimpse to be caught of it, except by intuition; you need not ring it, you but touch it, and you find it is gold.

Now it is that blackness in Hawthorne, of which I have spoken, that so fixes and fascinates me. It may be, nevertheless, that it is too largely developed in him. Perhaps he does not give us a ray of his light for every shade of his dark. But however this may be, this blackness it is that furnishes the infinite obscure of his back-ground,—that back-ground, against which Shakespeare plays his grandest conceits, the things that have made for Shakespeare his loftiest, but most circumscribed renown, as the profoundest of thinkers. For by philosophers Shakespeare is not adored as the great man of tragedy and comedy.—"Off with his head! so much for Buckingham!" this sort of rant, interlined by another hand, brings down the house,—those mistaken souls, who dream of Shakespeare as a mere man of Richard-the-Third humps, and Macbeth daggers. But it is those deep far-away things in him; those occasional flashings-forth of the intuitive Truth in him; those short, quick probings at the very axis of reality;—these are

2CALVINISTIC: Referring to the Protestant reformer John Calvin (1509–1564), whose theology formed the foundation of Puritan beliefs.

the things that make Shakespeare, Shakespeare. Through the mouths of the dark characters of Hamlet, Timon, Lear, and Iago,[3] he craftily says, or sometimes insinuates the things, which we feel to be so terrifically true, that it were all but madness for any good man, in his own proper character, to utter, or even hint of them. Tormented into desperation, Lear the frantic King tears off the mask, and speaks the sane madness of vital truth. But, as I before said, it is the least part of genius that attracts admiration. And so, much of the blind, unbridled admiration that has been heaped upon Shakespeare, has been lavished upon the least part of him. And few of his endless commentators and critics seem to have remembered, or even perceived, that the immediate products of a great mind are not so great, as that undeveloped, (and sometimes undevelopable) yet dimly-discernable greatness, to which these immediate products are but the infallible indices. In Shakespeare's tomb lies infinitely more than Shakespeare ever wrote. And if I magnify Shakespeare, it is not so much for what he did do, as for what he did not do, or refrained from doing. For in this world of lies, Truth is forced to fly like a scared white doe in the woodlands; and only by cunning glimpses will she reveal herself, as in Shakespeare and other masters of the great Art of Telling the Truth,—even though it be covertly, and by snatches.

But if this view of the all-popular Shakespeare be seldom taken by his readers, and if very few who extol him, have ever read him deeply, or, perhaps, only have seen him on the tricky stage, (which alone made, and is still making him his mere mob renown)—if few men have time, or patience, or palate, for the spiritual truth as it is in that great genius;— it is, then, no matter of surprise that in a contemporaneous age, Nathaniel Hawthorne is a man, as yet, almost utterly mistaken among men. Here and there, in some quiet arm-chair in the noisy town, or some deep nook among the noiseless mountains, he may be appreciated for something of what he is. But unlike Shakespeare, who was forced to the contrary course by circumstances, Hawthorne (either from simple disinclination, or else from inaptitude) refrains from all the popularizing noise and show of broad farce, and blood-besmeared tragedy; content with the still, rich utterances of a great intellect in repose, and which sends few thoughts into circulation, except they be arterialized at his large warm lungs, and expanded in his honest heart.

---

[3]HAMLET, TIMON, LEAR, AND IAGO: Characters from Shakespeare's plays. Hamlet is the haunted prince of Denmark in the tragedy that bears his name; Timon is a philosopher in the tragedy *Timon of Athens*; Lear is the tragic monarch who loses his family and throne in *King Lear*; and Iago is the treacherous villain of *Othello*.

Nor need you fix upon that blackness in him, if it suit you not. Nor, indeed, will all readers discern it, for it is, mostly, insinuated to those who may best understand it, and account for it; it is not obtruded upon every one alike.

Some may start to read of Shakespeare and Hawthorne on the same page. They may say, that if an illustration were needed, a lesser light might have sufficed to elucidate this Hawthorne, this small man of yesterday. But I am not, willingly, one of those, who, as touching Shakespeare at least, exemplify the maxim of Rochefoucault,[4] that "we exalt the reputation of some, in order to depress that of others";—who, to teach all noble-souled aspirants that there is no hope for them, pronounce Shakespeare absolutely unapproachable. But Shakespeare has been approached. There are minds that have gone as far as Shakespeare into the universe. And hardly a mortal man, who, at some time or other, has not felt as great thoughts in him as any you will find in Hamlet. We must not inferentially malign mankind for the sake of any one man, whoever he may be. This is too cheap a purchase of contentment for conscious mediocrity to make. Besides, this absolute and unconditional adoration of Shakespeare has grown to be a part of our Anglo Saxon superstitions. The Thirty Nine articles[5] are now Forty. Intolerance has come to exist in this matter. You must believe in Shakespeare's unapproachability, or quit the country. But what sort of a belief is this for an American, a man who is bound to carry republican progressiveness into Literature, as well as into Life? Believe me, my friends, that Shakespeares are this day being born on the banks of the Ohio. And the day will come, when you shall say who reads a book by an Englishman that is a modern? The great mistake seems to be, that even with those Americans who look forward to the coming of a great literary genius among us, they somehow fancy he will come in the costume of Queen Elizabeth's day,—be a writer of dramas founded upon old English history, or the tales of Boccaccio.[6] Whereas, great geniuses are parts of the times; they themselves are the times; and possess a correspondent coloring. It is of a piece with the Jews, who while their Shiloh[7] was meekly walking in their streets, were still praying for his magnificent coming; looking for him in a chariot, who was already among them

[4]ROCHEFOUCAULT: François de la Rochefoucauld (1613–1680), a French writer and moralist.
[5]THIRTY NINE ARTICLES: Originally the doctrines of the Church of England, but used here to mean any set of national beliefs.
[6]BOCCACCIO: Giovanni Boccaccio (1313–1375), an Italian poet and the author of *The Decameron*.
[7]SHILOH: Messiah.

on an ass. Nor must we forget, that, in his own life-time, Shakespeare was not Shakespeare, but only Master William Shakespeare of the shrewd, thriving, business firm of Condell, Shakespeare & Co., proprietors of the Globe Theatre in London; and by a courtly author, of the name of Greene, was hooted at, as an "upstart crow" beautified "with other birds' feathers." For, mark it well, imitation is often the first charge brought against real originality. Why this is so, there is not space to set forth here. You must have plenty of sea-room to tell the Truth in; especially, when it seems to have an aspect of newness, as America did in 1492, though it was then just as old, and perhaps older than Asia, only those sagacious philosophers, the common sailors, had never seen it before; swearing it was all water and moonshine there.

Now, I do not say that Nathaniel of Salem[8] is a greater than William of Avon,[9] or as great. But the difference between the two men is by no means immeasurable. Not a very great deal more, and Nathaniel were verily William.

This, too, I mean, that if Shakespeare has not been equalled, he is sure to be surpassed, and surpassed by an American born now or yet to be born. For it will never do for us who in most other things out-do as well as out-brag the world, it will not do for us to fold our hands and say, In the highest department advance there is none. Nor will it at all do to say, that the world is getting grey and grizzled now, and has lost that fresh charm which she wore of old, and by virtue of which the great poets of past times made themselves what we esteem them to be. Not so. The world is as young today, as when it was created; and this Vermont morning dew is as wet to my feet, as Eden's dew to Adam's. Nor has Nature been all over ransacked by our progenitors, so that no new charms and mysteries remain for this latter generation to find. Far from it. The trillionth part has not yet been said; and all that has been said, but multiplies the avenues to what remains to be said. It is not so much paucity, as superabundance of material that seems to incapacitate modern authors.

Let America then prize and cherish her writers; yea, let her glorify them. They are not so many in number, as to exhaust her good-will. And while she has good kith and kin of her own, to take to her bosom, let her not lavish her embraces upon the household of an alien. For believe it or not England, after all, is, in many things, an alien to us.

---

[8]NATHANIEL OF SALEM: Nathaniel Hawthorne was born in Salem, Massachusetts.
[9]WILLIAM OF AVON: William Shakespeare (1564–1616) was born in Stratford-on-Avon, England.

China has more bowels of real love for us than she. But even were there no Hawthorne, no Emerson,[10] no Whittier,[11] no Irving,[12] no Bryant,[13] no Dana,[14] no Cooper,[15] no Willis[16] (not the author of the "Dashes," but the author of the "Belfry Pigeon")—were there none of these, and others of like calibre among us, nevertheless, let America first praise mediocrity even, in her own children, before she praises (for everywhere, merit demands acknowledgment from every one) the best excellence in the children of any other land. Let her own authors, I say, have the priority of appreciation. I was much pleased with a hot-headed Carolina cousin of mine, who once said,—"If there were no other American to stand by, in Literature,—why, then, I would stand by Pop Emmons and his 'Fredoniad,'[17] and till a better epic came along, swear it was not very far behind the Iliad." Take away the words, and in spirit he was sound.

Not that American genius needs patronage in order to expand. For that explosive sort of stuff will expand though screwed up in a vice, and burst it, though it were triple steel. It is for the nation's sake, and not for her authors' sake, that I would have America be heedful of the increasing greatness among her writers. For how great the shame, if other nations should be before her, in crowning her heroes of the pen. But this is almost the case now. American authors have received more just and discriminating praise (however loftily and ridiculously given, in certain cases) even from some Englishmen, than from their own countrymen. There are hardly five critics in America; and several of them are asleep. As for patronage, it is the American author who now patronizes his country, and not his country him. And if at times some among them appeal to the people for more recognition, it is not always with selfish motives, but patriotic ones.

It is true, that but few of them as yet have evinced that decided originality which merits great praise. But that graceful writer,[18] who perhaps of all Americans has received the most plaudits from his own country

---

[10]EMERSON: Ralph Waldo Emerson (1803–1882), an American poet and essayist and a leader of the Transcendental movement.
[11]WHITTIER: John Greenleaf Whittier (1807–1892) was a poet and an American Quaker and reformer.
[12]IRVING: Washington Irving (1783–1859), an American author best known for his short stories.
[13]BRYANT: William Cullen Bryant (1794–1878), an American poet and social reformer.
[14]DANA: Richard Henry Dana (1787–1879), an American poet, essayist, and literary critic.
[15]COOPER: James Fenimore Cooper (1789–1851), an American novelist most famous for *The Deerslayer* (1841) and *The Last of the Mohicans* (1826).
[16]WILLIS: Nathaniel Parker Willis (1806–1867), an American author and journalist.
[17]POP EMMONS AND HIS 'FREDONIAD': Richard Emmons (1788–1834) wrote a four-volume epic poem entitled *The Fredoniad: or, independence preserved. An epick poem on the late war of 1812*. It was published in 1827.
[18]GRACEFUL WRITER: Melville refers to Washington Irving.

for his productions,—that very popular and amiable writer, however good, and self-reliant in many things, perhaps owes his chief reputation to the self-acknowledged imitation of a foreign model, and to the studied avoidance of all topics but smooth ones. But it is better to fail in originality, than to succeed in imitation. He who has never failed somewhere, that man can not be great. Failure is the true test of greatness. And if it be said, that continual success is a proof that a man wisely knows his powers,—it is only to be added, that, in that case, he knows them to be small. Let us believe it, then, once for all, that there is no hope for us in these smooth pleasing writers that know their powers. Without malice, but to speak the plain fact, they but furnish an appendix to Goldsmith,[19] and other English authors. And we want no American Goldsmiths; nay, we want no American Miltons.[20] It were the vilest thing you could say of a true American author, that he were an American Tompkins.[21] Call him an American, and have done; for you can not say a nobler thing of him.—But it is not meant that all American writers should studiously cleave to nationality in their writings; only this, no American writer should write like an Englishman, or a Frenchman; let him write like a man, for then he will be sure to write like an American. Let us away with this Bostonian leaven of literary flunkeyism towards England. If either must play the flunkey in this thing, let England do it, not us. And the time is not far off when circumstances may force her to it. While we are rapidly preparing for that political supremacy among the nations, which prophetically awaits us at the close of the present century; in a literary point of view, we are deplorably unprepared for it; and we seem studious to remain so. Hitherto, reasons might have existed why this should be; but no good reason exists now. And all that is requisite to amendment in this matter, is simply this: that, while freely acknowledging all excellence, everywhere, we should refrain from unduly lauding foreign writers and, at the same time, duly recognize the meritorious writers that are our own;—those writers, who breathe that unshackled, democratic spirit of Christianity in all things, which now takes the practical lead in this world, though at the same time led by ourselves—us Americans. Let us boldly contemn all imitation, though it comes to us graceful and fragrant as the morning; and foster all originality, though, at first, it be crabbed and ugly as our own pine knots. And

[19]GOLDSMITH: Oliver Goldsmith (1702–1774), an Irish author of the pre-Romantic period. Washington Irving was sometimes referred to as "the American Goldsmith."
[20]MILTON: John Milton (1608–1674), an English poet best known for his epic work *Paradise Lost* (1667).
[21]TOMPKINS: A British phrase meaning "anybody."

if any of our authors fail, or seem to fail, then, in the words of my enthusiastic Carolina cousin, let us clap him on the shoulder, and back him
against all Europe for his second round. The truth is, that in our point
of view, this matter of a national literature has come to such a pass with
us, that in some sense we must turn bullies, else the day is lost, or superiority so far beyond us, that we can hardly say it will ever be ours.

And now, my countrymen, as an excellent author, of your own flesh
and blood,—an unimitating, and, perhaps, in his way, an inimitable
man—whom better can I commend to you, in the first place, than
Nathaniel Hawthorne. He is one of the new, and far better generation
of your writers. The smell of your beeches and hemlocks is upon him;
your own broad praries are in his soul; and if you travel away inland into
his deep and noble nature, you will hear the far roar of his Niagara.
Give not over to future generations the glad duty of acknowledging him
for what he is. Take that joy to your self, in your own generation; and
so shall he feel those grateful impulses in him, that may possibly prompt
him to the full flower of some still greater achievement in your eyes.
And by confessing him, you thereby confess others; you embrace the
whole brotherhood. For genius, all over the world, stands hand in hand,
and one shock of recognition runs the whole circle round.

[1850]

Bartleby, the Scrivener:[1]
A Story of Wall Street

I am a rather elderly man. The nature of my avocations for the last thirty
years has brought me into more than ordinary contact with what would
seem an interesting and somewhat singular set of men, of whom as yet
nothing that I know of has ever been written:—I mean the law-copyists
or scriveners. I have known very many of them, professionally and privately, and if I pleased, could relate divers histories, at which good-
natured gentlemen might smile, and sentimental souls might weep. But
I waive the biographies of all other scriveners for a few passages in the
life of Bartleby, who was a scrivener the strangest I ever saw or heard

---

[1]SCRIVENER: A professional copyist responsible for replicating documents. According to the scholar
Jay Leyda, the law clerk Eli James Murdock Fly (1817–1854), a friend of Melville's, served as the
inspiration for the character of Bartleby.

of. While of other law-copyists I might write the complete life, of Bartleby nothing of that sort can be done. I believe that no materials exist for a full and satisfactory biography of this man. It is an irreparable loss to literature. Bartleby was one of those beings of whom nothing is ascertainable, except from the original sources, and in his case those are very small. What my own astonished eyes saw of Bartleby, *that* is all I know of him, except, indeed, one vague report which will appear in the sequel.

Ere introducing the scrivener, as he first appeared to me, it is fit I make some mention of myself, my *employées*, my business, my chambers, and general surroundings; because some such description is indispensable to an adequate understanding of the chief character about to be presented.

Imprimis[2]: I am a man who, from his youth upwards, has been filled with a profound conviction that the easiest way of life is the best. Hence, though I belong to a profession proverbially energetic and nervous, even to turbulence, at times, yet nothing of that sort have I ever suffered to invade my peace. I am one of those unambitious lawyers who never addresses a jury, or in any way draws down public applause; but in the cool tranquillity of a snug retreat, do a snug business among rich men's bonds and mortgages and title-deeds. All who know me, consider me an eminently *safe* man. The late John Jacob Astor,[3] a personage little given to poetic enthusiasm, had no hesitation in pronouncing my first grand point to be prudence; my next, method. I do not speak it in vanity, but simply record the fact, that I was not unemployed in my profession by the late John Jacob Astor; a name which, I admit, I love to repeat, for it hath a rounded and orbicular sound to it, and rings like unto bullion. I will freely add, that I was not insensible to the late John Jacob Astor's good opinion.

Some time prior to the period at which this little history begins, my avocations had been largely increased. The good old office, now extinct in the State of New York, of a Master in Chancery, had been conferred upon me. It was not a very arduous office, but very pleasantly remunerative. I seldom lose my temper; much more seldom indulge in dangerous indignation at wrongs and outrages; but I must be permitted to be rash here and declare, that I consider the sudden and violent abrogation of the office of Master in Chancery,[4] by the new Constitution, as a——premature act; inasmuch as I had counted upon a life-lease of the profits, whereas I only received those of a few short years. But this is by the way.

[2]IMPRIMIS: In the first place. (Latin)
[3]JOHN JACOB ASTOR: John Jacob Astor (1763–1848), a German-American merchant who became the world's wealthiest man through shrewd real estate transactions in Manhattan.
[4]MASTER IN CHANCERY: A court officer who verifies property titles for transfer.

My chambers were up stairs at No.—Wall-street.[5] At one end they looked upon the white wall of the interior of a spacious sky-light shaft, penetrating the building from top to bottom. This view might have been considered rather tame than otherwise, deficient in what landscape painters call "life." But if so, the view from the other end of my chambers offered, at least, a contrast, if nothing more. In that direction my windows commanded an unobstructed view of a lofty brick wall, black by age and everlasting shade; which wall required no spy-glass to bring out its lurking beauties, but for the benefit of all near-sighted spectators, was pushed up to within ten feet of my window panes. Owing to the great height of the surrounding buildings, and my chambers being on the second floor, the interval between this wall and mine not a little resembled a huge square cistern.

At the period just preceding the advent of Bartleby, I had two persons as copyists in my employment, and a promising lad as an office-boy. First, Turkey; second, Nippers; third, Ginger Nut. These may seem names, the like of which are not usually found in the Directory. In truth they were nicknames, mutually conferred upon each other by my three clerks, and were deemed expressive of their respective persons or characters. Turkey was a short, pursy[6] Englishman of about my own age, that is, somewhere not far from sixty. In the morning, one might say, his face was of a fine florid hue, but after twelve o'clock, meridian[7]—his dinner hour—it blazed like a grate full of Christmas coals; and continued blazing—but, as it were, with a gradual wane—till 6 o'clock, P.M. or thereabouts, after which I saw no more of the proprietor of the face, which gaining its meridian with the sun, seemed to set with it, to rise, culminate, and decline the following day, with the like regularity and undiminished glory. There are many singular coincidences I have known in the course of my life, not the least among which was the fact, that exactly when Turkey displayed his fullest beams from his red and radiant countenance, just then, too, at that critical moment, began the daily period when I considered his business capacities as seriously disturbed for the remainder of the twenty-four hours. Not that he was absolutely idle, or averse to business then; far from it. The difficulty was, he was apt to be altogether too energetic. There was a strange, inflamed, flurried, flighty recklessness of activity about him. He would be incautious in dipping his pen into his inkstand. All his blots upon my documents, were dropped there after twelve o'clock, meridian.

[5]WALL-STREET: In the lower part of Manhattan, the center of New York City's financial district.
[6]PURSY: Shortwinded from obesity.
[7]MERIDIAN: Noon.

Indeed, not only would he be reckless and sadly given to making blots in the afternoon, but some days he went further, and was rather noisy. At such times, too, his face flamed with augmented blazonry, as if cannel coal had been heaped on anthracite. He made an unpleasant racket with his chair; spilled his sand-box; in mending his pens, impatiently split them all to pieces, and threw them on the floor in a sudden passion; stood up and leaned over his table, boxing his papers about in a most indecorous manner, very sad to behold in an elderly man like him. Nevertheless, as he was in many ways a most valuable person to me, and all the time before twelve o'clock, meridian, was the quickest, steadiest creature too, accomplishing a great deal of work in a style not easy to be matched—for these reasons, I was willing to overlook his eccentricities, though indeed, occasionally, I remonstrated with him. I did this very gently, however, because, though the civilest, nay, the blandest and most reverential of men in the morning, yet in the afternoon he was disposed, upon provocation, to be slightly rash with his tongue, in fact, insolent. Now, valuing his morning services as I did, and resolved not to lose them; yet, at the same time made uncomfortable by his inflamed ways after twelve o'clock; and being a man of peace, unwilling by my admonitions to call forth unseemly retorts from him; I took upon me, one Saturday noon (he was always worse on Saturdays), to hint to him, very kindly, that perhaps now that he was growing old, it might be well to abridge his labors; in short, he need not come to my chambers after twelve o'clock, but, dinner over, had best go home to his lodgings and rest himself till tea-time. But no; he insisted upon his afternoon devotions. His countenance became intolerably fervid, as he oratorically assured me—gesticulating with a long ruler at the other end of the room—that if his services in the morning were useful, how indispensable, then, in the afternoon?

"With submission, sir," said Turkey on this occasion, "I consider myself your right-hand man. In the morning I but marshal and deploy my columns; but in the afternoon I put myself at their head, and gallantly charge the foe, thus!"—and he made a violent thrust with the ruler.

"But the blots, Turkey," intimated I.

"True,—but, with submission, sir, behold these hairs! I am getting old. Surely, sir, a blot or two of a warm afternoon is not to be severely urged against gray hairs. Old age—even if it blot the page—is honorable. With submission, sir, we *both* are getting old."

This appeal to my fellow-feeling was hardly to be resisted. At all events, I saw that go he would not. So I made up my mind to let him stay, resolving, nevertheless, to see to it, that during the afternoon he had to do with my less important papers.

Nippers, the second on my list, was a whiskered, sallow, and, upon the whole, rather piratical-looking young man of about five and twenty. I always deemed him the victim of two evil powers—ambition and indigestion. The ambition was evinced by a certain impatience of the duties of a mere copyist, an unwarrantable usurpation of strictly professional affairs, such as the original drawing up of legal documents. The indigestion seemed betokened in an occasional nervous testiness and grinning irritability, causing the teeth to audibly grind together over mistakes committed in copying; unnecessary maledictions, hissed, rather than spoken, in the heat of business; and especially by a continual discontent with the height of the table where he worked. Though of a very ingenious mechanical turn, Nippers could never get this table to suit him. He put chips under it, blocks of various sorts, bits of pasteboard, and at last went so far as to attempt an exquisite adjustment by final pieces of folding blotting-paper. But no invention would answer. If, for the sake of easing his back, he brought the table lid at a sharp angle well up towards his chin, and wrote there like a man using the steep roof of a Dutch house for his desk:—then he declared that it stopped the circulation in his arms. If now he lowered the table to his waistbands, and stooped over it in writing, then there was a sore aching in his back. In short, the truth of the matter was, Nippers knew not what he wanted. Or, if he wanted any thing, it was to be rid of a scrivener's table altogether. Among the manifestations of his diseased ambition was a fondness he had for receiving visits from certain ambiguous-looking fellows in seedy coats, whom he called his clients. Indeed I was aware that not only was he, at times, considerable of a ward-politician, but he occasionally did a little business at the Justices' courts, and was not unknown on the steps of the Tombs.[8] I have good reason to believe, however, that one individual who called upon him at my chambers, and who, with a grand air, he insisted was his client, was no other than a dun,[9] and the alleged title-deed, a bill. But with all his failings, and the annoyances he caused me, Nippers, like his compatriot Turkey, was a very useful man to me; wrote a neat, swift hand; and, when he chose, was not deficient in a gentlemanly sort of deportment. Added to this, he always dressed in a gentlemanly sort of way; and so, incidentally, reflected credit upon my chambers. Whereas with respect to Turkey, I had much ado to keep him from being a reproach to me. His clothes were apt to look oily and smell of eating-houses. He wore his pantaloons very

---

[8]TOMBS: The nickname for the Manhattan House of Detention for Men, built in 1840, so named for its architectural style, which resembled an Egyptian tomb. The narrator implies that Nippers is involved in questionable dealings with the types of people known to frequent the prison.
[9]DUN: Debt collector.

loose and baggy in summer. His coats were execrable; his hat not to be handled. But while the hat was a thing of indifference to me, inasmuch as his natural civility and deference, as a dependent Englishman, always led him to doff it the moment he entered the room, yet his coat was another matter. Concerning his coats, I reasoned with him; but with no effect. The truth was, I suppose, that a man with so small an income, could not afford to sport such a lustrous face and a lustrous coat at one and the same time. As Nippers once observed, Turkey's money went chiefly for red ink. One winter day I presented Turkey with a highly-respectable looking coat of my own, a padded gray coat, of a most comfortable warmth, and which buttoned straight up from the knee to the neck. I thought Turkey would appreciate the favor, and abate his rashness and obstreperousness of afternoons. But no. I verily believe that buttoning himself up in so downy and blanket-like a coat had a pernicious effect upon him; upon the same principle that too much oats are bad for horses. In fact, precisely as a rash, restive horse is said to feel his oats, so Turkey felt his coat. It made him insolent. He was a man whom prosperity harmed.

Though concerning the self-indulgent habits of Turkey I had my own private surmises, yet touching Nippers I was well persuaded that whatever might be his faults in other respects, he was, at least, a temperate young man. But indeed, nature herself seemed to have been his vintner, and at his birth charged him so thoroughly with an irritable, brandy-like disposition, that all subsequent potations were needless. When I consider how, amid the stillness of my chambers, Nippers would sometimes impatiently rise from his seat, and stooping over his table, spread his arms wide apart, seize the whole desk, and move it, and jerk it, with a grim, grinding motion on the floor, as if the table were a perverse voluntary agent, intent on thwarting and vexing him; I plainly perceive that for Nippers, brandy and water were altogether superfluous.

It was fortunate for me that, owing to its peculiar cause—indigestion—the irritability and consequent nervousness of Nippers, were mainly observable in the morning, while in the afternoon he was comparatively mild. So that Turkey's paroxysms only coming on about twelve o'clock, I never had to do with their eccentricities at one time. Their fits relieved each other like guards. When Nippers' was on, Turkey's was off; and *vice versa*. This was a good natural arrangement under the circumstances.

Ginger Nut, the third on my list, was a lad some twelve years old. His father was a carman,[10] ambitious of seeing his son on the bench instead of a cart, before he died. So he sent him to my office as student at law,

[10]CARMAN: Driver.

errand boy, and cleaner and sweeper, at the rate of one dollar a week. He had a little desk to himself, but he did not use it much. Upon inspection, the drawer exhibited a great array of the shells of various sorts of nuts. Indeed, to this quick-witted youth the whole noble science of the law was contained in a nut-shell. Not the least among the employments of Ginger Nut, as well as one which he discharged with the most alacrity, was his duty as cake and apple purveyor for Turkey and Nippers. Copying law papers being proverbially a dry, husky sort of business, my two scriveners were fain to moisten their mouths very often with Spitzenbergs[11] to be had at the numerous stalls nigh the Custom House and Post Office. Also, they sent Ginger Nut very frequently for that peculiar cake—small, flat, round, and very spicy—after which he had been named by them. Of a cold morning when business was but dull, Turkey would gobble up scores of these cakes, as if they were mere wafers—indeed they sell them at the rate of six or eight for a penny—the scrape of his pen blending with the crunching of the crisp particles in his mouth. Of all the fiery afternoon blunders and flurried rashnesses of Turkey, was his once moistening a ginger-cake between his lips, and clapping it on to a mortgage for a seal. I came within an ace of dismissing him then. But he mollified me by making an oriental bow, and saying—"With submission, sir, it was generous of me to find you in stationery on my own account."

Now my original business—that of a conveyancer and title hunter, and drawer-up of recondite documents of all sorts—was considerably increased by receiving the master's office. There was now great work for scriveners. Not only must I push the clerks already with me, but I must have additional help. In answer to my advertisement, a motionless young man one morning, stood upon my office threshold, the door being open, for it was summer. I can see that figure now—pallidly neat, pitiably respectable, incurably forlorn! It was Bartleby.

After a few words touching his qualifications, I engaged him, glad to have among my corps of copyists a man of so singularly sedate an aspect, which I thought might operate beneficially upon the flighty temper of Turkey, and the fiery one of Nippers.

I should have stated before that ground glass folding-doors divided my premises into two parts, one of which was occupied by my scriveners, the other by myself. According to my humor I threw open these doors, or closed them. I resolved to assign Bartleby a corner by the folding-doors, but on my side of them, so as to have this quiet man within easy call, in case any trifling thing was to be done. I placed his desk close

[11]SPITZENBERGS: A variety of apple with a red and yellow skin.

up to a small side-window in that part of the room, a window which originally had afforded a lateral view of certain grimy back-yards and bricks, but which, owing to subsequent erections, commanded at present no view at all, though it gave some light. Within three feet of the panes was a wall, and the light came down from far above, between two lofty buildings, as from a very small opening in a dome. Still further to a satisfactory arrangement, I procured a high green folding screen, which might entirely isolate Bartleby from my sight, though not remove him from my voice. And thus, in a manner, privacy and society were conjoined.

At first Bartleby did an extraordinary quantity of writing. As if long famishing for something to copy, he seemed to gorge himself on my documents. There was no pause for digestion. He ran a day and night line, copying by sun-light and by candle-light. I should have been quite delighted with his application, had he been cheerfully industrious. But he wrote on silently, palely, mechanically.

It is, of course, an indispensable part of a scrivener's business to verify the accuracy of his copy, word by word. Where there are two or more scriveners in an office, they assist each other in this examination, one reading from the copy, the other holding the original. It is a very dull, wearisome, and lethargic affair. I can readily imagine that to some sanguine temperaments it would be altogether intolerable. For example, I cannot credit that the mettlesome poet Byron[12] would have contentedly sat down with Bartleby to examine a law document of, say five hundred pages, closely written in a crimpy hand.

Now and then, in the haste of business, it had been my habit to assist in comparing some brief document myself, calling Turkey or Nippers for this purpose. One object I had in placing Bartleby so handy to me behind the screen, was to avail myself of his services on such trivial occasions. It was on the third day, I think, of his being with me, and before any necessity had arisen for having his own writing examined, that, being much hurried to complete a small affair I had in hand, I abruptly called to Bartleby. In my haste and natural expectancy of instant compliance, I sat with my head bent over the original on my desk, and my right hand sideways, and somewhat nervously extended with the copy, so that immediately upon emerging from his retreat, Bartleby might snatch it and proceed to business without the least delay.

In this very attitude did I sit when I called to him, rapidly stating what it was I wanted him to do—namely, to examine a small paper with me.

[12]BYRON: George Gordon, Lord Byron (1788–1824), an English poet known for his dramatic temper and passionate creativity.

Imagine my surprise, nay, my consternation, when without moving from his privacy, Bartleby in a singularly mild, firm voice, replied, "I would prefer not to."

I sat awhile in perfect silence, rallying my stunned faculties. Immediately it occurred to me that my ears had deceived me, or Bartleby had entirely misunderstood my meaning. I repeated my request in the clearest tone I could assume. But in quite as clear a one came the previous reply, "I would prefer not to."

"Prefer not to," echoed I, rising in high excitement, and crossing the room with a stride. "What do you mean? Are you moon-struck?[13] I want you to help me compare this sheet here—take it," and I thrust it towards him.

"I would prefer not to," said he.

I looked at him steadfastly. His face was leanly composed; his gray eye dimly calm. Not a wrinkle of agitation rippled him. Had there been the least uneasiness, anger, impatience or impertinence in his manner; in other words, had there been any thing ordinarily human about him, doubtless I should have violently dismissed him from the premises. But as it was, I should have as soon thought of turning my pale plaster-of-paris bust of Cicero out of doors. I stood gazing at him awhile, as he went on with his own writing, and then reseated myself at my desk. This is very strange, thought I. What had one best do? But my business hurried me. I concluded to forget the matter for the present, reserving it for my future leisure. So calling Nippers from the other room, the paper was speedily examined.

A few days after this, Bartleby concluded four lengthy documents, being quadruplicates of a week's testimony taken before me in my High Court of Chancery. It became necessary to examine them. It was an important suit, and great accuracy was imperative. Having all things arranged I called Turkey, Nippers and Ginger Nut from the next room, meaning to place the four copies in the hands of my four clerks, while I should read from the original. Accordingly, Turkey, Nippers and Ginger Nut had taken their seats in a row, each with his document in hand, when I called to Bartleby to join this interesting group.

"Bartleby! quick, I am waiting."

I heard a slow scrape of his chair legs on the uncarpeted floor, and soon he appeared standing at the entrance of his hermitage.

"What is wanted?" said he mildly.

[13]MOON-STRUCK: Deranged.

"The copies, the copies," said I hurriedly. "We are going to examine them. There"—and I held towards him the fourth quadruplicate.

"I would prefer not to," he said, and gently disappeared behind the screen.

For a few moments I was turned into a pillar of salt,[14] standing at the head of my seated column of clerks. Recovering myself, I advanced towards the screen, and demanded the reason for such extraordinary conduct.

"*Why* do you refuse?"

"I would prefer not to."

With any other man I should have flown outright into a dreadful passion, scorned all further words, and thrust him ignominiously from my presence. But there was something about Bartleby that not only strangely disarmed me, but in a wonderful manner touched and disconcerted me. I began to reason with him.

"These are your own copies we are about to examine. It is labor saving to you, because one examination will answer for your four papers. It is common usage. Every copyist is bound to help examine his copy. Is it not so? Will you not speak? Answer!"

"I prefer not to," he replied in a flute-like tone. It seemed to me that while I had been addressing him, he carefully revolved every statement that I made; fully comprehended the meaning; could not gainsay the irresistible conclusion; but, at the same time, some paramount consideration prevailed with him to reply as he did.

"You are decided, then, not to comply with my request—a request made according to common usage and common sense?"

He briefly gave me to understand that on that point my judgment was sound. Yes: his decision was irreversible.

It is not seldom the case that when a man is browbeaten in some unprecedented and violently unreasonable way, he begins to stagger in his own plainest faith. He begins, as it were, vaguely to surmise that, wonderful as it may be, all the justice and all the reason is on the other side. Accordingly, if any disinterested persons are present, he turns to them for some reinforcement for his own faltering mind.

"Turkey," said I, "what do you think of this? Am I not right?"

"With submission, sir," said Turkey, with his blandest tone, "I think that you are."

---

[14]PILLAR OF SALT: Frozen by shock. The origin of the phrase is Genesis 19, in which Lot's wife is turned into a pillar of salt for looking back during her flight from the doomed city of Sodom.

"Nippers," said I, "what do *you* think of it?"

"I think I should kick him out of the office."

(The reader of nice perceptions will here perceive that, it being morning, Turkey's answer is couched in polite and tranquil terms, but Nippers replies in ill-tempered ones. Or, to repeat a previous sentence, Nippers's ugly mood was on duty, and Turkey's off.)

"Ginger Nut," said I, willing to enlist the smallest suffrage in my behalf, "what do *you* think of it?"

"I think, sir, he's a little *luny*," replied Ginger Nut, with a grin.

"You hear what they say," said I, turning towards the screen, "come forth and do your duty."

But he vouchsafed no reply. I pondered a moment in sore perplexity. But once more business hurried me. I determined again to postpone the consideration of this dilemma to my future leisure. With a little trouble we made out to examine the papers without Bartleby, though at every page or two, Turkey deferentially dropped his opinion that this proceeding was quite out of the common; while Nippers, twitching in his chair with a dyspeptic nervousness, ground out between his set teeth occasional hissing maledictions against the stubborn oaf behind the screen. And for his (Nippers's) part, this was the first and the last time he would do another man's business without pay.

Meanwhile Bartleby sat in his hermitage, oblivious to every thing but his own peculiar business there.

Some days passed, the scrivener being employed upon another lengthy work. His late remarkable conduct led me to regard his ways narrowly. I observed that he never went to dinner; indeed that he never went any where. As yet I had never of my personal knowledge known him to be outside of my office. He was a perpetual sentry in the corner. At about eleven o'clock though, in the morning, I noticed that Ginger Nut would advance toward the opening in Bartleby's screen, as if silently beckoned thither by a gesture invisible to me where I sat. The boy would then leave the office jingling a few pence, and reappear with a handful of ginger-nuts which he delivered in the hermitage, receiving two of the cakes for his trouble.

He lives, then, on ginger-nuts, thought I; never eats a dinner, properly speaking; he must be a vegetarian then; but no; he never eats even vegetables, he eats nothing but ginger-nuts. My mind then ran on in reveries concerning the probable effects upon the human constitution of living entirely on ginger-nuts. Ginger-nuts are so called because they contain ginger as one of their peculiar constituents, and the final flavoring one. Now what was ginger? A hot, spicy thing. Was Bartleby hot and spicy? Not at all. Ginger, then, had no effect upon Bartleby. Probably he preferred it should have none.

Nothing so aggravates an earnest person as a passive resistance. If the individual so resisted be of a not inhumane temper, and the resisting one perfectly harmless in his passivity; then, in the better moods of the former, he will endeavor charitably to construe to his imagination what proves impossible to be solved by his judgment. Even so, for the most part, I regarded Bartleby and his ways. Poor fellow! thought I, he means no mischief; it is plain he intends no insolence; his aspect sufficiently evinces that his eccentricities are involuntary. He is useful to me. I can get along with him. If I turn him away, the chances are he will fall in with some less indulgent employer, and then he will be rudely treated, and perhaps driven forth miserably to starve. Yes. Here I can cheaply purchase a delicious self-approval. To befriend Bartleby; to humor him in his strange wilfulness, will cost me little or nothing, while I lay up in my soul what will eventually prove a sweet morsel for my conscience. But this mood was not invariable with me. The passiveness of Bartleby sometimes irritated me. I felt strangely goaded on to encounter him in new opposition, to elicit some angry spark from him answerable to my own. But indeed I might as well have essayed to strike fire with my knuckles against a bit of Windsor soap.[15] But one afternoon the evil impulse in me mastered me, and the following little scene ensued:

"Bartleby," said I, "when those papers are all copied, I will compare them with you."

"I would prefer not to."

"How? Surely you do not mean to persist in that mulish vagary?"[16]

No answer.

I threw open the folding-doors near by, and turning upon Turkey and Nippers, exclaimed:

"Bartleby a second time says, he won't examine his papers. What do you think of it, Turkey?"

It was afternoon, be it remembered. Turkey sat glowing like a brass boiler, his bald head steaming, his hands reeling among his blotted papers.

"Think of it?" roared Turkey; "I think I'll just step behind his screen, and black his eyes for him!"

So saying, Turkey rose to his feet and threw his arms into a pugilistic position. He was hurrying away to make good his promise, when I

---

[15]WINDSOR SOAP: A scented, usually brown soap.
[16]MULISH VAGARY: A stubborn departure from the expected course of conduct or decorum.

detained him, alarmed at the effect of incautiously rousing Turkey's combativeness after dinner.

"Sit down, Turkey," said I, "and hear what Nippers has to say. What do you think of it, Nippers? Would I not be justified in immediately dismissing Bartleby?"

"Excuse me, that is for you to decide, sir. I think his conduct quite unusual, and indeed unjust, as regards Turkey and myself. But it may only be a passing whim."

"Ah," exclaimed I, "you have strangely changed your mind then— you speak very gently of him now."

"All beer," cried Turkey; "gentleness is effects of beer—Nippers and I dined together to-day. You see how gentle *I* am, sir. Shall I go and black his eyes?"

"You refer to Bartleby, I suppose. No, not to-day, Turkey," I replied; "pray, put up your fists."

I closed the doors, and again advanced towards Bartleby. I felt additional incentives tempting me to my fate. I burned to be rebelled against again. I remembered that Bartleby never left the office.

"Bartleby," said I, "Ginger Nut is away; just step round to the Post Office, won't you? (it was but a three minutes walk) and see if there is any thing for me."

"I would prefer not to."

"You *will* not?"

"I *prefer* not."

I staggered to my desk, and sat there in a deep study. My blind inveteracy returned. Was there any other thing in which I could procure myself to be ignominiously repulsed by this lean, penniless wight?—my hired clerk? What added thing is there, perfectly reasonable, that he will be sure to refuse to do?

"Bartleby!"

No answer.

"Bartleby," in a louder tone.

No answer.

"Bartleby," I roared.

Like a very ghost, agreeably to the laws of magical invocation, at the third summons, he appeared at the entrance of his hermitage.

"Go to the next room, and tell Nippers to come to me."

"I prefer not to," he respectfully and slowly said, and mildly disappeared.

"Very good, Bartleby," said I, in a quiet sort of serenely severe self-possessed tone, intimating the unalterable purpose of some terrible retribution very close at hand. At the moment I half intended something of the kind. But upon the whole, as it was drawing towards my dinner-hour, I thought it best to put on my hat and walk home for the day, suffering much from perplexity and distress of mind.

Shall I acknowledge it? The conclusion of this whole business was, that it soon became a fixed fact of my chambers, that a pale young scrivener, by the name of Bartleby, had a desk there; that he copied for me at the usual rate of four cents a folio (one hundred words); but he was permanently exempt from examining the work done by him, that duty being transferred to Turkey and Nippers, out of compliment doubtless to their superior acuteness; moreover, said Bartleby was never on any account to be dispatched on the most trivial errand of any sort; and that even if entreated to take upon him such a matter, it was generally understood that he would prefer not to—in other words, that he would refuse point-blank.

As days passed on, I became considerably reconciled to Bartleby. His steadiness, his freedom from all dissipation, his incessant industry (except when he chose to throw himself into a standing revery behind his screen), his great stillness, his unalterableness of demeanor under all circumstances, made him a valuable acquisition. One prime thing was this,—*he was always there;*—first in the morning, continually through the day, and the last at night. I had a singular confidence in his honesty. I felt my most precious papers perfectly safe in his hands. Sometimes to be sure I could not, for the very soul of me, avoid falling into sudden spasmodic passions with him. For it was exceeding difficult to bear in mind all the time those strange peculiarities, privileges, and unheard of exemptions, forming the tacit stipulations on Bartleby's part under which he remained in my office. Now and then, in the eagerness of dispatching pressing business, I would inadvertently summon Bartleby, in a short, rapid tone, to put his finger, say, on the incipient tie of a bit of red tape with which I was about compressing some papers. Of course, from behind the screen the usual answer, "I prefer not to," was sure to come; and then, how could a human creature with the common infirmities of our nature, refrain from bitterly exclaiming upon such perverseness—such unreasonableness. However, every added repulse of this sort which I received only tended to lessen the probability of my repeating the inadvertence.

Here it must be said, that according to the custom of most legal gentlemen occupying chambers in densely-populated law buildings, there were several keys to my door. One was kept by a woman residing in the attic, which person weekly scrubbed and daily swept and dusted my apartments. Another was kept by Turkey for convenience sake. The third I sometimes carried in my own pocket. The fourth I knew not who had.

Now, one Sunday morning I happened to go to Trinity Church,[17] to hear a celebrated preacher, and finding myself rather early on the ground, I thought I would walk round to my chambers for a while. Luckily I had my key with me; but upon applying it to the lock, I found it resisted by something inserted from the inside. Quite surprised, I called out; when to my consternation a key was turned from within; and thrusting his lean visage at me, and holding the door ajar, the apparition of Bartleby appeared, in his shirt sleeves, and otherwise in a strangely tattered dishabille, saying quietly that he was sorry, but he was deeply engaged just then, and—preferred not admitting me at present. In a brief word or two, he moreover added, that perhaps I had better walk round the block two or three times, and by that time he would probably have concluded his affairs.

Now, the utterly unsurmised appearance of Bartleby, tenanting my law-chambers of a Sunday morning, with his cadaverously gentlemanly *nonchalance*, yet withal firm and self-possessed, had such a strange effect upon me, that incontinently I slunk away from my own door, and did as desired. But not without sundry twinges of impotent rebellion against the mild effrontery of this unaccountable scrivener. Indeed, it was his wonderful mildness chiefly, which not only disarmed me, but unmanned me, as it were. For I consider that one, for the time, is a sort of unmanned when he tranquilly permits his hired clerk to dictate to him, and order him away from his own premises. Furthermore, I was full of uneasiness as to what Bartleby could possibly be doing in my office in his shirt sleeves, and in an otherwise dismantled condition of a Sunday morning. Was any thing amiss going on? Nay, that was out of the question. It was not to be thought of for a moment that Bartleby was an immoral person. But what could he be doing there?—copying? Nay again, whatever might be his eccentricities, Bartleby was an eminently decorous person. He would be the last man to sit down to his desk in any state approaching to nudity. Besides, it was Sunday; and there was something about Bartleby that forbade the supposition that he would by any secular occupation violate the proprieties of the day.

Nevertheless, my mind was not pacified; and full of a restless curiosity, at last I returned to the door. Without hindrance I inserted my key, opened it, and entered. Bartleby was not to be seen. I looked round anxiously, peeped behind his screen; but it was very plain that he was gone. Upon more closely examining the place, I surmised that for an

[17]TRINITY CHURCH: Anglican church (founded 1696) that faces Wall Street on the west side of Broadway.

indefinite period Bartleby must have ate, dressed, and slept in my office, and that too without plate, mirror, or bed. The cushioned seat of a rickety old sofa in one corner bore the faint impress of a lean, reclining form. Rolled away under his desk, I found a blanket; under the empty grate, a blacking box and brush; on a chair, a tin basin, with soap and a ragged towel; in a newspaper a few crumbs of ginger-nuts and a morsel of cheese. Yes, thought I, it is evident enough that Bartleby has been making his home here, keeping bachelor's hall all by himself. Immediately then the thought came sweeping across me, What miserable friendlessness and loneliness are here revealed! His poverty is great; but his solitude, how horrible! Think of it. Of a Sunday, Wall-street is deserted as Petra[18]; and every night of every day it is an emptiness. This building too, which of week-days hums with industry and life, at nightfall echoes with sheer vacancy, and all through Sunday is forlorn. And here Bartleby makes his home; sole spectator of a solitude which he has seen all populous—a sort of innocent and transformed Marius brooding among the ruins of Carthage![19]

For the first time in my life a feeling of overpowering stinging melancholy seized me. Before, I had never experienced aught but a not-unpleasing sadness. The bond of a common humanity now drew me irresistibly to gloom. A fraternal melancholy! For both I and Bartleby were sons of Adam. I remembered the bright silks and sparkling faces I had seen that day, in gala trim, swan-like sailing down the Mississippi of Broadway; and I contrasted them with the pallid copyist, and thought to myself, Ah, happiness courts the light, so we deem the world is gay; but misery hides aloof, so we deem that misery there is none. These sad fancyings—chimeras, doubtless, of a sick and silly brain—led on to other and more special thoughts, concerning the eccentricities of Bartleby. Presentiments of strange discoveries hovered round me. The scrivener's pale form appeared to me laid out, among uncaring strangers, in its shivering winding sheet.

Suddenly I was attracted by Bartleby's closed desk, the key in open sight left in the lock.

I mean no mischief, seek the gratification of no heartless curiosity, thought I; besides, the desk is mine, and its contents too, so I will make bold to look within. Every thing was methodically arranged, the papers smoothly placed. The pigeon holes were deep, and removing the files of documents, I groped into their recesses. Presently I felt something there,

---

[18]PETRA: An ancient city carved into the red cliffs of Jordan's Edom desert.
[19]CARTHAGE: An ancient city and state in Northern Africa; Caius Marius (157–86 BCE), Roman general who fled Africa after being defeated by patrician forces and who saw his condition reflected in Carthage's ruins.

and dragged it out. It was an old bandanna handkerchief, heavy and knotted. I opened it, and saw it was a savings' bank.

I now recalled all the quiet mysteries which I had noted in the man. I remembered that he never spoke but to answer; that though at intervals he had considerable time to himself, yet I had never seen him reading— no, not even a newspaper; that for long periods he would stand looking out, at his pale window behind the screen, upon the dead brick wall; I was quite sure he never visited any refectory[20] or eating house; while his pale face clearly indicated that he never drank beer like Turkey, or tea and coffee even, like other men; that he never went any where in particular that I could learn; never went out for a walk, unless indeed that was the case at present; that he had declined telling who he was, or whence he came, or whether he had any relatives in the world; that though so thin and pale, he never complained of ill health. And more than all, I remembered a certain unconscious air of pallid—how shall I call it?—of pallid haughtiness, say, or rather an austere reserve about him, which had positively awed me into my tame compliance with his eccentricities, when I had feared to ask him to do the slightest incidental thing for me, even though I might know, from his long-continued motionlessness, that behind his screen he must be standing in one of those dead-wall reveries of his.

Revolving all these things, and coupling them with the recently discovered fact that he made my office his constant abiding place and home, and not forgetful of his morbid moodiness; revolving all these things, a prudential feeling began to steal over me. My first emotions had been those of pure melancholy and sincerest pity; but just in proportion as the forlornness of Bartleby grew and grew to my imagination, did that same melancholy merge into fear, that pity into repulsion. So true it is, and so terrible too, that up to a certain point the thought or sight of misery enlists our best affections; but, in certain special cases, beyond that point it does not. They err who would assert that invariably this is owing to the inherent selfishness of the human heart. It rather proceeds from a certain hopelessness of remedying excessive and organic ill. To a sensitive being, pity is not seldom pain. And when at last it is perceived that such pity cannot lead to effectual succor, common sense bids the soul be rid of it. What I saw that morning persuaded me that the scrivener was the victim of innate and incurable disorder. I might give alms to his body; but his body did not pain him; it was his soul that suffered, and his soul I could not reach.

I did not accomplish the purpose of going to Trinity Church that morning. Somehow, the things I had seen disqualified me for the time from

[20]REFECTORY: A dining hall.

church-going. I walked homeward, thinking what I would do with Bartleby. Finally, I resolved upon this;—I would put certain calm questions to him the next morning, touching his history, &c., and if he declined to answer them openly and unreservedly (and I supposed he would prefer not), then to give him a twenty dollar bill over and above whatever I might owe him, and tell him his services were no longer required; but that if in any other way I could assist him, I would be happy to do so, especially if he desired to return to his native place, wherever that might be, I would willingly help to defray the expenses. Moreover, if, after reaching home, he found himself at any time in want of aid, a letter from him would be sure of a reply.

The next morning came.

"Bartleby" said I, gently calling to him behind his screen.

No reply.

"Bartleby" said I, in a still gentler tone, "come here; I am not going to ask you to do any thing you would prefer not to do—I simply wish to speak to you."

Upon this he noiselessly slid into view.

"Will you tell me, Bartleby, where you were born?"

"I would prefer not to."

"Will you tell me *any thing* about yourself?"

"I would prefer not to."

"But what reasonable objection can you have to speak to me? I feel friendly towards you."

He did not look at me while I spoke, but kept his glance fixed upon my bust of Cicero,[21] which as I then sat, was directly behind me, some six inches above my head.

"What is your answer, Bartleby?" said I, after waiting a considerable time for a reply, during which his countenance remained immovable, only there was the faintest conceivable tremor of the white attenuated mouth.

"At present I prefer to give no answer," he said, and retired into his hermitage.

It was rather weak in me I confess, but his manner on this occasion nettled me. Not only did there seem to lurk in it a certain calm disdain, but his perverseness seemed ungrateful, considering the undeniable good usage and indulgence he had received from me.

Again I sat ruminating what I should do. Mortified as I was at his behavior, and resolved as I had been to dismiss him when I entered my office, nevertheless I strangely felt something superstitious knocking at my heart, and forbidding me to carry out my purpose, and denouncing

[21]CICERO: Marcus Tullius Cicero (106–43 BCE), Roman statesman, writer, and renowned orator.

me for a villain if I dared to breathe one bitter word against this forlornest of mankind. At last, familiarly drawing my chair behind his screen, I sat down and said: "Bartleby, never mind then about revealing your history; but let me entreat you, as a friend, to comply as far as may be with the usages of this office. Say now you will help to examine papers to-morrow or next day: in short, say now that in a day or two you will begin to be a little reasonable:—say so, Bartleby."

"At present I would prefer not to be a little reasonable," was his mildly cadaverous reply.

Just then the folding-doors opened, and Nippers approached. He seemed suffering from an unusually bad night's rest, induced by severer indigestion than common. He overheard those final words of Bartleby.

"*Prefer not*, eh?" gritted Nippers—"I'd *prefer* him, if I were you, sir," addressing me—"I'd *prefer* him; I'd give him preferences, the stubborn mule! What is it, sir, pray, that he *prefers* not to do now?"

Bartleby moved not a limb.

"Mr. Nippers," said I, "I'd prefer that you would withdraw for the present."

Somehow, of late I had got into the way of involuntarily using this word "prefer" upon all sorts of not exactly suitable occasions. And I trembled to think that my contact with the scrivener had already and seriously affected me in a mental way. And what further and deeper aberration might it not yet produce? This apprehension had not been without efficacy in determining me to summary measures.

As Nippers, looking very sour and sulky, was departing, Turkey blandly and deferentially approached.

"With submission, sir," said he, "yesterday I was thinking about Bartleby here, and I think that if he would but prefer to take a quart of good ale every day, it would do much towards mending him, and enabling him to assist in examining his papers."

"So you have got the word too," said I, slightly excited.

"With submission, what word, sir," asked Turkey, respectfully crowding himself into the contracted space behind the screen, and by so doing, making me jostle the scrivener. "What word, sir?"

"I would prefer to be left alone here," said Bartleby, as if offended at being mobbed in his privacy.

"*That's* the word, Turkey," said I—"*that's* it."

"Oh, *prefer*? oh yes—queer word. I never use it myself. But, sir, as I was saying, if he would but prefer—"

"Turkey," interrupted I, "you will please withdraw."

"Oh certainly, sir, if you prefer that I should."

As he opened the folding-doors to retire, Nippers at his desk caught a glimpse of me, and asked whether I would prefer to have a certain paper copied on blue paper or white. He did not in the least roguishly accent the word prefer. It was plain that it involuntarily rolled from his tongue. I thought to myself, surely I must get rid of a demented man, who already has in some degree turned the tongues, if not the heads of myself and clerks. But I thought it prudent not to break the dismission at once.

The next day I noticed that Bartleby did nothing but stand at his window in his dead-wall revery. Upon asking him why he did not write, he said that he had decided upon doing no more writing.

"Why, how now? what next?" exclaimed I, "do no more writing?"

"No more."

"And what is the reason?"

"Do you not see the reason for yourself," he indifferently replied.

I looked steadfastly at him, and perceived that his eyes looked dull and glazed. Instantly it occurred to me, that his unexampled diligence in copying by his dim window for the first few weeks of his stay with me might have temporarily impaired his vision.

I was touched. I said something in condolence with him. I hinted that of course he did wisely in abstaining from writing for a while; and urged him to embrace that opportunity of taking wholesome exercise in the open air. This, however, he did not do. A few days after this, my other clerks being absent, and being in a great hurry to dispatch certain letters by the mail, I thought that, having nothing else earthly to do, Bartleby would surely be less inflexible than usual, and carry these letters to the post-office. But he blankly declined. So, much to my inconvenience, I went myself.

Still added days went by. Whether Bartleby's eyes improved or not, I could not say. To all appearance, I thought they did. But when I asked him if they did, he vouchsafed no answer. At all events, he would do no copying. At last, in reply to my urgings, he informed me that he had permanently given up copying.

"What!" exclaimed I; "suppose your eyes should get entirely well—better than ever before—would you not copy then?"

"I have given up copying," he answered, and slid aside.

He remained as ever, a fixture in my chamber. Nay—if that were possible—he became still more of a fixture than before. What was to be done? He would do nothing in the office: why should he stay there? In plain fact, he had now become a millstone to me, not only useless as a necklace, but afflictive to bear. Yet I was sorry for him. I speak less than truth when I say that, on his own account, he occasioned me uneasiness. If he would but have named a single relative or friend, I would instantly have written, and urged their taking the poor fellow away to some convenient retreat. But he seemed alone, absolutely alone in the universe. A bit of wreck in the mid Atlantic. At length, necessities connected with my business tyrannized over all other considerations. Decently as I could, I told Bartleby that in six days' time he must unconditionally leave the office. I warned him to take measures, in the interval, for procuring some other abode. I offered to assist him in this endeavor, if he himself would but take the first step towards a removal. "And when you finally quit me, Bartleby," added I, "I shall see that you go not away entirely unprovided. Six days from this hour, remember."

At the expiration of that period, I peeped behind the screen, and lo! Bartleby was there.

I buttoned up my coat, balanced myself; advanced slowly towards him, touched his shoulder, and said, "The time has come; you must quit this place; I am sorry for you; here is money; but you must go."

"I would prefer not," he replied, with his back still towards me.

"You *must*."

He remained silent.

Now I had an unbounded confidence in this man's common honesty. He had frequently restored to me sixpences and shillings carelessly dropped upon the floor, for I am apt to be very reckless in such shirt-button affairs. The proceeding then which followed will not be deemed extraordinary.

"Bartleby," said I, "I owe you twelve dollars on account; here are thirty-two; the odd twenty are yours.—Will you take it?" and I handed the bills towards him.

But he made no motion.

"I will leave them here then," putting them under a weight on the table. Then taking my hat and cane and going to the door I tranquilly turned and added—"After you have removed your things from these offices, Bartleby, you will of course lock the door—since every one is now gone for the day but you—and if you please, slip your key underneath the mat, so that I may have it in the morning. I shall not see you again; so good-bye to you. If hereafter in your new place of abode I can be of any service to you, do not fail to advise me by letter. Good-bye, Bartleby, and fare you well."

But he answered not a word; like the last column of some ruined temple, he remained standing mute and solitary in the middle of the otherwise deserted room.

As I walked home in a pensive mood, my vanity got the better of my pity. I could not but highly plume myself on my masterly management in getting rid of Bartleby. Masterly I call it, and such it must appear to any dispassionate thinker. The beauty of my procedure seemed to consist in its perfect quietness. There was no vulgar bullying, no bravado of any sort, no choleric hectoring, and striding to and fro across the apartment, jerking out vehement commands for Bartleby to bundle himself off with his beggarly traps. Nothing of the kind. Without loudly bidding Bartleby depart—as an inferior genius might have done—I *assumed* the ground that depart he must; and upon that assumption built all I had to say. The more I thought over my procedure, the more I was charmed with it. Nevertheless, next morning, upon awakening, I had my doubts,—I had somehow slept off the fumes of vanity. One of the coolest and wisest hours a man has, is just after he awakes in the morning. My procedure seemed as sagacious as ever,—but only in theory. How it would prove in practice—there was the rub. It was truly a beautiful thought to have assumed Bartleby's departure; but, after all, that assumption was simply my own, and none of Bartleby's. The great point was, not whether I had assumed that he would quit me, but whether he would prefer so to do. He was more a man of preferences than assumptions.

After breakfast, I walked down town, arguing the probabilities *pro* and *con*. One moment I thought it would prove a miserable failure, and Bartleby would be found all alive at my office as usual; the next moment it seemed certain that I should find his chair empty. And so I kept veering about. At the corner of Broadway and Canal-street, I saw quite an excited group of people standing in earnest conversation.

"I'll take odds he doesn't," said a voice as I passed.

"Doesn't go?—done!" said I, "put up your money."

I was instinctively putting my hand in my pocket to produce my own, when I remembered that this was an election day. The words I had overheard bore no reference to Bartleby, but to the success or non-success of some candidate for the mayoralty. In my intent frame of mind, I had, as it were, imagined that all Broadway shared in my excitement, and were debating the same question with me. I passed on, very thankful that the uproar of the street screened my momentary absent-mindedness.

As I had intended, I was earlier than usual at my office door. I stood listening for a moment. All was still. He must be gone. I tried the knob. The door was locked. Yes, my procedure had worked to a charm; he indeed must be vanished. Yet a certain melancholy mixed with this: I was almost sorry for my brilliant success. I was fumbling under the door mat for the key, which Bartleby was to have left there for me, when accidentally my knee knocked against a panel, producing a summoning sound, and in response a voice came to me from within—"Not yet; I am occupied."

It was Bartleby.

I was thunderstruck. For an instant I stood like the man who, pipe in mouth, was killed one cloudless afternoon long ago in Virginia, by summer lightning; at his own warm open window he was killed, and remained leaning out there upon the dreamy afternoon, till some one touched him, when he fell.

"Not gone!" I murmured at last. But again obeying that wondrous ascendancy which the inscrutable scrivener had over me, and from which ascendancy, for all my chafing, I could not completely escape, I slowly went down stairs and out into the street, and while walking round the block, considered what I should next do in this unheard-of perplexity. Turn the man out by an actual thrusting I could not; to drive him away by calling him hard names would not do; calling in the police was an unpleasant idea; and yet, permit him to enjoy his cadaverous triumph over me,—this too I could not think of. What was to be done? or, if nothing could be done, was there any thing further that I could *assume* in the matter? Yes, as before I had prospectively assumed that Bartleby would depart, so now I might retrospectively assume that departed he was. In the legitimate carrying out of this assumption, I might enter my office in a great hurry, and pretending not to see Bartleby at all, walk straight against him as if he were air. Such a proceeding would in a singular degree have the appearance of a home-thrust. It was hardly possible that Bartleby could withstand such an application of the doctrine of assumptions. But upon second thoughts the success of the plan seemed rather dubious. I resolved to argue the matter over with him again.

"Bartleby," said I, entering the office, with a quietly severe expression, "I am seriously displeased. I am pained, Bartleby. I had thought better of you. I had imagined you of such a gentlemanly organization, that in any delicate dilemma a slight hint would suffice—in short, an assumption. But it appears I am deceived. Why," I added, unaffectedly starting, "you have not even touched that money yet," pointing to it, just where I had left it the evening previous.

He answered nothing.

"Will you, or will you not, quit me?" I now demanded in a sudden passion, advancing close to him.

"I would prefer *not* to quit you," he replied, gently emphasizing the *not*.

"What earthly right have you to stay here? Do you pay any rent? Do you pay my taxes? Or is this property yours?"

He answered nothing.

"Are you ready to go on and write now? Are your eyes recovered? Could you copy a small paper for me this morning? or help examine a few lines? or step round to the post-office? In a word, will you do any thing at all, to give a coloring to your refusal to depart the premises?"

He silently retired into his hermitage.

I was now in such a state of nervous resentment that I thought it but prudent to check myself at present from further demonstrations. Bartleby and I were alone. I remembered the tragedy of the unfortunate Adams and the still more unfortunate Colt[22] in the solitary office of the latter; and how poor Colt, being dreadfully incensed by Adams, and imprudently permitting himself to get wildly excited, was at unawares hurried into his fatal act—an act which certainly no man could possibly deplore more than the actor himself. Often it had occurred to me in my ponderings upon the subject, that had that altercation taken place in the public street, or at a private residence, it would not have terminated as it did. It was the circumstance of being alone in a solitary office, up stairs, of a building entirely unhallowed by humanizing domestic associations—an uncarpeted office, doubtless, of a dusty, haggard sort of appearance;—this it must have been, which greatly helped to enhance the irritable desperation of the hapless Colt.

But when this old Adam of resentment rose in me and tempted me concerning Bartleby, I grappled him and threw him. How? Why, simply by recalling the divine injunction: "A new commandment give I unto you, that ye love one another."[23] Yes, this it was that saved me. Aside from higher considerations, charity often operates as a vastly wise and prudent principle—a great safeguard to its possessor. Men have committed murder for jealousy's sake, and anger's sake, and hatred's sake, and selfishness' sake, and spiritual pride's sake; but no man that ever I heard of, ever committed a diabolical murder for sweet charity's sake. Mere self-interest, then, if no better motive can be enlisted, should, especially with high-tempered men, prompt all beings to charity and philanthropy. At any rate, upon the occasion in question, I strove to drown my exasperated feelings towards the scrivener by benevolently construing his

---

[22]THE TRAGEDY OF THE UNFORTUNATE ADAMS AND THE STILL MORE UNFORTUNATE COLT: In 1841, John C. Colt (brother of revolver inventor Samuel Colt), used a hatchet to murder Samuel Adams, a printer who had come to collect a debt. Colt crated the corpse and arranged to have it shipped out of Manhattan to New Orleans. He was discovered and convicted of the murder despite his protests that he had acted in self-defense. He killed himself just before he was to be publicly hanged. The crime scene was the second floor of a building at the corner of Broadway and Chambers Street, near where this story is set.

[23]THAT YE LOVE ONE ANOTHER: John 13:34.

conduct. Poor fellow, poor fellow! thought I, he don't mean any thing; and besides, he has seen hard times, and ought to be indulged.

I endeavored also immediately to occupy myself, and at the same time to comfort my despondency. I tried to fancy that in the course of the morning, at such time as might prove agreeable to him, Bartleby, of his own free accord, would emerge from his hermitage, and take up some decided line of march in the direction of the door. But no. Half-past twelve o'clock came; Turkey began to glow in the face, overturn his inkstand, and become generally obstreperous; Nippers abated down into quietude and courtesy; Ginger Nut munched his noon apple; and Bartleby remained standing at his window in one of his profoundest dead-wall reveries. Will it be credited? Ought I to acknowledge it? That afternoon I left the office without saying one further word to him.

Some days now passed, during which, at leisure intervals I looked a little into "Edwards on the Will," and "Priestley on Necessity."[24] Under the circumstances, those books induced a salutary feeling. Gradually I slid into the persuasion that these troubles of mine touching the scrivener, had been all predestinated from eternity, and Bartleby was billeted upon me for some mysterious purpose of an all-wise Providence, which it was not for a mere mortal like me to fathom. Yes, Bartleby, stay there behind your screen, thought I; I shall persecute you no more; you are harmless and noiseless as any of these old chairs; in short, I never feel so private as when I know you are here. At last I see it, I feel it; I penetrate to the predestinated purpose of my life. I am content. Others may have loftier parts to enact; but my mission in this world, Bartleby, is to furnish you with office-room for such period as you may see fit to remain.

I believe that this wise and blessed frame of mind would have continued with me, had it not been for the unsolicited and uncharitable remarks obtruded upon me by my professional friends who visited the rooms. But thus it often is, that the constant friction of illiberal minds wears out at last the best resolves of the more generous. Though to be sure, when I reflected upon it, it was not strange that people entering my office should be struck by the peculiar aspect of the unaccountable Bartleby, and so be tempted to throw out some sinister observations concerning him. Sometimes an attorney having business with me, and calling at my office, and finding no one but the scrivener there, would undertake to obtain some sort of precise information from him touching my whereabouts; but without

---

24"EDWARDS ON THE WILL," AND "PRIESTLEY ON NECESSITY": Puritan minister Jonathan Edwards (1703–1758) and English physicist Joseph Priestley (1733–1804). Both men promoted the theology of predestination, which instructs that God, owing to his infallible knowledge of the future, has appointed and ordained all events. Thus, humans have no free will, as all things are predetermined.

heeding his idle talk, Bartleby would remain standing immovable in the middle of the room. So after contemplating him in that position for a time, the attorney would depart, no wiser than he came.

Also, when a Reference[25] was going on, and the room full of lawyers and witnesses and business was driving fast; some deeply occupied legal gentlemen present, seeing Bartleby wholly unemployed, would request him to run round to his (the legal gentleman's) office and fetch some papers for him. Thereupon, Bartleby would tranquilly decline, and yet remain idle as before. Then the lawyer would give a great stare, and turn to me. And what could I say? At last I was made aware that all through the circle of my professional acquaintance, a whisper of wonder was running round, having reference to the strange creature I kept at my office. This worried me very much. And as the idea came upon me of his possibly turning out a long-lived man, and keep occupying my chambers, and denying my authority; and perplexing my visitors; and scandalizing my professional reputation; and casting a general gloom over the premises; keeping soul and body together to the last upon his savings (for doubtless he spent but half a dime a day), and in the end perhaps outlive me, and claim possession of my office by right of his perpetual occupancy: as all these dark anticipations crowded upon me more and more, and my friends continually intruded their relentless remarks upon the apparition in my room; a great change was wrought in me. I resolved to gather all my faculties together, and for ever rid me of this intolerable incubus.[26]

Ere revolving any complicated project, however, adapted to this end, I first simply suggested to Bartleby the propriety of his permanent departure. In a calm and serious tone, I commended the idea to his careful and mature consideration. But having taken three days to meditate upon it, he apprised me that his original determination remained the same; in short, that he still preferred to abide with me.

What shall I do? I now said to myself, buttoning up my coat to the last button. What shall I do? what ought I to do? what does conscience say I *should* do with this man, or rather ghost? Rid myself of him, I must; go, he shall. But how? You will not thrust him, the poor, pale, passive mortal,—you will not thrust such a helpless creature out of your door? you will not dishonor yourself by such cruelty? No, I will not, I cannot do that. Rather would I let him live and die here, and then mason up his remains in the wall. What then will you do? For all your coaxing, he will not budge. Bribes he leaves under your own paper-weight on your table; in short, it is quite plain that he prefers to cling to you.

---

[25]REFERENCE: The act of referring a matter in dispute to a referee.
[26]INCUBUS: Evil spirit.

Then something severe, something unusual must be done. What! surely you will not have him collared by a constable, and commit his innocent pallor to the common jail? And upon what ground could you procure such a thing to be done?—a vagrant, is he? What! he a vagrant, a wanderer, who refuses to budge? It is because he will *not* be a vagrant, then, that you seek to count him *as* a vagrant. That is too absurd. No visible means of support: there I have him. Wrong again: for indubitably he *does* support himself, and that is the only unanswerable proof that any man can show of his possessing the means so to do. No more then. Since he will not quit me, I must quit him. I will change my offices; I will move elsewhere; and give him fair notice, that if I find him on my new premises I will then proceed against him as a common trespasser.

Acting accordingly, next day I thus addressed him: "I find these chambers too far from the City Hall; the air is unwholesome. In a word, I propose to remove my offices next week, and shall no longer require your services. I tell you this now, in order that you may seek another place."

He made no reply, and nothing more was said.

On the appointed day I engaged carts and men, proceeded to my chambers, and having but little furniture, every thing was removed in a few hours. Throughout, the scrivener remained standing behind the screen, which I directed to be removed the last thing. It was withdrawn; and being folded up like a huge folio, left him the motionless occupant of a naked room. I stood in the entry watching him a moment, while something from within me upbraided me.

I re-entered, with my hand in my pocket—and—and my heart in my mouth.

"Good-bye, Bartleby; I am going—good-bye, and God some way bless you; and take that," slipping something in his hand. But it dropped upon the floor, and then,—strange to say—I tore myself from him whom I had so longed to be rid of.

Established in my new quarters, for a day or two I kept the door locked, and started at every footfall in the passages. When I returned to my rooms after any little absence, I would pause at the threshold for an instant, and attentively listen, ere applying my key. But these fears were needless. Bartleby never came nigh me.

I thought all was going well, when a perturbed looking stranger visited me, inquiring whether I was the person who had recently occupied rooms at No.—Wall-street.

Full of forebodings, I replied that I was.

"Then sir," said the stranger, who proved a lawyer, "you are responsible for the man you left there. He refuses to do any copying; he refuses to do any thing; he says he prefers not to; and he refuses to quit the premises."

"I am very sorry, sir," said I, with assumed tranquillity, but an inward tremor, "but, really, the man you allude to is nothing to me—he is no relation or apprentice of mine, that you should hold me responsible for him."

"In mercy's name, who is he?"

"I certainly cannot inform you. I know nothing about him. Formerly I employed him as a copyist; but he has done nothing for me now for some time past."

"I shall settle him then,—good morning, sir."

Several days passed, and I heard nothing more; and though I often felt a charitable prompting to call at the place and see poor Bartleby, yet a certain squeamishness of I know not what withheld me.

All is over with him, by this time, thought I at last, when through another week no further intelligence reached me. But coming to my room the day after, I found several persons waiting at my door in a high state of nervous excitement.

"That's the man—here he comes," cried the foremost one, whom I recognized as the lawyer who had previously called upon me alone.

"You must take him away, sir, at once," cried a portly person among them, advancing upon me, and whom I knew to be the landlord of No.— Wall-street. "These gentlemen, my tenants, cannot stand it any longer; Mr. B——" pointing to the lawyer, "has turned him out of his room, and he now persists in haunting the building generally, sitting upon the banisters of the stairs by day, and sleeping in the entry by night. Every body is concerned; clients are leaving the offices; some fears are entertained of a mob; something you must do, and that without delay."

Aghast at this torrent, I fell back before it, and would fain have locked myself in my new quarters. In vain I persisted that Bartleby was nothing to me—no more than to any one else. In vain:—I was the last person known to have any thing to do with him, and they held me to the terrible account. Fearful then of being exposed in the papers (as one person present obscurely threatened) I considered the matter, and at length said, that if the lawyer would give me a confidential interview with the scrivener, in his (the lawyer's) own room, I would that afternoon strive my best to rid them of the nuisance they complained of.

Going up stairs to my old haunt, there was Bartleby silently sitting upon the banister at the landing.

"What are you doing here, Bartleby?" said I.

"Sitting upon the banister," he mildly replied.

I motioned him into the lawyer's room, who then left us.

"Bartleby," said I, "are you aware that you are the cause of great tribulation to me, by persisting in occupying the entry after being dismissed from the office?"

No answer.

"Now one of two things must take place. Either you must do something, or something must be done to you. Now what sort of business would you like to engage in? Would you like to re-engage in copying for some one?"

"No; I would prefer not to make any change."

"Would you like a clerkship in a dry-goods store?"

"There is too much confinement about that. No, I would not like a clerkship; but I am not particular."

"Too much confinement," I cried, "why you keep yourself confined all the time!"

"I would prefer not to take a clerkship," he rejoined, as if to settle that little item at once.

"How would a bar-tender's business suit you? There is no trying of the eyesight in that."

"I would not like it at all; though, as I said before, I am not particular."

His unwonted wordiness inspirited me. I returned to the charge.

"Well then, would you like to travel through the country collecting bills for the merchants? That would improve your health."

"No, I would prefer to be doing something else."

"How then would going as a companion to Europe, to entertain some young gentleman with your conversation,—how would that suit you?"

"Not at all. It does not strike me that there is any thing definite about that. I like to be stationary. But I am not particular."

"Stationary you shall be then," I cried, now losing all patience, and for the first time in all my exasperating connection with him fairly flying into a passion. "If you do not go away from these premises before night, I shall feel bound—indeed I *am* bound—to—to—to quit the premises myself!" I rather absurdly concluded, knowing not with what possible threat to try to frighten his immobility into compliance. Despairing of all further efforts, I was precipitately leaving him, when a final thought occurred to me—one which had not been wholly unindulged before.

"Bartleby," said I, in the kindest tone I could assume under such exciting circumstances, "will you go home with me now—not to my office, but my dwelling—and remain there till we can conclude upon some convenient arrangement for you at our leisure? Come, let us start now, right away."

"No: at present I would prefer not to make any change at all."

I answered nothing; but effectually dodging every one by the sud-denness and rapidity of my flight, rushed from the building, ran up Wall-street towards Broadway, and jumping into the first omnibus was soon removed from pursuit. As soon as tranquillity returned I distinctly per-ceived that I had now done all that I possibly could, both in respect to the demands of the landlord and his tenants, and with regard to my own desire and sense of duty, to benefit Bartleby, and shield him from rude persecution. I now strove to be entirely care-free and quiescent; and my conscience justified me in the attempt; though indeed it was not so successful as I could have wished. So fearful was I of being again hunted out by the incensed landlord and his exasperated tenants, that, surren-dering my business to Nippers, for a few days I drove about the upper part of the town and through the suburbs, in my rockaway[27]; crossed over to Jersey City and Hoboken, and paid fugitive visits to Manhattanville and Astoria. In fact I almost lived in my rockaway for the time.

When again I entered my office, lo, a note from the landlord lay upon the desk. I opened it with trembling hands. It informed me that the writer had sent to the police, and had Bartleby removed to the Tombs as a vagrant. Moreover, since I knew more about him than any one else, he wished me to appear at that place, and make a suitable statement of the facts. These tidings had a conflicting effect upon me. At first I was indignant; but at last almost approved. The landlord's energetic, sum-mary disposition, had led him to adopt a procedure which I do not think I would have decided upon myself; and yet as a last resort, under such peculiar circumstances, it seemed the only plan.

As I afterwards learned, the poor scrivener, when told that he must be conducted to the Tombs, offered not the slightest obstacle, but in his pale unmoving way, silently acquiesced.

Some of the compassionate and curious bystanders joined the party; and headed by one of the constables arm in arm with Bartleby, the silent procession filed its way through all the noise, and heat, and joy of the roaring thoroughfares at noon.

The same day I received the note I went to the Tombs, or to speak more properly, the Halls of Justice. Seeking the right officer, I stated the pur-pose of my call, and was informed that the individual I described was indeed within. I then assured the functionary that Bartleby was a perfectly honest man, and greatly to be compassionated, however unaccountably

[27]ROCKAWAY: A carriage.

eccentric. I narrated all I knew, and closed by suggesting the idea of letting him remain in as indulgent confinement as possible till something less harsh might be done—though indeed I hardly knew what. At all events, if nothing else could be decided upon, the alms-house must receive him. I then begged to have an interview.

Being under no disgraceful charge, and quite serene and harmless in all his ways, they had permitted him freely to wander about the prison, and especially in the inclosed grass-platted yards thereof. And so I found him there, standing all alone in the quietest of the yards, his face towards a high wall, while all around, from the narrow slits of the jail windows, I thought I saw peering out upon him the eyes of murderers and thieves.

"Bartleby!"

"I know you," he said, without looking round,—"and I want nothing to say to you."

"It was not I that brought you here, Bartleby," said I, keenly pained at his implied suspicion. "And to you, this should not be so vile a place. Nothing reproachful attaches to you by being here. And see, it is not so sad a place as one might think. Look, there is the sky, and here is the grass."

"I know where I am," he replied, but would say nothing more, and so I left him.

As I entered the corridor again, a broad meat-like man, in an apron, accosted me, and jerking his thumb over his shoulder said—"Is that your friend?"

"Yes."

"Does he want to starve? If he does, let him live on the prison fare, that's all."

"Who are you?" asked I, not knowing what to make of such an unofficially speaking person in such a place.

"I am the grub-man. Such gentlemen as have friends here, hire me to provide them with something good to eat."

"Is this so?" said I, turning to the turnkey.

He said it was.

"Well then," said I, slipping some silver into the grub-man's hands (for so they called him). "I want you to give particular attention to my friend there; let him have the best dinner you can get. And you must be as polite to him as possible."

"Introduce me, will you?" said the grub-man, looking at me with an expression which seemed to say he was all impatience for an opportunity to give a specimen of his breeding.

Thinking it would prove of benefit to the scrivener, I acquiesced; and asking the grub-man his name, went up with him to Bartleby.

"Bartleby, this is Mr. Cutlets; you will find him very useful to you."

"Your sarvant, sir, your sarvant," said the grub-man, making a low salutation behind his apron. "Hope you find it pleasant here, sir; nice grounds—cool apartments, sir—hope you'll stay with us some time—try to make it agreeable. May Mrs. Cutlets and I have the pleasure of your company to dinner, sir, in Mrs. Cutlets' private room?"

"I prefer not to dine to-day," said Bartleby, turning away. "It would disagree with me; I am unused to dinners." So saying he slowly moved to the other side of the inclosure, and took up a position fronting the dead-wall.

"How's this?" said the grub-man, addressing me with a stare of astonishment. "He's odd, aint he?"

"I think he is a little deranged," said I, sadly.

"Deranged? deranged is it? Well now, upon my word, I thought that friend of yourn was a gentleman forger; they are always pale and genteel-like, them forgers. I can't help pity 'em—can't help it, sir. Did you know Monroe Edwards?"[28] he added touchingly, and paused. Then, laying his hand pityingly on my shoulder, sighed, "he died of consumption[29] at Sing-Sing.[30] So you weren't acquainted with Monroe?"

"No, I was never socially acquainted with any forgers. But I cannot stop longer. Look to my friend yonder. You will not lose by it. I will see you again."

Some few days after this, I again obtained admission to the Tombs, and went through the corridors in quest of Bartleby; but without finding him.

"I saw him coming from his cell not long ago," said a turnkey, "may be he's gone to loiter in the yards."

So I went in that direction.

"Are you looking for the silent man?" said another turnkey passing me. "Yonder he lies—sleeping in the yard there. 'Tis not twenty minutes since I saw him lie down."

The yard was entirely quiet. It was not accessible to the common prisoners. The surrounding walls, of amazing thickness, kept off all sounds behind them. The Egyptian character of the masonry weighed upon me with its gloom. But a soft imprisoned turf grew under foot. The heart

---

[28]MONROE EDWARDS: A colonel and American financier (1808–1847) who was convicted of forging letters of credit and stealing fifty thousand dollars from two Wall Street firms.
[29]CONSUMPTION: Pulmonary tuberculosis.
[30]SING-SING: A prison in Ossining, New York, on the Hudson River.

of the eternal pyramids, it seemed, wherein, by some strange magic, through the clefts, grass-seed, dropped by birds, had sprung.

Strangely huddled at the base of the wall, his knees drawn up, and lying on his side, his head touching the cold stones, I saw the wasted Bartleby. But nothing stirred. I paused; then went close up to him; stooped over, and saw that his dim eyes were open; otherwise he seemed profoundly sleeping. Something prompted me to touch him. I felt his hand, when a tingling shiver ran up my arm and down my spine to my feet.

The round face of the grub-man peered upon me now. "His dinner is ready. Won't he dine to-day, either? Or does he live without dining?"

"Lives without dining," said I, and closed the eyes.

"Eh!—He's asleep, aint he?"

"With kings and counsellors,"[31] murmured I.

There would seem little need for proceeding further in this history. Imagination will readily supply the meagre recital of poor Bartleby's interment. But ere parting with the reader, let me say, that if this little narrative has sufficiently interested him, to awaken curiosity as to who Bartleby was, and what manner of life he led prior to the present narrator's making his acquaintance, I can only reply, that in such curiosity I fully share, but am wholly unable to gratify it. Yet here I hardly know whether I should divulge one little item of rumor, which came to my ear a few months after the scrivener's decease. Upon what basis it rested, I could never ascertain; and hence, how true it is I cannot now tell. But inasmuch as this vague report has not been without a certain strange suggestive interest to me, however sad, it may prove the same with some others; and so I will briefly mention it. The report was this: that Bartleby had been a subordinate clerk in the Dead Letter Office[32] at Washington, from which he had been suddenly removed by a change in the administration. When I think over this rumor, hardly can I express the emotions which seize me. Dead letters! does it not sound like dead men? Conceive a man by nature and misfortune prone to a pallid hopelessness, can any business seem more fitted to heighten it than that of continually handling these dead letters, and assorting them for the

---

[31]WITH KINGS AND COUNSELLORS: A reference to Job 3:13–14: "For now should I have lain still and been quiet, I should have slept: then had I been at rest, / With kings and counsellors of the earth, which build desolate places for themselves."
[32]DEAD LETTER OFFICE: Letters that can neither be delivered to the addressee nor returned to the sender are kept on file (in the "dead letter office") for one year by the Post Office before they are destroyed.

flames? For by the cart-load they are annually burned. Sometimes from out the folded paper the pale clerk takes a ring:—the finger it was meant for, perhaps, moulders in the grave; a bank-note sent in swiftest charity:—he whom it would relieve, nor eats nor hungers any more; pardon for those who died despairing; hope for those who died unhoping; good tidings for those who died stifled by unrelieved calamities. On errands of life, these letters speed to death.

Ah Bartleby! Ah humanity!

[1853]

Benito Cereno

In the year 1799, Captain Amasa Delano,[1] of Duxbury, in Massachusetts, commanding a large sealer[2] and general trader, lay at anchor, with a valuable cargo, in the harbor of St. Maria—a small, desert, uninhabited island toward the southern extremity of the long coast of Chili. There he had touched for water.

On the second day, not long after dawn, while lying in his berth, his mate came below, informing him that a strange sail was coming into the bay. Ships were then not so plenty in those waters as now. He rose, dressed, and went on deck.

The morning was one peculiar to that coast. Everything was mute and calm; everything gray. The sea, though undulated into long roods of swells, seemed fixed, and was sleeked at the surface like waved lead that has cooled and set in the smelter's mold. The sky seemed a gray surtout.[3] Flights of troubled gray fowl, kith and kin with flights of troubled gray vapors among which they were mixed, skimmed low and fitfully over the waters, as swallows over meadows before storms. Shadows present, foreshadowing deeper shadows to come.

To Captain Delano's surprise, the stranger, viewed through the glass, showed no colors; though to do so upon entering a haven, however uninhabited in its shores, where but a single other ship might be lying, was the custom among peaceful seamen of all nations. Considering the lawlessness and loneliness of the spot, and the sort of stories, at that day,

---

[1]CAPTAIN AMASA DELANO: Amasa Delano (1763–1823), an American sea captain from Massachusetts who served in the American Revolution. He wrote of his experiences at sea in *Narrative of Voyages and Travels in the Northern and Southern Hemispheres, Comprising Three Voyages Round the World* (1817). Melville based his story on Delano's chapter 18, which describes the capture of a slave ship.
[2]SEALER: A ship engaged in hunting seals.
[3]SURTOUT: Long overcoat.

associated with those seas, Captain Delano's surprise might have deepened into some uneasiness had he not been a person of a singularly undistrustful good nature, not liable, except on extraordinary and repeated incentives, and hardly then, to indulge in personal alarms, any way involving the imputation of malign evil in man. Whether, in view of what humanity is capable, such a trait implies, along with a benevolent heart, more than ordinary quickness and accuracy of intellectual perception, may be left to the wise to determine.

But whatever misgivings might have obtruded on first seeing the stranger, would almost, in any seaman's mind, have been dissipated by observing that, the ship, in navigating into the harbor, was drawing too near the land; a sunken reef making out off her bow. This seemed to prove her a stranger, indeed, not only to the sealer, but the island; consequently, she could be no wonted freebooter on that ocean. With no small interest, Captain Delano continued to watch her—a proceeding not much facilitated by the vapors partly mantling the hull, through which the far matin[4] light from her cabin streamed equivocally enough; much like the sun—by this time hemisphered on the rim of the horizon, and apparently, in company with the strange ship, entering the harbor—which, wimpled by the same low, creeping clouds, showed not unlike a Lima intriguante's[5] one sinister eye peering across the Plaza from the Indian loop-hole of her dusk *saya-y-manta*.[6]

It might have been but a deception of the vapors, but, the longer the stranger was watched, the more singular appeared her maneuvers. Ere long it seemed hard to decide whether she meant to come in or no—what she wanted, or what she was about. The wind, which had breezed up a little during the night, was now extremely light and baffling, which the more increased the apparent uncertainty of her movements.

Surmising, at last, that it might be a ship in distress, Captain Delano ordered his whale-boat to be dropped, and, much to the wary opposition of his mate, prepared to board her, and, at the least, pilot her in. On the night previous, a fishing-party of the seamen had gone a long distance to some detached rocks out of sight from the sealer, and, an hour or two before day-break, had returned, having met with no small success. Presuming that the stranger might have been long off soundings, the good captain put several baskets of the fish, for presents, into his boat, and so pulled away. From her continuing too near the sunken

[4]MATIN: Early morning.
[5]LIMA INTRIGUANTE'S: A woman involved in secret plotting.
[6]SAYA-Y-MANTA: A shawl that can be drawn around the face.

reef, deeming her in danger, calling to his men, he made all haste to apprise those on board of their situation. But, some time ere the boat came up, the wind, light though it was, having shifted, had headed the vessel off, as well as partly broken the vapors from about her.

Upon gaining a less remote view, the ship, when made signally visible on the verge of the leaden-hued swells, with the shreds of fog here and there raggedly furring her, appeared like a white-washed monastery after a thunder-storm, seen perched upon some dun cliff among the Pyrenees. But it was no purely fanciful resemblance which now, for a moment, almost led Captain Delano to think that nothing less than a ship-load of monks was before him. Peering over the bulwarks were what really seemed, in the hazy distance, throngs of dark cowls; while, fitfully revealed through the open port-holes, other dark moving figures were dimly descried, as of Black Friars[7] pacing the cloisters.

Upon a still nigher approach, this appearance was modified, and the true character of the vessel was plain—a Spanish merchantman of the first class; carrying negro slaves, amongst other valuable freight, from one colonial port to another. A very large, and, in its time, a very fine vessel, such as in those days were at intervals encountered along that main; sometimes superseded Acapulco treasure-ships, or retired frigates of the Spanish king's navy, which, like superannuated Italian palaces, still, under a decline of masters, preserved signs of former state.

As the whale-boat drew more and more nigh, the cause of the peculiar pipe-clayed[8] aspect of the stranger was seen in the slovenly neglect pervading her. The spars, ropes, and great part of the bulwarks,[9] looked woolly, from long unacquaintance with the scraper, tar, and the brush. Her keel seemed laid, her ribs put together, and she launched, from Ezekiel's Valley of Dry Bones.[10]

In the present business in which she was engaged, the ship's general model and rig appeared to have undergone no material change from their original war-like and Froissart pattern.[11] However, no guns were seen.

The tops were large, and were railed about with what had once been octagonal net-work, all now in sad disrepair. These tops hung overhead like three ruinous aviaries, in one of which was seen perched, on a ratlin,[12]

---

[7]BLACK FRIARS: The Dominican monastic order.
[8]PIPE-CLAYED: Grayish-white.
[9]BULWARKS: The raised woodwork that runs along the sides of a ship above the deck.
[10]EZEKIEL'S VALLEY OF DRY BONES: Ezekiel 37:1: "The hand of the LORD was upon me, and carried me out in the spirit of the LORD, and set me down in the midst of the valley which was full of bones."
[11]FROISSART PATTERN: A medieval style; referring to French poet and historian Jean Froissart (1337–1410).
[12]RATLIN: Small ropes, forming the steps of a rope ladder.

a white noddy,[13] strange fowl, so called from its lethargic, somnambulistic character, being frequently caught by hand at sea. Battered and mouldy, the castellated forecastle seemed some ancient turret, long ago taken by assault, and then left to decay. Toward the stern, two high-raised quarter galleries—the balustrades here and there covered with dry, tindery sea-moss—opening out from the unoccupied state-cabin, whose dead lights, for all the mild weather, were hermetically closed and calked—these tenantless balconies hung over the sea as if it were the grand Venetian canal. But the principal relic of faded grandeur was the ample oval of the shield-like stern-piece, intricately carved with the arms of Castile and Leon,[14] medallioned about by groups of mythological or symbolical devices; uppermost and central of which was a dark satyr in a mask, holding his foot on the prostrate neck of a writhing figure, likewise masked.

Whether the ship had a figure-head, or only a plain beak, was not quite certain, owing to canvas wrapped about that part, either to protect it while undergoing a re-furbishing, or else decently to hide its decay. Rudely painted or chalked, as in a sailor freak, along the forward side of a sort of pedestal below the canvas, was the sentence, "*Seguid vuestro jefe*," (follow your leader); while upon the tarnished head-boards, near by, appeared, in stately capitals, once gilt, the ship's name, "SAN DOMINICK," each letter streakingly corroded with tricklings of copper-spike rust; while, like mourning weeds, dark festoons of sea-grass slimily swept to and fro over the name, with every hearse-like roll of the hull.

As at last the boat was hooked from the bow along toward the gangway amidship, its keel, while yet some inches separated from the hull, harshly grated as on a sunken coral reef. It proved a huge bunch of conglobated barnacles adhering below the water to the side like a wen; a token of baffling airs and long calms passed somewhere in those seas.

Climbing the side, the visitor was at once surrounded by a clamorous throng of whites and blacks, but the latter outnumbering the former more than could have been expected, negro transportation-ship as the stranger in port was. But, in one language, and as with one voice, all poured out a common tale of suffering; in which the negresses, of whom there were not a few, exceeded the others in their dolorous vehemence. The scurvy,[15] together with a fever, had swept off a great part

---

[13]WHITE NODDY: A seabird, found in tropical regions, resembling a tern.
[14]CASTILE AND LEON: Kingdoms of Spain; their carved arms featured a castle and a lion, respectively.
[15]SCURVY: A disease now known to be caused by a lack of vitamin C in the diet. It is characterized by wasting and bleeding under the skin and from the gums. If left untreated, it can be fatal.

of their number, more especially the Spaniards. Off Cape Horn,[16] they had narrowly escaped shipwreck; then, for days together, they had lain tranced without wind; their provisions were low; their water next to none; their lips that moment were baked.

While Captain Delano was thus made the mark of all eager tongues, his one eager glance took in all the faces, with every other object about him.

Always upon first boarding a large and populous ship at sea, especially a foreign one, with a nondescript crew such as Lascars or Manilla men,[17] the impression varies in a peculiar way from that produced by first entering a strange house with strange inmates in a strange land. Both house and ship, the one by its walls and blinds, the other by its high bulwarks like ramparts, hoard from view their interiors till the last moment; but in the case of the ship there is this addition; that the living spectacle it contains, upon its sudden and complete disclosure, has, in contrast with the blank ocean which zones it, something of the effect of enchantment. The ship seems unreal; these strange costumes, gestures, and faces, but a shadowy tableau just emerged from the deep, which directly must receive back what it gave.

Perhaps it was some such influence as above is attempted to be described, which, in Captain Delano's mind, heightened whatever, upon a staid scrutiny, might have seemed unusual; especially the conspicuous figures of four elderly grizzled negroes, their heads like black, doddered willow tops, who, in venerable contrast to the tumult below them, were couched sphynx-like, one on the starboard cat-head,[18] another on the larboard, and the remaining pair face to face on the opposite bulwarks above the main-chains. They each had bits of unstranded old junk in their hands, and, with a sort of stoical self-content, were picking the junk into oakum,[19] a small heap of which lay by their sides. They accompanied the task with a continuous, low, monotonous chant; droning and druling[20] away like so many gray-headed bag-pipers playing a funeral march.

The quarter-deck rose into an ample elevated poop, upon the forward verge of which, lifted, like the oakum-pickers, some eight feet above the general throng, sat along in a row, separated by regular spaces, the cross-legged figures of six other blacks; each with a rusty hatchet in his hand, which, with a bit of brick and a rag, he was engaged like

---

[16]CAPE HORN: The southern tip of South America.
[17]LASCARS OR MANILLA MEN: Sailors from east India and the Philippines, respectively.
[18]CAT-HEAD: A beam that projects horizontally from each side of a ship's bow, used to hoist and secure the anchor.
[19]OAKUM: Loose rope fibers used as calking.
[20]DRONING AND DRULING: Driveling.

a scullion[21] in scouring; while between each two was a small stack of hatchets, their rusted edges turned forward awaiting a like operation. Though occasionally the four oakum-pickers would briefly address some person or persons in the crowd below, yet the six hatchet-polishers neither spoke to others, nor breathed a whisper among themselves, but sat intent upon their task, except at intervals, when, with the peculiar love in negroes of uniting industry with pastime, two and two they sideways clashed their hatchets together, like cymbals, with a barbarous din. All six, unlike the generality, had the raw aspect of unsophisticated Africans.

But that first comprehensive glance which took in those ten figures, with scores less conspicuous, rested but an instant upon them, as, impatient of the hubbub of voices, the visitor turned in quest of whomsoever it might be that commanded the ship.

But as if not unwilling to let nature make known her own case among his suffering charge, or else in despair of restraining it for the time, the Spanish captain, a gentlemanly, reserved-looking, and rather young man to a stranger's eye, dressed with singular richness, but bearing plain traces of recent sleepless cares and disquietudes, stood passively by, leaning against the main-mast, at one moment casting a dreary, spiritless look upon his excited people, at the next an unhappy glance toward his visitor. By his side stood a black of small stature, in whose rude face, as occasionally, like a shepherd's dog, he mutely turned it up into the Spaniard's, sorrow and affection were equally blended.

Struggling through the throng, the American advanced to the Spaniard, assuring him of his sympathies, and offering to render whatever assistance might be in his power. To which the Spaniard returned, for the present, but grave and ceremonious acknowledgments, his national formality dusked by the saturnine mood of ill health.

But losing no time in mere compliments, Captain Delano returning to the gangway, had his baskets of fish brought up; and as the wind still continued light, so that some hours at least must elapse ere the ship could be brought to the anchorage, he bade his men return to the sealer, and fetch back as much water as the whale-boat could carry, with whatever soft bread the steward might have, all the remaining pumpkins on board, with a box of sugar, and a dozen of his private bottles of cider.

Not many minutes after the boat's pushing off, to the vexation of all, the wind entirely died away, and the tide turning, began drifting back the ship helplessly seaward. But trusting this would not long last, Captain Delano sought with good hopes to cheer up the strangers, feeling no small satisfaction that, with persons in their condition he could—thanks to

[21]SCULLION: A kitchen helper.

his frequent voyages along the Spanish main[22]—converse with some freedom in their native tongue.

While left alone with them, he was not long in observing some things tending to heighten his first impressions; but surprise was lost in pity, both for the Spaniards and blacks, alike evidently reduced from scarcity of water and provisions; while long-continued suffering seemed to have brought out the less good-natured qualities of the negroes, besides, at the same time, impairing the Spaniard's authority over them. But, under the circumstances, precisely this condition of things was to have been anticipated. In armies, navies, cities, or families, in nature herself, nothing more relaxes good order than misery. Still, Captain Delano was not without the idea, that had Benito Cereno been a man of greater energy, misrule would hardly have come to the present pass. But the debility, constitutional or induced by the hardships, bodily and mental, of the Spanish captain, was too obvious to be overlooked. A prey to settled dejection, as if long mocked with hope he would not now indulge it, even when it had ceased to be a mock, the prospect of that day or evening at furthest, lying at anchor, with plenty of water for his people, and a brother captain to counsel and befriend, seemed in no perceptible degree to encourage him. His mind appeared unstrung, if not still more seriously affected. Shut up in these oaken walls, chained to one dull round of command, whose unconditionality cloyed him, like some hypochondriac abbot he moved slowly about, at times suddenly pausing, starting, or staring, biting his lip, biting his finger-nail, flushing, paling, twitching his beard, with other symptoms of an absent or moody mind. This distempered spirit was lodged, as before hinted, in as distempered a frame. He was rather tall, but seemed never to have been robust, and now with nervous suffering was almost worn to a skeleton. A tendency to some pulmonary complaint appeared to have been lately confirmed. His voice was like that of one with lungs half gone, hoarsely suppressed, a husky whisper. No wonder that, as in this state he tottered about, his private servant apprehensively followed him. Sometimes the negro gave his master his arm, or took his handkerchief out of his pocket for him; performing these and similar offices with that affectionate zeal which transmutes into something filial or fraternal acts in themselves but menial; and which has gained for the negro the repute of making the most pleasing body servant in the world; one,

---

[22]SPANISH MAIN: The area near the mainland of North America adjacent to the Caribbean Sea, spanning the coast of the Isthmus of Panama to the mouth of the Orinoco River in Venezuela.

too, whom a master need be on no stiffly superior terms with, but may treat with familiar trust less a servant than a devoted companion.

Marking the noisy indocility of the blacks in general, as well as what seemed the sullen inefficiency of the whites, it was not without humane satisfaction that Captain Delano witnessed the steady good conduct of Babo.

But the good conduct of Babo, hardly more than the ill-behavior of others, seemed to withdraw the half-lunatic Don Benito from his cloudy langour. Not that such precisely was the impression made by the Spaniard on the mind of his visitor. The Spaniard's individual unrest was, for the present, but noted as a conspicuous feature in the ship's general affliction. Still, Captain Delano was not a little concerned at what he could not help taking for the time to be Don Benito's unfriendly indifference towards himself. The Spaniard's manner, too, conveyed a sort of sour and gloomy disdain, which he seemed at no pains to disguise. But this the American in charity ascribed to the harassing effects of sickness, since, in former instances, he had noted that there are peculiar natures on whom prolonged physical suffering seems to cancel every social instinct of kindness; as if forced to black bread themselves, they deemed it but equity that each person coming nigh them should, indirectly, by some slight or affront, be made to partake of their fare.

But ere long Captain Delano bethought him that, indulgent as he was at the first, in judging the Spaniard, he might not, after all, have exercised charity enough. At bottom it was Don Benito's reserve which displeased him; but the same reserve was shown towards all but his faithful personal attendant. Even the formal reports which, according to seausage, were, at stated times, made to him by some petty underling, either a white, mulatto or black, he hardly had patience enough to listen to, without betraying contemptuous aversion. His manner upon such occasions was, in its degree, not unlike that which might be supposed to have been his imperial countryman's, Charles V,[23] just previous to the anchoritish retirement of that monarch from the throne.

This splenetic disrelish of his place was evinced in almost every function pertaining to it. Proud as he was moody, he condescended to no personal mandate. Whatever special orders were necessary, their delivery was delegated to his body-servant, who in turn transferred them to their ultimate destination, through runners, alert Spanish boys or slave boys, like pages or pilot-fish[24] within easy call continually hovering round Don Benito. So that to have beheld this undemonstrative invalid gliding

---

[23]CHARLES V: King of Spain (1500–1558) and the Holy Roman Empire who lived out his final years in a monastery while still taking an active interest in politics.
[24]PILOT-FISH: A small silvery-blue tropical fish that was thought to act as a guide for sharks.

about, apathetic and mute, no landsman could have dreamed that in him was lodged a dictatorship beyond which, while at sea, there was no earthly appeal.

Thus, the Spaniard, regarded in his reserve, seemed as the involuntary victim of mental disorder. But, in fact, his reserve might, in some degree, have proceeded from design. If so, then here was evinced the unhealthy climax of that icy though conscientious policy, more or less adopted by all commanders of large ships, which, except in signal emergencies, obliterates alike the manifestation of sway with every trace of sociality; transforming the man into a block, or rather into a loaded cannon, which, until there is call for thunder, has nothing to say.

Viewing him in this light, it seemed but a natural token of the perverse habit induced by a long course of such hard self-restraint, that, notwithstanding the present condition of his ship, the Spaniard should still persist in a demeanor, which, however harmless, or, it may be, appropriate, in a well appointed vessel, such as the San Dominick might have been at the outset of the voyage, was anything but judicious now. But the Spaniard perhaps thought that it was with captains as with gods: reserve, under all events, must still be their cue. But more probably this appearance of slumbering dominion might have been but an attempted disguise to conscious imbecility—not deep policy, but shallow device. But be all this as it might, whether Don Benito's manner was designed or not, the more Captain Delano noted its pervading reserve, the less he felt uneasiness at any particular manifestation of that reserve towards himself.

Neither were his thoughts taken up by the captain alone. Wonted to the quiet orderliness of the sealer's comfortable family of a crew, the noisy confusion of the San Dominick's suffering host repeatedly challenged his eye. Some prominent breaches not only of discipline but of decency were observed. These Captain Delano could not but ascribe, in the main, to the absence of those subordinate deck-officers to whom, along with higher duties, is entrusted what may be styled the police department of a populous ship. True, the old oakum-pickers appeared at times to act the part of monitorial constables to their countrymen, the blacks; but though occasionally succeeding in allaying trifling outbreaks now and then between man and man, they could do little or nothing toward establishing general quiet. The San Dominick was in the condition of a transatlantic emigrant ship, among whose multitude of living freight are some individuals, doubtless, as little troublesome as crates and bales; but the friendly remonstrances of such with their ruder companions are of not so much avail as the unfriendly arm of the mate. What the San Dominick wanted was, what the emigrant ship has, stern superior officers. But on these decks not so much as a fourth mate was to be seen.

The visitor's curiosity was roused to learn the particulars of those mishaps which had brought about such absenteeism, with its consequences; because, though deriving some inkling of the voyage from the wails which at the first moment had greeted him, yet of the details no clear understanding had been had. The best account would, doubtless, be given by the captain. Yet at first the visitor was loth to ask it, unwilling to provoke some distant rebuff. But plucking up courage, he at last accosted Don Benito, renewing the expression of his benevolent interest, adding, that did he (Captain Delano) but know the particulars of the ship's misfortunes, he would, perhaps, be better able in the end to relieve them. Would Don Benito favor him with the whole story?

Don Benito faltered; then, like some somnambulist suddenly interfered with, vacantly stared at his visitor, and ended by looking down on the deck. He maintained this posture so long, that Captain Delano, almost equally disconcerted, and involuntarily almost as rude, turned suddenly from him, walking forward to accost one of the Spanish seamen for the desired information. But he had hardly gone five paces, when with a sort of eagerness Don Benito invited him back, regretting his momentary absence of mind, and professing readiness to gratify him.

While most part of the story was being given, the two captains stood on the after part of the main-deck, a privileged spot, no one being near but the servant.

"It is now a hundred and ninety days," began the Spaniard, in his husky whisper, "that this ship, well officered and well manned, with several cabin passengers—some fifty Spaniards in all—sailed from Buenos Ayres bound to Lima, with a general cargo, hardware, Paraguay tea and the like—and," pointing forward, "that parcel of negroes, now not more than a hundred and fifty, as you see, but then numbering over three hundred souls. Off Cape Horn we had heavy gales. In one moment, by night, three of my best officers, with fifteen sailors, were lost, with the mainyard; the spar snapping under them in the slings, as they sought, with heavers, to beat down the icy sail. To lighten the hull, the heavier sacks of mata[25] were thrown into the sea, with most of the water-pipes[26] lashed on deck at the time. And this last necessity it was, combined with the prolonged detentions afterwards experienced, which eventually brought about our chief causes of suffering. When——"

Here there was a sudden fainting attack of his cough, brought on, no doubt, by his mental distress. His servant sustained him, and drawing a cordial from his pocket placed it to his lips. He a little revived. But unwill-

[25]MATA: Cotton.
[26]WATER-PIPES: Kegs of water.

ing to leave him unsupported while yet imperfectly restored, the black with one arm still encircled his master, at the same time keeping his eye fixed on his face, as if to watch for the first sign of complete restoration, or relapse, as the event might prove.

The Spaniard proceeded, but brokenly and obscurely, as one in a dream. —"Oh, my God! rather than pass through what I have, with joy I would have hailed the most terrible gales; but——"

His cough returned and with increased violence; this subsiding, with reddened lips and closed eyes he fell heavily against his supporter.

"His mind wanders. He was thinking of the plague that followed the gales," plaintively sighed the servant; "my poor, poor master!" wringing one hand, and with the other wiping the mouth. "But be patient, Señor," again turning to Captain Delano, "these fits do not last long; master will soon be himself."

Don Benito reviving, went on; but as this portion of the story was very brokenly delivered, the substance only will here be set down.

It appeared that after the ship had been many days tossed in storms off the Cape, the scurvy broke out, carrying off numbers of the whites and blacks. When at last they had worked round into the Pacific, their spars and sails were so damaged, and so inadequately handled by the surviving mariners, most of whom were become invalids, that, unable to lay her northerly course by the wind, which was powerful, the unmanageable ship for successive days and nights was blown northwestward, where the breeze suddenly deserted her, in unknown waters, to sultry calms. The absence of the water-pipes now proved as fatal to life as before their presence had menaced it. Induced, or at least aggravated, by the less than scanty allowance of water, a malignant fever followed the scurvy; with the excessive heat of the lengthened calm, making such short work of it as to sweep away, as by billows, whole families of the Africans, and a yet larger number, proportionably, of the Spaniards, including, by a luckless fatality, every remaining officer on board. Consequently, in the smart west winds eventually following the calm, the already rent sails having to be simply dropped, not furled, at need, had been gradually reduced to the beggar's rags they were now. To procure substitutes for his lost sailors, as well as supplies of water and sails, the captain at the earliest opportunity had made for Baldivia, the southernmost civilized port of Chili and South America; but upon nearing the coast the thick weather had prevented him from so much as sighting that harbor. Since which period, almost without a crew, and almost without canvas and almost without water, and at intervals giving its added dead to the sea, the San Dominick had been battle-dored[27] about

[27]BATTLE-DORED: Tossed back and forth.

by contrary winds, inveigled by currents, or grown weedy in calms. Like a man lost in woods, more than once she had doubled upon her own track.

"But throughout these calamities," huskily continued Don Benito, painfully turning in the half embrace of his servant, "I have to thank those negroes you see, who, though to your inexperienced eyes appearing unruly, have, indeed, conducted themselves with less of restlessness than even their owner could have thought possible under such circumstances."

Here he again fell faintly back. Again his mind wandered: but he rallied, and less obscurely proceeded.

"Yes, their owner was quite right in assuring me that no fetters would be needed with his blacks; so that while, as is wont in this transportation, those negroes have always remained upon deck—not thrust below, as in the Guineamen—they have, also, from the beginning, been freely permitted to range within given bounds at their pleasure."

Once more the faintness returned—his mind roved—but, recovering, he resumed:

"But it is Babo here to whom, under God, I owe not only my own preservation, but likewise to him, chiefly, the merit is due, of pacifying his more ignorant brethren, when at intervals tempted to murmurings."

"Ah, master," sighed the black, bowing his face, "don't speak of me; Babo is nothing; what Babo has done was but duty."

"Faithful fellow!" cried Capt. Delano. "Don Benito, I envy you such a friend; slave I cannot call him."

As master and man stood before him, the black upholding the white, Captain Delano could not but bethink him of the beauty of that relationship which could present such a spectacle of fidelity on the one hand and confidence on the other. The scene was heightened by the contrast in dress, denoting their relative positions. The Spaniard wore a loose Chili jacket of dark velvet; white small clothes and stockings, with silver buckles at the knee and instep; a high-crowned sombrero, of fine grass; a slender sword, silver mounted, hung from a knot in his sash; the last being an almost invariable adjunct, more for ornament than utility, of a South American gentleman's dress to this hour. Excepting when his occasional nervous contortions brought about disarray, there was a certain precision in his attire, curiously at variance with the unsightly disorder around; especially in the belittered Ghetto,[28] forward of the main-mast, wholly occupied by the blacks.

[28]GHETTO: A thickly populated slum area. The term originally denoted the quarter of a city to which Jews were restricted, but in current usage it may apply to any area where a particular ethnic group lives closely together.

The servant wore nothing but wide trowsers, apparently, from their coarseness and patches, made out of some old topsail; they were clean, and confined at the waist by a bit of unstranded rope, which, with his composed, deprecatory air at times, made him look something like a begging friar of St. Francis.[29]

However unsuitable for the time and place, at least in the blunt-thinking American's eyes, and however strangely surviving in the midst of all his afflictions, the toilette of Don Benito might not, in fashion at least, have gone beyond the style of the day among South Americans of his class. Though on the present voyage sailing from Buenos Ayres, he had avowed himself a native and resident of Chili, whose inhabitants had not so generally adopted the plain coat and once plebeian pantaloons; but, with a becoming modification, adhered to their provincial costume, picturesque as any in the world. Still, relatively to the pale history of the voyage, and his own pale face, there seemed something so incongruous in the Spaniard's apparel, as almost to suggest the image of an invalid courtier tottering about London streets in the time of the plague.

The portion of the narrative which, perhaps, most excited interest, as well as some surprise, considering the latitudes in question, was the long calms spoken of, and more particularly the ship's so long drifting about. Without communicating the opinion, of course, the American could not but impute at least part of the detentions both to clumsy seamanship and faulty navigation. Eying Don Benito's small, yellow hands, he easily inferred that the young captain had not got into command at the hawse-hole,[30] but the cabin-window; and if so, why wonder at incompetence, in youth, sickness, and gentility united?

But drowning criticism in compassion, after a fresh repetition of his sympathies, Captain Delano having heard out his story, not only engaged, as in the first place, to see Don Benito and his people supplied in their immediate bodily needs, but, also, now further promised to assist him in procuring a large permanent supply of water, as well as some sails and rigging; and, though it would involve no small embarrassment to himself, yet he would spare three of his best seamen for temporary deck officers; so that without delay the ship might proceed to Conception, there fully to refit for Lima, her destined port.

Such generosity was not without its effect, even upon the invalid. His face lighted up; eager and hectic, he met the honest glance of his visitor. With gratitude he seemed overcome.

---

[29]BEGGING FRIAR OF ST. FRANCIS: A friar of the Order of Saint Francis.
[30]HAWSE-HOLE: A round hole in a ship's bow for a cable to run through. The term also means to begin a career from a low position (before the mast).

"This excitement is bad for master," whispered the servant, taking his arm, and with soothing words gently drawing him aside.

When Don Benito returned, the American was pained to observe that his hopefulness, like the sudden kindling in his cheek, was but febrile and transient.

Ere long, with a joyless mien, looking up towards the poop, the host invited his guest to accompany him there, for the benefit of what little breath of wind might be stirring.

As during the telling of the story, Captain Delano had once or twice started at the occasional cymballing of the hatchet-polishers, wondering why such an interruption should be allowed, especially in that part of the ship, and in the ears of an invalid; and moreover, as the hatchets had anything but an attractive look, and the handlers of them still less so, it was, therefore, to tell the truth, not without some lurking reluctance, or even shrinking, it may be, that Captain Delano, with apparent complaisance, acquiesced in his host's invitation. The more so, since with an untimely caprice of punctilio, rendered distressing by his cadaverous aspect, Don Benito, with Castilian bows, solemnly insisted upon his guest's preceding him up the ladder leading to the elevation; where, one on each side of the last step, sat for armorial supporters and sentries two of the ominous file. Gingerly enough stepped good Captain Delano between them, and in the instant of leaving them behind, like one running the gauntlet, he felt an apprehensive twitch in the calves of his legs.

But when, facing about, he saw the whole file, like so many organ-grinders, still stupidly intent on their work, unmindful of everything beside, he could not but smile at his late fidgety panic.

Presently, while standing with his host, looking forward upon the decks below, he was struck by one of those instances of insubordination previously alluded to. Three black boys, with two Spanish boys, were sitting together on the hatches, scraping a rude wooden platter, in which some scanty mess had recently been cooked. Suddenly, one of the black boys, enraged at a word dropped by one of his white companions, seized a knife, and though called to forbear by one of the oakum-pickers, struck the lad over the head, inflicting a gash from which blood flowed.

In amazement, Captain Delano inquired what this meant. To which the pale Don Benito dully muttered, that it was merely the sport of the lad.

"Pretty serious sport, truly," rejoined Captain Delano. "Had such a thing happened on board the Bachelor's Delight, instant punishment would have followed."

At these words the Spaniard turned upon the American one of his sudden, staring, half-lunatic looks; then relapsing into his torpor, answered, "Doubtless, doubtless, Señor."

Is it, thought Captain Delano, that this hapless man is one of those paper captains I've known, who by policy wink at what by power they cannot put down? I know no sadder sight than a commander who has little of command but the name.

"I should think, Don Benito," he now said, glancing towards the oakumpicker who had sought to interfere with the boys, "that you would find it advantageous to keep all your blacks employed, especially the younger ones, no matter at what useless task, and no matter what happens to the ship. Why, even with my little band, I find such a course indispensable. I once kept a crew on my quarter-deck thrumming mats for my cabin, when, for three days, I had given up my ship—mats, men, and all—for a speedy loss, owing to the violence of a gale, in which we could do nothing but helplessly drive before it."

"Doubtless, doubtless," muttered Don Benito.

"But," continued Captain Delano, again glancing upon the oakumpickers and then at the hatchet-polishers, near by. "I see you keep some at least of your host employed."

"Yes," was again the vacant response.

"Those old men there, shaking their pows[31] from their pulpits," continued Captain Delano, pointing to the oakum-pickers, "seem to act the part of old dominies to the rest, little heeded as their admonitions are at times. Is this voluntary on their part, Don Benito, or have you appointed them shepherds to your flock of black sheep?"

"What posts they fill, I appointed them," rejoined the Spaniard, in an acrid tone, as if resenting some supposed satiric reflection.

"And these others, these Ashantee[32] conjurors here," continued Captain Delano, rather uneasily eying the brandished steel of the hatchet-polishers, where in spots it had been brought to a shine, "this seems a curious business they are at, Don Benito?"

"In the gales we met," answered the Spaniard, "what of our general cargo was not thrown overboard was much damaged by the brine. Since coming into calm weather, I have had several cases of knives and hatchets daily brought up for overhauling and cleaning."

---

[31]POWS: Heads.
[32]ASHANTEE: Ashanti or Asante; of the Akan peoples from the area of Ghana, West Africa.

"A prudent idea, Don Benito. You are part owner of ship and cargo, I presume; but not of the slaves, perhaps?"

"I am owner of all you see," impatiently returned Don Benito, "except the main company of blacks, who belonged to my late friend, Alexandro Aranda."

As he mentioned this name, his air was heart-broken; his knees shook: his servant supported him.

Thinking he divined the cause of such unusual emotion, to confirm his surmise, Captain Delano, after a pause, said "And may I ask, Don Benito, whether—since awhile ago you spoke of some cabin passengers—the friend, whose loss so afflicts you at the outset of the voyage accompanied his blacks?"

"Yes."

"But died of the fever?"

"Died of the fever.—Oh, could I but—"

Again quivering, the Spaniard paused.

"Pardon me," said Captain Delano lowly, "but I think that, by a sympathetic experience, I conjecture, Don Benito, what it is that gives the keener edge to your grief. It was once my hard fortune to lose at sea a dear friend, my own brother, then supercargo. Assured of the welfare of his spirit, its departure I could have borne like a man; but that honest eye, that honest hand—both of which had so often met mine—and that warm heart; all, all—like scraps to the dogs—to throw all to the sharks! It was then I vowed never to have for fellow-voyager a man I loved, unless, unbeknown to him, I had provided every requisite, in case of a fatality, for embalming his mortal part for interment on shore. Were your friend's remains now on board this ship, Don Benito, not thus strangely would the mention of his name affect you."

"On board this ship?" echoed the Spaniard. Then, with horrified gestures, as directed against some specter, he unconsciously fell into the ready arms of his attendant, who, with a silent appeal toward Captain Delano, seemed beseeching him not again to broach a theme so unspeakably distressing to his master.

This poor fellow now, thought the pained American, is the victim of that sad superstition which associates goblins with the deserted body of man, as ghosts with an abandoned house. How unlike are we made! What to me, in like case, would have been a solemn satisfaction, the bare suggestion, even, terrifies the Spaniard into this trance. Poor Alexandro Aranda! what would you say could you here see your friend—who, on former voyages, when you for months were left behind, has, I dare say, often longed, and longed, for one peep at you—now transported with terror at the least thought of having you anyway nigh him.

At this moment, with a dreary graveyard toll, betokening a flaw, the ship's forecastle bell, smote by one of the grizzled oakum-pickers, proclaimed ten o'clock through the leaden calm; when Captain Delano's attention was caught by the moving figure of a gigantic black, emerging from the general crowd below, and slowly advancing towards the elevated poop. An iron collar was about his neck, from which depended a chain, thrice wound round his body; the terminating links padlocked together at a broad band of iron, his girdle.

"How like a mute Atufal moves," murmured the servant.

The black mounted the steps of the poop, and, like a brave prisoner, brought up to receive sentence, stood in unquailing muteness before Don Benito, now recovered from his attack.

At the first glimpse of his approach, Don Benito had started, a resentful shadow swept over his face; and, as with the sudden memory of bootless rage, his white lips glued together.

This is some mulish mutineer, thought Captain Delano, surveying, not without a mixture of admiration, the colossal form of the negro.

"See, he waits your question, master," said the servant.

Thus reminded, Don Benito, nervously averting his glance, as if shunning, by anticipation, some rebellious response, in a disconcerted voice, thus spoke:—

"Atufal, will you ask my pardon now?"

The black was silent.

"Again, master," murmured the servant, with bitter upbraiding eying his countryman, "Again, master; he will bend to master yet."

"Answer," said Don Benito, still averting his glance, "say but the one word *pardon*, and your chains shall be off."

Upon this, the black, slowly raising both arms, let them lifelessly fall, his links clanking, his head bowed; as much as to say, "no, I am content."

"Go," said Don Benito, with inkept and unknown emotion.

Deliberately as he had come, the black obeyed.

"Excuse me, Don Benito," said Captain Delano, "but this scene surprises me; what means it, pray?"

"It means that that negro alone, of all the band, has given me peculiar cause of offense. I have put him in chains; I—"

Here he paused; his hand to his head, as if there were a swimming there, or a sudden bewilderment of memory had come over him; but meeting his servant's kindly glance seemed reassured, and proceeded:—

"I could not scourge such a form. But I told him he must ask my pardon. As yet he has not. At my command, every two hours he stands before me."

"And how long has this been?"

"Some sixty days."

"And obedient in all else? And respectful?"

"Yes."

"Upon my conscience, then," exclaimed Captain Delano, impulsively, "he has a royal spirit in him, this fellow."

"He may have some right to it," bitterly returned Don Benito, "he says he was king in his own land."

"Yes," said the servant, entering a word, "those slits in Atufal's ears once held wedges of gold; but poor Babo here, in his own land, was only a poor slave; a black man's slave was Babo, who now is the white's."

Somewhat annoyed by these conversational familiarities, Captain Delano turned curiously upon the attendant, then glanced inquiringly at his master; but, as if long wonted to these little informalities, neither master nor man seemed to understand him.

"What, pray, was Atufal's offense, Don Benito?" asked Captain Delano; "if it was not something very serious, take a fool's advice, and, in view of his general docility, as well as in some natural respect for his spirit, remit him his penalty."

"No, no, master never will do that," here murmured the servant to himself, "proud Atufal must first ask master's pardon. The slave there carries the padlock, but master here carries the key."

His attention thus directed, Captain Delano now noticed for the first time that, suspended by a slender silken cord, from Don Benito's neck hung a key. At once, from the servant's muttered syllables divining the key's purpose, he smiled and said:—"So, Don Benito—padlock and key—significant symbols, truly."

Biting his lip, Don Benito faltered.

Though the remark of Captain Delano, a man of such native simplicity as to be incapable of satire or irony, had been dropped in playful allusion to the Spaniard's singularly evidenced lordship over the black; yet the hypochondriac seemed in some way to have taken it as a malicious reflection upon his confessed inability thus far to break down, at least, on a verbal summons, the entrenched will of the slave. Deploring this supposed misconception, yet despairing of correcting it, Captain

Delano shifted the subject; but finding his companion more than ever withdrawn, as if still sourly digesting the lees of the presumed affront above-mentioned, by-and-by Captain Delano likewise became less talkative, oppressed, against his own will, by what seemed the secret vindictiveness of the morbidly sensitive Spaniard. But the good sailor himself, of a quite contrary disposition, refrained, on his part, alike from the appearance as from the feeling of resentment, and if silent, was only so from contagion.

Presently the Spaniard, assisted by his servant, somewhat discourteously crossed over from his guest; a procedure which, sensibly enough, might have been allowed to pass for idle caprice of ill-humor, had not master and man, lingering round the corner of the elevated skylight, began whispering together in low voices. This was unpleasing. And more; the moody air of the Spaniard, which at times had not been without a sort of valetudinarian stateliness, now seemed anything but dignified; while the menial familiarity of the servant lost its original charm of simple-hearted attachment.

In his embarrassment, the visitor turned his face to the other side of the ship. By so doing, his glance accidentally fell on a young Spanish sailor, a coil of rope in his hand, just stepped from the deck to the first round of the mizzen-rigging.[33] Perhaps the man would not have been particularly noticed, were it not that, during his ascent to one of the yards, he, with a sort of covert intentness, kept his eye fixed on Captain Delano, from whom, presently, it passed, as if by a natural sequence, to the two whisperers.

His own attention thus redirected to that quarter, Captain Delano gave a slight start. From something in Don Benito's manner just then, it seemed as if the visitor had, at least partly, been the subject of the withdrawn consultation going on—a conjecture as little agreeable to the guest as it was little flattering to the host.

The singular alternations of courtesy and ill-breeding in the Spanish captain were unaccountable, except on one of two suppositions—innocent lunacy, or wicked imposture.

But the first idea, though it might naturally have occurred to an indifferent observer, and, in some respect, had not hitherto been wholly a stranger to Captain Delano's mind, yet, now that, in an incipient way, he began to regard the stranger's conduct something in the light of an intentional affront, of course the idea of lunacy was virtually vacated. But if not a lunatic, what then? Under the circumstances, would a gentleman,

[33]MIZZEN-RIGGING: The rigging securing the principal sail of the mizzen-mast of a ship.

nay, any honest boor, act the part now acted by his host? The man was an impostor. Some low-born adventurer, masquerading as an oceanic grandee; yet so ignorant of the first requisites of mere gentlemanhood as to be betrayed into the present remarkable indecorum. That strange ceremoniousness, too, at other times evinced, seemed not uncharacteristic of one playing a part above his real level. Benito Cereno—Don Benito Cereno—a sounding name. One, too, at that period, not unknown, in the surname, to supercargoes and sea captains trading along the Spanish Main, as belonging to one of the most enterprising and extensive mercantile families in all those provinces; several members of it having titles; a sort of Castilian Rothschild,[34] with a noble brother, or cousin, in every great trading town of South America. The alleged Don Benito was in early manhood, about twenty-nine or thirty. To assume a sort of roving cadetship[35] in the maritime affairs of such a house, what more likely scheme for a young knave of talent and spirit? But the Spaniard was a pale invalid. Never mind. For even to the degree of simulating mortal disease, the craft of some tricksters had been known to attain. To think that, under the aspect of infantile weakness, the most savage energies might be couched—those velvets of the Spaniard but the silky paw to his fangs.

From no train of thought did these fancies come; not from within, but from without; suddenly, too, and in one throng, like hoar frost; yet as soon to vanish as the mild sun of Captain Delano's good-nature regained its meridian.

Glancing over once more towards his host—whose side-face, revealed above the skylight, was now turned towards him—he was struck by the profile, whose clearness of cut was refined by the thinness incident to ill-health, as well as ennobled about the chin by the beard. Away with suspicion. He was a true off-shoot of a true hidalgo[36] Cereno.

Relieved by these and other better thoughts, the visitor, lightly humming a tune, now began indifferently pacing the poop, so as not to betray to Don Benito that he had at all mistrusted incivility, much less duplicity; for such mistrust would yet be proved illusory, and by the event; though, for the present, the circumstance which had provoked that distrust remained unexplained. But when that little mystery should have been cleared up, Captain Delano thought he might extremely regret it, did he allow Don Benito to become aware that he had indulged in ungen-

[34]CASTILIAN ROTHSCHILD: An allusion to the Rothschild German banking family, which became one of Europe's chief financial powers in the nineteenth century. Castile is an area of central and northern Spain.
[35]CADETSHIP: An apprentice-like position in which a young man of a wealthy family trains for a post of authority.
[36]HIDALGO: Son of riches or property, nobleman. (Spanish)

erous surmises. In short, to the Spaniard's black-letter text, it was best, for awhile, to leave open margin.

Presently, his pale face twitching and overcast, the Spaniard, still supported by his attendant, moved over towards his guest, when, with even more than his usual embarrassment, and a strange sort of intriguing intonation in his husky whisper, the following conversation began:—

"Señor, may I ask how long you have lain at this isle?"

"Oh, but a day or two, Don Benito."

"And from what port are you last?"

"Canton."[37]

"And there, Señor, you exchanged your seal-skins for teas and silks, I think you said?"

"Yes. Silks, mostly."

"And the balance you took in specie,[38] perhaps?"

Captain Delano, fidgeting a little, answered—

"Yes; some silver; not a very great deal, though."

"Ah—well. May I ask how many men have you, Señor?"

Captain Delano slightly started, but answered—

"About five-and-twenty, all told."

"And at present, Señor, all on board, I suppose?"

"All on board, Don Benito," replied the Captain, now with satisfaction.

"And will be to-night, Señor?"

At this last question, following so many pertinacious ones, for the soul of him Captain Delano could not but look very earnestly at the questioner, who, instead of meeting the glance, with every token of craven discomposure dropped his eyes to the deck; presenting an unworthy contrast to his servant, who, just then, was kneeling at his feet, adjusting a loose shoe-buckle; his disengaged face meantime, with humble curiosity, turned openly up into his master's downcast one.

The Spaniard, still with a guilty shuffle, repeated his question:—

"And—and will be to-night, Señor?"

"Yes, for aught I know," returned Captain Delano,—"but nay," rallying himself into fearless truth, "some of them talked of going off on another fishing party about midnight."

"Your ships generally go—go more or less armed, I believe, Señor?"

"Oh, a six-pounder or two, in case of emergency," was the intrepidly indifferent reply, "with a small stock of muskets, sealing-spears, and cutlasses, you know."

[37]CANTON: Kanton (formerly Canton) Island, in the central Pacific Ocean.
[38]SPECIE: Coin.

As he thus responded, Captain Delano again glanced at Don Benito, but the latter's eyes were averted; while abruptly and awkwardly shifting the subject, he made some peevish allusion to the calm, and then, without apology, once more, with his attendant, withdrew to the opposite bulwarks, where the whispering was resumed.

At this moment, and ere Captain Delano could cast a cool thought upon what had just passed, the young Spanish sailor before mentioned was seen descending from the rigging. In act of stooping over to spring inboard to the deck, his voluminous, unconfined frock, or shirt, of coarse woollen, much spotted with tar, opened out far down the chest, revealing a soiled under garment of what seemed the finest linen, edged, about the neck, with a narrow blue ribbon, sadly faded and worn. At this moment the young sailor's eye was again fixed on the whisperers, and Captain Delano thought he observed a lurking significance in it, as if silent signs of some Freemason[39] sort had that instant been interchanged.

This once more impelled his own glance in the direction of Don Benito, and, as before, he could not but infer that himself formed the subject of the conference. He paused. The sound of the hatchet-polishing fell on his ears. He cast another swift side-look at the two. They had the air of conspirators. In connection with the late questionings and the incident of the young sailor, these things now begat such return of involuntary suspicion, that the singular guilelessness of the American could not endure it. Plucking up a gay and humorous expression, he crossed over to the two rapidly, saying:—"Ha, Don Benito, your black here seems high in your trust; a sort of privy-counselor, in fact."

Upon this, the servant looked up with a good-natured grin, but the master started as from a venomous bite. It was a moment or two before the Spaniard sufficiently recovered himself to reply; which he did, at last, with cold constraint:—"Yes, Señor, I have trust in Babo."

Here Babo, changing his previous grin of mere animal humor into an intelligent smile, not ungratefully eyed his master.

Finding that the Spaniard now stood silent and reserved, as if involuntarily, or purposely giving hint that his guest's proximity was inconvenient just then, Captain Delano, unwilling to appear uncivil even to incivility itself, made some trivial remark and moved off; again and again turning over in his mind the mysterious demeanor of Don Benito Cereno.

---

[39]FREEMASON: Referring to the secret fraternal order known as the Free and Accepted Masons, or Ancient Free and Accepted Masons. Many people regarded Freemasons with suspicion due to their considerable political power and their secret practices, which included hand signals and symbols.

He had descended from the poop, and, wrapped in thought, was passing near a dark hatchway, leading down into the steerage, when, perceiving motion there, he looked to see what moved. The same instant there was a sparkle in the shadowy hatchway, and he saw one of the Spanish sailors prowling there hurriedly placing his hand in the bosom of his frock, as if hiding something. Before the man could have been certain who it was that was passing, he slunk below out of sight. But enough was seen of him to make it sure that he was the same young sailor before noticed in the rigging.

What was that which so sparkled? thought Captain Delano. It was no lamp—no match—no live coal. Could it have been a jewel? But how come sailors with jewels?—or with silk-trimmed under-shirts either? Has he been robbing the trunks of the dead cabin passengers? But if so, he would hardly wear one of the stolen articles on board ship here. Ah, ah—if now that was, indeed, a secret sign I saw passing between this suspicious fellow and his captain awhile since; if I could only be certain that in my uneasiness my senses did not deceive me, then—

Here, passing from one suspicious thing to another, his mind revolved the strange questions put to him concerning his ship.

By a curious coincidence, as each point was recalled, the black wizards of Ashantee would strike up with their hatchets, as in ominous comment on the white stranger's thoughts. Pressed by such enigmas and portents, it would have been almost against nature, had not, even into the least distrustful heart, some ugly misgivings obtruded.

Observing the ship now helplessly fallen into a current, with enchanted sails, drifting with increased rapidity seaward; and noting that, from a lately intercepted projection of the land, the sealer was hidden, the stout mariner began to quake at thoughts which he barely durst confess to himself. Above all, he began to feel a ghostly dread of Don Benito. And yet when he roused himself, dilated his chest, felt himself strong on his legs, and coolly considered it—what did all these phantoms amount to?

Had the Spaniard any sinister scheme, it must have reference not so much to him (Captain Delano) as to his ship (the Bachelor's Delight). Hence the present drifting away of the one ship from the other, instead of favoring any such possible scheme, was, for the time at least, opposed to it. Clearly any suspicion, combining such contradictions, must need be delusive. Beside, was it not absurd to think of a vessel in distress—a vessel by sickness almost dismanned of her crew—a vessel whose inmates were parched for water—was it not a thousand times absurd that such a craft should, at present, be of a piratical character; or her commander, either for himself or those under him, cherish any desire but for speedy relief and refreshment? But then, might not general distress, and thirst in particular, be affected? And might not that same undiminished Spanish crew, alleged to have perished off to a remnant, be at that very moment lurking in the hold? On heart-broken pretense of entreating a cup of cold water, fiends in human form had got into lonely dwellings, nor retired until a dark deed had been done. And among the Malay pirates, it was no unusual thing to lure ships after them into their treacherous harbors, or entice boarders from a declared enemy at sea, by the spectacle of thinly manned or vacant decks, beneath which prowled a hundred spears with yellow arms ready to upthrust them through the mats. Not that Captain Delano had entirely credited such things. He had heard of them—and now, as stories, they recurred. The present destination of the ship was the anchorage. There she would be near his own vessel. Upon gaining that vicinity, might not the San Dominick, like a slumbering volcano, suddenly let loose energies now hid?

He recalled the Spaniard's manner while telling his story. There was a gloomy hesitancy and subterfuge about it. It was just the manner of one making up his tale for evil purposes, as he goes. But if that story was not true, what was the truth? That the ship had unlawfully come into the Spaniard's possession? But in many of its details, especially in reference to the more calamitous parts, such as the fatalities among the seamen, the consequent prolonged beating about, the past sufferings from obstinate calms, and still continued suffering from thirst; in all these points, as well as others, Don Benito's story had corroborated not only the wailing ejaculations of the indiscriminate multitude, white and black, but likewise—what seemed impossible to be counterfeit—by the very expression and play of every human feature, which Captain Delano saw. If Don Benito's story was throughout an invention, then every soul on board, down to the youngest negress, was his carefully drilled recruit in the plot: an incredible inference. And yet, if there was ground for mistrusting his veracity, that inference was a legitimate one.

But those questions of the Spaniard. There, indeed, one might pause. Did they not seem put with much the same object with which the burglar or assassin, by day-time, reconnoitres the walls of a house? But, with ill purposes, to solicit such information openly of the chief person endangered, and so, in effect, setting him on his guard; how unlikely a procedure was that? Absurd, then, to suppose that those questions had been prompted by evil designs. Thus, the same conduct, which, in this instance, had raised the alarm, served to dispel it. In short, scarce any suspicion or uneasiness, however apparently reasonable at the time, which was not now, with equal apparent reason, dismissed.

At last he began to laugh at his former forebodings; and laugh at the strange ship for, in its aspect someway siding with them, as it were; and laugh, too, at the odd-looking blacks, particularly those old scissors-grinders, the Ashantees; and those bed-ridden old knitting-women, the oakum-pickers; and almost at the dark Spaniard himself, the central hob-globin of all.

For the rest, whatever in a serious way seemed enigmatical, was now good-naturedly explained away by the thought that, for the most part, the poor invalid scarcely knew what he was about; either sulking in black vapors, or putting idle questions without sense or object. Evidently, for the present, the man was not fit to be entrusted with the ship. On some benevolent plea withdrawing the command from him, Captain Delano would yet have to send her to Conception, in charge of his second mate, a worthy person and good navigator—a plan not more convenient for the San Dominick than for Don Benito; for, relieved from all anxiety, keeping wholly to his cabin, the sick man, under the good nursing of his servant, would probably, by the end of the passage, be in a measure restored to health, and with that he should also be restored to authority.

Such were the American's thoughts. They were tranquilizing. There was a difference between the idea of Don Benito's darkly pre-ordaining Captain Delano's fate, and Captain Delano's lightly arranging Don Benito's. Nevertheless, it was not without something of relief that the good seaman presently perceived his whale boat in the distance. Its absence had been prolonged by unexpected detention at the sealer's side, as well as its returning trip lengthened by the continual recession of the goal.

The advancing speck was observed by the blacks. Their shouts attracted the attention of Don Benito, who, with a return of courtesy, approaching Captain Delano, expressed satisfaction at the coming of some supplies, slight and temporary as they must necessarily prove.

Captain Delano responded; but while doing so, his attention was drawn to something passing on the deck below: among the crowd climbing the landward bulwarks, anxiously watching the coming boat, two blacks, to all appearances accidentally incommoded by one of the sailors, violently pushed him aside, which the sailor someway resenting, they dashed him to the deck, despite the earnest cries of the oakum-pickers.

"Don Benito," said Captain Delano quickly, "do you see what is going on there? Look!"

But, seized by his cough, the Spaniard staggered, with both hands to his face, on the point of falling. Captain Delano would have supported him, but the servant was more alert, who, with one hand sustaining his master, with the other applied the cordial. Don Benito restored, the black withdrew his support, slipping aside a little, but dutifully remaining within call of a whisper. Such discretion was here evinced as quite wiped away, in the visitors eyes, any blemish of impropriety which might have attached to the attendant, from the indecorous conferences before mentioned; showing, too, that if the servant were to blame, it might be more the master's fault than his own, since when left to himself he could conduct thus well.

His glance called away from the spectacle of disorder to the more pleasing one before him, Captain Delano could not avoid again congratulating his host upon possessing such a servant, who, though perhaps a little too forward now and then, must upon the whole be invaluable to one in the invalid's situation.

"Tell me, Don Benito," he added, with a smile—"I should like to have your man here myself—what will you take for him? Would fifty doubloons be any object?"

"Master wouldn't part with Babo for a thousand doubloons," murmured the black, overhearing the offer, and taking it in earnest, and, with the strange vanity of a faithful slave appreciated by his master, scorning to hear so paltry a valuation put upon him by a stranger. But Don Benito, apparently hardly yet completely restored, and again interrupted by his cough, made but some broken reply.

Soon his physical distress became so great, affecting his mind, too, apparently, that, as if to screen the sad spectacle, the servant gently conducted his master below.

Left to himself, the American, to while away the time till his boat should arrive, would have pleasantly accosted some one of the few Spanish seamen he saw; but recalling something that Don Benito had said touching their ill conduct, he refrained, as a ship-master indisposed to countenance cowardice or unfaithfulness in seamen.

While, with these thoughts, standing with eye directed forward towards that handful of sailors, suddenly he thought that one or two of them returned the glance and with a sort of meaning. He rubbed his eyes, and looked again; but again seemed to see the same thing. Under a new form, but more obscure than any previous one, the old suspicions recurred, but, in the absence of Don Benito, with less of panic than before. Despite the bad account given of the sailors, Captain Delano resolved forthwith to accost one of them. Descending the poop, he made his way through the blacks, his movement drawing a queer cry from the oakum-pickers, prompted by whom, the negroes, twitching each other aside, divided before him; but, as if curious to see what was the object of this deliberate visit to their Ghetto, closing in behind, in tolerable order, followed the white stranger up. His progress thus proclaimed as by mounted kings-at-arms, and escorted as by a Caffre[40] guard of honor, Captain Delano, assuming a good humored, off-handed air, continued to advance; now and then saying a blithe word to the negroes, and his eye curiously surveying the white faces, here and there sparsely mixed in with the blacks, like stray white pawns venturously involved in the ranks of the chess-men opposed.

While thinking which of them to select for his purpose, he chanced to observe a sailor seated on the deck engaged in tarring the strap of a large block, with a circle of blacks squatted round him inquisitively eying the process.

The mean employment of the man was in contrast with something superior in his figure. His hand, black with continually thrusting it into the tar-pot held for him by a negro, seemed not naturally allied to his face, a face which would have been a very fine one but for its haggardness. Whether this haggardness had aught to do with criminality, could not be determined; since, as intense heat and cold, though unlike, produce like sensations, so innocence and guilt, when, through casual association with mental pain, stamping any visible impress, use one seal—a hacked one.

Not again that this reflection occurred to Captain Delano at the time, charitable man as he was. Rather another idea. Because observing so singular a haggardness combined with a dark eye, averted as in trouble and shame, and then again recalling Don Benito's confessed ill opinion of his crew, insensibly he was operated upon by certain general notions, which, while disconnecting pain and abashment from virtue, invariably link them with vice.

If, indeed, there be any wickedness on board this ship, thought Captain Delano, be sure that man there has fouled his hand in it, even as now he fouls it in the pitch. I don't like to accost him. I will speak to this other, this old Jack here on the windlass.

He advanced to an old Barcelona tar,[41] in ragged red breeches and dirty night-cap, cheeks trenched and bronzed, whiskers dense as thorn hedges. Seated between two sleepy-looking Africans, this mariner, like his younger shipmate, was employed upon some rigging—splicing a cable—the sleepy-looking blacks performing the inferior function of holding the outer parts of the ropes for him.

---

[40]CAFFRE: A Kaffir (or Kafir) was a member of a South African people belonging to the great Bantu family.
[41]TAR: Seaman, sailor (from tarpaulin).

Upon Captain Delano's approach, the man at once hung his head below its previous level; the one necessary for business. It appeared as if he desired to be thought absorbed, with more than common fidelity, in his task. Being addressed, he glanced up, but with what seemed a furtive, diffident air, which sat strangely enough on his weather-beaten visage, much as if a grizzly bear, instead of growling and biting, should simper and cast sheep's eyes. He was asked several questions concerning the voyage, questions purposely referring to several particulars in Don Benito's narrative, not previously corroborated by those impulsive cries greeting the visitor on first coming on board. The questions were briefly answered, confirming all that remained to be confirmed of the story. The negroes about the windlass joined in with the old sailor, but, as they became talkative, he by degrees became mute, and at length quite glum, seemed morosely unwilling to answer more questions, and yet, all the while, this ursine air was somehow mixed with his sheepish one.

Despairing of getting into unembarrassed talk with such a centaur, Captain Delano, after glancing round for a more promising countenance, but seeing none, spoke pleasantly to the blacks to make way for him; and so, amid various grins and grimaces, returned to the poop, feeling a little strange at first, he could hardly tell why, but upon the whole with regained confidence in Benito Cereno.

How plainly, thought he, did that old whiskerando yonder betray a consciousness of ill-desert. No doubt, when he saw me coming, he dreaded lest I, apprised by his Captain of the crew's general misbehavior, came with sharp words for him, and so down with his head. And yet—and yet, now that I think of it, that very old fellow, if I err not, was one of those who seemed so earnestly eying me here awhile since. Ah, these currents spin one's head round almost as much as they do the ship. Ha, there now's a pleasant sort of sunny sight; quite sociable, too.

His attention had been drawn to a slumbering negress, partly disclosed through the lace-work of some rigging, lying, with youthful limbs carelessly disposed, under the lee of the bulwarks, like a doe in the shade of a woodland rock. Sprawling at her lapped breasts was her wide-awake fawn, stark naked, its black little body half lifted from the deck, crosswise with its dam's; its hands, like two paws, clambering upon her; its mouth and nose ineffectually rooting to get at the mark; and meantime giving a vexatious half-grunt, blending with the composed snore of the negress.

The uncommon vigor of the child at length roused the mother. She started up, at distance facing Captain Delano. But as if not at all concerned at the attitude in which she had been caught, delightedly she caught the child up, with maternal transports, covering it with kisses.

There's naked nature, now; pure tenderness and love, thought Captain Delano, well pleased.

This incident prompted him to remark the other negresses more particularly than before. He was gratified with their manners; like most uncivilized women, they seemed at once tender of heart and tough of constitution; equally ready to die for their infants or fight for them. Unsophisticated as leopardesses; loving as doves. Ah! thought Captain Delano, these perhaps are some of the very women whom Ledyard[42] saw in Africa, and gave such a noble account of.

These natural sights somehow insensibly deepened his confidence and ease. At last he looked to see how his boat was getting on; but it was still pretty remote. He turned to see if Don Benito had returned; but he had not.

To change the scene, as well as to please himself with a leisurely observation of the coming boat, stepping over into the mizzen-chains he clambered his way into the starboard quarter-gallery;[43] one of those abandoned Venetian-looking water-balconies previously mentioned; retreats cut off from the deck. As his foot pressed the half-damp, half-dry sea-mosses matting the place, and a chance phantom cats-paw—an islet of breeze, unheralded, unfollowed—as this ghostly cats-paw came fanning his cheek, as his glance fell upon the row of small, round dead-lights, all closed like coppered eyes of the coffined, and the state-cabin door, once connecting with the gallery, even as the dead-lights had once looked out upon it, but now calked fast like a sarcophagus lid, to a purple-black, tarred-over panel, threshold, and post; and he bethought him of the time, when that state-cabin and this state-balcony had heard the voices of the Spanish king's officers, and the forms of the Lima viceroy's daughters had perhaps leaned where he stood—as these and other images flitted through his mind, as the cats-paw through the calm, gradually he felt rising a dreamy inquietude, like that of one who alone on the prairie feels unrest from the repose of the noon.

He leaned against the carved balustrade, again looking off toward his boat; but found his eye falling upon the ribboned grass, trailing along the ship's water-line, straight as a border of green box; and parterres[44] of seaweed, broad ovals and crescents, floating nigh and far, with what seemed long formal alleys between, crossing the terraces of swells, and sweeping round as if leading to the grottoes below. And overhanging all was the

---

[42]LEDYARD: John Ledyard (1751–1789), an American traveler.
[43]QUARTER-GALLERY: A windowed balcony that projects from the aft part of a ship's sides.
[44]PARTERRES: Ornamental flowerbeds.

balustrade by his arm, which, partly stained with pitch and partly embossed with moss, seemed the charred ruin of some summer-house in a grand garden long running to waste.

Trying to break one charm, he was but becharmed anew. Though upon the wide sea, he seemed in some far inland country; prisoner in some deserted château, left to stare at empty grounds, and peer out at vague roads, where never wagon or wayfarer passed.

But these enchantments were a little disenchanted as his eye fell on the corroded main-chains. Of an ancient style, massy and rusty in link, shackle and bolt, they seemed even more fit for the ship's present business than the one for which she had been built.

Presently he thought something moved nigh the chains. He rubbed his eyes, and looked hard. Groves of rigging were about the chains; and there, peering from behind a great stay, like an Indian from behind a hemlock, a Spanish sailor, a marlingspike in his hand, was seen, who made what seemed an imperfect gesture towards the balcony, but immediately, as if alarmed by some advancing step along the deck within, vanished into the recesses of the hempen forest, like a poacher.

What meant this? Something the man had sought to communicate, unbeknown to any one, even to his captain. Did the secret involve aught unfavorable to his captain? Were those previous misgivings of Captain Delano's about to be verified? Or, in his haunted mood at the moment, had some random, unintentional motion of the man, while busy with the stay, as if repairing it, been mistaken for a significant beckoning?

Not unbewildered, again he gazed off for his boat. But it was temporarily hidden by a rocky spur of the isle. As with some eagerness he bent forward, watching for the first shooting view of its beak, the balustrade gave way before him like charcoal. Had he not clutched an outreaching rope he would have fallen into the sea. The crash, though feeble, and the fall, though hollow, of the rotten fragments, must have been overheard. He glanced up. With sober curiosity peering down upon him was one of the old oakum-pickers, slipped from his perch to an outside boom; while below the old negro, and, invisible to him, reconnoitering from a port-hole like a fox from the mouth of its den, crouched the Spanish sailor again. From something suddenly suggested by the man's air, the mad idea now darted into Captain Delano's mind, that Don Benito's plea of indisposition, in withdrawing below, was but a pretense: that he was engaged there maturing his plot, of which the sailor, by some means gaining an inkling, had a mind to warn the stranger against; incited, it may be, by gratitude for a kind word on first boarding the ship. Was it from foreseeing some possible interference like this, that Don

Benito had, beforehand, given such a bad character of his sailors, while praising the negroes; though, indeed, the former seemed as docile as the latter the contrary? The whites, too, by nature, were the shrewder race. A man with some evil design, would he not be likely to speak well of that stupidity which was blind to his depravity, and malign that intelligence from which it might not be hidden? Not unlikely, perhaps. But if the whites had dark secrets concerning Don Benito, could then Don Benito be any way in complicity with the blacks? But they were too stupid. Besides, who ever heard of a white so far a renegade as to apostatize[45] from his very species almost, by leaguing in against it with negroes? These difficulties recalled former ones. Lost in their mazes, Captain Delano, who had now regained the deck, was uneasily advancing along it, when he observed a new face; an aged sailor seated cross-legged near the main hatchway. His skin was shrunk up with wrinkles like a pelican's empty pouch; his hair frosted; his countenance grave and composed. His hands were full of ropes, which he was working into a large knot. Some blacks were about him obligingly dipping the strands for him, here and there, as the exigencies of the operation demanded.

Captain Delano crossed over to him, and stood in silence surveying the knot; his mind, by a not uncongenial transition, passing from its own entanglements to those of the hemp. For intricacy such a knot he had never seen in an American ship, or indeed any other. The old man looked like an Egyptian priest, making gordian knots for the temple of Ammon.[46] The knot seemed a combination of double-bowline-knot, treble-crown-knot, back-handed-well-knot, knot-in-and-out-knot, and jamming-knot.

At last, puzzled to comprehend the meaning of such a knot, Captain Delano addressed the knotter:—

"What are you knotting there, my man?"

"The knot," was the brief reply, without looking up.

"So it seems; but what is it for?"

"For some one else to undo," muttered back the old man, plying his fingers harder than ever, the knot being now nearly completed.

While Captain Delano stood watching him, suddenly the old man threw the knot towards him, saying in broken English,—the first heard

---

[45]APOSTATIZE: To renounce one's religious faith.

[46]AMMON: According to legend, the oracle of Jupiter Ammon predicted that Alexander the Great would conquer the world. It also prophesied that whoever could untie the complicated knot tied by King Gordius of Phrygia would rule Asia. When Alexander came to Phrygia, he severed the knot with one blow of his sword (hence the saying, "to cut the Gordian knot," meaning to solve a complex problem with a single and simple action).

in the ship,—something to this effect—"Undo it, cut it, quick." It was said lowly, but with such condensation of rapidity, that the long, slow words in Spanish, which had preceded and followed, almost operated as covers to the brief English between.

For a moment, knot in hand, and knot in head, Captain Delano stood, mute; while, without further heeding him, the old man was now intent upon other ropes. Presently there was a slight stir behind Captain Delano. Turning, he saw the chained negro, Atufal, standing quietly there. The next moment the old sailor rose, muttering, and, followed by his subordinate negroes, removed to the forward part of the ship, where in the crowd he disappeared.

An elderly negro, in a clout like an infant's, and with a pepper and salt head, and a kind of attorney air, now approached Captain Delano. In tolerable Spanish, and with a good-natured, knowing wink, he informed him that the old knotter was simple-witted, but harmless; often playing his odd tricks. The negro concluded by begging the knot, for of course the stranger would not care to be troubled with it. Unconsciously, it was handed to him. With a sort of congé,[47] the negro received it, and turning his back, ferreted into it like a detective Custom House officer after smuggled laces. Soon, with some African word, equivalent to pshaw, he tossed the knot overboard.

All this is very queer now, thought Captain Delano, with a qualmish sort of emotion; but as one feeling incipient sea-sickness, he strove, by ignoring the symptoms, to get rid of the malady. Once more he looked off for his boat. To his delight, it was now again in view, leaving the rocky spur astern.

The sensation here experienced, after at first relieving his uneasiness, with unforeseen efficacy, soon began to remove it. The less distant sight of that well-known boat—showing it, not as before, half blended with the haze, but with outline defined, so that its individuality, like a man's, was manifest; that boat, Rover by name, which, though now in strange seas, had often pressed the beach of Captain Delano's home, and, brought to its threshold for repairs, had familiarly lain there, as a Newfoundland dog; the sight of that household boat evoked a thousand trustful associations, which, contrasted with previous suspicions, filled him not only with lightsome confidence, but somehow with half humorous self-reproaches at his former lack of it.

"What, I, Amasa Delano—Jack of the Beach, as they called me when a lad—I, Amasa; the same that, duck-satchel in hand, used to paddle along the waterside to the school-house made from the old hulk;—I, little Jack

[47]CONGÉ: A bow as one formally parts company.

of the Beach, that used to go berrying with cousin Nat and the rest; I to be murdered here at the ends of the earth, on board a haunted pirate-ship by a horrible Spaniard?—Too nonsensical to think of! Who would murder Amasa Delano? His conscience is clean. There is some one above. Fie, fie, Jack of the Beach! you are a child indeed; a child of the second childhood, old boy; you are beginning to dote and drule,[48] I'm afraid."

Light of heart and foot, he stepped aft, and there was met by Don Benito's servant, who, with a pleasing expression, responsive to his own present feelings, informed him that his master had recovered from the effects of his coughing fit, and had just ordered him to go present his compliments to his good guest, Don Amasa, and say that he (Don Benito) would soon have the happiness to rejoin him.

There now, do you mark that? again thought Captain Delano, walking the poop. What a donkey I was. This kind gentleman who here sends me his kind compliments, he, but ten minutes ago, dark-lantern in hand, was dodging round some old grind-stone in the hold, sharpening a hatchet for me, I thought. Well, well; these long calms have a morbid effect on the mind, I've often heard, though I never believed it before. Ha! glancing towards the boat; there's Rover; good dog; a white bone in her mouth. A pretty big bone though, seems to me.—What? Yes, she has fallen afoul of the bubbling tide-rip there. It sets her the other way, too, for the time. Patience.

It was now about noon, though, from the grayness of everything, it seemed to be getting towards dusk.

The calm was confirmed. In the far distance, away from the influence of land, the leaden ocean seemed laid out and leaded up, its course finished, soul gone, defunct. But the current from landward, where the ship was, increased; silently sweeping her further and further towards the tranced waters beyond.

Still, from his knowledge of those latitudes, cherishing hopes of a breeze, and a fair and fresh one, at any moment, Captain Delano, despite present prospects, buoyantly counted upon bringing the San Dominick safely to anchor ere night. The distance swept over was nothing; since, with a good wind, ten minutes' sailing would retrace more than sixty minutes' drifting. Meantime, one moment turning to mark "Rover" fighting the tide-rip, and the next to see Don Benito approaching, he continued walking the poop.

Gradually he felt a vexation arising from the delay of his boat; this soon merged into uneasiness; and at last, his eye falling continually, as from a stage-box into the pit, upon the strange crowd before and below

[48]DRULE: Talk nonsense.

him, and by and by recognising there the face—now composed to indifference—of the Spanish sailor who had seemed to beckon from the main chains, something of his old trepidations returned.

Ah, thought he—gravely enough—this is like the ague[49]: because it went off, it follows not that it won't come back.

Though ashamed of the relapse, he could not altogether subdue it; and so, exerting his good nature to the utmost, insensibly he came to a compromise.

Yes, this is a strange craft; a strange history, too, and strange folks on board. But—nothing more.

By way of keeping his mind out of mischief till the boat should arrive, he tried to occupy it with turning over and over, in a purely speculative sort of way, some lesser peculiarities of the captain and crew. Among others, four curious points recurred.

First, the affair of the Spanish lad assailed with a knife by the slave boy; an act winked at by Don Benito. Second, the tyranny in Don Benito's treatment of Atufal, the black; as if a child should lead a bull of the Nile by the ring in his nose. Third, the trampling of the sailor by the two negroes; a piece of insolence passed over without so much as a reprimand. Fourth, the cringing submission to their master of all the ship's underlings, mostly blacks; as if by the least inadvertence they feared to draw down his despotic displeasure.

Coupling these points, they seemed somewhat contradictory. But what then, thought Captain Delano, glancing towards his now nearing boat,—what then? Why, Don Benito is a very capricious commander. But he is not the first of the sort I have seen; though it's true he rather exceeds any other. But as a nation—continued he in his reveries—these Spaniards are all an odd set; the very word Spaniard has a curious, conspirator, Guy-Fawkish[50] twang to it. And yet, I dare say, Spaniards in the main are as good folks as any in Duxbury, Massachusetts. Ah good! At last "Rover" has come.

As, with its welcome freight, the boat touched the side, the oakum-pickers, with venerable gestures, sought to restrain the blacks, who, at the sight of three gurried[51] water-casks in its bottom, and a pile of wilted pumpkins in its bow, hung over the bulwarks in disorderly raptures.

Don Benito with his servant now appeared; his coming, perhaps, hastened by hearing the noise. Of him Captain Delano sought permission

---

[49]AGUE: A form of malarial fever.
[50]GUY-FAWKISH: Resembling Guy Fawkes (1570–1606), a Catholic conspirator executed for plotting to blow up the English Parliament and King James I on November 5, 1605, the opening day of Parliament.
[51]GURRIED: Slimy.

to serve out the water, so that all might share alike, and none injure themselves by unfair excess. But sensible, and, on Don Benito's account, kind as this offer was, it was received with what seemed impatience; as if aware that he lacked energy as a commander, Don Benito, with the true jealousy of weakness, resented as an affront any interference. So, at least, Captain Delano inferred.

In another moment the casks were being hoisted in, when some of the eager negroes accidentally jostled Captain Delano, where he stood by the gangway; so that, unmindful of Don Benito, yielding to the impulse of the moment, with good-natured authority he bade the blacks stand back; to enforce his words making use of a half-mirthful, half-menacing gesture. Instantly the blacks paused, just where they were, each negro and negress suspended in his or her posture, exactly as the word had found them—for a few seconds continuing so—while, as between the responsive posts of a telegraph, an unknown syllable ran from man to man among the perched oakum-pickers. While the visitor's attention was fixed by this scene, suddenly the hatchet-polishers half rose, and a rapid cry came from Don Benito.

Thinking that at the signal of the Spaniard he was about to be massacred, Captain Delano would have sprung for his boat, but paused, as the oakum-pickers, dropping down into the crowd with earnest exclamations, forced every white and every negro back, at the same moment, with gestures friendly and familiar, almost jocose, bidding him, in substance, not be a fool. Simultaneously the hatchet-polishers resumed their seats, quietly as so many tailors, and at once, as if nothing had happened, the work of hoisting in the casks was resumed, whites and blacks singing at the tackle.

Captain Delano glanced towards Don Benito. As he saw his meager form in the act of recovering itself from reclining in the servant's arms, into which the agitated invalid had fallen, he could not but marvel at the panic by which himself had been surprised on the darting supposition that such a commander, who upon a legitimate occasion, so trivial, too, as it now appeared, could lose all self-command, was, with energetic iniquity, going to bring about his murder.

The casks being on deck, Captain Delano was handed a number of jars and cups by one of the steward's aids, who, in the name of his captain, entreated him to do as he had proposed: dole out the water. He complied, with republican impartiality as to this republican element, which always seeks one level, serving the oldest white no better than the youngest black; excepting, indeed, poor Don Benito, whose condition, if not rank, demanded an extra allowance. To him, in the first place,

Captain Delano presented a fair pitcher of the fluid; but thirsting as he was for it, the Spaniard quaffed not a drop until after several grave bows and salutes. A reciprocation of courtesies which the sight-loving Africans hailed with clapping of hands.

Two of the less wilted pumpkins being reserved for the cabin table, the residue were minced up on the spot for the general regalement. But the soft bread, sugar, and bottled cider, Captain Delano would have given the whites alone, and in chief Don Benito; but the latter objected; which disinterestedness not a little pleased the American; and so mouthfuls all around were given alike to whites and blacks; excepting one bottle of cider, which Babo insisted upon setting aside for his master.

Here it may be observed that as, on the first visit of the boat, the American had not permitted his men to board the ship, neither did he now; being unwilling to add to the confusion of the decks.

Not uninfluenced by the peculiar good humor at present prevailing, and for the time oblivious of any but benevolent thoughts, Captain Delano, who from recent indications counted upon a breeze within an hour or two at furthest, dispatched the boat back to the sealer with orders for all the hands that could be spared immediately to set about rafting casks to the watering-place and filling them. Likewise he bade word be carried to his chief officer, that if against present expectation the ship was not brought to anchor by sunset, he need be under no concern, for as there was to be a full moon that night, he (Captain Delano) would remain on board ready to play the pilot, come the wind soon or late.

As the two Captains stood together, observing the departing boat— the servant as it happened having just spied a spot on his master's velvet sleeve, and silently engaged rubbing it out—the American expressed his regrets that the San Dominick had no boats; none, at least, but the unseaworthy old hulk of the long-boat, which, warped as a camel's skeleton in the desert, and almost as bleached, lay pot-wise inverted amidships, one side a little tipped, furnishing a subterraneous sort of den for family groups of the blacks, mostly women and small children; who, squatting on old mats below, or perched above in the dark dome, on the elevated seats, were descried, some distance within, like a social circle of bats, sheltering in some friendly cave; at intervals, ebon flights of naked boys and girls, three or four years old, darting in and out of the den's mouth.

"Had you three or four boats now, Don Benito," said Captain Delano, "I think that, by tugging at the oars, your negroes here might help along matters some.—Did you sail from port without boats, Don Benito?"

"They were stove in the gales, Señor."

"That was bad. Many men, too, you lost then. Boats and men.—Those must have been hard gales, Don Benito."

"Past all speech," cringed the Spaniard.

"Tell me, Don Benito," continued his companion with increased interest, "tell me, were these gales immediately off the pitch of Cape Horn?"

"Cape Horn?—who spoke of Cape Horn?"

"Yourself did, when giving me an account of your voyage," answered Captain Delano with almost equal astonishment at this eating of his own words, even as he ever seemed eating his own heart, on the part of the Spaniard. "You yourself, Don Benito, spoke of Cape Horn," he emphatically repeated.

The Spaniard turned, in a sort of stooping posture, pausing an instant, as one about to make a plunging exchange of elements, as from air to water.

At this moment a messenger-boy, a white, hurried by, in the regular performance of his function carrying the last expired half hour forward to the forecastle, from the cabin time-piece, to have it struck at the ship's large bell.

"Master," said the servant, discontinuing his work on the coat sleeve, and addressing the rapt Spaniard with a sort of timid apprehensiveness, as one charged with a duty, the discharge of which, it was foreseen, would prove irksome to the very person who had imposed it, and for whose benefit it was intended, "master told me never mind where he was, or how engaged, always to remind him, to a minute, when shaving-time comes. Miguel has gone to strike the half-hour afternoon. It is *now*, master. Will master go into the cuddy?"[52]

"Ah—yes," answered the Spaniard, starting, somewhat as from dreams into realities; then turning upon Captain Delano, he said that are long he would resume the conversation.

"Then if master means to talk more to Don Amasa," said the servant, "why not let Don Amasa sit by master in the cuddy, and master can talk, and Don Amasa can listen, while Babo here lathers and strops."[53]

"Yes," said Captain Delano, not unpleased with this sociable plan, "yes, Don Benito, unless you had rather not, I will go with you."

"Be it so, Señor."

As the three passed aft, the American could not but think it another strange instance of his host's capriciousness, this being shaved with such uncommon punctuality in the middle of the day. But he deemed it more

---

[52]CUDDY: Small cabin.
[53]STROPS: To strop is to hone or sharpen a blade, such as a razor.

than likely that the servant's anxious fidelity had something to do with the matter; inasmuch as the timely interruption served to rally his master from the mood which had evidently been coming upon him.

The place called the cuddy was a light deck-cabin formed by the poop, a sort of attic to the large cabin below. Part of it had formerly been the quarters of the officers; but since their death all the partitionings had been thrown down, and the whole interior converted into one spacious and airy marine hall; for absence of fine furniture and picturesque disarray, of odd appurtenances, somewhat answering to the wide, cluttered hall of some eccentric bachelor-squire in the country, who hangs his shooting-jacket and tobacco-pouch on deer antlers, and keeps his fishing-rod, tongs, and walking-stick in the same corner.

The similitude was heightened, if not originally suggested, by glimpses of the surrounding sea; since, in one aspect, the country and the ocean seem cousins-german.[54]

The floor of the cuddy was matted. Overhead, four or five old muskets were stuck into horizontal holes along the beams. On one side was a claw footed old table lashed to the deck; a thumbed missal on it, and over it a small, meager crucifix attached to the bulkhead. Under the table lay a dented cutlass or two, with a hacked harpoon, among some melancholy old rigging, like a heap of poor friars' girdles. There were also two long, sharp-ribbed settees of malacca cane, black with age, and uncomfortable to look at as inquisitors' racks, with a large, misshapen arm-chair, which, furnished with a rude barber's crutch[55] at the back, working with a screw, seemed some grotesque engine of torment. A flag locker was in one corner, open, exposing various colored bunting, some rolled up, others half unrolled, still others tumbled. Opposite was a cumbrous washstand, of black mahogany, all of one block, with a pedestal, like a font, and over it a railed shelf, containing combs, brushes, and other implements of the toilet. A torn hammock of stained grass swung near; the sheets tossed, and the pillow wrinkled up like a brow, as if whoever slept here slept but illy, with alternate visitations of sad thoughts and bad dreams.

The further extremity of the cuddy, overhanging the ship's stern, was pierced with three openings, windows or port holes, according as men or cannon might peer, socially or unsocially, out of them. At present neither men nor cannon were seen, though huge ring-bolts and other rusty iron fixtures of the wood-work hinted of twenty-four-pounders.

Glancing towards the hammock as he entered, Captain Delano said, "You sleep here, Don Benito?"

---

[54]COUSINS-GERMAN: Related by descent from a common ancestor; having the same parents.
[55]CRUTCH: Headrest.

"Yes, Señor, since we got into mild weather."

"This seems a sort of dormitory, sitting-room, sail-loft, chapel, armory, and private closet all together, Don Benito," added Captain Delano, looking round.

"Yes, Señor; events have not been favorable to much order in my arrangements."

Here the servant, napkin on arm, made a motion as if waiting his master's good pleasure. Don Benito signified his readiness, when, seating him in the malacca arm-chair, and for the guest's convenience drawing opposite it one of the settees, the servant commenced operations by throwing back his master's collar and loosening his cravat.

There is something in the negro which, in a peculiar way, fits him for avocations about one's person. Most negroes are natural valets and hair-dressers; taking to the comb and brush congenially as to the castinets, and flourishing them apparently with almost equal satisfaction. There is, too, a smooth tact about them in this employment, with a marvelous, noiseless, gliding briskness, not ungraceful in its way, singularly pleasing to behold, and still more so to be the manipulated subject of. And above all is the great gift of good humor. Not the mere grin or laugh is here meant. Those were unsuitable. But a certain easy cheerfulness, harmonious in every glance and gesture; as though God had set the whole negro to some pleasant tune.

When to all this is added the docility arising from the unaspiring contentment of a limited mind, and that susceptibility of blind attachment sometimes inhering in indisputable inferiors, one readily perceives why those hypochondriacs, Johnson and Byron—it may be something like the hypochondriac, Benito Cereno—took to their hearts, almost to the exclusion of the entire white race, their serving men, the negroes, Barber and Fletcher.[56] But if there be that in the negro which exempts him from the inflicted sourness of the morbid or cynical mind, how, in his most prepossessing aspects, must he appear to a benevolent one? When at case with respect to exterior things, Captain Delano's nature was not only benign, but familiarly and humorously so. At home, he had often taken rare satisfaction in sitting in his door, watching some free man of color at his work or play. If on a voyage he chanced to have a black sailor, invariably he was on chatty, and half-gamesome terms with him. In fact, like most men of a good, blithe heart, Captain Delano took to

[56]JOHNSON AND BYRON...BARBER AND FLETCHER: William Fletcher was the valet of Lord Byron (1788–1824). Melville confuses him with the African servant of Byron's friend Edward Trelawny (1792–1881). Frank Barber was a servant of the English essayist and poet Samuel Johnson (1709–1784), who left him a large annuity.

negroes, not philanthropically, but genially, just as other men to Newfoundland dogs.

Hitherto the circumstances in which he found the San Dominick had repressed the tendency. But in the cuddy, relieved from his former uneasiness, and, for various reasons, more sociably inclined than at any previous period of the day, and seeing the colored servant, napkin on arm, so debonair about his master, in a business so familiar as that of shaving, too, all his old weakness for negroes returned.

Among other things, he was amused with an odd instance of the African love of bright colors and fine shows, in the black's informally taking from the flag-locker a great piece of bunting of all hues, and lavishly tucking it under his master's chin for an apron.

The mode of shaving among the Spaniards is a little different from what it is with other nations. They have a basin, specifically called a barber's basin, which on one side is scooped out, so as accurately to receive the chin, against which it is closely held in lathering; which is done, not with a brush, but with soap dipped in the water of the basin and rubbed on the face.

In the present instance salt-water was used for lack of better; and the parts lathered were only the upper lip, and low down under the throat, all the rest being cultivated beard.

The preliminaries being somewhat novel to Captain Delano, he sat curiously eying them, so that no conversation took place, nor for the present did Don Benito appear disposed to renew any.

Setting down his basin, the negro searched among the razors, as for the sharpest, and having found it, gave it an additional edge by expertly strapping it on the firm, smooth, oily skin of his open palm; he then made a gesture as if to begin, but midway stood suspended for an instant, one hand elevating the razor, the other professionally dabbling among the bubbling suds on the Spaniard's lank neck. Not unaffected by the close sight of the gleaming steel, Don Benito nervously shuddered, his usual ghastliness was heightened by the lather, which lather, again, was intensified in its hue by the contrasting sootiness of the negro's body. Altogether the scene was somewhat peculiar, at least to Captain Delano, nor, as he saw the two thus postured, could he resist the vagary, that in the black he saw a headsman, and in the white, a man at the block. But this was one of those antic conceits, appearing and vanishing in a breath, from which, perhaps, the best regulated mind is not always free.

Meantime the agitation of the Spaniard had a little loosened the bunting from around him, so that one broad fold swept curtain-like over the chair-arm to the floor, revealing, amid a profusion of armorial bars and ground-colors—black, blue, and yellow—a closed castle in a blood-red field diagonal with a lion rampant in a white.

"The castle and the lion," exclaimed Captain Delano—"why, Don Benito, this is the flag of Spain you use here. It's well it's only I, and not the King, that sees this," he added with a smile, "but"—turning towards the black,—"it's all one, I suppose, so the colors be gay;" which playful remark did not fail somewhat to tickle the negro.

"Now, master," he said, readjusting the flag, and pressing the head gently further back into the crotch of the chair; "now master," and the steel glanced nigh the throat.

Again Don Benito faintly shuddered.

"You must not shake so, master.—See, Don Amasa, master always shakes when I shave him. And yet master knows I never yet have drawn blood though it's true, if master will shake so, I may some of these times. Now master," he continued. "And now, Don Amasa, please go on with your talk about the gale, and all that, master can hear, and between times master can answer."

"Ah yes, these gales," said Captain Delano; "but the more I think of your voyage, Don Benito, the more I wonder, not at the gales, terrible as they must have been, but at the disastrous interval following them. For here, by your account, have you been these two months and more getting from Cape Horn to St. Maria, a distance which I myself, with a good wind, have sailed in a few days. True, you had calms, and long ones, but to be becalmed for two months, that is, at least, unusual. Why, Don Benito, had almost any other gentleman told me such a story, I should have been half disposed to a little incredulity."

Here an involuntary expression came over the Spaniard, similar to that just before on the deck, and whether it was the start he gave, or a sudden gawky roll of the hull in the calm, or a momentary unsteadiness of the servant's hand; however it was, just then the razor drew blood, spots of which stained the creamy lather under the throat; immediately the black barber drew back his steel, and remaining in his professional attitude, back to Captain Delano, and face to Don Benito, held up the trickling razor, saying, with a sort of half humorous sorrow, "See, master,—you shook so—here's Babo's first blood."

No sword drawn before James the First of England,[57] no assassination in that timid King's presence, could have produced a more terrified aspect than was now presented by Don Benito.

[57]JAMES THE FIRST OF ENGLAND: He (1566–1625) succeeded Elizabeth I and reigned from 1603 to 1625.

Poor fellow, thought Captain Delano, so nervous he can't even bear the sight of barber's blood; and this unstrung, sick man, is it credible that I should have imagined he meant to spill all my blood, who can't endure the sight of one little drop of his own? Surely, Amasa Delano, you have been beside yourself this day. Tell it not when you get home, sappy Amasa. Well, well, he looks like a murderer, doesn't he? More like as if himself were to be done for. Well, well, this day's experience shall be a good lesson.

Meantime, while these things were running through the honest seaman's mind, the servant had taken the napkin from his arm, and to Don Benito had said—"But answer Don Amasa, please, master, while I wipe this ugly stuff off the razor, and strop it again."

As he said the words, his face was turned half round, so as to be alike visible to the Spaniard and the American, and seemed by its expression to hint, that he was desirous, by getting his master to go on with the conversation, considerately to withdraw his attention from the recent annoying accident. As if glad to snatch the offered relief, Don Benito resumed, rehearsing to Captain Delano, that not only were the calms of unusual duration, but the ship had fallen in with obstinate currents; and other things he added, some of which were but repetitions of former statements, to explain how it came to pass that the passage from Cape Horn to St. Maria had been so exceedingly long, now and then mingling with his words, incidental praises, less qualified than before, to the blacks, for their general good conduct.

These particulars were not given consecutively, the servant at convenient times using his razor, and so, between the intervals of shaving, the story and panegyric went on with more than usual huskiness.

To Captain Delano's imagination, now again not wholly at rest, there was something so hollow in the Spaniard's manner, with apparently some reciprocal hollowness in the servant's dusky comment of silence, that the idea flashed across him, that possibly master and man, for some unknown purpose, were acting out, both in word and deed, nay, to the very tremor of Don Benito's limbs, some juggling play before him. Neither did the suspicion of collusion lack apparent support, from the fact of those whispered conferences before mentioned. But then, what could be the object of enacting this play of the barber before him? At last, regarding the notion as a whimsy, insensibly suggested, perhaps, by the theatrical aspect of Don Benito in his harlequin ensign, Captain Delano speedily banished it.

The shaving over, the servant bestirred himself with a small bottle of scented waters, pouring a few drops on the head, and then diligently rubbing; the vehemence of the exercise causing the muscles of his face to twitch rather strangely.

His next operation was with comb, scissors and brush; going round and round, smoothing a curl here, clipping an unruly whisker-hair there, giving a graceful sweep to the temple-lock, with other impromptu touches evincing the hand of a master; while, like any resigned gentleman in barber's hands, Don Benito bore all, much less uneasily, at least, than he had done the razoring; indeed, he sat so pale and rigid now, that the negro seemed a Nubian[58] sculptor finishing off a white statue-head.

All being over at last, the standard of Spain removed, tumbled up, and tossed back into the flag-locker, the negro's warm breath blowing away any stray hair which might have lodged down his master's neck; collar and cravat readjusted; a speck of lint whisked off the velvet lapel; all this being done; backing off a little space, and pausing with an expression of subdued self-complacency, the servant for a moment surveyed his master, as, in toilet at least, the creature of his own tasteful hands.

Captain Delano playfully complimented him upon his achievement; at the same time congratulating Don Benito.

But neither sweet waters, nor shampooing, nor fidelity, nor sociality, delighted the Spaniard. Seeing him relapsing into forbidding gloom, and still remaining seated, Captain Delano, thinking that his presence was undesired just then, withdrew, on pretense of seeing whether, as he had prophecied, any signs of a breeze were visible.

Walking forward to the mainmast, he stood awhile thinking over the scene, and not without some undefined misgivings, when he heard a noise near the cuddy, and turning, saw the negro, his hand to his cheek. Advancing, Captain Delano perceived that the cheek was bleeding. He was about to ask the cause, when the negro's wailing soliloquy enlightened him.

"Ah, when will master get better from his sickness; only the sour heart that sour sickness breeds made him serve Babo so; cutting Babo with the razor, because, only by accident, Babo had given master one little scratch; and for the first time in so many a day, too. Ah, ah, ah," holding his hand to his face.

Is it possible, thought Captain Delano; was it to wreak in private his Spanish spite against this poor friend of his, that Don Benito, by his sullen manner, impelled me to withdraw? Ah, this slavery breeds ugly passions in man—Poor fellow!

He was about to speak in sympathy to the negro, but with a timid reluctance he now reëntered the cuddy.

Presently master and man came forth; Don Benito leaning on his servant as if nothing had happened.

[58]NUBIAN: Nubia, region in Nile Valley, northeastern Africa.

But a sort of love-quarrel, after all, thought Captain Delano.

He accosted Don Benito, and they slowly walked together. They had gone but a few paces, when the steward—a tall, rajah-looking mulatto, orientally set off with a pagoda turban formed by three or four Madras handkerchiefs wound about his head, tier on tier—approaching with a saalam, announced lunch in the cabin.

On their way thither, the two Captains were preceded by the mulatto, who, turning round as he advanced, with continual smiles and bows, ushered them on, a display of elegance which quite completed the insignificance of the small bare-headed Babo, who, as if not unconscious of inferiority, eyed askance the graceful steward. But in part, Captain Delano imputed his jealous watchfulness to that peculiar feeling which the full-blooded African entertains for the adulterated one. As for the steward, his manner, if not bespeaking much dignity of self-respect, yet evidenced his extreme desire to please; which is doubly meritorious, as at once Christian and Chesterfieldian.[59]

Captain Delano observed with interest that while the complexion of the mulatto was hybrid, his physiognomy was European; classically so.

"Don Benito," whispered he, "I am glad to see this usher-of-the-golden-rod[60] of yours; the sight refutes an ugly remark once made to me by a Barbadoes planter; that when a mulatto has a regular European face, look out for him; he is a devil. But see, your steward here has features more regular than King George's of England; and yet there he nods, and bows, and smiles; a king, indeed—the king of kind hearts and polite fellows. What a pleasant voice he has, too?"

"He has, Señor."

"But, tell me, has he not, so far as you have known him, always proved a good, worthy fellow?" said Captain Delano, pausing, while with a final genuflexion the steward disappeared into the cabin; "come, for the reason just mentioned, I am curious to know."

"Francesco is a good man," a sort of sluggishly responded Don Benito, like a phlegmatic appreciator, who would neither find fault nor flatter.

"Ah, I thought so. For it were strange indeed, and not very creditable to us white-skins, if a little of our blood mixed with the African's, should, far from improving the latter's quality, have the sad effect of pouring vitriolic acid[61] into black broth; improving the hue, perhaps, but not the wholesomeness."

---

[59]CHESTERFIELDIAN: Characteristic of Philip Stanhope (1694–1773), the fourth Earl of Chesterfield, who wrote on issues relating to manners and etiquette.
[60]USHER-OF-THE-GOLDEN-ROD: Attendant who walks ceremoniously before a person of rank.
[61]VITRIOLIC ACID: Sulfuric acid.

"Doubtless, doubtless, Señor, but"—glancing at Babo—"not to speak of negroes, your planter's remark I have heard applied to the Spanish and Indian intermixtures in our provinces. But I know nothing about the matter," he listlessly added.

And here they entered the cabin.

The lunch was a frugal one. Some of Captain Delano's fresh fish and pumpkins, biscuit and salt beef, the reserved bottle of cider, and the San Dominick's last bottle of Canary.

As they entered, Francesco, with two or three colored aids, was hovering over the table giving the last adjustments. Upon perceiving their master they withdrew, Francesco making a smiling congé, and the Spaniard, without condescending to notice it, fastidiously remarking to his companion that he relished not superfluous attendance.

Without companions, host and guest sat down, like a childless married couple, at opposite ends of the table, Don Benito waving Captain Delano to his place, and, weak as he was, insisting upon that gentleman being seated before himself.

The negro placed a rug under Don Benito's feet, and a cushion behind his back, and then stood behind, not his master's chair, but Captain Delano's. At first, this a little surprised the latter. But it was soon evident that, in taking his position, the black was still true to his master; since by facing him he could the more readily anticipate his slightest want.

"This is an uncommonly intelligent fellow of yours, Don Benito," whispered Captain Delano across the table.

"You say true, Señor."

During the repast, the guest again reverted to parts of Don Benito's story, begging further particulars here and there. He inquired how it was that the scurvy and fever should have committed such wholesale havoc upon the whites, while destroying less than half of the blacks. As if this question reproduced the whole scene of plague before the Spaniard's eyes, miserably reminding him of his solitude in a cabin where before he had had so many friends and officers round him, his hand shook, his face became hueless, broken words escaped; but directly the sane memory of the past seemed replaced by insane terrors of the present. With starting eyes he stared before him at vacancy. For nothing was to be seen but the hand of his servant pushing the Canary over towards him. At length a few sips served partially to restore him. He made random reference to the different constitution of races, enabling one to offer more resistance to certain maladies than another. The thought was new to his companion.

Presently Captain Delano, intending to say something to his host concerning the pecuniary part of the business he had undertaken for him, especially—since he was strictly accountable to his owners—with reference to the new suit of sails, and other things of that sort; and naturally preferring to conduct such affairs in private, was desirous that the servant should withdraw; imagining that Don Benito for a few minutes could dispense with his attendance. He, however, waited awhile; thinking that, as the conversation proceeded, Don Benito, without being prompted, would perceive the propriety of the step.

But it was otherwise. At last catching his host's eye, Captain Delano, with a slight backward gesture of his thumb, whispered, "Don Benito, pardon me, but there is an interference with the full expression of what I have to say to you."

Upon this the Spaniard changed countenance; which was imputed to his resenting the hint, as in some way a reflection upon his servant. After a moment's pause, he assured his guest that the black's remaining with them could be of no disservice; because since losing his officers he had made Babo (whose original office, it now appeared, had been captain of the slaves) not only his constant attendant and companion, but in all things his confidant.

After this, nothing more could be said; though, indeed, Captain Delano could hardly avoid some little tinge of irritation upon being left ungratified in so inconsiderable a wish, by one, too, for whom he intended such solid services. But it is only his querulousness, thought he; and so filling his glass he proceeded to business.

The price of the sails and other matters was fixed upon. But while this was being done, the American observed that, though his original offer of assistance had been hailed with hectic animation, yet now when it was reduced to a business transaction, indifference and apathy were betrayed. Don Benito, in fact, appeared to submit to hearing the details more out of regard to common propriety, than from any impression that weighty benefit to himself and his voyage was involved.

Soon, his manner became still more reserved. The effort was vain to seek to draw him into social talk. Gnawed by his splenetic mood, he sat twitching his beard, while to little purpose the hand of his servant, mute as that on the wall, slowly pushed over the Canary.

Lunch being over, they sat down on the cushioned transom; the servant placing a pillow behind his master. The long continuance of the calm had now affected the atmosphere. Don Benito sighed heavily, as if for breath.

"Why not adjourn to the cuddy," said Captain Delano; "there is more air there." But the host sat silent and motionless.

Meantime his servant knelt before him, with a large fan of feathers. And Francesco coming in on tiptoes, handed the negro a little cup of aromatic waters, with which at intervals he chafed his master's brow; smoothing the hair along the temples as a nurse does a child's. He spoke no word. He only rested his eye on his master's, as if, amid all Don Benito's distress, a little to refresh his spirit by the silent sight of fidelity.

Presently the ship's bell sounded two o'clock; and through the cabin-windows a slight rippling of the sea was discerned; and from the desired direction.

"There," exclaimed Captain Delano, "I told you so, Don Benito, look!"

He had risen to his feet, speaking in a very animated tone, with a view the more to rouse his companion. But though the crimson curtain of the stern-window near him that moment fluttered against his pale cheek, Don Benito seemed to have even less welcome for the breeze than the calm.

Poor fellow, thought Captain Delano, bitter experience has taught him that one ripple does not make a wind, any more than one swallow a summer. But he is mistaken for once. I will get his ship in for him, and prove it.

Briefly alluding to his weak condition, he urged his host to remain quietly where he was, since he (Captain Delano) would with pleasure take upon himself the responsibility of making the best use of the wind.

Upon gaining the deck, Captain Delano started at the unexpected figure of Atufal, monumentally fixed at the threshold, like one of those sculptured porters of black marble guarding the porches of Egyptian tombs.

But this time the start was, perhaps, purely physical. Atufal's presence, singularly attesting docility even in sullenness, was contrasted with that of the hatchet-polishers, who in patience evinced their industry; while both spectacles showed, that lax as Don Benito's general authority might be, still, whenever he chose to exert it, no man so savage or colossal but must, more or less, bow.

Snatching a trumpet which hung from the bulwarks, with a free step Captain Delano advanced to the forward edge of the poop, issuing his orders in his best Spanish. The few sailors and many negroes, all equally pleased, obediently set about heading the ship towards the harbor.

While giving some directions about setting a lower stu'n'-sail, suddenly Captain Delano heard a voice faithfully repeating his orders. Turning, he saw Babo, now for the time acting, under the pilot, his original part of captain of the slaves. This assistance proved valuable. Tattered sails and warped yards were soon brought into some trim. And no brace or halyard was pulled but to the blithe songs of the inspirited negroes.

Good fellows, thought Captain Delano, a little training would make fine sailors of them. Why see, the very women pull and sing too. These must be some of those Ashantee negresses that make such capital soldiers, I've heard. But who's at the helm. I must have a good hand there.

He went to see.

The San Dominick steered with a cumbrous tiller, with large horizontal pullies attached. At each pully-end stood a subordinate black, and between them, at the tiller-head, the responsible post, a Spanish seaman, whose countenance evinced his due share in the general hopefulness and confidence at the coming of the breeze.

He proved the same man who had behaved with so shame-faced an air on the windlass.

"Ah—it is you, my man," exclaimed Captain Delano—"well, no more sheep's-eyes now;—look straightforward and keep the ship so. Good hand, I trust? And want to get into the harbor, don't you?"

The man assented with an inward chuckle, grasping the tiller-head firmly. Upon this, unperceived by the American, the two blacks eyed the sailor intently.

Finding all right at the helm, the pilot went forward to the forecastle, to see how matters stood there.

The ship now had way enough to breast the current. With the approach of evening, the breeze would be sure to freshen.

Having done all that was needed for the present, Captain Delano, giving his last orders to the sailors, turned aft to report affairs to Don Benito in the cabin; perhaps additionally incited to rejoin him by the hope of snatching a moment's private chat while the servant was engaged upon deck.

From opposite sides, there were, beneath the poop, two approaches to the cabin; one further forward than the other, and consequently communicating with a longer passage. Marking the servant still above, Captain Delano, taking the nighest entrance—the one last named, and at whose porch Atufal still stood—hurried on his way, till, arrived at the cabin threshold, he paused an instant, a little to recover from his eagerness. Then, with the words of his intended business upon his lips, he entered. As he advanced toward the seated Spaniard, he heard another footstep, keeping time with his. From the opposite door, a salver in hand, the servant was likewise advancing.

"Confound the faithful fellow," thought Captain Delano; "what a vexatious coincidence."

Possibly, the vexation might have been something different, were it not for the brisk confidence inspired by the breeze. But even as it was, he felt a slight twinge, from a sudden indefinite association in his mind of Babo with Atufal.

"Don Benito," said he, "I give you joy; the breeze will hold, and will increase. By the way, your tall man and time-piece, Atufal, stands without. By your order, of course?"

Don Benito recoiled, as if at some bland satirical touch, delivered with such adroit garnish of apparent good-breeding as to present no handle for retort.

He is like one flayed alive, thought Captain Delano; where may one touch him without causing a shrink?

The servant moved before his master, adjusting a cushion; recalled to civility, the Spaniard stiffly replied: "You are right. The slave appears where you saw him, according to my command; which is, that if at the given hour I am below, he must take his stand and abide my coming."

"Ah now, pardon me, but that is treating the poor fellow like an ex-king indeed. Ah, Don Benito," smiling, "for all the license you permit in some things, I fear lest, at bottom, you are a bitter hard master."

Again Don Benito shrank; and this time, as the good sailor thought, from a genuine twinge of his conscience.

Again conversation became constrained. In vain Captain Delano called attention to the now perceptible motion of the keel gently cleaving the sea; with lack-lustre eye, Don Benito returned words few and reserved.

By-and-by, the wind having steadily risen, and still blowing right into the harbor, bore the San Dominick swiftly on. Rounding a point of land, the sealer at distance came into open view.

Meantime Captain Delano had again repaired to the deck, remaining there some time. Having at last altered the ship's course, so as to give the reef a wide berth, he returned for a few moments below.

I will cheer up my poor friend, this time, thought he.

"Better and better, Don Benito," he cried as he blithely reëntered; "there will soon be an end to your cares, at least for awhile. For when, after a long, sad voyage, you know, the anchor drops into the haven, all its vast weight seems lifted from the captain's heart. We are getting on famously, Don Benito. My ship is in sight. Look through this side-light here; there she is; all a-taunt-o! The Bachelor's Delight, my good friend. Ah, how this wind braces one up. Come, you must take a cup of coffee with me this evening. My old steward will give you as fine a cup as ever any sultan tasted. What say you, Don Benito, will you?"

At first, the Spaniard glanced feverishly up, casting a longing look towards the sealer, while with mute concern his servant gazed into his face. Suddenly the old ague of coldness returned, and dropping back to his cushions he was silent.

"You do not answer. Come, all day you have been my host; would you have hospitality all on one side?"

"I cannot go," was the response.

"What? it will not fatigue you. The ships will lie together as near as they can, without swinging foul. It will be little more than stepping from deck to deck; which is but as from room to room. Come, come, you must not refuse me."

"I cannot go," decisively and repulsively repeated Don Benito.

Renouncing all but the last appearance of courtesy, with a sort of cadaverous sullenness, and biting his thin nails to the quick, he glanced, almost glared, at his guest; as if impatient that a stranger's presence should interfere with the full indulgence of his morbid hour. Meantime the sound of the parted waters came more and more gurglingly and merrily in at the windows; as reproaching him for his dark spleen; as telling him that, sulk as he might, and go mad with it, nature cared not a jot; since, whose fault was it, pray?

But the foul mood was now at its depth, as the fair wind at its hight.

There was something in the man so far beyond any mere unsociality or sourness previously evinced, that even the forbearing good-nature of his guest could no longer endure it. Wholly at a loss to account for such demeanor, and deeming sickness with eccentricity, however extreme, no adequate excuse, well satisfied, too, that nothing in his own conduct could justify it, Captain Delano's pride began to be roused. Himself became reserved. But all seemed one to the Spaniard. Quitting him, therefore, Captain Delano once more went to the deck.

The ship was now within less than two miles of the sealer. The whaleboat was seen darting over the interval.

To be brief, the two vessels, thanks to the pilot's skill, ere long in neighborly style lay anchored together.

Before returning to his own vessel, Captain Delano had intended communicating to Don Benito the smaller details of the proposed services to be rendered. But, as it was, unwilling anew to subject himself to rebuffs, he resolved, now that he had seen the San Dominick safely moored, immediately to quit her, without further allusion to hospitality or business. Indefinitely postponing his ulterior plans, he would regulate his future actions according to future circumstances. His boat was ready to receive him; but his host still tarried below. Well, thought

Captain Delano, if he has little breeding, the more need to show mine. He descended to the cabin to bid a ceremonious, and, it may be, tacitly rebukeful adieu. But to his great satisfaction, Don Benito, as if he began to feel the weight of that treatment with which his slighted guest had, not indecorously, retaliated upon him, now supported by his servant, rose to his feet, and grasping Captain Delano's hand, stood tremulous; too much agitated to speak. But the good augury hence drawn was suddenly dashed, by his resuming all his previous reserve, with augmented gloom, as, with half-averted eyes, he silently reseated himself on his cushions. With a corresponding return of his own chilled feelings, Captain Delano bowed and withdrew.

He was hardly midway in the narrow corridor, dim as a tunnel, leading from the cabin to the stairs, when a sound, as of the tolling for execution in some jail-yard, fell on his ears. It was the echo of the ship's flawed bell, striking the hour, drearily reverberated in this subterranean vault. Instantly, by a fatality not to be withstood, his mind, responsive to the portent, swarmed with superstitious suspicions. He paused. In images far swifter than these sentences, the minutest details of all his former distrusts swept through him.

Hitherto, credulous good-nature had been too ready to furnish excuses for reasonable fears. Why was the Spaniard, so superfluously punctilious at times, now heedless of common propriety in not accompanying to the side his departing guest? Did indisposition forbid? Indisposition had not forbidden more irksome exertion that day. His last equivocal demeanor recurred. He had risen to his feet, grasped his guest's hand, motioned toward his hat; then, in an instant, all was eclipsed in sinister muteness and gloom. Did this imply one brief, repentent relenting at the final moment, from some iniquitous plot, followed by remorseless return to it? His last glance seemed to express a calamitous, yet acquiescent farewell to Captain Delano forever. Why decline the invitation to visit the sealer that evening? Or was the Spaniard less hardened than the Jew, who refrained not from supping at the board of him whom the same night he meant to betray?[62] What imported all those day-long enigmas and contradictions, except they were intended to mystify, preliminary to some stealthy blow? Atufal, the pretended rebel, but punctual shadow, that moment lurked by the threshold without. He seemed a sentry, and more. Who, by his own confession, had stationed him there? Was the negro now lying in wait?

---

[62]NIGHT HE MEANT TO BETRAY: Referring to Judas Iscariot's betrayal of Jesus (Matthew 26).

The Spaniard behind—his creature before: to rush from darkness to light was the involuntary choice.

The next moment, with clenched jaw and hand, he passed Atufal, and stood unharmed in the light. As he saw his trim ship lying peacefully at anchor, and almost within ordinary call; as he saw his household boat, with familiar faces in it, patiently rising and falling on the short waves by the San Dominick's side; and then, glancing about the decks where he stood, saw the oakum-pickers still gravely plying their fingers; and heard the low, buzzing whistle and industrious hum of the hatchet-polishers, still bestirring themselves over their endless occupation; and more than all, as he saw the benign aspect of nature, taking her innocent repose in the evening; the screened sun in the quiet camp of the west shining out like the mild light from Abraham's tent,[63] as charmed eye and ear took in all these, with the chained figure of the black, clenched jaw and hand relaxed. Once again he smiled at the phantoms which had mocked him, and felt something like a tinge of remorse, that, by harboring them even for a moment, he should, by implication, have betrayed an atheist doubt of the ever-watchful Providence above.

There was a few minutes' delay, while, in obedience to his orders, the boat was being hooked along to the gangway. During this interval, a sort of saddened satisfaction stole over Captain Delano, at thinking of the kindly offices he had that day discharged for a stranger. Ah, thought he, after good actions one's conscience is never ungrateful, however much so the benefited party may be.

Presently, his foot, in the first act of descent into the boat, pressed the first round of the side-ladder, his face presented inward upon the deck. In the same moment, he heard his name courteously sounded; and, to his pleased surprise, saw Don Benito advancing—an unwonted energy in his air, as if, at the last moment, intent upon making amends for his recent discourtesy. With instinctive good feeling, Captain Delano, withdrawing his foot, turned and reciprocally advanced. As he did so, the Spaniard's nervous eagerness increased, but his vital energy failed; so that, the better to support him, the servant, placing his master's hand on his naked shoulder, and gently holding it there, formed himself into a sort of crutch.

When the two captains met, the Spaniard again fervently took the hand of the American, at the same time casting an earnest glance into his eyes, but, as before, too much overcome to speak.

[63]ABRAHAM'S TENT: Referring to the journeys of the biblical patriarch Abraham.

I have done him wrong, self-reproachfully thought Captain Delano; his apparent coldness has deceived me; in no instance has he meant to offend.

Meantime, as if fearful that the continuance of the scene might too much unstring his master, the servant seemed anxious to terminate it. And so, still presenting himself as a crutch, and walking between the two captains, he advanced with them towards the gangway; while still, as if full of kindly contrition, Don Benito would not let go the hand of Captain Delano, but retained it in his, across the black's body.

Soon they were standing by the side, looking over into the boat, whose crew turned up their curious eyes. Waiting a moment for the Spaniard to relinquish his hold, the now embarrassed Captain Delano lifted his foot, to overstep the threshold of the open gangway; but still Don Benito would not let go his hand. And yet, with an agitated tone, he said, "I can go no further; here I must bid you adieu. Adieu, my dear, dear Don Amasa. Go—go!" suddenly tearing his hand loose, "go, and God guard you better than me, my best friend."

Not unaffected, Captain Delano would now have lingered; but catching the meekly admonitory eye of the servant, with a hasty farewell he descended into his boat, followed by the continual adieus of Don Benito, standing rooted in the gangway.

Seating himself in the stern, Captain Delano, making a last salute, ordered the boat shoved off. The crew had their oars on end. The bowsman pushed the boat a sufficient distance for the oars to be lengthwise dropped. The instant that was done, Don Benito sprang over the bulwarks, falling at the feet of Captain Delano; at the same time, calling towards his ship, but in tones so frenzied, that none in the boat could understand him. But, as if not equally obtuse, three sailors, from three different and distant parts of the ship, splashed into the sea, swimming after their captain, as if intent upon his rescue.

The dismayed officer of the boat eagerly asked what this meant. To which, Captain Delano, turning a disdainful smile upon the unaccountable Spaniard, answered that, for his part, he neither knew nor cared; but it seemed as if Don Benito had taken it into his head to produce the impression among his people that the boat wanted to kidnap him. "Or else—give way for your lives," he wildly added, starting at a clattering hubbub in the ship, above which rang the tocsin[64] of the hatchet-polishers; and seizing Don Benito by the throat he added, "this plotting pirate means murder!" Here, in apparent verification of the words, the

[64]TOCSIN: Alarm signal, or bell.

servant, a dagger in his hand, was seen on the rail overhead, poised in the act of leaping, as if with desperate fidelity to befriend his master to the last; while, seemingly to aid the black, the three white sailors were trying to clamber into the hampered bow. Meantime, the whole host of negroes, as if inflamed at the sight of their jeopardized captain, impended in one sooty avalanche over the bulwarks.

All this, with what preceded, and what followed, occurred with such involutions of rapidity, that past, present, and future seemed one.

Seeing the negro coming, Captain Delano had flung the Spaniard aside, almost in the very act of clutching him, and, by the unconscious recoil, shifting his place, with arms thrown up, so promptly grappled the servant in his descent, that with dagger presented at Captain Delano's heart, the black seemed of purpose to have leaped there as to his mark. But the weapon was wrenched away, and the assailant dashed down into the bottom of the boat, which now, with disentangled oars, began to speed through the sea.

At this juncture, the left hand of Captain Delano, on one side, again clutched the half-reclined Don Benito, heedless that he was in a speechless faint, while his right foot, on the other side, ground the prostrate negro; and his right arm pressed for added speed on the after oar, his eye bent forward, encouraging his men to their utmost.

But here, the officer of the boat, who had at last succeeded in beating off the towing sailors, and was now, with face turned aft, assisting the bowsman at his oar, suddenly called to Captain Delano, to see what the black was about; while a Portuguese oarsman shouted to him to give heed to what the Spaniard was saying.

Glancing down at his feet, Captain Delano saw the freed hand of the servant aiming with a second dagger—a small one, before concealed in his wool—with this he was snakishly writhing up from the boat's bottom, at the heart of his master, his countenance lividly vindictive, expressing the centred purpose of his soul, while the Spaniard, half-choked, was vainly shrinking away, with husky words, incoherent to all but the Portuguese.

That moment, across the long-benighted mind of Captain Delano, a flash of revelation swept, illuminating in unanticipated clearness, his host's whole mysterious demeanor, with every enigmatic event of the day, as well as the entire past voyage of the San Dominick. He smote Babo's hand down, but his own heart smote him harder. With infinite pity he withdrew his hold from Don Benito. Not Captain Delano, but Don Benito, the black, in leaping into the boat, had intended to stab.

Both the black's hands were held, as, glancing up towards the San Dominick, Captain Delano, now with scales dropped from his eyes, saw the negroes, not in misrule, not in tumult, not as if frantically concerned for Don Benito, but with mask torn away, flourishing hatchets and knives, in ferocious piratical revolt. Like delirious black dervishes, the six Ashantees danced on the poop. Prevented by their foes from springing into the water, the Spanish boys were hurrying up to the topmost spars, while such of the few Spanish sailors, not already in the sea, less alert, were descried, helplessly mixed in, on deck, with the blacks.

Meantime Captain Delano hailed his own vessel, ordering the ports up, and the guns run out. But by this time the cable of the San Dominick had been cut; and the fag-end, in lashing out, whipped away the canvas shroud about the beak, suddenly revealing, as the bleached hull swung round towards the open ocean, death for the figure-head, in a human skeleton; chalky comment on the chalked words below, *"Follow your leader."*

At the sight, Don Benito, covering his face, wailed out: "'Tis he, Aranda! my murdered, unburied friend!"

Upon reaching the sealer, calling for ropes, Captain Delano bound the negro, who made no resistance, and had him hoisted to the deck. He would then have assisted the now almost helpless Don Benito up the side; but Don Benito, wan as he was, refused to move, or be moved, until the negro should have been first put below out of view. When, presently assured that it was one, he no more shrank from the ascent.

The boat was immediately dispatched back to pick up the three swimming sailors. Meantime, the guns were in readiness, though, owing to the San Dominick having glided somewhat astern of the sealer, only the aftermost one could be brought to bear. With this, they fired six times; thinking to cripple the fugitive ship by bringing down her spars. But only a few inconsiderable ropes were shot away. Soon the ship was beyond the guns' range, steering broad out of the bay; the blacks thickly clustering round the bow-sprit, one moment with taunting cries towards the whites, the next with upthrown gestures hailing the now dusky moors of ocean— cawing crows escaped from the hand of the fowler.

The first impulse was to slip the cables and give chase. But, upon second thoughts, to pursue with whale-boat and yawl seemed more promising.

Upon inquiring of Don Benito what fire arms they had on board the San Dominick, Captain Delano was answered that they had none that could be used; because, in the earlier stages of the mutiny, a cabin-passenger, since dead, had secretly put out of order the locks of what few muskets there were. But with all his remaining strength, Don Benito entreated the American not to give chase, either with ship or boat; for the negroes had already proved themselves such desperadoes, that, in case of a present assault, nothing but a total massacre of the whites could be looked for. But, regarding this warning as coming from one whose spirit had been crushed by misery, the American did not give up his design.

The boats were got ready and armed. Captain Delano ordered his men into them. He was going himself when Don Benito grasped his arm.

"What! have you saved my life, señor, and are you now going to throw away your own?"

The officers also, for reasons connected with their interests and those of the voyage, and a duty owing to the owners, strongly objected against their commander's going. Weighing their remonstrances a moment, Captain Delano felt bound to remain; appointing his chief mate—an athletic and resolute man, who had been a privateer's-man[65]—to head the party. The more to encourage the sailors, they were told, that the Spanish captain considered his ship good as lost; that she and her cargo, including some gold and silver, were worth more than a thousand doubloons. Take her, and no small part should be theirs. The sailors replied with a shout.

The fugitives had now almost gained an offing. It was nearly night; but the moon was rising. After hard, prolonged pulling, the boats came up on the ship's quarters, at a suitable distance laying upon their oars to discharge their muskets. Having no bullets to return, the negroes sent their yells. But, upon the second volley, Indian-like, they hurtled their hatchets. One took off a sailor's fingers. Another struck the whale-boat's bow, cutting off the rope there, and remaining stuck in the gunwale like a woodman's axe. Snatching it, quivering from its lodgment, the mate hurled it back. The returned gauntlet now stuck in the ship's broken quarter-gallery, and so remained.

The negroes giving too hot a reception, the whites kept a more respectful distance. Hovering now just out of reach of the hurtling hatchets, they, with a view to the close encounter which must soon come, sought to decoy the blacks into entirely disarming themselves of their most murderous weapons in a hand-to-hand fight, by foolishly flinging them, as missiles, short of the mark, into the sea. But ere long perceiving the stratagem, the negroes desisted, though not before many of them had to replace their lost hatchets with hand-spikes; an exchange which, as counted upon, proved in the end favorable to the assailants.

Meantime, with a strong wind, the ship still clove the water; the boats alternately falling behind, and pulling up, to discharge fresh volleys.

---

[65]PRIVATEER'S-MAN: One who has served on a privateer, an armed privately owned vessel with a commission from a government authorizing it to capture merchant ships from hostile nations.

The fire was mostly directed towards the stern, since there, chiefly, the negroes, at present, were clustering. But to kill or maim the negroes was not the object. To take them, with the ship, was the object. To do it, the ship must be boarded; which could not be done by boats while she was sailing so fast.

A thought now struck the mate. Observing the Spanish boys still aloft, high as they could get, he called to them to descend to the yards, and cut adrift the sails. It was done. About this time, owing to causes hereafter to be shown, two Spaniards, in the dress of sailors and conspicuously showing themselves, were killed; not by volleys, but by deliberate marksman's shots; while, as it afterwards appeared, by one of the general discharges, Atufal, the black, and the Spaniard at the helm likewise were killed. What now, with the loss of the sails, and loss of leaders, the ship became unmanageable to the negroes.

With creaking masts, she came heavily round to the wind; the prow slowly swinging, into view of the boats, its skeleton gleaming in the horizontal moonlight, and casting a gigantic ribbed shadow upon the water. One extended arm of the ghost seemed beckoning the whites to avenge it.

"Follow your leader!" cried the mate; and, one on each bow, the boats boarded. Sealing-spears and cutlasses crossed hatchets and hand-spikes. Huddled upon the long-boat amidships, the negresses raised a wailing chant, whose chorus was the clash of the steel.

For a time, the attack wavered; the negroes wedging themselves to beat it back; the half-repelled sailors, as yet unable to gain a footing, fighting as troopers in the saddle, one leg sideways flung over the bulwarks, and one without, plying their cutlasses like carters' whips. But in vain. They were almost overborne, when, rallying themselves into a squad as one man, with a huzza, they sprang inboard; where, entangled, they involuntarily separated again. For a few breaths' space, there was a vague, muffled, inner sound, as of submerged sword-fish rushing hither and thither through shoals of black-fish. Soon, in a reunited band, and joined by the Spanish seamen, the whites came to the surface, irresistibly driving the negroes toward the stern. But a barricade of casks and sacks, from side to side, had been thrown up by the mainmast. Here the negroes faced about, and though scorning peace or truce, yet fain would have had respite. But, without pause, overleaping the barrier, the unflagging sailors again closed. Exhausted, the blacks now fought in despair. Their red tongues lolled, wolf-like, from their black mouths. But the pale sailors' teeth were set; not a word was spoken; and, in five minutes more, the ship was won.

Nearly a score of the negroes were killed. Exclusive of those by the balls,[66] many were mangled; their wounds—mostly inflicted by the long-edged sealing-spears—resembling those shaven ones of the English at Preston Pans, made by the poled scythes of the Highlanders.[67] On the other side, none were killed, though several were wounded; some severely, including the mate. The surviving negroes were temporarily secured, and the ship, towed back into the harbor at midnight, once more lay anchored.

Omitting the incidents and arrangements ensuing, suffice it that, after two days spent in refitting, the ships sailed in company for Conception, in Chili, and thence for Lima, in Peru; where, before the vice-regal courts, the whole affair, from the beginning, underwent investigation.

Though, midway on the passage, the ill-fated Spaniard, relaxed from constraint, showed some signs of regaining health with free-will; yet, agreeably to his own foreboding, shortly before arriving at Lima, he relapsed, finally becoming so reduced as to be carried ashore in arms. Hearing of his story and plight, one of the many religious institutions of the City of Kings opened an hospitable refuge to him, where both physician and priest were his nurses, and a member of the order volunteered to be his one special guardian and consoler, by night and by day.

The following extracts, translated from one of the official Spanish documents, will it is hoped, shed light on the preceding narrative, as well as, in the first place, reveal the true port of departure and true history of the San Dominick's voyage, down to the time of her touching at the island of St. Maria.

But, ere the extracts come, it may be well to preface them with a remark.

The document selected, from among many others, for partial translation, contains the deposition of Benito Cereno; the first taken in the case. Some disclosures therein were, at the time, held dubious for both learned and natural reasons. The tribunal inclined to the opinion that the deponent, not undisturbed in his mind by recent events, raved of some things which could never have happened. But subsequent depositions of the surviving sailors, bearing out the revelations of their captain in several of the strangest particulars, gave credence to the rest. So that the tribunal, in its final decision, rested its capital sentences upon statements which, had they lacked confirmation, it would have deemed it but duty to reject.

66BALLS: Musket balls.
67HIGHLANDERS: Referring to the Battle of Preston Pans in Scotland in 1745, in which Prince Charles Edward (a.k.a. Bonnie Prince Charlie), claimant to the British throne and the grandson of King James II, led an army of Scottish Highlanders to victory over the royal forces.

I, Don Jose de Abos and Padilla, His Majesty's Notary for the Royal Revenue, and Register of this Province, and Notary Public of the Holy Crusade of this Bishopric, etc.

Do certify and declare, as much as is requisite in law, that, in the criminal cause commenced the twenty-fourth of the month of September, in the year seventeen hundred and ninety-nine, against the negroes of the ship San Dominick, the following declaration before me was made.

Declaration of the first witness, DON BENITO CERENO

The same day, and month, and year, His Honor, Doctor Juan Martinez de Rozas, Councilor of the Royal Audience of this Kingdom, and learned in the law of this Intendency, ordered the captain of the ship San Dominick, Don Benito Cereno, to appear; which he did in his litter, attended by the monk Infelez; of whom he received the oath, which he took by God, our Lord, and a sign of the Cross; under which he promised to tell the truth of whatever he should know and should be asked;—and being interrogated agreeably to the tenor of the act commencing the process, he said, that on the twentieth of May last, he set sail with his ship from the port of Valparaiso, bound to that of Callao; loaded with the produce of the country beside thirty cases of hardware and one hundred and sixty blacks, of both sexes, mostly belonging to Don Alexandro Aranda, gentleman, of the city of Mendoza; that the crew of the ship consisted of thirty-six men, beside the persons who went as passengers; that the negroes were in part as follows:

[Here, in the original, follows a list of some fifty names, descriptions, and ages, compiled from certain recovered documents of Aranda's, and also from recollections of the deponent, from which portions only are extracted.]

One, from about eighteen to nineteen years, named José, and this was the man that waited upon his master, Don Alexandro, and who speaks well the Spanish, having served him four or five years; ... a mulatto, named Francisco, the cabin steward, of a good person and voice, having sung in the Valparaiso churches, native of the province of Buenos Ayres, aged about thirty-five years. ... A smart negro, named Dago, who had been for many years a grave-digger among the Spaniards, aged forty-six years. ... Four old negroes, born in Africa, from sixty to seventy, but sound, calkers by trade, whose names are as follows:— the first was named Muri, and he was killed (as was also his son named Diamelo); the second, Nacta; the third, Yola, likewise killed; the fourth, Ghofan; and six full-grown negroes, aged from thirty to forty-five, all raw, and born

among the Ashantees—*Matiluqui, Yan, Lecbe, Mapenda, Yambaio, Akim;
four of whom were killed; ... a powerful negro named Atufal, who, being
supposed to have been a chief in Africa, his owners set great store by him.
... And a small negro of Senegal, but some years among the Spaniards,
aged about thirty, which negro's name was Babo; ... that he does not
remember the names of the others, but that still expecting the residue
of Don Alexandro's papers will be found, will then take due account of
them all, and remit to the court; ... and thirty-nine women and children of all ages.*

[The catalogue over, the deposition goes on:]

... *That all the negroes slept upon deck, as is customary in this navigation, and none wore fetters, because the owner, his friend Aranda, told
him that they were all tractable; ... that on the seventh day after leaving
port, at three o'clock in the morning, all the Spaniards being asleep except
the two officers on the watch, who were the boatswain, Juan Robles, and
the carpenter, Juan Bautista Gayete, and the helmsman and his boy, the
negroes revolted suddenly, wounded dangerously the boatswain and the
carpenter, and successively killed eighteen men of those who were sleeping upon deck, some with hand-spikes and hatchets, and others by throwing them alive overboard, after tying them; that of the Spaniards upon
deck, they left about seven, as he thinks, alive and tied, to manœuvre the
ship, and three or four more who hid themselves, remained also alive.
Although in the act of revolt the negroes made themselves masters of the
hatchway, six or seven wounded went through it to the cockpit, without
any hindrance on their part; that during the act of revolt, the mate and
another person, whose name he does not recollect, attempted to come up
through the hatchway, but being quickly wounded, were obliged to return
to the cabin; that the deponent resolved at break of day to come up the
companionway, where the negro Babo was, being the ringleader, and
Atufal, who assisted him and having spoken to them, exhorted them to
cease committing such atrocities, asking them, at the same time, what they
wanted and intended to do, offering, himself, to obey their commands; that,
notwithstanding this, they threw, in his presence, three men, alive and tied,
overboard; that they told the deponent to come up, and that they would
not kill him; which having done, the negro Babo asked him whether there
were in those seas any negro countries where they might be carried, and
he answered them. No; that the negro Babo afterwards told him to carry
them to Senegal, or to the neighboring islands of St. Nicholas; and he
answered, that this was impossible, on account of the great distance, the
necessity involved of rounding Cape Horn, the bad condition of the ves-*

*sel, the want of provisions, sails, and water; but that the negro Babo
replied to him he must carry them in any way; that they would do and conform themselves to everything the deponent should require as to eating and
drinking; that after a long conference, being absolutely compelled to please
them, for they threatened him to kill all the whites if they were not, at all
events, carried to Senegal, he told them that what was most wanting for
the voyage was water; that they would go near the coast to take it, and
thence they would proceed on their course; that the negro Babo agreed
to it; and the deponent steered towards the intermediate ports, hoping to
meet some Spanish or foreign vessel that would save them; that within
ten or eleven days they saw the land, and continued their course by it in
the vicinity of Nasca; that the deponent observed that the negroes were now
restless and mutinous, because he did not effect the taking in of water,
the negro Babo having required, with threats, that it should be done, without fail, the following day; he told him he saw plainly that the coast was
steep, and the rivers designated in the maps were not to be found, with
other reasons suitable to the circumstances; that the best way would be
to go to the island of Santa Maria, where they might water easily, it being
a solitary island, as the foreigners did; that the deponent did not go to
Pisco, that was near, nor make any other port of the coast, because the
negro Babo had intimated to him several times, that he would kill all the
whites the very moment he should perceive any city, town, or settlement
of any kind on the shores to which they should be carried: that having
determined to go to the island of Santa Maria, as the deponent had
planned, for the purpose of trying whether, on the passage or near the
island itself, they could find any vessel that should favor them, or whether
he could escape from it in a boat to the neighboring coast of Arruco; to
adopt the necessary means he immediately changed his course, steering for
the island; that the negroes Babo and Atufal held daily conferences, in
which they discussed what was necessary for their design of returning to
Senegal, whether they were to kill all the Spaniards, and particularly the
deponent; that eight days after parting from the coast of Nasca, the deponent being on the watch a little after day-break, and soon after the negroes
had their meeting, the negro Babo came to the place where the deponent
was, and told him that he had determined to kill his master, Don Alexandro
Aranda, both because he and his companions could not otherwise be sure
of their liberty, and that, to keep the seamen in subjection, he wanted to
prepare a warning of what road they should be made to take did they or
any of them oppose him; and that, by means of the death of Don
Alexandro, that warning would best be given; but, that what this last
meant, the deponent did not at time comprehend, nor could not, further*

than that the death of Don Alexandro was intended; and moreover, the negro Babo proposed to the deponent to call the mate Raneds, who was sleeping in the cabin, before the thing was done, for fear, as the deponent understood it, that the mate, who was a good navigator, should be killed with Don Alexandro and the rest; that the deponent, who was the friend, from youth, of Don Alexandro, prayed and conjured, but all was useless; for the negro Babo answered him that the thing could not be prevented, and that all the Spaniards risked their death if they should attempt to frustrate his will in this matter or any other; that, in this conflict, the deponent called the mate, Raneds, who was forced to go apart, and immediately the negro Babo commanded the Ashantee Martinqui and the Ashantee Lecbe to go and commit the murder; that those two went down with hatchets to the berth of Don Alexandro; that, yet half alive and mangled, they dragged him on deck; that they were going to throw him overboard in that state, but the negro Babo stopped them, bidding the murder be completed on the deck before him, which was done, when, by his orders, the body was carried below, forward; that nothing more was seen of it by the deponent for three days; ... that Don Alonzo Sidonia, an old man, long resident at Valparaiso, and lately appointed to a civil office in Peru, whither he had taken passage, was at the time sleeping in the berth opposite Don Alexandro's; that, awakening at his cries, surprised by them, and at the sight of the negroes with their bloody hatchets in their hands, he threw himself into the sea through a window which was near him, and was drowned, without it being in the power of the deponent to assist or take him up; ... that, a short time after killing Aranda, they brought upon deck his german-cousin, of middle-age, Don Francisco Masa, of Mendoza, and the young Don Joaquin, Marques de Aramboalaza, then lately from Spain, with his Spanish servant Ponce, and the three young clerks of Aranda, José Morairi, Lorenzo Bargas, and Hermenegildo Gandix, all of Cadiz; that Don Joaquin and Hermenegildo Gandix, the negro Babo for purposes hereafter to appear, preserved alive; but Don Francisco Masa, José Morairi, and Lorenzo Bargas, with Ponce the servant, beside the boatswain, Juan Robles, the boatswain's mates, Manuel Viscaya and Roderigo Hurta, and four of the sailors, the negro Babo ordered to be thrown alive into the sea, although they made no resistance, nor begged for anything else but mercy; that the boatswain, Juan Robles, who knew how to swim, kept the longest above water, making acts of contrition, and, in the last words he uttered, charged this deponent to cause mass to be said for his soul to our Lady of Succor; ... that, during the three days which followed, the deponent, uncertain what fate had befallen the remains of Don Alexandro, frequently asked the negro Babo where they were, and if still on board, whether they were to be preserved for interment ashore, entreating him so to order it; that the negro Babo answered nothing till the fourth day, when at sunrise, the deponent coming on deck, the negro Babo showed him a skeleton, which had been substituted for the ship's proper figure-head, the image of Christopher Colon, the discoverer of the New World; that the negro Babo asked him whose skeleton that was, and whether, from its whiteness, he should not think it a white's; that, upon his covering his face, the negro Babo, coming close, said words to this effect: "Keep faith with the blacks from here to Senegal, or you shall in spirit, as now in body, follow your leader," pointing to the prow; ... that the same morning the negro Babo took by succession each Spaniard forward, and asked him whose skeleton that was, and whether, from its whiteness, he should not think it a white's; that each Spaniard covered his face; that then to each the negro Babo repeated the words in the first place said to the deponent; ... that they (the Spaniards), being then assembled aft, the negro Babo harangued them, saying that he had now done all; that the deponent (as navigator for the negroes) might pursue his course, warning him and all of them that they should, soul and body, go the way of Don Alexandro if he saw them (the Spaniards) speak or plot anything against them (the negroes)—a threat which was repeated every day; that, before the events last mentioned, they had tied the cook to throw him overboard, for it is not known what thing they heard him speak, but finally the negro Babo spared his life, at the request of the deponent; that a few days after, the deponent, endeavoring not to omit any means to preserve the lives of the remaining whites, spoke to the negroes peace and tranquillity, and agreed to draw up a paper, signed by the deponent and the sailors who could write, as also by the negro Babo, for himself and all the blacks, in which the deponent obliged himself to carry them to Senegal, and they not to kill any more, and he formally to make over to them the ship, with the cargo, with which they were for that time satisfied and quieted.... But the next day, the more surely to guard against the sailors' escape, the negro Babo commanded all the boats to be destroyed but the long-boat, which was unseaworthy, and another, a cutter in good condition, which, knowing it would yet be wanted for towing the water casks, he had lowered down into the hold.

[Various particulars of the prolonged and perplexed navigation ensuing here follow, with incidents of a calamitous calm, from which portion one passage is extracted, to wit:]

—That on the fifth day of the calm, all on board suffering much from the heat, and want of water, and five having died in fits, and mad, the negroes became irritable, and for a chance gesture, which they deemed suspicious—though it was harmless—made by the mate, Raneds, to the deponent, in the act of handing a quadrant, they killed him; but that for this they afterwards were sorry, the mate being the only remaining navigator on board, except the deponent.

—That omitting other events, which daily happened, and which can only serve uselessly to recall past misfortunes and conflicts, after seventy-three days' navigation, reckoned from the time they sailed from Nasca, during which they navigated under a scanty allowance of water, and were afflicted with the calms before mentioned, they at last arrived at the island of Santa Maria, on the seventeenth of the month of August, at about six o'clock in the afternoon, at which hour they cast anchor very near the American ship, Bachelor's Delight, which lay in the same bay, commanded by the generous Captain Amasa Delano; but at six o'clock in the morning, they had already descried the port, and the negroes became uneasy, as soon as at distance they saw the ship, not having expected to see one there; that the negro Babo pacified them, assuring them that no fear need be had; that straightway he ordered the figure on the bow to be covered with canvas, as for repairs, and had the decks a little set in order; that for a time the negro Babo and the negro Atufal conferred; that the negro Atufal was for sailing away, but the negro Babo would not, and, by himself, cast about what to do; that at last he came to the deponent, proposing to him to say and do all that the deponent declares to have said and done to the American captain; ... that the negro Babo warned him that if he varied in the least, or uttered any word, or gave any look that should give the least intimation of the past events or present state, he would instantly kill him, with all his companions, showing a dagger, which he carried hid, saying something which, as he understood it, meant that that dagger would be alert as his eye; that the negro Babo then announced the plan to all his companions, which pleased them; that he then, the better to disguise the truth, devised many expedients, in some of them uniting deceit and defense; that of this sort was the device of the six Ashantees before named, who were his bravoes;[68] that them he stationed on the break of the poop, as if to clean certain hatchets (in cases, which were part of the cargo), but in reality to use them, and distribute them at need, and at a given word he told them that, among other devices, was the device of presenting Atufal, his right-hand

[68]BRAVOES: Hired assassins.

man, as chained, though in a moment the chains could be dropped;
that in every particular he informed the deponent what part he was
expected to enact in every device, and what story he was to tell on every
occasion, always threatening him with instant death if he varied in the
least: that, conscious that many of the negroes would be turbulent, the
negro Babo appointed the four aged negroes, who were calkers, to keep
what domestic order they could on the decks; that again and again
he harangued the Spaniards and his companions, informing them of his
intent, and of his devices, and of the invented story that this deponent
was to tell, charging them lest any of them varied from that story; that
these arrangements were made and matured during the interval of two
or three hours, between their first sighting the ship and the arrival on
board of Captain Amasa Delano; that this happened about half-past
seven o'clock in the morning, Captain Amasa Delano coming in his
boat, and all gladly receiving him; that the deponent, as well as he
could force himself, acting then the part of principal owner, and a free
captain of the ship, told Captain Amasa Delano, when called upon, that
he came from Buenos Ayres, bound to Lima, with three hundred
negroes; that off Cape Horn, and in a subsequent fever, many negroes
had died; that also, by similar casualties, all the sea officers and the
greatest part of the crew had died.

[And so the deposition goes on, circumstantially recounting the fictitious story dictated to the deponent by Babo, and through the deponent
imposed upon Captain Delano; and also recounting the friendly offers
of Captain Delano, with other things, but all of which is here omitted.
After the fictitious story, etc., the deposition proceeds:]

—that the generous Captain Amasa Delano remained on board all
the day, till he left the ship anchored at six o'clock in the evening, depo-
nent speaking to him always of his pretended misfortunes, under the fore-
mentioned principles, without having had it in his power to tell a single
word, or give him the least hint, that he might know the truth and state
of things; because the negro Babo, performing the office of an officious
servant with all the appearance of submission of the humble slave, did not
leave the deponent one moment; that this was in order to observe the depo-
nent's actions and words, for the negro Babo understands well the Spanish;
and besides, there were thereabout some others who were constantly on
the watch, and likewise understood the Spanish; .... that upon one occa-
sion, while deponent was standing on the deck conversing with Amasa
Delano, by a secret sign the negro Babo drew him (the deponent) aside,

the act appearing as if originating with the deponent; that then, he being drawn aside, the negro Babo proposed to him to gain from Amasa Delano full particulars about his ship, and crew, and arms; that the deponent asked "For what?" that the negro Babo answered he might conceive; that, grieved at the prospect of what might overtake the generous Captain Amasa Delano, the deponent at first refused to ask the desired questions, and used every argument to induce the negro Babo to give up this new design; that the negro Babo showed the point of his dagger; that, after the information had been obtained, the negro Babo again drew him aside, telling him that that very night he (the deponent) would be captain of two ships, instead of one, for that, great part of the American's ship's crew being to be absent fishing, the six Ashantees, without any one else, would easily take it; that at this time he said other things to the same purpose; that no entreaties availed; that, before Amasa Delano's coming on board, no hint had been given touching the capture of the American ship: that to prevent this project the deponent was powerless; ...—that in some things his memory is confused, he cannot distinctly recall every event; ...—that as soon as they had cast anchor at six of the clock in the evening, as has before been stated, the American Captain took leave to return to his vessel; that upon a sudden impulse, which the deponent believes to have come from God and his angels, he, after the farewell had been said, followed the generous Captain Amasa Delano as far as the gunwale, where he stayed, under pretense of taking leave, until Amasa Delano should have been seated in his boat; that on shoving off, the deponent sprang from the gunwale into the boat, and fell into it, he knows not how, God guarding him; that—

[Here, in the original, follows the account of what further happened at the escape, and how the San Dominick was retaken, and of the passage to the coast; including in the recital many expressions of "eternal gratitude" to the "generous Captain Amasa Delano." The deposition then proceeds with recapitulatory remarks, and a partial renumeration of the negroes, making record of their individual part in the past events, with a view to furnishing, according to command of the court, the data whereon to found the criminal sentences to be pronounced. From this portion is the following:]

—That he believes that all the negroes, though not in the first place knowing to the design of revolt, when it was accomplished, approved it. ... That the negro, José, eighteen years old, and in the personal service of Don Alexandro, was the one who communicated the information to *the negro Babo, about the state of things in the cabin, before the revolt; that this is known, because, in the preceding midnight, he used to come from his berth, which was under his master's, in the cabin, to the deck where the ringleader and his associates were, and had secret conversations with the negro Babo, in which he was several times seen by the mate; that, one night, the mate drove him away twice; ... that this same negro José, was the one who, without being commanded to do so by the negro Babo, as Lecbe and Martinqui were, stabbed his master, Don Alexandro, after he had been dragged half-lifeless to the deck; ... that the mulatto steward, Francisco, was of the first band of revolters, that he was, in all things, the creature and tool of the negro Babo; that, to make his court, he, just before a repast in the cabin, proposed, to the negro Babo, poisoning a dish for the generous Captain Amasa Delano; this is known and believed, because the negroes have said it; but that the negro Babo, having another design, forbade Francisco; ... that the Ashantee Lecbe was one of the worst of them; for that, on the day the ship was retaken, be assisted in the defense of her, with a hatchet in each hand, one of which he wounded, in the breast, the chief mate of Amasa Delano, in the first act of boarding; this all knew; that, in sight of the deponent, Lecbe struck, with a hatchet, Don Francisco Masa when, by the negro Babo's orders, he was carrying him to throw him overboard, alive; beside participating in the murder, before mentioned, of Don Alexandro Aranda, and others of the cabin-passengers; that, owing to the fury with which the Ashantees fought in the engagement with the boats, but this Lecbe and Yau survived; that Yau was bad as Lecbe; that Yau was the man who, by Babo's command, willingly prepared the skeleton of Don Alexandro, in a way the negroes afterwards told the deponent, but which he, so long as reason is left him, can never divulge; that Yau and Lecbe were the two who, in a calm by night, riveted the skeleton to the bow; this also the negroes told him; that the negro Babo was he who traced the inscription below it; that the negro Babo was the plotter from first to last; he ordered every murder, and was the helm and keel of the revolt; that Atufal was his lieutenant in all; but Atufal, with his own hand, committed no murder; nor did the negro Babo; ... that Atufal was shot, being killed in the fight with the boats, ere boarding; ... that the negresses, of age, were knowing to the revolt and testified themselves satisfied at the death of their master, Don Alexandro; that, had the negroes not restrained them, they would have tortured to death, instead of simply killing, the Spaniards slain by command of the negro Babo; that the negresses used their utmost influence to have the deponent made away with; that, in the various acts of murder, they sang songs and danced—not gaily, but solemnly; and before*

*the engagement with the boats, as well as during the action, they sang
melancholy songs to the negroes, and that this melancholy tone was more
inflaming than a different one would have been, and was so intended;
that all this is believed, because the negroes have said it. —that of the
thirty-six men of the crew exclusive of the passengers, (all of whom are
now dead), which the deponent had knowledge of, six only remained
alive, with four cabin-boys and ship-boys, not included with the crew;
... —that the negroes broke an arm of one of the cabin-boys and gave him
strokes with hatchets.*

[Then follow various random disclosures referring to various periods of time. The following are extracted:]

*—That during the presence of Captain Amasa Delano on board, some
attempts were made by the sailors, and one by Hermenegildo Gandix,
to convey hints to him of the true state of affairs; but that these attempts
were ineffectual, owing to fear of incurring death, and furthermore owing
to the devices which offered contradictions to the true state of affairs;
as well as owing to the generosity and piety of Amasa Delano incapable
of sounding such wickedness; ... that Luys Galgo, a sailor about sixty
years of age, and formerly of the king's navy, was one of those who sought
to convey tokens to Captain Amasa Delano; but his intent, though undiscovered, being suspected, he was, on a pretense, made to retire out of
sight, and at last into the hold, and there was made away with. This
the negroes have since said; ... that one of the ship-boys feeling, from
Captain Amasa Delano's presence, some hopes of release, and not having enough prudence, dropped some chance-word respecting his expectations, which being overheard and understood by a slave-boy with
whom he was eating at the time, the latter struck him on the head with
a knife, inflicting a bad wound, but of which the boy is now healing; that
likewise, not long before the ship was brought to anchor, one of the seamen, steering at the time, endangered himself by letting the blacks remark
some expression in his countenance, arising from a cause similar to the
above; but this sailor, by his heedful after conduct, escaped; ... that these
statements are made to show the court that from the beginning to the end
of the revolt, it was impossible for the deponent and his men to act otherwise than they did; ... —that the third clerk, Hermenegildo Gandix,
who before had been forced to live among the seamen, wearing a seaman's habit, and in all respects appearing to be one for the time; he,
Gandix, was killed by a musket-ball fired through a mistake from the
boats before boarding; having in his fright run up the mizzen-rigging,
calling to the boats—"don't board," lest upon their boarding the negroes*

should kill him; that this inducing the Americans to believe he some way favored the cause of the negroes, they fired two balls at him, so that he fell wounded from the rigging, and was drowned in the sea; ... —that the young Don Joaquin, Marques de Arambaolaza, like Hermenegildo Gandix, the third clerk, was degraded to the office and appearance of a common seaman; that upon one occasion when Don Joaquin shrank, the negro Babo commanded the Ashantee Lecbe to take tar and heat it, and pour it upon Don Joaquin's hands; ... —that Don Joaquin was killed owing to another mistake of the Americans, but one impossible to be avoided, as upon the approach of the boats, Don Joaquin, with a hatchet tied edge out and upright to his hand, was made by the negroes to appear on the bulwarks; whereupon, seen with arms in his hands and in a questionable attitude, he was shot for a renegade seaman; ... —that on the person of Don Joaquin was found secreted a jewel, which, by papers that were discovered, proved to have been meant for the shrine of our Lady of Mercy in Lima; a votive offering, beforehand prepared and guarded, to attest his gratitude, when he should have landed in Peru, his last destination, for the safe conclusion of his entire voyage from Spain; ... —that the jewel, with the other effects of the late Don Joaquin, is in the custody of the brethren of the Hospital de Sacerdotes, awaiting the disposition of the honorable court; ... —that, owing to the condition of the deponent, as well as the haste in which the boats departed for the attack, the Americans were not forewarned that there were, among the apparent crew, a passenger and one of the clerks disguised by the negro Babo; ... —that, beside the negroes killed in the action, some were killed after the capture and re-anchoring at night, when shackled to the ring-bolts on deck; that these deaths were committed by the sailors, ere they could be prevented. That so soon as informed of it, Captain Amasa Delano used all his authority, and, in particular with his own hand, struck down Martinez Gola, who, having found a razor in the pocket of an old jacket of his, which one of the shackled negroes had on, was aiming it at the negro's throat; that the noble Captain Amasa Delano also wrenched from the hand of Bartholomew Barlo, a dagger secreted at the time of the massacre of the whites, with which he was in the act of stabbing a shackled negro, who, the same day, with another negro, had thrown him down and jumped upon him; ... —that, for all the events, befalling through so long a time, during which the ship was in the hands of the negro Babo, he cannot here give account; but that, what he had said is the most substantial of what occurs to him at present, and is the truth under the oath which he has taken; which declaration he affirmed and ratified, after hearing it read to him.

He said that he is twenty-nine years of age, and broken in body and mind; that when finally dismissed by the court, he shall not return home to Chili, but betake himself to the monastery on Mount Agonia without; and signed with his honor, and crossed himself, and, for the time, departed as he came, in his litter, with the monk Infelez, to the Hospital de Sacerdotes.

DOCTOR ROZAS.   BENITO CERENO.

If the Deposition have served as the key to fit into the lock of the complications which precede it, then, as a vault whose door has been flung back, the San Dominick's hull lies open to-day.

Hitherto the nature of this narrative, besides rendering the intricacies in the beginning unavoidable, has more or less required that many things, instead of being set down in the order of occurrence, should be retrospectively, or irregularly given; this last is the case with the following passages, which will conclude the account:

During the long, mild voyage to Lima, there was, as before hinted, a period during which the sufferer a little recovered his health, or, at least in some degree, his tranquillity. Ere the decided relapse which came, the two captains had many cordial conversations—their fraternal unreserve in singular contrast with former withdrawments.

Again and again, it was repeated, how hard it had been to enact the part forced on the Spaniard by Babo.

"Ah, my dear friend," Don Benito once said, "at those very times when you thought me so morose and ungrateful, nay, when, as you now admit, you half thought me plotting your murder, at those very times my heart was frozen; I could not look at you, thinking of what, both on board this ship and your own, hung, from other hands, over my kind benefactor. And as God lives, Don Amasa, I know not whether desire for my own safety alone could have nerved me to that leap into your boat, had it not been for the thought that, did you, unenlightened, return to your ship, you, my best friend, with all who might be with you, stolen upon, that night, in your hammocks, would never in this world have wakened again. Do but think how you walked this deck, how you sat in this cabin, every inch of ground mined into honeycombs under you. Had I dropped the least hint, made the least advance towards an understanding between us, death, explosive death—yours as mine—would have ended the scene."

"True, true," cried Captain Delano, starting, "you saved my life, Don Benito, more than I yours; saved it, too, against my knowledge and will."

"Nay, my friend," rejoined the Spaniard, courteous even to the point of religion, "God charmed your life, but you saved mine. To think of some things you did—those smilings and chattings, rash pointings and gesturings. For less than these, they slew my mate, Raneds; but you had the Prince of Heaven's safe conduct through all ambuscades."[69]

"Yes, all is owing to Providence, I know; but the temper of my mind that morning was more than commonly pleasant, while the sight of so much suffering, more apparent than real, added to my good nature, compassion, and charity, happily interweaving the three. Had it been otherwise, doubtless, as you hint, some of my interferences might have ended unhappily enough. Besides, those feelings I spoke of enabled me to get the better of momentary distrust, at times when acuteness might have cost me my life, without saving another's. Only at the end did my suspicions get the better of me, and you know how wide of the mark they then proved."

"Wide, indeed," said Don Benito, sadly; "you were with me all day; stood with me, sat with me, talked with me, looked at me, ate with me, drank with me; and yet, your last act was to clutch for a monster, not only an innocent man, but the most pitiable of all men. To such degree may malign machinations and deceptions impose. So far may even the best man err, in judging the conduct of one with the recesses of whose condition he is not acquainted. But you were forced to it; and you were in time undeceived. Would that, in both respects, it was so ever, and with all men."

"You generalize, Don Benito; and mournfully enough. But the past is passed; why moralize upon it? Forget it. See, yon bright sun has forgotten it all, and the blue sea, and the blue sky; these have turned over new leaves."

"Because they have no memory," he dejectedly replied; "because they are not human."

"But these mild trades[70] that now fan your cheek, do they not come with a human-like healing to you? Warm friends, steadfast friends are the trades."

"With their steadfastness they but waft me to my tomb, señor," was the foreboding response.

"You are saved," cried Captain Delano, more and more astonished and pained; "you are saved; what has cast such a shadow upon you?"

"The negro."

There was silence, while the moody man sat, slowly and unconsciously gathering his mantle about him, as if it were a pall.

There was no more conversation that day.

---

[69]AMBUSCADES: Ambushes.
[70]MILD TRADES: Favorable tradewinds.

But if the Spaniard's melancholy sometimes ended in muteness upon topics like the above, there were others upon which he never spoke at all; on which, indeed, all his old reserves were piled. Pass over the worst, and, only to elucidate, let an item or two of these be cited. The dress so precise and costly, worn by him on the day whose events have been narrated, had not willingly been put on. And that silver-mounted sword, apparent symbol of despotic command, was not, indeed, a sword, but the ghost of one. The scabbard, artificially stiffened, was empty.

As for the black—whose brain, not body, had schemed and led the revolt, with the plot—his slight frame, inadequate to that which it held, had at once yielded to the superior muscular strength of his captor, in the boat. Seeing all was over, he uttered no sound, and could not be forced to. His aspect seemed to say, since I cannot do deeds, I will not speak words. Put in irons in the hold, with the rest, he was carried to Lima. During the passage Don Benito did not visit him. Nor then, nor at any time after, would he look at him. Before the tribunal he refused. When pressed by the judges he fainted. On the testimony of the sailors alone rested the legal identity of Babo.

Some months after, dragged to the gibbet at the tail of a mule, the black met his voiceless end. The body was burned to ashes; but for many days, the head, that hive of subtlety, fixed on a pole in the Plaza, met, unabashed, the gaze of the whites; and across the Plaza looked towards St. Bartholomew's church, in whose vaults slept then, as now, the recovered bones of Aranda; and across the Rimac bridge looked towards the monastery, on Mount Agonia without; where, three months after being dismissed by the court, Benito Cereno, borne on the bier, did, indeed, follow his leader.

[1855, 1856]

From Battle-Pieces: The Portent (1859)[1]

Hanging from the beam,
  Slowly swaying (such the law),
Gaunt the shadow on your green,
  Shenandoah![2]

---

[1]PORTENT: Omen. In 1859 the abolitionist John Brown (1800–1859) led a raid at Harpers Ferry, Virginia. The raid took place in October; Brown was hanged two months later.
[2]SHENANDOAH: River in northern Virginia that empties into the Potomac River at Harpers Ferry.

The cut is on the crown   5
(Lo, John Brown),
And the stabs shall heal no more.

Hidden in the cap
     Is the anguish none can draw;
So your future veils its face,   10
     Shenandoah!
But the streaming beard is shown
(Weird[3] John Brown),
The meteor of the war.

[1866]

From Battle-Pieces: The March into Virginia, Ending in the First Manassas[1] (July, 1861)

Did all the lets[2] and bars appear
     To every just or larger end,
Whence should come the trust and cheer?
     Youth must its ignorant impulse lend–
Age finds place in the rear.   5
     All wars are boyish, and are fought by boys,
The champions and enthusiasts of the state:
     Turbid ardors and vain joys
          Not barrenly abate–
Stimulants to the power mature,   10
     Preparatives of fate.

Who here forecasteth the event?
What heart but spurns at precedent
And warnings of the wise,
Contemned foreclosures of surprise?   15

---

[3]WEIRD: Unusual-looking, but here with the suggestion of fate or ill fortune.
[1]FIRST MANASSAS: Known in the North as the First Battle of Bull Run. On July 21, 1861, in the first major land engagement of the Civil War (1861–1865), the Union Army under General Irvin McDowell met the Confederate forces led by General Pierre G.T. Beauregard at Manassas Junction, Virginia. The Union retreated, losing nearly 3,000 soldiers. The Confederate forces suffered over 2,000 losses.
[2]LETS: A let is something that impedes.

The banners play, the bugles call,
The air is blue and prodigal.
   No berrying party, pleasure-wooed,
No picnic party in the May,
Ever went less loth than they   20
   Into that leafy neighborhood.
In Bacchic glee[2] they file toward Fate,
Moloch's[3] uninitiate;
Expectancy, and glad surmise
Of battle's unknown mysteries.   25
All they feel is this: 'tis glory,
A rapture sharp, though transitory,
Yet lasting in belaureled story.
So they gayly go to fight,
Chatting left and laughing right.   30

But some who this blithe mood present,
   As on in lightsome files they fare,
Shall die experienced ere three days are spent—
   Perish, enlightened by the vollied glare;
Or shame survive, and, like to adamant,   35
   The throe of Second Manassas[4] share.

[1866]

---

[2]BACCHIC GLEE: Frenzied intoxication, after Bacchus, the Roman god of wine.
[3]MOLOCH'S: The Canaanite sun god, to whom children were sacrificed (Leviticus 18:21).
[4]SECOND MANASSAS: The Second Battle of Bull Run (July 1862), like the first, was a victory for the Confederates. Generals Robert E. Lee and Thomas "Stonewall" Jackson drove back Union forces led by General John Pope.

Walt Whitman

(1819–1892)

*Walt Whitman was born on Long Island, New York, of working-class back-
ground (his father was a house-builder), and he took jobs in his youth as
an office boy, printer, and compositor. Later he taught school, edited a
newspaper on Long Island, and, during the 1840s, was a journalist, editor, essayist, and poet for several New York City papers.*

Whitman's passionate book Leaves of Grass *was published, at his
own expense, in 1855; a second edition appeared the following year,
and a third, much longer edition in 1860.* Leaves of Grass *was not a
success in the marketplace, and a number of reviewers and readers
criticized it as blasphemous and sexually scandalous. But Whitman
was undeterred, and* Leaves of Grass *became a lifelong project for him.
He added poems to it, revised and rearranged poems, and combined
and recombined them into various sections, until his death. The first
edition comprised 95 pages of poetry accompanied by a 10-page prose
Preface; the final edition, published in 1892, was 600 pages.*

*During the Civil War, Whitman cared for wounded and dying sol-
diers in Washington, D.C. He wrote memorable poems as well as prose
pieces about his Civil War experiences and the nation's bloody ordeal,
notably "When Lilacs Last in the Dooryard Bloom'd" (included below),
his haunting elegy on the death of Abraham Lincoln, struck down by
an assassin's bullet in April 1865. Whitman's most significant prose
work, describing his fears and hopes for the nation in the aftermath of
the war, is* Democratic Vistas *(1871), excerpted here.*

*Readers throughout the world have responded to Whitman's poetry
with great affection. It is highly accessible and deeply moving, and its
expansive lines and rhythms, and profound inquiries into love and
death, American identity and democracy, have inspired and influenced
countless writers, among them Carl Sandburg, Hart Crane, William
Carlos Williams, and Allen Ginsberg.*

Not many readers encountered the first edition of Leaves of Grass.
*Some who did were immediately scandalized. One reviewer condemned
it as "a mass of stupid filth." Emily Dickinson later commented that she
had never read Whitman because she had heard he was disgraceful.
But a few select readers recognized Whitman's provocative newness as
a writer—the vibrancy of his themes, the strangely compelling form
(lacking meter and rhyme, it did not seem like poetry), and the exuberant declamations (Whitman was a devotee of the opera) that his style
and voice featured.*

*Emerson, especially, was astounded by the book, a copy of which
Whitman had sent him; he replied to Whitman in a letter, dated July
21, 1855, that begins:*

> *Dear Sir—I am not blind to the worth of the wonderful gift of*
> *Leaves of Grass. I find it the most extraordinary piece of wit and*
> *wisdom that America has yet contributed. I am very happy in read-*
> *ing it, as great power makes us happy.*

A year later, Thoreau wrote to a friend about Leaves of Grass, *which had recently been published in a second edition:*

> *[Whitman] occasionally suggests something a little more than*
> *human. You can't confound him with the other inhabitants of*
> *Brooklyn or New York. How they must shudder when they read him!*
> *He is awfully good.*

Whitman thrills and excites readers even as he disconcerts and embarrasses them—and, it is sometimes said, embarrasses himself. The critic John Jay Chapman a century ago expressed something of the ambivalence many readers harbor toward Whitman when he said he found the poetry "repellent, divine, disgusting, extraordinary."

Crude, coarse, outrageous: the British writer D. H. Lawrence, in 1921, protested that there is something "overdone" and "wrong," forced and preachy, about Whitman. Yet Lawrence also described him as "the greatest of the Americans," a writer who "has gone further, in actual living expression, than any man." He immensely valued Whitman's poetry for its sensual and erotic daring, its zest and yearning for the rewards and challenges of "the open road" (one of Whitman's favorite phrases, which Lawrence rejoiced in), and its delvings into humanity's deepest sexual secrets and needs.

Whitman is the biggest of all American poets, a celebrant and prophet of American democracy and multicultural inclusiveness. Yet he is the most intimate of American poets too; he seeks to make contact individually with each of his readers, encouraging and fortifying them, making them feel their sheer value as persons—the goodness of their desiring selves and their desirability to others. He urges his readers to overcome hesitations and scruples, and, beyond that, to embrace the truth, as he sees it—that there is no death, no end to who we are, just endless transformations of life.

On this very point, the critic Harold Bloom has stated that Whitman gives consolation to us at moments of grievous loss when no other author is able to. Through the richness and radiance of his verse, Whitman may bestow upon us the precious hope that death does not exist after all.

Whitman contains multitudes, so he professes in "Song of Myself." He is sweet, obnoxious, touching, silly, extravagant, candid, evasive, solicitous, detached, presumptuous, wise, foolish, cockily pleased with himself, and winningly modest. Whitman is the most American of poets, proclaiming in the Preface he wrote for the first edition of Leaves of

Grass: *"Of all nations the United States with veins full of poetical stuff most need poets and will doubtless have the greatest and use them the greatest."* But he is also the American poet with the most international appeal; no poet in the American tradition has won a wider readership throughout the world. The Chilean poet Pablo Neruda (1904–1973), for instance, declared his debt to Whitman: *"I must start by acknowledging myself to be the humble servant of a poet who strode the earth with long, slow paces, pausing everywhere to love, to examine, to learn, to teach and admire."*

Whitman is selfless, a lover of brotherhood and sisterhood more than a lover of himself. But he does find himself endlessly fascinating, as he reflects on each and every dimension of himself in a grand, boisterous, and sometimes humorously self-absorbed fashion. As Richard Poirier, in an essay in The New Republic *(1995),* acutely noted, Whitman is the premier *"poet of democracy,"* but even in that role he is *"among the most elusive and foxiest and most manipulative of American writers."*

An important trend in Whitman scholarship has been the study of homosexuality and homoeroticism (or both) in his life and in the work. There is no question that Whitman loved men, and it is possible, maybe probable, that he had sexual relations with them, and perhaps with women—though clear evidence for any for this is hard to come by. Some of his most beautiful writing focuses on a male speaker describing his feelings for another man or men, as in the poems below, *"When I Heard at the Close of the Day"* and *"I Saw in Louisiana a Live-Oak Growing,"* both of which first appeared in the *"Calamus"* section (celebrating manly love) of the 1860 edition of Leaves of Grass. My gay and lesbian students and friends have told me of their sense of kinship with Whitman, whose sexual themes and intimacies strike a sympathetic chord.

Yet my heterosexual students and friends feel the same way about Whitman—they also feel close to and uplifted by him. This testifies to the amazing range and complexity of Whitman's sexuality, as he explores and expresses it in his poetry. Whitman is a great gay poet, one who wrote at a time when there was no defined conception of homosexuality. As M. Jimmie Killingsworth showed in *"Whitman and the Gay American Ethos"* (2000), *"the very word 'homosexuality' did not appear until the end of the nineteenth century....The word 'gay' may have been used in Whitman's day as an underground code term...but no solid evidence exists for this early dating, and the usage certainly had no public currency."* Killingsworth's central point is that Whitman *"participated in bringing gayness into history.... He helped to invent gayness."*

We perceive ideas and feelings in Whitman's poetry that he helped to give us a language for. During his own era, his poems about love *between men did not upset readers; those who were offended by Whitman instead pointed to his "obscene" poems dealing with sexual love between men and women. Men, it was assumed, could be affectionate friends and loving comrades; what Whitman was saying and suggesting was that men could be passionately sexual lovers of one another.*

Ultimately, however, Whitman is a great poet for the sexualized selves of everyone. He is the most sexually capacious writer in American literature, rivaled in the English literary tradition only by Shakespeare.

Whitman demands to be read and studied in large terms, for the scale of his claims, assertions, and ideas. But his skillful effects from line to line must not be overlooked. As the poet-critic Randall Jarrell observed in Poetry and the Age *(1953), Whitman "was no sweeping rhetorician, but a poet of the greatest and oddest delicacy and originality and sensitivity, so far as words are concerned....How inexhaustibly interesting the world is in Whitman!"*

The opening selection here is "Song of Myself," Whitman's most important and influential poem, first published, untitled, in the 1855 edition (which is the text used below) of Leaves of Grass. *It is followed by "Crossing Brooklyn Ferry," first published in 1856 and given its final form in 1881; as Richard Chase stated, this poem is remarkable for its "pathos and musing reflection," for the speaker's "meditative self-doubt" that he explores and seeks to resolve.*

Next are two of the Calamus *poems: "When I Heard at the Close of the Day" and "I Saw in Louisiana a Live-Oak Growing" (both 1860, 1867). Then, three poems that treat aspects of the Civil War: "Vigil Strange I Kept on the Field One Night" and "A Sight in Camp in the Daybreak Gray and Dim" (both 1865, 1867), and "When Lilacs Last in the Dooryard Bloom'd" (1865–1866, 1881), Whitman's elegy on Lincoln's death, a poem that blends the speaker's sense of personal loss and the nation's wound and grief.*

The final selection is an excerpt from the prose work Democratic Vistas *(1871), where Whitman assails rampant materialism among Americans and beckons for a spiritual force, an inspired and renewed commitment to democratic idealism, that will temper and contain it.*

For biography: Justin Kaplan, Walt Whitman: A Life *(1980); Philip Callow,* From Noon to Starry Night: A Life of Walt Whitman *(1992); Jerome Loving,* Walt Whitman: The Song of Himself *(1999); and Roy Morris Jr.,* The Better Angel: Walt Whitman in the Civil War *(2000).*

For analysis of Whitman's poetry and its literary and historical contexts, see Richard Chase, Walt Whitman Reconsidered *(1955); Paul Zweig,* Walt Whitman: The Making of a Poet *(1984); David Cavitch,* My Soul and I: The Inner Life of Walt Whitman *(1985); Kerry C. Larson,* Whitman's Drama of Consensus *(1988); Betsy Erkkila,* Whitman: The Political Poet *(1989); Michael Moon,* Disseminating Whitman: Revision and Corporeality in *Leaves of Grass* (1991); Byrne*

R. S. Fone, Masculine Landscapes: Walt Whitman and the Homoerotic Text *(1992); David S. Reynolds*, Walt Whitman's America *(1995);* Breaking Bounds: Whitman and American Cultural Studies, *ed. Betsy Erkkila and Jay Grossman (1996); and Vivian R. Pollak*, The Erotic Whitman *(2000).*

Song of Myself [1855]

[1]

I celebrate myself,[1]
And what I assume you shall assume,
For every atom belonging to me as good belongs to you.

I loafe and invite my soul,
I lean and loafe at my ease .... observing a spear of summer grass.   5

[2]

Houses and rooms are full of perfumes .... the shelves are crowded
    with perfumes,
I breathe the fragrance myself, and know it and like it,
The distillation would intoxicate me also, but I shall not let it.

The atmosphere is not a perfume ....i t has no taste of the distillation
    .... it is odorless,
It is for my mouth forever .... I am in love with it,   10
I will go to the bank by the wood and become undisguised and naked,
I am mad for it to be in contact with me.

The smoke of my own breath,
Echos, ripples, and buzzed whispers .... loveroot, silkthread, crotch
    and vine,
My respiration and inspiration .... the beating of my heart .... the
    passing of blood and air through my lungs,   15
The sniff of green leaves and dry leaves, and of the shore and
    darkcolored sea-rocks, and of hay in the barn,
The sound of the belched words of my voice .... words loosed to the
    eddies of the wind,
A few light kisses .... a few embraces .... a reaching around of arms,
The play of shine and shade on the trees as the supple boughs wag,

---

[1]MYSELF: For convenience, section numbers are inserted in brackets. Whitman used this numbering in later editions but not in 1855.

The delight alone or in the rush of the streets, or along the fields and
    hillsides,   20
The feeling of health .... the full-noon trill .... the song of me rising
    from bed and meeting the sun.

Have you reckoned a thousand acres much? Have you reckoned the
    earth much?
Have you practiced so long to learn to read?
Have you felt so proud to get at the meaning of poems?

Stop this day and night with me and you shall possess the origin of all
    poems,   25
You shall possess the good of the earth and sun .... there are millions
    of suns left,
You shall no longer take things at second or third hand .... nor look
    through the eyes of the dead .... nor feed on the spectres in books,
You shall not look through my eyes either, nor take things from me,
You shall listen to all sides and filter them from yourself.

[3]
I have heard what the talkers were talking .... the talk of the
    beginning and the end,   30
But I do not talk of the beginning or the end.

There was never any more inception than there is now,
Nor any more youth or age than there is now;
And will never be any more perfection than there is now,
Nor any more heaven or hell than there is now.   35

Urge and urge and urge,
Always the procreant urge of the world.

Out of the dimness opposite equals advance .... Always substance and
    increase,
Always a knit of identity .... always distinction .... always a breed of
    life.
To elaborate is no avail .... Learned and unlearned feel that it is so. 40

Sure as the most certain sure .... plumb in the uprights, well
    entretied,[2] braced in the beams,
Stout as a horse, affectionate, haughty, electrical,
I and this mystery here we stand.

[2]ENTRETIED: Cross-braced, reinforced.

Clear and sweet is my soul .... and clear and sweet is all that is not my
   soul.

Lack one lacks both .... and the unseen is proved by the seen,   45
Till that becomes unseen and receives proof in its turn.

Showing the best and dividing it from the worst, age vexes age,
Knowing the perfect fitness and equanimity of things, while they
   discuss I am silent, and go bathe and admire myself.

Welcome is every organ and attribute of me, and of any man hearty
   and clean,
Not an inch nor a particle of an inch is vile, and none shall be less
   familiar than the rest.   50

I am satisfied .... I see, dance, laugh, sing;
As God comes a loving bedfellow and sleeps at my side all night and
   close on the peep of the day,
And leaves for me baskets covered with white towels bulging the house
   with their plenty,
Shall I postpone my acceptation and realization and scream at my
   eyes,
That they turn from gazing after and down the road,   55
And forthwith cipher[3] and show me to a cent,
Exactly the contents of one, and exactly the contents of two, and
   which is ahead?

[4]
Trippers and askers surround me,
People I meet .... the effect upon me of my early life .... of the ward
   and city I live in .... of the nation,
The latest news .... discoveries, inventions, societies .... authors old
   and new,   60
My dinner, dress, associates, looks, business, compliments, dues,
The real or fancied indifference of some man or woman I love,
The sickness of one of my folks—or of myself .... or ill-doing .... or
   loss or lack of money .... or depressions or exaltations,
They come to me days and nights and go from me again,
But they are not the Me myself.   65

---

[3]CIPHER: Calculate; perform elementary arithmetic.

Apart from the pulling and hauling stands what I am,
Stands amused, complacent, compassionating, idle, unitary,
Looks down, is erect, bends an arm on an impalpable certain rest,
Looks with its sidecurved head curious what will come next,
Both in and out of the game, and watching and wondering at it.   70

Backward I see in my own days where I sweated through fog with
    linguists and contenders,
I have no mockings or arguments .... I witness and wait.

[5]

I believe in you my soul .... the other I am must not abase[4] itself to
    you,
And you must not be abased to the other.

Loafe with me on the grass .... loose the stop[5] from your throat,   75
Not words, not music or rhyme I want .... not custom or lecture, not
    even the best,
Only the lull I like, the hum of your valved voice.

I mind how we lay in June, such a transparent summer morning;
You settled your head athwart my hips and gently turned over upon me,
And parted the shirt from my bosom-bone, and plunged your tongue
    to my barestript heart,   80
And reached till you felt my beard, and reached till you held my feet.

Swiftly arose and spread around me the peace and joy and knowledge
    that pass all the art and argument of the earth;
And I know that the hand of God is the elderhand of my own,
And I know that the spirit of God is the eldest brother of my own,
And that all the men ever born are also my brothers .... and the
    women my sisters and lovers,   85
And that a kelson[6] of the creation is love;
And limitless are leaves stiff or drooping in the fields,
And brown ants in the little wells beneath them,
And mossy scabs of the wormfence, and heaped stones, and elder and
    mullen and pokeweed.[7]

[6]

A child said, What is the grass? fetching it to me with full hands;   90

[4]ABASE: Degrade.
[5]THE STOP: The knob that turns a set of organ pipes on and off.
[6]KELSON: A beam placed inside a ship along the floor-timbers and parallel with the keel; it was used
to fasten together the floorboards and the keel.
[7]POKEWEED: A branching shrub; mullen is a fuzzy-leafed weed, and elder is a low shrub known for
its berries.

How could I answer the child? .... I do not know what it is any more
than he.

I guess it must be the flag of my disposition, out of hopeful green stuff
woven.

Or I guess it is the handkerchief of the Lord,
A scented gift and remembrancer designedly dropped,
Bearing the owner's name someway in the corners, that we may see
and remark, and say Whose?   95

Or I guess the grass is itself a child .... the produced babe of the
vegetation.

Or I guess it is a uniform hieroglyphic,[8]
And it means, Sprouting alike in broad zones and narrow zones,
Growing among black folks as among white,
Kanuck, Tuckahoe, Congressman, Cuff,[9] I give them the same, I
receive them the same.   100

And now it seems to me the beautiful uncut hair of graves.

Tenderly will I use you curling grass,
It may be you transpire from the breasts of young men,
It may be if I had known them I would have loved them;
It may be you are from old people and from women, and from
offspring taken soon out of their mothers' laps,   105
And here you are the mothers' laps.

This grass is very dark to be from the white heads of old mothers,
Darker than the colorless beards of old men,
Dark to come from under the faint red roofs of mouths.

O I perceive after all so many uttering tongues!   110
And I perceive they do not come from the roofs of mouths for nothing.

I wish I could translate the hints about the dead young men and women,
And the hints about old men and mothers, and the offspring taken
soon out of their laps.

What do you think has become of the young and old men?
And what do you think has become of the women and children?   115

---

[8]HIEROGLYPHIC: Egyptian symbol-writing, or any cryptic symbol.
[9]KANUCK, TUCKAHOE, CONGRESSMAN, CUFF: Whitman groups "congressman" with three slang
terms for ethnicities: Kanuck for a French Canadian, Tuckahoe for tidewater Virginian, Cuff (Cuffee)
for an African American.

They are alive and well somewhere;
The smallest sprout shows there is really no death,
And if ever there was it led forward life, and does not wait at the end
    to arrest it,
And ceased the moment life appeared.

All goes onward and outward .... and nothing collapses,   120
And to die is different from what any one supposed, and luckier.

[7]

Has any one supposed it lucky to be born?
I hasten to inform him or her it is just as lucky to die, and I know it.

I pass death with the dying, and birth with the new-washed babe ....
    and am not contained between my hat and boots,
And peruse manifold objects, no two alike, and every one good,   125
The earth good, and the stars good, and their adjuncts all good.

I am not an earth nor an adjunct of an earth,
I am the mate and companion of people, all just as immortal and
    fathomless as myself;
They do not know how immortal, but I know.

Every kind for itself and its own .... for me mine male and female,   130
For me all that have been boys and that love women,
For me the man that is proud and feels how it stings to be slighted,
For me the sweetheart and the old maid .... for me mothers and the
    mothers of mothers,
For me lips that have smiled, eyes that have shed tears,
For me children and the begetters of children.   135

Who need be afraid of the merge?
Undrape .... you are not guilty to me, nor stale nor discarded,
I see through the broadcloth and gingham whether or no,
And am around, tenacious, acquisitive, tireless .... and can never be
    shaken away.

[8]

The little one sleeps in its cradle,   140
I lift the gauze and look a long time, and silently brush away flies with
    my hand.

The youngster and the redfaced girl turn aside up the bushy hill,
I peeringly view them from the top.

The suicide sprawls on the bloody floor of the bedroom.
It is so .... I witnessed the corpse .... there the pistol had fallen.   145

The blab of the pave .... .the tires of carts and sluff of bootsoles and
    talk of the promenaders,
The heavy omnibus, the driver with his interrogating thumb, the clank
    of the shod horses on the granite floor,
The carnival of sleighs, the clinking and shouted jokes and pelts of
    snowballs;
The hurrahs for popular favorites .... the fury of roused mobs,
The flap of the curtained litter—the sick man inside, borne to the
    hospital,   150
The meeting of enemies, the sudden oath, the blows and fall,
The excited crowd—the policeman with his star quickly working his
    passage to the centre of the crowd;
The impassive stones that receive and return so many echoes,
The souls moving along .... are they invisible while the least atom of
    the stones is visible?
What groans of overfed or half-starved who fall on the flags sunstruck
    or in fits,   155
What exclamations of women taken suddenly, who hurry home and
    give birth to babes,
What living and buried speech is always vibrating here .... what howls
    restrained by decorum,
Arrests of criminals, slights, adulterous offers made, acceptances,
    rejections with convex lips,
I mind them or the resonance of them .... I come again and again.

  [9]

The big doors of the country-barn stand open and ready,   160
The dried grass of the harvest-time loads the slow-drawn wagon,
The clear light plays on the brown gray and green intertinged,
The armfuls are packed to the sagging mow:
I am there .... I help .... I came stretched atop of the load,
I felt its soft jolts .... one leg reclined on the other,   165
I jump from the crossbeams, and seize the clover and timothy,[10]
And roll head over heels, and tangle my hair full of wisps.

  [10]

Alone far in the wilds and mountains I hunt,
Wandering amazed at my own lightness and glee,

[10]TIMOTHY: Grass.

In the late afternoon choosing a safe spot to pass the night,   170
Kindling a fire and broiling the freshkilled game,
Soundly falling asleep on the gathered leaves, my dog and gun by my
    side.

The Yankee clipper is under her three skysails .... she cuts the sparkle
    and scud,[11]
My eyes settle the land .... I bend at her prow or shout joyously from
    the deck.

The boatmen and clamdiggers arose early and stopped for me,   175
I tucked my trowser-ends in my boots and went and had a good time,
You should have been with us that day round the chowder-kettle.

I saw the marriage of the trapper in the open air in the farwest .... the
    bride was a red girl,
Her father and his friends sat near by crosslegged and dumbly[12]
    smoking .... they had moccasins to their feet and large thick
    blankets hanging from their shoulders;
On a bank lounged the trapper .... he was dressed mostly in skins ....
    his luxuriant beard and curls protected his neck,   180
One hand rested on his rifle .... the other hand held firmly the wrist of
    the red girl,
She had long eyelashes .... her head was bare .... her coarse straight
    locks descended upon her voluptuous limbs and reached to her feet.

The runaway slave came to my house and stopped outside,
I heard his motions crackling the twigs of the woodpile,
Through the swung half-door of the kitchen I saw him limpsey and
    weak,   185
And went where he sat on a log, and led him in and assured him,
And brought water and filled a tub for his sweated body and bruised feet,
And gave him a room that entered from my own, and gave him some
    coarse clean clothes,
And remember perfectly well his revolving eyes and his awkwardness,
And remember putting plasters on the galls[13] of his neck and ankles;   190
He staid with me a week before he was recuperated and passed north,
I had him sit next me at table .... my firelock[14] leaned in the corner.

---

[11]SCUD: Sea spray.
[12]DUMBLY: Mutely.
[13]PLASTERS ON THE GALLS: A plaster is a muslin or other cloth spread with an ointment and
applied to wounds and sores. A gall is a sore or blister.
[14]FIRELOCK: Rifle.

[11]

Twenty-eight young men bathe by the shore,
Twenty-eight young men, and all so friendly,
Twenty-eight years of womanly life, and all so lonesome.   195

She owns the fine house by the rise of the bank,
She hides handsome and richly drest aft the blinds of the window.

Which of the young men does she like the best?
Ah the homeliest of them is beautiful to her.

Where are you off to, lady? for I see you,   200
You splash in the water there, yet stay stock still in your room.

Dancing and laughing along the beach came the twenty-ninth bather,
The rest did not see her, but she saw them and loved them.

The beards of the young men glistened with wet, it ran from their long
    hair,
Little streams passed all over their bodies.   205

An unseen hand also passed over their bodies,
It descended tremblingly from their temples and ribs.

The young men float on their backs, their white bellies swell to the sun
    .... they do not ask who seizes fast to them,
They do not know who puffs and declines with pendant and bending
    arch,
They do not think whom they souse[15] with spray.   210

[12]

The butcher-boy puts off his killing-clothes, or sharpens his knife at
    the stall in the market,
I loiter enjoying his repartee and his shuffle and breakdown.[16]
Blacksmiths with grimed and hairy chests environ the anvil,
Each has his main-sledge .... they are all out .... there is a great heat
    in the fire.

From the cinder-strewed threshold I follow their movements,   215
The lithe sheer of their waists plays even with their massive arms,
Overhand the hammers roll—overhand so slow—overhand so sure,
They do not hasten, each man hits in his place.

---

[15]SOUSE: Drench.
[16]REPARTEE AND HIS SHUFFLE AND BREAKDOWN: Repartee is a lively, witty conversation.
Shuffle and breakdown were popular American country dances.

[13]

The negro holds firmly the reins of his four horses .... the block swags
    underneath on its tied-over chain,
The negro that drives the huge dray of the stoneyard .... steady and
    tall he stands poised on one leg on the stringpiece,   220
His blue shirt exposes his ample neck and breast and loosens over his
    hipband,
His glance is calm and commanding .... he tosses the slouch of his hat
    away from his forehead,
The sun falls on his crispy hair and moustache .... falls on the black of
    his polish'd and perfect limbs.

I behold the picturesque giant and love him .... and I do not stop there,
I go with the team also.   225

In me the caresser of life wherever moving .... backward as well as
    forward slueing,[17]
To niches aside and junior bending.

Oxen that rattle the yoke or halt in the shade, what is that you express
    in your eyes?
It seems to me more than all the print I have read in my life.

My tread scares the wood-drake and wood-duck on my distant and
    daylong ramble,   230
They rise together, they slowly circle around.
.... I believe in those winged purposes,
And acknowledge the red yellow and white playing within me,
And consider the green and violet and the tufted crown intentional;
And do not call the tortoise unworthy because she is not something
    else,   235
And the mockingbird in the swamp never studied the gamut,[18] yet
    trills pretty well to me,
And the look of the bay mare shames silliness out of me.

[14]

The wild gander leads his flock through the cool night,
Ya-honk! he says, and sounds it down to me like an invitation;
The pert[19] may suppose it meaningless, but I listen closer,   240
I find its purpose and place up there toward the November sky.

---

[17]SLUEING: Slogging; also, twisting or turning.
[18]GAMUT: Musical scale.
[19]PERT: Expert.

The sharphoofed moose of the north, the cat on the housesill, the
    chickadee, the prairie-dog,
The litter of the grunting sow as they tug at her teats,
The brood of the turkeyhen, and she with her halfspread wings,
I see in them and myself the same old law.   245

The press of my foot to the earth springs a hundred affections,
They scorn the best I can do to relate them.

I am enamoured of growing outdoors,
Of men that live among cattle or taste of the ocean or woods,
Of the builders and steerers of ships, of the wielders of axes and
    mauls, of the drivers of horses,   250
I can eat and sleep with them week in and week out.

What is commonest and cheapest and nearest and easiest is Me,
Me going in for my chances, spending for vast returns,
Adorning myself to bestow myself on the first that will take me,
Not asking the sky to come down to my goodwill,   255
Scattering it freely forever.

    [15]

The pure contralto[20] sings in the organloft,
The carpenter dresses his plank .... the tongue of his foreplane
    whistles its wild ascending lisp,
The married and unmarried children ride home to their thanksgiving
    dinner,
The pilot seizes the king-pin, he heaves down with a strong arm,   260
The mate stands braced in the whaleboat, lance and harpoon are
    ready,
The duck-shooter walks by silent and cautious stretches,
The deacons are ordained with crossed hands at the altar,
The spinning-girl retreats and advances to the hum of the big wheel,
The farmer stops by the bars of a Sunday and looks at the oats and
    rye,   265
The lunatic is carried at last to the asylum a confirmed case,
He will never sleep any more as he did in the cot in his mother's
    bedroom;
The jour printer[21] with gray head and gaunt jaws works at his case,
He turns his quid of tobacco, his eyes get blurred with the manuscript;

---

[20]CONTRALTO: In a sung musical piece, the contralto is the lowest female voice or voice part.
[21]JOUR PRINTER: Experienced printer.

The malformed limbs are tied to the anatomist's table,   270
What is removed drops horribly in a pail;
The quadroon[22] girl is sold at the stand .... the drunkard nods by the
   barroom stove,
The machinist rolls up his sleeves .... the policeman travels his beat
   .... the gate-keeper marks who pass,
The young fellow drives the express-wagon .... I love him though I do
   not know him;
The half-breed straps on his light boots to compete in the race,   275
The western turkey-shooting draws old and young .... some lean on
   their rifles, some sit on logs,
Out from the crowd steps the marksman and takes his position and
   levels his piece;
The groups of newly-come immigrants cover the wharf or levee,
The woollypates[23] hoe in the sugarfield, the overseer views them from
   his saddle;
The bugle calls in the ballroom, the gentlemen run for their partners,
   the dancers bow to each other;   280
The youth lies awake in the cedar-roofed garret and harks to the
   musical rain.
The Wolverine[24] sets traps on the creek that helps fill the Huron,
The reformer ascends the platform, he spouts with his mouth and
   nose,
The company returns from its excursion, the darkey brings up the rear
   and bears the well-riddled target,
The squaw wrapt in her yellow-hemmed cloth is offering moccasins
   and beadbags for sale,   285
The connoisseur peers along the exhibition-gallery with halfshut eyes
   bent sideways,
The deckhands make fast the steamboat, the plank is thrown for the
   shoregoing passengers,
The young sister holds out the skein, the elder sister winds it off in a
   ball and stops now and then for the knots,
The one-year wife is recovering and happy, a week ago she bore her
   first child,
The cleanhaired Yankee girl works with her sewing-machine or in the
   factory or mill,   290

---

[22]QUADROON: One-quarter African American—that is, having one black and three white grandparents.
[23]WOOLYPATES: Tight, curly hair.
[24]WOLVERINE: A native of the state of Michigan.

The nine months' gone[25] is in the parturition chamber, her faintness
  and pains are advancing;
The pavingman leans on his twohanded rammer—the reporter's lead[26]
  flies swiftly over the notebook—the signpainter is lettering with red
  and gold,
The canal-boy trots on the towpath—the bookkeeper counts at his
  desk—the shoemaker waxes his thread,
The conductor beats time for the band and all the performers follow
  him,
The child is baptised—the convert is making the first professions,   295
The regatta is spread on the bay .... how the white sails sparkle!
The drover watches his drove, he sings out to them that would stray,
The pedlar sweats with his pack on his back—the purchaser higgles
  about the odd cent,
The camera and plate are prepared, the lady must sit for her
  daguerreotype,[27]
The bride unrumples her white dress, the minutehand of the clock
  moves slowly,   300
The opium eater reclines with rigid head and just-opened lips,
The prostitute draggles her shawl, her bonnet bobs on her tipsy and
  pimpled neck,
The crowd laugh at her blackguard oaths, the men jeer and wink to
  each other,
(Miserable! I do not laugh at your oaths nor jeer you,)
The President holds a cabinet council, he is surrounded by the great
  secretaries,   305
On the piazza walk five friendly matrons with twined arms;
The crew of the fish-smack pack repeated layers of halibut in the hold,
The Missourian crosses the plains toting his wares and his cattle,
The fare-collector goes through the train—he gives notice by the
  jingling of loose change,
The floormen are laying the floor—the tinners are tinning the roof—
  the masons are calling for mortar,   310
In single file each shouldering his hod pass onward the laborers;
Seasons pursuing each other the indescribable crowd is gathered .... it
  is the Fourth of July .... what salutes of cannon and small arms!

---

[25]NINE MONTHS' GONE: A pregnant woman about to give birth.
[26]LEAD: Pencil.
[27]DAGUERREOTYPE: A portrait made with an early form of photography invented by the French
painter and physicist Louis-Jacques Mandé Daguerre (1789–1851) in 1839.

Seasons pursuing each other the plougher ploughs and the mower
   mows and the wintergrain falls in the ground;
Off on the lakes the pikefisher watches and waits by the hole in the
   frozen surface,
The stumps stand thick round the clearing, the squatter strikes deep
   with his axe,   315
The flatboatmen make fast toward dusk near the cottonwood or
   pekantrees,
The coon-seekers go now through the regions of the Red river, or through
   those drained by the Tennessee, or through those of the Arkansas,
The torches shine in the dark that hangs on the Chattahoochee or
   Altamahaw[28];
Patriarchs sit at supper with sons and grandsons and great grandsons
   around them,
In walls of adobie, in canvass tents, rest hunters and trappers after
   their day's sport.   320
The city sleeps and the country sleeps,
The living sleep for their time .... the dead sleep for their time,
The old husband sleeps by his wife and the young husband sleeps by
   his wife;
And these one and all tend inward to me, and I tend outward to them,
And such as it is to be of these more or less I am.   325

    [16]

I am of old and young, of the foolish as much as the wise,
Regardless of others, ever regardful of others,
Maternal as well as paternal, a child as well as a man,
Stuffed with the stuff that is coarse, and stuffed with the stuff that is
   fine,
One of the great nation, the nation of many nations—the smallest the
   same and the largest the same,   330
A southerner soon as a northerner, a planter nonchalant and
   hospitable,
A Yankee bound my own way .... ready for trade .... my joints the
   limberest joints on earth and the sternest joints on earth,
A Kentuckian walking the vale of the Elkhorn in my deerskin leggings,
A boatman over the lakes or bays or along coasts .... a Hoosier, a
   Badger, a Buckeye,[29]
A Louisianian or Georgian, a poke-easy from sandhills and pines, 335

[28]CHATTAHOOCHEE OR ALTAMAHAW: Rivers in Georgia.
[29]HOOSIER, A BADGER, A BUCKEYE: Natives of Indiana, Wisconsin, and Ohio, respectively.

At home on Canadian snowshoes or up in the bush, or with fishermen
    off Newfoundland,
At home in the fleet of iceboats, sailing with the rest and tacking,
At home on the hills of Vermont or in the woods of Maine or the Texan
    ranch,
Comrade of Californians .... comrade of free northwesterners, loving
    their big proportions,
Comrade of raftsmen and coalmen—comrade of all who shake hands
    and welcome to drink and meat;   340
A learner with the simplest, a teacher of the thoughtfulest,
A novice beginning experient of myriads of seasons,
Of every hue and trade and rank, of every caste and religion,
Not merely of the New World but of Africa Europe or Asia .... a
    wandering savage,
A farmer, mechanic, or artist .... a gentleman, sailor, lover or quaker, 345
A prisoner, fancy-man, rowdy, lawyer, physician or priest.
I resist anything better than my own diversity,
And breathe the air and leave plenty after me,
And am not stuck up, and am in my place.

The moth and the fisheggs are in their place,   350
The suns I see and the suns I cannot see are in their place,
The palpable is in its place and the impalpable is in its place.

    [17]
These are the thoughts of all men in all ages and lands, they are not
    original with me,
If they are not yours as much as mine they are nothing or next to
    nothing,
If they do not enclose everything they are next to nothing,   355
If they are not the riddle and the untying of the riddle they are
    nothing,
If they are not just as close as they are distant they are nothing.

This is the grass that grows wherever the land is and the water is,
This is the common air that bathes the globe.

This is the breath of laws and songs and behaviour,   360
This is the tasteless water of souls .... this is the true sustenance,
It is for the illiterate .... it is for the judges of the supreme court .... it
    is for the federal capitol and the state capitols,
It is for the admirable communes of literary men and composers and
    singers and lecturers and engineers and savans,
It is for the endless races of working people and farmers and seamen.

[18]

This is the trill of a thousand clear cornets and scream of the octave
    flute and strike of triangles.   365

I play not a march for victors only .... I play great marches for
    conquered and slain persons.

Have you heard that it was good to gain the day?
I also say it is good to fall .... battles are lost in the same spirit in
    which they are won.

I sound triumphal drums for the dead .... I fling through my
    embouchures[30] the loudest and gayest music to them,
Vivas to those who have failed, and to those whose war-vessels sank in
    the sea, and those themselves who sank in the sea,   370
And to all generals that lost engagements, and all overcome heroes, and
    the numberless unknown heroes equal to the greatest heroes known.

[19]

This is the meal pleasantly set .... this is the meat and drink for
    natural hunger,
It is for the wicked just the same as the righteous .... I make
    appointments with all,
I will not have a single person slighted or left away,
The keptwoman and sponger and thief are hereby invited .... the
    heavy-lipped slave is invited .... the venerealee[31] is invited,   375
There shall be no difference between them and the rest.

This is the press of a bashful hand .... this is the float and odor of hair,
This is the touch of my lips to yours .... this is the murmur of
    yearning,
This is the far-off depth and height reflecting my own face,
This is the thoughtful merge of myself and the outlet again.   380

Do you guess I have some intricate purpose?
Well I have .... for the April rain has, and the mica on the side of a
    rock has.

Do you take it I would astonish?
Does the daylight astonish? or the early redstart twittering through the
    woods?
Do I astonish more than they?   385

[30]EMBOUCHURES: Puckering of the lips to play a woodwind instrument.
[31]VENEREALEE: A person with a venereal disease.

This hour I tell things in confidence,
I might not tell everybody but I will tell you.

[20]

Who goes there! hankering, gross, mystical, nude?
How is it I extract strength from the beef I eat?

What is a man anyhow? What am I? and what are you?   390
All I mark as my own you shall offset it with your own,
Else it were time lost listening to me.

I do not snivel that snivel the world over,
That months are vacuums and the ground but wallow and filth,
That life is a suck and a sell, and nothing remains at the end but
    threadbare crape and tears.   395

Whimpering and truckling fold with powders[32] for invalids ....
    conformity goes to the fourth-removed,
I cock my hat as I please indoors or out.

Shall I pray? Shall I venerate and be ceremonious?

I have pried through the strata and analyzed to a hair,
And counselled with doctors and calculated close and found no
    sweeter fat than sticks to my own bones.   400

In all people I see myself, none more and not one a barleycorn less,
And the good or bad I say of myself I say of them.

And I know I am solid and sound,
To me the converging objects of the universe perpetually flow,
All are written to me, and I must get what the writing means.   405

And I know I am deathless,
I know this orbit of mine cannot be swept by a carpenter's compass,
I know I shall not pass like a child's carlacue[33] cut with a burnt stick
    at night.

I know I am august,
I do not trouble my spirit to vindicate itself or be understood,   410
I see that the elementary laws never apologize,
I reckon I behave no prouder than the level I plant my house by
    after all.

---

[32]POWDERS: Powdered medicine.
[33]CARLACUE: Curlique; a fancy twist or twirl.

I exist as I am, that is enough,
If no other in the world be aware I sit content,
And if each and all be aware I sit content.   415

One world is aware, and by far the largest to me, and that is myself,
And whether I come to my own today or in ten thousand or ten
    million years,
I can cheerfully take it now, or with equal cheerfulness I can wait.

My foothold is tenoned and mortised in granite,[34]
I laugh at what you call dissolution,   420
And I know the amplitude of time.

[21]

I am the poet of the body,
And I am the poet of the soul.

The pleasures of heaven are with me, and the pains of hell are with
    me,
The first I graft and increase upon myself …. the latter I translate into
    a new tongue.   425

I am the poet of the woman the same as the man,
And I say it is as great to be a woman as to be a man,
And I say there is nothing greater than the mother of men.

I chant a new chant of dilation or pride,
We have had ducking[35] and deprecating about enough,   430
I show that size is only development.

Have you outstript the rest? Are you the President?
It is a trifle …. they will more than arrive there every one, and still
    pass on.

I am he that walks with the tender and growing night;
I call to the earth and sea half-held by the night.   435

Press close barebosomed night! Press close magnetic nourishing night!
Night of south winds! Night of the large few stars!
Still nodding night! Mad naked summer night!

---

[34]TENONED AND MORTISED IN GRANITE: Wedge-cuts in separate pieces of wood that form a
tight joint when fitted together.
[35]DUCKING: A form of punishment used since the Middle Ages in which the offender was tied to a
chair or stool and dunked in a river or pond.

Smile O voluptuous coolbreathed earth!
Earth of the slumbering and liquid trees!   440
Earth of departed sunset! Earth of the mountains misty-topt!
Earth of the vitreous pour of the full moon just tinged with blue!
Earth of shine and dark mottling the tide of the river!
Earth of the limpid gray of clouds brighter and clearer for my sake!
Far-swooping elbowed earth! Rich apple-blossomed earth!   445
Smile, for your lover comes!

Prodigal! you have given me love! .... therefore I to you give love!
O unspeakable passionate love!

Thruster holding me tight and that I hold tight!
We hurt each other as the bridegroom and the bride hurt each other.[36] 450

[22]

You sea! I resign myself to you also .... I guess what you mean,
I behold from the beach your crooked inviting fingers,
I believe you refuse to go back without feeling of me;
We must have a turn together .... I undress .... hurry me out of sight
    of the land,
Cushion me soft .... rock me in billowy drowse,   455
Dash me with amorous wet .... I can repay you.

Sea of stretched ground-swells!
Sea breathing broad and convulsive breaths!
Sea of the brine of life! Sea of unshovelled and always-ready graves!
Howler and scooper of storms! Capricious and dainty sea!   460
I am integral with you .... I too am of one phase and of all phases.

Partaker of influx and efflux .... extoler of hate and conciliation,
Extoler of amies[37] and those that sleep in each others' arms.

I am he attesting sympathy;
Shall I make my list of things in the house and skip the house that
    supports them?   465

I am the poet of commonsense and of the demonstrable and of
    immortality;
And am not the poet of goodness only .... I do not decline to be the
    poet of wickedness also.

[36]EACH OTHER: Whitman did not include these two lines in later editions.
[37]EXTOLER OF AMIES: One who praises his or her friends.

Washes and razors for foofoos[38] .... for me freckles and a bristling beard.

What blurt is it about virtue and about vice?
Evil propels me, and reform of evil propels me .... I stand
    indifferent,   470
My gait is no faultfinder's or rejecter's gait,
I moisten the roots of all that has grown.

Did you fear some scrofula[39] out of the unflagging pregnancy?
Did you guess the celestial laws are yet to be worked over and rectified?

I step up to say that what we do is right and what we affirm is right
    .... and some is only the ore of right,   475
Witnesses of us .... one side a balance and the antipodal side a balance,
Soft doctrine as steady help as stable doctrine,
Thoughts and deeds of the present our rouse and early start.

This minute that comes to me over the past decillions,
There is no better than it and now.   480

What behaved well in the past or behaves well today is not such a
    wonder,
The wonder is always and always how there can be a mean man or an
    infidel.[40]

[23]
Endless unfolding of words of ages!
And mine a word of the modern .... a word en masse.[41]

A word of the faith that never balks,   485
One time as good as another time .... here or henceforward it is all the
    same to me.

A word of reality .... materialism first and last imbueing.
Hurrah for positive science! Long live exact demonstration!
Fetch stonecrop and mix it with cedar and branches of lilac;
This is the lexicographer or chemist .... this made a grammar of the
    old cartouches,[42]   490
These mariners put the ship through dangerous unknown seas,
This is the geologist, and this works with the scalpel, and this is a
    mathematician.

[38]FOOFOOS: Persons of no significance, fools.
[39]SCROFULA: A tubercular disease usually affecting the young and spread via the unpasteurized milk of infected cows.
[40]INFIDEL: Nonbeliever; a term usually applied to non-Christians.
[41]EN MASSE: All at once.
[42]CARTOUCHES: Oblong characters representing the names of ancient Egyptian rulers or deities.

Gentlemen I receive you, and attach and clasp hands with you,
The facts are useful and real .... they are not my dwelling .... I enter
    by them to an area of the dwelling.

I am less the reminder of property or qualities, and more the reminder
    of life,   495
And go on the square for my own sake and for others' sakes,
And make short account of neuters and geldings, and favor men and
    women fully equipped,
And beat the gong of revolt, and stop with fugitives and them that plot
    and conspire.

    [24]

Walt Whitman, an American, one of the roughs, a kosmos,[43]
Disorderly fleshy and sensual .... eating drinking and breeding,   500
No sentimentalist .... no stander above men and women or apart from
    them .... no more modest than immodest.

Unscrew the locks from the doors!
Unscrew the doors themselves from their jambs!

Whoever degrades another degrades me .... and whatever is done or
    said returns at last to me,
And whatever I do or say I also return.   505

Through me the afflatus[44] surging and surging .... through me the
    current and index.

I speak the password primeval .... I give the sign of democracy;
By God! I will accept nothing which all cannot have their counterpart
    of on the same terms.

Through me many long dumb voices,

Voices of the interminable generations of slaves,   510
Voices of prostitutes and of deformed persons,
Voices of the diseased and despairing, and of thieves and dwarfs,
Voices of cycles of preparation and accretion,
And of the threads that connect the stars—and of wombs, and of the
    fatherstuff,
And of the rights of them the others are down upon,   515
Of the trivial and flat and foolish and despised,
Of fog in the air and beetles rolling balls of dung.

[43]KOSMOS: The harmonious system of the universe.
[44]AFFLATUS: Inspiration.

Through me forbidden voices,
Voices of sexes and lusts .... voices veiled, and I remove the veil,
Voices indecent by me clarified and transfigured.   520

I do not press my finger across my mouth,
I keep as delicate around the bowels as around the head and heart,
Copulation is no more rank to me than death is.

I believe in the flesh and the appetites,
Seeing hearing and feeling are miracles, and each part and tag of me
    is a miracle.   525

Divine am I inside and out, and I make holy whatever I touch or am
    touched from;
The scent of these arm-pits is aroma finer than prayer,
This head is more than churches or bibles or creeds.

If I worship any particular thing it shall be some of the spread of my
    body;
Translucent mould of me it shall be you,   530
Shaded ledges and rests, firm masculine coulter,[45] it shall be you,

Whatever goes to the tilth[46] of me it shall be you,
You my rich blood, your milky stream pale strippings of my life;
Breast that presses against other breasts it shall be you,
My brain it shall be your occult convolutions,   535
Root of washed sweet-flag, timorous pond-snipe, nest of guarded
    duplicate eggs, it shall be you,
Mixed tussled hay of head and beard and brawn it shall be you,
Trickling sap of maple, fibre of manly wheat, it shall be you;
Sun so generous it shall be you,
Vapors lighting and shading my face it shall be you,   540
You sweaty brooks and dews it shall be you,
Winds whose soft-tickling genitals rub against me it shall be you,
Broad muscular fields, branches of liveoak, loving lounger in my
    winding paths, it shall be you,
Hands I have taken, face I have kissed, mortal I have ever touched, it
    shall be you.

I dote on myself .... there is that lot of me, and all so luscious,   545
Each moment and whatever happens thrills me with joy.

---

[45]COULTER: The iron blade fixed in front of the share in a plough that makes a vertical cut in the soil.
[46]TILTH: Tilled soil.

I cannot tell how my ankles bend .... nor whence the cause of my
faintest wish,
Nor the cause of the friendship I emit .... nor the cause of the
friendship I take again.

To walk up my stoop is unaccountable .... I pause to consider if it
really be,
That I eat and drink is spectacle enough for the great authors and
schools,   550
A morning-glory at my window satisfies me more than the
metaphysics of books.

To behold the daybreak!
The little light fades the immense and diaphanous shadows,
The air tastes good to my palate.

Hefts of the moving world at innocent gambols,[47] silently rising,
freshly exuding,
Scooting obliquely high and low.   555

Something I cannot see puts upward libidinous prongs,
Seas of bright juice suffuse heaven.

The earth by the sky staid with .... the daily close of their junction,
The heaved challenge from the east that moment over my head,   560
The mocking taunt, See then whether you shall be master!

[25]

Dazzling and tremendous how quick the sunrise would kill me,
If I could not now and always send sunrise out of me.

We also ascend dazzling and tremendous as the sun,
We found our own my soul in the calm and cool of the daybreak.   565
My voice goes after what my eyes cannot reach,
With the twirl of my tongue I encompass worlds and volumes of worlds.

Speech is the twin of my vision .... it is unequal to measure itself.

It provokes me forever,
It says sarcastically, Walt, you understand enough .... why don't you
let it out then?   570

Come now I will not be tantalized .... you conceive too much of
articulation.

[47]GAMBOLS: Leaps about playfully; typically applied to young animals and children.

Do you not know how the buds beneath are folded?
Waiting in gloom protected by frost,
The dirt receding before my prophetical screams,
I underlying causes to balance them at last,   575
My knowledge my live parts .... it keeping tally with the meaning of
    things,
Happiness .... which whoever hears me let him or her set out in search
    of this day.

My final merit I refuse you .... I refuse putting from me the best I am.

Encompass worlds but never try to encompass me,
I crowd your noisiest talk by looking toward you.   580

Writing and talk do not prove me,
I carry the plenum[48] of proof and every thing else in my face,
With the hush of my lips I confound the topmost skeptic.

[26]

I think I will do nothing for a long time but listen,
And accrue what I hear into myself .... and let sounds contribute
    toward me.   585

I hear the bravuras[49] of birds .... the bustle of growing wheat ....
    gossip of flames .... clack of sticks cooking my meals.

I hear the sound of the human voice .... a sound I love,
I hear all sounds as they are tuned to their uses .... sounds of the city
    and sounds out of the city .... sounds of the day and night;
Talkative young ones to those that like them .... the recitative of fish-
    pedlars and fruit-pedlars .... the loud laugh of workpeople at their
    meals,
The angry base of disjointed friendship .... the faint tones of the sick, 590
The judge with hands tight to the desk, his shaky lips pronouncing a
    death-sentence,
The heave'e'yo of stevedores unlading ships by the wharves .... the
    refrain of the anchor-lifters;
The ring of alarm-bells .... the cry of fire .... the whirr of swift-
    streaking engines and hose-carts with premonitory tinkles and
    colored lights,
The steam-whistle .... the solid roll of the train of approaching cars;

[48]PLENUM: Fullness.
[49]BRAVURAS: Musical passages that require skill and spirit in their execution.

The slow-march played at night at the head of the association,   595
They go to guard some corpse …. the flag-tops are draped with black
    muslin.

I hear the violincello or man's heart's complaint,[50]
And hear the keyed cornet or else the echo of sunset.

I hear the chorus …. it is a grand-opera …. this indeed is music!

A tenor large and fresh as the creation fills me,   600
The orbic flex of his mouth is pouring and filling me full.

I hear the trained soprano …. she convulses me like the climax of my
    love-grip;[51]
The orchestra whirls me wider than Uranus flies,
It wrenches unnamable ardors from my breast,
It throbs me to gulps of the farthest down horror,   605
It sails me …. I dab with bare feet …. they are licked by the indolent
    waves,
I am exposed …. cut by bitter and poisoned hail,
Steeped amid honeyed morphine …. my windpipe squeezed in the
    fakes[52] of death,
Let up again to feel the puzzle of puzzles,
And that we call Being.   610

[27]

To be in any form, what is that?
If nothing lay more developed the quahaug and its callous shell were
    enough.

Mine is no callous shell,
I have instant conductors all over me whether I pass or stop,
They seize every object and lead it harmlessly through me.   615

I merely stir, press, feel with my fingers, and am happy,
To touch my person to some one else's is about as much as I can stand.

[28]

Is this then a touch? …. quivering me to a new identity,
Flames and ether making a rush for my veins,

---

[50]COMPLAINT: Lament.
[51]SHE…LOVE-GRIP: Not included in later editions.
[52]THE FAKES: Coiled ropes.

Treacherous tip of me reaching and crowding to help them,   620
My flesh and blood playing out lightning, to strike what is hardly
  different from myself,
On all sides prurient provokers stiffening my limbs,
Straining the udder of my heart for its withheld drip,
Behaving licentious toward me, taking no denial,
Depriving me of my best as for a purpose,   625
Unbuttoning my clothes and holding me by the bare waist,
Deluding my confusion with the calm of the sunlight and pasture fields,
Immodestly sliding the fellow-senses away,
They bribed to swap off with touch, and go and graze at the edges of me,
No consideration, no regard for my draining strength or my anger,   630
Fetching the rest of the herd around to enjoy them awhile,
Then all uniting to stand on a headland and worry me.

The sentries desert every other part of me,
They have left me helpless to a red marauder,
They all come to the headland to witness and assist against me.   635

I am given up by traitors;
I talk wildly .... I have lost my wits .... I and nobody else am the
  greatest traitor,
I went myself first to the headland .... my own hands carried me there.

You villain touch! what are you doing? .... my breath is tight in its throat;
Unclench your floodgates! you are too much for me.   640

  [29]
Blind loving wrestling touch! Sheathed hooded sharptoothed touch!
Did it make you ache so leaving me?

Parting tracked by arriving .... perpetual payment of the perpetual loan,
Rich showering rain, and recompense richer afterward.

Sprouts take and accumulate .... stand by the curb prolific and vital,   645
Landscapes projected masculine full-sized and golden.

  [30]
All truths wait in all things,
They neither hasten their own delivery nor resist it,
They do not need the obstetric forceps of the surgeon,
The insignificant is as big to me as any,   650
What is less or more than a touch?

Logic and sermons never convince,
The damp of the night drives deeper into my soul.

Only what proves itself to every man and woman is so,
Only what nobody denies is so.   655

A minute and a drop of me settle my brain;
I believe the soggy clods shall become lovers and lamps,
And a compend of compends[53] is the meat of a man or woman,
And a summit and flower there is the feeling they have for each other,
And they are to branch boundlessly out of that lesson until it becomes
      omnific,[54]   660
And until every one shall delight us, and we them.

      [31]

I believe a leaf of grass is no less than the journeywork of the stars,
And the pismire[55] is equally perfect, and a grain of sand, and the egg
      of the wren,
And the tree-toad is a chef-d'oeuvre for the highest,
And the running blackberry would adorn the parlors of heaven,   665
And the narrowest hinge in my hand puts to scorn all machinery,
And the cow crunching with depressed head surpasses any statue,
And a mouse is miracle enough to stagger sextillions of infidels,
And I could come every afternoon of my life to look at the farmer's girl
      boiling her iron tea-kettle and baking shortcake.

I find I incorporate gneiss[56] and coal and long-threaded moss and
      fruits and grains and esculent roots,   670
And am stucco'd with quadrupeds and birds all over,
And have distanced what is behind me for good reasons,
And call any thing close again when I desire it.

In vain the speeding or shyness,
In vain the plutonic rocks send their old heat against my approach, 675
In vain the mastodon retreats beneath its own powdered bones,
In vain objects stand leagues off and assume manifold shapes,
In vain the ocean settling in hollows and the great monsters lying low,
In vain the buzzard houses herself with the sky,

---

[53]COMPENDS: A compendium is an abridgement of a larger work; a compend of compends would
therefore be the most concise of abstracts.
[54]OMNIFIC: All-creating.
[55]PISMIRE: Ant.
[56]GNEISS: Metamorphic rock.

In vain the snake slides through the creepers and logs,   680
In vain the elk takes to the inner passes of the woods,
In vain the razorbilled auk sails far north to Labrador,
I follow quickly .... I ascend to the nest in the fissure of the cliff.

[32]

I think I could turn and live awhile with the animals .... they are so
    placid and self-contained,
I stand and look at them sometimes half the day long.   685

They do not sweat and whine about their condition,
They do not lie awake in the dark and weep for their sins,
They do not make me sick discussing their duty to God,
Not one is dissatisfied .... not one is demented with the mania of
    owning things,
Not one kneels to another nor to his kind that lived thousands of years
    ago,   690
Not one is respectable or industrious over the whole earth.

So they show their relations to me and I accept them;
They bring me tokens of myself .... they evince them plainly in their
    possession.

I do not know where they got those tokens,
I must have passed that way untold times ago and negligently dropt
    them,   695
Myself moving forward then and now and forever,
Gathering and showing more always and with velocity,
Infinite and omnigenous[57] and the like of these among them;
Not too exclusive toward the reachers of my remembrancers,
Picking out here one that shall be my amie,[58]   700
Choosing to go with him on brotherly terms.

A gigantic beauty of a stallion, fresh and responsive to my caresses,
Head high in the forehead and wide between the ears,
Limbs glossy and supple, tail dusting the ground,
Eyes well apart and full of sparkling wickedness .... ears finely cut
    and flexibly moving.   705

His nostrils dilate .... my heels embrace him .... his well built limbs
    tremble with pleasure .... we speed around and return.

---

[57]OMNIGENOUS: Of all kinds.
[58]AMIE: A female friend. (French) But note the next line.

I but use you a moment and then I resign you stallion .... and do not
    need your paces, and outgallop them,
And myself as I stand or sit pass faster than you.

[33]

Swift wind! Space! My Soul! Now I know it is true what I guessed at;
What I guessed when I loafed on the grass,   710
What I guessed while I lay alone in my bed .... and again as I walked
    the beach under the paling stars of the morning.

My ties and ballast leave me .... I travel .... I sail .... my elbows rest in
    the sea-gaps,
I skirt the sierras .... my palms cover continents,
I am afoot with my vision.

By the city's quadrangular houses .... in log-huts, or camping with
    lumbermen,   715
Along the ruts of the turnpike .... along the dry gulch and rivulet bed,
Hoeing my onion-patch, and rows of carrots and parsnips .... crossing
    savannas .... trailing in forests,
Prospecting .... gold-digging .... girdling the trees of a new purchase,
Scorched ankle-deep by the hot sand .... hauling my boat down the
    shallow river;
Where the panther walks to and fro on a limb overhead .... where the
    buck turns furiously at the hunter,   720
Where the rattlesnake suns his flabby length on a rock .... where the
    otter is feeding on fish,
Where the alligator in his tough pimples sleeps by the bayou,
Where the black bear is searching for roots or honey .... where the
    beaver pats the mud with his paddle-tail;
Over the growing sugar .... over the cottonplant .... over the rice in its
    low moist field;
Over the sharp-peaked farmhouse with its scalloped scum and slender
    shoots from the gutters;   725
Over the western persimmon .... over the longleaved corn and the
    delicate blueflowered flax;
Over the white and brown buckwheat, a hummer and a buzzer there
    with the rest,
Over the dusky green of the rye as it ripples and shades in the breeze;
Scaling mountains .... pulling myself cautiously up .... holding on by
    low scragged limbs,

Walking the path worn in the grass and beat through the leaves of the
    brush;   730
Where the quail is whistling betwixt the woods and the wheatlot,
Where the bat flies in the July eve .... where the great goldbug drops
    through the dark;
Where the flails keep time on the barn floor,
Where the brook puts out of the roots of the old tree and flows to the
    meadow,
Where cattle stand and shake away flies with the tremulous
    shuddering of their hides,   735
Where the cheese-cloth hangs in the kitchen, and andirons straddle the
    hearth-slab, and cobwebs fall in festoons from the rafters;
Where triphammers[59] crash .... where the press is whirling its
    cylinders;
Wherever the human heart beats with terrible throes out of its ribs;
Where the pear-shaped balloon is floating aloft .... floating in it myself
    and looking composedly down;
Where the life-car[60] is drawn on the slipnoose .... where the heat
    hatches pale-green eggs in the dented sand,   740
Where the she-whale swims with her calves and never forsakes them,
Where the steamship trails hindways its long pennant of smoke,
Where the ground-shark's fin cuts like a black chip out of the water,
Where the half-burned brig is riding on unknown currents,
Where shells grow to her slimy deck, and the dead are corrupting
    below;   745
Where the striped and starred flag is borne at the head of the regiments;
Approaching Manhattan, up by the long-stretching island,
Under Niagara, the cataract falling like a veil over my countenance;
Upon a door-step .... upon the horse-block of hard wood outside,
Upon the race-course, or enjoying pic-nics or jigs or a good game of
    base-ball,   750
At he-festivals with blackguard jibes and ironical license and bull-
    dances and drinking and laughter,
At the cider-mill, tasting the sweet of the brown sqush .... sucking the
    juice through a straw,
At apple-pealings, wanting kisses for all the red fruit I find,
At musters and beach-parties and friendly bees and huskings and
    house-raisings;

59TRIPHAMMERS: Massive machine hammers.
60LIFE-CAR: A sea-rescue boat.

Where the mockingbird sounds his delicious gurgles, and cackles and
  screams and weeps,   755
Where the hay-rick stands in the barnyard, and the dry-stalks are
  scattered, and the brood cow waits in the hovel,
Where the bull advances to do his masculine work, and the stud to the
  mare, and the cock is treading the hen,
Where the heifers browse, and the geese nip their food with short jerks;
Where the sundown shadows lengthen over the limitless and lonesome
  prairie,
Where the herds of buffalo make a crawling spread of the square miles
  far and near;   760
Where the hummingbird shimmers .... where the neck of the longlived
  swan is curving and winding;
Where the laughing-gull scoots by the slappy shore and laughs her
  near-human laugh;
Where beehives range on a gray bench in the garden half-hid by the
  high weeds;
Where the band-necked partridges roost in a ring on the ground with
  their heads out;
Where burial coaches enter the arched gates of a cemetery;   765
Where winter wolves bark amid wastes of snow and icicled trees;
Where the yellow-crowned heron comes to the edge of the marsh at
  night and feeds upon small crabs;
Where the splash of swimmers and divers cools the warm noon;
Where the katydid[61] works her chromatic reed on the walnut-tree over
  the well;
Through patches of citrons and cucumbers with silver-wired leaves,   770
Through the salt-lick or orange glade .... or under conical firs;
Through the gymnasium .... through the curtained saloon .... through
  the office or public hall;
Pleased with the native and pleased with the foreign .... pleased with
  the new and old,
Pleased with women, the homely as well as the handsome,
Pleased with the quakeress as she puts off her bonnet and talks
  melodiously,   775
Pleased with the primitive tunes of the choir of the whitewashed church,
Pleased with the earnest words of the sweating Methodist preacher, or
  any preacher .... looking seriously at the camp-meeting;

---

[61]KATYDID: A large longhorn grasshopper common in the eastern and central United States.

Looking in at the shop-windows in Broadway the whole forenoon ....
  pressing the flesh of my nose to the thick plate-glass,
Wandering the same afternoon with my face turned up to the clouds;
My right and left arms round the sides of two friends and I in the
  middle;   780
Coming home with the bearded and dark-cheeked bush-boy .... riding
  behind him at the drape of the day;
Far from the settlements studying the print of animals' feet, or the
  moccasin print;
By the cot in the hospital reaching lemonade to a feverish patient,
By the coffined corpse when all is still, examining with a candle;
Voyaging to every port to dicker and adventure;   785
Hurrying with the modern crowd, as eager and fickle as any,
Hot toward one I hate, ready in my madness to knife him;
Solitary at midnight in my back yard, my thoughts gone from me a
  long while,
Walking the old hills of Judea[62] with the beautiful gentle god by my side;
Speeding through space .... speeding through heaven and the stars,   790
Speeding amid the seven satellites and the broad ring and the
  diameter of eighty thousand miles,
Speeding with tailed meteors .... throwing fire-balls like the rest,
Carrying the crescent child that carries its own full mother in its belly;
Storming enjoying planning loving cautioning,
Backing and filling, appearing and disappearing,   795
I tread day and night such roads.

I visit the orchards of God and look at the spheric product,
And look at quintillions[63] ripened, and look at quintillions green.

I fly the flight of the fluid and swallowing soul,
My course runs below the soundings of plummets.   800

I help myself to material and immaterial,
No guard can shut me off, no law can prevent me.

I anchor my ship for a little while only,
My messengers continually cruise away or bring their returns to me.

I go hunting polar furs and the seal .... leaping chasms with a pike-
  pointed staff .... clinging to topples of brittle and blue.   805

---

[62]JUDEA: Biblically, an area in southern Israel.
[63]QUINTILLIONS: A million squared; 1,000,000,000,000,000,000,000.

I ascend to the foretruck .... I take my place late at night in the crow's
  nest .... we sail through the arctic sea .... it is plenty light enough,
Through the clear atmosphere I stretch around on the wonderful
  beauty,
The enormous masses of ice pass me and I pass them .... the scenery is
  plain in all directions,
The white-topped mountains point up in the distance .... I fling out
  my fancies toward them;
We are about approaching some great battlefield in which we are soon
  to be engaged,   810
We pass the colossal outposts of the encampments .... we pass with
  still feet and caution;
Or we are entering by the suburbs some vast and ruined city .... the
  blocks and fallen architecture more than all the living cities of the
  globe.

I am a free companion .... I bivouac by invading watchfires.

I turn the bridegroom out of bed and stay with the bride myself,   815
And tighten her all night to my thighs and lips.

My voice is the wife's voice, the screech by the rail of the stairs,
They fetch my man's body up dripping and drowned.

I understand the large hearts of heroes,
The courage of present times and all times;
How the skipper saw the crowded and rudderless wreck of the
  steamship, and death chasing it up and down the storm,   820
How he knuckled tight and gave not back one inch, and was faithful
  of days and faithful of nights,
And chalked in large letters on a board, Be of good cheer, We will not
  desert you;
How he saved the drifting company at last,
How the lank loose-gowned women looked when boated from the side
  of their prepared graves,
How the silent old-faced infants, and the lifted sick, and the sharp-
  lipped unshaved men;   825
All this I swallow and it tastes good .... I like it well, and it becomes
  mine,
I am the man .... I suffered .... I was there.

The disdain and calmness of martyrs,
The mother condemned for a witch and burnt with dry wood, and her
  children gazing on;

The hounded slave that flags in the race and leans by the fence,
    blowing and covered with sweat,   830
The twinges that sting like needles his legs and neck,
The murderous buckshot and the bullets,
All these I feel or am.

I am the hounded slave …. I wince at the bite of the dogs,
Hell and despair are upon me …. crack and again crack the
    marksmen,   835
I clutch the rails of the fence …. my gore dribs thinned with the ooze
    of my skin,
I fall on the weeds and stones,
The riders spur their unwilling horses and haul close,
They taunt my dizzy ears …. they beat me violently over the head
    with their whip-stocks.

Agonies are one of my changes of garments;   840
I do not ask the wounded person how he feels …. I myself become the
    wounded person,
My hurt turns livid upon me as I lean on a cane and observe.

I am the mashed fireman with breastbone broken …. tumbling walls
    buried me in their debris,
Heat and smoke I inspired[64]…. I heard the yelling shouts of my comrades,
I heard the distant click of their picks and shovels;   845
They have cleared the beams away …. they tenderly lift me forth.

I lie in the night air in my red shirt …. the pervading hush is for my sake,
Painless after all I lie, exhausted but not so unhappy,
White and beautiful are the faces around me …. the heads are bared
    of their fire-caps,
The kneeling crowd fades with the light of the torches.   850

Distant and dead resuscitate,
They show as the dial or move as the hands of me …. and I am the
    clock myself.

I am an old artillerist, and tell of some fort's bombardment …. and am
    there again.

Again the reveille of drummers …. again the attacking cannon and
    mortars and howitzers,[65]
Again the attacked send their cannon responsive.   855

[64]INSPIRED: Breathed in.
[65]HOWITZERS: A lightweight missile engine, designed to fire shells horizontally.

I take part .... I see and hear the whole,
The cries and curses and roar .... the plaudits[66] for well aimed shots,
The ambulanza slowly passing and trailing its red drip,
Workmen searching after damages and to make indispensible repairs,
The fall of grenades through the rent roof .... the fan-shaped
   explosion,   860
The whizz of limbs heads stone wood and iron high in the air.

Again gurgles the mouth of my dying general .... he furiously waves
   with his hand,
He gasps through the clot .... Mind not me .... mind .... the
   entrenchments.

[34]

I tell not the fall of Alamo[62] .... not one escaped to tell the fall of
   Alamo,
The hundred and fifty are dumb yet at Alamo.   865

Hear now the tale of a jetblack sunrise,
Hear of the murder in cold blood of four hundred and twelve young men.
Retreating they had formed in a hollow square with their baggage for
   breastworks,
Nine hundred lives out of the surrounding enemy's nine times their
   number was the price they took in advance,
Their colonel was wounded and their ammunition gone,   870
They treated for an honorable capitulation, received writing and seal,
   gave up their arms, and marched back prisoners of war.

They were the glory of the race of rangers,
Matchless with a horse, a rifle, a song, a supper, or a courtship,
Large, turbulent, brave, handsome, generous, proud and affectionate,
Bearded, sunburnt, dressed in the free costume of hunters,   875
Not a single one over thirty years of age.

The second Sunday morning they were brought out in squads and
   massacred .... it was beautiful early summer,
The work commenced about five o'clock and was over by eight.

None obeyed the command to kneel,
Some made a mad and helpless rush .... some stood stark and straight, 880

66PLAUDITS: Applause.
67I TELL NOT THE FALL OF ALAMO: After the fall of the Alamo in San Antonio, Texas, in 1836,
the Mexican general Santa Anna (1794–1876) had 330 Texas revolutionaries executed. The heroic
resistance by those at the Alamo roused many Texans to fight back ("Remember the Alamo!"), and
six weeks later they defeated the Mexicans at San Jacinto.

A few fell at once, shot in the temple or heart .... the living and dead
    lay together,
The maimed and mangled dug in the dirt .... the new-comers saw
    them there;
Some half-killed attempted to crawl away,
These were dispatched with bayonets or battered with the blunts of
    muskets;
A youth not seventeen years old seized his assassin till two more came
    to release him,   885
The three were all torn, and covered with the boy's blood.

At eleven o'clock began the burning of the bodies;
And that is the tale of the murder of the four hundred and twelve
    young men,
And that was a jetblack sunrise.

    [35]
Did you read in the seabooks of the oldfashioned frigate-fight?[68]   890
Did you learn who won by the light of the moon and stars?

Our foe was no skulk in his ship, I tell you,
His was the English pluck, and there is no tougher or truer, and never
    was, and never will be;
Along the lowered eve he came, horribly raking us.

We closed with him .... the yards entangled .... the cannon touched, 895
My captain lashed fast with his own hands.
We had received some eighteen-pound shots under the water,
On our lower-gun-deck two large pieces had burst at the first fire,
    killing all around and blowing up overhead.

Ten o'clock at night, and the full moon shining and the leaks on the
    gain, and five feet of water reported,
The master-at-arms loosing the prisoners confined in the after-hold to
    give them a chance for themselves.   900

The transit to and from the magazine was now stopped by the
    sentinels,
They saw so many strange faces they did not know whom to trust.

---

[68]FRIGATE-FIGHT: A reference to the sea battle between captain John Paul Jones's ship the
Bonhomme Richard and the British ship *Serapis* in 1779, during the American Revolution. When
asked if the Americans would surrender, Jones told the captain of the British vessel, "Sir, I have not yet
begun to fight." The *Serapis* later surrendered, and Jones's crew boarded it as the extensively damaged
Bonhomme Richard sank. Whitman's great-grandfather served under Jones.

Our frigate was afire …. the other asked if we demanded quarters? if
   our colors were struck and the fighting done?

I laughed content when I heard the voice of my little captain,
We have not struck, he composedly cried, We have just begun our part
   of the fighting.   905

Only three guns were in use,
One was directed by the captain himself against the enemy's mainmast,
Two well-served with grape and canister silenced his musketry and
   cleared his decks.

The tops alone seconded the fire of this little battery, especially the
   maintop,
They all held out bravely during the whole of the action.   910

Not a moment's cease,
The leaks gained fast on the pumps …. the fire eat toward the
   powder-magazine,
One of the pumps was shot away …. it was generally thought we were
   sinking.

Serene stood the little captain,
He was not hurried …. his voice was neither high nor low,   915
His eyes gave more light to us than our battle-lanterns.

Toward twelve at night, there in the beams of the moon they
   surrendered to us.

   [36]
Stretched and still lay the midnight,
Two great hulls motionless on the breast of the darkness,
Our vessel riddled and slowly sinking …. preparations to pass to the
   one we had conquered,   920
The captain on the quarter deck coldly giving his orders through a
   countenance white as a sheet,
Near by the corpse of the child that served in the cabin,
The dead face of an old salt with long white hair and carefully curled
   whiskers,
The flames spite of all that could be done flickering aloft and below,
The husky voices of the two or three officers yet fit for duty,   925
Formless stacks of bodies and bodies by themselves …. dabs of flesh
   upon the masts and spars,
The cut of cordage and dangle of rigging …. the slight shock of the
   soothe of waves,

Black and impassive guns, and litter of powder-parcels, and the strong
    scent,
Delicate sniffs of the seabreeze .... smells of sedgy grass and fields by
    the shore....death-messages given in charge to survivors,
The hiss of the surgeon's knife and the gnawing teeth of his saw,   930
The wheeze, the cluck, the swash of falling blood .... the short wild
    scream, the long dull tapering groan,
These so .... these irretrievable.

    [37]

O Christ! My fit is mastering me!
What the rebel said gaily adjusting his throat to the rope-noose,
What the savage at the stump, his eye-sockets empty, his mouth
    spirting whoops and defiance,   935
What stills the traveler come to the vault at Mount Vernon,[69]
What sobers the Brooklyn boy as he looks down the shores of the
    Wallabout and remembers the prison ships,
What burnt the gums of the redcoat at Saratoga[70] when he
    surrendered his brigades,
These become mine and me every one, and they are but little,
I become as much more as I like.   940

I become any presence or truth of humanity here,
And see myself in prison shaped like another man,
And feel the dull unintermitted pain.

For me the keepers of convicts shoulder their carbines and keep watch,
It is I let out in the morning and barred at night.   945

Not a mutineer walks handcuffed to the jail, but I am handcuffed to
    him and walk by his side,
I am less the jolly one there, and more the silent one with sweat on my
    twitching lips.

Not a youngster is taken for larceny, but I go up too and am tried and
    sentenced.
Not a cholera patient lies at the last gasp, but I also lie at the last gasp,
My face is ash-colored, my sinews gnarl .... away from me people
    retreat.   950

[69]MOUNT VERNON: The home and burial place in Virginia of the Revolutionary War general and
first president of the United States, George Washington (1732–1799).
[70]SARATOGA: A decisive battle of the American Revolution in which American General Horatio Gates
(1727–1806) defeated the British forces at Saratoga, New York, on October 17, 1777.

Askers embody themselves in me, and I am embodied in them,
I project my hat and sit shamefaced and beg.

   [38]

I rise extatic through all, and sweep with the true gravitation,
The whirling and whirling is elemental within me.
Somehow I have been stunned. Stand back!   955
Give me a little time beyond my cuffed head and slumbers and dreams
      and gaping,
I discover myself on a verge of the usual mistake.

That I could forget the mockers and insults!
That I could forget the trickling tears and the blows of the bludgeons
      and hammers!
That I could look with a separate look on my own crucifixion and
      bloody crowning!   960

I remember …. I resume the overstaid fraction,
The grave of rock multiplies what has been confided to it …. or to any
      graves,
The corpses rise …. the gashes heal …. the fastenings roll away.

I troop forth replenished with supreme power, one of an average
      unending procession,
We walk the roads of Ohio and Massachusetts and Virginia and
      Wisconsin and New York and New Orleans and Texas and Montreal
      and San Francisco and Charleston and Savannah and Mexico,   965
Inland and by the seacoast and boundary lines …. and we pass the
      boundary lines.

Our swift ordinances are on their way over the whole earth,
The blossoms we wear in our hats are the growth of two thousand
      years.

Eleves[71] I salute you,
I see the approach of your numberless gangs …. I see you understand
      yourselves and me,   970
And know that they who have eyes are divine, and the blind and lame
      are equally divine,
And that my steps drag behind yours yet go before them,
And are aware how I am with you no more than I am with everybody.

[71]ELEVES: Students. (French)

[39]

The friendly and flowing savage .... Who is he?
Is he waiting for civilization or past it and mastering it?   975

Is he some southwesterner raised outdoors? Is he Canadian?
Is he from the Mississippi country? or from Iowa, Oregon or
     California? or from the mountains? or prairie life or bush-life? or
     from the sea?

Wherever he goes men and women accept and desire him,
They desire he should like them and touch them and speak to them
     and stay with them.

Behaviour lawless as snow-flakes .... words simple as grass ....
     uncombed head and laughter and naivete;   980
Slowstepping feet and the common features, and the common modes
     and emanations,
They descend in new forms from the tips of his fingers,
They are wafted with the odor of his body or breath .... they fly out of
     the glance of his eyes.

[40]

Flaunt of the sunshine I need not your bask .... lie over,
You light surfaces only .... I force the surfaces and the depths also.   985

Earth! you seem to look for something at my hands,
Say old topknot![72] what do you want?

Man or woman! I might tell how I like you, but cannot,
And might tell what it is in me and what it is in you, but cannot,
And might tell the pinings I have .... the pulse of my nights and days. 990

Behold I do not give lectures or a little charity,
What I give I give out of myself.

You there, impotent, loose in the knees, open your scarfed chops till I
     blow grit within you,
Spread your palms and lift the flaps of your pockets,
I am not to be denied .... I compel .... I have stores plenty and to spare, 995
And any thing I have I bestow.

I do not ask who you are .... that is not important to me,
You can do nothing and be nothing but what I will infold you.

[72]TOPKNOT: A tuft of hair on the crown of the head.

To a drudge of the cottonfields or emptier of privies I lean .... on his
    right cheek I put the family kiss,
And in my soul I swear I never will deny him.   1000

On women fit for conception I start bigger and nimbler babes,
This day I am jetting the stuff of far more arrogant republics.

To any one dying .... thither I speed and twist the knob of the door,
Turn the bedclothes toward the foot of the bed,
Let the physician and the priest go home.   1005

I seize the descending man .... I raise him with resistless will.

O despairer, here is my neck,
By God! you shall not go down! Hang your whole weight upon me.

I dilate you with tremendous breath .... I buoy you up;
Every room of the house do I fill with an armed force .... lovers of me,
    bafflers of graves: 1010
Sleep! I and they keep guard all night;
Not doubt, not decease shall dare to lay finger upon you,
I have embraced you, and henceforth possess you to myself,
And when you rise in the morning you will find what I tell you is so.

[41]

I am he bringing help for the sick as they pant on their backs,   1015
And for strong upright men I bring yet more needed help.

I heard what was said of the universe,
Heard it and heard of several thousand years;
It is middling well as far as it goes .... but is that all?

Magnifying and applying come I,   1020
Outbidding at the start the old cautious hucksters,
The most they offer for mankind and eternity less than a spirt of my
    own seminal wet,
Taking myself the exact dimensions of Jehovah73 and laying them away,
Lithographing Kronos and Zeus his son, and Hercules his grandson,74

73JEHOVAH: The English and common European phrasing, since the sixteenth century, for the
Hebrew divine name "Yhwh"; God.
74KRONOS AND ZEUS HIS SON, AND HERCULES HIS GRANDSON: In Greek mythology, Kronus
was the youngest of the twelve Titans. With his Titan wife Rhea, he sired Demeter, Hestia, Hera,
Hades, Poseidon, and Zeus. Zeus became supreme ruler of Mount Olympus and of its pantheon of
gods. Hercules (the Roman equivalent of the Greek Heracles), known for his great strength and
courage, was the son of Zeus and Alcmene.

Buying drafts of Osiris and Isis[75] and Belus and Brahma[76] and
 Adonai,[77]   1025
In my portfolio placing Manito[78] loose, and Allah[79] on a leaf, and the
 crucifix engraved,
With Odin,[80] and the hideous-faced Mexitli,[81] and all idols and images,
Honestly taking them all for what they are worth, and not a cent more,
Admitting they were alive and did the work of their day,
Admitting they bore mites as for unfledged birds who have now to rise
 and fly and sing for themselves,   1030
Accepting the rough deific sketches to fill out better in myself ....
 bestowing them freely on each man and woman I see,
Discovering as much or more in a framer framing a house,
Putting higher claims for him there with his rolled-up sleeves, driving
 the mallet and chisel;
Not objecting to special revelations .... considering a curl of smoke or
 a hair on the back of my hand as curious as any revelation;
Those ahold of fire-engines and hook-and-ladder ropes more to me
 than the gods of the antique wars,   1035
Minding their voices peal through the crash of destruction,
Their brawny limbs passing safe over charred laths .... their white
 foreheads whole and unhurt out of the flames;
By the mechanic's wife with her babe at her nipple interceding for
 every person born;
Three scythes at harvest whizzing in a row from three lusty angels
 with shirts bagged out at their waists;
The snag-toothed hostler with red hair redeeming sins past and to
 come,   1040
Selling all he possesses and traveling on foot to fee lawyers for his
 brother and sit by him while he is tried for forgery;
What was strewn in the amplest strewing the square rod about me,
 and not filling the square rod then;
The bull and the bug never worshipped half enough,

[75]OSIRIS AND ISIS: Osiris was the Egyptian god of the underworld. He was married to Isis, the goddess of the sky.
[76]BELUS AND BRAHMA: Belus is the Latin name for the Semitic god Baal, a Canaanite fertility deity.
In the Hindu pantheon, Brahma is the senior member of the Trimurti (triad) of the great gods
(Brahma, Vishnu, and Shiva).
[77]ADONAI: The Hebrew word for "my lord, my master." It is used verbally to replace the written
Yhwh (see note 68).
[78]MANITO: Manitou, from the Native American Algonquin word for Great Spirit.
[79]ALLAH: The sole deity of Islam.
[80]ODIN: The chief divinity of the Norse pantheon, Odin is the god of war and death, poetry and wisdom.
[81]HIDEOUS-FACED MEXITLI: The principal god of the Aztecs, now usually called Huitzilopochtli.
He was the god of war, and hundreds of people were sacrificed to him annually.

Dung and dirt more admirable than was dreamed,
The supernatural of no account .... myself waiting my time to be one
    of the supremes,   1045
The day getting ready for me when I shall do as much good as the
    best, and be as prodigious,
Guessing when I am it will not tickle me much to receive puffs out of
    pulpit or print;
By my life-lumps! becoming already a creator!
Putting myself here and now to the ambushed womb of the shadows!

    [42]

    .... A call in the midst of the crowd,   1050
My own voice, orotund sweeping and final.

Come my children,
Come my boys and girls, and my women and household and intimates,
Now the performer launches his nerve .... he has passed his prelude on
    the reeds within.

Easily written loosefingered chords! I feel the thrum of their climax
    and close.   1055

My head evolves on my neck,
Music rolls, but not from the organ .... folks are around me, but they
    are no household of mine.

Ever the hard and unsunk ground,
Ever the eaters and drinkers .... ever the upward and downward sun
    .... ever the air and the ceaseless tides,
Ever myself and my neighbors, refreshing and wicked and real,   1060
Ever the old inexplicable query .... ever that thorned thumb—that
    breath of itches and thirsts,
Ever the vexer's hoot! hoot! till we find where the sly one hides and
    bring him forth;
Ever love .... ever the sobbing liquid of life,
Ever the bandage under the chin .... ever the tressels[82] of death.

Here and there with dimes on the eyes walking,   1065
To feed the greed of the belly the brains liberally spooning,
Tickets buying or taking or selling, but in to the feast never once going;
Many sweating and ploughing and thrashing, and then the chaff for
    payment receiving,
A few idly owning, and they the wheat continually claiming.

---

[82]TRESSELS: Frameworks for support; here, to transport a coffin.

This is the city .... and I am one of the citizens;   1070
Whatever interests the rest interests me .... politics, churches,
    newspapers, schools,
Benevolent societies, improvements, banks, tariffs, steamships,
    factories, markets,
Stocks and stores and real estate and personal estate.

They who piddle and patter here in collars and tailed coats .... I am
    aware who they are .... and that they are not worms or fleas,
I acknowledge the duplicates of myself under all the scrape-lipped and
    pipe-legged concealments.   1075

The weakest and shallowest is deathless with me,
What I do and say the same waits for them,
Every thought that flounders in me the same flounders in them.

I know perfectly well my own egotism,
And know my omniverous words, and cannot say any less,   1080
And would fetch you whoever you are flush with myself.

My words are words of a questioning, and to indicate reality;
This printed and bound book .... but the printer and the printing-
    office boy?
The marriage estate and settlement .... but the body and mind of the
    bridegroom? also those of the bride?
The panorama of the sea .... but the sea itself?   1085
The well-taken photographs .... but your wife or friend close and solid
    in your arms?
The fleet of ships of the line and all the modern improvements .... but
    the craft and pluck of the admiral?
The dishes and fare and furniture .... but the host and hostess, and
    the look out of their eyes?
The sky up there .... yet here or next door or across the way?
The saints and sages in history .... but you yourself?   1090
Sermons and creeds and theology .... but the human brain, and what
    is called reason, and what is called love, and what is called life?

[43]

I do not despise you priests;
My faith is the greatest of faiths and the least of faiths,
Enclosing all worship ancient and modern, and all between ancient
    and modern,
Believing I shall come again upon the earth after five thousand
    years,   1095

Waiting responses from oracles …. honoring the gods …. saluting the
sun,
Making a fetish of the first rock or stump …. powowing with sticks in
the circle of obis,[83]
Helping the lama[84] or brahmin as he trims the lamps of the idols,
Dancing yet through the streets in a phallic procession …. rapt and
austere in the woods, a gymnosophist,[85]
Drinking mead from the skull-cup …. to shasta and vedas[86] admirant
…. minding the koran,[87]   1100
Walking the teokallis,[88] spotted with gore from the stone and knife—
beating the serpent-skin drum;
Accepting the gospels, accepting him that was crucified, knowing
assuredly that he is divine,
To the mass kneeling—to the puritan's prayer rising—sitting patiently
in a pew,
Ranting and frothing in my insane crisis—waiting dead-like till my
spirit arouses me;
Looking forth on pavement and land, and outside of pavement and
land,   1105
Belonging to the winders of the circuit of circuits.

One of that centripetal and centrifugal gang,
I turn and talk like a man leaving charges before a journey.

Down-hearted doubters, dull and excluded,
Frivolous sullen moping angry affected disheartened atheistical,   1110
I know every one of you, and know the unspoken interrogatories,
By experience I know them.

How the flukes splash!
How they contort rapid as lightning, with spasms and spouts of blood!

Be at peace bloody flukes of doubters and sullen mopers,   1115
I take my place among you as much as among any;
The past is the push of you and me and all precisely the same,
And the day and night is for you and me and all,
And what is yet untried and afterward is for you and me and all.

---

[83]OBIS: Obeah; magical amulets and charms of African origin used in a mixture of religion and
voodoo practices in the Caribbean.
[84]LAMA: Buddhist priest.
[85]GYMNOSOPHIST: A member of a sect of Hindu philosophers who wore little or no clothing, followed strict vegan diets, and spent their days in mystical contemplation.
[86]SHASTA AND VEDAS: Hindu scriptures.
[87]KORAN: The sacred book of Islam, recording the revelations of Muhammad.
[88]TEOKALLIS: Aztec temples where human sacrifices were performed.

I do not know what is untried and afterward,   1120
But I know it is sure and alive, and sufficient.

Each who passes is considered, and each who stops is considered, and
   not a single one can it fail.
It cannot fail the young man who died and was buried,
Nor the young woman who died and was put by his side,
Nor the little child that peeped in at the door and then drew back and
   was never seen again,   1125
Nor the old man who has lived without purpose, and feels it with
   bitterness worse than gall,
Nor him in the poorhouse tubercled by rum and the bad disorder,
Nor the numberless slaughtered and wrecked .... nor the brutish
   koboo,[89] called the ordure[90] of humanity,
Nor the sacs merely floating with open mouths for food to slip in,
Nor any thing in the earth, or down in the oldest graves of the earth, 1130
Nor any thing in the myriads of spheres, nor one of the myriads of
   myriads that inhabit them,
Nor the present, nor the least wisp that is known.

[44]

It is time to explain myself .... let us stand up.

What is known I strip away .... I launch all men and women forward
   with me into the unknown.

The clock indicates the moment .... but what does eternity indicate? 1135

Eternity lies in bottomless reservoirs .... its buckets are rising forever
   and ever,
They pour and they pour and they exhale away.

We have thus far exhausted trillions of winters and summers;
There are trillions ahead, and trillions ahead of them.

Births have brought us richness and variety,   1140
And other births will bring us richness and variety.

I do not call one greater and one smaller,
That which fills its period and place is equal to any.

Were mankind murderous or jealous upon you my brother or my sister?
I am sorry for you .... they are not murderous or jealous upon me; 1145

[89]KOBOO: Indonesian tribesman.
[90]ORDURE: Filth.

All has been gentle with me .... I keep no account with lamentation;
What have I to do with lamentation?
I am an acme of things accomplished, and I am encloser of things to be.

My feet strike an apex of the apices[91] of the stairs,
On every step bunches of ages, and larger bunches between the steps, 1150
All below duly traveled—and still I mount and mount.

Rise after rise bow the phantoms behind me,
Afar down I see the huge first Nothing, the vapor from the nostrils of
    death,
I know I was even there .... I waited unseen and always,
And slept while God carried me through the lethargic mist,   1155
And took my time .... and took no hurt from the foetid[92] carbon.

Long I was hugged close .... long and long.

Immense have been the preparations for me,
Faithful and friendly the arms that have helped me.

Cycles ferried my cradle, rowing and rowing like cheerful boatmen;   1160
For room to me stars kept aside in their own rings,
They sent influences to look after what was to hold me.

Before I was born out of my mother generations guided me,
My embryo has never been torpid .... nothing could overlay it;
For it the nebula cohered to an orb .... the long slow strata piled to
    rest it on .... vast vegetables gave it sustenance,   1165
Monstrous sauroids[93] transported it in their mouths and deposited it
    with care.

All forces have been steadily employed to complete and delight me,
Now I stand on this spot with my soul.

[45]

Span of youth! Ever-pushed elasticity! Manhood balanced and florid
    and full!

My lovers suffocate me!   1170
Crowding my lips, and thick in the pores of my skin,
Jostling me through streets and public halls .... coming naked to me at
    night,

---

[91]APICES: Plural of apex.
[92]FOETID: Fetid, stinking.
[93]SAUROIDS: Lizards.

Crying by day Ahoy from the rocks of the river .... swinging and
    chirping over my head,
Calling my name from flowerbeds or vines or tangled underbrush,
Or while I swim in the bath .... or drink from the pump at the corner
    .... or the curtain is down at the opera .... or I glimpse at a
    woman's face in the railroad car;   1175
Lighting on every moment of my life,
Bussing my body with soft and balsamic busses,[94]
Noiselessly passing handfuls out of their hearts and giving them to be
    mine.

Old age superbly rising! Ineffable grace of dying days!

Every condition promulges[95] not only itself .... it promulges what
    grows after and out of itself,   1180
And the dark hush promulges as much as any.

I open my scuttle[96] at night and see the far-sprinkled systems,
And all I see, multiplied as high as I can cipher, edge but the rim of
    the farther systems.

Wider and wider they spread, expanding and always expanding,
Outward and outward and forever outward.   1185

My sun has his sun, and round him obediently wheels,
He joins with his partners a group of superior circuit,
And greater sets follow, making specks of the greatest inside them.

There is no stoppage, and never can be stoppage;
If I and you and the worlds and all beneath or upon their surfaces,
    and all the palpable life, were this moment reduced back to a
    pallid float, it would not avail in the long run,   1190
We should surely bring up again where we now stand,
And as surely go as much farther, and then farther and farther.

A few quadrillions of eras, a few octillions of cubic leagues, do not
    hazard the span, or make it impatient,
They are but parts .... any thing is but a part.

See ever so far .... there is limitless space outside of that,   1195
Count ever so much .... there is limitless time around that.

Our rendezvous is fitly appointed .... God will be there and wait till
    we come.

---

[94]BUSSES: Kisses.
[95]PROMULGES: Proclaims.
[96]SCUTTLE: Small opening in a roof or wall furnished with a lid.

[46]

I know I have the best of time and space—and that I was never
measured, and never will be measured.

I tramp a perpetual journey,
My signs are a rain-proof coat and good shoes and a staff cut from the
woods;   1200
No friend of mine takes his ease in my chair,
I have no chair, nor church nor philosophy;
I lead no man to a dinner-table or library or exchange,
But each man and each woman of you I lead upon a knoll,
My left hand hooks you round the waist,   1205
My right hand points to landscapes of continents, and a plain public
road.

Not I, not any one else can travel that road for you,
You must travel it for yourself.

It is not far .... it is within reach,
Perhaps you have been on it since you were born, and did not know,   1210
Perhaps it is every where on water and on land.

Shoulder your duds, and I will mine, and let us hasten forth;
Wonderful cities and free nations we shall fetch as we go.

If you tire, give me both burdens, and rest the chuff of your hand[97] on
my hip,
And in due time you shall repay the same service to me;   1215
For after we start we never lie by again.

This day before dawn I ascended a hill and looked at the crowded
heaven,
And I said to my spirit, When we become the enfolders of those orbs
and the pleasure and knowledge of every thing in them, shall we
be filled and satisfied then?
And my spirit said No, we level that lift to pass and continue
beyond.

You are also asking me questions, and I hear you;   1220
I answer that I cannot answer .... you must find out for yourself.

Sit awhile wayfarer,
Here are biscuits to eat and here is milk to drink,

[97]CHUFF OF YOUR HAND: The fleshy part of the hand.

But as soon as you sleep and renew yourself in sweet clothes I will
    certainly kiss you with my goodbye kiss and open the gate for your
    egress hence.

Long enough have you dreamed contemptible dreams,   1225
Now I wash the gum from your eyes,
You must habit yourself to the dazzle of the light and of every moment
    of your life.

Long have you timidly waded, holding a plank by the shore,
Now I will you to be a bold swimmer,
To jump off in the midst of the sea, and rise again and nod to me and
    shout, and laughingly dash with your hair.   1230

[47]

I am the teacher of athletes,
He that by me spreads a wider breast than my own proves the width
    of my own,
He most honors my style who learns under it to destroy the teacher.

The boy I love, the same becomes a man not through derived power
    but in his own right,
Wicked, rather than virtuous out of conformity or fear,   1235
Fond of his sweetheart, relishing well his steak,
Unrequited love or a slight cutting him worse than a wound cuts,
First rate to ride, to fight, to hit the bull's eye, to sail a skiff, to sing a
    song or play on the banjo,
Preferring scars and faces pitted with smallpox over all latherers and
    those that keep out of the sun.

I teach straying from me, yet who can stray from me?   1240
I follow you whoever you are from the present hour;
My words itch at your ears till you understand them.

I do not say these things for a dollar, or to fill up the time while I wait
    for a boat;
It is you talking just as much myself .... I act as the tongue of you,
It was tied in your mouth .... in mine it begins to be loosened.   1245

I swear I will never mention love or death inside a house,
And I swear I never will translate myself at all, only to him or her who
    privately stays with me in the open air.

If you would understand me go to the heights or water-shore,
The nearest gnat is an explanation and a drop or the motion of waves
    a key,
The maul the oar and the handsaw second my words.   1250

No shuttered room or school can commune with me,
But roughs and little children better than they.

The young mechanic is closest to me .... he knows me pretty well,
The woodman that takes his axe and jug with him shall take me with
    him all day,
The farmboy ploughing in the field feels good at the sound of my
    voice,   1255
In vessels that sail my words must sail .... I go with fishermen and
    seamen, and love them,
My face rubs to the hunter's face when he lies down alone in his
    blanket,
The driver thinking of me does not mind the jolt of his wagon,
The young mother and old mother shall comprehend me,
The girl and the wife rest the needle a moment and forget where they
    are,   1260
They and all would resume what I have told them.

[48]

I have said that the soul is not more than the body,
And I have said that the body is not more than the soul,
And nothing, not God, is greater to one than one's-self is,
And whoever walks a furlong without sympathy walks to his own
    funeral, dressed in his shroud,   1265
And I or you pocketless of a dime may purchase the pick of the earth,
And to glance with an eye or show a bean in its pod confounds the
    learning of all times,
And there is no trade or employment but the young man following it
    may become a hero,
And there is no object so soft but it makes a hub for the wheeled
    universe,
And any man or woman shall stand cool and supercilious before a
    million universes.   1270

And I call to mankind, Be not curious about God,
For I who am curious about each am not curious about God,

No array of terms can say how much I am at peace about God and
about death.

I hear and behold God in every object, yet I understand God not in the
least,
Nor do I understand who there can be more wonderful than myself.   1275

Why should I wish to see God better than this day?
I see something of God each hour of the twenty-four, and each
moment then,
In the faces of men and women I see God, and in my own face in the
glass;
I find letters from God dropped in the street, and every one is signed
by God's name,
And I leave them where they are, for I know that others will
punctually come forever and ever.   1280

[49]

And as to you death, and you bitter hug of mortality …. it is idle to
try to alarm me.
To his work without flinching the accoucheur[98] comes,
I see the elderhand pressing receiving supporting,
I recline by the sills of the exquisite flexible doors …. and mark the
outlet, and mark the relief and escape.

And as to you corpse I think you are good manure, but that does not
offend me,   1285
I smell the white roses sweetscented and growing,
I reach to the leafy lips …. I reach to the polished breasts of melons.

And as to you life, I reckon you are the leavings of many deaths,
No doubt I have died myself ten thousand times before.

I hear you whispering there O stars of heaven,   1290
O suns …. O grass of graves …. O perpetual transfers and promotions
…. if you do not say anything how can I say anything?

Of the turbid pool that lies in the autumn forest,
Of the moon that descends the steeps of the soughing[99] twilight,
Toss, sparkles of day and dusk …. toss on the black stems that decay
in the muck,
Toss to the moaning gibberish of the dry limbs.   1295

[98]ACCOUCHEUR: Midwife.
[99]SOUGHING: Murmuring, rustling.

I ascend from the moon .... I ascend from the night,
And perceive of the ghastly glitter the sunbeams reflected,
And debouch[100] to the steady and central from the offspring great or
small.

[50]

There is that in me .... I do not know what it is .... but I know it is in me.

Wrenched and sweaty .... calm and cool then my body becomes;   1300
I sleep .... I sleep long.

I do not know it .... it is without name .... it is a word unsaid,
It is not in any dictionary or utterance or symbol.

Something it swings on more than the earth I swing on,
To it the creation is the friend whose embracing awakes me.   1305

Perhaps I might tell more .... Outlines! I plead for my brothers and sisters.

Do you see O my brothers and sisters?
It is not chaos or death .... it is form and union and plan .... it is
eternal life .... it is happiness.

[51]

The past and present wilt .... I have filled them and emptied them,
And proceed to fill my next fold of the future.   1310

Listener up there! Here you .... what have you to confide to me?
Look in my face while I snuff the sidle[101] of evening,
Talk honestly, for no one else hears you, and I stay only a minute longer.

Do I contradict myself?
Very well then .... I contradict myself;   1315
I am large .... I contain multitudes.

I concentrate toward them that are nigh .... I wait on the door-slab.

Who has done his day's work and will soonest be through with his
supper?
Who wishes to walk with me?

Will you speak before I am gone? Will you prove already too late?   1320

[52]

The spotted hawk swoops by and accuses me .... he complains of my
gab and my loitering.

[100]DEBOUCH: Emerge.
[101]SNUFF THE SIDLE: Snuff means to scent or smell; sidle is a furtive advance, a move or turn sideways.

I too am not a bit tamed …. I too am untranslatable,
I sound my barbaric yawp over the roofs of the world.

The last scud of day holds back for me,
It flings my likeness after the rest and true as any on the shadowed
wilds,   1325
It coaxes me to the vapor and the dusk.

I depart as air …. I shake my white locks at the runaway sun,
I effuse my flesh in eddies and drift it in lacy jags.

I bequeath myself to the dirt to grow from the grass I love,
If you want me again look for me under your bootsoles.   1330

You will hardly know who I am or what I mean,
But I shall be good health to you nevertheless,
And filter and fibre your blood.

Failing to fetch me at first keep encouraged,
Missing me one place search another,   1335
I stop some where waiting for you[102]

[1855]

Crossing Brooklyn Ferry

1

Flood-tide below me! I see you face to face!
Clouds of the west—sun there half an hour high—I see you also face
to face.

Crowds of men and women attired in the usual costumes, how curious
you are to me!
On the ferry-boats the hundreds and hundreds that cross, returning
home, are more curious to me than you suppose,
And you that shall cross from shore to shore years hence are more to
me, and more in my meditations, than you might suppose.   5

2

The impalpable sustenance of me from all things at all hours of the day,
The simple, compact, well-join'd scheme, myself disintegrated, every
one disintegrated yet part of the scheme,
The similitudes of the past and those of the future,
The glories strung like beads on my smallest sights and hearings, on
the walk in the street and the passage over the river,

---

[102]YOU: Whitman did not place a period at the end of the final line in the 1855 edition.

The current rushing so swiftly and swimming with me far away,   10
The others that are to follow me, the ties between me and them,
The certainty of others, the life, love, sight, hearing of others.

Others will enter the gates of the ferry and cross from shore to shore,
Others will watch the run of the flood-tide,
Others will see the shipping of Manhattan north and west, and the
    heights of Brooklyn to the south and east,   15
Others will see the islands large and small;
Fifty years hence, others will see them as they cross, the sun half an
    hour high,
A hundred years hence, or ever so many hundred years hence, others
    will see them,
Will enjoy the sunset, the pouring-in of the flood-tide, the falling-back
    to the sea of the ebb-tide.

3

It avails not, time nor place—distance avails not,   20
I am with you, you men and women of a generation, or ever so many
    generations hence,
Just as you feel when you look on the river and sky, so I felt,
Just as any of you is one of a living crowd, I was one of a crowd,
Just as you are refresh'd by the gladness of the river and the bright
    flow, I was refresh'd,
Just as you stand and lean on the rail, yet hurry with the swift current,
    I stood yet was hurried,   25
Just as you look on the numberless masts of ships and the thick-
    stemm'd pipes of steamboats, I look'd.

I too many and many a time cross'd the river of old,
Watched the Twelfth-month[1] sea-gulls, saw them high in the air
    floating with motionless wings, oscillating their bodies,
Saw how the glistening yellow lit up parts of their bodies and left the
    rest in strong shadow,
Saw the slow-wheeling circles and the gradual edging toward the south,30
Saw the reflection of the summer sky in the water,
Had my eyes dazzled by the shimmering track of beams,
Look'd at the fine centrifugal spokes of light round the shape of my
    head in the sunlit water,
Look'd on the haze on the hills southward and south-westward,
Look'd on the vapor as it flew in fleeces tinged with violet,   35
Look'd toward the lower bay to notice the vessels arriving,

[1]TWELFTH-MONTH: December; winter.

Saw their approach, saw aboard those that were near me,
Saw the white sails of schooners and sloops, saw the ships at anchor,
The sailors at work in the rigging or out astride the spars,
The round masts, the swinging motion of the hulls, the slender
    serpentine pennants,   40
The large and small steamers in motion, the pilots in their pilot-houses,
The white wake left by the passage, the quick tremulous whirl of the
    wheels,
The flags of all nations, the falling of them at sunset.
The scallop-edged waves in the twilight, the ladled cups, the
    frolicsome crests and glistening,
The stretch afar growing dimmer and dimmer, the gray walls of the
    granite storehouses by the docks,   45
On the river the shadowy group, the big steam-tug closely flank'd on
    each side by the barges, the hay-boat, the belated lighter,[2]
On the neighboring shore the fires from the foundry chimneys burning
    high and glaringly into the night,
Casting their flicker of black contrasted with wild red and yellow light
    over the tops of houses, and down into the clefts of streets.

    4

These and all else were to me the same as they are to you,
I loved well those cities, loved well the stately and rapid river,   50
The men and women I saw were all near to me,
Others the same—others who looked back on me because I look'd
    forward to them,
(The time will come, though I stop here to-day and to-night.)

    5

What is it then between us?
What is the count of the scores or hundreds of years between us?   55

Whatever it is, it avails not—distance avails not, and place avails not,
I too lived, Brooklyn of ample hills was mine,
I too walk'd the streets of Manhattan island, and bathed in the waters
    around it,
I too felt the curious abrupt questionings stir within me,
In the day among crowds of people sometimes they came upon me,   60
In my walks home late at night or as I lay in my bed they came
    upon me,
I too had been struck from the float forever held in solution,

---

[2]LIGHTER: A barge used to unload a larger cargo ship.

I too had receiv'd identity by my body,
That I was I knew was of my body, and what I should be I knew I
    should be of my body.

6

It is not upon you alone the dark patches fall,   65
The dark threw its patches down upon me also,
The best I had done seem'd to me blank and suspicious,
My great thoughts as I supposed them, were they not in reality
    meagre?
Nor is it you alone who know what it is to be evil,
I am he who knew what it was to be evil,   70
I too knitted the old knot of contrariety,
Blabb'd, blush'd, resented, lied, stole, grudg'd,
Had guile, anger, lust, hot wishes I dared not speak,
Was wayward, vain, greedy, shallow, sly, cowardly, malignant,
The wolf, the snake, the hog, not wanting in me,   75
The cheating look, the frivolous word, the adulterous wish, not wanting,
Refusals, hates, postponements, meanness, laziness, none of these
    wanting,
Was one with the rest, the days and haps of the rest,
Was call'd by my nighest name by clear loud voices of young men as
    they saw me approaching or passing,
Felt their arms on my neck as I stood, or the negligent leaning of their
    flesh against me as I sat,   80
Saw many I loved in the street or ferry-boat or public assembly, yet
    never told them a word,
Lived the same life with the rest, the same old laughing, gnawing,
    leeping,
Play'd the part that still looks back on the actor or actress,
The same old role, the role that is what we make it, as great as we like,
Or as small as we like, or both great and small.   85

7

Closer yet I approach you,
What thought you have of me now, I had as much of you—I laid in
    my stores in advance,
I consider'd long and seriously of you before you were born.

Who was to know what should come home to me?
Who knows but I am enjoying this?   90
Who knows, for all the distance, but I am as good as looking at you
    now, for all you cannot see me?

8

Ah, what can ever be more stately and admirable to me than mast-
hemm'd Manhattan?
River and sunset and scallop-edg'd waves of flood-tide?
The sea-gulls oscillating their bodies, the hay-boat in the twilight, and
the belated lighter?
What gods can exceed these that clasp me by the hand, and with
voices I love call me promptly and loudly by my nighest name as I
approach?   95
What is more subtle than this which ties me to the woman or man that
looks in my face?
Which fuses me into you now, and pours my meaning into you?

We understand then do we not?
What I promis'd without mentioning it, have you not accepted?
What the study could not teach—what the preaching could not
accomplish is accomplish'd, is it not?   100

9

Flow on, river! flow with the flood-tide, and ebb with the ebb-tide!
Frolic on, crested and scallop-edg'd waves!
Gorgeous clouds of the sunset! drench with your splendor me, or the
men and women generations after me!
Cross from shore to shore, countless crowds of passengers!
Stand up, tall masts of Mannahatta![3] stand up, beautiful hills of
Brooklyn!   105
Throb, baffled and curious brain! throw out questions and answers!
Suspend here and everywhere, eternal float of solution!
Gaze, loving and thirsting eyes, in the house or street or public assembly!
Sound out, voices of young men! loudly and musically call me by my
nighest name!
Live, old life! play the part that looks back on the actor or actress!   110
Play the old role, the role that is great or small according as one
makes it!
Consider, you who peruse me, whether I may not in unknown ways be
looking upon you;
Be firm, rail over the river, to support those who lean idly, yet haste
with the hasting current;
Fly on, sea-birds! fly sideways, or wheel in large circles high in the air;

[3]MANNAHATTA: Variation of the Native American word for Manhattan.

Receive the summer sky, you water, and faithfully hold it till all
    downcast eyes have time to take it from you!   115
Diverge, fine spokes of light, from the shape of my head, or any one's
    head, in the sunlit water!
Come on, ships from the lower bay! pass up or down, white-sail'd
    schooners, sloops, lighters!
Flaunt away, flags of all nations! be duly lower'd at sunset!
Burn high your fires, foundry chimneys! cast black shadows at
    nightfall! cast red and yellow light over the tops of the houses!
Appearances, now or henceforth, indicate what you are,   120
You necessary film, continue to envelop the soul,
About my body for me, and your body for you, be hung our divinest
    aromas,
Thrive, cities—bring your freight, bring your shows, ample and
    sufficient rivers,
Expand, being than which none else is perhaps more spiritual,
Keep your places, objects than which none else is more lasting.   125

You have waited, you always wait, you dumb, beautiful ministers,
We receive you with free sense at last, and are insatiate henceforward,
Not you any more shall be able to foil us, or withhold yourselves from us,
We use you, and do not cast you aside—we plant you permanently
    within us,
We fathom you not—we love you—there is perfection in you also,   130
You furnish your parts toward eternity,
Great or small, you furnish your parts toward the soul.

                                   [1856, 1881]

When I Heard at the Close of the Day

When I heard at the close of the day how my name had been receiv'd
    with plaudits in the capitol, still it was not a happy night for me
    that follow'd;
And else, when I carous'd, or when my plans were accomplish'd, still I
    was not happy;
But the day when I rose at dawn from the bed of perfect health,
    refresh'd, singing, inhaling the ripe breath of autumn,

When I saw the full moon in the west grow pale and disappear in the
    morning light,
When I wander'd alone over the beach, and undressing, bathed,
    laughing with the cool waters, and saw the sun rise,   5
And when I thought how my dear friend, my lover, was on his way
    coming, O then I was happy;
O then each breath tasted sweeter—and all that day my food
    nourish'd me more—and the beautiful day pass'd well,
And the next came with equal joy—and with the next, at evening,
    came my friend;
And that night, while all was still, I heard the waters roll slowly
    continually up the shores,
I heard the hissing rustle of the liquid and sands, as directed to me,
    whispering, to congratulate me,   10
For the one I love most lay sleeping by me under the same cover in the
    cool night,
In the stillness, in the autumn moonbeams, his face was inclined
    toward me,
And his arm lay lightly around my breast—and that night I was happy.

[1860, 1867]

I Saw in Louisiana a
Live-Oak Growing

I saw in Louisiana a live-oak growing,
All alone stood it, and the moss hung down from the branches;
Without any companion it grew there, uttering joyous leaves of dark
    green,
And its look, rude, unbending, lusty, made me think of myself;
But I wonder'd how it could utter joyous leaves, standing alone there,
    without its friend, its lover near—for I knew I could not;   5
And I broke off a twig with a certain number of leaves upon it, and
    twined around it a little moss,
And brought it away—and I have placed it in sight in my room;
It is not needed to remind me as of my own dear friends,

(For I believe lately I think of little else than of them;)
Yet it remains to me a curious token—it makes me think of manly love;10
For all that, and though the live-oak glistens there in Louisiana,
    solitary, in a wide flat space,
Uttering joyous leaves all its life, without a friend, a lover, near,
I know very well I could not.

[1860, 1867]

Vigil Strange I Kept on the Field One Night

Vigil strange I kept on the field one night;
When you my son and my comrade dropt at my side that day,
One look I but gave which your dear eyes return'd with a look I shall
    never forget,
One touch of your hand to mine O boy, reach'd up as you lay on the
    ground,
Then onward I sped in the battle, the even-contested battle,   5
Till late in the night reliev'd to the place at last again I made my way,
Found you in death so cold dear comrade, found your body son of
    responding kisses, (never again on earth responding,)
Bared your face in the starlight, curious the scene, cool blew the
    moderate night-wind,
Long there and then in vigil I stood, dimly around me the battle-field
    spreading,
Vigil wondrous and vigil sweet there in the fragrant silent night,   10
But not a tear fell, not even a long-drawn sigh, long, long I gazed,
Then on the earth partially reclining sat by your side leaning my chin
    in my hands,
Passing sweet hours, immortal and mystic hours with you dearest
    comrade—not a tear, not a word,
Vigil of silence, love and death, vigil for you my son and my soldier,
As onward silently stars aloft, eastward new ones upward stole,   15
Vigil final for you brave boy, (I could not save you, swift was your death,
I faithfully loved you and cared for you living, I think we shall surely
    meet again,)
Till at latest lingering of the night, indeed just as the dawn appear'd,

My comrade I wrapt in his blanket, envelop'd well his form,
Folded the blanket well, tucking it carefully over head and carefully
    under feet,   20
And there and then and bathed by the rising sun, my son in his grave,
    in his rude-dug grave I deposited,
Ending my vigil strange with that, vigil of night and battle-field dim,
Vigil for boy of responding kisses, (never again on earth responding,)
Vigil for comrade swiftly slain, vigil I never forget, how as day brighten'd,
I rose from the chill ground and folded my soldier well in his blanket, 25
And buried him where he fell.

[1865, 1867]

A Sight in Camp in the Daybreak Gray and Dim

A sight in camp in the daybreak gray and dim,
As from my tent I emerge so early sleepless,
As slow I walk in the cool fresh air the path near by the hospital tent,
Three forms I see on stretchers lying, brought out there untended lying,
Over each the blanket spread, ample brownish woolen blanket,   5
Gray and heavy blanket, folding, covering all.

Curious I halt and silent stand,
Then with light fingers I from the face of the nearest the first just lift
    the blanket;
Who are you elderly man so gaunt and grim, with well-gray'd hair,
    and flesh all sunken about the eyes?
Who are you my dear comrade?   10

Then to the second I step—and who are you my child and darling?
Who are you sweet boy with cheeks yet blooming?

Then to the third—a face nor child nor old, very calm, as of beautiful
    yellow-white ivory;
Young man I think I know you—I think this face is the face of the
    Christ himself,
Dead and divine and brother of all, and here again he lies.   15

[1865, 1867]

When Lilacs Last in the Dooryard Bloom'd[1]
from Memories of President Lincoln

1

When lilacs last in the dooryard bloom'd,
And the great star early droop'd in the western sky in the night,
I mourn'd, and yet shall mourn with ever-returning spring.

Ever-returning spring, trinity sure to me you bring,
Lilac blooming perennial and drooping star in the west,[2]   5
And thought of him I love.

2

O powerful western fallen star!
O shades of night—O moody, tearful night!
O great star disappear'd—O the black murk that hides the star!
O cruel hands that hold me powerless—O helpless soul of me!   10
O harsh surrounding cloud that will not free my soul.

3

In the dooryard fronting an old farm-house near the white-wash'd
    palings,[3]
Stands the lilac-bush tall-growing with heart-shaped leaves of rich green,
With many a pointed blossom rising delicate, with the perfume strong
    I love,
With every leaf a miracle—and from this bush in the dooryard,   15
With delicate-color'd blossoms and heart-shaped leaves of rich green,
A sprig with its flower I break.

4

In the swamp in secluded recesses,
A shy and hidden bird is warbling a song.

[1]WHEN LILACS LAST IN THE DOORYARD BLOOM'D: This poem was written as part of a cluster of poems titled "President Lincoln's Burial Hymn." Abraham Lincoln (1809–1865), the sixteenth president of the United States, was assassinated on April 14, 1865. Lilacs bloom in mid-April in the Washington, D.C., area.
[2]DROOPING STAR IN THE WEST: The planet Venus, a bright "western star" and emblematic of Lincoln.
[3]PALINGS: Fence planks.

Solitary the thrush,   20
The hermit withdrawn to himself, avoiding the settlements,
Sings by himself a song.

Song of the bleeding throat,
Death's outlet song of life, (for well dear brother I know,
If thou wast not granted to sing thou would'st surely die.)   25

5

Over the breast of the spring, the land, amid cities,
Amid lanes and through old woods, where lately the violets peep'd
    from the ground, spotting the gray debris,
Amid the grass in the fields each side of the lanes, passing the endless
    grass,
Passing the yellow-spear'd wheat, every grain from its shroud in the
    dark-brown fields uprisen,
Passing the apple-tree blows[4] of white and pink in the orchards,   30
Carrying a corpse to where it shall rest in the grave,
Night and day journeys a coffin.[5]

6

Coffin that passes through lanes and streets,
Through day and night with the great cloud darkening the land,
With the pomp of the inloop'd flags with the cities draped in black,   35
With the show of the States themselves as of crape-veil'd women
    standing,
With processions long and winding and the flambeaus[6] of the night,
With the countless torches lit, with the silent sea of faces and the
    unbared heads,
With the waiting depot, the arriving coffin, and the sombre faces,
With dirges[7] through the night, with the thousand voices rising strong
    and solemn,   40
With all the mournful voices of the dirges pour'd around the coffin,
The dim-lit churches and the shuddering organs—where amid these
    you journey,
With the tolling tolling bells' perpetual clang,

[4]BLOWS: Blossoms.
[5]NIGHT AND DAY JOURNEYS A COFFIN: Lincoln's body was transported by train to his home in
Springfield, Illinois, for burial on May 4, 1865. His assassination shocked a nation already grieving
from the toll taken by the Civil War. Streets were draped in black crepe, and citizens wore mourning
clothes as the coffin passed through many towns along its journey.
[6]FLAMBEAUS: Torches.
[7]DIRGES: Funeral songs; songs of mourning.

Here, coffin that slowly passes,
I give you my sprig of lilac.   45

    7

(Nor for you, for one alone,
Blossoms and branches green to coffins all I bring,
For fresh as the morning, thus would I chant a song for you O sane
    and sacred death.

All over bouquets of roses,
O death, I cover you over with roses and early lilies,   50
But mostly and now the lilac that blooms the first,
Copious I break, I break the sprigs from the bushes,
With loaded arms I come, pouring for you,
For you and the coffins all of you O death.)

    8

O western orb sailing the heaven,   55
Now I know what you must have meant as a month since I walk'd,
As I walk'd in silence the transparent shadowy night,
As I saw you had something to tell as you bent to me night after night,
As you droop'd from the sky low down as if to my side, (while the
    other stars all look'd on,)
As we wander'd together the solemn night, (for something I know not
    what kept me from sleep,)   60
As the night advanced, and I saw on the rim of the west how full you
    were of woe,
As I stood on the rising ground in the breeze in the cool transparent
    night,
As I watch'd where you pass'd and was lost in the netherward[8] black
    of the night,
As my soul in its trouble dissatisfied sank, as where you sad orb,
Concluded, dropt in the night, and was gone.   65

    9

Sing on there in the swamp,
O singer bashful and tender, I hear your notes, I hear your call,
I hear, I come presently, I understand you,
But a moment I linger, for the lustrous star has detain'd me,
The star my departing comrade holds and detains me.   70

[8]NETHERWARD: Downward.

10

O how shall I warble myself for the dead one there I loved?
And how shall I deck my song for the large sweet soul that has gone?
And what shall my perfume be for the grave of him I love?

Sea-winds blown from east and west,
Blown from the Eastern sea and blown from the Western sea, till there
    on the prairies meeting,   75
These and with these and the breath of my chant,
I'll perfume the grave of him I love.

11

O what shall I hang on the chamber walls?
And what shall the pictures be that I hang on the walls,
To adorn the burial-house of him I love?   80

Pictures of growing spring and farms and homes,
With the Fourth-month eve at sundown, and the gray smoke lucid and
    bright,
With floods of the yellow gold of the gorgeous, indolent, sinking sun,
    burning, expanding the air,
With the fresh sweet herbage under foot, and the pale green leaves of
    the trees prolific,
In the distance the flowing glaze, the breast of the river, with a wind-
    dapple[9] here and there,   85
With ranging hills on the banks, with many a line against the sky, and
    shadows,
And the city at hand with dwellings so dense, and stacks of chimneys,
And all the scenes of life and the workshops, and the workmen
    homeward returning.

12

Lo, body and soul—this land,
My own Manhattan with spires, and the sparkling and hurrying tides,
    and the ships,   90
The varied and ample land, the South and the North in the light,
    Ohio's shores and flashing Missouri,
And ever the far-spreading prairies cover'd with grass and corn.

Lo, the most excellent sun so calm and haughty,
The violet and purple morn with just-felt breezes,

---

[9]WIND-DAPPLE: A dappled effect on the surface of water caused by wind.

The gentle soft-born measureless light,   95
The miracle spreading bathing all, the fulfill'd noon,
The coming eve delicious, the welcome night and the stars,
Over my cities shining all, enveloping man and land.

13

Sing on, sing on you gray-brown bird,
Sing from the swamps, the recesses, pour your chant from the bushes, 100
Limitless out of the dusk, out of the cedars and pines.

Sing on dearest brother, warble your reedy song,
Loud human song, with voice of uttermost woe.

O liquid and free and tender!
O wild and loose to my soul—O wondrous singer!   105
You only I hear—yet the star holds me, (but will soon depart,)
Yet the lilac with mastering odor holds me.

14

Now while I sat in the day and look'd forth,
In the close of the day with its light and the fields of spring, and the
    farmers preparing their crops,
In the large unconscious scenery of my land with its lakes and forests, 110
In the heavenly aerial beauty, (after the perturb'd winds and the
    storms,)
Under the arching heavens of the afternoon swift passing, and the
    voices of children and women,
The many-moving sea-tides, and I saw the ships how they sail'd,
And the summer approaching with richness, and the fields all busy
    with labor,
And the infinite separate houses, how they all went on, each with its
    meals and minutia of daily usages,   115
And the streets how their throbbings throbb'd, and the cities pent—lo,
    then and there,
Falling upon them all and among them all, enveloping me with the
    rest,
Appear'd the cloud, appear'd the long black trail,
And I knew death, its thought, and the sacred knowledge of death.

Then with the knowledge of death as walking one side of me,   120
And the thought of death close-walking the other side of me,
And I in the middle as with companions, and as holding the hands of
    companions,

I fled forth to the hiding receiving night that talks not,
Down to the shores of the water, the path by the swamp in the dimness,
To the solemn shadowy cedars and ghostly pines so still.   125

And the singer so shy to the rest receiv'd me,
The gray-brown bird I know receiv'd us comrades three,
And he sang the carol of death, and a verse for him I love.

From deep secluded recesses,
From the fragrant cedars and the ghostly pines so still,   130
Came the carol of the bird.

And the charm of the carol rapt[10] me,
As I held as if by their hands my comrades in the night,
And the voice of my spirit tallied the song of the bird.

Come lovely and soothing death,   135
Undulate round the world, serenely arriving, arriving,
In the day, in the night, to all, to each,
Sooner or later delicate death.

Prais'd be the fathomless universe,
For life and joy, and for objects and knowledge curious,   140
And for love, sweet love—but praise! praise! praise!
For the sure-enwinding arms of cool-enfolding death.

Dark mother always gliding near with soft feet,
Have none chanted for thee a chant of fullest welcome?
Then I chant it for thee, I glorify thee above all,   145
I bring thee a song that when thou must indeed come, come
    unfalteringly.

Approach strong deliveress,
When it is so, when thou hast taken them I joyously sing the dead,
Lost in the loving floating ocean of thee,
Laved in the flood of thy bliss O death.   150

From me to thee glad serenades,
Dances for thee I propose saluting thee, adornments and feastings for
    thee,
And the sights of the open landscape and the high-spread sky are fitting,
And life and the fields, and the huge and thoughtful night.

---

[10]RAPT: Enraptured.

The night in silence under many a star,   155
The ocean shore and the husky whispering wave whose voice I know,
And the soul turning to thee O vast and well-veil'd death,
And the body gratefully nestling close to thee.

Over the tree-tops I float thee a song,
Over the rising and sinking waves, over the myriad fields and the
  prairies wide,   160
Over the dense-pack'd cities all and the teeming wharves and ways,
I float this carol with joy, with joy to thee O death.

15

To the tally of my soul,
Loud and strong kept up the gray-brown bird,
With pure deliberate notes spreading filling the night.   165

Loud in the pines and cedars dim,
Clear in the freshness moist and the swamp-perfume,
And I with my comrades there in the night.

While my sight that was bound in my eyes unclosed,
As to long panoramas of visions.   170

And I saw askant[11] the armies,
I saw as in noiseless dreams hundreds of battle-flags,
Borne through the smoke of the battles and pierc'd with missiles I saw
  them,
And carried hither and yon through the smoke, and torn and bloody,
And at last but a few shreds left on the staffs, (and all in silence,) 175
And the staffs all splinter'd and broken.

I saw battle-corpses, myriads of them,
And the white skeletons of young men, I saw them,
I saw the debris and debris of all the slain soldiers of the war,
But I saw they were not as was thought,   180
They themselves were fully at rest, they suffer'd not,
The living remain'd and suffer'd, the mother suffer'd,
And the wife and the child and the musing comrade suffer'd,
And the armies that remain'd suffer'd.

---

[11]ASKANT: Off to the side.

16

Passing the visions, passing the night,	185

Passing the visions, passing the night, 185
Passing, unloosing the hold of my comrades' hands,
Passing the song of the hermit bird and the tallying song of my soul,
Victorious song, death's outlet song, yet varying ever-altering song,
As low and wailing, yet clear the notes, rising and falling, flooding the
   night,
Sadly sinking and fainting, as warning and warning, and yet again
   bursting with joy, 190
Covering the earth and filling the spread of the heaven,
As that powerful psalm in the night I heard from recesses,
Passing, I leave thee lilac with heart-shaped leaves,
I leave thee there in the door-yard, blooming, returning with spring.

I cease from my song for thee, 195
From my gaze on thee in the west, fronting the west, communing with
   thee,
O comrade lustrous with silver face in the night.

Yet each to keep and all, retrievements out of the night,
The song, the wondrous chant of the gray-brown bird,
And the tallying chant, the echo arous'd in my soul, 200
With the lustrous and drooping star with the countenance full of woe,
With the holders holding my hand nearing the call of the bird,
Comrades mine and I in the midst, and their memory ever to keep, for
   the dead I loved so well,
For the sweetest, wisest soul of all my days and lands—and this for his
   dear sake,
Lilac and star and bird twined with the chant of my soul, 205
There in the fragrant pines and the cedars dusk and dim.

[1865–1866]

From Democratic Vistas

Repeating our inquiry, what, then, do we mean by real literature? especially the democratic literature of the future? Hard questions to meet.
The clues are inferential, and turn us to the past. At best, we can only
offer suggestions, comparisons, circuits.

It must still be reiterated, as, for the purpose of these memoranda, the deep lesson of history and time, that all else in the contributions of a nation or age, through its politics, materials, heroic personalities, military eclat,[1] &c., remains crude, and defers, in any close and thorough-going estimate, until vitalized by national, original archetypes in literature. They only put the nation in form, finally tell anything—prove, complete anything—perpetuate anything. Without doubt, some of the richest and most powerful and populous communities of the antique world, and some of the grandest personalities and events, have, to after and present times, left themselves entirely unbequeath'd. Doubtless, greater than any that have come down to us, were among those lands, heroisms, persons, that have not come down to us at all, even by name, date, or location. Others have arrived safely, as from voyages over wide, century-stretching seas. The little ships, the miracles that have buoy'd them, and by incredible chances safely convey'd them, (or the best of them, their meaning and essence,) over long wastes, darkness, lethargy, ignorance, &c., have been a few inscriptions—a few immortal compositions, small in size, yet compassing what measureless values of reminiscence, contemporary portraitures, manners, idioms and beliefs, with deepest inference, hint and thought, to tie and touch forever the old, new body, and the old, new soul! These! and still these! bearing the freight so dear—dearer than pride—dearer than love. All the best experience of humanity, folded, saved, freighted to us here. Some of these tiny ships we call Old and New Testament,[2] Homer,[3] Eschylus,[4] Plato,[5] Juvenal,[6] &c. Precious minims![7] I think, if we were forced to choose, rather than have you, and the likes of you, and what belongs to, and has grown of you, blotted out and gone, we could better afford, appaling as that would be, to lose all actual ships, this day fasten'd by wharf, or floating on wave, and see them, with all their cargoes, scuttled and sent to the bottom.

Gather'd by geniuses of city, race or age, and put by them in highest of art's forms, namely, the literary form, the peculiar combinations

---

[1]ECLAT: Successes.
[2]OLD AND NEW TESTAMENT: The two primary divisions of the Bible.
[3]HOMER: Considered the greatest Greek poet (c. 850 BCE) of classical antiquity, to whom the epics the *Iliad* and the *Odyssey* are attributed.
[4]ESCHYLUS: Eschylus (525–456 BCE) was an Athenian tragic dramatist. He is best known for his tragic trilogy the *Oresteia*.
[5]PLATO: Plato (427?–347 BCE) was a Greek philosopher whose works highly influenced western literature and thought. His middle dialogues are considered his best works, including the *Republic*, *Phaedo*, *Symposium*, *Phaedrus*, *Timaeus*, and *Philebus*.
[6]JUVENAL: Decimus Junius Juvenalis was a Roman poet who lived around the first century CE.
[7]MINIMS: Pen strokes.

and the outshows of that city, age, or race, its particular modes of the universal attributes and passions, its faiths, heroes, lovers and gods, wars, traditions, struggles, crimes, emotions, joys, (or the subtle spirit of these,) having been pass'd on to us to illumine our own selfhood, and its experiences—what they supply, indispensable and highest, if taken away, nothing else in all the world's boundless storehouses could make up to us, or ever again return.

For us, along the great highways of time, those monuments stand—those forms of majesty and beauty. For us those beacons burn through all the nights. Unknown Egyptians, graving hieroglyphs; Hindus, with hymn and apothegm and endless epic; Hebrew prophet, with spirituality, as in flashes of lightning, conscience like red-hot iron, plaintive songs and screams of vengeance for tyrannies and enslavement; Christ, with bent head, brooding love and peace, like a dove; Greek, creating eternal shapes of physical and esthetic proportion; Roman, lord of satire, the sword, and the codex;[8] —of the figures, some far off and veil'd, others nearer and visible; Dante,[9] stalking with lean form, nothing but fibre, not a grain of superfluous flesh; Angelo,[10] and the great painters, architects, musicians; rich Shakespeare, luxuriant as the sun, artist and singer of feudalism in its sunset, with all the gorgeous colors, owner thereof, and using them at will; and so to such as German Kant[11] and Hegel,[12] where they, though near us, leaping over the ages, sit again, impassive, imperturbable, like the Egyptian gods. Of these, and the like of these, is it too much, indeed, to return to our favorite figure, and view them as orbs and systems of orbs, moving in free paths in the spaces of that other heaven, the kosmic intellect, the soul?

Ye powerful and resplendent ones! ye were, in your atmospheres, grown not for America, but rather for her foes, the feudal and the old—while our genius is democratic and modern. Yet could ye, indeed, but breathe your breath of life into our New World's nostrils—not to enslave us, as now, but, for our needs, to breed a spirit like your own—perhaps, (dare we to say it?) to dominate, even destroy, what you yourselves have left! On your plane, and no less, but even higher and wider, must we mete and measure for to-day and here. I demand races of orbic bards, with unconditional uncompromising sway. Come forth, sweet democratic despots of the west!

[8]CODEX: The Latin codex, the Roman legal code, issued in 438 by the Roman emperor of the eastern empire Theodosius II.
[9]DANTE: Dante Alighieri (1265–1321), Italian poet and author of the *Divine Comedy*.
[10]ANGELO: Michelangelo Buonarroti (1475–1564), Italian sculptor, painter and architect.
[11]KANT: German metaphysician and philosopher Immanuel Kant (1724–1804).
[12]HEGEL: German philosopher Georg Wilhelm Friedrich Hegel (1770–1831).

By points like these we, in reflection, token what we mean by any land's or people's genuine literature. And thus compared and tested, judging amid the influence of loftiest products only, what do our current copious fields of print, covering in manifold forms, the United States, better, for an analogy, present, than, as in certain regions of the sea, those spreading, undulating masses of squid, through which the whale swimming, with head half out, feeds?

Not but that doubtless our current so-called literature, (like an endless supply of small coin,) performs a certain service, and may-be, too, the service needed for the time, (the preparation-service, as children learn to spell.) Everybody reads, and truly nearly everybody writes, either books, or for the magazines or journals. The matter has magnitude, too, after a sort. But is it really advancing? or, has it advanced for a long while? There is something impressive about the huge editions of the dailies and weeklies, the mountain stacks of white paper piled in the press-vaults, and the proud, crashing, ten-cylinder presses, which I can stand and watch any time by the half hour. Then, (though the States in the field of imagination present not a single first-class work, not a single great literatus,) the main objects, to amuse, to titillate, to pass away time, to circulate the news, and rumors of news, to rhyme and read rhyme, are yet attain'd, and on a scale of infinity. To-day, in books, in the rivalry of writers, especially novelists, success, (so-call'd,) is for him or her who strikes the mean flat average, the sensational appetite for stimulus, incident, persiflage,[13] &c., and depicts, to the common calibre, sensual, exterior life. To such, or the luckiest of them, as we see, the audiences are limitless and profitable; but they cease presently. While this day, or any day, to workmen portraying interior or spiritual life, the audiences were limited, and often laggard—but they last forever.

Compared with the past, our modern science soars, and our journals serve—but ideal and even ordinary romantic literature, does not, I think, substantially advance. Behold the prolific brood of the contemporary novel, magazine-tale, theatre-play, &c. The same endless thread of tangled and superlative love-story, inherited, apparently from the Amadises[14] and Palmerins[15] of the 13th, 14th, and 15th centuries over there in Europe. The costumes and associations brought down to date, the seasoning hotter and more varied, the dragons and ogres left out—but the

13PERSIFLAGE: The frivolous treatment of subject matter.
14AMADISES: A reference to *Amadis de Gaule*, a prose romance of chivalry dating from the thirteenth- or fourteenth-century.
15PALMERINS: A sixteenth-century chivalric romance featuring the hero Palmerin.

thing, I should say, has not advanced—is just as sensational, just as strain'd—remains about the same, nor more, nor less.

What is the reason our time, our lands, that we see no fresh local courage, sanity, of our own—the Mississippi, stalwart Western men, real mental and physical facts, Southerners, &c., in the body of our literature? especially the poetic part of it. But always, instead, a parcel of dandies and ennuyees,[16] dapper little gentlemen from abroad, who flood us with their thin sentiment of parlors, parasols, piano-songs, tinkling rhymes, the five-hundredth importation—or whimpering and crying about something, chasing one aborted conceit after another, and forever occupied in dyspeptic amours with dyspeptic women. While, current and novel, the grandest events and revolutions, and stormiest passions of history, are crossing to-day with unparallel'd rapidity and magnificence over the stages of our own and all the continents, offering new materials, opening new vistas, with largest needs, inviting the daring launching forth of conceptions in literature, inspired by them, soaring in highest regions, serving art in its highest, (which is only the other name for serving God, and serving humanity,) where is the man of letters, where is the book, with any nobler aim than to follow in the old track, repeat what has been said before—and, as its utmost triumph, sell well, and be erudite or elegant?

Mark the roads, the processes, through which these States have arrived, standing easy, henceforth ever-equal, ever-compact, in their range to-day. European adventures? the most antique? Asiatic or African? old history—miracles—romances? Rather, our own unquestion'd facts. They hasten, incredible, blazing bright as fire. From the deeds and days of Columbus down to the present, and including the present—and especially the late Secession war—when I con them, I feel, every leaf, like stopping to see if I have not made a mistake, and fall'n on the splendid figments of some dream. But it is no dream. We stand, live, move, in the huge flow of our age's materialism—in its spirituality. We have had founded for us the most positive of lands. The founders have pass'd to other spheres—but what are these terrible duties they have left us?

Their politics the United States have, in my opinion, with all their faults, already substantially establish'd, for good, on their own native, sound, long-vista'd principles, never to be overturn'd, offering a sure basis for all the rest. With that, their future religious forms, sociology, literature, teachers, schools, costumes, &c., are of course to make a compact whole, uniform, on tallying principles. For how can we remain,

[16]ENNUYEES: Those who feel weary, bored, dissatisfied.

divided, contradicting ourselves, this way?[17] I say we can only attain harmony and stability by consulting ensemble and the ethic purports, and faithfully building upon them. For the New World, indeed, after two grand stages of preparation-strata, I perceive that now a third stage, being ready for, (and without which the other two were useless,) with unmistakable signs appears. The First stage was the planning and putting on record the political foundation rights of immense masses of people—indeed all people—in the organization of republican National, State, and municipal governments, all constructed with reference to each, and each to all. This is the American programme, not for classes, but for universal man, and is embodied in the compacts of the Declaration of Independence, and, as it began and has now grown, with its amendments, the Federal Constitution—and in the State governments, with all their interiors, and with general suffrage; those having the sense not only of what is in themselves, but that their certain several things started, planted, hundreds of others in the same direction duly arise and follow. The Second stage relates to material prosperity, wealth, produce, labor-saving machines, iron, cotton, local, State and continental railways, intercommunication and trade with all lands, steamships, mining, general employment, organization of great cities, cheap appliances for comfort, numberless technical schools, books, newspapers, a currency for money circulation, &c. The Third stage, rising out of the previous ones, to make them and all illustrious, I, now, for one, promulge, announcing a native expression-spirit, getting into form, adult, and through mentality, for these States, self-contain'd, different from others, more expansive, more rich and free, to be evidenced by original authors and poets to come, by American personalities, plenty of them, male and female, traversing the States, none excepted—and by native superber tableaux and growths of language, songs, operas, orations, lectures, architecture—and by a sublime and serious Religious Democracy sternly taking command, dissolving the old, sloughing off surfaces, and from its own interior and vital principles, reconstructing, democratizing society.

For America, type of progress, and of essential faith in man, above all his errors and wickedness—few suspect how deep, how deep it really strikes.

---

[17]THIS WAY: Of this section Whitman notes, "To-day, an instructive, curious spectacle and conflict. Science, (twin, in its fields, of Democracy in its)—Science, testing absolutely all thoughts, all works, has already burst well upon the world—a sun, mounting, most illuminating, most glorious—surely never again to set. But against it, deeply entrench'd, holding possession, yet remains, (not only through the churches and schools, but by imaginative literature, and unregenerate poetry,) the fossil theology of the mythic-materialistic, superstitious, untaught and credulous, fable-loving, primitive ages of humanity."

The world evidently supposes, and we have evidently supposed so too, that the States are merely to achieve the equal franchise, an elective government—to inaugurate the respectability of labor, and become a nation of practical operatives, law-abiding, orderly and well off. Yes, those are indeed parts of the task of America; but they not only do not exhaust the progressive conception, but rather arise, teeming with it, as the mediums of deeper, higher progress. Daughter of a physical revolution—other of the true revolutions, which are of the interior life, and of the arts. For so long as the spirit is not changed, any change of appearance is of no avail.

The old men, I remember as a boy, were always talking of American independence. What is independence? Freedom from all laws or bonds except those of one's own being, control'd by the universal ones. To lands, to man, to woman, what is there at last to each, but the inherent soul, nativity, idiocrasy,[18] free, highest-poised, soaring its own flight, following out itself?

At present, these States, in their theology and social standards, (of greater importance than their political institutions,) are entirely held possession of by foreign lands. We see the sons and daughters of the New World, ignorant of its genius, not yet inaugurating the native, the universal, and the near, still importing the distant, the partial, and the dead. We see London, Paris, Italy—not original, superb, as where they belong—but second-hand here, where they do not belong. We see the shreds of Hebrews, Romans, Greeks; but where, on her own soil, do we see, in any faithful, highest, proud expression, America herself? I sometimes question whether she has a corner in her own house.

Not but that in one sense, and a very grand one, good theology, good art, or good literature, has certain features shared in common. The combination fraternizes, ties the races—is, in many particulars, under laws applicable indifferently to all, irrespective of climate or date, and, from whatever source, appeals to emotions, pride, love, spirituality, common to humankind. Nevertheless, they touch a man closest, (perhaps only actually touch him,) even in these, in their expression through autochthonic[19] lights and shades, flavors, fondnesses, aversions, specific incidents, illustrations, out of his own nationality, geography, surroundings, antecedents, &c. The spirit and the form are one, and depend far more on association, identity and place, than is supposed. Subtly interwoven with the materiality and personality of a land, a race—Teuton,[20] Turk, Californian, or what not—there is always some-

---

[18]IDIOCRASY: That is, idiosyncracy; here, temperment.
[19]AUTOCHTHONIC: Native, indigenous.
[20]TEUTON: German.

thing—I can hardly tell what it is—history but describes the results of it—it is the same as the untellable look of some human faces. Nature, too, in her stolid forms, is full of it—but to most it is there a secret. This something is rooted in the invisible roots, the profoundest meanings of that place, race, or nationality; and to absorb and again effuse it, uttering words and products as from its midst, and carrying it into highest regions, is the work, or a main part of the work, of any country's true author, poet, historian, lecturer, and perhaps even priest and philosoph. Here, and here only, are the foundations for our really valuable and permanent verse, drama, &c.

But at present, (judged by any higher scale than that which finds the chief ends of existence to be to feverishly make money during one-half of it, and by some "amusement," or perhaps foreign travel, flippantly kill time, the other half,) and consider'd with reference to purposes of patriotism, health, a noble personality, religion, and the democratic adjustments, all these swarms of poems, literary magazines, dramatic plays, resultant so far from American intellect, and the formation of our best ideas, are useless and a mockery. They strengthen and nourish no one, express nothing characteristic, give decision and purpose to no one, and suffice only the lowest level of vacant minds.

Of what is called the drama, or dramatic presentation in the United States, as now put forth at the theatres, I should say it deserves to be treated with the same gravity, and on a par with the questions of ornamental confectionery at public dinners, or the arrangement of curtains and hangings in a ball-room—nor more, nor less. Of the other, I will not insult the reader's intelligence, (once really entering into the atmosphere of these Vistas,) by supposing it necessary to show, in detail, why the copious dribble, either of our little or well-known rhymesters, does not fulfil, in any respect, the needs and august occasions of this land. America demands a poetry that is bold, modern, and all-surrounding and kosmical, as she is herself. It must in no respect ignore science or the modern, but inspire itself with science and the modern. It must bend its vision toward the future, more than the past. Like America, it must extricate itself from even the greatest models of the past, and, while courteous to them, must have entire faith in itself, and the products of its own democratic spirit only. Like her, it must place in the van, and hold up at all hazards, the banner of the divine pride of man in himself, (the radical foundation of the new religion.) Long enough have the People been listening to poems in which common humanity, deferential, bends low, humiliated, acknowledging superiors. But America listens to no such poems. Erect, inflated, and fully self-esteeming be the chant; and then America will listen with pleased ears.

Nor may the genuine gold, the gems, when brought to light at last, be probably usher'd forth from any of the quarters currently counted on. To-day, doubtless, the infant genius of American poetic expression, (eluding those highly-refined imported and gilt-edged themes, and sentimental and butterfly flights, pleasant to orthodox publishers—causing tender spasms in the coteries, and warranted not to chafe the sensitive cuticle of the most exquisitely artificial gossamer delicacy,) lies sleeping far away, happily unrecognized and uninjur'd by the coteries, the art-writers, the talkers and critics of the saloons, or the lecturers in the colleges—lies sleeping, aside, unrecking itself, in some western idiom, or native Michigan or Tennessee repartee, or stump-speech—or in Kentucky or Georgia, or the Carolinas—or in some slang or local song or allusion of the Manhattan, Boston, Philadelphia or Baltimore mechanic[21]—or up in the Maine woods—or off in the hut of the California miner, or crossing the Rocky mountains, or along the Pacific railroad—or on the breasts of the young farmers of the northwest, or Canada, or boatmen of the lakes. Rude and coarse nursing-beds, these; but only from such beginnings and stocks, indigenous here, may haply arrive, be grafted, and sprout, in time, flowers of genuine American aroma, and fruits truly and fully our own.

I say it were a standing disgrace to these States—I say it were a disgrace to any nation, distinguish'd above others by the variety and vastness of its territories, its materials, its inventive activity, and the splendid practicality of its people, not to rise and soar above others also in its original styles in literature and art, and its own supply of intellectual and esthetic masterpieces, archetypal, and consistent with itself. I know not a land except ours that has not, to some extent, however small, made its title clear. The Scotch have their born ballads, subtly expressing their past and present, and expressing character. The Irish have theirs, England, Italy, France, Spain, theirs. What has America? With exhaustless mines of the richest ore of epic, lyric, tale, tune, picture, &c., in the Four Years' War;[22] with, indeed, I sometimes think, the richest masses of material ever afforded a nation, more variegated, and on a larger scale—the first sign of proportionate, native, imaginative Soul, and first-class works to match, is, (I cannot too often repeat), so far wanting.

Long ere the second centennial arrives, there will be some forty to fifty great States, among them Canada and Cuba. When the present century

21ECHANIC: A manual laborer.
22FOUR YEARS' WAR: The American Civil War (1861–1865) between the Northern states and the Southern states that seceded from the Union.

closes, our population will be sixty or seventy millions. The Pacific will be ours, and the Atlantic mainly ours. There will be daily electric communication with every part of the globe. What an age! What a land! Where, elsewhere, one so great? The individuality of one nation must then, as always, lead the world. Can there be any doubt who the leader ought to be? Bear in mind, though, that nothing less than the mightiest original non-subordinated SOUL has ever really, gloriously led, or ever can lead. (This Soul—its other name, in these Vistas, is LITERATURE)

[1871]

Emily Dickinson

(1830–1886)

Except for brief trips in her youth to Boston, Worcester, and Cambridge, Massachusetts, a longer visit to Washington, D.C., and Philadelphia in 1855, and a few weeks in Cambridge in 1864 for treatment of an eye disorder, Emily Dickinson spent her entire life in Amherst, Massachusetts. She was capable of warmth, affection, and playful humor, but, especially as she became older, Dickinson made sure that she alone established (and secured) the terms for interacting with other people. She had no desire for any kind of public life or career; she had no interest in politics or reform movements; and, however fervent her feelings for both men and women may have been, she had no sexual relationship or sustained romance with anyone. She rigorously maintained her privacy in the family home; she dressed in white all the time and allowed a doctor to examine her only as she walked by a door cracked open to an adjoining room.

Self-sentenced to confinement in her Amherst house, Dickinson baked bread, spent time in the garden, made brief appearances in this or that room or hallway, and then vanished through a door or up a stairway. She sent many heightened, exuberant, often mirthful, and sometimes enigmatic notes and letters, above all to her sister-in-law, Sue Gilbert, who lived next door.

Dickinson was complicatedly connected to the members of her family and to a few friends. There was, for example, her ambitious, aloof father, Edward Dickinson, who was an attorney, the treasurer of Amherst College, and a one-term U.S. congressman, and her melancholy, detached, but wryly humorous mother, Emily Norcross. There was also the young lawyer B. F. Newton (who gave her a copy of Ralph Waldo Emerson's poems); the literary journalists and editors Josiah Holland and Samuel Bowles; Charles Wadsworth, a married Presbyterian minister and almost certainly the man, addressed as "Master," to whom Dickinson wrote passionate letters; the radical reformer and essayist Thomas Wentworth Higginson, with whom Dickinson corresponded about her poetry and who visited her in 1870 (he told his wife, "I never was with anyone who drained my nerve power so much"); and Otis Phillips Lord, a crusty Whig politician and Massachusetts judge, two decades older than Dickinson, with whom she exchanged ardent letters late in her life.

Emotionally and intellectually (she felt special kinship with Shakespeare, Charlotte Bronte, Elizabeth Barrett Browning, and George Eliot), Dickinson was supercharged, as the nearly 1,800 poems she composed—many of which she neatly sewed into booklets and hid in the drawers of her bureau—demonstrate with a stunning, even shocking thematic brilliance and technical daring. Extremely con-

densed in syntax and structure, idiosyncratic in punctuation, and
breathtaking in imagery and phrasing, Dickinson's poems (and many of
her letters, too) catch our attention immediately. Yet many of the poems
are so inward-looking and private that they ultimately resist our
attempts to understand their meaning. Indeed, as the biographer Alfred
Habegger suggests, Dickinson may not have wanted to be understood.

Only a handful of Dickinson's poems were published in her lifetime,
all of them anonymously and probably without her consent. Through
her father's friends and acquaintances, and familiar as she was with
literary journals and papers, she could have published more, and in
her own name, if publication had been a goal. But, in Habegger's view,
Dickinson understood poetry as writing to be done for oneself and in
certain instances to be shared with friends and family members, as was
the case with the poems she sent to Sue Gilbert. She saved her poems
and assembled many of them into bundles, but, Habegger acknowledges, she left not a single "explicit statement as to what the massive
project meant to her."

Dickinson made her sister and brother promise that after her death
they would burn all of her papers. As instructed, Lavinia proceeded to
destroy all of the letters that Dickinson had saved. The poems, which
were a revelation to her, she preserved, and many of them were published in the 1890s and in subsequent decades, though in editions that
often revised and tampered with the wording and structure of the texts.
Modern scholars, led by Thomas H. Johnson and R. W. Franklin, have
restored the poems to the versions that Dickinson herself prepared. It is
unnerving to realize that we know (and now can read in correct form)
Dickinson's thrilling poems because of a broken promise. Possessed as
she was with a fierce, ironic intelligence, Dickinson would have understood deeply both the love and betrayal her sister's act displayed.

The text of the poems below is from The Poems of Emily Dickinson
(1960), edited by Thomas H. Johnson.

Illuminating studies include Richard B. Sewall, The Life of Emily
Dickinson (2 vols., 1974); Cynthia Griffin Wolff, Emily Dickinson
(1986); and Alfred Habegger, My Wars Are Laid Away in Books: The
Life of Emily Dickinson (2001).

130 [These are the days when Birds come back—]

These are the days when Birds come back—
A very few—a Bird or two—
To take a backward look.

These are the days when skies resume
The old—old sophistries of June—   5
A blue and gold mistake.

Oh fraud that cannot cheat the Bee—
Almost thy plausibility
Induces my belief.

Till ranks of seeds their witness bear—   10
And softly thro' the altered air
Hurries a timid leaf.

Oh Sacrament of summer days,
Oh Last Communion in the Haze—
Permit a child to join.   15

Thy sacred emblems to partake—
Thy consecrated bread to take
And thine immortal wine!

[c. 1859]

199 [I'm "wife"—I've finished that—]

I'm "wife"—I've finished that—
That other state—
I'm Czar—I'm "Woman" now—
It's safer so—

How odd the Girl's life looks   5
Behind this soft Eclipse—
I think that Earth feels so
To folks in Heaven—now—

This being comfort—then
That other kind—was pain—   10
But why compare?
I'm "Wife"! Stop there!

[c. 1860]

214 [I taste a liquor never brewed—]

I taste a liquor never brewed—
From Tankards scooped in Pearl—
Not all the Frankfort Berries[1]
Yield such an Alcohol!

Inebriate of Air—am I—   5
And Debauchee of Dew—
Reeling—thro endless summer days—
From inns of Molten Blue—

When "Landlords" turn the drunken Bee
Out of the Foxglove's door—   10
When Butterflies—renounce their "drams"—
I shall but drink the more!

Till Seraphs[2] swing their snowy Hats—
And Saints—to windows run—
To see the little Tippler   15
From Manzanilla[3] come!

[c. 1860]

216 [Safe in their Alabaster Chambers—]

Safe in their Alabaster Chambers—
Untouched by Morning
And untouched by Noon—
Sleep the meek members of the Resurrection—
Rafter of satin,   5
And Roof of stone.

[1]FRANKFORT BERRIES: Referring to German (Rhine) wine.
[2]SERAPHS: Seraphim; angels of the highest order, as seen by the prophet Isaiah in a vision as hovering above the throne of God.
[3]MANZANILLA: A pale, dry sherry.

Light laughs the breeze
In her Castle above them—
Babbles the Bee in a stolid Ear,
Pipe the Sweet Birds in ignorant cadence—   10
Ah, what sagacity perished here!

[1859]

241 [I like a look of Agony,]

I like a look of Agony,
Because I know it's true—
Men do not sham Convulsion,
Nor simulate, a Throe—

The Eyes glaze once—and that is Death—   5
Impossible to feign
The Beads upon the Forehead
By homely Anguish strung.

[c. 1861]

249 [Wild Nights—Wild Nights!]

Wild Nights—Wild Nights!
Were I with thee
Wild Nights should be
Our luxury!

Futile—the Winds—   5
To a Heart in port—
Done with the Compass—
Done with the Chart!

Rowing in Eden—
Ah, the Sea!   10
Might I but moor—Tonight—
In Thee!

[c. 1861]

258 [There's a certain Slant of light,]

There's a certain Slant of light,
Winter Afternoons—
That oppresses, like the Heft
Of Cathedral Tunes—

Heavenly Hurt, it gives us—   5
We can find no scar,
But internal difference,
Where the Meanings, are—

None may teach it—Any—
'Tis the Seal Despair—   10
An imperial affliction
Sent us of the Air—

When it comes, the Landscape listens—
Shadows—hold their breath—
When it goes, 'tis like the Distance   15
On the look of Death—

[c. 1861]

280 [I felt a Funeral, in my Brain,]

I felt a Funeral, in my Brain,
And Mourners to and fro
Kept treading—treading—till it seemed
That Sense was breaking through—

And when they all were seated,   5
A Service, like a Drum—
Kept beating—beating—till I thought
My Mind was going numb—

And then I heard them lift a Box
And creak across my Soul   10
With those same Boots of Lead, again,
Then Space—began to toll,

As all the Heavens were a Bell,
And Being, but an Ear,
And I, and Silence, some strange Race   15
Wrecked, solitary, here—

And then a Plank in Reason, broke,
And I dropped down, and down—
And hit a World, at every plunge,
And Finished knowing—then—   20

[c. 1861]

303 [The Soul selects her own Society—]

The Soul selects her own Society—
Then—shuts the Door—
To her divine Majority—
Present no more—

Unmoved—she notes the Chariots—pausing—   5
At her low Gate—
Unmoved—an Emperor be kneeling
Upon her Mat—

I've known her—from an ample nation—
Choose One—   10
Then—close the Valves of her attention—
Like Stone—

[c. 1862]

324 [Some keep the Sabbath going to Church—]

Some keep the Sabbath going to Church—
I keep it, staying at Home—

With a Bobolink[1] for a Chorister—
And an Orchard, for a Dome—

Some keep the Sabbath in Surplice[2]—   5
I just wear my Wings—
And instead of tolling the Bell, for Church,
Our little Sexton[3]—sings.

God preaches, a noted Clergyman—
And the sermon is never long,   10
So instead of getting to Heaven, at last—
I'm going, all along.

[c. 1860]

341 [After great pain, a formal feeling comes—]

After great pain, a formal feeling comes—
The Nerves sit ceremonious, like Tombs—
The stiff Heart questions was it He, that bore,
And Yesterday, or Centuries before?

The Feet, mechanical, go round—   5
Of Ground, or Air, or Ought—
A Wooden way
Regardless grown,
A Quartz contentment, like a stone—

This is the Hour of Lead—   10
Remembered, if outlived,
As Freezing persons, recollect the Snow—
First—Chill—then Stupor—then the letting go—

[c. 1862]

---

[1]BOBOLINK: A North American songbird.
[2]SURPLICE: A loose robe of white linen with wide sleeves usually worn by members of a chorus.
[3]SEXTON: Church employee responsible for maintenance, bell-ringing, and gravedigging.

348 [I dreaded that first Robin, so,]

I dreaded that first Robin, so,
But He is mastered, now,
I'm some accustomed to Him grown,
He hurts a little, though—

I thought if I could only live   5
Till that first Shout got by—
Not all Pianos in the Woods
Had power to mangle me—

I dared not meet the Daffodils—
For fear their Yellow Gown   10
Would pierce me with a fashion
So foreign to my own—

I wished the Grass would hurry—
So—when 'twas time to see—
He'd be too tall, the tallest one   15
Could stretch—to look at me—

I could not bear the Bees should come,
I wished they'd stay away
In those dim countries where they go,
What word had they, for me?   20

They're here, though; not a creature failed—
No Blossom stayed away
In gentle deference to me—
The Queen of Calvary[1]—

Each one salutes me, as he goes,   25
And I, my childish Plumes,
Lift, in bereaved acknowledgement
Of their unthinking Drums—

                                                    [c. 1862]

---

[1]QUEEN OF CALVARY: Referring to the crucifixion of Christ at Calvary—in this case, one who has experienced great suffering.

441 [This is my letter to the World]

This is my letter to the World
That never wrote to Me—
The simple News that Nature told—
With tender Majesty

Her Message is committed   5
To Hands I cannot see—
For love of Her—Sweet—countrymen—
Judge tenderly—of Me

[c. 1862]

448 [This was a Poet— It is That]

This was a Poet—It is That
Distills amazing sense
From ordinary Meanings—
And Attar so immense

From the familiar species   5
That perished by the Door—
We wonder it was not Ourselves
Arrested it—before—

Of Pictures, the Discloser—
The Poet—it is He—   10
Entitles Us—by Contrast—
To ceaseless Poverty—

Of Portion—so unconscious—
The Robbing—could not harm—
Himself—to Him—a Fortune—   15
Exterior—to Time—

[c. 1862]

465 [I heard a Fly buzz— when I died—]

I heard a Fly buzz—when I died—
The Stillness in the Room
Was like the Stillness in the Air—
Between the Heaves of Storm—

The Eyes around—had wrung them dry—   5
And Breaths were gathering firm
For that last Onset—when the King
Be witnessed—in the Room—

I willed my Keepsakes—Signed away
What portion of me be   10
Assignable—and then it was
There interposed a Fly—

With Blue—uncertain stumbling Buzz—
Between the light—and me—
And then the Windows failed—and then   15
I could not see to see—

[c. 1862]

501 [This World is not Conclusion.]

This World is not Conclusion.
A Species stands beyond—
Invisible, as Music—
But positive, as Sound—
It beckons, and it baffles—   5
Philosophy—dont know—
And through a Riddle, at the last—
Sagacity, must go—
To guess it, puzzles scholars—
To gain it, Men have borne   10
Contempt of Generations
And Crucifixion, shown—
Faith slips—and laughs, and rallies—

Blushes, if any see—
Plucks at a twig of Evidence—   15
And asks a Vane, the way—
Much Gesture, from the Pulpit—
Strong Hallelujahs roll—
Narcotics cannot still the Tooth
That nibbles at the soul—   20

[c. 1862]

520 [I started Early— Took my Dog—]

I started Early—Took my Dog—
And visited the Sea—
The Mermaids in the Basement
Came out to look at me—

And Frigates—in the Upper Floor   5
Extended Hempen Hands—
Presuming Me to be a Mouse—
Aground—upon the Sands—

But no Man moved Me—till the Tide
Went past my simple Shoe—   10
And past my Apron—and my Belt
And past my Bodice—too—

And made as He would eat me up—
As wholly as a Dew
Upon a Dandelion's Sleeve—   15
And then—I started—too—

And He—He followed—close behind—
I felt His Silver Heel
Upon my Ancle—Then my Shoes
Would overflow with Pearl—   20

Until We met the Solid Town—
No One He seemed to know—
And bowing—with a Mighty look—
At me—The Sea withdrew—

[c. 1862]

632 [The Brain—is wider than the Sky—]

The Brain—is wider than the Sky—
For—put them side by side—
The one the other will contain
With ease—and You—beside—

The Brain is deeper than the sea—   5
For—hold them—Blue to Blue—
The one the other will absorb—
As Sponges—Buckets—do—

The Brain is just the weight of God—
For—Heft them—Pound for Pound—   10
And they will differ—if they do—
As Syllable from Sound—

[c. 1862]

650 [Pain—has an Element of Blank—]

Pain—has an Element of Blank—
It cannot recollect
When it begun—or if there were
A time when it was not—

It has no Future—but itself—   5
Its Infinite contain
Its Past—enlightened to perceive
New Periods—of Pain.

[c. 1862]

709 [Publication— is the Auction—]

Publication—is the Auction
Of the Mind of Man—

Poverty—be justifying
For so foul a thing

Possibly—but We—would rather   5
From Our Garret go
White—Unto the White Creator—
Than invest—Our Snow—

Thought belong to Him who gave it—
Then—to Him Who bear   10
It's Corporeal[1] illustration—Sell
The Royal Air—

In the Parcel—Be the Merchant
Of the Heavenly Grace—
But reduce no Human Spirit   15
To Disgrace of Price—

[c. 1863]

712 [Because I could not stop for Death—]

Because I could not stop for Death—
He kindly stopped for me—
The Carriage held but just Ourselves—
And Immortality.

We slowly drove—He knew no haste   5
And I had put away
My labor and my leisure too,
For His Civility—

We passed the School, where Children strove
At Recess—in the Ring—   10
We passed the Fields of Gazing Grain—
We passed the Setting Sun—

Or rather—He passed Us—
The Dews drew quivering and chill—

[1]CORPOREAL: Of the body, as opposed to of the spirit.

For only Gossamer,[1] my Gown—
My Tippet[2] only Tulle[3]—   15

We paused before a House that seemed
A Swelling of the Ground—
The Roof was scarcely visible—
The Cornice—in the Ground—   20

Since then—'tis Centuries—and yet
Feels shorter than the Day
I first surmised the Horses Heads
Were toward Eternity—

[c. 1863]

754 [My Life had stood— a Loaded Gun—]

My Life had stood—a Loaded Gun—
In Corners—till a Day
The Owner passed—identified—
And carried Me away—

And now We roam in Sovereign Woods—   5
And now We hunt the Doe—
And every time I speak for Him—
The Mountains straight reply—

And do I smile, such cordial light
Upon the Valley glow—   10
It is as a Vesuvian[1] face
Had let its pleasure through—

And when at Night—Our good Day done—
I guard My Master's Head—
'Tis better than the Eider-Duck's[2]   15
Deep Pillow—to have shared—

---

[1]GOSSAMER: Soft, sheer gauzy fabric.
[2]TIPPET: A covering for the shoulders.
[3]TULLE: A fine, starched net of silk, especially for veils and gowns.
[1]VESUVIAN: Referring to Mount Vesuvius, the active volcano on the eastern shore of the Bay of Naples in Italy, known for the eruption that buried the towns of Pompeii and Herculaneum in 79 CE. Here, metaphorically, a face that could abruptly erupt.
[2]EIDER-DUCK'S: Eider is a large northern sea duck; its soft down was used for pillows and comforters.

To foe of His—I'm deadly foe—
None stir the second time—
On whom I lay a Yellow Eye—
Or an emphatic Thumb—   20

Though I than He—may longer live
He longer must—than I—
For I have but the power to kill,
Without—the power to die—

[c. 1863]

986 [A narrow Fellow in the Grass]

A narrow Fellow in the Grass
Occasionally rides—
You may have met Him—did you not
His notice sudden is—

The Grass divides as with a Comb—   5
A spotted shaft is seen—
And then it closes at your feet
And opens further on—

He likes a Boggy Acre
A Floor too cool for Corn—   10
Yet when a Boy, and Barefoot—
I more than once at Noon
Have passed, I thought, a Whip lash
Unbraiding in the Sun
When stooping to secure it   15
It wrinkled, and was gone—

Several of Nature's People
I know, and they know me—
I feel for them a transport
Of cordiality—   20

But never met this Fellow
Attended, or alone
Without a tighter breathing
And Zero at the Bone—

[c. 1865]

1129 [Tell all the Truth but tell it slant—]

Tell all the Truth but tell it slant—
Success in Circuit lies
Too bright for our infirm Delight
The Truth's superb surprise
As Lightning to the Children eased   5
With explanation kind
The Truth must dazzle gradually
Or every man be blind—

[c. 1868]

1545 [The Bible is an antique Volume—]

The Bible is an antique Volume—
Written by faded Men
At the suggestion of Holy Spectres—
Subjects—Bethlehem[1]—
Eden[2]—the ancient Homestead—   5
Satan[3]—the Brigadier—
Judas[4]—the Great Defaulter—
David[5]—the Troubadour[6]—
Sin—a distinguished Precipice
Others must resist—   10
Boys that "believe" are very lonesome—
Other Boys are "lost"—
Had but the Tale a warbling Teller—
All the Boys would come—
Orpheus'[7] Sermon captivated—   15
It did not condemn—

[c. 1882]

[1]BETHLEHEM: The birthplace of Jesus.
[2]EDEN: The garden where Adam and Eve lived before their fall from grace; paradise.
[3]SATAN: The fallen angel, Satan, waged war against God.
[4]JUDAS: Judas Iscariot, who betrays Jesus for thirty pieces of silver (Matthew 26:14–15).
[5]DAVID: A biblical king of Israel to whom the Book of Psalms is traditionally attributed.
[6]TROUBADOUR: A medieval lyric poet from southern France.
[7]ORPHEUS: Orpheus—the son, in Greek myth, of the Muse Calliope, and the only nonbiblical person in the poem—had the gift of music. His lyre (harp) could charm wild beasts and even make the rocks and trees sway.

1732 [My Life closed twice before its close—]

My life closed twice before its close—
It yet remains to see
If Immortality unveil
A third event to me

So huge, so hopeless to conceive   5
As these that twice befell.
Parting is all we know of heaven,
And all we need of hell.

[pub. 1896]

From *Letters of Emily Dickinson*

[APRIL 15, 1862.]

MR. HIGGINSON,
Are you too deeply occupied to say if my Verse is alive?
The Mind is so near itself— it cannot see, distinctly— and I have none to ask—
Should you think it breathed—and had you the leisure to tell me, I should feel quick gratitude—
If I make the mistake—that you dared to tell me—would give me sincerer honor—toward you—
I enclose my name—asking you, if you please—Sir—to tell me what is true?
That you will not betray me—it is needless to ask— since Honor is its own pawn—

[APRIL 25, 1862.]

MR. HIGGINSON,
Your kindness claimed earlier gratitude—but I was ill—and write today from my pillow.
Thank you for the surgery—it was not so painful as I supposed. I bring you others—as you ask—though they might not differ—

While my thought is undressed—I can make the distinction; but when I put them in the gown—they look alike and numb.

You asked how old I was? I made no verse—but one or two—until this winter—Sir—

I had a terror—since September—I could tell to none—and so I sing, as the boy does of the burying Ground—because I am afraid—You inquire my books— For Poets—I have Keats—and Mr. and Mrs. Browning. For prose, Mr. Ruskin— Sir Thomas Browne—and the *Revelations*. I went to school—but in your manner of the phrase—had no education. When a little Girl, I had a friend who taught me Immortality—but venturing too near, himself—he never returned—Soon after, my Tutor died—and for several years my Lexicon—was my only companion—Then I found one more—but he was not contented I be his scholar—so he left the Land.

You ask of my Companions Hills—Sir—and the Sundown—and a Dog—large as myself, that my Father bought me—They are better than Beings—because they know—but do not tell—and the noise in the Pool, at Noon—excels my Piano.

I have a Brother and Sister—My Mother does not care for thought—and Father, too busy with his Briefs—to notice what we do—He buys me many Books— but begs me not to read them—because he fears they joggle the Mind. They are religious—except me—and address an Eclipse, every morning—whom they call their "Father." But I fear my story fatigues you—I would like to learn— Could you tell me how to grow—or is it unconveyed—like Melody—or Witchcraft?

You speak of Mr. Whitman—I never read his book—but was told that he was disgraceful—

I read Miss Prescott's "Circumstance,"[1] but it followed me in the Dark—so I avoided her—

Two Editors of Journals came to my Father's House this winter—and asked me for my Mind—and when I asked them "Why" they said I was penurious—and they, would use it for the World—

I could not weigh myself—Myself—

My size felt small—to me—I read your Chapters in The Atlantic—and experienced honor for you—I was sure you would not reject a confiding question—

Is this—Sir—what you asked me to tell you?

> Your friend,
> E—DICKINSON.

[1]CIRCUMSTANCE: A story by Harriet Prescott Spofford (1835–1921), published in the *Atlantic Monthly* in May 1860.

Rebecca Harding Davis

(1831–1910)

The journalist and fiction writer Rebecca Harding Davis was born in Washington, Pennsylvania, raised until age five in Big Spring (later Huntsville), Alabama, and then taken to Wheeling, Virginia (later West Virginia), an industrial town. She was tutored at home and attended Washington Female Seminary, a school in Pennsylvania, from which she graduated first in the class of 1848.

A devout Christian and the eldest of five children, Davis lived at home, caring for other members of her family and continuing to read her favorite authors, such as John Bunyan, Sir Walter Scott, Elizabeth Gaskell, and Nathaniel Hawthorne, whose choice of common subject matter and psychological insight she admired. But with the publication in April 1861 in the prestigious Atlantic Monthly *of her long story "Life in the Iron Mills," based on her observations of mill and iron workers in Wheeling, Davis suddenly became a sought-after author.*

At Davis's request, and in keeping with the journal's practice, "Life in the Iron Mills" was published anonymously. The editor, James T. Fields, paid her fifty dollars, a good fee for that era, and through him she met Hawthorne and his wife Sophia, Ralph Waldo Emerson, the Transcendentalist author and educator Amos Bronson Alcott (the father of Louis May Alcott), and the physician and writer Oliver Wendell Holmes.

Seeking to "dig into this commonplace, this vulgar American life, and see what is in it," Davis continued her treatment of the impact of industrialism in a novel, Margaret Howth: A Story of Today *(1862). Married in 1863 to L. Clarke Davis, a lawyer and journalist in Philadelphia, and the mother of three children (one of whom, Richard, became a famous short-story writer and journalist), she nonetheless remained active (if uneven in quality) as a writer, producing 100 stories, ten novels, and many essays and journalistic pieces. Among her significant works are* Waiting for the Verdict *(1868), about race relations in the aftermath of the abolition of slavery;* Earthen Pitchers *(1873–1874), about the challenges faced by a woman writer struggling to make a living and enjoy personal freedom; and* John Andross *(1874), which examines political corruption in Pennsylvania.*

The critic Steven Frye has noted that Davis, above all as the author of "Life in the Iron Mills," occupies a notable place in American literary history: she falls between Emerson and Whitman, with their affirmation of human worth and potential, and Stephen Crane, Frank Norris, Theodore Dreiser, and others in the later realist and naturalist traditions. Her story (apparently the first she ever wrote) shows with grim clarity the degradation of the mind and spirit caused by arduous labor and poverty. Davis delves into the crushing

*burden of working conditions in a society becoming ever more industri-
alized, and weaves into her account an evocative presentation of the
role of women and the place of art.*

*For biography and critical interpretation: William Frazer
Grayburn,* The Major Fiction of Rebecca Harding Davis *(1965); Sharon
M. Harris,* Rebecca Harding Davis and American Realism *(1991); Jane
Atteridge Rose,* Rebecca Harding Davis *(1993); and Jean Pfaelzer,*
Parlor Radical: Rebecca Harding Davis and the Origins of American
Social Realism *(1996).*

Life in the Iron Mills

"Is this the end?
O Life, as futile, then, as frail!
What hope of answer or redress?"[1]

A cloudy day: do you know what that is in a town of iron-works?[2]
The sky sank down before dawn, muddy, flat, immovable. The air is
thick, clammy with the breath of crowded human beings. It stifles me.
I open the window, and, looking out, can scarcely see through the rain
the grocer's shop opposite, where a crowd of drunken Irishmen are puffing Lynchburg tobacco[3] in their pipes. I can detect the scent through
all the foul smells ranging loose in the air.

The idiosyncrasy of this town is smoke. It rolls sullenly in slow folds
from the great chimneys of the iron-founderies, and settles down in
black, slimy pools on the muddy streets. Smoke on the wharves, smoke
on the dingy boats, on the yellow river,—clinging in a coating of greasy
soot to the house-front, the two faded poplars, the faces of the passers-
by. The long train of mules, dragging masses of pig-iron[4] through the
narrow street, have a foul vapor hanging to their reeking sides. Here,
inside, is a little broken figure of an angel pointing upward from the
mantel-shelf; but even its wings are covered with smoke, clotted and
black. Smoke everywhere! A dirty canary chirps desolately in a cage

---

[1]WHAT HOPE OF ANSWER OR REDRESS? An adaptation of "In Memoriam A. H. H." (1850), a
poem by Alfred, Lord Tennyson (1809–1892), 12:4: "And saying; 'Comes he thus, my friend? / Is
this the end of all my care?' / And circle moaning in the air: / Is this the end? Is this the end?"; and
56:7: "O life as futile, then, as frail! / O for thy voice to soothe and bless! / What hope of answer, or
redress? / Behind the veil, behind the veil."
[2]IRON-WORKS: Davis does not name the town, but it could be her hometown of Wheeling, West
Virginia, on the Ohio River.
[3]LYNCHBURG TOBACCO: Cheap tobacco from Lynchburg, Virginia.
[4]PIG-IRON: Cast iron in pigs or ingots (oblong blocks).

beside me. Its dream of green fields and sunshine is a very old dream,— almost worn out, I think.

From the back-window I can see a narrow brick-yard sloping down to the river-side, strewed with rain-butts and tubs. The river, dull and tawny-colored, (la belle rivière![5]) drags itself sluggishly along, tired of the heavy weight of boats and coal-barges. What wonder? When I was a child, I used to fancy a look of weary, dumb appeal upon the face of the negro-like river slavishly bearing its burden day after day. Something of the same idle notion comes to me to-day, when from the street-window I look on the slow stream of human life creeping past, night and morning, to the great mills. Masses of men, with dull, besotted faces bent to the ground, sharpened here and there by pain or cunning; skin and muscle and flesh begrimed with smoke and ashes; stooping all night over boiling caldrons of metal, laired by day in dens of drunkenness and infamy; breathing from infancy to death an air saturated with fog and grease and soot, vileness for soul and body. What do you make of a case like that, amateur psychologist? You call it an altogether serious thing to be alive: to these men it is a drunken jest, a joke,—horrible to angels perhaps, to them commonplace enough. My fancy about the river was an idle one: it is no type of such a life. What if it be stagnant and slimy here? It knows that beyond there waits for it odorous sunlight,—quaint old gardens, dusky with soft, green foliage of apple-trees, and flushing crimson with roses,—air, and fields, and mountains. The future of the Welsh puddler[6] passing just now is not so pleasant. To be stowed away, after his grimy work is done, in a hole in the muddy graveyard, and after that,— not air, nor green fields, nor curious roses.

Can you see how foggy the day is? As I stand here, idly tapping the window-pane, and looking out through the rain at the dirty back-yard and the coal-boats below, fragments of an old story float up before me,— a story of this house into which I happened to come to-day. You may think it a tiresome story enough, as foggy as the day, sharpened by no sudden flashes of pain or pleasure.—I know: only the outline of a dull life, that long since, with thousands of dull lives like its own, was vainly lived and lost: thousands of them,—massed, vile, slimy lives, like those of the torpid lizards in yonder stagnant water-butt.—Lost? There is a curious point for you to settle, my friend, who study psychology in a lazy, dilettante[7] way. Stop a moment. I am going to be honest. This is what I want you to do. I want you to hide your disgust, take no heed to your

[5]LA BELLE RIVIÈRE: The beautiful river. (French)
[6]PUDDLER: A worker who puddles iron, stirring it into a vat of molten pig iron to make wrought iron.
[7]DILETTANTE: Amateur.

clean clothes, and come right down with me,—here, into the thickest of the fog and mud and foul effluvia. I want you to hear this story. There is a secret down here, in this nightmare fog, that has lain dumb for centuries: I want to make it a real thing to you. You, Egoist,[8] or Pantheist,[9] or Arminian,[10] busy in making straight paths for your feet on the hills, do not see it clearly,—this terrible question which men here have gone mad and died trying to answer. I dare not put this secret into words. I told you it was dumb. These men, going by with drunken faces, and brains full of unawakened power, do not ask it of Society or of God. Their lives ask it; their deaths ask it. There is no reply. I will tell you plainly that I have a great hope; and I bring it to you to be tested. It is this: that this terrible dumb question is its own reply; that it is not the sentence of death we think it, but, from the very extremity of its darkness, the most solemn prophecy which the world has known of the Hope to come. I dare make my meaning no clearer, but will only tell my story. It will, perhaps, seem to you as foul and dark as this thick vapor about us, and as pregnant with death, but if your eyes are free as mine are to look deeper, no perfume-tinted dawn will be so fair with promise of the day that shall surely come.

My story is very simple,—only what I remember of the life of one of these men,—a furnace-tender in one of Kirby & John's rolling-mills,—Hugh Wolfe. You know the mills? They took the great order for the lower Virginia railroads there last winter; run usually with about a thousand men. I cannot tell why I choose the half-forgotten story of this Wolfe more than that of myriads of these furnace-hands. Perhaps because there is a secret, underlying sympathy between that story and this day with its impure fog and thwarted sunshine,—or perhaps simply for the reason that this house is the one where the Wolfes lived. There were the father and son,—both hands, as I said, in one of Kirby & John's mills for making railroad-iron,—and Deborah, their cousin, a picker[11] in some of the cotton-mills. The house was rented then to half a dozen families. The Wolfes had two of the cellar-rooms. The old man, like many of the puddlers and feeders[12] of the mills, was Welsh,—had spent half of his life in the Cornish tin-mines. You may pick the Welsh emigrants, Cornish miners, out of

---

[8]EGOIST: A person devoted to his or her self-interest.

[9]PANTHEIST: One who believes the doctrine that God is everything and everything is God and especially in the presence of the deity in nature.

[10]ARMINIAN: One who follows the teachings of James Arminius (1560–1609), a Dutch Reformed theologian who opposed the Calvinist doctrine of predestination (the doctrine that instructs that God, owing to his infallible knowledge of the future, has appointed and ordained all events).

[11]PICKER: A worker in a cotton mill who runs a machine that pulls apart raw cotton.

[12]FEEDERS: Ironworkers who pour molten metal into casts.

the throng passing the windows, any day. They are a trifle more filthy; their muscles are not so brawny, they stoop more. When they are drunk, they neither yell, nor shout, nor stagger, but skulk along like beaten hounds. A pure, unmixed blood, I fancy, shows itself in the slight angular bodies and sharply-cut facial lines. It is nearly thirty years since the Wolfes lived here. Their lives were like those of their class: incessant labor, sleeping in kennel-like rooms, eating rank pork and molasses, drinking— God and the distillers only know what; with an occasional night in jail, to atone for some drunken excess. Is that all of their lives?—of the portion given to them and these their duplicates swarming the streets to-day?—nothing beneath?—all? So many a political reformer will tell you,—and many a private reformer, too, who has gone among them with a heart tender with Christ's charity, and come out outraged, hardened.

One rainy night, about eleven o'clock, a crowd of halfclothed women stopped outside of the cellar-door. They were going home from the cotton-mill.

"Good-night, Deb," said one, a mulatto, steadying herself against the gas-post. She needed the post to steady her. So did more than one of them.

"Dah's a ball to Miss Potts' to-night. Ye 'd best come."

"Inteet, Deb, if hur'll come, hur'll hef fun," said a shrill Welsh voice in the crowd.

Two or three dirty hands were thrust out to catch the gown of the woman, who was groping for the latch of the door.

"No."

"No? Where's Kit Small, then?"

"Begorra![13] on the spools.[14] Alleys behint, though we helped her, we dud. An wid ye! Let Deb alone! It's ondacent frettin' a quite body. Be the powers, an' we'll have a night of it! there'll be lashin's o' drink,—the Vargent[15] be blessed and praised for't!"

They went on, the mulatto inclining for a moment to show fight, and drag the woman Wolfe off with them; but, being pacified, she staggered away.

Deborah groped her way into the cellar, and, after considerable stumbling, kindled a match, and lighted a tallow dip, that sent a yellow glimmer over the room. It was low, damp,—the earthen floor covered with a green, slimy moss,—a fetid air smothering the breath. Old Wolfe lay asleep on a heap of straw, wrapped in a torn horse-blanket. He was a pale,

[13]BEGORRA!: An Irish variation of the expletive "by God!"
[14]SPOOLS: Spindles on which cotton is wound by the spinning machine.
[15]VARGENT: The Virgin Mary.

meek little man, with a white face and red rabbit-eyes. The woman Deborah was like him; only her face was even more ghastly, her lips bluer, her eyes more watery. She wore a faded cotton gown and a slouching bonnet. When she walked, one could see that she was deformed, almost a hunchback. She trod softly, so as not to waken him, and went through into the room beyond. There she found by the half-extinguished fire an iron saucepan filled with cold boiled potatoes, which she put upon a broken chair with a pint-cup of ale. Placing the old candlestick beside this dainty repast, she untied her bonnet, which hung limp and wet over her face, and prepared to eat her supper. It was the first food that had touched her lips since morning. There was enough of it, however: there is not always. She was hungry,—one could see that easily enough,—and not drunk, as most of her companions would have been found at this hour. She did not drink, this woman,—her face told that too,—nothing stronger than ale. Perhaps the weak, flaccid wretch had some stimulant in her pale life to keep her up,—some love or hope, it might be, or urgent need. When that stimulant was gone, she would take to whiskey. Man cannot live by work alone. While she was skinning the potatoes, and munching them, a noise behind her made her stop.

"Janey!" she called, lifting the candle and peering into the darkness. "Janey, are you there?"

A heap of ragged coats was heaved up, and the face of a young girl emerged, staring sleepily at the woman.

"Deborah," she said, at last, "I'm here the night."

"Yes, child. Hur's welcome," she said, quietly eating on.

The girl's face was haggard and sickly; her eyes were heavy with sleep and hunger: real Milesian[16] eyes they were, dark, delicate blue, glooming out from black shadows with a pitiful fright.

"I was alone," she said, timidly.

"Where's the father?" asked Deborah, holding out a potato, which the girl greedily seized.

"He's beyant,—wid Haley,—in the stone house." (Did you ever hear the word jail from an Irish mouth?) "I came here. Hugh told me never to stay me-lone."

"Hugh?"

"Yes."

A vexed frown crossed her face. The girl saw it, and added quickly,—

---

[16]MILESIAN: Irish, after the mythical Irish King Milesius.

"I have not seen Hugh the day, Deb. The old man says his watch lasts till the mornin'."

The woman sprang up, and hastily began to arrange some bread and flitch[17] in a tin pail, and to pour her own measure of ale into a bottle. Tying on her bonnet, she blew out the candle.

"Lay ye down, Janey dear," she said, gently, covering her with the old rags. "Hur can eat the potatoes, if hur's hungry."

"Where are ye goin', Deb? The rain's sharp."

"To the mill, with Hugh's supper."

"Let him bide till th' morn. Sit ye down."

"No, no,"—sharply pushing her off. "The boy'll starve."

She hurried from the cellar, while the child wearily coiled herself up for sleep. The rain was falling heavily, as the woman, pail in hand, emerged from the mouth of the alley, and turned down the narrow street, that stretched out, long and black, miles before her. Here and there a flicker of gas lighted an uncertain space of muddy footwalk and gutter; the long rows of houses, except an occasional lagerbier[18] shop, were closed; now and then she met a band of millhands skulking to or from their work.

Not many even of the inhabitants of a manufacturing town know the vast machinery of system by which the bodies of workmen are governed, that goes on unceasingly from year to year. The hands of each mill are divided into watches that relieve each other as regularly as the sentinels of an army. By night and day the work goes on, the unsleeping engines groan and shriek, the fiery pools of metal boil and surge. Only for a day in the week, in half-courtesy to public censure, the fires are partially veiled; but as soon as the clock strikes midnight, the great furnaces break forth with renewed fury, the clamor begins with fresh, breathless vigor, the engines sob and shriek like "gods in pain."

As Deborah hurried down through the heavy rain, the noise of these thousand engines sounded through the sleep and shadow of the city like far-off thunder. The mill to which she was going lay on the river, a mile below the citylimits. It was far, and she was weak, aching from standing twelve hours at the spools. Yet it was her almost nightly walk to take this man his supper, though at every square she sat down to rest, and she knew she should receive small word of thanks.

Perhaps, if she had possessed an artist's eye, the picturesque oddity of the scene might have made her step stagger less, and the path

[17]FLITCH: Salt pork.
[18]LAGERBIER: Light beer.

seem shorter; but to her the mills were only "summat deilish[19] to look at by night."

The road leading to the mills had been quarried from the solid rock, which rose abrupt and bare on one side of the cinder-covered road, while the river, sluggish and black, crept past on the other. The mills for rolling iron are simply immense tent-like roofs, covering acres of ground, open on every side. Beneath these roofs Deborah looked in on a city of fires, that burned hot and fiercely in the night. Fire in every horrible form: pits of flame waving in the wind; liquid metal-flames writhing in tortuous streams through the sand; wide caldrons filled with boiling fire, over which bent ghastly wretches stirring the strange brewing; and through all, crowds of half-clad men, looking like revengeful ghosts in the red light, hurried, throwing masses of glittering fire. It was like a street in Hell. Even Deborah muttered, as she crept through, "'T looks like t' Devil's place!" It did,—in more ways than one.

She found the man she was looking for, at last, heaping coal on a furnace.[20] He had not time to eat his supper; so she went behind the furnace, and waited. Only a few men were with him, and they noticed her only by a "Hyur comes t' hunchback, Wolfe."

Deborah was stupid with sleep; her back pained her sharply; and her teeth chattered with cold, with the rain that soaked her clothes and dripped from her at every step. She stood, however, patiently holding the pail, and waiting.

"Hout, woman! ye look like a drowned cat. Come near to the fire,"— said one of the men, approaching to scrape away the ashes.

She shook her head. Wolfe had forgotten her. He turned, hearing the man, and came closer.

"I did not think; g'me my supper, woman."

She watched him eat with a painful eagerness. With a woman's quick instinct, she saw that he was not hungry,—was eating to please her. Her pale, watery eyes began to gather a strange light.

"Is't good, Hugh? T' ale was a bit sour, I feared."

"No, good enough." He hesitated a moment. "Ye're tired, poor lass! Bide here till I go. Lay down there on that heap of ash, and go to sleep."

He threw her an old coat for a pillow, and turned to his work. The heap was the refuse of the burnt iron, and was not a hard bed; the half-smothered warmth, too, penetrated her limbs, dulling their pain and cold shiver.

[19]SUMMAT DELISH: Somewhat devilish.
[20]FURNACE: Area where ingots are shaped into case rails.

Miserable enough she looked, lying there on the ashes like a limp, dirty rag,—yet not an unfitting figure to crown the scene of hopeless discomfort and veiled crime: more fitting, if one looked deeper into the heart of things,—at her thwarted woman's form, her colorless life, her waking stupor that smothered pain and hunger,—even more fit to be a type of her class. Deeper yet if one could look; was there nothing worth reading in this wet, faded thing, half covered with ashes? no story of a soul filled with groping, passionate love, heroic unselfishness, fierce jealousy? of years of weary trying to please the one human being whom she loved, to gain one look of real heart-kindness from him? If anything like this were hidden beneath the pale, bleared eyes, and dull, washed-out-looking face, no one had ever taken the trouble to read its faint signs: not the halfclothed furnace-tender, Wolfe, certainly. Yet he was kind to her: it was his nature to be kind, even to the very rats that swarmed in the cellar: kind to her in just the same way. She knew that. And it might be that very knowledge had given to her face its apathy and vacancy more than her low, torpid life. One sees that dead, vacant look steal sometimes over the rarest, finest of women's faces,—in the very midst, it may be, of their warmest summer's day; and then one can guess at the secret of intolerable solitude that lies hid beneath the delicate laces and brilliant smile. There was no warmth, no brilliancy, no summer for this woman; so the stupor and vacancy had time to gnaw into her face perpetually. She was young, too, though no one guessed it; so the gnawing was the fiercer.

She lay quiet in the dark corner, listening, through the monotonous din and uncertain glare of the works, to the dull plash of the rain in the far distance,—shrinking back whenever the man Wolfe happened to look towards her. She knew, in spite of all his kindness, that there was that in her face and form which made him loathe the sight of her. She felt by instinct, although she could not comprehend it, the finer nature of the man, which made him among his fellow-workmen something unique, set apart. She knew, that, down under all the vileness and coarseness of his life, there was a groping passion for whatever was beautiful and pure,—that his soul sickened with disgust at her deformity, even when his words were kindest. Through this dull consciousness, which never left her, came, like a sting, the recollection of the dark blue eyes and lithe figure of the little Irish girl she had left in the cellar. The recollection struck through even her stupid intellect with a vivid glow of beauty and of grace. Little Janey, timid, helpless, clinging to Hugh as her only friend: that was the sharp thought, the bitter thought, that drove into the glazed eyes a fierce light of pain. You laugh at it? Are pain and jealousy less savage realities down here in this place I am taking you to than in your own house or your own heart,—your heart, which they clutch at sometimes? The note is the same, I fancy, be the octave high or low.

If you could go into this mill where Deborah lay, and drag out from the hearts of these men the terrible tragedy of their lives, taking it as a symptom of the disease of their class, no ghost Horror would terrify you more. A reality of soul-starvation, of living death, that meets you every day under the besotted faces on the street,—I can paint nothing of this, only give you the outside outlines of a night, a crisis in the life of one man: whatever muddy depth of soul-history lies beneath you can read according to the eyes God has given you.

Wolfe, while Deborah watched him as a spaniel its master, bent over the furnace with his iron pole, unconscious of her scrutiny, only stopping to receive orders. Physically, Nature had promised the man but little. He had already lost the strength and instinct vigor of a man, his muscles were thin, his nerves weak, his face (a meek, woman's face) haggard, yellow with consumption. In the mill he was known as one of the girl-men: "Molly Wolfe" was his sobriquet.[21] He was never seen in the cockpit,[22] did not own a terrier, drank but seldom; when he did, desperately. He fought sometimes, but was always thrashed, pommelled to a jelly. The man was game enough, when his blood was up: but he was no favorite in the mill; he had the taint of school-learning on him,—not to a dangerous extent, only a quarter or so in the free-school in fact, but enough to ruin him as a good hand in a fight.

For other reasons, too, he was not popular. Not one of themselves, they felt that, though outwardly as filthy and ash-covered; silent, with foreign thoughts and longings breaking out through his quietness in innumerable curious ways: this one, for instance. In the neighboring furnace-buildings lay great heaps of the refuse from the ore after the pig-metal is run. Korl we call it here: a light, porous substance, of a delicate, waxen, flesh-colored tinge. Out of the blocks of this korl, Wolfe, in his off-hours from the furnace, had a habit of chipping and moulding figures,—hideous, fantastic enough, but sometimes strangely beautiful: even the mill-men saw that, while they jeered at him. It was a curious fancy in the man, almost a passion. The few hours for rest he spent hewing and hacking with his blunt knife, never speaking, until his watch came again,—working at one figure for months, and, when it

---

[21]SOBRIQUET: Nickname.
[22]COCKPIT: The arena where fighting cocks are thrown in order to fight until the death. Bets are placed on the outcome of the fight.

was finished, breaking it to pieces perhaps, in a fit of disappointment. A morbid, gloomy man, untaught, unled, left to feed his soul in grossness and crime, and hard, grinding labor.

I want you to come down and look at this Wolfe, standing there among the lowest of his kind, and see him just as he is, that you may judge him justly when you hear the story of this night. I want you to look back, as he does every day, at his birth in vice, his starved infancy; to remember the heavy years he has groped through as boy and man,—the slow, heavy years of constant, hot work. So long ago he began, that he thinks sometimes he has worked there for ages. There is no hope that it will ever end. Think that God put into this man's soul a fierce thirst for beauty,— to know it, to create it; to be—something, he knows not what,—other than he is. There are moments when a passing cloud, the sun glinting on the purple thistles, a kindly smile, a child's face, will rouse him to a passion of pain,—when his nature starts up with a mad cry of rage against God, man, whoever it is that has forced this vile, slimy life upon him. With all this groping, this mad desire, a great blind intellect stumbling through wrong, a loving poet's heart, the man was by habit only a coarse, vulgar laborer, familiar with sights and words you would blush to name. Be just: when I tell you about this night, see him as he is. Be just,—not like man's law, which seizes on one isolated fact, but like God's judging angel, whose clear, sad eye saw all the countless cankering days of this man's life, all the countless nights, when, sick with starving, his soul fainted in him, before it judged him for this night, the saddest of all.

I called this night the crisis of his life. If it was, it stole on him unawares. These great turning-days of life cast no shadow before, slip by unconsciously. Only a trifle, a little turn of the rudder, and the ship goes to heaven or hell.

Wolfe, while Deborah watched him, dug into the furnace of melting iron with his pole, dully thinking only how many rails the lump would yield. It was late,—nearly Sunday morning; another hour, and the heavy work would be done,—only the furnaces to replenish and cover for the next day. The workmen were growing more noisy, shouting, as they had to do, to be heard over the deep clamor of the mills. Suddenly they grew less boisterous,—at the far end, entirely silent. Something unusual had happened. After a moment, the silence came nearer; the men stopped their jeers and drunken choruses. Deborah, stupidly lifting up her head, saw the cause of the quiet. A group of five or six men were slowly approaching, stopping to examine each furnace as they came. Visitors often came to see the mills after night: except by growing less noisy, the men took no notice of them. The furnace where Wolfe worked was near the bounds of the works; they halted there hot and tired: a walk over one of these great founderies is no trifling task. The woman, drawing out of sight, turned over to sleep. Wolfe, seeing them stop, suddenly roused from his indifferent stupor, and watched them keenly. He knew some of them: the overseer, Clarke,—a son of Kirby, one of the mill-owners,—and a Doctor May, one of the town-physicians. The other two were strangers. Wolfe came closer. He seized eagerly every chance that brought him into contact with this mysterious class that shone down on him perpetually with the glamour of another order of being. What made the difference between them? That was the mystery of his life. He had a vague notion that perhaps to-night he could find it out. One of the strangers sat down on a pile of bricks, and beckoned young Kirby to his side.

"This is hot, with a vengeance. A match, please?"—lighting his cigar. "But the walk is worth the trouble. If it were not that you must have heard it so often, Kirby, I would tell you that your works look like Dante's Inferno."[23]

Kirby laughed.

"Yes. Yonder is Farinata himself[24] in the burning tomb,"—pointing to some figure in the shimmering shadows.

"Judging from some of the faces of your men," said the other, "they bid fair to try the reality of Dante's vision, some day."

Young Kirby looked curiously around, as if seeing the faces of his hands for the first time.

"They're bad enough, that's true. A desperate set, I fancy. Eh, Clarke?"

The overseer did not hear him. He was talking of net profits just then,—giving, in fact, a schedule of the annual business of the firm to a sharp peering little Yankee, who jotted down notes on a paper laid on the crown of his hat: a reporter for one of the city papers, getting up a series of reviews of the leading manufactories. The other gentlemen had accompanied them merely for amusement. They were silent until the notes were finished, drying their feet at the furnaces, and sheltering their faces from the intolerable heat. At last the overseer concluded with—

"I believe that is a pretty fair estimate, Captain."

"Here, some of you men!" said Kirby, "bring up those boards. We may as well sit down, gentlemen, until the rain is over. It cannot last much longer at this rate."

---

[23]DANTE'S INFERNO: Dante Alighieri (1265–1321), an Italian poet and the author *The Divine Comedy*, the first part of which is *Inferno* (Hell).
[24]FARINATA HIMSELF: In Canto 10 of the *Inferno*, Farinata degli Uberti, a nobleman of Florence, is described as trapped in a red-hot coffin, the lid of which is suspended over him until Judgment Day.

"Pig-metal,"—mumbled the reporter,—"um!—coal facilities,—um!—hands employed, twelve hundred,—bitumen,—um!—all right, I believe, Mr. Clarke;—sinking-fund,[25]—what did you say was your sinking-fund?"

"Twelve hundred hands?" said the stranger, the young man who had first spoken. "Do you control their votes, Kirby?"

"Control? No." The young man smiled complacently. "But my father brought seven hundred votes to the polls for his candidate last November. No force-work, you understand,—only a speech or two, a hint to form themselves into a society, and a bit of red and blue bunting to make them a flag. The Invincible Roughs,—I believe that is their name. I forget the motto: 'Our country's hope,' I think."

There was a laugh. The young man talking to Kirby sat with an amused light in his cool gray eye, surveying critically the half-clothed figures of the puddlers, and the slow swing of their brawny muscles. He was a stranger in the city,—spending a couple of months in the borders of a Slave State, to study the institutions of the South,—a brother-in-law of Kirby's,—Mitchell. He was an amateur gymnast,—hence his anatomical eye; a patron, in a blasé way, of the prize-ring; a man who sucked the essence out of a science or philosophy in an indifferent, gentlemanly way; who took Kant, Novalis, Humboldt,[26] for what they were worth in his own scales; accepting all, despising nothing, in heaven, earth, or hell, but one-idead men; with a temper yielding and brilliant as summer water, until his Self was touched, when it was ice, though brilliant still. Such men are not rare in the States.

As he knocked the ashes from his cigar, Wolfe caught with a quick pleasure the contour of the white hand, the blood-glow of a red ring he wore. His voice, too, and that of Kirby's, touched him like music,—low, even, with chording cadences. About this man Mitchell hung the impalpable atmosphere belonging to the thoroughbred gentleman. Wolfe, scraping away the ashes beside him, was conscious of it, did obeisance to it with his artist sense, unconscious that he did so.

The rain did not cease. Clarke and the reporter left the mills; the others, comfortably seated near the furnace, lingered, smoking and talking in a desultory way. Greek would not have been more unintelligible to the furnace-tenders, whose presence they soon forgot entirely. Kirby drew out a newspaper from his pocket and read aloud some article, which

[25]SINKING-FUND: Revenue set aside to pay off a company debt.
[26]KANT, NOVALIS, HUMBOLDT: Immanuel Kant (1724–1804), a German metaphysician and philosopher; Friedrich von Hardenberg (1772–1801), the German poet who used the pseudonym Novalis; Alexander von Humboldt (1769–1859), a German naturalist who explored parts of Asia and South America.

they discussed eagerly. At every sentence, Wolfe listened more and more like a dumb, hopeless animal, with a duller, more stolid look creeping over his face, glancing now and then at Mitchell, marking acutely every smallest sign of refinement, then back to himself, seeing as in a mirror his filthy body, his more stained soul.

Never! He had no words for such a thought, but he knew now, in all the sharpness of the bitter certainty, that between them there was a great gulf[27] never to be passed. Never!

The bell of the mills rang for midnight. Sunday morning had dawned. Whatever hidden message lay in the tolling bells floated past these men unknown. Yet it was there. Veiled in the solemn music ushering the risen Saviour was a key-note to solve the darkest secrets of a world gone wrong,—even this social riddle which the brain of the grimy puddler grappled with madly to-night.

The men began to withdraw the metal from the caldrons. The mills were deserted on Sundays, except by the hands who fed the fires, and those who had no lodgings and slept usually on the ash-heaps. The three strangers sat still during the next hour, watching the men cover the furnaces, laughing now and then at some jest of Kirby's.

"Do you know," said Mitchell, "I like this view of the works better than when the glare was fiercest? These heavy shadows and the amphitheatre of smothered fires are ghostly, unreal. One could fancy these red smouldering lights to be the half-shut eyes of wild beasts, and the spectral figures their victims in the den."

Kirby laughed. "You are fanciful. Come, let us get out of the den. The spectral figures, as you call them, are a little too real for me to fancy a close proximity in the darkness,—unarmed, too."

The others rose, buttoning their overcoats, and lighting cigars.

"Raining still," said Doctor May, "and hard. Where did we leave the coach, Mitchell?"

"At the other side of the works.—Kirby, what's that?"

Mitchell started back, half-frightened, as, suddenly turning a corner, the white figure of a woman faced him in the darkness,—a woman, white, of giant proportions, crouching on the ground, her arms flung out in some wild gesture of warning.

---

[27]GREAT GULF: From the parable of the beggar Lazarus in Luke 16:26. Lazarus is a poor man who begs in vain for crumbs from a rich man's table. Lazarus dies and goes heaven while the rich man goes to hell. The rich man begs that Lazarus be returned to earth to warn the rich man's surviving brothers of their folly. Abraham, in heaven, denies the request, explaining that the errand would be futile: "And beside all this, between us and you there is a great gulf fixed: so that they which would pass from hence to you cannot; neither can they pass to us, that would come from thence."

"Stop! Make that fire burn there!" cried Kirby, stopping short. The flame burst out, flashing the gaunt figure into bold relief. Mitchell drew a long breath.

"I thought it was alive," he said, going up curiously.

The others followed.

"Not marble, eh?" asked Kirby, touching it.

One of the lower overseers stopped.

"Korl, Sir."

"Who did it?"

"Can't say. Some of the hands; chipped it out in off-hours."

"Chipped to some purpose, I should say. What a flesh-tint the stuff has! Do you see, Mitchell?"

"I see."

He had stepped aside where the light fell boldest on the figure, looking at it in silence. There was not one line of beauty or grace in it: a nude woman's form, muscular, grown coarse with labor, the powerful limbs instinct with some one poignant longing. One idea: there it was in the tense, rigid muscles, the clutching hands, the wild, eager face, like that of a starving wolf's. Kirby and Dr. May walked around it, critical, curious. Mitchell stood aloof, silent. The figure touched him strangely.

"Not badly done," said Doctor May. "Where did the fellow learn that sweep of the muscles in the arm and hand? Look at them! They are groping,—do you see?—clutching: the peculiar action of a man dying of thirst."

"They have ample facilities for studying anatomy," sneered Kirby, glancing at the half-naked figures.

"Look," continued the Doctor, "at this bony wrist, and the strained sinews of the instep! A working-woman,—the very type of her class."

"God forbid!" muttered Mitchell.

"Why?" demanded May. "What does the fellow intend by the figure? I cannot catch the meaning."

"Ask him," said the other, dryly. "There he stands,"—pointing to Wolfe, who stood with a group of men, leaning on his ash-rake.

The Doctor beckoned him with the affable smile which kind-hearted men put on, when talking to these people.

"Mr. Mitchell has picked you out as the man who did this,—I'm sure I don't know why. But what did you mean by it?"

"She be hungry."

Wolfe's eyes answered Mitchell, not the Doctor.

"Oh-h! But what a mistake you have made, my fine fellow! You have given no sign of starvation to the body. It is strong,—terribly strong. It has the mad, half-despairing gesture of drowning."

Wolfe stammered, glanced appealingly at Mitchell, who saw the soul of the thing, he knew. But the cool, probing eyes were turned on himself now,—mocking, cruel, relentless.

"Not hungry for meat," the furnace-tender said at last.

"What then? Whiskey?" jeered Kirby, with a coarse laugh.

Wolfe was silent a moment, thinking.

"I dunno," he said, with a bewildered look. "It mebbe. Summat to make her live, I think,—like you. Whiskey ull do it, in a way."

The young man laughed again. Mitchell flashed a look of disgust somewhere,—not at Wolfe.

"May," he broke out impatiently, "are you blind? Look at that woman's face! It asks questions of God, and says, 'I have a right to know.' Good God, how hungry it is!"

They looked a moment; then May turned to the millowner:—

"Have you many such hands as this? What are you going to do with them? Keep them at puddling iron?"

Kirby shrugged his shoulders. Mitchell's look had irritated him.

"*Ce n'est pas mon affaire.*[28] I have no fancy for nursing infant geniuses. I suppose there are some stray gleams of mind and soul among these wretches. The Lord will take care of his own; or else they can work out their own salvation. I have heard you call our American system a ladder which any man can scale. Do you doubt it? Or perhaps you want to banish all social ladders, and put us all on a flat table-land,—eh, May?"

The Doctor looked vexed, puzzled. Some terrible problem lay hid in this woman's face, and troubled these men. Kirby waited for an answer, and, receiving none, went on, warming with his subject.

"I tell you, there's something wrong that no talk of '*Liberté*' or '*Egalité*'[29] will do away. If I had the making of men, these men who do the lowest part of the world's work should be machines,—nothing more,—hands. It would be kindness. God help them! What are taste, reason, to creatures who must live such lives as that?" He pointed to Deborah, sleeping on the ash-heap. "So many nerves to sting them to pain. What if God had put your brain, with all its agony of touch, into your fingers, and bid you work and strike with that?"

"You think you could govern the world better?" laughed the Doctor.

"I do not think at all."

"That is true philosophy. Drift with the stream, because you cannot dive deep enough to find bottom, eh?"

---

[28]*CE N'EST PAS MON AFFAIRE*: It's none of my business. (French)
[29]*LIBERTÉ* OR *EGALITÉ*: Liberty or Equality (French); slogans of the French Revolution.

"Exactly," rejoined Kirby. "I do not think. I wash my hands of all social problems,—slavery, caste, white or black. My duty to my operatives has a narrow limit,—the payhour on Saturday night. Outside of that, if they cut korl, or cut each other's throats, (the more popular amusement of the two,) I am not responsible."

The Doctor sighed,—a good honest sigh, from the depths of his stomach.

"God help us! Who is responsible?"

"Not I, I tell you," said Kirby, testily. "What has the man who pays them money to do with their souls' concerns, more than the grocer or butcher who takes it?"

"And yet," said Mitchell's cynical voice, "look at her! How hungry she is!"

Kirby tapped his boot with his cane. No one spoke. Only the dumb face of the rough image looking into their faces with the awful question, "What shall we do to be saved?" Only Wolfe's face, with its heavy weight of brain, its weak, uncertain mouth, its desperate eyes, out of which looked the soul of his class,—only Wolfe's face turned towards Kirby's. Mitchell laughed,—a cool, musical laugh.

"Money has spoken!" he said, seating himself lightly on a stone with the air of an amused spectator at a play. "Are you answered?"—turning to Wolfe his clear, magnetic face.

Bright and deep and cold as Arctic air, the soul of the man lay tranquil beneath. He looked at the furnace-tender as he had looked at a rare mosaic in the morning; only the man was the more amusing study of the two.

"Are you answered? Why, May, look at him! *De profundis clamavi.* [30] Or, to quote in English, 'Hungry and thirsty, his soul faints in him.' And so Money sends back its answer into the depths through you, Kirby! Very clear the answer, too!—I think I remember reading the same words somewhere:—washing your hands in Eau de Cologne,[31] and saying, 'I am innocent of the blood of this man. See ye to it!'"[32]

Kirby flushed angrily.

"You quote Scripture freely."

"Do I not quote correctly? I think I remember another line, which may amend my meaning: 'Inasmuch as ye did it unto one of the least of these,

[30]*DE PROFUNDIS CLAMAVI*: From Psalm 130:1: "Out of the depths have I cried unto thee, O Lord." (Latin)
[31]EAU DE COLOGNE: Cologne water. (French)
[32]I AM INNOCENT OF THE BLOOD OF THIS MAN, SEE YE TO IT: The words of Roman governor Pontius Pilate as he renounces responsibility for the crucifixion of Jesus. "When Pilate saw that he could prevail nothing, but that rather a tumult was made, he took water, and washed his hands before the multitude, saying, I am innocent of the blood of this just person: see ye to it." (Matthew 27:24)

ye did it unto me.'[33] Deist?[34] Bless you, man, I was raised on the milk of the Word. Now, Doctor, the pocket of the world having uttered its voice, what has the heart to say? You are a philanthropist, in a small way,— *n'est ce pas?*[35] Here, boy, this gentleman can show you how to cut korl better,—or your destiny. Go on, May!"

"I think a mocking devil possesses you to-night," rejoined the Doctor, seriously.

He went to Wolfe and put his hand kindly on his arm. Something of a vague idea possessed the Doctor's brain that much good was to be done here by a friendly word or two: a latent genius to be warmed into life by a waited-for sunbeam. Here it was: he had brought it. So he went on complacently:—

"Do you know, boy, you have it in you to be a great sculptor, a great man?—do you understand?" (talking down to the capacity of his hearer: it is a way people have with children, and men like Wolfe)—"to live a better, stronger life than I, or Mr. Kirby here? A man may make himself anything he chooses. God has given you stronger powers than many men,—me, for instance."

May stopped, heated, glowing with his own magnanimity. And it was magnanimous. The puddler had drunk in every word, looking through the Doctor's flurry, and generous heat, and self-approval, into his will, with those slow, absorbing eyes of his.

"Make yourself what you will. It is your right."

"I know," quietly. "Will you help me?"

Mitchell laughed again. The Doctor turned now, in a passion,—

"You know, Mitchell, I have not the means. You know, if I had, it is in my heart to take this boy and educate him for"—

"The glory of God, and the glory of John May."

May did not speak for a moment; then, controlled, he said,—

"Why should one be raised, when myriads are left?—I have not the money, boy," to Wolfe, shortly.

"Money?" He said it over slowly, as one repeats the guessed answer to a riddle, doubtfully. "That is it? Money?"

"Yes, money,—that is it," said Mitchell, rising, and drawing his furred coat about him. "You've found the cure for all the world's diseases.—

---

[33]YE DID IT UNTO ME: Matthew 25:37–40: "Then shall the righteous answer him, saying, Lord, when saw we thee a hungered, and fed thee? or thirsty, and gave thee drink? / When saw we thee a stranger, and took thee in? or naked, and clothed thee? / Or when saw we thee sick, or in prison, and came unto thee? / And the King shall answer and say unto them, Verily I say unto you, Inasmuch as ye have done it unto one of the least of these my brethren, ye have done it unto me."
[34]DEIST: One who believes that God created the universe but does not exercise any further control over it.
[35]*N'EST CE PAS?*: Isn't it so? (French)

Come, May, find your good-humor, and come home. This damp wind chills my very bones. Come and preach your Saint-Simonian doctrines[36] to-morrow to Kirby's hands. Let them have a clear idea of the rights of the soul, and I'll venture next week they'll strike for higher wages. That will be the end of it."

"Will you send the coach-driver to this side of the mills?" asked Kirby, turning to Wolfe.

He spoke kindly: it was his habit to do so. Deborah, seeing the puddler go, crept after him. The three men waited outside. Doctor May walked up and down, chafed. Suddenly he stopped.

"Go back, Mitchell! You say the pocket and the heart of the world speak without meaning to these people. What has its head to say? Taste, culture, refinement? Go!"

Mitchell was leaning against a brick wall. He turned his head indolently, and looked into the mills. There hung about the place a thick, unclean odor. The slightest motion of his hand marked that he perceived it, and his insufferable disgust. That was all. May said nothing, only quickened his angry tramp.

"Besides," added Mitchell, giving a corollary to his answer, "it would be of no use. I am not one of them."

"You do not mean"—said May, facing him.

"Yes, I mean just that. Reform is born of need, not pity. No vital movement of the people's has worked down, for good or evil; fermented, instead, carried up the heaving, cloggy mass. Think back through history, and you will know it. What will this lowest deep—thieves, Magdalens,[37] negroes—do with the light filtered through ponderous Church creeds, Baconian theories,[38] Goethe schemes?[39] Some day, out of their bitter need will be thrown up their own light-bringer,—their Jean Paul,[40] their Cromwell,[41] their Messiah."[42]

---

[36]SAINT-SIMONIAN DOCTRINES: Beliefs of the Count of Saint-Simon (1760–1825), founder of French socialism.
[37]MAGDALENS: Harlots.
[38]BACONIAN THEORIES: Theories proposed by the English essayist and political philosopher Francis Bacon (1561–1626) in his utopian work *The New Atlantis*, left unfinished and posthumously published in 1627.
[39]GOETHE SCHEMES: Johann Wolfgang von Goethe (1749–1832), the German poet, dramatist, and novelist best known for his dramatic poem *Faust*. Goethe had great faith in the promise of science and technology.
[40]JEAN PAUL: Johann Paul Friedrich (pseudonym Jean-Paul) Richter (1763–1825), a German novelist whose works were known for their *Sturm und Drang* ("storm and stress," a movement in German literature).
[41]CROMWELL: Oliver Cromwell (1599–1658), Lord Protector of England during the Commonwealth (1649–1658).
[42]MESSIAH: Savior.

"Bah!" was the Doctor's inward criticism. However, in practice, he adopted the theory; for, when, night and morning, afterwards, he prayed that power might be given these degraded souls to rise, he glowed at heart, recognizing an accomplished duty.

Wolfe and the woman had stood in the shadow of the works as the coach drove off. The Doctor had held out his hand in a frank, generous way, telling him to "take care of himself, and to remember it was his right to rise." Mitchell had simply touched his hat, as to an equal, with a quiet look of thorough recognition. Kirby had thrown Deborah some money, which she found, and clutched eagerly enough. They were gone now, all of them. The man sat down on the cinder-road, looking up into the murky sky.

"'T be late, Hugh. Wunnot hur come?"

He shook his head doggedly, and the woman crouched out of his sight against the wall. Do you remember rare moments when a sudden light flashed over yourself, your world, God? when you stood on a mountain-peak, seeing your life as it might have been, as it is? one quick instant, when custom lost its force and every-day usage? when your friend, wife, brother, stood in a new light? your soul was bared, and the grave,—a foretaste of the nakedness of the Judgment-Day? So it came before him, his life, that night. The slow tides of pain he had borne gathered themselves up and surged against his soul. His squalid daily life, the brutal coarseness eating into his brain, as the ashes into his skin: before, these things had been a dull aching into his consciousness; to-night, they were reality. He gripped the filthy red shirt that clung, stiff with soot, about him, and tore it savagely from his arm. The flesh beneath was muddy with grease and ashes,—and the heart beneath that! And the soul? God knows.

Then flashed before his vivid poetic sense the man who had left him,—the pure face, the delicate, sinewy limbs, in harmony with all he knew of beauty or truth. In his cloudy fancy he had pictured a Something like this. He had found it in this Mitchell, even when he idly scoffed at his pain: a Man all-knowing, all-seeing, crowned by Nature, reigning,— the keen glance of his eye falling like a sceptre on other men. And yet his instinct taught him that he too—He! He looked at himself with sudden loathing, sick, wrung his hands with a cry, and then was silent. With all the phantoms of his heated, ignorant fancy, Wolfe had not been vague in his ambitions. They were practical, slowly built up before him out of his knowledge of what he could do. Through years he had day by day made this hope a real thing to himself,—a clear, projected figure of himself, as he might become.

Able to speak, to know what was best, to raise these men and women working at his side up with him: sometimes he forgot this defined hope in the frantic anguish to escape,—only to escape,—out of the wet, the pain, the ashes, somewhere, anywhere,—only for one moment of free air on a hill side, to lie down and let his sick soul throb itself out in the sunshine. But to-night he panted for life. The savage strength of his nature was roused; his cry was fierce to God for justice.

"Look at me!" he said to Deborah, with a low, bitter laugh, striking his puny chest savagely. "What am I worth, Deb? Is it my fault that I am no better? My fault? My fault?"

He stopped, stung with a sudden remorse, seeing her hunchback shape writhing with sobs. For Deborah was crying thankless tears, according to the fashion of women.

"God forgi' me, woman! Things go harder wi' you nor me. It's a worse share."

He got up and helped her to rise; and they went doggedly down the muddy street, side by side.

"It's all wrong," he muttered, slowly,—"all wrong! I dunnot understan'. But it'll end some day."

"Come home, Hugh!" she said, coaxingly; for he had stopped, looking around bewildered.

"Home,—and back to the mill!" He went on saying this over to himself, as if he would mutter down every pain in this dull despair.

She followed him through the fog, her blue lips chattering with cold. They reached the cellar at last. Old Wolfe had been drinking since she went out, and had crept nearer the door. The girl Janey slept heavily in the corner. He went up to her, touching softly the worn white arm with his fingers. Some bitterer thought stung him, as he stood there. He wiped the drops from his forehead, and went into the room beyond, livid, trembling. A hope, trifling, perhaps, but very dear, had died just then out of the poor puddler's life, as he looked at the sleeping, innocent girl,—some plan for the future, in which she had borne a part. He gave it up that moment, then and forever. Only a trifle, perhaps, to us: his face grew a shade paler,—that was all. But, somehow, the man's soul, as God and the angels looked down on it, never was the same afterwards.

Deborah followed him into the inner room. She carried a candle, which she placed on the floor, closing the door after her. She had seen the look on his face, as he turned away; her own grew deadly. Yet, as she came up to him, her eyes glowed. He was seated on an old chest, quiet, holding his face in his hands.

"Hugh!" she said, softly.

He did not speak.

"Hugh, did hur hear what the man said,—him with the clear voice? Did hur hear? Money, money,—that it wud do all?"

He pushed her away,—gently, but he was worn out; her rasping tone fretted him.

"Hugh!"

The candle flared a pale yellow light over the cobwebbed brick walls, and the woman standing there. He looked at her. She was young, in deadly earnest; her faded eyes, and wet, ragged figure caught from their frantic eagerness a power akin to beauty.

"Hugh, it is true! Money ull do it! Oh, Hugh, boy, listen till me! He said it true! It is money!"

"I know. Go back! I do not want you here."

"Hugh, it is t' last time. I'll never worrit hur again."

There were tears in her voice now, but she choked them back.

"Hear till me only to-night! If one of t' witch people wud come, them we heard of t' home, and gif hur all hur wants, what then? Say, Hugh!"

"What do you mean?"

"I mean money."

Her whisper shrilled through his brain.

"If one of t' witch dwarfs wud come from t' lane moors to-night, and gif hur money, to go out,—out, I say,—out, lad, where t' sun shines, and t' heath grows, and t' ladies walk in silken gownds, and God stays all t' time,—where t' man lives that talked to us to-night,—Hugh knows,—Hugh could walk there like a king!"

He thought the woman mad, tried to check her, but she went on, fierce in her eager haste.

"If I were t' witch dwarf, if I had t' money, wud hur thank me? Wud hur take me out o' this place wid hur and Janey? I wud not come into the gran' house hur wud build, to vex hur wid t' hunch,—only at night, when t' shadows were dark, stand far off to see hur."

Mad? Yes! Are many of us mad in this way?

"Poor Deb! poor Deb!" he said, soothingly.

"It is here," she said, suddenly jerking into his hand a small roll. "I took it! I did it! I shall be hanged! I shall be burnt in hell, if anybody knows I took it! Me, me! not hur! Out of his pocket, as he leaned against t' bricks. Hur knows?"

She thrust it into his hand, and then, her errand done, began to gather chips together to make a fire, choking down hysteric sobs.

"Has it come to this?"

That was all he said. The Welsh Wolfe blood was honest. The roll was a small green pocket-book containing one or two gold pieces, and a check for an incredible amount, as it seemed to the poor puddler. He laid it down, hiding his face again in his hands.

"Hugh, don't be angry wud me! It's only poor Deb,—hur knows?"

He took the long skinny fingers kindly in his.

"Angry? God help me, no! Let me sleep. I am tired."

He threw himself heavily down on the wooden bench, stunned with pain and weariness. She brought some old rags to cover him.

It was late on Sunday evening before he awoke. I tell God's truth, when I say he had then no thought of keeping this money. Deborah had hid it in his pocket. He found it there. She watched him eagerly, as he took it out.

"I must gif it to him," he said, reading her face.

"Hur knows," she said with a bitter sigh of disappointment. "But it is hur right to keep it."

His right! The word struck him. Doctor May had used the same. He washed himself, and went out to find this man Mitchell. His right! Why did this chance word cling to him so obstinately? Do you hear the fierce devils whisper in his ear, as he went slowly down the darkening street?

The evening came on, slow and calm. He seated himself at the end of an alley leading into one of the larger streets. His brain was clear to-night, keen, intent, mastering. It would not start back, cowardly, from any hellish temptation, but meet it face to face. Therefore the great temptation of his life came to him veiled by no sophistry, but bold, defiant, owning its own vile name, trusting to one bold blow for victory.

He did not deceive himself. Theft! That was it. At first the word sickened him; then he grappled with it. Sitting there on a broken cart-wheel, the fading day, the noisy groups, the church-bells' tolling passed before him like a panorama, while the sharp struggle went on within. This money! He took it out, and looked at it. If he gave it back, what then? He was going to be cool about it.

People going by to church saw only a sickly mill-boy watching them quietly at the alley's mouth. They did not know that he was mad, or they would not have gone by so quietly: mad with hunger; stretching out his hands to the world, that had given so much to them, for leave to live the life God meant him to live. His soul within him was smothering to death; he wanted so much, thought so much, and knew—nothing. There was nothing of which he was certain, except the mill and things there. Of God and heaven he had heard so little, that they were to him what fairy-land is to a child: something real, but not here; very far off. His brain, greedy, dwarfed, full of thwarted energy and unused powers, questioned these men and women going by, coldly, bitterly, that night. Was it not his right to live as they,—a pure life, a good, true-hearted life, full of beauty and kind words? He only wanted to know how to use the strength within him. His heart warmed, as he thought of it. He suffered himself to think of it longer. If took the money?

Then he saw himself as he might be, strong, helpful, kindly. The night crept on, as this one image slowly evolved itself from the crowd of other thoughts and stood triumphant. He looked at it. As he might be! What wonder, if it blinded him to delirium,—the madness that underlies all revolution, all progress, and all fall?

You laugh at the shallow temptation? You see the error underlying its argument so clearly,—that to him a true life was one of full development rather than self-restraint? that he was deaf to the higher tone in a cry of voluntary suffering for truth's sake than in the fullest flow of spontaneous harmony? I do not plead his cause. I only want to show you the mote in my brother's eye: then you can see clearly to take it out.[43]

The money,—there it lay on his knee, a little blotted slip of paper, nothing in itself; used to raise him out of the pit; something straight from God's hand. A thief! Well, what was it to be a thief? He met the question at last face to face, wiping the clammy drops of sweat from his forehead. God made this money—the fresh air, too—for his children's use. He never made the difference between poor and rich. The Something who looked down on him that moment through the cool gray sky had a kindly face, he knew,—loved his children alike. Oh, he knew that!

There were times when the soft floods of color in the crimson and purple flames, or the clear depth of amber in the water below the bridge, had somehow given him a glimpse of another world than this,—of an infinite depth of beauty and of quiet somewhere,—somewhere,—a depth of quiet and rest and love. Looking up now, it became strangely real. The sun had sunk quite below the hills, but his last rays struck upward, touching the zenith. The fog had risen, and the town and river were steeped in its thick, gray damp; but overhead, the sun-touched smoke-clouds opened like a cleft ocean,—shifting, rolling seas of crimson mist, waves of billowy silver veined with blood-scarlet, inner depths unfathomable of glancing light. Wolfe's artist-eye grew drunk with color. The gates of that

[43]I ONLY WANT TO SHOW YOU THE MOTE IN MY BROTHER'S EYE: THEN YOU CAN SEE CLEARLY TO TAKE IT OUT: From Jesus' Sermon on the Mount, Matthew 7:3–4: "And why beholdest thou the mote that is in thy brother's eye, but considerest not the beam that is in thine own eye? / Or how wilt thou say to thy brother, Let me pull out the mote out of thine eye; and, behold, a beam is in thine own eye?" A *mote* is a particle of dust, and a *beam* is a roof timber.

other world! Fading, flashing before him now! What, in that world of Beauty, Content, and Right, were the petty laws, the mine and shine, of mill-owners and mill-hands?

A consciousness of power stirred within him. He stood up. A man,— he thought, stretching out his hands,—free to work, to live, to love! Free! His right! He folded the scrap of paper in his hand. As his nervous fingers took it in, limp and blotted, so his soul took in the mean temptation, lapped it in fancied rights, in dreams of improved existences, driffing and endless as the cloud-seas of color. Clutching it, as if the tightness of his hold would strengthen his sense of possession, he went aimlessly down the street. It was his watch at the mill. He need not go, need never go again, thank God!—shaking off the thought with unspeakable loathing.

Shall I go over the history of the hours of that night? how the man wandered from one to another of his old haunts, with a half-consciousness of bidding them farewell,—lanes and alleys and back-yards where the mill-hands lodged,—noting, with a new eagerness, the filth and drunkenness, the pig-pens, the ash-heaps covered with potatoskins, the bloated, pimpled women at the doors,—with a new disgust, a new sense of sudden triumph, and, under all, a new, vague dread, unknown before, smothered down, kept under, but still there? It left him but once during the night, when, for the second time in his life, he entered a church. It was a sombre Gothic pile, where the stained light lost itself in far-retreating arches; built to meet the requirements and sympathies of a far other class than Wolfe's. Yet it touched, moved him uncontrollably. The distances, the shadows, the still, marble figures, the mass of silent, kneeling worshippers, the mysterious music, thrilled, lifted his soul with a wonderful pain. Wolfe forgot himself, forgot the new life he was going to live, the mean terror gnawing underneath. The voice of the speaker strengthened the charm; it was clear, feeling, full, strong. An old man, who had lived much, suffered much; whose brain was keenly alive, dominant; whose heart was summer-warm with charity. He taught it to-night. He held up Humanity in its grand total; showed the great world-cancer to his people. Who could show it better? He was a Christian reformer; he had studied the age thoroughly; his outlook at man had been free,world-wide, over all time. His faith stood sublime upon the Rock of Ages;[44] his fiery zeal guided vast schemes by which the Gospel was to be preached to all nations. How did he preach it to-night? In burning, light-laden words he painted Jesus, the incarnate Life, Love, the universal Man: words that became reality in the lives of these people,—that

---

[44]ROCK OF AGES: Christ, as the eternal foundation. The famous hymn "Rock of Ages" was composed in the late eighteenth-century.

lived again in beautiful words and actions, trifling, but heroic. Sin, as
he defined it, was a real foe to them; their trials, temptations, were his.
His words passed far over the furnace-tender's grasp, toned to suit
another class of culture; they sounded in his ears a very pleasant song
in an unknown tongue. He meant to cure this world-cancer with a steady
eye that had never glared with hunger, and a hand that neither poverty
nor strychnine-whiskey[45] had taught to shake. In this morbid, distorted
heart of the Welsh puddler he had failed.

Wolfe arose at last, and turned from the church down the street. He
looked up; the night had come on foggy, damp; the golden mists had vanished, and the sky lay dull and ash-colored. He wandered again aimlessly
down the street, idly wondering what had become of the cloud-sea of
crimson and scarlet. The trial-day of this man's life was over, and he
had lost the victory. What followed was mere drifting circumstance,—a
quicker walking over the path,—that was all. Do you want to hear the
end of it? You wish me to make a tragic story out of it? Why, in the police-
reports of the morning paper you can find a dozen such tragedies; hints
of shipwrecks unlike any that ever befell on the high seas; hints that here
a power was lost to heaven,—that there a soul went down where no tide
can ebb or flow. Commonplace enough the hints are,—jocose[46] sometimes, done up in rhyme.

Doctor May, a month after the night I have told you of, was reading
to his wife at breakfast from this fourth column of the morning-paper:
an unusual thing,—these police-reports not being, in general, choice
reading for ladies; but it was only one item he read.

"Oh, my dear! You remember that man I told you of, that we saw
at Kirby's mill?—that was arrested for robbing Mitchell? Here he is;
just listen:—'Circuit Court. Judge Day. Hugh Wolfe, operative in Kirby
& John's Loudon Mills. Charge, grand larceny. Sentence, nineteen years
hard labor in penitentiary.'—Scoundrel! Serves him right! After all our
kindness that night! Picking Mitchell's pocket at the very time!"

His wife said something about the ingratitude of that kind of people, and then they began to talk of something else.

Nineteen years! How easy that was to read! What a simple word for
Judge Day to utter! Nineteen years! Half a lifetime!

Hugh Wolfe sat on the window-ledge of his cell, looking out. His
ankles were ironed. Not usual in such cases; but he had made two desperate efforts to escape. "Well," as Haley, the jailer, said, "small blame
to him! Nineteen years' imprisonment was not a pleasant thing to look

45STRYCHNINE-WHISKEY: A dangerous, sometimes lethal, whiskey made from redistilling left-
over mash.
46JOCOSE: Playfully joking.

forward to." Haley was very good-natured about it, though Wolfe had fought him savagely.

"When he was first caught," the jailer said afterwards, in telling the story, "before the trial, the fellow was cut down at once,—laid there on that pallet like a dead man, with his hands over his eyes. Never saw a man so cut down in my life. Time of the trial, too, came the queerest dodge[47] of any customer I ever had. Would choose no lawyer. Judge gave him one, of course. Gibson it was. He tried to prove the fellow crazy; but it would n't go. Thing was plain as daylight: check found on him. 'T was a hard sentence,—all the law allows; but it was for 'xample's sake. These mill-hands are gettin' onbearable. When the sentence was read, he just looked up, and said the money was his by rights, and that all the world had gone wrong. That night, after the trial, a gentleman came to see him here, name of Mitchell,—him as he stole from. Talked to him for an hour. Thought he came for curiosity, like. After he was gone, thought Wolfe was remarkable quiet, and went into his cell. Found him very low; bed all bloody. Doctor said he had been bleeding at the lungs. He was as weak as a cat; yet, if ye'll b'lieve me, he tried to get a-past me and get out. I just carried him like a baby, and threw him on the pallet. Three days after, he tried it again: that time reached the wall. Lord help you! he fought like a tiger,—giv' some terrible blows. Fightin' for life, you see; for he can't live long, shut up in the stone crib down yonder. Got a death-cough now. 'T took two of us to bring him down that day; so I just put the irons on his feet. There he sits, in there. Goin' tomorrow, with a batch more of 'em. That woman, hunchback, tried with him,—you remember?—she's only got three years. 'Complice. But she's a woman, you know. He's been quiet ever since I put on irons: giv' up, I suppose. Looks white, sick-lookin'. It acts different on 'em, bein' sentenced. Most of 'em gets reckless, devilish-like. Some prays awful, and sings them vile songs of the mills, all in a breath. That woman, now, she's desper't'. Been beggin' to see Hugh, as she calls him, for three days. I'm a-goin' to let her in. She don't go with him. Here she is in this next cell. I'm a-goin' now to let her in."

He let her in. Wolfe did not see her. She crept into a corner of the cell, and stood watching him. He was scratching the iron bars of the window with a piece of tin which he had picked up, with an idle, uncertain, vacant stare, just as a child or idiot would do.

"Tryin' to get out, old boy?" laughed Haley. "Them irons will need a crowbar beside your tin, before you can open 'em."

Wolfe laughed, too, in a senseless way.

---

[47]QUEEREST DODGE: Strangest strategy.

"I think I'll get out," he said.

"I believe his brain's touched," said Haley, when he came out.

The puddler scraped away with the tin for half an hour. Still Deborah did not speak. At last she ventured nearer, and touched his arm.

"Blood?" she said, looking at some spots on his coat with a shudder.

He looked up at her. "Why, Deb!" he said, smiling,—such a bright, boyish smile, that it went to poor Deborah's heart directly, and she sobbed and cried out loud.

"Oh, Hugh, lad! Hugh! dunnot look at me, when it wur my fault! To think I brought hur to it! And I loved hur so! Oh, lad, I dud!"

The confession, even in this wretch, came with the woman's blush through the sharp cry.

He did not seem to hear her,—scraping away diligently at the bars with the bit of tin.

Was he going mad? She peered closely into his face. Something she saw there made her draw suddenly back,—something which Haley had not seen, that lay beneath the pinched, vacant look it had caught since the trial, or the curious gray shadow that rested on it. That gray shadow,— yes, she knew what that meant. She had often seen it creeping over women's faces for months, who died at last of slow hunger or consumption. That meant death, distant, lingering: but this— Whatever it was the woman saw, or thought she saw, used as she was to crime and misery, seemed to make her sick with a new horror. Forgetting her fear of him, she caught his shoulders, and looked keenly, steadily, into his eyes.

"Hugh!" she cried, in a desperate whisper,—"oh, boy, not that! for God's sake, not that!"

The vacant laugh went off his face, and he answered her in a muttered word or two that drove her away. Yet the words were kindly enough. Sitting there on his pallet, she cried silently a hopeless sort of tears, but did not speak again. The man looked up furtively at her now and then. Whatever his own trouble was, her distress vexed him with a momentary sting.

It was market-day. The narrow window of the jail looked down directly on the carts and wagons drawn up in a long line, where they had unloaded. He could see, too, and hear distinctly the clink of money as it changed hands, the busy crowd of whites and blacks shoving, pushing one another, and the chaffering[48] and swearing at the stalls. Somehow, the sound, more than anything else had done, wakened him up,—made the whole real to him. He was done with the world and the business of

---

[48]CHAFFERING: Buying and selling, haggling about the price.

it. He let the tin fall, and looked out, pressing his face close to the rusty bars. How they crowded and pushed! And he,—he should never walk that pavement again! There came Neff Sanders, one of the feeders at the mill, with a basket on his arm. Sure enough, Neff was married the other week. He whistled, hoping he would look up; but he did not. He wondered if Neff remembered he was there,—if any of the boys thought of him up there, and thought that he never was to go down that old cinder-road again. Never again! He had not quite understood it before; but now he did. Not for days or years, but never!—that was it.

How clear the light fell on that stall in front of the market! and how like a picture it was, the dark-green heaps of corn, and the crimson beets, and golden melons! There was another with game: how the light flickered on that pheasant's breast, with the purplish blood dripping over the brown feathers! He could see the red shining of the drops, it was so near. In one minute he could be down there. It was just a step. So easy, as it seemed, so natural to go! Yet it could never be—not in all the thousands of years to come—that he should put his foot on that street again! He thought of himself with a sorrowful pity, as of some one else. There was a dog down in the market, walking after his master with such a stately, grave look!—only a dog, yet he could go backwards and forwards just as he pleased: he had good luck! Why, the very vilest cur, yelping there in the gutter, had not lived his life, had been free to act out whatever thought God had put into his brain; while he—No, he would not think of that! He tried to put the thought away, and to listen to a dispute between a countryman and a woman about some meat; but it would come back. He, what had he done to bear this?

Then came the sudden picture of what might have been, and now. He knew what it was to be in the penitentiary,—how it went with men there. He knew how in these long years he should slowly die, but not until soul and body had become corrupt and rotten,—how, when he came out, if he lived to come, even the lowest of the mill-hands would jeer him,—how his hands would be weak, and his brain senseless and stupid. He believed he was almost that now. He put his hand to his head, with a puzzled, weary look. It ached, his head, with thinking. He tried to quiet himself. It was only right, perhaps; he had done wrong. But was there right or wrong for such as he? What was right? And who had ever taught him? He thrust the whole matter away. A dark, cold quiet crept through his brain. It was all wrong; but let it be! It was nothing to him more than the others. Let it be!

The door grated, as Haley opened it.

"Come, my woman! Must lock up for t' night. Come, stir yerself!"

She went up and took Hugh's hand.

"Good-night, Deb," he said, carelessly.

She had not hoped he would say more; but the tired pain on her mouth just then was bitterer than death. She took his passive hand and kissed it.

"Hur'll never see Deb again!" she ventured, her lips growing colder and more bloodless.

What did she say that for? Did he not know it? Yet he would not be impatient with poor old Deb. She had trouble of her own, as well as he.

"No, never again," he said, trying to be cheerful.

She stood just a moment, looking at him. Do you laugh at her, standing there, with her hunchback, her rags, her bleared, withered face, and the great despised love tugging at her heart?

"Come you!" called Haley, impatiently.

She did not move.

"Hugh!" she whispered.

It was to be her last word. What was it?

"Hugh, boy, not THAT!"

He did not answer. She wrung her hands, trying to be silent, looking in his face in an agony of entreaty. He smiled again, kindly.

"It is best, Deb. I cannot bear to be hurted any more."

"Hur knows," she said, humbly.

"Tell my father good-by; and—and kiss little Janey."

She nodded, saying nothing, looked in his face again, and went out of the door. As she went, she staggered.

"Drinkin' to-day?" broke out Haley, pushing her before him. "Where the Devil did you get it? Here, in with ye!" and he shoved her into her cell, next to Wolfe's, and shut the door.

Along the wall of her cell there was a crack low down by the floor, through which she could see the light from Wolfe's. She had discovered it days before. She hurried in now, and, kneeling down by it, listened, hoping to hear some sound. Nothing but the rasping of the tin on the bars. He was at his old amusement again. Something in the noise jarred on her ear, for she shivered as she heard it. Hugh rasped away at the bars. A dull old bit of tin, not fit to cut korl with.

He looked out of the window again. People were leaving the market now. A tall mulatto girl, following her mistress, her basket on her head, crossed the street just below, and looked up. She was laughing; but, when she caught sight of the haggard face peering out through the bars, suddenly grew grave, and hurried by. A free, firm step, a clear-cut olive face, with a scarlet turban tied on one side, dark, shining eyes, and on the head the basket poised, filled with fruit and flowers, under which the scarlet turban and bright eyes looked out half-shadowed. The picture caught his eye. It was good to see a face like that. He would try to-morrow, and cut one like it. To-morrow! He threw down the tin, trembling, and covered his face with his hands. When he looked up again, the daylight was gone.

Deborah, crouching near by on the other side of the wall, heard no noise. He sat on the side of the low pallet, thinking. Whatever was the mystery which the woman had seen on his face, it came out now slowly, in the dark there, and became fixed,—a something never seen on his face before. The evening was darkening fast. The market had been over for an hour; the rumbling of the carts over the pavement grew more infrequent: he listened to each, as it passed, because he thought it was to be for the last time. For the same reason, it was, I suppose, that he strained his eyes to catch a glimpse of each passer-by, wondering who they were, what kind of homes they were going to, if they had children,—listening eagerly to every chance word in the street, as if—(God be merciful to the man! what strange fancy was this?)—as if he never should hear human voices again.

It was quite dark at last. The street was a lonely one. The last passenger, he thought, was gone. No,—there was a quick step: Joe Hill, lighting the lamps. Joe was a good old chap; never passed a fellow without some joke or other. He remembered once seeing the place where he lived with his wife. "Granny Hill" the boys called her. Bedridden she was; but so kind as Joe was to her! kept the room so clean!—and the old woman, when he was there, was laughing at "some of t' lad's foolishness." The step was far down the street; but he could see him place the ladder, run up, and light the gas. A longing seized him to be spoken to once more.

"Joe!" he called out of the grating. "Good-by, Joe!"

The old man stopped a moment, listening uncertainly; then hurried on. The prisoner thrust his hand out of the window, and called again, louder; but Joe was too far down the street. It was a little thing; but it hurt him,—this disappointment.

"Good-by, Joe!" he called, sorrowfully enough.

"Be quiet!" said one of the jailers, passing the door, striking on it with his club.

Oh, that was the last, was it?

There was an inexpressible bitterness on his face, as he lay down on the bed, taking the bit of tin, which he had rasped to a tolerable degree of sharpness, in his hand,—to play with, it may be. He bared his arms, looking intently at their corded veins and sinews. Deborah, listening in the next cell, heard a slight clicking sound, often repeated. She shut her lips tightly, that she might not scream; the cold drops of sweat broke over her, in her dumb agony.

"Hur knows best," she muttered at last, fiercely clutching the boards where she lay.

If she could have seen Wolfe, there was nothing about him to frighten her. He lay quite still, his arms outstretched, looking at the pearly stream of moonlight coming into the window. I think in that one hour that came then he lived back over all the years that had gone before. I think that all the low, vile life, all his wrongs, all his starved hopes, came then, and stung him with a farewell poison that made him sick unto death. He made neither moan nor cry, only turned his worn face now and then to the pure light, that seemed so far off, as one that said, "How long, O Lord? how long?"

The hour was over at last. The moon, passing over her nightly path, slowly came nearer, and threw the light across his bed on his feet. He watched it steadily, as it crept up, inch by inch, slowly. It seemed to him to carry with it a great silence. He had been so hot and tired there always in the mills! The years had been so fierce and cruel! There was coming now quiet and coolness and sleep. His tense limbs relaxed, and settled in a calm languor. The blood ran fainter and slow from his heart. He did not think now with a savage anger of what might be and was not; he was conscious only of deep stillness creeping over him. At first he saw a sea of faces: the mill-men,—women he had known, drunken and bloated,—Janey's timid and pitiful,—poor old Debs: then they floated together like a mist, and faded away, leaving only the clear, pearly moonlight.

Whether, as the pure light crept up the stretched-out figure, it brought with it calm and peace, who shall say? His dumb soul was alone with God in judgment. A Voice may have spoken for it from far-off Calvary, "Father, forgive them, for they know not what they do!"[49] Who dare say? Fainter and fainter the heart rose and fell, slower and slower the moon floated from behind a cloud, until, when at last its full tide of white splendor swept over the cell, it seemed to wrap and fold into a deeper stillness the dead figure that never should move again. Silence deeper than the Night! Nothing that moved, save the black, nauseous stream of blood dripping slowly from the pallet to the floor!

There was outcry and crowd enough in the cell the next day. The coroner and his jury, the local editors, Kirby himself, and boys with their

---

[49]FATHER, FORGIVE THEM, FOR THEY KNOW NOT WHAT THEY DO: Words spoken by Jesus during the crucifixion, Luke 23:34: "Then said Jesus, Father, forgive them; for they know not what they do. And they parted his raiment, and cast lots."

hands thrust knowingly into their pockets and heads on one side, jammed into the corners. Coming and going all day. Only one woman. She came late, and outstayed them all. A Quaker, or Friend, as they call themselves. I think this woman was known by that name in heaven. A homely body, coarsely dressed in gray and white. Deborah (for Haley had let her in) took notice of her. She watched them all—sitting on the end of the pallet, holding his head in her arms—with the ferocity of a watch-dog, if any of them touched the body. There was no meekness, no sorrow, in her face; the stuff out of which murderers are made, instead. All the time Haley and the woman were laying straight the limbs and cleaning the cell, Deborah sat still, keenly watching the Quaker's face. Of all the crowd there that day, this woman alone had not spoken to her,—only once or twice had put some cordial to her lips. After they all were gone, the woman, in the same still, gentle way, brought a vase of wood-leaves and berries, and placed it by the pallet, then opened the narrow window. The fresh air blew in, and swept the woody fragrance over the dead face. Deborah looked up with a quick wonder.

"Did hur know my boy wud like it? Did hur know Hugh?"

"I know Hugh now."

The white fingers passed in a slow, pitiful way over the dead, worn face. There was a heavy shadow in the quiet eyes.

"Did hur know where they'll bury Hugh?" said Deborah in a shrill tone, catching her arm.

This had been the question hanging on her lips all day.

"In t' town-yard? Under t' mud and ash? T' lad'll smother, woman! He wur born on t' lane moor, where t' air is frick[50] and strong. Take hur out, for God's sake, take hur out where t' air blows!"

The Quaker hesitated, but only for a moment. She put her strong arm around Deborah and led her to the window.

"Thee sees the hills, friend, over the river? Thee sees how the light lies warm there, and the winds of God blow all the day? I live there,— where the blue smoke is, by the trees. Look at me." She turned Deborah's face to her own, clear and earnest. "Thee will believe me? I will take Hugh and bury him there to-morrow."

Deborah did not doubt her. As the evening wore on, she leaned against the iron bars, looking at the hills that rose far off, through the thick sodden clouds, like a bright, unattainable calm. As she looked, a shadow of their solemn repose fell on her face: its fierce discontent faded into a pitiful, humble quiet. Slow, solemn tears gathered in her eyes: the poor

[50]FRICK: Fresh.

weak eyes turned so hopelessly to the place where Hugh was to rest, the grave heights looking higher and brighter and more solemn than ever before. The Quaker watched her keenly. She came to her at last, and touched her arm.

"When thee comes back," she said, in a low, sorrowful tone, like one who speaks from a strong heart deeply moved with remorse or pity, "thee shall begin thy life again,—there on the hills. I came too late; but not for thee,—by God's help, it may be."

Not too late. Three years after, the Quaker began her work. I end my story here. At evening-time it was light. There is no need to tire you with the long years of sunshine, and fresh air, and slow, patient Christ-love, needed to make healthy and hopeful this impure body and soul. There is a homely pine house, on one of these hills, whose windows over-look broad, wooded slopes and clover-crimsoned meadows,—niched into the very place where the light is warmest, the air freest. It is the Friends' meetinghouse.[51] Once a week they sit there, in their grave, earnest way, waiting for the Spirit of Love to speak, opening their simple hearts to receive His words. There is a woman, old, deformed, who takes a humble place among them: waiting like them: in her gray dress, her worn face, pure and meek, turned now and then to the sky. A woman much loved by these silent, restful people; more silent than they, more humble, more loving. Waiting: with her eyes turned to hills higher and purer than these on which she lives,—dim and far off now, but to be reached some day. There may be in her heart some latent hope to meet there the love denied her here,—that she shall find him whom she lost, and that then she will not be all-unworthy. Who blames her? Something is lost in the passage of every soul from one eternity to the other,—something pure and beau-tiful, which might have been and was not: a hope, a talent, a love, over which the soul mourns, like Esau deprived of his birthright.[52] What blame to the meek Quaker, if she took her lost hope to make the hills of heaven more fair?

Nothing remains to tell that the poor Welsh puddler once lived, but this figure of the mill-woman cut in korl. I have it here in a corner of my library. I keep it hid behind a curtain,—it is such a rough, ungainly thing. Yet there are about it touches, grand sweeps of outline, that show a master's hand. Sometimes,—to-night, for instance,—the curtain is acci-

---

[51]FRIENDS' MEETINGHOUSE: The Quaker meetinghouse.
[52]ESAU DEPRIVED OF HIS BIRTHRIGHT: Genesis 25:34: "Then Jacob gave Esau bread and pot-tage of lentils; and he did eat and drink, and rose up, and went his way: thus Esau despised his birthright."

dentally drawn back, and I see a bare arm stretched out imploringly in the darkness, and an eager, wolfish face watching mine: a wan, woful face, through which the spirit of the dead korl-cutter looks out, with its thwarted life, its mighty hunger, its unfinished work. Its pale, vague lips seem to tremble with a terrible question.

"Is this the End?"—they say,—"nothing beyond?—no more?" Why, you tell me you have seen that look in the eyes of dumb brutes,—horses dying under the lash. I know.

The deep of the night is passing while I write. The gas-light wakens from the shadows here and there the objects which lie scattered through the room: only faintly, though; for they belong to the open sunlight. As I glance at them, they each recall some task or pleasure of the coming day. A half-moulded child's head; Aphrodite[53]; a bough of forest-leaves; music; work; homely fragments, in which lie the secrets of all eternal truth and beauty. Prophetic all! Only this dumb, woful face seems to belong to and end with the night. I turn to look at it. Has the power of its desperate need commanded the darkness away? While the room is yet steeped in heavy shadow, a cool, gray light suddenly touches its head like a blessing hand, and its groping arm points through the broken cloud to the far East, where, in the flickering, nebulous crimson, God has set the promise of the Dawn.

[1861]

---

[53]APHRODITE: In Greek myth, the goddess of love.

A Chronology of Works and Events That Shaped American Literature 1492 to 1870

1492	Christopher Columbus lands in the Bahamas
1552	Bartolomé de Las Casas, *The Very Brief Relation of the Devastation of the Indies*
1565	Spanish settlement in St. Augustine, Florida
1607	Colony established in Jamestown, Virginia
1613	Pocahontas is first Indian convert to Christianity in Virginia
1616	Smallpox epidemic strikes Native Americans in New England
1616	John Smith, *A Description of New-England*
1620	Plymouth Colony founded
1624	Dutch settlement in Manhattan
1630	Massachusetts Bay Colony established
1630	William Bradford, *Of Plymouth Plantation* (1630–50); John Winthrop, *A Model of Christian Charity*
1636	Harvard College founded
1638	First printing press, Massachusetts Bay Colony
1637	Pequot War between Native Americans and settlers in Connecticut Valley
1640	*The Bay Psalm Book*
1643	First restaurant opens in Boston
1654	Twenty-four Jewish immigrants arrive in New Amsterdam (s. Manhattan)
1650	Anne Bradstreet, *The Tenth Muse Lately Sprung Up in America*
1670s–1680s	Edward Taylor, poems
1673	Regular mail service begins between Boston and New York
1675–76	King Philip's War between New England colonists and Native Americans
1678	Anne Bradstreet, *Poems*
1682	Mary Rowlandson, *A Narrative of the Captivity and Restoration of Mrs. Mary Rowlandson*
1683	*The New England Primer* (school book)
1689	First public school, Philadelphia
1692	Salem witch trials; nineteen persons tried, convicted, and executed
1693	William and Mary College (Virginia) founded
1693	Cotton Mather, *The Wonders of the Invisible World*
1700	Population in the colonies, 275,000; population of Boston, 7000
1702	Cotton Mather, *Magnalia Christi Americana*
1714	Tea is introduced in the colonies; other popular drinks are chocolate and rum

1727	Benjamin Franklin establishes *Junto*, scientific and philosophical society
1728	First synagogue, New York City
1731	Benjamin Franklin begins a circulating library, Philadelphia
1730–1740s	Great Awakening, religious revival
1733	Benjamin Franklin, *Poor Richard's Almanack* (1733–57)
1740	Jonathan Edward, "Personal Narrative"
1741	Jonathan Edwards, "Sinners in the Hands of an Angry God"
1742	1000 ships working in New England fishing industry
1754–63	French and Indian War fought over control of North America; French and Indian allies battle British, American colonists, and Indian allies
1756–72	John Woolman, *Journal*
1768	British troops arrive in Boston
1771	Benjamin Franklin begins *Autobiography*
1773	Boston Tea Party, colonists protest Tea Act
1773	310 street lamps installed in Boston
1773	Phillis Wheatley, *Poems*
1774	First Continental Congress
1775	Second Continental Congress establishes postal system; Benjamin Franklin is appointed postmaster general
1775–83	American Revolution
1776	Declaration of Independence
1776	Thomas Paine, *Common Sense*
1778	Articles of Confederation, first national constitution, adopted 1781, replaced by new Constitution in 1787–88
1782	J. Hector St. John de Crèvecoeur, *Letters from an American Farmer*
1782	First Catholic parochial school, Philadelphia
1782	New England discontinues use of scarlet letter for adulterers
1783	Treaty of Paris between Great Britain and American colonies; the United States recognized as independent nation
1783	Noah Webster, *The American Spelling Book*
1786-87	Shays' Rebellion, Massachusetts, insurrection by farmers in western Massachusetts against state government
1787	Constitutional Convention
1787	Thomas Jefferson, *Notes on the State of Virginia*; *The Federalist* (1787–88)
1788	U. S. Constitution ratified
1789	George Washington takes oath of office as first President

1790	U. S. population, 3,893,874; African American population, 757,000; 698,000 are slaves
1791	Bill of Rights
1791	Susanna Rowson, *Charlotte Temple*
1792	U. S. Stock Exchange organized
1793	Eli Whitney invents the cotton gin
1793	Yellow fever epidemic in Philadelphia (population, 28,500) kills 5000
1794	Thomas Paine, *The Age of Reason*
1795	Philip Freneau, *Poems*
1799	Charles Brockden Brown, *Edgar Huntly*
1800	Washington, D.C., becomes capital of the United States.
1800	U. S. population, 5,236,631
1800	Thomas Jefferson elected the 3rd President
1802	U. S. military academy established at West Point, New York
1803	U. S. purchases Louisiana Territory from France
1804–6	Lewis and Clark expedition to the west
1810	U.S. population, 7,036,491
1811	First steamboat navigates down the Mississippi river
1812–15	War of 1812, fought against Great Britain
1814	British troops burn Washington D. C.
1814	"Star-Spangled Banner" written by Francis Scott Key during British bombardment of Fort McHenry, Baltimore
1816	First savings banks, in Boston and Philadelphia
1817	American Society for the Return of Negroes to Africa established, in Richmond, Virginia
1817–25	Erie Canal constructed in New York, connects Buffalo with Albany and the Hudson River
1817	William Cullen Bryant, "Thanatopsis"
1819	Washington Irving, "Rip Van Winkle"
1820	Missouri Compromise, prohibits slavery in the territory of Louisiana Purchase north of 36°30'N latitude (southern boundary of Missouri)
1820	U. S. population, 10,037,323; largest state, Pennsylvania, 1,549,458; second largest, New York, 1,372,812; smallest, Delaware, 24,057
1820	Washington Irving, "The Legend of Sleepy Hollow"
1823	President James Monroe declares U. S. opposition to European intervention in the Americas ("Monroe Doctrine")
1826	James Fenimore Cooper, *The Last of the Mohicans*

1827	*Freedom's Journal*, first African-American newspaper
1827	Catherine Sedgwick, *Hope Leslie*
1828	Andrew Jackson elected 7th President
1828	*Cherokee Phoenix* in Georgia, first Indian newspaper
1828	Noah Webster, *American Dictionary of the English Language*
1829	First modern hotel, the Tremont, opens in Boston
1829	First school for the blind opens in Boston
1829	Cherokee Memorials
1830	Joseph Smith founds the Church of Jesus of Latter-Day Saints (Mormons), Fayette, New York
1831	New England Anti-Slavery Society
1831	Nat Turner slave rebellion, Virginia, sixty whites killed
1831	Edgar Allan Poe, "To Helen"
1833	William Apess, "An Indian's Looking-Glass for the White Man"
1835	Samuel Colt designs rapid-fire hand-sized revolver
1835	Nathaniel Hawthorne, "Young Goodman Brown"
1835–42	Seminole War between U. S. military and native Americans in Florida
1836	Battle of the Alamo, San Antonio, Texas
1836	Ralph Waldo Emerson, *Nature*
1837	Financial panic and depression
1837	John Deere invents steel plow
1837	Ralph Waldo Emerson, "The American Scholar"
1838	Cherokee Indians' "Trail of Tears"
1838	Underground Railroad, antislavery network aiding fugitive slaves
1840	First recorded use of expression "O.K." (from Old Kinderhook, New York, birthplace of President Martin Van Buren)
1840	Edgar Allan Poe, *Tales of the Grotesque and Arabesque*
1841	Ralph Waldo Emerson, *Essays: First Series*
1842	Showman, circus master, and entrepreneur P. T. Barnum's American Museum opens in New York City
1842	Edgar Allan Poe, "The Raven"
1844	First message sent by telegraph
1845	U. S. annexation of Texas
1845	Alexander Cartwright, in New York City, establishes first formal set of rules for baseball
1845	Edgar Allan Poe, *The Raven and Other Poems*; Frederick Douglass, *Narrative*; Margaret Fuller, *Woman in the Nineteenth Century*
1846	Smithsonian Institution established

1846–1848	Mexican War
1846	Nathaniel Hawthorne, *Mosses from an Old Manse*
1847	First use of adhesive postage stamps
1848	California Gold Rush begins
1848	Women's rights convention, Seneca Falls, New York
1848	Steam power used to provide "air conditioning" in Broadway Theater, New York City
1849	Francis Parkman, *The Oregon Trail*; Henry David Thoreau, "Resistance to Civil Government" ("Civil Disobedience")
1850	California 31st state admitted to the Union
1850	Fugitive Slave Act requires northerners to assist in recapture of runaway slaves
1850	Population, 23,054,152
1850	Nathaniel Hawthorne, *The Scarlet Letter*
1851	Herman Melville, *Moby-Dick*; Sojourner Truth, "Ain't I a Woman?"
1852	Harriet Beecher Stowe, *Uncle Tom's Cabin*
1853	Herman Melville, "Bartleby, the Scrivener"
1854	Kansas-Nebraska Act allows residents of Kansas and Nebraska territories to decide for themselves whether they will permit slavery
1854	Arrival of 13,000 Chinese immigrants
1854	Henry David Thoreau, *Walden*
1855	Herman Melville, "Benito Cereno"; Henry Wadsworth Longfellow, *The Song of Hiawatha*; Walt Whitman, *Leaves of Grass*
1856	First "street trains," pulled by steam engines, in Boston and Cambridge
1856	Patent issued for a pencil with an eraser attached
1857	Dred Scott decision: Supreme Court rules that African Americans, free or slave, could not be citizens and thus have no rights under the Constitution
1857	Celebration of Mardi Gras begins, New Orleans
1858	Abraham Lincoln/Stephen A. Douglas debates, in campaign for U. S. Senate seat, Illinois; election won by Douglas
1858	Religious revivals spread across nation
1858	Macy's Department Store, New York City, opens
1859	First passenger elevator installed, Fifth Avenue Hotel, New York City
1859	Abolitionist John Brown's raid on Harpers Ferry, Virginia; Brown tried, found guilty of treason and conspiracy, executed December 2nd
1860	Abraham Lincoln elected 16th President (receives no electoral votes from the slave states)

1860	South Carolina secedes from the Union
1860	Ralph Waldo Emerson, *The Conduct of Life*; Nathaniel Hawthorne, *The Marble Faun*
1861	Vassar College, Poughkeepsie, New York, established for women
1861	Confederate States of America formed
1861	First federal income tax (3% on incomes over $800)
1861	Rebecca Harding Davis, "Life in the Iron Mills"; Julia Ward Howe, "The Battle Hymn of the Republic"; Harriet Jacobs, *Incidents in the Life of a Slave Girl*
1861–65	Civil War
1863	First Union "conscription act," all men age 20 to 35, and all unmarried men to age 45, subject to military service
1863	Emancipation Proclamation grants freedom to slaves in southern states
1863	Abraham Lincoln, "The Gettysburg Address"
1865	Abraham Lincoln, "Second Inaugural Address"
1865	Abraham Lincoln assassinated
1865	Civil War casualties: North—362,000 dead, 278,000 wounded; South—261,000 dead, 194,000 wounded; total U. S. population in 1860—31,183,582
1865	Union Stockyards, for meat-producing and meat-packing, opens in Chicago
1865	Thirteenth Amendment abolishes slavery
1865	Walt Whitman, "When Lilacs Last in the Dooryard Bloom'd"; Mark Twain, "The Notorious Jumping Frog of Calaveras County"
1866	Ku Klux Klan organized, white supremacist organization
1867	First elevated railway begins operating in New York City
1867	U. S. purchases Alaska territory from Russia
1868	Louisa May Alcott, *Little Women*
1869	Transcontinental Railroad completed in Utah
1869	Bret Harte, "The Outcasts of Poker Flat"
1870	Great Atlantic and Pacific Tea Company (the A & P) begins chain of grocery stores
1870	John D. Rockefeller forms Standard Oil Company of Ohio;
1870	Population: 38,155,505; Native born: 32,675,877; Foreign born: 5,479,628; White population: 33,242,349; "colored" (i. e., black) population: 4,835,562

Credits

Adams, John, "The Letters of John and Abigail Adams," "John Adams to Abigail Adams (July 3, 1776)," *Reflections on the Declaration of Independence.*

Apess, William, *On Our Own Ground: The Complete Writings of William Apess, A Pequot,* Copyright ©1992 by The University of Massachusetts Press. Edited by Barry O'Connell, The University of Massachusetts Press, 1992.

Bradford, William, Of Plymouth Plantation, Book I, Chapter IX; Of Their Voyage and How They Passed the Sea; and of Their Safe Arrival at Cape Cod, Book I; Chapter X. Showing How They Sought Out a Place of Habitation; and What Befell Thereabout, Book II; Chapter XI. The Remainder of Anno 1620, [The Mayflower Compact], Book II; Chapter XII. *Anno 1621 First Thanksgiving.*

Bradstreet, Anne, "The Prologue, The Author to Her Book Before the Birth of One of Her Children," *To My Dear and Loving Husband.*

Bryant, William Cullen, *Thanatopsis; The Prairies.*

Cherokee Memorials, The. Memorial of the Cherokee Citizens, December 18, 1829.

Columbus, Christopher, "Regarding the First Voyage (February 15, 1493)" from *Letter to Luis de Santangel.* "Regarding the Fourth Voyage (July 7, 1503)" from *Letter to Ferdinand and Isabella*

Cooper, James Fenimore, *The American Democrat* (excerpt).

Crèvecoeur, J. Hector St. John de, *Letters from an American Farmer, Letter III. What Is an American?*

Davis, Rebecca Harding. *Life in the Iron-Mills.*

de Las Casas, Bartolomé, "The Very Brief Relation of the Devastation of the Indies," from *Hispaniola* (excerpt).

Dickinson, Emily, Poems 130, 199, 214, 216, 241, 249, 258, 280, 303, 324, 341, 348, 441, 448, 465, 501, 520, 632, 650, 709, 712, 754, 986, 1129, 1545, 1732, Reprinted by permission of the publishers and the Trustees of Amherst College from *The Poems of Emily Dickinson,* Thomas H. Johnson, ed., Cambridge, Mass.: The Belknap Press of Harvard University Press, Copyright (c) 1951, 1955, 1979 by the President and Fellows of Harvard College.

Dickinson, Emily, *Letters of Emily Dickinson,* ed. by Mabel Loomis Todd, 1931, Harper & Brothers. Boston Public Library/Rare Books Department. Courtesy of the Trustees.

Douglass, Frederick, *The Narrative and Selected Writings,* ed. by Michael Meyer, The Modern Library (Random House), 1984.

Edwards, Jonathan, *Personal Narrative, Sinners in the Hands of an Angry God.*

Emerson, Ralph Waldo, *The American Scholar; Self-Reliance; Concord Hymn; The Rhodora.*

Franklin, Benjamin, *The Way to Wealth; Remarks Concerning the Savages of North America; The Autobiography* (Part One) (excerpt, from Part Two).

Freneau, Philip, *The Indian Burying Ground; On the Religion of Nature.*

Fuller, Margaret, "The Great Lawsuit: Man vs. Men and Woman vs. Women," *Dial,* July, 1843.

Hawthorne, Nathaniel, *Young Goodman Brown; The May-Pole of Merry Mount; The Minister's Black Veil; The Scarlet Letter.*

Iroquois Creation Story, The. Version by David Cusick

Irving, Washington, *Rip Van Winkle.*

Jacobs, Harriet Ann, *Incidents in the Life of a Slave Girl.*

Jefferson, Thomas, from *The Autobiography of Thomas Jefferson* and from *The Declaration of Independence.*

Lincoln, Abraham, *Abraham Lincoln: His Speeches and Writings.*

Longfellow, Henry Wadsworth, *The Poetical Works of Henry Wadsworth Longfellow in Six Volumes, Volume III,* 1880, Houghton Mifflin Co.

Madison, James, *The Federalist.* No. 10

Mather, Cotton, *The Wonders of the Invisible World,* [A People of God in the Devil's Territories]; *The Trial of Martha Carrier.*

Melville, Herman, *Bartleby, the Scrivener. A Story of Wall-street.*

Melville, Herman, *The March into Virginia.*

Melville, Herman, *The Portent.*

Paine, Thomas, *Common Sense, Introduction III; Thoughts on the Present State of American Affairs; The Crisis; No. 1.*

Poe, Edgar Allan, *The Complete Works of Edgar Allan Poe,* ed. by James A. Harrison, AMS Press, Inc., 1965, 1979.

Rowlandson, Mary, *A Narrative of the Captivity and Restoration of Mrs. Mary Rowlandson* (excerpt).

Sigourney, Lydia Howard Huntley, *The Indian's Welcome to the Pilgrim Fathers.*

Smith, John, from *A Description of New England* (excerpt).

Stowe, Harriet Beecher, *Uncle Tom's Cabin.*

Taylor, Edward, *Preparatory Meditations, Meditation 22* (First Series), *Meditation 38* (First Series).

Thoreau, Henry David, "Resistance to Civil Government," *Aesthetic Papers.*

Thoreau, Henry David, *Collected Essays and Poems,* ed. by Elizabeth Hall Witherell, The Library of America, 2001.

Timrod, Henry, "Ode", ed. *Yale Book of American Verse.* New Haven: Yale University Press, 1912.

Wheatley, Phillis, "On the Death of Reverend Mr. George Whitefield," "On Being Brought from Africa to America," "To S.M., A Young African Painter, on Seeing His Works," "To His Excellency General Washington," "Letters: To Rev. Samson Occom (February 11, 1774)," from *The Natural Rights of Negroes.*

Whitman, Walt, "Song of Myself," "When I Heard at the Close of Day;" "I Saw in Louisiana a Live-Oak Growing;" "When Lilacs Last in the Dooryard Bloom'd," *Leaves of Grass,* Philadelphia: David McKay, [1900].

Whitman, Walt, *Prose Works,* Philadelphia: David McKay, 1892.

Winthrop, John, *A Model of Christian Charity.*

Woolman, John, *Some Considerations on the Keeping of Negroes, [Part One].*

Index of Authors, Titles, and First Lines of Poems

Map of the United States

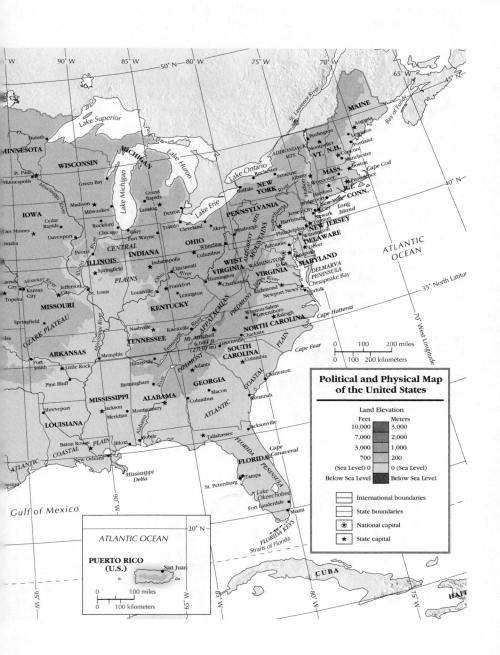

Political and Physical Map of the United States

Land Elevation

Feet		Meters
10,000		3,000
7,000		2,000
3,000		1,000
700		200
(Sea Level) 0		0 (Sea Level)
Below Sea Level		Below Sea Level

International boundaries

State boundaries

⊛ National capital

★ State capital

Additional Titles of Interest

Note to Instructors: Any of these Penguin-Putnam, Inc. titles can be packaged with this book at a special discount. Contact your local Longman sales representative for details on how to create a Penguin-Putnam, Inc. Value Package.

Albee, Edward, *Three Tall Women*
Alger, Horatio, *Ragged Dick and Struggling Upward*
Allison, Dorothy, *Bastard out of Carolina*
Alvarez, Julia, *How the Garcia Girls Lost Their Accent*
Bellamy, Edward, *Looking Backward*
Bellow, Saul, *The Adventures of Augie March*
Boyle, T.C., *The Tortilla Curtain*
Cather, Willa, *My Antonia*
Cather, Willa, *O Pioneers!*
Chopin, Kate, *The Awakening*
Delillo, Don, *White Noise*
Dos Passos, John, *Three Soldiers*
Du Bois, W.E.B., *The Souls of Black Folk*
Guthrie, Woody, *Bound for Glory*
Hansberry, Lorraine, *A Raisin in the Sun*
Hwang, David Henry, *M. Butterfly*
Jen, Gish, *Typical American*
Karr, Mary, *The Liars' Club*

Kerouac, Jack, *On the Road*
Kesey, Ken, *One Flew Over the Cuckoo's Nest*
King, Jr., Martin Luther, *Why We Can't Wait*
Lewis, Sinclair, *Babbitt*
McBride, James, *The Color of Water*
Miller, Arthur, *The Crucible*
Miller, Arthur, *Death of a Salesman*
Morrison, Toni, *Beloved*
Morrison, Toni, *The Bluest Eye*
Morrison, Toni, *Sula*
Naylor, Gloria, *The Women of Brewster Place*
Silko, Leslie Marmon, *Ceremony*
Sinclair, Upton, *The Jungle*
Steinbeck, John, *The Grapes of Wrath*
Steinbeck, John, *Of Mice and Men*
Steinbeck, John, *The Pearl*
Twain, Mark, *Adventures of Huckleberry Finn*
Wilson, August, *Fences*